GALE ENCYCLOPEDIA OF U.S. ECONOMIC HISTORY

GALE ENCYCLOPEDIA OF U.S. ECONOMIC HISTORY

VOLUME 1 A–K

THOMAS CARSON, EDITOR
MARY BONK, ASSOCIATE EDITOR

GALE GROUP

Detroit
San Francisco
London
Boston
Woodbridge, CT

Editor: Thomas Carson
Coeditor: Mary Rose Bonk
Assistant Editors: Talitha A. Jean, Nancy Matuszak, R. David Riddle
Contributing Editors: Pamela A. Dear, Michael Reade
Permissions Team Leader: Maria Franklin
Permissions Specialist: Margaret Chamberlain
Cataloger: Mary K. Grimes
Junior Cataloger: Leitha Etheridge-Sims
Research Manager: Victoria B. Cariappa
Research Specialist: Maureen Richards
Production Director: Mary Beth Trimper
Assistant Production Manager: Evi Seoud
Senior Buyer: Wendy Blurton
Production Design Manager: Cynthia Baldwin
Art Director: Michelle DiMercurio
Graphic Services Manager: Barbara Yarrow
Image Database Supervisor: Randy Bassett
Digital Imaging Specialist: Christine O'Bryan

TRADEMARKS AND PROPRIETARY RIGHTS

Library of Congress Catalog
Gale encyclopedia of U.S. economic history / Thomas Carson, editor
cm.
    Includes bibliographical references and index.
        ISBN 0-7876-3888-9 (set). - ISBN 0-7876-3889-7 (vol. 1)
0-7876-3890-0 (vol.2)
        1. United States—Economic conditions Encyclopedias.   I. Carson,
Thomas.   II. Title: Gale encyclopedia of US economic history.
HC102.G35 1999
        330.973'003—dc21   99-39623
                                            CIP

Printed in the United States of America
10 9 8 7 6 5 4 3 2

Table of Contents

Advisory Board

Charles K. Hyde Ph.D.
Subject-Area Specialist
Professor of History
Wayne State University
Detroit, Michigan

Brian Carey
Brother Rice High School
Bloomfield Hills, Michigan

Norma Coleman
Roosevelt High School
Gary, Indiana

Maria Gallo
Truman High School
Bronx, New York

Kenneth E. Hendrickson, Jr. Ph.D.
Chair—History Department

Midwestern State University
Wichita Falls, Texas

Michael Leahy Ph.D.
Eastern High School
Bristol, Connecticut

Gene McCreadie
Foundation for Teaching Economics
Mentor Teacher
Temple City High School
Temple City, California

Linda Karen Miller Ed. D.
Fairfax High School
Fairfax, California

Thomas C. Mackey Ph.D.
Department of History
University of Louisville
Louisville, Kentucky

Photo and Illustration Credits

Addams, Jane: p.2, The Library of Congress; **American troops during World War I gas attack, 1918, France:** p.1130, Corbis-Bettmann. Reproduced by permission; **Asian laborers, cheering as railroad enters station:** p.153, 19th century, engraving. Archive Photos. Reproduced by permission; **Assembly line workers at Ford Motor Company, Detroit, Michigan:** p.61, The Library of Congress; **Astor, John Jacob:** p.62, National Portrait Gallery; **Atomic explosion:** p.58, UPI/Corbis-Bettmann. Reproduced by permission; **Australian indenture termination document:** p.473, issued to Francis Neill, 1838. Archive Photos. Reproduced by permission; **Banisch, Al, of Heinz ketchup:** p.431, 1997. AP/Wide World Photos. Reproduced by permission; **Bar graph, Gross Output of WWII in Billions, 1939-1943:** p.241, illustration by George Barille. The Gale Group; **Bar graph, Public Assistance Payments by the Government:** p.1099, illustration by Smith & Santori. The Gale Group; **Bar graph, Rise of Suburbs, 1901-1960:** p.971, illustration by George Barille. The Gale Group; **Bar graph, Rise of the Steel Industry, 1867-1915:** p.960, illustration by George Barille. The Gale Group; **Bar graph, England's Colonial Population, 1700:** p.910, illustration by George Barille. The Gale Group; **Bar graph, Budget Deficit during presidencies, 1970-1995:** p.125, illustration by George Barille. The Gale Group; **Bar graph, gallons of alcohol consumed during Prohibition, 1910-1929:** p.829, illustration by George Barille. The Gale Group; **Bar graph, Southern Farm Production, 1850-1890:** p.179, illustration by George Barille. The Gale Group; **Bar graph, Tax Receipts, 1923-1932:** p.227, illustration by Smith & Santori. The Gale Group; **Bar graph, The Graying of America:** p.393, illustration by George Barille. The Gale Group; **Bar graph, American Troops in Vietnam, 1965-1973:** p.1064, illustration by George Barille. The Gale Group; **Bar graph, King Cotton, 1800-1860:** p.538, illustration by Smith & Santori. The Gale Group; **Bar graph, Total European Immigration to the United States, 1866-1925:** p.466, illustration by Smith & Santori. The Gale Group; **Couple at**

Morningstar Commune: p.1054, Occidental, California, 1971, AP/Wide World Photos. Reproduced by permission; **Barnum, P.T.:** p.80, Archive Photos. Reproduced by permission; **Battles of Korea, 1950, map:** p.545, UPI/Corbis-Bettmann. Reproduced by permission; **Bell, Alexander Graham:** p.86, U.S. National Aeronautics and Space Administration; **Berlin Wall being dismantled, Germany:** p.186, Corbis-Bettmann. Reproduced by permission; **Bethune, Mary McLeod:** p.90, by Carl Van Vechten. The Estate of Carl Van Vechten. Reproduced by permission; **Hershey's chocolate bar miniatures:** p.433, 1998. AP/Wide World Photos. Reproduced by permission; **Boeing 747:** p.104, Archive Photos. Reproduced by permission; **Boone, Daniel:** p.108, The Library of Congress; **Boston Tea Party:** p.113, lithograph by Sarony and Major. National Archives and Records Administration; **Boy laborers:** p.304, National Archives and Records Administration; **Brandeis, Louis Dembitz:** p.116, The Library of Congress; **Bunzey, Kenneth, Adrian Nelson working inside turbine generator:** p.365, Schenectady, New York, 1955. AP/Wide World Photos. Reproduced by permission; **Burnham, Daniel Hudson:** p.129, The Library of Congress; **Carnegie, Andrew:** p.139, AP/ Wide World Photos. Reproduced by permission; **Cars lined up at a Standard gas station:** p.752, UPI/Corbis-Bettmann. Reproduced by permission; **Carver, George Washington:** p.142, AP/Wide World Photos. Reproduced by permission; **Chart, The Articles of Confederation v. The Constitution:** p.10, illustration by George Barille. The Gale Group; **Chart, Financing a New Nation, 1789-1791:** p.1079, illustration by George Barille. The Gale Group; **Chart, Exchange Rates:** p.298, illustration by George Barille. The Gale Group; **Chart, the Federal Reserve System:** p.313, illustration by George Barille. The Gale Group; **Chart, Slaves and Slaveholders, 1860:** p.927, illustration by Smith & Santori. The Gale Group; **Chavez, Cesar:** p.157, AP/Wide World Photos. Reproduced by permission; **Child worker at the Turkey Knob Mine in West Virginia:** photograph by Lewis Hine; **Child,**

seated at computer ("INTERNET" on screen): p.488, Archive Photos. Reproduced by permission; **Chrysler, Walter P:** p.167, Reproduced by permission of American Automobile Association; **Confederate currency, five dollars:** p.201, Archive Photos. Reproduced by permission; **Cook, Jane, Fred Stier (looking at first United States patent grant):** p.776, Washington D.C., 1955, AP/Wide World Photos. Reproduced by permission; **Cooke, Jay:** p.215, portrait. Archive Photos. Reproduced by permission; **Corn piled high outside, Magnolia, Minnesota, 1995:** p.389, photograph by Jim Mone. AP/Wide World Photos. Reproduced by permission; **Cotton Gin:** p.219, Corbis-Bettmann Newsphotos. Reproduced by permission; **Couch, Paula (lifting tobacco plants), Simpsonville, Kentucky, 1998:** p.1006, photograph by Tony Gutierrez. AP/Wide World Photos. Reproduced by permission; **Cowboy with lasso during roundup on the Sherman Ranch, Genessee, Kansas:** p.222, National Archives and Records Administration; **Death of General Wolfe:** p.347, engraving. Archive Photos. Reproduced by permission; **Deere, John:** p.232, Ward/Corbis-Bettmann. Reproduced by permission; **Destitute sharecroppers, family of nine:** p.912, Corbis-Bettmann. Reproduced by permission; **Diagram titled Aggregate Demand:** p.14, illustration by Smith & Santori. The Gale Group; **Disney, Walt, "Mickey Mouse" (on Disney's knee), "Donald Duck" (on table), Miami, Florida, 1941:** p.247, AP/Wide World Photos. Reproduced by permission; **Dix, Dorothea:** p.250, AP/Wide World Photos. Reproduced by permission; **Dow, Charles:** p.252, AP/Wide World Photos. Reproduced by permission; **du Pont, Éleuthère Irénée:** p.260, The Library of Congress; **Eastman, George (sitting in stateroom, holding camera):** p.271, Corbis-Bettmann Newsphotos. Reproduced by permission; **Edison, Thomas (with his tinfoil phonograph):** p.277, Washington D. C., AP/Wide World Photos. Reproduced by permission; **Erie Canal Opening, 1825, engravings:** p.295, Archive Photos. Reproduced by permission; **Family posed with covered wagon, Loup Valley, Nebraska, 1886:** p.221, National Archives and Records Administration; **Family watching television, 1948:** p.286, AP/Wide World Photos. Reproduced by permission; **Female workers examining textiles for imperfections, 1912:** p.1000, Boston, Massachusetts, Corbis-Bettmann. Reproduced by permission; **Field, Marshall:** p.315, Archive Photos. Reproduced by permission; **Food stamps paying for milk, bread and eggs, 1980:** p.328, UPI/Corbis-Bettmann. Reproduced by permission; **Ford, Henry I (sitting in car):** p.330, Library of Congress; **Franke, Ernest A. (sitting in a Model T Ford):** p.651, Washington DC, 1938. AP/Wide World Photos. Reproduced

by permission; **Franklin, Benjamin:** p.338, painting. The Library of Congress; **Freedman's Bureau (man wearing military uniform, standing between groups):** p.343, Harper's Weekly; **Fuller, R. Buckminster (standing next to Playsphere):** p.352, Cambridge, Massachusetts, 1962, AP/Wide World Photos. Reproduced by permission; **Gates, Bill (holding Microsoft Money software):** p.361, New York, NY, 1991, photograph by David A. Cantor. AP/Wide World Photos. Reproduced by permission; **Gerber baby food, Detroit, Michigan, 1994:** p.371, photograph by Bill Waugh. AP/Wide World Photos. Reproduced by permission; **Gold Rush (California, African American gold miner standing, holding shovel):** p.379, Archive Photos. Reproduced by permission; **Gompers, Samuel (wearing tuxedo and glasses):** p.383, The Library of Congress; **Goodyear, Charles:** p.384, sketch. The Library of Congress; **Gould, Jay (in light suit and vest):** p.387, Archive Photos. Reproduced by permission; **Graph, Real Gross Domestic Product in Constant 1992 Dollars, 1959-1998:** p.407, illustration by Smith & Santori. The Gale Group; **Graph, birth rate, Baby Boom, 1940-1960:** p.71, illustration by George Barille. The Gale Group; **Graph, Total Trolley Coach Passengers, 1928-1970:** p.968, illustration by Smith & Santori. The Gale Group; **Graph, "Trustbusting" Administrations, 1891-1920:** p.1026, illustration by Smith & Santori. The Gale Group; **Great Railway Strike, cavalry on horses escorting train, drawn:** p.401, drawing by G. W. Peters from a sketch by G. A. Coffin. Library of Congress; **Great Serpent Mound:** p.402, The Library of Congress; **Greenspan, Alan (right hand in pocket, left on back of chair):** p.406, 1989, photograph by Dennis Cook. AP/Wide World Photos. Reproduced by permission; **Guggenheim, Daniel:** p.409, AP/Wide World Photos. Reproduced by permission; **Hammer, Armand:** p.414, The Library of Congress; **Harley Davidson motorcycle:** p.418, Archive Photos. Reproduced by permission; **Hauling a harpooned whale aboard Norwegian whaling vessel:** p.1112, photograph by Morgan, Greenpeace. Reproduced by permission; **Haymarket Square Riot:** p.427, painting. The Library of Congress; **Hearst, William Randolph:** p.429, The Library of Congress; **Hill, James Jerome:** p.435, drawing. Archive Photos. Reproduced by permission; **"His Master's Voice" ('Nipper' the dog sitting with phonograph):** p.861, painting by Francis Barraud. AP/Wide World Photos. Reproduced by permission; **Hoffa, James (sitting behind microphones):** p.439, Washington, DC., 1967, AP/Wide World Photos. Reproduced by permission; **"Hooverville" outside a factory during the Depression:** p.445, Archive Photos/American Stock. Reproduced by permission; **Hughes, Howard (standing** behind pilot's seat): p.451, 1947. AP/Wide World Photos. Reproduced by permission; **Iacocca, Lee, speaking at a Chrysler function:** p.456, 1992. Archive Photos. Reproduced by permission; **Industrial breweries, man filling kegs:** p.118, Archive Photos. Reproduced by permission; **Jackson, Andrew, drawing:** p.503, The Library of Congress; **Jefferson, Thomas (head and shoulders, turned slightly to his right), engraving:** p.509, The National Portrait Gallery/Smithsonian Institution; **Kelley, Florence:** p.525, UPI/Corbis-Bettmann. Reproduced by permission; **King, Dr. Martin Luther, Jr., Andrew Young, Ralph Abernathy, Eva Gracelemon, Aritha Willis (King's arms around girls), Grenada, Mississippi:** p.539, 1966, AP/Wide World Photos. Reproduced by permission; **Klu Klux Klan:** p.551, Corbis-Bettmann. Reproduced by permission; **Kroc, Ray (holding hamburger in front of a McDonald's):** p.549, AP/Wide World Photos. Reproduced by permission; **Los Angeles police officer:** p. 460, UPI/Corbis-Bettmann. Reproduced by permission; **Landing at Ellis Island, people walking across bridge:** p.281, The Library of Congress; **Langbo, Arnold, Tony the Tiger, shaking hands, Kellogg's Frosted Flakes:** p.527, 1996. Archive Photos. Reproduced by permission; **Lease, Mary E.,(wearing dark dress with high ruffled collar):** p.569, The Library of Congress; **Lewis, John L.:** p.577, The Library of Congress; **Line graph, Balance of Trade (deficit, 1976-1994):** p.73, illustration by George Barille. The Gale Group; **Line graph, Unemployment and Inflation, 1960-1985:** p.951, illustration by George Barille. The Gale Group; **Line graph, Embargo Act of 1807 (tonnage, foreign trade in U.S. ports, 1790-1815):** p.284, illustration by George Barille. The Gale Group; **Line graph, Growing Opposition to the War, 1965-1973:** p.814, illustration by George Barille. The Gale Group; **Line graph, Radios in Homes, 1922-1929:** p.852, illustration by George Barille. The Gale Group; **Line graph, Railroads (miles of track laid per year, 1830-1930):** p.854, illustration by George Barille. The Gale Group; **Line graph, Rate of Inflation, 1960-1994:** p.483, illustration by George Barille. The Gale Group; **Line graph, Stock Market Prices, 1920-1932:** p.397, illustration by George Barille. The Gale Group; **Line graph, The Labor Movement (union density for years 1930-1978):** p.554, illustration by George Barille. The Gale Group; **Line graph, Merger Movement, 1895-1904:** p.622, illustration by George Barille. The Gale Group; **Living room furniture in showroom:** p.355, c. 1950. Archive Photos. Reproduced by permission; **Loggers working in forest:** p.592, Archive Photos. Reproduced by permission; **Long, Huey P.:** p.583, The Library of Congress;

Long Island, New York (houses): p.574, Corbis-Bettmann. Reproduced by permission; **Man breaking open a barrel of liquor during Prohibition:** p.279, The Library of Congress; **Man cooling off after Chicago fire:** p.159, Chicago, Illinois, 1871, photograph by G.N. Barnard. AP/Wide World Photos. Reproduced by permission; **Man writing sign ("No Work Tomorrow"):** p.395, National Archives and Records Administration; **Map of western United States showing route of Lewis and Clark's exploration of the West:** p.587, illustration by XNR Productions. Gale Research; **Marshall Field's State Street store, 1879, Chicago, Illinois, painting:** p.239, Dayton Hudson Corporation. Reproduced by permission; **McCormick, Cyrus H.:** p.614, engraving. The Library of Congress; **McDevitt, William (displaying Susan B. Anthony dollars), Philadelphia:** p.642, 1979. AP/Wide World Photos. Reproduced by permission; **Men on boat, pulling in net of fish:** p.319, photograph by Robert Visser, Greenpeace. Reproduced by permission; **Men working in television station control room, Burbank, California:** p.682, 1955. AP/Wide World Photos. Reproduced by permission; **Microsoft Corporate headquarters:** p.633, Microsoft Corporation. Reproduced by permission; **Migrant worker with her five children, Fresno, California:** p.396, 1937. AP/Wide World Photos. Reproduced by permission; **Missionaries in camp on way to the Klondike, c. 1897, Alaska Territory:** p.542, photograph by LaRoche. Corbis. Reproduced by permission; **Morgan, J. P.:** p.663, Archive Photos. Reproduced by permission; **Morse, Samuel Finley Breese (standing by invention), painting:** p.667, The Library of Congress; **Nebraska Gas Company pipeline:** p.146, Archive Photos. Reproduced by permission; **New York City slums, five youngsters playing, New York City:** p.373, 1950. AP/Wide World Photos. Reproduced by permission; **New York Stock Exchange, balloons being released, New York City:** p.722, 1997. photograph by Emile Wamsteker. AP/Wide World Photos. Reproduced by permission; **Nielson, A.C., Sr.:** p.723, UPI/Corbis-Bettmann. Reproduced by permission; **Nolan, Mary in "Shanghai Lady:"** p.41, Corbis-Bettmann. Reproduced by permission; **Nuclear power plant complex (cooling tower at left):** p.740, photograph by Robert J. Huffman. Field Mark Publications. Reproduced by permission; **Panama Canal, foot gate slightly open, Panama, 1904-1914:** p.766, Archive Photos. Reproduced by permission; **Perkins, Frances:** p.784, AP/Wide World Photos. Reproduced by permission; **Pike's Peak, evergreen tree in foreground:** p.793, 1956. AP/Wide World Photos. Reproduced by permission; **Pinkham, Lydia Estes (oval format, cameo pinned to jabot):** p.798, Archive Photos. Reproduced by permission; **Porter scratching head, looking at rows of shoes:** p.121, Archive Photos. Reproduced by permission; **Post, Charles:** p.807, The Library of Congress; **Powderly, Terence Vincent (sitting at desk, writing):** p.817, The Library of Congress; **Pulitzer, Joseph (wearing pince-nez, thick dark hair and beard):** p.838, Archive Photos. Reproduced by permission; **Pullman strike, 1894, workmen pulling spikes from railway switches, train approaching men, engraving:** p.842, Archive Photos. Reproduced by permission; **Rand, Ayn (standing on city streets):** p.858, 1962. AP/Wide World Photos. Reproduced by permission; **Rath & Wright's buffalo hide yard, 1878, Dodge City, Kansas:** p.126, National Archives and Records Administration; **Reagan, Ronald (looking front, smiling, dotted tie):** p.862, 1981. The Library of Congress; **Reaper:** p.615, Corbis-Bettmann Newsphotos. Reproduced by permission; **Recruitment sign of Uncle Sam, "I want You," Washington:** p.908, 1961, AP/Wide World Photos. Reproduced by permission; **"Repeal the 18th Amendment" (woman putting sign on spare tire):** p.1030, The Library of Congress; **Reuther, Walter, and George Meany, New York:** p.34, 1955. UPI/Corbis-Bettmann. Reproduced by permission; **Revere, Paul (on horseback), illustration:** p.874, National Archives and Records Administration; **Robinson, Jackie (toeing home plate), 1955 World Series.:** p.82, AP/Wide World Photos. Reproduced by permission. **Rockefeller, John D. (wearing tweed suit, patterned vest):** p.881, Archive Photos. Reproduced by permission; **Roosevelt, Franklin (smiling into radio microphones):** p.883, The Library of Congress; **Rosie the Riveter (woman using a rivet gun):** p.884, Archive Photos. Reproduced by permission; **Rubber Pressing Machines:** p.1042, Archive Photos. Reproduced by permission; **Sacajawea (pointing), Meriwether Lewis, William Clark:** p.575, drawing by Alfred Russell. Corbis-Bettmann. Reproduced by permission; **Segregation sign (officer placing segregation sign), Jackson, Mississippi:** p.802, 1956, AP/Wide World Photos. Reproduced by permission; **Shays' Rebellion (two men fighting), Massachusetts, c. 1786, engraving:** p.913, Archive Photos. Reproduced by permission; **Silent movie theater with orchestra pit, illustration:** p.671, Archive Photos. Reproduced by permission; **Singer, Isaac Merritt:** p.922, illustration; **"Southern Industry" (black man standing with bag of picked cotton), c. 1850, engraving:** p.9, Corbis-Bettmann. Reproduced by permission; **Stanford, Amasa Leland (wearing dark three piece Regency style suit), engraving:** p.955, Archive Photos. Reproduced by permission; **States, maps of** The Gale Group; **Stock Market Crash (man selling car):** p.965, UPI/Corbis-Bettmann. Reproduced by

permission; **Studebaker, couple outside, women inside:** p.970, AP/Wide World Photos. Reproduced by permission; **Sunset over Appalachians, Stone Mountain, Virginia:** p.50, 1998. Photograph by Amy Sancetta. AP/Wide World Photos. Reproduced by permission; **Taft, William Howard:** p.977, The Library of Congress; **Tarbell, Ida M. (flowers in her lap and on her dress):** p.980, The Library of Congress; **Tecumseh, lithograph:** p.985, National Portrait Gallery. Reproduced by permission; **Telephone operators, connecting calls at switchboard:** p.1122, ca. 1940, AP/Wide World Photos. Reproduced by permission; **The original Colt Revolver:** p.195, Corbis-Bettmann. Reproduced by permission; **Three demonstrators seated at lunch counter while crowd harasses them:** p.171, AP/Wide World Photos. Reproduced by permission; **Trans-Alaska pipeline and pump station, Fairbanks, Alaska:** p.30, photograph by Al Grillo. AP/Wide World Photos. Reproduced by permission; **Transcontinental railroad line, two engineers shaking hands, Promontory Summit, Utah:** p.1015, 1869. photograph by Andrew J. Russell. AP/Wide World Photos. Reproduced by permission; **Truman, Harry (holding copy of Chicago Tribune with headline "Dewey Defeats Truman"):** p.1021, AP/Wide World Photos. Reproduced by permission; **Two children in dust storm (pumping water), Springfield, Colorado:** p.265, 1935. AP/ Wide World Photos. Reproduced by permission; **U.S.S. Shaw exploding at Pearl Harbor, December 7, 1941:** p.1132, National Archives and Records Administration; **Unemployed lining up outside a relief kitchen opened in New York City:** p.240, AP/Wide World Photos. Reproduced by permission; **Universal stock ticker:** p.964, AP/Wide World Photos. Reproduced by permission; **Vanderbilt, Cornelius (white hair, formal dress), print:** p.1057, The Library of Congress; **Wall Street, Christmas tree in front of New York Stock Exchange:** p.1074, 1997. photograph by Mark Lennihan. AP/Wide World Photos. Reproduced by permission; **Washington, Booker T. (seated at a desk):** p.1093, The Library of Congress; **Washington, George, at Valley Forge, engraving:** p.36, National Archives and Records Administration; **Wilson, Woodrow:** p.1117, The Library of Congress; **Women marching for the right to vote:** p.1125, Archive Photos/Hackett Collection. Reproduced by permission; **Women workers assembling aircraft (long rows of glass domes):** p.442, National Archives and Records Administration; **Wright, Frank Lloyd (standing, model of Guggenheim Museum):** p.1136, New York City, 1945, AP/Wide World Photos. Reproduced by permission; **Young girl standing by a power loom:** p.161, National Archives and Records Administration.

Contents by Era

Many topics do not fit easily into the categories that we have created for them. Companies are placed in the era in which they were founded. Industries and people are placed in the era when they first flourished. Geographic terms have been placed in eras only when it seemed logical to do so. No attempt has been made to list historical economic terms. The reader is advised to use the index for terms that cannot be found in this table of contents.

WAR AND COMMERCIAL INDEPENDENCE, 1790–1815 . . . . **v2**, 1078

EARLY REPUBLIC TO CIVIL WAR, 1815–1860 . . . . **v1**, 267

CIVIL WAR AND INDUSTRIAL EXPANSION, 1860–1897

AN ERA OF ECONOMIC INSTABILITY, 1897–1920

Preface

The *Gale Encyclopedia of U.S. Economic History* offers to students comprehensive coverage of American economic history from the Paleolithic Age to the present with an emphasis on the nineteenth and twentieth centuries. The topics selected for inclusion by our board of advisors have been chosen to support most textbooks on American history, and this work should be a useful tool for juniors and seniors in high school and first- and second-year college students who are beginning an investigation of the subject. The student will find articles on the Aztec, Maya, and Inca, because many texts begin with a chapter on the early history of our southern neighbors. The history of Native Americans has also been included, so articles can be found on Mound Builders, Plains Indians, Five Civilized Tribes, the Trail of Tears and many other topics. Successful women and minority leaders are also to be found. There is, of course, a wealth of material on the rise of the United States as an industrial power. Brilliant inventors, labor unionizers, robber barons, reformers, political leaders, and manufacturers of products as disparate as Colt revolvers and modern computer software can all be found on these pages.

The articles in this book have been selected by a distinguished board of nine advisors that represents both university and high school teachers and librarians. It includes people from different regions of the country and varied ethnic backgrounds. Five of them have doctorates in American History or a related area. Professor Charles K. Hyde, a specialist in U.S. Economic History from Wayne State University, not only helped in the selection of topics, but also read and commented on every article in the book. The encyclopedia is immeasurably stronger because of his contribution.

Professor Hyde divided American history into ten eras. We have had a research scholar write an overview essay for each of these eras, and we expect that these overviews will help the beginning student place the whirl of facts presented in this book into its proper context. These eras will also provide the basis of organization for our table of contents and our chronology.

The book includes 1,003 articles; about half are economic terms and historical and geographic definitions. These articles are somewhat shorter than the others, and they include no bibliography. They will give rather concise explanations of such terms as Prairie, Cumberland Gap, Santa Fe Trail, or Knights of Labor. About 200 of these terms are economic in character, defining such concepts as Laissez Faire, Aggregate Demand, and Pay Equity. It is hoped that their addition will make this book useful to the student of economics as well as the student of history.

The remaining half of the book consists of overviews, issues, biographies, state economic histories, historical events, and company and industry histories. Each of these entries have a ''Further Reading'' section that will direct the student toward other works on the subject and may serve as the basis for writing research papers. The ''Further Reading'' will average about five citations, ranging from on-line encyclopedia articles to scholarly monographs. The Issues essays, a special feature of this book, contain discussions of topics that are currently a subject of public debate, like the flat tax, or have been so in the past, like slavery. Matters of current scholarly dispute, such as whether the Spanish or the English treated Native Americans better, are also included among the Issues.

The book is organized in word-by-word alphabetical order. Most articles can be found under the full name of the entity and not the acronym. For example, IBM will be found under ''International Business Machines'' and not ''IBM.'' The exceptions to this rule are few. In some cases the acronym has become the company name, like the AT&T Corporation or RCA Victor. The OPEC Oil Embargo is our only instance of an event that contains an acronym, and it has been allowed to stand. A student who knows only the acronym should check the index to find the full name of the institution.

Introduction

Beginning students of American economic history and their teachers will find this encyclopedia to be a valuable source of information on the complex mosaic of people, businesses, industries, single events, and longer-lived movements and trends that together comprise the economic and social history of the United States. In teaching U.S. economic history over the past quarter-century, I have concluded that students struggle with the subject matter more than with other varieties of history. What makes the field difficult is the requirement that students learn basic economic concepts and at the same time come to grips with long-term, complex historical developments and trends. Students must also familiarize themselves with a long list of individuals and institutions, which were important forces in American economic and social history. In bringing all of this information together into a single reference work for the first time, this encyclopedia will be a valuable helpmate to students and teachers alike.

This encyclopedia has a variety of distinctive types of entries which is its real strength as a reference tool. The **Era Overviews** provide an overall chronological and thematic framework for more than four hundred years of American economic history. They help readers identify the major long-term economic changes within each era, providing a ''big picture'' focus. A second type of entry, **Issues in Economic History**, also emphasize long-term influences and policy issues, such as the role of immigrants in the national economy or the use of child labor. These entries remind the reader that issues or problems in economic history can extend beyond the boundaries of narrow chronological periods.

Students interested in the economic history of a particular colony or state will find the **Geographical Profiles** of great value. There is often a natural interest in the economic history of one's own state or even a requirement that students learn their state's history.

Textbooks sometimes discuss the economic development of individual colonies during the eighteenth century, but seldom carry that history into the nineteenth or twentieth centuries.

The more specific developments in U.S. economic history are analyzed using several complementary approaches. Entries that focus on **Key Events and Movements** take a broad approach to the causes and effects of major developments, while the **Biographies** emphasize the importance of the human actors in economic history. The **Historic Business and Industry Profiles** focus on the importance of profit-seeking firms or corporations and some of the key industries in the shaping of the economy over time.

Finally, the inclusion of **Economic Concepts and Terms** greatly aids the student who has little or no background in basic economics. American economic history textbooks for colleges and high schools typically assume that the student has completed at least one economics course and therefore is familiar with basic economic concepts. These textbooks rarely include a glossary.

The multiple approaches to U.S. economic history employed in this encyclopedia are its greatest strength. By including company and industry histories, biographies, key events and movements, critical issues in economic and social history, state economic histories, and the major eras in American economic development, these volumes enable the student to try various intellectual strategies in considering almost any topic. This encyclopedia will not only allow students to better understand materials presented in class and in readings, but will also serve as a basic resource and guide to further research.

Charles K. Hyde
Professor of History
Wayne State University

Chronology

SETTLEMENT AND ECONOMIC DEVELOPMENT: THE COLONIES TO 1763

50,000–5000 B.C.: During the last Ice Age, a migration of hunting and gathering peoples from Siberia cross over the "land bridge" (called Beringia) to North America. This land bridge is the result of the lower water levels caused by the large amount of water taken up in the glaciers. This migration of Paleo-Indians (ancient Indian people) disperses throughout the Western Hemisphere and develops different food cultures.

15,000–8000 B.C.: Among the Paleo-Indian people living in what later comes to be North America some develop a characteristic stone spear point called the clovis point. It is used for hunting large animals.

400 B.C.–A.D. 1700: Mound Builders occupy portions of eastern and central North America. They grow out of an older culture known to archaeologists as Mississippian. The early Mississippian built centers of a large trade network. The Mound Builders, without the aid of horses or mules, transport hundreds of tons of dirt to build burial mounds shaped like flat-topped pyramids. Some of these mounds are shaped like animals, such as the Great Serpent Mound of Adena, constructed in about A.D. 1000, near what becomes Cincinnati, Ohio. The Hopewell are also mound builders; they live in the area later known as eastern Ohio. The Cahokia mounds near what becomes St. Louis, Missouri, house a city of 40,000 people. Their peak development is around A.D. 1200.

800 B.C.: The Maya civilization in the southeast Yucatan peninsula of the land that becomes Mexico reaches its height.

1000: The Norse establish a settlement at L'Anse aux Meadows in Newfoundland.

1325: The Aztec build the city of Tenochtitlán, a site on what later becomes Mexico City.

1492: On his first exploratory voyage west across the Atlantic Ocean, Christopher Columbus encounters islands in the Caribbean Sea, mistakes them for the east Indies, and claims them for Spain.

1494: Spain and Portugal divide the New World between them in the Treaty of Tordesillas.

1497: John Cabot explores the coast of North America, up to the Delaware River.

1513: Vasco Núñez de Balboa crosses the isthmus of Panama and discovers the Pacific Ocean.

1513: Juan Ponce de León explores the coast of what comes to be the state of Florida.

ca.1500–late 1800s: Pandemics of European diseases for which the native populations of the Western Hemisphere have no immunity—smallpox, influenza, typhus, measles, etc.—run rampant through the Native American populations, killing as many as 95 percent of the people and reappearing periodically.

1518–1519: Spanish conquistador Hernando Cortés invades Mexico, enters Tenochtitlán with an army, and takes Aztec emperor Montezuma II prisoner.

1530s: Bartolomé de Las Casas, a Spanish priest and bishop in southern Mexico, criticizes the Spanish regime of exploitation, land theft, and murder of Native Americans.

1531–1533: Spanish conquistador Francisco Pizarro subjugates the Inca civilization of Peru in the quest for gold.

1535: French explorer Jacques Cartier discovers the St. Lawrence River while looking for a northwest passage to Asia.

1539–1540: Spanish conquistador Hernando de Soto explores the southeastern region of what would become the United States and discovers the Mississippi River.

1540–1541: Spanish conquistador Francisco Vásquez de Coronado, at the head of a large expeditionary force, explores the southwestern region of what becomes the United States.

1542: Spain reforms its *encomienda* system. The Spanish *conquistadores* are no longer allowed to enslave Indian people in the New World, but they may still receive tribute in money and crops from the Indian population.

1550s–1560s: The English attempt to subdue Ireland through a brutal occupation and expropriation of Irish land. The English colonizers are led by a handful of adventurers—Sir Humphrey Gilbert, Sir Walter Raleigh, and Sir Richard Grenville—who believe the Irish to be savages. Their genocidal conduct of the war in Ireland shapes their attitudes towards the indigenous people that they meet in the New World.

1565: St. Augustine, Florida, is founded by the Spanish explorer Pedro Menéndez de Avilés.

1585–1603: A privateering war takes place between England and Spain.

1587: England establishes the lost colony of Roanoke off the Chesapeake coast. The expedition, composed of families, vanishes, leaving behind the cryptic inscription ''CROATOAN'' (the name of a nearby island) carved on a piece of wood.

1588: England—with the help of a big storm—defeats the great Spanish Armada.

1607: One hundred and four men and boys form an English settlement at Jamestown, Virginia; approximately one-half of the inhabitants die before the end of the year. Jamestown becomes the second oldest town in North America, after St. Augustine, and the first permanent British settlement.

1608: The French succeed in establishing a permanent settlement in Quebec.

1609: Henry Hudson explores the Hudson River.

1610: The Spanish establish Santa Fe in the northern Mexico territory.

1612: Jamestown planter John Rolf begins experimenting with growing tobacco. Tobacco cultivation is soon thriving in Virginia.

1610–1680: During these years, most of the labor needs in the tobacco-growing Chesapeake are filled by indentured servants (who work for a landowner for a set period of time, usually seven years, after which they are free to settle anywhere they can find land to buy).

1616–1618: The ''head-right'' system, by which 50 acres are awarded to any person who pays for and sponsors transportation of a new worker to the Virginia plantations, is introduced to encourage immigration to Virginia.

1619: Carried aboard a Dutch vessel, approximately two dozen African people are transported to Virginia, possibly employed as indentured servants; other early African settlers on the English mainland colonies are most probably enslaved.

1619: The Virginia House of Burgesses (the colonial legislature) meets for the first time.

1620: Anchored on the *Mayflower* off of what becomes Cape Cod, Massachusetts, William Bradford and 41 Separatist Puritan heads of households sign the Mayflower Compact, establishing a community with the authority to make laws as necessary.

1621: The Puritans celebrate their first Thanksgiving at Plymouth.

1622: A Powhatan Indian confederation under the leadership of Opechancanough attacks English settlements along the James River in Virginia, killing about one quarter of the English colonists. The attack is prompted by the expansion of English settlement. It is the first large Indian attack against English settlers.

1624: The Dutch found the colony of New Amsterdam, which is later renamed New York.

1630: John Winthrop and the Massachusetts Bay Company, composed of English Puritans, sail to Massachusetts Bay and establish a colony.

1634: James I grants the Calvert family a proprietary charter for Maryland. The Calverts, who are Catholic, establish freedom of religion in the colony.

1635: Roger Williams escapes deportation to England for championing the rights of the Native Americans. Williams takes the public position that the English king has no right to grant land to Englishmen when the land already belongs to the Indians. Williams is expelled from Massachusetts. He founds Rhode Island and its first town, Providence, and drafts its first constitution, which declares the separation of church and state and the freedom of religious expression.

1636: The colony of Connecticut is founded.

1630–1640: There is a "great migration" of English peasants to the New World. These peasants are frequently the wandering refugees of the enclosure movement of the sixteenth and seventeenth centuries, when the peasants' leases to English farmland are terminated and the land is enclosed by hedges and turned over to sheep pasturage. Rather than starve, the peasants often become outlaws or "sturdy beggars," given to larceny, robbery, and poaching on the local lords' land. Parliament passes harsh laws and the peasants, when caught in some misbehavior, are sometimes given the option of being hanged or being transported to Virginia as indentured servants.

1636: Harvard College is founded in Massachusetts.

1636–1637: Pequot Indians attack the new settlement of Wethersfield and kill a handful of English settlers. A detachment of Massachusetts citizens and their Narragansett Indian allies attack a Pequot town on the Mystic River, killing upwards of 400 Pequots, mostly women and children.

1638: Anne Huchinson is banished from Massachusetts for professing an inner awareness of God and of the certainty of salvation.

1642–1648: The English Civil War, fought ostensibly as a struggle of different religious groupings (Catholics, Anglicans, and various strains of Puritans) to dominate the English government, also reflects a social revolution going on in England in which a non-titled gentry and merchant class demand a greater say in the running of government.

1644: Indians again attack English settlements in Virginia. This marks the second great Indian attack against settlers in the region.

1649: As the concluding act of the English Civil War, Catholic King Charles II is beheaded and Oliver Cromwell, the military leader of the Puritans, becomes the "Protector" of the nation and rules England until his death in 1658.

1651, 1660: The English Parliament passes the first of the Navigation Acts, which stipulate that the trade between New England and England has to be shipped on English or colonial ships. Granting this monopoly

to colonial merchant ships, the Parliament went on to rule that certain exports from the colonies could only be traded with England, not with other European nations. The other main Navigation Acts are passed in 1663 and 1676. They refine the rules of trade between the mainland colonies, England, Europe, the West Indies, and Africa.

1652–1654: A trade war between the English and the Dutch begins.

1660: Charles II (and the House of Stuart) is restored to the English throne after the conclusion of the English Civil War and Cromwell's Protectorate.

1662: The Puritan notion of town government includes a religious dimension of active participation in the church. The "selectmen"—those who take care of the town government between elections—are generally strong church members. But the Puritan notion of the church is that it is a community of "saints" who have already experienced God's grace and are assured of salvation. As the towns' populations grow, there is a diminishing proportion of the population who can say that they have had this religious experience. Especially among the younger people, Puritans seem to be more interested in working on their farms and in raising their families than in church life. This leads to a change in the Puritan doctrine about the church. Solomon Stoddard, a theologian and pastor in Northampton, Massachusetts, proposes the "Halfway Covenant" in 1662. It holds that a person's profession of faith, rather than his or her experience of God's grace, is sufficient to become a member of the church and that their offspring can be baptized.

1663: The Carolina colony is chartered. Most of its white settlers are the so-called adventurers from Barbados and other West Indies islands whose slave economies rest mainly on sugar cane production and refining.

1664: The Dutch colony of New Netherlands is seized by an English fleet and renamed New York.

1670s: Indentured servitude is on the decline; slavery rises in the Chesapeake and in the South.

1675–1676: King Philip's War (or Metacomet's War) begins in outlying parts of Massachusetts as the Wampanoag Indian tribe reacts to English encroachment on their land. The two-year conflict results in great loss of life and destruction for both sides. Twelve New England towns are leveled, and for every 10 white men of fighting age, one loses his life or is captured. The Indians, however, are overrun within a few months and their power is broken.

1676: Bacon's Rebellion pits Virginia's small frontier farmers against Governor William Berkeley. At issue is the attempt of Governor Berkeley and the English administration to restrain the incursions of the frontier farmers into Indian land. The short-lived rebellion reveals the tensions between the land-hungry small farmers, many of whom were former indentured servants, and the well-to-do tidewater colonial elite and British administration.

1680: The Pueblo revolt against the Spanish presence in northern Mexico.

1681: Charles II grants William Penn a proprietary charter in the land between Maryland and New York. Penn establishes his Frame of Government, which allows for the creation of an assembly, council, and governor's office in Pennsylvania.

1686: As part of the War of the Spanish Succession (1702–1713), known as Queen Anne's War in America, James Moore, the English governor of South Carolina, attacks Saint Augustine, Florida, burning outposts and missions in Apalachee, or northern Florida.

1688: During the bloodless Glorious Revolution the English Parliament deposes Stuart King James II and installs Mary (James' Protestant daughter) and her husband William (of the Dutch House of Orange) as limited monarchs, subordinate to Parliament.

1689: John Locke publishes *Concerning Toleration*, a key issue in the English Civil War.

1690s: South Carolina develops a strong economy in rice production.

1691: John Locke publishes *Two Treatises of Civil Government*, in which he argues that men establish governments and thus they can change or abolish governments. He says that both in a state of nature and in a civil society man has the absolute right to protect his life, liberty, and property. The revolutionary implication in this is that if the political system threatens life, liberty, or property, man has the right to overthrow it.

1692: Witchcraft trials take place in the town of Salem, Massachusetts. Nineteen people, mostly older women, are thought to be witches and are executed.

1696: A 15-member Board of Trade and Plantations, answerable to the king's ministers, is established in England to oversee commercial (trade and fishing) and political (powers of appointment and legislative review) matters in the American colonies.

1699: The French found Mobile, New Orleans, and Pensacola settlements on the Gulf coast.

1701: Sieur de Cadillac, a French explorer, founds Detroit on a strategically valuable narrow section of the sailing route through the Great Lakes.

1704: The first regular newspaper—*The Boston Newsletter*—makes its appearance in the colonies.

1720: Slave rebellion breaks out in New York City. Nine whites die and 21 slaves are executed.

1732: The Georgia colony is chartered.

1730s–1740s: In order to forestall the secular and non-religious direction of culture in the colonies, theologians and church leaders set out to inject a new evangelical religious message into the popular culture. Circuit riding preachers cover the colonies in nighttime camp meetings and the emotional preaching spreads like wildfire, especially among the poor white farmers, sometimes seated in the same audiences with slaves, who are also powerfully affected by the message of redemption. Preachers from England like George Whitfield evangelize on the grace of God to those who would take their own salvation seriously. Others, like Jonathan Edwards of Massachusetts hold forth on the depravity of sinners and the horrors of hell. The movement is called the Great Awakening, and it becomes an important aspect of early American life which links the colonies together in a shared culture.

1739: The Stono slave rebellion breaks out, the first major slave uprising in the southern mainland English colonies. The rebellion kills 25 whites. Over 30 slaves are executed.

1740s: South Carolina begins to cultivate indigo.

1754–1763: The French and Indian War is fought between Great Britain, its colonies and European and Indian allies, versus France and its Indian and European allies.

1754: The Albany Plan, formulated by Benjamin Franklin, is rejected. It would have joined the colonies in a defense against the French and would have established an inter-colonial council to handle relations with the Native Americans..

1759: During the war with France the British capture Quebec.

1760: The French army surrenders to the British in Montreal.

1763: The Treaty of Paris is signed, concluding the French and Indian War; Britain is given Canada and all French territory east of the Mississippi River and Florida.

THE AGE OF REVOLUTION, 1763–1790

1763: England issues the Proclamation of 1763. This document prohibits English colonists from settling on the western side of the Appalachian watershed. It is meant to prevent unnecessary friction between the colonists and the Indian tribes. It also makes it easier to tax the colonists. The declaration itself, however, is frequently violated and a robust farming culture springs up in the Ohio valley.

1765: To defray the cost of the French and Indian War in North America, the British impose the Stamp Act on the American colonies as a means of raising tax revenue.

1765: Protests and riots break out in response to the Stamp Act.

1766: Parliament repeals the Stamp Act.

1767–1781: ''Regulator Movements'' in South Carolina and North Carolina protest the lack of representation of poorer, back country farmers in the colonial assemblies, which are dominated by the established, well-to-do plantation owners of the tidewater coastal plains.

1767: The Townshend Acts are passed in Parliament. They establish new import taxes on trade goods like paper, glass, and tea. Unlike previous import taxes on the colonies, the Townshend Acts are levied against items shipped from England, rather than from the European mainland. The money that they raised was to be used to pay the salaries of the royal officials stationed in the colonies.

1770: The Boston Massacre occurs, in which British troops fire on a Boston mob that is pelting them with icy snowballs in retaliation for the British troops' practice of supplementing their meager wages by ''moonlighting'' after-hours on laborer jobs, thus taking employment away from American workers.

1773: Members of the protest group the Sons of Liberty, dressed as Indians, sneak aboard a British merchant ship lying at anchor and dump its cargo of 90,000 pounds of tea into Boston Harbor.

1773: The Committees of Correspondence publicize the grievances of the colonial population and discuss the options open to the colonists.

1774: The Coercive (or Intolerable) Acts pass in England and close Boston Harbor, attacking Massachusetts' right to self-rule and subjecting the populace to the indignities of the Quartering Act, which gives the military authorities the right to require colonial subjects to house their troops and horses. Instead of abandoning Massachusetts to fend for itself, the rest of the colonies send delegates to the First Continental Congress in Philadelphia to debate the means of resistance open to them. They also draft a Declaration of Rights and Grievances which combines a feigned submission to England's authority with a clear determination to obey only those acts of Parliament that they judge to be ''in the mutual interest of both countries,'' an unforgivable act of insolence in British eyes.

April 1775: The British decide to raid a site where the colonial rebels were said to have stored weapons. They march from Boston to Lexington and Concord, Massachusetts, initially dispersing the rag-tag American defenders, but they are unable to defend themselves against the sniping that wears on throughout the day.

May 1775: The Second Continental Congress meets and calls for the creation of an army to resist the British.

1775–1781: A war of national self-determination breaks out between the British and the Americans. The war is marked by the British attempt to corner the Americans and fight large battles to determine the outcome of the war. Instead, under the command of British-trained General George Washington, the Americans fight a war of mobility and harassment, with few large battles. Canada elects to remain loyal to the British crown.

1776: Thomas Paine publishes *Common Sense*, an immensely successful propaganda tract urging separation from England.

1776: Thomas Jefferson drafts the *Declaration of Independence* for the Second Continental Congress.

1776–1777: The first state constitutions emphasize the distrust of the Americans for a system of strong central government, which they had experienced under British rule. For instance, the authors of the

Pennsylvania state constitution refuse to create the office of governor.

1777: The Continental Congress drafts the Articles of Confederation, which accords little authority to the central government and vests most governing power (including the right to tax) in the states.

October 1777: In the Battle of Saratoga, New England militiamen surround the British army under General Burgoyne and force its surrender. This convinces the French that the Americans might actually win the war. Their long-term enmity with the British leads them to render important aid to the Americans, both in military provisions and in the use of the French fleet and the participation of French volunteers like General LaFayette.

1780: Pennsylvania becomes the first state to abolish slavery.

September 1781: General George Washington maneuvers the British, under the leadership of General Cornwallis, into a trap. Supported by French soldiers and by the French fleet at Yorktown, Cornwallis is forced to surrender his army of 7,000 soldiers and the British Parliament sues for peace.

1781: The *Articles of Confederation* are ratified.

1783: Under the Treaty of Paris the British recognize American independence.

1784, 1785, 1787: The Northwest Ordinances devise a systematic way to divide up and sell the land and to bring new states into the nation out of the Old Northwest territory east of the Mississippi River and north of the Ohio River, which Britain gave up in the Treaty of Paris.

1786: Thomas Jefferson authors the *Virginia Statute for Religious Freedom*, establishing ''freedom of conscience'' as the basis of the protection of all religious beliefs.

1786: Shays' Rebellion grows out of a post-war economic depression, caused in part by war-time inflation and England's dumping of manufactured goods on the American market once the war was over. This hurts the infant manufacturing industry. In addition, the shaky financial markets and the collapsing monetary system lead the state and local governments to raise taxes. Small farmers—many of them veterans of the Revolutionary War—begin losing their farms for non-payment of loans and taxes. In western Massachusetts they raise a rebellion, which the weak central government of the Articles of Confederation finds itself almost unable to put down.

1787: The new nation's political elite meet in Philadelphia, Pennsylvania, in February 1787, to write a *Constitution* devising a stronger national government. The resulting document operates on the principle of ''checks and balances'' between the branches of government and between the state and national governments.

1787–1788: Debate rages over whether the *Constitution* should be ratified. Anti-Federalists fear that the *Constitution* gives too much power to the central government and threatens democracy. Some Anti-Federalists call for a bill of rights guaranteeing specific individual liberties. James Madison, widely regarded as the ''architect of the *Constitution*,'' collaborates with Alexander Hamilton and John Jay in a series of articles collectively known as the *Federalist Papers*. These argue that the country is large enough that no single faction will be able to lord over the others, and that the variety and vitality of the economy require a strong central government to assure the stability of a representative democracy. Madison drafts the Bill of Rights, which become the first ten amendments to the *Constitution* in December 1791.

1787: Delaware, Pennsylvania and New Jersey ratify the *Constitution* and join the Union.

1788: Georgia, Connecticut, Massachusetts, Maryland, South Carolina, New Hampshire, Virginia, and New York join the Union.

1789: North Carolina becomes a state.

1789: The Judiciary Act of 1789 becomes law. The act defined the basic structure of the federal judicial system consisting of the Supreme Court, the District Courts, and the Circuit Courts.

1789: The *Constitution* is ratified by 11 of 13 states. George Washington is elected President of the United States.

1789: The French Revolution begins.

WAR AND COMMERCIAL INDEPENDENCE, 1790–1815

1790: Secretary of the Treasury Alexander Hamilton's proposals for federal funding of the states' Revolutionary War debt and for creating a national bank both become law. The proposals encounter opposition from Thomas Jefferson and James Madison, but do help the two to define their Republican, agrarian, states' rights politics.

1790: The District of Columbia is created.

1790: Rhode Island joins the Union.

1791: Vermont becomes the fourteenth state.

1791: Alexander Hamilton submits his *Report on Manufactures.* This part of his program advocates aid and protection for U.S. manufactures. The legislation does not meet with favor in Congress, although much of it later becomes law.

1792: Kentucky becomes the fifteenth state.

1792: President Washington is reelected.

1793: The Fugitive Slave Act passes through Congress and is signed into law, making it a crime to harbor a fugitive slave or to interfere with his or her arrest.

1793: Eli Whitney invents a workable version of the cotton gin (engine) to remove seeds from cotton.

1793: France enters a more radical phase of the French Revolution and begins guillotining (beheading) its internal enemies, including King Louis XVI. It soon becomes involved in war with England, Holland, and Spain, who are determined to stamp out the revolution before it spreads to their soil. France begins to exert pressure on the United States for support against England, arguing that France's support had been invaluable to the success of the American Revolution against England and that the United States was obligated under the Alliance of 1778 to help France. Washington and the Federalist government grant diplomatic recognition to France but issue a Neutrality Proclamation declaring the U.S. intention to remain uncommitted to either side but to trade with all.

1793: The French send Edmond Genêt to try to convince the Americans to reciprocate with military aid. Rather than presenting himself in Philadelphia to President Washington, Genêt lands in Charleston, South Carolina, and goes about contracting with United States citizens to engage in a privateer war against England. Although Thomas Jefferson and the Republicans favor supporting France and create the "Democratic-Republican Societies" in support of France, the relations between France and the United States remain cool.

1794: The Jay Treaty, the Federalist attempt to normalize relations with Great Britain, is signed. The United States wants British troops to vacate its frontier posts, and it also wants British assaults on U.S. shipping to cease. The British comply with the first item and ignore the second. The treaty is unpopular in the United States, especially among Jefferson and the Republicans.

1794: The Whiskey Rebellion breaks out in western Pennsylvania in reaction to the federal government's levying a tax on whiskey. President George Washington and Secretary of the Treasury Alexander Hamilton lead a federal force of 15,000 soldiers to disperse the rebels.

1794: At the Battle of Fallen Timbers west of what later becomes Toledo, Ohio, General Anthony Wayne, supported by the British (who held a fort in the vicinity), defeats the formidable Miami Indians.

1795: Pinkney's Treaty is signed. With this treaty Spain gives U.S. citizens the right to navigate the Mississippi River and to use the facilities in New Orleans to off-load river boats and reload onto ocean-going ships. The treaty also fixes the northern boundary of Florida at the 31st parallel and Spain promises to restrain Indian attacks across the border.

1796: John Adams is elected president.

1796: Tennessee becomes a state.

1796–1797: Relations between the United States and France deteriorate to the point that the French navy begins to waylay U.S. merchant ships and imprison the crews. The French also refuse to receive U.S. diplomat Charles Cotesworth Pinckney and, when Cotesworth is joined by John Marshall and Elbridge Gerry to negotiate these disagreements with the French government (called the "Directory"), they are solicited for a bribe by three French officials before negotiations could begin. The Americans refuse and the issue becomes known as the XYZ affair, after the acronym given the three French ministers in a report that U.S. President John Adams turns over to Congress. In spite of the sympathy to the French cause on the part of the Republicans as well as the fact that the relations between the United States and England are equally tense, U.S. public outrage against France is widespread. Hostile naval encounters occur between the French and the United States navies. This period (1798–1799) is called the Quasi War with France.

1798: Following the leadership of the Federalist Party, Congress passes the Naturalization Act, making it more difficult to become a U.S. citizen. Congress also passes the Alien and Sedition Acts, repressing political opposition.

1798: Jefferson and Madison write the Virginia and Kentucky Resolutions, successfully arguing for the limited and delegated nature of the federal government's power under the *Constitution.*

1800: Thomas Jefferson is elected president. It marks the first time that political power changes hands from one party to another and is peacefully accomplished. The Republican Congress repeals the Alien and Sedition Acts.

1800: President Adams sends another three-man commission to Paris to negotiate an end to the Quasi War. The new First Consul of France, Napoleon Bonaparte, receives the Americans and composes a new treaty relieving the U.S. of any obligations dating from the Alliance of 1778 and facilitating trade between France and the United States.

1801–1815: The Barbary Wars are fought.

1803: England and France become embroiled in the Napoleonic Wars.

1803: Chief Justice John Marshall rules in *Marbury v. Madison* that the Judiciary Act of 1799 is unconstitutional. This establishes a precedent—the power of judicial review over legislation. The federal judiciary, including the Supreme Court, now successfully asserts the power of ruling a law unconstitutional. This increases the power of the judiciary in the system of ''checks and balances'' between the different branches of government.

1803: Napoleon sells a vast expanse of land to the United States in the Louisiana Purchase, almost doubling the size of the nation.

1803: Ohio becomes a state.

1804: By order of President Jefferson, William Clark and Meriwether Lewis begin a long expedition into the territory recently acquired in the Louisiana Purchase. They return two-and-a-half years later with copious notes and observations of the Great Plains and the Oregon territory.

1804: Jefferson is elected for a second term as president.

1805: Both England and France begin to stop and board U.S. merchant ships to check for deserting members of their own nation's merchant marine (called impressment).

1807: Robert Fulton builds the steamboat *Clermont.* This changes shipping patterns, as shallow draft, paddle wheeler steamboats ply the rivers with bulk loads of staple products, livestock, and people. By the 1810s steam locomotion is applied to ocean-going packet ships, a development which quickens the pace of international commerce and alters immigration patterns.

1807: The *Chesapeake* affair, in which a U.S. Navy ship is fired on, stopped, and boarded by the British frigate the *Leopard*, occurs. The British remove a handful of American sailors, charge them as deserters of the British Navy and hang one of them. Between 1803 and 1812 over 6,000 American sailors are similarly subject to impressment.

1807: Faced with the problem of stopping impressment when the United States did not have sufficient naval forces to prevent it from happening, Jefferson calls for a total embargo on all U.S. shipping. This causes a major unemployment crisis, especially in the New England ports.

1809: Jefferson introduces the Non-intercourse Act, which declares the United States is ready to trade with any nation other than Great Britain and France and pledges to resume shipping with either England or France if they stop violating U.S. shipping rights.

1811: William Henry Harrison's army wins an important battle at Tippecanoe, in land that later becomes the state of Indiana. This victory disrupts the plans of the Shawnee leader called Tecumseh to form an Indian confederation to resist white incursions onto Indian land.

1812: Louisiana joins the Union.

1812: Congress declares war on Britain, which is already preoccupied with a larger war against Napoleon in Europe. In the War of 1812 neither the Americans nor the British are able to win a definitive victory.

1812: The British successfully blockade the Chesapeake and Delaware Bays. By 1813 the blockade extends to all the New England ports and the southern ports on the Gulf of Mexico.

1813: The Boston Manufacturing Company, under the leadership of Francis Cabot Lowell, installs a power loom for manufacturing textiles at Waltham, Massachusetts.

1813: The Americans, led by Commander Oliver Perry, win a naval victory on Lake Erie, gaining control of the Northwest Territory. Tecumseh sides with the British, captures Detroit, and is killed in the Battle of the Thames, in Ontario, but the Americans are unable to break Canada off from the British Empire.

1814: The British defeat Napoleon and are able to concentrate their attention on the war with the United States. In 1814 they raid and burn Washington, D.C., but are unable to take Fort McHenry in the Baltimore harbor.

1815: U.S. forces, under the command of General Andrew Jackson, win the concluding military encounter in the Battle of New Orleans.

EARLY REPUBLIC TO CIVIL WAR: 1815–1860

1816: Indiana becomes the 19th state to enter the Union.

1816: Connecticut abolishes the property qualification for white male voters.

1817–1818: General Andrew Jackson fights a two-year campaign against Florida Indians.

1817: Mississippi becomes a new state.

1817: The Rush-Bagot Treaty limits the number of warships that the United States and Canada can have on the Great Lakes.

1817: Construction begins on the Erie Canal in New York.

1818: The National Road reaches Wheeling, Virginia.

1818: The Convention of 1818 establishes a border between Canada and the United States from the Lake of the Woods in Minnesota west to the Rocky Mountains.

1818: Illinois becomes the 21st state to join the Union.

1819: The Panic of 1819 occurs.

1819: John Quincy Adams negotiates the Adams-Onís Treaty, in which Spain cedes Florida to the United States and the boundary between Spanish and U.S. land is defined all the way to the Pacific Ocean.

1819: Alabama becomes a state.

1820: Maine becomes a state.

1820: The order of admission to statehood in relation to balancing the pro- and anti-slavery forces in the Republic results in a crisis over the admission of Missouri as a slave state. Henry Clay devises a compromise in which Missouri joins the Union as a slave state; Maine is split off from Massachusetts and admitted as a free state, and no future slave states can be admitted north of Missouri's southern border.

1821: Missouri joins the Union.

1821: After an 8-year guerilla war of national liberation, Spain recognizes Mexico's independence.

1822: Founded in 1816 as a philanthropic precursor to the Abolitionist Movement, the American Colonization Society begins resettling freed African American former slaves to the West African country of Liberia in 1822 on land purchased from local tribes.

1823: Prompted by Secretary of State John Quincy Adams, President James Monroe announces the Monroe Doctrine, forbidding further European intervention in the emerging nations of the Western Hemisphere.

1825: The Erie Canal is completed.

1828: The Tariff of Abominations spawns a controversy between the North and South: Congress passes a tariff bill which strikes the political leadership of the South as contributing to high prices for consumer goods with no provisions to soften the impact on the agrarian South.

1830: The Baltimore and Ohio Railroad opens for operation.

1831–1838: The Trail of Tears becomes the name for a forced migration of the Cherokee Indian Nation from Georgia to Indian Territory west of the Mississippi River.

1831: William Lloyd Garrison begins to publish the Abolitionist newspaper, *The Liberator.*

1831: Nat Turner's bloody uprising in the southeastern part of Virginia kills 57 whites and results in the death of 200 slaves.

1831: Cyrus McCormick brings out the first mechanical reaping machine.

1832: Controversy brews between Andrew Jackson and Nicolas Biddle over the re-chartering of the Second National Bank.

1832: The Nullification Crisis pits North against South in a contest over states' rights versus national sovereignty.

1834: Women workers at the Lowell, Massachusetts, textile mills go on strike.

1834: The British Empire abolishes slavery.

1836–1842: The Seminole Indians are forced to migrate from Florida to land west of the Mississippi River.

1836: White Americans living in Texas secede and fight Mexican General Santa Anna. Victorious at San Jacinto in 1836, Texas declares itself a Republic.

1836: Arkansas becomes a state.

1837: Michigan becomes a state.

1841: Frederick Douglass begins his abolitionist lecturing career.

1841: The first wagon train bound for California leaves Independence, Missouri.

1844: A telegraph line links Baltimore, Maryland, and Washington, D.C.

1845: Texas joins the Union, precipitating the Mexican-American War.

1844–1848: Tensions build between the United States and Mexico, and, in 1846, the Mexican War breaks out. American General Winfield Scott captures Mexico City and the Mexican forces are defeated in 1847. Signed in 1848, the Treaty of Guadalupe Hidalgo cedes New Mexico and California to the United States.

1845: Florida joins the Union.

1845: The Irish potato famine begins, stimulating mass immigration to the United States.

1846: Iowa joins the United States.

1846: Brigham Young leads the trek of Mormons to Utah.

1847: In Missouri, the slave Dred Scott files a lawsuit against his owner to secure his freedom, using the argument that his master had taken him into free territory, at which point he was no longer a slave.

1848: Wisconsin becomes the 30th state to join the Union.

1848: Regularly scheduled steamship service is established between New York and Liverpool, England.

1849: The California gold rush begins.

1850: California joins the Union.

1850: Henry Clay and, later, Stephen Douglas devise the Compromise of 1850 to resolve the sectional crisis over slavery resulting from the Mexican War. A series of practical trade-offs are arranged, but they do not resolve the root causes of the contention, and the country does no more than buy itself another decade of peace.

1850s: The Abolitionist Movement gains powerful support from women like Sojourner Truth, Harriet Tubman, and Harriet Beecher Stowe, who in 1852 publishes her novel, *Uncle Tom's Cabin*, depicting the plight of slaves in the South.

1854: In return for the support of a block of southern senators for the Kansas-Nebraska Act, authorizing a transcontinental railroad line, Illinois Democrat Stephen Douglas agrees to include language repealing the Missouri Compromise by opening up the western territories of Kansas and Nebraska as possible slave states. Douglas agrees to have the slave or free labor status of these new states determined by popular sovereignty by way of a vote on the permissibility of slavery in state constitutions. This creates a fire-storm of protest in the North and leads many northerners to renounce their membership in the Democratic Party.

1854–1855: Free labor and slave labor supporters flock to Kansas, where the state constitution referendum on slavery becomes a mini-civil war. Five thousand armed pro-slavery ''Border ruffians'' from Missouri stuff the ballot boxes, while 1,000 antislavery ''Free Soil'' settlers, armed and supported by the abolitionist New England Immigrant Aid Society, refuse to abide by the fraudulent result. Two sets of competing state capitals and forts are established. Pro-slavery supporters establish a base at Lecompton, while antislavery advocates set up in Lawrence. Topeka remains the territory's central city. Raids, arson, and murder characterize the subsequent campaigns and the several votes on the constitution, none of which support slavery.

1854: The Republican Party is founded and builds its membership out of the disintegration of the Whig Party, the northern Democratic Party, the Free Soil Party, and the anti-immigrant ''Know Nothing''

Party. The Republican Party has no support in the South. It picks up northern anti-slavery forces who defect from the Democratic Party over the Dred Scott decision and the Kansas-Nebraska Act.

1857: The Panic of 1857 and falling prices for agricultural products aggravate sectional tensions between the North and the South.

1857: Roger Taney, Chief Justice of the Supreme Court, writes the majority opinion in the Dred Scott case, holding that Dred Scott, as a slave and, moreover, as a Negro, had ''no rights which the white man was bound to respect.''

1858: Minnesota becomes a member of the Union.

1859: Oregon becomes a state.

1859: Abolitionist John Brown, his sons, and a few other supporters briefly seize the Harpers Ferry Federal Armory, convinced that this act will precipitate a massive slave rebellion across the South, bringing an end to slavery. A detachment of federal forces led by Colonel Robert E. Lee captures Brown, who is hanged.

1860: Abraham Lincoln, the leader of the Republican Party, running on a platform of confining slavery to the states in which it is already established, is elected to the presidency.

CIVIL WAR AND INDUSTRIAL EXPANSION, 1860–1897

1861: Seven southern states secede from the Union and form the Confederate States of America. Four additional states join the Confederacy after the firing on Fort Sumter in Charleston (South Carolina) Bay.

1861: Kansas becomes the 34th state to join the Union.

1861–1865: The Civil War demonstrates both the skill of southern military leadership and the overwhelming strength of the northern economy, which slowly grinds the secessionist movement into the ground.

1862–1864: Freed from the presence of southern members of Congress, absent now in secession, the Republican Party passes its program—the Homestead Act granting government land to small farmers; the Morrill Land Grant Act setting aside government land to fund agricultural and engineering colleges; the raising of protective tariffs to shield U.S. industry from foreign competition; the National

Bank Act establishing a national system of banks to enforce standards on state banks and to restrict the circulation of state banks' currency notes; the passage of the first income tax and other war taxes; and the railroad acts subsidizing the transcontinental railroad. This monumental legislative accomplishment sets forth the economic agenda that facilitates the industrialization of the country.

1863: Composed of a population of mostly antislavery small white farmers with a tradition of hostility to Virginia's plantation-based political elite, West Virginia secedes from confederate Virginia and becomes the 35th state to join the Union.

1863: President Lincoln's executive order issued in the summer of 1862, becomes effective on January 1, 1863, declaring that all slaves in the states in rebellion are henceforth and forever free. It says nothing about slavery in other states.

1863: In his December 1863 Proclamation of Amnesty and Reconstruction President Lincoln announces a mild program of bringing the South back into the Union. This was the ''10 percent plan'' by which (with the temporary exception of military or political leaders) he would pardon all white southerners and readmit each southern state back into the Union whenever 10 percent of the number of voters in the 1860 election swore allegiance to the Union. The states also had to pass laws guaranteeing African Americans their freedom and providing for their education.

1863–1865: General William Tecumseh Sherman engages in ''total war,'' involving civilian populations through laying waste to southern agricultural resources in his ''March to the Sea.''

1864: President Lincoln vetoes the Wade-Davis Bill, a more stringent process of readmission of the Confederate states to the Union than Lincoln preferred.

1864: Nevada is admitted to the Union.

1865: The Commander of the Confederate Armies, Robert E. Lee, surrenders his forces to General Ulysses S. Grant at Appomatox Courthouse, ending the rebellion.

1865: President Lincoln is assassinated in April 1865. Vice President Andrew Johnson becomes president.

1865: The Freedman's Bureau is established to educate, feed, locate families of, and oversee the labor relations of former slaves. The Bureau also helps the most destitute of the white population.

1865: Congress reconvenes in December 1865 and refuses to seat Southern representatives. It establishes the Joint Committee on Reconstruction and passes the Thirteenth Amendment, ending slavery.

1865–1890: Sharecropping grows in the South, where the tenant farmer rents land for shares of the crop.

1865–1890: A crop-lien system of credit extends itself into the South, a region with too few credit institutions. The local merchant extends high-interest credit to small farmers. Often the small farmer owes more at the end of the harvest than he had at the beginning of the sowing season. If the farmer gets too far behind in his payments the merchant may repossess his land. Many small farmers, both African American and white, lost land in this manner and became tenant farmers on land they once owned.

1866: Congress passes its Civil Rights bill over President Johnson's veto. This ends the period of presidential Reconstruction and begins the period of congressional Reconstruction, in which the Republican Party, led by the "radical Republicans," tries to continue and complete the revolution that the Civil War had brought on in the South.

1866: The Ku Klux Klan organizes secretly to terrorize African Americans or "scalawag" white Republicans who try to vote. Southern legislatures begin passing "black codes" based on segregation laws imposed on freed slaves in the pre-Civil War South. These black codes restrict African Americans to agricultural labor and clamp down on their mobility.

1866: Congress passes the Fourteenth Amendment, defining citizenship and seeking to preserve the rights of ex-slaves to "due process of law."

1867: The National Grange is founded.

1867: The Military Reconstruction Act passes Congress as part of a package of legislation outlining the congressional plan for Reconstruction.

1867: Nebraska becomes the 37th state to join the Union.

1867: Congress passes the Tenure of Office Act to cut back on President Andrew Johnson's ability to obstruct congressional Reconstruction.

1868: Most of the southern states are readmitted to Congress under the congressional Reconstruction plan.

1868: President Andrew Johnson is impeached, but not convicted, and he remains in office.

1868: Ulysses S. Grant is elected president.

1868: The open-hearth steel production technique is first used in the United States.

1869: Congress passes the Fifteenth Amendment, guaranteeing that voting can not be denied because of "race, color, or previous condition of servitude."

1869: The Knights of Labor is founded.

1869: The first transcontinental railroad is completed at Promontory Point in Utah.

1870: Mississippi becomes the last southern state readmitted to the Union.

1870: New York City begins operation of an elevated railway system.

1870: John D. Rockefeller founds the Standard Oil Company.

1871: The Ku Klux Klan Act represses the Klan and drives it underground.

1871: Chicago experiences a great fire, devastating the city.

1872: The Freedman's Bureau is dismantled.

1873: Barbed wire is invented and puts an end to open-range cattle drives.

1873: The U.S. economy enters a quarter century of instability marked by recurrent panics and brief recoveries.

1874: The Women's Christian Temperance Society is founded.

1875: The Specie Resumption Act, which seeks to retire the inflationary Civil War "greenback" currency, is passed by Congress. This pleases bankers and creditors, but angers workers, small farmers, and debtors.

1875: The Whiskey Ring scandal embarrasses the Grant administration. Grant's Attorney General discovers that members of his department were cheating the government out of taxes on distilled alcohol. This recalls several other Grant-era scandals. One was the Crédit Mobilier scandal. It comes to light in 1872 that the Crédit Mobilier construction company paid bribes to Congress and to members of Grant's Cabinet to cover up fraudulent contracts awarded in the construction of the Union Pacific Railroad. Grant's vice president, Schuyler Colfax, resigns in disgrace.

1876: Alexander Graham Bell invents the telephone.

1876: Chief Sitting Bull and 2,500 Sioux and Cheyenne Indians kill General George Armstrong Custer and his entire regiment at the Battle of Little Bighorn.

1876: Colorado joins the Union.

1876: Almost 82 percent of eligible voters cast ballots in a disputed election resulting from the Compromise of 1877. Republican candidate Rutherford B. Hayes is declared the winner. The South receives various favors including control of the federal patronage in their region, federal aid for the Texas and Pacific Railroad, and the withdrawal of the last of the federal troops. After the departure of the federal troops African Americans in the South enter a period of political repression and social degradation.

1877: Mine owners and Pinkerton agents hang 11 Molly Maguires. A group of Irish miners in the coal mines around Scranton, Pennsylvania, the Molly Maguires use violence and the threat of violence in the struggle with management.

1877: Railroad workers go on the first nation-wide strike.

1878: Some African Americans, unwilling to live under the increasingly repressive social segregation of the New South, migrate to the North or, like the Exodusters, to Kansas or other western states.

1879: The California state constitution is amended to outlaw the hiring of Chinese laborers.

1879: Thomas A. Edison invents the incandescent light bulb.

1880: The Chinese Exclusion Act, which limits the number of Chinese allowed to enter the country, is passed by Congress.

1881: The Tuskegee Institute is founded by Booker T. Washington.

1880s: In the face of movement towards political alliance between African Americans and white Farmers' Alliances (also called Populists), southern state legislatures pass voter registration laws such as the grandfather clause, the poll tax, and the literacy test, which disenfranchise African American voters and disrupt the class-based politics of the early Populists.

1883: The Pendleton Act is passed by Congress, creating the civil service as an alternative to political patronage.

1883: The Supreme Court rules that the Fourteenth Amendment forbids state governments from discrimination, but does not apply to individuals or private organizations, such as businesses.

1884: The first skyscraper is built in Chicago.

1886: A bomb blast during a riot in the Chicago Haymarket Square kills seven police officers. Police open up with gunfire and four people are killed. The state rounds up eight anarchists and hangs four of them.

1886: Cigar worker Samuel Gompers helps form the American Federation of Labor, an organization of trades unions which believes in strikes and contracts, but does not advocate political or social change.

1887: The Interstate Commerce Act, meant to regulate the railroads, passes Congress.

1887: The Dawes Severalty Act passes Congress. This legislation attempts to convert the reservation Indians into small farmers by abolishing the tradition of communally-owned land.

1889: In Chicago, Jane Addams founds Hull House, the first ''settlement house'' center of food, shelter, and assimilation for the urban immigrant poor.

1889: North Dakota and South Dakota join the Union on the same day, November 2.

1889: Montana and Washington become the 41st and 42nd states, respectively, to be admitted to the Union.

1890: Idaho and Wyoming join the Union in July 1890.

1890: The Sherman Anti-Trust Act becomes law.

1890: At the last major confrontation between U.S. troops and Native Americans in the Battle of Wounded Knee in South Dakota, U.S. Army troops of the Seventh Calvary (Custer's old regiment) use machine guns to kill 200 Ogalala Sioux Indians. Twenty nine U.S. soldiers also die.

1890s: ''Jim Crow'' laws enforcing social segregation are passed by southern state legislatures, and in the 1890s the lynching (execution without trial) of African Americans averages 187 per year.

1890: Congress passes the Sherman Silver Purchase Act.

1892: Striking workers at the Carnegie Steel Company in Homestead, Pennsylvania, win a battle against the strike-breaking Pinkerton Detective Agency, but they lose the strike, and the Amalgamated Association of Iron and Steel Workers disbands.

1893: Severe economic depression resulting from agricultural and manufacturing over-production and financial panic settles in for the next four years.

1893: Historian Frederick Jackson Turner writes an article speculating on the meaning of the fact that, according to the Census Bureau, the frontier, as a continuous line of development, no longer exists.

1894: Jacob S. Coxey, an Ohio small businessman, leads ''Coxey's Army'' of unemployed on a futile march to Washington, D.C., to pressure Congress to enact legislation that will employ the jobless to improve and maintain public works.

1894: The Pullman strike is put down by federal judges.

1895: Booker T. Washington, an African American spokesman for self-improvement, gives his 1895 Atlanta Exposition speech in which he tries to convince his (mostly white) audience that if they hire African Americans, employers will find them to be good and grateful workers who will not make any demands on the political system or on the race etiquette of the South.

1896: The Populist Movement, which adopts the ''fusion'' strategy of supporting the Democratic Party's presidential candidate, William Jennings Bryan, goes down in defeat as Republican William McKinley wins the presidential election.

1896: Utah becomes the 45th state admitted to the Union.

1896: In *Plessy v. Ferguson* the Supreme Court rules that social segregation of the races in interstate travel is not in conflict with any constitutional amendment or federal statute as long as equal facilities exist for the African Americans.

1896: The Alaskan gold rush begins.

AN ERA OF ECONOMIC INSTABILITY, 1897–1920

1897: President William McKinley offers to mediate Spain's war against the Cuban forces of national self-determination. Spain declines the offer.

1898: In part due to articles that appear in the sensationalist ''yellow journalism'' press, the U.S. public registers disgust with the repressive policy of the Spanish government towards its colony, Cuba, which is fighting a guerilla war of national liberation led, until his death in battle in 1895, by José Martí. To emphasize its displeasure with the bloody counter-insurgency, the United States sends the battleship *Maine* to Havana. While at anchor in Havana harbor the *Maine* blows up. The United States promptly goes to war with Spain.

1898: The United States mounts an amateurish, but successful campaign against the demoralized Spanish forces occupying Cuba. Assistant Secretary of the Navy Theodore Roosevelt quits his post, organizes an irregular cavalry regiment called the Rough Riders, and participates in an assault on Kettle Hill. Meanwhile, the United States attacks the Spanish south Pacific colony of the Philippines. Here, Commodore George Dewey and the U.S. fleet destroys the Spanish fleet.

1898–1902: The Philippines becomes the site of another guerilla war of independence against Spain. When the United States proceeds to set up its own colonial administration, the Philippine movement for national liberation and its guerilla army led by Emilio Aguinaldo, resolves to expel the new invaders.

1898: The Treaty of Paris ends the Spanish-American War. It cedes Puerto Rico and the Philippines to the United States and recognizes Cuban independence.

1898: In reaction to the U.S. acquisition of an empire as a result of the war with Spain, the Anti-Imperialist League develops. Although never strong enough to deter the U.S. policies of imperial aggrandizement, the Anti-Imperialist League, including such personages as Jane Addams, Andrew Carnegie, Samuel Gompers, Mark Twain, and former President Grover Cleveland, stakes out a position of opposition to empire (frequently mixed with isolationism).

1899: In an attempt to make up for the fact that the United States had not participated in carving China up into spheres of influence like the other European trading powers had, Secretary of State John Hay releases the Open Door notes, advocating that each nation trading with China should afford equal trading rights within its sphere of influence to all other trading nations. The Europeans receive this proposal with skepticism.

1900: Although the roots of muckraking stretch back well into the nineteenth century, this genre of social exposé becomes more popular and more influential in suggesting targets of Progressive reform. Prominent muckrakers include Lincoln Steffens, Ida Tarbell, and, on the issue of lynching, African American journalist Ida B. Wells.

1900: The Social Gospel movement establishes a link between religious culture (mainly Protestant) and social reform. It imbues a crusade-like quality to Progressive era reform struggles. In addition to the Settlement House movement, its manifestations include the Salvation Army. By 1900 the Salvation Army has over 20,000 volunteers in service to the urban poor.

1900: The Boxer Rebellion breaks out against foreign trading powers in China. The Boxers are a secret martial arts society and a focal point for Chinese nationalist resentments against imperialist European policies. During the summer the Boxers besiege the foreign diplomatic compound in Beijing. Five thousand U.S. troops join an expeditionary force to help rescue the diplomats. The experience converts the European trading powers in China (especially England and Germany) into accepting the American Open Door policy.

1901: President McKinley is assassinated. Vice President Theodore Roosevelt becomes president, causing some consternation in business circles where Roosevelt is regarded as an impulsive "cowboy."

1901: When Cuba attempts to compose its own constitution after Spain is expelled, the United States intervenes with the Platt Amendment. This U.S.-suggested addendum to the Cuban constitution restricts Cuba's right to enter into treaty relations with nations other than the United States. It also grants the United States the right to intervene in Cuban affairs to protect U.S. life and property and grants the United States the right to naval stations on Cuban territory.

1901: Robert LaFollette is elected governor of Wisconsin. He introduces many progressive reforms such as the regulation of the railroads, increasing the proportion of state workers under the civil service, the direct election of senators, and the measures of initiative, referendum, and recall.

1902: The Bureau of the Census is created.

1902: The Reclamation Act of 1902 is enacted, which sets aside money from the sale of public land to irrigate portions of the south and the west, an example

of the progressive approach to "managing" the nation's natural resources.

1902: President Theodore Roosevelt directs his Justice Department to file an anti-trust lawsuit against the Northern Securities Company, a railroad holding company assembled by financier J.P. Morgan.

1903: The Women's Trade Union League is founded.

1903: The Roosevelt administration creates the departments of Labor and of Commerce.

1903: Congress passes the Elkins Act, which gives the Interstate Commerce Commission the right to end railroad rebates, a reform endorsed by the railroads.

1903: After Colombia refuses to accept the U.S. offer of $10 million plus $225,000 per year for the 100-year lease of a 6-mile-wide canal zone spanning the isthmus of Panama, a "revolution" against Colombia takes place, and the new nation of Panama is promptly recognized by the United States. The United States signs the same deal with Panama that the Colombians had rejected and continues the construction of the Panama Canal.

1904: Theodore Roosevelt runs for reelection as president (and wins) on the platform of the Square Deal, which promises a kind of class-neutral politics and a determination to use the powers of the federal government to bring about reform where it is justified.

1904: As friction begins to build between Germany and its debtor nation, Venezuela, President Theodore Roosevelt announces the Roosevelt Corollary to the Monroe Doctrine. It says that if any newly emerging Latin American republic fails to meet its financial obligations to European creditors the United States will step in to reorganize that country's economy so that it can pay its debts, rather than witness the violation of the Monroe Doctrine (which in 1823 warned European powers to refrain from interfering in the affairs of any new nation in the Western Hemisphere).

1906: The Hepburn Railroad Regulation Act is passed by Congress and signed into law.

1906: In his novel *The Jungle*, Sinclair Lewis exposes conditions in the meat-packing industry.

1907: Overproduction of agricultural and industrial goods results in the Panic of 1907. The power of the financial establishment is illustrated when financier J.P. Morgan moves adequate assets into several New

York City banks to prevent their closure and thus props up public confidence in the financial system.

1907: The "Great White Fleet," consisting of 16 white battleships symbolizing U.S. economic and military strength, embarks on a world tour, including Japan.

1907: Oklahoma becomes the 46th state to join the Union.

1907: Congress passes the Pure Food and Drug Act.

1908: Henry Ford begins production of the Model T automobile.

1908: Seeking to avoid the militaristic foreign policy of his predecessors and asserting the mutually beneficial results of commerce between developed and undeveloped nations, President Howard Taft develops the foreign policy of Dollar Diplomacy.

1909: The National Association for the Advancement of Colored People is formed and is led in its early years by W.E.B. DuBois.

1910s: The clubwomen movement comes into existence, as urbanization and middle-class family culture afford a moderate degree of leisure to some women. The clubwomen usually support reform movements, such as restrictions on child labor or the campaign against poor conditions of work for women employed in factories. Some women also become active in the anti-lynching movement and in the campaign for women's suffrage.

1910: Responding to stories in the press concerning immoral conditions in the cities and the danger to young single women of being abducted and exploited by "white slave trade" prostitution rings, Congress passes the Mann Act, making it a federal crime to transport women across state lines for immoral purposes.

1911: One hundred and forty-six workers die in the Triangle Shirtwaist Factory fire.

1911: The Taft Justice Department files an anti-trust suit against the United States Steel Company.

1911: Although the roots of the anti-alcohol movement stretch back decades into the early Republic period, the temperance movement reaches a crescendo of activism in this period. In 1911 the Women's Christian Temperance Society claims 245,000 members, the largest organization of women to this point in U.S. history.

1912: The New Mexico territory is admitted to the Union.

1912: In the presidential election of 1912 Democrat Woodrow Wilson, running under the slogan of the New Freedom, bests both Republican William Howard Taft and Theodore Roosevelt, who runs under the slogan of New Nationalism and the banner of the newly formed Bull Moose Progressive Party.

1912: Arizona joins the Union.

1913: The Sixteenth Amendment to the *Constitution* passes, giving Congress the power to levy an income tax.

1913: With the Underwood-Simmons Tariff the Wilson administration succeeds in passing a reduced tariff. This fulfills one of the pledges of the New Freedom, in that it would bring more competition and cheaper goods. It creates the conditions for more trade. It also lowers the amount of revenue that the tariff brings in. In order to off-set this revenue decline, the Congress includes a provision for a moderate income tax in the Underwood-Simmons Tariff.

1913: The Federal Reserve Act passes Congress, creating a dozen regional Federal Reserve banks, owned and controlled by the banks in the district.

1913: Implementing a demand of the Populist Movement twenty years before, the Seventeenth Amendment to the *Constitution* replaces the election of senators by state legislatures with the direct election of senators.

1914: The Clayton Anti-Trust Act is passed. This version of anti-trust legislation explicitly excludes labor unions from prosecution as trusts engaged in restricting the free flow of commerce. Samuel Gompers calls it "the Magna Carta of Labor."

1914: The Panama Canal opens.

1914: When the Western Federation of Miners stage a strike in the coal fields of Ludlow, Colorado, the state militia and the strike-breakers attack the workers' tent colony with rifle fire, causing the death of 39 people, including eleven children.

1914: President Woodrow Wilson creates the Federal Trade Commission, a bipartisan body to oversee commerce and insure orderly competition.

1914: Henry Ford begins to manufacture automobiles through the use of the moving assembly line.

1914: World War I begins in Europe.

1914: The war-time boom begins.

1915: President Wilson declares the U.S. neutrality towards the war in Europe.

1915: Germany's submarine warfare, affecting U.S. vessels, brings the United States very close to war, but when Wilson delivers an ultimatum on the subject, the German high command pledges to stop sinking neutral vessels.

1915: The Great Migration of African American people from the rural south to the urban north begins.

1916: Running on the slogan, "He kept us out of war," Wilson wins a second presidential term.

1916: The Keating-Owen child labor law is enacted, forbidding the use of child labor in any goods shipped across state lines.

1916: Margaret Sanger organizes the New York Birth Control League.

1917: Congress legislates literacy tests for immigrants.

1917: The British intercept and decode the "Zimmerman telegram," sent by the German Kaiser's foreign secretary to the German ambassador in Mexico, offering to furnish Mexico with military supplies for an invasion of the southwest United States and promising that Mexico would regain the territory that it had lost to the United States in the Mexican War. This, along with the fact that the German U-boats resume unrestricted submarine warfare, leads Wilson to ask Congress for a declaration of war against Germany.

1917: In a series of events with profound implications for the history of the United States and the world, the Russian Revolution begins. The utopian fantasy of communism, which had occasionally expressed itself in American intellectual circles, now becomes a reality as the Russian Communist Party, taking advantage of the extreme social crisis precipitated by World War I, seizes control of Russia.

1917: The War Industries Board is created and in March 1918, Wilson turns it over to the leadership of Wall Street financier Bernard Baruch. Its mission is to allocate resources between the war effort and the civilian economy and to plan all aspects of the economy. It makes some important contributions in this area, but is generally too cumbersome and inefficient to fulfill its mission.

1917: Congress passes the Espionage, Sabotage, and Sedition Acts, severely restricting the rights of free speech.

1918: Wilson releases his Fourteen Points, emphasizing the democratic and peaceable nature of U.S. war aims.

1918: The National War Labor Board promises workers the right to join unions, grants equal pay for women doing equal work, and concedes the 8-hour day in return for a no-strike pledge for the duration of the war.

1918: Eugene V. Debs, formerly head of the American Railway Union and leader of the American Socialist Party, makes a speech against World War I and is jailed.

1918: The Eighteenth Amendment, prohibiting the production, transportation, and sale of alcohol, is adopted.

1918: At the end of World War I, President Wilson sends an "expeditionary force" of American troops into the Soviet Union. During the three years of the Russian civil war the U.S. troops engage in limited supportive actions for the "White Army" of the old Russian regime. Gradually, however, the Bolshevik Party (led by Vladimir Ilyich Lenin) and the Red Army (led by Leon Trotsky) consolidate Soviet control over Russia and over the nations that made up the Russian Empire. Unable to decisively influence the course of events, the American troops withdraw by 1920. The actions of the American expeditionary force create a climate of mistrust between the United States and the Soviet Union.

1919: The peace treaty of Versailles is negotiated and signed, but Wilson cannot convince the Senate to accept the League of Nations as a forum for international conflict, a concept in which Wilson had personally invested much of his energy. Wilson succumbs to a stroke while on a speaking tour in an attempt to "go over the Senate's head" and rally support for the Versailles treaty among the American people.

1919: The conclusion of the war brings both an increased level of class conflict, with massive strikes in steel, meatpacking, and shipyards, and an alarming increase in racial violence, including race riots in East St. Louis and Chicago.

1919: Alfred Sloan introduces the installment plan with the General Motors Acceptance Corporation. Consumer credit arrangements begin to play a prominent role in marketing.

1920: Alarmed at the level of class conflict, the anarchist bombings, and the increasingly radical rhetoric of working class leaders, A. Mitchell Palmer, the Progressive Attorney General under Wilson, and his assistant, J. Edgar Hoover, lead the Palmer Raids in early January. Mostly directed against immigrants, the Palmer raids, arrest about 6,000 people. Five hundred are eventually deported.

1920: The Nineteenth Amendment is ratified, granting women the right to vote.

PROSPERITY DECADE, 1920–1929

1920: The economy goes into recession.

1920: The first commercial radio broadcast airs.

1920: Warren Harding, running on a platform of ''normalcy,'' is elected to the presidency.

1920: Two anarchists, Bartolomeo Vanzetti and Nicola Sacco, are arrested and convicted of murder in Braintree, Massachusetts, in what most observers believe is a politically motivated case.

1920s: The Ku Klux Klan, the ''night riders'' of Reconstruction fifty years earlier, revive in 1915 and flourish during the 1920s, a manifestation of the culture war between the urban and rural sections of the country. Membership peaks in 1924.

1920s: Poor farming management and ignorance of erosion causes the topsoil in several western states to erode during the 1920s. Dust storms result, devastating the remaining topsoil and turn everyday life into an ordeal. Many farmers migrate to the west coast.

1920: A bumper crop causes farm prices, already in decline, to drop further.

1921: The National Association of Manufacturers and the Chamber of Commerce mount an anti-union campaign called the American Plan. They attack the union shop, in which workers have to belong to a union to get a job. Under the American Plan workers sign ''yellow dog contracts'' in which they pledge not to join or aid the union movement.

1921: The first issue of the *Reader's Digest* appears. This publication is for busy people who do not have enough time to read many books. It purports to condense the essential significance of a book into a few pages.

1921: The economy is in mild recession although productivity is rising rapidly.

1921: Congress passes immigration restriction legislation which sets the total limit of immigration at 350,000 per year distributed on the basis of three percent of the number of each nationality living in the United States in 1910.

1921: Secretary of the Treasury Andrew Mellon encourages Congress to repeal the excess-profits tax on corporations.

1921–1922: The Washington Naval Disarmament Conference is hosted by U.S. Secretary of State Charles Evans Hughes, who proposes that the naval powers of the world should freeze production of battleships and maintain the presently existing ratio of ships in the water. Initially meeting with enthusiastic approval from the delegates of the different nations, the resulting Five-Power Agreement proves unable to stem the building of cruisers, submarines, destroyers, and eventually, aircraft carriers. It is still an important diplomatic event as the first disarmament conference and treaty.

1922: Congress passes a higher protective tariff with the Fordney-McCumber Tariff.

1922: Italian fascist rebel Benito Mussolini's Brownshirts march on Rome, Italy.

1923: The Teapot Dome scandal and several other scandals besmirch the reputation of the Harding administration.

1923: Calvin Coolidge becomes president when Harding dies in office.

1923: The stock market enters a six-year expansion.

1923: *Time* magazine begins publication.

1924: Nellie Taylor Ross of Wyoming and Miriam Ferguson of Texas become the first women to be elected U.S. governors.

1924: Businessman Charles Dawes puts forward a plan to have American bankers fund the reparation payments that Germany is required to pay other European nations after World War I. The recipients of the reparations use the funds to pay off the war debt that they owe the United States.

1924: Congress passes the Indian Citizenship Act, which makes all Native Americans citizens of the United States.

1924: The National Origins Act reduces the total immigration to 150,000 per year and apportions it on the basis of the numbers of each nationality immigrating in 1890, thus favoring northwest Europe over southeastern Europe.

1924: Senator Charles McNary and Representative Gilbert Haugen pass a bill to sell farm surpluses abroad. President Calvin Coolidge vetoes the bill in 1924 and again in 1927.

1925: John Scopes is convicted of teaching evolution in a Tennessee high school.

1925: F. Scott Fitzgerald publishes *The Great Gatsby*.

1925: The Brotherhood of Sleeping Car Porters is founded by A. Philip Randolph.

1926: Treasury Secretary Mellon convinces Congress to cut income and estate taxes in half and to eliminate the gift tax.

1927: "Lucky Lindy," Charles Lindbergh, sets a record for the first transatlantic solo airplane flight.

1927: Despite an international protest movement in their behalf, Sacco and Vanzetti are executed.

1927: The first "talky" film, *The Jazz Singer*, is released.

1927: Amelia Earhart becomes the first woman to fly an airplane solo over the Atlantic Ocean.

1927: In *Nixon v. Herndon* the Supreme Court uses the Equal Protection Clause to strike down a Texas law barring African Americans from voting in Democratic Party primaries.

1928: The highly speculative Miami real estate market collapses.

1928: Al Smith, a Catholic New York City Democrat, sets a precedent by obtaining the Democratic Party nomination to run for president. He loses to Herbert Hoover, an engineer and an able Republican Progressive who had coordinated the aid to European refugees during World War I and had served as Secretary of Commerce in the Coolidge administration.

1928: In the Kellogg-Briand Pact the major military powers of the world (except for the Soviet Union) sign an agreement outlawing war as a means of conflict resolution. Unfortunately, it has no enforcement provisions.

DEPRESSION AND WORLD WAR II, 1929–1945

1929: The decline of the stock market in October 1929 marks the beginning of the public awareness of the Great Depression, although the agricultural sector of the economy had been suffering from depressed prices and profits for almost ten years.

1930: The Smoot-Hawley Tariff is enacted. This extremely high tariff depressed foreign trade at the very moment the economy needed to be pulled out of depression.

1930: Novelist John Dos Passos brings out the *U.S.A.* trilogy. With its "newsreel" actualities and its evocation of a complex and dynamic national culture, this portrait of American life in the late 1910s catches the United States on the edge of modernity.

1931: The Federal Reserve System raises interest rates. This depresses business investment at a time when it needs to be stimulated.

1931: The economic crisis spreads to Europe. Burdened by reparations or loan repayments after World War I, the governments of Europe (especially Germany) are tempted to print money. Although some observers call for the United States to cancel its debts, others like President Calvin Coolidge refuse to consider this measure and expect full repayment. This, plus high tariffs and an isolationist attitude of seeking to avoid involvement in Europe's problems, reduce the ability of the United States to play a constructive role in the growing European political crisis of the 1930s.

1931: The Scottsboro affair, in which eight African American teenagers are sentenced to death for supposedly raping two white women on a boxcar in which they were all traveling, creates controversy. The lack of evidence and the nature of the testimony indicates the innocence of the accused, and the International Labor Defense, a Communist Party legal support committee, defends the "Scottsboro boys" and eventually gains their freedom.

1931: The U.S. Communist Party stages an unemployment march on Washington, D.C.

1931: Japan invades Manchuria.

1931: Secretary of State Henry Stimson is instructed by President Hoover to withhold diplomatic recognition of any territorial boundary change as a result of Japanese aggression in Asia. This becomes known as the Stimson Doctrine, and it has little effect. Japan continues to assert itself in the region.

1932: The Reconstruction Finance Corporation is established.

1932: The Farmers' Holiday Association forms in Iowa.

1932: Twenty thousand Bonus Marchers, veterans who in 1924 had been awarded a $1,000 "bonus" by Congress for their service in World War I, rally in Washington, D.C., and demand that the bonus be distributed immediately. (It was payable in 1945.) President Hoover refuses, violence breaks out between the marchers and the Washington police force, and Hoover sends in the U.S. Army to clear the marchers out of their tent city. The violence leaves at least two marchers and one baby dead.

1932: Herbert Hoover runs for a second term as president, but the paralysis that has seized the economy, plus Hoover's lack of warmth as a campaigner, leads the American people to vote in overwhelming numbers (57.4 percent) for Franklin Delano Roosevelt, a member of the New York Hudson Valley aristocracy and a distant cousin of former president Theodore Roosevelt. Franklin Roosevelt gives no clear indication of his program, other than to promise in his speech accepting the Democratic Party nomination that he pledged a "New Deal" for Americans.

1933: In February 1933 bank depositors begin withdrawing their savings. The movement accelerates and becomes a panic when banks begin running out of funds to meet the depositors' demands.

1933: The following New Deal programs are passed by Congress and signed by the president: the Emergency Banking Act; the Economy Act; the Civilian Conservation Corps; the Agricultural Adjustment Act; the Tennessee Valley Authority; the National Industrial Recovery Act; the Federal Emergency Relief Act; the Homeowners' Refinancing Act; the Civil Works Administration; and the Federal Securities Act.

1933: Adolph Hitler is elected Chancellor of Germany.

1933: Francis Townsend, retired California physician, proposes the "Townsend Plan" of "priming the pump" of consumer spending through a government pension to senior citizens.

1933: The United States recognizes the Soviet Union, and the two establish diplomatic ties.

1934: The Southern Tenant Farmers' Union is organized by members of the Socialist Party of America. Convinced that the economic depression is an aspect of the worldwide unraveling of capitalism and committed to the strategy of building a biracial coalition of poor people to bring about change, the American Socialist and Communist Parties during the 1930s "point the way" towards reform, but lose members to the Democratic Party and its popular standard-bearer, Franklin Roosevelt.

1934: Brought on by several years of drought, as well as the mechanization of agriculture (with tractors and disk plows disrupting the root systems of plains grasses which normally retain moisture in the soil), twenty-two giant dust storms ravage the west and the south. The storms carry away tons of soil and ruin agriculture until the early 1940s, when the rains return and the demand for agricultural goods once again brings the planting of crops.

1934: The following New Deal programs are created in 1934: the National Housing Act; the Securities and Exchange Act; and the Homeowners' Loan Act.

1934: Conservative critics of Roosevelt form the Liberty League.

1934: Huey Long, governor of Louisiana, originally supported Franklin Roosevelt but now demands the redistribution of wealth with the "Share-Our-Wealth" Societies.

1935: Father Charles Coughlin, the "radio priest" who had supported the New Deal, now finds President Roosevelt too mild and establishes the National Union for Social Justice. Eventually, Coughlin drifts into support for fascism.

1935: John L. Lewis, head of the United Mine Workers, takes his union out of the craft-conscious American Federation of Labor in order to lead the unionization of the semi-skilled workers in mass production industries.

1935: The following New Deal programs are passed by Congress and signed by the President in 1935: Works Progress Administration; National Youth Administration; Social Security Act; National Labor Relations Act; Public Utilities Holding Company Act; Resettlement Administration; Rural Electrification Administration; Revenue Act ("Wealth Tax").

1935: In an attempt to avoid in the future what some believed to be a connection between the profit motives of U.S. armament producers and the U.S.

entry into war, the Congress passes Neutrality Acts in 1935, 1936, and 1937. They prohibit the sale of arms to belligerent nations and direct the president to inform American travelers of the possibility of harm as a result of traveling near war zones.

1935: The Supreme Court rules that the National Industrial Recovery Act is unconstitutional.

1935: Huey Long is assassinated.

1935: Italy invades Ethiopia.

1936: Franklin Roosevelt signs the Soil Conservation and Domestic Allotment Act.

1936: John L. Lewis and like-minded labor leaders form the Congress of Industrial Organizations (CIO) to "organize the unorganized" and aggressively expand the union movement with the adoption of innovative organizing tactics, such as the sit-down strike.

1936: Roosevelt wins a record 61 percent of the votes for president in 1936.

1936: The Spanish Civil War begins. Fascist Germany and Italy supply weapons and volunteers to the right-wing rebellion of the Falange under Ferdinand Franco. The United States, as well as the nations of western Europe, refuses to intervene on the side of the democratic socialist Spanish loyalist forces. Only the Soviet Union and its allies send aid. A volunteer army of International Brigades, including the 3,000 Americans in the Abraham Lincoln Brigade, travel to Spain to fight, but although they suffer high casualties (about a third of the Americans die in Spain), the Franco rebellion overwhelms its opposition.

1936: Germany reoccupies the Rhineland, which France has held since World War I.

1937: In order to defeat the conservatives on the U.S. Supreme Court, Roosevelt proposes to expand the size of the court, which would have allowed him to appoint a number of new justices. This infuriates his opponents and distresses his allies and he drops the idea, but his administration is sullied by the act.

1937: Japan invades China.

1937: Roosevelt signs the Farm Security Administration and the National Housing Acts into law.

1937: In a bitter strike of the Steel Workers' Organizing Committee against the "Little Steel" companies, a Memorial Day picnic and march to the Republic Steel plant in Chicago is fired upon by police. Ten workers are killed. Known as the Memorial Day Massacre, this act of state violence on behalf of the employer effectively breaks the strike.

1938: Germany annexes Austria.

1938: Congress passes and Roosevelt signs into law the Second Agricultural Adjustment Act and the Fair Labor Standards Act.

1938: At a Munich conference, British Prime Minister Neville Chamberlain tries to appease Hitler by allowing German troops to occupy a German-speaking portion of Czechoslovakia.

1938: As the economy seems to have rebounded in 1937, the Roosevelt administration reduces government allocation of funds for the Works Progress Administration and other programs. The economy slips back into recession (called the Roosevelt Recession) and does not pull out of it until the threat of World War II prompts hiring at the factories engaged in the 1940 military build-up.

1939: Fearing that the west European powers are maneuvering to set up a bloody war between Germany and the Soviet Union, a scenario in which the western democracies could "pick up the pieces" after the combatants had bled themselves dry, Stalin stuns the world by signing a non-aggression pact with Hitler. This allows the Soviets to industrialize and to build up its stock of military hardware, but it confuses and demoralizes the communist parties of western Europe and the United States.

1939: Germany invades the whole of Czechoslovakia.

1939: Germany invades Poland. World War II begins in Europe.

1939: John Steinbeck's *The Grapes of Wrath* is published and tells the story of the "Okies" and the trek of migrant farmers from the drought-plagued great plains to California.

1939–1940: The Soviet Union invades Finland, Estonia, Latvia, and Lithuania.

1940: Germany rolls across western Europe in a mechanized warfare called the "Blitzkrieg."

1941: The lend-lease plan gives aid to Great Britain while still maintaining neutrality.

1941: Germany invades the Soviet Union.

1941: Although the United States is not yet at war, Churchill and Roosevelt meet on a British destroyer near Newfoundland and outline a set of shared goals, including the ''destruction of Nazi tyranny.'' The charter also calls for the national self-determination of colonial holdings, a goal that Churchill embraces with much less enthusiasm.

1941: A. Philip Randolph threatens to bring thousands of African Americans to a march on Washington, D.C., protesting discrimination against African American workers in the defense industry. As a result of this demand, Franklin Roosevelt creates the Fair Employment Practices Commission, which handles these complaints and impresses on employers the need to project the spirit of the ''double 'V','' victory against fascism abroad and against racism at home.

1941: Roosevelt imposes an embargo on petroleum and scrap iron shipping to Japan.

1941: Japan bombs Pearl Harbor, Hawaii, largely destroying the U.S. Pacific fleet. The next day, the United States declares war on Japan, Germany, and Italy.

1941: Work on the Manhattan Project (the atomic bomb) begins.

1942: The Office of Price Administration is created to fight inflation by freezing prices, wages, and rents.

1942: The War Production Board (WPB) is created to coordinate the production of military goods. In part because of the daunting nature of this mission, and also because of the ineffectual performance of its leaders, the WPB is generally unsuccessful in this goal, although the economy does manage to produce a huge output of weapons and other materiel.

1942: The Japanese take the Philippines.

1942: Japanese American citizens are locked up in concentration camps as Americans begin to imagine that citizens of Japanese descent constitute a ''fifth column'' of saboteurs and spies for Japan. Their private possessions are often stolen when they are forced into the camps.

1942: The Congress on Racial Equality (CORE) is founded.

1943: Racial confrontations occur between African Americans and whites in Detroit and between Mexican Americans and white sailors in Los Angeles.

1944: The Allied amphibious invasion of Normandy takes place.

1944: The United States retakes the Philippines.

1944: In a meeting at Bretton Woods, New Hampshire, the United States and other western powers discuss post-war recovery programs. They create the International Monetary Fund and the International Bank for Reconstruction and Development, also known as the World Bank.

1944: In the summer of 1944 the Allies meet at Dumbarton Oaks to plan the structure of the proposed United Nations.

1945: Western European and American troops meet the Red Army in Berlin, as the German army is destroyed.

1945: After a three month siege, the United States captures Okinawa, Japan, at a cost of 11,000 U.S. and 80,000 Japanese lives.

1945: The United States drops the atomic bomb on Hiroshima and Nagasaki.

1945: The United Nations Organization meets in San Francisco to plan its post-war future.

POSTWAR PROSPERITY, 1945–1973

1945: In February 1945, Joseph Stalin, Winston Churchill, and Franklin Roosevelt meet in Yalta, a resort on the Black Sea, to discuss the outlines of post-war Europe. They all agree to partition Germany. Stalin agrees that, once Germany is defeated, the Red Army will help the United States defeat Japan. In return, the Soviet Union will repossess the Kurile Islands, north of Japan, as well as southern Sakhalin Island and Port Arthur, which Russia lost to Japan in the Russo-Japanese War (1905). The Allies, however, fail to reach agreement on the shape of post-war Europe.

1945: Franklin D. Roosevelt dies; Harry Truman becomes president.

1945: The Potsdam Conference between Churchill, Stalin, and Truman, is held in a Berlin suburb in July 1945, and confirms what the Yalta Conference already revealed in February of the same year: there are serious disagreements between the Allies. One is over the Polish question. The Red Army occupies Poland and, intent on acquiring a set of ''buffer states'' to prevent future invasion from the West, Stalin has already installed a pro-Soviet government. At Yalta, Stalin agreed to a vague date sometime in the future for holding free elections in Poland, but he never does so. Instead, in the weeks after Yalta, the Soviets proceed to create more buffer states in Eastern Europe. In light of the U.S. possession of a working nuclear bomb, President Truman adopts an aggressive stance and ''talks tough'' to the Soviet diplomats at Potsdam, but without gaining any concessions.

1945: Japan surrenders on August 14, 1945.

1946: Post-war inflation and the desire to ''catch up'' with the substantial price increases during the war prompt U.S. railroad workers and the coal miners to go on nation-wide strikes.

1946: The Philippines are given independence by the United States.

1946: The dominance of the Democratic Party in national politics since 1933 is finally broken as the Republicans gain control of Congress.

1946: Dr. Benjamin Spock publishes *Baby and Child Care*, the ''Bible'' for baby boomer infants and children's home diagnosis.

1946: Truman submits a domestic program called the Fair Deal. The name recalls the powerful New Deal program and the coalition that supported it. But, although the specifics of the Fair Deal—an expansion of Social Security benefits, public housing, federal aid for the St. Lawrence Seaway, and a national health plan—recall the New Deal, the drift of post-war politics is in a conservative direction and most elements of the program fail to win enough votes for passage.

1946: George F. Kennan, a career diplomat stationed in Moscow in 1946, sends a ''long telegram'' to the State Department in which he discusses ''the sources of Soviet conduct.'' Later published as an article in *Foreign Affairs* under the pseudonym Mr. X., Kennan's argument is that historical circumstances have made the Soviet Union expansionist and that Marxism-Leninism has provided a rationale for this behavior. He says that the best way to deal with Soviet expansionism is to quarantine the U.S.S.R.

until it runs out of revolutionary energy and settles down to a consumer-based economy.

1946: In a speech at Fulton, Missouri, the former Prime Minister of Great Britain Winston Churchill predicts that the world to come will be marked by the struggle between democratic and totalitarian systems of government. He notes that Eastern bloc nations are being turned into satellites of the Soviet Union, and he uses the image of an ''iron curtain'' that is descending across Europe.

1947: President Harry Truman reformulates George Kennan's arguments and presents them in a speech to Congress as the Truman Doctrine, the essence of which is that the United States will henceforth ''support free peoples who are resisting attempted subjugation by armed minorities or by outside pressures.''

1947: Secretary of State George C. Marshall unveils the Marshall Plan, a $12 billion package of aid to a devastated Western Europe, as a way to decrease the attractiveness of socialism.

1947: The Brooklyn Dodgers sign Jackie Robinson, the first African American to play in a regular position in Major League baseball.

1947: The National Security Act passes Congress and is signed into law. The Act creates the National Security Council (NSC), which advises the president on foreign policy, and the Central Intelligence Agency (CIA), which coordinates the intelligence apparatus and also engages in extra-legal covert activity in foreign lands to forward the interests of the United States.

1947: The first suburban tract housing at Levittown, New York, is built.

1947: Puerto Rico is given commonwealth status.

1947: The House Un-American Activities Committee begins holding hearings to investigate the charge leveled by some members of Congress that the federal government has been lax in allowing communists to infiltrate the government.

1947: The Truman administration institutes loyalty review programs to insure the patriotism of government employees and to weed out subversive elements that might have become ensconced in government jobs. By 1951 over 2,200 government workers have either resigned or been terminated.

1947: The Taft-Harley Act is passed, making it harder to organize and maintain unions, a result of language such as Section 14-B, which permits states to pass ''right to work'' laws outlawing union shops (where a worker is required to join the union after being hired).

1948: The Soviets react to the merger of the U.S., British, and French sectors of Germany into one zone, ''West Germany,'' by blockading shipments of food and other necessities to the western zones of Berlin. (Berlin lies inside East Germany.) Rather than try to open up the land corridors by force, the Western powers agree on a closely coordinated airlift of supplies to the city. For ten months the Berlin airlift successfully provisions the city, until the East Germans open the corridors again.

1948: The United Nations partitions Palestine and establishes the state of Israel.

1948: Alger Hiss, a New Deal liberal and formerly a valued member of the State Department, is accused of being part of a ring that passed classified information to the Soviet Union in 1937 and 1938. Hiss sues his accuser, former communist Whittaker Chambers, for libel and loses the case, at which point he is convicted of perjury. He goes to jail for several years and the incident casts a shadow over the reputation and the careers of many New Deal liberals, including members of the movie industry like the ''Hollywood Ten,'' the directors who refuse to answer the House Un-American Activities Committee's inquiries concerning their politics.

1948: The United Automobile Workers' Union and General Motors agree to an automatic cost-of-living factor in the calculation of wages.

1948: The New Deal political coalition comes under considerable stress as the Democratic Party splits into three parties—the conservative States' Rights, or Dixiecrat Party in the South, led by Strom Thurmond, the left-wing Progressive Party, under the leadership of Henry Wallace, and the mainstream Democratic Party under Truman. In spite of this division, labor mobilizes behind Truman, who wins an upset election.

1949: Twelve nations sign the North Atlantic Treaty Organization (NATO), a mutual defense pact and a standing military force in Western Europe, to guard against aggression by the Soviet Union. The U.S. Senate ratifies the treaty. The Soviets spearhead their own mutual defense organization, the Warsaw Pact.

1949: President Truman issues an executive order ending racial segregation in the U.S. military.

1949: The Soviet Union explodes its first atomic bomb years earlier than expected, and the United States loses its monopoly on nuclear weapons.

1949: The Chinese Communist Revolution takes place, and the former government of China flees to Taiwan.

1950: The National Security Council issues its report, NSC-68, which recommends that the United States assume the leadership of the forces opposed to the expansion of the Soviet bloc. This means that wherever such an expansion appears likely, the United States must take up the struggle against it. To do this, the United States must provide itself with a strong and flexible defense capability, not just a nuclear deterrent.

1950: North Korea invades South Korea in late June 1950. The peninsula was partitioned at the end of World War II. Syngman Rhee runs a corrupt government in the South. Kim Il Sung, the North Korean head of state, builds a Spartan, dictatorial, socialist state and introduces land reform, which wins him the support of the peasantry. The North Korean invasion brings a coordinated response from members of the Security Council of the United Nations (minus the Soviet Union, which is boycotting the Security Council sessions to protest communist China's exclusion from the body). U.N. forces battle North Korea and its Chinese allies until a treaty is signed in 1953. The treaty produces a limited victory, with an armistice line at the 38th parallel that must be patrolled at considerable expense in the future.

1950: President Truman relieves General Douglas MacArthur of command in Korea for publicly criticizing Truman's handling of the war. MacArthur flies home to a ticker-tape parade and addresses Congress; his popularity considerably exceeds Truman's. Still, Truman's action comes to be understood as a stand in favor of the subordination of military to civilian authority.

1950: In a speech at a rally in Wheeling, West Virginia, Wisconsin Senator Joseph McCarthy begins leveling the charge that the federal government is rife with communists.

1950: Congress passes the McCarran Internal Security Act, requiring all communist organizations to register with the government and publish their records. Truman vetoes the bill, but Congress overrides the veto.

1951: Two members of the Communist Party, Julius and Ethel Rosenberg, are sentenced to death for leaking secrets concerning the atomic bomb to the Soviet Union. Two years later, after massive worldwide protests reminiscent of the Sacco and Vanzetti case in the 1920s, the Rosenbergs are executed by electrocution.

1952: Dwight D. Eisenhower, military hero and head of NATO forces, is elected president on the Republican ticket.

1953: The economy slips into a recession.

1953: The CIA collaborates in the overthrow of Mohammed Mossadegh, the prime minister of Iran, who may have been maneuvering towards the nationalization of the oil industry in Iran. Mossadegh is replaced by the shah of Iran, Mohammed Reza Pahlavi, who cooperates with the West in the development of his country's oil resources.

1953: Stalin dies.

1954: In *Brown v. Board of Education* the U.S. Supreme Court rules that "separate" can never be "equal" in school systems and directs the Topeka School Board to move "with all deliberate speed" to integrate its schools.

1954: After Senator Joseph McCarthy continues to make unsubstantiated accusations against individuals and even against the U.S. Army, the fact that his committee hearings are televised help to turn the investigation into a revelation of his own bullying tactics and character assassination. He loses most of the support that he enjoyed earlier in the 1950s. Congress censures him, and within a few years he dies from the effects of alcoholism.

1954: In Guatemala the CIA helps to overthrow the newly elected Jacobo Arbenz Guzman, a leftist with whom the United Fruit Company (an American firm with extensive plantations in Guatemala) does not feel entirely comfortable.

1954: The Vietnamese nationalist forces, the Viet Minh, defeat the French army at Dien Bien Phu.

1955: The industrial unions of the CIO rejoin the trade unions in the AFL. George Meany heads the united organization, the AFL-CIO.

1955: The Montgomery Bus Boycott, a year-long struggle, begins when African American seamstress and Secretary of the Alabama NAACP, Rosa Parks, refuses to move from her seat in the front of a bus in order to let a white man sit down. Dr. Martin Luther King, Jr., emerges from the struggle with a reputation as a formidable speaker and charismatic leader, urging the rank and file civil rights adherents to practice the discipline of passive resistance and creative non-violence.

1956: The Federal Highway Act is passed and signed by President Eisenhower.

1956: The Hungarian Revolution is repressed by the Soviet Union. Although the Radio Free Europe (West European broadcasts into Soviet dominated East Europe) had encouraged the rebellion, the West was not in a position to do anything when the Russian tanks rolled across Hungary.

1956: One hundred and one southern congressmen pledge "massive resistance" to the Supreme Court rulings on desegregation.

1956: U.S. Secretary of State John Foster Dulles suspends a loan to Egypt for financing of the Aswan Dam project on the Nile River. Dulles takes the action to punish the Egyptians for their friendly relations with the Soviet Union. This prompts Egyptian leader Gamal Abdel Nasser to seize the Suez Canal and use its revenues to build the dam. This, in turn, leads Israel, Great Britain, and France to attack Egypt. The United States fears the attack on Egypt might alienate other oil rich Arab states so it supports a Soviet-sponsored U.N. resolution condemning the attack. Nasser, like a number of Third World leaders after him, learns the technique of playing the United States and its allies off against the Soviet Union and its allies.

1957: The Civil Rights Act of 1957 is passed. More a declaration of principles than a serious piece of legislation, the law has few enforcement powers.

1957: President Eisenhower orders the National Guard into Little Rock, Arkansas, to assist in desegregating a high school.

1957: The Southern Christian Leadership Conference forms under the leadership of Martin Luther King.

1957: The post-World War II baby boom peaks.

1957: The U.S. economy slips into recession again.

1957: The Teamsters are investigated for corruption.

1957: The Soviet Union launches *Sputnik*, the first earth orbiting satellite. This feat also alerts the United States to the fact that the Soviet Union possesses extremely powerful booster rockets.

1958: The National Defense Education Act is passed, providing broad support for education.

1958: The John Birch Society, a grass roots anticommunist organization, is formed.

1958: The National Aeronautics and Space Administration (NASA) is formed.

1959: Alaska becomes the 49th state to be admitted to the Union.

1959: In line with a call from the Comintern to the colonial and underdeveloped world to engage in wars of national liberation against colonialism and imperialism, the National Liberation Front in Vietnam is formed.

1959: Hawaii becomes the 50th state to enter the Union.

1959: Fidel Castro and the 26th of May Movement seizes power in Cuba.

1959: Soviet leader Nikita Khrushchev visits the United States.

1960: A U.S. U-2 spy airplane is shot down over the Soviet Union, embarrassing President Eisenhower and destroying a planned U.S.-Soviet summit meeting in Paris, France.

1960: John F. Kennedy is elected president.

1961: In his farewell address Eisenhower warns of the growth of the ''military-industrial complex.''

1961: The Congress on Racial Equality (CORE) calls for ''freedom rides'' to establish the right of African American people to have access to a racially integrated public transportation system. On May 14 a Greyhound bus carrying freedom riders near Anniston, Alabama, is surrounded by an angry white mob that burns the bus and beats its occupants. The local hospitals refuse to treat the injured freedom riders.

1961: The Alliance for Progress is created by President Kennedy.

1961: East Germany erects the Berlin Wall to stop the escape of its citizens to the West.

1962: The stunning failure of the United States-backed invasion at the Bay of Pigs by Cuba's anticommunist exiles embarrasses American policy makers. Their belief that most Cuban people are looking for an opportunity to overthrow the Castro regime is disproved.

1962: Michael Harrington publishes *The Other America*.

1962: Students for a Democratic Society (SDS) form at a UAW recreation center in Port Huron, Michigan.

1962: In order to protect themselves from the threat of another U.S. backed invasion similar to the Bay of Pigs attack, Cuba accepts the Soviet Union's aid in building nuclear missile silos in Cuba. In what becomes known as the Cuban Missile Crisis, U.S. president John F. Kennedy faces down Soviet leader Nikita Khrushchev and the missiles are withdrawn. The possibility of a large nuclear war has a sobering effect on both the Americans and the Soviets.

1962: Rachel Carson publishes *Silent Spring*, a manifesto of the environmental movement.

1963: Medgar Evans, head of the Mississippi NAACP, is assassinated in the front yard of his home.

1963: John F. Kennedy proposes a strong Civil Rights Bill.

1963: The Civil Rights March on Washington, D.C., along with Martin Luther King's ''I Have a Dream'' speech legitimizes the Civil Rights Movement in the eyes of many Americans for the first time.

1963: In Vietnam the large protest demonstrations led by Buddhist monks, some of whom engage in self-immolation (dousing themselves with gasoline and setting themselves on fire) plus the South Vietnamese government's brutal repression of political dissent leads to the CIA-approved assassination of Ngo Dinh Diem. This sets off a series of coups in South Vietnam that further delegitimize the South Vietnamese political leadership.

1963: Betty Frieden's *The Feminine Mystique* is published.

1963: President John F. Kennedy is assassinated in Dallas, Texas. Lyndon Johnson is sworn in as president.

1963-1966: Lyndon Johnson's Great Society programs are approved by Congress.

1964: President Johnson initiates tax cuts, following through on a promise of President Kennedy's.

1964: Johnson announces the War of Poverty.

1964: The Volunteers in Service to America (VISTA) is created.

1964: Lyndon Johnson goes before Congress to speak in favor of federal protection of civil rights, publicizing his support to the American people.

1964: The Economic Opportunity Act passes Congress.

1964: The "freedom summer" of 1964 brings volunteers, both African American and white, from the north to Mississippi in a drive to register African Americans to vote. White repression of this campaign leads to a number of murders of both African American and white volunteers.

1964: The British rock group The Beatles make a tour of the United States. Their immense success highlights the growing importance in the economy of the youth culture of the baby boomers.

1964: Responding to pressure from Lyndon Johnson, Congress breaks a southern filibuster and passes the Civil Rights Act of 1964, the first such effective show of congressional power on the civil rights issue since Reconstruction.

1964: After being told that North Vietnamese PT boats had attacked the destroyer *Maddox* with torpedoes in international waters, Congress passes the Gulf of Tonkin Resolution, which gives the American president the power to engage in hostile action to protect American lives. President Johnson uses this resolution to justify a massive commitment of troops and a huge bombing campaign (called Rolling Thunder) in North as well as in South Vietnam. The Gulf of Tonkin Resolution becomes known as the "blank check."

1964: Lyndon Johnson wins the presidential election of 1964, convincingly beating Republican candidate Barry Goldwater.

1964: The Berkeley campus of the University of California is the site of the Free Speech Movement.

1965: The Immigration Reform Act does away with the national origins aspects of previous immigration acts. Under the new law, all candidates for immigration are evaluated equally without regard to the nation from which they came.

1965: The race riot in the Watts neighborhood of Los Angeles tellingly describes the change in race relations as the Civil Rights Movement moves out of the south and into the north and west of the country.

1965: For the first time since Reconstruction the Voting Rights Act of 1965 gives federal protection to people trying to register to vote or to exercise their right to vote.

1965: Teach-ins on the war in Vietnam are staged on college campuses.

1965: The United States sends combat troops to Vietnam and begins a build-up which will peak in 1969 at well over half a million troops.

1965: Ralph Nader publishes *Unsafe at Any Speed*, an exposé of the General Motors Corporation and the Corvair automobile.

1965: Anti-war protests begin on college campuses.

1965: Malcolm X is assassinated in New York City.

1966: Medicaid is enacted.

1966: Huey P. Newton and a handful of other militants in Oakland, California, form the Black Panther Party.

1966: Senator J. William Fulbright, chairman of the Senate Foreign Relations Committee, begins to hold open hearings on the war in Vietnam.

1966: Partly in reaction to the disturbances on the state's college campuses and in the ghettos, Ronald Reagan is elected governor of California.

1966: The National Organization for Women is formed.

1966: The U.S. Supreme Court decides *Miranda v. State of Arizona*, defining new standards for the protection of the rights of criminal suspects.

1967: Thurgood Marshall becomes a justice on the U.S. Supreme Court.

1967: An anti-war march on the Pentagon takes place.

1967: A police raid on an after-hours tavern leads to a race riot in Detroit, in which 43 people die, mostly from rifle fire by National Guard troops.

1967: Martin Luther King, Jr., speaks on Vietnam. This transforms King into more than a spokesman on civil rights. By linking the war with the situation of African American people King may have been elaborating a platform from which to address the entire nation.

1968: The Tet offensive by Viet Cong communist guerillas in South Vietnam occurs, taking the United States and South Vietnam by surprise. Although a military catastrophe for the Viet Cong, the Tet offensive demonstrates the will of communists in

Vietnam to continue fighting and successfully undermines support for the war in the United States.

1968: The Youth International Party (YIPPIES) is founded. The YIPPIES' threats to run naked through the streets of Chicago during the national Democratic Convention and to spike the Chicago water supply with hallucinogenic drugs struck most mainstream Americans as both incomprehensible and outrageous.

1968: Skewered by his inability to extricate the country from the twin crises of Vietnam and mounting racial antagonism, on March 31, 1968, President Lyndon Johnson announces his decision to not seek the Democratic Party nomination for reelection.

1968: The My Lai massacre of 200 Vietnamese civilians becomes public knowledge. The killing of women, children, and the elderly by U.S. soldiers under the command of Lieutenant William Calley is brought to light through the actions of a helicopter pilot who intervened to prevent further bloodshed and an army photographer who took pictures of the carnage.

1968: Martin Luther King, Jr., is assassinated.

1968: Robert Kennedy, brother of John F. Kennedy and a candidate for the Democratic nomination for president, is assassinated.

1968: The Democratic National Convention in Chicago takes place in the midst of a violent confrontation between thousands of anti-war demonstrators and the Chicago police department, some of which is broadcast on live television.

1968: George Wallace founds the American Independent Party and in the election of 1968 pulls votes away from Hubert Humphrey, the Democratic Party candidate for president.

1968: Richard M. Nixon is elected president.

1969: President Nixon begins withdrawing U.S. troops from Vietnam.

1969: The Woodstock rock festival takes place.

1969: Senator George McGovern is appointed head of the Democratic Party's Internal Rules Reform Committee.

1969: Neil Armstrong, a U.S. astronaut, becomes the first human being to walk on the moon.

1969: The Stonewall riot in New York City signals the beginning of the openly public gay rights movement.

1970: President Nixon authorizes the invasion of Cambodia to constrict supply lines from North Vietnam to South Vietnam.

1970: At Kent State University in Ohio, National Guard troops fire on Vietnam war protesters, killing four. At Jackson State University in Mississippi, two African American civil rights protesters are shot to death by police.

1970: The Environmental Protection Agency is created.

1970: The Occupational Safety and Health Agency (OSHA) is created.

1971: The *New York Times* publishes the *Pentagon Papers*. They reveal that during the Johnson administration the Department of Defense deliberately lied to the public about the effectiveness of U.S. policy in Vietnam.

1970–1971: To curb inflation, President Nixon submits the Economic Stabilization Act of 1970 to Congress; the act imposes a ninety-day freeze on all wages and prices.

1972: President Nixon begins revenue sharing.

1972: Congress approves the Equal Rights Amendment.

1972: The Committee to Re-elect the President (CREEP) is formed.

1972: The SALT I treaty is signed. This treaty between the United States and the Soviet Union freezes the total number of intercontinental ballistic missiles at existing levels. The treaty says nothing about the implementation of new types of weapons such as missiles with multiple warheads or missiles on submarines.

1972: President Nixon visits communist China, an historic first which not only opens the possibility of exporting consumer durable goods to this vast new market, but also offers the strategic opening of further splintering the Sino-Soviet bloc.

1972: The United States risks a hostile Soviet reaction with the mining of Haiphong Harbor in North Vietnam.

1972: A break-in is discovered at the Democratic Party headquarters in the Washington, D.C., Watergate office complex.

1972: President Nixon is reelected.

1972: President Nixon orders an unusually heavy bombing of North Vietnam during the Christmas holidays.

1973: A woman's right to end pregnancy by abortion is upheld by the Supreme Court in *Roe v. Wade*.

1973: Vice President Spiro Agnew resigns, leaving office under a cloud of suspicion concerning his involvement in bribery and kickback deal while in the office of vice president and while governor of Maryland.

1973: The Vietnam Peace Treaty signed.

THE CONTEMPORARY WORLD, 1973-PRESENT

1973: Members of the American Indian Movement (AIM) hold a demonstration at Wounded Knee.

1973: The Paris Peace Accords allow the United States to withdraw from Vietnam, but fighting continues between the South Vietnamese government and the communists.

1973: The Yom Kippur War occurs. Israel is able to recover from the surprise attack and defeat the Egyptian forces in the Sinai peninsula. The United States intervenes to re-establish balance in the region, rather than support an unqualified Israeli victory.

1973: In response to the Yom Kippur War, the Oil Producing and Exporting Countries (OPEC) cartel imposes an embargo on shipments of oil to the United States from 1973 to 1974. This embargo forces the United States to confront its dependence on foreign sources of oil.

1973: The Watergate scandal turns into a national crisis of authority.

1974: Gerald Ford is appointed to fill the unfinished term of President Nixon's previous vice president, Spiro Agnew.

1974: Congress begins impeachment proceedings against President Nixon for participating in a cover-up of the Watergate burglary of the National Democratic Party headquarters in 1972.

1974: OPEC raises the price of crude oil.

1974: President Nixon resigns and Gerald Ford becomes president. President Ford soon pardons Nixon of any crimes he may have committed.

1974: The Supreme Court rules in *Bradley v. Milliken* that cross-district school busing is not a proper remedy for segregation in the schools.

1974: Inflation and unemployment (''stagflation'') begin to plague the U.S. economy.

1975: South Vietnam is defeated by communist forces and the nation is reunited under the leadership of the Communist Party of Vietnam.

1976: Democrat Jimmy Carter wins the presidential election against Republican Gerald Ford.

1976: Chinese communist leader Mao Zedong dies.

1977: President Carter pardons Vietnam-era draft resisters.

1977: The Department of Energy is created.

1977: President Carter negotiates the end of the 100-year lease on the Panama Canal and the return of the canal to the government of Panama.

1978: The Supreme Court rules on affirmative action in the case of *Bakke v. University of California*. The ruling does not terminate affirmative action, but it does limit the use of quotas to attain affirmative action goals.

1978: Proposition 13, a referendum rolling back property taxes, passes in California, signifying the arrival of a grassroots tax revolt.

1978: The Panama Canal Treaty is ratified.

1978: In October 1978 Congress passes and President Carter signs the Airline Deregulation Act. This act is a sign of the general move towards deregulating industries that had prospered for decades under the protective wing of the regulated sector of the economy. The result of airline deregulation, as was also the case in trucking and telecommunications, was the sudden destabilization of rates and carriers and labor relations in the airline industry.

1978: The federal government bails out the ailing Chrysler Corporation with a $1.5 billion loan. The company recovers and pays the loan back early.

1978: The United States normalizes diplomatic relations with China, which is now led by Deng Xiaoping.

1978–1979: President Jimmy Carter acts as a go-between in the Camp David talks between Egyptian President Anwar Sadat and Israeli Prime Minister Menachem Begin. The talks produce the Camp David Accords, a peace treaty between Israel and

Egypt that ends 31 years of warfare. The achievement also solidifies the reputation of Jimmy Carter as a skilled negotiator.

1979: The Three Mile Island nuclear power plant suffers an accident and damages the public perception of the safety of nuclear power.

1979: The shah of Iran, a long-time U.S. ally, is deposed by Islamic fundamentalists. Islamic militants soon seize 53 hostages at the American embassy. The hostage takers demand the return of the shah to face trial. The shah, who is undergoing unsuccessful cancer treatment in the United States, is exactly the kind of westernized and cosmopolitan national leader that the Islamic militants despise. The hostage crisis continues to the end of Carter's presidency.

1979: President Carter negotiates SALT II, a second arms limitation agreement with the Soviet Union.

1979: The first national march on Washington, D.C., for gay and lesbian rights attracts 100,000 participants.

1979: In Nicaragua, the leftist Sandinista rebels succeed in driving the Somoza family from power and set up a reform-minded regime with close ties to Cuba.

1979: The Soviet Union invades Afghanistan in what many Americans see as an attempt to secure access to the massive oil supplies of the Persian Gulf. The invasion leads President Carter to withdraw the SALT II treaty from the Senate without ratification, and contributes to an already worsening relationship between the United States and the Soviet Union.

1980: During the 1980s the number of Asian legal immigrants to the United States exceeds the number of Hispanic legal immigrants.

1980: Cuban ''boat people,'' the *Marielitos*, flood Florida.

1980: The United States boycotts the 1980 Olympics in Moscow.

1980: Ronald Reagan beats Jimmy Carter in the 1980 presidential election.

1981: On the same day Ronald Reagan is inaugurated as president, the American hostages in Iran are released.

1981: Ronald Reagan fires the air traffic controller members of the PATCO union for going on strike, citing the fact that as civil service employees they did not have the right to strike. This action encourages a ''get tough'' attitude which became the hallmark

of labor-management relations during the Reagan years.

1981: Sandra Day O'Connor is appointed to the U.S. Supreme Court as its first female justice.

1981: Reagan convinces Congress to agree to substantial tax reductions and to also cut the federal budget in many areas. Defense spending is increased substantially, however, leading to large budget deficits throughout the Reagan administration.

1981: The United States begins supporting the *Contra* anticommunist rebels in Nicaragua.

1981: The AIDS epidemic makes its first appearance in the United States.

1982: The Equal Rights Amendment to the Constitution fails to be ratified by the states.

1982: The economy falls into deep recession.

1982: National unemployment reaches 11 percent.

1982: The United States invades Grenada when a leftist group of rebels with ties to Cuba seizes control of the state.

1982: The recession brings inflation down as a weak market depresses prices; subsequently, interest rates begin to drop, and the economy rejuvenates itself with fresh inflows of capital.

1982: The nuclear freeze movement builds upon a popular fear of nuclear war.

1982: United States troops are killed in a truck bombing in Beirut, Lebanon.

1982: President Reagan strongly advocates the development of a so-called ''Star Wars'' nuclear defense system (orbiting satellites with laser guns to shoot down incoming ballistic missiles before they reenter the Earth's atmosphere). Despite scientific criticism, billions of dollars are spent on the Strategic Defense Initiative during the Reagan administration. The program fails to produce a working defense system.

1983: A pastoral letter on nuclear war is released by the Catholic bishops in the United States.

1983: The unemployment level stands at 10.2 percent.

1984: Unemployment is at 7.1 percent.

1984: The fear of urban violence and the availability of handguns leads to more urban violence. When four African American youths try to shake down Bernard Goetz in a New York City subway, he pulls out a gun and shoots them.

1984: Geraldine Ferraro receives the Democratic Party's nomination for the vice presidency.

1984: Reagan is reelected president, defeating Democrat Walter Mondale.

1985: Mikhail Gorbachev becomes head of the Communist Party and the Soviet government. He ushers in the period of *glasnost* (open discussion) in the Soviet Union.

1985: Homeless ''street people'' become a familiar sight in most big cities.

1985: Crack cocaine becomes the drug of choice on the U.S. illegal drug market.

1986: The Iran-Contra scandal, in which Iran was supplied with U.S. weapons in return for the Iranian contribution to the right-wing Contra rebels fighting a guerilla war against Nicaragua's Sandinista government is revealed.

1987: U.S. bombers strike Libya in an effort to ''take out'' Libyan President Muammar al Qaddafi, widely held to be engaged in state-supported terrorism.

1987: The Iran-Contra hearings determine that President Reagan was not involved in the Iran-Contra dealings, but several of his senior staff members are prosecuted. The scandal undermines public confidence in government.

1987: Although the economy is recovering from recession, investor psychology is still shaky, and a 508-point drop occurs on the New York stock market in one day.

1988: Republican George Bush and his running mate, Dan Quayle, defeat Democrat Michael S. Dukakis and Geraldine Ferraro in the 1988 presidential election.

1988: The Soviets agree to withdraw from Afghanistan.

1989: Germany begins to reunify as the Cold War grinds to an end. The Berlin Wall is dismantled, and the communist parties of Eastern and Central Europe are weakened. Rather than maintain the safety net features of socialist societies, these nations attempt the difficult transition to free-market economies.

1989: On March 1989 the Exxon oil tanker *Exxon Valdez* runs aground in Prince William Sound, Alaska.

Eleven million gallons of oil befoul 728 miles of coastline.

1989: Pro-democracy demonstrators in Tiananmen Square in Beijing, China, are shot down at the order of the Chinese government.

1989: After Panamanian troops harass several U.S. soldiers and kill one of them, the Bush administration sends 12,000 U.S. troops to Panama to arrest its dictatorial leader, Manuel Noriega, a former informant for the CIA, so that he can be tried on drug trafficking charges.

1990: The system of apartheid begins to fall apart in South Africa. The United States has taken a strong position against apartheid since the U.S. Civil Rights Movement demanded, in protest, that U.S. companies divest themselves of stock in South African companies.

1990: Congress passes and the president signs the Americans with Disabilities Act.

1990: In spite of his campaign promise, ''Read My Lips: No New Taxes,'' and in light of burgeoning budget deficits, President George Bush raises taxes.

1990: The U.S. economy slips into recession.

1991: In the Persian Gulf War, the United States and its allies rain destruction on the armed forces of Iraq. The small but oil-rich nation of Kuwait which Iraq had occupied, is liberated.

1991: President George Bush nominates African American conservative jurist Clarence Thomas to the Supreme Court, only to be confronted with the testimony of Anita Hill, who alleges that in a previous job Thomas persistently subjected her to sexual harassment. Most senators vote to confirm Thomas.

1992: After the beating of an African American motorist, Rodney King, by Los Angeles police, and after the accused police officers are acquitted by an all-white suburban jury, the city goes up in flames. In the resulting race riot, the largest and bloodiest in the twentieth century United States, over 50 people die.

1992: Democrat William Jefferson Clinton defeats George Bush in the presidential election.

1993: Congress raises taxes to shrink the federal deficit.

1993: Congress ratifies the North American Free Trade Agreement (NAFTA) which lowers tariffs, principally with Mexico and Canada.

1994: Congress rejects President Clinton's plan for a national health care system.

1994: For the first time since 1952, the election of 1994 gives the majority of both houses of Congress to the Republican Party and brings in many new Republican legislators pledged to shake up the Washington establishment and to pass tax reductions and term limits. Led by Congressman Newt Gingrich of Georgia, the Republican Congress engages in many political battles with President Clinton, including one that shuts down the government for several weeks.

1995: Perhaps as a result of a booming economy and low levels of unemployment, the national crime rate declines significantly.

1995: Congress passes and the president signs bills on welfare-to-work, a minimum wage increase, and minor reforms in the health care system.

1997: The Justice Department files an anti-trust lawsuit against the Microsoft Corporation.

1998: Already under investigation for possible sexual harassment and illegal real estate deals, President Clinton denies reports that he engaged in a sexual relationship with Monica Lewinsky, a former White House intern. If true, the reports would mean that Clinton lied under oath during investigations into the sexual harassment suit brought by Paula Jones.

1998: President Clinton admits to having engaged in a relationship with Monica Lewinsky which was ''not appropriate,'' but denies that he lied under oath.

1998: Accusing him of perjury and obstruction of justice, the U.S. House of Representatives votes along party lines to impeach President Clinton.

1999: President Clinton is acquitted by the Senate, which cannot muster a majority to convict him and remove him from office—much less the required two-thirds vote. The vote is largely along party lines. No Democrat votes to convict.

ABOLITION

The Abolition movement wanted to put an end to (abolish) slavery. The success of the anti-slavery campaign in Great Britain, which prohibited the slave trade in 1807, significantly strengthened the cause in the United States. The U.S. government outlawed slave trade the following year, and in the 1830s the revival of evangelical religion in the North gave the movement to emancipate African American slaves an even stronger impetus. Those Abolitionists believed that it violated Christian beliefs for one human being to own another. They called for an end to slavery, although the system was crucial to the agrarian economy of the southern states.

Leaders of the abolition movement included journalist William Lloyd Garrison (1805–79), founder of an influential anti-slavery journal; Theodore Dwight Weld (1803–95), leader of student protests and organizer of the American and Foreign Anti-Slavery Society; and brothers Arthur and Lewis Tappan (1786–1865; 1788–1873), prominent New York merchants who co-founded the American Anti-Slavery Society. Writers such as Harriet Beecher Stowe (1811–96), author of *Uncle Tom's Cabin* (1851–52), helped strengthen the abolitionist cause and were instrumental in swaying public opinion. But the nation remained mostly split along North-South lines. A middle ground was occupied by the Free-Soilers, who would tolerate slavery in the South but believed it should not be extended into new parts of the country. The slavery controversy deepened with the Compromise of 1850, which proved a poor attempt to assuage tensions. The legislation was prompted by the question of whether slavery should be extended into Texas and into territories gained in the Mexican War (1846–48). The Congressional compromise allowed for Texas to be a slave state. California was to be admitted as a free state (slavery was prohibited). Voters in New Mexico and Utah would decide the slavery question themselves, while the slave trade was to be prohibited in Washington, DC. Congress also passed a strict fugitive slave

law. The question arose again in 1854 when Kansas and Nebraska were added to the Union. Kansas became a proving ground for both sides, but the slavery question remained unresolved. In the hands of some activists the abolition movement became violent: In 1859 ardent abolitionist John Brown (1800–59) led a raid on the armory at Harper's Ferry (in present-day West Virginia), which failed to emancipate slaves by force. The slavery question for the South was not answered until President Abraham Lincoln (1861–65) issued the Emancipation Proclamation in January 1863. The Thirteenth Amendment, passed by Congress in January 1865, banned slavery throughout the United States.

See also: **Emancipation Proclamation, Fugitive Slave Act, Harpers Ferry Armory, Kansas-Nebraska Act, Slavery, Thirteenth Amendment**

ADAMS-ONIS TREATY

The Adams-Onis Treaty, officially called the Transcontinental Treaty, was signed in 1819 by the United States and Spain. The treaty, which was ratified on February 21, 1821, settled boundary disputes between the two countries. The terms of the earlier Louisiana Purchase (1803) failed to specify fully the boundaries of the territory that the United States had acquired from France. Britain and the United States soon disagreed over the Louisiana Territory's northern boundary. Spain and the United States reached an impasse over where the boundary lay between the U.S. territory and Spanish America—Spain's possessions in Florida, along the Gulf Coast, and in the Southwest. The terms of the Adams-Onis Treaty were negotiated by U.S. Secretary of State (later elected president) John Quincy Adams (1767–1848) and Spanish Minister to the United States Luis de Onis (1762–1827). The treaty established the line of demarcation between the new republic and Spanish territorial claims. The countries agreed that the western boundary of the United States began at the mouth of the Sabine River (which today forms the border between western Louisiana and eastern Texas). From there the boundary ran at a northwest angle until it reached 42 degrees north latitude. It then followed this line of latitude west to the Pacific Ocean. Territory lying east and north of this line belonged to the United States; territory lying west and south of this line belonged to Spain. By this treaty the United States gained all of Florida and a southern strip of Alabama and Mississippi (collectively called the Old Southwest). Spain retained its claim to the Southwest, which was roughly the area of present-day Texas, New Mexico, Colorado, Utah, Arizona, Nevada, and California. As part of the treaty, the United States agreed to pay $5 million in claims of U.S. citizens against Spain. The claims were made by people who had settled Florida, predominately the panhandle (then called West Florida), while it was still a possession of Spain.

See also: **Convention of 1818, Louisiana Purchase, Manifest Destiny, Old Southwest**

ADDAMS, (LAURA) JANE

(Laura) Jane Addams (1860–1935), a social reformer, internationalist, and feminist, was the first American woman to win the Nobel prize for peace. Best known as the founder of Chicago's Hull House, one of the first social settlements in North America, she was widely recognized for her numerous books and articles, social activism, and international efforts for world peace.

Addams was born in Cedarville, Illinois, on September 6, 1860, the eighth of nine children of Sarah and John Huy Addams. When she was only two, her mother died in childbirth. Her father, a prosperous businessman and Illinois state senator, was a friend of President Abraham Lincoln and a widely respected leader in the community.

In 1881 Addams graduated from Rockford College (then Rockford Women's Seminary), the valedictorian of a class of 17. Over the next six years, while intermittently studying medicine, she traveled and studied in Europe, battled an illness characterized by chronic exhaustion, and underwent surgery for a congenital spinal defect.

Confronted with the limited career opportunities available to women in the late nineteenth century, Addams searched for a way to be of service to society. In 1888, at age 27, during a second tour of Europe, she and a college friend, Ellen Gates Starr, visited a pioneering settlement house called Toynbee Hall in a desperately poor area of London. This visit crystallized

Jane Addams.

in their minds the idea of opening a similar facility in one of Chicago's most underprivileged working-class neighborhoods.

The two friends returned home to a city that Lincoln Steffens, a famous writer of the period, described as ''loud, lawless, unlovely, ill-smelling, new; an overgrown gawk of a village, the teeming tough among cities.'' In 1889 Addams acquired a large, vacant mansion built by Charles Hull in 1856 at the corner of Halsted and Polk Streets. She and Ellen Starr moved in and opened the doors of Hull House on September 18, 1889.

The settlement house was an immediate success. By the end of its second year, Hull House was host to two thousand people every week and was soon famous throughout the country. Journalists, educators, and researchers came to observe its operations, well-to-do young women gave their time and effort, and well-known social workers and reformers lived at the settlement and assisted in its activities.

Hull House eventually included 13 buildings and a playground as well as a camp near Lake Geneva,

Wisconsin. Facilities included a day nursery, a gymnasium, a community kitchen, and a boarding club for working women. Among the services provided were the city's first kindergarten and day care center. Hull House also offered college-level courses in various subjects; training in art, music, and crafts; and the nation's first little theater group, the Hull House players. An employment bureau, an art gallery, and libraries and social clubs for men, women, and children were among other services and cultural opportunities offered to the largely immigrant population of the neighborhood.

As her reputation increased, Addams expanded her vision to focus on many crucial social issues of the time. Local activities at Hull House gave way to national activities on behalf of the underprivileged. In 1906 she became the first woman president of the National Conference of Charities and Corrections. She led investigations on midwifery, narcotics consumption, milk supplies, and sanitary conditions. In 1910 she received the first honorary degree ever awarded to a woman by Yale University.

In 1914, at the onset of World War I (1914–1918), Addams worked for peace, refusing to endorse American participation in the war. For her opposition, she was expelled from the Daughters of the American Revolution and widely attacked in the press. She devoted herself to providing relief supplies of food to the women and children of the enemy nations. In 1915 she accepted the chairmanship of the Women's Peace Party and, four months later, was named president of the International Congress of Women. That organization later became the Women's International Peace League for Peace and Freedom, of which Addams remained president until her death.

In 1931, with Nicholas Murray Butler, Addams was named a cowinner of the Nobel prize for peace. Hospitalized for heart problems at the time of the award ceremony, she was unable to deliver the Nobel lecture in Oslo. She died in 1935 of cancer; appropriately, her funeral service took place in the courtyard of Hull House.

See also: **Tenements**

FURTHER READING

Addams, Jane. *Democracy and Social Ethics*. Cambridge: Belknap Press of Harvard University Press, 1964.

———. *Twenty Years at Hull House*. New York: MacMillan Press, 1910.

Farrell, John C. *Beloved Lady: A History of Jane Addams's Ideas on Reform and Peace*. New York: John Hopkins Press, 1967.

Tims, Margaret. *Jane Addams of Hull House, 1860–1935*. London: Allen & Unwin, 1961.

Nash, Roderick. *From These Beginnings: A Biographical Approach to American History*, vol. 2. New York: Harper Press, 1984, s.v. "Jane Addams."

ADVERTISING INDUSTRY

The earliest forms of advertising included simple signs that merchants put over their doors to inform the public about what was for sale inside. Posters, pamphlets, and handbills began appearing in England following the invention of movable type in Germany around 1450. Advertising became a part of newspapers when they first appeared in England in the seventeenth century and in America at the beginning of the eighteenth century. Magazine advertising followed in the early nineteenth century.

During the 1700s Great Britain made great advances in advertising. Handbills and trade cards were common. A wide variety of goods were advertised. For example, one of the most exciting subjects of advertising was the New World. Historians have commented that posters and handbills lauding the wonders of the New World may have hastened emigration there.

During the eighteenth century advertising could be found in the British colonies in America—a practice that, centuries later, achieved a great level of refinement and popularity in the new nation. Advertising in the colonies, however, initially had little impact. Since America was predominantly wilderness and farm country, many people lived in comparative isolation. In addition, ads appearing in newspapers were often illegible and poorly written.

Improvements in printing technology and a new advertising philosophy led to advances in U.S. advertising in the larger cities during the 1820s and 1830s. New York's penny press newspapers began to make their advertising more understandable and accessible to common readers. Finally in 1848 the *New York Herald* began changing the newspaper's ads daily. This expansion created a need for advertising agencies.

Advertising agencies began to emerge in the United States in the 1840s. They sold space in newspapers and magazines for commission. The commission system allowed the agency to collect a fee for placing an ad in a given newspaper or journal. It became established that agencies were compensated by their clients, that is, agencies represented the newspapers and periodicals in which advertising appeared. In 1875 George Rowell, who pioneered buying advertising space in bulk, announced that he would reverse the relationship and act on behalf of the advertisers. Soon F.W. Ayer introduced a new arrangement, the "open contract," in which terms were vague, and the agency was permitted to represent the advertiser over an indefinite period of time. It created a dynamic, long-term relationship between advertiser and agency that was generally healthy for the industry.

Changes in the American marketing system in the 1880s made modern advertising models possible. Previously the market was dominated by wholesalers who purchased goods in large lots and sold them in smaller lots for a profit. During the 1880s, however, manufacturers of packaged goods began to package, brand, and distribute their products throughout the country. This change introduced a need for advertising on a national level. These advertisers provided agencies with a new set of clients with higher standards than those who sold to only local markets. For example, packaged goods manufacturers wanted their advertising to create a bond of trust with the consumer, so their advertising needed to be more truthful.

Throughout the nineteenth century the most widely advertised products were patent medicines. Even as late as 1893 more than half of all advertisers who spent more than $50,000 annually on advertising were patent medicine manufacturers.

For firms making durable and non-durable goods advertising served many purposes. It helped introduce new products and suggested new uses for those already existing. It could also reach new audiences to inform them about established products that were unfamiliar to them. Heavily advertised products were safer to stock and easier to sell because advertising created consumer demand and brand loyalty.

During the 1890s the advertising industry grew dramatically. By 1897 more than 2,500 companies were conducting large-scale advertising campaigns. This expansion was the result of the increased use of brand names and trademarks and growing newspaper distribution. Copywriters also contributed to the growth. In 1892 N.W. Ayer & Son agency in Philadelphia hired its first copywriter to create an advertisement. Previously it had simply bought advertising space from newspapers and magazines and sold it to advertisers. Now agencies could provide both art and copy for their clients.

In 1900 the major agencies included J. Walter Thompson, N. W. Ayer & Son, and Lord & Thomas. In the nineteenth century J. Walter Thompson had persuaded several literary magazines to carry advertising, and by 1900 his agency was creating ads for thirty of the most popular women's and general interest monthly periodicals. J. Walter Thompson can be credited with transforming magazines into an advertising medium.

The Chicago agency Lord & Thomas, which later became Foote, Cone & Belding, is credited with developing a now-common form of advertising that stressed salesmanship. It originated with Albert Davis Lasker, who joined the agency in 1898 and was its sole owner from 1912 to 1942. Lasker, along with copywriter John E. Kennedy, were the founders of the "reason-why" school of advertising. Until its advent, the industry was mainly concerned with keeping the client's name before the public. Lasker innovated by adding the element of persuasion (stressing benefits to the consumer). He argued that an advertisement must give the consumer a specific reason for buying a product. This new approach later earned him the title, "the father of modern advertising."

During the 1920s the introduction of radio in the United States gave advertising an impetus that carried it through the Great Depression (1929–1939) and World War II (1939–1945). When radio was first introduced, many people felt that radio advertising should be prohibited. This view was supported by then Secretary of Commerce Herbert Hoover (1874–1964). By the end of the decade, however, advertisers began to use radio's advantages as an advertising medium by injecting elements such as drama and immediacy into commercials.

With the formation of the NBC and CBS radio networks in 1926 and 1927, respectively, radio became an important medium for advertisers. Ad agencies created nighttime radio programs as a way to communicate their client's message. They also created daytime radio dramas that became known as "soap operas" (a term that was first applied to the dramas created for consumer product giant Proctor & Gamble).

During the 1920s advertising agencies were transformed into professional organizations offering specialized services. Market research was used to gain a better understanding of the prospective audience, and agencies developed separate departments and operating units, including research and art departments (which were added to complement copy-writing services). Ad budgets soared.

Following World War II, the introduction of television laid the foundation for an advertising boom in the 1950s. By 1948 one million U.S. homes had television sets; the first coast-to-coast network was established in 1951. It was a period marked by numerous changes: ad agencies added more staff; new agencies were formed; mergers strengthened those already existing. From 1950 to 1980 advertising expenditures increased tenfold.

After World War II the U.S. advertising industry began spread throughout the world. American companies began to sell again to markets that they had entered before the war and compete in new ones. Offices were set up abroad, and the major agencies became multinational to serve their multinational clients such as Coca-Cola, Ford Motor Company, Eastman Kodak, General Foods, and many others. In the 1980s and 1990s, U.S. advertising came to dominate the international market. There were, however, some notable exceptions. For example, London's Saatchi & Saatchi, became a giant by acquiring smaller shops located in strategic cities around the world. The Dentsu agency was the principal company in Japan. France also had its own dominant agencies.

By 1980 U.S. advertising expenditures were more than $55 billion, or about two percent of the gross national product. Sears, Roebuck and Co. was the nation's largest advertiser, spending $700 million in national and local advertising. From 1976 to 1988 U.S. spending on advertising grew faster than the economy as a whole. TV advertising was mainly responsible for this growth. In 1988, as the country began slipping into an economic recession, there was a slowdown in advertising spending. U.S. ad spending would not recover until 1993, when U.S. advertising spending reached $140.6 billion.

At the time of the economic recession industry analysts began to question the effectiveness of traditional advertising to sell products and services. They offered several possible explanations: consumers were becoming less receptive to the continual barrage of advertising messages, and they grew more price conscious and less brand loyal.

Technological innovations also had an impact on traditional advertising. The proliferation of alternative communication, including the rise of cable television, changed the way advertisers could reach their audience. Advanced market research techniques allowed companies to gather a wealth of data about their customers and consumers in general. This data could be effectively used to create a database marketing program. Direct marketing increased in usage and

popularity. In addition to traditional advertising, clients began demanding agencies provide integrated marketing programs that combined a variety of elements such as direct mail, direct response, database marketing, coupon redemption, in-store promotions, and other, similar techniques. Although large advertising agencies could offer their clients a range of marketing services, smaller agencies seemed better able to adjust to the changing marketing needs of their clients. This ability made smaller agencies the fastest-growing segment of the advertising industry in the early 1990s.

In spite of the growth of smaller agencies, advertising in the 1990s was dominated by large marketing conglomerates that owned several well-known advertising agencies. These conglomerates were formed through acquisitions and mergers. The largest included WPP Group PLC (which, among others, owned ad agencies J. Walter Thompson and Ogilvy & Mather); Omnicom Group Inc. (which held BBDO Worldwide Network and DDB Needham Worldwide Network and several independent agencies); Interpublic Group of Companies (whose holdings included McCann-Erickson Worldwide, Lintas: Worldwide, Dailey & Associates, and The Lowe Group); and True North Communications Inc. (which, among other agencies, owned Foote, Cone & Belding and Bozell, Jacobs, Kenyon, & Eckhardt Inc.).

FURTHER READING

Applegate, Edd. *Personalities and Products: A Historical Perspective on Advertising in America*. Westport, CT: Greenwood Press, 1998.

Fox, Stephen. *The Mirror Makers: A History of American Advertising and its Creators*. New York: Morrow, 1984.

Goldsborough, Robert. ''The Postwar Era, 1945–1950.'' *Advertising Age*, July 31, 1995.

Lears, Jackson. *Fables of Abundance: A Cultural History of Advertising in America*. New York: Basic Books, 1994.

Lockwood, Lisa. ''The Image Makers.'' *WWD*, September 28, 1998.

Norris, James D. *Advertising and the Transformation of American Society, 1865–1920*. New York: Greenwood Press, 1990.

Perlongo, Bob. *Early American Advertising*. New York: Art Direction Book Co., 1985.

Sivulka, Juliann. *Soap, Sex, and Cigarettes: A Cultural History of American Advertising*. Belmont, CA: Wadsworth Publishing Co., 1997.

AFFIRMATIVE ACTION *(ISSUE)*

In 1996 a majority of Californians voted for Proposition 209, a state law which attacked affirmative action programs by stating that race, sex, color, ethnicity, or national origin could not be used to "grant preferential treatment" in the areas of "public employment, public education, or public contracting." The Civil Rights Initiative (CCRI) organized the campaign. A member of the University of California Board of Regents argued that affirmative action programs, in place since the 1960s, have hurt more than helped African Americans.

Clearly, the political atmosphere had changed dramatically in the United States since the Civil Rights Act of 1964 and the Voting Rights Act of 1965. These measures inaugurated a massive campaign to dismantle legal segregation and to protect the rights of African Americans under federal law. A decade earlier the Supreme Court handed down the landmark case of *Brown v. Board of Education* (1954). In the *Brown* case a unanimous Court ruled that state and local governments could no longer maintain racially segregated educational institutions. The Court argued that schools separated by race would always create inferior institutions for black children because isolation "generates a feeling of inferiority as to their status in the community that may affect their hearts and minds in a way unlikely ever to be undone."

In a commencement address at Howard University in June 1965, President Lyndon B. Johnson (1963–1969) stated that guaranteeing basic equal freedoms was not enough; the nation also had to work toward an "equality of result." However, in a legislative compromise, the actual Civil Rights Act of 1964 disavowed using quotas as an anti-discrimination measure. In September 1965, President Johnson issued Executive Order (EO) 11246, which required employers to search aggressively for qualified minority applicants through such methods as advertising and recruitment in minority communities. It did not establish a means of enforcement to ensure candidates were now considered in a "color-blind" pool of applicants. In addition, EO 11246 did not include gender discrimination, which would be added a few years later.

The willingness of the public to provide a level playing field to the disadvantaged was again undermined in the 1970s and 1980s when economic recessions created a tight labor market. More of the nation began to view job opportunities as a zero-sum game. This perspective suggested that when an individual belonging to a minority was hired under affirmative action, someone else, probably a white male, was disqualified. As this kind of attitude towards affirmative action became more pervasive, the Supreme Court in 1977 took up a case that addressed "reverse discrimination:" *Regents of the University of California v. Bakke* (1977). Allen Bakke and other higher-ranked white applicants were rejected from the University of California Davis Medical School and argued they had been discriminated against in order to fill a given number of slots with minority applicants. In a majority decision the Supreme Court struck down U.C.-Davis's racial-quota system and ordered Bakke admitted. However, the Court also found that it was acceptable to take race into account as a positive factor in admissions as a way to create a diverse student body. Affirmative action as a system remained intact although institutions were no longer allowed to blatantly use quotas to enforce desegregation.

Some critics of affirmative action want it abolished altogether. They argue that the programs hurt those they intend to help by implying the inferiority of African Americans through the hiring or admitting of less qualified black candidates to jobs and colleges. Opponents of affirmative action claim that these programs lead African Americans to think of themselves as victims of past racial injustices rather than to encourage self-reliance. In addition, critics claim that the country needs "color-blind" policies. In their eyes, affirmative action has already done away with the discriminatory policies and practices that existed prior to the concrete gains of the Civil Rights Movement of the 1960s. Other scholars, such as William Julius Wilson, argue that we need "race-neutral" affirmative action. Rather than help the majority of poor African Americans, Wilson claims affirmative action aids mostly upper stratum African Americans and other minorities. He argues that programs based on socio-economic status would provide opportunities to those who most need it in U.S. society including poor whites.

Critics often misrepresent affirmative action in the heated debate. First, the public debate about the issue has been misrepresented solely as a "black and white" issue, even though women and Latinos are important beneficiaries of the opportunities afforded under affirmative action programs as well. In addition, anecdotal evidence is usually used when instances of reverse discrimination are noted. However, in general, companies and colleges often have to decide between white men and African Americans or women who are equally qualified, and race and gender serves as a tiebreaker.

On the other side of the debate, affirmative action supporters provide four major reasons why affirmative action is not only necessary but needs to be strengthened. They say African Americans in the United States were historically harmed by racism and slavery. Historical oppression makes it necessary to give African Americans a head start, leveling the playing field and providing everyone with a fair opportunity. In a 1965 speech President Lyndon Johnson (1963–1969) supported this position, making an analogy to a running event, saying that if one runner got ahead of another whose legs were shackled together, it would be unfair merely to remove the shackles. Instead, in order to ensure a fair race, the shackled runner must be allowed to make up the ''40 yards'' he lost while in chains.

IN A COMMENCEMENT ADDRESS AT HOWARD UNIVERSITY IN JUNE 1965, PRESIDENT LYNDON B. JOHNSON STATED THAT GUARANTEEING BASIC EQUAL FREEDOMS WAS NOT ENOUGH; THE NATION ALSO HAD TO WORK TOWARD AN "EQUALITY OF RESULT."

Another argument in support of affirmative action is that it is needed to overcome the racism still evident in the workplace and education system. Although the number of wealthy and middle class African Americans has increased greatly since the 1960s, a ''glass ceiling'' still remains as an obstacle to the advancement beyond entry-level jobs for most black men and women.

The third reason given for the need for affirmative action is that it increases diversity at jobs and colleges. By working and studying next to people from diverse backgrounds, some corporate leaders and college admissions officers argue, workers become more productive and students learn more from experiencing different perspectives and cultures. Supporters of affirmative action also suggest that companies can serve their customers better by including more personnel with diverse backgrounds in their decisions.

The fourth argument for these programs is that a social need is addressed by hiring minorities through affirmative action. For example, an African American doctor who grew up in a poor neighborhood might decide to go back and serve the community with his or her medical degree. A good example is the doctor who was admitted to medical school in the place of Allen Bakke. Dr. Patrick Chavis is an obstetrician gynecologist with a practice that serves mostly Medicaid patients in a poor neighborhood in Los Angeles. Another example of the way social needs may be met is that an African American female scientist is more likely to pursue research interests that may improve the health of black women, historically neglected as research subjects, than would a white researcher.

Several conclusions can be drawn about affirmative action despite its controversial nature. First, discrimination and racism still operate in the workplace and the education system in the United States. Second, countless African Americans, women, and Latinos have benefited from a higher education and higher income by taking advantage of affirmative action programs. Third, the benefits to society in raising the income and educational level of minorities outweigh the rarer instances of ''reverse discrimination'' which take place.

On the other hand, since the original purpose of the civil rights movement was to remove barriers based on race, creed, etc., affirmative action seems to many like a step backward that breeds its own injustice. They maintain that it is as unfair to discriminate against European Americans as it was to discriminate against African Americans, and the children are not responsible for the sins of their parents. It is not the state's job to redress the wrongs of history but to provide equal justice for all. According to this view, society is best served by treating everyone impartially, and in the long run talent will receive its reward. This argument has had the better of it in the public debate, because the national trend since the 1980s has been to reverse policies which overtly favor minorities, women, and the disadvantaged.

See also: **Civil Rights Movement, Jim Crow Laws**

FURTHER READING

Beckwith, Francis J., and Todd E. Jones, eds. *Affirmative Action: Social Justice or Reverse Discrimination*. Amherst, NH: Prometheus Books, 1997.

Bowen, William G., and Derek Bok. *The Shape of the River: Long Term Consequences of Considering Race in College and University Admissions*. Princeton, NJ: Princeton University Press, 1998.

Hacker, Andrew. *Two Nations: Black and White, Separate, Hostile, Unequal*. New York: Ballantine Books, 1995.

Omi, Michael, and Howard Winant. *Racial Formation in the United States From the 1960s to the 1990s*, 2nd ed. New York: Routledge, 1994.

Wilson, William Julius. *The Truly Disadvantaged: The Inner City, the Underclass, and Public Policy*. Chicago: University of Chicago Press, 1987.

AFRICANS ARRIVE IN VIRGINIA, 1619

One stormy day in August of 1619 a Dutch man-of-war with about 20 Africans on board entered port at the English colony of Jamestown, Virginia. Little is known of these newly arrived people: the first Africans to set foot on the North American continent. At this time the slave trade between Africa and the English colonies had not yet been established, and it is unlikely that the 20 or so newcomers became slaves upon their arrival. They were perhaps considered indentured servants, who worked under contract for a certain period of time (usually seven years) before they were granted freedom and the rights accorded to other settlers. Their historic arrival, however, marked the beginning of an atrocious trend in colonial America, in which the people of Africa were taken unwillingly from their motherland and consigned to lifelong slavery. The robust economic growth of the English colonies was caused largely by this exploitative institution.

Many scholars agree that the captain and crew of the Dutch ship stole their valuable human cargo from the San Juan Bautista, a Portuguese merchant-slaver that had been making its way from the West African port town of Luanda, Angola to Vera Cruz. The raid of the Portuguese ship took place on the high seas and when the Dutch adventurers arrived in Virginia they traded the Africans to Jamestown settlers in exchange for food. If these Africans indeed hailed from Luanda, which was then the newly established capital of the Portuguese colony of Angola, it is likely that they had been trading with Europeans for years, that they spoke a language in common with these Europeans, and that they were Christians. It is possible that these characteristics enabled them to escape a life of slavery, which was to become the fate of the more ethnically and linguistically diverse groups of Africans that arrived in North America in later years.

The social status of the first Africans in Jamestown was confusing, and perhaps deliberately ambiguous. Records from 1623 and 1624 list the black inhabitants of the colony as servants, not slaves. In these same records, however, white indentured servants are listed along with the year in which they were to attain freedom; no such year accompanies the names of black servants. Freedom was the birthright of William Tucker, the first African born in the colonies. Yet court records show that at least one African had been declared a slave by 1640, the year that slavery was officially instituted in Jamestown. After the legalization of slavery by the Virginia colony, the African population began to rise slowly and steadily. The

> Whatever the status of these first Africans to arrive at Jamestown, it is clear that by 1640, at least one African had been declared a slave. This African was ordered by the court "to serve his said master or his assigns for the time of his natural life here or elsewhere."
>
> **PBS Online, *Africans in America: America's Journey Through Slavery*, 1998**

number of blacks increased from 23 in 1625 to approximately three hundred in 1650.

Economic interests propelled the rise of slavery throughout the seventeenth century in colonial Virginia, where tobacco was the cash crop that held the promise of wealth. At first settlers in the colonies looked to England for workers. Arriving from overseas English laborers cleared the fields for the planting and harvesting of tobacco, which sold for a high price in the 1620s and 1630s. The influx of a British workforce, however, did not last; in the 1660s the price of tobacco plummeted, and the Great Plague diminished England's population. After a fire devastated London, the reconstruction of the city created jobs for laborers, who preferred to remain at home. When these events led the colonial settlers to look elsewhere for field workers, they resorted to the slave trade, which had been active in Europe since the Portuguese first explored the African coast in the fifteenth century.

Tobacco, coffee, sugar, and rice were the colonies' chief exports, and the production of these cash crops required a hearty and dependable workforce. Meanwhile the contracts of indentured servants were expiring, depleting the plantations of laborers. Attempts were made to enslave Native Americans, but these were largely unsuccessful. The settlers found it difficult to subdue the Native American people, who knew the land and who lived in unified communities that had the means of self-defense. The European slave trade provided New World settlers with culturally disparate African captives who had been forcibly uprooted from their homeland and stripped of their ability to defend themselves. Although many Africans rebelled and resisted enslavement, most found themselves unable to escape the bondage that was to be their tragic fate.

Less than one hundred years after the arrival of the first Africans in Virginia the institution of slavery was firmly in place. By the turn of the eighteenth century more than a thousand Africans were arriving each year via merchant-slave ships. Sea routes were established: Sailors voyaged from England to Africa, where they

The first Africans arrived in the American colonies in 1619. By 1640, the institution of slavery was officially established in at least one of the colonies.

offered goods in exchange for slaves, then departed for the New World colonies where settlers purchased the slaves and put them to work. While colonial America profited from the Africans' labor, the slave trade became a tremendously lucrative business in itself. At the expense of a people held captive, colonial America's plantation economy and the slave trade industry flourished for many years to come.

See also: **Slavery, Sugar, Tobacco, Triangular Trade**

FURTHER READING

"Africans in America: America's Journey Through Slavery," [cited April 19, 1999], available on the World Wide Web @ www.pbs.org/wgbh/aia/.

"Chronology on the History of Slavery, 1619 to 1789," [cited March 3, 1999], available from the World Wide Web @ innercity.org/holt/slavechron.html/.

The Columbia Encyclopedia, 5th ed. New York: Columbia University Press, 1993, s.v. "Slavery."

"First Africans in America" [cited April 19, 1999], available from the World Wide Web @ www.msstate.edu/listarchives/afrigeneas/ 199902/msg00612.html/.

Thornton, John. "The African Experience of the '20, and odd Negroes' Arriving in Virginia in 1619." *The William and Mary Quarterly*, July 1998.

THE AGE OF REVOLUTION, 1763–1790 *OVERVIEW*

At the end of the French and Indian War (1754–1763), British North America was a scattered patchwork of individual colonies that had been allowed to develop their own economic and political systems during a previous 40-year period of neglect by the government in London. By 1790, Americans had worked together to end British rule, cooperated to form a political union, created a centralized federal constitution, and were beginning to deal with the huge economic consequences and responsibilities of being a united nation. In order to undergo such a transition, Americans had to fight a bitter revolution and to endure difficult economic changes that would shape their country for decades to come.

Although the American colonies were primarily agricultural, farming varied from region to region. In the southern colonies, slave labor produced a large surplus of tobacco and wheat for overseas trade, frequently handled by wealthy Scottish merchants (called "factors")who held monopolies licensed by the British crown. Slavery was present in the South and in some of the northern colonies, like New York. It had a different function there, however—many of the slaves in New York City worked as domestic servants. In general, slavery was much less important in other colonies, like Pennsylvania, where smaller family farms that produced goods mainly for their own use were the norm.

With the exception of some areas of the mid-Atlantic colonies, ordinary Americans owned land in numbers that far exceeded their counterparts in Europe. Merchants in New England and in the port cities of the middle colonies enriched themselves (and their British counterparts) by importing and exporting rum, ship masts, sugar, and tea, among other trade goods. During the early 1700s the British government had been content to let colonial economies develop on their own because, even though the colonists dodged many taxes, the mother country profited from colonial economic activity and the colonies played an important

THE ARTICLES OF CONFEDERATION VS. THE CONSTITUTION

The Federal Government is Empowered to:	Under the Articles of Confederation:	Under the United States Constitution:
Declare War and make peace	Yes	Yes
Control foreign affairs	Yes	Yes
Create a postal system	Yes	Yes
Coin money	Yes	Yes
Impose taxes	No	Yes
Utilize state militia	No	Yes
Trade regulation	No	Yes
Organize a court system	No	Yes
Protect copyrights	No	Yes
Take other necessary actions to manage the federal government	No	Yes

This table highlights the different powers given to the federal government by the Articles of Confederation and the U.S. Constitution. The Articles of Confederation created a weak central government, unable to deal with the nation's economy.

part of the economic theory of mercantilism that defined the relationship between governments and their colonies.

The close of the French and Indian War brought Great Britain's "benign neglect" to an end. The British government spent more than one million pounds on colonial defense during the war, and a series of new activist Prime Ministers decided that the colonies should bear a fair share of the taxes that would be needed to pay back Britain's war debt. Although the colonials paid taxes that were at least 25 times lower than the British living in England and only one-fifth that of the Irish, they did not react well to attempts to raise their taxes over the next ten years. The vast majority of the colonial population were loyal British citizens, but they had grown used to levying their own taxes in local assemblies for the upkeep and improvement of the colony.

Economic resistance sparked a movement for political change as colonists protested an increasingly strict series of commercial laws and taxes passed by the British Parliament between 1764 and 1774. The British government attempted not only to control trade (which

they had done since the first Navigation Acts in 1651 and 1660). They also tried to raise taxes to pay off the shortfalls in the British Exchequer and they passed restrictions on colonial paper money that was virtually worthless in Britain. The Sugar Act (1764) and the Tea Act (1773) tried to increase revenue by taxing these vital imports and they tried to stop smuggling. To do all this they appointed Customs Agents and founded Admiralty Courts. Another set of laws—the Stamp Act (1765), the Townshend Revenue Acts (1767), and the Declaratory Act (1766)—placed duties on a wide variety of goods, such as legal documents, glass, and lead. Parliament also restricted American trade outside the British empire and declared Parliament's authority to legislate for the colonies "in all cases whatsoever."

Colonists resisted all of these measures through a variety of means. Intellectuals like Philadelphia lawyer John Dickinson wrote pamphlets denouncing Parliament's right to tax without colonial representatives giving their consent. Merchants and workingmen formed paramilitary clubs called the Sons of Liberty. Crowds of ordinary men and women harassed individual tax collectors, held public protest meetings, and even resorted to dumping East India Company tea into Boston Harbor in December 1773 at the Boston Tea Party. The "Committees of Correspondence" encouraged communication among resistance leaders in different colonies, and after 1774 the First Continental Congress organized boycotts of British luxury items like tea and silk cloth.

Disagreements over economic issues led Americans to begin to question the rationale of political authority of Great Britain. When Parliament dissolved the Massachusetts legislature, closed Boston Harbor, shut down colonial courts, and quartered troops in private homes in 1774, some Americans prepared to take resistance to a higher level. The restrictive economic policies, even though several of them had been repealed, inspired colonists to work together as never before, and reaction spread far beyond Massachusetts. In the Quebec Act of 1774 the British tried to enforce a previous restriction on American settlement west of the Allegheny Mountains (designed to keep settlers from clashing with Native Americans and to facilitate the collection of taxes). This raised the ire of the frontier population who, to that point, were largely indifferent to the quarrels of their city cousins.

Though not all Americans agreed that greater resistance was necessary, some colonists began to stockpile weapons and to train for war. The conflict turned violent on April 19, 1775, when British troops were dispatched to capture weapons and agitators in Lexington and Concord, Massachusetts. They met armed resistance from citizen militias. Meanwhile, a revolutionary assembly called the Continental Congress mobilized for armed conflict, and the American Revolution (1775–1783) began.

In 1775 the Second Continental Congress—not yet a proper national legislature—was ill-prepared to finance a war. Although the Congress on July 4, 1776 produced a stirring Declaration of Independence based on the ideas of representative government that had been advanced by British philosopher John Locke, the American Revolution had to confront a serious financial challenge. Seven years of warfare created both economic problems and opportunities as the upheaval of war affected the circumstances of individual Americans. Loyalists who opposed the war and the secession from Great Britain often found their property confiscated or destroyed by unsympathetic ''mobs'' or by local governments. One hundred and eighty thousand men volunteered for military service in the Continental Army or the state militias. Women assumed control of businesses and farms in unprecedented numbers while their fathers or husbands were away. African American slaves freed themselves from bondage by seeking protection from the British Army or joining the American armed forces themselves. Farmers faced confiscation of their property by foraging armies, especially as the war shifted to the middle states and to the South. Some city dwellers carried on business under enemy occupation.

The government faced constant conflict over how to finance the war and supply the military. The Continental Congress had no powers to enforce state tax contributions to pay for the war, so they mainly solved their financial difficulties through securing loans and by printing money. Congress and the states ordered almost $400 million worth of paper money to be printed, despite the fact that hard currency reserves (the gold and silver that was supposed to back up paper currency at the time) probably never exceeded $30 million. The unfortunate result of so much paper currency was inflation, which continued throughout the war. Financial problems persisted, although foreign loans flowed in after France signed a treaty of alliance with the United States in 1779. The national government was almost bankrupt by 1780, and troops threatened to mutiny over lack of pay just as the fighting grew fiercer. Prominent Philadelphia merchant Robert Morris was appointed superintendent of finance in early 1781, and his efforts to shore up national credit as well as his advocacy of a charter for the Bank of North America probably helped the American army triumph at the climactic Battle of Yorktown in October 1781.

Morris remained at the helm of the national economy until the war was formally concluded in 1783.

Some individuals, such as ''privateers'' who were commissioned to capture British ships and keep the profits for themselves, or merchants who charged outrageous prices for food, profited from the war. Others, mainly the poor or the Loyalists (who abandoned their houses and fled the country), suffered from high prices or from the disruption that the war caused to the agricultural economy. The British imposed a blockade on the eastern seaboard and both imports and exports declined. This led some enterprising merchants in cities like Philadelphia to consider founding a manufacturing sector to produce goods that could no longer be imported. State controls on prices and wages did little to even out the economic effects of the war.

The relative weakness of the central government, which Americans had chosen in reaction to British rule, caused many financial difficulties during the American Revolution that continued after the war. The Articles of Confederation, which were proposed in 1777 as the United States' first national written constitution, called for a Congress in which each state had one equal vote. But the problems with such an arrangement became clear when the document itself was not accepted by all the states until 1781. Under the Articles, the national government controlled credit and could charter banks, but could not directly tax American citizens. Realizing that taxation would be necessary to pay off war debt, Morris proposed an amendment to the Articles that would have allowed Congress to impose a 5 percent tax or ''impost'' on imports. Even though by 1782 twelve states had ratified the amendment, the proposal failed because Rhode Island, the smallest state, refused to agree. Constant squabbling among the states, over western land claims and other issues, contributed to continued financial chaos throughout the 1780s.

The fact that the Revolution was not only a successful rejection of British rule but also contained elements of a social revolution became clear when, after the war a new breed of leaders came to power in the United States, particularly in state legislatures. Businessmen, merchants, and even tradesmen who had acquired a comfortable standard of living now questioned the traditional authority of the landed elite that, in tandem with the British officials, had controlled colonial American society. In the South, the slaveholding class grew worried as the first organized antislavery movement in American history took aim at the basis of their wealth. Tenants in western New York revolted against their landlords and demanded equal opportunity to buy land. But although the Revolution was "made" through the blood and the sweat of ordinary Americans, it was led by a class of entrepreneurs—the commercial and financial elite of New England and Philadelphia as well as the rich, slave-holding farmers of the South. These leaders of the economy argued that the pursuit of profit was not incompatible with the "virtuous" American political ideal.

Inflation continued after the war, and some people began to view paper currency as almost worthless. Other people, small farmers mostly, found it easier to pay the mortgages with cheap money. Meanwhile, a trade imbalance with Great Britain plunged the United States, which still relied on the former "mother country" for the majority of its imports and exports, into a depression. While the national government under the Articles of Confederation could not impose taxes to pay off debt, many individuals were heavily taxed by their states. Veterans who received western land grants in return for wartime service often sold off their claims to land speculators, who in turn drove up prices for those who chose to relocate to the west. Urban poverty increased in every region. When creditors began to demand that individual debtors pay their bills in hard currency, dramatic social unrest resulted. The most famous incident occurred in 1786 when Revolutionary veteran Daniel Shays led a band of unhappy debtors who took over a government arms depot in western Massachusetts. Shays's rebels was put down by the Massachusetts militia, and conservatives all over the country worried that financial unrest might cause the downfall of the nation.

Ultimately, political leaders were convinced that the national government needed to be revamped in order to solve the country's economic problems. Delegates from each state met in Philadelphia in May 1787 to discuss a possible alteration of the Articles of Confederation, but by the time the convention had concluded in September, they had debated and drafted a whole new Constitution. This Constitution proposed a more powerful federal government that would exercise authority over internal and external trade, taxation, national debt, and the money supply. The Constitution created a two-branch legislature (as well as an executive and judicial branch), and provided an easier mechanism for amendments.

When the Confederation Congress sent the document to the states for ratification, its supporters, the Federalists, claimed that the new government was necessary to resolve the nation's financial ills. Alexander Hamilton, James Madison, and John Jay urged the

public to accept a powerful central government. On the other side of the issue stood a loose group, the Anti-Federalists, who opposed ratification and wished to maintain the power of the states. The Anti-Federalists, including Samuel Adams and John Hancock, disliked the Constitution for different reasons, one of which was the lack of a bill of rights. After Federalists promised to add a bill of rights, the conventions in 11 of the 13 states (the necessary two-thirds margin) approved the Constitution by June 1788.

George Washington, leader of the army during the American Revolution, took office as he first president of the United States in 1789. As a member of Virginia's slave-holding elite, Washington was just the type of man who had exercised the greatest economic power in colonial America. Now he came into office as the democratically elected head of a republic. The country still faced financial instability, and it was unclear whether the new Constitution would solve all of the economic challenges posed by the American Revolution, but the citizens of the United States could look forward to economic opportunities never dreamt of by colonial subjects of the British crown.

See also: **American Revolution, Articles of Confederation, Boston Massacre, Boston Tea Party, French and Indian Wars, Proclamation of 1763, Stamp Act, Sugar Act, George Washington**

FURTHER READING

Carp, E. Wayne. *To Starve the Army at Pleasure: Continental Army Administration and American Political Culture, 1775–1783.* Chapel Hill: University of North Carolina Press, 1984.

Christie, Ian, and Benjamin Labaree. *Empire or Independence: 1760–1776.* New York: W.W. Norton, 1977.

Jensen, Merrill. *The New Nation: A History of the United States During the Confederation, 1781–1789.* New York: Alfred A. Knopf, 1950.

Kulidoff, Allan. *Tobacco and Slaves: The Development of Southern Cultures in the Chesapeake, 1680–1800.* Chapel Hill: University of North Carolina Press, 1986.

McCusker, John, and Russell Menard. *The Economy of British America, 1607–1789.* Chapel Hill: University of North Carolina Press, 1985.

AGGREGATE DEMAND

Aggregate demand is the total amount of goods and services that U.S. consumers and businesses are willing to buy at specific price levels. As prices for goods and services fall, consumers, businesses, and government agencies tend to buy more. In addition to the consumption of goods and services aggregate demand includes the money consumers and firms invest in government expenditures and net exports (that is, exports minus imports). When aggregate demand increases aggregate supply generally rises to keep up with it. Aggregate supply is the total output or production of goods and services.

Aggregate demand increases when consumers spend more or save less, when businesses believe the profitability of their investments will increase, or when the government spends more or lowers taxes. Aggregate demand will also rise when foreign consumers or businesses increase their purchases of U.S. products, when U.S. consumers buy fewer imports and more U.S. products, and when the money supply is increased. Because each of these factors can change fairly quickly, aggregate demand is more unpredictable than aggregate supply.

Aggregate demand can also be more easily shaped by government policy than aggregate supply can. British economist John Maynard Keynes (1883–1946) popularized the view that the best way to increase aggregate demand is to raise government spending or cut taxes. On the other hand so-called monetarists like Milton Friedman (b. 1912) argue that aggregate demand is best stimulated by lowering interest rates or loosen the supply of money circulating in the economy. Keynes believed that the Great Depression was caused by the federal government's failure to come to the rescue of an inherently unstable U.S. economy. Friedman argued that the Depression would never have occurred if the government had not sharply tightened the money supply in the late 1920s and early 1930s.

Between 1945 and 1990 the U.S. Federal Reserve never allowed the U.S. money supply to shrink as dramatically as it had just before and during the Great Depression. During this forty-five year period there were no major depressions. Those who followed Keynes argued that fiscal policy rather than money supply was the best way to pump up aggregate demand. But when the administration of President Ronald Reagan (1981–89) sharply lowered income tax rates in the early 1980s, aggregate demand remained largely unaffected.

See also: Federal Reserve System, Milton Friedman, John Maynard Keynes, Keynesian Economic Theory, Ronald Reagan

AGGREGATE SUPPLY

Aggregate supply is the total amount of goods and services that U.S. businesses are prepared to produce for sale to buyers at various price levels. When the demand for businesses' products increases, the prices they charge for those products tend to rise. Businesses will then increase the supply of those goods. When the prices for goods and services fall, aggregate supply also tends to fall.

With a constantly growing U.S. population the demand for goods and services generally rises over time. Aggregate supply rises to meet that demand. But aggregate supply is affected by more than just prices and demand. The number of businesses competing in a market, the effects of technology on worker productivity, the costs of paying workers or buying raw materials, and even the weather can affect the total amount of goods and services businesses produce for sale. For example, a drought can destroy wheat farmers' crops, lowering the supply of wheat they can bring to market. The federal government can stimulate the growth of aggregate supply by spending less than it takes in taxes. This frees up money to be invested in opening new businesses and factories. The government can also implement tax policies that reward businesses and individuals for investing, or that lower the costs of doing business.

In 1929 the wealth of many consumers and businesses was wiped out by a stock market crash. The United States experienced the worst drop in aggregate supply in its history. This process resulted in the Great Depression. Demand for goods and services fell, prices dropped, and businesses cut back the production of goods because they could not make a profit on them. All these events were the result of consumers and businesses having less money to spend on goods and services. After World War II aggregate supply skyrocketed. According to some economists, this happened because the federal government's huge spending on the war effort had resulted in surplus wealth among consumers and businesses. Businesses increased aggregate supply to meet this new demand. During the energy crises of the 1970s U.S. aggregate supply fell

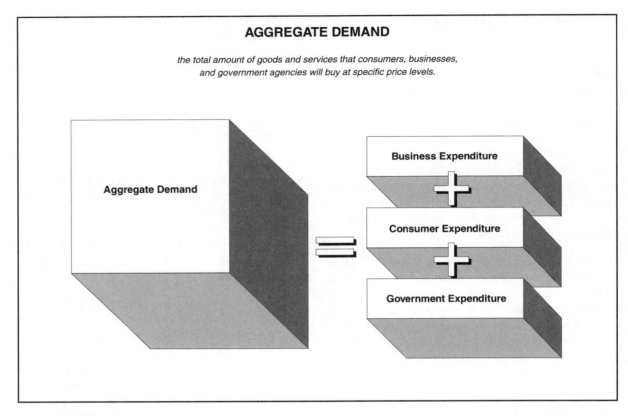

AGGREGATE DEMAND

the total amount of goods and services that consumers, businesses, and government agencies will buy at specific price levels.

Aggregate Demand = Business Expenditure + Consumer Expenditure + Government Expenditure

The table illustrates aggregate demand, the total amount of goods and services businesses, consumers, and government agencies will buy at specific prices.

because the rising price of oil increased the costs to businesses of producing goods and services.

See also: **OPEC Oil Embargo, Stock Market Crash**

AGRICULTURAL EQUIPMENT INDUSTRY

The mechanization of agricultural equipment in the mid-nineteenth century began a period of rapid change and advancement for the agricultural industry. Mechanization made the processes of planting and harvesting quicker and reduced the industry's reliance on manual labor. Until mechanization began in the 1850s, farmers used hand tools made of wood or iron. The industrial revolution and the modernization of equipment sometimes brought rebellions by rural workers who feared machines would eliminate their jobs.

These fears were not completely unfounded. By using machine work in place of many tasks traditionally done by laborers, mechanized equipment did lessen the agricultural industry's dependence on manual labor. In 1850, the first threshing machines were created

independently by Cyrus McCormick (1809–1884) in the United States and Patrick Bell in Scotland. Plow improvements enabled farmers to work easily in different types of soil, while technological advances mechanized the planting and measurement of corn. An early breakthrough came in the 1850s, in Galesburg, Illinois, when George W. Brown developed the first semi-mechanized method of corn planting using a horse-drawn machine that manually dropped seed. These first innovations stimulated further inventions. For example, "furrow openers" or shoes were placed on the front of the vehicle to prepare the soil. Seed-dropping became more refined, which allowed the vehicle operator to pay closer attention to where the corn was placed. Hay rakes, hay-loaders, harvesting machines, and milking machines also appeared at about this time.

Steam power, which came to be used on farms in the 1860s, made mechanized equipment a vital part of the farming industry. It rapidly turned the curve of development upward by expanding into so many areas of farming technology that in 1860 the U.S. Patent Office issued hundreds of new patents. Among these were patents for harvesters, shellers, huskers, cultivators, and cob crushers for corn, as well as smut machines and seed drills.

When the first gasoline-powered tractor was built in 1901, most American farmers could not afford it, but in 1917 automobile entrepreneur Henry Ford offered his Fordson tractor for $397, a price that made the product much more accessible to farmers. Seven years later International Harvester introduced its versatile Farmall tractor with removable attachments. One such attachment was the cultivator, which could penetrate the soil at different depths. Other attachments included rotary hoes that could chop up weeds, and spraying devices that could spray in circles of up to 100 feet. Gasoline-driven tractors came into wider use during the 1920s and 1930s, increasingly replacing the horse for farm labor. Between 1940 and 1960, five million tractors replaced an estimated twelve million horses.

The era of the western and southern farmer coincided with the era of the railroad, as it was the rail system during the second half of the nineteenth century that allowed the farmer to get his crop to market. Advancements in the transportation industry in the early twentieth century had a profound impact on agriculture. The truck and the airplane both significantly contributed to the production and transportation of farm products. After they first appeared on farms between 1913 and 1920, trucks changed the marketing and production patterns of farm products. Their importance to harvesting the fields was paramount because they could haul items such as fertilizer, feed, crops, and livestock. Later on, the development of portable refrigeration units allowed trains and trucks to carry freshly slaughtered meat to market. Trucks also carried pigs to centralized meatpacking centers in the cities.

Farmers found many uses for the airplane in farm work. In the early twentieth century, one of the first uses for the airplane was to scatter poison dust over cotton fields infected by the pink mollworm. Other early tasks included dusting against disease and insects, spreading fertilizer, transporting breeding livestock, and dropping bales of hay to livestock stranded in snowstorms. The use of the truck and the airplane helped alleviate many problems faced by agricultural workers, such as crop failure due to disease or insects.

At the same time improvements in steam power and gasoline-driven vehicles continued. The versatile Farmall tractor in the early 1900s replaced the steam-driven reaping and threshing machine that was first introduced in the 1880s. Despite wide use of the Allis Chalmers' All-Crop Harvester as early as 1936, however, crop harvester advancements were delayed because of World War II (1939–1945). The All-Crop was a diesel-driven combine with a capacity for mass-harvesting, but consumers still preferred the more affordable picker-sheller machines, which were more

affordable if less advanced. The use of silos and improved storage methods eventually gave the All-Crop Harvester an unbeatable advantage in the farm implement market.

The advancements in agricultural equipment slowed in the latter half of the twentieth century and some of the industry's old standbys began to weaken. During the 1980s, American farmers bought about 50,000 large tractors, but by the 1990s only a little over 20,000 were purchased. Combine harvesters also began to lose their appeal. Only 130,000 were sold during the 1980s compared to 300,000 in the 1970s. This trend continued into the 1990s. Showroom viewing of new farm equipment became less popular, creating a swollen inventory in early 1991. Farmers were also subject to a variety of short-term hazards like the old problem of excess yields, which caused prices to drop. Also, high interest rates brought many farm bankruptcies in 1991.

Tied to the always shaky farming sector, the economic highs and lows of the agricultural equipment market also continued to affect employment in the farm implement industry. In the early 1990s tractor and industrial truck manufacturing was concentrated in 139 factories in the five-state region of Michigan, Wisconsin, Indiana, Ohio and Illinois. The manufacturing of farm machinery generated large revenues and employed a substantial number of people. In 1993 Deere & Company, a leader in the industry, employed 36,500 and had sales of $7 billion. Another industry leader, J.I. Case, employed 7,000 and generated sales of $3.7 billion.

See also: **Agriculture Industry, Cyrus McCormick**

FURTHER READING

Brandon, Hembree. ''Machinery Sales Pace Quickens.'' *Implement and Tractor*, November/December 1993.

Brezonick, Mike. ''How Deere Designed Its New Ag Tractors.'' *Diesel Progress Engines and Drivers*, April 1993.

Little, Dale L. ''Legacy of Science.'' *Farm Chemicals*, July 1993.

Semling, Harold V. ''Commerce Predicts Good MH Sales Year.'' *Material Handling Engineering*, March 1982.

Witt, Clyde E. ''Partnering Gets Lift from Crane Manufacturers.'' *Material Handling Engineering*, January 1992.

AGRICULTURE INDUSTRY

From the founding of Virginia in 1607 until the late 1890s agriculture played a predominant economic role in the United States. The early settlers adopted the Native American practices of growing corn, squash, and tobacco. Initially corn was the primary food crop, while tobacco was exported to earn foreign exchange. In New England most farmers raised multiple food crops as well as livestock, producing enough for their family needs with some surplus goods for sale.

Agriculture in the South became more specialized and commercialized than in the North. By the late seventeenth century tobacco, rice, and indigo became major commercial crops. Production expanded rapidly in conjunction with the plantation system that utilized the labor of African American slaves. Cotton became an important commercial crop with the invention of the cotton gin in 1793 by Eli Whitney (1765–1825).

At the beginning of the nineteenth century significant changes occurred in the farming sector of the economy. Tens of thousands of settlers migrated west to settle in the Ohio and Mississippi valleys between the time of the American Revolution (1775-1783) and the American Civil War (1861–1865). This produced the vast productive potential of grain and livestock farmers. By 1860 the United States had 2,044,077 farms. The U.S. government actively supported the farming community by promoting liberal public land policies, developing canal and rail transportation and reallocating choice farmland from Native Americans to prospective settlers.

Prior to the American Civil War the introduction of animal power and labor-saving machinery provided one of the greatest advances in agricultural history. Innovations such as iron plows, threshing machines, grain drills, and cultivators became common. The McCormick agricultural equipment company in Chicago led the mechanization of farming. In 1800 it took approximately 56 man-hours to plant and harvest one acre of wheat. By 1840, with mechanization the same acre of wheat took only 35 man-hours to achieve the same result.

Agriculture became the engine behind the U.S. economic development in the first half of the nineteenth century. By 1860 the two million farms in the United States produced 838 million bushels of corn, 172 million bushels of wheat, 5.4 million bales of cotton, and millions of pounds of tobacco. Increasingly farmers began to sell their produce to purchase manufactured goods. In 1860 farm products comprised 82 percent of U.S. exports. This helped support the foreign exchange used for investment in U.S. manufacturing and transportation.

IN 1800 IT TOOK APPROXIMATELY 56 MAN-HOURS TO PLANT AND HARVEST ONE ACRE OF WHEAT. BY 1840, WITH MECHANIZATION THE SAME ACRE OF WHEAT TOOK ONLY 35 MAN-HOURS TO ACHIEVE THE SAME RESULT.

Following the American Civil War agricultural expansion accelerated at an even higher rate with the migration of farmers to the Great Plains. Further, with the end of slavery, African American sharecroppers worked on hundreds of thousands of small farms in the South. Between 1860 and 1916 the number of farms grew from two million to 6.4 million. Farm acreage doubled from 407 million to 879 million acres. With the increased acreage and the introduction of better machinery, the production of commercial crops continued to increase tremendously. The great deflationary crisis of the last third of the nineteenth century stemmed from precisely this ''crisis of over-production'' in agriculture. Productivity on the farm had outstripped the market demand for farm produce. From about 1873 to the end of the century, this glutted farm commodity market became a drag on the rest of the economy. It also produced a strong protest movement in the Farmers' Alliance movements and the Populist challenge. Farmers did not always know what lay behind their distress. At different points they blamed the railroads, the elevator (crop storage facilities) companies, and the bankers. But they eventually focused on the need for ''parity,'' a government subsidy for a fair return on their outlay of labor and capital.

By World War I (1914–1918) the agricultural landscape of the United States settled into regional patterns. Farmers in the Northeast focused on dairy, poultry, and fruits and vegetables for the urban market. In the Midwest grain crops such as wheat, corn, and barley supported a thriving cattle and hog business. The region of the Great Plains from Texas to the Canadian border became known as the nation's breadbasket, with wheat being the primary commercial crop. Agriculture in the Rocky Mountain States focused on cattle and sheep raising, while most of the crops in the Far West depended on irrigation. In the South cotton continued to be the main cash crop until after World War II (1939–1945).

After World War I the overproduction crisis continued to trouble American agriculture, with farm prices generally in decline. None of the measures taken by the U.S. Government solved the problem of low returns to farmers. However in 1933, during the Great Depression, Congress passed the Agricultural Adjustment Act, which introduced a wide range of federal programs to help the farmer. These programs—which involved paying farmers to leave their land fallow in order to create a shortage in farm commodities and an upturn in prices—continued throughout the rest of the twentieth century. Government payments to farmers in 1934 totaled $134 million; by 1961 payments increased to $1.5 billion and by 1987 to $22 billion.

In the 1930s agriculture underwent significant changes due to the advancements in technology and the introduction of science to farming. The use of the gasoline tractor ended the horse age of farming shortly after World War II. The continued development of better machinery made the farming industry less labor-intensive. The contribution from science included the growing use of chemicals for fertilizers and insecticides, and the breeding of hybrid strains producing better crops and healthier livestock. These and other developments increased the nation's agricultural productivity without a proportionate increase in acreage. The amount of farmland in use remained constant at about 1 billion acres between 1930 and 1980. However crop production increased dramatically. For example, corn production increased from 20 bushels an acre in 1930 to about 110 bushels half a century later. In 1980 one-third of farm production was sold overseas and agricultural exports made up about 20 percent of the nation's foreign sales.

By the end of the twentieth century, new trends emerged in agriculture. These include organic farming and the reduced use of chemicals in response to health and environmental issues. Crop and livestock production has also changed as farmers made increased use of biotechnology and genetic engineering. Farmers continue to have increased capabilities to cultivate more land and handle more livestock with less labor. This resulted in a sharp increase in the average size of farms and a rapid decline in the number of farmers. In 1940 there were 6.1 million farms averaging 215 acres in size. By 1980 only 2.4 million farms remained, averaging 431 acres. In spite of this trend over 90 percent of farms in the United States continue to be operated by families rather than agricultural corporations.

Throughout U.S. history farming was an important economic activity. By the end of the twentieth century it became a business that required skilled labor, capital, and good management. In addition, most people in the United States had little direct contact or involvement with this industry. By the 1980s the number of people living on farms had declined to less than 2.5 percent of the population. Agriculture had shifted from a simple commercial venture to a specialized business.

See also: **Agricultural Equipment Industry, Populist Movement, Subsistence Agriculture**

FURTHER READING

Ferleger, Lou, ed. *Agriculture and National Development: Views on the Nineteenth Century.* Ames, IA: Iowa State University Press, 1990.

Foner, Eric and John Garraty, eds. ''Agriculture.'' In *The Reader's Companion to American History*, Boston, MS: Houghton Mifflin Co., 1991.

Hurt, Douglas R. *American Farms: Exploring their History.* Malabar, FL: Krieger Pub. Co., 1996.

Peterson, Trudy Huskamp, ed. *Farmers, Bureaucrats, and Middlemen: Historical Perspectives on American Agriculture.* Washington, DC: Howard University Press, 1980.

Taylor, Carl. *The Farmer's Movement, 1620–1920.* Westport, CT: Greenwood Press, 1971.

AIR TRAFFIC CONTROLLER STRIKE

With dramatic increases in commercial airline traffic following World War II (1939–45), Congress established the Federal Aviation Agency in 1958, which it later renamed the Federal Aviation Administration (FAA). Congress entrusted the agency with many responsibilities related to air travel in the United States, including the control of both civil and military use of U.S. airspace for purposes of safety and efficiency. To fulfill its charge, the FAA established and operated a network of airport control towers and 20 air route control centers spaced across the nation. Air traffic controllers manning the towers and centers guided planes from takeoff to landing by using of radar and verbal communication with pilots. As air travel steadily grew, air traffic controllers were increasingly subjected to high levels of stress, since they directed numerous airliners carrying thousands of persons in an crowded sky.

By passing the Airline Deregulation Act in 1978, Congress lifted broad federal controls over airlines including approving new carriers, setting ticket prices, and limiting air routes. A surge of new airlines and air routes further taxed the already stretched air control system. Increasingly tight airline schedules placed more pressures on the controllers themselves. The FAA employed more than 16,000 controllers by the end of the 1970s. Finally, in August of 1981, in protest of the stressful working conditions, and demanding higher salaries, 11,000 air traffic controllers went on strike. Their union, Professional Air Traffic Controllers Organization (PATCO), organized the work stoppage. As public employees they were forbidden to strike and PATCO's action was deemed illegal. The strike threatened to have a major economic impact on the nation and international trade as well. Consequently, President Ronald Reagan (1981–89) gave the strikers three days to return to work or be fired. When most striking controllers refused to return, they were fired and PATCO dissolved. In the wake of the firing, the FAA quickly imposed new restrictions on air traffic flow. The agency temporarily reduced the number of flights by one third to ease demands on overworked centers and answer public fears of safety concerns. In desperate need of experienced controllers, for more than a decade the FAA hired retired former employees in areas with critical personnel shortages.

BUT REPLACING THE AIR TRAFFIC CONTROLLERS WASN'T ONLY MEANT TO SAVE MONEY. IT ALSO LET MANAGERS IN EVERY INDUSTRY KNOW THAT IT WAS O.K. TO FIRE STRIKERS. AND WORD GOT OUT, AS GREYHOUND, PHELPS DODGE AND EASTERN AIRLINES BROKE MAJOR STRIKES BY HIRING REPLACEMENTS.

"A Day in the Life," *The Nation*, February 19, 1996

The shortage of fully skilled and experienced air traffic controllers significantly affected airline operations. It was difficult to increase the number of full-performance level controllers since many of those who were not fired retired or moved up into management positions. During the summer and fall of 1984 significant disruption of airline schedules occurred. The understaffed system inspired policies that would rather error on the side of caution during times of bad weather, but the airlines found this conservative approach very expensive. Airlines claimed flight delays caused by undermanned controller facilities and outdated equipment was costing the industry a fortune. Traffic bottlenecks at major airports, such as New York and Chicago, were frequent and led to flight disruptions across the country.

As new airlines attempted to break into the larger markets in the aftermath of airline deregulation, they found the restrictions associated with the rebuilding of the controller work force a difficult hurdle. Some argued that it would have been less costly and less

disruptive to air travel over the long term to give the controllers the raise they were requesting in 1981. Nonetheless, since air traffic continued to boom, others believed that President Reagan was right to uphold the principle that government workers are forbidden to strike. More than a decade later, President Bill Clinton (1993–) invited the previously fired air traffic controllers to apply for their jobs.

Following the firings, the FAA had also pledged to overhaul and modernize the air traffic control system. The agency developed the National Airspace System Plan, which had estimated budget of almost 16 billion dollars for implementation. Although some new hardware, such as Aircraft Situation Display computers, was installed by 1990, the aging system remained only partially updated with newer equipment despite approximately a half billion dollars spent. Although a largely computer-automated system was in the development stage during the 1990s to address the ever increasing air traffic levels of commercial flight, the FAA was accused of moving too slowly in developing and approving new flight control systems.

Repercussions of the 1981 mass firing may have significantly extended into the U.S. labor movement. The actions by Reagan sent a message to private industry that firing striking workers and hiring replacements was an acceptable practice. Some observers considered the firing of the controllers a watershed event in U.S. labor relations. Statistics on union activism indicated that between 1960 and 1981, approximately 275 strikes occurred in the United States annually and involved 1.3 million workers each year. Between 1981 and 1992, the annual number of strikes fell to 56 and involved just over 400,000 workers annually. The peak era of labor strikes was clearly the early 1970s.

See also: **Ronald W. Reagan**

FURTHER READING

Campagna, Anthony S. *The Economy in the Reagan Years: The Economic Consequences of the Reagan Administrations.* Westport, CT: Greenwood Press, 1994.

Nordlund, Willis J. *Silent Skies: The Air Traffic Controllers' Strike.* Westport, CT: Praeger, 1998.

Northrup, Herbert R., and Amie D. Thornton. *The Federal Government as Employer: The Federal Labor Relations Authority and the PATCO Challenge.* Philadelphia: Industrial Research Unit, Wharton School, University of Pennsylvania, 1988.

Shostak, Arthur B., and David Skocik. *The Air Controllers' Controversy: Lessons from the PATCO Strike.* New York: Human Sciences Press, 1986.

Wickens, Christopher D., Anne S. Mavor, and James P. McGee, eds. *Flight to the Future: Human Factors in Air Traffic Control.* Washington, DC: National Academy Press, 1997.

AIRLINE DEREGULATION

The first airlines began appearing in the United States following World War I (1914–1918). By the 1930s the federal government had granted exclusive rights to domestic airmail routes to four airlines: American Airlines, United Air Lines, Eastern Air Lines, and TransWorld Airlines (TWA). (Also among the first of U.S. airlines, Pan American was granted rights for international mail routes.) Government regulation of airlines began in 1938 when Congress created the Civil Aeronautics Board (CAB) to set fares, select routes, and license new carriers. Meanwhile airline passenger loads escalated from fewer than 6,000 passengers annually in the 1930s to a total of 200 million by the mid-1970s. But discount fares were nonexistent and flying continued to be a luxury. For four decades no new major airlines were licensed and few newly proposed routes approved as the four airlines managed to hold onto their lucrative contracts and routes. Competition was intentionally muted to ensure stability for both airlines and passengers.

By the 1970s high inflation, low national economic growth, escalating fuel costs, and rising labor costs hit the airline industry hard. Deregulation supporters claimed that it was decades of inefficient regulation by the CAB that was taking its toll. The near monopoly held by the five major airlines originally charted in the U.S., they argued, had to end. In October 1978, Congress passed the Airline Deregulation Act. With the intent of promoting competition in the industry, the act gave airlines virtually unlimited freedom to establish new routes and drop existing routes, to merge and form alliances, and to enter or exit the market without CAB approval. The airlines were also free to raise or lower rates as they chose and service standards were eliminated. Only safety regulations remained. On top of this, the deregulation era also created the opening for hard-nosed management to pursue a much more aggressive—some might say union-busting—policy. Some observers pointed to Eastern Airlines' chief executive officer Frank Lorenzo as an example of this trend.

The effects of deregulation of the airline industry were immediately felt as airfares dropped in some cases to record low levels and passenger loads increased. Newly formed no-frills airlines appeared, such as People Express. But with the formation of the Middle East oil cartel in 1979 the price of jet fuel skyrocketed and airline profits dropped. In 1981, struggling under the demands of significantly more daily flights, air traffic controllers went on strike for higher pay and better working conditions. In response President Ronald Reagan (1981–1989) suddenly fired 11,000 controllers and requested that airlines temporarily reduce their number of flights by a third. Fuel prices and the controllers' firing greatly reduced opportunities for new airlines to break into the larger markets.

When new airlines managed to enter the smaller air traffic market, they entered a hostile business climate. The larger companies lowered prices to artificially low levels and drove out competition. Thus increased competition—the goal that convinced Congress to deregulate—was thwarted by such monopolistic pricing strategies. Charges of unfair business practices escalated. Some airlines went heavily into debt and teetered on the edge of financial disaster. Fears rose concerning air safety being compromised as airlines sought to cut expenses by skimping on maintenance costs and hiring less experienced pilots. In 1990 Eastern Airlines was indicted for poor and dishonest aircraft maintenance practices. The following year the company went out of business.

Deregulation continued to transform the industry: nonstop flights from coast to coast were no longer as profitable. Instead, the major airlines established "hubs," or central points, at certain cities—United in Chicago, American in Dallas-Ft. Worth, Northwest in Minneapolis-St. Paul, and Delta in Atlanta. By 1992 twelve major hubs existed; competition was dampened further because at these localities the dominant carrier greatly influenced flight choices for transferring passengers. Approximately 80 percent of transferring passengers rode the same airline for their entire journey. One strategy of larger airlines was to set ticket prices for flights out of smaller airports at rates as much as 20 percent lower than at hubs. Such fare discounts tended to drive out new start–up carriers; later prices would often rise to hub–level fares once competition was removed.

Deregulation also spurred computerization of reservations and "frequent–flier" programs. Because of anti–trust concerns, the government required each airline to create its own reservation system rather than a single, shared system. This requirement further reduced competition by limiting the access of information to passenger and booking agents. The major airlines also introduced "frequent flier" offers to attract and maintain customers. Such programs gave large, broadly–based airlines the opportunity to offer loyal customers bonus rides for flying a single airline extensively. Sometimes, such practices significantly reduced airline revenues and often eliminated competition (which also drove up fares).

Between 1989 and 1992 industry instability peaked as some large carriers (notably Pan American) ceased operations; a number of mergers took place as well. Airline earnings fluctuated wildly. Some airlines, such as Continental and TWA, reorganized under bankruptcy. Still others, including Northwest, received cash infusions from foreign airlines. In some cases, unions helped companies avoid financial disaster by accepting wage reductions in return for part ownership of the airline. At one carrier, United Airlines, employees gained majority control in return for major pay and benefits cuts. Stability returned in 1993 when new airlines began to appear that did not attempt to compete with the major airlines and their hub systems.

By the end of the twentieth century, debate still raged over the impact of deregulation on airline competition, service, profitability, and safety. Some smaller commuter airlines serving hubs, often in a restrictive alliance with a major airline, proved they could survive in the deregulation era, but mid-level carriers were largely uncompetitive with the big airlines. Smaller communities suffered economically from declining air service and increasing prices due to the anti–competitive strategies of the large carriers who, for their part, often found it unprofitable to compete in these communities. Business fares for all routes significantly increased through the 1990s. Some degree of new regulation for the industry and subsidies for smaller carriers was sought by deregulation critics to stimulate competitive pricing, guarantee safety, and better serve a broader range of communities.

See also: **Air Traffic Controllers Strike, Airline Industry**

FURTHER READING

Brown, Anthony E. *The Politics of Airline Deregulation.* Knoxville: University of Tennessee Press, 1987.

Dempsey, Paul S. *Flying Blind: The Failure of Airline Deregulation.* Washington, DC: Economic Policy Institute, 1990.

Heppenheimer, T. A. *Turbulent Skies: The History of Commercial Aviation.* New York: John Wiley and Sons, Inc., 1998.

Morrison, Steven A., and Clifford Winston. *The Evolution of the Airline Industry.* Washington, DC: Brookings Institution, 1994.

Peterson, Barbara S. and James Glab. *Rapid Descent: Deregulation and the Shakeout in the Airlines.* New York: Simon and Schuster, 1994.

Reynolds-Feighan, Aisling J. *The Effects of Deregulation on U.S. Air Networks.* New York: Springer-Verlag, 1992.

AIRLINE INDUSTRY

On December 17, 1913, in St. Petersburg, Florida, the first airline contract in United States history was signed. Salesman and motorboat racer Percival E. Fansler knew that the city of St. Petersburg was dependent upon the winter tourist trade for its economic survival. In order to reach St. Petersburg from Tampa, tourists had a choice of travelling two hours across Tampa Bay by steamer, a 12-hour train ride, or a day trip by automobile over rough terrain. Fansler believed that by air, the trip from Tampa to St. Petersburg would only take 20 minutes. Fansler shared his idea with a pioneer aircraft manufacturer, Thomas W. Benoist. Enthusiastic St. Petersburg business and civil leaders signed a contract with Benoist to operate an air travel business with two flying ''boats'' and pilots. On January 1, 1914, the first day of operation, thousands of people turned out for a downtown parade. In a short speech Fansler boldly stated, ''What was impossible yesterday is an accomplishment today, while tomorrow heralds the unbelievable.'' Pilot Anthony H. Jannus then pushed the aircraft throttle to full and lifted off from the water, soaring into history.

On May 15, 1918, the nation's first scheduled air mail service began between Washington, DC, and New York, using military pilots as part of the armed forces' wartime training program. By August a civilian-operated U.S. Air Mail Service was initiated by Otto Praeger, second assistant postmaster general in charge of all mail transportation. In 1919 the Post Office took on the monumental task of supplying an overnight airmail service by flying 755 miles from New York to Chicago. The government's expert body on aviation, the National Advisory Committee for Aeronautics (NACA), stated in its annual report that the Post Office was making ''a substantial contribution in the practical development of commercial aviation.''

The best coast-to-coast mail record of 72 hours was shattered on February 22–23, 1921, when airmail pilots made the transcontinental crossing in 33 hours and 20 minutes. The push for faster airmail service with aircraft not as technologically advanced came with a human price tag—twelve postal airmen were killed in 1920. The *New York Times*, however, observed in 1921: "There are critics who think that the Post Office Department's air mail service is dangerous and costly, but nothing ventured, nothing gained. The modern world demands efficiency and speed; aviation is international and competitive. The United States has distanced all countries in transportation of mails through the air."

When Congress passed the Air Mail (Kelly) Act of 1925, it helped give private airlines the opportunity, through competitive bidding, to serve as mail carriers. The Air Commerce Act of 1926 would designate and establish airways, license pilots and aircraft, investigate accidents, and maintain aids to air navigation. These acts drew businessmen and financiers into aviation, which led to the creation of new air transportation companies. The U.S. government's involvement in the industry came in the form of regulatory agencies, congressional acts, and appointed commissions.

The dramatic transatlantic solo flight of Charles A. Lindbergh (1902–1974) on May 20–21, 1927, captured the fascination of the American people. Amid new public enthusiasm there was a frenzy to get in on the ground floor of the aviation industry. Early airplane manufacturers such as William Boeing (1881–1956), Claud Ryan, and Donald Douglas (1892–1981), began manufacturing airplanes designed specifically for passenger travel. Air transportation continued to develop, and by 1930, there were 43 scheduled airlines in the United States. Better radio communications, revolving beacon lights, and more accurate weather services improved airway facilities and safety records. Air traffic and profits increased during the early 1950s. The American economy flourished as passenger sales rose dramatically from $17.3 million in 1950 to $38 million in 1955. The airliner was well on its way to replacing the train and the ocean liner in long distance travel.

Thirty years after the end of World War II (1939–1945), the American airframe and engine industry enjoyed a prosperous period with the jet-propelled airliners of Boeing, McDonnell-Douglas, Lockheed, and other U.S. firms. Passenger transportation became the largest source of airline revenue, followed by freight and mail. Intense competition arose from the cost-per-seat-per-mile afforded to each passenger. The giant carriers, United, American, TWA, and Eastern Airlines continued their domination of the industry and accounted for more than half the seat-mile productivity of the entire industry. Jumbo jets were introduced in the 1970s, and seated 400 to 500 tourist-class passengers. The wide-bodied jets also contributed to the chronic congestion at many airports. By the mid-1970s the airline industry was plagued by shifts in regulatory procedure, labor unrest, high fuel costs, corporate mismanagement, airport congestion, crowded skies, and public concerns ranging from safety and service to air and noise pollution. The Airline Deregulation Act of 1978 removed governmental control of routes and fare pricing with the intention of encouraging competition and increasing efficiency. Some effects of deregulation were felt immediately, as heavy competition led to lower ticket prices.

Unprepared for the effects of an inflation-ridden world economy and the lowest boarding rate in 50 years, airlines throughout the world suffered financial losses in the early 1980s. Scrambling to increase passenger numbers, airlines began to overbook flights in an attempt to fill every seat. Budgets were cut in the quality and quantity of passenger food, as well. Although these tactics did cut airline costs, customer satisfaction reached an all-time low. This trend continued into the late 1990s, as many airlines struggled to find a solution to financial difficulties, and some failed. The number of people traveling by air, however, continued to increase, and for those airlines that can survive the competition the future looks bright.

As aerospace technology develops, significant changes and advances in design, safety, electronics, and computer science evolve. The airline industry also benefits in all aspects from high-tech communication technology. More than eight decades ago, salesman and motorboat racer Percival E. Fansler's novel idea of "a real commercial line, running from somewhere to somewhere else" took flight, and despite its difficulties, became what is perhaps the most important technological innovation in history.

See also: **Air Traffic Controllers Strike, Airline Deregulation, Boeing**

FURTHER READING

Leary, William M., ed. *Encyclopedia of American Business History and Biography*. New York: Facts On File, s.v. "The Airline Industry."

Foner, Eric and John A. Garraty, eds. *The Reader's Companion to American History*. Boston: Houghton Mifflin Co., 1991.

Morrison, Steven. *The Evolution of the Airline Industry*. Washington, DC: Brookings Institution, 1995.

Heppenheimer, T.A. *Turbulent Skies: The History of Commercial Aviation*. New York: J. Wiley & Sons, 1995.

Meyer, John Robert. *Airline Deregulation: The Early Experience*. Boston, MA: Auburn House Publishing Co., 1981.

Hillstrom, Kevin, and Mary K. Ruby, eds. *Encyclopedia of American Industries*. Farmington Hills, MI: The Gale Group, vol. 2, s.v. "Service and Non-Manufacturing Industries."

ALABAMA

Alabama, traditionally one of the nation's poorest states, has survived the demise of a one-crop economy, the upheaval of a civil war, a revolution in race relations, and the challenges of a modern industrial economy. While the state still has many difficulties to overcome, it continues to be an important contributor to the nation's economy.

The first Europeans to arrive in Alabama found the land inhabited by Creek, Cherokee, and Chickasaw Indians. The Spanish first entered Mobile Bay during the sixteenth century. Hernando de Soto (c.1496–1542) entered the Mobile Delta via Tennessee in 1540. In the early 1700s French explorers established the first permanent settlement at Mobile. The British took over the territory by terms of the Treaty of Paris in 1763 but lost it again to Spain in 1780. The United States did not gain title to the land until after the War of 1812 (1812–1814). In 1814 a force led by Andrew Jackson (1767–1845) drove off most of the remaining Indian tribes, opening up the territory to white settlement. After this time many immigrants from southern states poured into Alabama in hopes of acquiring good land on which to grow cotton, a newly profitable crop in the South. Though still sparsely populated, Alabama became a state in 1819.

Alabama remained an almost entirely agricultural state for some decades to come. Cotton was the major crop though sorghum, corn, oats, vegetables, and livestock also were important. The farm economy, particularly on large plantations, was based on slave labor. By 1860 the number of slaves in the state constituted 45 percent of the population. Large planters, only about one percent of the total, owned 28 percent of all of the state's wealth and wielded the most power in the state legislature both before and after the American Civil War (1860–1865). They lived in columned mansions, which according to historian Virginia Van der Veer Hamilton, "betray[ed] their owners as among America's conspicuous consumers, free from Puritan scruples about showiness and lavish expenditure even when heavily in debt."

Small farmers, by contrast, led a hardscrabble life in Alabama at this time. In his *Journey in the Back Country*, Frederick Law Olmsted, a New York journalist who toured the South in 1853, noted that these farmers were hardworking yet reaped only minimal crops for their efforts. "They are very ignorant," he said. "The agriculture is wretched and the work hard."

The large planters led the movement to secede from the Union, and Alabama joined the Confederate States of America in 1861. Montgomery served as the Confederate capital until it was moved to Richmond in May of 1861, and Alabama native Jefferson Davis was elected president. After the South's defeat in 1865, a Reconstruction (1865–1877) government ruled the state for six years. It aroused the hatred of most Alabama whites, who resented both the radical Republicans and the blacks they placed in positions of power.

Although cotton was still "king" after the Civil War, many readjustments were necessary in Alabama. Without the free labor provided by slavery, landowners had to rely on landless farmers called sharecroppers who paid rent in cotton for the land they worked. This system tended to perpetuate a culture of dependency and deep divisions between wealthy landowners and poor sharecroppers.

The state attempted to diversify the economy in the 1880s and 1890s by encouraging industry, particularly the iron industry, in cities like Birmingham. The presence of coal fields and veins of iron in the state made this industry possible. In the early days in the iron mills, according to Hamilton, "Hammers rose and fell eighty strokes a minute, their steady throb audible for four to five miles on still days." Labor unrest, along with controversy over the leasing of convicts to work in the factories, plagued the iron business. The 1894 strike at Birmingham's Tennessee Coal, Iron, and Railroad Company (TCI) ended with capitulation by the workers. Thereafter labor made few strides in the state until the mid-1930s. In 1907 U.S. Steel, the country's largest steel maker, bought-out TCI. Birmingham, like its sister city in England, had become an important manufacturing city by this time.

Cotton milling also became a vital industry, employing mostly poor farm people who had lost their land after the war and were forced to work long hours

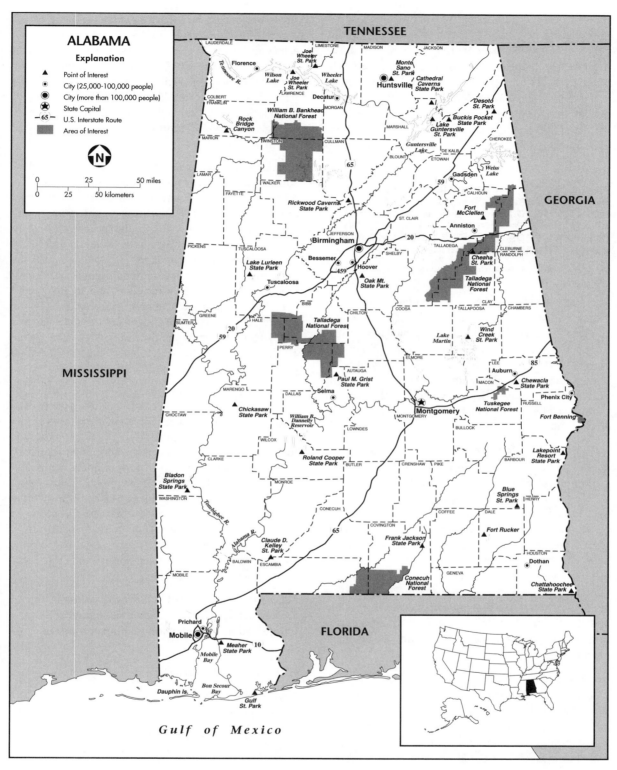

ALABAMA

Explanation

▲   Point of Interest

⊙   City (25,000-100,000 people)

◎   City (more than 100,000 people)

★   State Capital

—65—   U.S. Interstate Route

▨   Area of Interest

N

0   25   50 miles

0   25   50 kilometers

TENNESSEE

LAUDERDALE

Florence

LIMESTONE

MADISON

JACKSON

Joel Wheeler St. Park

Monte Sano St. Park

Cathedral Caverns State Park

Huntsville

Wilson Lake

Wheeler Lake

Tennessee R.

COLBERT FRANKLIN

Joe Wheeler St. Park

LAWRENCE

Wheeler Lake

Decatur

MORGAN

MARSHALL

Desoto St. Park

Buckis Pocket State Park

Lake Guntersville St. Park

DE KALB

CHEROKEE

Rock Bridge Canyon

MARION

William B. Bankhead National Forest

CULLMAN

Guntersville Lake

BLOUNT

ETOWAH

Weiss Lake

LAMAR

WINSTON

65

WALKER

Gadsden

59

CALHOUN

GEORGIA

FAYETTE

Rickwood Caverns State Park

ST. CLAIR

Fort McClellen

Anniston

PICKENS

TUSCALOOSA

JEFFERSON

Birmingham

20

TALLADEGA

Cheaha St. Park

CLEBURNE RANDOLPH

Lake Lurleen State Park

Bessemer

459

Hoover

SHELBY

Talladega National Forest

GREENE

Tuscaloosa

BIBB

Oak Mt. State Park

CLAY

SUMTER

20

HALE

Talladega National Forest

CHILTON

COOSA

TALLAPOOSA

CHAMBERS

59

PERRY

Lake Martin

Wind Creek St. Park

MARENGO

DALLAS

AUTAUGA

Paul M. Grist State Park

ELMORE

LEE

85

Auburn

Chewacla State Park

Selma

MACON

RUSSELL

Phenix City

CHOCTAW

Chickasaw State Park

William B. Dannelly Reservoir

LOWNDES

Montgomery

MONTGOMERY

Tuskegee National Forest

Fort Benning

CLARKE

WILCOX

Roland Cooper State Park

BUTLER

CRENSHAW

PIKE

BULLOCK

BARBOUR

Lakepoint Resort State Park

Bladon Springs State Park

MONROE

Tombigbee R.

WASHINGTON

CONECUH

COFFEE

DALE

Blue Springs St. Park

HENRY

Claude D. Kelley St. Park

65

Frank Jackson State Park

COVINGTON

Fort Rucker

HOUSTON

Dothan

Alabama R.

BALDWIN

ESCAMBIA

Conecuh National Forest

GENEVA

Chattahoochee State Park

Prichard

Mobile

Meaher State Park

10

FLORIDA

Mobile Bay

Dauphin Is.

Bon Secour Bay

Gulf St. Park

Gulf   of   Mexico

State of Alabama.

for low wages. By 1900 nearly 9,000 workers, including children, were employed in Alabama mills. Episcopal rector Edgar Gardner Murphy led a reform movement to prevent the exploitation of child workers, who often worked 12 hours a day for as little as 15 cents a day. In 1907 the Alabama legislature set the minimum age for workers at 12, limited the work week for children to 60 hours, and forbade those under 16 from working all night.

> **WHEN [RURAL ELECTRIFICATION] FINALLY REACHED HER, A RURAL [ALABAMA] HOUSEWIFE EXPRESSED HER HEARTFELT GRATITUDE: "WONDER OF WONDERS, THIS DELIVERY FROM THE PRISON OF ISOLATION AND DARKNESS AND DRUDGERY."**
>
> Carl Elliott, *Annals of Northwest Alabama*, 1958

The increasing number of tenant farms in the state led to unrest among farmers in the late nineteenth century. In the 1890s many farmers joined the Grange, a cooperative organization for farmers, and, along with factory workers, supported the Populist Party in a vain attempt to overthrow longtime Democratic rule. Both African Americans and poor whites were becoming more and more disenfranchised by state Democratic administrations.

During the Great Depression of the 1930s Alabama was harder hit than most other states. One-third of the population was out of work, and private charities were overburdened. The New Deal programs of President Franklin D. Roosevelt (1933–1945) helped Alabama, one of the most destitute states, even though the federal government was viewed with suspicion by the people of Alabama. This period saw the shortening of the workweek, reform of child labor practices, and guarantees of the right to join a union. The Tennessee Valley Authority made many new industries possible, and the Rural Electrification Act brought people in remote areas from subsistence living into the twentieth century.

World War II (1939–1945) revived Alabama's industry, but the postwar period saw another relapse. War plants stood empty, and many blamed the labor and marketing practices of U.S. Steel for Birmingham's failure to compete successfully with plants in the East. In the late 1940s the Interstate Commerce Commission equalized freight rates, making it again profitable to produce steel in Birmingham.

The civil rights struggle of the mid-twentieth century brought white Alabama citizens into direct conflict with the national government. The first in a series of protests by African Americans—the Montgomery bus boycott of 1955—took the form of an economic boycott. The young African American preacher Dr. Martin Luther King, Jr. rose to prominence during this time of social change. Since the 1960s African Americans in Alabama have gained some of the political and civil rights they sought. Their economic status, while improved, remains much behind that of whites.

Alabama has resisted progressive changes such as education, health care, and the taxation that would pay for these social programs and bring the state to the level of most other states. The tax system is regressive and even exempts from taxation the property of giant lumber companies at their market value. No property taxes go toward education, putting Alabama near the bottom of all the states in funding schools. Infant mortality is also high in the state, and in 1990 more than 20 percent of the people in Alabama lived below the federal poverty level. Citizens of the state also had difficulty recovering from the serious recessions of the 1970s and 1980–1982, which caused the loss of 39,000 jobs in manufacturing.

Alabama, however, made some important economic strides during the last few decades of the twentieth century. The economy diversified from its heavy dependence on steel. Alabama employment opened up for thousands of workers in the food, textile, metal, electronic equipment, and transportation equipment industries in the 1990s. Birmingham's U.S. Steel spent well over one billion dollars in 1984 to improve the Fairfield steel plant, and in 1997 Mercedes Benz began producing a sport utility vehicle in the town of Vance. The state provides a number of tax incentives for new businesses, and the Alabama Development Office provides assistance in financing.

See also: **Civil Rights, Civil War (Economic Causes of), Civil War (Economic Impact of), King Cotton, Reconstruction, Sharecropping**

FURTHER READING

Agee, James, and Walker Evans. *Let Us Now Praise Famous Men*. New York: Ballantine Books, 1966.

Armes, Ethel. *The Story of Coal and Iron in Alabama*. Birmingham, UK: Book-keepers Press, 1972.

Lofton, J. Mack. *Voices from Alabama: A Twentieth-Century Mosaic*. Tuscaloosa, AL: University of Alabama Press, 1993.

Olmsted, Frederick Law. *A Journey in the Back Country*. New York: Schocken Books, 1970.

Van der Veer Hamilton, Virginia. *Alabama: A Bicentennial History*. New York: Norton, 1977.

ALABAMA CLAIMS

During the Civil War, the Confederacy contracted with private ship builders in Liverpool England to refurbish ships for combat. The *Alabama* was one such ship. Although the British Foreign Enlistment Act of 1819 had forbidden the construction of foreign warships, the American Confederacy was still able to evade the letter of the law and purchase a number of cruisers from Britain. Confederate cruisers destroyed or captured more than 250 American merchant ships and caused the conversion of 700 more to foreign flags. By the end of the war, the U.S. Merchant Marine had lost half of its ships.

The Alabama Claims were brought against Great Britain by the United States for the damage caused by several Confederate warships, including the *Alabama* and the *Florida*. Recognizing that the affair might be used against Great Britain in some future conflict British Foreign Minister, the Earl of Clarendon, met with American ambassador Reverdy Johnson, and determined to submit the claims to arbitration.

When the Johnson-Clarendon Convention came before the U.S. Senate, Charles Sumner (1811–1874), chairman of the Committee on Foreign Affairs, opposed it on the ground that British encouragement of the Confederacy had been responsible for prolonging the war for two years, and that this cost should also be assessed against Britain. These "indirect claims," which Sumner did not name, were variously estimated at more than $2 billion, and Sumner implied they might be settled by the cession of Canada to the United States. The British refused to recognize the validity of the indirect claims, and the problem remained unsettled until 1871, when the Alabama claims were referred to an arbitration tribunal by the Treaty of Washington. Meeting in Geneva, the arbitrators excluded the indirect claims, but they awarded the United States $15.5 million for the losses caused by the Confederate vessels.

The Geneva Arbitration was praised by many nations for establishing a precedent for the peaceable settlement of international disputes. Most historians today believe that the raider warships' worst effect, rather than prolonging the course of the American Civil War, was on the U.S. Merchant Marine, which was not able to regain its pre-war standing for many years.

See also: **Arbitration, Civil War (Economic Impact of)**

FURTHER READING

Cook, Adrian. *The Alabama Claims: American Politics and Anglo-American Relations, 1865–1872*. Ithaca: Cornell University Press, 1975.

Great Historical Documents of America. New York: P.F. Collier & Son, 1910.

Hackett, Frank Warren. *Reminiscences of the Geneva Tribunal of Arbitration, 1872, The Alabama Claims*. Boston: Houghton Mifflin, 1911.

McCullough, Robert Hason. *The Alabama Claims and the Origin of the American Arbitration Policy*. Thesis (M.A.) University of Detroit, 1936.

ALASKA

At first, dismissed as a foolish venture, the purchase of Alaska from Russia in the 1870s was little more than a curiosity to most people in the United States. The idea that an ice-ridden territory so far from mainland United States could have any future value to the nation was not widely accepted. But the discovery of gold on the territory, and later oil, put a new light on the possibilities of Alaska. Those willing to brave the Alaska frontier in search of valuable resources eventually established permanent settlements, which formed the basis of what became the 49th state.

Ages after the ancestors of America's aboriginal people crossed a land bridge which then connected northern Siberia with Alaska, Russian explorers came to the area in the 1700s. The first permanent Russian settlement was on Kodiak Island; by the early 1800s, the Russian American Company was given control over the region, with headquarters at Sitka. The Russians had great difficulty with Indian uprisings, the depletion of the sea otter, and changes in the fur trade. Viewing the Alaskan colonies as a drain on their resources, the Russians agreed to sell them to the United States for $7.2 million in 1867. Some U.S. citizens were not at all impressed with Secretary of State William H. Seward's (1801–1872) success in acquiring Alaska, calling it "Seward's folly" or "Seward's icebox." The territory was at first administered by the U.S. Army and then by the U.S. Customs Service.

The economic potential of "Seward's icebox" was first apparent when gold was discovered at Juneau in 1880. After prospectors moved into the eastern

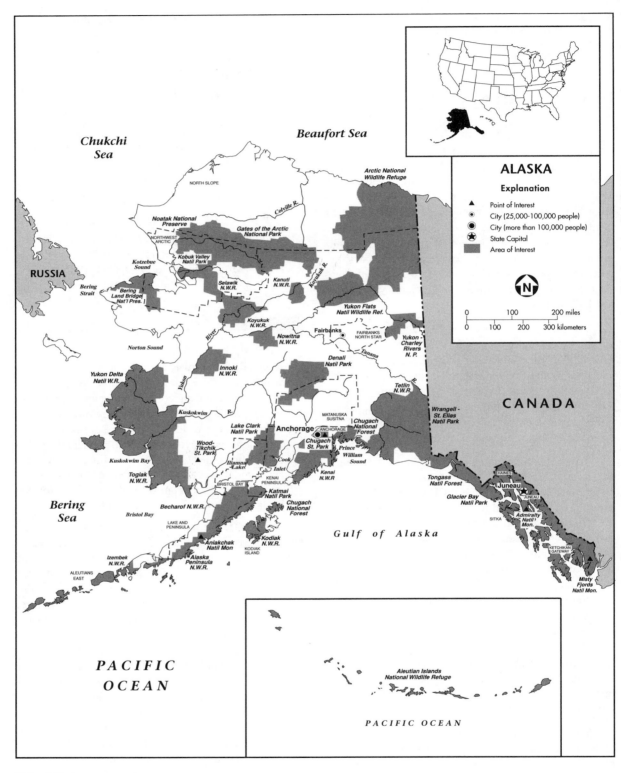

State of Alaska.

interior, they also discovered gold on Forty-Mile River and at Circle. The most important gold strike, however, was in the Klondike region of Canada in 1896; soon a stampede of prospectors was crossing Alaska's Yukon and other regions. They established some of the first permanent towns in the interior.

Still a wild country with few transportation networks, Alaska nonetheless began to develop its considerable fishing and timber resources. These industries benefited when the Alaska Railroad, started in 1914, connected Anchorage and Fairbanks with Seward, a newly created ice-free port. As more and more people moved into Alaska Congress voted to grant it territorial status in 1912.

Gold continued to be mined in the territory though at a slower pace. The population began to decline in the second decade of the century and the territory saw a general state of depression throughout the 1920s. World War II (1939–1945) showed the nation that Alaska, with its proximity to Japan and the Soviet Union, was important strategically. Federal construction and military installations were increased in the territory even after the war.

Development in Alaska was accelerated considerably when the U.S. government built the Alaska Highway, an extension of the Alaska Railroad, and other facilities such as docks and airfields. These wartime and postwar improvements brought many more military personnel and civilians into Alaska. Wanting the same rights as other U.S. citizens, the newcomers pressured Congress to make Alaska a state. In 1959 they succeeded, when Alaska became the 49th state, the first one not contiguous to the lower 48 states.

The use and allocation of lands in Alaska have always been sources of controversy. The 1971 Native Claims Settlement Act provided extensive land grants to aboriginal residents of the state but did not end the controversy over land use and ownership. The discovery of oil in 1968 and in 1974 caused another economic boom in the state but also aroused the anger of environmentalists who feared damage to the state's delicate ecosystem from a proposed Alaska oil pipeline. In 1970 after an oil crisis brought on by Middle East suppliers panicked the U.S. public, much of the opposition melted; the Trans-Alaska Pipeline was built, taking oil from Prudhoe Bay to Valdez and establishing Alaska as one of the leading energy sources for the United States.

The boom created by oil enabled the state to decrease its dependence on the federal government,

increase services to its citizens, and abolish the state income tax. Other private industries did not develop as fast as the state had hoped, however. Moreover, since 82 percent of the state's revenue came from oil, Alaska was highly susceptible to the vicissitudes of the oil market. This became evident in the mid-1980s, when Middle East oil overproduction drove Alaska oil prices down from $36.00 to $13.50 a barrel. Alaska lost 20,000 jobs in the four years after 1985, and the state government lost two-thirds of its revenue. At the same time oil reserves in the state were being rapidly depleted.

Further damage to Alaska's oil industry occurred on March 24, 1989, when the oil tanker *Exxon Valdez* ran aground in Prince William Sound, contaminating 1,285 miles of shoreline, including the sound and its wildlife refuge, the Gulf of Alaska, and the Alaska Peninsula. After a long series of suits by the federal and state governments, Alaska received a $1.025 billion settlement from Exxon. Exxon claims that the Prince William Sound sustained no permanent damage; Alaska's citizens, who maintain there is still visible evidence of oil contamination, are less convinced even after years of cleanup efforts.

A modest economic recovery occurred in the early 1990s, with significant growth in the fishing industry. An important segment of Alaska's economy, the seafood industry accounted for wholesale values of three billion dollars in 1990. Oil and gas production, however, continued to decline, reducing mining jobs by 11 percent in 1992; and by 1997 the decreasing supply of timber caused log exports to decline by 50 percent. During the 1990s Alaska was also engaged in a battle with the federal government over the rights to revenues from mineral leasing on federal land. Despite economic setbacks Alaska still ranked nineteenth among all states in 1996 in per capita personal income. This distinction was offset, however, by a cost of living 25-35 percent higher than the average for the other states.

As oil production declined in Prudhoe Bay in the early 1990s the state government again was forced to cut back state services. The governor of Alaska, Toby Knowles, pressured Congress to open a new area in the Arctic National Wildlife Refuge to oil and gas exploration. Again, environmentalists loudly disputed the wisdom of such a move, despite the favorable attitude of the Republican Congress. President Bill Clinton (1993—) said he would veto any such legislation. In 1998 another controversy erupted in Congress over a proposed road over a marshy wilderness from King Cove to an airstrip on Cold Bay. Proponents called it a boon to development; opponents called it a threat to the environment.

Alaska remained highly dependent on its limited network of transportation links at the end of the twentieth century. Though the Alaska Railroad with 480 miles of track was not connected to any other North American line, it was accessible to other rail routes by rail-barge service. Crude oil and other freight from Alaska was shipped mostly from Valdez, Kenai/Nikishka, and Anchorage. The Alaska Marine Highway System provided ferry service to 32 communities in southeast and southwest Alaska. Most of the consumer goods used by Alaskans were shipped from the port of Seattle; though freight costs were still high, they were smaller than by overland routes. The Alaska Highway was the only major road link with the rest of the United States. Other roads within the state were sparse and often unimproved. Many small airports across Alaska accommodated travelers seeking other ways of traversing the state.

See also: **Alaska Pipeline, Alaska Purchase, Environmentalism, Exxon Corporation**

FURTHER READING

Gruening, Ernest. *State of Alaska*. New York: Random House, 1968.

Hedin, Robert, and Gary Holthaus, eds. *The Great Land: Reflections on Alaska*. Tucson, AZ: University of Arizona Press, 1994.

Hunt, William R. *Alaska: A Bicentennial History*. New York: Norton, 1976.

Naske, Claus M., and Herman E. Slotnick. *Alaska: A History of the 49th State*, 2nd ed. Norman, OK: University of Oklahoma, 1987.

Ryan, Alan, ed. *The Reader's Companion to Alaska*. San Diego, CA: Harcourt Brace, 1997.

ALASKA PURCHASE

In the mid-nineteenth century, the most economically advanced and powerful nations of Europe, such as Britain, France, and Spain, began to scramble for colonies in Asia and Africa. They shared similar motivations—to increase their economic strength through expanding trade networks and to extend their political clout through a worldwide presence. The relatively untapped resources of products and people in Asia and Africa created a trading boom for European imperial nations and increased their international prestige. In the face of growing European imperialism, the relatively young United States began to look about for its own expansion opportunities.

The opportunity was found in the United States' backyard. The region of Alaska had for years been a Russian territory. As early as 1854 and 1860 the United States and Russia had been involved in unsuccessful attempts to arrange a purchase of the land, which spanned 586,400 square miles. U.S. westward expansion, once propelled by the doctrine of manifest destiny, had cooled with the additions of Texas, California, and the Oregon territory. Improvements in transportation, including a growing network of roads, canals, and railroads, made settlement and trade in the U.S. states and territories easier. Though some political friction remained over Russian enforcement of an 1824 treaty forbidding Americans from direct trade with the Alaskan natives, Americans frequently visited the Russian harbors in Alaska, to the profit of both sides.

Alaska was explored and claimed by Russia in the mid-eighteenth century and contained numerous coastal cities with busy trading businesses. Russian population in the region, however, was low and concentrated mainly along the coastline. One of the more advanced coastal cities was Sitka. Settled in 1830, Sitka was known for its commerce and culture, and was the seat of a lucrative fur trade. Aleuts from the nearby islands gave the land the name Alaska and provided pelts for export. A multitude of Indians, Aleuts, Eskimos, and Russians worked in Sitka's warehouses, shops, flour mill, bakery, tannery, arsenal, and shipyard. Cities similar to Sitka lined Alaska's coastline.

The California gold rush in the early 1850s led to a surge in America's western population. Trade out of coastal cities such as San Francisco prospered, and American pioneers and traders soon turned their attention northward. They came to Alaska to investigate its resources and found a wealth of timber, coal, copper, gold, and oil, as well as the world's richest salmon fishing grounds. These discoveries reinvigorated U.S. interest in the area.

After 100 years of poor management and regular indifference on the part of the Russians, the territory's profitability had declined markedly by the time of the American purchase. Russia, having turned its attention to East Asia and fresh from defeat in the Crimean War of 1854, needed revenue and was willing to part with its North American territory to get it. The Russian minister to Washington, D.C., Edouard de Stoecki, and U.S. Secretary of State William H. Seward successfully arranged the 1867 purchase of Alaska for the bargain amount of two cents an acre—a total of $7.2 million. Both sides thought they were getting the better deal.

Though the land was rich in natural resources and would prove to be a boon in fisheries and fur, the purchase met a dubious response from the American public. Critics of the purchase referred to it as Seward's Folly or Seward's Icebox. American pioneers and traders, however, did not hesitate. Between the purchase date in 1867 and the final Alaskan gold rush in the Klondike tributaries (1896–1897), people flocked to the region, looking to make their fortunes. With the first discovery of gold in Juneau in 1881, there was never a dearth of gold seekers. Large gold strikes at Nome brought more people in a gold rush fever and, behind them, came suppliers of physical and mining needs, who also profited from the region's booming resources. Others came to Alaska to break through the mountain barriers and explore its interior, mapping the Upper Yukon, stringing telegraph line, exploring northern Alaska to the Arctic Ocean, and discovering the glacier-lined shores of 40-mile-long Glacier Bay.

CRITICS OF THE PURCHASE REFERRED TO IT AS SEWARD'S FOLLY OR SEWARD'S ICEBOX. AMERICAN PIONEERS AND TRADERS, HOWEVER, DID NOT HESITATE. BETWEEN THE PURCHASE DATE IN 1867 AND THE FINAL ALASKAN GOLD RUSH IN THE KLONDIKE TRIBUTARIES (1896–1897), PEOPLE FLOCKED TO THE REGION, LOOKING TO MAKE THEIR FORTUNES.

Almost completely disorganized from a governmental standpoint, the human stampede to Alaska finally resulted in the passage of the 1884 Organic Act, which placed Alaska under a collection of federal laws and Oregon state laws. Congress enacted a second Organic Act in 1912, providing for land ownership, mail service, and civil government (as the Territory of Alaska). This form of government prevailed until 1959, when Alaska became the forty-ninth state in the federal union.

See also: **Alaska, Alaska Pipeline, Manifest Destiny**

FURTHER READING

Chevigny, Hector. *Russian America: The Great Alaskan Adventure, 1741–1867.* New York: Viking Press, 1965

Hunt, William R. *Alaska; A Bicentennial History.* New York: W.W. Norton Co., Inc., 1976.

Naske, Claus M. and Herman E. Slotnick. *Alaska: A History of the 49th State.* Norman: University of Oklahoma Press, 1979.

Wharton, Keith. *The Alaskans.* Alexandria, VA: Time Life Books, Inc., 1977.

ALASKAN PIPELINE, BUILDING OF

Native Eskimos in the Alaska territory first showed oil samples to Russians, who were looking for a northwest passage through the land in the early eighteenth century. The United States acquired the Alaska territory from Russia in 1867, and many American pioneers came to the land to take advantage of its vast natural resources, including fur, fishing, and gold. But it wasn't until the mid-twentieth century that the significance of Alaska's oil reserves were fully realized. In 1968 the oil company Atlantic Richfield discovered a large oil field in Prudhoe Bay, Alaska. Once the word was out, other companies flocked to the area. British Petroleum and Humble Oil companies joined Atlantic Richfield to coordinate their efforts as a single discovery unit. Other coalitions soon followed. Oil exploration experts projected Alaskan oil reserves on the same scale as the Middle East giants.

The best method to access Alaska's vast reserves was a pipeline which, though expensive, would allow for non-stop use of the product. A preliminary study outlined problems of constructing a pipeline across the state. One of the major stumbling blocks to its construction was the presence of permafrost, which covered much of the projected near-800 mile route. In addition, the pipeline would have to contend with severe climatic conditions, ranging from minus 70 F in the winter season to plus 90 F in the summer, as well as logistical problems in transporting and maintaining workers and equipment in a bleak, inhospitable terrain.

Alaska's North Shore yielded the largest oil reserves, and in September 1969 the state held a sale on oil leases in that area. Around 40 oil companies participated. Bidders were allowed one year to carry out exploration work, decide the value of the leases offered, and place a bid. Alaska gained $900,040,000 from the lease sales, equaling a historically high average rate of $2,180 per acre of oil. Most white Alaskans were thrilled with the sale. Native Alaskans and Eskimos, however, were not. They felt the transaction ignored their ownership of the land. Sympathetic environmentalists, fearing destruction of the land's natural landscape and habitat, joined in their opposition and successfully persuaded the courts to put a five year freeze on the development of the oil-rich land.

Native and environmentalist concerns about the use of the land resulted in several developments. Under the Alaska Native Claims Settlement (1971), aboriginal owners—native Alaskans and Eskimos—were accorded rights to the land, and eight oil companies paid for the privilege of working this land. Forty million acres

The 800 mile Trans-Alaska pipeline carries a peak flow of 1.2 million barrels worth of crude oil a day. This is a pumping station north of Fairbanks, Alaska.

were placed into 13 native-owned-and-administered, profit-making regional corporations. Conservationists also won a provision according 80 million acres to the creation of new national parks, forests, wildlife refuges, and preserve, wild scenic rivers.

Meanwhile, oil companies geared up for production and formed the Alyeska Pipeline Service Company, a consortium to build and operate the Trans-Alaska Pipeline System (TAPS). At the same time, the oil-producing nations of the Middle East determined to take control of the oil trade. With the 1973 OPEC oil embargo, petroleum became a precious commodity. The United States looked for ways to alleviate the affects of the hard-hitting embargo. Alaska held the answer. The legal logjam on the development of Alaska's oil resources were overridden by congressional authorization, and construction on the Trans-Alaska Pipeline System began.

A U.S. Interior Department environmental impact study resulted in about 200 technical and environmental stipulations in the right-of-way agreements signed by the oil companies, the State of Alaska, and the Interior Department. These restrictions, combined with the rugged terrain, required the most sophisticated pipeline ever designed. A master of engineering, the Trans-Alaska Pipeline System cost $9 billion, paid for by private industry. It runs from Prudhoe Bay, on Alaska's northern Arctic Circle Coast, and zigzags southwest across nearly 800 miles to the seaport of Valdez on the Gulf of Alaska.

Before actual construction could begin, crews selected the route through aerial mapping and ground surveys. The state granted permits allowing a pipeline width of 50 to 200 feet (15 to 61 meters), maintaining restrictions in accordance to conservation laws. A highway was built to transport manpower (20,000 people at the height of construction) and supplies along the construction route. A main concern in constructing the pipeline was to protect it from erosion. Towards this end, corrosion-resistant aluminum and plastic pipe were used to construct the pipeline, which was then pointed with asphalt and wrapped in a blanket of protective material. Refrigerated brine pumped through pipes four miles below the pipeline protects it from permafrost. Bulldozers dug trenches in the spring of

1974, and sideboom tractors laid the pipe, long sections of which were welded together to form a continuous conduit, which was tested under hydraulic pressure to ensure it could handle the traffic of oil. Parts of the pipeline necessarily ran underwater. Barges lowered this section of the pipeline underwater and weighted it with concrete or steel anchors to overcome buoyancy. To address environmental concerns, 400 underpasses and pathways were provided over buried pipeline for migrating wildlife.

The Trans-Alaska Pipeline System travels for almost 800 miles, 425 feet of which run on a high-rise ditch above ground, made from 78,000 eighteen-inch diameter vertical supports planted in permafrost so delicate that a one-degree temperature increase could upset its balance. The remainder of the pipeline runs underground or under water. The pipeline is subject to incredible air temperature stress (ranging from 60 F to minus 60 F). Friction generated from pumping oil at a pressure of up to 1,180 pounds per square inch keeps the oil heated to 135 F. In addition, heavy insulation can maintain the oil at a pumpable temperature for as long as 21 days, in case of a winter stoppage.

Several precautions were devised to protect the pipeline from the environment and the environment from the pipeline. Violent earthquakes have struck within 50 miles of the pipeline's route, so it was designed to withstand shocks of 8.5 on the Richter scale. In addition, should a break occur in the pipeline, over 140 automatic or remote-controlled valves are in place to eliminate an average of 15,000 barrels worth of oil spills.

Individual wells pump crude oil to a central location along the route. From Prudhoe Bay, which has a sea level height of 4,800 feet (1,463 meters) in the Brooks Range, the long distance pipeline crosses 34 major rivers and streams, traversing the Alaska Range at 3,500 feet (1,067 meters) before descending to Valdez. Once oil arrives there, tankers carry it primarily to West Coast and to Japanese refineries.

The oil began flowing in 1977, travelling through pipes controlled by devices and valves operated mainly from points hundreds of miles away. Eight pumping stations, located 50 to 75 miles (80 to 120 kilometers) apart along trunk lines, maintain the flow of oil at desired velocities. Communication to stations along the pipeline occur through radio, teletype, telephone and voice amplifiers and enable the entire system to be shut down within ten minutes if necessary. Peak flow through the Trans-Alaska Pipeline System amounts to 1.2 million barrels of crude oil daily.

See also: **Alaska, Alaska Purchase, Petroleum Industry**

FURTHER READING

Cooper, Bryan. *Alaska: The Last Frontier*. New York: William Morrow & Co., Inc., 1973.

Federal Field Committee for Development Planning in Alaska. *Alaska Natives and the Land*. Washington, D.C.: U.S. Government Printing Office, 1971.

Hodgson, Bryan. ''The Pipeline: Alaska's Troubled Colossus.'' *National Geographic*, November 1976.

Judge, Joseph. ''Alaska: Rising Northern Star.'' *National Geographic*, June 1975.

Marc, B.D. Dela, ed. *Advance in Off-Shore Oil and Gas Pipeline Technology*. New York: Gulf, 1985.

ALLEN, PAUL GARDNER

Businessman-billionaire Paul Allen (1953–) recalled in 1995, ''I remember having pizza at Shakey's in Vancouver, Washington in 1973 and talking about the fact that eventually everyone is going to be on-line and have [electronic] access to newspapers and stuff.'' Paul Allen realized that vision when he and his childhood friend, Bill Gates (1955–), co-founded the Microsoft Corporation in 1975. Their motto was ''a computer on every desktop and Microsoft software in every computer.''

Paul Allen was born in Seattle, Washington in 1953. His parents were both librarians and they helped both he and his sister Jody develop a wide variety of interests. From a young age, Paul Allen visited museums, art galleries, and concerts of every kind. Allen attended Lakeside School in Seattle, where he met Bill Gates. When a teletype terminal that was connected to a remote mainframe computer was installed in the school, Allen and a group of other high school kids became addicted to this early computer technology. Alongside Bill Gates, Allen became one of the first ''computer nerds.'' Allen and his friends spent their free time around the computer and spent their money exploring the machine's possibilities. Allen later said, ''I was just in love with the technology and wanted to understand it.''

In 1971 Paul Allen and Bill Gates started their first computer business venture in Seattle, the Traf-O-Data Co. They developed a computerized way to analyze traffic volume data. When Intel Corp. introduced the 8008 microprocessor chip in 1972, Allen recognized that this chip could help them build smaller and more efficient traffic-counting computers. With that advance in technology Allen and Gates now had the idea and the tool (the microchip) to build computers for a fraction of the cost of using conventional electronics components.

Allen pursued some college during the early 1970s but became bored. He tried to convince Bill Gates to work with him in the computer business, but Gates, then a student at Harvard University, was still unconvinced of the computer's future.

PAUL ALLEN AND BILL GATES CREATED MORE WEALTH THAN ANY BUSINESS PARTNERS IN THE HISTORY OF CAPITALISM.

Brent Schlender, *Fortune*, October 2, 1995

Then, in 1975, the cover story of *Popular Electronics* magazine featured a new computer called the Altair 8800, which was to be manufactured by a company in Albuquerque, New Mexico, called MITS, and sold at a low price. This computer would be low priced. Allen and Gates recognized that anyone who bought an Altair would need one essential component: software. Without a predetermined set of commands and operations, programming the Altair would be a nightmare. Working day and night in a garage in Albuquerque, Allen and Gates adapted the application they had developed for their Traf-O-Data computers and created a new software program to operate the Altair. Their software was inexorably linked to the success of the hardware it was designed to operate, a practice that became a standard formula for success at Microsoft Corporation.

By the late 1970s Allen and Gates' new company, Microsoft Corp., was flooded with business. They moved operations to the Seattle suburb of Bellevue, Washington. At their new business location they invented the personal home computer. According to Brent Schlender in *Fortune* magazine (October 2, 1995) their invention "created more wealth than any business partners in the history of American capitalism."

In 1982, Paul Allen was diagnosed with Hodgkin's disease, a form of cancer. He spent two months receiving radiation therapy. Then, at age 30, he dropped out of active participation in Microsoft. The cancer caused Allen to reconsider his life. He traveled widely, spent time with his family and, instead of returning to Microsoft, he decided to pursue other business ventures. In 1997, Allen officially left Microsoft and his position as its resident "idea man." At the same time he was listed in *Forbes* magazine as one of the three richest men in the world. (One of the two leading him on the list was his old friend Bill Gates.)

By 1997, Allen had invested nearly two billion dollars (part of which he received upon leaving Microsoft) in broad investment allocations ranging from software companies, multi-media and electronic entertainment companies, and others. Allen hoped to use his money to pursue software development and businesses that would help "wire the world" for computers. He also invested a sizeable amount in the Seattle Seahawks football team.

In addition to his entrepreneurial pursuits, Allen also engaged in philanthropy. He helped establish a popular music museum in Seattle and created the Experience Music Project [EMP] Foundation, which funds music and arts projects in the Pacific Northwest. Other philanthropic foundations he created include organizations devoted to community service, medical research, and forest preservation.

See also: **Computer Industry, Bill Gates, Microsoft Corporation**

FURTHER READING

Egan, Timothy. "Engineer of the Electronic Era." *The Financial Times*, December 31, 1994.

Kirkpatrick, David. "Over the Horizon with Paul Allen." *Fortune*, July 11, 1994.

Lesly, Elizabeth, and Cathy Rebello. "Paul Allen: New Age Media Mogul." *Business Week*, November 18, 1996.

Schlender, William. "Bill Gates and Paul Allen Talk." *Fortune*, October 2, 1995.

"The Wired World of Paul Allen," [cited June 13, 1997] available from the World Wide Web @ www.paulallen.com.

ALLOCATE

In economics, the idea of allocation is directly related to the ideas of demand and scarcity. Generally speaking, consumers' demands usually exceed the resources that society has available to satisfy those demands. Moreover, western economists largely agree that while people's desires are, by nature, unlimited; the resources available to meet those desires are limited. The economy or marketplace must therefore find a way to "decide" which resources should be allocated to meet particular consumer desires.

The term *allocation* refers to the efficient distribution of a society's economic assets (capital, raw materials, human resources) to satisfy the demands of consumers for various products and services. An example of an economy where resources are allocated inefficiently could be a marketplace in which television manufacturers made many more black-and-white televisions, (which consumers do not want) than color televisions (which consumers do want).

In an economy like that of the United States, however, resources are usually allocated efficiently. If consumer demand for seventeen-inch computer monitors, for example, grows stronger, the marketplace will automatically transfer the resources and materials away from other uses to meet that demand. Taking a cue from the prices that consumers are willing to pay, the marketplace "knows" when to begin making more seventeen-inch monitors and fewer fifteen-inch monitors. Consumer demand for seventeen-inch monitors increase if consumers are willing to pay more for a seventeen-inch monitor than they would have in the past. When companies realize that, they can make more profit for seventeen-inch monitors than they were able to in the past; in turn, companies allocate their resources to make more seventeen-inch monitors to meet the changing demand.

The Scottish economist Adam Smith (1723–90) is credited with being the first to explain how the changing preferences of individual self-interested consumers could, like an "invisible hand," force the marketplace to spontaneously and efficiently reallocate resources to meet consumer demand. Even at the inception of a U.S. economy, technological advances and changing consumer demand has forced the marketplace to allocate resources away from once popular products to new uses. Wooden teeth, hoop skirts, flintlock rifles, steam locomotives, gas lamps, vacuum tube radios, and 78 RPM phonograph records are only a few of the thousands of the once-commonplace goods that vanished from the market because the economy's productive assets were reallocated to different products.

See also: **Laissez-Faire, Scarcity, Adam Smith**

AMERICAN FEDERATION OF LABOR (AFL)

The American Federation of Labor (AFL) was originally founded in 1881 as the Federation of Organized Trade and Labor Unions. Trade union leaders representing some fifty thousand members in the United States and Canada formed the group in Pittsburgh,

Pennsylvania. As a part of reorganizing in 1886, the association of unions changed its name to the American Federation of Labor and elected their president, Samuel Gompers (1850–1924). For nearly forty-years he shaped the AFL by fostering a policy that allowed member unions autonomy.

Unlike the open-membership policy of the Knights of Labor (from whom the AFL gained numerous members in 1886), the AFL decided to organize by craft. This decision, however, was no inhibition to growth, since its member unions included a total of 140,000 skilled laborers. Similarly, the AFL departed from pursing long-term, abstract goals such as Knights leader Terence Powderly's objective of making "every man his own master—every man his own employer." Instead, the AFL focused its efforts on specific, short-term goals such as higher wages, shorter hours, and the right to bargain collectively (when an employer agrees to negotiate with worker representatives, usually labor union representatives).

In the 1890s the AFL was weakened by labor violence which raised public fears over labor unions. A July, 1892, strike at the Carnegie Steel plant in Homestead, Pennsylvania, turned into a riot between angry steelworkers and Pinkerton guards. The militia was called in to monitor the strike; five months later, the strike ended in failure for the AFL-affiliated steelworkers. Nevertheless, membership of the AFL grew to more than one million by 1901 and to 2.5 million by 1917. At that time the AFL included 111 national unions and 27,000 local unions.

The AFL inaugurated many important advances on behalf of laborers. By collecting dues from its members, the federation was able to create a fund to aid striking workers. By avoiding party politics, they were able to seek out and gain the support of labor advocates regardless of political affiliation. The AFL worked to support the establishment of the U.S. Department of Labor (1913) which, in turn, administered and enforced statutes promoting the welfare and advancement of the American work force. The AFL also supported the passage of the Clayton Anti–Trust Act (1914), an important piece of legislation which protected the interests of organized labor in three important ways. Price fixing was outlawed (the practice of pricing below cost to eliminate a competitive product). Executives could no longer manage two or more competing companies (a practice called interlocking directorates). And corporations were prohibited from owning stock in a competing corporation.

See also: **Clayton Anti-Trust Act, Congress of Industrial Organizations (CIO), Samuel**

AFL president George Meany (*left*) and CIO president Walter Reuther (*right*) officially opened the AFL-CIO convention on December 5, 1955, that joined these historically divergent organizations.

Gompers, Homestead Strike, Knights of Labor, Labor Movement, Labor Unionism, Trade Unions

AMERICAN PLAN

The American Plan was an employer offensive against unions in the years immediately following World War I. Spawned in the conservative reaction to the great changes that accompanied the First World War, this anti-union drive was promoted by the National Association of Manufacturers and driven by the anti-foreign violence of nationalist groups like the American Legion and the American Protective League. The American Plan included anti-boycott associations, the open shop drive, and the general message that unions were un-American havens of immigrant radicals.

The American Plan received impetus from the Red Scare, a government campaign against war-time dissent. This campaign peaked with the government's

reaction to a huge wave of strikes and anti-capitalist violence that broke out in 1919. Like the American Plan, the Red Scare identified radicalism with immigrants and unions. A. Mitchell Palmer, Attorney General under President Woodrow Wilson, and his ambitious assistant, J. Edgar Hoover, orchestrated the ''Palmer Raids,'' a round-up of immigrants on New Year's Day, 1920.

The combined result of this repressive atmosphere of the American Plan plus the Red Scare was the shrinking of the size of the labor movement. The number of unionized workers, which had grown by 1.5 million from 1917 to 1919, fell again from a total of 5 million in 1920 to less than 3 million in 1929.

See also: **Woodrow Wilson**

AMERICAN PLANTS

American plants are broadly defined as those plants native to North, Central, and South America as well as the Caribbean islands. When the Europeans first arrived in the Western Hemisphere in 1492, they discovered an abundance of indigenous foods unknown to Europe. Many of these plants had been cultivated by the Native Americans for hundreds of years and had provided for their subsistence. Some of these indigenous plants became staples in European and U.S. diets such as maize (corn), sweet potatoes, potatoes, peppers, plantains, pineapples, wild rice, squash, tomatoes, cacao (chocolate beans), peanuts, cashews, and tobacco. Moreover, because early explorers transported these plants back to Europe, their cultivation spread to suitable climates around the world.

See also: **Corn, Potatoes, Rice, Tobacco**

AMERICAN RAILWAY UNION (ARU)

Founded in June 1893 by labor organizer Eugene Debs (1855–1926), the American Railway Union (ARU) was an industrial union for all railroad workers. The union grew quickly and met with early success before its demise a few years later. Within a year of its founding, the ARU established 125 locals, and membership increased daily. In April 1894, ARU workers at the Great Northern Railroad voted to strike in response to wage cutting. The strike shut down the railroad for 18 days before the company agreed to restore wages. The union triumphed.

Later that same year workers at the Pullman Palace Car Company, which manufactured railcars in Pullman, Illinois (near Chicago), went on strike, protesting a significant reduction in their wages. In 1894, Pullman was a model ''company town'' where the company founder George W. Pullman (1831–1897) owned all the land and buildings and ran the school, bank, and utilities. In 1893, in order to maintain profits following declining revenues, the Pullman company cut workers' wages by 25 to 40 percent, but did not adjust rent and prices in the town, forcing many employees and their families into deprivation. In May 1894 a labor committee approached the Pullman company management to resolve the situation. The company, which had always refused to negotiate with employees, responded by firing committee members. The firings incited a strike of all 3,300 Pullman workers.

Pullman leaders were able to break the strike by attaching their cars to U.S. Mail trains. Since it was illegal to interfere with the delivery of the mail, Pullman workers now broke federal law when they obeyed

their leader Eugene Debs and refused to return to work. President Grover Cleveland (1893–1897) ordered federal troops to insure the passage of the mail trains. Government intervention led to violent confrontations, and the strike was broken.

The American Railway Union was destroyed by the Pullman strike failure. Despite public protest, Eugene Debs was tried for contempt of court and conspiracy and was imprisoned for six months in 1895.

See also: **Eugene Debs, Pullman Palace Car Company, Pullman Strike**

AMERICAN REVOLUTION

The American Revolution (1775–1783) was a rebellion of 13 of Great Britain's North American colonies. The colonies won their independence from the British crown and went on to form the United States of America. Although the revolution began as a civil war, France, Spain, and the Netherlands eventually joined the American side, transforming the struggle into an international conflict.

The revolution had not only national but also global significance: it defined the character of the modern political system by establishing a pattern of rule based on democratic constitutional governance. At the time, the American Revolution was a lone and fragile challenge to the prevailing monarchical and autocratic systems of rule on the European continent and elsewhere. By the twentieth century, however, the American model of governance achieved global currency. Virtually all governments—democratic or otherwise—now attempted to legitimate their rule by invoking the ''the will of the people.'' Even avowedly authoritarian governments usually argued that the suppression of democratic freedoms was only temporary.

The decision to go to war stemmed from fundamental differences between Britain and the American colonies over the legislative and fiscal authority of the British Parliament—specifically, the power of the parliament to tax the colonies without their representation in that institution. The conflict came to a head as Britain set out to levy new taxes on the colonies to meet the costs of the French and Indian War (1754–1763). Although Britain was victorious in the war, which concluded with the Treaty of Paris in 1763, its treasury was significantly depleted. The fiscal burden grew even larger when Britain decided to keep its forces at near full strength in the colonies in the event of renewed hostilities with France. Britain expected the

Washington and the main American force settled into winter quarters at Valley Forge, Pennsylvania. The privations endured by the troops that winter were extensive, and many died from starvation and exposure to the elements.

colonies to help pay its war debts and to support its standing armies in North America.

Through a number of acts—including the Sugar Act (1764), the Stamp Act (1765), and the Townshend Duties (1767)—the British Parliament sought to raise revenue in the colonies. Americans vehemently responded to these impositions, arguing that their colonial legislatures alone had the authority to levy such taxes since the colonists enjoyed no representation in Parliament. Britain remained adamant. Increased colonial resistance led to the imposition of the Coercive Acts in 1774. These were attempts by Parliament to restrict the power of local colonial government, particularly in Massachusetts, a hot-bed of revolutionary agitation. This effort at repression had the opposite effect, mobilizing the other colonies to join Massachusetts in protest. While at the beginning most colonists were willing to remain British subjects, as the conflict escalated they became convinced that full independence was necessary. The colonies began to prepare for armed resistance.

The success of colonial arms against the British owed much to the leadership of George Washington (1732–1799) and to the intervention of France. In June 1775 the delegates to the Second Continental Congress unanimously approved Washington's appointment as commander in chief of the newly created Continental Army. This decision was based in part on political considerations. Northern revolutionaries, who had dominated thus far in the struggle against the British, saw Washington's appointment as a means to bind the South to the perilous venture. The fact that Washington did not display aggressive political ambitions and did not seem likely to use his military powers for political purposes also weighed heavily in his favor. The delegates also understood that Washington's military training and experience, together with his personal authority, were unmatched assets to the insurgent colonies.

Washington now faced a Herculean task. The colonials stood alone against the enormous power and prestige of Britain's armed forces, fielding only a ragtag collection of national volunteers ("Continentals") and inexperienced state militias that served for only months at a time. There was no coherent system to produce and distribute munitions, supplies, and clothing, all of which remained in grievous shortage throughout the war. To make matters worse, there was no legitimate and effective national government that might improve these perilous conditions. Instead, Washington had to deal with a weak Continental Congress and 13 fractious state governments that jealously guarded their rights and prerogatives.

Against all odds Washington overcame these crippling disabilities. Skillfully maneuvering amid domestic political and economic obstacles and periodic opposition from within the Continental Congress, he forged an army that eventually stood toe-to-toe with British regulars, either winning the field or retreating in good order.

The road to this outcome was long and hard. The heady first encounters with the Redcoats at Bunker's and Breed's Hill, and then the British evacuation of Boston under American pressure in March 1776, were followed by a string of defeats. Yet Washington was at his best when disaster seemed unavoidable. He turned the seemingly endless and demoralizing retreat from New York and through New Jersey into victory in late 1776 when he forded the partly frozen Delaware River and defeated superior British and mercenary forces at Trenton (December 1776) and Princeton (January 1777). These bold and unexpected victories energized the American army and public, as did the victory of American forces under Horatio Gates at Saratoga in October 1777.

Despite these successes, the future still appeared bleak. Washington and the main American force settled into winter quarters at Valley Forge, Pennsylvania, after suffering important (and humiliating) defeats at Brandywine (September 1777) and Germantown (October 1777). The privations endured by the troops that winter were extensive, and many died from starvation and exposure to the elements. The army was further decimated by desertions and a widespread failure to re-enlist. Nevertheless, the Continental Army emerged rejuvenated in the spring of 1778. Under Washington's supervision, Baron Friedrich von Steuben transformed what remained of Washington's force into a disciplined and effective fighting weapon.

Equally important, the stalwart resistance and dogged survival of American arms (especially the American victory at Saratoga in New York state) convinced the French in May 1778 that the colonial forces had a good chance of winning the war. This led them to lend vital support to Americans in their struggle. Now France would have a chance to defeat its old rival, after being ousted from so many of its colonial possessions by Britain in the French and Indian War. Ironically, Washington, who had fought with the British against France, now became a willing instrument of the French attempt to knock Britain from the global chessboard. The coup de grace for the British came in October 1781 with a masterstroke by Washington. Commanding the combined American and French forces, Washington brilliantly maneuvered to envelop Yorktown, Virginia, by land and by sea, trapping British General Lord Cornwallis and forcing him to surrender. The independence of the colonies was now assured. As the opponents met at Yorktown to discuss Washington's terms of surrender, the shock and enormity of the American victory was poignantly underlined by the British band as it played "The World Turned Upside Down."

See also: **Townsend Acts, George Washington**

FURTHER READING

Bell, Rudolph. *Party and Faction in American Politics*. Westport, CT: Greenwood Press, 1973.

Carman, Harry J., Harold C. Syrett, and Bernard W. Wishy. *A History of the American People*. Vol. 1. New York: Knopf, 1964.

Draper, Theodore. *Struggle for Power: The American Revolution*. New York: Vintage Books, 1997.

Emery, Noemie. *Washington*. New York: G.P. Putnam, 1976.

Flexner, James Thomas. *Washington: The Indispensable Man*. Boston: Little, Brown, 1969.

———. *George Washington and the New Nation*, Boston: Little, Brown, 1970.

Simmons, Richard C. *The American Colonies: From Settlement to Independence*. New York: W.W. Norton, 1981.

Ward, Harry. *The American Revolution: Nationhood Achieved, 1763–1788*. New York: St. Martin's Press, 1995.

Wood, Gordon. *The Radicalism of the American Revolution*. New York: Random House, 1993.

AMERICAN REVOLUTION, LOYALTY TO GREAT BRITAIN DURING *(ISSUE)*

From a potential pool of about 800,000 men, the Continental Army was never able to attract more than 20,000 during the American Revolution (1775–1783). One important reason for the discrepancy in numbers was that the American Revolution had few ideological supporters. On one side, an educated group of middle-class patriots composed of lawyers, merchants, and planters led an underclass of farmers and urban laborers who were enticed by radical ideas regarding the evils of aristocratic privilege. On the other side were loyalists, a less vocal group of Crown civil servants, landed wealth, and Anglican clergy. Caught in the middle were the majority of colonists with no perceived economic interest or political loyalty. These colonists acted as a buffer between patriots and loyalists, maintained economic production purely out of self-interest; their presence perhaps prevented an all-out, ''total'' war during the American Revolution.

Even those patriots who were quick to bear arms during the early years of the War were not fighting for independence—they were fighting for their rights as Englishmen within the British Empire. Although many did believe that independence would inevitably come, most colonists maintained loyalty to King George III of England who, they assumed, was being misled by corrupt court ministers conspiring to enslave the colonies. Even as late as May, 1775, when the Second Continental Congress met in Philadelphia, the assembly insisted that the colonies were protecting themselves from these ministerial ''conspirators'' and that reconciliation would occur as soon as the King restrained his advisers. For many American colonists, the benefits of membership in the British Empire had offset its costs. Naval protection, access to a large free-trading area, easy credit, cheap manufactures, and restricted foreign competition had all contributed to a strong sense of loyalty to Britain and the Crown.

EVEN THOSE PATRIOTS WHO WERE QUICK TO BEAR ARMS DURING THE EARLY YEARS OF THE WAR WERE NOT FIGHTING FOR INDEPENDENCE—THEY WERE FIGHTING FOR THEIR RIGHTS AS ENGLISHMEN WITHIN THE BRITISH EMPIRE.

As many as twenty thousand Loyalists fought with the British. In New York, the Tory Rangers and the Royal Greens, and in the Southern states, Tarleton's Legion and Rawdon's Volunteers all fought bravely for the British Crown. But their numbers were never as great as was expected. In the Mohawk, Wyoming, and Cherry valleys and at King's Mountain and Hanging Rock their organization and training didn't match their courage.

One of the most visible signs of British loyalty before and during the war was land. Before 1775 British officials in the colonies had obtained large estates granted by the crown. Sir John Wentworth, governor of New Hampshire had extensive land in that colony. In 1775 Sir John Johnson inherited 200,000 acres in New York from his father while the Van Cortlandt, Smith, De Lancey, Bayard, and Philipse families owned as much as three hundred square miles of land. Sir William Peperrell guarded a thirty mile tract of land along Maine's coast while Sir James

Wright, royal governor of Georgia held twelve plantations totaling more than 19,000 acres and worth over $160,000.

By 1781 the tide had already changed in favor of the patriot cause. Anyone still remaining neutral was likely to be mistaken for a Loyalist, which by that time, carried serious consequences and costly penalties. Loyalist homes were attacked, their jobs lost, and all legal action was denied them. In order to raise money to meet the escalating costs of war, many states began confiscating land once owned by loyalists. Those serving in Britain's armed forces or leaving a state under the protection of British troops were likely to have their land, homes, and estates seized and sold at public auction. Beginning in 1777 states began the practice of banishing prominent Loyalists and everywhere Loyalists ran the risk of being tarred and feathered.

By 1783, it is estimated that as many as eighty thousand Loyalists went into exile. A thousand left Boston in 1776 with British Commander William Howe while four thousand left Philadelphia in 1778 with Commander Henry Clinton. A few thousand left Charleston and New York with the British at the end. Most went to Florida, Jamaica, Saint John, Halifax, and Britain.

The state of New York raised about $3,100,000 from sale of some 2,500,000 acres from 59 loyalists. After the war, 2,560 loyalists petitioned the British government to compensate for property losses By the terms of the Treaty of Paris (1783), Congress was not to oppose the collection of debts and the states were urged to restore Loyalists property. The Loyalists received awards amounting to 3,292,000 pounds sterling from the British government but none from the states themselves who refused to ''make good'' on their promises.

Historians have failed to adequately recognize the significance of the size and fate of the loyalist element in the American economy. Their disappearance was immensely important not only in terms of the large estates they left behind, but also with respect to the void their absence made within the social and economic structures of the old colonial aristocracy. The vacuum left room at the top for a new generation and a new class of newly-rich U.S. citizens.

See also: **American Revolution**

FURTHER READING

Atack, Jeremy and Peter Passel. *A New Economic View of American History from Colonial Times to 1940,*

2nd ed. New York: W. W. Norton and Company, 1994.

McCusker, John J. and Russell R. Menard. *The Economy of British America: 1607–1789.* Chapel Hill, NC: University of North Carolina Press, 1985.

Nettels, Curtis P. *The Emergence of a National Economy: 1775–1815.* New York: Holt, Rinehart and Winston, 1962.

Smith, Paul. ''The American Loyalists: Notes on their Organization and Numerical Strength.'' *William and Mary Quarterly*, XXIV (2), 1968.

Van Tyne, Claude Halstead. *The Loyalists of the American Revolution.* New York: The Macmillan Company, 1902.

AMERICAN SMELTING AND REFINING COMPANY

Meyer Guggenheim (1828–1905) a man of humble beginnings, arrived in Philadelphia from Switzerland in 1847. Struggling to support his family, he sold household goods in the coal towns of northeast Pennsylvania. Peddling goods led Guggenheim to manufacture a polish for stoves. Realizing the profits to be made from manufacturing, Guggenheim began to produce and sell lye, a synthetic coffee, and other goods. Guggenheim eventually built a prosperous wholesale business in household goods. By 1868, Meyer Guggenheim had fathered seven sons, whom he trained to become one of the best management teams in the nation.

Sending two sons overseas, Guggenheim established machine-made lace factories in Switzerland, which enabled him to import and sell fine laces and embroideries into the United States under the firm name of ''M. Guggenheim's Sons.'' In 1879, at the age of 51, Meyer Guggenheim had amassed a fortune. After acquiring interests in Colorado lead and silver mines in 1881, Guggenheim invested $20,000 for operational costs. These proved to be some of the richest mines in the area. By 1888 they were producing approximately $750,000 a year. The Guggenheim metal empire had just begun.

Meyer Guggenheim became aware that smelters generated more profit than the mining of ore. In 1888 he built a smelter in Pueblo, Colorado, and started the Philadelphia Smelting and Refining Company. With his next step, Guggenheim consolidated some of his various businesses, including his share of Philadelphia Smelting, under the name of ''M. Guggenheim's Sons.'' Guggenheim then delegated various duties among his seven sons.

The Guggenheims had been importing ore from Mexican mines for their Pueblo smelter. With the introduction of the McKinley Tariff Act of 1890, this proved to be a far more expensive venture. The Guggenheims went on to build two smelters in Mexico, taking advantage of the cheaper Mexican labor rates, and they were able to avoid the tariffs. With the passing of the Sherman Silver Purchase Act (where the U.S. Treasury Department agreed to buy four million ounces of silver every month) in 1890, the price of silver rose sharply. In 1895, in addition to being one of Mexico's largest industrial giants, the Guggenheim smelter operations were producing in excess of $1 million a year.

In an attempt to dominate the nonferrous metal industry, Henry H. Rogers (1840–1909) along with William Rockefeller and brothers Adolph and Leonard Lewisohn formed the United Metals Selling Company in the 1890s. The even larger launch of the American Smelting and Refining Company (officially renamed ASARCO in 1975) was assembled in 1899. This included the amalgamation of 23 other smelters. The Guggenheims refused an invitation to join the American Smelting and Refining Company. Instead, they formed the Guggenheim Exploration Company. With the assistance of son Daniel Guggenheim (1856–1930), the Guggenheims had mining operations in all parts of the world by the end of the nineteenth century.

Problems arose for American Smelting in 1900; mineworkers were striking against 12-hour days and the company's capital was estimated at too high an amount. American Smelting began to flounder. Daniel Guggenheim's strategy to drive the price of lead and silver down by flooding the market, worked. As ASARCO stock prices fell, Daniel Guggenheim bought it up. In April 1901, under the Guggenheim's terms, American Smelting and Refining Company and the Guggenheim family, merged. With the Guggenheims having controlling interest, Daniel Guggenheim became chairman of the board and president of ASARCO; Solomon Guggenheim became treasurer; and Isaac, Murray and Simon Guggenheim were named as members of the board. Expansion and acquisitions continued as Daniel Guggenheim increased the family business holdings to include mines in Bolivia, Chile, Alaska, and the Congo. When Daniel Guggenheim resigned as president in 1919, Simon Guggenheim assumed leadership of American Smelting and Refining Company.

Murray and Solomon Guggenheim, also gave up their board positions, at that time.

At the start of the Great Depression (1929–1939), American Smelting and Refining Company was the largest refiner of nonferrous metals in the world with a net income of about $22 million. Business declined though, and by 1932 ASARCO had suffered a $4.5 million deficit. ASARCO continued to expand, despite hard times, and acquired a huge source of scrap metal with the purchase of Federated Metals Incorporated. In 1934, ASARCO invested $8 million in a mine at Mount Isa, Australia, which supplied copper during World War II (1939–1945). The huge extent of the mine's copper deposit was not known until 20 years later.

Upon the death of Simon Guggenheim in 1941, ASARCO's bylaws were changed to make the of chairman of the board into the chief executive officer. Francis H. Brownell, already chairman in 1941, was in charge until Roger Straus, son-in-law of Daniel Guggenheim, took over in 1947. A member of the Guggenheim family was always at the helm of ASARCO until 1958, when John D. MacKenzie became the chief executive officer.

A prolonged copper strike in 1959 kept ASARCO's 13 U.S. smelters and refineries shut down for one hundred and thirteen days. Due to the decline in lead and zinc prices, ASARCO focused on copper mining, entering the 1960s still the world's leading custom smelter. By 1963, ASARCO was the forth-largest copper producer behind Kennecott, Anaconda, and Phelps Dodge. Copper comprised nearly two-thirds of ASARCO's revenue in the early 1970s, with aggregates, lead, molybdenum, silver, specialty chemicals, and zinc taking up the balance. From 1974 to 1978, labor problems, market fluctuations, and anti-pollution regulations, impeded the growth of ASARCO. Despite the high demand for copper in the early 1980s, the price was dropping due to a copper glut on the market—ASARCO lost $304 million in 1984. Richard J. Osborne stepped in as CEO and chairman of the board in 1985. Osborne restructured, renegotiated, and redeveloped ASARCO's financial health, and by 1987, ASARCO had bounded back.

ASARCO increased its copper holdings and continued to diversify with the purchase of two more chemical companies. The mining operations were suspended at two silver mines in 1992, due to a drop in the price of silver. In 1994, ASARCO sold its gold-mining operations in Australia. A leader in mining, refining, and smelting of nonferrous metals, ASARCO's interest in mined copper reached one billion pounds, for the first time in 1996, indicating that this company's firm hold on the copper industry would continue well into the 21st century.

See also: **Daniel Guggenheim**

FURTHER READING

"ASARCO: The Metal Maker." New York: ASARCO Incorporated, 1981.

Davis, John H. *The Guggenheims (1848–1988): An American Epic.* New York: William Morrow and Company, 1978.

Encyclopedia of World Biography. Farmington Hills: The Gale Group, 1998, s.v. "Meyer Guggenheim."

"Guggenheim Family Page," [cited April 5, 1999] available from the World Wide Web @ www.gf.org/.

"Guggenheim Family," [cited April 5, 1999] available from the World Wide Web @ www.optonline.com/comptons/ceo/02017_A.html/.

Hoover's Company Profiles. Austin, TX: Hoovers Incorporated, 1999, s.v. "ASARCO Incorporated."

AMERICAN SYSTEM OF MANUFACTURES

The American System of Manufactures was an innovative method for producing finished goods. In essence, the American System of Manufactures relied on precision machining of parts so that the total product was standardized and featured interchangeable parts. The earliest practitioners of the American System were small arms manufacturers.

It was earlier thought that Eli Whitney, who designed the cotton gin, was responsible for the innovation regarding the interchangeability of parts in small arms manufacturer. This claim was erroneous, however. Most scholars now believe that another inventor by the name of Simeon North deserves credit for that advance. In 1798 the U.S. federal government awarded an order of five hundred "horse pistols" to North, who organized production so that one individual did only one operation.

This innovation of using the division of labor in manufacture was important, but it was only one element of the American System. In 1808 North received another order from the federal government—this one for twenty thousand pistols. The contract stipulated that the parts were to be interchangeable: "the component parts of pistols, are to correspond so exactly that any limb or part of one pistol may be fitted to any other pistol of the twenty thousand." (Hounshell, 28)

The system had far-reaching effects on American industry. It spelled the end of the handicraft methods of cottage industry and accelerated the move of American laborers from their home enterprises to factories. It made for more reliable repair of the finished product. It also allowed industrial managers to hire unskilled labor to produce a great number of goods at once, rather than one at a time. By the mid-1800s the system had revolutionized manufacturing. New technologies combined with the nation's plentiful raw materials and an ever-growing number of laborers to transform the United States into a leading manufacturing society.

See also: **Mass Production**

FURTHER READING

Hounshell, David A. *From the American System to Mass Production, 1800-1932.* Baltimore: Johns Hopkins University Press, 1984.

AMERICAN TOBACCO COMPANY

The story of the American Tobacco Company begins with Confederate veteran Washington Duke, a tobacco trader in North Carolina during the post–Civil War period. In 1878 Duke and his two sons, James Buchanan Duke (1856–1925) and Benjamin N. Duke (1855–1929), founded W. Duke, Sons & Co. It was part of a plan that eventually enabled them to have corporate control over almost the entire U.S. tobacco industry. In 1890 the Duke family created a trust, known as the American Tobacco Company, the result of a merger of the five principal cigarette manufacturers of this era: Goodwin & Co., Williams S. Kimball & Co., Kinney Tobacco Co., Allen & Ginter, and W. Duke, Sons & Co.

In 1911 the U.S. Court of Appeals determined that this tobacco trust was in violation of the Sherman Anti-Trust Act. The trust was ordered to break down into 16 separate corporations. The emerging leaders were Liggett & Myers, R.J. Reynolds, Lorillard, and the American Tobacco Company—which retained the title of the now defunct trust.

In 1912 Percival Hill, an assistant to James B. Duke, became president of the American Tobacco Company. Because of his gentle manner and his preference for being a follower instead of a leader the company lost ground under his guidance. His son, George Washington Hill, became president of the company in 1925. He was a more aggressive and efficient leader and is credited with introducing more

Cigarette smoking became extremely popular among women during the 1920s. The direct advertisement campaigns featuring beautiful women contributed to this increase in female smokers.

people to smoking than anyone else in history. Between 1917 and 1938, Hill spent approximately $250 million in advertising. Hill also made cigarette smoking extremely popular among women during the 1920s The slogan "Reach for a Lucky instead of a sweet" inspired many women to switch from eating candy to smoking cigarettes. It also seemed to appeal to weight-conscious women who believed that smoking was a healthful practice. Advertisements featured beautiful young women smoking Lucky Strike cigarettes, the most recognized brand in the United States by the 1930s. During this time many show business and news personalities, including Rita Hayworth, Frank Sinatra, and Jack Benny, were paid to promote Lucky Strikes on the radio.

The American Tobacco Company made financial gains during the 1920s and 1930s, finally attaining market leadership in 1940. Brilliant examples of product promotion occurred during World War II (1939–1945). The war effort needed dyes and Hill transformed this into a windfall for the company. Eliminating the need for dyes in product packaging, Hill changed the Lucky Strike packages from green to white and came up with the slogan ''Lucky Strike Green has gone to war.'' He also developed the slogan LS/MFT (Lucky Strike Means Fine Tobacco)—which was clicked in Morse code over the radio. These strategies succeeded in introducing more people to smoking.

The death of George Washington Hill in 1944 signaled the end of the American Tobacco Company as a leader in the cigarette industry. An increasing amount of people were switching to filter-tip cigarettes, but the American Tobacco Company still relied heavily on the popularity of its Lucky Strike and Pall Mall brands, which did not have filter-tips until 1963, long after the other important manufacturers had converted. In the 1950s, the British Medical Resource Council and the American Cancer Society published reports claiming that tobacco was a danger to heavy smokers. Further suggestions from the medical community implied that smoking could lead to high blood pressure, heart disease, lung cancer, and numerous other health problems. On January 1, 1966, cigarette packaging was required to carry health warnings. Cigarette advertising on television was prohibited in the United States on January 1, 1971. As a result of these developments, Lucky Strikes and the American Tobacco Company continued to decline both financially and in the public's eyes.

In order to avoid financial disaster, the American Tobacco Company began to diversify. It purchased Sunshine Biscuits and James Beam Distilling in 1966, followed by Bell Brand Foods and Duffy-Mott in 1968. The company changed its name to American Brands in 1970, and that same year bought a variety of office equipment companies. Franklin Life Insurance was purchased in 1979.

By 1998, the company was known as Fortune Brands, Inc. and had extended its reach worldwide, with offices as far as Hong Kong, Singapore, and Buenos Aires, Argentina. Products offered included distilled spirits, office supplies, hardware, golfing equipment, cigarettes, and home improvement goods. The company's sales surpassed $5 billion in 1998.

See also: **James Buchanan Duke, Tobacco Industry, Tobacco Trust**

FURTHER READING

Aaker, David A. *Building Strong Brands*. New York: Free Press, 1996.

Petrone, Gerard S. *Tobacco Advertising: The Great Seduction*. PA: Schiffer Publishing Limited, 1996.

Tate, Cassandra. *Cigarette Wars: The Triumph of 'the Little White Slaver.'* New York: Oxford University Press, 1999.

Kluger, Richard. *Ashes to Ashes: America's Hundred-Year Cigarette War, the Public Health, and the Unabashed Triumph of Philip Morris*. New York: Vintage Books, 1997.

''Fortune Brands.'' [cited April 19, 1999] available from the World Wide Web @ www.ambrands.com.

AMERICANS WITH DISABILITIES ACT (ADA)

The Americans with Disabilities Act (ADA) is a revolutionary piece of civil rights legislation. The law is designed to protect the civil rights of people who have physical and mental disabilities, in a manner similar to the way that previous civil rights laws have protected people who are of various races, religions, and ethnic backgrounds. The ADA mandates changes in the way that both private businesses and the government conduct employment practices and provide products and services to the general public to ensure that all Americans have full access to, and can fully participate in, all aspects of society. It was the first federal law that required privately-financed businesses to provide physical accessibility in existing buildings. The ADA requires the removal of barriers that deny individuals with disabilities equal opportunity and access to jobs, public accommodations, government services, public transportation, and telecommunications. On July 26, 1990, President George Bush signed the ADA into law.

The legal structure of the ADA is based on those of the Civil Rights Act of 1964 and the Rehabilitation Act of 1973, and much of its wording is taken directly from these earlier Acts.

AMES, OAKES

Oakes Ames (1804–1873) was a U.S. manufacturer and five-term member of the United States House of Representatives. He was the principal financier of the Union Pacific Railroad, the eastern half of the first transcontinental railroad. Unfortunately, in his zeal to complete this railroad project, Ames made several errors in judgment. His questionable business practices eventually led to his censure by Congress.

Oakes Ames was the eldest son of Oliver Ames, Sr. and Susannah Angier, born on January 10, 1804, in Easton, Massachusetts. His father was a socially prominent manufacturer who owned a well-known shovel factory. Ames attended local schools until he was sixteen and then spent some months at the Dighton Academy.

Ames had an early interest in business. As a teenager he and his younger brother, Oliver, Jr. (1807–1877), began working for their father as general laborers. They started at the bottom of the company and worked long hours at a variety of tasks. Both boys worked their way up to management positions. When their father retired in 1844, Oakes and Oliver, Jr. reorganized the company under the name Oliver Ames and Sons and served as co-presidents.

The Ames brothers rapidly expanded the already successful business. The California gold rush, the settlement on the Western frontier, and the growth of the railroad industry all fueled demand for their products. In addition, the company was awarded several government contracts to supply equipment during the American Civil War (1861–1865). By 1865 Oliver Ames and Sons was worth over $8 million.

A successful businessman, Oakes Ames became involved in politics as a member of the Republican Party when he was in his fifties. He served as a close business advisor to the governor of Massachusetts. In 1862, at age of fifty-eight, Ames ran successfully for the Massachusetts second district seat in the United States House of Representatives. He was reelected four times and served in Congress until his death. As a Congressman Ames served on committees related to manufacturing and railroads.

The Ames brothers shared an interest in railroads and, in 1865, extended that interest to business ventures. Oliver Ames and Sons built the four-mile long Easton Branch Railroad. It began at a shovel works in Stoughton, Massachusetts, and continued to a connection with a line bound to Boston. Railroad-related business pursuits continued. In 1865, the brothers became interested in the Union Pacific Railroad, the eastern half of the first transcontinental railroad under construction. They joined a company called the Crédit Mobilier, the construction company and investment project for the railroad.

The Crédit Mobilier was organized by T.C. Durant, vice president of the Union Pacific to solve the railroad's financial difficulties and to complete the building of the railroad. It was a complex and corrupt scheme in which a small group of financiers contracted with themselves or their associates to construct the railroad, charging exorbitant prices for their services. Durant and his cronies pocketed huge profits for construction that was often faulty.

Dissention within the ranks of the Crédit Mobilier led to a reorganization of the company and its railroad interests. Oakes Ames stepped into the leadership of the Crédit Mobilier and his brother Oliver became president of Union Pacific Railroad. Oakes Ames won contracts to construct the Union Pacific railroad line. He then reassigned the contracts to trustees who served as stockholders of the Crédit Mobilier. The Union Pacific gave cash to the Crédit Mobilier to construct the railroad. The Crédit Mobilier instead used much of the money to buy stocks and bonds in Union Pacific at face value. These were later sold in the open market at a large profit for the investors, who all served the Crédit Mobilier company.

Thus, while the Union Pacific railroad line was slowly being built, the Crédit Mobilier investors were getting rich. This labyrinthine way of doing business garnered large profits for the investors. It was a cutthroat way of doing business, but was not uncommon at the time. The practices, however, did draw the attention of the United States Congress. As a Congressman, Oaks Ames was expected to support free market activities. In reality, his business practices appeared more like that of a monopoly. When Congress started to raise questions about this practice Ames sold Union Pacific stock to other members of Congress, also at face value. When this was revealed he was then accused of buying political support for his business interests.

In 1872 two Congressional committees were formed to investigate whether or not the government had been defrauded by the Crédit Mobilier. Certain members of

Congress wanted Ames expelled for illegal business practices. Ames defended himself by claiming his motives were purely patriotic because the railroad was important for the development of the country. He also argued that he had not become wealthy from the business dealings because the railroad was $6 million in debt at the time of its completion. Many members of Congress and the public agreed that while Ames had compromised legal principles he was not consciously corrupt. However, his desire to complete the Union Pacific project had clouded his ethical judgment. In the end Ames was not expelled from Congress, but he was censured.

After the Crédit Mobilier scandal, Ames returned to his hometown, depressed and in poor health. He suffered a stroke and died a few days later, on May 8, 1873. The memorial hall in North Easton was dedicated to him in 1881, and in 1883 the Union Pacific erected a monument in his name in Sherman Summit, Wyoming.

See also: **Oliver Ames, Railroad Industry, Transcontinental Railroad, Union Pacific Railroad**

FURTHER READING

Crawford, Jay Boyd. *The Crédit Mobilier of America.* Boston: C.W. Calkins and Company, 1880.

Foner, Eric and John A. Garraty, eds. *The Reader's Companion to American History.* Boston: Houghton Mifflin, 1991.

McComb, H.S. "The King of Frauds." *New York Sun,* September 4, 1872.

Oakes Ames: A Memoir. Cambridge: Riverside Press, 1883.

Union Pacific Railway Archives, Fact Figures and History. Massachusetts, 1997.

Utley, Robert H. "Golden Spike: Chapter 2: Building the Pacific Railroad." *US History,* September 1, 1990.

AMES, OLIVER

Oliver Ames (1807–1877) was a successful manufacturer, businessman, and politician. He is best known for his role as director of the Union Pacific Railroad, the eastern half of the first transcontinental railroad. Ames helped finance the project and oversaw its construction.

Oliver Ames was born on November 5, 1807 in Plymouth, Massachusetts, one of six sons born to Oliver Ames and Susanna Angier. His father owned a successful shovel manufacturing company in Bridgewater, Massachusetts. Ames was raised in North Easton, 20 miles south of Boston. At the age of 21 he went to study law at the Franklin Academy at North Andover. He studied there for 18 months and worked briefly in an attorney's office. After this short introduction to law, Ames decided that he did not enjoy working in an office and joined his father's company.

Oliver Ames and his brother Oakes Ames joined their father at the Ames Shovel Works. They entered the company at the bottom, working 10-hour days, six days a week. By the early 1840s, both boys had worked their way up to management positions. In 1844, Oliver Sr. retired and Oliver Jr. and Oakes reorganized the company as Oliver Ames and Sons. The boys served as co-presidents of the firm.

The company owned a water-powered plant that produced several types of tools, but specialized in shovels. They established a foothold in the market by creating a lighter shovel. At first the new product was thought to be less durable than the older, heavier shovels. But the lighter shovels allowed workers to be more productive and the product proved a great success. The company supplied shovels to thousands of western settlers and California gold miners. In addition, the growth of the railroad industry fueled the demand for the Ames' products. By 1860 the company was worth over 4 million dollars.

Oliver Ames also had an interest in politics. In 1852 he was appointed as a Whig to the Massachusetts State Senate. In 1857 he was popularly elected to the same position. His stint in politics, however, was brief. After his second term, Ames chose not to run for reelection and instead returned to his business interests.

In the 1850s Oliver and his brother became increasingly interested in the budding railroad industry. In 1855 they built the four-mile Easton Branch Railroad from the shovel works in Stoughton, Massachusetts, to a point where it connected to a Boston-bound line. Ames later served as director of the Old Colony and Newport Railroad, which took control of the Easton Branch Railroad.

During the American Civil War (1861–65) Oliver Ames and Sons won several government contracts to supply shovels, swords, and other equipment. By 1865 the firm's worth had increased to 8 million dollars and the Ames brothers had surplus money for investing. They decided to invest their money in the railroad industry, particularly in the Union Pacific Railroad, which was the eastern half of the first transcontinental railroad. Oliver and Oakes purchased large quantities of stock in the Union Pacific Crédit Mobilier, a construction company and investment project for the Union Pacific. Ames was able to invest a large amount of money in the project. He invested more than 1 million dollars of his own money into the railroad and raised an additional 1.5 million dollars on the credit of the family business. In addition, the Ames brothers placed the resources of their factories at the disposal of the railroad.

In 1866 Oliver Ames became acting president of the Union Pacific Railroad and was elected as president from 1868 to 1871. With Oliver's careful management and financial backing, the railroad flourished., Four-fifths of the line was built during his tenure as president. Despite engineering difficulties, rough terrain, and labor problems, the project was finally completed on May 10, 1869, when the Union Pacific Railroad met with the Central Pacific Railroad at Promontory, Utah. The company's success, however, was marred by a financial and political scandal involving Oakes Ames and the Crédit Mobilier. While Oliver Ames was never directly involved in the affair, the events occurred during his presidency of the company. In one sense it was tribute to him that the railroad was completed in spite the enormous loss of revenue because of graft.

In 1871 Ames left the presidency of Union Pacific, though he remained a director until his death. He returned his attention to the shovel company, which was on the verge of bankruptcy because of the extensive financing of the railroad. Oliver put that company back in order and also pursued business interests with banks and other railroads.

Ames was not only a successful businessman, but also a philanthropist. He was a devout Unitarian and donated a large sum of money for a new Unity church and parsonage in North Easton. He also contributed funds for a Catholic church and a Methodist meeting house. In his will Ames left money for a library, public schools, and local roads in his hometown of North Easton. Oliver Ames died in that town on March 9, 1877.

See also: **Oakes Ames, Central Pacific Railroad, Union Pacific**

FURTHER READING

Galloway, John Debo. *The First Transcontinental Railroad: Central Pacific, Union Pacific.* New York: Simmons-Boardman, 1950.

Garraty, John A., and Mark C. Carnes. *American National Biography*, Volume 1. New York: Oxford University Press, 1999.

Griswold, Wesley S. *A Work of Giants: Building the First Transcontinental Railroad.* New York: McGraw Hill, 1962.

Union Pacific Railway Archives, Fact Figures and History. Massachusetts, 1997.

Utley, Robert H. "Golden Spike: Chapter 2: Building the Pacific Railroad," *US History*, September 1, 1990.

AMUSEMENT PARKS

Amusement parks developed in the United States during the last decade of the 1800s. In 1893 Chicago hosted the World's Columbian Exposition, the equivalent of a world's fair. One of the highlights of the event was a "pleasure wheel," built by American mechanical engineer George W. Gale Ferris (1859–96). Measuring 250 feet (76 meters) in diameter, the ride could carry sixty people at a time. The excitement and success of the Chicago fair inspired businessmen to build permanent outdoor carnivals elsewhere.

The first sizeable park was built at Coney Island in Brooklyn, New York, which had been a recreation area since the mid-1800s. In 1897 it opened under the name of Steeplechase Park. In addition to a roller coaster, it included New York's first Ferris wheel. When New York City extended its subway in the 1920s to reach Coney Island, the resort became accessible to the masses, with whom it was very popular. It offered an escape from the monotony of daily life and showed that American industry could produce machines that were just plain fun.

Coney Island became the model for amusement parks around the country. In 1906 the Dream City amusement park opened in Pittsburgh, Pennsylvania. As a byproduct of an increase in American leisure time (between 1890 and 1920 the average work week in manufacturing dropped from 60 hours to 47.4 hours), recreation areas were part of the mass culture that was beginning to emerge in the United States at the turn of the century.

The model for amusement parks was reinvented in July, 1955, by American entrepreneur and entertainment mogul Walt Disney (1901–66), who opened Disneyland, a multi-acre theme park in Anaheim, California. The park included rides based on Disney

The "Pleasure Wheel" as built by G. W. G. Ferris contributed to the excitement and success of American Amusement Parks.

movies, featured roving movie characters such as Mickey Mouse and Donald Duck, and held daily parades on Main Street. Music, stage shows, and shops were all included in the price of admission—all entertainment was geared toward amusement for the whole family. In the decades that followed, carnival-like amusement parks gave way to theme parks inspired by Disneyland.

See also: **Baseball, Bicycles, Walt Disney**

ANASAZI INDIANS

Anasazi is a Navajo word meaning "ancient peoples." These early Native Americans settled throughout the canyon and mesa (flat-topped hill) country of the Southwest. Their culture had emerged in the Four Corners region (Arizona, New Mexico, Colorado, and Utah) by A.D. 400.

The Anasazi moved from subterranean dwellings (called pit-houses) and constructed aboveground masonry buildings, some with more than 1,200 rooms. Ruins at Mesa Verde (Colorado), Chaco Canyon (New Mexico), and Montezuma Castle (near Flagstaff, Arizona) are examples of distinctive Anasazi dwellings that were built into the sides of canyons and mesas. For this reason the Anasazi are commonly called Cliff Dwellers.

The Anasazi, who also produced a distinctive pottery, were one of the three major cultures of Southwestern Indians. (The others were the Mogollon and the Hohokam.) People of the modern Pueblos of Arizona and New Mexico descended from different branches of the Anasazi. Among the Anasazi descendants are the Pueblo, Hopi, and Zuni American Indian tribes.

See also: **Pueblo Indians, Southwestern Indians**

ANDERSEN, ARTHUR EDWARD

Arthur Andersen (1885–1947) was the founder and senior partner of Arthur Andersen and Company, the Chicago-based accounting firm that grew to become an international company known for its many services, including auditing, tax services, and specialty consulting in areas such as technology applications. Andersen established his company's focus on maintaining a strong organization through education, training, enlightened corporate policies, and a fundamental understanding of economic and business trends.

Born in 1885, Andersen achieved early success. In 1908, at age twenty-three, Andersen was the youngest Certified Public Accountant (CPA) in Illinois and one of only 2200 CPAs in the country. The previous year he had joined Price Waterhouse and Co. as a senior accountant, a position he held until 1911, when he joined Jos. Schlitz Brewing Company as controller.

While working as an accountant in the private sector, Andersen was also teaching accounting at the college level. At just twenty-seven years of age he was asked to head the department of accounting at Northwestern University. He received his Bachelor's degree from Northwestern five years later in 1917.

In 1913 Andersen and a partner, Clarence DeLany, founded their own accounting firm, Andersen, DeLany and Company. The firm soon had important corporate clients, including ITT, Briggs and Stratton, Colgate-Palmolive, and Parker Pen. Delany left the firm in 1918 when it adopted its current name, Arthur Andersen and Company. Under Andersen's direction the firm, which was licensed in most states to offer accounting and auditing services, grew quickly.

Andersen considered himself an educator—he continued to teach at Northwestern for a decade after the founding of Andersen, DeLany and Company. Simultaneously, he continued his work as an accountant. In 1953, when he was elected to the Accounting Hall of Fame at Ohio State University, he was cited for his "contributions as an educator and outstanding practitioner."

Throughout his career, Andersen emphasized a broad view of the accountant's role: "The thoroughly trained accountant must have a sound understanding of the principles of economics, of finance, and of organization. It has been the view of accountants up to this time that their responsibility begins and ends with the certification of the balance sheet and statement of earnings. I maintain that the responsibility of the public accountant begins, rather than ends, at this point.'' Under the motto ''Think Straight-Talk Straight,'' Andersen challenged traditional accounting practices by going beyond the balance sheet to understand the effect of sheer numbers on a particular business. Thus, members of the firm were encouraged to use their auditing skills to contribute to a client's overall success.

UNDER THE MOTTO "THINK STRAIGHT-TALK STRAIGHT," ANDERSEN CHALLENGED TRADITIONAL ACCOUNTING PRACTICES BY GOING BEYOND THE BALANCE SHEET TO UNDERSTAND THE EFFECT OF SHEER NUMBERS ON A PARTICULAR BUSINESS.

Anderson's reputation grew and he was invited in 1938 to become the first salaried president of the New York Stock Exchange. He declined the offer in order to devote his energies to his expanding accounting practice. By the end of the twentieth century Arthur Andersen and Co. was among the largest of the nation's Big Six accounting firms.

Throughout his life Arthur Andersen was active in professional organizations, civic and community services, and education. He wrote numerous articles for professional journals and several pamphlets on economic issues. He was widely recognized as an authority on financial affairs and was often called upon to provide expert analysis in legal cases and advice as a member of various boards. He served as chairman of the board of Certified Public Accountant examiners for the state of Illinois; director of the State Bank and Trust Company of Evanston, Illinois; trustee for Chicago's Century of Progress, and president of the board of trustees at Northwestern University. Arthur Andersen died in 1947.

FURTHER READING

''About Arthur Andersen,'' [cited April 5, 1999] available from the World Wide Web @ www.arthurandersen.com/.

The First Sixty Years. Chicago: Arthur Andersen and Co., 1974.

''Arthur Edward Andersen,'' [cited April 5, 1999] available from the World Wide Web @ www.cob.ohio-state.edu/.

National Cyclopaedia of American Biography. New York: James T. White, 1949, XXXV: 98–99, s.v. ''Andersen, Arthur.''

Spaak, Leonard. *The Growth of Arthur Andersen and Co. 1928–1973.* New York: Garland Publishing, 1989.

ANDREESEN, MARC

The creative mind behind Netscape Communications Corporation, Marc Andreesen (1971–) became a Silicon Valley legend and a multimillionaire well before his thirtieth birthday. The explosive growth of Internet commerce in the last decade of the twentieth century was directly attributable to his co-invention of the first widely used browser for finding and retrieving Internet information. In 1998, just five years after its founding, American Online, Inc. (AOL) acquired Netscape in a $9.6 billion deal. As part of the merger Andreesen, still only twenty-seven, signed on as chief technology officer of AOL.

Born in 1971, Marc Andreesen grew up in New Lisbon, Illinois. As a boy, Andreesen was fascinated with computers. Before he was ten he had taught himself BASIC programming by reading a book. In the seventh grade his parents gave him his first computer. While a student in computer science at the University of Illinois, Andreesen was introduced to the Internet. In the early 1990s the Internet was primarily used by scientists who could navigate through its complex codes.

In 1992, while working part-time at the National Center for Supercomputing Applications (NCSA) at the university, Andreesen and a friend, Eric Bina, began to speculate on the potential of the World Wide Web. Working nights and weekends the two developed a program, eventually named *Mosaic*, that incorporated elements of Web navigation, text display, and sound.

When Mosaic was demonstrated in January 1993 it was an immediate hit, and by the time Andreesen graduated in December of that year, several million free copies of NCSA Mosaic had been distributed over the Internet. Andreesen recognized the commercial applications of the project, but NCSA was not prepared to take commercial advantage of the program it owned copyright for.

Following graduation Andreesen took a job in Silicon Valley, but a legendary e-mail message soon changed his life. The message was from James H.

Clark, co-founder of Silicon Graphics Inc., one of the computer industry's early success stories. Clark had resigned from his company and was looking for a new venture. He asked Andreesen if he would be interested in forming a company to create a commercially viable, improved version of the Mosaic browser.

In April 1994 Clark invested some $3 million in the new firm, which began with three employees with offices in Mountain View, California. The new company was first called Mosaic Communications Corporation, but after the University of Illinois contested the use of the name, the fledgling firm was christened Netscape Communications.

By December 1994 Netscape had released its revolutionary browser, the Netscape Navigator. Almost immediately the new browser became the industry standard. Within only a few months Netscape claimed 70 percent of the browser market. It offered users speed, sophisticated graphics, and a special encryption code that secured their credit card transactions on the Web.

When Netscape made an initial public stock offering of 3.5 million shares in August 1995, an unprecedented stock frenzy ensued. Investors bought the stock in record numbers. Opening at $28 a share, the stock closed at $58 1/2, making Netscape's market value $2.3 billion. With Netscape's continuing strong showing on the booming stock market of the late 1990s, Clark, Andreesen, and many of the company's employees became extremely wealthy. Four years later electronic commerce had transformed the way the nation did business. Nearly every advertisement, for example, included a web address. Banking and investing, travel arrangements, and personal shopping on the Internet had become routine. Automobile and home purchases could be negotiated on-line. Some analysts predicted that Internet commerce could reach $3.2 trillion, or 5 percent of all sales worldwide by 2003.

At first the new browser faced virtually no competition, but in 1995 Microsoft Corporation introduced the Explorer, which it bundled free with its popular Windows software. In the last years of the twentieth century, as Netscape and Microsoft battled for the browser market and in the courts, Netscape began to lose its market share. A landmark federal anti-trust trial began involving Microsoft's alleged attempts to obstruct Netscape from competing for a fair share of the lucrative browser business. In late 1998, before that trial was completed, Netscape was purchased by AOL.

See also: **Computer Industry, Information Superhighway, Internet, Netscape**

FURTHER READING

1997 Current Biography Yearbook. New York: H.W. Wilson, 1997, s.v. "Andreesen, Marc."

Barksdale, Jim. "A Winning Company for the 21st Century," [cited April 6, 1999] available from the World Wide Web @ netscape.com/.

Cusumano, Michael A. *Competing on Internet Time: Lessons from Netscape and its Battle with Microsoft.* New York: Free Press, 1998.

Lohr, Steve and John Markoff. "AOL Sees Netscape Purchase as Step Toward Ambitious Goals." *New York Times*, November 24, 1998.

Quittner, Joshua. *Speeding the Net: The Inside Story of Netscape and How it Challenged Microsoft.* New York: Atlantic Monthly Press, 1998.

Swartz, Jon. "Netscape's Andreesen Joining Ranks of AOL." *San Francisco Chronicle*, January 18, 1999.

Tetzeli, Rick. "What It's Really Like to be Marc Andreessen." *Fortune*, December 9, 1996.

ANTI-IMMIGRATION LAWS

Anti-immigration laws are congressional acts that regulate the conditions under which residents of foreign countries may enter the U.S. to live permanently. Such laws usually contain provisions that have the effect of discouraging or prohibiting certain classes of persons from immigrating. Vested with almost total authority over immigration, Congress initially began stemming the tide of immigrants in the late nineteenth century. Between 1865 and 1890 a great wave of immigrants came to the U.S., mostly from northwest Europe (especially England, Ireland, Wales, Germany, and Scandinavia). In 1875 Congress passed the first restrictive immigration statute, barring criminals, anarchists, polygamists, and prostitutes from entry. Other anti-immigration laws passed in 1882 and 1892 barred admission to persons who were insane, had a loathsome or contagious disease, or were likely to become dependent on governmental assistance. Congress passed a series of Alien Contract Labor laws in 1885, 1887, 1888, and 1891, which precluded immigrants from entering the U.S. to work under contracts made before their arrival and prohibited U.S. employers from advertising job opportunities in other countries.

Between 1890 and 1914 a second wave of 15 million people immigrated to the U.S., mostly coming from eastern and southern Europe (Poland, Russia, Ukraine, Slovakia, Croatia, Slovenia, Hungary, Greece,

Rumania, and Italy). By World War I (1914–1918) there was a growing belief that the country was becoming overcrowded. Many Americans complained that new immigrants were taking good jobs and depressing wages by working for little money. Congress responded by passing immigration laws in 1917, 1921, and 1924. The 1917 law created literacy, physical, and economic standards for aliens seeking admission, and barred immigration from many of the Asian and Pacific islands. The 1921 law established a quota system, under which the total number immigrants from any one nation in a given year could not exceed three percent of the number of foreign-born residents of that nationality living in the U.S. during 1910. The 1924 law lowered the cap to two percent. Immigration slowed dramatically during the Great Depression, as economic opportunities in the U.S. dwindled. In some years during this period the number of Americans emigrating from the U.S. actually exceeded the number of foreigners seeking admission. Immigration did not pick up again until after World War II (1939–1945), when Congress recognized two new categories of immigrants: wives and children of American citizens who had served abroad in the U.S. armed forces.

See also: **Chinese Exclusion Act, Immigration**

APPALACHIAN MOUNTAINS

Named for the Apalachee Indians, the Appalachian Mountains form a great continental divide which runs roughly parallel to the eastern seaboard of the Unites States. On the eastern side of the mountains waterways drain into the Atlantic Ocean; on the western side they drain into the Gulf of Mexico. The Appalachians extend 1,500 miles (2,400 kilometers), from Quebec's Gaspe Peninsula to Birmingham, Alabama. The chief ranges include the Notre Dame (in Quebec), the White Mountains (in New Hampshire), the Green Mountains (in Vermont), and the Catskills (in New York). South of New York the Appalachians divide into three sections: farthest to the east lie the Blue Ridge Mountains (which include the Appalachians' tallest peaks, in the Black Mountains of North Carolina); the middle section is called the Great Valley (which includes the Cumberland, Lehigh, and Shenandoah valleys); the western-most section is the Ridge-and-Valley Province (whose western boundary is formed by the Cumberland and Allegheny mountains).

Although the mountain range was a barrier to the settlement of the country, British acquisition of the territory west of the Appalachians in 1763 prompted people to cross the mountains and move into the fertile land beyond them. In the late 1700s settlers followed the Great Valley south to the Cumberland Gap near the intersection of North Carolina, Kentucky, and Tennessee. They followed the narrow trails forged by Native Americans—widening them for wagons. The chief trail was the Wilderness Road forged by U.S. pioneer Daniel Boone (c. 1734–1820). Settlers also followed a western route to the Ohio River through the river valleys of Pennsylvania and into Pittsburgh. In 1811 construction of a federal route called the National Road began. The northernmost westward trail was the Mohawk, which ran through New York state. It followed the southern shores of the Great Lakes. In 1825 the completion of New York's Erie Canal aided westward movement. By the 1840s railroads crossed the mountain range.

On this frontier farmers cultivated crops in the valleys. Settlers were mostly Scots-Irish, English, and German. The principal products in the northern regions included apples, barley, hay, potatoes, wheat, and dairy. Chief products in the South included corn, tobacco, and poultry. Trees from the Appalachians were cut for the U.S. furniture industry, centered in North Carolina. Approximately 50,000 square miles (130,000 square kilometers) of the mountains were rich in coal and other mineral deposits. These resources were important to the economies of Alabama, Kentucky, Pennsylvania, Virginia, and West Virginia.

See also: **Back Country , Cumberland Gap, Erie Canal, National Road, Maysville Road, Subsistence Agriculture, Wilderness Road**

APPRECIATION

The term *appreciation* has several specific uses in economics but in general it refers to an increase in value over time. At the level of macroeconomics (or the study of entire economic systems), appreciation is often used to describe the rise of the value of one currency *vis-à-vis* (in relation to) another. For example, when U.S. travelers can buy more foreign goods with their dollar in one year than they could in an earlier year, we say that the dollar has "appreciated" in comparison to the foreign currency. It is also possible for the U.S. dollar to appreciate vis-à-vis one currency but depreciate relative to another. For example, between January 1979 and January 1981 the U.S. dollar appreciated in value relative to the German mark (U.S. travelers could buy more marks with their dollar than earlier); during the same period the U.S. dollar depreciated relative to the British pound (the dollar bought

The setting sun over the Appalachian Mountains, at Stone Mountain, Virginia. The Appalachian Mountains extend 1,500 miles forming the eastern continental divide of the U.S.

fewer pounds). (Note that the terms *revaluation* and *devaluation* are used instead of *appreciation* and *depreciation* when referring to changes in a currency's value brought about by the action of that currency's government. For example, if country A's currency has appreciated relative to other global currencies, the country's government may "devalue" its currency so its goods will be more attractively priced in the international marketplace.)

Appreciation is also used to describe the increase in market value of an asset such as a home or a stock over time. For example, buying a home is considered an excellent investment because individual homes often appreciate in value when the property values in their neighborhood rise, even if the individual homeowner made no improvements to his or her own home. Similarly, the value of the stocks of many large corporations appreciated in value since the bull market of 1982 began. For example, investors who bought $1000 in the stock of computer storage firm EMC Corp. in 1991 (but no additional stock) saw their $1000 appreciate in value to more than $18,000 five years later.

See also: **Currency, Depreciation**

ARBITRATION

Arbitration is the process by which two parties agree to submit a dispute they cannot settle on their own to a third party, or arbitrator, whose decision is final and binding on both sides. Disputing parties resort to arbitration when they have reached a point where the only alternative is a lawsuit or a strike. In some cases arbitration is required by law. Arbitration is common in disputes over construction contracts, landlord-tenant contracts, and even salary disagreements in professional sports. After evaluating the dispute, the arbitrator either sides with one of the parties or tries to find a solution that is fair to both. He may be appointed by the two parties or assigned by a court. The arbitrator may be a respected individual or panel of individuals or a professional arbitrator hired through organizations like the American Arbitration Association.

Arbitration proceedings differ from lawsuits. They are faster and cheaper, and arbitrators have greater flexibility than law courts because they do not have to assign "blame" to one of the parties. Arbitration proceedings are ideally suited to complex disputes where the arbitrator has specialized expertise in the subject matter of the dispute, and they enable the disagreeing parties to maintain greater privacy over the arbitration process.

Commercial or contract arbitration arose in medieval Europe to settle disputes when the law was no help because the disputing merchants lived in different political or legal systems. By the nineteenth century the United States had developed a voluntary arbitration system in which workers and owners freely submitted their labor disputes to an "umpire" for resolution. In 1926 the American Arbitration Association was established to create a trained pool of professional arbitrators. Nine years later, the National Labor Relations Act was passed, making it easier for workers to use arbitration to bargain collectively for better labor agreements. The need for quick resolution of labor disputes during World War II (1939–1945) increased the number of arbitrated labor disputes. The passage of the Arbitration Acts of 1947, 1970, and 1990 strengthened the process of arbitrating commercial disputes, made the process more uniform, and established procedures for resolving disputes with foreign companies. In 1960 the landmark "Steelworkers' Trilogy" Supreme Court case limited the role of the courts in overturning arbitration cases, paving the way for today's independent, legally binding arbitration decisions.

See also: **Collective Bargaining, Strike**

ARIZONA

Arizona is known to most people in the United States as a haven for vacationers and retirees. With its hot, arid climate and scenic wonders, it offers many advantages to those seeking unusual terrain or refuge from northern winters. The state, however, is much more than just a refuge. For over a hundred years it has been an important source of livestock and minerals. Moreover, after waters from its rivers were diverted into the rest of the state, Arizona has emerged as an important producer of manufactured goods and farm crops.

The first Spanish explorers in Arizona found a number of Native American tribes subsisting on hunting, gathering, and limited farming. Four Spanish expeditions set out between 1539 and 1605 across the upland plateau and lower desert in failed attempts to find riches. Franciscan friars also came to proselytize among the Hopi and Pima Indians, establishing a large mission at the site of present-day Tucson. The first important European settlement was a military outpost at Tubac, north of Nogales; this outpost was moved to Tucson in 1776. The Spaniards treated most of the outposts in the territory as merely way stations to California, thought to be a more desirable area for colonization.

When war started between Mexico and the United States in 1846, over the U.S. annexation of Texas, Col. Stephen W. Kearny and Lt. Philip Cooke led troops across Arizona on their way to California. With the defeat of Mexico in the Mexican War (1846–1848) most of present-day Arizona became part of the United States as part of the Mexican Cession. Thousands of U.S. citizens passed through the region during the California Gold Rush of 1849. In 1850 Arizona was formally organized as part of the territory of New Mexico, with a southern strip added by the terms of the Gadsden Purchase in 1853.

By the early 1860s the federal government was planning road and railroad routes through Arizona in an effort to provide better links to California. The Army put up forts to protect travelers from the Indians, and the government established overland mail service. Citizens of Arizona unsuccessfully tried to join with southern New Mexico in a new territory when they became dissatisfied with their territorial government at Santa Fe. The region was declared part of the Confederacy during the American Civil War (1861–1865), but Union troops occupied the region. The U.S. Congress declared Arizona an official territory in 1863.

Gold and silver mining were the mainstays of Arizona's economy during the 1850s and 1860s. Jackson Snively first discovered gold on the Gila River, 20 miles above the Colorado. Those who rushed in to pan for gold earned as much as $125 a day for their efforts, and Gila City soon became a boom town with gambling halls, saloons, and temporary dwellings for the prospectors. Gold mines were also established along the Colorado and in the interior mountains, and silver was discovered in Tombstone and other districts.

As military posts sprung up to protect the influx of people and the towns they created, the cattle industry benefited from the increased demand for beef. Irrigated farming developed and Phoenix became an agricultural center. Cattle ranching continued to expand in the 1870s after the Apache Indian threat subsided. At first driven in from Texas and Mexico to supply the armies that protected Arizona, cattle soon became a major source of income. Along with lumbering and mining, cattle ranching flourished when the Southern Pacific Railroad reached Tucson in 1880; the Atlantic and Pacific (later merged with the Santa Fe) offered service to California through Flagstaff in 1883. Copper mining became more profitable than silver mining by the 1890s.

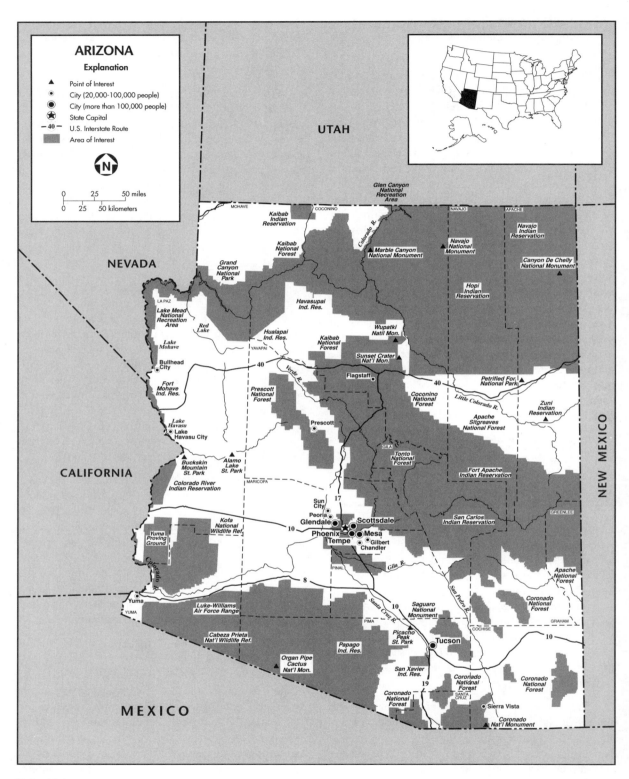

State of Arizona.

During the late nineteenth century political power responded to the needs of the merchants and capitalists with strong ties to California and the East, such as the mining and railroad interests, by calling for statehood for Arizona. The movement for statehood was slow to attract interest on the federal level but in 1912 Arizona finally became the 48th state.

During World War I (1914–1918) the copper industry continued to grow. Problems with the lack of water were partially solved in 1917 when the Salt River Valley Project was opened, providing enough water for agricultural development in central Arizona. The Goodyear Tire and Rubber Company soon established large farms in the Salt River Valley to produce pima cotton. Labor unrest followed much of this expansion. More than one thousand striking miners were deported from the cities of Bisbee and Jerome in 1917. In the 1920s a general depression closed banks, discouraged agriculture, and shut down mines. Local promoters tried to bring relief by encouraging highway building and tourist resorts.

In the 1930s Arizona suffered from the Great Depression (1929–1939), as did the rest of the country. A copper tariff brought some relief to the mining industry and federal relief and recovery funds also helped through the initiation of irrigation and public works projects. During World War II (1939–1945) recovery occurred rapidly as camps were built in the state for military troops, prisoners of war, and displaced Japanese Americans. The meat, cotton, and copper industries thrived, and many processing and assembly plants were built in the state.

Following the war Arizona developed a truly modern economy. Wartime production was replaced by peacetime manufacturing, which soon became the major source of income in the state, especially in the Phoenix and Tucson areas. The state made itself attractive to industry with a favorable tax structure, plenty of electric power, an available labor pool, and low land costs. The advent of air conditioning also made business and living more bearable in Arizona's torrid heat.

Like the rest of the southwest ''sun belt'' states, Arizona grew phenomenally during the 1970s and 1980s, increasing in population by 39 percent between 1973 and 1983. During the same period total employment grew by 49 percent and personal income by 218 percent. The most prosperous areas were the populous Maricopa and Pima counties, with a far lower income level in most other counties. This distribution of wealth in large part overlapped the ethnic composition of the state, with much of Arizona's large Mexican American population among the poorest citizens of the state.

Despite this fact, Arizona politics were traditionally conservative, a political characteristic reinforced by the presence of many retirees. Statewide in 1995, only about eight percent of its workers belonged to labor unions.

The problem of water supply continued to plague Arizona in the late twentieth century. To address this issue, in 1985 the Central Arizona Project (CAP) was built, diverting water from the Colorado River to the rest of the state. This project included a $3 billion dollar network of canals, tunnels, dams, and pumping stations. CAP was controversial; many felt that the water supply exceeded demand and that the water was of poor quality.

Modern Arizona's major products include electronic components, non-electrical machinery, copper, cattle, and cotton. Some of the important electronics and technology-related industries in the state include Motorola, Allied Signal Aerospace, Honeywell, Hughes Missile Systems, and Intel. Next to the technology industry, the state's biggest employer is tourism. Twenty-two national parks and monuments are located within the state, the most popular of which is Grand Canyon National Park. Lake Mead and other lakes created during water reclamation projects attract vacationers, as do Indian reservations and dude ranches. In 1996 the state ranked 36th among the 50 states in per capita personal income.

See also: **Mexican Cession, Sun Belt**

FURTHER READING

Council of State Governments. *The Book of the States, 1994–1995 Edition*, Vol. 30. Lexington, KY: Council of State Governments, 1994.

Fireman, Bert M. *Arizona: Historic Land*. New York: Knopf, 1982.

Peck, Anne Merriman. *The March of Arizona History*. Tucson, AZ: Arizona Silhouettes, 1962.

Powell, Lawrence C. *Arizona: A Bicentennial History*. New York: Norton, 1976.

Sheridan, Thomas E. *Arizona: A History*. Tucson, AZ: University of Arizona Press, 1995.

ARKANSAS

Arkansas has maintained a certain backwoods reputation in spite of its attempts to modernize and industrialize. At first totally dependent on the cotton crop grown on slaveholding plantations, the state was

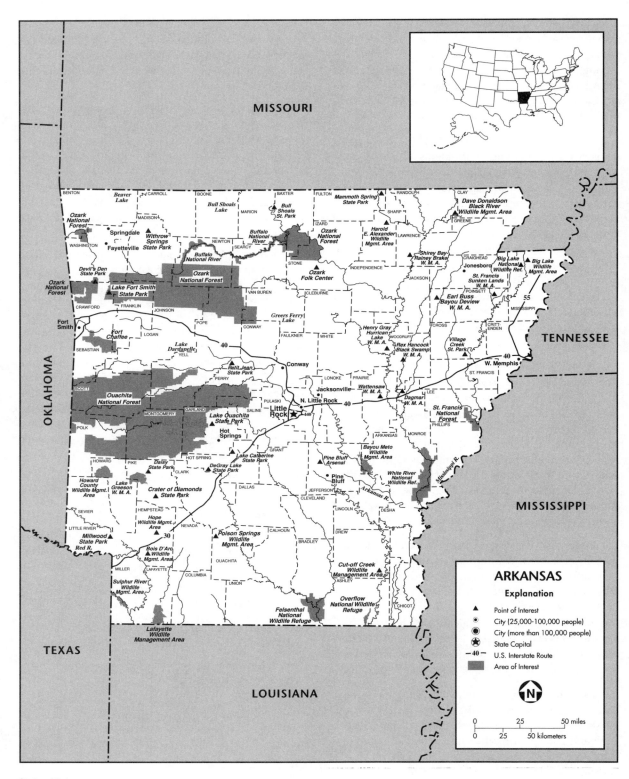

State of Arkansas.

forced to diversify its agriculture after the Civil War. Today agriculture is only a small part of the state's economic output; such sectors as manufacturing, mining, and services are far more important to the state's economy. Arkansas continues to struggle to provide employment for its poorest citizens, many of whom lack education and job skills.

Hernando de Soto (c.1496–1592) led the first Spanish expedition into Arkansas in 1541. In 1673 a French expedition headed by Father Jacques Marquette (1637–1675) and Louis Jolliet (1645–1700) entered the territory, as did Robert Cavelier, Sieur de la Salle (1643–1687) in 1682. La Salle claimed the whole Mississippi valley for France. The first permanent European settlement was at Arkansas Post, at the confluence of the Arkansas and White Rivers. France held onto the territory until 1762 when it was ceded to Spain, although it was later returned to French control. The French sold Arkansas to the United States as part of the Louisiana Purchase in 1803. Initially, part of the Missouri Territory, Arkansas, became an independent territory in 1819 and entered the Union as a slave state in 1836.

Southern and eastern Arkansas fast became cotton-growing areas, with the large plantations run by slave labor which characterized other southern states. The northern and western counties in the Ozark and Ouachita mountains were populated by smaller, poorer white farmers.

DEEP IN THE ARKANSAS CONSCIOUSNESS IS A TRAGIC SENSE THAT ACROSS THREE CENTURIES OF EXISTENCE AS A COLONY, TERRITORY, AND STATE ITS PEOPLE HAVE BEEN MISUNDERSTOOD AND PUT UPON.

Harry S. Ashmore, *Arkansas: A Bicentennial History*, 1978

In the mid-nineteenth century the state was beset by credit problems. The state's two largest banks failed in the 1840s, the government defaulted on bonds issued by one of the banks. A measure of the fatalism and distrust of banks on the part of the rural population is evident in the fact that the state constitution was amended to prohibit all banking in the state. After the American Civil War (1861–1865) banking was restored, but the state again defaulted on its obligations to pay off railroad bonds. Until 1917 Arkansas securities were not honored by New York banks.

Transportation was slow to develop in Arkansas. Before the Civil War, commerce developed along the rivers where freight was shipped by hand-propelled keelboats and later, by steamboat. Thus the major towns in the state, such as Little Rock, Camden, Fort Smith, and Pine Bluff, grew along the waterways. Little Rock boasted over 300 steamboats docking in 1859. In the later nineteenth century towns were founded not only by the rivers but also in the interior. This happened in the 1870s, when the railroads begin to traverse the state, laying 2,200 miles of track by 1890.

In 1861 after a period of hesitation the state voted to secede from the Union. After the South's defeat in 1865 a Reconstruction (1865–1877) government was established that was led by Governor Powell Clayton and other northern Republican politicians. The people in Arkansas hated the corruption and exploitation they suffered under these profiteering outsiders, whom they called carpetbaggers. They ruled the state until 1874 and left such a bad reputation that after Reconstruction, the Democratic Party was in power for many decades to come.

When the Confederacy collapsed property values in the South deflated rapidly. In order to restore agricultural productivity in Arkansas after the war a system of "sharecropping" was developed. According to historian Harry S. Ashmore "It would prove a blight to whites and blacks alike in the years to come, and at its worst it properly could be condemned as the replacement of slavery with a form of peonage. But it provided a means of survival for both races in a desperate time. . . ."

After Reconstruction Arkansas railroads promoted immigration from other states and from abroad, hoping for settlers to establish themselves on the land the railroads had received through government grants. The railroads also controlled large stands of virgin timber. By the 1880s the two largest landowners in Grant County were the St. Louis and Iron Mountain Railroad and the Muskegon Lumber Company of Michigan—the latter evidence that most of the lumbering profits were going out of state.

Arkansas was slow to modernize and did not really emerge from its agricultural past until after the Great Depression (1929–1939). Its farm economy gradually changed from total dependence on cotton to the growing of crops like rice and soybeans and the production of poultry. Cotton, formerly grown only on large plantations, began to appear in the northwest hill country. Tenant farming was the norm for several decades after the Civil War. Coal mining began in the late nineteenth century; the state also mined bauxite and produced oil. Lumbering was important until around 1909, when it decreased until reforestation began in the 1920s. Pulaski County's industrial development was slowed down by the controversy over school integration in Little Rock in 1957, but development continued in the following decades.

In 1966 Winthrop Rockefeller became the first Republican governor since Reconstruction, bringing a new, businesslike image to the state. Though he warred constantly with a Democratic legislature he did encourage investment in the state. In the early 1970s the Arkansas River navigation system opened up a water route between the Mississippi River and Oklahoma, helping to promote industrial expansion in several river ports along the Arkansas River. By this time the tenant farmer economy had been virtually eliminated by farm mechanization and industrialization.

A later governor, William Jefferson Clinton, who became U.S. President in 1992, brought a number of reforms to the state in areas such as health insurance, education funding, and investment tax credits for corporations. Arkansas's constitution, however, requires a two-thirds majority vote of the legislature for new state income taxation and this had hampered the state government's efforts to improve the state's standard of living.

In the mid-1990s Arkansas's important industries were manufacturing, especially lumber and wood products, agriculture, forestry, and tourism. Over 40 percent of the state's annual gross product was now based on commercial, financial, and professional services. Some industries such as chicken processing, enjoyed close relations with the state's regulatory system. The state's per capita income was under $17,000 in 1996, ranking it only 47th in the nation. Although a number of important labor reforms were passed at the beginning of the century Arkansas is not a strong union state, with only eight percent of workers claiming union membership.

See also: **Keelboats, Reconstruction, Sharecropping, Steamboats**

FURTHER READING

Ashmore, Harry S. *Arkansas: A Bicentennial History.* New York: Norton, 1978.

Du Vall, Leland. *Arkansas: Colony and State.* Little Rock, AR: Rose, 1973.

Fletcher, John Gould. *Arkansas.* Fayetteville, AR: University of Arkansas Press, 1989.

Gatewood, Willard B., and Jeannie Whayne, eds. *The Arkansas Delta: Land of Paradox.* Fayetteville, AR: University of Arkansas Press, 1993.

Whayne, Jeannie M. *A New Plantation South: Land, Labor, and Federal Favor in Twentieth-Century Arkansas.* Fayetteville, AR: University of Arkansas Press, 1983.

ARMS RACE

Arms race is a term that refers to the intensely competitive and belligerent manner in which the United States and the Soviet Union developed their nuclear weapons systems between 1945 and 1989. When the U.S. dropped two atomic bombs (A-bombs) on Japan to end World War II (1939–1945), Soviet Premier Joseph Stalin (1879–1953) immediately assembled a team of physicists to begin work on a Russian A-bomb. Tripling the scientific budget, Stalin made clear that the team was to proceed expeditiously without regard to cost. Four years later, on August 29, 1949, the Soviets astounded the world by detonating their first A-bomb far ahead of schedule. The United States responded by beginning work on a bigger, more powerful bomb known as a hydrogen bomb (H-bomb). Detonated on November 1, 1952, America's first H-bomb exploded with a yield of 10.4 megatons, or a thousand times more powerful than the bomb dropped on Hiroshima, Japan. This time it only took the Soviet Union 9 months to catch up, as they tested their first H-bomb on August 12, 1953. Although the Russian bomb was a comparatively small device of 400 kilotons, a sampling of its radioactive cloud produced traces of lithium, an element the United States had not yet technologically harnessed. President Dwight D. Eisenhower (1953–1961) suggested replacing the escalating Superpower competition with nuclear cooperation, but opponents accused him of being soft on Communism.

In 1954 the Soviets tested the world's first H-bomb dropped from a bomber airplane. Three years later the arms race reached outer space, when the Soviets launched Sputnik. A group of satellites designed to measure the temperature and density of the earth's upper atmosphere, Sputnik was powered by intercontinental ballistic missiles (IBMs) that could reach the American soil in a few hours. Now fearful that it was losing the arms race, the U.S. government began investing heavily in national defense and technology. The National Aeronautics and Space Administration (NASA) was established in 1958, the same year that college students were offered millions of dollars in loans and grants to major in science, engineering, and mathematics. The United States also began stockpiling its nuclear arsenal. By 1962 the United States had over 27,000 nuclear weapons, 500 long-range bombers, and

> It shall be the policy of this nation to regard any nuclear missile launched from Cuba against any nation in the western hemisphere as an attack by the Soviet Union on the United States, requiring full retaliatory response. . . . I call upon Chairman [Nikita] Khrushchev to halt and eliminate this clandestine, reckless, and provocative threat to world peace. . . . He has an opportunity now to move the world back from the abyss of destruction.
>
> **President John F. Kennedy, Television Address, October 22, 1962**

2,500 mid-range bombers that were at a constant state of full military readiness. The year 1962 also marked a turning point in the arms race. In October the Soviets began installing IBM launchers in Cuba, only 1,100 miles away from Washington, D.C. Although the United States already had nuclear warheads pointed at the Soviet Union from Western Europe, a U.S. naval blockade of Cuba and the nation's seeming willingness to go to war over the issue forced the Soviet Union to dismantle the missile launchers and remove them from the western hemisphere.

Having teetered on the brink of annihilation during the Cuban Missile Crisis, fewer people in the United States believed that a nuclear war was winnable. Instead, more Americans became convinced that a policy of Mutual Assured Destruction (MAD) was the most effective deterrent against either side launching a first strike. For the next 25 years both nations made efforts at arms control through bilateral accords, but fear, mistrust, and cheating on both sides got in the way. It was not until the Soviet Union itself collapsed in 1989 that the arms race between the two countries officially came to an end. The arms race cost Americans approximately $5.5 trillion dollars, and contributed to the federal government's $4 trillion debt in the 1980s, when spending on nuclear weapons systems skyrocketed. At the same time, the collapse of Communist Bloc countries in Eastern Europe has been largely attributed to the Soviet Union's failed efforts to keep its economy afloat while attempting to accelerate development of its own nuclear forces during this period.

FURTHER READING

Manchester, William. *The Glory and the Dream: A Narrative History of America, 1932–1972*. New York: Bantam Books, 1974.

Johnson, Paul. *A History of the American People*. New York: Harper Collins Publishers, 1997.

Bailyn, Bernard, David Brion Davis, David Herbert Donald, John L. Thomas, Robert H. Wiebe, and Gordon S. Wood. *The Great Republic: A History of the American People*. Lexington, MA: D.C. Heath and Company, 1981.

Isaacs, Jeremy, and Taylor Downing. *Cold War: An Illustrated History, 1945–1991*. New York: Little, Brown, and Company, 1998.

ARSENAL OF DEMOCRACY

Arsenal of Democracy was a phrase used by President Franklin D. Roosevelt (1882–1945) to describe the United States as he tried to arouse popular support for sending military aid to nations fighting against the Axis powers (Germany, Italy, and Japan, among others) during World War II (1939–1942). Re-elected to an unprecedented third term in November of 1940, Roosevelt had made an unqualified campaign pledge to keep the U.S. out of the war. But by the end of the year Great Britain lacked sufficient capital to pay for war materials necessary to defend itself against German air and naval attack. Roosevelt, speaking to the nation during a fireside radio broadcast on December 29, 1940, told the American people how their country's security hinged on the survival of Great Britain. The president explained that the United States must become ''the great arsenal of democracy'' in the struggle against global tyranny and dictatorship. In March 1941 Congress passed the Lend-Lease Act, which gave the chief executive broad authority to provide Britain and its allies with munitions, petroleum, industrial materials, agricultural products, and miscellaneous other goods and services that deemed in the interest of U.S. national defense. Over the next four years the United States provided the Allied cause with 44 million rounds of ammunition, 20 million machine guns and pistols, two million trucks, 107,000 tanks, and 93,000 ships.

See also: **Lend-Lease Act, Franklin D. Roosevelt, World War II**

ARTICLES OF CONFEDERATION

The Articles of Confederation comprised the governing document that was the forerunner to the *Constitution of the United States* (1789). Drafted by the

The July 26, 1946 atomic bomb test at the Bikini Atoll in the South Pacific. The development of nuclear weapons was an important aspect of the Cold War.

Second Continental Congress at York, Pennsylvania, on November 15, 1777, the Articles of Confederation went into effect on March 1, 1781, when the last state (Maryland) ratified the document.

The Articles provided the original thirteen states (Connecticut, Delaware, Georgia, Maryland, Massachusetts, New Hampshire, New Jersey, New York, North Carolina, Pennsylvania, Rhode Island, South Carolina, and Virginia) with more power than the central government. Each state was given sovereignty and one vote in Congress. Congress, unable to levy taxes, had to rely on the states to do so. It was also left to the states to carry out the acts of Congress, whose powers were limited to declaring war and peace, managing foreign relations, commanding the military (an army and a navy), and issuing and borrowing money. But Congress had no authority to regulate commerce and each state was free to set up its own taxes, tariffs, and trade policies.

The inadequacies of the Articles of Confederation became clear in the first few years after they went into effect. In particular, as the post-war economy suffered a depression, the non-payment of farm mortgages and of taxes led to courts seizing the property of their citizens. This enraged the farming population, many of whom were veterans of the American Revolution (1775–1783). Many of these hard pressed farmers decided that the present government was no better than the British had been.

The most significant manifestation of this discontent was Shay's Rebellion (1786–1787). Daniel Shays, who had been a captain in the Continental Army, led a band of several thousand disgruntled farmers throughout western Massachusetts stopping the courts from seizing land for non-payment of taxes. The money to put down the rebellion had to be loaned to the Continental Congress by Boston bankers. This crisis convinced many of the political leaders of the new nation to conclude that the Articles of Confederation had to be revised. Once the process of revision was underway, the entire document was replaced by the Constitution.

James Madison (1751–1736) was among those who realized that the Articles made for a weak national government. He and others such as Alexander Hamilton (1755–1804) led the movement to change that orientation even at the expense of the states. Eventually, Hamilton and Madison won the backing of the other leaders like George Washington (1732–1799), John Jay (1745–1829), and Thomas Jefferson (1743–1836). Thus, political consensus among the political elite of the new nation led to the Philadelphia Constitutional Convention (1787), where the U.S. Constitution was drawn up.

One lasting provision of the Articles of Confederation was the Ordinance of 1787. Adopted early in the era of westward expansion, the ordinance established guidelines for how the nation could enlarge itself. Un-surveyed wilderness would eventually attract settlers. A legislature would be elected as soon as the population included five thousand voting citizens (men only) and the territory would be eligible for statehood once its population had reached sixty thousand.

See also: **Constitution, Continental Congress (Second), Alexander Hamilton, Thomas Jefferson, Shays' Rebellion, George Washington**

ASIAN FINANCIAL CRISIS

The Asian financial crisis in the late 1990s had its roots in private sector borrowing. In years recent to that time, most of the afflicted countries ran budget surpluses or small budget deficits while private sector borrowing increased heavily, especially short-term and from abroad. For example, loans to Thai corporations from international banks doubled from 1988 to 1994. By 1997, Thai foreign debt stood at $89 billion—four-fifths of the amount owed by private corporations. Most disturbingly, one-half of Thailand's debt was short-term, falling due all within one year.

The Asian economies collapsed when their export boom came to a halt and their short-term loans came due. In 1996 Thai exports stagnated because of a decline in demand from First World countries, especially from recession-ridden Japan. Also, opening domestic markets to outside money (under an early round of pressure from the International Monetary Fund) brought a deluge of short-term foreign investment and spurred heavy short-term borrowing from abroad, fueling a building boom. By the mid-1990s, speculative investments in everything from high-rise office towers to golf courses accounted for nearly 40 percent of growth in Thailand.

Thailand's bubble was not the only one to burst, for in 1998, the entire region endured a painful and extended drying-out process. Southeast Asian exports, from autos to computer chips, from steel to textiles, glutted international markets. The crisis was made worse by intensifying competition from Chinese exports. Foreign financial capital fled; domestic spending collapsed; banks failed at an unprecedented rate, and unemployment climbed. Suffering increased as large numbers of people across the region fell into poverty.

Most economists agreed that the Asian capital markets failed in three critical ways. First, there was too much capital. Lured by the prospect of continued double-digit growth, investors continued to put money into uncertain markets in spite of the widespread financial instability. Second, the capital markets and the banking system could not channel these funds into productive uses. Too much money went into real estate, and too little went into productive investments

likely to sustain the export boom. Third, there was no commitment. Too much capital rushed out too quickly. The excessive inflow of capital reversed itself at the first sign of trouble and fled with little regard for the actual strength of a particular economy.

As the 1990s drew to a close, most financial conservatives argued that international markets were stable, if subject to periodic excesses. These excesses could be traced back to a misguided interference in market economy. Conservatives believed the problem varied with the situation: industrial policy, crony capitalism (political connections guiding private sector investment decisions), or fixed exchange rates. But in each case, conservatives contended that the economies of Southeast Asia ran into trouble because non-market forces had a hand in allocating credit and economic resources better left to the financiers. Their solution was to end the non-market allocations of resources. Alan Greenspan (1926—), the chair of the U.S. Federal Reserve, concluded the Asian crisis would root out ''the last vestiges'' of artificially inflated and poorly managed markets and will ultimately be regarded as a milestone in the triumph of market capitalism.

Liberals disagreed. They contended that none of the leading economies of the region relied on government-managed industrial policies to direct economic growth. They maintained that crony capitalism was a constant, not a new element in the Southeast Asian economic mix; that it was just as present in the boom as it was in the crisis; and that there was no evidence that cronyism was responsible for turning investment in its speculative direction. They also contended that there was no reason to believe that greater transparency in financial transactions would have done anything to extinguish the speculative frenzy. For liberals, the root cause for the economic crisis of Southeast Asia, which threatened the onslaught of a worldwide depression, was the abrupt reversal of the excessively fast rise of capital inflows and the falling global demand for the exports from that region.

Liberals insisted that some sort of public policy that regulates capital, whatever its national origins, is most needed in Southeast Asia. They believed that only regulation demanding genuine accountability from both the cronies and the capitalists offered the prospect of genuine reform. They conceded that the crunch of economic losses and slack labor markets made reform more difficult. But they maintained that as long as the myth of infallible markets was punctured, movements organized, and the opposition to free markets was strengthened, the Asian financial crisis offered the opportunity and the potential to regulate capital.

Surprisingly, the U.S. economy survived the crisis and remained relatively unharmed by it, despite significant drops in exports to Japan, South Korea, Thailand, and Indonesia. Economists pointed to three important factors contributing to the strength of the American economy. First, the Federal Reserve remained relatively passive during the crisis, which helped produce large gains in residential construction and commercial real estate. Second, the resiliency of the U.S. equity market boosted foreign demand for U.S. financial assets. Third, the fall of global commodity prices and U.S. import prices helped boost consumer real income in the United States by lowering inflation.

See also: **Capital, Exchange Rates, International Monetary Fund, Recession, Speculation, Unemployment**

FURTHER READING

Bosworth, Barry. ''The Asian Financial Crisis: What Happened and What Can We Learn from It.'' *Brookings Review*, Summer 1998.

Hale, David D. ''Dodging the Bullet—This Time: The Asian Crisis and U.S. Economic Growth During 1998.'' *Brookings Review*, Summer 1998.

Lincoln, Edward J. ''End of the Miracle: Exploring the Asian Financial Crisis.'' *Brookings Review*, Summer 1998.

Parker, Stephen. ''Out of the Ashes? Southeast Asia's Struggle Through Crisis.'' *Brookings Review*, Summer 1998.

Sivy, Michael. ''Will Asia's Financial Crisis Sink the U.S. Stock Market?'' *Money*, July 1998.

ASSEMBLY LINE

Developed in the early twentieth century, assembly line methods greatly increased the efficiency and productivity of manufacturing. The moving assembly line is a highly mechanized process that breaks manufacturing tasks down to the smallest detail. A product moves along a conveyor belt that is lined with workers. Each laborer performs one simple operation in the production process, so that by the time the product reaches the end of the line, it has undergone many different operations and is completely finished.

This method of mass product manufacturing can be done by largely unskilled laborers. It is an early example of the growing interaction between human laborers and machines in the workplace. The increased

production and efficiency not only allowed businesses to put more of their product on the market, but it also lowered the costs of production. This, in turn, decreased the cost of the product to consumers.

The assembly line was first used by the brewing, canning, milling, and meatpacking industries. The most successful early use of the assembly line is in the automobile industry. In 1913, Henry Ford (1863–1947) began to use the assembly line at his Ford Motor Company in Highland Park, Michigan. Ford used the method in the assembly of the flywheel magneto, a part of the automobile's electrical system. It showed such promise that a year later, in 1914, Ford introduced an electrically driven endless-chain conveyor to move entire auto chassis down the line for production. It was a success. Production increased from 475 cars in a nine-hour day to over 1200 cars in an eight-hour day. By using the moving assembly line, Ford Motor Company tripled production and reduced labor time per vehicle by almost 90 percent.

Since Henry Ford's success, the assembly line process has continued to grow. One development is the modular assembly. This process strives to increase efficiency by having parts of a whole product produced on subassembly lines before joining the main line for final production. For example, in the automobile industry the chassis, interior, and body would each be produced on their own subassembly line before joining together at the final stages of production.

The new assembly line methods being developed all aim to refine its original goal—to improve the production process by reducing the amount of time workers and machines spend on specific tasks.

See also: **Automobile Industry, Colt Manufacturing, Ford Motor Company**

ASSET

Assets are items that have value, which can be measured monetarily. There are two types of assets: tangible and intangible. Tangible assets, or touchable assets, are real, physical objects such as equipment, raw materials, furniture, and land. Intangible assets may represent something of economic value that is not cash or a physical item or place. Examples include patents, copyrights, trademarks, franchises, leases, technical expertise, and goodwill. Intangible assets represent long-term rights that have future value to a business. For instance, a copyright gives the owner the right to publish a literary or artistic work for the life of the creator plus 50 years. Goodwill is an intangible

Assembly line workers put the finishing touches on automobiles being manufactured at a Ford Motor Company plant in Detroit, Michigan.

asset because it represents the amount of money over the fair market value paid by the buyer to the seller in expectation of the ability of a business to generate higher than normal earnings.

Assets can also be divided in two ways—current and non-current. A current asset is cash or something that can be converted quickly into cash (usually under one year). Current assets may include marketable securities, notes receivable (formal written promises to receive a fixed amount of money at a future date of less than one year) and accounts receivable (money due from customers for services rendered) less allowance for uncollectables, inventory, supplies and prepaid items.

A non-current asset can be either tangible or intangible. A non-current tangible asset is something of value such as land, equipment, machinery, furnishings, or buildings, which is used to produce a good or service. The benefit of a non-current asset usually extends more than a year and cannot be quickly liquidated. The value of a non-current intangible asset such as a patent is spread out over a number of years. This cost is called amortization. An asset is no longer an asset when it stops being economically viable to its owner.

FURTHER READING

Emery, Douglas R., and John D. Finnerty. *Principles of Finance with Coroprate Applications*. New York: West Publishing Company, 1991.

Hillman, A. Douglas *et.al.. Principles of Accounting.* Sixth Ed. New York: The Dryden Press/Harcourt Brace Jonanovich College Publishers, 1991.

Marshall, David H. *A Survey of Accounting: What the Numbers Mean.* Second edition. Boston: Richard D. Irwin, Inc., 1993.

Montgomery, A. Thompson. *Financial Accounting Information: An Introduction to Its Preparation and Use.* Reading, PA: Addison-Wesley Publishing Company, 1982.

Rachlin, Harvey. *The Money Encyclopedia*. New York: Harper & Row, Publishers, 1984.

ASTOR, JOHN JACOB

The life of John Jacob Astor (1763–1848), a fur trader who became one of the wealthiest individuals in U.S. history, is a classic example of a rags-to-riches story. Born to a poor butcher in Waldorf, Germany, in 1762, he died 85 years later in New York with a fortune estimated in 1998 dollars at $78 billion.

At age seventeen, Astor left Germany for England, where he learned English and worked for his brother, a musical instruments craftsman. After three years, John Astor had saved enough money to immigrate to the United States. In March 1784, after a long trans-Atlantic crossing, he arrived in New York with seven flutes and $25. During the voyage, young Astor befriended a fellow German emigrant who had previously worked as a fur trader in the United States. The information that he gleaned from his new friend convinced him to make his career in the fur trade.

Starting out in the fur business as a clerk, Astor quickly moved on to work for himself. In 1786 he married Sarah Todd and, with the help of her $300 dowry, opened a store on Water Street in New York where he sold musical instruments and bought furs. Both Astors were very involved in the new business and lived very frugally. Astor often left the shop in his wife's care when he traveled to what was then the U.S. frontier in search of furs. In 1789 Astor purchased his first Manhattan property: two lots on the Bowery Lane for $625.

By 1800 Astor was worth $250,000, and he was the leading fur dealer in the United States. Following a trip to London, England, in 1799, where he obtained a license to ship to any East India Company port, Astor became involved in trade with the Orient. He began expanding the scope of his business by shipping furs to China and importing Chinese silks and teas. A part of his profits from these ventures immediately went into real estate purchases in New York.

The success of the Lewis and Clark expedition in 1806 opened up the great fur lands of the U.S. Northwest. Astor was determined to establish an outpost on the Pacific Ocean. In the spring of 1811, the ship *Tonquin* arrived at the mouth of the Columbia River. A fort was built and the settlement was named Astoria. For once however, Astor's timing was poor; during the War of 1812 (1812–1814), his agent was forced by the

John Jacob Astor.

British to sell the outpost to Canada's Northwest Company for $58,000.

Astor emerged from the war wealthier than ever. With a consortium of other businessmen, he bought $2 million in bonds from the hard-pressed U.S. government, paying only 88 cents on the dollar. By the 1820s Astor's Manhattan properties had also become prime real estate; one of his holdings would include the famous intersection of 42nd Street and Broadway. When he saw the fur trade begin to decline, he sold out his commercial interests and turned his strong intellect and acquisitive instincts toward his real estate investments, buying up land in sparsely inhabited northern sections of Manhattan.

Astor did not sell off his land when prices soared; instead, he developed his properties by building commercial buildings and apartments on them. In the hands of his descendants, it was the Astor real estate in Manhattan that was critical to the spectacular growth of the family fortune, which reached $200 million before 1900.

Astor, grieving over the death of his wife, spent his last 14 years administering to his estate and managing his properties. When he died in 1848 he was the richest man in the United States, leaving an estate of some $20 million. His only public bequest was a comparatively insignificant $400,000 to found a public library, the Astor Library, which was later consolidated with other libraries as the New York Public Library in 1895. He left the remainder of his wealth to secure his family's immense fortune for the next century.

FURTHER READING

''The American heritage 40: a ranking of the forty wealthiest Americans of all time.'' *American Heritage*, October 1998.

Baida, Peter. ''Poor Jacob.'' *Forbes*, October 26, 1987.

Cordtz, Dan. ''Land Lords.'' *Financial World*, November 12, 1991.

Haeger, John D. *John Jacob Astor: Business and Finance in the Early Republic*. Detroit: Wayne State University Press, 1991.

Stokesbury, James L. ''John Jacob Astor: A Self-Invented Money-Making Machine.'' *American History*, December 1997.

AT&T CORPORATION

The AT&T story is the saga of a giant ''natural monopoly'' compelled to engage in periodic massive reorganizations in order to comply with the swings in government policy from non-regulation to regulation to de-regulation. The American Telephone and Telegraph Company (AT&T) was established by the American Bell Telephone Company in 1885 as its long-distance subsidiary. At the time the U.S. telephone system consisted primarily of unconnected local networks; Bell wanted to put a long-distance network in place before its patents expired in 1894. Theodore J. Vail, Bell's general manager since 1879, was named president of AT&T, but he left in 1887 over differences with Bell's Boston-based financiers.

As AT&T discovered it would be more expensive to lay underground cables for a long-distance telephone network, the company raised funds by selling bonds to public investors. Throughout its history, AT&T would raise money from the public through the sale of stocks and bonds, and for many years AT&T stock was the most widely held in the world. The need to attract investors disciplined AT&T to be an efficiently run company, even though it faced little competition for much of its history.

In 1892 the company completed a New York-Chicago long-distance line, and the following year Boston-Chicago and New York-Cincinnati lines were introduced. When Bell's patents expired in 1894, the company faced increasing competition from independent telephone companies, especially in the West and Midwest. Bell was forced to expand more rapidly than it had planned, growing from 240,000 telephones in 1892 to 800,000 in 1899.

The rapid expansion in the last decade of the nineteenth century forced Bell to raise more capital. American Bell was based in Massachusetts, which imposed more regulatory interference to Bell's plans than did New York, where AT&T was based. As a result, the company reorganized and made AT&T the parent company of the Bell System, which it remained until the breakup of the company in 1984.

AT&T aggressively met the challenge from independent telephone companies, which were unable to compete with it for very long. Telephone systems sprouted like weeds in rural areas, increasing from 267,000 in 1902 to 1.4 million in 1907, a year in which independent phone companies operated 51 percent of all phones. AT&T's response was to slash phone rates, emphasize customer service, and buy out the failing independent companies. The company often used its political and financial clout to make it hard for the competition to survive.

As AT&T grew in the first decade of the twentieth century, its finances weakened, allowing financier J.P. Morgan to gain control of the company in 1907. Morgan and his investor group brought back Vail as president for the purpose of creating a comprehensive, nationwide communications system. At the time Vail took over AT&T's operations, it had more than three million telephones in service, but was plagued with a bad public image, low morale, poor service, numerous debts, and serious technological problems.

Vail was one of the first U.S. business leaders who knew how to balance the profit motive with the need to please customers. Within a decade he turned AT&T around and made it a model of corporate success. He improved the company's finances by selling bonds at a discount to shareholders. He increased the amount of research and development and laid the foundation for what would become Bell Labs in 1925.

Although Vail and Morgan were monopolists, they were unable to make AT&T the sole supplier of U.S. telecommunications services. After acquiring a controlling interest in Western Union in 1910 and buying out numerous independent telephone companies, Vail decided to sell Western Union in 1913 and allow the independents access to AT&T's long-distance lines. These decisions were made in response to growing anti-monopoly sentiments against AT&T and resulted in a better image for the company.

In 1915 AT&T completed the first coast-to-coast long-distance line from New York to San Francisco. Thus, AT&T dramatized their linkup when Alexander Graham Bell and Thomas Watson re-enacted their famous first-ever telephone conversation between the two cities. AT&T was also able to send the first transatlantic message in 1915. With the telephone becoming a matter of national interest, pressure for federal regulation was growing.

AT&T provided significant support to the military during World War I (1914-1918) when its telephone network was used for military communications. It also set up radio and telephone communication lines in France. In 1918 the U.S. government took control of AT&T, making it a branch of the U.S. Post Office for the duration of the war. Once the government had control of the nation's telephone lines, however, it began to raise rates and introduce service connection charges. Popular support for government ownership quickly faded and in August 1919 the government gave up control of AT&T. Vail retired that same year.

With telephone communications made exempt from the Sherman Antitrust Act by the Graham Act of 1921, AT&T prospered during the 1920s. It expanded into side businesses, including radio and film. By 1932 AT&T had the second largest financial interest in the film industry which it sold in 1936; its national network of 17 radio stations was sold in the mid-1920s. In 1925 Bell Labs became a separate company, jointly funded by AT&T and Western Electric (AT&T's telephone equipment manufacturing subsidiary). Walter S. Gifford, who became president of the company and would serve in that capacity until 1948, exerted a strong influence on the growing telephone industry.

AT&T suffered during the first years of the 1930s when the Great Depression forced many families to give up their phones because they could no longer afford them. Sales at Western Electric fell from 411 million dollars in 1929 to 70 million dollars in 1933, and revenues from subscribers dropped from 1.05 billion dollars to 853 million dollars for the same period.

Americans soon found, however, that the telephone had become a necessity, not just a convenience and by 1937, phone connections exceeded pre-Depression levels. By 1939 AT&T controlled 5 billion dollars in assets—more capital than any other company had controlled up to that time. The immense size of AT&T prompted the newly formed Federal Communications Commission (FCC) to investigate AT&T's competitive practices. There were renewed concerns over AT&T's monopoly of telephone service. While the FCC's final report was ignored as World War II (1939-1945) broke out, the findings would have an impact on the company later on.

AT&T AGGRESSIVELY MET THE CHALLENGE FROM INDEPENDENT TELEPHONE COMPANIES, WHICH WERE UNABLE TO COMPETE WITH IT FOR VERY LONG. . . . THE COMPANY OFTEN USED ITS POLITICAL AND FINANCIAL CLOUT TO MAKE IT HARD FOR THE COMPETITION TO SURVIVE.

During World War II, Western Electric and Bell Labs concentrated on military work. This government subsidized research turned into a cornucopia of invention with vast implications for the company in the post-war world. Research brought about patented ''spin-off'' inventions and technological innovations, like radar and microwave radio relay systems. Other applications based on war-time research included coaxial cable to carry television signals and the invention of the transistor, which eventually replaced the vacuum tube.

In 1949, following up on the FCC's investigation, the U.S. Department of Justice, filed a suit seeking to split Western Electric from AT&T. However, Western Electric's work during the 1950s on Nike anti-aircraft missiles, the air defense radar system, and other defense projects gave AT&T some leverage with the Justice Department. In 1956 AT&T settled the antitrust suit by agreeing to limit its business to providing common carrier service and to confine Western Electric to providing equipment to the Bell System.

During the 1950s AT&T improved telephone communications and lowered long-distance rates by making it possible to dial directly to other cities without using an operator. In 1955 it laid the first transatlantic telephone cable, which it owned jointly with the British Post Office and the Canadian Overseas Telecommunications Corporation. As the nation's economy boomed in the late 1950s, telephone usage reached unprecedented levels. Private lines replaced party lines, and telephone based services became more common. AT&T was in enviable financial shape.

AT&T became involved in satellite communications when it formed Bellcom to supply most of the communications and guidance systems for the U.S. space program from 1958 to 1969. The first AT&T satellite, Telstar, was launched in 1962. That same year Comsat was launched as a half public, half private company to handle U.S. satellite communications; AT&T owned a 27.5 percent interest at a cost of 58 million dollars.

AT&T spent more than 500 million dollars to develop another communications innovation, an electronic switching system, during the 1950s and 1960s. As the United States became more of an information-based society, the speed and automation of the system made possible huge increases in telephone hardware efficiency during the 1970s and 1980s,.

AT&T's dominance in the communications industry again prompted concern about its monopoly status. In 1974 the company faced two antitrust lawsuits. One suit, brought by long-distance provider MCI, claimed AT&T was preventing it from competing in long-distance calling. The second suit, brought by the Department of Justice, called for the dismemberment of AT&T, charging that it had used its dominant position to stifle competition. As the Department of Justice suit dragged on, AT&T earned record profits in 1980 and 1981.

When the Department of Justice suit came to trial in 1981, both sides wanted to settle the case. AT&T wanted to enter the computer and information services business but was prevented from doing so by the 1956 consent decree. In 1982 AT&T was forced to set up a separate, unregulated subsidiary called American Bell to sell equipment and enhanced services. In January 1982 AT&T and the Justice Department reached an agreement to break up the Bell System, leaving AT&T free to compete in non-long-distance businesses such as computers. Final approval to the AT&T breakup was given in August 1983 by Federal Judge Harold Greene and the breakup became effective January 1, 1984.

At the time of the breakup, AT&T was the largest corporation in the world with 155 billion dollars in assets (even more than General Motors). After the breakup its assets were reduced to 34 billion dollars and net income dropped from 7.1 billion dollars to 2.1 billion dollars. Its 22 regional operating companies were divided into seven regional holding companies and AT&T was prohibited from using the Bell name.

The company was then organized in two major groups: AT&T Communications, which handled the company's long-distance services, and AT&T Technologies, which manufactured and marketed telecommunications equipment. The latter began concentrating on switching and transmission systems for telephone companies, an area in which AT&T was losing ground to competitors. American Bell became AT&T Information Systems and began investing heavily in computers.

In 1986 James E. Olson became chairman of AT&T, and Robert E. Allen became president. AT&T's computer operations lost 1.2 billion dollars in 1986, due to the lack of acceptance of AT&T's newly developed Unix operating system. After Unix made some progress in 1986 and 1987, AT&T formed a consortium of Unix manufacturers that included Unisys and Sun Microsystems. AT&T won two major government contracts, including one to build a new government telephone system. When Olson died in 1988, Allen became chairman and CEO until 1997, when he was replaced by C. Michael Armstrong, former chairman of Hughes Electronics.

AT&T reported its first-ever loss in 1988, a staggering 1.7 billion dollars. Then in 1989 it had a 2.7 billion dollars profit, the largest since the breakup. With AT&T losing market share in long-distance services, regulators gave the company permission to match the low prices of its long-distance competitors such as MCI and U.S. Sprint. Long-distance service was the company's primary source of revenue, but it used its financial and information resources to enter other businesses. In 1990 it introduced its Universal Card, which combined the features of credit and calling cards. In 1993 it acquired McCaw Cellular for 11.5 billion dollars, making it the dominant provider of wireless communication services. AT&T's structure as an integrated services, equipment, and computer company was no longer appropriate for the rapidly changing industry;

In September of 1995, AT&T announced that it would be splitting into three companies. One, a "new" AT&T, would concentrate on providing communications services. A second company, Lucent Technologies, would work in the area of research and development of communications technologies. The third new company, NCR, acquired in 1996 for an exchange of stock valued at 7.3 billion dollars, would focus on transaction-intensive computing. NCR and Lucent Technologies became separate, independent companies, leaving telecommunications and long-distance services AT&T's core business.

AT&T itself split into three main divisions addressing specific markets: business markets, consumer markets, and wireless services. For 1997, business markets generated 22.03 billion dollars in revenue, consumer markets brought in 23.52 billion dollars, and wireless services generated 4.43 billion dollars. The company's net income was 4.6 billion dollars, down from the 5.9 billion dollars net income in 1996. Other businesses and divisions that remained attached to AT&T included AT&T Solutions (an integrated partner of the business markets division); the local services division (which led the company's efforts to enter local service markets); and AT&T Universal Card Services (the company's credit card unit). These divisions were supported by Network and Computing Services, which ensured the reliability of AT&T products and services, and AT&T Labs, which created new technologies, products, and services.

Throughout its history, AT&T's financial strength allowed it to grow, improve, and make acquisitions. Its accomplishments included the multi-billion-dollar digitization of its entire network as well as its entrance into the international market in more than 200 countries. AT&T launched WorldNet to meet competition from the Internet arena and it also introduced DIRECTV, a television satellite system. At the end of 1998 AT&T announced it would acquire IBM's Global Network business for 5 billion dollars in cash. The IBM Global Network served large global companies, mid-sized businesses, and individual Internet users in 59 countries. At the beginning of 1999 AT&T acquired cable television giant, TCI (Tele-Communications Inc.), for 46 billion dollars, giving it 12.5 million cable subscribers who were also potential customers for local telephone service, a market AT&T was interested in developing. As the twentieth century drew to a close, AT&T's prospects looked bright. It continued to be on the cutting edge of technology and product development. As a polymorphous entity that acquired and divested itself of huge subsidiaries, it had outlasted the public's limited attention span and survived the threat of government regulation. Maybe it was a monopoly and maybe it wasn't. One thing was sure: the phone bills kept going up.

See also: **Interstate Commerce Commission**

FURTHER READING

"AT&T Corporate History," available from the World Wide Web @ http://www.att.com/factbook/co_history.html

"AT&T Corporate Structure," available from the World Wide Web @ http://www.att.com/factbook/co_overview.html

"AT&T Shareowners Vote in Favor of TCI Merger," available from the World Wide Web @ http://www.att.com/press/

"AT&T to Acquire IBM's Global Data Network," available from the world wide web @ http://www.att.com/globalnetwork/

Coll, Steve. *The Deal of the Century: The Breakup of AT&T.* New York: Simon & Schuster, 1986.

Dellinger, Margaret. *AT&T's Total Quality Approach.* Indianapolis: AT&T Customer Information Center, 1992.

Greenwald, John. "AT&T's Second-Chance CEO: Hughes Electronics Boss C. Michael Armstrong Takes the Top Job a Year after Turning it Down." *Time*, October 27, 1997.

Kahaner, Larry. *On the Line: How MCI Took on AT&T—and Won!* New York: Warner Books, 1987.

"Dialing for Dollars (Purchase of TCI)." *Fortune*, March 1, 1999.

Smith, George D. *The Anatomy of a Business Strategy: Bell, Western Electric, and the Origins of the American Telephone Industry.* Baltimore: Johns Hopkins University Press, 1985.

Stone, Alan. *Wrong Number: The Breakup of AT&T.* New York: Basic Books, 1989.

AUTOMOBILE INDUSTRY

Few industries have had a larger impact on the U.S. economy as the automobile industry. The development of the motor vehicle brought significant changes in twentieth century U.S. culture and society. The auto industry provided progressively easier and faster travelling and shipping and it spurred the development of elaborate highway systems linking cities and states. It also stimulated the creation of suburbs around major cities. The average person could now afford to travel easily from city to city and to commute to work from an outlying area. Owning an automobile became an indicator of financial success; some type of vehicle was within the reach of all but the poorest citizens. Autos were also one of the first products available for purchase on a payment plan, a financial arrangement that became a marketing mainstay of the U.S. economy. In the cities buses allowed large numbers of people to move easily from place to place at a low price. It also became commonplace to bus children to schools. The automobile also sparked the development of other industries such as petroleum and steel, as well as other support businesses such as gas stations, repair shops, and automobile dealerships. Emergency systems also depended on automobiles for getting people to hospitals and for putting out fires.

Not all of these improvements, however, met with success. For example, tractors and harvesters eventually became so sophisticated and expensive (including improvements that made the work less onerous, like air conditioning and tape players) that it ran many farmers out of business. In general, farm implement technology based on internal combustion reduced the overall cost of harvesting crops such as corn or wheat by using machinery that did the work of several farmers in a fraction of the time. This, however, drove farm families off of their small farms and into the city.

The development of the automobile in the late nineteenth century had its foundations in the invention of the steam engine a century earlier. By the middle of the nineteenth century certain types of farm equipment had utilized the steam engine as a source of propulsion. Inventor Sylvester H. Roper developed and tested several steam carriages, which were shown in the East and the Midwest. In addition to the steam engine, other inventors tested electric and gasoline powered engines. Frank and Charles Duryea tested a gasoline-powered wagon in 1893. The development of these vehicles grew out of the carriage industries. Many bicycle companies also became involved in this process of improving automotive technology by providing parts such as ball bearings, wheels, and tires.

By the early part of the twentieth century, the gasoline internal combustion engine became the favorite choice for providing power to carriages, especially after the 1912 Cadillac combined the engine with the ease of an electric self starter. While electric and steam-powered motor vehicles remained popular for a while longer in the East, the Midwest became the home for many of the producers of gasoline powered autos. Ranson E. Olds (1864–1950) of Lansing, Michigan, switched from steam engines to the gasoline engine by the late 1890s, building the first in 1896. Production of his cars was limited until 1899, when Olds Motor Works was formed, a company that eventually became known as General Motors' Oldsmobile Division. Olds expanded production and in 1904 about 5000 were assembled, an impressive feat for the time. Many Olds employees, machinists and parts suppliers eventually left to form their own companies, such as Maxwell, the Reo Company, Hudson, Cadillac, and Dodge.

By 1903 the Ford Motor Company emerged as a rival to Olds by creating a sturdy but low-priced car which became very popular. The Model T, sold from 1908 through 1927, became one of the most famous cars of all time. With Ford's utilization of the moving assembly line, (c 1913–1914,) automobile yearly production soared to numbers in the millions by the 1920s.

World War I (1914–1918) caused a shortage in the materials used to produce automobiles, but production resumed in full as soon as the war ended. However, the bottom fell out of the automobile market as the country entered a depression era (1920–1923). Many independent or smaller automobile companies went out of business. Larger companies struggled as well. Maxwell and Chalmers became part of a new company named Chrysler Corporation in 1925. In 1928 the Dodge Company also became a part of Chrysler. By the late 1920s most smaller companies had either disappeared or had been absorbed into one of the three major companies: Ford, General Motors, and Chrysler, known as The Big Three. General Motors, a leader of the industry during this time, developed some very successful managerial and marketing strategies, such as improvements in offering consumers installment credit, producing models in various price ranges that encouraged car owners to trade in for a more expensive model, and changing car designs yearly. Ford fell behind by holding on to the Model T until it had been long outdated; the company continued to struggle until the 1950s. Chrysler remained a strong second place to General Motors throughout the 1930s.

In the later 1930s automobile workers—both skilled and unskilled workers—turned to unions to protect their jobs. By the early 1940s the industry was fully unionized, but not without several violent confrontations. From 1937 to 1941 a bitter war of sorts was waged between the Ford Motor Company and the United Auto Workers. Several acts of violence occurred, fostering the animosity between auto workers and the large corporations.

During World War II (1939–1945) automotive factories were put to use producing vehicles, airplanes, airplane engines, and other related items for use in the war. At the end of the war consumer production was again booming as buyers replaced their aging autos. The Big Three continued to dominate automobile production throughout the mid-twentieth century. During the 1960s and 1970s laws were passed to improve safety, including the requirement of seat belts and a reduction in allowable automobile emissions. Fuel efficiency soon became an important issue because of the jump in gasoline prices in the mid-1970s. The automotive industry tried to break its habit of producing big cars and turned to the design and manufacture of smaller "economy" cars.

By the late 1950s foreign automobile manufacturers began to export cars such as Volkswagens, Hondas, Toyotas, and Datsuns. These cars became popular because of their efficient fuel consumption, contemporary design, and quality of construction. They soon became a threat to U.S. manufacturers. By 1980 Japan had become the primary producer of automobiles for the entire world. U.S. auto makers rose to the challenge, revamping, restructuring, modernizing, "downsizing" and even giving concessions to the auto companies in the effort to protect jobs. The restructuring of the U.S. auto industry meant more machines and fewer workers, a prescription, which led to layoffs. Moreover, U.S. automobile companies bought into the foreign competition and thus became morally implicated in the erosion of the U.S. "middle class" standard of living.

The final decade of the twentieth century found the major automobile companies striving to please a demanding American consumer while asking for concessions from its unions and trying to compete with the foreign competition. New innovations included: the development and successful marketing of the sport utility vehicle (a lighter version of the truck that could be used both on and off the road), air conditioner coolant that would not pollute, and plans by General Motors to produce an electric car. At the end of the 1990s it remained to be seen whether these innovations would revitalize the U.S. automotive industry.

See also: **Assembly Line, Walter Chrysler, Chrysler Corporation, Henry Ford, Ford Motor Company, General Motors, Model T, Alfred Sloan, United Auto Workers**

FURTHER READING

Compton's Encyclopedia and Fact Index, Ani-Az. Chicago: Compton's Learning Co., 1985, s.v. "Automobile Industry."

Encyclopedia of American Business History and Biography. New York: Bruccoli Clark Layman, 1990, s.v. "The Automotive Industry, 1896–1920."

Encyclopedia of American Business History and Biography. New York: Bruccoli Clark Layman, 1989, s.v. "The Automotive Industry, 1920–1980."

Foner, Eric, and John A. Garraty, eds. *The Reader's Companion to American History*. Boston: Houghton Mifflin Co., 1991, s.v. "Automobiles."

Hillstrom, Kevin, ed. *Encyclopedia of American Industries, Volume 1: Manufacturing Industries*. New York: Gale Research, Inc.

Johnston, James D. *Driving America: Your Car, Your Government, Your Choice*. Washington, D.C.: AEI Press, 1997.

Scharchburg, Richard P. *Carriages Without Horses: J. Frank Duryea and the Birth of the American Automobile Industry*. Warrendale, PA: Society of Automotive Engineers, 1993.

St. Clair, David James. *The Motorization of American Cities*. New York: Praeger, 1986.

Wolf, Winfried. *Car Mania: A Critical History of Transport*. Chicago, IL: Pluto Press, 1996.

AUTOMOBILE, ORIGIN OF

The automobile was a four-wheeled vehicle powered by an internal combustion engine and used primarily for the transportation of people. It was the result of a series of inventions which began in 1769 when French military engineer Nicolas-Joseph Cugnot (1725–1804) built a steam-powered road vehicle. In the early 1800s other inventors also experimented with this idea and the steam-powered vehicle was put into production in Europe and the United States. A breakthrough in developing gas-powered automobiles came in 1860, when an internal combustion engine was patented in France. But a prototype of the twentieth century automobile wasn't "born" until 1885 when Germans Gottlieb Daimler (1834–1900) and Carl Benz (1844–1929) (working independently of each other) developed the forerunners of the gas engines used today. In 1891–1892 a French company Panhard et Levassor designed a front-engine, rear-wheel drive automobile. This concept remained relatively unchanged for nearly one hundred years. In 1896 the Duryea Motor Wagon Company turned out the United States' first production motor vehicle. The gas-powered cars were available for purchase that same year. Until 1900 Europeans led the world in the development and production of automobiles. But the first decades of the 1900s saw the U.S. auto industry take the lead, establishing Detroit, Michigan, as Motor City, U.S.A.

In 1908 Ford Motor Company (established 1903) produced the first dependable, easily maintained, and widely affordable automobile—the Model T. American consumers bought 17,000 Model Ts the year they were introduced at the price of $850. The popularity of the "Tin Lizzie" (it was also nicknamed the "Flivver") was met by stepped-up production: In 1917 Ford produced 700,000 Model Ts. The innovation of the moving assembly line (1914) steadily improved production time. This resulted in lowering of manufacturing costs and the decrease of the price of the car to the consumer (in 1924 the Model T sold for just $295). Model T now became accessible to working class families. In the 1920s automobile registration in the U.S. climbed from eight million to 23 million.

The impact of the automobile on American life was profound and lasting. Public safety officials stepped up to the ever-increasing demands of traffic control. Roads had to be improved and extended (in 1921 Congress passed the Federal Highway Act which provided federal aid for state roads; in 1923 a national highway system was conceived of). The oil industry worked to keep pace with soaring demand for petroleum and motor oils. Suburbs grew rapidly and businesses rushed to take advantage of the car craze. America's romance with the automobile launched related industries including roadside eateries, drive-in movies, motels, and billboard advertising along highways. The car transformed America into a mobile society. By the end of the twentieth century most Americans viewed the automobile as a necessity of life.

See also: **Automobile Industry, Henry Ford, Ford Motor Company, Model T**

AZTEC

The Aztec were a nomadic Native American people who settled in central Mexico during the fourteenth century. In 1325, they founded the city of Tenochtitlan (the site of present-day Mexico City). The Aztec were a poor tribe but during the 1400s they conquered neighboring peoples to build a powerful empire that dominated the region for two centuries.

Although they were hunters (primarily deer, rabbit, and fowl), their economy was based on agriculture. Among other crops, they cultivated corn, beans, squash, sweet potatoes, papayas, cotton, rubber, and cacao (the chocolate bean). They cleared forests by a slash-and-burn method and dug trenches to create irrigation systems. They also practiced step-farming in the highlands by cutting terraces into mountainsides to create arable (farmable) tracts of land.

The marketplace was central to Aztec life, and trade flourished. But since the Aztec had no form of money, merchants bartered rather than sold their goods.

They worshiped many gods, including the god of the Sun and the god of the Moon, for whom they built terraced pyramids at Teotihuacan, in central Mexico. The tallest pyramid, built to honor the Sun, reaches a height of 216 feet (66 meters). Their chief god was Quetzalcoatl, who represented the forces of good and light.

According to legend Quetzalcoatl would return one day from over the sea. This belief at first worked in the favor of Spanish conquistador Hernan Cortes (1485–1547) who arrived in central Mexico in November 1519. Aztec emperor Montezuma (1466–1520) initially mistook Cortes and his group for heavenly hosts and presented the Spaniards with gifts.

The impressive city of Tenochtitlan bedazzled the European explorers. Besides being a marvel of engineering (with a system of causeways, canals, bridges, and aqueducts), it was home to an estimated quarter of a million people (more densely populated than any Spanish city at that time). It was also a thriving trade and cultural center. The Spanish explorers called it a Venice of the New World.

When the Aztec revolted in 1520, Cortes put down the insurrection and went on to conquer them, claiming Mexico for the Spanish in August 1521. Mexico City became the seat of the viceroyalty (a province governed by a representative of the king or queen) of New Spain. This designation remained throughout the colonial period.

See also: **Inca, Mesoamerica, Native Americans (Treatment of), New Spain (Viceroyalty of)**

BABY BOOM

Baby Boom is a term that describes the explosion of childbirths in the United States between 1946 and 1964. The annual birthrate jumped 13 percent in 1946 to 3.4 million, and then climbed fairly steadily to a peak of 4.3 million in 1957. Thereafter the national birth rate leveled to approximately 4 million per year through 1964. In 1965 America experienced its first year of a "baby bust," as births fell below 3.8 million. The national birth rate continued to decline until 1977 when Baby Boomers themselves started having children. Seventy-seven million children were born during the Baby Boom, as compared with 63 million during the previous generation (1909–1945) and 52 million in the subsequent generation (1965–1978). Several reasons have been proposed to explain the Baby Boom. First, millions of American servicemen returned home after World War II (1939–1945) ready to embrace life, settle down, and start families. Second, the U.S. to which these men came home was the most prosperous and powerful nation in the world, providing its citizens with an unprecedented degree of economic and physical security. Third, society traditionally encouraged American women to be homemakers. Fourth, both American men and women felt a sense of urgency in making the most of life, as they faced the uncertainties of the atomic age and recalled the painful memories of the Great Depression and World War II.

See also: **Post-War Boom, Suburbs (Rise of)**

BACK COUNTRY

Back country is a geographic term that dates back to the American colonial period. Sometimes also referred to as upcountry, the region called back country designated the lands that lie west of the Atlantic coastal areas where the Europeans first settled.

In the late 1600s and into the first half of the 1700s, immigrants landing at eastern seaboards did not

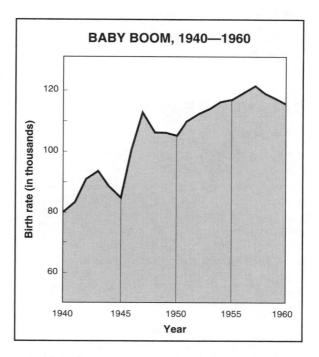

The annual number of births per thousand women 15–44 years old, 1940–1960. Following WWII there was a "Baby Boom," so called because of the record increase of birth rates.

always integrate into the coastal and near-inland settlements of New England, the Mid-Atlantic, and the South. Many of these newly landed immigrants were Scotch-Irish and German who chose to make their homes in the interior—in the woods of New England, the foothills of the Appalachian Mountains, and the Piedmont of the Carolinas.

The back country regions soon flooded with newcomers, and the colonies were faced with the problem of how to extend their governments, schools, and churches to the new settlements. Because back country settlers were highly independent people, however, they sometimes rejected outside authority. Conflicts arose between the established societies to the east and the new settlements of the frontier. (Such differences were felt even during the American Revolution [1775–1783]; back country settlers tended to remain loyal to Great Britian, because they felt they had little in common with the eastern establishment.)

Clashes between the old guard and the new arrivers in the Carolinas resulted in the Regulator movement (1765–1771), in which extremists became determined to bring law and order to the back country by their own hand. A direct conflict never ensued because the colonial governors pacified the lawless frontier by giving the back country settlers legislative representation and establishing schools in the interior.

See also: **North Carolina, South Carolina, Tidewater**

BALANCE OF PAYMENTS

The balance of payments is similar to the balance sheets bookkeepers maintain to keep track of their companies' credits and debits. But it does not focus on the cash flow of a single company. The balance of payments records the credits and debits of the entire U.S. economy with its foreign trading partners. If U.S. consumers, businesses, or the government spend more in foreign economies than those economies spend in the United States, the balance of payments is "in deficit." If the reverse is true, the U.S. balance of payments is "in surplus."

The balance of payments is not the same as the balance of trade. The balance of trade is only one of two major components in the balance of payments. The first component is the "current account." The "current account" is roughly the same as the balance of trade, and includes all short-term imports and exports of goods and services. The second component is the "capital account", which includes long-term investments and loans between the United States and foreign economies.

Before 1933 the United States and most of the industrialized world was on the gold standard. Applying this standard meant that all international currencies were valued in terms of how much gold they represented. Because of the Great Depression, Great Britain abandoned the gold standard in the early 1930s, but it was not until the Bretton Woods Agreement of 1944 that a new system based on the U.S. dollar instead of gold was implemented. Under this system a country could always "devalue" its currency relative to other countries' currencies if its balance-of-payments deficit became dangerously large. This would wipe out much of the deficit. The United States was the only country

that could not devalue its currency to lower its balance-of-payments deficit. That restriction was applied because the Bretton Woods system valued all currencies against the U.S. dollar. President Richard Nixon (1913–94) abandoned the Bretton Woods Agreement in 1973, which enabled the United States to devalue the dollar when necessary. Since then all world currencies including the dollar may be exchanged freely on the world market at whatever rate the market will bear. The United States continues to accumulate balance-of-payment deficits, when the value of the dollar is strong compared to other currencies. Foreign goods and services are inexpensive relative to U.S. goods and services. The U.S. government offsets these deficits by selling U.S. government bonds to foreign investors attracted to the stable dollar.

See also: **Bretton Woods Agreement, Gold Standard, Richard Nixon**

BALANCE OF TRADE

As individuals, private businesses, and government agencies buy and sell goods and services around the world, they create a balance of trade. International trade is composed of exports and imports. (Exports are the goods and services produced within a country and sold to foreign countries. Imports are the goods and services that a country buys from other countries.) A country's balance of trade represents the difference between the value of its exports and imports. If a country has a trade surplus, or a favorable balance, then it is exporting more goods than it is importing. On the other hand, a nation may experience a trade deficit or unfavorable balance when its imports are greater than its exports. Because the balance of trade is a result of foreign trade, a surplus is called the foreign trade surplus and a deficit is called the foreign trade deficit. The balance of trade is considered a key component of a country's economic health. Soaring trade deficits slow economic growth because as more goods are imported, demand for domestic products falls.

During the 1980s and 1990s the balance of trade became a major issue in the United States. In 1975 the United States had a foreign trade surplus of $10.4 billion, but afterwards it experienced foreign trade deficits. Although deficits are rarely good, it was not until 1983 that they became a serious problem. In that year, the U.S. foreign trade deficit started rising, going from $38 billion in 1982 to $170 billion in 1987. While the deficit decreased over the next five years it remained more than $100 billion each year. The U.S. foreign-trade deficit rose in 1993 to $115.8 billion. The

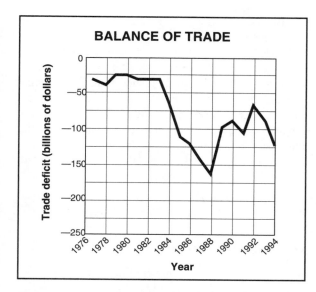

BALANCE OF TRADE

A trade deficit exists when a country imports more goods than it exports. There was a persistent trade deficit in the U.S. between 1976 and 1994.

top two trading partners for the United States were Canada and Japan; they, accounted for $70 billion of the trading deficit that year. The United States had a $10.7 billion trading deficit with Canada and a $59.3 billion trading deficit with Japan. In 1993 the United States had trading surpluses with the United Kingdom and the Netherlands—$4.7 billion and $7.4 billion, respectively.

BALANCED BUDGET AMENDMENT

The creation of the U.S. federal government's annual budget is a lengthy, complex process. The process became even more complicated in the 1990s as some congressional members called upon Congress to enact a Balanced Budget Amendment to halt a growing federal deficit. The movement for a Balanced Budget Amendment, a Republican-backed initiative, gained steam after the 1994 elections that ushered in a Republican-controlled Congress. The Republican Party promoted an anti-tax and anti-spending platform and saw the amendment as a curb to federal spending. For four years in a row, however, the amendment failed to gain the necessary votes in Congress. (Even if the measure had won congressional approval it would have needed to be ratified by the states before it could become a Constitutional amendment.)

The proposed amendment called for the federal budget to be balanced by 2002 and would have required the president and Congress to weigh proposed total spending against proposed total potential income. Opponents to the amendment believed that it would have restricted Congress from being able to deal with unforeseen situations such as a military crisis. However the amendment had a provision that a three-fifths majority of Congress could waive the requirement of a balanced budget in any given year. Critics also felt that balancing the budget should be accomplished through presidential and congressional restraint in the budget-planning stage.

The call for a balanced budget was not a new theme. Congress had passed many measures over the years to try to mandate a balanced budget with varying or little success. In 1986 the U.S. Supreme Court struck down a provision of the Gramm-Rudman-Hollings Act, which was passed by Congress in 1985. The act required the federal budget to be balanced within five years and failing that, there would be automatic across-the-board spending cuts. The Court ruled that this budget-slashing measure was in violation of the Constitution's doctrine of separation of powers.

See also: **Budget Deficit**

BALDRIDGE, MALCOLM HOWARD

Malcolm Baldridge (1922–1987) served as Secretary of Commerce for President Ronald Reagan (1981–1989). Once a successful manufacturing executive, he became a highly respected trade negotiator for the United States known for his straightforward, plain-spoken style. As Commerce Secretary he backed protectionist policies against countries that maintained restrictive import regulations against the United States. He also promoted free trade policies and business deregulation.

Baldridge was born October 4, 1922, in Omaha, Nebraska. He graduated from Yale University in 1944 with a Bachelor of Arts in English. Baldridge enlisted in the U.S. Army the year before his graduation from college and fought in World War II. Serving with the 27th Infantry Division, he participated in combat against the Japanese at Okinawa.

After Baldridge was released from the Army in 1946, he took a job as an iron worker for the Eastern Malleable Iron Company in Connecticut, where by 1960 he had worked his way up to company president. In 1962 the Scovill Manufacturing Company (later Scovill Inc.) hired him as an executive vice-president. He was later promoted president and Chief Executive Officer (CEO), and then finally to Chairman of the

Board of Directors. Under Baldridge's leadership, the company sold its brass milling operations and began to focus solely on manufacturing and distribution of household products such as Hamilton Beach appliances, Nutone remodeling products, Shrader hardware, and Dritz sewing notions. The company prospered under Baldridge's management, earning annual revenues of around $950 million.

The U.S. Senate confirmed Baldridge as Secretary of Commerce on January 22, 1981. Since he had served in Connecticut as campaign chairman for then–Vice President George Bush (1981–1989) during the 1980 presidential primary election, Baldridge's appointment was viewed as a special gesture to the Vice President. Within a year he markedly increased the influence of the Department of Commerce and was eventually considered the most influential Commerce Secretary since former president Herbert Hoover (1929–1933) held the position.

Baldridge was a respected trade negotiator and participated in talks around the world. He was admired in the White House for treating all staff members with equal consideration. A straightforward communicator, he expressed himself simply and succinctly. Within his own department he discouraged the use of complicated bureaucratic language and issued a widely reprinted memo instructing Department of Commerce staff to use active verbs and avoid unnecessary adjectives and adverbs in letters and memos. During his term in office he slashed 30 percent from the department's budget and, while boosting productivity, also cut personnel costs by 25 percent.

With the U.S. trade deficit approaching $170 billion in the 1980s Baldridge advocated an aggressive approach to deal with foreign trading partners who maintained unfair import policies. Although he advocated free trade and deregulation he did not hesitate to press for "fair trade" or protectionist policies when he felt such action was warranted. For example, Baldridge was at the forefront of the Reagan Administration's move to restrict Japanese imports, including automobiles. His position differed from that of other Reagan advisors, who initially were concerned that protectionist policies would raise prices for American consumers and have a negative impact on foreign relations. In efforts to increase trade Baldridge was a key figure in talks with China and the Soviet Union. He paved the way for U.S. companies in the global marketplace by opening up technology transfers with China, India, and what was then the Soviet Union. At home he was considered an influential negotiator between the administration and Congress.

Baldridge's Cabinet service was tragically cut short when he was killed in a rodeo accident on July 25, 1987. He was an experienced amateur rodeo rider and was practicing calf roping before a competition when his horse reared, fell, and crushed him. He suffered internal injuries to the heart and pancreas and died within a few hours of the accident. His death was a personal and professional loss to the entire Reagan administration. A month after Secretary Baldridge's death, the Malcolm Baldridge National Quality Award was established in his honor.

See also: **Free Enterprise, Free Trade, Protectionism, Protective Tariff, Ronald Reagan**

FURTHER READING

Abrahamson, Peggy. "Malcolm Baldridge Award Encourages U.S. Industry's Quest for Quality." *Business America*, May 22, 1989.

Carey, John, Robert Neff, and Lois Therrien. "The Prize and the Passion." *Business Week*, October 25, 1991.

Farnsworth, Clyde H. "Administration Mourns Baldridge, Skilled master of Its Trade Policy." *New York Times*, July 27, 1987.

Farnsworth, Clyde H. "The Quiet Cowboy." *New York Times*, July 26, 1987.

Johnston, David. "Malcolm Baldridge, Cabinet Member: Businessman with a Love for Rodeo." *New York Times*, July 26, 1987.

BALTIMORE AND OHIO RAILROAD

In February 1827 the Baltimore and Ohio was charted as the first railroad company in the United States of America by a group of Baltimore businessmen. Its establishment was a response to an emerging commercial rivalry and to a complex series of social, economic, and technological changes that were transforming the country in the first half of the nineteenth century. The settling of the agriculturally rich Ohio Valley and the rapid expansion of the population on the eastern seaboard, which generated chronic food shortages, demanded that a swift means of transportation be found to ship produce from the Midwest to the coast. The construction of the Erie Canal in 1825 gave New York City a gateway to the interior and a decided edge on Baltimore in their struggle for U.S. economic supremacy. In the 1820s Baltimore was a thriving commercial center of about 80,00 people with an aspiration to become the nation's leading emporium. Until then it had depended upon the National Road to gain access to markets, but turnpikes were slow and expensive compared to water routes.

In 1826 two brothers, Evan and Philip Thomas, who were important members of Baltimore society, began to solicit support for the establishment of a railroad. In 1827 they were able to convince a number of leading businessmen to "construct a railway between the city of Baltimore and some suitable city upon the Ohio River." The Maryland legislature approved the incorporation of this enterprise on February 21, 1827. The $3 million needed to support the venture was to be raised by the sale of 15,000 shares of stock at $100.00 a share. Ten thousand would be offered by the state of Maryland and 5,000 by the city of Baltimore. The entire subscription was sold out in 12 days, and almost every family in Maryland brought shares in the company. Philip Thomas was its first president.

It was originally envisioned that either horses or the wind would provide the power for the train. On January 7, 1830, when the Baltimore and Ohio made first run, teams of horses pulled the cars, which ran on a narrow gauge track, the width of an English carriage. Evan Thomas, however, had been inspired to build a railway by the success of the Stockton and Darlington, an English company that in 1825 became the first to use a steam-powered locomotive to carry freight. Its performance impressed him on a trip abroad. So the Baltimore and Ohio began to experiment with steam engines almost from its inception. Peter Cooper built the first American-built steam locomotive, the Tom Thumb, in the shops of the B & O, and in August 1830 he demonstrated his invention on the company's tracks. Steam power soon became the standard means of propulsion, and as steam engines improved rapidly in the 1840s and 1850s, the cost of transporting freight dropped significantly.

In spite of its willingness to innovate, the Baltimore and Ohio had a rather slow start because of political problems and difficulties in laying track. It planned a 380-mile route that would cross the Allegheny Mountains and connect Baltimore with Wheeling, West Virginia, a city on the Ohio River. Although experts were hired to help with this difficult engineering project, there were many delays. By August of 1830 the line stretched only 13 miles to Elliot Mills, and Washington D. C. was not reached until 1835. The line did not arrive at Wheeling until 1852.

The rail line grew rapidly in the second half of the nineteenth century. Its extension to Parkersburg, West Virginia in 1857 allowed the railway to connect with local lines and gain access to Columbus, Cincinnati, and St. Louis. Coal from Ohio and West Virginia now became an important cargo, the hauling of which was responsible for a third of the company's revenue by 1860. The Baltimore and Ohio served the Union well during the Civil War (1861–65), and although it sustained damage, it recovered rapidly and continued to expand after the war. The 521 miles of track that existed in 1865 grew to 1,700 in 1885. The B & O was hurt in the panic of 1893 and went bankrupt in 1896. But, the Pennsylvania Railroad bought the majority of its stock and it was able to reorganize successfully. It regained its independence in 1906, when the Pennsylvania Railroad, fearing anti-trust action on the part of the government, sold its controlling interest. Daniel Willard, who was president of the company from 1910 to 1941, improved equipment and service, and by 1935 the B & O possessed about 6,350 miles of track, its high-water mark.

From the 1930s to the 1970s, however, the Baltimore and Ohio, like many railroads, had a difficult time. The Depression, the popularity of the automobile, and the rise of the trucking industry, all contributed to its demise. Except for a brief period of prosperity during World War II (1939–45), track mileage and profits declined, while inflation and the demands of strong unions increased labor costs. Between 1932 and 1952 no dividends were paid on its common stock. In the mid-1950s the Baltimore and Ohio petitioned the public service commissions of New York and Maryland to suspend its service between Baltimore and New York because of the "enormous deficits" that this route was generating.

As the Baltimore and Ohio continued to lose money, it began to seek a financially sound company with which to merge. After previously having received permission from the Interstate Commerce Commission, another railroad with roots deep in American history, the Chesapeake and Ohio formally took control of the company on February 4, 1963. The combined railroads became the Chessie System in 1972.

In spite of the setbacks that afflicted the industry in the first half of this century, American railroads were far from dead. Since a single railway line can be as productive as a ten-lane expressway, trains remain an efficient way to carry large quantities of bulk products, like ore, coal or grain. The use of large containers to hold finished products and flatcars that can transport piggyback truck trailers helped the railroads compete with other means of transport. The financial atmosphere improved, and the Chessie System attained revenues of $1.5 billion by 1978. In order to gain access to the booming southeastern United States, it merged in

1982 with Seaboard Coastline Industries, Inc., which was then the eighth largest railroad in the United States, and a component of which, the Petersburg Railroad, was charted in 1830. The Chessie System and Seaboard formed the CSX Corporation, a holding company that controlled one of the largest rail systems in the country. Coincidentally, like the B & O in 1860, the CSX Corporation earned a third of its revenue in 1990 by hauling coal.

See also: **Coal Industry, Erie Canal, Interstate Commerce, Maryland, National Road, Railroad Industry**

FURTHER READING

Douglas, George H. *All Aboard!: The Railroad in American Life*. Seattle: Superior, 1958.

Fishlow, Albert. *American Railroads and the Transformation of the Ante-Bellum Economy*. Cambridge, Mass.: Harvard University Press, 1965.

Fogel, Robert W. *Railroads and American Economic Growth: Essays in Econometric History*. Baltimore: The Johns Hopkins University Press, 1964.

Hungerford, Edward. *The Story of the Baltimore and Ohio Railroad*. New York: G.P. Putnam's Sons, 1928.

Stover, John F. *American Railroads*. Chicago: University of Chicago Press, 1961.

BANK OF THE UNITED STATES (FIRST NATIONAL BANK)

The nation's founding fathers differed on whether a national bank should be created when they drafted the U.S. Constitution (1788) and established the federal government. This split led to the formation of the two major political parties. The first Secretary of the Treasury Alexander Hamilton (1755–1804) led the Federalist Party. The Federalists believed that the government could use all powers except those expressly denied by the Constitution. Hamilton promoted the establishment of a national bank, arguing it would strengthen the government and promote economic growth. Secretary of State Thomas Jefferson (1743–1826) headed the Democratic-Republicans. They argued that powers not specifically mentioned in the Constitution could not be exercised. Jefferson regarded the national bank as a potential monopoly that could infringe upon civil liberties in the United States.

In 1791 the Federalists won the argument and the First Bank of the United States was established. Eighty percent of its stock was privately held. The other 20 percent was owned by the U.S. government. Its capital was $10 million (two million dollars of which was supplied by the U.S. government). The bank had eight branches in U.S. cities. The bank could issue notes, hold deposits, and make loans. It also paid the salaries of public officials and monitored the states' issuance of bank notes (promissory notes issued by a bank which had to be paid—converted to coin—by the bank on demand of the holder). The government's involvement in the bank was short-lived: In 1802 it sold its interest to private investors at a profit. When the charter for the bank came up for renewal it was allowed to expire and the bank ceased to exist in 1811.

See also: **Bank of the United States (Second National Bank), Thomas Jefferson**

BANK OF THE UNITED STATES (SECOND NATIONAL BANK)

After the First National Bank ceased to exist in 1811 U.S. currency and state bank notes became unstable. They could not be converted to gold or silver coins. Bank notes had become a common means of payment by that time. Inflation increased when the holders of these notes could not exchange them at face value. The economic situation was worsened by the War of 1812 (1812–14), which the United States fought against Britain because of its interference in U.S. shipping. In 1816 the federal government created the Second Bank of the United States, which had an initial capitalization of 35 million. Since the U.S. government owned 20 percent of the institution (just as it did with the First Bank), it deposited $7 million in start-up capital. With branches across the country the bank's powers were similar to those of the First Bank: it could issue notes, hold deposits, make loans, pay the salaries of public officials, and monitor the states' issuance of bank notes (to ensure they could be converted to coin). U.S. banker Langdon Cheves (1776–1857) became president of the Second Bank of the United States in 1819. He rescued it from the brink of disaster by building up its resources, reorganizing it, and reducing the number of speculative loans it made. Cheves was followed as the bank's president in 1823 by U.S. financier Nicholas Biddle (1786–1844). Under Biddle the bank further restricted credit, sold branch drafts enabling business people to send money from state to state, managed foreign payments, and prevented state banks from issuing notes they could not pay. Biddle's advocates in Congress moved for renewal of the bank's charter in 1832. Since President Andrew Jackson (1767–1845) viewed the bank with suspicion, he vetoed the bill. The U.S. government removed its deposits from the bank and its federal charter was allowed to expire in 1836. The state of Pennsylvania granted the institution a charter that year, but the bank failed in 1841.

See also: **Bank of the United States (First National Bank), Bank War, Nicholas Biddle, Andrew Jackson**

BANK WAR

President Andrew Jackson's (1829–37) struggle against the Second Bank of the United States, known as the "Bank War," was the major national financial issue during his tenure in office. The Second Bank's policies were blamed for starting the economic crisis known as the Panic of 1819, while its dissolution by Jackson was blamed for the Panic of 1837. At odds with the Bank's president, Nicholas Biddle (1786–1844), Jackson decided to remove federal funds from the Second Bank of the United States and put them on deposit with selected state banks. This action led to accusations that Jackson was using his powers arbitrarily and acting contrary to the Constitution. On March 28, 1834, the U.S. Senate formally voted to censure Jackson for his actions.

The Second Bank of the United States was chartered by the U.S. government in 1816, partly to help manage the federal debt left by the War of 1812 (1812–14), and partly to curb inflation brought on by unregulated state banks. In the early nineteenth century there was no standardized national currency. Instead, because most banks were privately owned and operated for commercial purposes, they issued their own paper money. (In reality, this paper money was imprinted with a promise to pay in gold or silver on demand—an action known in financial markets as specie.) These banks were necessary in order to supply the credit needed to buy land, finance businesses, and create economic growth. However, they tended to lend more paper "money" than they had the specie to cover. Thus, if several large creditors demanded payment in cash at the same time, the result was called a "run" and usually led to the bank's failure. If several banks failed at the same time the result was a financial panic, such as the panics of 1819 and 1837. Both of these events led to high rates of inflation and national depressions.

Because of the large cash resources available through federal deposits, the Second Bank of the

United States could discipline state banks and force them to limit the credit they supplied to borrowers to the amount of specie they kept in their vaults. The Second Bank also competed with state banks by agreeing to pay in specie any of its drafts, no matter where the draft was originally issued. For that reason it was unpopular with shareholders in the state banks, who felt the national bank limited their ability to profit from their investments. The Bank's competition with state–chartered institutions also led to a celebrated Supreme Court case: *McCullough v. Maryland* (1819), in which Chief Justice John Marshall (1755-1835) established that Congress had the right to charter a national bank and that states had no power to tax federal institutions.

The Second Bank of the United States faced many of the problems that plagued state institutions. Between 1816 and 1818, for instance, dishonest managers of the Baltimore, Maryland, branch of the Second Bank swindled investors out of more than $1 million before they were caught. The following year this scandal forced the resignation of Bank President William Jones. The reputation of the Second Bank was restored by Jones' successor, a South Carolina lawyer named Langdon Cheves. Cheves brought discipline to the Bank's dealings, sharply reducing the number of loans issued and aggressively pursuing individuals and banks that defaulted on loans. Cheves' policies helped place the Bank on a sound financial footing, however, they also caused a number of bank failures that led directly to the Panic of 1819.

> **(THE SECOND BANK OF THE UNITED STATES IS) . . .UNAUTHORIZED BY THE CONSTITUTION, SUBVERSIVE OF THE RIGHTS OF THE STATES, AND DANGEROUS TO THE LIBERTIES OF THE PEOPLE.**
>
> President Andrew Jackson, Veto message to Congress 1832

When Jackson was elected president in 1828 the Second Bank, under Nicholas Biddle, was exercising considerable influence over the nation's financial affairs. By 1828 the Bank had built up a surplus of $1.5 million and it was paying its stockholders an annual dividend of seven percent. It also helped stabilize a national currency and provided credit and cash in areas of the West and South where financial resources were scarce. By doing so it made development on the American frontier easier and faster. However, to President Jackson the Bank was a tool of Eastern economic privilege, which enabled speculators, monopolists, and moneyed interests to take advantage of farmers and mechanics. Jackson also believed, despite Chief Justice Marshall's ruling in *McCullough v. Maryland*, that

Congress had no right under the Constitution to charter a bank.

In 1832—a presidential election year—Henry Clay and Daniel Webster, two of Jackson's most vocal opponents in Congress, decided to challenge the president. Even though the Bank's charter was not due to expire for four years, they promoted a bill that renewed the charter of the Second Bank of the United States. Clay and Webster believed that, whether Jackson signed the bill into law, the president would alienate a significant number of voters and risk his chance of a second term. Jackson vetoed the bill on July 10, 1832, in one of the most strongly worded messages ever sent to Congress. Although Clay tried to make the veto an issue in his campaign for the presidency later that year, Jackson easily won reelection, defeating Clay by a margin of 219 electoral votes to 49.

Jackson believed his reelection represented a mandate from the American people to destroy the Second Bank of the United States. In 1833 he instructed his Secretary of the Treasury, Louis McLane, to prepare for the expiration of the Bank's charter by removing the government's deposits to certain state institutions, known as "pet banks." McLane refused and was moved to the position of Secretary of State. His successor, William Duane, also refused and resigned. Jackson did not find a pliable Secretary of the Treasury until former Attorney General Roger B. Taney (1777–1864) took the position.

The removal of the government's deposits brought Jackson into conflict with Nicholas Biddle, who was as strong–willed as the president. Biddle felt that Jackson's actions exceeded his constitutional authority and tried to force the president to renew the Second Bank's charter by sharply reducing the number of loans and also by vigorously collecting outstanding debts. Biddle's actions, however, failed to deter the president. Biddle succeeded only in causing a financial crisis for American business in the summer and autumn of 1834. Worse, he alienated some of his strongest supporters.

Despite Biddle and censure by the Senate, Jackson continued his policy of placing funds in state–chartered banks. When Biddle discovered his policies were ineffective, he reversed himself and launched an even more extensive program of lending. For his part, Jackson made a determined effort to eliminate the extension of credit by forbidding banks with federal deposits from issuing banknotes of less than $5 denominations. In 1836 he issued the presidential order known as the Specie Circular, which required purchasers of public lands to pay in cash. By the time Jackson left office the Second Bank of the United States credit system had been severely crippled.

The Specie Circular was the final salvo in the Bank War, which ended in victory for Jacksonian principles. When the Bank's charter expired in 1836, it sought and received a charter from Pennsylvania, the state in which the main branch of the Bank had always been housed. It then operated under the name of the United States Bank of Pennsylvania. In 1839 the Bank found itself with too little specie to cover its loans. It went into receivership and was dissolved in 1841.

Jackson's victory left a questionable legacy. A boom in public works, such as canal construction, manufacturing, cotton production, and land sales, followed Jackson's decision to remove funds from the Second Bank of the United States. However, soon after his hand–picked successor Martin Van Buren took over in 1837, the country experienced a severe depression, marked by high rates of inflation and large public debt that lasted for nearly a decade. Many historians argue that by eliminating the Second Bank of the United States, Jackson removed an institution that might have eased the Panic of 1837.

See also: **Nicholas Biddle, Panic of 1819, Panic of 1837, Bank of the United States (Second National Bank), Specie, War of 1812**

FURTHER READING

McFaul, John M. *The Politics of Jacksonian Finance.* Ithaca, NY: Cornell University Press, 1972.

Redlich, Fritz. *The Molding of American Banking: Men and Ideas.* New York: Johnson Reprint Corp., 1968.

Rockoff, Hugh. *The Free Banking Era.* New York: Arno Press, 1975.

Timberlake, Richard H., Jr. *The Origins of Central Banking in the United States.* Cambridge, MA: Harvard University Press, 1978.

Wilburn, Jean Alexander. *Biddle's Bank: The Crucial Years.* New York: Columbia University Press, 1967.

BARBARY STATES

From the mid-1500s to the mid-1800s the North African countries of Morocco, Algiers (present-day Algeria), Tunis (now Tunisia), and Tripoli (in northwestern Libya) were called the Barbary States. The name was derived from the Turkish leader and pirate Barbarossa, whose name means "red beard" in Italian.

Barbarossa's original name was Khayr ad-Din (c. 1483–1546).

Barbarossa seized Spanish-occupied Algiers in 1518. He placed Algiers and three other states he later captured in the hands of the Ottoman Turks. Under Turkish leadership the region became a center for pirates who raided Spanish and Portuguese ships on the Mediterranean Sea and along Africa's Atlantic coast. The pirates (also called corsairs) demanded payment in the form of loot or slaves.

At the same time the Barbary States extorted money from European nations and the United States. They required the governments of these countries to pay tribute for protecting their merchant marine from seizure by the corsairs. By 1800 the United States had paid Tripoli alone an estimated $2 million. After Thomas Jefferson (1743–1826) became president of the United States in 1801 Tripoli increased the amount of the tribute. Jefferson had complained bitterly about these payments since his days as U.S. minister to France (1785–89). He preferred to fight the rogue states rather than concede to their demands.

The next 15 years saw intermittent conflict between the United States and Tripoli. The U.S. Navy won important battles along the North African coast. In 1815 the leaders of Algiers, Tunis, and Tripoli signed treaties that obligated them to cease collecting tribute or ransom from the United States. European military initiatives placed further pressure on the Barbary States to end their acts of piracy by 1835.

See also: **Thomas Jefferson**

BARBED WIRE

Barbed wire (or barbwire) was commercially developed in 1874 by American inventor Joseph Glidden (1813–1906). The invention consisted of steel wires that were twisted together to make sharp points resembling thorns. Barbed wire was predominantly used in the West to construct fences. Because trees were scarce on the Great Plains, farmers had lacked the materials to erect wooden fences. Instead they resorted to planting prickly shrubs as a way of defining their lands and confining livestock. This method, however, was not always effective. With the advent of barbed wire farmers were able to fence in their acreage. But small farmers who put up barbed wire angered cattle owners who had previously allowed livestock to roam the open plain. Fearing depletion of grazing lands, ranchers also began using barbed wire to fence tracts, whether or not they could claim legal title to them. Disputes arose

between ranchers and between ranchers and farmers. In 1885 President Grover Cleveland (1885–1889) brought an end to illegal fencing by ordering officials to remove barbed wire from public lands and Indian reservations. Thus, Cleveland helped determine what constituted legal use of barbed wire for defining land claim boundaries. That move also brought the demise of the open range and helped speed the agricultural development of the prairie.

See also: **Cattle Drives, Cowboys, Open Range**

BARNUM, PHINEAS TAYLOR

P. T. Barnum (1810–1891) portrayed himself as the ''Prince of Humbugs'' to characterize many outrageous stunts and exhibits that were part of his exploits as a showman. His tours, lectures, museum, and autobiography made him famous and a millionaire long before he entered the circus business and formed the innovative Barnum and Bailey Circus in the 1880s. Although he probably never said, ''There's a sucker born every minute,'' as is widely believed, he did act as if his audiences hoped to be fooled or, as he said, ''humbugged.''

Barnum was only 15 years old when his father died. He was forced to find the means to support his mother and five brothers and sisters. After trying his hand at various jobs he bought a weekly newspaper in his hometown of Bethel, Connecticut, called the *Herald of Freedom*. Over the course of several years he was arrested three times for libel and once spent 60 days in jail. In 1834 Barnum moved to New York City and became a shopkeeper.

Shortly afterward, Barnum was transformed from shopkeeper to showman when he discovered an elderly black woman, Joice Heth, who claimed to be George Washington's (1789–1797) nurse. A showman in Philadelphia had promoted Heth as the first president's 161-year-old nurse without much financial success. Under Barnum's management and sensational advertising, Heth toured the country telling her fabricated memories of the president's childhood. After her death, an autopsy showed her to be only 80 years old. A canny Barnum played to the public and claimed that he himself was also the victim of a hoax.

The Heth experience convinced Barnum that there was a market for satisfying the public's taste for the outrageous and improbable on a much larger scale. He bought John Scudder's American Museum in New York City which, at the time, housed conventional exhibits of stuffed animals and wax figures. Barnum

Phineas Taylor Barnum.

transformed the museum into a place of lively entertainment and bizarre attractions, open to the public for 25 cents admission. The five–story museum, which he operated for more than twenty–five years, housed some 50,000 curiosities including strange objects, unusual animals, and assorted people. Some of his most popular attractions were "freaks," such as the Siamese twins Chang and Eng; Anna Swan, the tallest girl in the world; Annie Jones, the bearded lady; and 26-inch-tall Charles S. Stratton, who became internationally famous as "General Tom Thumb." Equally important to the success of the museum were advertising and the imaginative stunts Barnum created to publicize his exhibits.

Although his policy of exhibiting humans as freaks may dismay current sensibilities, Barnum's exhibits were not intended solely for the masses. With Tom Thumb acting as his calling card, the showman was received by many heads of state, including President Abraham Lincoln (1809–65) and England's Queen Victoria (1819–1901). His European tours were tremendously successful, as were his lectures on such topics as "The Science of Money Making and the Philosophy of Humbug." In the 1850s he staked his entire fortune on his most legitimate endeavor: importing Swedish soprano Jenny Lind, "the Swedish Nightingale," for a tour of the United States. After a publicity campaign that topped all the great showman's previous efforts, he made immense profits for himself and the singer.

> **BARNUM'S OBSESSION WITH PUBLICITY WAS SO STRONG THAT WHEN HE BECAME SERIOUSLY ILL AT THE AGE OF 80, HE ASKED A NEW YORK NEWSPAPER TO RUN HIS OBITUARY IN ADVANCE SO THAT HE COULD READ IT HIMSELF.**

Barnum was well past 60 when he entered the circus business. With a partner, James A. Bailey (1847–1906), he transformed a small, poorly-run, often fraudulent, wagon-based circus show into a railroad-travelling, three-ring, electrically-lit giant extravaganza that was fun for the entire family. Typically, he made the show a success with his relentless promotion of the Barnum and Bailey Circus as "the greatest show on earth."

Barnum also publicized his own life and career in an autobiography. It was designed to entertain as much as inform. *The Life of P. T. Barnum, Written by Himself* was published in 1855 and was repeatedly revised and supplemented by the showman. Barnum claimed sales of a million copies for the work and, presumably with the hope of even greater exposure, he eventually placed the book in the public domain. Barnum's obsession with publicity was so strong that when he became seriously ill at the age of 80 he asked a New York newspaper to run his obituary in advance so that he could read it himself. Two weeks later he died at his home in Connecticut.

See also: **Entertainment Industry**

FURTHER READING

Farnham, Alan. "America's Original Huckster." *Fortune*, February 5, 1996.

Harris, Neil. *Humbug: The Art of P. T. Barnum.* Chicago: University of Chicago Press, 1981.

Kunhardt Jr., Philip B., Philip B. Kunhardt 3rd, and Peter W. Kunhardt. "For an America that Loved Freaks." *New York Times Magazine*, August 20, 1995.

Saxon, Arthur. *P. T. Barnum: The Legend and the Man.* New York: Columbia University Press, 1989.

Wallace, Irving. *The Fabulous Showman: The Life and Times of P. T. Barnum.* New York: Knopf, 1959.

BARTER

Barter is the exchange of goods and services without the use of money. The technique has been used in commercial transactions since ancient times. More recently, U.S.-based multinational companies have used a form of bartering called countertrade when selling large-value items, such as jet aircraft, overseas. Bartering allows a company to dispose of excess inventory, use surplus production capacity, and obtain necessary raw materials when a cash shortage exists. In addition, the technique also enables firms to gain access to new production channels and customers, resulting in increased sales volume.

BARUCH, BERNARD MANNES

Bernard M. Baruch (1870–1965) used his extraordinary talent as a stock market speculator to amass a sizable fortune at an early age. A generous contributor to the Democratic Party, he achieved influence and renown as an informal, and formal, consultant and adviser to the White House.

Born in Camden, South Carolina, in 1879, Baruch was the son of a doctor in the Confederate Army, and a descendant of one of the few Jewish families in South Carolina. The family moved to New York City when Baruch was eleven. He attended public schools and, in 1889, graduated from the College of the City of New York.

Baruch's interests in business and finance were evident early. He began his Wall Street career in the 1890s, as a runner for the firm A.A. Houseman & Co., which later merged into what became Merrill Lynch. He ventured out entirely on his own in his late twenties, and by the age of 30 he was on his way the becoming a very wealthy man. Baruch made his money as a speculator, often by selling short. Shrewdly and boldly playing the markets in copper, railroads, and sugar, sometimes with the help of insider tips, Baruch accumulated a $15 million fortune by the outbreak of World War I (1914–1918).

As his fortune increased, Baruch became more cautious and, in some instances, tended to sell early.

During the stock market crash of 1929, his financial assets fell from more than $22 million to about $16 million, but his maxim, ''run quickly'' enabled him to escape Wall Street's free fall relatively unscathed. He continued to invest in the stock market throughout his life. Though he continued to build on his substantial wealth, he never became, as many believed from Baruch's very effective self-promotion, one of the richest men in America.

Baruch's wealth did not blind him to the world outside the stock market. He played an active role in the great events of his time. For most of his long life, he dedicated much of his time and efforts to public service. Still in his early thirties in 1912, Baruch became an informal adviser to President Woodrow Wilson (1913–1921). In 1916 Wilson appointed him to the Advisory Commission of the Council of National Defense, and then made him chairman of the War Industries Board in 1917. In 1919, following the end of World War I, Baruch was appointed to the Supreme Economic Council at the Versailles Peace Conference, a meeting of world leaders to set the terms of the German surrender, and he advised Wilson on terms of the peace.

In the 1930s, with the Democrats back in the White House, Baruch maintained a long, but not close, relationship with President Franklin Roosevelt (1933–1945). When World War II (1939–1945) broke out, Roosevelt called on the expertise Baruch developed through his running of the War Industries Board during World War I to advise the government on wartime economic mobilization. Among his other contributions to the war effort, Baruch was instrumental in a successful effort to overcome bottlenecks between the United States and several South American countries, obtaining rubber imports vital to the war effort.

In 1946, after World War II ended, Baruch was asked by President Harry Truman to head the American delegation to the United Nations Atomic Energy Commission, a group representing the major world powers, established to find international control mechanisms for the use and proliferation of nuclear energy. His proposal to control atomic energy, known as the Baruch Plan, required that any agreement on atomic weapons must contain veto-proof sanctions on offenders and include provisions for inspection of all atomic facilities. The then-Soviet Union could not accept these conditions, and Baruch's plan was rejected by a United Nations vote on New Year's Eve 1946.

Baruch's 40-year career as a close adviser to U.S. presidents gave him a reputation as ''the parkbench sage,'' and he was one the most respected men of his time. When he died at age 94 in 1965, he had come to represent to many Americans the personification of the term "elder statesman."

See also: **Council of National Defense, Speculation, Wall Street, War Industries Board, World War I, World War II**

FURTHER READING

Baruch, Bernard. *My Own Story.* New York: Holt, 1957

Brimelow, Peter. "Bernard Baruch (book review)," *Fortune*, February 20, 1984.

Colt, Margaret L. *Mr. Baruch.* Boston: Houghton Mifflin, 1957.

Field, Carter. *Bernard Baruch, Park Bench Statesman.* New York: McGraw-Hill, 1944.

Grant, James. *Bernard Baruch: The Adventures of a Wall Street Legend.* New York: Simon & Schuster, 1984.

Schwartz, Jordan. *The Speculator: Bernard M. Baruch in Washington.* Chapel Hill: University of North Carolina Press, 1981.

BASEBALL

Baseball, a stick-and-ball sport played with four bases arranged in a diamond, was first organized in the mid-1800s in the United States. In June 1846 two amateur teams of nine players played each other in a ball game on the Elysian Fields in Hoboken, New Jersey, just across the Hudson River from New York City. The game was umpired by U.S. sportsman, Alexander J. Cartwright (1820–1892), who established the rules of play. The game is similar in some ways to the English games of Cricket and Rounders. A legend grew up that baseball's beginnings on U.S. soil dated to 1839 when U.S. Army officer Abner Doubleday (1819–1893) invented the game in Cooperstown, New York. Though Doubleday helped popularize games resembling modern baseball, there is little evidence that he developed the game that people in the United States know today, which became a favorite pastime during the late 1800s.

The first baseball club, the Knickerbocker Base Ball Club, was organized by Alexander Cartwright (1820–1892) in 1842 in New York City. By 1845 the

The great Jackie Robinson slides into home plate as Yogi Berra reaches to tag him out. Jackie Robinson broke the "color line" in 1942 by signing on as second baseman for the Brooklyn Dodgers.

team developed a set of twenty rules which included specifications for where the bases are to be positioned, how runners can be tagged as out, and defined a field of play, outside of which balls are declared "foul." The so-called "New York Game" spread in popularity after the 1846 Hoboken match. By 1860 there were at least fifty ball clubs. Pick-up games were played in fields across the country. Union soldiers helped spread the game during the American Civil War (1861–1865). Its popularity increased during the last three decades of the nineteenth century.

The first professional baseball team was the Cincinnati Red Stockings formed in 1869. In 1876 the National League of Professional Baseball Clubs was founded; it included teams in Boston, Chicago, Cincinnati, Hartford, Louisville, New York, Philadelphia, and St. Louis. By the 1880s the sport became big business: an 1887 championship series between St. Louis and Detroit drew 51,000 paying spectators. The American League was formed in 1901 and two years later the American and National leagues staged a championship between their teams. In 1903 the Boston Red Socks beat the Pittsburgh Pirates in the first World Series.

During the early decades of its existence as an organized sport, baseball reflected the racism of U.S. society by excluding African American players. When one all-black team applied for admittance in 1876 the National League adopted an unwritten "gentlemen's agreement" denying entry to any baseball club with black players. For the most part this exclusionary clause was effective in segregating baseball, but African American players occasionally found positions in the minor leagues.

The unfairness of excluding excellent players solely because of their skin color occasionally led to challenges of the color line. Catcher Moses Fleetwood (''Fleet'') Walker was actually the first black player to break into the major leagues. In 1883 Fleet and his Toledo teammates (Toledo then had a team that belonged to the American League) won the pennant. Still most black baseball players were relegated to the Negro leagues. Because of their limited audience, the Negro leagues had difficulty in establishing themselves. However in 1920 Rube Foster, a talented black pitcher and manager for the Chicago American Giants, formed the Negro National League. A number of African American teams and leagues were formed in the 1920s and the Negro leagues flourished for about 25 years, mostly in Mid-western cities. The Negro leagues fielded some excellent players, including Satchel Paige, Ray Dandridge, and John Henry ''Pop'' Lloyd. Paige was so devastating as a pitcher that he would often call his outfielders in and have them sit down in the infield while he retired the side. The color line was definitively broken when in 1947 Brooklyn Dodger Manager Branch Rickey (1881–1965) signed second baseman Jackie Robinson (1919–1972). Although he had to put up with ostracism from many of his teammates and cat-calls from the crowds Robinson eventually won acceptance and respect. Once Robinson became a hero to the general audience, African American players were signed by other major league teams, and the Negro leagues died.

The rise of organized professional sports is tied to the greater affluence that an industrialized society provided. People now had more money to spend, and an overall increase in leisure time as the workweek declined allowed baseball to become the national sport. Played on an open field, the game recalled the nation's agrarian roots. But with standardized rules, reliance on statistics, and the larger audience provided by radio and television, baseball looked forward to a modern, industrialized future.

See also: **Amusement Parks, Bicycles**

BEAN, LEON LEONWOOD

Tired of returning from hunting trips with cold, wet feet, Leon Leonwood (''L.L.'') Bean (1872–1967) designed a new type of boot that combined lightweight leather tops with waterproof bottoms. In 1912, the success of his practical footwear launched a company with annual sales that reached more than $1 billion by the end of the twentieth century.

Bean was born and brought up in rural Maine. Since his parents died when he was twelve, he and his brothers and sister lived with relatives in various remote ''Down East'' (Maine) villages. Early in life Bean developed a passion for hunting, fishing, and roaming the outdoors. He worked at odd jobs to support himself, his wife, and three children.

In 1911, at age 39, Bean invented what he claimed were the first modern lightweight, warm, and dry boots. He called his boots the ''Maine Hunting Shoe,'' and in 1912, while helping his brother run a small dry goods store in Freeport, Maine, he decided to sell the handmade footwear by mail order. His first step was to obtain a copy of the publicly available list of persons holding Maine hunting licenses—the natural market for his boots. Bean sent each of the licensed hunters his first mail order catalog, a three-page brochure, extolling the virtues of his new boots and guaranteeing 100 percent satisfaction.

SELL GOOD MERCHANDISE AT A REASONABLE PROFIT, TREAT YOUR CUSTOMERS LIKE HUMAN BEINGS, AND THEY'LL ALWAYS COME BACK FOR MORE.
L.L. Bean

He had to make good on that guarantee almost immediately. Ninety of the first 100 boots sprung leaks when the stitching holding the leather tops pulled out of the soft rubber bottoms. Without hesitation Bean refunded the purchase price of the boots to his disgruntled, but impressed, customers. He borrowed additional capital, improved the boot's design, and began to manufacture the improved footwear on a much greater scale. The Maine Hunting Shoe soon became a necessity for anyone seeking to hunt or fish in the Northeast wilderness.

By 1917 Bean's business had outgrown his brother's dry goods shop and Bean moved to a showroom across the street where customers could drop by to purchase his products in person. By 1925, with hand knit stockings and other associated items (such as shoelaces) added to his product line, Bean employed 25 people in his operation, and yearly sales had reached $135,000. Customers were attracted by the practical nature of L.L. Bean products and by the quirky, folksy tone of the catalogs Bean wrote himself. Most attractive, however, was Bean's reputation for honesty. Customers liked the old fashioned style and character of L.L. Bean, where the boss's motto for success was: ''Sell good merchandise at a reasonable profit, treat your customers like human beings, and they'll always come back for more.'' Bean's guarantee was unconditional. No matter how long a customer owned a product, it could always be exchanged for a replacement or a refund.

Throughout the 1920s and 1930s, L.L. Bean continued to expand its mail-order business and product line; the company was incorporated on July 1, 1934. During World War II (1939–1945), Bean served as a consultant on boot design for the U.S. Army and Navy, and his company received several contracts for military versions of hunting boots and other outdoor products. By the late 1940s, L.L. Bean had become a household word, attracting regular visits from political leaders, sports and other celebrities and had added casual apparel, gear for many outdoor sports, and additional footwear to its line.

Throughout the last years of his life, in semi-retirement in Florida, Bean held his company relentlessly to his old fashioned business practices, limiting growth, and only slowly accommodating modern technology. By 1967, when its founder died at age 94, L.L. Bean was in danger of retreating into a comfortable, but constricted, niche market.

Under Bean's grandson, Leon A. Gorman (1934–), who became president in 1967, L.L. Bean was drastically modernized. The company grew into one of the world's leading international mail order concerns, with sales of over $1 billion per year. L.L. Bean sells more than 16,000 products through catalogs, the Internet, a retail operation in Freeport, Maine, eight retail stores in Japan, and 90 factory outlet stores. The Freeport store, opened in 1951, is open 24 hours a day, 365 days a year, and remains one of Maine's most popular tourist destinations. More than 3.5 million people visit the store each year. Over 4.5 million customers place orders from all over the world; as many as 180,000 orders a day are received by phone. Despite the company's phenomenal growth in the past three decades of the century, however, it has retained its founder's strong commitment to product quality, customer satisfaction, and love of the outdoors.

See also: **Leon Gorman, Mail-Order Houses**

FURTHER READING

''Bean Sticks To His Backyard.'' *Economist Magazine*, August 4, 1990.

Brubach, Holly. ''Mail Order America.'' *New York Times Magazine*, November 21, 1993.

Montgomery, M.R. *In Search of L.L. Bean.* Boston: Little, Brown, 1984.

''Obituary.'' *New York Times.* February 7, 1967.

Skow, John. ''Using the Old Bean.'' *Sports Illustrated*, December 2, 1985.

The Company Behind the Catalog: The Story of L.L. Bean [cited March 4, 1999] available from the World Wide Web @ www.llbean.com/.

BEAR AND BULL MARKETS

The terms *bear* and *bull* refer to two opposing attitudes about the future of the economy. The meanings of the terms are symbolized in their names. Bears tend to be overbearing and push prices down. They believe that stock prices, currencies, commodities, or other financial investments will fall. Viewing the future pessimistically, bears are cautious investors and may quickly sell their holdings to avoid the losses they are certain will come. Bulls, however, run fast with their heads (and horns) high; they want to grab stocks and push prices upward. Bulls believe stock and other investment prices will rise. This optimism leads them to confidently invest in the stock market, believing their investments will increase in value.

Bear markets tend to coincide with recessions or downturns in the business cycle, while bull markets coincide with ''boom'' periods of high growth. The greatest bear market in U.S. history occurred after the stock market crash of 1929 when, over a period of two months, the Dow Jones index of industrial stocks lost 50 percent of its value. Because investors had little faith that the economy would rebound they avoided buying stocks and sold their investments before all their value was lost. This bear market existed until the end of World War II (1939–1945). In fact, it was not until the early 1950s that the Dow Jones Industrial Average regained its high of September 1929.

The terms *bear* and *bull* were already being used in the United States in the mid-1800s, when they were often used to refer to investors who sold and bought purely speculative stocks (called ''fancy stocks'') of companies that had little chance of ever earning a profit. Before the Great Depression, the decade of the ''Roaring Twenties'' was the greatest bull market the United States had ever seen. Between 1921 and 1929 the stocks on the New York Stock Exchange grew more than 800 percent in value. The next great bull market occurred between 1954 and 1969, but this time investors' optimism was based not on speculation (risk taking with the stocks of companies the investor knows little about) but on real growth in the profits of U.S. corporations. In the 1970s, runaway inflation, higher oil prices, and political turmoil led to the first extended bear market since the 1930s. Beginning in 1982, however, the U.S. economy began to enjoy the longest and most dramatic bull market in its history. The Dow Jones Industrial Average stood at 831 in 1982, but in early 1999 it crossed the 10,000 level for the first time ever.

See also: **Business Cycle, Dow Jones Industrial Average, New York Stock Exchange, Recession, Speculation, Stock, Stock Market Crash of 1929**

BECHTEL, STEPHEN DAVISON

Stephen D. Bechtel (1900–89), a man who directed some of the twentieth century's greatest construction feats, possessed extraordinary imagination and organizational abilities. Beginning with his work on the Hoover Dam in the 1930s, he thrived on surmounting nearly impossible challenges. In naming him one of its 100 most influential persons of the twentieth century, *Time* magazine said, "Only a man who thought on the grandest scale could build the world's biggest engineering projects. . . . Thinking big was Steve Bechtel's forte."

Young Bechtel spent school vacations working with his father and brothers on rugged railroad construction projects throughout the West. During World War I Bechtel served in France with the Twentieth Engineers, American Expeditionary Force. After the war he attended the University of California at Berkeley but left before graduation to join his father in the construction business.

Bechtel's father founded the W. A. Bechtel Company in California in 1925 and appointed his son its vice president. The company built many of the roads, tunnels, bridges, pipelines, and dams that fueled West Coast economic growth in the twentieth century. In 1931 the elder Bechtel organized six companies in a successful bid to build one of the largest construction projects in history, the Hoover Dam. When his father died suddenly in 1933, Bechtel became president of the family company and chief executive of the dam project.

The Hoover Dam, which eventually transformed the economy of much of the West, was completed in a remarkably short five years, at a cost of $54 million.

The scale of the project was immense. The dam, which rises 70 feet in the air, required 4.4 million cubic yards of concrete to build. 5,000 workers at a time toiled on the project, excavating 3.7 million cubic yards of rock.

Bechtel followed the success of the Hoover Dam project with the 8.2-mile San Francisco–Oakland Bay Bridge. In 1936 he joined with steel executive John A. McCone (1909–1991), who later became director of the CIA, to form Bechtel-McCone Corporation, a firm concentrating on designing and building petroleum refineries and chemical plants. During World War II, Bechtel's companies and joint ventures turned their efforts to supporting U.S. defense efforts. The shipyards his companies organized built 560 vessels between 1941 and 1945. Bechtel's companies also guided the work of aircraft modification plants and constructed naval bases and other key defense facilities.

In 1946, following the war, Bechtel consolidated his various companies into the Bechtel Corporation and began to build many of the world's oil pipelines, including the 1,600-mile Alaska pipeline and, beginning in 1947, the Trans-Arabian (1,068 miles) pipeline that opened up Mideast oil reserves to the world.

Bechtel was widely recognized as a man of unusual vision. In his last years he was actively engaged in building a new city, Jubail, on the site of a former fishing village in Saudi Arabia. He pioneered the concept of "turnkey" projects—projects that remained entirely under his company's supervision and responsibility until they were completed. Coordinating the work of several contractors with Bechtel as project manager was another of his initiatives that took root and helped his company to flourish.

Bechtel resigned as president and CEO of Bechtel Corporation in 1960. He remained active in the company's affairs until his death in 1989 (at age 88), first as chairman of the board and later as senior director. He had built the company from revenues of less than $20 million when he took it over in 1936 to $463 million when he retired in 1960. By 1997 the company was posting annual revenues of $11.3 billion. Since 1898 four generations of the Bechtel family have guided the family-owned business through 19,000 projects which included transit systems in San Francisco, Washington, D.C., and Athens, Greece, the Boston expressway project, and the Hong Kong airport.

FURTHER READING

Church, George J. "Stephen Bechtel, Global Builder." *Time*, December 7, 1998.

Current Biography 1957. New York: H.W. Wilson, 1957, s.v. ''Bechtel, Stephen D(avison).''

McCartney, Laton. *Friends in High Places: The Bechtel Story: The Most Secret Corporation and How It Engineered the World*. New York: Simon and Schuster, 1988.

''Stephen D. Bechtel'' [cited March 15, 1999] available from the World Wide Web @ www.bechtel.com/aboutbech/stephenSr.html/.

BELL, ALEXANDER GRAHAM

In 1876 Alexander Graham Bell (1847–1922), at age twenty-nine, invented the telephone. A year later he founded the Bell Telephone Company, which later became the American Telephone and Telegraph Company (AT&T). Throughout the remainder of his long and productive life, Bell continued his work as an inventor, eventually securing eighteen patents in his name. In addition he maintained a lifelong commitment to the education of the deaf.

Bell was born in 1847 Edinburgh, Scotland, to a family of eminent speech educators and musicians. His father, Alexander Melville Bell, taught speech to the deaf and the mute and wrote textbooks on correct speech. Bell's mother was a portrait painter and an accomplished musician. Bell received his early education at home and graduated at age fourteen from the Royal High School, Edinburgh. He then enrolled as a student teacher at Weston House, a nearby boys' school, where he taught music and speech and in turn received instruction in other subjects. Bell also studied briefly at Edinburgh University. In his late teens, Bell worked as an assistant to his father, promoting ''visible'' speech, a system developed by his father that shows the articulation of sound on the lips, tongue, and throat. Bell became deeply interested in the study of sound, especially as it affects hearing and speech, and he followed this interest throughout his life.

When young Bell's two brothers died of tuberculosis, their father took the family to the healthier climate of Ontario, Canada, in 1870. Bell soon moved to Boston, Massachusetts, and in 1872 opened his own school for training teachers of the deaf. In 1873 he became a professor of vocal physiology at Boston University.

Bell's interest in speech and communication led him to investigate the transmission of sound over wires. Backed financially in his investigations by

Alexander Graham Bell testing his new telephone invention.

Gardiner Hubbard and Thomas Sanders, grateful fathers of two of his deaf pupils, he experimented with developing the harmonic telegraph, a device that could send multiple messages at the same time over a single wire. Using vibrating membranes and an actual human ear in his tests, Bell also investigated the possibility of transmitting the human voice by wire.

MR. WATSON, COME HERE, I WANT YOU!

Alexander Graham Bell, first words spoken on the telephone, March 10, 1876

Early in 1874 Bell met Thomas A. Watson (1854–1934), a young machinist and technician with expertise in electrical engineering. Watson became Bell's indispensable assistant and the two spent endless hours together experimenting with transmitting sound. In the summer of 1874 Bell developed the basic concept of the telephone using a varying but unbroken electric current to transmit the sound waves of human speech. However, at the urging of his financial backers, who were more interested in the potential of the harmonic telegraph, Bell did not pursue the idea for several months. He resumed work on the telephone in 1875 and by September began to write the required patent specifications.

Bell's patent, U.S. Patent No. 174,465, was granted on March 7, 1876, and on March 10, the first message transmitted by telephone passed from Bell to Watson in their workshop: ''Mr. Watson, come here, I want you!'' After a year of refining the new device Watson and Bell, along with their two backers Hubbard and Sanders, formed the Bell Telephone Company in 1877. Soon afterwards Bell married Mabel Hubbard, his former speech student and daughter of his new partner, and sailed to England for a yearlong honeymoon.

Bell's claim to have invented the telephone was challenged in more than 600 lawsuits. The courts eventually upheld Bell's patent, and the Bell Company's principal competitor, Western Union Telegraph, agreed to stay out of the telephone business. The Bell Company, in turn, stayed away from the telegraph. In 1878, with the sale of the Bell Company to a group of investors, Bell's financial future was secure and he could devote the rest of his life to his work as an inventor. Bell won France's Volta Prize for his telephone invention and received 50,000 francs in prize money. With this reward he established the Volta Laboratory in Washington, D.C., primarily for research on deafness. Among the new devices he and his fellow scientists at the laboratory invented were the graphophone, a device for recording sound on wax cylinders or disks (an advance that made Thomas Edison's (1847–1931) phonograph commercially viable); the photophone, used for transmitting speech on a beam of light; a telephone probe, used in surgery until the discovery of the X-ray; an audiometer; and an induction balance for detecting metal within the human body.

Working with collaborators at the Volta Laboratory and at another scientific facility he established near Baddeck, Nova Scotia, Bell invented a prototype air conditioning system, an improved strain of sheep, an early iron lung, solar distillation of water, and the sonar detection of icebergs. The possibility of flight fascinated Bell. He built tetrahedral kites capable of carrying a human being and supported pioneering experiments in aviation. He also designed a hydrofoil boat that set the world water speed record in 1918.

Bell retained his dual interests in education of the deaf and invention throughout his later life. He became a naturalized U.S. citizen in 1882 and established several organizations to support teaching of the deaf, including the American Association to Promote the Teaching of Speech to the Deaf in 1890, later known as the Alexander Graham Bell Association for the Deaf. He was also influential in the founding of *Science* magazine and the National Geographic Society. Bell died in 1922.

See also: **American Telephone and Telegraph**

FURTHER READING

Mackay, James A. *Alexander Graham Bell: A Life.* New York: J. Wiley, 1997.

Grosvenor, Edwin S. *Alexander Graham Bell: The Life and Times of the Man who Invented the Telephone.* New York: Harry Abrams, 1997.

Bruce, Robert V. *Bell: Alexander Graham Bell and the Conquest of Solitude.* Boston: Little, Brown, 1973.

Costain, Thomas B. *The Chord of Steel: The Story of the Invention of the Telephone.* Garden City, N.Y.: Doubleday, 1960.

''The Papers of Alexander Graham Bell: An Introduction,'' [cited March 3, 1999] available from the World Wide Web @ memory.loc.gov/ammem/atthtml/bell_ms.html

BENNETT, JAMES GORDON

James Gordon Bennett (1795–1872), in many ways the father of modern journalism, shaped the American newspaper as it is today. At the time of the American Civil War (1861–1865), Bennett's newspaper, the *New York Herald*, had the largest circulation of any newspaper in the world and it wielded great national influence. Reportedly the only paper that President Abraham Lincoln (1861–65) read daily, the *Herald* made Bennett one of the wealthiest men in America.

Bennett was the first newspaper publisher to exploit rail and steamboat transportation and use the telegraph to speed the delivery of news. He joined Horace Greeley (1811–1872) and Charles Dana (1819–1897) to become one of the three giants of journalism and publishing in America in the nineteenth century.

Born and raised in Scotland, Bennett grew up in a devout Catholic family in a overwhelmingly Presbyterian community. He received a classical education in a local school and later at a Catholic seminary in Aberdeen. In 1817, at age 24, he sailed to America, landing in Nova Scotia with just five pounds sterling in his pocket. By the time he reached Boston, he was penniless and actually went two days without food until he found a job as a clerk with a book selling and publishing firm. After working for the firm as a proofreader and learning many of the details of the publishing business, Bennett moved on to New York where he sought work as a freelancer.

Bennett's next important job was with the very influential Charleston, South Carolina, *Courier*. Its editor, Aaron Smith Wellington, was ahead of his time in believing that speed and timeliness were crucial to a newspaper's success. For example, Wellington scooped the rest of the country with the first news of the Treaty of Ghent, which ended the War of 1812 (1812–1814). Bennett's job at the *Courier* was to translate articles from French and Spanish newspapers that were brought by ships into Charleston's busy seaport. Although he learned the tenets of deadline journalism in Charleston, Bennett's poor social skills hampered his ability to participate in the city's active social life. At the end of ten months he returned to New York.

For the next few years, until 1827, Bennett supported himself precariously as a lecturer and freelance writer. In 1827 he was hired by the *New York Enquirer* and became the first Washington correspondent in history. Over the next few years he worked for a series of newspapers as a reporter. Twice he tried to start his own paper and both times he failed.

Finally, in 1835, with $500 in capital, he founded the *New York Herald*. The newspaper's offices were in a cellar furnished with planks and barrels and Bennett was its publisher, reporter, and advertising and circulation manager. At the time New Yorkers already had a choice of more than a dozen daily newspapers, and the *Herald*'s chances for success were poor.

But in the next 37 years Bennett built the *Herald* into the newspaper with the largest circulation in the world. He accomplished this by introducing several enduring innovations. Among them were listing the closing prices of stocks traded each day on the New York Stock Exchange, hiring as many as 63 correspondents to cover the battles of the Civil War, printing the first illustration accompanying a news story, establishing correspondents in Europe, and introducing a society column. Bennett was the first newspaper publisher to use the telegraph to obtain a full report of a major political speech and was also the first to narrate a sensational murder in great detail.

Whatever resources were demanded, Bennett was determined to cover stories ahead his rivals. Speed in newsgathering became his watchword. Even the most successful of his competitors were sometimes forced to copy stories from the *Herald*. He early realized and exploited the communications potential opened up by the telegraph, the ever-faster steamships crossing the Atlantic from Europe, and the new railroads which began to connect American cities. During the Mexican War and the Civil War, the *Herald* usually received stories from the battlefield days ahead of the dispatches that were sent to the War Department in Washington.

The *Herald* in the mid-nineteenth century was among the most profitable newspapers in the world. Bennett's salary of about $400,000 a year made him one of the wealthiest Americans of his time. Politically independent, reported on deadline, and aimed at the widest possible audience, the *New York Herald* was the first mass circulation newspaper that was essential reading for the country's opinion makers and political leaders.

FURTHER READING

Carlson, Oliver. *The Man Who Made News: James Gordon Bennett*. New York: Duell, Sloan and Pearce, 1942.

Crouthamel, James L. *Bennett's New York Herald and the Rise of the Popular Press*. Syracuse, N.Y.: Syracuse University Press, 1989.

Gordon, John Steele. ''The man who invented mass media.'' *St. Louis Journalism Review*, March, 1996.

Herd, Harold. *Seven Editors*. Westport, CT: Greenwood Press, 1977.

Stewart, Kenneth, and John Tebbell. *Makers of Modern Journalism*. Englewood Cliffs, NJ, Prentice-Hall, 1952.

Tebbell, John and Sarah Miles Watts. *The Press and the Presidency*. New York: Oxford University Press, 1985.

BERINGIA

Beringia is the land bridge thought to have existed over the Bering Strait, the waterway that separates Asia (Russia) from North America (Alaska). Scholars believe that a natural bridge was formed across the strait either by ice or by dropping sea levels that exposed land masses during the late ice age (known as the Pleistocene glacial epoch, which ended around 10,000 B.C.)

Asian peoples are believed to have migrated over Beringia as they pursued large game. They arrived in North America as early as 50,000 B.C. These people were the Paleo-Indians, the first inhabitants of the Western Hemisphere. Many American Indian groups that were encountered by the Europeans in the early 1500s were descendants of the migratory Paleo-Indians.

The Bering Strait, which connects the Arctic Ocean and the Bering Sea, is 53 miles (85 kilometers) across at its most narrow point. The first European to traverse the Bering Strait (in 1728) was Danish navigator Vitus Bering (1681–1741), from whom it takes its name. He had been employed by Russian Czar Peter the Great to determine whether Asia and North America were connected.

See also: **Paleo-Indians**

BESSEMER PROCESS

The Bessemer process was the first method for making steel cheaply and in large quantities, developed during the early 1850s. It was named after British engineer Henry Bessemer (1813–1898), who invented the process. The process was also developed independently in the United States by William Kelly (1811–1888), who received a patent for it in 1857.

Bessemer and Kelly experimented with injecting air into molten pig iron (crude iron); the oxygen in the air helped rid the iron of its impurities (such as manganese, silicon, and carbon), converting the iron to molten steel, which was then poured into molds. The process was introduced to the U.S. steel manufacturing industry in 1864. Alloys were also added to the refining process to help purify the metal. Within two decades the method was used to produce more than 90 percent of the nation's steel; it was eventually implemented throughout the industrialized world.

In the mid-1800s rich iron ore deposits were discovered in the Upper Peninsula of Michigan along Lake Superior. The discovery of the minerals and the innovation of the Bessemer process combined to create a thriving steel industry in the United States. There was a growing market for the material; railroads needed iron to make rail gauges and the new auto manufacturing industry used steel to make cars. As a result annual U.S. steel production increased by a factor of 20 between 1880 and 1910.

One of the early industry leaders was Andrew Carnegie (1835–1919). In 1873 Carnegie founded the nation's first large-scale steel plant at Braddock, Pennsylvania. In 1901 he sold the plant and other steel mills to the United States Steel Corporation (later to become the USX Corporation, the largest steel producer in the United States). The Bessemer process continued to be used until after World War II (1939–1945). The open-hearth method of refining gradually replaced it.

See also: **Andrew Carnegie, Steel Industry**

BETHUNE, MARY MCLEOD

Mary McLeod Bethune (1875–1955) was an educator and activist who founded a college in Florida for African-American women. She promoted education for African Americans at the national level and served on many presidential committees. Involved in the women's movement, Bethune founded and led organizations that represented African-American women in the United States.

Mary McLeod Bethune was born on July 10, 1875, near Mayesville, South Carolina. She was the fifteenth of seventeen children born to former slaves. As a child, she worked in a cotton field, where she developed a strong work ethic and an appreciation for manual labor. Because of her strong desire to learn how to read and write, Bethune was allowed to attend the one-room schoolhouse in Mayesville. Her teacher recognized her talent for learning and recommended her for a scholarship to attend Scotia Seminary in Concord, North Carolina. Bethune graduated from the seminary in 1894 and then won a scholarship to the Moody Bible Institute in Chicago.

Bethune started her career as a teacher's assistant in 1896, at the same Mayesville school she had attended. Next she received an appointment from the Presbyterian Board of Education to teach at the Haines Normal and Industrial Institute in Augusta, Georgia. Under the direction of Lucy Craft Laney, Bethune learned a great deal about how to administer a girls' school with primary, grammar, normal, and industrial courses. In 1898 Bethune was transferred to the Kendell Institute in Sumpter, South Carolina, where she met her husband-to-be, Albertus Bethune. The couple married in May 1898, and Bethune gave birth to their son, Albertus McLeod Bethune, Jr., in February 1899.

While living with her new family in Savannah, Georgia, Bethune met Reverent C.J. Uggans, a Presbyterian minister from Palatka, Florida, who encouraged her to found a school in Palatka. Bethune took the opportunity and spent the next five years there. Not only did she start a community school, but she also worked in the jails, sawmills, and clubs teaching and doing missionary work. A few years later, she was encouraged by Reverend S.P. Pratt to move to Daytona and start a new school. In 1904 Bethune opened the Daytona Normal and Industrial Institute for Negro Girls. Bethune worked tirelessly at the school to develop its academic program and earn regional accreditation. In addition, because she had no assets with which to fund the school, Bethune spent a considerable amount of time soliciting contributions from both the African American and white communities. In 1923 Bethune's

Mary McLeod Bethune.

school merged with the Cookman Institute for Men, then in Jacksonville, and in 1929 the institution became known as the Bethune-Cookman College in Daytona Beach. Bethune served as president of the college until 1947. The college awarded its first four-year degrees in teacher education in 1943.

Bethune was not only an educator, but also a leader and an activist. In 1924 she became the eighth president of the National Association of Colored Women's (NACW) clubs, and in that position she helped establish a national headquarters for the organization in Washington, D.C. In addition, Bethune also served on many presidential committees. In 1928 she attended President Calvin Coolidge's (1923–1929) Child Welfare Conference. During President Herbert Hoover's (1929–1933) administration she attended the National Commission for Child Welfare and served on the Hoover Commission on Home Building and Home Ownership. She was appointed to the Planning Committee of the Federal Office of Education of Negroes in 1933.

WE MUST GAIN FULL EQUALITY IN EDUCATION . . . IN THE FRANCHISE . . . IN ECONOMIC OPPORTUNITY, AND FULL EQUALITY IN THE ABUNDANCE OF LIFE.

Mary McLeod Bethune, *Chicago Defender*, May 1954

Aside from her work with the NACW, Bethune was active in other aspects of the women's movement during the 1920s and 1930s. In 1935 she founded the National Council of Negro Women in New York City, and remained president of that organization until 1949. Through the activities with the women's movement Bethune came to the attention of Eleanor Roosevelt (1884–1962), who invited her to attend a luncheon for leaders of the National Council of Women in the United States. Bethune was appointed administrator of the National Youth Administration (NYA) by President Franklin D. Roosevelt (1933–1945), a position she held from 1935 to 1944. During her tenure with the NYA, Bethune was instrumental in encouraging African Americans to join the Democratic Party, and she traveled around the country promoting Roosevelt's New Deal policies. In addition, Bethune founded the Federal Council on Negro Affairs, a group of prominent African American administrators in Washington during the Roosevelt administration who became known as the "black cabinet."

The NYA was abolished in 1943, and Bethune returned to Daytona Beach. She was, however, still involved in national affairs. Bethune lobbied the United States War Department in 1942 to commission

black women officers in the Women's Army Auxiliary Corps (WAAC). Two years later she became the national commander of the Women's Army for National Defense, an African American women's organization founded by Lovonia H. Brown. After World War II (1939–1945), Bethune became involved in international activities, traveling to Haiti, Liberia, and Switzerland.

Mary McLeod Bethune died of a heart attack on May 18, 1955. Her legacy lives on not only through the Bethune-Cookman College, but also through the Mary McLeod Bethune foundation. In addition, her home, "The Retreat," was made a National Historic Landmark by the National Park Services in 1975.

See also: **Women's Movement**

FURTHER READING

Bethune, Mary McLeod. *Mary McLeod Bethune Papers: The Bethune-Cookman College Collection, 1922-1955*. Bethesda, MD: University Publications of America, 1995.

Height, Dorothy I. "Remembering Mary McLeod Bethune." *Essence*, February 1994.

McCluskey, Audrey Thomas. "Multiple Consciousness in the Leadership of Mary McLeod Bethune." *NWSA Journal*, 6, Spring 1994.

Norment, Lynn. "10 Most Unforgettable Black Women." *Ebony*, February 1990.

Smith, Elaine M. "Mary McLeod Bethune's 'Last Will and Testament': A Legacy for Race Vindication." *The Journal of Negro History*, 81, Winter-Fall 1996.

BEVERIDGE, ALBERT JEREMIAH

Albert Jeremiah Beveridge (1862–1927) was one of the leading political progressives in the United States, and a highly respected historian. He was a champion of U.S. economic growth, but he also sought to protect U.S. workers and consumers.

Albert Beveridge was born on October 6, 1862 in Highland County, Ohio, to Thomas and Frances Beveridge. He had a difficult childhood because of family financial problems. In 1865 his father lost his property and moved the family to a farm in Illinois. Beveridge went to work as a child to help support the family. He worked as a plowboy at age twelve, as a railroad hand at age fourteen, and as a logger at age fifteen. When he was sixteen Beveridge was able to attend high school. After graduating in 1881, he borrowed $50 from a friend to attend Asbury College (now De Pauw University) in Greencastle, Indiana. Beveridge managed to finance the rest of his college education with prize money from oratorical competitions.

Beveridge graduated from college in 1885 and was admitted to the bar in 1887. He then opened his own law practice in Indianapolis, where he built a successful business over the next twelve years. Beveridge continued to use his skills as an orator, this time for the Republican Party. During the late 1880s and early 1890s he became known as one of the party's most capable and enthusiastic campaigners. He quickly became a skilled lawyer and cultivated many friendships among the city's leading political figures.

In 1889 there was a deadlock among the leading Republican candidates for senator and the legislative caucus turned to Beveridge as a compromise candidate. At the age of thirty-six, Beveridge was elected as the youngest member of the United States Senate. In his first term Beveridge spoke out as a firm believer in U.S. imperialism and passionately championed the expansion of United States domination in Canada, Mexico, and the Philippines. He supported an aggressive foreign policy, advocating strong protectionist tariffs for the United States, the annexation of Cuba, and increased economic domination for what he considered to be "backward" societies. He declared that he was for: "American first! Not only America first, but American only!"

In 1905 Beveridge was reelected to the Senate. As the country's overseas interests diminished, Beveridge turned his attention to domestic matters and allied himself with Republican President Theodore Roosevelt (1901–1909). Beveridge became involved in the party insurgency of the time that led to the formation of the Progressive Party. In particular, Beveridge supported equal industrial opportunities, antitrust legislation, government regulation of public service, a strong navy, and the conservation of natural resources.

Beveridge is best known for two pieces of important legislation that he advocated during his second term in the Senate. In 1906 he was strongly influenced by Upton Sinclair's (1878–1968) book *The Jungle*, which exposed the public to the horrors of unsanitary food preparation in the U.S. meat packing industry. Beveridge fervently fought for the passage of the Pure Food and Meat Inspection Acts aimed at curbing the abuses of this industry. The second important piece of

legislation with which Beveridge was actively involved was the Keating-Owen bill, a child labor protection act passed in 1916. Beveridge worked tirelessly for a national child labor law to stop the victimization of children in U.S. factories, and the law was eventually passed five years after Beveridge's term as senator ended.

Because of his outspoken position on some rather controversial issues Beveridge lost his bid for the Senate in 1911. He then joined Roosevelt and the Progressive Party in 1912 and was the keynote speaker at the party's first national convention. In 1914 he ran for Senate as a Progressive but again lost the bid. Beveridge and Roosevelt both rejoined the Republican Party in 1916.

Beveridge was never again elected to political office. While he remained active in politics, he also pursued a career as a historian. He wrote several books throughout his lifetime, but his most influential works came during his later years. Between 1916 and 1919 Beveridge authored a four-volume series on *The Life of John Marshall*, a biography of the Chief Justice of the Supreme Court. The work was awarded a Pulitzer Prize. Beveridge then began another four-volume work, this time on the life of Abraham Lincoln. However, he finished only two volumes before his death on April 27, 1927.

See also: **Upton Sinclair**

FURTHER READING

American Academy of Arts and Letters. *Commemorative Tributes to Beveridge*. New York: The American Academy of Arts and Letters, 1929.

Bowers, Claude Gernade. *Beveridge and the Progressive Era*. New York: The Literary Guild, 1932.

Braeman, John. *Albert J. Beveridge: American Nationalist*. Chicago: University of Chicago Press, 1971.

Findling, John E. *Dictionary of American Diplomatic History*, Second Edition. New York: Greenwood Press, 1989.

B.F. GOODRICH

Benjamin Franklin Goodrich (1841–1888) was a businessman and a physician by profession. He served as an assistant surgeon in the Union Army during the American Civil War (1861–1865). When the war ended his interest turned to primarily business dealings and he formed a real estate partnership with John P.

Morris of New York City. In 1869 they invested in the Hudson River Rubber Company. Soon they acquired complete ownership of the company and Goodrich became president.

The Hudson River Rubber Company was struggling financially in New York at the time. Goodrich felt that by moving the company westward he could take advantage of the promise of a growing population and new opportunity for advancement and prosperity. In 1870 a new two-story factory was built on the banks of the Ohio Canal. Its products included billiard cushions, bottle stoppers, rubber rings for canning jars, and fire hoses. It was the first rubber company west of the Allegheny Mountains.

The company reorganized internally several times and finally secured a loan in 1880 from George W. Crouse, an original investor. The Hudson River Rubber Company now became the B.F. Goodrich Company and was incorporated in the state of Ohio. In 1896 the first automobile tires in the United States were produced by Goodrich. The B.F. Goodrich Tire Company devoted its entire energies to rubber technology. Inventions and products included the first rubber sponge in 1902 and aircraft tires in 1909. All aircraft used in World War I (1914–1918) had B.F. Goodrich tires. The *Spirit of St. Louis* piloted by Charles Lindbergh (1902–1974) sported tires manufactured by B.F. Goodrich.

During World War II (1939–1945) Japan controlled the supply of natural rubber. Goodrich invented synthetic rubber to supply the war needs of the United States. Tubeless tires came into being in 1947. Because of this invention the tires on all new cars were much safer. The first American in space, Alan Shepard, wore a space suit designed by Goodrich. The popular 1960s children's sneakers P-F Flyers also came from this innovative company.

In 1979 the new B.F. Goodrich chairman John Ong began diverting the company's focus from tires to chemical and aerospace concerns. By 1986, the merger of B.F. Goodrich and Uniroyal created the Uniroyal Goodrich Tire Company. In 1990 Michelin purchased this new company and B.F Goodrich was out of the tire business.

Ong diverted research money back into the chemical and aerospace businesses. He acquired British companies, because although they had low productivity, they generally had sound research and good products and were relatively easy to reorganize into profitable ventures. This investment strategy generally worked well because of its long-term growth potential. B.F. Goodrich chemicals were eventually used in everything from textiles to Turtle Wax.

Ong retired in 1997 and was succeeded by David L. Burner. B.F. Goodrich continued to focus on making profitable acquisitions around the world. These acquisitions were chosen because they meshed well with current holdings and improved their returns.

See also: **Tire and Rubber Industry**

FURTHER READING

"B.F. Goodrich," [cited April 23, 1999] available from the World Wide Web @ www.bfgoodrich.com/default.asp/.

Low, Chris. "Goodrich Gaining in Confidence." *Gannett News Service*, November 6, 1997.

Mavrigina, Mike. *Performance Wheels and Tires*. H.P. Books, 1998.

Neely, William. *Tire Wars: Racing With Goodyear*. Tucson, AZ: Aztex Corporation, 1993.

Rodengen, Jeffrey L. *The Legend of Goodyear: The First 100 Years*. Ft. Lauderdale, FL: Write Stuff Syndicate, 1997.

BICYCLES

A series of inventions during the 1800s resulted in the introduction of the safety bicycle in 1876. It was the direct ancestor of the modern bike and the first commercially successful bicycle. It had wheels that were equal in size, making it easier and safer to ride than its "high-wheeler" predecessor. The industry proliferated and by 1900 more than 10 million people in the United States owned bicycles. In the years preceding the U.S. manufacture of automobiles (which began around 1900) the bicycle became an important means of transportation and recreation.

As with other inventions, the bicycle was a result of the work of several innovators. In 1817 German Baron Karl von Drais de Sauerbrun developed a device that resembled a scooter, the *drasienne*. The device was later improved by Scotsman Kirkpatrick Macmillan (1813–1878), who in 1839 added pedals to the vehicle, creating the world's first real bicycle. In 1870 English inventor James Starley (1830–1881) designed a bicycle with a large front wheel and a small rear wheel. He named it the Ariel. The invention was also called a "penny-farthing" (after two different-sized British coins), the "high-wheeler," and the "ordinary." Though the bicycle was easier to pedal and faster (one revolution of the pedals turned the front wheel once), its high center of gravity made it unstable and even dangerous. The innovation of the tricycle, or velocipede, improved the design of the Ariel by giving it the added stability of the third wheel.

But it was not until the safety bike was developed in 1876 that the bicycle's popularity began to rise. Invented by Englishman H.J. Lawson, the bicycle had wheels of equal size and a bike chain (to drive the rear wheel). This practical design was improved again in 1895 when air-filled tires were added. Mass production of the safety bicycle began in 1885.

After the advent of the automobile the bicycle continued to figure prominently in American life. Bicycle riding became a leisure pursuit that rivaled baseball in popularity. Cycling clubs emerged. The tandem, a bicycle built for two, allowed American youths an opportunity for courtship. The bicycle industry yielded some of the great innovators in transportation, including bicycle designer Charles Edward Duryea (1861–1938). Duryea demonstrated the first successful gas-powered car in the United States with his brother Frank (1869–1967). Brothers Wilbur and Orville Wright (1867–1912; 1871–1948), who owned a bicycle shop in Dayton, Ohio, used their skill they learned at their trade to build the first airplane.

See also: **Automobile**

BIDDLE, NICHOLAS

Nicholas Biddle (1786–1844) established the Bank of the United States as a prototype of the modern central banking system. Using the power of the bank to expand and contract the money supply, Biddle played a prominent role in creating a stable currency and in bringing order to the chaotic American marketplace. A true American aristocrat, he read classics in their original language and collected art. Following his retirement from banking, he helped establish Girard College in Philadelphia and held literary salons at Andalusia, his country estate.

Biddle was born in Philadelphia, the son of Charles Biddle and Hannah Shepard. Biddle's mother was the daughter of a North Carolina merchant; his father was a successful merchant. Biddle was a precocious student and was admitted to the University of Pennsylvania when he was ten years old. His parents took a keen interest in his education. At age thirteen they had him transferred to Princeton University as a sophomore. He graduated in September 1801. At the age of fifteen, Biddle was the highest ranking student in his class.

In 1804 Biddle went to France as a member of the American legation, where he worked on claims resulting from the Louisiana Purchase. After one year, he took a tour of Europe and Greece, then settled in London where he worked for two years as secretary for future President James Monroe (1817–1875). During the time he spent overseas, Biddle acquired valuable insights into the problems and techniques of international finance.

In 1810 Biddle met and later married Jane Craig, whose father's estate was one of the largest in Philadelphia. That same year he was elected to the Pennsylvania legislature. The highlight of his term was an eloquent defense of the First Bank of the United States.

USING THE POWER OF THE BANK TO EXPAND AND CONTRACT THE MONEY SUPPLY, BIDDLE PLAYED A PROMINENT ROLE IN CREATING A STABLE CURRENCY AND IN BRINGING ORDER TO THE CHAOTIC AMERICAN MARKETPLACE.

In 1822 Biddle assumed the presidency of the Second Bank of the United States—the first effective central bank in U.S. history. The bank carried out regular commercial functions, and also acted as a collecting and disbursing agent for the federal government. Under Biddle's guidance, the bank expanded to twenty-nine branches and controlled one-fifth of the country's loans and bank notes in circulation.

Biddle was a brilliant administrator who maintained complete control over the Bank of the United States. His political instincts, however, were less astute: He believed that any reasonable person must agree with him on the value of the bank to the nation's economy. His hard—headed convictions proved disastrous for the bank.

By 1828 the central bank was under attack from President Andrew Jackson (1829–1837) whose personal experience had given him a deep mistrust of financial institutions. Uncertain of the bank's future, Biddle decided to press for re-chartering the bank in 1832, four years before the bank's original charter required the action. Jackson vetoed the move, publicly denouncing the bank as a monopoly that was under foreign influence. Though the reputation of the bank had improved under Biddle's leadership, public opinion favored Jackson's position.

Bolstered by his supporters, Jackson resolved to destroy the bank. He directed the removal of almost $10 million in government deposits, which were placed in state or ''pet banks.'' Biddle responded by curtailing loans. Though the move may have been necessary to protect the bank, the restriction of credit dealt a serious blow to the US economy. Bankruptcies multiplied while wages and prices declined. These hardships turned people against the bank.

The bank's federal charter was terminated in 1836, but it was granted a state charter to operate as the Bank of the United States of Pennsylvania. The frenzied speculation that followed the loss of stability that the central bank had provided the Panic of 1837. Biddle, however, was still the most prominent banker in the country. As President of the Bank of the United States of Pennsylvania, Biddle played an important role in trying to shore up the nation's banking system. He also intervened heavily in the cotton market to prevent its collapse.

With order seemingly restored, Biddle resigned his position in March 1839. The bank continued to operate, but due to falling cotton prices and mismanagement by the bank's directors, its plight grew steadily worse. The bank collapsed in February 1841, taking Biddle's personal fortune with it. During his final years, Biddle faced many lawsuits. Although arrested on charges of criminal conspiracy in 1842, he was exonerated. Legal problems continued to pursue him until his death in 1844.

See also: **Bank of the United States (First National Bank), Bank of the United States (Second National Bank), Bank War, Central Bank, Andrew Jackson, Panic of 1837**

FURTHER READING

Govan, Thomas Payne. *Nicholas Biddle: Nationalist and Public Banker, 1786–1844*. Chicago: University of Chicago Press, 1959.

Hammond, Bray. *Banks and Politics in America from the Revolution to the Civil War*. Princeton, New Jersey: Princeton University Press, 1957.

McFaul, John M. *The Politics of Jacksonian Finance*. Ithaca, New York: W.W. Norton and Co., 1968.

Temin, Peter. *The Jacksonian Economy*. New York: W.W. Norton and Co., 1969.

Weisberger, Bernard A. "The bank war." *American Heritage*, July–August 1997.

Wilburn, Jean Alexander. *Biddle's Bank: The Crucial Years*. New York: Columbia University Press, 1967.

BIG STICK DIPLOMACY

"Speak softly and carry a big stick—you will go far." With these words President Theodore Roosevelt (1901–1909) described his approach to foreign policy.

The press characterized Roosevelt as a menacing ogre brandishing a club as his aggressive policies bullied smaller nations into conforming to U.S. desires. Indeed, the "big stick" was a sizable naval force (the "white fleet") sent on a world tour by Roosevelt to display the controlled might of the United States. One important consideration of U.S. policy makers was the sugar market. At the time Europe was the global leader in sugar production. The United States saw an opportunity to promote American economic interests in this market through Cuba's sugar production.

A second issue involved Venezuela and Santo Domingo (now known as the Dominican Republic). These two countries had incurred debts to several European countries—debts that they could not pay. In December 1902, British and German ships blockaded Venezuelan ports in an effort to force payment. Known as the Venezuela Affair, this action violated the cornerstone document of U.S. foreign policy—the Monroe Doctrine. Promulgated in 1823, the Monroe Doctrine warned European powers to stay clear of further involvement in the affairs of smaller nations in the Western Hemisphere. Though Roosevelt stepped in and settled the dispute without bloodshed, he realized that something more needed to be done to prevent such actions by Europe in the future. This led to the Roosevelt Corollary to the Monroe Doctrine.

The Roosevelt Corollary was published on December 6, 1904 as an amendment to the Monroe Doctrine. It stated that the United States may be forced "in flagrant cases of . . . wrongdoing or impotence, to the exercise of an international police power" in the Caribbean, Central America, or South America. Roosevelt clearly had the power at his command. In 1902 he had obtained congressional approval to strengthen the U.S. Navy with 10 new battleships and four cruisers. He reasoned that the expanded fleet would gain the United States greater clout in international affairs.

To maximize this clout, the fleet needed to be readily available in both the Atlantic and Pacific Oceans. Roosevelt opened negotiations with the Republic of Columbia to secure the right to build a canal across Panama. This canal could be used not only as a military passage, but also for commercial shipping, an important point to U.S. farmers, manufacturers, and shippers looking to expand their markets. However, the Colombian Senate rejected a treaty giving the U.S. a 99-year lease on a canal corridor across the Isthmus of Panama. Roosevelt defied the U.S. Congress and bent the rules of international law by backing a revolution in Panama. Panama seceded from Colombia, becoming the Republic of Panama. Within two weeks the United States had recognized the new "nation of Panama" and Panama had signed a treaty with the U.S. and a lease that allowed the construction of the Panama Canal.

Contemporary critics of Roosevelt's somewhat muscular policies denounced them as imperialist. Roosevelt did not flinch from the term. He rather reveled in the idea of an American empire. But, like the "dollar diplomacy" of his successor, William Howard Taft, Teddy Roosevelt was not anxious to administer a traditional European-style empire. Administering the Philippines—a task left over from the Spanish-American War—was more than enough trouble. For Roosevelt, it was a matter that the small nations of the Western Hemisphere engaged in international trade should pay their bills so that the U.S. might avoid going to war with a European creditor nation over violation of the Monroe Doctrine. Roosevelt's own words seem to confirm this: "No independent nation in [Latin] America need have fear of aggression from the United States. It behooves each one to maintain order within its own borders. When this is done, they can rest assured that, they have nothing to dread from outside interference." And in his own, less formal style Roosevelt had this to say about U.S. interest in the Dominican Republic: "I have about as much desire to annex it as a gorged boa constrictor might have to swallow a porcupine wrong-end-to."

Big Stick Diplomacy continued to be a dominant aspect of U.S. foreign policy through the 1980s. From President Woodrow Wilson's (1913–1921) intervention in the Mexican Revolution to the U.S. funding of the anti-Communist Contra guerillas in Nicaragua, the United States continues to employ impressive military strength and covert action in its Caribbean sphere of influence.

See also: **Dollar Diplomacy, Imperialism, Monroe Doctrine, Panama Canal Treaty**

FURTHER READING

Grant, George E. *Carry a Big Stick: The Uncommon Heroism of Theodore Roosevelt.* Nashville, TN: Cumberland House, 1997.

Collin, Richard H. "Symbiosis versus Hegemony: New Directions in the Foreign Relations Historiography of Theodore Roosevelt and William Howard Taft." *Diplomatic History*, vol. 19, Number 3, 1995.

"Big Stick Diplomacy Can Work," [cited March 12, 1999] available from the World Wide Web @ cynews.com/October/14/editoria1014.htm/.

"Teddy-the bear in the bully pulpit: Theodore Roosevelt Could Be Brash and Outrageous, But He Shaped the Modern Presidency," [cited March 12, 1999] available from the World Wide Web @ web4.iac-insite.com/.

The World Book Multimedia Encyclopedia. Chicago: World Book, Incorporated, 1998, s.v. "Roosevelt, Theodore."

BIRDS OF PASSAGE

Between 1881 and 1920 a wave of immigration brought more than 23 million new arrivals to the United States. They were largely from eastern and southern Europe. But not all of them planned to stay. "Birds of passage," also known as round-trippers, were usually young male immigrants who intended to make money in the United States and then return to their native countries. After leaving their families behind they traveled to the United States in search of employment, most often during the summer. They were usually hired to work on farms, in mines, and in construction. If work was scarce (as it was following the Panic of 1907) the temporary immigrants often lacked money to pay for the return trip. If work was plentiful the young migrant workers chose to settle in the United States. They became naturalized citizens and brought their families over from their home country. Between 1908 and 1914 U.S. immigration recorded nearly seven million new arrivals and just over two million departures. Many of the two million who departed were considered birds of passage.

See also: **Immigration**

BLACK & DECKER CORPORATION

Under its original name—the Black & Decker Manufacturing Company—the Black & Decker Corporation was founded in September 1910 when S. Duncan Black and Alonzo G. Decker joined forces to set up a machine shop in a rented warehouse in Baltimore, Maryland. After several years of contract manufacturing such products as a milk bottle cap machine and a cotton picker, Black and Decker began to design and manufacture their own electric powered tools in 1916. Black and Decker designed a universal motor—the first for electric tool use—which used either alternating or direct current, and also a trigger switch modeled after the mechanism in the Colt revolver. The first tool incorporating these innovative elements was a 1/2–inch portable drill with the innovative ''pistol grip and trigger switch'' that have remained standard for electric drills ever since.

In 1917 the company was awarded patents for its pistol grip and trigger switch and it constructed a factory on the outskirts of Towson, Maryland. By 1918 sales surpassed $1 million. Immediately after World War I (1914–1918), additional portable electric tools were introduced, including a 3/8–inch drill, a grinder, and a screwdriver.

Black & Decker used aggressive salesmanship and product services to build its client base. The company's first service centers were opened in Boston and New York in 1918. Black & Decker also organized clinics to teach distributors how to use and sell the tools. The firm began its first mass media campaign in the *Saturday Evening Post* in 1921.

Despite significant layoffs, Black & Decker nearly went bankrupt during the Great Depression. Only loyal employees, some of whom worked without pay, and a large influx of capital from outside investors kept the company afloat. During World War II (1939–1945) Black & Decker switched to the production of fuses, shells, and other products that contributed to the war effort.

After World War II Black & Decker became very successful. The company founders, who led Black & Decker into the 1950s, anticipated the postwar economic boom and targeted the consumer market, then a largely unexplored niche. In 1946 Black & Decker introduced the world's first power tools for the consumer market: the inexpensive Home Utility line of 1/4–inch and 1/2–inch drills and accessories. In the first five years one million 1/4–inch drills were produced. This success led to the addition of other products to the Home Utility line. A set of circular saws was introduced in 1949, and a finishing sander and jigsaw in 1953. It was through these and other new products that Black & Decker established itself as the firm most responsible for the creation of the post-World War II consumer market for power tools.

During the 1960s and 1970s Black & Decker diversified its product line. Through the 1960 acquisition of DeWalt, the company added radial arm saws and other woodworking equipment. Black & Decker entered the lawn and garden care field in the late 1950s, with the debut of electric lawn edgers and hedge trimmers in 1957. The first electric lawn mowers were unveiled in 1966, while a cordless model went into production three years later. In 1973 the Workmate portable worktable and accessories were first marketed

in England, and they soon proved very successful around the world.

By the early 1980s the firm's future looked dim in the face of growing competition from Japanese and German toolmakers offering lower-priced, high quality tools. Black & Decker responded in part by diversifying still further into the area of small household appliances. The company had already achieved an immediate success in this area through the 1978 introduction of the Dustbuster cordless vacuum cleaner. It was the 1984 acquisition of the small appliance operations of General Electric, however, that placed Black & Decker squarely in this new market niche. Through this purchase Black & Decker gained the largest U.S. producer of irons, toaster ovens, portable mixers, coffeemakers, and hairdryers. This line of small appliances was subsequently expanded to include the Spacemaker series of under-the-cabinet kitchen appliances and additional cordless appliances, including a mixer and an electric knife. To help emphasize its transformation, the company in 1985 revamped its hexagonal trademark and changed its name to the Black & Decker Corporation. The change was meant to help the marketing and sales side of the company.

In 1989 Black & Decker expanded still further through the $2.7 billion acquisition of Emhart Corporation, a conglomerate that included True Temper lawn and garden tools, Kwikset locks, GardenAmerica sprinkler systems, Price Pfister faucets, and various fastening systems. In 1992 Black & Decker relaunched the DeWalt brand as a line of professional power tools. The company was now able to offer the low-end Black & Decker line of power tools aimed at do-it-yourselfers and the high-end DeWalt line aimed at professional contractors. This strategy was immensely successful and the company's share of the domestic professional power tool market increased from eight percent in 1991 to more than 40 percent in 1995.

With the DeWalt line proving so successful, Black & Decker again decided to emphasize power tools, and in 1998 it sold the bulk of its household appliance operations. At the turn of the twenty-first century, Black & Decker continues to be one of the world's leading producers of power tools, electric lawn and garden tools, and building products.

FURTHER READING

''A.G. Decker of Black & Decker,'' *Nation's Business,* December, 1969.

Barrett, Amy. ''Home Improvement at Black & Decker.'' *Business Week,* May 11, 1998.

Black & Decker Corporation. *Highlights of Progress.* Towson, MD: Black & Decker Corporation, 1987.

Huey, John. "The New Power in Black and Decker." *Fortune*, January 2, 1989.

Saporito, Bill. "Ganging Up on Black & Decker." *Fortune*, December 23, 1985.

Schifrin, Matthew. "Cut–and–Build Archibald." *Forbes*, September 23, 1996.

Weber, Joseph, and Brian Bremner. "The Screws Are Tightening at Black & Decker." *Business Week*, September 23, 1991.

BLACK CODES

Black codes were state laws passed in the South during Reconstruction (1865–1877), the period of rebuilding that followed the American Civil War (1861–1865). The laws were intended to restrict the civil rights of African Americans. Though they varied by state the codes were usually written to prevent land ownership by African Americans and limit their freedom of movement. Some prevented them from owning weapons. The enactment of the codes prompted the U.S. Congress to pass the Civil Rights Acts of 1866 and 1875 to protect African American citizens in the South. President Andrew Johnson (1865–1869) opposed the 1866 measure enacted during his administration. However, the radical Republican-led Congress was able to overturn presidential vetoes to determine Reconstruction policy. Under the watchful eye of Congress and federal military administrators who were sent to the South to reorganize the states for readmission to the Union, two African American men, Hiram Rhoades Revels (1822–1901) and Blanche Kelso Bruce (1841–1898), became U.S. senators. Fifteen other African Americans were elected to the U.S. House of Representatives.

But after the withdrawal of federal troops from the South (1877) racial discrimination intensified despite ratification of the Fourteenth Amendment (1868). The amendment protected the rights of all citizens regardless of race. Black codes were strengthened by Supreme Court decisions in the 1880s and 1890s. One of these was *Plessy vs. Ferguson* (1896), which upheld the constitutionality of a Louisiana law requiring separate-but-equal facilities for whites and blacks in railroad cars. Such policies of strict segregation were called "Jim Crow laws": Jim Crow was the stereotype of a black man described in a nineteenth century song-and-dance act. As the social, political, and economic climate in the South worsened for African Americans many of them migrated north to urban centers. Some of them went west to settle towns and establish farms on the open plains. African American farmers joined the Populist (People's party) movement during the late 1800s, which worked to improve conditions for growers and laborers. The system of segregation born out of the Black Codes prevailed until the mid-1900s. Most segregation laws were overturned by decisions of the Supreme Court during the Civil Rights Movement of the 1950s and 1960s.

See also: **Civil Rights Acts of 1866 and 1875, Jim Crow Laws, Nineteenth Amendment, Plessy v. Ferguson, Reconstruction, Thirteenth Amendment**

BLACK GOLD

Black gold is an informal term for oil or petroleum—black because of its appearance when it comes out of the ground, and gold because it made everyone involved in the oil industry rich. The oil industry in the United States began in 1859 when retired railroad conductor Edwin L. Drake (1819–1880) drilled a well near Titusville, Pennsylvania. His drill was powered by an old steam engine. Oil from animal tallow and whales were used as lubricants since colonial times. A process for deriving kerosene from coal oil was not patented until 1854. (Kerosene is a clean-burning and easy-lighting fuel.)

After Drake's Titusville well produced shale oil the substance was analyzed for its properties and it was determined to be an excellent source of kerosene. Soon others began prospecting for "rock oil" and western Pennsylvania became an important oil-producing region. Wagons and river barges transported barrels to market, though later the railroad reached into the region and, by 1875, a pipeline was built to carry the oil directly to Pittsburgh. Petroleum soon replaced whale oil as a fluid for illumination. During the 1880s the states of Ohio, Kentucky, Illinois, and Indiana also produced oil. In 1901 the famous Spindletop field in eastern Texas provided the nation's first "gusher" (a site where oil literally shoots out of the earth.) During the next decade California and Oklahoma joined Texas as leaders of the nation's oil industry. U.S. oil production boomed: while only 2000 barrels of oil were produced in 1859, more than 64 million barrels were produced annually by the turn of the century.

The second half of the 1800s saw an increase in the use of oil. The fuel was being used for lighting, heating, and lubrication (principally of machinery and tools). The advent of the automobile with its central role in the life of the twentieth-century United States made the oil industry even richer. Demand soon exceeded the nation's supply of petroleum, prompting the United States to increasingly rely on imported oil for fuel.

See also: **Andrew Mellon, Kerosene, Petroleum Industry**

BLACK HAWK WAR (1832)

The Black Hawk War—named after the Indian leader Black Hawk (1767–1838)—was the last of the Indian wars that took place in the Old Northwest Territory, north of the Ohio and east of the Mississippi rivers. The conflict completed the grab for Indian territory that started before the American Revolution (1775–1783), continued through the Indian wars of the 1790s, and reached a peak just after the War of 1812 (1812–14). Black Hawk's struggle to keep the last traces of Sac and Fox lands in what is now western Illinois led directly to the forced expulsion of his group of Native Americans from their traditional territory.

Black Hawk had a history of grievances with white Americans dating back over a quarter of a century. In 1804 he had signed a treaty that—he thought—conveyed only some hunting rights in Sac and Fox lands to white Americans. When he found that he had in fact ceded some 50 million acres to the U.S. government, Black Hawk joined the Shawnee leader Tecumseh and the British in opposing American expansion during the War of 1812.

After the war Black Hawk returned to his homeland, but he was confronted with increasing numbers of white settlers. In 1829 one family entered his home when he was away on a hunting trip and dispossessed him. Protests to U.S. Indian agents only resulted in suggestions that he and his supporters (known as the ''British Band'' of Sac and Fox) find new lands west of the Mississippi River. He was also informed by the General Land Office that his homelands were to be opened to white settlement. Black Hawk responded by dividing his time between summer camps in his homeland and winter camps, in what is now Iowa, west of the Mississippi.

The outbreak of the Black Hawk War had less to do with direct disagreements between the Native American leader and white Americans than it did with internal politics among the Sac and Fox themselves. Black Hawk's opposition to the U.S. government was countered by another Sac and Fox chief called Keokuk. Keokuk favored negotiations with the government. During 1831–32 he ceded the Rock River country in

what is now northwestern Illinois—the heart of Sac and Fox territory—to the Americans in exchange for an annuity and promises of lands west of the Mississippi. When Black Hawk and the British Band of Sac and Fox rejected the agreement and crossed the Mississippi in April of 1832—accompanied by a scattering of Winnebagos and Potawatomis. It was Keokuk who warned the whites of Blackhawk's approach.

General Henry Atkinson appealed to Illinois governor John Reynolds to raise 3,000 militiamen to augment his small force of 220 regular soldiers. Reynolds, however, was only able to pull together about 1,700 raw, untrained troops, including a young Abraham Lincoln. On April 28, 1832, Atkinson and his men set off in pursuit of Black Hawk and the British Band. Major Isaac Stillman's militia unit caught up with them on May 14 at the mouth of the Kyte River. Black Hawk had discovered that neither the Potawatomis nor the Winnebagos were willing to support him against the soldiers and had decided to surrender. The militia, which had been drinking heavily, panicked at the sight of Black Hawk's emissaries and fired on them, killing two. With only 40 warriors to call upon, Black Hawk set up an ambush and, in a battle known as Stillman's Run, routed Major Stillman's force of 275 men.

The comparatively easy defeat of the militia emboldened Blackhawk and his followers. On May 20 a group made up mostly of Black Hawk's Potawatomi supporters attacked a farmstead at Indian Creek, killed 15 men, women, and children, and kidnapped two girls (who were later ransomed). The Indian Creek Massacre roused the frontier. By mid-June Atkinson had the 3,000 militia he had originally wanted, plus 400 regular soldiers. President Andrew Jackson (1828–36) ordered Major General Winfield Scott to gather 800 soldiers at Chicago and move west in support of Atkinson. Lieutenant James W. Kingsbury, commanding the steamboat *Warrior*, was also ordered to proceed up the Mississippi to cut off Black Hawk from possible escape to the West.

I TOUCHED THE GOOSE QUILL TO THE TREATY . . . NOT KNOWING, HOWEVER, THAT BY THAT ACT I CONSENTED TO GIVE AWAY MY VILLAGE.

Black Hawk, Sac Indian leader, 1831

By August 1, 1832, Black Hawk had abandoned any hope of regaining his homelands. His followers were trying to cross the Mississippi River in handmade canoes or rafts when the *Warrior* found them and, after negotiations failed, fired on them. Two days later the militia units under Colonel Henry Dodge and Atkinson arrived and captured or killed many of the remaining Sacs and Foxes. Those who escaped across the Mississippi—about 200—were captured by Sioux who were allied with the U.S. government. Black Hawk himself was turned over to the Americans by the Winnebagos, among whom he had sought refuge.

On September 19, 1832, General Scott brought the Black Hawk War to an end by concluding a treaty with the remaining Sacs and Foxes. The treaty ceded to the U.S. government a strip of Sac and Fox land running along the western bank of the Mississippi River—almost the entire length of Iowa's Mississippi riverbank—and reaching 50 miles inland. The territory, comprising a total of about six million acres, was to be vacated entirely by the Sacs and Foxes by June 1, 1833. The U.S. government paid $660,000 for this concession.

See also: **Andrew Jackson, Tecumseh, War of 1812**

FURTHER READING

Black Hawk. *Black Hawk: An Autobiography*. Edited by Donald Jackson. Urbana, IL: University of Illinois Press, 1955.

Eby, Cecil D. *"That Disgraceful Affair:" The Black Hawk War*. New York: W. W. Norton, 1973.

Gurko, Miriam. *Indian America: The Black Hawk War*. New York: Crowell, 1970.

Hagan, William T. *The Sac and the Fox Indians*. Norman, OK: University of Oklahoma Press, 1958.

Weeks, Philip. *Farewell, My Nation: The American Indian and the United States, 1820–1890*. Arlington Heights, IL: H. Davidson, 1990.

BLACK MARKET

The "black market" refers to the persistence of economic activity outside the bounds of the legitimate economy. Since colonial days there has always been a stratum of society that resisted being drawn into the formal market economy. The earliest black market involved virtually the entire existence of runaways—the enslaved American Indians, abused indentured servants, and newly arrived African slaves—who sometimes escaped into the backwoods and reverted to a life of hunting and gathering or subsistence farming. During the "market revolution" of the early 1800s when ordinary settlers began using currency within the broad social division of labor, there were whole families that picked up and moved with the frontier—they trapped, shot, fished or otherwise raised their own food and made their own clothes.

The reasons that they avoided being drawn into mainstream American economy were various. Some faded into the woods to avoid serving out the terms of their indenture or to escape enslavement; some feared being conscripted into the army; others objected to paying taxes or having anything at all to do with the economic elite of the country or its institutions. Some, no doubt, just reveled in the bounty of the land and in the life of independence.

But remaining outside the market was sometimes ruled illegal. One example was the "Proclamation of 1763," in which the British government ruled that colonial whites could not move west of the Appalachian watershed. The motive for this was to prevent hostile encounters with the Native Americans and to integrate the European population into a colonial workforce. But the proclamation was a futile gesture: with no one to stop them the settlers kept coming over the mountains at the Cumberland Gap or at other crossings and they spread out into the Ohio basin.

Even after the War of Independence, the government of the United States tried to corral this population. In 1794 the "Whiskey Rebellion" in western Pennsylvania broke out over the government's attempt to tax corn whiskey. For a few months the rebels terrorized the "revenuers," or tax collectors. The rebellion was put down in the summer of 1794 with an extraordinary display of force, when President Washington and Alexander Hamilton (who, as secretary of the treasury, had recommended the tax in 1791) raised an army of 12,900 militia men, marched across Pennsylvania and dispersed the rebels.

This episode illustrates the relationship between the black market and the mainstream American economy. By refusing to pay the tax on liquor, the farmers were defending the black market, or the "informal economy," of barter and pseudo currency. The black market services social needs that the legal market cannot meet. Every time that the government passes laws making ordinary activity illegal, the boundaries of the "black market" expand to include this illegal activity. This happened in the 1920s when the 18th amendment to the Constitution ruled alcohol illegal. In more recent decades the same story has been repeated in the case of marijuana cultivation or the smuggling of cigarettes.

See also: **Illegal Drugs, Prohibition, Whiskey Rebellion**

FURTHER READING

Nash, Gary B. *Red, White, and Black: the People of Early America*. Englewood Cliffs, N. J.: Prentice Hall, 1982.

Sellers, Charles. *The Market Revolution: Jacksonian America, 1815–1846*. New York: Oxford University Press, 1991.

Tindall, George Brown and David E. Shi. *America: A Narrative History*. New York: Norton, 1999.

BLACKWELL, HENRY BROWN

Henry Brown Blackwell (1825–1909) was an English immigrant who became an activist for many reform issues in the United States including the anti-slavery movement. He is best known as an advocate for women's suffrage and was married to feminist Lucy Stone (1818–1893). Together the couple founded a women's suffrage organization and a women's journal.

Henry Brown Blackwell was born May 4, 1825 in Bristol, England. He was the second of five children born to Samuel and Hannah Blackwell. His father was a successful businessman in the sugar refinery industry and a community activist. Samuel Blackwell taught his children to treat people equally, regardless of race, sex, or social class. Through his examples he also taught his children to act on their beliefs.

The Blackwells emigrated to the United States in 1832 after an accidental fire destroyed the family business in England. Henry Blackwell was seven years old when the family moved to the United States, and he spent his childhood years in New York. The family became actively involved in the anti-slavery movement, and their Long Island home often served as a refuge for persecuted abolitionists. Financially the Blackwells were not as successful in the United States as they had been in England. Their sugar business struggled until the financial panic of 1837 destroyed it completely. In the same year the family moved to Cincinnati, Ohio for a fresh start. Soon after the move Samuel Blackwell died, plunging the family into a financial crisis.

In response to the poor financial situation, the Blackwell women opened a day school for girls, and Henry Blackwell and his brother found office jobs. A few years later, the boys opened their own hardware business. During this time Henry Blackwell continued to be involved in the anti-slavery movement in Ohio and became interested in other humanitarian movements. While watching his older sister Elizabeth struggle to become the first female doctor in the United States, Blackwell took an interest in the women's suffrage movement. In 1853 he made his first public speech in support of women's suffrage at a convention in Cleveland, Ohio. Later that same year he attended a legislative meeting in Massachusetts, where Lucy Stone, an ardent feminist, spoke in support of a women's suffrage petition.

After that first meeting, Blackwell began to court Stone. He promised her he would devote himself to the suffrage movement and after a two-year courtship, the two activists married. On their wedding day the couple signed a pact of equality, agreeing, among other things, that Stone would keep her maiden name. The couple also made a public statement against the inequalities of marriage law at that time, especially with respect to property rights for married women.

Soon after their marriage Blackwell and Stone moved to New Jersey, where Blackwell started a book-selling business. He also had some business interests in real estate and sugar refinery and was able to make money with each venture. The couple then moved to Boston, Massachuetts, where they helped organize the American Women's Suffrage Association in 1869. The organization was devoted to promoting women's rights at the state, rather than the federal, level. Because of his earlier business successes, Blackwell was financially secure and able to devote much of his time to this cause. In 1896 he spoke before the United States House of Representatives on behalf of the American Women's Suffrage Association stating that: ''It is as much for the interest of men as women, as much the duty of men as women to advocate [the women's suffrage] cause.''

A year later Blackwell and Stone started their next venture together. In 1870 the couple founded the *Woman's Journal* in Boston, a magazine devoted primarily to professional women. Blackwell financed most of the project and jointly edited the weekly magazine with his wife. When Stone died in 1893 Blackwell continued to edit the journal with their daughter, Alice Stone Blackwell.

While the women's movement occupied much of Blackwell's life, he was actively involved in other causes as well. For example Blackwell publicly opposed the deportation of political refugees, the Armenian massacres of 1895, and the Russian pogroms. Blackwell died in Boston on September 7, 1909, eleven years before women were granted suffrage in the United States.

See also: **Women's Movement**

FURTHER READING

Ashby, Ruth, and Doborah Gore Ohrn, eds. *Herstory: Women Who Changed the World.* New York: Viking Childrens' Books, 1995.

Blackwell, Alice Stone. *Growing Up in Boston's Gilded Age: The Journal of Alice Stone Blackwell, 1972–1874.* New Haven, CT: Yale University Press, 1990.

Jolliffe, Lee. "Women's Magazines in the 19th Century." *Journal of Popular Culture*, 27 (Spring 1994): 125-140.

Stone, Lucy. *Loving Warriors: Selected Letters of Lucy Stone and Henry B. Blackwell, 1853 to 1893.* New York: Dial Press, 1981.

"The National American Women's Suffrage Association Collection, 1848–1921," [cited July 5, 1999] available from the World Wide Web @ rs6.loc.gov/ammem/ndlpedu/naw/nawintro.html.

BLAND-ALLISON ACT

The Bland-Allison Act was a piece of legislation passed by the U.S. Congress in 1878, which required the U.S. Treasury to buy silver bullion and to mint $2 to $4 million worth of silver coin per month. The bill was introduced by Representative Richard Bland (1835–1899) of Missouri and was amended by Representative William Allison (1829–1908) of Iowa. Their constituents included many farmers who preferred the government to mint the coins. The U.S. economy went through a depression during the 1870s. While some clamored for the government to alleviate the situation by printing more greenbacks (paper currency issued to finance the Civil War), others advocated the coinage of silver. President Rutherford B. Hayes (1877–1881) vetoed the Bland-Allison Act. He feared that the re-monetarization of silver would cause inflation because U.S. currency had been based on the gold standard since 1874. But Congress was able to muster enough votes to overturn the veto and pass the bill into law. Under the act silver coins were minted on a standard of 16 ounces of silver per one ounce of gold.

In January 1879 the U.S. Treasury began paying gold for greenbacks; as a result the coinage of silver (which never exceeded $2 million per month) only had a mild inflationary effect. The Free Silver forces in the West advocated an unlimited coinage of silver versus the $2 to $4 million provided for in the legislation. On the other hand the gold standard forces called for an abandonment of silver coinage altogether. Both of them tried to replace the Bland-Allison Act. The Free Silver alliance won the day: In 1890 Congress repealed the Bland-Allison Act. It passed the Sherman Silver Purchase Act, doubling government purchase of silver to increase the money in circulation. The resumption of silver as a monetary standard had increased the activities of silver prospectors in the West. Mines began overproducing silver, causing prices to collapse. People in the United States responded by trading their silver dollars for gold dollars, draining federal reserves. In 1893 the Sherman Silver Purchase Act was repealed and the United States returned to the gold standard, which it retained until April 1933.

See also: **Cross of Gold Speech, Free Silver, Gold Standard, Sherman Silver Purchase Act**

BLEEDING KANSAS

"Bleeding Kansas" describes a conflict over slavery in the state of Kansas during the 1850s, immediately preceding the American Civil War (1861–65). The Kansas-Nebraska Act of 1854 created two new territories (Kansas and Nebraska). The U.S. Congress ruled that the question of slavery in each should be decided by popular sovereignty. Nebraska's population primarily consisted of people opposed to slavery, but settlers from both the North and the South settled Kansas. The territory became the scene of a showdown between the Free State advocates (who formed the Free State party to oppose slavery) and the pro-slavery contingent.

In 1855 territorial elections were held, and the vote was swung to the pro-slavery side. This was partly due to Missourians who crossed the border and cast votes in the neighboring territory. Slavery supporters soon dominated the Kansas legislature and passed laws favorable to their own interests. Tensions were heightened and violence broke out between the two sides. Most of the conflicts clustered around the border with Missouri, a state where slavery was legal. In one incident on May 24, 1856 ardent abolitionist John Brown (1800–1859) led an attack in which five pro-slavery men were brutally murdered in their sleep. The act was carried out in retribution for earlier killings of freemen at Lawrence, Kansas. Brown claimed his was a mission from God. Newspapers dubbed the series of violent conflicts "Bleeding Kansas," after they claimed more than 50 lives. The situation proved that the doctrine of popular sovereignty would not solve the nation's deep ideological differences.

In Kansas the Free State party eventually regained control of the territorial government and wrote a constitution abolishing slavery. Kansas was admitted to the Union as a free state on January 29, 1861. By that time the states of South Carolina, Mississippi, Florida, Alabama, Georgia, and Louisiana had already seceded from the Union.

See also: **Kansas, Slavery**

BLOCKADE

Blockades were a specific kind of warfare in which one country attempted to reduce its opponent's economic ability to wage war by cutting its ports off from seagoing trade with other nations. Historically, nations at war have used either close blockades or long-range blockades to stifle their enemy's trade. In close blockades, ships were stationed within miles of the enemy's port, forming an impregnable ring through which no trading ship could pass unseen. If that kind of blockade was impractical, however, the blockading ships could be positioned far off of the coast, or along the entire coastline—safe from enemy interference but still close enough to stop blockade-running vessels.

Over time international laws and treaties were developed to govern the use of blockades. For example under the Declaration of London of 1909, any neutral country that traded with the enemy of a blockading country had to be officially notified in advance that its ships would be stopped if they tried to run the blockade. Similarly, blockades had to be applied equally to the vessels of all countries, and blockades could only be established at ports occupied by the blockading country's enemy—a neutral country's port could not be blockaded.

Because seagoing trade with other countries had always played a major role in the U.S. economy, blockades had been a common feature of its history. During the War of 1812 (1812–1814) the United States was the victim of a very effective British blockade that almost totally stifled U.S. trade with neutral countries. During the American Civil War (1861–1865), the North implemented an effective if costly blockade of 3,500 miles along the Confederate coast. By the war's end the blockade had closed off every Southern port except for the one at Galveston, Texas.

The invention of submarines, airplanes, and missiles made it virtually impossible for any nation to maintain a traditional close blockade of an enemy's port. In the twentieth century, blockades took a more informal form, such as Germany's loose submarine blockade of Great Britain in World War I (1914–1918). The blockade became particularly important to the United States when a German submarine sank the passenger ship *Lusitania* in 1915. One hundred and twenty-eight U.S. citizens were killed, and the United States moved a significant step closer to entering the war against Germany. Later on, President John Kennedy (1961–63) initiated a successful blockade of Cuba. During the height of the Cold War in 1962, he ordered the U.S. Navy to prevent Soviet ships from delivering to Cuba nuclear missiles that were to be pointed at U.S. cities.

BOEING COMPANY

The Boeing Company is a manufacturer of commercial jetliners and military aircraft, and one of the largest aerospace companies in the world. Its primary competitors are: Airbus; Bombardier; Daimler-Benz; Lockheed Martin; Raytheon; Rockwell International, and Thiokol.

Boeing has been the leading aircraft manufacturer in the world for 30 consecutive years. The company's primary businesses are commercial aircraft construction, defense and space, and computer services. The company successfully juggled the continuing need for commercial passenger airliners with its defense contracts, which account for an estimated 30 percent of its business as a result of the company's merger with McDonnell Douglas in 1997. Boeing works with companies such as Lockheed Martin, Sikorsky, and Bell Helicopter Textron, and is the leading contractor for NASA.

The idea for The Boeing Company was born on a lake in Seattle on July 4, 1914, when William E. Boeing, a lumber company executive from Michigan, took a ride on a Curtiss seaplane with a barnstormer named Terah Maroney. His friend, Navy Commander Conrad Westervelt, also came along. Neither man knew anything about aircraft design, but both were fascinated with airplanes. Boeing asked Westervelt to design a plane, which Boeing would build. The result was Model 1, the B&W, a utility airplane, which they named after themselves. It was 27 feet 6 inches long. The fuselage was built in a hanger on Seattle's Lake Union. The wings and floats were produced at the Heath Shipyard on Puget Sound's Elliot Bay, which was owned by Boeing to service his yacht. Finally, on July 15, 1916, Boeing tested his aircraft and incorporated his company as the Pacific Aero Products Company.

The popular commercial airliner, the Boeing 747 jumbo jet.

The New Zealand government, the company's first customer, bought the plane for mail delivery and pilot training.

Renamed The Boeing Airplane Company in April, 1917, it built Curtiss HS-2L flying boats for the Navy in World War I (1914–1918). After the war ended, the Navy canceled half of its order and Boeing returned to making furniture and cabinets to keep the company afloat. Contracts with the Navy to rebuild the De Havilland DH-4 aircraft and with the army to build a new army designed plane kept the company in business. By 1922 Boeing had successfully negotiated a number of contracts with the military, and the company was financially solvent.

Between world wars, the company embarked on air mail service. When Congress forced the Post Office to pay private companies to fly mail between distant cities, commercial aviation was born. Boeing with his new partner, Edward Hubbard, created Boeing Air Transport Company and got the contract to carry mail between Chicago and San Francisco. Boeing Air Transport Company also established the first international airmail route between Seattle and neighboring British Columbia. Boeing developed a new plane, Model 40, specifically for this market. It could carry four passengers and 1000 pounds of mail. The Kelly Airmail Act of 1925 resulted in the formation of a number of companies, which developed airmail routes. Boeing soon bought up a number of these small companies

which together formed the basis of the original United Airlines. Bill Boeing and Frederick Rentschler combined their businesses in 1929 into a firm called United Aircraft and Transport. The advent of regulations for airmail services led to the formation of United Airlines, and Boeing Airplane continued as an aircraft manufacturer.

Boeing and Rentschler formed a holding company called the Boeing Aircraft and Transportation Company and Bill Boeing engaged in some serious capital manipulation which made him at least \$12 million through stock flotation. Though this was legal, Boeing was incensed at being investigated by the U.S. government and sold all of his aviation stocks. In 1934 the Boeing Aircraft and Transportation Company was forced to break up by government regulation. Everything east of the Mississippi became United Aircraft and was run by Fred Rentschler. The Boeing Airplane Company remained in Seattle run by Phil Johnson and exclusively manufactured airplanes. United Airlines was based in Chicago at Old Orchard Airport (later O'Hare) and was run by Pat Patterson. Bill Boeing was never active in the aviation business again.

In the 1930's, Boeing developed single-wing airplanes constructed completely of metal, which made them stronger and faster. They also created more efficient aerodynamic designs as well as retractable landing gears and better wings, multiple power plant technology, and directional radios, which allowed for better navigation and night flying.

Boeing was well situated to become a major player in airplane production during World War II (1939–1945). Some of the most famous planes used during the war came from Boeing, including the B-17 ''Flying Fortress.'' Sixteen B-17's were turned out every 24 hours by June, 1944. The B-29 ''Super Fortress'' was also on line by 1944 and one nicknamed the *Enola Gay* dropped the atomic bombs on Hiroshima and Nagasaki in August, 1944. After the war Boeing produced a number of bombers, including the B-47, B-50, and the famous B-52.

Boeing, which changed its name to the Boeing Company in 1961, has also seen American consumers through the birth and adolescence of commercial passenger airline travel. The company built many of the most popular commercial airliners between 1935 and 1965 including the PanAm 314 Clipper, the 707, 727, 737, and the 747 Jumbo Jet. The 747 was so expensive to develop that it almost drove the company into bankruptcy. Boeing also brought the first pressurized cabin to market, the Model 307 Stratoliner. The jumbo jets reduced the cost of air travel and made it affordable for everyone. Jeans and sneakers replaced suits and furs and a new era had arrived.

Every American president from Franklin Delano Roosevelt (1933–1945) to Bill Clinton (1993—) flew in Boeing or Douglas airplanes. Roosevelt was the first when the Navy purchased a *Douglas Dolphin* flying yacht. A DC-54 Skymaster, a military version of the DC-4, replaced the Dolphin with the advent of World War II. Roosevelt, however, preferred to fly a Boeing 314 Clipper to Africa for a 1943 meeting with Allied leaders. Boeing 707's, also known as *Air Force One* when the President was on board, carried presidents from Dwight D. Eisenhower (1953–1961) to George Bush (1989–1993), until two Boeing 747-200's replaced them.

The downsizing and consolidation within the modern aircraft industry affected Boeing, which integrated competitor companies into its operations. Boeing and Rockwell completed a merger of their defense and aerospace units in 1996, and Boeing completed its merger with McDonnell Douglas Corporation on August 1, 1997.

Boeing experienced some difficulties getting approval from Europe on its merger with McDonnell Douglas. The European Union was concerned about Airbus Industrie, a French consortium and Boeing's only major competitor, and its continued viability if the merger went through. Boeing did finally get approval from the European Union Commission. However, the company had to sign nonexclusive contracts with any airlines for the next decade in order to do so.

The aircraft industry has been cyclical in nature from the beginning when Boeing had to return to the furniture business after World War 1 to keep afloat. In 1969, Boeing reduced its workforce from 105,000 to 38,000. Labor problems led to a strike that lasted 69 days in 1995, resulting in $2 billion in financial losses to the company as well as substantial trickle-down losses to the numerous subcontractors and communities in which Boeing operates. By the middle of 1999, however, Boeing was back on track and earnings were high again.

Boeing operated through four divisions in the 1990's. Boeing Commercial Airplane Company manufactured and sold civilian aircraft. Boeing Vertol Company produced helicopters for the military, including CH-46 and CH-47 (Chinook) helicopters. Boeing Aerospace developed space products as well as strategic and tactical missiles, including cruise missiles. Boeing Military Airplane Company manufactured bombers, tankers, and high-technology surveillance aircraft, including the 3-E Airborne Warning and Control System aircraft (AWACs).

From almost the very beginnings of the American space program, Boeing was there. Boeing's involvement began in earnest in 1960 when its Delta II rocket was launched, carrying the Echo 1A satellite into orbit. Then in 1966 and 1967, the Boeing-built Lunar Orbiters circled the moon, photographing the surface in order to help NASA choose a safe landing site for the Apollo 11 astronauts. The astronauts reached the moon with the help of the 363-foot-tall Saturn V rocket. Its development was integrated by Boeing, which also made the first stage booster. It was 138 feet high and had 7.5 million pounds of thrust; the equivalent of 130 of today's most powerful jet engines. The Saturn V was used 13 times and did not fail once.

Boeing not only helped the astronauts get to the moon, it also helped them get around once they got there. The Lunar Roving Vehicles, built by Boeing in only 17 months, were used on the last three Apollo missions. The rovers looked like modified dune buggies and enabled the astronauts to travel more than 20 miles from the landing site. The vehicles operated without a problem in temperatures that ranged from minus 200 to plus 200 Fahrenheit degrees. To this day the rovers are still parked on the lunar surface.

Boeing's involvement in the lunar missions might have been its most spectacular moment, yet it remains heavily involved in the space program to this day. It continues to launch Delta rockets, and it has a large role to play in the Space Shuttle operations. Boeing processes all space suits and equipment, and McDonnell Douglas, with which it merged in 1997, developed the aft propulsion pods and structural parts of the boosters used to get the shuttles into orbit In the late 1990's, Boeing began working in cooperation with sixteen countries as the main contractor on the International Space Station which is expected to be completed by 2004.

See also: **Airline Industry**

FURTHER READING

Banks, Howard. "Slow Learner." *Forbes*, May 1998.

"Boeing Corp. Moving Ahead and Flying High." *The Online Investor,* [cited August 4, 1997] Available on the World Wide Web @ www.investhelp.com/ba_spotlight.shtml/.

"Boeing Earnings Soar to $469 Million." *The Detroit News*, April 16, 1999.

"Common Heritage." The Boeing Company, 1999. Available from the World Wide Web @ www.boeing.com/companyoffices/history/.

Company Profile. Seattle, WA: The Boeing Company, 1995.

Hackney, Holt. "Boeing: Back on Course." *Financial World*, January 18, 1994.

Kepos, Paula. Ed. *International Directory of Company Histories*, vol. 10. New York: St. James Press, 1995, s.v. "Boeing Company."

Redding, Robert and Bill Yenne. *Boeing: Planemaker to the World.* Greenwich: Bison Books Corp., 1983.

BOLL WEEVIL INFESTATION

Boll weevils, small grey-brown beetles (about one-quarter inch, or six millimeters, long) feed off of the fibers in cotton seed pods (bolls). Female boll weevils lay their eggs inside cotton plant buds; once their larvae hatch, worm-like grubs are produced. The offspring consume the boll fibers, causing the bolls to fall off of the plants.

The beetles spread from Central America and Mexico to Texas in the 1890s, first arriving there in 1894. During the following decade they moved eastward into other cotton-growing areas of the United States, reaching the Atlantic coast by 1916. The infestation devastated cotton crops throughout the South.

By 1904, the boll weevil was costing Texas cotton farmers $50 million a year; after 1908, cotton farmers in Mississippi lost 75 percent of their crops. The destruction prompted some farmers to again diversify their crops, and encouraged the "Great Migration" (1915–29) of African Americans out of the South to the more industrialized cities of the North.

After the American Civil War (1861–65), cotton was the easiest crop to convert to cash; demand was so great that growers could readily sell their harvest at a fair to good price. With Southern farmers hungry for cash, too many growers began to rely solely on the cotton crop. Supply soon exceeded demand, prices dropped, and farmers lost money.

Responses to boll weevil infestation were varied. Some farmers began cultivating different plants, while others simply planted less cotton. Farmers spaced rows farther apart so that each plant got more direct sunlight; the additional heat killed developing weevils. Various forms of insecticides (including arsenic) were found to be effective in managing boll weevil infestation. During the 1920s, the cotton industry recovered but the recovery did not last long, as all farmers were severely affected by the Great Depression, the worldwide economic crisis of the 1930s.

See also: **Great Depression, Great Migration (1910–1920), King Cotton, Sharecropping**

BONANZA FARMS

Bonanza farms were large, extremely successful farms, principally on the Great Plains and in the West, that emerged during the second half of the 1800s. The term "bonanza," which is derived from Spanish and literally means "good weather," was coined in the mid-1800s; thus, "bonanza" came to mean a source of great and sudden wealth.

Large-scale bonanza farming was aided by the development of machinery that greatly increased production, especially of wheat and other grains. The innovations included reapers, invented by Cyrus Hall McCormick (1809–84) and Obed Hussey (1792–1860), and steel plows developed by John Deere (1804–86).

In particular, promotion of westward settlement in the nineteenth century furthered farming interests west of the Mississippi River. Congress passed the Homestead Act (1862), which allowed for ready and cheap acquisition of vast tracts of land. Settlers could buy land for as little as $1.25 per acre or they could live on a tract and farm it for a period of five years, at the end of which they were granted 160 acres (65 hectares). In

1872 the Northern Pacific Railroad was extended to Fargo, North Dakota, allowing farmers to ship their products greater distances. Another important agricultural innovation also contributed to development of large-scale farming. Dry farming techniques (in which fields lie fallow every other year in order to support future crops by regaining their nutrients and moisture) proved a successful method for growing in the Great Plains, which were previously thought to be too dry for cultivating crops.

Deliberate government promotion of westward expansion and advances in farming turned some western farms into ''bonanzas''—sources of great wealth for their owners. Encouraged by stories of success, settlers poured into the West. But not all farmers fared well, and many were severely hit by the Panic of 1873. In the 1880s a drought in the Plains states caused farm prices to drop, further hurting western farmers.

See also: **John Deere, Dry Farming, Homestead Act, McCormick Reaper, Panics of the Late Nineteenth Century**

BONDS

When a business or the government needs to raise a large amount of money for, say, corporate expansion or to build a new sports facility, it sells bonds to the public. A bond, then, is a financial instrument that represents a binding promise to pay the buyer of the bond the face or ''par'' value of the bond plus a definite rate of interest (known as the ''coupon'' rate) within a specific period of time (normally ten to thirty years). When a business or government issues a bond it is asking the public to lend it money, and in return for that loan it promises to pay bond holders interest, usually twice a year until the bond is paid back (known as reaching ''maturity''). While a stock represents a piece of actual ownership in the company that can grow or shrink as much as the company underlying it does, a bond is an obligation to pay back a finite loan that the bondholder made to the company when he or she bought the bond. Bonds are a cheaper way to raise money because they are tax deductible.

Bonds have always played a critical role in the U.S economy. Because it issued war bonds, for example, the U.S. government was able to retire its debt established during the American Revolution (1775–1783) by 1835. Local governments began issuing municipal bonds in the nineteenth century as U.S. communities built canals and public highways. By the end of the American Civil War (1861–1865), 75 percent of the

U.S. government's war debt was in the form of war bonds and similar instruments. A bull market in bonds lasted from the end of the Civil War until World War I (1914–1918), during which the government sold more than $21 billion in ''Liberty loans'' to U.S. citizens. This was the first time many Americans had ever owned paper securities (bonds or stocks), and it paved the way for a new group of middle-class investors who participated in the bull market of the 1920s. After the Japanese attacked Pearl Harbor in 1941, the U.S. Treasury quickly sold $2.5 billion in war bonds to U.S. citizens, and by 1944 alone it was selling $53 billion annually in war bonds. Both the government and corporate bond markets continued to grow and diversify after World War II (1939–1945), and today investors can own dozens of different bonds through bond mutual funds.

See also: **Bear and Bull Markets, Interest, Liberty Bonds, Stock**

BOONE, DANIEL

Few people reach legendary status in a society in their own lifetime. Daniel Boone (1734–1820) was one of them. In fact the legend of Daniel Boone has become difficult to separate from the real Daniel Boone. Many unauthorized biographies and books appeared trumpeting his accomplishments and promoting various causes and points of view. However, the truth about Boone is just as fascinating as the stories.

Daniel Boone was born on November 2, 1734, near what is known today as Reading, Pennsylvania. Boone was the sixth of eleven children. From their log cabin home his Quaker family ran a small farm, a blacksmith shop, and a weaving establishment. Daniel tended cows as a child and began hunting at the age of twelve. He had little formal schooling, but he did learn to read and write.

Boone excelled at skills required to survive in the woods. He developed a keen eye and an accurate shot with his long rifle, and with those skills he kept the family in meat. He traded animal skins for lead, gunpowder, salt, and other needed items. In 1750 the Boone family moved to North Carolina along the Yadkin River. In 1755 Boone volunteered to drive a supply wagon in a British military expedition to seize Fort Duquesne from the French. Another driver in the expedition was trader John Findley, who thrilled Boone with tales of a rich hunter's paradise beyond the Appalachian Mountains.

Daniel Boone.

The military expedition was cut short by a surprise attack of French and Indians and the British troops fled. Boone returned home to marry neighbor Rebecca Bryan. Rebecca had ten children with Daniel and followed him through all his moves and exploring, a true pioneer woman.

BOONE LIVED THE LIFE OF EXPLORER AND HUNTER—A LIFE EXTOLLED IN PRINT MANY TIMES WHILE BOONE WAS STILL ALIVE. OVER 175 YEARS AFTER HIS DEATH THE LEGEND HAS CONTINUED TO GROW.

Findley told Boone of the Cumberland Gap, a pass through the mountains, and of the Warriors' Path, a trail that led to Kentucky. Boone took his first trip through the Cumberland Gap in 1767 with his brother Squire and his friend William Hill. They reached what is now Floyd County in Kentucky before winter weather discouraged them. In the spring they returned home. A year later John Findley came to Boone and described a route to Kentucky along the Ohio River and the two made the journey in 1769. Boone's party was attacked by Indians and he was briefly captured. He spent two

years exploring Kentucky and hunting. Years later he was to say of Kentucky, ''I have never found but one Kentucky—a spot of earth where nature seems to have concentrated all her bounties.''

After his return to his family in North Carolina, Boone led a group of friends and family to Kentucky in 1773 with the intention of staying. Indians attacked settler groups. Boone's oldest son, James, was captured, tortured, and killed. Against Boone's desires, the entire party returned to North Carolina. In 1775 Boone helped Judge Richard Henderson buy a huge tract of land from the Cherokee Indians. Boone led a group of thirty woodsmen into the heart of Kentucky to connect Indian trails and buffalo paths and prepare the region for settlement. The paths were to be known as the Wilderness Road. Boone built a fort, called Boonesborough, at a site by the Kentucky River, just south of present-day Lexington. Boone's wife and daughter, whom Boone brought when the building was finished, were the first white women to see the heart of Kentucky.

Life in the wilderness was hard. Boone's daughter and two female friends were captured by Indians in 1776 and held for several days until Boone rescued them. In 1778 Boone himself was captured by the Shawnee and held captive. Chief Blackfish adopted Boone and made him a Shawnee brave. When he learned of a planned attack on Boonesborough, Boone escaped and led the successful defense of his fort. Troubles with the Indians continued and Boone lost another son, Israel, to Indian attacks in 1782.

Boone became one of the wealthiest men in Kentucky in terms of land, but he was naive in the ways of business and never held clear title to the land. Eventually, he lost all his claims of land ownership in Kentucky. In 1789 Boone moved to Point Pleasant on the Ohio River, where he supplied meat and grain to the U.S. military. In 1799 Boone led a group of settlers into Missouri at the invitation of the Spanish governor, who granted Boone 850 acres of land near St. Louis. Boone lost this land when the Louisiana Purchase in 1803 brought the area under U.S. control. However, the U.S. Congress restored his 850 acres in 1814 as a reward for his services in opening the West.

Boone served as a lieutenant colonel in the Virginia militia during the American Revolution (1775–1783). He was elected to the state legislature in 1781, 1787, and 1791. He ran several businesses, but he was always most at home hunting and exploring in the deep woods. Boone's business ventures usually failed and he was often in debt. His land ownership was normally based on unfiled claims. At one point in his late 1760s, Boone was even arrested for bad debts.

Boone died at his son Nathan's home on September 26, 1820, at the age of 85. The remains of Daniel and Rebecca Boone were moved to Frankfort, Kentucky, in 1845. Boone lived the life of explorer and hunter—a life extolled in print many times while Boone was still alive. Over 175 years after his death the legend has continued to grow.

See also: **Cumberland Gap, Louisiana Purchase, Wilderness Road**

FURTHER READING

Bakeless, John E. *Daniel Boone: Master of the Wilderness*. Lincoln, NE: University of Nebraska Press, 1939.

Lofaro, Michael A. *The Life and Adventures of Daniel Boone*. Lexington, KY: University Press of Kentucky, 1986.

The World Book Multimedia Encyclopedia. Chicago: World Book, Inc., 1998, s.v. "Boone, Daniel."

Snodgrass, Mary Ellen, *Encyclopedia of Frontier Literature*. Santa Barbara: ABC-CLIO, Inc., 1997, s.v. "Boone, Daniel."

Snodgrass, Mary Ellen, *Encyclopedia of Southern Literature*. Santa Barbara: ABC-CLIO, Inc., 1997, s.v. "Boone, Daniel."

BORDEN, INC.

The company was founded by Gail Borden Jr., an amateur inventor, who was born in 1801 in Norwich, New York. On a trip back from London in 1851 he saw several children on board ship die after drinking contaminated milk. Because no one yet knew how to keep milk fresh, spoiled and even poisonous milk was not uncommon. Borden knew that the Shakers (members of a religious sect) used vacuum pans to preserve fruit, and he began experimenting with a similar apparatus in search of a way to preserve milk.

After much tinkering, he discovered he could prevent milk from souring by evaporating it over a slow heat in a vacuum. Believing that it resisted spoilage because its water content had been removed, he called his revolutionary product "condensed milk." As French chemist and microbiologist Louis Pasteur

(1822–1895) later demonstrated, however, it was the heat Borden used in his evaporation process that kept the milk from spoiling because it killed the bacteria in fresh milk.

After receiving a patent from the U.S. Patent Office on August 19, 1856, Borden started a small processing operation near a dairy farm in Wolcottville, Connecticut, and opened a sales office in New York City. Consumers, however, took little notice of canned milk. Undaunted by sluggish sales, he resumed production in 1857 in Burrville, Connecticut, under the name Gail Borden, Jr., and Company.

The second enterprise also struggled financially until Borden met Jeremiah Milbank, a wholesale grocer, banker, and railroad financier. With Milbank's funding they formed a partnership in 1858 known as the New York Condensed Milk Company. Another stroke of fortune came when Borden decided to advertise in an issue of *Leslie's Illustrated Weekly,* which coincidentally contained an article condemning the unsanitary conditions at city dairies and the practice by many unscrupulous dairymen of adding chalk and eggs to enhance their "swill milk," as it was called. Soon after the magazine appeared, the New York Condensed Milk Company was delivering condensed milk throughout lower Manhattan and in Jersey City, New Jersey.

In 1861 the U.S. government ordered 500 pounds of condensed milk for troops fighting in the American Civil War (1861–1865). As the conflict grew, government orders increased, until Borden had to license other manufacturers to keep up with demand. After the war, the New York Condensed Milk Company had a ready-made customer base among both Union and Confederate veterans. To distinguish this product from its new competitors, Borden adopted the American bald eagle as his trademark.

Gail Borden Jr. died in 1874, leaving the management of the thriving company to his sons, John Gail and Henry Lee, who presided from 1874 to 1884 and 1884 to 1902, respectively. In 1875 the company diversified by offering delivery of fluid milk in New York and New Jersey. Ten years later, it pioneered the use of easily decontaminated glass bottles for milk distribution. In 1892 Borden's fluid-milk business was expanded to Chicago and the Chicago branch also manufactured evaporated milk.

Seven years later, Henry Lee Borden opened the first foreign branch, in Ontario, Canada, bringing to 18 the number of branch facilities. In 1899, as fresh and condensed milk sales generated profits of $2 million, the company was incorporated as the Borden Condensed Milk Company.

Management of the company passed outside the Borden family for the first time in 1919 when the company changed its name to the Borden Company. During a late 1920s, Borden bought more than 200 companies around the country and became the nation's largest distributor of fluid milk. In the process, it also entered five new fields: ice cream, cheese, powdered milk, mincemeat, and adhesives.

The move into adhesives was particularly important as it formed the basis for the Borden chemical business which developed rapidly from the 1930s through the 1950s. The company expanded into formaldehyde, printing inks, fertilizers, and polyvinyl chloride. By the 1960s a key Borden product was the brand name adhesive, Elmer's Glue-All. Meantime, Borden expanded through the acquisition of several brand-name food manufacturers in the late 1950s and 1960s, including Wyler's bouillon and Wise potato chips.

After a period of slow growth in the 1970s and a major restructuring in the early 1980s, Borden once again stepped up its acquisitions activities in the later 1980s. From 1986 through 1991 the company spent $1.9 billion to purchase 91 companies, with an emphasis on pasta and snack foods. The 1987 purchase of the Prince Company made Borden the undisputed leader in U.S. pasta sales. Its nine pasta companies accounted for nearly one-third of the U.S. pasta market.

But Borden was a troubled company by the early 1990s, and huge losses posted in 1992 and 1993 led to a takeover by Kohlberg Kravis Roberts & Co. (KKR) in 1995. Under KKR, Borden was dramatically restructured, with the most notable development being the 1997 divestment of the Borden dairy business, severing the link to the company's condensed milk roots. Borden, Inc. of the late 1990s was a diversified producer of pasta, pasta sauces, snacks, bouillon and dry soup, consumer adhesives (including the Elmer's and Krazy Glue brands), and industrial resins, coatings, and adhesives.

See also: **Civil War**

FURTHER READING

Alster, Norm. "Remaking Elsie." *Forbes*, December 25, 1989.

Collins, James H. *The Story of Condensed Milk*. New York: Borden Co., 1922.

Deveny, Kathleen, and Suein L. Hwang. "'Elsie's Bosses: A Defective Strategy of Heated Acquisitions Spoils Borden Name." *Wall Street Journal*, January 18, 1994.

Frantz, Joe Bertram. *Gail Borden: Dairyman to a Nation*. Norman: University of Oklahoma Press, 1951.

Lesly, Elizabeth. "Why Things Are So Sour at Borden." *Business Week*. November 22, 1993.

Schifrin, Matthew. "Last Legs?" *Forbes*, September 12, 1994.

Wade, Mary Dodson. *Milk, Meat Biscuits, and the Terraqueous Machine: The Story of Gail Borden*. Austin, Tex.: Eakin Press, 1987.

BOSTON MASSACRE

On the snowy evening of Monday, March 5, 1770, a mob of more than one hundred Bostonians confronted a band of nine British soldiers near a sentry box outside the Boston Custom House. Despite the best efforts of Captain Thomas Preston, commander of the squad, tensions between the civilians and the soldiers quickly escalated. Within the space of a few minutes the soldiers began firing, killing or fatally wounding five civilians. Among those who died in the Massacre are Crispus Attucks, a former slave turned sailor; James Caldwell, another sailor; Patrick Carr, an immigrant Irishman who made leather trousers; Samuel Gray, a rope maker; and Samuel Maverick, the brother–in–law of mob leader Ebenezer Mackintosh. Six other colonists were wounded, some of them innocent bystanders who had not been part of the mob.

Lieutenant Governor Thomas Hutchinson and his supporters worked through the night to avoid further bloodshed. Tensions were partially relieved by the arrest of Preston and his eight men early the following morning. The event, which became known as the Boston Massacre, helped convince both radical patriots and conservative loyalists that Parliament's efforts to tax the colonists against their will could only end in violence.

The roots of the Boston Massacre lay in the resistance to the Townshend Acts, passed by Parliament in 1767. Parliament's Secretary for American Affairs, Wills Hill, Lord Hillsborough, ordered four British regiments be stationed in Boston after a crowd mobbed customs officers who, on suspicion of smuggling, had seized a merchant ship owned by (radical patriot) John Hancock. On August 1, 1768, the Massachusetts General Court responded. Led by representative Samuel Adams it adopted a Nonimportation Agreement that placed a boycott on imported British goods. The radical patriots hoped that this measure would put economic pressure on Parliament to repeal the

Townshend Acts. Although the boycott, later adopted by several other colonies, eventually persuaded Parliament to repeal the acts, it also prolonged the hard times many of Boston's poorest citizens were experiencing. The aftermath of the French and Indian War (1754–63) brought a prolonged economic depression to the colonies. Jobs were especially scarce for unskilled laborers. Many of the colonists who formed part of the Boston mob competed directly with the soldiers for these jobs. Others, such as the sailors Crispus Attucks and James Caldwell, held jobs that were affected by the boycott. They may have been prepared to take their frustrations out on the soldiers who represented the British government.

From the time the soliders arrived in Boston, there were bad feelings between the military and the town's citizens. Soldiers broke into private shops and stole goods. Citizens took soldiers' equipment. Others encouraged soldiers to desert their units and seek refuge from their officers in the surrounding countryside. Sometimes the differences between the groups came out in violent confrontations that were made worse by the colonial courts' bias in favor of the citizenry. On July 13, 1769, for instance, a private soldier named John Riley exchanged blows with a grocer named Jonathan Winship. Winship complained to Justice of the Peace Edmund Quincy, obtained a warrant for Riley's arrest, and had the soldier arrested and fined. When Riley did not pay the fine Quincy ordered him to jail. Riley was rescued from the courthouse by several members of his regiment, who fought off the court's constable. In another incident, on October 24, British Ensign John Ness was charged with assaulting a colonial official named Robert Pierpoint and stealing his cargo of wood. On his way to answer the charges before a Justice of the Peace, Ness and his men were mobbed, and several of the soldiers were injured. On February 22, 1770, loyalist sympathizer Ebenezer Richardson was attacked in his home by a mob of stone–throwing radical patriots. One of the stones hit Richardson's wife and, in a rage, he seized a gun and fired into the crowd, killing an eleven-year-old boy named Christopher Seider. All these events increased tensions between the radical patriots and the supporters of the Crown.

Events that led directly to the March 5 confrontation began on Friday, March 2, 1770. Around noon that day, hoping to find work during his off–duty hours, Private Patrick Walker approached rope maker John Gray's ropeworks around noon on that day. He was insulted by worker William Green, who invited Walker to ''clean out my shithouse.'' More citizens and soldiers joined the exchange, and it broke out into a fight.

The fighting spread on Saturday, resulting in a fractured skull and arm for one of the soliders. Rumors of armed and angry townspeople looking for an excuse to fight spread throughout the town on Sunday and Monday. On the evening of March 5, Private Hugh White was threatened by a crowd made up largely of the working poor of Boston—day laborers, apprentices, and merchant seamen. White called for assistance and was supported by a squad of eight soldiers, including Captain Preston and two soldiers who had been involved in the fight at the ropeworks the previous day. The mob began pelting the soldiers with mud, ice, and snow. Although Preston tried to maintain order, his soldiers panicked and began firing into the crowd.

AFTER ALL THE FIRING CAPTAIN PRESTON PUT UP THE GUN OF A SOLDIER WHO WAS GOING TO FIRE AND SAID, "FIRE NO MORE, YOU HAVE DONE MISCHIEF ENOUGH."
Edward Hill, Witness for the defense of Captain Thomas Preston, 1770

Preston and his soldiers were arrested and taken into custody. They had to wait until the following October, however, before Lieutenant Governor Hutchinson concluded that they could receive a fair trial. His decision was based in part on a popular (and inaccurate) print of the massacre by silversmith Paul Revere. Most Bostonians believed Preston and his soldiers deliberately fired into the crowd. The nine were threatened with lynching while they awaited their trials. After a three-day trial, defense lawyer John Adams won Preston's acquittal. Of the eight other soldiers, six were found not guilty. Two, however, were convicted of manslaughter and were branded on their thumbs before being returned to their regiments.

Captain Preston's acquittal and the relatively light sentences given to the two soldiers were due in part to the desire of the radical patriot faction to make martyrs out of the victims of the Boston Massacre. However, there was also an economic motive to these events. By the autumn of 1770, the Townshend Acts had largely been repealed and merchants in New York, Boston, and elsewhere were no longer observing the Nonimportation Agreement. As a result, jobs were more plentiful, work for unskilled laborers was easier to find, and the crowds of unemployed urban poor that made up the mobs of citizens melted away. Nonetheless, these very same working poor would return at the outbreak of the American Revolution (1775–83).

See also: **American Revolution, French and Indian War, Paul Revere**

FURTHER READING

Ferling, John. *John Adams*. New York: Henry Holt, 1992.

Hoerder, Dick. *Crowd Action in Revolutionary Massachusetts*. New York: Academic Press, 1977.

Maier, Pauline R. *From Resistance to Revolution: Colonial Radicals and the Development of Opposition to Britain, 1765–1776*. New York: Knopf, 1972.

Tyler, John W. *Smugglers and Patriots: Boston Merchants and the Advent of the American Revolution*. Boston, MA: Northeastern University Press, 1986.

Zobel, Hiller B. *The Boston Massacre*. New York: W. W. Norton, 1970.

BOSTON TEA PARTY (1773)

At nine o'clock on the night of December 16, 1773, a band of Bostonians disguised as Native Americans boarded the British merchant ship *Dartmouth* and two companion vessels anchored at Griffin's Wharf in Boston harbor. The Americans, who numbered around 70, shared a common aim: to destroy the ships' cargo of British East India Company tea. Many years later George Hewes, a 31–year–old shoemaker and participant, recalled ''We then were ordered by our commander to open the hatches and take out all the chests of tea and throw them overboard. And we immediately proceeded to execute his orders, first cutting and splitting the chests with our tomahawks, so as thoroughly to expose them to the effects of the water.'' Urged on by a crowd of cheering townspeople, the disguised Bostonians destroyed 342 chests of tea estimated to be worth between £10,000 and £18,000. Their actions, which became known as the Boston Tea Party, set in motion events that led directly to the American Revolution (1775–83).

The Boston Tea Party was one of a long series of conflicts between the American colonies and the English government after the British victory in the French and Indian War (1754–63). The French and Indian War was the last and most expensive of almost a century of colonial wars between France and England. Since a lot of this money was spent to protect the American colonists from French Canadians and their Native American allies, the British government felt the Americans should help pay for the war. They also wanted the colonists to pay some of the future costs of stationing soldiers at forts scattered over the new Western frontier. The Americans, for their part, saw little sense in sending money to England to pay for troops that were needed much closer to home.

During the 1760s Parliament passed a series of acts designed to reduce the British national debt and to finance the costs of keeping regular soldiers on the American frontier. The most notorious of these was the Stamp Act (1765), which placed a tax on almost every public piece of paper in the colonies, including newspapers, pamphlets, diplomas, licenses, packs of cards, almanacs, and dice. The colonists fiercely resisted these taxes, organizing public protests and intimidating tax collectors. The Stamp Act resistance was the most widespread and best organized inter–colonial protest before the tea crisis of the 1770s. In the face of such widespread opposition the British Parliament backed down. It repealed the Stamp Act and its companion taxes in 1766.

The following year Parliament tried another means of raising money, through the Townshend Duties or Revenue Acts (1767), so named after Chancellor of the Exchequer Charles ''Champagne Charlie'' Townshend. Instead of placing a direct tax on materials that colonists bought and sold, these acts made certain important items such as lead, glass, paint, paper, and tea more expensive. The colonists responded by refusing to buy those products. Nonimportation agreements were signed throughout the American colonies. Citizens at all levels of society either refused to drink tea or bought black-market varieties that came from Dutch colonies. Faced with widespread American opposition, the British government backed down. The Townshend Duties were repealed on March 5, 1770, with the exception of a three penny duty on tea, kept to prove that Parliament had the right to tax the colonies. However, although this piece of legislation is credited with causing the Boston Tea Party, it had nothing to do with the American colonies.

The duty on tea mandated by the Townshend Duties act was meant to save the old British East India Company from bankruptcy. Until the Townshend Duties were first passed the Company had made much of its money transporting tea from India to England, where it was sold first to English wholesalers and then to American wholesalers before being sold to the colonial public. The American boycott of British tea, combined with intensive smuggling of Dutch tea, cut into Company profits. In an attempt to revive the East India Company, Prime Minister Lord Charles

The colonists protested Great Britain's tax on tea by throwing 15,000 pounds of it into the Boston Harbor, on December 16,1773.

North(1770–1782) persuaded Parliament to pass the Tea Act (1773). This legislation effectively cut the wholesalers out and allowed the East India Company to sell tea directly to agents in America. It gave the Company a monopoly on the sale of tea in the colonies.

The monopoly hurt colonists at all levels of society. Because the Tea Act allowed the East India Company to name its own sales agents to distribute the tea in American ports, business for local merchants and middlemen decreased. The Act offended politicians and patriots, who saw it as an attempt by Parliament to tax them without their consent. Even smugglers—who included wealthy merchants such as John Hancock (1737–1793)—were hurt because it made East India tea competitive with or cheaper than Dutch tea. Other Americans sought to profit from the Act. Governor Thomas Hutchinson of Massachusetts (1771–74), for example, used his influence to get his sons Thomas and Elisha named East India Company sales agents.

In September of 1773 the East India Company readied 600,000 pounds of tea in 2,000 chests for shipment to the colonies. The cargoes arrived at major colonial ports a month and a half later and met with hostile receptions. In New York and Philadelphia angry crowds forced local officials to send the tea ships

> **IN ABOUT THREE HOURS FROM THE TIME WE WENT ON BOARD, WE HAD . . . BROKEN AND THROWN OVERBOARD EVERY TEA CHEST TO BE FOUND IN THE SHIP, WHILE THOSE IN THE OTHER SHIPS WERE DISPOSING OF THE TEA IN THE SAME WAY, AT THE SAME TIME.**
>
> George Hewes, Shoemaker and Participant

back to England without unloading their cargoes. In Annapolis, Maryland, demonstrators burned a tea ship, and in New Jersey arsonists set fire to a warehouse where unloaded tea was stored. In Massachusetts, however, Governor Hutchinson decided to face down the demonstrators. When Boston citizens, led by patriot Samuel Adams (1722–1803), refused to allow the tea ships to unload, Hutchinson called on the Royal Navy to blockade Boston harbor so that the ships could not leave port. He knew that British law required a ship to unload its cargo after 20 days in port and he planned to use this law to sidestep Adams and his patriot followers.

The 20 day waiting period ended for the *Dartmouth* on December 16. On that day Sam Adams and his party tried to contact Governor Hutchinson to convince him to let the ships leave harbor. Hutchinson refused and, at five o'clock in the afternoon, the meeting of Boston citizens broke up. Some of them followed George Hewes' example, by dressing up as Native Americans. Carrying tomahawks and clubs, they marched to Griffin's Wharf. Hewes and his companions took great pains that nothing but the tea was destroyed and that no one profited from the destruction. "One Captain O'Connor, whom I well knew, came on board [to steal some tea], and when he supposed he was not noticed, filled his pockets, and also the lining of his coat," Hewes recalled. "But I had detected him and gave information to the captain of what he was doing. We were ordered to take him into custody, and just as he was stepping from the vessel, I seized him by the skirt of his coat, and in attempting to pull him back, I tore it off; but, springing forward by a rapid effort he made his escape."

The Boston Tea Party led almost directly to the American Revolution. To punish the city of Boston for its role in the destruction of so much East India Company property, the British Parliament passed a series of laws known collectively as the Coercive Acts (1774). These laws closed the port of Boston until the citizens paid for the destroyed tea, dismantled Massachusetts's colonial charter, expanded the powers of the king's governor, and made it harder to convict royal officials of crimes. In the Quebec Act (1774), Parliament also took away lands that had been claimed by the American colonies since their founding. In reply the Americans formed the First Continental Congress to organize and coordinate their response. Sixteen months after the tea finally sank in Boston harbor, the first shots of the American Revolution were fired.

See also: **American Revolution, French and Indian War, John Hancock, Stamp Act, Townshend Act**

FURTHER READING

Labaree, Benjamin Woods. *The Boston Tea Party.* New York: Oxford University Press, 1968.

McCusker, John J., and Menard, Russell R. *The Economy of British North America, 1607–1789.* Chapel Hill: University of North Carolina Press,1985.

"Recollections of George Hewes," in *A Retrospective of the Boston Tea Party, 1843.* Reprinted in Commager, Henry Steele, and Morris, Richard B., editors. *The Spirit of 'Seventy-Six: The Story of the American Revolution as Told by Participants.* Volume I. Indianapolis: Bobbs-Merrill Co., Inc., 1958.

BOYCOTT

A boycott is an organized, deliberate effort by consumers, workers, or businesses to avoid trade that benefits another group, business, or an entire country whose policies they disagree with. For example, in the 1950s and 1960s civil rights groups boycotted businesses in the American South that discriminated against African Americans. The goal of such boycotts was not only to protest nonviolently but also to coerce the targeted businesses to change their policies by directly affecting their revenues. The term *boycott* is derived from a nineteenth century British estate manager named Charles Boycott (1832–1897). During the potato famine of 1880, Irish tenant farmers on Boycott's land told Boycott he had to reduce their rents so they could survive the famine. Boycott refused, and the farmers joined together to refrain from any interaction that might benefit Boycott and his sympathizers. Boycott never backed down, but he eventually moved out of Ireland.

A strike by workers against a business for higher wages or an embargo of one country by another are both boycotts intended to force change. Consumers who band together to avoid a store known for its high prices are practicing a boycott, as are companies that begin doing business with a new vendor to get their former partner to lower its prices. So-called primary boycotts are direct boycotts against the targeted business or group. For example, the civil-rights protestors of the 1950s and 1960s directly boycotted the very storeowners who refused to serve them. Secondary boycotts are directed against a third party who does business with the targeted business or group. For example, citizens protesting South Africa's formerly racist social policies boycotted U.S. companies that did business in South Africa. In the nineteenth century United States it was quite common for farmers to boycott railroads to get them to lower their freight haulage rates. U.S. labor unions also frequently told their members to avoid purchasing products from non-unionized businesses, and non-unionized businesses used the reverse tactic on unionized firms. During the Great Depression (1929–1939), for example, the National Metal Trades Association encouraged its member firms to boycott metal firms whose workforce had unionized or was considering doing so. In a landmark 1921 ruling, *Duplex Printing Press v. Deering*, the Supreme Court decided that unions could be sued for the damages caused by their secondary boycotts. In 1947 the Taft-Hartley Act outlawed secondary boycotts and strikes completely.

See also: **Taft-Hartley Act**

BRAND NAMES

Many grocery stores today carry common products like pizza, toothpaste, or cola that are easily spotted on the shelves because of their unflashy packaging and very low prices compared to the more recognizable products displayed next to them. These lower-priced products are called "generics" for a reason. Even though they may be made with exactly the same ingredients and in exactly the same way (and sometimes even in the same factory) as their more expensive cousins they lack one important quality: brand name. Brand name is more than the memorable, sometimes very famous name given to a product, more than the color and design of its label, and more than the tune or slogan that pops into your mind when you think of its latest commercial. Brand name is what makes consumers spend a little more to know they are getting a certain product that is like no other, that will taste or perform exactly the same every time they use it, and that they associate with positive qualities like good taste, excitement, reliability, or high quality. Corporations spend many millions of dollars to build and preserve their products' brand names, and they use complicated financial formulas and highly trained experts to tell them exactly how much a brand name they own or want to own is really worth. Companies register their brand names with government agencies as trademarks, which give the name a legally protected status. The cost and time required to build a genuinely international brand is so great that many companies are willing to pay several times the value of a target company's physical assets just to acquire an already established brand name.

The word *brand* comes from a root word meaning "burn" and is directly related to the hot branding irons ranchers use to mark their ranch's symbol on cattle. Although manufacturers have used identifying marks on everything from pottery, metal ware, and guns for centuries, it wasn't until the growth of the railroad and development of mass production in the nineteenth century that brand names became as powerful as they are today. When products could be identically produced and transported rapidly all over the world, brand names became more than just identifying marks. They became the foundation on which corporations presented themselves to the consuming public. Many of the world's first major brand names were American, and several of those, including Campbell's, Heinz, Wrigley's, and Goodyear, are still dominant today. In the early 1990s it was estimated that of the world's ten strongest brand names, the top seven (Coca-Cola, Kellogg's, McDonald's, Kodak, Marlboro, IBM, and American Express) were U.S. firms. In the last half of the twentieth century the development of sophisticated advertising and promotional techniques, led by television ads, has created truly international brands that are recognized in every corner of the world. Although brand names were first associated with physical products, since the early 1960s powerful brand names have also been developed in service industries (such as Allstate, United Parcel Service, and Sprint).

See also: **Trademark**

BRANDEIS, LOUIS DEMBITZ

The appointment of Louis Brandeis (1856–1941) to the U.S. Supreme Court made him the first Jewish Supreme Court Associate Justice in the nation's history. Before his appointment, Brandeis led a varied and successful professional life as a public advocate, a progressive lawyer, and a Zionist. Brandeis served the nation's highest court from 1916 until his retirement in 1939.

Louis Dembitz Brandeis was born November 13, 1856, in Louisville, Kentucky. His parents, Adolph and Frederika Dembitz Brandeis, were Czechoslovakian refugees who fled the failed liberal Revolution of 1848. Brandeis was raised in a family atmosphere that was intellectual, open-minded, progressive, and dedicated to freedom. This had positive impact on his character throughout his life.

Adolph Brandeis was a prosperous grain merchant. Although Louis attended public schools in Louisville, his father's wealth enabled him to spend three years in Germany where he studied at the Annen Realschule in Dresden. At the age of 18, Brandeis entered Harvard Law School, where he completed a three-year program in two years. He graduated with the highest grades received to that date in the law school's history.

After a brief period in St. Louis, Missouri, Brandeis returned to Boston in 1879 and soon established a profitable law practice. He argued and won his first U.S. Supreme Court case in 1889 on behalf of the Wisconsin Central Railroad. He also became known as "the people's lawyer" because of his *pro bono* (without pay) advocacy in cases involving the public interest.

In 1890 Brandeis and his former partner Samuel Warren jointly published a path-breaking article in the *Harvard Law Review*, "The Right to Privacy." From

Louis Dembitz Brandeis.

IT IS ONE OF THE HAPPY INCIDENTS OF THE FEDERAL SYSTEM THAT A SINGLE COURAGEOUS STATE MAY, IF ITS CITIZENS CHOOSE, SERVE AS A LABORATORY; AND TRY NOVEL SOCIAL AND ECONOMIC EXPERIMENTS WITHOUT RISK TO THE REST OF THE COUNTRY.

Louis Brandeis, *New State Ice Company of Oklahoma City vs. Liebman*, 1932

the bench, Brandeis would later support this new legal concept which his article helped promote.

By the mid-1890s Brandeis's law practice was earning more than $70,000 a year, an enormous amount by the standards of the day. In 1891 Brandeis married his second cousin, Alice Goldmark, and the two dedicated themselves to public service. Through their frugal living and careful investments, they became millionaires before 1900. As their wealth grew, so did their generosity. Between 1905 and 1939, they gave away approximately $1.5 million.

In 1908, arguing before the Supreme Court in *Muller vs. Oregon*, Brandeis defended the constitutionality of an Oregon statute limiting the labor of women in factories to ten hours a day. In a precedent-setting brief, he included a mass of legislative and statistical data relating to the condition of women in industry along with his legal arguments. As a result, the court was forced to consider its decision in light of both the law and contemporary economic reality. Brandeis's brief became a legal model for those lawyers, judges, and social welfare proponents who were determined to humanize industrial working conditions. Associate Supreme Court Justice Felix Frankfurter wrote several years later, ''The *Muller* case is epoch-making, not because of its decision [the Court upheld the Oregon statute], but because of the authoritative recognition by the Supreme Court that the way in which Mr. Brandeis presented the case . . . laid down a new technique for counsel charged with the responsibility of arguing such constitutional questions, and an obligation upon courts to insist upon such method of argument before deciding the issue.''

Before *Muller*, Brandeis had tried for years to minimize what writer and sociologist Thorstein Veblen called ''the discrepancy between law and fact.'' The law, Brandeis argued, often did not correspond to the economic and social circumstances in America. The danger, he said, was that ''a lawyer who has not studied economics and sociology is very apt to become a public enemy.''

Brendeis spent ten years acting as counsel for persons advocating and defending progressive laws throughout the country. His work caught the attention of the current presidential administration. On January 28, 1916, President Woodrow Wilson (1856–1924) nominated Brandeis, then 59, to the U.S. Supreme Court. His activism, however, made confirmation difficult. Two years before his nomination, Brandeis had published two influential books: *Other People's Money and How the Bankers Use It* (1914) and *Business, a Profession* (1914). Both books were critical of business practices of the time, particularly those of investment bankers. For over four months the Senate Judiciary Committee heard heated testimony for and against Brandeis's nomination to the nation's highest court for more than four months. Some considered Brandeis's nomination to be a radical threat to the American legal system, but his appointment was finally confirmed by a 47 to 22 vote. The appointment broke an unwritten ban that had kept Jews from serving on the Supreme Court or in high positions of government.

Brandeis served on the high court through the Great Depression and post–World War I period. In his major judicial opinions Brandeis often concurred with the dissenting opinions of the great jurist Oliver Wendell Holmes. Many of their dissents were in defense of the First Amendment guarantees relating to freedom of speech. Following World War I (1914–1918), in several decisions upholding the Espionage Act of 1918, the Court, with only Justices Holmes and Brandeis dissenting, denied the right of free speech based on the argument that certain statements or opinions might provoke violent acts. For example, in *Abrams v. United States*, the Court upheld a 20-year jail sentence imposed on five Russian immigrants who had published two booklets protesting U.S. actions in their native land. The booklets contained a few quoted phrases from the Communist Manifesto. The Court, again with Brandeis in dissent, also held that pacifism on religious grounds was a legitimate cause for barring U.S. citizenship to an individual.

In a famous dissent from the *New State Ice Company of Oklahoma City vs. Liebman*, Brandeis summed up his philosophy: ''It is one of the happy incidents of the federal system that a single courageous State may, if its citizens choose, serve as a laboratory; and try novel social and economic experiments without risk to the rest of the country. This Court has the power to prevent an experiment. We may strike down the state law, which embodies it on the ground that, in our opinion, the measure is arbitrary, capricious or unreasonable. But in the exercise of this high power, we must be ever on our guard, lest we erect our prejudices into legal principles. If we would guide by the light of reason, we must let our minds be bold.''

Justice Brandeis resigned from the Supreme Court in February 1939. He died in 1941.

See also: **Liberalism**

FURTHER READING

Abraham, Henry J. *Justices and Presidents: A Political History of Appointments to the Supreme Court.* 2d ed. New York: Oxford University Press, 1985.

Bates, Ernest Sutherland. *The Story of the Supreme Court.* Indianapolis: Bobbs Merrill, 1938.

Burt, Robert A. *Two Jewish Justices: Outcasts in the Promised Land.* Berkeley and Los Angeles: University of California Press, 1988.

Konefsky, Samuel J. *The Legacy of Holmes and Brandeis: A Study in the Influence of Ideas.* New York: The Macmillan Company, 1956.

Mason, Alpheus Thomas. *Brandeis: A Free Man's Life.* New York: Viking Press, 1946.

Strum, Philippa. *Brandeis: Beyond Progressivism.* Lawrence, Kan.: University Press of Kansas, 1993.

BRETTON WOODS AGREEMENT

In July of 1944, representatives from 44 nations met at Bretton Woods, New Hampshire, for an international monetary conference. There, they developed the groundwork to establish of two international organizations, the International Money Fund (IMF), and the International Bank for Reconstruction and Development, in assist in the creation of a stable economic foundation in the post–World War II (1939–1945) world. The measures detailed at Bretton Woods were adopted by the United States and other participating nations in 1945, officially creating the IMF and the International Bank.

The function of the IMF is to maintain orderly currency practices in international trade. The function of the International Bank is to facilitate the extension of long-term investments for specified purposes, such as development and structural improvements in a nation. Amendments were made to the initial agreement in 1969 and in 1978, enhancing the role of the IMF and establishing ''Special Drawing Rights'' (SDRs) that are used by the IMF as legal guidelines for all of its currency transfers. The IMF monitors compliance and assists nations in defending their officially established exchange rates. If a country's foreign exchange problems prove to be more than temporary, the IMF advises the country to devalue its currency and to undertake domestic actions designed to stem further declines in the value of its currency.

BREWING INDUSTRY

Historians have traced the origin of the brewing of beer to the early history of ancient Mesopotamia and Egypt. Grain, most likely barley, was soaked in water until fermentation occurred. Although this method was quite crude, it remained the essential foundation for brewing throughout history.

The pilgrims brought the art of brewing to America in the early 1600s. Dutch settlers brewed ale in New York (then known as New Amsterdam) soon after their arrival in 1624. Early brewing was a small scale subsistence enterprise—just enough beer was produced for the neighborhood barter market.

As the colonies expanded, and the number of breweries increased. Partly because of the problem of finding potable (pure) water, early American per capita consumption of alcohol (including hard cider, which

The art of brewing came to the U.S. with the pilgrims in 1620 and was a cottage industry in 1630, when the first American commercial brewery opened in New Amsterdam. The brewing of alcoholic beverages continued to rise as an American industry, except for the years of prohibition (1920–1933).

actually surpassed beer in popularity in the eighteenth century) was about double what it was in the late twentieth century. As in Europe, differing flavors developed in different regions—mostly because of varied ingredients. Ales and stouts were (and still are) made with a yeast that rises during the fermentation process; this gives the brew a dark, cloudy look. American brews were decidedly different in taste from English ale because of their short fermentation time and the need to import barley, which could not be grown locally in the colonies. Large amounts of English ale were imported for most of the eighteenth century. This practice, however, came to an end in 1770, when George Washington (1732–1799) proclaimed a boycott on imported English ale in order to boost sales for ailing American breweries. The American Revolution (1775–1783) and the subsequent break with Great Britain finalized what Washington had begun five years earlier. In 1789 the U.S. House of Representatives strengthened commercial brewing by limiting the tax on beer. The success of this measure led to the expansion of the industry; by 1810 there were

approximately 132 breweries operating in the United States.

Throughout the mid–1800s, a new type of beer revolutionized the U.S. brewing industry. Brought to the United States in 1840 by Bavarian brewer Johann Wagner, lager utilized a different type of yeast during fermentation that sank—leaving the beer clear and light instead of cloudy. This process required a cool environment. Recognizing the importance of this yeast, brewer George Manger purchased a quantity and set up America's first commercial lager brewery in Philadelphia.

In the mid-nineteenth century, an influx of German immigrants introduced a new type of lager to the United States: the pilsner. Some of these immigrants set up breweries on the shore of Lake Michigan. Many famous breweries arose from this period, including Schlitz, Pabst, and Miller. By 1860 the number of breweries in the United States had swollen to 1,269—mostly lager brewers. As in the case of other commodities, the development of a national economy required distribution in larger markets. Milwaukee breweries attained good reputations in part because of Milwaukee's large German population (in which beer had long been part of the national culture) and in part through the accident of the Great Chicago Fire (1871). Damage to Chicago's water supply and breweries gave Milwaukee brewers temporary access to a huge, new market.

By 1873 there were 4,131 breweries in the United States; nine million barrels of beer were produced per year. This year also saw the birth of what would become two of the country's most prominent breweries: Coors and Anheuser-Busch. To improve the taste of his beer, Adolphus Busch (1839–1913) studied the work of scientist Louis Pasteur (1822–1895). The pasteurization of the brew to kill bacteria, coupled with the invention of the crown bottle cap in 1892, extended the shelf life of beer, which made shipping of beer to remote areas possible. By using these new techniques to make beer, Busch began to produce and market Budweiser, creating the empire of Anheuser-Busch. The ability to manufacture ice, the growth of the railway lines, and European immigration gave birth to the first nationally recognized brands of beer: Pabst, Schlitz, and Anheuser-Busch. Facing competition on this scale, smaller breweries began to consolidate or go out of business.

By 1910 only 1,568 breweries remained in the United States, and these were about to be dealt a serious economic blow. Fueled by anti-German sentiment during World War I (1914–1918), Protestant morality, and the agitation of the Anti-Saloon League, the production and consumption of alcoholic beverages was outlawed by the Eighteenth Amendment to the Constitution, which become law in 1920. Larger breweries survived by making malt for the food industry, ice cream, soft drinks, industrial alcohol, and non-alcoholic beer. Organized crime produced the now-illegal beer and hard liquor.

In 1933, Congress passed the Twenty-first Amendment repealing Prohibition. In the grip of the Great Depression (1929–1939), the sale of bottled beer helped the brewing industry stay afloat. With the advent of cans, dominated by the American Can Company in 1935, beer found a new container—one that would not break and would protect the beverage from the damaging effects of light. Take-home packaging was also developed. Now beers could be purchased six to a pack.

During World War II (1939–1945), fifteen percent of brewery output went to the military. The anti-German sentiment that had afflicted the German-dominated brewing industry during the World War I did not occur this time. In fact, there was a substantial increase in brewing. Due to a shortage of malt during this period, lighter styles of beer became popular. Lighter beers would characterize the American brewing industry until the late 1980s.

After the war the major brewers in Milwaukee and St. Louis began to expand. Both Pabst and Schlitz owned breweries in New York by 1949. In 1951, Anheuser-Busch constructed a new brewery in Newark, New Jersey. Anheuser-Busch and Schlitz continued expansion, both building breweries in Los Angeles, California (1954), and Tampa, Florida (1959). By 1957 Anheuser-Busch had taken the lead in sales and remained the number one selling brewery in the United States through the 1990s. Though Anheuser-Busch's Tampa brewery would eventually be shut down, the location became the site of the popular Busch Gardens theme park.

During the 1970s a series of mergers occurred. Philip Morris, known primarily for its tobacco products, purchased Miller Brewing Company. Philip Morris reasoned that beer was not unlike cigarettes in that it was an agriculturally based item dependent on advertising for consumer awareness. Mergers were happening on a smaller scale as well. Regional breweries joined forces to form national concerns with bigger markets.

Advertising had become as important as the beer itself to the breweries' success. Competition was fierce.

In 1975 America's breweries produced 147 million barrels of beer and spent $140 million dollars in advertising. By 1994, total beer production had increased by almost 37 percent while the amount spent on advertising skyrocketed to $700 million, an increase of five hundred percent.

Part of this growth was caused by expected competition. The late 1980s brought the rebirth of the regional brewery (now known as the micro-brewery) and the homebrewer. A large number of beer drinkers had grown weary of pilsner. Micro-breweries offered American-made stouts, porters, ales, bocks, and other brews, all with a taste specific to the region in which they were brewed. Homebrew supply shops popped up across the country and beer enthusiasts began making beer with ingredients of their own choosing. In the late 1990s it was legal for individuals to brew up to one hundred gallons of beer for personal consumption per year.

Does this spell the end of the national brewery? Hardly. Sensing the change in the market, Anheuser-Busch began producing a wide variety of flavors, including a honey-blond ale, a stout, and many others. This gambit paid off. In 1998 Anheuser-Busch reaped the profit from the sale of over ninety million barrels of brew and their flagship product—Budweiser—was the number one selling beer in the world.

See also: **Adolphus Busch, Eighteenth Amendment, Prohibition, Twenty-First Amendment**

FURTHER READING

Baron, Stanley. *Brewed In America: The History of Beer and Ale In the United States.* New York: Little, Brown, and Co., 1962.

Papazian, Charlie. *The New Complete Joy of Home Brewing.* New York: Avon Books, 1991.

Van Munching, Philip. *Beer Blast: The Inside Story of the Brewing Industry's Bizarre Battles for Your Money.* New York: Times Books, 1997.

"Beer Institute Online," [cited April 12, 1999] available from the World Wide Web @ www.beerinst.org/.

"Breweries and Brands," [cited April 12, 1999] available from the World Wide Web @ dir.yahoo.com/ Business_and_Economy/Companies/Beverages/ Alcohol_and_Spirits/Beer/Breweries_and_Brands/.

BROOK FARM

Brook Farm was an experimental commune and agricultural cooperative in West Roxbury, Massachusetts (now part of Boston). It was established in 1841 by Unitarian minister and author George Ripley (1802–80), a leader of the Transcendental movement. Transcendentalists rejected the conventional doctrines of the Calvinist Church and the rationalism of the Unitarian Church. They were influenced by German philosopher Immanuel Kant (1724–1804) as well as English poets Samuel Taylor Coleridge (1772–1834) and William Wordsworth (1770–1850). Transcendentalist philosophy held that an individual's intuition, as opposed to the five senses, is the highest source of knowledge. The senses are therefore to be transcended. They also emphasized self-reliance and intellectual stimulation. These beliefs spawned an American literary movement, which flourished between 1836 and 1860, and was epitomized by the works of American writer and former Unitarian minister Ralph Waldo Emerson (1803–82) and his protegee author Henry David Thoreau (1817–62). The movement's philosophy was also captured in the transcendentalist journal *The Dial*.

At Brook Farm the transcendentalists strove to establish social harmony. They followed French philosopher Charles Fourier's (1772–1837) ideas that small communities (preferably of 1,620 people) should form an economic unit, share a communal dwelling, and divide work among themselves. Since labor was shared each community member was theoretically allowed ample time for artistic and literary pursuits. But the utopian experiment was short-lived: Brook Farm's central building caught fire and was destroyed in 1846; by the following year the commune had disbanded.

Other notable figures who were associated with Brook Farm included American writer Nathaniel Hawthorne (1804–64), whose novel *Blithedale Romance* (1852) was inspired by his years at the commune; and American feminist and writer Margaret Fuller (1810–50), editor of *The Dial*. The utopian community was also visited by American newspaper editor Horace Greeley (1811–72), founder of the highly influential *New York Tribune*.

See also: **Utopia, Utopian Communties**

BROOKLYN BRIDGE

The Brooklyn Bridge, which spans New York's East River to connect Manhattan and Brooklyn, was completed in 1883. Extending 1595 feet (486 meters), it was the longest suspension bridge in the world when it was finished. The bridge hangs from steel cables that are almost 16 inches (41 centimeters) thick. The cables are suspended from stone and masonry towers that are 275 feet (84 meters) tall. Upon opening, the span was celebrated as a feat of modern engineering and, with its twin gothic towers, as an architectural landmark of considerable grace and beauty.

The Brooklyn Bridge was conceived of and designed by German American engineer John Augustus Roebling (1806–1869) who first proposed the project in 1857. Roebling's earlier accomplishments included a span over Pittsburgh, Pennsylvania's Monongahela River (1846) and one over the Niagara River at Niagara Falls (1855), between New York and Ontario. The engineer's plans for the Brooklyn Bridge (officially called the East River Bridge) were approved in 1869; Roebling died one month later. He was succeeded by his son, Washington Augustus Roebling (1837–1926), who took on the role of chief engineer. Specially designed watertight chambers allowed for the construction of the two towers whose bases were built on the floor of the East River. The project proved to be an enormous and dangerous undertaking. Underwater workers, including Roebling, suffered from the bends—a serious and potentially fatal blood condition caused by the decrease in pressure that results from rising from the water's depth too quickly. But man prevailed against the elements, and after fourteen laborious years, on May 24, 1883, the Brooklyn Bridge was inaugurated. Five years later Brooklyn became a borough of New York City. In 1964 the bridge was designated a national historic landmark.

See also: **John Augustus Roebeling**

BROTHERHOOD OF SLEEPING CAR PORTERS

Founded in 1925, the Brotherhood of Sleeping Car Porters (BSCP), now part of the Brotherhood of Railway and Airline Clerks, was a critical institution linking together the African American community in the south and in the north. The union, composed entirely of the African American porters and maids who worked on the railway trains that traversed the nation, was a strategic institution in the African American community. It served as the "eyes and ears" of the black community. During the period of migration of African American people to the north following World War II, the Brotherhood of Sleeping Car Porters carried news

Passengers placed their shoes outside their train berths, to be collected and shined by the attending car porter.

about the conditions in the north: the availability of jobs and housing and generally what the migrants could expect from the authorities in the north. It was also a network of news about the civil rights movement in the south.

The members of the union, such as Mr. E.D. Nixon, a Pullman Porter who lived in Montgomery, Alabama and served as the president of the Alabama National Association for the Advancement of Colored People (NAACP) in the 1950s, often became leaders of the Civil Rights Movement. This had to do with the fact that the Porters literally had "broader horizons" due to the mobility associated with their jobs. E.D. Nixon helped provide leadership in the Montgomery Bus Boycott of 1955–1956.

The BSCP was organized in Harlem, New York City, in 1925 by Asa Philip Randolph (1889–1979). Randolph was the publisher of *The Messenger*, a New York monthly devoted to black politics and culture. He was a member of the Socialist Party and he believed that unions provided the best opportunity for black workers to secure a fair wage and to defend their rights.

Randolph led the union from 1925 until he retired in 1968. His union was not large—at its height it represented only about 12,000 workers, but it was strategically placed. Randolph also served as vice president of the American Federation of Labor and the Congress of Industrial Organizations (AFL-CIO) in 1957.) As a labor leader, Randolph made many advances, both on the part of the union and on behalf of black Americans.

Initially, the Brotherhood of Sleeping Car Porters (BSCP) had to deal with the Pullman Company because the company not only built the railway coaches (in its factory located in a suburb of Chicago), it also furnished to the railroads the personnel who served as porters and maids on the trains. As leader of the Brotherhood of Sleeping Car Porters, Randolph organized these workers and bargained for union recognition and the right to negotiate labor contracts on their behalf with the Pullman Company. Randolph also secured inclusion of railway porters and maids in the language of the Railway Labor Act (1926). The act was designed to settle disputes through negotiation, mediation, arbitration, and to establish a protocol for the investigation and recommendations of an emergency fact-finding board.

Randolph worked for increases in wages for members of the brotherhood. The National Labor Relations Board certified the Brotherhood of Sleeping Car Porters as the legitimate representative of the porters and maids in 1935. In 1941, Randolph pressured the federal government to provide blacks with equal access to jobs in the defense industries. Randolph threatened President Franklin Roosevelt with a large protest march unless Roosevelt established a policy of non-discrimination for African American workers and founded a national watchdog apparatus known as the Fair Employment Practices Committee (FEP). Franklin Roosevelt (1882–1945) agreed to this demand because the stated war goals of the United States included the fight against fascism and racism. In 1963, Randolph also figured prominently in directing the March on Washington for Jobs and Freedom, the largest civil rights demonstration in American history.

See also: **Civil Rights Movement, Asa Philip Randolph**

BRUNSWICK CORPORATION

Born 1819 in Switzerland, John Moses Brunswick emigrated to the United States at age fourteen. Having opened a woodworking shop in Cincinnati, Ohio, in 1845 to make carriages, Brunswick soon expanded into the manufacture of billiard tables. In the late 1860s three firms dominated the U.S. billiards market: J. M. Brunswick and Brothers, Julius Balke's Cincinnati-based Great Western Billiard Manufactory, and New York-based Phelan and Collender. In 1873 Brunswick merged with Balke to form J. M. Brunswick and Balke Company. Then in 1884 Phelan and Collender merged with Brunswick and Balke to form the Brunswick-Balke-Collender Company.

Following John Brunswick's death in 1866, the company's new leadership aggressively expanded the firm's product line. Since many billiard tables were being sold to taverns, the company also developed a line of carved wooden back bars. Back bars covered the wall behind a bar and served a functional and decorative purpose. They were intricate and elaborate status symbols and also greatly enhanced Brunswick's image as craftsmen. Before long Brunswick bars were installed across the United States and Canada.

In the 1880s Brunswick added another product line—bowling pins and bowling balls. Taverns had begun to install lanes, interest in bowling seemed to be growing, and the Brunswick-Balke-Collender was determined to be ready for this new market. The company actively promoted bowling as a participatory sport and helped to standardize the game. The company's president was also instrumental in organizing the American Bowling Congress, the sport's governing body. Although Brunswick continued to expand its markets and product lines, bowling was to become the financial backbone of the firm.

In the 1910s the temperance movement (which advocated prohibition of the sale and consumption of alcohol) threatened not only the fixtures and bar business but also billiards and bowling. In 1912 Brunswick suspended its bar-fixtures operations, which accounted for one-fourth of annual sales, and sought to replace it with automobile tires and the world's first hard-rubber toilet seats. Rubber products best utilized the firm's existing facilities. By 1921 the company was producing two thousand tires a day. When the price of rubber tripled in 1922, Brunswick sold its tire line to B.F. Goodrich, who began to manufacture tires under the Brunswick name as the Brunswick Tire Company.

Brunswick then began to manufacture wood piano cases, phonograph cabinets, and phonographs. In 1922 the company also began producing records under its own label. Jazz greats such as Duke Ellington, Cab Calloway, and Benny Goodman and classical artists such as Irene Pavlovska and Leopold Godowsky all recorded on the Brunswick label. In 1924 Brunswick became a publicly traded company.

Even with the repeal of Prohibition in 1933 and the popularity of pool halls, the Great Depression (1929–1939) was hard on Brunswick. Nonetheless the company marketed a line of tabletop refrigerators called the Blue Flash and a successful line of soda fountains to replace its once thriving bar and fixture business.

During World War II (1939–1945) Brunswick found new markets and new products and once again prospered. United Service Organizations (USO) centers and military bases eagerly purchased billiard and bowling equipment. Brunswick also made wartime products, including mortar shells, flares, assault boats, fuel cells, floating mines, aircraft instrument panels, and aluminum stretchers.

In the postwar period, Brunswick expanded widely. In the mid-1950s the company successfully developed an automatic pinsetter for bowling alleys, which, along with a competing machine made by the rival American Machine and Foundry Company (better known as AMF), helped revolutionize the sport. Brunswick's policy of selling pinsetters on credit, along with an aggressive advertising campaign, combined with suburban expansion to make bowling centers enormously popular in the late 1950s. After the introduction of the pinsetter the company prospered as never before. Sales, which had been $33 million in 1954, jumped to $422 million in 1961.

Fueled by this revenue rise, Brunswick made several acquisitions in the late 1950s and early 1960s. Through these purchases the company became a major provider of equipment for golf, roller-skating, fishing, and boating. Brunswick's most important purchase proved to be the 1961 acquisition of the Kiekhaefer Corporation, which built Mercury outboard motors and formed the basis for the company's marine business, which became increasingly important over succeeding decades. In 1960 the company changed its name to Brunswick Corporation.

Brunswick also expanded well beyond the recreation area in the 1960s and 1970s, adding medical supply operations and various industrial manufacturing units. The 1980s and 1990s, however, saw Brunswick exit from these businesses in order to focus exclusively on recreation. A series of acquisitions in 1986 and 1988 made Brunswick the world's largest manufacturer of pleasure boats and marine engines. In the 1990s the company expanded its recreational offerings to include bicycles, wagons, sleds, camping equipment, ice chests, and exercise equipment.

FURTHER READING

Bettner, Jill. "Bowling for Dollars." *Forbes*, September 12, 1983.

Kogan, Rick. *Brunswick: The Story of an American Company: The First 150 Years*. Lake Forest, IL: Brunswick Corporation, 1995.

Melcher, Richard A. "Brunswick Wades into New Waters." *Business Week*, June 2, 1997.

Rodengen, Jeffrey L. "A Great American Empire." *Boating*, September 1987.

Slutsker, Gary. "Toes in the Water." *Forbes*, March 15, 1993.

BRYAN, WILLIAM JENNINGS

William Jennings Bryan (1860–1925) was a great populist orator who unsuccessfully ran for the U.S. presidency three times. He was born and brought up in Illinois. Following graduation from law school he practiced law in Jacksonville, Illinois, from 1883 to 1887, but his heart was never in his work. In 1887 he moved his family to Lincoln, Nebraska, where he ran for Congress in 1890. Bryan won his Congressional seat as a Democrat by 7,713 votes, a substantial margin in a strongly Republican district.

During his first term in the House of Representatives, Bryan attracted wide attention when he gave a masterful three-hour speech in defense of the "free silver cause." In the late 19th century the United States was in the throes of depression. Unemployment and farm failures were common. The country was divided over the hard money vs. the so-called question of bimetallism. Advocates of free silver were mainly southern and western farmers. They argued that the gold standard resulted in an unfavorable economic bias against the common man. Free silver partisans believed they were being exploited. They favored the circulation of silver currency and other inflationary policies that would cheapen the value of money in order to ease personal and business debts. Bryan's simplistic solution for the depressed economy that followed the Panic of 1893 was the unlimited coinage of silver at a ratio to gold of 16 to 1. He claimed lawmakers had to decide between a policy supported by financiers and wealthy industrialists and the justified demands of the downtrodden masses.

Bryan's two Congressional terms and his growing reputation as a dynamic public speaker helped make his name as "the boy orator from the Platte." His national renown did not help him back home in Nebraska, however, and he failed in his bid to become a U.S. senator in 1894. Bryan spent the next two years as an editor of the *Omaha World-Herald* and conducted a vigorous public campaign in favor of the free silver cause.

At the 1896 Democratic presidential convention in Chicago 36 year-old Bryan dazzled the assembled delegates, newspaper reporters, and the public with a famous address known today as the "Cross of Gold" speech. Delivering a carefully planned and rehearsed text as if it were a spontaneous outpouring, he said, "We have petitioned, and our petitions have been scorned; we have entreated, and our entreaties have been disregarded; we have begged, and they have mocked us when our calamity came. We beg no longer, we entreat no more; we petition no more. We defy them." Bryan went on to declare the farms could survive without the cities, but cities could not survive without the farms. He summed up his defiance of gold standard supporters: "Having behind us the producing masses of this nation and the world, supported by the laboring interests and the toilers everywhere, we will answer their demand for a gold standard by saying to them: You shall not press down upon the brow of labor this crown of thorns; you shall not crucify mankind on a cross of gold."

WE HAVE PETITIONED, AND OUR PETITIONS HAVE BEEN SCORNED; WE HAVE ENTREATED, AND OUR ENTREATIES HAVE BEEN DISREGARDED; WE HAVE BEGGED, AND THEY HAVE MOCKED US WHEN OUR CALAMITY CAME. WE BEG NO LONGER, WE ENTREAT NO MORE; WE PETITION NO MORE. WE DEFY THEM.

William Jennings Bryan, Cross of Gold speech, 1896

The next day Bryan was nominated as the Democratic Party's presidential candidate. He also received the nomination of the Populist Party and the National Silver Party and was supported by those Republicans who favored free silver. The Republican candidate was the affable and well-financed William McKinley (1897–1901). Bryan embarked on a campaign that covered more than 18,000 miles in 27 states. For some of the spectators his oratory bordered on demagoguery, but to many of his listeners Bryan was a hero. He inspired listeners with his wonderful voice and dramatic delivery. However, Bryan ultimately failed to convert eastern workers to the free silver cause. Industrialists convinced their employees that Bryan was a radical, even a revolutionary. McKinley narrowly won the popular vote (51 percent to 46 percent) but dominated in the electoral college (271 to 176 votes), which is the deciding vehicle in an election.

The 1896 campaign was the high point of Bryan's political career. Though he ran for president in 1900 and in 1908, he was unsuccessful. He did succeed in seeing many of his central ideas enacted into law. This included the popular election of senators, the income tax, the creation of the Department of Labor, prohibition, and women's right to vote. In 1912 President Woodrow Wilson (1913–1921) appointed Bryan to be his Secretary of State. Bryan had earlier helped Wilson win the Democratic nomination and the presidency. Bryan was a pacifist at heart, and he was effective in spearheading several treaties designed to forestall the coming war in Europe. He resigned when Wilson used stronger language than Bryan thought acceptable after Germany sank the British liner *Lusitania* and 128 U.S. citizens were killed. He nevertheless loyally supported the United States when war was finally declared and the country entered World War I (1914–1918).

Following the war Bryan championed Prohibition and served as the president of the National Dry Federation in 1918. He was known for serving grape juice rather than wine at diplomatic functions while he was Secretary of State. Bryan continued to advocate Prohibition until it was ratified in 1919 when the 18th Amendment to the U.S. Constitution was passed.

Bryan's last great crusade was against the Darwinian theory of evolution. He was a prosecutor of John T. Scopes in what has become known as the "Monkey Trial." The case brought Bryan head-to-head with renowned Chicago lawyer Clarence Darrow. The trial was great theater and attracted worldwide notoriety as a duel between fundamentalism and the theory of the evolutionary origin of man. Scopes was eventually found guilty, but the trial took a great toll on Bryan. He died in 1925, five days after its conclusion.

See also: **Free Silver, Cross of Gold Speech, Gold Standard, Gold Standard Act, Prohibition,**

FURTHER READING

Ashby, LeRoy. *William Jennings Bryan: Champion of Democracy*. Boston: Twayne, 1987.

Cherny, Robert W. *A Righteous Cause: The Life of William Jennings Bryan*. Boston: Little, Brown, 1985.

Coletta, Paolo E. *William Jennings Bryan: I. Political Evangelist, 1860–1908; II. Progressive Politician and Moral Statesman, 1909–1915; III. Political Puritan, 1915–1925*. Lincoln: University of Nebraska Press, 1964–69.

Koenig, Louis W. *Bryan: A Political Biography of William Jennings Bryan*. New York: Putnam, 1971.

Ranson, Edward. "Electing a President, 1896." *History Today*, October, 1996.

Springen, Donald K. *William Jennings Bryan: Orator of Small-Town America*. New York: Greenwood Press, 1991.

BUDGET DEFICIT

A budget is an estimate of expected income and expenses for a specific period of time. Governments, private businesses, and individuals use the budget-making process to establish financial goals. The completed budget is then used as a blueprint to monitor the progress toward those goals. If income or expenses are equal, a budget is in balance. But, depending on financial objectives, a budget might have a surplus or deficit. A surplus is created when an individual or organization has more income than expenses for a given time period and decides to set some of this money aside. For instance, an individual might make monthly payments into a college-savings plan that will be used in the future. A deficit is just the opposite and occurs when expenses are greater than income. As a consequence, money is borrowed from an outside source. For example, an individual who wants to buy a car may lack the necessary cash and so takes out a loan to cover the cost. If a deficit continues over a long period of time, it is called a chronic deficit.

During much of the 1970s, '80s, and '90s, the U.S. federal government had annual budget deficits that often exceeded $100 billion. In 1992, the federal government had an annual budget deficit of $290 billion. The result of these years of deficit spending was that by 1999, the United States had a national debt of approximately $5.5 trillion and paid $240 billion annually in interest to finance the debt. The purpose of the federal budget is to collect and spend the funds needed to carry out social, military, and economic policies. According to the Employment Act of 1946, the federal government has the responsibility to promote maximum employment, fight inflation, and encourage economic stability and growth. To achieve these aims, the federal government might spend more money than it receives in order to stimulate the economy. This type of fiscal policy creates a budget deficit. The federal government reversed this budget deficit spending in the late 1990s and began passing surplus budgets. By 2008, the federal government's annual budget is expected to reach a surplus of $251 billion. However, unless these annual surpluses are used to pay

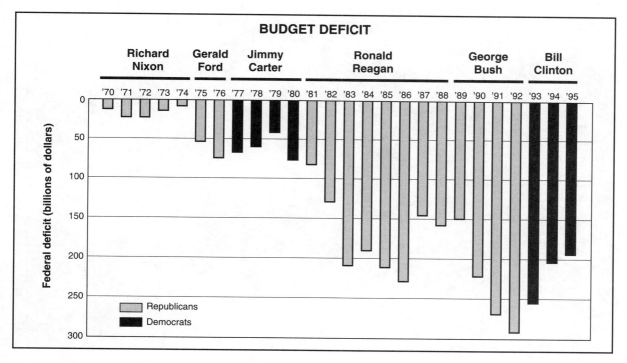

BUDGET DEFICIT

The annual federal budget deficit for each year from 1970–1995 is shown on this bar graph. The budget deficit was greatest while George Bush was in office and began to decline after the election of Bill Clinton.

off the accumulated debt, the country will have an estimated federal debt of $6.3 trillion in 2003.

See also: **Inflation**

BUFFALO, EXTERMINATION OF

In the early nineteenth century great herds of buffalo, more appropriately called American bison, roamed the Great Plains. Then over 50 million buffalo existed (perhaps as many of 75 million). A number of early accounts described awesome sights of the enormous herds. Lewis and Clark commented in 1806 that in what later became South Dakota ''The moving multitude . . . darkened the whole plains.'' Others wrote that, when viewing a herd from a distance, it appeared the entire prairie was in motion. Army major Richard Dodge commented as late as 1871 that it took five days to pass one herd.

The buffalo was central to the Plains Indian economy and remained central to their spiritual world even as late as the twentieth century. Bison provided a variety of foodstuffs, hides for clothing and shelter, bladders for pouches, gall and blood for paints, bones for utensils, droppings for fuel and heat, and skulls for

sacred ceremonies. The ox-like grazing mammal had woolly hair and pronounced shoulder hump and was well adapted to the short-grass prairies of the Plains. Though weighing almost 2000 pounds each, the buffalo were surprisingly agile and fast and actually make lighter use of the fragile prairie landscapes than domestic livestock. Buffalo also could withstand more extreme weather conditions than cattle. They tended not to congregate near water sources. In earlier times their native range covered much of North America, but by the mid-nineteenth century the primary range extended from West Texas northward through Alberta, Canada and west from the Mississippi River to the Rockies.

At the end of the American Civil War (1861–1865), the U.S. military's attention turned again to American Indian relations. Since U.S. settlements expanded further west, troops entered the Great Plains region to protect American settlers and the pending railroad development which would extend well into the central Plains.

The military was keenly aware that a substantial decline in buffalo would pose a serious setback to the Indians' ability to resist U.S. expansion. It would also spell an end to their seemingly nomadic lifestyle and force their move to reservations. Some believe the military made concerted efforts to exterminate the buffalo, both by direct actions and with logistical

In 1878, the Rath and Wright's buffalo hide yard in Dodge City, Kansas, stored 40,000 buffalo hides.

assistance provided to private hunting expeditions. Given the nature of the animals sometimes to not stampede when fired on, a marksman could shoot a hundred buffalo in an hour standing in one spot. Often only the buffalo tongues and other choice cuts were taken and most of the animal was left to rot. Sometimes they were killed purely for sport. Fencing by new settlers also took its toll by restricting buffalo from traditional watering holes and rich grazing areas.

By 1871 the slaughter of buffalo escalated further. A Pennsylvania tannery developed an industrial method to convert buffalo hides into inexpensive commercial leather for harnesses and machine belts. With hides worth between $1 and $3 each, hunters invaded the Plains. The Kansas Pacific and the Santa Fe railroads carried the hides to eastern markets. As the Kansas herds vanished rapidly, the decimation extended southward to the Texas panhandle. Because the buffalo herds sometimes blocked trains, railroad companies hired hunters to clear the tracks and guard watering holes. An estimated 15 million buffalo in 1865 decreased by 1872 to seven million.

Congress grew alarmed and passed legislation in 1874 regulating the killing of buffalo. Non-Indians could not kill female buffalo and were prohibited from killing no more than needed for food. However, President Ulysses S. Grant (1869–1877) vetoed the measure. The Texas state legislature also unsuccessfully introduced a buffalo protection bill in 1875.

In 1880 the Northern Pacific Railroad reached the Dakota-Montana border in the central area of the traditional buffalo range. Thousands of buffalo hides were shipped from the Montana Territory and Yellowstone River area. The following year the railroad reached Miles City, Montana. Two years later, in 1883, a herd of 10,000 in Montana were exterminated in a few days time.

By the 1890s less than a thousand buffalo remained in scattered areas, mostly on private ranches. Perhaps a scant twenty to fifty buffalo had sought refuge in Yellowstone National Park. In 1908 Congress created a national bison range west of Flathead Lake in Montana.

Hide hunters as well as thrill seekers in combination with the growing railroad network doomed the once massive herds. The herds on the central plains were exterminated by the early 1870s; they were eliminated from the southern plains later in the 1870s; and they vanished from the northern plains in the early 1880s. To the Plains Indians the wasteful mass killing of the buffalo herds was perhaps the most disheartening act of all by the white intruders. Their economy was shattered and the native groups were forced to live on government handouts. The demise of the great buffalo herds also marked the transition of the extensive grasslands into agricultural production. The prairie itself eventually disappeared under the plow.

See also: **Lewis and Clark Expedition, Plains Indians, Westward Expansion**

FURTHER READING

Callenbach, Ernest. *Bring Back the Buffalo!: A Sustainable Future for America's Great Plains.* Washington, DC: Island Press, 1996.

Dary, David A. *The Buffalo Book: The Full Saga of the American Animal.* Athens, OH: Ohio University Press, 1989.

Josephy, Alvin M. *Now That the Buffalo's Gone: A Study of Today's American Indians.* Norman, OK: University of Oklahoma Press, 1984.

Milner, Clyde A., II, Carol A. O'Connor, and Martha A. Sandweiss, eds. *The Oxford History of the American West.* New York: Oxford University Press, 1994.

Paul, Rodman W. *The Far West and the Great Plains in Transition, 1859–1900.* New York: Harper and Row, 1988.

BUFFETT, WARREN

Regarded by many as America's most brilliant investor and recognized as one of the richest men in the United States during the late twentieth century, Warren Buffett (1930–) has become a legend during his lifetime. Buffett's folksy pronouncements along with his long-time home address in Omaha, Nebraska, mask a shrewd and aggressive approach to business. When he was a boy Buffett had the life goal of being "very, very rich" as he once put it. He certainly achieved that goal by becoming a multi-billionaire.

Buffett was born in Omaha on August 30, 1930. While he was still a boy Buffet often accompanied his father to work. His father's stockbrokerage firm, became a familiar haunt for the boy. Before he reached his teenage years Buffett was already doing routine duties around the office. He chalked stock prices on the office blackboard and charted performance records of various equities. In 1942 the family moved to Fredericksburg, Virginia. They lived there while his father served Nebraska as a U.S. Congressman. According to Robert Lenzner writing in *Forbes* magazine (18 October 1993), Buffett credits his father as an important role model: "I have never known a better human being than my Dad."

When he was only sixteen, Buffett enrolled at the University of Pennsylvania where he studied mathematics and statistics. At age twenty he received a Bachelor's from the University of Nebraska. He then entered Columbia University's Graduate School of Business where he obtained an MBA.

After working briefly for his father in Omaha, Buffett joined the New York investment firm of his mentor Benjamin Graham. Buffett later claimed that the great turning point in his life and career came when he met Graham. Graham identified undervalued companies by avoiding the use of annual reports. He concentrated instead on exacting analyses of balance sheets and profit and loss statements. Buffett's facility in math and statistics enabled him to become adept at this analysis. However, he later realized that although statistical bargains often turned out to be winners, it made sense to also look for companies that were undervalued for other reasons.

When Graham closed his Wall Street firm in 1956, Buffett left New York and returned to Omaha. There he started an investment partnership that he managed until 1969. To drum up business he gave seminars for doctors and other professionals seeking advice on how to invest their money. Many of them decided to put their savings under Buffett's management after they heard him speak. Other investors in his partnership were either former business school classmates or Wall Street financiers. Several of Buffett's early backers now hold stock portfolios worth tens of millions.

In a joint interview with Microsoft Corporation chairman Bill Gates in *Fortune* (20 July 1998) Buffett explained why he eventually terminated the investment partnership: "[I] closed it up because I couldn't find anything. I hadn't lost the ability to value companies; there just weren't any left that were cheap enough, and I wasn't in the business of shorting stocks." Within a decade, however, the situation had changed. As Buffett said: ". . . in the mid-1970s, every security you looked at was really dramatically undervalued."

Buffett preached that the key to making money in the stock market was to pick good stocks at good prices and to stay with a company as long as it continued to be well-managed. He left frenetic trading to others and hung on to stocks even if they became overvalued. Buffett bought stock in companies that made products he understood and felt comfortable with. His major holdings, for example, included Coca Cola Company and Gillette Company. He also had three major media holdings: The Washington Post, Capital Cities/ABC, and the Buffalo News. He never invested heavily in technology stocks or in foreign companies because these were not market categories with which he was familiar. According to Lenzner in *Forbes* Buffett's basic rule was "Don't put too many eggs in your basket and pick them carefully."

In the mid-1960s Buffett bought controlling interest in Berkshire Hathaway, a failing textile business in New Bedford, Mass. He briefly attempted to maintain Berkshire Hathaway as a textile company and simultaneously continue his investment activities. In the end he liquidated the textile business but retained its name for his investment company. He used his base in the company to buy stocks in the wildly under priced market of the 1970s and 1980s. Between 1977 and 1991, according to Michael Lewis in *The New Republic* (17 February 1992), Berkshire Hathaway grew from a pool of $180 million in risk capital to one of more than $11 billion.

During the 1980s Buffett also developed a very lucrative "white knight" strategy. Using this strategy he saved certain businesses from being bought out by competition. He often stepped in to save a business by infusing it with the cash it needed to fend off takeovers. In exchange, he expected a return on his investment in the form of preferred stock that guaranteed a healthy dividend whether or not the company performed well.

Buffett summed up his views on investment in *Fortune* magazine: "What you want to do was attract shareholders who were very much like you, with the same time horizons and expectations. We don't talk about quarterly hearings, we don't have an investor relations department, and we don't have conference calls with Wall Street analysts, because we don't want people who were focusing on what's going to happen next quarter or even next year. We want people to join us because they want to be with us until they die."

See also: **Wall Street**

FURTHER READING

Buffett, Mary. *Buffettology: The Previously Unexplained Techniques That Have Made Warren Buffett the World's Most Famous Investor*. New York: Rawson Associates, 1997.

Lewis, Michael. "The Temptation of St. Warren: Buffet's Principles—and Wall Street's." *The New Republic*, February 17, 1992.

Lenzner, Robert. Warren Buffett's Idea of Heaven." *Forbes*, October 18, 1993.

———. "The Berkshire Bunch." *Forbes*, October 12, 1998.

Serwer, Andrew. "Buffett's Growth Plan: Another $58 Billion." *Fortune*, July 20, 1998.

Lowenstein, Roger. *Buffett: The Making of an American Capitalist*. New York: Random House, 1995.

BURNHAM, DANIEL HUDSON

Daniel H. Burnham (1846–1912), one of America's most important architects, helped to rebuild Chicago after the Chicago Fire of 1871. Burnham made important contributions to the development of the skyscraper. Long after his death, his visionary ideas about urban and regional planning remained influential as a way to accommodate work, home, and recreation in close proximity to each other. His 1909 plan to transform Chicago into a beautiful, functional city was the first comprehensive urban plan in the United States.

Daniel Burnham was born near New York City on September 4, 1846. His family moved to Chicago when he was nine. He graduated from a public high school in Chicago but failed to obtain admission to college. In his early adulthood, Burnham worked as retail clerk, mined for gold in Nevada, and ran unsuccessfully for a seat in the Illinois State Senate. Still in his early twenties, Burnham was accepted as an apprentice by a leading Chicago architect, William Le Baron Jenney.

In 1872 Burnham, age twenty-six, moved to the firm of Carter, Drake, and Wight, where he worked as a draftsman. A year later he went into partnership with a fellow draftsman at the firm, John Wellborn Root. The partnership turned out to be a profitable one. Root was creative and versatile; Burnham, practical and businesslike, was a superb administrator. They prospered after the Great Chicago Fire, which decimated downtown Chicago. Between 1873 and 1891 the firm designed 165 private residences and 75 buildings of various types.

Most of these buildings were European in influence: their exterior decorations echoed ancient Greek and Roman monuments. In 1891 Burnham and Root adapted modern techniques to meet the demand for more centralized office space in Chicago. Three of their buildings have been designated landmarks. The Rookery (1886) and the Reliance Building (1890) both used a skeleton frame construction. The sixteen-story

Daniel H. Burnham.

Monadnock building (1891) was the last and tallest American masonry skyscraper.

In 1893, two years after the death of his partner, Burnham became chief of construction and chief consulting architect for the World's Columbian Exposition in Chicago. Burnham teamed with architectural firms from all over the eastern United States to create an eclectic "White City"—a community of buildings and landscapes that combined boulevards, gardens and classical facades. The Colombian Exposition was a triumph and it made Burnham famous. That year he received honorary architectural degrees from Harvard and Yale Universities, and he was elected president of the American Institute of Architects.

The "White City" became the nucleus of Burnham's 1909 plan to transform Chicago into a beautiful city. Critics have said that Burnham ignored the social side of urban planning in his zeal for a visually attractive and smoothly functioning city. He was also accused of failing to realize that boulevards lined with offices would be deserted at night. Despite these criticisms, much of his great plan was put into effect. Some $300 million worth of architectural projects were built before the Great Depression called it to a halt in the 1930s.

Burnham was also faulted for trying to make Chicago into another Paris, France. The neoclassical architecture, broad avenues, and public gardens he favored echoed those of the French capital. Famed Chicago architect Louis Sullivan (1856–1924) was said to have complained that Burnham's designs set American architecture back by 50 years. Notwithstanding these attacks, many of Burnham's ideas have stood the test of time and influenced city planners across the country.

One great legacy was Burnham's vision of making the Lake Michigan lakefront a recreational resource. His plan proposed the creation of a string of landfill islands and peninsulas, which would provide protection against natural erosion and storms and would also be an attractive site for pleasure boating, picnics, and other outdoor activities. Although only one island was built, the Lincoln Park shoreline was extended with five miles of landfill. Legacies of Burnham's plan also included Lakeshore Drive and Grant Park. A ring of forest preserves surrounding the city provided the greenbelt that Burnham anticipated in 1907, long before the waves of population growth in the twentieth century transformed the city.

In 1923 Burnham's recommendation for a complex of railroad stations west of the Loop (the historic center of the city) resulted in the construction of Union Station. In addition, Chicago's expressway system followed Burnham's plan for regional highways, though he could not have anticipated the effect of the automobile on American cities.

Burnham was asked to serve as a planning consultant by many other major American cities, including San Francisco, Detroit, and Cleveland. In 1905 he was consulted by then-Secretary of War William Howard Taft (1857–1930) for advice on a plan to rebuild and modernize Manila in the Philippines. In addition to his work as an urban planner, by the time of his death in 1912 Burnham was responsible for the design of several important buildings, including the Flatiron Building, New York (1901); Union Station, Washington, D.C. (1909); and Filene's Store, Boston (1912). Each of these buildings had a lasting influence on the twentieth century cityscape, and through them, Daniel Burnham's vision endures.

See also: **Chicago Fire of 1871, Reinforced Concrete**

FURTHER READING

Hines, Thomas S. *Burnham of Chicago: Architect and Planner.* New York: Oxford University Press, 1974.

Hitchcock, Henry R. *Architecture: Nineteenth and Twentieth Centuries*, 4th ed. New York: Penguin Books, 1977.

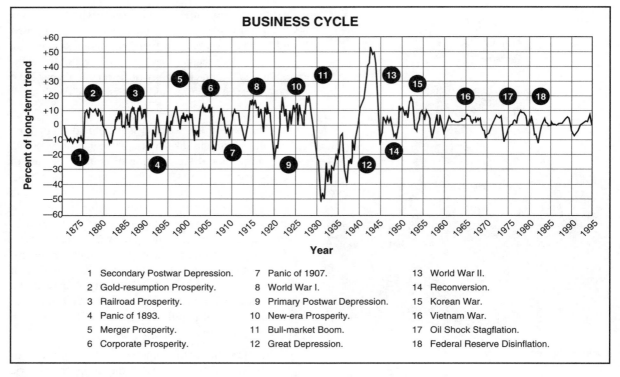

BUSINESS CYCLE

1 Secondary Postwar Depression.	7 Panic of 1907.	13 World War II.
2 Gold-resumption Prosperity.	8 World War I.	14 Reconversion.
3 Railroad Prosperity.	9 Primary Postwar Depression.	15 Korean War.
4 Panic of 1893.	10 New-era Prosperity.	16 Vietnam War.
5 Merger Prosperity.	11 Bull-market Boom.	17 Oil Shock Stagflation.
6 Corporate Prosperity.	12 Great Depression.	18 Federal Reserve Disinflation.

When an economy declines over a sustained period, it is in recession, then when it grows, it is in expansion. From 1875 to 1995, there were 18 contributing factors to the country's growth and shrinkage.

Hoffman, Donald. *The Architecture of John Root.* Baltimore, MD: Johns Hopkins University Press, 1973.

Moore, Charles. *Daniel H. Burnham, Architect, Planner of Cities.* Boston: Houghton Mifflin Co., 1921.

Reps, John W. *The Making of Urban America: A History of City Planning in the United States.* Princeton, NJ: Princeton University Press, 1965.

BUSCH, ADOLPHUS

Adolphus Busch (1839–1913) was a German immigrant to the United States who used his inheritance funds to launch his career with a small brewing supply company. He went on to found one of the largest and most successful breweries in the United States.

Busch was born in Kastel, near Mainz, Germany, one of 22 children. His father was a prosperous merchant, innkeeper and landowner. At age eighteen Busch emigrated to St. Louis, Missouri after completing his education. There he worked first as a clerk in riverfront businesses and then in the wholesale supply house of William Hainrichschofen. In 1859 he received his inheritance and in partnership with Ernst Wattenberg formed a brewer's supply company which would become Adolphus Busch & Co.

In 1861 Busch married Lilly Anheuser. Her father Eberhard Anheuser was a successful St. Louis businessman who bought a struggling local brewery in 1860. In 1864 he convinced his son-in-law to join the company as a salesman. Busch eventually became a full partner and president of the company. He was credited with transforming the fledgling enterprise into an industry giant and is generally considered the founder of Anheuser-Busch, the largest beer maker in the United States and the world's largest brewer.

Busch was known as an innovator and an accomplished marketer. When he joined the brewery the firm's storage capacity was limited by how much beer it could hold in its caves. Busch pioneered the new technology of artificial refrigeration that enabled the company to store a much larger quantity of its product. Within five years of joining his father-in-law's brewery Busch doubled its storage capacity.

Among the innovations he introduced to the U.S. brewing industry was the process of pasteurization. This process enabled beer to withstand temperature fluctuations and substantially expanded its shelf life. As a result his beer could now be shipped far beyond St. Louis. To distribute the beer nationally, Busch decided to use refrigerated freight cars. His fleet ultimately totaled 850 of these specialized railroad cars. He also built a network of ice houses that were located adjacent to railroad transportation; beer could be kept cool there until it was needed in a local market.

Together with St. Louis restaurateur Carl Conrad, Busch developed a light beer called Budweiser. He believed that consumers would prefer it to the darker brews then available. Budweiser was an immediate success and became the company's flagship brand.

In 1879 the company was renamed the Anheuser-Busch Brewing Association. When Eberhard died in 1880 Busch became company president. By 1901 the company was the nation's largest brewery with an annual production rate of 1,000,000 barrels of beer. The company during Busch's 33-year presidency marketed 19 different brands of beer. These included Michelob, introduced in 1896 as a specialty beer for Connoisseurs.

To maintain Budweiser's market dominance Busch came up with countless promotional campaigns. Among the most famous was a lithograph of Custer's Last Stand. It was prominently displayed in bars everywhere with its Budweiser logo.

Busch believed in developing product loyalty through quality control. His strict insistence on quality resulted in Budweiser's winning numerous gold medals at world fairs and exhibitions throughout the nation and the world. He was also keenly aware of market preferences. As early as 1889 when the forces of Prohibition were only beginning to gather strength he marketed beer as "the true temperance beverage." He initiated product development of nonalcoholic beverages. He was also ahead of his time in focusing on international markets. When Prohibition went into effect in the United States in 1920 Anheuser-Busch had established 125 markets in 44 countries on six continents. This was seven years after Busch's death in 1913.

In 1899 Busch wrote to a friend: "Only by fair, sociable and liberal treatment can you create a lasting attachment between brewery and its trade. What is a great brewery anyway? It is an immense complex of buildings filled with machinery, casks and general equipment costing millions of dollars, and what is such investment worth if there is not an adequate trade for its capacity? A large plant with only trade to consume one half to three quarters of its capacity in output is bound to run into bankruptcy; therefore the most valuable assets we posses in our brewery are our trade and the loyalty of all those with whom we are in business connection."

That operating philosophy served Busch well. At the time of his death in 1913 his personal fortune was estimated at $60 million. Management of the business he founded remained in the family for several generations after his death. In addition to Budweiser, Michelob, and Busch beers Anheuser-Busch today makes and distributes several specialty beers. As of the late 1990s the company had joint ventures in China, Japan, Mexico, several South American countries, and throughout Europe and operated theme and water parks.

See also: **Brewing Industry, Prohibition**

FURTHER READING

"A Legacy of Quality" [cited February 10, 1999] available from the World Wide Web @www.anheuser-busch.com/.

"Anheuser-Busch History" [cited February 10, 1999] available from the World Wide Web @www.anheuser-busch.com.

"Anheuser-Busch Companies, Inc.," [cited February 10, 1999] available from the World Wide Web @www.hoovers.com/index.html

Anheuser-Busch Historical Archives. St. Louis, Missouri.

Hernon, Peter and Terry Ganey. *Under the Influence: The Unauthorized Story of the Anheuser-Busch Dynasty.* New York: Simon and Schuster, 1991.

Plavchan, Ronald Jan. *A History of Anheuser-Busch, 1852–1933.* New York: Arno Press, 1976.

BUSINESS CYCLE

Business cycle is the name given to the tendency of all economies to go through periods of economic weakness followed by periods of economic growth. When employment, income, trade, and the production of goods and services declines the economy is said to be in a "recession" or a "contraction." If this downturn is particularly harsh, this part of the business cycle is known as a "depression." Conversely, when employment, income, trade, and the production of goods and services grows over a sustained period of time, the economy is said to be enjoying an "expansion." Thus, the term *business cycle* describes the full process of economic growth and shrinkage—of "boom" followed by "bust"—that every economy experiences. The causes for changes in the business cycle are as complex as the economy itself, but important factors are over investment, under consumption of goods and services, and the amount of money circulating in the economy. Business cycles can differ greatly in their length, in the number of industries they affect, and in their harshness. Today economists use dozens of statistical measures to try to identify when a business cycle has ended or begun. These include, among others, new factory orders, number of business bankruptcies, stock market performance, new home building, and length of average work week.

Between 1790 and 1990 the United States experienced 44 complete business cycles, each of which lasted about four and a half years (i.e., including both a recessionary period and an expansionary period). In the nineteenth century the recessionary period of the business cycle was usually accompanied by a financial panic in which stock prices fell and banks and businesses went bankrupt. The longest recession in U.S. history during the nineteenth century was between 1873 and 1879. The most severe recession was the Great Depression, which lasted from 1929 to 1939. To understand how disastrous the Great Depression was one should consider that during the recession of 1973–1975 the gross national product fell six percent, while during the Great Depression it fell a staggering 50 percent. Since World War II (1939–1945), however, the business cycle has become much more mild because economists and government leaders know much more about the role the money supply and government fiscal policy can play in affecting the business cycle. When the economy begins to contract, for example, the Federal Reserve can quickly lower interest rates to encourage lending, which stimulates economic growth.

See also: **Federal Reserve System, Financial Panic, Recession**

CALIFORNIA

California is so large and so diverse that it is difficult to characterize. Native American, Spanish, and Mexican influences marked its earlier centuries. White settlers who came to exploit its various resources (from sea otter to beavers and gold) led it into statehood. Now an agricultural and manufacturing giant, the state has experienced many economic booms but has also weathered its share of harsh times.

European economic interest in California began in the sixteenth century, when Spanish explorers in their search for a western passage to the East discovered Baja California (now a part of Mexico). Believing there was a transcontinental canal, Juan Rodriquez de Cabrillo first landed in Upper (or Alta) California in 1542, at the bay now known as San Diego. Until the late eighteenth century, however, Europeans were little interested in the region. Spurred on by its economic rivals in 1769, Spain sent Father Junipero Serra (1713–1784) and military leader Gaspar de Portol to establish the first permanent European settlement in California. Franciscan friars established some 21 missions along the coast to convert the Native American population and also built four military outposts called *presidios*. San Jose de Guadalupe was the first civilian settlement in California.

Having done little to strengthen its California outposts, Spain lost control of the territory after the Mexican Revolution of 1821. The Mexicans gradually began redistributing the vast lands and herds owned by the missions to Mexican private citizens, who established huge *ranchos* (ranches) that produced grain and large herds of cattle. The *rancheros* (ranch owners) traded hides and tallow for manufactured products from foreign traders along the coast. They assigned most of the manual labor on the ranchos to Indian workers.

U.S. citizens first came to California in pursuit of the sea otter, whose pelts were shipped to China at profitable rates. Others came to exploit the hide and tallow trade, and inland explorers profited from the hunting of beavers. U.S. interest in California began to grow and during the administration of President James K. Polk (1845–1849) war was waged on Mexico. By the terms of the Treaty of Guadalupe-Hidalgo in 1848, California was ceded to the United States.

By far the largest effect on the economy of the new territory was the Gold Rush of 1849, which began with the discovery of gold along the American River. Thousands of prospectors poured into California, and by 1852, $80 million in gold was being mined in the state. The state's population quadrupled during the 1850s and grew at two times the national rate in the 1860s and 1870s. California became the thirty-first state in 1851.

WE THIS DAY WORKED OUR MACHINE. OH CHRISTMAS, WHERE ARE THE JOYS AND FESTIVITIES? NOT IN CALIFORNIA SURELY.

Joseph Wood, Miner, Christmas Day, 1849

Racial discrimination and racial divisions marked the first years of statehood, as white citizens attempted to put down the state's growing ethnic populations. New tax laws were passed to discourage Latin American and Chinese miners, and efforts were made to displace the original Mexican owners of large *ranchos*.

The completion of the transcontinental railroad in 1869 brought California into extensive contact with the rest of the country. The directors of the Central Pacific railroad—Leland Stanford (1824–1893), Collis P. Huntington (1821–1900), Charles Crocker (1822–1888), and Mark Hopkins (1814–1878)—wielded tremendous political and economic influence in the state, creating a transportation and land monopoly. Considerable opposition to this monopoly was expressed by novelist Frank Norris in his 1901 novel *The Octopus*.

In the late nineteenth century irrigation projects made it possible for agriculture to replace gold and silver mining as the mainstay of the economy. Orange and lemon groves began to supply most of the nation

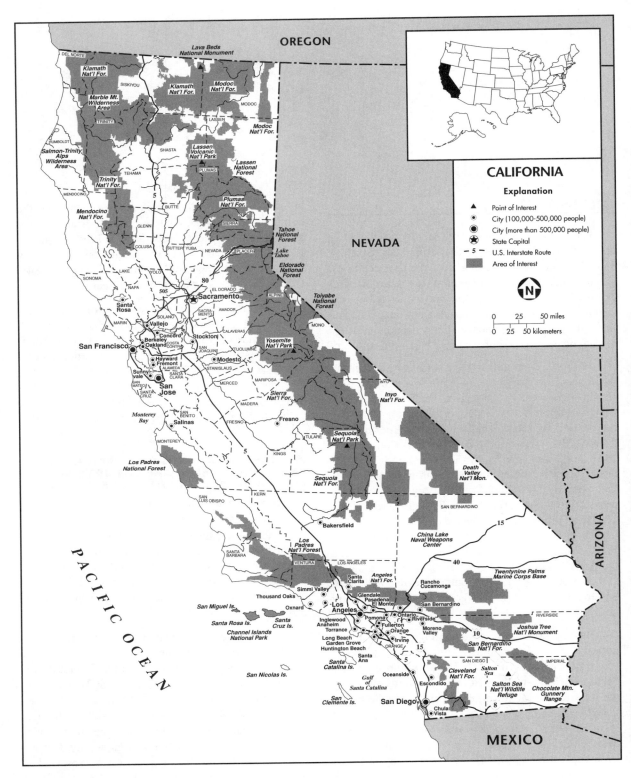

State of California.

with citrus fruit. In the 1870s the state became the top cattle-raising state and the second-highest producer of wheat. California's population burgeoned in the 1880s because of the success of the citrus industry, the increasing popularity of the state as a destination for invalids, and a railroad rate war which made transportation cheap. The urban population grew rapidly during the early twentieth century. The San Francisco earthquake of 1906 brought a halt to that city's amazing success story, but only for a few years.

Los Angeles and San Francisco, the two major urban areas, were each at about one million people in 1920. The two cities increasingly vied with one another for water rights, vital to a growing population. Over the objections of conservationists, San Francisco created a reservoir by damming the Tuolumne River at the Hetch Hetchy Valley. Los Angeles angered farmers along the Owens Valley by diverting nearly all the water in the Owens River through an aqueduct. Manufacturing in the urban areas soon began to outstrip mining and agriculture as the major employer in the state.

California continued to boom throughout the 1920s as people were drawn to the state's favorable climate, natural beauty, and economic opportunities. Oil was discovered in the Los Angeles Basin, placing the state for a time in first place in crude oil production. By 1930 the size of Los Angeles had more than doubled, growing to over 2.2 million. The city also became known for its expanding network of highways and its large number of motor cars, a distinction that would plague Los Angeles in the traffic-clogged years to come.

Like other states California suffered during the Great Depression (1929–1939), but also gained in some areas. People from all over the United States, especially from the dust bowl of the southern Great Plains, fled to California in search of a better life. The California film industry grew as well, giving people in the United States movies that helped them escape from their worries during the 1930s. By 1940 the United States boasted more movie theaters than banks.

IF IT WERE AN INDEPENDENT NATION WITH THE SAME GROSS PRODUCT, CALIFORNIA WOULD RANK WITH THE GREATEST POWERS OF THE EARTH IN WEALTH.

Ralph J. Roske, *Everyman's Eden: A History of California*, 1968

1930s politics in the state were marked by several socialist-oriented ideas, such as the Townsend Plan and the ''Ham 'n' Eggs'' Plan, which promised cash payments for the elderly. A candidate for governor in 1934, author Upton Sinclair (1878–1968, also a well-known socialist) promised to ''end poverty in California,'' but he lost to the Republican incumbent. Only World War II (1939–1945) brought the state to real economic health by expanding the number of military installations, aircraft factories, and shipyards in the state. Along with this expansion came the increasing importance of ethnic minorities in California, particularly Mexican and Japanese Americans.

Throughout the 1950s and early 1960s California continued to grow rapidly, reaching the top population ranking among all states in 1963. The 1970s saw a slowdown in growth after a number of industries, particularly aerospace, experienced a downturn. The military buildup during Californian Ronald Reagan's presidency (1981–1989), however, helped the economy bounce back in the 1980s. It declined again in the late 1980s and early 1990s as defense spending decreased, real estate became expensive, and environmental regulations discouraged business. By 1992 the state's unemployment rate had reached 10.1 percent, with jobs in aerospace and manufacturing dropping by 24 percent. Another San Francisco earthquake in 1989 caused extreme economic stress in that city, with $5 to $7 billion in property damage. Still another earthquake northwest of Los Angeles in 1994 caused $13 to $20 million in property damage.

California felt the economic stress of illegal immigration more than most states and also struggled more with its treatment of ethnic minorities. Proposition 187, passed in 1994, banned illegal immigrants from welfare, education, and non-emergency health care. In 1995 Governor Pete Wilson issued an executive order banning the use of affirmative action in state hiring and contracting and in university admissions.

By the 1990s California had the largest work force in the nation and the greatest number of employed workers. In 1995, 49 percent of the total of employees in the guided missile and space vehicle industry were located in California. In 1995 nearly 18 percent of all workers were members of labor unions. The organizing of migrant farm workers has been the most difficult task. During the 1960s labor activist Cesar Chavez (1927–1993) mobilized migrants to secure bargaining rights in the grape, lettuce, and berry fields of the San Joaquin Valley. An organized nationwide boycott of these products helped this effort. After surviving a challenge from the Teamsters Union, the United Farm Workers gained the right to free elections among farm workers.

California led the nation in economic output and total income in the late 1990s, with per capita income at over $25,000 in 1996. It had quite a diversified econo-my, including manufacturing, technology, retail trade, banking, finance, and personal services. Not to be forgotten is the growth of the California wine industry, which became both a prestigious consumer commodity and a source of tourist dollars in the Napa and Sonoma valleys and in other grape-growing areas of the state. Tourism was a major contributor to the state's econo-my in many other areas of California, including San Francisco, Los Angeles, and the many national and state parks, as well as on the spectacular coastline.

See also: **Gold Rush of 1849, Mexican Cession, James Polk**

FURTHER READING

Bean, Walton, and James J. Rawls. *California: An Interpretive History*, 4th ed. New York: McGraw-Hill, 1982.

Caughey, John W. *California: A Remarkable State's Life-History*, 4th ed. Englewood Cliffs, NJ: Pren-tice-Hall, 1982.

Kahrl, William L. *Water and Power: The Conflict over Los Angeles's Water Supply in the Owens Valley*. Berkeley and Los Angeles: University of California Press, 1982.

Roske, Ralph J. *Everyman's Eden: A History of Cali-fornia*. New York: Macmillan, 1968.

Watkins, T.H. *California: An Illustrated History*. New York: Outlet, 1983.

CAMPBELL SOUP COMPANY

The roots of the Campbell Soup Company can be traced back to 1860, when Abraham Anderson opened a small canning factory in Camden, New Jersey. In 1869 Philadelphia produce merchant Joseph Campbell became Anderson's partner, forming Anderson and Campbell. The company canned vegetables, mince-meat, jams and jellies, and a variety of soups. In 1876 Anderson and Campbell dissolved their partnership and Campbell bought Anderson's share of the busi-ness, changing the business name to the Joseph A. Campbell Preserve Company. In 1882 a partnership was formed between Campbell's son-in-law, Walter S. Spackman; Campbell's nephew, Joseph S. Campbell; and Arthur Dorrance, Spackman's personal friend, who brought more cash to the partnership. At this time,

the company was renamed the Joseph Campbell Pre-serving Company.

In 1896 the company built a large factory in Camden and expanded its product line to include prepared meats, sauces, canned fruits, ketchup, and plum pudding. In 1897 Arthur Dorrance hired his nephew, John Thompson Dorrance, a chemical engi-neer and organic chemist who invented a method of successfully canning condensed soup. This innovation helped Campbell surpass its competitors. While others were still shipping heavy, uncondensed soup, Camp-bell was able to ship and sell its product at one-third the cost. As the company began increasing the variety of soups it offered, it canned fewer produce products. John Dorrance became director of the company in 1900 and soon after, the company was renamed the Joseph Campbell Company.

With the help of advertising that featured the Campbell Kids, Campbell's soup began finding its way into more and more American kitchens at a time when the prepared-food industry was growing rapidly. By 1904 the company sold 16 million cans of soup a year; and with 21 varieties of soup produced by 1905, Campbell began to eye a bigger market. In 1911 Campbell expanded its business into California, and became one of the first companies to serve the entire nation. Campbell's soup also had an impact on the way Americans prepared meals; as early as 1916, recipes using condensed soup as an ingredient appeared in cookbooks.

The company was incorporated as the Campbell Soup Company in 1922. Although Campbell diversi-fied into other food categories during the remainder of the twentieth century, soup remained the company's core product. By the late 1990s, Campbell accounted for 75 percent of all soup sold in the United States.

FURTHER READING

"Campbell: Now It's M-M-Global." *Business Week*, March 15, 1993.

Campbell Soup Company. A History. Camden, N.J.: Campbell Soup Company, 1988.

Collins, Douglas. *America's Favorite Food: The Sto-ry of Campbell Soup Company*. New York: Abrams, 1994.

Dwyer, Steve. "Red Alert: The Soup's Back On." *Prepared Foods*, September 1997.

Pehanich, Mike. "Brand Power." *Prepared Foods*, mid-April 1993.

Saporito, Bill. "Campbell Soup Gets Piping Hot." *Fortune*, September 9, 1991.

Sim, Mary B. *History of Commercial Canning in New Jersey*. Trenton, NJ: New Jersey Agricultural Society, 1951.

CANNING

Canning was a process for preserving food (vegetables, fruits, meats, and fish) by heating and sealing it in airtight containers. The method was developed by French candy-maker Nicolas-Francois Appert (c. 1750–1841) in 1809, though he did not understand why the process worked. Some fifty years later, the pioneering French chemist and microbiologist Louis Pasteur (1822–1895) explained that heating was necessary to the canning process since it killed bacteria (microorganisms) that would otherwise spoil the food.

Canning was introduced to the U.S. consumer market in stages. In 1821 the William Underwood Company began a canning operation in Boston, Massachusetts. Oyster canning began in Baltimore, Maryland in the 1840s. In 1853 U.S. inventor Gail Borden (1801–1874) developed a way to condense and preserve milk in a can and he founded the Borden Company four years later. In 1858 U.S. inventor John Landis Mason (1832–1902) developed a glass jar and lid suited to home-canning.

Early commercial canning methods in the United States did not ensure a safe product; as such, many female consumers avoided canned convenience foods. Nevertheless, the canning industry grew rapidly, due in part to the male market—cowboys in particular. Between 1860 and 1870 the U.S. canning industry increased output from five million to thirty million cans.

Convenience and long shelf life of canned foods helped them to catch on even though the canning process changed food flavor, color, and texture. Improvements in the manufacturing process during the 1870s helped eliminate the chance that cans would burst. By the end of the 1800s a wide variety of canned foods were available at increasingly lower prices and were common in the urban diet. Companies such as Franco-American advertised in women's magazines, promoting their "delicacies in tins." An outbreak of botulism in the 1920s prompted the U.S. canning industry to make further improvements to its preservation processes, but consumer demand for canned products persisted.

See also: **Borden**

CAPITAL

Capital is an underlying component of an economy. As a collective body, capital includes resources such as cash, equipment, investments, and property that are used to operate a business. Capital can be categorized in several ways. For instance, it can be either fixed or circulating. Fixed capital is durable in nature and is expected to have a long life. Plants (buildings/factories) and equipment are examples of fixed capital. Circulating capital refers to nonrenewable resources, such as raw material or oil. Capital can also be liquid, or readily able to be converted to cash. For instance finished goods that are in inventory are liquid capital. Frozen capital consists of resources that cannot be easily converted to cash, as is the case with buildings or machinery.

Capital assets, or fixed assets, can be sold. Capital gains or losses represent the profit or loss from the sale of capital assets. The gain or loss is the difference between the selling price and the original cost of the asset. Capitalization is the conversion of something into financial capital. As an example, capitalization occurs when a company sells stocks to gain cash. Over the years the term capital has changed in its meaning. To economists in the nineteenth century capital referred to the business income that resulted from industry. Income that was generated from natural resources such as oil deposits was called rent. Economists no longer recognize this distinction and use capital to refer to all resources that can produce goods or services, and hence create future income for a business.

CAPITAL GAIN

If you buy a piece of land or a company's stock in January and then sell it the next January for a higher amount, you have realized a capital gain on that asset. (If the value of that land or stock has gone down between the time you bought and sold it you have experienced a capital loss.) Capital gains are controversial because they usually accrue to people in higher-income tax brackets. The reason for this is simply that higher-income people generally have more money to set aside for stock market investments or real estate speculation. However, between 1921, when the federal government first began taxing capital gains, and 1987, capital gains were always taxed at a *lower* rate than regular income. In other words, while the U.S. government taxes 100 percent of a person's ordinary work income every tax year, it has traditionally taxed only 20 to 40 percent of long-term capital gains (depending in part on your income level and how long you have held the asset). Critics call this unfair. Why should the ordinary income that every working person makes be fully taxed while the capital gains that mostly upper-income people make is only partly taxed?

Defenders of lower tax rates for capital gains usually cite two main reasons. First, capital gains tax rate only applies to that portion of income that is plowed back into the economy in the form of job-creating capital investment. Second, suppose you hold a stock for ten years and in the eleventh year sell it for a capital gain of $50,000. If your capital gain were taxed as ordinary income, your income during that eleventh year would shoot up by $50,000. This would probably put you in a higher income tax bracket and force you to pay much higher taxes on your $50,000 than if you had paid taxes on your stock every year as it was growing. In other words, if you had to pay ordinary taxes on your $50,000 in capital gains you might think twice about selling your stock—and you might even hold onto a stock that had begun to fall in price just to avoid a big tax penalty. During the 1990s, more ordinary Americans than ever before bought stocks (often by investing in mutual funds) and enjoyed capital gains. This made it more politically palatable for Congress to pass the Taxpayer Relief Act of 1997 which lowered the capital gains tax rate to 20 percent for assets held for more than eighteen months.

See also: **Asset, Stock**

CAPITAL GOODS

Capital goods include goods such as tools and machinery that businesses use to produce consumer products and services. Capital goods are distinguished from consumer goods, which are not used in the production process and are intended for personal consumption. Capital goods use resources in such a way that they increase the capability of the production process. As a result they help to make more goods available to society than would ordinarily exist. For this reason some economists believe that capital goods represent an efficient use of the earth's limited resources. Capital goods can be considered fixed goods, that is, assets that are necessary to carry on a business. Fixed goods cannot be readily converted to cash and include equipment, buildings, and land. Capital goods are often called productive capital because they represent the potential capacity to produce future consumer goods.

See also: **Consumer Goods**

CAPITALISM

Capitalism is an economic system in which capital, or wealth, is put to use in order to create more capital. The system is characterized by private ownership of land and the means of production and distribution, which are used to make a profit with little or no government control. Capitalism provides the freedom to engage in economic activities based on the supply of resources and the market demand for goods; it promotes ingenuity and entrepreneurship. A capitalistic economy is also distinguished by a high degree of technological innovation due to several factors: competition, wages, and prices are based on market conditions; profit is the key consideration when making economic decisions; banking, insurance and credit systems are well-developed. Because of the element of competition, capitalism also results in the creation of wealth by the most cost-effective method, which lowers costs and prices, increases demand and production, and creates further economic opportunities.

Capitalism had its start in Western Europe in the seventeenth century with the discovery of new lands and colonization. Early capitalists were primarily merchants who dramatically increased their wealth through overseas trade. By the eighteenth century capitalism was the dominant economic system in England and the United States. Vast amounts of capital were being invested in machinery for factories, which eventually resulted in the Industrial Revolution. Industrialists replaced merchants as the primary figures in capitalistic societies. One of the greatest advocates of capitalism at the time was British economist Adam Smith (1723–90). In his work, *An Inquiry into the Nature and Causes of the Wealth of Nations*, Smith reasoned that economies operated best under a ''natural law,'' which was primarily competition, and that they would be disrupted by government intervention. In the last decades of the nineteenth century and through the twentieth century, capitalism has taken another turn with a shift from ownership and management of industry by individuals to corporations.

See also: **Capital, Entrepreneurship, Laissez Faire, Adam Smith**

CARNEGIE, ANDREW

Andrew Carnegie (1835–1919) was a Scottish-born steel magnate in the United States known for his extraordinary philanthropy as well as his great wealth. He was born in Dunfermline, Scotland, the son of a handloom weaver. When a power loom was introduced

Andrew Carnegie.

in Dunfermline, the family became impoverished and decided to emigrate to the United States. Arriving in 1848, they settled in Allegheny, Pennsylvania. At age 13, Carnegie went to work as a bobbin boy in a cotton mill. He educated himself by reading voraciously and attending night school where he learned double-entry bookkeeping.

The young Carnegie worked in the cotton mill for barely a year before he landed a job as a telegraph messenger in 1849. He advanced quickly. By 1851 he was a telegraph operator. Only two years later he became secretary and personal telegrapher to Tom Scott, the superintendent of the Pennsylvania Railroad's Pittsburgh division.

Carnegie spent twelve years working for the railroad. When Scott was promoted to vice-president of the company in 1859, he chose his young secretary to succeed him as superintendent. During the American Civil War (1861–1865) Carnegie assisted in the management of railroad and telegraph services for the Union.

As railroad superintendent Carnegie invested in the Woodruff Sleeping Car Company and introduced the first successful sleeping car on American railroads. While still working for Scott, he began to invest in stocks. Carnegie made shrewd investments in industrial concerns. These included the Keystone Bridge Company, the Superior Rail Mill and Blast Furnaces, the

Union Iron Mills, and the Pittsburgh Locomotive Works. In 1865 Carnegie left the Pennsylvania Railroad to manage the Keystone Bridge Company (where he had become the dominant shareholder), and a principal Keystone supplier, the Union Iron Mills.

In the early 1870s Carnegie decided to concentrate his efforts on steel. He founded the J. Edgar Thomson Steel Works, named after the president of the Pennsylvania Railroad, which eventually became the Carnegie Steel Company. The company built the first steel plants in the United States that used the Bessemer steel-making process, a revolutionary industrial development in which steel was made from pig iron by using a blast of air forced through molten metal to burn out carbon and other impurities.

Carnegie also pioneered other major technological innovations that enabled his company to quickly become a model of productive efficiency. He kept costs down with detailed cost-and-production accounting procedures. By the 1890s, Carnegie's mills had introduced the basic open-hearth furnace process to American steel-making.

THE MAN WHO DIES THUS RICH DIES DISGRACED.

Andrew Carnegie

At the same time Carnegie and his unusually capable group of managers purchased vast acres of coal fields and iron-ore deposits that furnished the raw materials needed for steel-making. They also purchased ships and railroads needed to transport these supplies to the mills. By the end of the nineteenth century, the Carnegie Steel Company controlled all the elements it used in the steel production process and dominated the American steel industry.

Carnegie was less adept at labor-management relations than he was at building an industry. The Homestead Strike of 1892 resulted from his company's efforts to lower the minimum wage and eliminate the union as the exclusive bargaining agent in Carnegie's Homestead Works. The confrontation between labor and management turned violent when local management at the Homestead plant called in Pinkerton guards in an attempt to break the union.

By the turn of the century company profits reached $40 million; Carnegie's own share was $25 million. In 1901, at the age of 65, Carnegie sold his empire to the newly formed United States Steel Corporation, headed by financier J.P. Morgan. Carnegie's personal share of the proceeds from the sale came to about $230 million. After he sold the company Carnegie devoted his life to philanthropic activities and writing. He authored 8 books and 70 magazine articles.

Although he was an enthusiastic proponent of the capitalist ethic, Carnegie was concerned about some of the social ills that came about as byproducts of a market economy. A two part article entitled "Wealth" appeared in the 1889 *North American Review*. (It was later published in book form in 1900 as *The Gospel of Wealth*.) In this piece Carnegie addressed the problem of the "proper administration of wealth" and outlined his vision of a socially responsible capitalist. He argued that it was the duty of the rich to administer their surplus wealth for the common benefit. "The man who dies thus rich dies disgraced," he wrote.

Carnegie backed up his words with deeds. He eventually funded 2,509 public libraries throughout the English-speaking world, built the famous Carnegie Hall in New York, and founded the Carnegie Institute of Technology, which later became Carnegie-Mellon University. In 1905 he established the Carnegie Foundation for the Advancement of Teaching and in 1910 the Carnegie Endowment for International Peace. In 1911 he founded the Carnegie Corporation of New York, which continued his philanthropic legacy after his death. Throughout his lifetime Carnegie distributed some $350 million towards the public good.

See also: **Bessemer Process, Homestead Strike, J.P. Morgan, Pinkerton National Detective Agency, Robber Barons, United States Steel Company**

FURTHER READING

Bridge, James Howard. *The Inside History of the Carnegie Steel Company: A Romance of Millions*. Pittsburgh: University of Pittsburgh Press, 1992.

Chernow, Ron. "Blessed Barons." *Time*, December 7, 1998.

Livesay, Harold. *Andrew Carnegie and the Rise of Big Business*. New York: Harper Collins, 1975.

Wall, Joseph Frazier. *Andrew Carnegie*. New York: Oxford University Press, 1970.

Wall, Joseph Frazier, ed. *The Andrew Carnegie Reader*. Pittsburgh: University of Pittsburgh Press, 1992.

CARPETBAGGERS

Carpetbaggers was a derisive term that referred to northern merchants who arrived in the South in the early days of Reconstruction (1865–1877), the twelve-year period of rebuilding that followed the American Civil War (1861–1865). Carpetbaggers were so named because many of them carried carpetbags as luggage. Some Southerners even quipped that these northerners could carry all of their belongings in a carpetbag—implying that carpetbaggers were nothing more than transients.

Many northern businessmen who migrated to the South settled there, but Southerners viewed the newcomers as outsiders and, worse, as opportunists who only intended to make a quick profit before returning North. Nevertheless, carpetbaggers played an important role during Reconstruction. Some, aided by the African American vote, were elected to public office and impacted state and local policy. But others proved to be corrupt. Because of the latter, the term "carpetbagger" became synonymous with a meddling, opportunistic outsider.

See also: **Reconstruction, Scalawags**

CARRIER, WILLIS HAVILAND

Willis H. Carrier (1876–1950) invented the equipment that made air conditioning possible and founded the company that brought cooler homes, factories, and movie theaters to much of the United States. Air conditioning, invented by Carrier in 1902, has been credited with making possible the booming economic development of the Sun Belt in the last half of the twentieth century.

Carrier was born near rural Angola, New York, and grew up as an only child in a poor farm family. He worked his way through high school and taught for three years before he could enroll at Cornell University where he was awarded a full scholarship. After graduating from Cornell in 1901 with a Master's in engineering, Carrier took a job for $10 a week with the Buffalo Forge Company, a firm that manufactured heating and exhaust systems.

One of the young engineer's first assignments was to solve a dilemma that was vexing a Brooklyn, New York, printing plant. Fluctuations in heat and humidity in the plant caused the printer's paper supply to expand and contract. As a result, colored inks were not accurately applied to the paper. In 1902, just a year after graduating from college, Carrier designed a heat and humidity control system that stabilized the atmosphere in the factory. His patent for "Apparatus for Treating Air" (Patent No. 808,897) was awarded in 1906. It was the first of more than 80 patents he was to receive over a lifetime of inventions. At the time, Carrier predicted his invention would be used in homes as well as factories.

In 1911 Carrier announced his "Rational Psychrometric Formulae" to the American Society of Mechanical Engineers. Fundamental calculations in air conditioning technology are still made according to these formulas. Carrier discovered these formulae as he struggled with the problems they entailed one foggy night on a railroad platform. By the time the train arrived, he understood the relationship between temperature, humidity, and dew point.

In 1915, together with six other engineers from Buffalo Forge, Carrier founded the Carrier Engineering Corp. with starting capital of $35,000. In 1921 he patented the first safe, low-pressure centrifugal refrigeration machine that used nontoxic, noninflammable refrigerant. Many historians mark this invention as the beginning of the air-conditioning era. In 1924, shoppers came in droves to a Detroit department store after three of Carrier's chillers were installed. Soon movie theaters were advertising that they were "cooled by refrigeration," and the summer film business boomed.

In 1928 Carrier developed the first air conditioner for home use. Private sales of air conditioners were slow during the Great Depression, but the business rapidly expanded when home units again became available after World War II (1939–1945). Some cultural historians have claimed that the prevalence of air conditioning in many parts of the country drastically changed U.S. society in the last half of the twentieth century. They contend that, along with television, air conditioning has kept Americans within their own homes and lessened the hours of social interaction that formerly took place on country porches and city front stoops. Cities in the South and Southwest, once considered nearly impossible to live in during the warm summer months, suddenly became very attractive locations in which to live and work. The Sun Belt was born.

Willis Carrier died in 1950, but his invention has left almost no area of contemporary American life untouched. Climate control enabled the growth of the computer industry, made deep mining for gold, silver, and other metals possible, saved many valuable manuscripts for posterity, and kept meat, fish, fruit and vegetables fresh and cool in supermarkets throughout the country. Hospitals, schools, airports, and office buildings were maintained at optimum temperature and humidity by air conditioning. Within a century, a device invented to solve a printing problem transformed an entire society.

See also: **Sun Belt**

FURTHER READING

Bellis, Mary. "The Father of Cool," [cited March 19, 1999] available from the World Wide Web @ www.inventors.miningco.com/

Friedman, Robert. "The air-conditioned century: the story of how a blast of cool dry air changed America." *American Heritage*, August-September, 1984.

Holt, Donald D. "The Hall of Fame for Business Leadership." *Fortune*, March 23, 1981.

Ingels, Margaret. *Willis Haviland Carrier, Father of Air Conditioning*. New York: Arno Press, 1972.

Ivins, Molly. "King of Cool: Willis Carrier." *Time*, December 7, 1998.

"Willis Haviland Carrier," [cited March 19, 1999] available from the World Wide Web @ www.invent.org/.

CARTEL

A cartel is a group of independently owned businesses that attempts to regulate pricing, production, and distribution within an industry. To accomplish this, cartel members agree to act together rather than compete against each other. As a result the cartel does not allow market forces to determine prices; instead the cartel decides how much to charge, how much to produce, and how to divide the market. The term cartel is usually applied to agreements that regulate business in the international marketplace. (Collaborative arrangements on a national level are called trusts.)

Cartels originated in Germany and date back to the 1870s. In the early years of the twentieth century the German government encouraged companies to join cartels as a way to increase Germany's export trade. During that same period the aluminum industry was entirely controlled by a cartel made up of four companies from the United States, France, Germany, and Great Britain.

After World War I (1914–1918) cartels flourished, and by the start of World War II (1939–1945) there were an estimated 200 international cartels. These cartels controlled 30 percent of worldwide trade in industries such as rubber, steel, chemicals, and tin. More recently, oil-exporting nations formed cartels in the 1970s to establish market prices for crude oil. These oil cartels, operating under the auspices of the

Organization of Petroleum Exporting Countries (OPEC), initially enjoyed success in controlling the world's oil supply and prices. However as oil prices went up demand for oil decreased; by the 1980s OPEC's influence eroded. While antitrust laws make collusive agreements illegal in the United States, national cartels are common in Japan, where businesses operate under a system of managed competition.

See also: **OPEC Oil Embargo**

CARVER, GEORGE WASHINGTON

Agricultural chemist George Washington Carver (1861?–1943) devoted his life to developing industrial applications for farm products. His research developed hundreds of products from peanuts, sweet potatoes and pecans. Although many of these products could be mass-produced more successfully from other materials and none were a commercial success, Carver's work helped liberate the economy of the South from an excessive dependence on cotton.

Carver was born during the American Civil War (1861–1865) near Diamond Grove, Missouri, the son of a slave woman. He was only an infant when he and his mother were sent to Arkansas where slaveholding was still legal. After the war, the young boy, now an orphan and a frail, sickly child, was returned to his former master's plantation where he was nursed back to health. He spent much of his boyhood wandering through the nearby woods and studying the plants he found there.

Carver's ability to have himself educated was remarkable when one considers the bias that African Americans faced in the early years after the Civil War. Although he was a gifted child, he had to spend his early youth working at a succession of menial jobs, and he did not complete high school until he was in his twenties. Although he was accepted by a Presbyterian college in Kansas, he was refused admission upon arrival because of his race. In 1890, Carver became the first black student admitted to Simpson College in Indianola, Iowa. Impressed by the young man's talent with plants, an art teacher at Simpson advised Carver to transfer to the Iowa State College of Agriculture, where he received a degree in agricultural science in 1894. Two years later he earned a Master's degree in science. He then became a member of the faculty in

George Washington Carver.

charge of the school's bacterial laboratory work in the systematic botany department.

In 1896 Carver received an invitation from Booker T. Washington (1856–1915), the most respected black educator in the country, to establish an agricultural school and experiment station at Tuskegee Institute. Carver's acceptance began for him a special relationship with Tuskegee. In 1940 he used his life savings to endow there the Carver Research Foundation, which would carry on his work in agricultural research. Carver remained on the faculty at Tuskegee until his death in 1943.

[CARVER'S] RESEARCH DEVELOPED HUNDREDS OF PRODUCTS FROM PEANUTS, SWEET POTATOES, AND PECANS. . . . [AND] HIS WORK HELPED LIBERATE THE ECONOMY OF THE SOUTH FROM AN EXCESSIVE DEPENDENCE ON COTTON.

Carver found his true calling in working on projects designed to help Southern agriculture. When he arrived in Alabama much of the state's soil had been exhausted and eroded by extensive single-crop cotton cultivation. To replace cotton, the longtime staple of Southern agriculture, Carver experimented with sweet potatoes and black-eyed peas. He also introduced crops new to Alabama like soybeans and alfalfa. None of these crops became as popular with farmers or caught the public's fancy as much as the peanut. Recognizing its value in restoring nitrogen to depleted soil, Carver encouraged farmers to grow the lowly ''goober.'' Carver research on the peanut was at the forefront of a revolution underway in Southern agriculture. Peanut production increased from 3.5 million bushels in 1889 to more than 40 million bushels in 1917. By 1940 peanuts became the South's second cash crop (after cotton). Ultimately, his research resulted in 325 products derived from peanuts, 75 products from pecans, and 108 applications for sweet potatoes.

Carver's work also reflected his commitment to poor, African-American farmers. Initially Carver advised them to work hard and use natural resources wisely rather than invest in expensive machinery or fertilizers they could not afford. Yet, his research into the commercial uses for the South's agricultural products and natural resources enabled them to better their lives.

His success also brought him an national and international recognition. In 1923 he received the Spingarn Medal, awarded each year by the National Association for the Advancement of Colored People (NAACP) to the person who made the greatest contribution to the advancement of his or her race. In 1928, he received an honorary doctorate from Simpson College and was made a member of England's Royal Society of Arts. U.S. presidents visited him. Mohandas K. Gandhi (1869–1948) and Henry Ford (1863–1947) were friends of Carver. Foreign leaders sought his advice. In 1943 President Franklin Delano Roosevelt (1933–1945) dedicated the first national monument honoring an African American to Carver's memory.

Both during and after his lifetime Carver captured a special place in folk history. According to Linda McMurray in her biography, *George Washington Carver, Scientist and Symbol*, ''The romance of his life story and the eccentricities of his personality led to his metamorphosis into a kind of folk saint. . . [and] he was readily appropriated by many diverse groups as a symbol of myriad causes.'' Segregationists approved of his apparent acceptance of their ''separate but equal'' society and used his accomplishments as an example of how a talented black individual could excel under those conditions. Many African Americans and others saw Carver as a needed example of black success and intellectual achievement. Americans of all races struggling through the Great Depression saw in his career the realization that hard work and talent could prevail no matter how daunting the odds.

See also: **Agriculture Industry**

FURTHER READING

Carwell, Hattie. *Blacks in Science: Astrophysicist to Zoologist.* Hicksville, N.Y.: Exposition Press, 1977.

Haber, Louis. *Black Pioneers in Science and Invention.* New York: Harcourt, Brace and World, 1970.

Holt, Rackham. *George Washington Carver, An American Biography.* Garden City, N.Y.: Doubleday, 1963.

McMurray, Linda O. *George Washington Carver, Scientist and Symbol.* New York: Oxford University Press, 1981.

''George Washington Carver, Jr.: Chemurgist?'' [cited February 15, 1999] available from the World Wide Web @ www.lib.lsu.edu/lib/chem/display/carver.html

CASE, STEPHEN M.

Under Stephen M. Case (1958–), America Online, Inc. (AOL)—the consumer-oriented on-line service company he co-founded in 1985—became the undisputed leader in its market throughout the twentieth century. AOL's user membership regularly doubled throughout the 1990s, to more than 14 million subscribers by late 1998. Case's tireless efforts to broaden the service's appeal and build a majority market share pushed the company's earnings past the billion-dollar mark in 1996, making AOL the first new-media company to reach this milestone.

AOL's success vaulted Case to the top ranks of executive pay. In 1998 alone, according to the *New York Times*, his direct compensation was $16.4 million and the value of his stock options in the company grew by $324.5 million.

Case was born in 1958, and was raised in Honolulu, Hawaii. An entrepreneur at an early age, he and his brother, Dan, had a neighborhood juice stand and delivered newspapers. In their teens, however, the Case brothers went beyond the usual boyhood enterprises and began to operate a direct-mail and a door-to-door sales business.

Stephen Case studied political science at Williams College. After graduation, he worked first with Proctor and Gamble and then for Pizza Hut. In 1983 he took a position as a marketing assistant with Control Video Corporation which was introducing an on-line gaming service. The firm soon ran into financial problems and fired its management. Jim Kimsey, a successful entrepreneur and restaurateur, was appointed chief executive officer. Kimsey retained Case to help redefine Control Video's business objectives and to seek out new venture capital.

In 1985 Kimsey and Case renamed the company Quantum Computer Services, Inc., and began offering on-line services to owners of then popular Commodore computers. In addition, they expanded their market by producing software for Apple and Tandy computers, and for DOS and Windows systems. The company's separate divisions merged in 1991, and the corporation was renamed America On-line, Inc. (AOL).

In 1992, when Kimsey became chairman of the new company, he named Case as chief executive officer. At the time, AOL's market share trailed far behind the leading on-line services, CompuServe and Prodigy. Case instituted an ambitious marketing campaign designed to close the gap. The company mailed thousands of floppy diskettes to potential customers, offering free trials of the service and lowered subscription fees. The strategy worked almost too well. By the end of the year, AOL was finding it difficult to handle the influx of new business.

> [T]HOSE OF US IN THE INTERNET COMMUNITY HAVE FOUND OURSELVES ON A MISSION. IT'S A MISSION TO MAKE THIS NEW MEDIUM AS CENTRAL TO PEOPLE'S LIVES AS THE TELEVISION AND THE TELEPHONE, AND EVEN MORE VALUABLE.
>
> Stephen Case, Jupiter Communications Annual Conference, 1998

Over the next few years, Case worked hard to provide a mix of products and services that would appeal to a wide variety of subscribers. The company offered its customers access to the Internet, opportunities to communicate in chat rooms and on bulletin boards, and a reliable electronic mail service. Case made deals and formed partnerships with companies such as NBC, the *New York Times*, and Hachette magazines to provide the content necessary to attract new business. An Internet browser was added to AOL's services in 1994 with the acquisition of a company called BookLink. Case also began to investigate high-speed cable connections with business partners such as Intel and Viacom.

Although competing services were owned by corporate giants, Case was determined to keep AOL independent. He was, however, not averse to alliances and acquisitions. In February 1995 he announced that AOL had formed a $100 million joint venture with the German media conglomerate Bertelsmann AG, in order to expand overseas. The following year Case struck a deal with AT&T for its new Internet access business. In late 1998, in a $4.21 billion purchase, AOL took over Netscape Communications Corporation, a pioneer in the Internet browser market, and acquired Moviefone for $388 million in 1999.

AOL's road to dominance in its market was not always smooth. In August 1996, problems encountered during a routine maintenance of the AOL network resulted in a 19-hour service blackout. More serious customer complaints resulted from the company's decision in December 1996 to move from a tiered payment system to an unlimited flat-fee-pricing plan. AOL's customers, who then numbered over seven million, began to stay on-line for longer periods, creating logjams in the system. Subscribers became increasingly frustrated at the unreliable service and turned to attorneys general in more than 30 states for help. As part of a settlement reached in early 1997, Case agreed to cease advertising until his company was able to handle customer demand.

In a 1998 speech to the Jupiter Communications annual conference titled "Ten Commandments for Building the Medium: Setting Priorities," Case said, "[T]hose of us in the Internet community have found ourselves on a mission. It's a mission to make this new medium as central to people's lives as the television and the telephone, and even more valuable. And perhaps the most important thing for all of us to remember about this mission, in order for us to succeed, is how far we still are from realizing it." At the end of the twentieth century, Stephen Case continued to lead his business towards realizing this goal.

See also: **Internet, Netscape**

FURTHER READING

Abelson, Reed. "Silicon Valley Aftershocks." *New York Times*, April 4, 1999.

Current Biography Yearbook 1996. New York: H.W. Wilson, 1996, s.v. "Case, Steve."

Hansell, Saul. "Mr. Moviefone is Hooking up with the "You've got Mail" Man." *New York Times*, February 2, 1999.

Lohr, Steve and John Markoff. "AOL Sees Netscape Purchase as Step Toward Ambitious Goals." *New York Times*, November 24, 1998.

Swisher, Kara. *AOL.COM: How Steve Case beat Bill Gates, Nailed the Netheads and Made Millions in the War for the Web.* New York: Times Business, 1998.

CASH CROP

A cash crop is any crop that a farmer sells for money, rather than holding it for use by his own family, or to feed livestock, or for bartering with others. For example if a farmer grows corn, wheat and soybeans, but sells only wheat on the open market for cash while feeding his corn to his livestock and bartering his soybeans for other goods, the wheat is his cash crop. Economists may also use the term to refer to any crop that is easily sold on the open market, such as wheat, cotton or tobacco, or to one that historically has produced a high rate of return on the grower's investment.

CATERPILLAR INC.

Caterpillar Tractor Company (the original name for Caterpillar Inc.) was formed in 1925 through the merger of companies founded by Daniel Best and Benjamin Holt. After arriving in California in 1859, Best observed that many farmers transported their grain to special cleaning stations to make it suitable for market. Best thought there was a way to clean grain by machine at the same time as it was being harvested to avoid the costly step of transporting it to another site. By 1871 Best had patented his first grain cleaner, which he manufactured and sold with great success. By the 1880s Best owned manufacturing centers in Oregon and Oakland, California.

Holt arrived in California in 1863 and with his brothers operated the Stockton Wheel Company, which manufactured wooden wheels. It marked the firm's first experience with the vehicular products that would be the company's strength in the years to come. In the 1880s inventors were tinkering with the combined harvester and thresher, known as the combine, which revolutionized grain farming through its ability to cut and thresh, and later to clean and sack grain in vast quantities. It accomplished these processes in far less time than was previously needed. The Holt brothers' Link Belt Combined Harvester, developed in 1886, advanced agricultural technology further by using flexible chain belts rather than gears to transmit power from the ground wheels to the working parts of the machine. This innovation cut down on machine breakage.

Near the end of the nineteenth century the major bottleneck in the progress of agricultural technology was the need for animal power. The combine had made large farms profitable, but the cost of housing and feeding large horse teams and the men who drove them cut into earnings. Both the Holts and Daniel Best were interested in solving this problem by using steam-driven engines to supply tractor power.

The Holts built a steam-driven tractor that could haul 50 tons of freight at three miles per hour. The Stockton Wheel Company was then incorporated as Holt Manufacturing Company in 1892. In the same period Daniel Best refined his steam-engine tractor into one of the finest available during this period. Throughout the 1890s steam-powered tractors were used for hauling freight and plowing fields, as well as for harvesting grain.

In the early 1900s the Holt brothers turned their ingenuity to another farming problem. The land around Stockton, California, where the Holt Company was headquartered, was boggy and became impassable when wet. To overcome this limitation the Holts produced the first "caterpillar"-style tractor, or crawler. It was built on tracks instead of wheels, and the "Cat" could negotiate any terrain short of a swamp. It soon allowed farmers to reclaim thousands of acres of land previously thought useless. In 1906 a steam-powered crawler was perfected, and caught on quickly because of its ability to work on ground that all but swallowed other machines.

In 1908 the engineers who were building the 230-mile Los Angeles Aqueduct used a gas-powered crawler to transport materials across the Mojave Desert. The machine worked so well that 25 more tractors were purchased for further work on the aqueduct, thus giving the Holt tractor credibility with the public and a substantial boost to sales. Also in 1908 Daniel Best sold out to the Holts, after decades of individual success. Best's son, C. W. Best, was taken on as company superintendent, but after two years, formed his own company and advanced the state of tractor technology even further on his own.

In 1909 Charles Holt, who had been looking for a new manufacturing plant in the eastern half of the

The Caterpillar Company specializes in heavy machinery built to perform specific tasks such as laying pipelines as shown here.

United States, bought the abandoned but relatively new plant of a tractor company that had failed. After this plant in Peoria, Illinois, opened, Holt continued to improve his tractor and expand its range of applications. He experimented with several different materials for the body to achieve a heavy-duty tractor that was not excessively heavy. Holt knew that his tractors could be used for even more rugged chores than agriculture or hauling freight, and fitted adjustable blades onto his tractors. He then hired them out to grade roads or move soil and rocks at construction sites.

Soon after World War I (1914–1918) broke out, thousands of troops were caught in trench warfare, marked by the lethal combination of sharp-edged concertina wire plus machine-gun emplacements. Observing the futility of mounting attacks in such terrain, a British lieutenant colonel, Ernest Swinton, recognized the usefulness of an armored machine that could resist automatic machine-guns and also negotiate the war-scarred battlefield. His requirements resulted in the invention in 1916 of an experimental tank, based on the track-laying tractors designed by Holt and others. A year later the tank was used with such telling effect that it is credited with winning the Battle of Cambrai, in

France, for the Allies. Some historians point to this battle as the turning point of the war. Germany had investigated the military applications of the track-laying vehicle well before anyone else and mistakenly concluded that tractors were without military significance.

Holt tractors themselves served the war effort by hauling artillery and supplies. In all, more than 10,000 Holt vehicles served the Allied forces, and the international exposure that the Holt tractor received during the war did much to popularize the tracked vehicle.

In 1925 Holt and C. W. Best's companies merged, this time to form the Caterpillar Tractor Company. The company relocated its headquarters from California to Peoria three years later. By 1931, the diesel tractor engine, which had been used before but not widely, was perfected for common use by Caterpillar. Previously, diesels had been too heavy and undependable for commercial use. The Diesel-60 tractor, however, made the diesel the staple engine for heavy-duty vehicles, as it is to this day.

Caterpillar's contributions to World War II (1939–1945) were many and varied. One was the conversion of a gasoline airplane engine into a dependable diesel engine. In 1942 Caterpillar unveiled the new RD-1820 radial diesel engine, which was used to power the M-4 tank. The company manufactured other engines, as well, and even artillery shells for the war effort. Caterpillar tractors worked in battle zones repairing damaged roads, building new ones, and bulldozing tank traps. Because the Cat was usually seen doing such roadwork with a bulldozer blade attached, the term ''bulldozer'' came to be used for Caterpillar products.

In the postwar period, Caterpillar experienced enormous growth, because of the massive rebuilding campaigns begun both in Europe and Japan. From the 1950s through the end of the century, the company (which was renamed Caterpillar Inc. in 1986) grew to become the world's largest manufacturer of earth-moving machinery. In addition to its tractors, trucks, graders, excavators, scrapers, and other heavy machinery used in the construction, mining, and agriculture industries, the Caterpillar of the late 1990s also made diesel and gas engines used in medium- and heavy-duty trucks, electric power generation equipment, locomotives, and other industrial equipment. During a long and bitter strike by the United Automobile Workers union during much of the 1990s, Caterpillar successfully resisted the union's demands and ''rolled over'' its opposition as if the company's labor relations strategy were mounted on tractor treads.

FURTHER READING

Bremner, Brian. ''Can Caterpillar Inch Its Way Back into Heftier Profits?'' *Business Week*, September 25, 1989.

Caterpillar Inc. *The Caterpillar Story*. Peoria, Ill.: Caterpillar Inc., 1990.

———. *Century of Change: Caterpillar Special World Historical Edition*. Peoria, Ill.: Caterpillar Inc., 1984.

Dubashi, Jagannath. ''Cat-apult: The Cheap Dollar Helped, but Caterpillar's Turnaround Was Engineered in Peoria.'' *Financial World*, November 23, 1993.

Gibson, Paul, and Barbara Rudloph. ''Playing Peoria to Perfection.'' *Forbes*, May 11, 1981.

Kelly, Kevin. ''Cat Is Purring, but They're Hissing on the Floor.'' *Business Week*, May 16, 1994.

Naumann, William L. *The Story of Caterpillar Tractor Co.* New York: Newcomen Society in North America, 1977.

Weimer, De'Ann. ''A New Cat on the Hot Seat.'' *Business Week*, March 9, 1998.

CATTLE DRIVES

Cattle drives moved large herds of livestock to market, to shipping points, or to find fresh pasturage. The practice was introduced to North America early during European colonization. As early as 1540, Spaniards established a cattle industry and began driving herds northward from central Mexico, as they looked for good pasturage. The cattle culture of the early American Southwest borrowed heavily from the South American and Central American cowboys, who were called ''gauchos.'' These gauchos developed the chaps, spurs, saddles, and the techniques of horsemanship and cattle handling associated with the cowboy. By 1690 cattle were brought as far north as Texas. Having little commercial value, cattle were left to roam freely in the open range, and by the early 1800s hundreds of thousands of wild longhorns populated the region.

Cattle drives were also known in the newly established United States. Cattle were driven several hundred miles from Tennessee to Virginia in the 1790s. It was not until the 1830s, however, that cattle driving became a steady occupation. Drives took place from Texas to the port at New Orleans. Further west, some herds were even driven from California to Oregon in the 1830s. In the 1840s, most drives continued to originate in Texas, bringing beef northward to various Missouri market points. They even extended to California to feed the gold miners following the Gold Rush of 1849. With the outbreak of the American Civil War (1861–1865), the focus of Texas cattle drives shifted dramatically to feed Confederate troops in the South.

After the Civil War the market for Texas cattle vanished and ranchers were left holding several million head. Drives toward the north began again in 1866, but with little financial gain. Fortunately for the cattlemen, the close of the Civil War also marked a major transition in U.S. meat–consumption patterns. A national preference for pork abruptly gave way to beef. Cattle worth four dollars a head in Texas might be sold at 40 dollars a head in Missouri or Kansas. In addition, a ready workforce was already in place: the de-commissioned horsemen of the Confederate cavalry plus freed ex-slaves and Mexican gauchos combined to provide a ready supply of skilled horsemen. Responding to the demand for beef, James G. McCoy established a cattle market in Abilene, Kansas in 1867, and

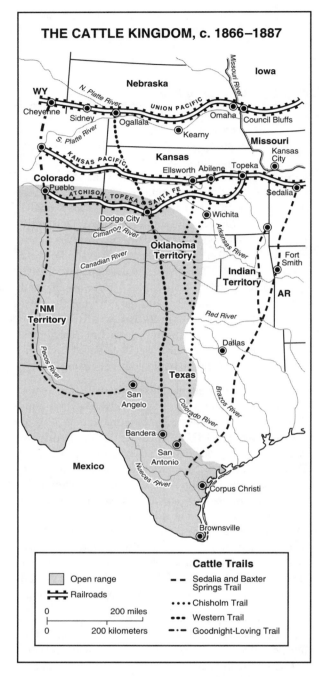

THE CATTLE KINGDOM, c. 1866–1887

Cattle Trails

- Open range
- Railroads
- 0 — 200 miles
- 0 — 200 kilometers
- – – Sedalia and Baxter Springs Trail
- •••• Chisholm Trail
- •–•– Western Trail
- –•–• Goodnight-Loving Trail

Due to a shortage of beef in the northern states after the Civil War, it became more profitable to drive the herds north along these cattle trails. This practice continued from 1866 to 1886.

much as 50 miles wide in some stretches. Typically rivers and Indian lands had to be crossed, but good grazing, relatively level terrain, and higher prices waiting at the destination made the hazards worthwhile. Drives were cost–effective too—a drive of two thousand or more cattle usually required only a trail boss and a dozen cowhands.

In 1867 the Goodnight–Loving Trail opened markets for Texas cattle in Colorado and New Mexico. The booming demand for beef drew many more settlers to Texas and the Southwest. Cattle ranching had become big business and attracted Eastern investors. In 1869 more than 350,000 head of cattle were driven along the Chisholm Trail. By 1871 more than 700,000 head were driven along the route. The practice of branding made it easy to identify the owners. The extermination of buffalo on the Great Plains during the 1870s opened more grasslands for livestock grazing and the Texas longhorn was the first to fill the void. Local economies of towns along the frequently used routes benefited substantially. Fort Worth, Texas, served as a provisioning stop on the Chisholm Trail. Merchants would send out individuals with gifts to entice cowhands into to town to spend their money.

In the mid–1870s farming crept westward and barbed wire fencing threatened the cattle drives. The Chisholm Trail detoured 100 miles westward to Dodge City, Kansas. Cattlemen petitioned Congress to designate a National Cattle Trail. Envisioned as a several mile wide strip from the Red River to Canada, the proposal never came to fruition.

The longhorn was the preferred trail–herd breed for cattle drives until the late 1880s. A descendent of Andalusian cattle that the Spaniards had let run wild in the Southwest, the lean, hardy, lanky animals were the product of three centuries of interbreeding. They thrived on buffalo grass and needed less water than other species. Though often dangerous in a herd and not good beef producers—their meat was stringy and tough—the longhorn was readily available and provided a means to establish a cattle industry in the more arid Southwest. Eventually as cattle drives became less frequent, longhorns were interbred with Durhams and Herefords to create more plump and docile varieties.

By the mid–1880s the great days of the cattle drives were about over. The farmers and their barbed wire were blocking the right–of–way of the drives. Even with branding, the presence of cattle rustlers lowered the profit margin and made the drives more dangerous. The herds sometimes suffered from ''Texas Fever,'' a disease transmitted by ticks. Also, the extension of railroad tracks in the south and west

the era of massive cattle drives began. Soon others saw the wild Texas herds as a ready means to tap into the lucrative northern market with little start–up capital.

The famous Chisholm Trail became a major route. The trail was established in 1865 by Jesse Chisholm and ran 600 miles from San Antonio, Texas, to Abilene, Kansas. More a corridor than a trail, the route was as largely did away with the need for drives. In addition, abnormally harsh winters during 1885–1886 and 1886–1887 devastated the cattle industry. The drives continued into the 1890s with herds being driven from the Texas panhandle to Montana, but by 1895, the era of cattle drives finally ended as new homestead laws further spurred settlement. With the decline of the open range cattle industry, Southwest ranches became large, fenced livestock farms safe from the westward expansion of civilization.

Some communities, such as Fort Worth, became points where herds were assembled for shipping by rail. Packing plants were built and stockyards grew at the turn of the century. The cattle drive lives on in western legend, however, and remains integrally associated with the economic history of Texas.

See also: **Barbed Wire, Chisholm Trail, Cowboy, Cow Towns, Longhorn Cattle**

FURTHER READING

Beckstead, James H. *Cowboying: A Tough Job in a Hard Land.* Salt Lake City: University of Utah Press, 1991.

Cusic, Don. *Cowboys and the Wild West: An A–Z Guide from the Chisholm Trail to the Silver Screen.* New York: Facts on File, 1994.

Eggen, John E. *The West That Was.* West Chester, PA: Schiffer Publishing, 1991.

Hamner, Laura V. *Short Grass and Longhorns.* Norman: University of Oklahoma Press, 1943.

Jordan, Terry G. *North American Cattle–Ranching Frontiers: Origins, Diffusion, and Differentiation.* Albuquerque: University of New Mexico Press, 1993.

McLoughlin, Denis. *Wild and Woolly: An Encyclopedia of the Old West.* Garden City, NY: Doubleday and Company, 1975.

Slatta, Richard W. *Cowboys of the Americas.* New Haven: Yale University Press, 1990.

CATTLE INDUSTRY

Cattle have been domesticated for thousands of years. Since approximately 4000 B.C. cattle have been utilized for their meat, blood, milk, and skin, and have also been used as draft animals. The two most prevalent species of cattle are *Bos taurus*, found mainly in the Western world, and *Bos indicus*, which includes the Brahman cattle found in India and other Middle and Far Eastern countries. Cattle are ruminants, eating grasses and grains.

The modern cattle industry had its earliest beginnings in eighteenth century Europe. Farmers began to selectively breed cattle to try to increase the quantity or quality of their cattle products, or to produce cattle that were hardier and better suited to their geographic area. An Englishman, Robert Bakewell (1725–1795), is credited as being the first to promote selective animal breeding, a successful practice which continued throughout the twentieth century. Eventually, cattle societies and registries were formed to keep track of new breeds of purebred cattle. Crossing two or more breeds together was also done to improve specific attributes. In the late 1990s, the numerous popular cattle breeds for producing beef included the Charolais, Hereford, Angus, Shorthorn, and Brahman. Dairy cattle breeds included the Holstein, Jersey, and Guernsey.

Christopher Columbus (1451–1506) introduced cattle to the New World in 1494, on his second voyage. Early colonists brought cows to Jamestown, Virginia, in 1611 and to the Plymouth Colony in 1624. Most of these cattle were English Shorthorn, a breed used to produce several types of cattle products. Pioneers traveling west often used oxen to pull wagons and plow, and herded cattle along as well. By the mid-nineteenth century, cattle production was an important industry in the Mid-West, and by the 1880s it had expanded westward to the Pacific.

It was during this time that the cowboy came into being in the American West. Cowboys were responsible for gathering cattle and moving them from place to place to graze on public lands. They also put together long cattle drives, where cattle from the Southern states were driven to markets for shipment by rail north for slaughter. Prices for beef were very competitive in the Northern States because the end of the American Civil War (1861–1865) had caused a shortage. Most of the large cattle drives occurred from 1866 to 1886. Driving cattle was a dangerous and difficult job. Cowboys faced the prospects of stampedes, lightening storms, and other hazards such as encounters with outlaws, Native Americans, and farmers who did not want cattle to pass near their herds, fearful of the deadly cattle disease known as "Texas fever." According to Cecil K. Hutson in a study of the Texas fever in Kansas, "collectively, with blizzards, drought, barbed wire, railroad expansion, settlement, foreign embargoes, and a more sophisticated urban palate, this cattle plague brought an end to the era of the long cattle drives."

Beginning in 1886, two years of severe drought interspersed with freezing winters put most of the remaining cattle ranchers out of business. After 1888, barbed wire fences prevented the open grazing that had been allowed previously. Cattle were more and more often contained to individual ranches, where windmills drew water for the herds. This was the beginning of the modern cattle industry in the United States.

In 1995, the U.S. Department of Agriculture (USDA) listed the United States as fourth in the world in the number of cattle and buffalo. The production of beef had become a systematized process in the United States. Cattle had to be raised and fattened, then shipped to slaughterhouses for processing; distributors would then sell and transport the meat to supermarkets and restaurants for retail sale to consumers. According to the USDA, in 1994 cattle products were "the leading commodity in 18 states." The January 1, 1997 Cattle Inventory Report, NDSS/USDA, stated that Texas was the 1995 leader in income from cattle, with Kansas second, and Nebraska a close third. The amount of beef produced in the United States rose steadily from 1993 to 1996.

Cattle production in the 1990s was the single largest contributor to American agriculture, with sales accounting for over $30 billion in 1995 alone. America was also a leading exporter of beef and cattle products, second in the world only to Argentina. In 1995, about sixty-four percent of all exported beef went to Japan, making the American cattle industry a key player in reducing the international trade deficit.

See also: **Agriculture Industry, Barbed Wire, Cattle Drives, Cow Town, Cowboy, Westward Expansion**

FURTHER READING

"Beef Economics," [cited January 12, 1999] available from the World Wide Web @ www.beef.org/libbref/beefhand/econ1.html#3.

Academic American Encyclopedia. Danbury, Ct.: Grolier Inc., 1995, s.v. "Cattle and Cattle Raising," Neumann, Alvin L.

"Beef Organizations Page." National Cattlemen's Beef Association, [cited January 12, 1999] available from the World Wide Web @ www.beef.org/organs.htm.

Ewing, Sherm. *The Ranch: a Modern History of the North American Cattle Industry*. Missoula: Mountain Press Publishing Co., 1995.

Foner, Eric, and John A. Garraty, eds. *The Reader's Companion to American History*. Boston: Houghton Mifflin Co., 1991, s.v. "Cattle."

CENTRAL BANK *(ISSUE)*

The idea of the central bank in the newly formed United States arose as the dusk of eighteenth-century mercantilism turned into the dawn of nineteenth-century laissez-faire economics. Its existence raised numerous issues of states rights, federal power, and the national currency. After Andrew Jackson's determination to put an end to the Second Bank of the United States during his "Bank War" of 1832 and the Panic of 1837 a few years later, the question of a central bank wasn't seriously raised again until the financial insecurities and social displacements of industrialization at the beginning of the twentieth century forced the government to establish the Federal Reserve Bank in 1913.

But for well over a century, the dispute raged between advocates of a decentralized banking system and proponents of a strong central bank. The former argued that a national bank was dangerous because it concentrated the power of granting loans and expanding currency into the hands of a relatively small group of men who would follow private rather than national interests. They argued that a large number of small state or commercial banks would better serve the nation, its people, and the economy by responding to local conditions while preventing the concentration of such powers. But proponents of a central bank disagreed. They argued that a central bank was necessary to enlarge the national manufacturing base, maintain a stable currency, and keep up with the demands of a country whose boundaries and peoples increasingly pushed westward. For them, a central bank could keep the amount of currency in circulation flexible and provide the capital and credit needed to meet the demands of population increases, territorial expansion, and heavy industrialization.

Largely through the efforts of Alexander Hamilton, the First Bank of the United States, modeled after the Bank of England, was established in 1791 and was chartered for a period of twenty years. It was a private corporation with $10 million in capital, governed by twenty-five directors, and like other commercial banks, could print notes and exchange them for borrowers' interest-bearing promises to pay. It could also extend loans to individuals and companies. But unlike other private banks, the federal government was a central partner in the enterprise. The government owned 20 percent of the Bank's holdings while the Bank served as a fiscal agent for the government. The Bank held tax receipts, paid government bills, and performed various other financial tasks. It lent money to the government and provided convenient depositories in the leading seaports like New York, Boston, Baltimore, and Charleston, where most of the federal revenues were collected. It also served the Treasury by transferring funds safely and cheaply from place to place, and facilitated the payment of taxes by increasing the supply of currency. As a partner, the government granted it special privileges unique among other state banks. It kept its cash as deposits with the Bank, giving it a huge financial base. The government borrowed from the Bank, paid it interest for the use of its notes, and also shared its profits.

According to its charter, the Bank was allowed to operate in all states, which gave it a considerable edge over state banks that could only operate in the states that chartered them. Because of this large banking network in various parts of the country and in its role as creditor, the Bank was able to hold as assets more notes issued by state banks than those banks held of their own.

THE TENDENCY OF A NATIONAL BANK IS TO INCREASE PUBLIC AND PRIVATE CREDIT. INDUSTRY IS INCREASED, COMMODITIES ARE MULTIPLIED, AGRICULTURE AND MANUFACTURING FLOURISH, AND HEREIN CONSISTS THE TRUE WEALTH AND PROSPERITY OF A STATE.

Alexander Hamilton, *Second Report on Public Credit*, January 1790

Overall, the First Bank was profitable averaging 8 percent per year rate of return for those that invested in it. It succeeded in maintaining the stability of currency, in meeting government expenses, and in preventing the drain of specie from the country.

But even so, in 1812 opposition from various quarters was strong enough to prevent it from being rechartered. Thomas Jefferson and John Randolph from Virginia questioned its constitutionality, and Henry Clay from Kentucky feared the concentration of financial power. Others feared that it posed serious hurdles to the growth and spread of state banks, while an increasingly large faction criticized the growing influence that foreign investment placed on the Bank. In the end, the Bank's charter was revoked in the Senate by a tie-breaking 18-17 vote.

But within five years, federal debt associated with the War of 1812 and inflation caused in part by the rise of unregulated state banks forced Congress to reconsider its earlier decision. The Second Bank of the United States was chartered in 1816 along the same lines that the first had been. Eighty percent of its $35 million capital was private, paid in specie, 20 percent

was federal, paid in government bonds, and the Bank was made the depository of government funds and also the fiscal agency of the United States. Note issues could not exceed total capital, were receivable in all payments to the United States, and were redeemable in specie on demand. It was intended that state banks would have to resume specie payments or their notes would be driven out of circulation. After the Bank's charter was granted, additional legislation was enacted to help promote specie resumption in general: all payments to the government after February 20, 1817 had to be made in coin, Treasury notes, United States Bank notes, or other convertible bank notes.

Politicians in many of the states blamed the Second Bank for the Panic of 1819. Maryland, Tennessee, Georgia, North Carolina, Kentucky and Ohio enacted laws to tax branches of the Bank out of existence. But in two Supreme Court decisions, *McCulloch v. Maryland (1819)* and *Osborne v. United States Bank (1824)*, Chief Justice John Marshall declared the state acts unconstitutional.

Under the presidency of Langdon Cheves (1819-1823) and Nicholas Biddle (1823-1836), the Second Bank recaptured the standing that the First once had within the banking community. Under Biddle, the Bank and its twenty-nine branches became an effective regulator of the expanding economy. The Bank marketed government bonds, served as a reliable depository for government funds, and its bank notes provided the country with a sound paper currency. But because the Bank forced state banks to back their notes with adequate specie reserves, many, especially President Andrew Jackson, believed that this was too much power. They were afraid that the Bank's control over short-term credit was not subjected to sufficient government regulation, and that state banks risked termination under such a system. By the time of Andrew Jackson's presidency, the Bank had antagonized both those who favored ''soft money'' (more state-bank notes) and those who favored ''hard money'' (only gold and silver coins). ''Soft money'' proponents including land-speculators, small entrepreneurs, and anyone who was in debt felt their needs were best served with an abundant paper currency while Eastern workingmen resented receiving their wages in paper of uncertain value. On the other hand, many ''hard money'' advocates were hostile to banks of any kind, state or national, that issued bank notes and they tended to look upon banking in general as a parasitic enterprise.

During the Bank War, Biddle was unable to prevail over President Jackson and renew the Bank's charter with the federal government. He was, however, able to obtain a charter from the state of Pennsylvania. But during the Panic of 1837 the reorganized bank suspended specie payment and failed completely in 1841. In its absence, the number state banks rose dramatically across the country. The victorious Andrew Jackson termed these banks his "pet banks."

The charter of the Second Bank did not assign to it the public responsibilities of a central bank, as did the legislation that created the Federal Reserve System a century later. Instead, the Second Bank was responsible to its own investors, and its chief function was to earn dividends for them. Many state banks resented it not only because it forced them to maintain adequate specie reserves but also because its federal charter gave it a considerable competitive edge.

By the time that the Federal Reserve System was established under the Woodrow Wilson administration in 1913, the financial anarchy of an unregulated banking system had settled the question of the legitimacy of the central bank. In constructing the modern banking system, the Federal Reserve, established after the Panic of 1907, had two basic functions. Along with other federal agencies, it helped to investigate and insure the financial soundness of private banks. As lender of last resort, it protected banks against insufficient funds (liquid assets) when those banks were forced to cover the withdrawal demands of their depositors. This lessened the self-fulfilling fear of "bank runs," when depositors lost faith in the ability of the banking system to cover their deposits. The Federal Reserve also monitored and controlled the national money supply. It could order changes in the percentages of bank assets held as reserve. This, in turn, controlled the ability of the nation's banking system to create money by making loans. It could also affect the money supply directly by buying and selling government bonds in the market. This gave the federal government an extremely important ability to encourage growth in a sluggish economy (by creating credit) or to slow down an inflationary economy (by restricting credit). Thomas Jefferson and Andrew Jackson might not have approved, but Alexander Hamilton and Nicolas Biddle got the last laugh.

See also: **Bank War, Nicolas Biddle, Federal Reserve System, Alexander Hamilton, Andrew Jackson, Thomas Jefferson**

FURTHER READING

Hammond, Bray. *Banks and Politics in America from the Revolution to the Civil War*. Princeton: Princeton University Press, 1957.

Redlich, Fritz. *The Molding of American Banking: Men and Ideas*. New York, Johnson Reprint Corp., 1968.

Timberlake, Richard H., Jr. *The Origins of Central Banking in the United States*. Cambridge: Harvard University Press, 1978.

White, Eugene. "The Membership Problem of the National Banking System." *Explorations in Economic History*, 19, 1982.

———. *The Regulation and Reform of the American Banking System, 1900–1929*. Princeton: Princeton University Press, 1983.

CENTRAL PACIFIC RAILROAD

The Central Pacific Railroad was conceived by engineer Theodore Dehone Judah, whose idea won the financial backing of four California merchants: Collis P. Huntington, Leland Stanford, Mark Hopkins, and Charles Crocker. These men envisioned an immensely profitable railway that would connect the western frontier to eastern trade; they founded the Central Pacific Railroad Company in 1861. They were engaged in a contest to lay the most track in national railway history, and a rivalry arose between Central Pacific and the Union Pacific Railroad Company. Their systems would link populations and commodities of Missouri with those of Sacramento, California.

The conflict between the Central Pacific and Union Pacific companies was not the only one surrounding the transcontinental railways' beginnings. Before the American Civil War (1861–1865), U.S. Congressmen fought over whether the tracks should be laid on Northern or Southern soil. The project's approval was subsequently delayed in Congress until President Abraham Lincoln (1861–1865) signed the Pacific Railway Act in 1862.

The Railway Act sought to establish support for the project and resolve the conflicts in Congress and between the rival companies. This legislation was an important boost to the railways, and it dramatically shaped the future of the frontier. The Act authorized specific routes for the rival Central Pacific and Union Pacific companies and resolved that the tracks of the two railways would eventually meet and connect. The right of way through large tracts of public land—200 feet on each side of the entire railroad—was granted to the companies for passage, any buildings necessary to the railroad's operation, and materials such as timber and stone. Additionally, in alternate sections of public land along the railroad, the land allotment extended

Chinese laborers celebrated the successful laying of 1,800 miles of track. In order to reach their goal they had to blast nine tunnels through the Sierra Nevada Mountains and endure severe weather conditions.

from 200 feet to 10 miles. To further expand the amount of public land available to the railway companies, the legislation also sanctioned the United States to renege on government treaties it had signed with Native Americans. The legislation proclaimed: ''The United States shall extinguish as rapidly as may be the Indian titles to all lands falling under the operation of this act.''

With nearly limitless support of the government, track was laid eastward from Sacramento in 1863. Chinese laborers faced mountain winters and desert heat, and the obstacle of the Sierra Nevada Mountains, where nine tunnels had to be blasted through. On May 10, 1869, 1,800 miles (2,900 km) of new tracks had been laid, and the rail lines met at Promontory Summit, Utah. A luxurious celebration was planned during which two locomotives coming from either end of the railroad would touch noses and wealthy friends of the railroads' founders would be the first passengers. The plan faced some near disasters, including a mid-track labor uprising for the Union Pacific car, which delayed its arrival to the celebration by two days.

Political and economic opportunism of the government and founding business partners triumphed in opening up U.S. trade by rail. The new railroad could move cargo more quickly than wagons or boats. The railroad also opened territory for settlers seeking to become large-scale landowners.

The railroad expanded by acquiring additional lines and through mergers and leasing relationships with other companies. Soon after the completion of the main railroad, the company began building new lines, and also procured existing lines in California. Some of these additional lines were established under the umbrella of the Southern Pacific Company of California. Later, the railroad acquired existing tracks along southern routes to Texas and New Orleans. The Central Pacific Railroad Company was leased to a new holding company, the Southern Pacific (incorporated in 1884). The two companies merged in 1959.

The founders of the Central Pacific Railroad Company became fabulously wealthy. They obtained enormous financial and political support from the U.S. government even as the Union was warring with itself. They would be remembered for their contributions to the nation's first transcontinental railway and for having further secured the nation's movement and settlement westward. But this was not progress for everyone affected by the railroad. Government and owner policies toward immigrant workers cost many lives as the railroad was constructed. The seizure of lands by breaking U.S. governmental treaties with the Native Americans, and the slaughter of buffalo herds to open up land and expand industry, further circumscribed American existence and permanently scarred the relationship between indigenous peoples living under U.S. government authority.

See also: **Union Pacific Railroad**

FURTHER READING

Athey, Jean. ''Transcontinental Train Wreck.'' *Boy's Life*, June, 1998.

Blumberg, Rhoda. *Full Steam Ahead: The Race to Build a Transcontinental Railroad*. Washington, DC: National Geographic Society, 1996.

Laughlin, Rosemary. *The Great Iron Link: The Building of the Central Pacific Railroad*. Greensboro, NC: Morgan Reynolds, 1996.

''The Pacific Railway Act'' [cited April 6,1999] available on the World Wide Web @ www.pbs.org/weta/thewest/wpages/wpgs650/railact.htm/.

CHAIN STORE

A chain store consists of two or more retail outlets, operated by the same company, which sell the same kind of merchandise. The innovation of the chain store was conceived by American businessmen George Gilman (1830?–1901) and George Huntington Hartford (1833–1917) who, in 1859, set up the Great Atlantic & Pacific Tea Company in New York City. Better known as A&P, the stores proliferated rapidly, and other chain stores opened their doors for business, such as W.P. Woolworth (established 1879) and J. C. Penney (1902). The early twentieth century saw tremendous growth of the chain stores: Between 1910 and 1931, the number of A&P stores grew from 200 to more than 15,000. Department stores, also a byproduct of the late-1800s, catered to middle and upper class customers. Chain stores, including Woolworth's ''Five-and-Dimes'' (which sold many items at low prices), served lower-income consumers.

Chain stores offer consumers many advantages and operate within all major retailing categories (including grocery stores, department stores, drugstores, as well as apparel and food outlets). Their system of centralized, mass buying allows them to acquire merchandise from manufacturers and wholesalers at reduced costs. Savings are passed along to the consumer, who pays less for the item. Further, chain stores can economize on advertising: A single ad placement promotes all the stores within the chain. During the 1920s independent retailers rallied against the chain stores, claiming they had unfair advantages. This argument has resurfaced off and on throughout the twentieth century as chain stores entered into more and more retailing sectors including hardware, jewelry, furniture, music, and books. But the only federal legislation that constructively attempted to regulate the chain stores came in 1936: the Robinson-Patman Act, which tried to control competition. Today chain stores account for roughly one-third of all American retail sales.

See also: **Department Store, Mail-Order House**

CHANDLER, ALFRED DUPONT

Alfred DuPont Chandler (1918–) is a U.S. historian, specializing in the history of business. A Harvard graduate and professor *emeritus*, Chandler wrote and edited numerous books and articles about business history and famous businesspeople. Over the course of five decades he helped establish this field of study and earned a reputation as a business expert.

Alfred Chandler was born September 15, 1918, in Guyencourt, Delaware, to Alfred Dupont and Carol Remsay Chandler. He studied at Harvard University, where he earned his Bachelor of Arts in 1940. After graduation Chandler joined the Navy, where he served until 1945. He then returned to Harvard to study history and earned his Master of Arts in 1947, and his Ph.D. in 1952.

In 1950 Chandler began working as a research associate at the Massachusetts Institute of Technology (M.I.T.). He also began his first editing project that year, working as an assistant editor for Elting M. Morison and John M. Blum on *The Letters of Theodore Roosevelt*. Once he earned his doctorate, he became a faculty member at M.I.T. and remained there until 1963. Chandler wrote his first book in 1956, *Henry Varnum Poor: Business Editor, Analyst, and Reformer*, which highlighted his interest in the field of business history.

Chandler's second book, *Strategy and Structure: Chapters in the History of the Industrial Enterprise*, was a study in organizational behavior. The work was highly regarded, and Chandler won a Newcomen Award for it in 1962. Chandler began to establish a reputation as a respected business historian. In 1963 he left M.I.T. to join the faculty at Johns Hopkins University, where he became director of the Center for Study of Recent American History and department chairman in 1966.

During this time, Chandler also wrote his next book, *Giant Enterprises: Ford, General Motors, and the Automotive Industry*, and edited a book called *The Railroads*. Chandler's expertise as a historian landed him a position as the chairman of the Historical Advisory Committee of the United States Atomic Energy Commission in 1969, a post he held until 1977.

> **NO OTHER AUTHOR IN OUR FIELD OF STUDIES HAS OFFERED US SO MUCH BOTH IN TERMS OF RESEARCH RESULTS AS WELL AS TOOLS FOR THE ANALYSIS AND DEFINITION OF THE GLOBAL CHARACTERISTICS OF THE MODERN LARGE ENTERPRISE.**
>
> Franco Amatori, *Business History Review*, Summer 1997

The 1970s were a prolific period for Chandler. He started off the decade with his five-volume series on *The Papers of Dwight David Eisenhower*. In 1970 Chandler was the Thomas Henry Carroll Ford Foundation Visiting Fellow at Harvard University, and he was also a member of the National Advertising Council's Committee on Educational and Professional Development. Although he was also a visiting scholar at All Souls, Oxford University, and the European Institute in Washington, D.C., Chandler stayed at Harvard as the Isidor Strauss Professor of Business History in the Graduate School of Business. In 1971 he co-authored two books with Stephen Salsbury, *Pierre S. du Pont* and *The Making of the Modern Corporation*.

Chandler's most popular book, *The Visible Hand: The Managerial Revolution in American Business* appeared in 1977. The book's focus on managers and institutions was well received by the public. The *New Republic* called *The Visible Hand* "a triumph of creative synthesis." Robert L. Heilbroner of the *New York Review of Books* said the book was "a major contribution to economics, as well as to business history, because it provides powerful insights into the ways in which the imperatives of capitalism shaped at least one aspect of the business world—its tendency to grow into giant companies in some industries but not in others." The book was such a success it won Chandler both the Pulitzer and the Bancroft prizes in 1978.

Chandler continued to write about business and economic markets in the 1980s. In 1988 he published *The Essential Alfred Chandler: Essays Toward a Historical Theory of Big Business*, which contains a biographical introduction by editor Thomas McCraw. The next year Chandler retired from the Harvard Business School, but he continued his research and writing. In 1990 he published *Scale and Scope: The Dynamics of Industrial Capitalism*, with the assistance of Takashi Hikino. In that book Chandler examined the history of 600 top firms in the United States, the United Kingdom, and Germany for three-quarters of the twentieth century. He evaluated the significance of what was considered an indispensable historical reference. In 1991 *Financial World* dubbed Chandler the "dean of American business history."

Since the publication of *Scale and Scope*, Chandler wrote many articles on the history of the firm, the logic of industrial success, and corporate structure. He also edited and co-edited several more books, including *Big Business and the Wealth of Nations* and *The Dynamic Firm: The Role of Technology, Strategy, Organizations, and Regions*. Even after a decade of retirement, Chandler continued to maintain a leading role in the field of business history through the end of the twentieth century.

FURTHER READING

Alford, B.W.E. "Chandlerism, the New Orthodoxy of US and European Corporate Development." *Journal of European Economic History*, 23, Winter 1994.

Amatori, Franco. "Reflections on Global Business and Modern Italian Enterprise by a Stubborn 'Chandlerian.'" *Business History Review*, 71, Summer 1997.

Chandler, Alfred Dupont. *The Essential Alfred Chandler: Essays Toward a Historical Theory of Big Business*. Boston, MA: Harvard Business School Press, 1988.

———. *The Visible Hand: The Managerial Revolution in American Business*. Cambridge, MA: Belknap Press, 1977.

"A Chat with the Dean of American Business History." *Financial World*, 160, June 25, 1991.

Parker, William N. "The Scale and Scope of Alfred D. Chandler, Jr." *The Journal of Economic History*, 51, December, 1991.

CHASE, SALMON PORTLAND

Salmon Portland Chase (1808–1873) was a lawyer who was deeply devoted to the antislavery movement. This cause led him to political life, where he became the first Republican governor of Ohio. Though he tried unsuccessfully to run for president several times, he did serve as Secretary of the Treasury and Chief Justice of the Supreme Court.

Salmon Chase was born in Cornish, New Hampshire, on January 13, 1808. He attended public school at Keene, New Hampshire, and then attended private school in Vermont. When he was nine years old, Chase's father passed away and his uncle, Philander Chase, an early leader of the American Episcopal Church, raised him. Chase pursued classical and religious studies at his uncle's church school near Columbus, Ohio. His uncle then became president of Cincinnati College, and Chase studied there as well for a brief time. Later, Chase entered Dartmouth College, where he graduated in 1826.

After graduation, Chase worked briefly as the headmaster of a boys' school in Washington, DC, and privately studied law. In 1829 he was admitted to the bar and soon returned to Cincinnati to practice law. The city, located on the northern bank of the Ohio River, was a busy trade port whose opposite bank bordered slave territory. Chase held deeply rooted moral opinions stemming from his upbringing and was strongly opposed to slavery. He quickly entrenched himself in the antislavery cause and soon earned a reputation as the "attorney for runaway Negroes."

Chase had a rather sad private life. His first wife died a year after their marriage, his second wife died after five years, and his third wife after six years. Of his six children, only two daughters grew to adulthood. These tragic experiences deepened his religious fervor.

In public life, however, Chase was quite successful. His strong sentiments for the antislavery movement shaped his political associations. In 1840 he helped organize the Liberty Party and then became active in the Free Soil Party in 1848. It was on the Free Soil ticket that Chase was elected to a six-year term in the United States Senate in 1849. He continued his fight against slavery as a Senator and opposed the Missouri Compromise of 1850 and the Kansas-Nebraska Act of 1854.

In 1854 Chase helped establish the Republican Party in Ohio. Three years later he was elected the first Republican governor of the state. Chase was re-elected in 1857 and was widely considered a potential presidential candidate. Because of his fluid party affiliations, however, Chase could not garner enough support from one party to run for president. When Abraham Lincoln (1861–1865) won the presidency, Chase was appointed to Lincoln's Cabinet as Secretary of the Treasury.

In this position Chase faced the difficult task of organizing the country's finances during the American Civil War (1861–1865). Large sums of money had to be borrowed, bonds marketed, and the national currency kept as stable as possible. Chase was even forced to issue paper currency, or "greenbacks," to help finance the war, although he personally favored hard currency. Despite these challenges Chase also managed to develop a national banking system, which opened a market for bonds and stabilized currency.

While Chase was successful in his position as Secretary of the Treasury, he was often in disagreement with the president and with other members of the Cabinet. Chase was disappointed with the Emancipation Proclamation, believing its stand against slavery was too weak. In 1864 he resigned as Secretary of the Treasury and sought the Republican nomination for president. His bid was unsuccessful, however, because of Lincoln's intense popularity with the public. Instead, Chase made several speeches on Lincoln's behalf during the campaign. When Lincoln again won the presidency, he appointed Chase Chief Justice of the Supreme Court.

Chase presided over the Supreme Court during the troubled Reconstruction period (1865–1877). His important tasks were to restore the Southern judicial system and uphold the law against congressional invasion. Chase also supported the Radical Republicans, who believed that African Americans should be guaranteed their civil rights before the southern states could be readmitted to the Union. Chase's most memorable role as Chief Justice was presiding over the impeachment proceedings of President Andrew Johnson (1865–1869), for which he commended for his fairness and devotion to justice during the proceedings.

Even while serving as Chief Justice, Chase still sought the post of U.S. President, hoping to become Lincoln's successor. He tried to secure the Democratic nomination in 1868 and the Liberal Republican nomination in 1872, but was unsuccessful both times. Chase died of a stroke in 1873.

See also: **Emancipation Proclamation, Kansas-Nebraska Act, Missouri Compromise, Slavery**

FURTHER READING

Blue, Frederick J. *Salmon P. Chase: A Life in Politics*. Kent, OH: Kent State University Press, 1987.

Chase, Salmon P. *The Salmon P. Chase Papers*. Kent, OH: Kent State University Press, 1993.

Middleton, Stephen. *Ohio and the Antislavery Activities of Attorney Salmon Portland Chase, 1830–1849*. New York: Garland, 1990.

Niven, John. *Salmon P. Chase: A Biography.* New York: Oxford University Press, 1995.

Niven, John, and Frederick J. Blue. "Salmon P. Chase." *The Journal of American History*, 82, December 1995.

CHAVEZ, CESAR ESTRADA

Cesar Chavez (1927–1993) was raised in Arizona as the son of a farming family. He devoted his life to union organizing and nonviolent social activism on behalf of laborers in the fields and vineyards of the Southwest. The founder of the United Farm Workers (UFW), Chavez planted the seeds of a broadly–based civil rights movement among Hispanic Americans. As a deeply religious man he drew from the teachings of his Roman Catholic heritage. He was also deeply influenced by the nonviolent activism of Martin Luther King, Jr. (1929–1968), Mohandas Gandhi (1869–1948), and the tactics of radical community activist, Saul Alinsky.

Cesar Chavez was barely ten years old when a bank repossessed his family's farm. With his parents and four siblings, he became one of thousands of migrant workers roving from one crop harvest to another. They all worked to earn a marginal existence during the Great Depression.

Chavez was twelve when the Congress of Industrial Organizations (CIO) began organizing dried-fruit industry workers. His father and uncle actively supported unions. In this way the boy learned firsthand about strikes, picket lines and organizing operations. Most efforts, however, failed to organize farm workers in those days. After long and brutally exhausting days in the field, there was little time to attend meetings. The labor force was constantly shifting from place to place, and many of the Mexican immigrants feared personal retribution by farm owners if they joined together to protest working conditions.

Chavez's family moved from one migrant labor camp to another; Chavez later said that though he attended 65 schools, he never graduated from high school. He served in the U.S. Navy for two years during World War II (1939–1945). When the war was over he returned to working in the fields. Three years later he married Helen Fabela, a fellow migrant worker. They shared strong religious beliefs and a commitment to investing farm workers with hope and dignity.

In 1952 Chavez began actively organizing workers in the fields. He was recruited and trained for his

Cesar E. Chavez.

work by the California-based Community Service Organization (CSO). During the next ten years Chavez built new chapters of CSO, led voter registration drives, and helped Mexican-Americans confront issues of police and immigration abuse. In 1958 he became general director of CSO. He resigned four years later to found the National Farm Workers Association (NFWA) with $1,200 of his own savings.

Organizing farm workers was agonizingly slow work, but by 1965 Chavez had organized a union with a membership of 1700 workers. The staff was composed mostly of Roman Catholic clerics and lay people. In September of that year Chavez led California grape pickers on a five-year strike. Grape growers fought back, but gradually the nation's consumers swung to the workers' side and stopped buying grapes. By 1968 there was a nationwide boycott of California grapes, and the growers were forced to negotiate.

Chavez went on to wage a successful boycott of iceberg lettuce. Like Gandhi, he dramatized his fights against grape growers and lettuce producers by fasting and inviting arrest. He picketed alongside his workers and did jail time with them. By the late 1960s the movement had been baptized *La Causa* (The Cause).

In 1966 Chavez's union merged with the AFL-CIO Agricultural Workers Organizing Committee. It became the United Farm Workers Organizing Committee (UFWOC). By May 1970 farmer after farmer signed contracts with UFWOC, but problems arose three years later when it was time for these contracts to be renewed. The UFWOC—now renamed the United

Farm Workers of America (UFW)—found itself challenged by the National Teamsters Union. Backed by growers who saw an opportunity to weaken or break the UFW, the Teamsters were moderately successful in luring workers away from the UFW. After years of conflict between the two unions an agreement was signed giving UFW the sole right to organize farm workers.

In the final years of Chavez's life the UFW and *La Causa* were troubled with internal dissension. Union membership fell from a peak 100,000 members to 20,000 agricultural workers. This represented a small precentage of the actual number of men and women working in the fields. Many of Chavez's key lieutenants resigned in protest against his increasingly eccentric behavior and autocratic management of the UFW's affairs. But among his followers and supporters Chavez remained respected and admired. *La Causa* continued to attract nuns, priests, ministers, rabbis and other veterans of the nonviolent civil rights and antiwar movements.

Chavez's self-sacrifice and personal devotion to the cause of liberating farm workers from exploitation was an inspiration to millions. He brought the nation's attention to the plight of desperately poor migrant workers. His legacy does not consist only of the increases in pay, eligibility for medical insurance, employer-paid pensions, and unemployment benefits that UFW members received. He was responsible for *La Causa*, the birth of the Hispanic American civil rights movement. When Chavez died in his sleep on April 23, 1993, at age 66, he was on the road in Arizona working for his union.

See also: **Agriculture Industry, American Federation of Labor, Congress of Industrial Organizations, United Farm Workers**

FURTHER READING

Barr, Evan T. "Sour Grapes: Cesar Chavez 20 Years Later." *The New Republic*, 25 November 1985.

Cletus, Daniel. "Cesar Chavez and the Unionization of California Farm Workers." In *Labor Leaders in America*, edited by Melvin Dubofsky and Warren Van Tine. Urbana and Chicago: University of Illinois Press, 1987.

Ferriss, Susan, and Ricardo Sandoval. *The Fight in the Fields: Cesar Chavez and the Farmworkers Movement*. New York: Harcourt Brace, 1997.

Jones, Arthur. "Millions Reaped What Cesar Chavez Sowed." *National Catholic Reporter*, May 7, 1993.

Kannellos, Nicholas, ed. *Hispanic-American Almanac*. Detroit: Gale Research, 1993.

Tardiff, Joseph, and L. Mpho Mabunda, ed. *Dictionary of Hispanic Biography*. Detroit: Gale Research, 1994.

Taylor, Ronald B. *Chavez and the Farm Workers*. Boston: Beacon Press, 1975.

CHICAGO FIRE OF 1871

At about 9 o'clock on the night of October 8, 1871, a fire started in a cowshed behind a Chicago home. It had been an unusually dry summer and the flames jumped quickly from house to house, then from street to street. The blaze raced along from the southwest to the northeast, enveloping the business district and leaping over the Chicago River, dying out only when it reached Lake Michigan almost thirty hours later. Never before had the prosperous American city seen such devastation and upheaval. At the time, many feared the metropolis would not be able to regain its standing as an industrial and economic center. But Chicago recovered swiftly, reaffirming its citizen's faith in their city's perseverance and resilience.

There are several theories about how the Chicago Fire of 1871 began. Rumors spread almost as rapidly as the flames, most of them based on stories about Patrick and Catherine O'Leary and their dairy cow, which was said to have kicked over a lantern that sparked the conflagration. Other explanations range from the accidental—a spark blown from a chimney, or a matchstick dropped —to the intentional—arson, or even the wrath of an angry God. To this day, however, colorful myths surround the tragic event, and the unsolved mystery remains a subject of speculation and debate.

Less ambiguous to historians is what made the fire grow to a size and ferocity that were uncontainable. At the onset of the blaze, local firefighters struggled to pin down its location; by the time they reached the O'Leary's residence, the barn was engulfed in flames. A smaller fire had swept through four of Chicago's city blocks the day before and the fire department's hoses and pumps were worn out from that effort. Once the barnyard blaze raged out of control, the surrounding buildings and the entire city were at risk.

Then the lumber capital of the world, Chicago was a city built primarily of wood. Its houses, storefronts, and factories—even its sidewalks and streets—were made of this versatile yet flammable material. Drought, which had plagued the region for months, left all of this

This Chicago bank was devastated by the 1871 fire.

wood dry, brittle, and particularly vulnerable to flame. The fire enveloped the city's most ornate mansions and its humblest shacks. Gusts of wind carried ''fire devils,'' chunks of flaming wood, which rapidly spread the destruction.

> **NEVER SHALL I FORGET THE SIGHT AS I LOOKED BACK ON THE BURNING CITY. ON THE BRIDGE, A MAN HURRYING ALONG SAID, "THIS IS THE END OF CHICAGO," BUT WITH ASSURANCE THE THIRTEEN-YEAR-OLD REPLIED, "NO, NO, SHE WILL RISE AGAIN."**
>
> **Bessie Bradwell, Memoir sent to the Chicago Historical Society, 1926**

Pandemonium erupted in the streets as families abandoned their homes. Many people seized valuables from the blazing buildings and looting broke out as vandals took advantage of the confusion. In his article ''The Great Chicago Fire,'' John Pauly described how businessmen trundled their families off to safe havens, then risked their lives to reach downtown offices, hoping to salvage money, records, and equipment. Some felt safe enough to stand back and watch the bright, awesome conflagration. ''It was a grand sight, and yet and awful one,'' wrote William Gallagher, a theological student, in a letter to his sister preserved by the Chicago Historical Society. ''[T]he business part of

Chicago was unexcelled by any of our cities in beauty of architecture, handsome and costly warehouses, and convenience of arrangement.''

Chicago's business district was indeed impressive. With the development of the railroad and the economic boom that followed the American Civil War (1861–1865), the city thrived. But the fire raged through four square miles of the metropolis; it demolished factories, stores, railroad depots, hotels, theaters, and banks. Flames burned ships in the Chicago River and consumed nearly all the city's publishing and printing. In the end property damage totaled $192 million. Nearly 300 people died in the blaze and 100,000 were made homeless. Millionaires became paupers overnight, their businesses destroyed.

At first, the damage seemed irreparable. The fire not only halted but also erased much of the progress the city had made in recent years. Chaos reigned in the days following the catastrophe, as civil unrest and looting continued. Mayor Roswell B. Mason declared martial law to preserve peace in the ravaged city. But help was on the way, and with dispatches sent via telegraph, Chicagoans were able to maintain contact with nearby cities that would assist in the rescue, rebuilding, and recovery efforts. Many businesses in other cities had economic interests to protect in Chicago—New York vendors, for example, conducted trade with interior states through Chicago merchants. The support of businesses in other cities helped the city to emerge from the ashes of the great fire.

The rebuilding of Chicago was a tremendous endeavor. Insurance companies in America and Europe rose to the occasion, producing the sums they were obliged to pay for the damages. Cities in America and abroad sent $5 million in relief funds and thousands of donated books replenished Chicago's libraries. Fortunately much of the city's infrastructure—its grain elevators, railroad lines, water supply, and sewage systems—remained intact. The city was able to resurrect itself quickly on this underlying framework. Before long Chicago began to attract entrepreneurs, businessmen, and well-known architects, who found ways to profit from the reconstruction efforts.

Chicagoans' greatest fear was never realized: Their city did not perish. Rather, the rebuilt metropolis reemerged, years later stronger than before, with buildings and homes constructed under new fire regulations. The world's first steel frame skyscraper, the Home Insurance Building, was erected in 1885, and by 1890 Chicago was the second largest city in America. The 1871 fire marked an interruption—but fortunately, not a termination—in the period of economic growth that Chicago, along with other American cities, experienced during the post-Civil War years.

See also: **Illinois**

FURTHER READING

"A Dairy Tale: History Buff Richard Bales Says Mrs. O'Leary's Cow Did Not Kick-Start the Chicago Fire of 1871." *People Weekly*, September 22, 1997.

Burgan, Michael. "The Great Chicago Fire." *National Geographic World*, September, 1998.

"The Great Chicago Fire and the Web of Memory" [cited March 27, 1999], available from the Chicago Historical Society Site on the World Wide Web @ www.chicagohs.org/fire/intro/.

"The Great Chicago Fire of 1871" [cited March 27, 1999], available on the World Wide Web @ www.umi.com/hp/Support/K12/GreatEvents/Chicago.html.

The New Encyclopedia Britannica. Chicago: Encyclopedia Britannica, Inc., 19TK, s.v. "Chicago: History."

Pauly, John. "The Great Chicago Fire as a National Event." *American Quarterly*. Winter 1984.

CHILD LABOR *(ISSUE)*

Using children to perform manual labor is probably as old as the human race. European settlers brought this practice to North America, where it was expected that children would help their parents with the family enterprise, which was usually the farm. The modern summer vacation from school hearkens back to such an era. The expectation that children can provide an economic benefit to their families was transferred from farm work to factory labor when the nation began to industrialize. Many parents desperately needed the extra income their offspring could earn, and some would omit their children's names from school lists when education became compulsory. Samuel Slater, a pioneer in the New England textile industry, thought it natural to hire children to work in his cotton mill in 1793, because their small hands could manipulate the machines more easily. This practice aroused no outrage. Slater was remembered as a philanthropist, and President Andrew Jackson (1828-1836) respectfully referred to him as the "father of American manufactures."

> Breaker boys, some as young as nine or ten, worked in the mines, crouched for ten-hour shifts picking slate from coal chutes, breathing clouds of coal dust. All too often boys were pulled into machinery and mangled to death. Others worked underground in mud on fourteen-hour shifts as mule drivers.

As the nation continued to industrialize, many children were forced to work under conditions that were increasingly harsh. Boys would be expected to stand near hot furnaces, molding glass for hours on end, or they would sort coal by hand in the mines, where they might catch black lung disease or other illnesses associated with a dirty, damp, and cold environment. Children in factories were often mangled or killed, as they worked with or near heavy industrial machines. Even in the best of conditions, working children were denied their right to an education.

As the nineteenth century progressed, there was a reaction against this form of child abuse. Workmen's associations often protested child labor because it kept wages low and compromised job security, but there was also a growing appreciation that children should be defended and protected for their own sake. At first the response was rather mild. In 1842 the Massachusetts legislature passed a law that limited children under 12 to working no more than ten hours a day. Many other states passed legislation that restricted child labor, but the laws were often toothless. Certainly they were not uniform and offered industry no definite guidelines on how to curb the practice. The number of children in the workplace continued to expand.

In 1904 a group of reformers established the National Child Labor Committee, whose purpose was to investigate the problem and lobby state-by-state for legislation to end the abuse. It was not effective because each state feared restrictive legislation could give other states a competitive advantage in recruiting industry. In 1907 a federal law against child labor, sponsored by Senator Alan Beveridge of Ohio (1899-1911) went down to defeat. In 1910 there were still an estimated two million children employed in industry.

In 1912 a Children's Bureau was established as an agency of the Department of Commerce and Labor. Its mandate was to examine "all matters pertaining to the welfare of children," which included child labor, and it was led by Julia C. Lathrop, the first woman to head a

Children were often used to perform menial tasks, such as running this loom, during the early industrialization America. In 1842 the Massachusetts legislature was the first to pass many laws to protect children from this form of abuse.

federal agency. Progress, however, was still slow. In 1916 senators Robert L. Owen and Edward Keating sponsored a bill that restricted child labor, which passed both houses of Congress with the strong support of President Woodrow Wilson. The law was based on a recommendation of the National Child Welfare Committee, but it only prevented the interstate shipment of goods produced in factories by children under 14 and materials processed in mines by children under 16. It also limited their workday to eight hours. In 1918 the Supreme Court declared this law unconstitutional, because it was directed toward the regulation of working conditions, not the control interstate commerce. In 1919 Congress passed the Child Labor Act, which placed a tax on companies that used child labor, but the court too overturned it. In 1924 there was an attempt to amend the Constitution to prohibit child labor, but it never received approval from the required number of states.

In spite of these failures, the national mood was clearly against child labor. As educational requirements became more stringent and truancy laws more strictly enforced, it became harder for companies to depend on child labor. Also demands within industry for a better skilled, more highly trained labor force inhibited the hiring of children. By 1920 child labor was in decline nationally.

President Franklin Delano Roosevelt's domestic reforms in the 1930s, which are known collectively as the New Deal, also attacked child labor and settled the legality of the issue. The National Labor Relations Act of 1935 prohibited the use of boys under 16 and girls under 18 on projects where the U.S. government contributed $10 thousand or more. Another bill, the Fair Labor Standards Act, which was passed in 1938, remains the major piece of federal legislation directed against child labor. It prevented children, including the offspring of migrant workers, from taking jobs that would interfere with their education, health or general well being. It forbade the full-time employment of those 16 and under, and this prohibition could be raised to include those 18 and under for work in dangerous or unhealthy industries. The law also provided for certain exemptions. Children 14 and over could be employed after school hours. Young people were able to work in a family-owned business or at home, or deliver newspapers or act. The Fair Labor Standards Act also established a minimum wage, which further discouraged the employment of children, because low wages was an important inducement for hiring them. A Supreme Court to which Roosevelt had appointed five members upheld the constitutionality of the law in 1941.

Federal legislation is now also supplemented by modern more comprehensive state laws, which also aim to safeguard children by restricting the type of job they may hold and the number of hours they may work. Although there are isolated incidents, child labor in the United States is no longer a major problem, and the remaining domestic issue concerns the morality of importing goods that were produced by child labor abroad.

The international situation regarding child labor is discouraging. In 1973 the United Nations called upon the countries of the world to ratify a convention that established 15 as the minimum age for work. Children as young as 13 would be permitted to do light work, but only those who reached 18 could hold a hazardous job. The reform has not been effective in the developing countries, where poverty forces many children into the workforce to help their families. In 1997, the International Labor Office estimated that 250 million children are working in jobs that may cause physical or emotional damage.

FURTHER READING

Bernstein, Irving. *The New Deal, the Worker, and the Great Depression*. Boston: Houghton Mifflin, 1985.

Cameron, E.H. *Samuel Slater, Father of American Manufactures*. Freeport, Maine: Bond Wheelwright Company, 1960.

Semonche, John E. *Charting the Future: The Supreme Court Responds to a Changing Society*. Westport, Conn.: Greenwood Press, 1978.

Tentler, Leslie. *Wage-Earning Women: Industrial Work and Family Life in the United States, 1900-1930*. New York: Oxford University Press, 1979.

Wilcox, Claire. *Public Policies toward Business*. 3d ed. Homewood, Ill.: Richard D. Irwin, 1966.

CHINESE EXCLUSION ACT

When gold was discovered in California in 1848, few laborers were available for the new mining industry and many looked to China as a ready source of workers. Inexpensive transportation across the Pacific Ocean, acceptance of low wages, willingness to tackle dangerous jobs, and a strong work ethic made the Chinese attractive to mine operators. Brokers paid

> At least a thousand (Chinese) perished in building the (Central Pacific) roadbed. . . . But they worked so hard and so well that hundreds more were hired. In 1869 a group of Chinese and Irish workers laid a record ten miles of track in just under 12 hours, though the Chinese and their sacrifice were barely mentioned in the flossy speeches that year when the historic meeting of the rails was celebrated.
>
> **Donald D. Jackson, *Smithsonian*, February 1991**

passage expenses for the Chinese laborers' transportation and the laborers repaid them from their earnings. In 1852 alone more than 20,000 Chinese arrived in California almost exclusively from the Guangdong province of southern China (including the city of Canton.) Within a few years of the gold discovery, the Chinese population was an important part of California's labor force. On their own initiative, the Chinese reworked the spoils left by earlier mining operations, recovering previously overlooked gold .

Other work became available in the ensuing years, including construction of the transcontinental railroad and increased employment in agriculture and manufacturing. By the 1880s approximately 100,000 Chinese were in the United States, more than 90 percent of them males. The vast majority sent their wages home regularly, maintaining a goal of eventually returning to their homeland and families.

As the white population grew in the West, particularly after completion of the railroad, competition for jobs increased and hostility from whites mounted. A downturn in the economy during the early 1870s led to declining wages; persecution of the Chinese escalated. New trade unions devised tags for goods to identify those made by white laborers and those made by Chinese. Violence directed towards Chinese also increased; nineteen Chinese were killed in a mob incident in Los Angeles in 1871 and more were killed in 1877 during a San Francisco riot. Later in 1877, San Francisco businessman Denis Kearney (who was himself an immigrant from Ireland) formed the Workingman's Party of California which spearheaded the anti-Chinese movement.

Although Chinese comprised far less than one percent of the U.S. population, politicians reacted to voter demands by joining those who blamed the immigrants for economic ills. Seeking to restrict further

competition from Chinese workers, Congress passed the Fifteen Passenger Act limiting Chinese immigration in 1879. However, President Rutherford B. Hayes (1877–1881) vetoed the bill claiming it violated the 1868 Burlingame Treaty with China. The following year the United States negotiated a new treaty with China, permitting immigration restrictions for laborers but exempting foreign travelers, students, teachers, and merchants.

With the new treaty in place, Congress passed the Chinese Exclusion Act of 1882 suspending Chinese labor immigration for ten years and making Chinese immigrants ineligible for U.S. citizenship. The act was the first major law restricting immigration of a specific nationality into the United States. Chinese in the United States unsuccessfully challenged the new law as discriminatory. Persecution continued and 28 Chinese mine workers, refusing to join a strike, were killed in Rock Springs, Wyoming, in September of 1885. Congress extended the Exclusion Act in 1892 for another ten years, and in 1902 made the exclusion indefinite following a new, more restrictive treaty with China in 1894. In 1904 China refused to renew the 1894 treaty. Continuing immigration restrictions by the United States led to a boycott of U.S. goods in China in 1905.

The series of exclusion acts proved very effective in limiting immigration. The Chinese population substantially declined. The immigration acts were supplemented with other laws restricting the work activity of Chinese living in the country. In 1913 California passed a law prohibiting Chinese from owning land. Chinese people still entered the country but in smaller numbers, often using fraudulent papers to pose as merchants. Another ''loophole'' allowed Chinese-born children of U.S. citizens to gain entrance and citizenship. From 1910 to 1940, San Francisco's Angel Island was a point of entry where U.S. immigration officials examined ''papers'' of tens of thousands of Chinese trying to enter the country, much as Ellis Island in New York City served to process European immigrants.

The Chinese population quietly persevered through generations of persecution and consistently avoided conflict. Socioeconomic effects of the persecution included formation of self-contained communities, insulated from the dominant white Western society. ''Chinatowns'' grew within several large cities of the West and the Chinese established their own schools, printed their own newspapers, and formed their own banks. But the overall effectiveness of the Exclusion Acts led to later efforts to restrict immigration of other groups as well, including East Indians, Japanese, and Middle Easterners.

World War II (1939–1945) was a key catalyst in changing sixty years of discriminatory U.S. policies against the Chinese. China was an ally of the United States throughout the war. China's leader, General Chiang Kai-shek (1887–1975), was highly respected and the United States supported Chiang in his fight against internal (Mao Zedong and the Communists) and external (Japan) threats. This closer relationship helped change U.S. policy at home regarding Chinese-Americans.

Higher paying industrial employment opened up to the Chinese-Americans, whose population numbered 60,000 in the 1930s. With anti-Chinese sentiment dissipating, Congress repealed the Exclusion Act in 1943. It was immediately replaced with strict quotas limiting Chinese immigration in favor of Europeans, but these quotas were repealed in 1965 as the status of Chinese-Americans continued to improve. By 1970 most working Chinese-Americans held white-collar jobs and were well integrated into the U.S. economy.

See also: **Ellis Island, Immigration, Transcontinental Railroad**

FURTHER READING

Chan, Sucheng, ed. *Entry Denied: Exclusion and the Chinese Community in America, 1882–1943*. Philadelphia: Temple University Press, 1991.

Gyory, Andrew. *Closing the Gate: Race, Politics, and the Chinese Exclusion Act*. Chapel Hill, NC: University of North Carolina Press, 1998.

McKee, Delber L. *Chinese Exclusion Versus the Open Door Policy, 1900–1906: Clashes Over China Policy in the Roosevelt Era*. Detroit: Wayne State University Press, 1977.

Takaki, Ronald T. *Strangers from a Different Shore: A History of Asian Americans*. Boston: Little Brown, 1989.

Wong, K. Scott, and Sucheng Chan, eds. *Claiming America: Constructing Chinese American Identities During the Exclusion Era*. Philadelphia: Temple University Press, 1998.

CHISHOLM TRAIL

The Chisholm Trail originated in southern Texas and ran about 1,000 miles (1,600 kilometers) to its end at Abilene, Kansas. In 1866 the route was first traveled by American frontiersman Jesse Chisholm (1806?–1868?) as he drove a wagon from the Mexican border, through Texas, and across Indian Territory (present-day Oklahoma) to a trading post in Kansas. The following year, the Union Pacific Railroad reached Abilene. Cattle ranchers in Texas hired cowboys to round up their livestock on the open range and drive their herds to the depot. Cowboys followed Chisholm's path to Abilene. There the herds were loaded onto trains and transported to markets in the eastern United States, where the demand for beef increased growth in the cattle industry after the American Civil War (1861–1865). Between 1867 and 1870 cowboys drove about 1.5 million cattle along the Chisholm Trail. As the railways pushed westward, so did the route of the trail drive. At the ends of the trails, cities including Abilene and Dodge City, Kansas, became cow towns. As the railroad continued to expand into previously remote areas, the use of the trails declined.

See also: **Cattle Drives, Cow Towns, Cowboys, Open Range**

CHOCTAW

The Choctaw were Eastern Woodlands Indians who lived in central and southern Mississippi. They spoke Muskogean, a language in the same family as Iroquoian. Choctaw were known as successful farmers: they enjoyed a long growing season and ample rainfall. The Choctaw were also known as one of the Five Civilized Tribes of the Southeast, who were so named for their adoption of European customs.

When the Spaniards arrived in the early 1500s, the Choctaw were one of fifteen remaining tribes descended from the Mississippian (Mound Builders). When the French settled the region (by 1699) only the Choctaw, Chickasaw, and Natchez tribes remained. In 1830 the Removal Act forced the Choctaw to give up their lands and in 1832 they were moved west into Indian Territory (Oklahoma).

See also: **Eastern Woodlands Indians, Five Civilized Tribes, Mound Builders, Native American Policy**

CHRYSLER CORPORATION

Chrysler Corporation is the number three auto maker in the United States behind General Motors

(GM) and Ford Motor Company, producing nearly 3 million vehicles a year. After its $38 billion merger with German luxury carmaker Daimler-Benz in 1998, Chrysler is now known as DaimlerChrysler Corp., a North American Subsidiary of DaimlerChrysler AG. With joint headquarters in Auburn Hills, Michigan, and Stuttgart, Germany, the newly formed business is Europe's number one industrial company, and the fifth largest car manufacturer in the world. It employs over 200,000 persons worldwide, and sells vehicles in over 140 countries.

Chrysler Corporation was originally founded by Walter Percy Chrysler (1875–1940) in 1925. Chrysler, a former vice president at GM, designed Maxwell Motor Corporation's original Chrysler automobile in 1924. The car was enormously popular in its first year, selling approximately 32,000 units at a profit of $4 million. The next year Walter Chrysler took over Maxwell and renamed the corporation after himself.

In 1926 Chrysler introduced a series of models that could travel between 50 and 80 mph. It called the cars the "Model 50," "Model 60," etc. Until then, most of the fast motor vehicles in North America were expensive luxury cars, but since Chrysler's fast cars were mid-priced, they were more accessible to consumers. In 1928 Chrysler increased the size of its company fivefold by acquiring the Dodge Corporation. That year also marked Chrysler's introduction of the low-priced Plymouth and the more extravagant DeSoto. Chrysler's emphasis on innovation and research helped increase the company's market share during the Great Depression (1929–1939) and surpass Ford in sales in 1933. Since Chrysler bought more components from parts manufacturers than its competitors, it had greater flexibility than its rivals, but it was a flexibility born of necessity. It did not have the financial resources to make everything within the company and had to pay more for them. In 1937 Chrysler followed the lead of General Motors in signing a labor contract with its workers, represented by the United Automobile Workers (UAW).

During World War II (1939–1945), Chrysler's focus turned to military production, manufacturing tanks, trucks, bomber engines, submarine nets, antiaircraft guns, and small-arms ammunition for the Allied forces. Chrysler's efforts during the war earned the company a special Army-Navy award for reliability and prompt delivery.

But, Chrysler began encountering problems almost immediately after the war. Its relationship with its workers was not always smooth because of Chrysler's sometimes sloppy maintenance and unsafe plants. These problems stemmed from Chrysler's lack of resources; its pockets were not as deep as Ford's or GM's. Even when it managed to placate the leadership of the union, the company was often the target of "wildcat strikes" by disaffected rank and file workers. The company also seemed to have lost some of its earlier ambition and design innovation. Other manufacturers started introducing new cars with more features, while Chrysler's line remained largely static. Chrysler was soon out of step with consumer tastes. During the 1950s the company was selling larger, boxier automobiles when most Americans were buying sleeker cars from Ford and GM. In the 1960s Chrysler introduced a line of smaller cars just as Americans wanted power and luxury. When the OPEC oil embargo of the early 1970s tightened America's wallet, Chrysler maintained its line of inefficient large cars. By 1979 Chrysler's share of the U.S. car market was just nine percent, a decline of 12 points from 1952.

Teetering on the brink of bankruptcy, Chrysler turned to Lee Iacocca (1924—) and the federal government for help. Iacocca, a former executive with Ford, had been named president and chief executive officer of Chrysler in 1978. In 1980 Iacocca convinced Congress to guarantee $1.5 billion in loans to Chrysler, stressing his company's historical role in car manufacturing and its importance to the economy.

The billion-dollar bailout was unpopular with many Americans. But that did not prevent the charismatic Iacocca from trying to revitalize Chrysler. He took his case to the American people, starring in 61 television commercials, exhorting consumers to "buy American," staking his reputation on every Chrysler that left the plant, and otherwise personalizing the company. After suffering losses of $1.1 billion in 1979, $1.7 billion in 1980, and $475 million in 1981, Chrysler started turning a profit in 1982. In 1983 Chrysler repaid all of its federal loans, seven years before they were due.

Chrysler's recovery was stimulated by a successful new line of cars. The K-car debuted in 1981, and in 1982 Chrysler downsized the New Yorker, which introduced a six-cylinder Fifth Avenue model. In 1984 Chrysler pioneered one of the first mini-vans, a prototype of the Dodge Caravan. Over the next fifteen years the Caravan was the best-selling vehicle of its type. In 1986 Chrysler entered a joint venture to sell Mitsubishi cars in the United States, and the next year it purchased American Motors Company, maker of Eagle cars and four-wheel drive Jeeps.

But Chrysler's recovery was not one of uninterrupted success. In 1987 Chrysler laid off workers at two plants while reducing inventory. In 1991 the company lost $795 million because of a recession and weak consumer demand. Three years later the company suffered through a series of embarrassing recalls, including 115,000 Jeep Cherokees with flawed steering columns. In 1997 nearly 2000 engine-plant workers went on strike for a month, Chrysler's longest work-stoppage in 30 years.

Regardless of its success or failure in any particular year, Chrysler developed a reputation of investing heavily in the people and communities that surround its corporate plants. When Chrysler returned to South Africa in 1996, it donated $1 million to President Nelson Mandela's Children's Fund. From 1995 to 1997 Chrysler donated $13 million to Detroit area arts and cultural organizations. In 1998 it gave another $1 million to a pre-college engineering program for minority students in Michigan.

At the same time, Chrysler's merger with Daimler-Benz caused some thorny public-relations problems. A substantial number of Jewish shareholders opposed the deal because of the German company's links with Nazis during World War II (1939–1945). After DaimlerChrysler incorporated in Stuttgart, Standard & Poor's 500 announced that it would not allow the company into its elite group of businesses traded on the New York Stock Exchange, since it was no longer technically an American business. By March, 1999, German shareholders owned 60 percent of the company, with the ratio of American-owned shares dropping from 44 to 25 percent in five months.

See also: **Automobile Industry, Walter P. Chrysler, Lee Iacocca**

FURTHER READING

Babson, Steve. *Working Detroit*. Detroit: Wayne State University Press, 1984.

"DaimlerChrysler AG." Hoover's Online, [cited April 20, 1999] available on the World Wide Web @ www.hoovers.com.

"DaimlerChrysler," [cited April 12, 1999] available on the World Wide Web @ www.daimlerchrysler.com.

Konrad, Rachel, "Germans Surpass Americans as Major Stockholders in DaimlerChrysler." *Knight-Ridder Tribune Business News*, March 16, 1999.

"Chrysler Corporation." Microsoft Encarta Online Encyclopedia, 1999. Available on the World Wide Web @ encarta.msn.com/EncartaHome.asp.

Vlasic, Bill, "DaimlerChrysler era begins: Legal work closes stock swap, creating new company, but official start is Tuesday." *The Detroit News*, November 12, 1998.

CHRYSLER, WALTER PERCY

Walter Percy Chrysler (1875–1940) was an industrialist who began his career in the railroad industry. He later became involved in the automotive industry and was largely responsible for the Buick division of General Motors. He went on to found his own company, Chrysler Motors, which quickly rivaled its competitors General Motors and Ford Motor Company.

Walter Chrysler was born in Ellis, Kansas, in 1875. His father was an engineer for the Union Pacific Railroad. As a boy, Chrysler worked at various odd jobs, as a farm hand, a grocery boy, and a silverware salesman. At the age of seventeen he joined his father and became an apprentice at the Union Pacific shops. Chrysler earned five cents per hour and was eager to learn every aspect of his craft. He earned his journeyman's certificate and then worked as a machinist in several railroad shops throughout the Midwest.

Chrysler gradually moved up into positions of greater responsibility. At the age of thirty-three he became superintendent of the Chicago and Great Western Railroad system. During this time, Chrysler and his family lived in Oelwein, Iowa. He began to notice the new automobiles on the streets of town. He became more interested in them when he attended the 1905 Chicago automobile show and saw the Locomobile. The car cost $5,000; Chrysler borrowed more than $4,000 to purchase it. He took it home to Oelwein, but did not drive it around town. Instead, he took the car apart and put it together again several times.

His position at Great Western was an impressive job for a young man, but Chrysler aspired to move up the corporate ladder. He realized that he would have few opportunities to do so in the mechanical branch of railroading, so he switched industries. In 1910 Chrysler became the works manager of the American Locomotive Company in Pittsburgh at a starting salary of $8,000 per year. During the same year, Charles W. Nash, who was just made president of General Motors Corporation, became aware of Chrysler's efficient management of American Locomotive. In 1912 Nash persuaded Chrysler to take a salary cut and accept the position of works manager of Buick in Flint, Michigan.

Walter P. Chrysler stands proudly with his 1925 Chrysler.

IT DEVOLVES UPON THE UNITED STATES TO HELP MOTORIZE THE WORLD.

Walter P. Chrysler, September 1928

Since cars at Buick were being made by slow, handwork methods, Chrysler quickly reorganized the shops into efficient units, introducing Henry Ford's assembly line method of production. Output levels soared. From 1911 to 1919, when Chrysler was in charge of Buick, car production rose from 40 to 550 cars per day; the company's profits increased just as dramatically.

In 1916 William C. Durant (1861–1947) returned as president of General Motors and appointed Chrysler president of Buick at an annual salary of $500,000 dollars. Chrysler, however, was unhappy under Durant's leadership. He disapproved of Durant's management decisions and felt he was interfering unnecessarily in Buick's business affairs. In 1920 Chrysler decided to resign from General Motors and planned to retire.

Chrysler's retirement plans were short-lived as he was quickly persuaded by Chase National Bank to rescue the automotive company of Willys-Overland from bankruptcy. Chrysler's salary for this project was a yearly $1 million. Chrysler soon took on a similar task of reorganizing the Maxwell Motor Company. With the help of three talented engineers from Willys-Overland, Fred Zeder, Owen Skelton, and Carl Breer, Chrysler designed and produced his first car, the Chrysler, in June of 1925, at the Maxwell plant. In 1924 the Maxwell Company was rechartered as the Chrysler Corporation.

Popular demand for the Chrysler fueled the company's growth. First-year sales were 19,960; by 1926 sales had jumped to 129,572 The business grew when Chrysler introduced the Plymouth and the DeSoto in July of 1928. In the same month he purchased the Dodge Brothers manufacturing company and became the second largest automobile producer in the world, with business interests valued at approximately $432 million. In 1928 Chrysler Corporation became Chrysler Motors. The relatively new company was a major player in the automotive industry. The strength of the Chrysler Corporation challenged the traditional competition between Ford Motor Company and General Motors—the "Big Three" became a reality.

During the Great Depression, Chrysler adopted a survival strategy which focused on reducing debt and improving the existing line of cars—the Chrysler, DeSoto, and Plymouth. When the demand for cars began to rise again in 1937, the company was in a secure position and soon resumed its growth. Much of Chrysler's success was due to his ability to grow with his job. He became as skillful with finance and marketing as he was with production. Walter Chrysler retired in 1935 and died five years later.

See also: **Automobile Industry, Assembly Line, Chrysler Corporation, Ford Motor Company, General Motors**

FURTHER READING

Breer, Carl. *The Birth of Chrysler Corporation and Its Engineering Legacy.* Warrendale, PA: Society of Automotive Engineers, c1995.

Dammann, George H. *Seventy Years of Chrysler.* Glen Ellyn, IL: Crestline Publishers, 1974.

Fucini, Joseph J., and Suzy Fucini. *The Men and Women Behind Famous Brand Names and How They Made It.* Boston: G.K. Hall and Company, 1985.

Karwatka, Dennis. ''Walter Percy Chrysler.'' *Tech Directions*, September 1993.

Taylor III, Alex, Jurgen Schrempp, and Robert Eaton. ''Daimler-Chrysler: Gentlemen Start Your Engines.'' *Fortune*, June 8, 1998.

''Walter P.'s Road to Success Apparently Was One Way.'' *Automotive News*, April 24, 1996.

CIRCULAR FLOW OF ECONOMIC ACTIVITY

The basic tenet of the circular flow of economic activity is, ''What goes around comes around.'' The circular flow begins with the spending habits of consumers. How much and how fast consumers spend then drives the amount of investments that businesses make in resources to produce goods. These investments in turn affect the number of jobs that are available and the general economic health of a region. As more jobs become available, consumers have more money to spend. Conversely, as employment levels drop, consumers have less money to spend on goods and services. Consumer spending also determines the kinds and quantities of products that businesses produce.

The circular flow theory was first advanced by the physiocrats, a school of economics in the 1700s. The major proponent of the physiocratic view, Francois Quesnay (1694–1774), wrote in 1758 that the circular flow was a natural order in economics and self-sustaining. Quesnay proposed that the flow had an inherent self-correcting mechanism and therefore did not need to be directed by government. The circular flow created a balance by automatically decreasing and increasing consumer spending levels and business investments when needed.

See also: **Business Cycle**

CITY PLANNING

City planning is a process by which the growth and organization of a city is determined by some rational method. Roads, bridges, factories, and homes are built to take best advantage of the environment and provide a high quality of life. Even ancient cities were designed according to some sort of plan, some of which are quite beautiful and take good advantage of their natural resources.

During the eighteenth and nineteenth centuries in Europe and the United States, planners were concerned with creating monumental plazas, parks, boulevards, and other great public spaces. Paris, France, and Washington, D.C., with their notable plazas and great avenues radiating out from a central point, typified this kind of city planning. In the United States this impetus toward building attractive public areas became known as the City Beautiful Movement.

In the twentieth century, the concept of zoning developed out of a concern for the quality of life of ordinary citizens. Certain districts or zones were set aside for different types of development, with homes in one area, shops in another, and high-rise office buildings in a third. The impetus behind the development of zoning was a desire to shield urban residents from the harmful effects of pollution from factories, which were placed in special industrial districts. Thus, city planning developed into a complex process that involved economic, sociological, and political concerns, among others. Elements as diverse as race relations, traffic flow, noise pollution, and the economic well-being of citizens all play a part in modern city planning.

CIVIL RIGHTS ACTS OF 1866, 1875

The civil rights acts of 1866 and 1875 were passed by the U.S. Congress in an effort to make full citizens of and guarantee the rights of the freed slaves. The Thirteenth Amendment (1865) had abolished slavery throughout the nation, and Congress was faced with how to enfranchise this population. Both pieces of legislation proved to be controversial.

Early in 1866 Congress approved an act which stated that states could not infringe on the rights of their citizens. But President Andrew Johnson (1808–75) vetoed it. When the South seceded from the Union in 1861, Johnson, then a senator from Tennessee, remained in Washington, D.C.; he believed the act of secession was unconstitutional. When President Abraham Lincoln (1861–65) ran for a second term in 1864, he chose the southern Democrat as his running mate in an effort to heal the nation's wounds. Having won the election, Lincoln had just begun his second term when he was assassinated (April 1865); Johnson succeeded him in office. When the Civil Rights Act arrived on his desk, Johnson refused to sign it; he had always been a firm believer in the rights of states to regulate their own affairs. For the first time in history, Congress mustered enough votes to overturn a presidential veto and enacted the law anyway. It was the first of numerous veto overturns that came during the years of Reconstruction (1865–77), as Congress and the president squared off over how to restore the Union.

In June 1866 Congress proposed the Fourteenth amendment, which gave citizenship to all African Americans and guaranteed that all laws (both federal and state) applied equally to African Americans and whites. Congress further required that no southern state could be readmitted to the Union (at the time, none had been readmitted) without first ratifying the Fourteenth Amendment. The amendment was ratified in 1868—replacing the earlier, disputed legislation.

The Act of 1875, passed by Congress on March 1 of that year, aimed to protect all citizens from discrimination in places of public accommodation. In part it stated that, "All persons within the jurisdiction of the United States shall be entitled to the full and equal enjoyment of the accommodations, advantages, facilities, and privileges of inns, public conveyances [transportation] on land or water, theaters, and other places of public amusement . . . and applicable alike to citizens of every race and color." Eight years later, the legislation was struck down as unconstitutional by the U.S. Supreme Court, which stated that Congress does not have the authority to regulate the prevalent social mores of any state. The ground covered by the Civil Rights Act of 1875 was later covered anew by Congress in the Civil Rights Act of 1964, which bans discrimination based on a person's color, race, national origin, religion, or sex.

See also: **Thirteenth Amendment, Fifteenth Amendment**

CIVIL RIGHTS MOVEMENT

The civil rights movement was a "freedom struggle" by African Americans in the 1950s and 1960s to gain equality. The goals of the movement were freedom from discrimination; equal opportunity in employment, education, and housing; the right to vote; and equal access to public facilities.

Motivation for the movement came from an earlier period. During Reconstruction (1865–1877) the North attempted to force economic and social change on the South and at times exploited the region mercilessly. A broad-based reaction in Southern states led to creation of a legal system of discrimination against African Americans known as Jim Crow laws. The laws largely nullified recognition of citizenship and voting rights and equal protection under the law according to the Fourteenth and Fifteenth Amendments. Jim Crow laws persisted through the first half of the twentieth century.

Organized efforts to combat Jim Crow laws led to establishment of the National Association for the Advancement of Colored People (NAACP) in 1909. The NAACP pursued a lobbying and litigation strategy that challenged segregation and discrimination. The NAACP, however, had few successes before World War II (1939–45). At the close of the war returning African American servicemen expressed impatience with the segregation laws and policies that they found at home.

The 1954 U.S. Supreme Court decision *Brown v. Board of Education* proved to be the landmark event that struck down segregation in public elementary schools. The Court's decision effectively closed the door on the "separate-but-equal" doctrine that supported Jim Crow policies. Legal groundwork was laid for a more concerted nationwide effort to eliminate racial barriers in the United States.

African-American activism forced the government to extend racial reform beyond *Brown* to other aspects of life. The Civil Rights Movement would become more than just a protest against segregation in the schools. In December of 1955 Rosa Parks, the secretary of the Alabama NAACP, was arrested in Montgomery, Alabama; she had refused to give up her seat on a city bus to a white man as required by city law. In reaction to this arrest a group of black women called for a boycott of city buses. A rally was held at the Holt Street Baptist Church in Montgomery. The decision to pursue the boycott followed an inspirational speech by

> Eighteen days after the euphoria of the March on Washington, four hundred worshipers crowded into the Sixteenth Street Baptist Church in Birmingham for Sunday services. . . . A group of young girls had just finished a Sunday school lesson and were in the basement changing into their choir robes . . . at 10:19 A.M., fifteen sticks of explosives blew apart the church basement and the children in the changing room.
>
> **Henry Hampton and Steve Fayer,** *Voices of Freedom***, 1990**

a young, 27-year-old preacher, Martin Luther King, Jr. (1929–68), who preached the tactics of nonviolent, civil disobedience in contrast the NAACP's legal approach. The boycott lasted almost a year during which King's home was bombed. But the violence only served to garner additional support for the movement from people regardless of ethnicity. Late in 1956 the Supreme Court's *Gayle v. Browder* decision ruled the Montgomery bus law unconstitutional.

King founded the Southern Christian Leadership Conference (SCLC) in 1957 to provide leadership to a movement that was gaining momentum. The Klan, along with other racists, responded by beginning a terrorist campaign of murders and bombings. Other highly publicized confrontations followed. In 1957 President Dwight D. Eisenhower (1953–61) dispatched federal troops to Little Rock, Arkansas' Central High School to assist nine African-American students who tried to enroll. (Central High was a segregated school that did not accept African American.) In 1962 President John F. Kennedy (1961–63) sent federal troops to the University of Mississippi when James Meredith attempted to enroll.

The movement proceeded on a number of fronts. A campaign to register African American voters grew throughout the South, often at great personal risk to those involved. Other protesters targeted "whites-only" lunch counters, where they would take a seat and refuse to move until they were forcibly evicted, thereby introducing the non-violent tactic of "sit-ins." They often withstood considerable abuse while maintaining their nonviolent conduct.

Another strategy was Freedom Rides targeting the segregation on interstate buses and in bus stations. In 1961 a group of civil rights activists boarded segregated interstate buses that traveled from Washington, DC into the South. These activists, who were beaten at various Southern stops, were deliberately violating segregationist policies that the Supreme Court had earlier ruled unconstitutional in the 1960 *Boynton v. Virginia* decision. The fire bombing of one of these buses in Alabama forced President Kennedy to send U.S. Marshals to protect the riders. In September of 1961 the Interstate Commerce Commission implemented the *Boynton* decision by abolishing all remaining interstate transportation segregation policies.

The high point of the civil rights movement occurred on August 28, 1963, when 250,000 thousand persons participated in a March on Washington urging the federal government to support desegregation and protect voting rights. Martin Luther King Jr. gave his now-famous "I Have a Dream" speech espousing nonviolent direct action and voter registration. President Kennedy, who had earlier tried to discourage the march, decided to use it to promote the passage of what became the Civil Rights Act of 1964. Kennedy's successor, Lyndon Johnson, used the outpouring of grief after Kennedy's assassination in the fall of 1963 to get the 1964 Civil Rights Act passed by Congress. The sweeping act shattered the legal foundation of segregation by prohibiting discrimination in places of public accommodation, including lunch counters, motels, theaters, and service stations. It denied federal funding to programs with discrimination or segregation policies and it also established the Equal Employment Opportunity Commission. It outlawed discrimination in private businesses with 25 or more employees, as well as in labor unions. The act, however, did not address voting rights.

Violence continued. In 1963 Medgar Evers, the field secretary of the NAACP in Mississippi, was shot and killed in Jackson, Mississippi while organizing a boycott protesting voter discrimination. (Ironically, as a veteran of the World War II invasion at Omaha Beach Evers was buried in Arlington National Cemetery.) Yet the issue of civil rights did not come to the fore of public consciousness until in June 1964 two young white civil rights workers, Andrew Goodman and Michael Schwerner, were murdered along with an African-American companion, James Chaney, for promoting African American voter registration in Mississippi. In 1965 King led a march from Selma to Montgomery, Alabama, protesting voting restrictions. After first being attacked by mounted police using tear gas and clubs, the march was finally held with court permission. Protected by 3,000 federal troops, over 25,000 people joined the march; it was the largest and last major civil rights protest of the 1960s. Congress responded with the Voting Rights Act of 1965. The act expanded voting rights to blacks by prohibiting use of

Civil rights activists held lunch counter "sit-ins" to protest segregation. Although faced with threats of violence, harassment and verbal abuse, demonstrators remained steadfast.

literacy tests and other forms of discriminatory qualifications. In addition, the act established federal oversight of state voting laws.

Despite these successes, dissatisfaction with King's message of nonviolence grew among blacks. New, more radical groups formed, including the Black Muslims. For some of them black separatism rather than integration was an objective. Urban riots across the country in 1965, including Watts in Los Angeles, drew greater attention to these groups.

King, who had received the Nobel Peace Prize in 1964 for his leadership role in the movement, was assassinated in 1968 while supporting a strike by city sanitation workers in Memphis, Tennessee. Riots erupted the following week in 125 cities. Six days after King's assassination Congress passed the Fair Housing Act which banned discrimination in most housing. The leader of the civil rights movement, however, was gone and organizational unity was no longer evident; thus, the civil rights movement's national thrust faded.

No other twentieth century social movement in the United States posed as profound a challenge to political and legal institutions as the civil rights movement. The movement altered fundamental relationships between state and federal governments and compelled federal courts to protect constitutional civil liberties more effectively. U.S. citizens of all ethnic groups benefited from the movement's gains in social justice, especially women, the disabled and other victims of discrimination. Despite large legal gains, however, substantial racial discrimination persisted throughout the remainder of the twentieth century.

See also: **Jim Crow Laws, Discrimination, Martin Luther King, Jr., Reconstruction**

FURTHER READING

Branch, Taylor. *Pillar of Fire: America in the King Years, 1963–65*. New York: Simon and Schuster, 1998.

Eskew, Glenn T. *But for Birmingham: The Local and National Movements in the Civil Rights Struggle.* Chapel Hill: University of North Carolina Press, 1997.

Robinson, Cedric J. *Black Movements in America.* New York: Routledge, 1997.

Robnett, Belinda. *How long? How long?: African-American Women in the Struggle for Civil Rights.* New York: Oxford University Press, 1997.

Salmond, John A. *My Mind Set on Freedom: A History of the Civil Rights Movement, 1954–1968.* Chicago: Ivan R. Dee, 1997.

Young, Andrew. *An Easy Burden: The Civil Rights Movement and the Transformation of America.* New York: Harper Collins Publishers, 1996.

CIVIL SERVICE ACT

Early advocates of a civil service believed that it was necessary to reform the spoils system, a process by which an individual who supported the election of a candidate was rewarded with a position in the government. Rather than personal favors, these reformers wanted some type of test of merit, or required qualifications for persons appointed to non-elected positions in government. Reform supporters won a victory in 1871 when legislation, adopted as a rider to an appropriation act, authorized the establishment of regulations for admission into the civil service with regard to knowledge, ability, and other job performance factors. President Ulysses S. Grant (1869–1877) appointed George William Curtis as chairman of an Advisory Board of the Civil Service, later called the Civil Service Commission. But after two years of significant pioneer work by the commission, Congress failed to grant additional funds for its support. Nonetheless President Rutherford B. Hayes (1877–1881), Grant's successor, continued to encourage the reformers, who regrouped in 1880 to organize the Civil Service Reform Association.

The problem was highlighted in 1881, when a deranged office seeker assassinated President James A. Garfield. Civil Service reformers exploited the president's death by convincing the public that the spoils system was responsible for his murder. The Civil Service Act of 1883—also known as the Pendleton Act after its sponsor, Senator George H. Pendleton—established a bipartisan commission to oversee a merit system of examinations for specific public service positions. About 13,000 positions, less than ten percent of the civilian positions in the federal government at that time, were classified under the merit system, and applicants for these positions were subject to competitive examinations.

The Pendleton Act transformed the civil service and greatly affected the organization of political parties. By 1900, government workers were becoming more professional and better educated, and in the matter of their selection, political influence was being replaced by business skill and overall competency. Other legislation followed the Civil Service Act of 1883. In 1903, extensive rule changes were made; in 1920 the Civil Service Retirement Act was adopted; the Classification Act was passed in 1923, defining grades, qualifications, and salary ranges; and in 1940, the Hatch Act limited the political activity of federal officials.

A series of executive orders was also important in shifting the emphasis from a necessary political reform to a positive search for better procedures and personnel. Some of the more important of these directives reflected the changing nature of national life, its economy, and its values. After the Great Depression began in 1929, for example, the federal government expanded its activities and its personnel. To facilitate policy formulation, a 1931 executive order established a Council for Personnel Administration to link the new personnel services of the federal departments to the Civil Service Commission. By 1938 the number of federal employees had increased greatly, and an executive order in that year provided for better personnel management, on-the-job training, and extension of the merit system.

As the tensions that led to World War II (1939–1945) increased, the government tightened its personnel procedures to secure greater efficiency in the face of the developing threat of war. In 1939 President Franklin D. Roosevelt (1933–1945) issued an executive order establishing the Liaison Office for Personnel Management, directly under presidential control. When World War II expanded the civil service to 3.8 million people, the merit system was virtually abandoned, but it was revived at the end of the war.

The exposure of the corruption in the Watergate scandal under President Richard M. Nixon (1969–1974) prompted further reform. During the administration of President Jimmy Carter (1977–1981), Congress passed the Civil Service Reform Act of 1978, the most sweeping reform legislation since the Pendleton Act in 1883. It abolished the Civil Service Commission and split its functions among an Office of Personnel Management, a Federal Labor Relations Authority, and an independent quasi-judicial Merit System Protection Board.

See also: **Spoils System**

FURTHER READING

Hoogenboom, Ari. *Outlawing the Spoils: A History of the Civil Service Reform Movement, 1865–1883.* Urbana: University of Illinois Press, 1961.

Rose, Jonathan. ''From Spoils to Merit: 195 Years of the U.S. Civil Service.'' *Scholastic Update*, September 20, 1985.

Van Riper, Paul. *History of the United States Civil Service.* Westport, CT: Greenwood Press, 1958.

Weisenberger, Bernard A. ''Reinventing Government, 1882.'' *American Heritage*, February/March 1994.

CIVIL WAR AND INDUSTRIAL EXPANSION, 1860–1897 (OVERVIEW)

The period between the American Civil War (1861–65) and the end of the nineteenth century in the United States was marked by tremendous expansion of industry and agriculture as well as the spread of settlement across the continent. The population of the United States more than doubled during this period. In its report on the 1890 census the Bureau of the Census declared the frontier closed. Most of the economic growth was concentrated in the Northeast, Midwest, and plains states. The South remained largely agricultural, its total industrial production totaling about half that of New York State. The Northeast clearly emerged as the industrial core of the nation with 85 percent of the nation's manufacturing, processing raw materials from the Midwest and West.

For several decades prior to the Civil War, the North was forced to delay or compromise several of its national economic policy objectives due to Southern opposition and the strong position the Southern states held in the Senate. As soon as the Southern states seceded Congress began enacting this delayed agenda. The Morrill Tariff of 1861 raised rates to 20 percent on average, ending more than 30 years of declining tariffs. Funding for three transcontinental railroads was enacted in the Transcontinental Railroad Act. The Morrill Land Grant Act (1862) established agricultural and mechanical colleges by allotting each state that remained in the Union 30,000 acres of land for each

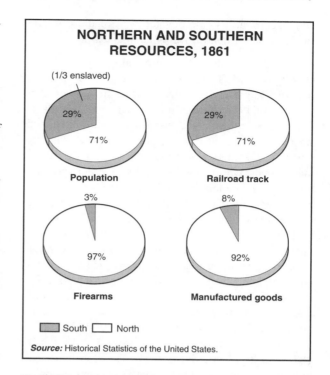

NORTHERN AND SOUTHERN RESOURCES, 1861

(1/3 enslaved)

Population — South 29%, North 71%

Railroad track — South 29%, North 71%

Firearms — South 3%, North 97%

Manufactured goods — South 8%, North 92%

☐ South ☐ North

Source: Historical Statistics of the United States.

The North had a great advantage over the South at the beginning of the Civil War. The roots of these advantages can be found in the diverse economy of the industrialized North, as opposed to the agricultural economy of the South.

member of Congress. The Homestead Act (1862) provided 160 acres (a quarter section) in western territories free to anyone who settled on it for five years and declared their intention to become a citizen. Each of these policies profoundly shaped the development of the U.S. economy for the rest of the century.

The American Civil War devastated the South. Most of the war was fought in the South and much of the region's infrastructure was destroyed. Confederate bonds and currency became worthless, depriving the region of a great proportion of its wealth. Emancipation of the slaves also destroyed a large part of the South's capital, creating the need for a new labor system. There was little capital available in the South to finance reconstruction. The sharecrop system that had replaced slavery had few incentives for innovation and the region remained capital poor and population growth was slow. The South failed to attract large numbers of immigrants because of limited opportunities. Its slowly growing population did not create a demand for expanded infrastructure, one of the factors driving the rapid expansion of the national economy outside the former Confederate states. For at least two generations after the American Civil War the South remained predominantly agricultural and largely outside the industrial expansion of the national economy.

One exception was the development of the iron and steel industry around Birmingham, Alabama.

Northern control of Congress after the War led to ever higher tariffs, reaching an average of 57 percent with the Dingle Tariff of 1897. These rates remained in effect until 1913. Behind the protective wall of these tariffs U.S. industry grew and agriculture expanded westward to feed the growing populations of industrial cities. The United States was the largest free trade market in the world. Northern and Midwestern populations grew much faster than those of the South and the expansion of the nation's railroad system tied those two regions closely together. A large part of the industrial expansion during the post Civil War years was based on connecting the industrial northeast with the farm and grazing areas of the Midwest and Plains states and completing the transcontinental railroads. Railroad mileage in the United States doubled between 1865 and 1873 and increased by an additional 50 percent between 1873 and 1881. Transported freight increased from 2.16 billion ton/mile in 1865 to 7.48 billion in 1873 and 16.06 billion in 1881. The iron and steel industry was one direct beneficiary of the expansion of the railroad system. Steel production increased from 19,643 long tons in 1867 to 198,796 long tons in 1873 and 1,588,314 in 1881. In 1874 the United States was second to Great Britain in pig iron production. By 1900 the U.S. produced four times as much as Britain. Carnegie Steel alone produced more than the British. The expansion of iron and steel production led to comparable increases in iron and coal mining.

An important part of the tremendous economic growth following the Civil War was innovation. The number of patents issued by the Patent Office increased steadily. In 1815 the agency issued 173 patents, while 1,045 were issued in 1844 and 7,653 in 1860. After the Civil War the rate of innovation increased tremendously. At least 15,000 patents were issued annually during this period and 45,661 patents were issued in 1897. While not every patent represented a useful product, many of them did, such as the typewriter, cash register, calculating and adding machines, and the Kodak camera. Other patents were for improvements in industrial machinery such as faster spindles and looms in textiles, new processes for making steel, and the application of electricity to industrial production. In 1876 Alexander Graham Bell (1847–1922) patented the telephone. By 1895 there were 310,000 phones in the United States. The American Telephone and Telegraph Company (AT&T) was formed in 1885 to consolidate all of Bell's patents. Thomas Alva Edison (1847–1931) invented the electric light. He also made invention and industrial innovation a process, creating new products and improving existing ones on a regular basis. His Menlo Park, New Jersey facility was the first modern industrial research lab. Edison became a national hero. Nikola Tesla (1856–1943) developed systems for the transmission of high voltage electricity over long distances. He also developed the electric motor, which had a wide range of uses in the economy, especially in the street car and the electric railroad car. Tesla also developed the electric sewing machine for home and industrial use, and a wide array of industrial applications for electricity. Gustavus Swift developed the disassembly line, applying industrial production systems to meat processing in 1870. New products led to new industries, and new methods and techniques reshaped old industries.

The backbone of the rapid industrial growth of the U.S. economy during these years was the nation's natural resources. The United States had huge reserves of coal, iron ore, copper and other metals, petroleum, timber, and water power, as well as fertile land for agriculture. Iron reserves in northern Minnesota and along the Michigan–Wisconsin border were developed to augment those on the south shore of Lake Superior. Coal reserves in the Appalachian Mountains in West Virginia, Virginia, Kentucky, and Tennessee were developed. Silver and gold mines were developed in Nevada and Colorado. Copper found in Montana replaced that of Michigan as the main source of this increasingly important metal needed for the transport of electricity. An expanding range of uses for petroleum was discovered, its many components being used as lubricants and cleaning solvents. Its use as a fuel began only at the very end of the period. There was little in the way of raw material necessary for industrial expansion at this time that was not abundantly available in the United States.

The expanding economy needed an ever increasing work force, and large numbers of immigrants came to the United States during this period. During the first years of the Civil War immigration declined, but by 1863 it had rebounded to 176,282 new arrivals. Throughout the 1870s, 1880s, and 1890s hundreds of thousands entered the country each year, nearly 800,000 in 1882 alone. Toward the end of the period the immigration patterns changed with more immigrants coming from Scandinavia and southern and eastern Europe.

The growing scale of the economy bought several structural changes. The larger scale of industrial plants and companies and the more complex technology they used made their financing more complicated and more expensive. Investment bankers played an increasingly important role in the economy, supplying the capital that fueled growth. J. P. Morgan was among the more visible of these new players in the nation's economy. The resources banks had were a reflection of a high savings and investment rate among U.S. citizens after the Civil War. By 1880 banks held approximately $819 million in savings and by 1900 just under $2.5 billion. Foreign investment also flowed into the economy, increasing from about $1.4 billion in 1870 to $3.6 billion by 1900, much of it in railroads and utilities as well as municipal bonds.

A second change in the economy was the emergence of monopolies in major industries and the trust as a way of managing them. In the petroleum industry John D. Rockefeller (1839–1937) established the Standard Oil Company in 1863 when the industry was in its infancy. He began by consolidating control of refining through acquisition of competitors. He then moved to ''vertically integrate'' by controlling transportation and distribution. By 1879 he controlled 90 percent of the nation's refining capacity and in 1882 he reorganized the Standard Oil Company as a trust to operate and manage the near monopoly. When he retired from active business in 1897 Rockefeller's personal fortune was estimated at $900 million. Similar concentrations developed in nearly every industry. In each industry no more than a handful of firms dominated, often one or two. Seven companies controlled two–thirds of the railroad mileage in the country by 1900.

The economy was, on a larger scale, prone to periodic downturns due to what has been called the business cycle; periods of increased investment activity and expansion followed by periods of consolidation and slower growth. During the periods of consolidation, unemployment and business failures increased. There was a major panic (as such periods were called) from 1873 to 1879 that saw business failures double, and half the nation's capacity for producing steel remain idle. There was an even sharper drop in economic activity in 1893, but it was shorter in duration and by 1897 the economy was well into a recovery.

In the years between the American Civil War and the end of the nineteenth century the modern U.S. industrial economy developed and took a clear shape. The United States emerged as one of the major economies in the world. Its growth rate, vast reserves of natural resources, and stable political system positioned it well for continuing growth.

FURTHER READING

George, Peter. *The Emergence of Industrial America: Strategic Factors in American Economic Growth since 1870.* Albany: State University of New York Press, 1982.

Heilbroner, Robert, and Aaron Singer. *The Economic Transformation of America, 1600–Present*, 4th edition. New York: Harcourt Brace Jovanovich, 1998.

Jones, Howard Mumford. *The Age of Energy: Varieties of American Experience, 1865–1915*. New York: Viking, 1970.

Wiebe, Robert H. *Search for Order, 1877–1920*. New York: Hill and Wang, 1967.

Zunz, Olivier. *Making America Corporate, 1870–1920*. Chicago: University of Chicago Press, 1990.

CIVIL WAR, ECONOMIC CAUSES OF *(ISSUE)*

The economic roots of the Civil War reach almost to the beginning of English settlement in North America. The development of an economy based on the use of slave labor to produce staple crops through a plantation system in the South and a more diverse economy in the North based on free labor set the stage for the development of two economies within one country. Increasingly after 1800 the needs of these two economies were incompatible.

Southern plantations focused initially on tobacco in Virginia, and later in Maryland and North Carolina, and rice, indigo, and livestock in South Carolina. Africans were the major source of labor after 1619 in the Chesapeake and the system of inherited life slavery developed in Virginia and Maryland by 1660 and quickly spread to the rest of the South. In South Carolina Africans were important not only as a source of labor but for their knowledge of cattle herding in the subtropical climate as well as their knowledge of the cultivation of rice. Tobacco was a crop that was hard on the soil, and from the beginning expansion into new land was an important part of the tobacco economy.

Cotton appeared in the South as a decorative, novelty plant during the colonial era. But, it was well suited for the Southern climate, and the potential market for cotton began to expand dramatically as first Great Britain and then the United States began to industrialize in the eighteenth century. Large-scale cotton farming was not economically viable, however, because of the difficulties involved in separating the seeds from the fiber. The job was extremely labor intensive and the dark, oily seeds easily stained the fiber.

In 1793 Eli Whitney invented a machine that separated the seeds and the fiber quickly and efficiently. Whitney's cotton engine, or gin, made cotton an economically viable crop for the South and revitalized

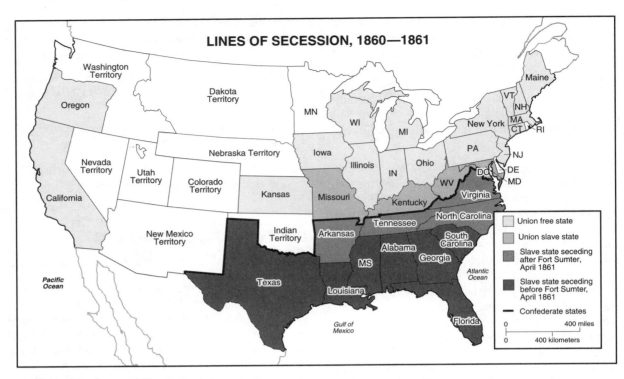

LINES OF SECESSION, 1860—1861

Legend:
- Union free state
- Union slave state
- Slave state seceding after Fort Sumter, April 1861
- Slave state seceding before Fort Sumter, April 1861
- Confederate states

The Lines of Secession were drawn between the Southern states, whose economy was based on staple crop production and slave labor, and the Northern states, whose economy was more diversified and relied less on slave labor.

slavery, which had been declining due to the decline of tobacco. Responding to the demand for cotton from the rapidly developing textile industry in both the U.S. and Britain, cotton plantations spread quickly across the lower South. Cotton, too, proved to be a hard crop on the soil and constant expansion into new lands became an essential part of the prosperity of the cotton culture.

The northern economy had moved in a very different direction from the South. While all of the northern colonies allowed slavery and merchants from several played important roles in the slave trade until it was abolished in 1808, slave labor was not a major element in any northern colony's economy. Northern climate and topography were ill suited for the use of slave labor and the system never became an essential part of the economy.

New England quickly focused its energies on shipbuilding and mercantile shipping, fishing, finance, and other urban occupations. These industries thrived and led to the accumulation of capital that for investment in an increasingly diversified economy. In Pennsylvania there was a staple crop, wheat, but it was ill suited for slave labor. Pennsylvania also diversified its economy rapidly - processing its wheat into flour and developing its own merchant shipping industry. Throughout the northern colonies there were small-scale industrial operations, many of the using water

power in traditional ways. While the South was constantly plowing its earned capital back into new land or additional labor, the North was accumulating capital that was invested in a wide variety of activities and northern investors were always looking for new areas in which to invest.

In 1790 Samuel Slater, an English millwright, offered such an opportunity to Moses Brown. Using Brown's capital and Slater's knowledge of the revolutionary new textile machinery that had transformed the industry in England, they built a textile mill at the great falls of the Pawtucket River in Woonsocket, Rhode Island. Quickly the new industry spread through New England and the Mid Atlantic states. Within a generation steam power became widely available and industry was free to locate wherever there were raw materials and labor. While industrialization began with the textile industry, many other industries emerged. Increased demand led to major advances in the iron industry, including the development of new technology for making steel and the development of coal as a fuel to replace charcoal, first in making iron and steel and later in industry generally. The railroad and the steam boat brought steam power to transportation.

The northern economy quickly became industrial during the first few decades of the nineteenth century, just as the South was becoming increasingly committed to cotton cultivation. The industrial economy attracted large numbers of people who sought work in the mills. Industrialists needed a reliable source of cheap food for this new industrial work force. The Midwest became the breadbasket of the industrial northeast, especially after the Erie Canal and, later, the railroad made it possible to move bulk cargoes east efficiently. The expansion of the industrial northeast required more and more territory for food—primarily wheat, corn, and beef. None of which were well suited to slave labor. These divergent economies were the basis for increasing sectional conflict over the territories in the West which both sections saw as essential to their continued development.

The tariff caused sectional conflict prior to conflict over territorial expansion. When Alexander Hamilton proposed the first tariff in 1790 it was not clearly a sectional issue. As the North industrialized, however, and the South became increasingly committed to cotton and other staple cultivation, the tariff was seen clearly as more beneficial to the North than the South. In response to large scale dumping of British manufactured goods in the United States after the War of 1812 (1812–1814), Northern manufacturers pushed for higher and higher tariffs as protection. Southern opposition grew slowly at first, but accelerated rapidly after 1820 as tariff duties pushed higher.

The tariff remained a long-standing bone of contention between North and South. For the North, tariffs protected its industries and jobs from foreign competition. For the South the tariff was little more than a transfer of wealth from them to the north through the higher prices for manufactured goods, both foreign and domestic. Thus they called the 1824 Tariff the "Tariff of Abominations."

Southern anger over tariff policies became issue that sparked a new and threatening weapon of southern states' rights advocates: nullification. Led by John C. Calhoun, South Carolina nullified the Tariff of 1832." Nullification was a states' rights solution to a contentious issue within the Republic. According to its southern advocates, if the leadership of a state found that it could not abide the imposition of a particular piece of legislation, it had the right to call a state convention and to "nullify" the act. This would take the act out of operation until Congress could debate the matter and add an amendment to the Constitution specifically allowing the act to become law. If this happened, the protesting state then had the right to peacefully secede from the Union.

The nullification crisis came to a head when Congress passed a tariff increase in 1832. South Carolina nullified the law and tried to convince the other southern states to support its position. But President Andrew Jackson, who on other issues favored the states' rights position, perceived nullification to be a threat to the sovereignty of the federal government, however, and moved quickly to quash the rebellion. This was a dicey issue because the leading theorist of nullification was John Calhoun from South Carolina, Jackson's Vice President.

Even though the tariff issue produced the theory of nullification, opposition to the tariff was never as volatile as the issue of the expansion of the slave or the wage labor system into new territories and the formation of slave- or wage-labor states. This was because the creation of new states—slave or free states—was on the order of a foot-race between the competing labor systems. If the states adhering to one labor system became more numerous than the other, Congress could conceivably pass laws that would abolish the labor system of the less numerous block of states. This became the nightmare of the Republic.

It was during the debate over the Missouri Compromise of 1820 that the nation confronted the whole issue of this equilibrium between slave and free states for the first time. The Missouri Compromise allowed Missouri to enter the Union as a slave state (and balanced that admission with the recognition of Maine as a free state) but prohibited future slave states north of Missouri's southern boundary. This was the first limitation on slavery in the territories since the emergence of cotton as a major crop and the revitalization of slavery that had followed from that. The Northwest Ordinance of 1785 had prohibited slavery north of the Ohio River, but it had been passed when the economic future of slavery was questionable and debate over the institution acceptable within the South. By 1820 the economic future of slavery appeared strong, provided new land for cotton could be brought into the system.

The territories were becoming increasingly important to the South after 1830 as the North's population surged past the South's and the North gained control of the House of Representatives (whose members were apportioned by population). The industrial economy of the North was attracting immigrants, while the South was not. The limitations on slavery that had been acceptable in 1820, when the populations of the two sections were more in balance and the economic potential of cotton still unclear, were no longer acceptable in the 1840s and 1850s. Cotton had proven very profitable and the demand for slaves in cotton producing areas provided economic benefits to older southern states where slaves were bred for sale to these new areas to supplement income.

The opposition between the North and South was becoming consolidated over more issues. Economically the slave economy needed as much room to expand as possible. Some southern leaders toyed with the idea of turning the Gulf of Mexico into a reserve for future slave states. The same thinking informed their view of expansion into the West. Balance was seen as necessary in the face of increasing opposition to slavery in the North on moral as well as economic grounds. As long as the number of slave states equaled the number of wage-labor states in the Senate, the South could block any Northern action to eliminate slavery.

The North, however, was also increasingly unwilling to compromise on the expansion of slavery. A plentiful supply of cheap cotton was desirable, but the cotton textile industry was only one of a large number of expanding industries. A dependable source of cheap food was more important and the railroad would soon be allowing the development of territory ever further west. The Spanish had used slaves to mine silver back in the sixteenth century. Would the South employ slave labor in western mining? Southern opposition served as a brake on tariff increases and held up approval of subsidies for further expansion of the railroad system. But compromise with the South was increasingly unpopular in the North.

In 1854 opposition to compromise with the South led to the formation of the Republican Party. Republicans represented the economic interests of the North and Mid-West, supporting higher tariffs, subsidies for railroad expansion, and uncompromising opposition to the expansion of slavery in the territories. The differences between the two sections over the tariff, railroad policy, and the expansion of slavery into the territories became more sharply drawn with every election. Each section saw its future economic prosperity threatened by the other's political success. The election of Republican Abraham Lincoln (1861-1865) as president in 1860 on a platform that was entirely pledged to support northern economic needs convinced Southern states that secession was their only hope to preserve their economies. Lincoln and the North's refusal to accept secession led directly to the Civil War.

See also: **Andrew Jackson, Missouri Compromise, Samuel Slater, Tariff of Abominations, Eli Whitney**

FURTHER READING

Barney, William L. *The Road to Secession: A New Perspective on the Old South*. New York: Praeger, 1972.

Potter, David. *The Impending Crisis 1848–1861*. New York: Harper and Row, 1976.

Stampp, Kenneth M., ed. *The Imperiled Union: Essays on the Background of the Civil War*. New York: Oxford University Press, 1980.

———. *America in 1857: A Nation on the Brink*. New York: Oxford University Press, 1990.

Wyatt-Brown, Bertram. *Yankee Saints and Southern Sinners*. Baton Rouge: Louisiana State University Press, 1985.

CIVIL WAR, ECONOMIC IMPACT OF *(ISSUE)*

The economic consequences of the American Civil War (1861–1865) are largely due to Northern control of the federal government during and for several decades after the War. During the sectional debates over the tariff and the expansion of slavery that characterized the thirty years before the War, the North had been forced to forgo or compromise several of its national economic policy objectives because of Southern opposition and the strong position the Southern states held in the Senate. As soon as the Southern states seceded and the legislators resigned their seats in Congress, the legislators from the North and West began enacting this delayed agenda, while simultaneously prosecuting the War. Northern victory in the War insured their continuing control of the federal government and implementation of their economic policies.

There were four pieces of legislation that passed during the Civil War which were critical to Northern economic development during the decades after the War. The Morrill Tariff of 1861 raised rates to 20 percent on average, ending more than thirty years of declining rates. Funding for three transcontinental railroads was enacted in the Transcontinental Railroad Act. The Morrill Land Grant Act (1862) established agricultural and mechanical colleges by allotting each state that remained in the Union 30,000 Acres of land for each member of Congress. The National Bank Act of 1863 created a set of standards for the banking system. Finally, the Homestead Act (1862) provided 160 Acres (a quarter section) in western territories free to anyone who settled on it for five years and declared their intention to become a citizen. Each of these

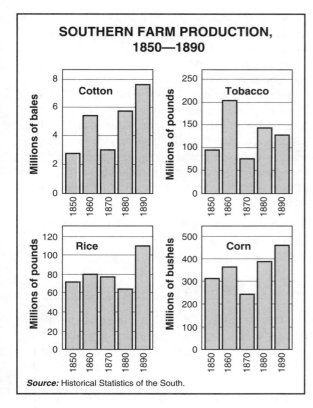

SOUTHERN FARM PRODUCTION, 1850—1890

Source: Historical Statistics of the South.

These graphs highlight the significant decreases in southern farm crop production following the Civil War.

policies profoundly shaped the development of the American economy for the rest of the century.

Another Civil War development with powerful implications for the nation's economy was the wartime devastation visited on the South. The war had been mostly fought in the South and much of its wealth had been destroyed. In South Carolina before the war, for instance, there were 965,000 hogs. After the surrender of the Confederate Army in 1865 at Appomatox, the hog population in South Carolina had dropped to 150,000. Confederate bonds and currency were now worthless, depriving the region of a great proportion of its wealth. Emancipation of the slaves also destroyed a large part of the South's capital, as well as creating the need for a new labor system. (The slaves accounted for the lion's share of capital investment in the South, more expensive than the very land.) The war had destroyed virtually all the banks in the South. There was little capital available to finance reconstruction.

By 1877, when Reconstruction ended with the withdrawal of the Union Army, native white rule returned in every former Confederate state. The South, however, remained largely agricultural, producing staple crops for northern factories or for export. Economic recovery in the South was slow. Cotton did not reach its

1859 level of production until 1879. As cotton production increased, however, the price fell. Tobacco, the other major cash crop in the South, followed a similar pattern. The sharecropping system that replaced slavery had few incentives for soil conservation innovation or the cultivation of new crops. The region remained capital poor and grew slowly in population. In 1860 the population of the slave slates was 11,133,361 compared to 12,288,020 in 1870, an increase of only about 10 percent, compared with a 29 percent increase for the rest of the country.

The South failed to attract many immigrants after the War because of limited economic opportunities. Its reliance on staple crop agriculture and slowly growing population did not create demand for expanded infrastructure, one of the factors driving the rapid expansion of the national economy outside the former Confederate states. For at least two generations after the Civil War the South remained predominantly agricultural and largely outside the industrial expansion of the national economy.

The Compromise of 1877 which ended Reconstruction solidified Northern control of Congress. This control led to ever higher tariffs, reaching an average of 57 percent with the Dingle Tariff of 1897, and a continuation of government subsidies for railroad expansion. Behind the protective wall of these tariffs U.S. industry grew and agriculture expanded ever westward to feed the growing populations of the industrial cities. Northern and Midwestern populations grew much faster than that of the South and the expansion of the nation's railroad system tied the two regions ever more closely together. A large part of the industrial expansion of the immediate post Civil War years was based on connecting the industrial northeast with the farm and grazing area of the Midwest and plains states and completing the transcontinental railroads. Railroad mileage in the U.S. doubled between 1865 and 1873 and increased by an additional 50 percent between 1873 and 1881. Freight carried increased from 2.16 billion ton/miles in 1865 to 7.48 in 1873 and 16.06 in 1881. The iron and steel industry was one direct beneficiary of the expansion of the railroad system. Steel production increased from 19,643 long tons in 1867 to 198,796 in 1873 and 1,588,314 in 1881. The expansion of steel led to comparable increases in mining and other basic industries.

The North and Midwest attracted growing numbers of immigrants, drawn by the promise of economic opportunity and inexpensive land. The growing population spurred construction of housing and infrastructure, which in turn attracted more immigrants in a circular process that continued until the Panic of 1893, which slowed the economy. The economy after the Civil War was initially driven by the construction of railroads connecting the industrial communities of the northeast and the agricultural regions of the Midwest and plains. In 1886, the railroads standardized the gauge (width) of the track, bringing the South into a national railway system. As it matured the industrial area expanded to include communities in the Midwest with an expansion of agricultural regions further west. The economy that developed after the Civil War was still sharply divided regionally along the same lines as the antebellum economy had been.

See also: **Civil War (Economic Causes of), Homestead Act**

FURTHER READING

Ayers, Edward L. *The Promise of the New South: Life after Reconstruction.* New York: Oxford University Press, 1992.

Higgs, Robert.*The Transformation of the American Economy, 1865–1914.* New York: Oxford University Press, 1971

Jones, Howard Mumford. *The Age of Energy: Varieties of American Experience, 1865-1915.* New York: Viking, 1971.

Vatter, H. C. *The Drive to Industrial Maturity: The U.S. Economy, 1860-1914.* New York: Oxford University Press, 1975.

Wright, Gavin. *Old South, New South: Revolutions in the Southern Economy Since the Civil War.* New York: Basic Books, 1982.

CIVILIAN CONSERVATION CORPS

Civilian Conservation Corps (CCC) was a federal agency created in 1933 as part of the New Deal program of President Franklin D. Roosevelt (1882–1945). Originally called Emergency Conservation Work, CCC had its name formally changed to Civilian Conservation Corps in 1937, when Congress extended its period of operation. To minimize the effects of the Great Depression, CCC was given responsibility for conserving the nation's resources, in particular timber, soil, and water. CCC was designed to provide jobs for unmarried men between the ages of 17 and 25, who would receive a base pay of $30 per month for a six-month stint. Normally, $25 of their monthly pay was sent home to the workers' families. Food, clothing, and shelter were provided to CCC workers at no charge.

Although the men who served in the CCC were required to live in work camps run by the Department of War, they were not subject to military control. Conservation training included instruction on how to plant trees, build dams, and fight forest fires. Approximately 3 million men served in 2,600 camps during CCC's ten years of existence, with enrollment peaking at about 500,000. With the outbreak of World War II (1939–1945), the production of industrial materials and munitions was emphasized at the expense of resource conservation. In 1942 Congress voted to abolish CCC, and the president's order for liquidation followed within six months.

See also: **Great Depression, New Deal, Franklin Delano Roosevelt**

CLAY, HENRY

Henry Clay (1777–1852) was a paradox. An eloquent speaker known for charm and generosity, Clay served in the U.S. House of Representatives and the U.S. Senate, as well as U.S. Secretary of State. He also ran for the presidency five times and lost each time. Clay was a leader of the "War Hawks"—a group that pushed Congress to declare war against Britain in 1812—but he opposed the war against Mexico and did much to avoid civil war in the United States. Though Clay was a slave owner and often spoke in support of the slavery dominated South, he also helped craft the compromise that kept slavery out of new U.S. territories.

The son of Reverend John Clay, a Baptist minister, and Elizabeth Hudson Clay, Henry Clay was born on April 12, 1777, in Hanover County, Virginia. British and Loyalist soldiers raided the area during the American Revolution (1775–1783) and looted the Clay home in 1781. That year, the elder Clay also died. Henry Clay's mother remarried when he was fourteen. Clay's stepfather moved the family to Richmond. With only three years of formal schooling, Clay began working as a store clerk at his stepfather's recommendation.

From 1793 to 1797, Clay worked as secretary to George Wythe, chancellor of the High Court of Chancery. As secretary, Clay copied and transcribed records. Wythe encouraged Clay to continue his education, and in 1796 Clay took up the study of law under the Attorney General of Virginia, Robert Brooke. At age twenty, Clay graduated and immediately relocated to Kentucky, where his mother had moved. Frontier land disputes were fertile territory for a young lawyer, and Clay became well known as a defense attorney. He married into a leading family when he wed Lucretia Hart in 1799; they had 11 children. Clay prospered, and eventually owned a 600-acre estate, which he called ''Ashland.''

Henry Clay was tall and slim, with an expressive face, warm spirit, and personal charm. He had an excellent speaker's voice and became well known for his skill as an orator. Clay fought duels in 1809 and 1826. He lived the life of a frontiersman, and was prone to drinking and gambling. John Quincy Adams (1767–1848) noted that Clay was ''half-educated,'' but that he possessed ''all the virtues indispensable to a popular man.''

Clay eventually became involved in politics. He participated in the constitutional convention for Kentucky in 1799, and in 1803 was elected to the Kentucky Legislature. He was appointed to two terms in the U.S. Senate, first from 1806 to 1807 and again from 1810 to 1811. Clay was elected to the U.S. House of Representatives in 1811 and was immediately chosen to be Speaker of the House, a position he held six times during his tenure in the House, which lasted until 1821. In that year, Clay made his first bid for the presidency. From 1825 to 1826 he served as Secretary of State in the Cabinet of President John Quincy Adams (1825–1829). He was elected to the U.S. Senate in 1831, where he served until 1842.

Clay was a lifetime advocate for business and protectionism. He pushed for federal support of infrastructure such as roads and canals. He developed the ''American System,'' a program to improve home manufacturing and business. It was Clay's intention to unite the commercial and manufacturing interests of the East with the agricultural and entrepreneurial interests of the West. The American System was intended to establish protection for U.S. industries against foreign competition and also centralize financial control in the U.S. Bank. Clay backed the Tariff of 1816 and the annexation of West Florida by President James Madison (1809–1817). His protectionism reached its peak in the Tariff of Abominations in 1828.

As a nationalist and an expansionist, Clay advocated war with Britain in 1812 due to the British trampling of U.S. rights on the high seas. The ''War Hawks'' as they were known, supported the War in 1812 (1812–1814). Clay supported the Latin American rebellions against the Spanish, and the Greek rebellion against the Turks. He was not in favor of war with Mexico, but supported the government nonetheless, losing one of his sons in the Battle of Buena Vista (1847).

Clay worked hard but unsuccessfully in the Kentucky constitutional convention to abolish slavery in the new state. He never reconciled his attitudes over slavery, defending the southern states on the one hand and owning slaves himself, but working hard for slavery's abolition on the other hand. At his death, his 50 slaves were willed to his family, but with the provision that all children of these slaves after January 1, 1850, be liberated and transported to Liberia. Clay was a founder of the American Colonization Society in 1816—a society that advocated the repatriation of slaves to Africa.

As an expansionist Clay worked for the addition of states and territories to the Union. A lifelong proponent of the ideals of the American Revolution (1775–1783), he worked for the preservation of the Union. He supported the Missouri Compromise, which allowed Missouri to enter the Union as a slave state while preventing slavery above the 36th parallel. He personally acquired the assurance of the Missouri Legislature that it would not pass any laws that would affect the rights and privileges of U.S. citizens. During the Missouri debates, Clay argued the side of the southern States, continuing the dualism that would be present throughout his life—advocating the rights of slave states while working at the same time to abolish slavery.

In 1849, aligned with statesman Daniel Webster (1782–1852), Clay advocated the Compromise of 1850, which was credited as postponing the American Civil War (1861–1865) for a decade. The compromise was actually a series of proposals that admitted California to the Union as a free state, abolished slavery in the District of Columbia, set up the territories of New Mexico and Utah without slavery, and established a more rigorous fugitive slave law.

Clay ran unsuccessfully for the presidency five times. He was a fearless fighter for his ideas, even if his positions on issues were primarily based on his own self interests. He was devoted to the Union, even if his compromises only postponed an inevitable clash between the North and the South. He considered himself an advocate of Jeffersonian democracy and was involved in party politics, including the establishment of the Whig party. He owned slaves, advocated the removal of blacks from the United States, and worked continuously for the abolition of slavery. As such a self-contradictory individual, Clay had as many fervent supporters as he did enemies.

Henry Clay was well respected by ordinary citizens. In his old age Clay was considerably in debt and when it became known that he was thinking of selling his beloved estate Ashland, common people donated enough money to clear his debts. Few of Clay's children survived him; many did not live to maturity. His son Thomas was ambassador to Guatemala under President Abraham Lincoln (1861–1865). His son James was charge d'affairs at the U.S. embassy in Portugal under President Zachary Taylor (1849–1850). Clay left no surviving descendents, however, when he died in Washington, DC, on June 29, 1852.

See also: **Protectionism, Slavery, Tariff of Abominations**

FURTHER READING

Clay, Henry. *The Papers of Henry Clay*. Lexington, KY: University Press of Kentucky, 1959–88.

Hewsen, Robert H., and Anne Commire, eds. *Historic World Leaders*. Detroit, MI: Gale Research, Inc. 1994, s.v. "Clay, Henry."

Howe, Daniel Walker, *The World Book Multimedia Encyclopedia*. Chicago: World Book, Inc., 1998, s.v. "Clay, Henry."

Encyclopedia of World Biography, 2nd ed. Detroit, MI: Gale Research, Inc., 1998, s.v. "Clay, Henry."

CLAYTON ANTI-TRUST ACT

Passed by Congress in 1914, the Clayton Anti-Trust Act strengthened the legislation of the Sherman Anti-Trust Act of 1890. The Clayton Act thus provided the government with more power to prosecute trusts (large business combinations that conspired to limit competition and monopolize a market). The Sherman legislation declared as illegal every "contract, combination, or conspiracy in restraint of interstate and foreign trade." The Clayton legislation outlawed price fixing (the practice of pricing below or above cost to eliminate a competitive product), made it illegal for the same executives to manage two or more competing companies (a practice called interlocking directorates), and prohibited any corporation from owning stock in a competing corporation. The price-cutting provision was later strengthened (in 1936) by the passage of the Robinson-Patman Act. The Clayton Act also exempted labor unions from prosecution under the Sherman Anti-Trust Act; before the 1914 legislation, businesses had invoked, with some success, the Sherman legislation when labor strikes affected business in more than one state, citing the interruption as a conspiracy of interstate trade. Since organized labor had not been the target of the Sherman legislation, lawmakers exempted them from the antitrust legislation of 1914.

Between 1880 and the early 1900s, corporate trusts proliferated in the United States, becoming powerful business forces. The vague language of the Sherman Anti-Trust legislation and the courts' reluctance to prosecute big business based on that act did little to break up the monopolistic giants. The tide turned against corporate trusts when Theodore Roosevelt (1901–1909) became president in September 1901, after President William McKinley (1897–1901) was assassinated. Roosevelt launched a "trust-busting" campaign; through the attorney general's office, his administration launched some 40 lawsuits against American corporations such as American Tobacco Company, Standard Oil Company, and American Telephone and Telegraph (AT&T). Government efforts to break up the monopolies were strengthened in 1914, during the presidency of Woodrow Wilson (1913–1921), when Congress passed the Clayton Anti-Trust legislation and created the Federal Trade Commission (FTC), which is responsible for keeping business competition free and fair. Trust busting declined during the prosperity of the 1920s, but was again vigorously pursued during the 1930s by the administration of Franklin Roosevelt (1933–1945)

See also: **Monopolies, Theodore Roosevelt, Sherman Anti-Trust Act, Tobacco Trust, Trust-Busting, Woodrow Wilson**

CLIPPER SHIPS

To accommodate increasing overseas trade, North American shipbuilders developed fast sailing vessels called clipper ships in the mid-1800s. With their slender hulls and numerous sails (as many as 35), these swift ships were said to "clip off the miles." The first true clipper ship, The *Rainbow*, debuted in 1845. The vessel was designed by American naval architect John W. Griffiths (1809–82) who, the next year, launched another famous clipper, the *Sea Witch*. Another clipper, the *Flying Cloud*, was launched in 1851 by Canadian-American shipbuilder Donald McKay (1810–80). This ship sailed from New York's East River, around the tip of South America to San Francisco in just under 90 days—a record. Clipper ships transported settlers to the west (including those who made the trip as part of the California Gold Rush). They were fast, but carried relatively little freight. As a result, they were used only for high value cargo, such as silk, spices, and tea. Clipper ships carried goods and people from as far away as China and Australia, and were used by slave traders to outrun British ships that were on patrol for them in the Atlantic.

The construction of canals around the globe shortened most sea trade routes and virtually eliminated the need for the swift clippers. They were replaced by square riggers, which were slower but could carry larger loads. Eventually steam-powered ships proved to be more dependable and quicker than any wind-powered craft.

See also: **Steamboats**

CLOSED SHOP

A closed shop was a workplace in which anyone who hoped to gain employment had to first join a labor union. Closed shop requirements remained one of the most aggressive methods a labor union could use to maintain its power among a company's workforce. A less radical form was a "union shop," in which nonunion workers could join the workforce provided they joined the union within a certain period of time. Conversely, a workplace where workers freely belonged to a union or remained nonunionized was called an "open shop."

Labor unions first became powerful during the Industrial Revolution of the nineteenth century when workers banded together for improved pay and working conditions. During the Great Depression of the 1930s, economic conditions became so difficult that the federal government passed laws such as the National Industrial Recovery Act of 1933 and the National Labor Relations Act of 1935. These acts gave workers the right to bargain collectively (as a single group) with management and required management to negotiate with duly elected union officials. However, during the remainder of the 1930s and in the 1940s some unions in the Northeast and Midwest, the regions with the most heavy industries and the most unions, began requiring that prospective employees be union members before a company could hire them.

After World War II (1939–45) and the damaging labor strikes of 1946, attempts were made to rein in the growing power of the U.S. labor union, culminating in the Taft-Hartley Act of 1947. The act sharply limited the circumstances in which closed shops were legal and enabled state governments to outlaw union shops if they chose. However, even after the Taft-Hartley Act became law many workplaces continued to be informal closed shops. In such workplaces there was no "union only" requirement written anywhere in the labor agreement, but only workers who were already members of the union were ever hired. In some workplaces union workers would simply refuse to work with anyone who was not already a member of the union—this practice

is a "de facto" closed shop. Closed shops are most common in industries where the company allowed the union to hire workers and where workers were employed by a specific company for a short time, as in the construction industry or among longshoremen.

See also: **Labor Movement, Labor Unionism, National Industrial Recovery Act, National Labor Relations Act, Taft-Hartley Act**

CLOVIS POINT

Clovis point is a particular kind of spear point, used by Paleo-Indians (the first inhabitants of North America) to hunt large game such as the now-extinct mastodon and mammoth. The Clovis point was made of stone and had a leaf-like shape, fluted edges, lengthwise channels on each side, and a long, slender point. Named for Clovis, New Mexico, where it was first discovered by archeologists, the spear point is believed to have been widely used throughout what is today the mainland United States. There lived a hunting people that was dominant in North America from about 15,000 to 8000 B.C.. Archeologists and scholars refer to this people as a Clovis culture or civilization.

The Clovis groups were succeeded by the Folsom culture, which began to emerge around 9200 B.C.. The Folsom culture is named for its own distinctive spear point, also found in New Mexico. The Folsom point was smaller than the Clovis, had a concave (rounded inward) base, and a lengthwise groove on each side. This spear point was used to hunt smaller animals (such as deer and rodents) and was used primarily on the east side of the Rocky Mountains, particularly in the Great Plains. The Folsom groups did not rely as heavily on hunting as did their predecessors. They began to better exploit their natural environments, turning to both foraging and fishing for sustenance.

See also: **Paleo-Indians**

COAL INDUSTRY

Coal is a rock that is made up mostly of carbon. Because it is combustible, it is used as a fuel that can provide light, heat, and power. Most coal was formed during the Carboniferous Period and the Permian Period, approximately 250-to 350-million years ago. Warm moist swampy areas became covered with vegetation that decomposed into peat, which in time and under pressure turned into different types of coal, depending on the exact conditions. There are four major grades of coal (from softest to hardest): lignite, subbituminous, bituminous, and anthracite. Bituminous coal is the type most often produced in the United States.

The use of coal may trace back to China around 1000 B.C.. The Romans may have used coal in the fifth century A.D., and there references to the use of coal in medieval Europe. However, there was no widespread use of coal until the Englishman Abraham Darby began to burn it as fuel for his furnace. The invention of the steam engine provided another important use for this product.

By 1745 coal began to be commercially mined in North America, but it was not until the American Revolution(1775–83) brought a halt to the importation of coal from Europe that the American coal industry began to expand at a rapid pace. By the 1840s there were numerous small mining companies in the northeastern United States. The development of the steam locomotive in the second half of the nineteenth century improved transportation and distribution of coal over long distances. The Industrial Revolution also contributed greatly to the expansion of the coal mining industry in the United States.

By the 1920s the coal industry experienced a decline in coal processing, largely because of overexpansion. Many mines closed and as many as 150,000 coal mining related jobs were lost. As other fuels such as petroleum and natural gas became popular, coal continued to drop in price. An act of Congress called the Bituminous Coal Act (1937) attempted to improve the stability of the coal industry.

The 1940s saw the conversion of steam locomotives to diesel fuel, but the loss of this use of coal was replaced by greater use of coal in electric power plants. Throughout the rest of the twentieth century, electric power plants continued to be a major consumer of coal. More efficient methods of shipping coal by train that were introduced in the 1960s allowed greater quantities to be moved across the country. Oil shortages in 1973–74 also caused the demand for coal to increase. Several developments in the 1970s limited productivity and profits although they forced coal operators to become better corporate citizens. Among them were stricter federal regulations on safety, labor practices, and environmental pollution, all areas where coal companies had a questionable reputation. In addition, other fuel resources such as nuclear power came into use as alternatives to coal.

Two very common ways to mine coal on the surface are strip mining and auger mining. However, the most hazardous method to mine coal is underground. Coal mining was always a dangerous undertaking and some of the early coal operators took advantage of mine workers. Dangers included mineshaft collapse, explosions, and exposure to coal dust, which could cause ''black-lung disease.'' In 1890 miners banded together to found their own union, the United Mine Workers (UMW), to improve safety and working conditions. The union also improved wages; the UMW remained active through the end of the twentieth century. However, though automation and advancements in technology reduced the dangers, elements of risk would always be present.

The 1980s saw some profit increases for coal producing companies through advancements in technology that improved efficiency and productivity. In the 1990s growth in coal production remain slow but steady, although the numbers of people employed in the coal industry continued to drop. The major use of coal in the United States continued to be the production of electric power. In the 1990s coal resources in the United States were projected to last for another 250 years. According to these estimations, this natural resource would continue to be utilized as a means of power for generations to come.

See also: **United Mine Workers**

FURTHER READING

Heil, Scott, and Terrance W. Peck, eds. *Encyclopedia of American Industries*, 2nd ed., Vol 2. Detroit: Gale Research, 1997.

Stearns, Peter N., and John H. Hinshaw. *The ABC-CLIO World History Companion to the Industrial Revolution*. Santa Barbara, CA: ABC-CLIO, Inc., 1996, s.v. ''Coal Miners.''

Stearns, Peter N., and John H. Hinshaw. *The ABC-CLIO World History Companion to the Industrial Revolution*. Santa Barbara, CA: ABC-CLIO, Inc., 1996, s.v. ''United Mine Workers.''

''Assessing the Coal Resources of the United States,'' [cited February 1, 1999] available from the World Wide Web @ energy.usgs.gov/factsheets/nca/nca.html/.

The Business of Coal. Chicago: Arthur Andersen and Company, 1981.

COCA-COLA BEVERAGES

Coca-Cola Beverages is the world's largest soft drink producer and distributor, holding 47 percent of the global market. The company produces several beverages other than Coke and owns a line of food products. About 90 percent of the company's revenues come from beverage sales, while the balance comes from food sales. Despite its popularity and presence in the United States, 68 percent of Coca-Cola's soft drink products are sold outside North America.

Coca-Cola Beverages is regarded as one of the best managed companies in the world. In *Fortune Magazine*'s 1997 Annual Survey of corporate reputations the Coca-Cola company ranked first based on its strong marketing skills, financial soundness, corporate and environmental responsibility, quality products and services, and overall business performance. In the same survey corporate executives rated Coca-Cola as America's most admired corporation.

The company traces its origins to May 8, 1886, when the Coca-Cola soft drink (Coke) was invented by pharmacist Dr. John Styth Pemberton in Atlanta, Georgia. Experimenting with a three-legged brass kettle in his backyard, Pemberton mixed caramel colored, cane sugar syrup with carbonated water, caffeine, and extracts from kola nuts and coca leaves. Pemberton's bookkeeper, Frank M. Robinson, suggested the name Coca-Cola. Robinson also created the product's distinctive handwritten logo.

Coke generated profits of only $50 in its first year of sales. Pemberton had to sell two-thirds of his pharmacy business in 1888 to cover his losses. In 1891 Asa Candler, an Atlanta druggist, acquired total control of Coca-Cola for $2300. In 1892 Candler and his partners formed the Coca-Cola Company. That same year Candler spent $11,000 on an advertising campaign that placed the Coke logo on common, everyday household items like calendars and drinking glasses. Candler was among the first businessmen in the United States who used coupons to entice customers to try his product. In 1893 Candler registered Coca-Cola as a patented trademark.

Coke was initially sold as a soda fountain drink. In 1899 Candler sold the rights to bottle his product to two Tennessee lawyers who established an extensive bottling franchise system that still exists today. In 1915 the Root Glass Company designed a contoured glass bottle for the soft drink that was shaped in the form of a coca bean. This bottle design quickly became nationally associated with Coke. During World War I (1914–1918) sugar rationing measures temporarily slowed the company's growth; however, a revolutionary process was invented whereby fuel could be saved by mixing sugar and water without heat.

In 1919 the Candler family sold the Coca-Cola Company to Georgia businessman Ernest Woodruff for $25 million. The Woodruff family presided over the company until 1955 and made a lasting impression on the product's marketing. Under the Woodruffs the familiar slogan "Coke is the real thing" and the six-pack carton of Coke were developed. During World War II (1939–1945) Coca-Cola boosted its image by promising to provide a free Coke to every U.S. soldier. The company also took risks with its image by continuing to distribute Coke from its plant inside Nazi Germany. In the 1950s Coca-Cola took another risk by featuring African Americans in advertisements before the Civil Rights Movement had taken hold.

During the next decade Coca-Cola began to diversify, merging with the Minute Maid Corporation in 1960 and Duncan Foods in 1964. In 1969 Coca-Cola acquired Belmont Springs Water Company. The 1960s also marked the debut of canned Coke and the introduction of four new soft drinks in the United States: Fanta, an orange soda, Sprite, a lemon-lime soda, Fresca, a grapefruit-flavored soda, and Tab, a diet cola. From the 1970s Coke has been packaged in two-liter plastic bottles. In 1982 Coca-Cola introduced Diet Coke, which has outsold all other soda products almost since its inception.

Two years later, in 1984, Coca-Cola began experimenting with its recipe. Concerned by indications that its main competitor Pepsi-Cola had drawn even in market share, Coca-Cola introduced New Coke, a sweeter cola that tasted much like its competition. But the American public rejected the modified recipe, and Coca-Cola returned to producing Coke with its original flavor under the name Coca-Cola Classic. Every year since the change in recipes Coca-Cola has increased its share of the soft drink market. Nonetheless, Coca-Cola still sells New Coke, renamed Coke II, in a number of states.

In the 1990s Coca-Cola continued to challenge itself and the competition. Attempting to reduce Gatorade's dominance of the sport drink market, Coca-Cola rolled out a fruit punch flavored beverage called PowerAde. In 1994 it introduced Fruitopia, a line of fruit juices and teas. The next year Coca-Cola bought Barq's root beer. At the 1996 Olympics in Atlanta, Georgia, Coca-Cola launched a successful $250 million advertising campaign, which spurred sales at double the competition's rate. In 1997 the company began selling Surge, a soft drink marketed as containing higher levels of caffeine and sugar than ordinary soda.

Still headquartered in Atlanta, Georgia, the Coca-Cola Company shows no signs of slowing. Its stock is traded on the New York Stock Exchange and the company is listed on the prestigious Dow Jones Industrial Average Index of blue chip companies. As the century approached its conclusion, Coca-Cola announced that Coke was sold in more than 200 countries at a pace of nearly one billion eight-ounce servings per day.

See also: **Charles Hires, Trademark**

FURTHER READING

Business News Briefs, ''Coca-Cola Buys Barq's.'' *The Arizona Republic*, March 30, 1995.

Cox News Service, ''Coke Sells Near 1 Billion Per Day.'' *The Grand Rapids Press*, March 3, 1998.

Maupin, Melissa. *The Story of Coca-Cola.* Mankato, Minn.: Smart Apple Media, 1999.

Roush, Chris, ''Coca-Cola's outlay for ads rises 41% in Olympic year.'' *The Atlanta Journal/The Atlanta Constitution*, March 20, 1997.

''The Coca-Cola Company,'' [cited April 10, 1999] available from the World Wide Web @ http://www.hoovers.com/.

COLD WAR

Never reaching a direct military conflict, the Cold War was a 45-year rivalry between the Western powers, led by the United States, and the Soviet Union. Beginning after World War II (1939–1945) and lasting until 1990, this worldwide conflict grew from the ideological differences between communism and capitalist democracy.

The United States and the Soviet Union shared a mutual distrust that existed years before the onset of the Cold War. After a century-long friendship, the United States and Russia competed over the economic development of Manchuria in the 1890s. Following the 1917 Bolshevik Revolution in Russia, the competition turned into an ideological rivalry that pitted U.S. capitalist democracy against Russian Communism. Although the United States and Russia became allies against the Axis nations (Germany, Italy, and Japan) in 1941 during World War II, friction arose within their

The Berlin Wall being dismantled in 1990, ending a 45 year rivalry between the Western powers and the Soviet Union.

alliance. Throughout the war the Soviets disagreed with the United States and Great Britain over military strategies and postwar plans for Germany.

After two German invasions into Russia and nearly 25 million Soviet casualties, Soviet leader Joseph Stalin (1879–1953) was determined to use his Red Army to control Poland and to keep Germany from ever regaining its strength. In the United States, President Harry S. Truman (1945–1953) was determined to ensure an open, capitalist, international economy—starting with the rebuilding of Europe's economic infrastructure, which included West Germany. After the war, the United States and other Western powers saw the expansion of the Soviet Union as a threat, while the Soviets feared that the powerful Western capitalist nations would overthrow their Communist regime. The Cold War began.

FROM STETTIN IN THE BALTIC TO TRIESTE IN THE ADRIATIC, AN IRON CURTAIN HAS DESCENDED ACROSS THE CONTINENT.

Winston Churchill, Iron Curtain Speech, 1946

Following World War II, Europe was devastated and in a severe economic crisis. Between 1945 and 1947, the Soviets seized power over much of Eastern Europe with the might of its Red Army and supported communist and Soviet-friendly regimes throughout the

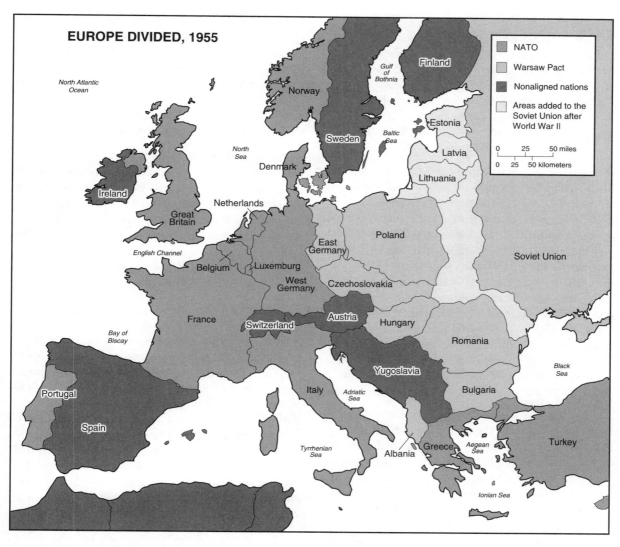

EUROPE DIVIDED, 1955

NATO

Warsaw Pact

Nonaligned nations

Areas added to the Soviet Union after World War II

In 1949 the U.S. and 11 European nations formed the North Atlantic Treaty Organization (NATO), with intentions of safeguarding against Communist expansion. The Communist Bloc responded in 1955 with the Warsaw Pact.

region. Alarmed by the rise of communism in Europe and wanting to contain its spread, the United States initiated a European recovery program known as the Marshall Plan, which helped restore war-ravaged Western Europe's economic growth. Wary of capitalist intrusion, the Soviet Union and other Eastern European nations strongly opposed the American plan.

Fearing the threat of a revived Germany, the Soviet Union restricted access into West Berlin (which it was overseeing in the post-war period) in 1948 by setting up road, train, and canal blockades into the city, but the United States flew supplies into Berlin until the blockades were removed in the following year. When the United States denied the Soviet Union war reparations in the form of West German factories, the Soviets secured East Germany as a communist state. Great

Britain's Winston Churchill criticized Moscow for barricading the new Soviet Empire with an "iron curtain."

The Western bloc developed a policy of containment, which was aimed at containing the Soviet-backed states within their current borders and preventing any further spread of communism. U.S. officials sought to strengthen their alliance with other nations and increase military defense spending. When the Soviets detonated their first atomic bomb in August 1949, President Truman ordered U.S. engineers to develop a hydrogen bomb. Also in 1949, the United States joined 11 other nations to form the North Atlantic Treaty Organization (NATO). To counterbalance NATO, the Communist bloc formed the Warsaw Treaty Organization military pact, or the Warsaw Pact, in 1955.

The Cold War spread into Asia in 1950, the year the Soviet Union negotiated an alliance with China, and Communist North Korean forces attacked South Korea, starting the Korean War (1950–1953). Communist China supported guerrillas in Cambodia, Laos, and Vietnam. In response, the United States helped establish the Southeast Asia Treaty Organization and provided neutral Asian nations tremendous military support, though guerrilla warfare persisted.

After Joseph Stalin's death in 1953, a relaxation in Soviet policy led to optimism for cooperation between the Soviet Union and the West. A permanent ban on nuclear weapons seemed likely. The launching of the Sputnik satellite in 1957, however, demonstrated the Soviet Union's technological capabilities, spurring a new race in space exploration and missile production. Both Soviet Prime Minister Nikita Khrushchev (1958–1964) and U.S. officials threatened "massive retaliation" for any aggression on the other's part. Meanwhile, the Cold War struggle continued in Southeast Asia, Africa, the Middle East, and Latin America. Vying for the allegiance of these neutral Third World regions, the two superpowers each provided military and financial aid to support often brutal regimes.

In 1961 the East German government built the Berlin Wall to prevent the emigration of East Germans to the West. In 1962 American intelligence discovered Soviet missile bases in Cuba, where a Communist allegiance had formed in 1959, following Fidel Castro's revolution. When President John F. Kennedy (1961–1963) sent U.S. ships to intercept Soviet vessels carrying rockets to Cuba, Khrushchev ordered a retreat. After this incident, known as the Cuban Missile Crisis—one of the few direct confrontations to take place during the Cold War—the United States and the Soviet Union both made careful efforts to avoid nuclear war and subsequently agreed to ban nuclear testing.

Meanwhile, the two superpowers had begun to weaken. In Europe, France considered withdrawing its presence from NATO, while Romania departed from its allegiance with the Soviet Union. In 1968 a Czechoslovakian reform movement was terminated by Soviet leader Leonid Brezhnev (1977–1982). The once friendly Soviet and Chinese troops began to battle one another along their common border, and heavy military expenditures damaged the Soviet economy. American involvement in the Vietnam War (1964–1975) was a controversial example of Western determination to achieve the goals of the containment policy, as the United States went to long efforts to assist the South Vietnamese government in resistance against the aggressive communist North.

In the early 1970s U.S. President Richard Nixon (1969–1974) signed the SALT I treaty with Soviet President Brezhnev to reduce the need for spending on strategic weapons, and an agreement was made to strengthen American and Soviet economic bonds. Shortly afterward, however, tensions resurfaced when political clashes erupted in the Middle East, Angola, and Chile, and the two superpowers rivaled for influence.

American President Ronald Reagan (1981–1989) heightened Cold War antagonism in the early 1980s by calling the Soviet Union the "evil empire," increasing military spending, intensifying the nuclear arms race, and imposing economic sanctions to protest Brezhnev's recent crackdown on Poland. Relations between the United States and the Soviet Union deteriorated until tensions were the worst they had been since the height of the Cold War in the late 1940s.

Tensions began to ease in 1985 after Mikhail Gorbachev (1988–1981) took control in Moscow. Aware that the Soviet economy was failing, he made major reforms that called for economic restructuring, openness, and democracy within Communist bloc countries. Gorbachev meant his reforms to be a slow and mild effort. In fact, his policies resulted in the fall of the Berlin Wall, the reunification of Germany, the disintegration of Soviet military forces, and nuclear disarmament. The United States accepted military arms and economic agreements. In 1989 Gorbachev declared that the postwar period had ended, and Washington officials concurred that the world had outgrown Cold War policies.

By 1990 Gorbachev's reform policies and a Soviet economic collapse led to the overthrow of communist governments in Czechoslovakia, East Germany, Hungary, Poland, and Romania. The downfall of the Soviet Union officially ended the Cold War.

See also: **Korean War, Marshall Plan, Space Race, World War II**

FURTHER READING

Foner, Eric and John A. Garraty, eds. *The Readers Companion to American History*. Boston: Houghton Mifflin Co., 1991.

Issacs, Jeremy. *Cold War: An Illustrated History, 1945–1991*. New York: Little Brown & Company, 1998.

Kort, Michael. *The Cold War*. Brookfield, CT: Millbrook Press, 1994.

Lafeber, Walter. *America, Russia, and the Cold War 1945–1996 (America in Crisis)*. New York: McGraw Hill College, 1996.

The Cold War, 1945–1991. Detroit: The Gale Group, 1993.

COLLATERAL

Collateral is anything accepted as security for a loan. It works like this: when a lender loans money to someone, the borrower is obliged to repay the loaned sum. But, in addition to a spoken or written promise to repay, a lender often demands some collateral (such as property) so that if the borrower fails to repay, the lender will at least have the collateral. For example, if a borrower put up his or her home as collateral and then failed to repay the loan, the lender has the right to take the house. Other common types of collateral include stocks and bonds. (The borrower does not necessarily have to give the collateral to the lender until a loan is repaid. It is sometimes enough that the lender has the legal right to take the collateral if the borrower defaults on his or her obligation.)

COLLECTIVE BARGAINING

Collective bargaining is a formal negotiation process in which representatives of labor (employees) and management (employers) meet to hammer out a written, binding labor agreement. The purpose of labor agreements is to find common ground on such issues as wages, benefits, seniority, job security, grievance resolution, and working conditions. Collective bargaining offers labor and management a way to resolve differences so as to avoid a strike or lockout. By bargaining as a group rather than individually, workers no longer have to compete against each other for improved pay and benefits and can push for such improvements without fear of losing their jobs. Collective bargaining may take place between a single firm and labor organization, between the workers and management of an entire industry, or at the national level between the employees and management of several industries. The agreement produced by collective bargaining may be several hundred pages in length and remains in effect for a limited, specified period of time. If labor and management cannot come to agreement on their own

they may submit their dispute to a third party in an arbitration proceeding.

The term collective bargaining first came into use in the United States at the end of the nineteenth century, when America's national labor unions were organizing to win decent wages and working conditions in an era that was characterized by low pay, long hours, and harsh work environments. The Clayton Anti-Trust Act of 1914 gave labor the legal right to strike, but it took the devastating effects of the Great Depression to highlight the need for fundamental labor reform. The National Labor Relations Act of 1935 established a set of laws to encourage labor and management to resolve labor issues peacefully and ''in good faith,'' and it explicitly gave labor the right to form unions and bargain collectively for better wages and working conditions. This act also established the National Labor Relations Board (NLRB) to ensure that union elections were fair, to determine who could bargain on behalf of employees, and to promote equitable labor practices. By creating a formal, legal, defined system for negotiating differences between labor and management, collective bargaining has generally improved wages, benefits, and working conditions for U.S. workers and made them more uniform across industries and regions of the United States.

See also: **Clayton Anti-Trust Act, Closed Shop, Labor Movement, Labor Unionism**

COLONIES, CORPORATE

The British colonies of North America were founded as either corporate colonies or as proprietary colonies. Corporate colonies had a charter that the English monarch granted to stockholders, but they were essentially governed by the monarch. King James I (1603–25) granted corporate charters for the settlement of Virginia (founded 1607) and Massachusetts (1620). The charters stipulated that the king appoint the colonial governor who arrived in America with a royal commission and a set of instructions from the British Board of Trade. Each colony would have its own legislature made up of a crown-appointed council (of important citizens) and an elected assembly. The assembly was empowered to pass laws that had to be approved by the royal government of England before they could go into effect.

There were many problems with this system. While England regarded the royal commission given to each governor as absolute, the colonists often lacked reverence for the commissions, viewing them as impractical instructions. Colonial governors were supposed to serve the interests of the king as well as the interests of the colonists. These concerns were often in opposition to each other. Because the legislative assembly had control over all money bills, if it was in opposition to the governor, it could delay appropriations bills favored by the governor and it could even refuse to pay the governor's salary. The governor, on the other hand, could veto assembly legislation he did not favor. He could also, with the approval of the council (advisory board), appoint judges and other officers, issue paper money, establish martial law, and summon the assembly.

In the mid-1600s the English crown began converting the American colonies from either corporate or proprietary status to a third type of colony—royal. Eight of the 13 became royal colonies. In the process power was gradually taken away from the governors. Between 1689 and 1702 the king resumed control of all British warships in the colonies. The power to appoint officials was revoked; instead, the crown sent its appointees to the colonies. In 1755 the king dispatched a commander in chief to North America to control royal troops centrally and to rescind any military authority from the governors. Civil authority in the colonies had also been seriously diminished. This contributed to the colonists' growing political dissatisfaction with England.

Three other colonies were founded as self-governing corporate colonies: the Plymouth Colony (1620; it was merged with Massachusetts in 1691), Rhode Island (1636), and Connecticut (1636). The latter two remained self-governing throughout the colonial period and were not converted to royal colony status.

See also: **Colonies (Proprietary)**

COLONIES, DISTRIBUTION OF WEALTH IN *(ISSUE)*

By studying the way wealth was distributed in the American colonies, we can learn a great deal about their economy, like the relationship of the social structure to economic opportunity. The diversity of the regional economies and the uneven quality of statistical information from the period make broad generalizations difficult, but there are some general trends that can be identified, and it is possible to characterize the distribution of wealth in different colonies and the colonies as a whole.

After an initial period of extreme difficulty, known in the Chesapeake as the starving time, each of the colonies offered their settlers relatively high incomes and more opportunity to become wealthy than was the case in England or continental Europe. The accumulation of wealth was generally more rapid in the seventeenth century than in the eighteenth and in newer areas rather than those settled initially, reflecting the maturing of the colonial economy and the greater opportunity available to early arrivals.

It is important to distinguish between the colonial regions since there were sharp differences in climates and economies as well as in the composition of wealth. Among the mainland colonies, the white southerners were the richest, on average, with about twice the wealth of New England or the Middle Atlantic region. If we include the West Indies as one of the colonial areas, then its thriving sugar industry made it the wealthiest. Slavery was not the only reason for this difference. Confining our scope to the mainland colonies, we find that Southerners owned twice as much land as the average inhabitant of the other areas. The other regions were not poor, however, both income and the standard of living were generally higher in North America than in England by the end of the colonial period.

In New England, land was the most important component of wealth from first settlement through the American Revolution (1775–1783). In nearly all of New England, large-scale commercial agriculture was not possible because of climate, topography, and the quality of the soil. In the interior farming predominated (supplemented, early on, by trapping) but most of these farms were engaged in subsistence agriculture that provided, at most, a small surplus for their owners. The distribution of land was fairly egalitarian in nearly all of New England because of the custom of dividing land among heirs. Over time, however, there was social stratification as a result of land speculation.

But the quality of life in New England, especially in the early period, was good, compared to the Chesapeake and, even more, to England. The first European New Englanders were healthy and lived a long time. In contrast to the predominantly male Chesapeake colonies (which tended to be marked by a high level of violence), there were roughly equal numbers of men and women in New England. Their society was based on farm families and on a common Puritan religion. In the coastal communities of New England the economy was much more complex, for in addition to farming there was mercantile trade, shipbuilding, and a variety of service industries related to shipping. As a result New England developed substantial numbers of propertyless adult men and a wide range of incomes and wealth holdings. The income gap between merchants and master craftsmen and laborers increased throughout the colonial period.

The Middle Colonies, specifically New York and Pennsylvania, were similar to New England in that they had commercial communities with diverse economies and a broad range of incomes and wealth and a large number of farming communities with a higher degree of property ownership. These trends were most pronounced in New York City and Philadelphia. In New York there were large farms in the lower Hudson Valley. These were extensive tracts of land, some dating back to the holdings of the Dutch patroons (wealthy landholders). Tenants farmed these vast tracts of land.

Since William Penn offered land to all comers on generous terms, Pennsylvania had perhaps the easiest access to ownership of land for those who could afford their own passage to America. It also had the largest number of indentured servants whose passage from England was paid for and who worked off the debt with up to seven years of labor. Indentured servants were severely exploited, but the custom was to grant them money or land after they completed their period of service. As the price of land in the settled portions of Pennsylvania increased, however, they found themselves forced to the fringes of the settlement.

In the Southern colonies land was also an important component of wealth, but after 1660, slaves also contributed greatly to the income of their white masters. The climate and soil of the South were well suited to the cultivation of staple crops—tobacco in Virginia, Maryland, and North Carolina and rice in coastal South Carolina and Georgia. Success was linked both to the ownership of land and control of labor in the form first of indentured servants and later of African slaves. Slave owners possessed the majority of wealth in the Southern colonies; those who could not afford slaves or land found themselves pushed into the interior, where lack of access to transportation made commercial farming less profitable.

See also: **New Netherlands, New Sweden, Slavery, Subsistance Agriculture**

FURTHER READING

Goodfriend, Joyce D. *Before the Melting Pot: Society and Culture in Colonial New York City, 1664-1730.* Princeton, NJ: Princeton University Press, 1992.

Jones, Alice Hanson. *American Colonial Wealth: Documents and Methods*, 3 vols. New York: Arno Press, 1977.

Lemon, James T. *The Best Poor Man's Country: A Geographical Study of Early Southeastern Pennsylvania.* Baltimore: Johns Hopkins University Press, 1972.

Main, Jackson Turner. *The Social Structure of Revolutionary America.* Princeton, NJ: Princeton University Press, 1965.

Walton, Gary M. and James F. Shepherd. *The Economic Rise of Early America.* Cambridge, Eng.: Cambridge University Press, 1979.

McCusker, John J. and Russell R. Menard. *The Economy of British America: (1607–1789).* Chapel Hill: University of North Carolina Press, 1991.

COLONIES, PROPRIETARY

The British colonies of North America were founded as either proprietary colonies or as corporate colonies. A proprietary colony was a gift made by the king to a trading company or an individual, who then privately owned it. This type of colony was administered by a colonial governor, who was elected by the owner or owners and supposed to serve in their best interest. The legislature comprised a council, which was chosen by the owners and an elected assembly.

Maine (founded 1623), New Hampshire (1623), New York (1624), New Jersey (1624), Maryland (1634), Pennsylvania (1638), Delaware (1664), North and South Carolina (1665), and Georgia (1733) were all founded as proprietary colonies. In an effort to preserve its empire, in the mid-1600s England began converting its American colonies to royal colonies—regardless of whether they had been founded as corporate or proprietary. Of the proprietary colonies, only Maryland, Delaware, and Pennsylvania remained as such; they were not converted to royal colonies. In the others, the crown exerted its authority at the expense of the royal governors and the legislatures. The military and navy were brought under the central control of the crown. The situation greatly contributed to the outbreak of the American Revolution (1775–83).

See also: **Colonies (Corporate), Colonies (Proprietary), Delaware, Distribution of Wealth in the Colonies, Georgia, Maryland, New Hampshire, New Jersey, New York, North Carolina, Pennsylvania, South Carolina**

COLORADO

Mention the state of Colorado and Americans still conjure up images of freewheeling gold and silver mining towns, rugged mountains, open spaces, health spas, and ski resorts. To a large extent, all of these stereotypes correctly describe aspects of the state and its history. First developed by prospectors looking for riches in gold and silver, the state also discovered its agricultural potential and promoted its many tourist attractions. Contemporary Colorado has a healthy industrial base, as well as a steadily growing population attracted by the state's many amenities.

In the early 1600s, Spanish conquistadors arrived in Colorado, finding a number of warring Native American tribes. French fur traders were not much interested in what was called the Colorado region, which then included most of the area east of the Rocky Mountains. France ceded the territory to Spain in 1763, then regained it in 1801. In 1803 the area east of the Rockies became part of the Louisiana Purchase when France ceded it to the United States.

In 1806 Lt. Zebulon M. Pike (1779–1813) set out to explore the southwestern border of the territory, and he unsuccessfully attempted to scale the peak that now bears his name. In 1819 the United States and Spain established a boundary along the Arkansas River, then north to the Continental Divide. Stephen Long (1784–1864) soon arrived to explore the new border, and Dr. Edwin James was the first to climb Pikes Peak. Western and southern Colorado became U.S. territory after the Mexican War (1846–1848). John C. Frémont (1813–1890) led five expeditions into eastern Colorado between 1842 and 1853.

THE PIKES PEAKERS CREATED [THE COLORADO TERRITORY], PROPELLED BY FAITH, GREED, AMBITION, AND ZEST FOR ACHIEVING THE IMPOSSIBLE.

Marshall Sprague, *Colorado: A Bicentennial History*, 1976

It was an exaggerated report of the discovery of gold at Cherry Creek (now Denver), however, which brought thousands of prospectors into the territory beginning in 1858. The so-called ''Pikes Peakers'' sent home glowing reports of fortunes to be made in Colorado. A number of mining towns sprang up, and by 1860 the population of Colorado was more than 30,000. In 1861 Colorado formally became a territory, with Denver becoming the capital in 1867.

Expansion and settlement of the Colorado region was not without its difficulties. The early history of the territory was marked by serious conflict between white settlers and Native Americans. Cheyenne and Arapaho Indians, who had been pushed onto reservations, began to rebel, raiding towns and attacking travelers. After a brutal massacre of the Indians at Sand Creek in 1864, more warfare followed; but most of the Plains Indians were eventually moved to reservations in the Oklahoma territory. In 1873 the Ute Indians were forced from their large reservation, supposedly forever given to them by the U.S. government, when gold and silver were discovered there. After a number of unsuccessful attempts, Colorado finally entered the Union in 1876 as the thirty-eighth state.

More people trekked to Colorado during the 1870s and 1880s to seek their fortunes in the silver and lead mines, and farmers were attracted to the High Plains. At first bypassed by the transcontinental railroads, Colorado soon had rail access from Denver to the Union Pacific rail station at Cheyenne, Wyoming. Early tourism was also important to the economy of the new state. Resorts developed around the many mineral springs, and narrow-gauge trains brought travelers to the scenic mountain areas. Colorado Springs, one of the most important early spas, attracted thousands of tourists during this period, as did Denver. Unfortunately, this boom in the economy ended abruptly with a depression during the early 1890s. Silver became a glut on the market when the U.S. government adopted a gold standard in 1893. In addition, a severe drought caused many to abandon their farms.

California mineral miners experienced a number of violent disturbances during the last two decades of the nineteenth century. The Knights of Labor led around 35 strikes against mine owners between 1881 and 1886; and the Western Federation of Miners struck at Telluride and Cripple Creek. The United Mine Workers shut down operations at a number of mines in the early 1900s; a particularly violent episode occurred at Ludlow in 1914, when several women and children were killed after the governor called out the militia.

In the early twentieth century, farmers began returning to the land after a period of farm depression. Many German and Russian immigrants planted sugar beets in the Colorado, Arkansas, and South Platte river valleys. Cattle barons from Texas also drove their longhorns to Colorado's public lands for grazing. Later local farmers began to fence their land to produce the more popular shorthorns and Herefords. Water, always in short supply in the semiarid state, was made more available during this period by large reclamation projects. Tourism also increased as more roads were built in the mountain areas.

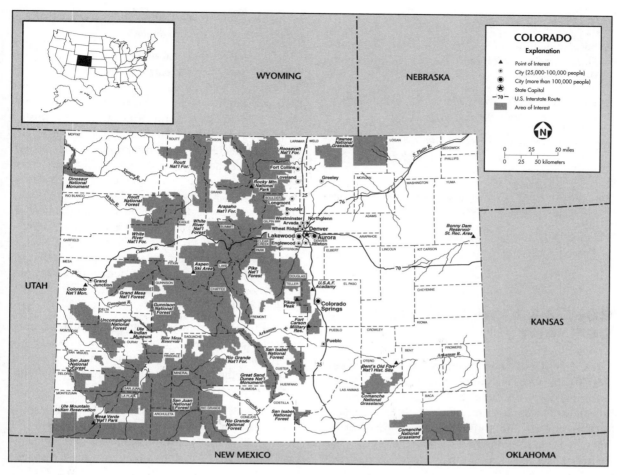

State of Colorado.

The state's economy fell after World War I (1914–1918), when mining and agriculture went into decline. The population growth rate in the state also declined, as did employment. During World War II (1939–1945) a number of military bases brought jobs, as did postwar expansion of federal facilities. Colorado Springs benefited from the placement of the North American Air Defense Command, the U.S. Air Force Academy, and the Air Force Space Operations Center. Between 1960 and 1983 Colorado grew twice as fast as the rest of the nation; by 1983 the state ranked ninth in per capita income.

In the 1970s and early 1980s Colorado's economy boomed as the oil, mining, and electronic industries continued to expand. In the mid-1980s, however, a drop in oil prices and the closing of several mines brought a recession, with the number of new businesses dropping 23 percent between 1987 and 1988. An upturn, however, occurred in the late 1980s and early 1990s. The state continues to face challenges, including air pollution, overcrowding on the eastern slopes of the Rockies, water shortages, and unemployment caused by cuts in defense spending.

Though agriculture and mining continue to be important economic sectors in Colorado, more jobs were created in trade, government, and manufacturing between 1975 and 1985. The service sector now accounts for more than 50 percent of the state's gross product. The companies that grew the fastest in Colorado during the 1980s and early 1990s were high-technology concerns such as IBM, Hewlett-Packard, Apple Computer, and MCI Telecommunications. Tourism generates more than $6 billion each year for the state. Ski resorts, such as Vail and Aspen, and tourist attractions, such as the Air Force Academy and Colorado's rugged mountains, continue to bring thousands of visitors to the state during all seasons. The per capita income of Colorado in 1996 was nearly $25,000, placing thirteenth in the nation. Denver ranked thirtieth among the most important metropolitan areas in income.

See also: **Louisiana Purchase, Pike's Expedition**

FURTHER READING

Abbott, Carl. *Colorado: A History of the Centennial State*. Boulder: Colorado Associated University Press, 1994.

Athearn, Robert G. *The Coloradans*. Albuquerque: University of New Mexico Press, 1982.

Aylesworth, Thomas G. *The Southwest: Colorado, New Mexico, Texas*. Chicago: Chelsea House Publishers, 1996.

Sprague, Marshall. *Colorado: A Bicentennial History*. New York: Norton, 1976.

Ubbelohde, Carol, et al. *A Colorado History*. Boulder: Pruett, 1982.

COLT'S MANUFACTURING COMPANY

Colt's Manufacturing Company is located in Hartford, Connecticut. Incorporated in 1855, Colt's Manufacturing produced and sold firearms for the law enforcement and sporting industries. Colt had produced firearms for the military since the early years of the republic. This relationship with the U.S. military can be traced back to the company's founder, Samuel Colt (1814–1862), who was fascinated for many years with revolvers and other types of weaponry. While on a voyage to Asia, Colt developed his now famous "revolving pistol." The crucial design aspect of this invention was that the revolving cartridge advanced the chambers each time that the trigger was pulled. The Colt revolver represented greatly increased firepower.

While the flintlock pistol was only able to fire one or two shots at a time, Colt's pistol was able to fire up to six shots before reloading. In 1832 Colt attempted to obtain a patent for his pistol from the U.S. government. He was also interested in marketing his revolver pistol among ordinary citizens as well as military procurement officials. By the late 1830's Colt's pistol had been tested and had gained wide acceptance with the military. The Colt pistol was quite effective in the Seminole Indian conflict (1835–1842) and the Texas War of Independence (1832–1836). Colt, however, was unable to expand sales with the gun-buying public because of their unfamiliarity with the basic concept of the revolver. More frustrating for Colt was his inability to get a sales contract with the federal government, even after the positive performance of the revolver in Florida and Texas. In 1842, Colt's economic condition became so dismal that he had no alternative but to leave the firearms industry altogether.

To meet his financial obligations that same year Colt had to sell the U.S. patent on the revolver that he had received back in 1836. Nevertheless, there were those in the military establishment who were favorably impressed with the performance of Colt's new invention in the Texas War of Independence. In particular, Captain Samuel H. Walker encouraged Colt and helped him improve the revolver design. Unlike the earlier model, the "Walker" was simpler and more easily manufactured. More important, Captain Walker was able to secure for Colt a United Sates Ordinance Department purchase contract for a thousand Walkers. With the help of his friend, Eli Whitney, Jr., Colt was able to produce and deliver this order by the middle of 1847. The United States Army demonstrated the superiority of the Walker in the war with Mexico (1846–1848).

Further achievement of success was due not only to the effectiveness of Colt's weaponry, but to his efforts in the area of marketing. Traveling across Europe and the United States, Colt succeeded in touting the superiority of the Colt revolver.

In 1855, Colt opened a huge plant in Hartford, Connecticut in which he was able to manufacture 150 guns per day. That year Colt named his new company the Colt's Patent Firearms Manufacturing Company. By the beginning of the American Civil War (1861–1865), Colt employed 1,000 workers and reporting yearly revenue of 250,000 dollars. Upon his early death on January 10, 1862 Colt left his business to his wife, Elizabeth Jarvis Colt. From 1862 to 1901 the Colt manufacturing company was a family firm.

Colt's original factory was destroyed by fire in 1864. Elizabeth Colt saw to it that the new structure was as fireproof as possible. Another significant development for the Colt company was the contribution of another firearms designer, John Browning. After the Civil War Browning helped develop and produce a "gas-operated" machine gun. Unlike the hand crank-operated Gattling machine-gun, the Browning version used the escaping muzzle gases to help power the mechanism. Colt Firearms also developed and produced the Browning designed Automatic Rifle and the Colt 45 semi-automatic pistol.

Early in the twentieth century, Colt Firearms enjoyed a secure relationship with the U.S. military. Its Colt 45 semi-automatic weapon was widely used both in World War I (1914–1918) and World War II (1939–1945). The Second World War generated enough orders to maintain an employment level of about 15,000

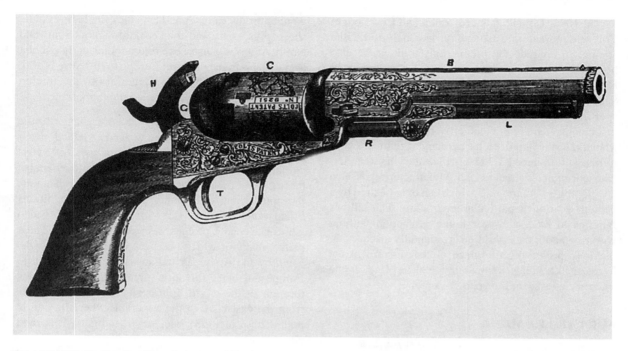

The original "Colt's Revolver," greatly increased firepower by enabling six shots to be fired before reloading. The revolving cartridge advanced the chambers each time the trigger was pulled.

in its Hartford factories. Its fate hinged on being able to maintain government orders for its weaponry. Following the end of World War II, the U.S. government lost confidence in Colt's aging factories and production techniques. Also, as Colt's workers were now unionized, so the payroll expenses increased. While the Colt business gained some financial ground during the Korean War (1950–1953), U.S. Government sales dramatically declined at the end of that conflict.

In the year of its centennial, 1955, Colt Firearms needed cash. It merged with Penn-Texas Corporation, led by Leopold D. Silberstein. Penn-Texas was a holding company that ran subsidiary companies. Colt Firearms was one of many other subsidiaries. In 1959 a block of stockholders ousted Silberstein and took control of the business under the new title of Fairbanks Whitney. Under this new leadership, Colt Firearms improved its standing with the U.S. military by developing new weaponry. In 1960 Colt came out with the M-16 full-automatic rifle. With the U.S. fighting in the Vietnam War (1959–1975), there were heavy demands on Colt to supply arms for the troops. By the end of the 1960s Colt had produced one million M-16s which had become standard issue for U.S. soldiers.

In the 1970s, the Vietnam War came to a formal close. Colt Firearms then confronted the challenge of peacetime production. During this period its management turned to variety of novel markets in the gun industry. For example Colt Firearms turned its ingenuity to the development and production of sporting guns and rifles. Colt also focused its marketing skills on those who collect rare and unique firearms. In 1976 Colt opened the Custom Gun Shop. The Custom Gun Shop produced and sold copies, for example, of the Walker and the 1860 Army revolver. As the 1970s came to an end, Colt's Custom Gun Shop was reporting yearly revenue of three million dollars.

Despite the success of the Custom Gun Shop, however, Colt was still in a slump. Unable to overcome its financial difficulties, Colt Firearms laid off about 700 employees between 1982 and 1983. Facing an uncertain future, the remaining employees, members of the United Automobile Workers union (UAW), went on strike in 1986. The situation for Colt management was made even more tenuous when it lost its contract on the M-16 in 1988.

The company, however, survived and business began to turn around. In 1989 C.F. Holding Corporation bought Colt Firearms for $100 million. Renamed Colt's Manufacturing Company, it was able to end the UAW strike in 1990. Under the terms of the agreement, Colt Manufacturing hired back its workers and gave the union three seats on the board of directors. Furthermore the state of Connecticut assumed 47 percent ownership of the company. Colt Manufacturing proved unable to compete successfully in the gun market, however, and in 1992 the company declared bankruptcy.

In 1994, Donald Zilka (of Zilka and Co.) bought Colt's Manufacturing Company. Not only did Zilka attempt to upgrade the production facilities, he also bought out some of the competition that produced firearms and other types of weaponry. Zilka bought Saco Defense, which produced and sold military and sporting weaponry. Saco Defense produced the M-60 machinegun and the Weatherby rifle. In 1998 Colt Manufacturing finalized an agreement with the U.S. military to produce the M4A1 rifle. In trying to anticipate consumer demand, Colt Manufacturing is also developing a ''smart gun'' which can only be fired by a person wearing a particular microchip. This allows families to have guns for home protection without worrying about their children accidentally discharging them. In preserving the place of the sidearm in the home, Zilka hopes to maintain Colt's place in the firearms industry in the years to come.

FURTHER READING

Edwards, William B. *The Story of Colt's Revolver: The Biography of Colonel Samuel Colt*. Harrisburg, PA: The Stockpole, Co., 1953.

Ellis, John. *The Social History of the Machine Gun*. Baltimore, MD: Johns Hopkins University Press, 1975.

Grant, Ellisworth. *The Colt Legacy: The Colt Armory in Hartford, 1855–1980*. Providence, RI: Mowbray Co., 1982.

Haven, Charles T. and Frank A. Belden. *A History of the Colt Revolver and other Arms Made by Colt's Patent Firearms Manufacturing Company from 1836 to 1940*. New York: Bonanza Books, n.d.

Kennett, Lee and James La Verne Anderson. *Contributions in American History*, Number 37. London, UK: Greenwood Press, 1975.

COLUMBIAN EXCHANGE

Columbian Exchange refers to the great changes that were initiated by Spanish explorer Christopher Columbus (1451–1506) as he and other Europeans voyaged from Europe to the New World and back during the late 1400s and in the 1500s. When Columbus landed at Hispaniola (present-day Dominican Republic) in 1492, he brought with him horses and cattle. These were the first animals of their kind seen in the Western Hemisphere; the American Indians had no beasts of burden prior to the arrival of the Europeans. In subsequent trips Columbus and other explorers would introduce horses and livestock (including cattle, sheep, pigs, goats, and chickens) throughout South and North America. Diseases were another early—albeit accidental—transport from Europe to the New World. Native inhabitants had no immunities to the foreign illnesses and, once exposed, died in numbers.

While Europe carried its seeds of change to the Western Hemisphere, the new lands yielded many plants unknown in Europe. On Columbus's 1492 voyage he became the first European to discover maize (corn), sweet potatoes, capsicums (peppers), plantains, pineapples, and turtle meat. Subsequent expeditions found potatoes, wild rice, squash, tomatoes, cacao (chocolate beans), peanuts, cashews, and tobacco. These plants, many of which had been developed and cultivated by the American Indians, were carried back to Europe and their cultivation spread to suitable climates throughout the world. Europeans later carried plants from the east back to the Americas where they took hold. These included rice, sugar, indigo, wheat, and citrus fruits.

The discovery of new lands in the west set off waves of migration which have ebbed and flowed ever since. But the discovery also resulted in exchanges of plants, animals, diseases, and even knowledge that brought dramatic changes to the world: it transformed the way people dressed, ate, traveled, and provided for themselves and their families.

See also: **Corn, Horses, Potatoes, Rice, Sugar, Tobacco**

COMMAND ECONOMY

A command economy is one based on centralized decision making by government authorities rather than private individuals, and such decisions are not dictated by market conditions. The centrally planned economy requires a formal administrative hierarchy staffed on many bureaucratic levels. Basic decisions are grounded in ideologies and political imperatives. Key decisions involve all aspects of a firm's activity and are issued by commands, directives, and regulatory guides based on a national plan of inputs and outputs. The government determines what will be produced, production targets, investment in plant equipment, coordination between firms, use of natural resources, and how products will be distributed to the populace. Capital and national resources are property of the state rather than private persons. Prices and wages are centrally controlled and frequently remain at fixed levels for long periods of time.

Advantages of a command economy may be: (1) maximum mobilization of resources toward an urgent national objective, such as rapid industrialization of an underdeveloped economy or in times of war; (2) coordinated economic activity reducing wasteful duplication; (3) production of needed and desirable commodities; (4) reducing unemployment and idle capacity; and, (5) protection of the economy from the outside world.

Disadvantages of a centrally planned economy stem from the enormous amount of information required to achieve efficiency and the necessity of coordinating large numbers of components and decision makers at each level of the economic process. The supply of reliable information to all factions is generally not efficient enough to allow a high level of coordination or flexibility. Rigidity, exacerbated by a large organization or bureaucracy, leads to resource allocation which does not necessarily match resource availability, a nation's requirements, or consumer wishes. Manifestations include persistent shortages of some goods combined with surpluses of others. Throughout the decision process problems of accountability, self-serving behaviors, decisions made on inappropriate parameters, interference by party and other authorities, and divergent interests complicate the procedure. To alleviate inefficiencies, underground economies develop and lead to widespread corruption.

The Union of Soviet Socialist Republics (USSR) and Eastern European nations served as models of highly centralized command economies until the collapse of many of these Communist-styled governments in 1989 and 1990. Dissatisfaction with the failure of planned systems to deliver goods was partially to blame for the upheaval. Those economies have since moved to more decentralized systems based on competition and market demands. The People's Republic of China remained an example of a command economy in the 1990s.

COMMODITY

A commodity is a basic good, material, or product that is produced in very large quantities and is usually sold in raw or only partly processed form. The most common commodities are essential agricultural products such as wheat, sugar, rubber, and coffee and basic mineral-derived products like copper, tin, or silver. On a more general level, a commodity may also be any manufactured product—for example, computer chips—that has become so common or inexpensive in design or manufacture that it is almost impossible to tell the difference between two producers' versions of that commodity.

Commodities are bought and sold in three markets: the spot market, the forward market, and the futures market. When an individual or company wants to buy (or sell) a commodity right away, they do so on the spot market, where they can negotiate the price, quantity, and other conditions with the seller (or buyer) immediately. When an individual or company wants to prearrange a purchase or sale of a commodity for a specific future date, they turn to the forward market where they can finalize a commodity transaction in advance and according to their requirements without having to wait and see what market conditions will be like months down the road. Both the spot market and the forward market are called the "actuals" market because actual commodities are bought and sold. The third commodities market, the futures market, involves the buying and selling of contracts or "bets" on the future price of commodities rather than the commodities themselves. For example, if the price that a commodities trader is planning to pay for a ton of wheat in six months is lower than the current price for that commodity, he or she may buy a futures contract on wheat that acts as a kind of insurance "bet" that the price of wheat six months from now will be *higher*. If the price of wheat goes down, the trader can buy the wheat at the price he or she desired. However, if the price of wheat goes higher the trader will win his or her insurance "bet" and make money anyway.

The earliest market or exchange for buying and selling commodities in the United States was a produce exchange operated in New York City during the 1750s. In the nineteenth century, Chicago emerged as the major U.S. commodities market because it was the primary hub for shipping Midwestern farmers' grain to the east coast and beyond. By the time the Chicago Board of Trade (the world's largest commodities exchange) was established in 1848, cotton, tobacco, lumber, and sugar were also being bought and sold there, and new commodities exchanges were being opened in New Orleans, Minneapolis, Duluth, and St. Louis.

COMPARATIVE ADVANTAGE

The idea of comparative advantage is one of the most fundamental arguments in favor of international trade between nations. In his revolutionary book *The Wealth of Nations* the Scottish philosopher Adam Smith (1723—90) argued that it is more efficient for a business to have each of its workers specialize in making a specific part for a product than to have each worker make the entire product from start to finish. According to Smith, this division of labor also applies to international trade: the wealth of all nations can be improved if each country specializes in making the products it is best at making. Similarly, a country should import the products it makes less efficiently. However, critics argued that Smith's idea of a "division of labor" among nations was flawed. What if a country (for example, Portugal) can make *every product* more efficiently than another country (for example, England)? In this case, Smith's critics argued, Portugal would have no reason to trade with England because it could make all products more efficiently on its own, and England would have no reason to trade with Portugal because the more efficiently made Portuguese products would overwhelm England's economy. In some cases, Smith's critics contended, a country's best interests were best served if it stopped trading internationally and instead strived for self-sufficiency.

Writing 41 years after Smith, the British economist David Ricardo (1772—1823) refuted Smith's critics. Ricardo used a hypothetical example in which Portugal could make both cloth and wine more efficiently than England, giving Portugal an "absolute advantage" over England in both these goods. In Ricardo's example, however, the increase in efficiency that England would enjoy by specializing only in cloth production would be greater than the increase in efficiency Portugal would gain by specializing only in wine production. Thus, if Portugal specialized only in wine production and England specialized only in cloth production England would have a "comparative advantage" over Portugal because it would gain the greatest boost in efficiency. For Ricardo and the defenders of international trade, Portugal should let England specialize in the goods that result in the greatest increases in efficiency because Portugal would then be free to specialize in the products where it enjoys the greatest efficiency gains. If economies produce only the goods that utilize their workforces most efficiently, the living standards of all countries increase.

See also: **Balance of Trade, Division of Labor, David Ricardo, Adam Smith**

COMPETITION

Competition is the term used by economists to describe the nature of the relationship between businesses vying against each other to sell their goods and services to consumers. McDonald's and General Motors do not compete with each other because a consumer's decision to buy a hamburger has no affect on his or her decision to buy a car. However, McDonald's and Burger King are competitors because a consumer's decision to dine at one involves a de facto decision not to dine at the other.

Economists have defined three major types of competition: perfect, monopolistic, and oligopolistic. The trout fishing industry is an example of perfect competition because trout are interchangeable as products, so trout fishing firms can only compete with each other by lowering prices. The computer operating system industry is an example of monopolistic competition because consumers purchase software programs that can only work on a single (firm's) computer operating system, (e.g., Windows, OS/2, Linex, etc). The automotive industry is an example of oligopolistic competition because there are only a handful of competing firms, the cost to break into the industry is prohibitive, and if one firm lowers its prices the others will automatically lower theirs. Oligopolistic firms, therefore, compete through advertising and customer loyalty.

Prior to 1815, U.S. businesses cooperated with each other to compete against the market outside the United States. Because of their religious beliefs, the harsh conditions of colonial life, and the socially-oriented economic philosophy the United States had inherited from England, early U.S. entrepreneurs banded together to work out a "fair" price for their goods. From about 1815 to the end of the nineteenth century, however, advances in manufacturing, communication, and transportation technologies created economic capitals like New York and Chicago. Powerful new industries were born that opened up a huge new national marketplace where competing firms could gain advantage by undercutting each other's prices. This long period of industrial, price-driven competition led to the third age of U.S. competition and the birth of the corporation. By combining oil and steel firms, industrial leaders like J. P. Morgan (1837–1913), John D. Rockefeller (1839–1937), and Andrew Carnegie (1835–1919) built huge monopolistic enterprises that sought to manage prices and control competitive chaos. In the twentieth century, the federal government played a significant role in breaking up these monopolies and managing the economy. Of note, the emergence of the personal computer and Internet industries during the 1980s and 1990s seemed to herald a partial return to the spirit of competition of the nineteenth century.

See also: **Capitalism, Andrew Carnegie, Free Enterprise, Monopolies, J. P. Morgan, John D. Rockefeller, Trusts**

COMPUTER INDUSTRY

Computers have become a useful and necessary part of modern society. They have been used in all types of businesses ranging from mail order and retail sales, to communications such as phone lines and internet access. Computers are prevalent in hospitals and supermarkets, universities and malls, restaurants and government agencies. By 1998, over 40% of all families in the United States had a personal computer.

The earliest type of machine used for computing was the abacus, dating back to possibly 3000 B.C. in Babylon. Still used in the 1990s, it was a simple system of beads that slid on wires. The next major improvement was made by Blaise Pascal (1623–1662) in 1642, when he developed a ''mechanical adding machine'' he called the Pascaline. In 1694, Gottfried Wilhem von Leibniz (1646–1716) made changes to the Pascaline so it could multiply as well. An Englishman named Charles Babbage (1791–1871) designed the first modern computer. Named the Analytical Engine, it used punched cards. American Herman Hollerith (1860–1929) used the punched card technique to make a machine for use in tabulating results of the U.S. Census in 1890. He founded the Tabulating Machine Co. in 1896, which became International Business Machines (IBM) in 1924. Dr. John V. Atanasoff and assistant Clifford Berry developed the first electronic computer circuits using Boolean algebra in 1940. In 1944, IBM finished the Mark I computer, which used electromagnetic signals.

From this point, computer history was marked by ''generations.'' The first generation of computers featured the use of vacuum tubes, which contributed to their characteristically huge size. Another limitation was their programming language. This period lasted roughly from the late 1940s to the mid-1950s. The second generation, approximately mid- to late-1950s to the early-1960s, saw the use of the transistor instead of the large vacuum tubes. This led to smaller, more efficient, and less costly machines. Improvements in programming language gave them greater flexibility. This generation of hardware generated new jobs in the computer industry such as programmers and software developers.

The third generation, mid-1960s to 1971, was based on the innovation of the semiconductor which replaced transistors, reducing heat and also the size of the computers. Another new development was the use of the operating system, which used one central program to control access to numerous other programs. Also, a new programming language called BASIC was developed by two Dartmouth professors. The fourth generation of computers began in 1971 and continued into the late 1990s with the new development of large-scale integrated circuits. This again reduced the size and price of computers. In 1975, the first personal computer, the Altair 8800, was introduced by Micro Instrumentation and Telemetry Systems (MITS). IBM released its version in 1981 which used the Disk Operating System (DOS) developed by Bill Gates of Microsoft, one of the most prominent software companies. Apple brought out its Macintosh computer in 1984. By 1986 there were over 30 million computers in the United States.

Other important computer businesses that began during the 1980s were Compaq Computers, Sun Microsystems, and Unisys Corporation. In the late 80s, Texas Instruments and Motorola marketed new microprocessors. Microsoft's Windows, 1985, Windows 3.0, 1990, Windows NT, 1993, Windows 95, and Windows 98 became extremely popular operating systems due to the use of graphics which made them easy to use. In 1997, Microsoft's Office 97 for businesses saw sales totaling $78.8 million. Other very popular software in the 1990s were computer games, such as ''Riven: The Sequel to Myst,'' the top seller in 1997.

The Internet or World Wide Web came about due to the efforts of Tim Berners-Lee. In 1989 he helped develop a system of ''hyperlinks'' that could be used to get access to related information, and by August 1991, that system was being used on the Internet, greatly improving the sharing of data. E-mail was a popular way to exchange messages on the Internet. The number of Internet users grew vastly throughout the 1990s, and by 1998 about 5 million people were using the Web.

Trends in the computer industry in the late-1990s included rental or lease options on computer systems, numerous models of personal computers in the below $1,000 price range, portable laptop computers, and a change in popularity from the large mainframe business computers to a ''client/server system'' which used a set of smaller, faster, and cheaper computers. Another innovation was ''e-commerce,'' where consumers could browse through on-line catalogs and then place an order. Goods were purchased directly on-line, and banking and investments were controlled through the Internet. By the late-1990s, it was estimated that there were over 400,000 businesses world wide with web sites.

The end of the twentieth century had seen the personal computer become a part of the average citizen's daily life. The demand for workers with computer skills was expected to increase as the computer industry continued to play an important role in the strength of the American economy.

See also: **Paul Allen, Steve Case, Bill Gates, Internet, Microsoft, Netscape, Stephen Wozniak**

FURTHER READING

Dvorak, John C. "What Ever Happened to . . . the First Computer?" [cited January 12, 1999] available from the World Wide Web @ web3.insitepro.com/insite_pro/sess.

McConnell, Stacy A., ed., and Linda D. Hall, assoc. ed. *Dun & Bradstreet/Gale Industry Reference Handbooks: Computers and Software.* Detroit: Gale, 1998.

"A Chronology of Computer History," [cited January 12, 1999] available from the World Wide Web (or On Line) @ www.cyberstreet.com/hcs/museum/chron.htm.

"Computers: History and Development," [cited January 12, 1999] available from the World Wide Web (or On Line) @ www.digitalcentury.com/encyclo/update/comp_hd.html.

Stearns, Peter N., and John H. Hinshaw. *The ABC–CLIO World History Companion to the Industrial Revolution.* Santa Barbara, Ca.: 1996, s.v. "Computers."

COMSTOCK LODE

The richest silver mine in the United States, the Comstock Lode also contained a large amount of gold. The ore deposit was found in 1857 at Mount Davidson in western Nevada, about 16 miles (26 kilometers) southeast of Reno. The discoverers Ethan Allen Grosh and Hosea Ballou Grosh, however, died before they could record the claim. Prospector Henry T.P. Comstock (1820–1870) laid claim to the lode in 1859, but later he sold it for an insignificant amount compared to what it was worth. The mine flourished until 1865 and again between 1873 and 1882—when the "Big Bonanza," a super-rich ore vein, yielded more than $100 million. By 1882, near the end of the Comstock Lode's greatest activity, it had yielded $397 million in ore and had produced half of the United States' silver output during the period.

Western Nevada became a hotbed of mining activity, attracting numerous prospectors. Among those who made their fortune from the Comstock Lode was mining magnate and future senator George Hearst (1820–1891). He used his fortune to buy the *San Francisco Examiner* in 1880, which was taken over by his son, newspaper publisher William Randolph Hearst (1863–1951), seven years later. Virginia City, established in 1859 at the site of the discovery, became one of the West's boomtowns during the late 1800s. By 1898 the mines at Comstock Lode were all but abandoned; wasteful mining methods and the demonetizations of silver brought about the mine's demise.

See also: **Gold Rush of 1848, Westward Expansion**

CONFEDERATE DOLLAR

Confederate dollars were the paper money issued by the Confederacy (of Southern States) to help fund the war against the Union. After the South seceded early in 1861, fighting broke out on April 12 at Fort Sumter, South Carolina: It was the first battle of the American Civil War (1861–65).

The North held much of the nation's wealth, and so the newly formed Confederacy was faced with the problem of financing its war effort. The South's agricultural economy made it difficult to raise taxes and the large sums of money required to make war against the Union. In need of funds the provisional government of the Confederacy issued $100 million in paper currency in August 1861. As the war continued, the Confederacy was forced to print more paper money. Because there was nothing to back up the currency, the dollars quickly lost value and became almost worthless.

As the currency became devalued, inflation climbed: In 1861 the price per bushel of salt was eighty cents in Confederate currency; by the end of the following year this price rose to 30 Confederate dollars per bushel. By January 1865 wartime inflation had reduced the value of Confederate paper money to $1.70 per $100 (or just under two cents to the dollar).

The South's inability to raise the capital it needed to wage war was a major factor in its eventual defeat. While funding the war was also a struggle for the Union, the industrial-based economy of the northern states helped the country sustain, and eventually win the conflict. On April 9, 1865, General Robert E. Lee (1807–70) surrendered his ragged Confederate troops to Union General Ulysses S. Grant (1822–85) at old Appomattox Court House, Virginia.

A Confederate five dollar bill.

See also: **Civil War (Economic Causes of), Civil War (Economic Impact of), Greenbacks, Inflation, National Bank Act of 1863**

CONGRESS OF INDUSTRIAL ORGANIZATIONS (CIO)

Congress of Industrial Organizations (CIO) was an organization of trade unions that represented all workers in major mass-production industries. Formed in 1935 by John L. Lewis (1880–1969), the CIO was initially called the Committee for Industrial Organizations, a collection of eight unions within the American Federation of Labor (AFL). But differences soon presented themselves between the AFL and the CIO. Except for miners and textile workers, the AFL was divided into craft unions. Boilermakers, machinists, upholsters, painters, and other trades were separated into local unions by the type of skills required to make their products. The CIO advocated an industrial unionism, whereby workers would be organized according to the nature of their products (their industry). Steelworkers would have one union, for example, and the building trades another. The CIO also had an open-door policy to African Americans and other classes of society rejected by the AFL. In 1938 the eight unions represented by the Committee for Industrial Organizations left the AFL, and reorganized themselves under the name Congress of Industrial Organizations. The CIO faced formidable opposition in its early days. The AFL collaborated with local unions and state and federal legislators to brand the CIO a communist

organization. Employers murdered, gassed, beat, and intimidated their workers to demoralize the CIO's unionizing efforts. World War II (1939–1945) pulled the AFL and CIO closer together, as both organizations supported governmental efforts to mobilize industry for military production. During the Korean War (1950–1953) the AFL and CIO formed a joint committee to deal with federal labor policies. This committee facilitated the formal merger of the two organizations in December 1955.

See also: **American Federation of Labor, Labor Movement, Labor Unionism**

CONGRESS OF RACIAL EQUALITY

Although World War II (1939–1945) signaled the end of the Great Depression for many Americans, the new age of prosperity largely bypassed African Americans. The Civil War amendments to the Constitution that guaranteed equal rights to African Americans were circumvented by Jim Crow laws throughout the South, and segregation remained common. This deprived blacks of access to education, jobs, and decent housing. In 1942, an interracial group founded the Congress of Racial Equality (CORE) to work for social change through nonviolent means. CORE members worked with black organizations, such as the Southern Christian Leadership Conference (SCLC) and the Student Nonviolent Coordinating Committee (SNCC), to bring national attention to issues such as segregation and voting rights.

One of the most effective strategies against segregation was the sit-in, the first of which occurred on January 31, 1960, when a group of black college students sat down at the "white only" section of the Woolworth's lunch counter in Greensboro, North Carolina. The students refused to leave, drawing attention to the injustice of segregation statutes. Soon, protesters were engaging in other sit-ins throughout the South. Many participants were beaten and arrested.

In 1961, CORE, with the help of SNCC, organized "freedom rides." These sent busloads of northern blacks and whites on rides to various cities and town in the South. The riders expected to encounter hostility in the region, but racial discrimination on interstate buses was illegal and the participants planned to demand that the U.S. attorney general's office protect their right to travel together. The Freedom Riders were frequently attacked by white mobs; in Birmingham, Alabama, police officers conspired to allow Ku Klux Klansmen to beat them without intervening. In some places, freedom riders' buses were burned. Attorney General Robert F. Kennedy (1925–1968) finally authorized federal protection for the freedom riders against mob violence, but not from illegal arrest. Freedom rides and other actions helped to galvanize support throughout the country for the growing Civil Rights movement. Though the slow pace of change through the 1960s drew some African Americans toward more extremist groups, such as the Black Panthers or the Black Muslims, CORE remained dedicated to nonviolent confrontation and continued to include white members.

See also: **Civil Rights Movement, Jim Crow Laws, Sit-Down Strikes**

CONNECTICUT

A colony established by no–nonsense Puritans and pushed forward by so–called "Yankee ingenuity," Connecticut has become an economic success story. Before the middle of the nineteenth century the state was well on its way to becoming an industrial powerhouse. Despite occasional downturns, changes in its population base, and fluctuations in its industrial character over a period of years, the state remains one the wealthiest in the United States.

Early Dutch settlers in Connecticut were dislodged by the large migration of English Puritans who came to the colony between 1630 and 1642. The Puritans established settlements all along the Connecticut River and formed a colony in 1639. After several years of friendly relations with the English, the situation deteriorated, and by 1770 the Native Americans of Connecticut had been largely driven out. Connecticut received legal recognition as a colony in 1662 and after it had a number of years of bitter border disputes with Massachusetts, Rhode Island, New York, and Pennsylvania. A relatively autonomous colony, Connecticut was a strong supporter of the American Revolution (1775–81). During the war Connecticut was known as the Provisions State because it supplied so much food to General George Washington's army. Connecticut ratified the new U.S. Constitution in 1788.

By the mid–nineteenth century Connecticut was unable to support itself through farming alone. Several important industries developed, including shipbuilding and whaling. In whaling ports the city of New London ranked behind only Nantucket and New Bedford in Massachusetts. The state has also led the insurance industry since the 1790s.

The inventiveness of early Connecticut manufacturers was a boon to the small state. Eli Whitney invented his famous cotton gin there and developed a system of interchangeable parts for rifles. Charles Goodyear developed a vulcanizing process for rubber, which later gave rise to the Goodyear Tire and Rubber Company. Linus Yale and his son created locks that still bear their name. Samuel Colt produced the rifles which had such an important effect on the winning of the American Civil War (1861–65), and Elias Howe invented the sewing machine. Clockmakers, like Eli Terry and Seth Thomas, made Connecticut a leader in clock and watch making.

Known as a conservative state, Connecticut was rather slow to develop railroads. They did not appear until the 1840s. After some opposition from turnpike and steamboat companies, the first railroad connected Hartford and New Haven, and later Northhampton, Massachusetts. By the 1850s a number of routes connected Hartford with other eastern Connecticut cities. The most important Connecticut railroad was the New York, New Haven, and Hartford.

This network of railroads, along with a healthy industrial base, made Connecticut an important contributor to the Union cause during the Civil War. A longtime antislavery state, Connecticut sent some 55,000 men to fight and provided large amounts of war materials. Gun manufacturers, such as Colt and Winchester, along with manufacturers of textiles, brass, and rubber, sent much–needed supplies to the war front. The war consolidated Connecticut's place as an industrially strong state. This development was made possible not only by the presence of railroads, but by abundant water power, sufficient capital from the many banks

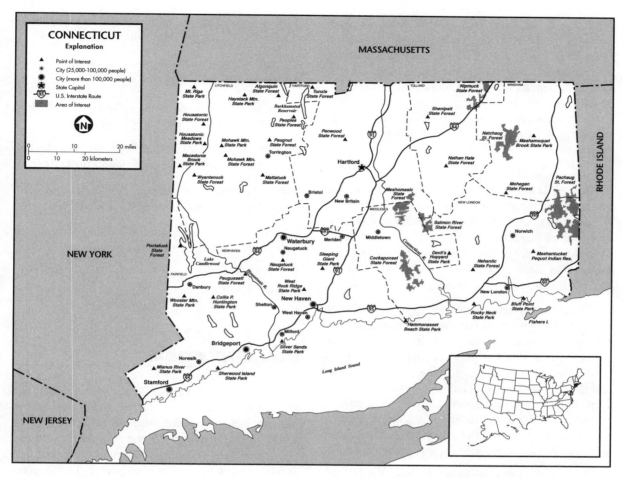

State of Connecticut.

and insurance companies, and the technological and marketing skills of Connecticut's citizens.

Around the turn of the century Connecticut was an important producer of products like electrical fixtures, machine tools, hardware, hats, and typewriters. Connecticut produced $50 million in textiles (ranking it sixth in the nation in 1900), and it was soon putting out four–fifths of the U.S. supply of ammunition and one–fifth of its firearms (not including governmental production). In addition to the increased urbanization brought on by industry, population patterns began to change as well. By 1910 the foreign–born, attracted by the prospect of employment, made up 30 percent of the population. Most came from Ireland, Italy, Germany, and Austria.

During World War I (1914–18) Connecticut supplied not only men but also substantial monetary contributions and war materiel. Liberty Loan drives in the state netted $437 million, more than any other state collected. The firearms produced in Connecticut, among them Enfield and Browning rifles, were invaluable to

the war effort. Other war–related products produced in the state included silk for parachutes, woven articles, and military hats.

Except for a brief recession just after the war, Connecticut's economy continued to boom in the 1920s. Factories churned out specialty parts for airplanes, automobiles, and the electric power industry. Hartford's Pratt and Whitney Company made the state a leader in the aviation industry, increasing the number of employees to over 2,000 by 1935. At the same time the textile industry in eastern Connecticut was declining, as more and more factories moved to the low–wage southern states.

The Great Depression of the 1930s brought hard times to the state, with thousands jobless and local and state governments struggling to find operating funds. In 1930 in Bridgeport, for example, 22,000 people applied for relief, and the city had to borrow $500,000 to pay for jobless benefits. This desperation led the state's voters to elect a Democratic governor for the first time in years. Connecticut then began to take advantage of the many federal work relief programs provided by the federal government under President Franklin D. Roosevelt (1933–45). According to historian David M. Roth, ''Out of the misery of the Depression there came a progressive political tide such as had never been experienced in the state, a tide that enabled Connecticut not only to weather the Depression but to emerge as a far more liberal society than it had ever been before.''

The renewed manufacturing activity brought by World War II (1939–45), however, was the real catalyst to economic revitalization. Defense contracts in Connecticut totaled $8 billion by 1945, and industrial employment increased by 200,000 between 1939 and 1944. Major products sent to the war front from Connecticut included submarines, Navy Corsair fighter aircraft, helicopters, ball bearings, and small arms.

After the war the state retained its economic health by diversifying its industrial base and relying more on the service industry. Urban problems began to plague the state in the 1950s as more and more middle–class whites fled to the suburbs, leaving ethnic minorities and the poor in the central part of cities like Hartford, New Haven, and Bridgeport. Housing in particular remained a problem in these areas. In addition, because Connecticut repeatedly rejected a state income tax, the state's taxes were among the highest in the nation.

During the 1980s, however, Connecticut boasted the highest per capita income in the United States, based largely on the expansion of defense contracts. This optimistic trend was threatened, however, when the Cold War began to defuse in the late 1980s, and manufacturing employment dropped by 25 percent. In 1991 defense–related contracts had dropped 37.7 percent from the year before. Pratt and Whitney and General Dynamics's Electric Boat Division announced major layoffs in 1992. Though service sector jobs increased by 23 percent, the total number of jobs in the state had dropped by 10 percent in 1992. Strapped for funds, the state passed a controversial personal income tax in 1991.

In the early 1990s the wide discrepancy between the standards of living of white suburbanites and inner city, ethnic populations was quite evident in Connecticut. Governor Lowell L. Weicker (1990–94) attempted to alleviate this situation by channeling more funds to urban communities. The employment outlook in the state had improved by the mid-1990s. By 1996 the state again ranked first in per capita income, at $33,189, and less than 10 percent of the population fell below the federal poverty level. To encourage business the state offers a number of tax incentives and it has begun to reduce its high corporate tax rate.

FURTHER READING

Bingham, Harold J. *History of Connecticut*, 4 vols. New York: Lewis, 1962.

Connecticut Secretary of State. *Register and Manual, 1999*. Hartford, CT: State of Connecticut, 1999.

Janick, Herbert F. *A Diverse People: Connecticut, 1914 to the Present*. Chester, CT: Pequot Press, 1975.

Roth, David M. *Connecticut: A Bicentennial History*. New York: Norton, 1979.

Van Dusen, Albert E. *Connecticut*. New York: Random House, 1961.

CONSERVATISM

Although conservatism in the United States did not become a generally coherent intellectual movement until the close of the American Revolution (1775–1783), it had strong roots in the colonial era nonetheless. The planter societies of Virginia, Maryland, and South Carolina, especially, were governed for the most part by principles that were solidly conservative—respect for religious establishments, aristocratic constitutions, a recognition of corresponding rights and duties, and guarantees for the protection of property, particularly property in land. Even the colonies founded upon dissent, such as the New England settlements and Pennsylvania, became relatively conservative very shortly after they acquired considerable population and wealth.

At their core, ''conservative'' debates in the colonies were really disputes between two political factions of Whigs, both attached to the Whig idea of liberty, but differing over views of the colonies' relationship with the Crown (England). For both of these groups, fears of political excesses, economic egalitarianism (equal rights and privileges for all), and cultural vulgarity defined conservatism politically and culturally. Neither of these factions was radical, although some leveling elements were contained in the faction that, at the time of the American Revolution, came to be known as ''Patriots.'' The triumph of the Patriots in the Revolution expelled from America what little Toryism (support for allegiance with Britain) had existed there, and along with it some of the moderate Whigs. Many scholars view the American Revolution as simply a War of Independence—a revolution, in the words of consummate conservative Edmund Burke, "not made, but prevented."

In general, the United States Constitution retained a fundamentally conservative core. It expressed principles intended to conserve justice, order, and liberty in the United States: arrangement of political checks and balances, restrictions upon power, respect for individuality, and protection for private property and the rights minorities. James Madison (1751–1836), the primary author of the Constitution, feared mass tyranny and spoke of the danger of majoritarian rule and elective tyranny.

For the most part, the political contests of the early years of the Republic were long and often times heated debates between two conservative interests—the mercantile and industrial interests of the North, and the agricultural interest of the South. President John Adams (1797–1801) in the North and President James Madison (1809–1817) in the South, dominated these political interests during the early national period. But gradually, Jacksonian democracy and the slavery debate began to divide the nation and tear at the conservative core. Statesman John Randolph (1773–1833) and politician John C. Calhoun (1782–1850) spoke eloquently for the agricultural interest, while orator and statesman Daniel Webster (1782–1852) spoke for Northern conservatism.

During the Gilded Age (the period after the American Civil War through the 1920s), political principles were often neglected in the face of growing materialism. But things began to change quickly during the Progressive era. The term "progressive" captured the sentiment of the age, and represented to many what was best about the nation. But what counted as "progressive" politically was debated. Conservatives, insurgents, socialists, and modern liberals all claimed to be progressive. By the 1910s, however, the predominant political usage of the term came to be associated with political reformers who supported the expansion of the regulatory powers of government as a means to lessen societal problems. Conservatives believed their programs offered the best hope for true political progress. John William Burgess, a political scientist at Columbia University, and his colleague, Nicholas Murray Butler, argued that "limitations on the power of government" were themselves progressive and that relaxing those limitations (as the progressives desired) would be at the expense of individual civil liberties. Freedom of choice, Butler maintained, could only

be maximized through restrictions on governmental activism.

The American Liberty League became the greatest voice of political conservatism during the New Deal era. During its six-year existence, the American Liberty League gained support from some of the wealthiest businessmen and professionals in the United States. Among them were Irénée du Pont of the Du Pont Company; Nathan Miller, head of U.S. Steel Co.; Edward F. Hutton of General Foods; and John Jacob Rascob, former director of General Motors and one-time head of the Democratic Party. Among other disillusioned Democrats active in the League were two former Democratic presidential candidates: John W. Davis, who lost to Calvin Coolidge in 1924, and Alfred E. Smith, who lost to Herbert Hoover in 1928. The American Liberty League offered conservative criticism of the New Deal. Its stated purpose was "to defend and uphold the Constitution . . . [and] to teach the duty of government to protect individual and group initiatives. . . ." Claiming that the New Deal threatened the constitutional system of checks and balances by concentrating power in the chief executive, the American Liberty League also opposed the New Deal's monetary policy, its deficit spending, its progressive taxation of businesses, and its efforts to enlarge government in general. Though the American Liberty League suffered from its popular image as a club for millionaires and did not gain wide popular support, its membership reached almost 125,000 at its height in 1936. The League fell apart after President Franklin D. Roosevelt's (1933–1945) decisive electoral victory that year.

With the emergence of the United States as a global power after World War II and the rise of the Soviet Union as a nuclear threat, the conservative movement shifted its focus. It abandoned its isolationist position in foreign policy, which was incompatible with its militant anti-communism views. The right was also critical of foreign aid and distrustful of American involvement in the United Nations. It was libertarian in its view of economics, opposing taxes, government regulation of business, government spending, and social programs. It was also socially traditional, stressing moral order and maintenance of the community.

After the election of Ronald Reagan (1981-1989), a conservative president, the right found itself in a position of power that it had not held for decades. Its advocates, like William Buckley Jr., became television personalities, and the movement gained a respectability that it lacked in the 1960s, when its presidential candidate Barry Goldwater was successfully branded as a dangerous extremist. Later, even a Democratic president William Clinton (1993-) declared that ''the age of big government is over,'' an essentially conservative message. It was during Clinton's first term that the Republicans, the more conservative of the two major parties, took control of both houses of Congress. Conservatives also saw the fall of the Soviet Union in 1989 and nearly worldwide rejection of socialism that followed as their victories. Nevertheless success also brought dissention. Conservatism became divided into two camps. There were libertarians who emphasized a laissez-faire economic policy, and social conservatives, who felt strongly about issues like abortion. The ability of these two groups to find common ground will be an important factor in the future of the movement.

See also: **Laissez Faire**

FURTHER READING

Bennett, David H. *The Party of Fear: From Nativist Movements to the New Right in American History*. Chapel Hill: University of North Carolina Press, 1988.

Forster, Arnold, and Benjamin R. Epstein. *Danger on the Right*. New York: Random House, 1964.

Himmelstein, Jerome L. *To the Right: The Transformation of American Conservatism*. Berkeley: University of California Press, 1990.

Kirk, Russell. *The Conservative Mind: From Burke to Eliot*. Washington, DC: Regnery Gateway, 1986.

CONSOLIDATION

The growth and expansion of economic activity in the United States over time was due, in large part, to businesses joining together or combining under single ownership or control. The two most common ways businesses combine were by consolidation and merger. Consolidation was the joining of two or more companies on relatively equal terms to form a new composite company. Frequently, company titles were maintained. For example, when Chase National Bank and Bank of Manhattan consolidated, the new organization became known as Chase Manhattan Bank. Conversely, a merger was the absorption of one company by another so that the absorbed company lost its identity. In both consolidations and mergers, shareholders agreed to exchange their stock holdings in the old company for shares in the new company, thereby combining capital to form a single new company.

Consolidations and mergers are horizontal combinations involving competitors who produce the same product or provide the same service. Vertical combinations take place when businesses performing different steps in an industrial process came together. A classic vertical example is the U.S. Steel Corporation, which combined with companies that mine, ship, and smelt ore, and fashion the resulting steel into various products. The terms consolidation and merger in practicality are used interchangeably. A third variation on the consolidation evolved in the mid-1960s: the conglomerate. A conglomerate is an organization of previously independent firms with dissimilar activities brought under the same management and control of a corporate holding company.

Four main waves of business consolidation have occurred in U.S. history. A consolidation wave rolled through U.S. industry between 1895 and 1904 producing giant twentieth century corporations, such as U.S. Steel, American Tobacco, DuPont, and Anaconda Copper. Likewise the 1920s, a high economic growth period with a relaxed government attitude toward mergers, experienced a sharp increase in consolidation of industrial power among large firms. In these first two periods of heavy merger activity, horizontal combinations predominated with a principle purpose of controlling output and prices to end cutthroat competition. During the 1960s conglomerates emerged as the chief form of consolidation. A prime conglomerate example was International Telephone and Telegraph (ITT) which owned such diverse firms as Wonder Bread, Sheraton Hotels, Hartford Insurance, and Burpee Lawn and Garden Products. In the 1980s, under a prevailing national *laissez faire* philosophy and driven by the increased need to compete in foreign markets, another wave of mergers occurred.

See also: **Laissez Faire, Merger, Tobacco Trust**

CONSTITUTION, ECONOMIC BENEFITS OF THE *(ISSUE)*

The basis of the discussion in the constitutional convention during the summer of 1787 was the economic rights and the political liberties of the American people. In other words, the Constitution was an attempt to define the terms and the relationship of freedom and property. This generation saw no contradiction between the two. In 1775 Arthur Lee of Virginia summed up this reciprocal relationship of economic rights and personal freedom, stating that "[t]he right of property is the guardian of every other right, and to deprive a people of this, is in fact to deprive them of their liberty." This, undoubtedly, was the perspective of people who owned some property. The slaves in the South might be forgiven for disputing this equation. For them, after all, the property interest of the slave-holder negated their own liberty.

Following the American Revolution (1775–1783) in the mid-1780s, during the period of the Articles of Confederation (1777–1788), the states assumed the burden of government. The central government was little more than a loose and impotent alliance between the states. The Articles of Confederation reserved to the states the power to tax and regulate commerce among the states. But the states could do little to fix the underlying economic problems of the 1780s, which included trade and tax disputes among the states, an influx of cheap British goods that threatened to devastate an infant manufacturing capacity, and a lack of common currency.

These problems, as well as the threat of popular uprisings of bankrupt farmers (like Shay's Rebellion in western Massachusetts in 1787) who faced bankruptcy during the post-war depression in the mid-1780s. The Constitutional Convention, held from May to September 1787, initially set out to revise the Articles of Confederation. Soon it became clear that most of the delegates favored a complete revamping of the document. Thus was born the U.S. Constitution, which was not ratified by all states until 1788. The new government began operation in 1789.

The Constitution spoke directly to economic issues. Article 1, section 8 stated that "Congress shall have Power To Lay and collect Taxes, Duties, Imposts, and Excises"; and further gave Congress the power "[t]o regulate Commerce with foreign Nations, and among the several States." These two clauses outline a new rationale for federal power. The authors of the Constitution looked on central government to trouble-shoot and regulate economic life, rather than fearing that the federal government might dominate economic and political life. The same section goes on to give the central government the power to standardize the rules of bankruptcy and to invest the federal government with the powers to coin and borrow money, to declare war, and to provide for armies and navies.

Article 1, section 10 prohibits the states from passing any law "impairing the obligation of contracts" or imposing its own imposts or duties on

THE CONSTITUTION SPOKE DIRECTLY TO ECONOMIC ISSUES. ARTICLE 1, SECTION 8 STATED THAT "CONGRESS SHALL HAVE POWER TO LAY AND COLLECT TAXES, DUTIES, IMPOSTS, AND EXCISES"; AND FURTHER GAVE CONGRESS THE POWER "[T]O REGULATE COMMERCE WITH FOREIGN NATIONS, AND AMONG THE SEVERAL STATES."

imports or exports. Moreover, to ensure that southern states ratified the Constitution, the constitutional convention approved protection for slave owners. The Constitution clearly regards slaves as "chattel," or property. The three key clauses addressing slavery are article 1, section 2—the three-fifths clause dealing with representation; article 1, section 9—the international slave trade clause, which stopped the international slave trade in 1808; and article 4, section 2—the fugitive slave clause, which provided a federal guarantee of the return of runaway slaves.

Much of the legal history of the United States is the history of state and federal laws enacted to encourage and regulate economic development. Over the years new legislation—new trade regulations, for example, and the rise of tort (wrongful act) law in the nineteenth century—illustrate the way that the Constitution supports and shapes the economy. This relationship is apparent in the numerous Supreme Court decisions made during the terms of two Chief Justices, John Marshall (1803—1835) and Roger B. Taney (1836—1864). During the Marshall years, the Supreme Court held the states to their contractual promises, in *Fletcher v. Peck* (1810), and the Court ruled that the contract clause of the Constitution protected private corporations from state interference, in *Dartmouth College v. Woodward* (1819). Marshall also upheld the validity of state bankruptcy statutes in the absence of federal regulations in the 1819 case of *Sturges v. Crowninshield*.

Perhaps no case better exemplifies the close relation between the law, the Constitution, and the economy than the 1824 steamboat case of *Gibbons v. Ogden*. In this decision, Marshall's Supreme Court held that the commerce clause of the Constitution provided Congress, not the states, with the power to establish regulations for commerce among the states. In effect, *Gibbons* established a national free-trade zone throughout the United States, allowing merchants to ship goods into and through various states without obstruction from the states. States could still regulate intrastate commerce (commerce wholly within their borders), but trade of this nature disappeared as the national market economy expanded over the course of the nineteenth century.

Chief Justice Taney's 1837 decision in *Charles River Bridge v. Warren Bridge* provides another example of the relationship between constitutional law and the economy. In this decision Taney struck down a restrictive understanding of property rights and upheld a more risk-oriented view of property rights. Taney established a legal environment that allowed for the release of entrepreneurial energies—an environment that mirrored the risk-taking values of his era. Both *Charles River Bridge* and *Gibbons* illustrate the way that constitutional law has fostered an energetic U.S. economy.

The era of the American Civil War (1861–1865) brought changes to the Constitution, shifted power away from the states and toward the federal government. In *Dred Scott v. Sandford* (1857) Chief Justice Taney was finally faced with having to choose between property rights and individual human liberty. He came down on the side of protecting the property rights of the slaveholder by denying the humanity of the slave, Dred Scott. In doing this, he also sought to ''federalize'' the question and to abolish whatever discrepancy might exist between the various states' interpretation of the law. This decision was swept away by the Civil War and the Thirteenth and Fourteenth Amendments explicitly affirm both the humanity of the ex-slave and the civil rights of all citizens, including the ex-slaves. One common theme that these judgments share with Tawney's ruling on Dred Scott is that they ''nationalize'' the legal condition of black people. No longer could the civil rights of black people be a function of whatever state they might live in. These post–Civil War pronouncements guarantee full civil rights to all citizens.

That industrialism took deep root in American culture is due in large part to the judicial deference to property and a willingness of Congress, the federal courts, and the states to promote corporate expansion. With the Great Depression of the late 1920s and 1930s Congress and the courts employed the language of the Fourteenth Amendment to support the rise of the social welfare state. This new approach, beginning with the New Deal's numerous regulatory boards and administrative laws, has lasted to the current day. Using the reach of the commerce clause, Congress and the administrative agencies regulate almost every aspect of the U.S. economy, theorizing that a national economy demands national regulations. Conservative states' rights advocates may not like it, but, for most Americans, the interconnected character of modern American society leads them to expect the government to assist in the development of the economy. In a reciprocal relationship, the Constitution benefits the economy and the economy is bolstered by the constitutional system.

FURTHER READING

Benson, Paul R., Jr. *The Supreme Court and the Commerce Clause, 1937–1970.* New York: Dunellen, 1970.

Ely, James W., Jr. *The Guardian of Every Other Right: A Constitutional History of Property Rights.* New York: Oxford University Press, 1998.

Kelly, Alfred H., Winfred A. Harbison, and Herman Belz, *The American Constitution: Its Origins and Development*, 7th ed. New York: W.W. Norton & Co., 1991.

Kutler, Stanley I. *Privilege and Creative Destruction: The Charles River Bridge Case.* Baltimore: The Johns Hopkins University Press, 1990.

Sunstein, Cass R. *After the Rights Revolution: Reconceiving the Regulatory State.* Cambridge: Harvard University Press, 1990.

CONSUMER GOODS

Consumer goods are goods or services that are ready for consumption by individuals, social groups, or governmental bodies. Consumer goods are the final result of the production process. Because consumer goods are purchased for personal use, they serve a different purpose than capital goods, which are used by businesses to manufacturer or produce more goods. Consumer goods can be categorized as either durable or non-durable. Durable goods have a long life and are not easily used up or destroyed. Examples of durable goods include stoves, cars, and computers. Generally, durable goods have an expected useful life of more than three years. Durable goods are sometimes called hard goods. By contrast, consumers can easily use up or discard non-durable goods, which are usually perishable in nature. Food, clothing, gasoline, and hairstyling services are all considered to be non-durable. Because of the short-term life of non-durable goods, they need to be purchased frequently.

See also: **Capital Goods, Consumption, Durable Goods**

CONSUMER PRICE INDEX

The Consumer Price Index (CPI) is a continually updated statistical survey of the prices consumers are paying for various basic goods and services. The Bureau of Labor Statistics (BLS) defines the prices it wants to track of a group or "basket" of about 2,400 typical consumer goods and services. (The "contents" of a basket can be quite varied, e.g., medical care, transportation, housing prices, or the current prices of entertainment, clothing, and food.)

Hundreds of BLS field representatives visit an average of 24,000 to 29,000 families and thousands of retail stores in 85 representative cities to determine the current prices paid and charged for each specific good. (A typical example of BLS inquiry might include, "Men's high work shoes, elk upper, Goodyear welt, size range 6 to 11.") During the next 20 days which follow visitations, government analysts use computers and complex computer programs to combine, sort, and refine all their price data, taking into account the fact that some goods play a more important role in the economy and in household budgets than others. (A change in the price of gasoline, for example, will have a much greater impact on a family budget than will a change in the price of toothpaste.) About the middle of every month, the Bureau publishes the CPI for the previous month. A typical BLS news release begins: "The CPI for all urban consumers rose 0.1 percent in February 1999 . . . to a level of 164.5 (1982–84 = 100). . . . For the 12-month period ended in February, the CPI has increased 1.6 percent."

The first attempt in the United States to use an index to compare price changes was prepared for the U.S. Senate in 1893. When labor and management began meeting to hammer out labor agreements in the early years of the twentieth century, they needed an accurate, official CPI so workers would receive automatic wage increases that kept pace with inflation. During World War I (1914–18), inflation accelerated, and an accurate CPI became more important than ever.

When Keynesian economic theory gained acceptance during the 1930s, the CPI became a tool government economists could use to fine-tune fiscal policy. For example, if the CPI showed that prices were falling, the government might become concerned that demand was weak and could lower taxes to stimulate consumer spending. As the twentieth century closed, the CPI remained one of the most closely watched measures of the health of the U.S. economy. Besides determining appropriate wage increases, the index was

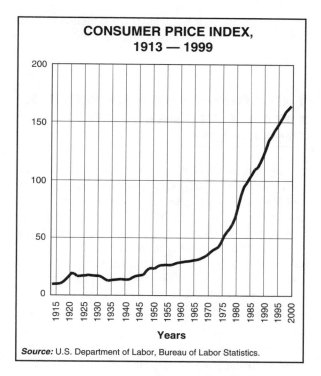

CONSUMER PRICE INDEX, 1913 — 1999

Source: U.S. Department of Labor, Bureau of Labor Statistics.

The Consumer Price Index is a statistical survey of commonly used goods and services. The constant rise of the Consumer Price Index for the last quarter of the century is depicted.

also used to calculate Social Security payment adjustments and income tax brackets.

See also: **Inflation, Keynesian Economic Theory**

CONSUMPTION

Consumption refers to the using up of goods and service by consumers. In fact, consumption of goods is considered to be the final step in the production process and the ultimate purpose of production. While the term consumption can include both capital consumption and nonproductive consumption, it generally is restricted to mean nonproductive consumption. Nonproductive consumption is when goods or services are not used in any further production processes. This is different than capital consumption, which refers to the use of goods and services to produce more goods and services. An example of capital consumption is the use of factory equipment to make products such as running shoes. Nonproductive consumption, on the other hand, occurs when individuals or families purchase personal-use items or services such as cars, computers, paper clips, or manicures. Governmental bodies can also engage in nonproductive consumption. An example of this might be the decision of a city or town to build a public facility, such as a school or library. Therefore, nonproductive consumption most often includes consumption by private individuals, social groups, and the public.

THE CONTEMPORARY WORLD, 1974 TO THE PRESENT *(OVERVIEW)*

During the 1970s Americans became preoccupied with questions of economic well-being. Despite the fact that the United States still possessed the world's largest gross national product, a fear of decline overtook American culture. The public had lost confidence in New Deal policies that valued stability and equitable distribution of wealth over opportunities for growth and upward mobility. Concerns over prosperity became the guiding force in American politics.

In the 1970s Presidents Gerald Ford (1974–1977) and Jimmy Carter (1977–1981) responded by initiating a policy of deregulation, which was an effort to minimize government intervention in the market economy. While the initial efforts of deregulation were applied to government's relations with businesses, the logic of deregulation extended to government intervention in the economic lives of individual citizens. Presidents Ronald Reagan (1981–1989), George Bush (1989–1993), and Bill Clinton (1993—) all sought to diminish the influence of the federal government over the economy. The result has been a public policy designed to permit every business and every citizen to succeed or fail without government intervention.

A reassessment of the definition of monopoly has been key to this process of deregulation. Presidential administrations began to tolerate consolidations in industry. Congress abandoned the assumption that monopolies are only safe when they are regulated as a public utility. The federal courts became reluctant to interfere with market forces. The result has been a revolution in economic competition.

The elements involved in reconstructing the relationship between government and business came together in the antitrust prosecution of American Telephone and Telegraph (AT&T). Until the initiation of this case in 1974 the government had supported AT&T's monopoly over both local and long distance telephone service and encouraged its dominance over research and development of telephone technology. In exchange for high profits on long distance service, AT&T guaranteed affordable local service to every household and state of the art technology. In 1984 the federal courts reversed this arrangement and separated AT&T long

distance from its local service providers (the "baby bells"). Since the AT&T decision other public service monopolies, most notably in the electrical generating industry, have been forced into open competition.

While breaking down public utility monopolies, the government became more tolerant of corporate consolidation. As a result corporate mergers in industries as varied as banking and oil refining have constructed business enterprises of a power and efficiency not seen in America since the nineteenth century. A small, regional bank in North Carolina (National Bank of North Carolina) was unchallenged in its transformation into the fifth largest bank in the United States (First Union). The unification of Mobil and Exxon resulted in a coordination of production that rivaled Standard Oil Corporation before Taft's (1909–1913) administration's antitrust prosecutions.

This acceptance of large scale corporations has been accompanied by a consistent policy of deregulation of industry. New Deal regulatory policies, which guaranteed reasonable corporate profits in exchange for an end to destructive competition, fell under attack and disappeared within a generation. The restrictions of the Glass-Steagall Act (1933), which were designed to promote banking stability and prevent the concentration of capital, were abandoned. Limits on interest rates, mergers, and establishment of new branches were eliminated. Successful American banks became better capitalized and could provide customers with a wider range of services; unsuccessful banks disappeared, with some spectacular collapses in the savings and loan industry. The airline industry, once protected by a Federal Aviation Administration's system that traded high passenger fares for strict controls on distributing profitable and unprofitable markets, was thrown open to competition with the Airline Deregulation Act of 1978. While air fares, fell new airlines emerged and the service to major airports expanded. Scheduling delays increased, airlines went bankrupt, and service to small cities diminished. This pattern of deregulation extended to agricultural production. Like the banking and airline industries, agriculture had benefited from the New Deal policy of guaranteeing profitability in exchange for limits on competition. The federal price support mechanisms of the Department of Agriculture limited the production of key commodities and prevented food processing industries from also owning farms. The Freedom to Farm Act of 1996 eliminated those restrictions in an effort to lower federal subsidies and promote greater efficiency on American farms.

Although the general pattern of government-business relations has been to dismantle regulation of business activity, a notable exception has emerged in the area of environmentalism. Since the establishment of the Environmental Protection Agency in 1970, the government has expanded its authority over standards of air and water pollution, introduced the concept of environmental clean up as a precondition of further industrial development, and curbed development in fragile ecological zones. The American public has accepted the idea that the general need for environmental safety outweighs corporate profit interests.

Deregulation and the reassessment of monopolies were designed to improve efficiency. As industries were forced into higher levels of competition, they had to become more productive. Improvements in productivity could be achieved by either introduction of new technology or a more effective use of labor. However, as corporations were adjusting to this new climate of regulation, they were suddenly hit by the disruptive impact of the embargo by the Organization of Petroleum Exporting Countries (OPEC). During the 1970s OPEC raised the price of crude oil, more than doubling the average price of energy in the United States. Corporations were forced to spend more money on energy, leaving less for the purchase of new technology or wage packages that would raise worker morale. The economic pressures felt by businessmen were also experienced by workers. The increasing cost of gasoline and home heating fuel raised the cost of living at a time when wages stagnated. The net result was frustration for managers, workers, and consumers.

Not only did the OPEC price shocks damage the patterns of corporate investment, they illuminated important weaknesses in the American economy. Businessmen in Germany and Japan adopted computer and robotics technology in the 1960s and early 1970s. By the mid 1970s American factory managers realized they needed to catch up, but were reluctant to modernize when rising energy costs had depleted their profit margins. German and Japanese firms were poised to challenge American corporations in their own domestic markets.

IT'S THE ECONOMY, STUPID.

**James Carville, Clinton presidential campaign
manager, 1992**

By the end of the 1970s the American economy was mired in stagflation (simultaneous high unemployment and high inflation). Despite efforts to improve productivity through deregulation, American manufacturing continued to be eclipsed by competition from Japan and Germany. Public morale continued to falter as consumer costs remained high, wage rates

stagnated, and long–term unemployment became common place. Once the epicenter of the American economy, the urban strip that began in Chicago and followed through Detroit, Cleveland, Pittsburgh, and to Philadelphia became known as "the rust belt."

Reaganomics emerged as the political solution to this problem. The process of deregulation begun under Presidents Ford and Carter was supplemented by the adoption of an aggressive anti–inflation policy and a decision to push money into the private sector through severe cuts in federal taxes. The Reagan and Bush administrations argued that deregulation, combined with lower taxes, would improve productivity. Clearly businesses would benefit from such a policy, but advocates of Reaganomics also argued that the benefits of improved productivity would "trickle down" to workers and consumers.

The Reagan and Bush policies coincided with important technological breakthroughs. Just as businesses were encouraged to restructure and invest in new processes, major innovations were made, including the development of desk–top computing and high speed digital transmission.

The adoption of new technology made American corporations more effective competitors in the world economy. Without federal curbs on the formation of monopolies, corporations could absorb rivals and divest unprofitable subsidiaries. These more powerful corporations sought to enlarge their operations in foreign markets. To support these corporate efforts, the United States government negotiated to eliminate tariff barriers. The most successful of these negotiations resulted in the North American Free Trade Agreement (NAFTA), which was designed to stimulate commerce among the United States, Canada, and Mexico.

The experience of American corporations had important ramifications for the American labor force. During the 1970s American business increased its use of part–time and temporary workers. This trend was particularly profitable for employers; wage costs could be lowered, and, in addition, benefits such as health insurance and pension plans could be dropped. The increasing reliance on part–time and temporary workers continued into the Reagan-Bush years. This pattern held important implications for worker-management relations.

The traditional power of labor unions rested in manufacturing. However, poor productivity in the 1970s triggered layoffs and forced unions to focus on the equitable distribution of remaining jobs in unionized plants. Workers with little seniority were pushed out of union jobs, often into service sector work or self-employment. The adoption of new technologies during the Reagan-Bush era reduced the number of employees needed in manufacturing and continued this process of moving workers away from unionized shop floors.

The movement of workers out of a collective bargaining process weakened organized labor. The leadership of the large national organizations such as the American Federation of Labor-Congress of Industrial Organizations (AFL-CIO) called for prudence and cooperation with management for the protection of jobs. But increasing numbers of workers participated in spontaneous strikes to protest the adoption of new technologies or proposals to utilize part-time or contract workers. Because they did not have the full support of the national union leadership, these job actions had limited success. This weakness of labor authority in the workplace was magnified by changes in federal policy toward labor. The National Labor Relations Board, the federal agency that supervises management-worker relations, became more sympathetic to business concerns. During the Reagan presidency this skepticism toward labor interests solidified, as demonstrated by the federal intervention against striking air traffic controllers in 1981.

Without strong labor unions to defend worker interests, market forces became the predominant factor in setting wage rates and working conditions. Skills that were useful to the reorganization of American business earned high wages and generous benefits packages. Computer literacy was one of the most sought after qualities of workers. Those who clung to older standards of training risked being left behind as the economy was transformed.

An important divide emerged in the American standard of living. The distribution of American wealth concentrated in the hands of fewer people. According to the U.S. Bureau of the Census, in 1993 the richest 20 percent of the American population controlled 46.2 percent of the wealth (as compared to controlling 40.4 percent in 1967). This gain of wealth among rich families occurred at the expense of the bottom 60 percent of the American population. Higher salaries and the added benefits of annual bonuses and stock options raised incomes for those Americans in the upper 20 percent of the population. These higher rates of earning were augmented by substantial tax cuts in the 1980s and 1990s, which permitted the wealthy to retain a larger share of their income.

Families that were not wealthy began to compensate for their diminishing earning power by working more. These families became increasingly reliant on pay checks from both the husband and wife. An income study done by the U.S. Bureau of the Census demonstrated that families with two members in the paid labor force experienced a .76 percent improvement in their annual incomes between 1970 and 1993. On the other hand, families with only one income experienced a decline in their standard of living. Families in areas where jobs were more plentiful benefited most from this pattern. Geographical patterns of poverty were magnified because the distribution of jobs was not even. During the 1970s and 1980s most new jobs were created on the East and West Coasts. In addition, jobs were more likely to be created in suburban areas. Those living in the suburbs of Washington, D.C., or San Diego found a different set of opportunities than those living in Detroit or rural Wyoming.

The desire to lower taxes and free money for investment spurred a search for government spending cuts in the 1980s and 1990s. Welfare reform became a primary objective. Politicians first limited the dollar amounts granted to poor citizens, and then the length of time for eligibility. As federal support for welfare, public health programs, and housing assistance diminished, the poor witnessed a diminishing quality of life.

The push for efficiency and productivity has carried mixed consequences. National chain stores like Walmart have provided lower prices to consumers, but have driven out locally based businesses. The introduction of computers and robotics in manufacturing has saved companies from bankruptcy, but has reduced the number of blue–collar jobs. Extraordinary wealth coexists with grotesque poverty. The gross national product of the United States is still the envy of the world, but the landscape of the American economy has completely changed.

See also: **Airline Deregulation, AT&T, North American Free Trade Agreement (NAFTA), OPEC Embargo, Savings and Loan Failures**

FURTHER READING

Bernstein, Michael A. and David E. Adler. *Understanding American Economic Decline.* New York: Cambridge University Press, 1994.

Burroughs, Bryan and John Helyar. *Barbarians at the Gate: The Fall of RJR Nabisco.* New York: Harper and Row, 1990.

Levy, Frank. *The New Dollars and Dreams: American Incomes and Economic Change.* New York: Russell Sage Foundation, 1998.

Nye, Joseph. *Bound to Lead: The Changing Nature of American Power.* New York: Basic Books, 1990.

Phillips, Kevin. *The Politics of Rich and Poor: Wealth and the American Electorate in the Reagan Aftermath*. New York: Random House, 1990.

Stein, Herbert. *Presidential Economics*. New York: Simon and Schuster, 1984.

Vietor, Richard H. K. *Contrived Competition: Regulation and Deregulation in America*. Cambridge: Harvard University Press, 1994.

Wilson, William Julius. *The Truly Disadvantaged: The Inner City, the Underclass, and Public Policy*. Chicago: University of Chicago Press, 1987.

CONTINENTAL CONGRESS (SECOND)

The Second Continental Congress convened in Philadelphia's Independence Hall on May 10, 1775, shortly after the first fighting broke out in the American Revolution (1775–1783). England had rebuffed the proposals of the First Continental Congress (1774). In response, colonial delegates met again as the Second Continental Congress and began preparing for the fight against the Mother Country. Many of these delegates ultimately became known as founding fathers of the United States—George Washington (1732–1799), John Hancock (1737–1793), Thomas Jefferson (1743–1826), and Benjamin Franklin (1706–1790).

The Second Continental Congress created the Continental Army and named George Washington commander in chief. Although armed conflict was underway, Congress moved cautiously toward proclaiming independence from Britain. On July 10, 1775, two days after issuing a declaration to take up arms, Congress made a last appeal to England's King George III (1738–1820). They hoped their appeal would settle the conflict without further combat. The attempt failed. The Second Continental Congress responded by forming committees to draft the Declaration of Independence.

In their Declaration of Independence the thirteen American colonies declared their freedom from Britain and forwarded reasons for doing so. They named the ''causes which impel them to the separation'' and objected to the British government's violations of individual rights (''the history of the present King of Great Britain is a history of repeated injuries and usurpations'' aimed at establishing ''an absolute Tyranny over these States''). The opening paragraphs stated that an ideal government existed for the benefit of the people and that ''all men are created equal.''

Thomas Jefferson, the chairman of the Second Continental Congress committee that prepared the Declaration, wrote and presented the first draft to the Congress. The Declaration was approved July 4, 1776. The thirteen colonies had proclaimed themselves the United States of America.

While the American Revolution raged, the Second Continental Congress acted as the new nation's central government. This role continued until March 1, 1781, when the Articles of Confederation, the forerunner of the U.S. Constitution (1789), were adopted. After declaring independence, the primary objective of the Second Continental Congress was financing the war. The Congress issued paper money (called Continentals), urged each of the colonies to set up its own republican government, and actively sought the support of other countries in its battle against the powerful British Empire. But since a formal constitution had not been written, the Second Continental Congress stopped short of collecting taxes from the colonies.

See also: **Articles of Confederation, Continentals, European Loans, Thomas Jefferson**

CONTINENTALS

Continentals were the paper money issued by the United States government during the American Revolution (1775–83). After the Declaration of Independence (1776) was made and before the Articles of Confederation (1781) were approved, the Second Continental Congress governed the new nation and ran the war effort against Great Britain. The governing body did not have the power to levy taxes, since no constitution had been drawn up yet. The Congress appealed to each state to contribute to the war fund. However, states that did not face imminent danger—those in which there was no fighting—often did not answer the call. Many of the new nation's most prominent citizens remained loyal to the British and refused to contribute money to the American patriotic cause. Yet money was needed to buy supplies, ammunition, and pay soldiers. In order to finance the Revolution, Congress was compelled to issue paper bills that promised holders future payment in silver. But as Congress issued more Continentals, the currency became devalued. There was not enough silver to back up promised payments. By 1780 there were so many Continentals in circulation that they had become almost worthless. The phrase ''not worth a continental'' was used by Americans to describe anything that had no value. To help solve the financial crisis, some patriotic citizens contributed sums of money; in exchange, they received interest-bearing securities from the U.S. government. But funds remained scarce. The problem of funding the revolutionary effort was not solved until foreign powers stepped in to aid the fledgling nation in its fight against the powerful British. European loans to the United States were instrumental in the American victory in the revolutionary war.

See also: **American Revolution, Articles of Confederation, European Loans, Rag Money**

CONVENTION OF 1818

On October 20, 1818, a convention was signed by the United States and Britain which established part of the present-day border between the United States and Canada. The agreement stipulated that 49 degrees north latitude (or the 49th parallel) would mark the boundary, from Lake of the Woods (in present-day northern Minnesota, southwestern Ontario, and southeastern Manitoba) west to the Rocky Mountains (in present-day Montana and Alberta). The two countries further agreed that for 10 years they would jointly occupy the Pacific Northwest territories—the area that begins at 42 degrees north latitude (the southern boundary of present-day Oregon) and extends north to 54 degrees 40 minutes north latitude (in present-day British Columbia). However, even before the agreement was made, and even before the United States and Britain had fought the War of 1812 (1812–1814), American expansionists had begun to demand the seizure of Canada from Great Britain. Thus, after the eastern boundary had been established by the Convention of 1818, expansionists began to suggest that the Pacific Northwest territories ought to be part of a strategic claim made by the United States.

See also: **Expansionists, Oregon Country Cession, War of 1812**

COOKE, JAY

Jay Cooke (1821–1905) was the foremost investment banker in the United States during the mid-nineteenth century. He pioneered new ways of mobilizing the savings of Americans for productive ends, most significantly to fund the Union effort during the American Civil War (1861–1865). For this reason he was known as the "Financier of the Union."

Jay Cooke.

Born in Sandusky, Ohio, Cooke attended public school until the age of 14. He then ended his formal education and took a job as a clerk in a general store. In 1838 he obtained work with his brother-in-law's canal transport company in Philadelphia, but the firm failed shortly after Cooke's arrival in the city. Cooke returned to Sandusky. Two years later he was lured back to Philadelphia by a job offer as an office boy with banker F. W. Clark. Cooke worked in the Clark banking house from 1839 to 1857. He rose quickly in the firm, and in three years, at the age of twenty-one, he became a partner.

F.W. Clark's profits derived from dealing in "domestic exchange." This meant the firm bought and sold bank notes from various parts of the country, pricing them according to risk. The nation in those days had no official government currency except metallic money. Private bankers provided the paper medium of daily exchange. With the bank notes of so many banks in circulation, a banker had to be shrewd when it came to judging the worth of paper that often purported to be "good as gold."

In the 1850s Cooke began to invest his own money in ventures outside of banking. One of his investments included a land speculation deal in Iowa and Minnesota that involved obtaining land from the government at prices below $1.25 an acre. The land was then resold to incoming farmers at $3.00 and $4.00 an acre. The land speculation scheme made Cooke very wealthy.

Growing restless as a junior partner at F.W. Clark and Company, Cooke left the firm in 1857. For the next few years he devoted his attention to private investing, particularly in railroads. He decided to reenter the banking business on the eve of the American Civil War. On January 1, 1861, he opened Jay Cooke and Company.

When Abraham Lincoln (1809–1865) took office he found the U.S. Treasury nearly empty. In order to finance the Union effort in the Civil War, the government was faced with three methods: taxation, borrowing, or printing paper money. Unlike the opposing Confederate States of America, Lincoln chose to borrow money to pay the war, a strategy that worked largely because of the efforts of Jay Cooke. Conversely, the Confederate government in Richmond chose to print paper money. This created an inflation rate of 5000 percent by the end of the war.

The traditional method of government finance was to offer government bonds to private bankers at competitive auction. In 1861 many bankers were unsure whether the Union would survive to pay the debt. Secretary of the Treasury Salmon P. Chase insisted on selling the bonds at par (one hundred cents on the dollar), but most bankers considered them to be too risky at that price. Cooke approached Chase and proposed marketing bonds directly to the public. Chase initially rejected the idea. But as the war turned against the Union in the summer of 1862, he became more receptive. He appointed Jay Cooke and Company as sole agent to sell $50 million in government bonds at 6 percent interest. The bonds were due in 20 years but the government could redeem them in five; hence, they were popularly called ''5-20s.''

Cooke promised one million dollars worth of daily sales in 5-20s. He also took a fee of 1/2 percent on the first $10 million he sold and 3/8 percent on the remaining bonds. His strategy exceeded all expectations. In 1865 he repeated his earlier success by helping the government finance a new issue of bonds. These were the so-called ''7-30s'' (bonds due in 30 years but redeemable in seven).

After the war Jay Cooke and Company engaged in further government debt financing, but by 1869 the government finance business had wound down and opportunities for profit appeared elsewhere. Cooke agreed to be the banker and agent for the Northern Pacific Railway Company. The rail line was projected to connect Lake Superior with Puget Sound on the Pacific coast, promising to become the largest construction project in U.S. history.

Originally financing for the Northern Pacific was earmarked to build the line westward. To finance further construction and service the debt, money was raised from fees charged to traffic along the first completed sections of the track and from the sale of a congressional land grant worth $50 million. With great difficulty Cooke managed in 1870 to raise $5 million for construction. He then initiated a public campaign to sell $100 million in Northern Pacific bonds at 7.3 percent interest. His goal was to raise enough money from small investors to complete construction of the railroad, but the results were disappointing. He only sold about $16 million worth of bonds in 1871 and 1872. Like major American and European bankers, small investors, were wary despite the high interest rate offered and regardless of Cooke's reputation for reliability.

Poor sales of Northern Pacific bonds and a tightening of the money market forced Jay Cooke and Co. to declare bankruptcy in 1873. Cooke lost most of his vast fortune and spent the next several years trying to satisfy his creditors. In 1880 he resumed business as an investor in Western mining ventures and was able to make a second fortune before his death.

Jay Cooke changed the nature of investment banking by reaching out to hundreds of thousands of Americans and asking them to invest their small holdings to support the Union cause during the Civil War. In the following century Wall Street would follow Cooke's lead by devoting itself to attracting the savings of the individual investor.

Clearly, Cooke's ideas created more than a new way of doing business on Wall Street. His innovative financing methods also kept the U.S. government afloat during crisis. In fact, without the millions of dollars invested by individuals of modest means, the financing of government debt and major industries in the late nineteenth and twentieth centuries might well have been unimaginable.

See also: **Bonds, Salmon P. Chase, Inflation**

FURTHER READING

Gates, Paul Wallace, ed. *The Fruits of Land Speculation.* New York: Arno Press, 1979.

Gordon, John Steele. ''Paying for War.'' *American Heritage*, March 1990.

Hammond, Bray. *Sovereignty and an Empty Purse: Banks and Politics in the Civil War.* Princeton, New Jersey: Princeton University Press, 1970.

Larson, Henrietta M. *Jay Cooke: Private Banker.* Cambridge, Massachusetts: Harvard University Press, 1936.

Minnigerode, Meade. *Certain Rich Men.* New York: G.P. Putnam's Sons, 1927.

Oberholtzer, Ellis Paxton. *Jay Cooke: Financier of the Civil War.* Philadelphia: George W. Jacobs and Co., 1907.

Trescott, Paul B. *Financing American Enterprise: The Story of Commercial Banking.* New York: Harper and Row, 1961.

CORN

Corn was first cultivated in Mexico where early Indians grew grasses that were the grain's ancestors. These grasses were steadily improved between 5000 B.C. and 2000 B.C.. By the time of the Aztec (c. 1325), corn had become the primary food source in central Mexico. As the Aztec came into contact with other Indian peoples, the cultivation of corn spread—reaching the Maya in southern Mexico and Central America, the Inca in South America, the native peoples in the Caribbean, and as far as the Canadian tribes in the north.

The grain was unknown to Europeans at this time. It was Christopher Columbus (1451–1506) who, upon his arrival in Cuba in 1492, discovered corn and took it with him when he returned home. By the end of the sixteenth century corn was well established as a crop and a primary food source in southern Europe, Africa, the Middle East, and Asia. During the next century corn became a staple of the colonial diet. European settlers in America learned from the Indians how to cultivate, harvest, and process the grain. In the late 1500s Virginia farmers planted their fields according to the Indian method, producing a much higher yield per acre (200 versus 40 bushels). From cornmeal colonists made mush (also known as hasty pudding), grits, hoecake (an unleavened cake), and bread. Hominy (a dish made of softened corn), succotash (a corn and bean casserole), and roasted corn were also widely consumed. Bourbon whiskey was made out of corn in Kentucky in 1789 and its popularity soon eclipsed that of brandy or rum in the American colonies.

To keep up with growing demand for this versatile grain, growers became commercialized during the 1800s.

They were aided by the development of the mechanical planter and other farm machinery. In 1870 U.S. corn production topped one billion bushels for the first time. This figure doubled in the next 15 years so that in 1885 production stood at two billion bushels. Still, more uses for corn were yet to be found. By the end of the nineteenth century corn would be mixed with oats to produce a superior feed for livestock. It was also added to pancake mix. Corn was made into flakes in a breakfast cereal introduced by American physician and entrepreneur John H. Kellogg (1852–1943). Throughout the twentieth century new uses combined with a growing population to produce an ever-increasing demand.

See also: **Aztec, Inca, Kellogg Company, Maya**

CORPORATE RESTRUCTURING

Many companies are more successful that their rivals because they are able to take advantage of new technology and produce, market, and distribute their products quicker and more cheaply than their rivals. They are able to provide services and products more efficiently. Conversely, companies that have failed to incorporate these improvements have lost the ability to compete effectively, resulting in losses in market share and profit margin. These companies must reorganize the way they do business in order to raise quality, lower costs and speed the production of their product. This process of reorganization is called restructuring. Parts of the company that are not profitable or not necessary to the principal business are sold or closed down, with the proceeds used to invest in improvements in the core business.

These improvements commonly involve increased automation and better, more efficient organization and processes, often resulting in the elimination of jobs. The combination of spinning off non-core businesses and reducing employment is referred to as "downsizing," or "right-sizing." In fact, the operative factor is often improved skill matching, where people with outmoded job skills are replaced by people with skills that are better matched to new business processes. This typically means workforce reduction as new, more efficient processes allow consolidation of job functions. During the 1980s, many companies in service and manufacturing sectors restructured in response to increased competition, both from within the domestic economy and from foreign competitors able to enter new markets because of the progressive removal of trade barriers.

CORPORATION

Along with sole proprietorships and partnerships, corporations were one of the three basic ways of organizing a business. Virtually all of the largest and most powerful businesses in the United States were corporations, and thousands of many very small businesses were as well.

Corporations had specific legal rights and characteristics that made them ideal for engaging in major economic enterprises. The owners of a corporation were not legally liable for more than their own investment in the corporation. In contrast, if the business of a sole proprietor accumulated massive debts the proprietor was personally, legally responsible for all of them. Corporations were thus also known as "limited liability companies." The corporation also did not have to reincorporate or legally reorganize itself every time one of its owners transferred his or her ownership. The buying, selling, and transferring of the ownership shares (called stock) in a corporation did not affect the corporation's legal identity. More, a corporation was a legal "person" in the sense that it could establish contracts, sue (and be sued), and own property just like an individual person. Finally, a corporation would continue to exist even if all the people who originally incorporated it died or ceased to participate in it. Corporations could raise huge amounts of capital by "going public," that is, selling ownership shares to anyone who wanted them. However, even private corporations, owned by only a small group of people (sometimes a family), enjoyed tax advantages that made incorporating an efficient way to organize a business.

The first U.S. corporations began to appear in the early nineteenth century and represented a new version of three older types of business organization: the joint stock company, the monopoly chartered by a monarch, and the medieval corporation (such as universities and trade guilds). The growing American economy needed large, financially strong organizations to build expensive highways, canals, and railroads. At first, individual states issued thousands of special "charters" to establish these new corporations. After the American Civil War (1861–65), states began to compete with each other to attract corporations by writing incorporation laws that offered corporations an increasingly generous range of powers and advantages. Beginning with the Sherman Anti-Trust Act in 1890 the federal government successfully curtailed the power of the big corporations. A century later, this consumer protection process against the corporation was enacted again when the U.S. government sued Microsoft Corporation for "monopolistic" practices.

See also: **Civil War (Economic Impact of), Microsoft, Monopolies, Sherman Anti-Trust Act**

COST OF LIVING INDEX

The Cost of Living Index is a term used to describe a method by which the government measures the rise and fall of prices in the economy. Such measures are important because much government policy, such as the amount paid to senior citizens in Social Security checks, is adjusted according to changes in the cost of living. The Consumer Price Index (CPI), known informally as the cost of living index, is the best known of the government's measures of price changes. The CPI is calculated by tracking changes in the price of a set of consumer items (such as gasoline, housing, dairy products, clothing, etc). The average price increase or decrease for this list is expressed in terms of a percentage change; for example, "the cost-of-living index rose two percent last year" means that consumer prices, on average, rose by two percent. The index is designed to reflect, as realistically as possible, the actual price changes that households face in daily life.

Since a process of steadily rising prices is known as inflation, the rate of change in the CPI is often called the inflation rate. The CPI is one of the most closely watched of all economic indicators. The CPI is the basis for calculating changes in many types of benefit payments, such as pensions. In addition, the government uses the CPI to help set economic policy. A sharply rising CPI may lead the government to restrain economic growth, either by raising taxes or raising interest rates. A very low CPI, in turn, means that inflation remains in check, and the government may decide to stimulate economic activity by cutting taxes or lowering interest rates.

Economists debate how accurately the CPI measures price changes. Some economists contend that the CPI may be somewhat inaccurate because, they argue, it may put too much emphasis on some consumer items, such as milk or gasoline, or not enough on others, such as computers or movie tickets. It is also important to note that the CPI probably will not reflect the experience of any one family. A family that is very careful about how it shops may have a lower cost-of-living index than a family that pays little heed to price changes.

The government agency that calculates the CPI is the Bureau of Labor Statistics. The CPI is issued monthly.

See also: **Consumer Price Index, Inflation, Price**

COTTON GIN

American inventor Eli Whitney (1765–1825) is credited with developing the cotton gin, a machine that removes cottonseeds from cotton fibers. A simple cotton gin (called the *churka*) dates back to ancient India (300 B.C.). But Whitney's gin would prove to be far superior. In 1792 Whitney, who had recently graduated from Yale University, was visiting the Georgia plantation owned by Katherine Greene, widow of American Revolution hero General Nathaniel Greene (1742–1786). Whitney observed that short-staple (or upland) cotton, which has green seeds that are difficult to separate from the fiber, differs from long-staple (also called Sea Island) cotton, which has black seeds that are easily removed. The latter was the staple of American commerce at the time.

In 1793 Whitney, who is described as a mechanical genius, completed an invention that could be used to clean bolls of short-staple cotton of their seeds. He patented it the next year. The machine worked by turning a crank, which caused a cylinder covered with wire teeth to revolve; the teeth pulled the cotton fiber, carrying it through slots in the cylinder as it revolved; since the slots were too small for the seeds, they were left behind; a roller with brushes then removed the fibers from the wire teeth.

The cotton gin revolutionized the American textile industry which was then but a fledgling concern. The increase in the production of processed cotton was phenomenal. One large gin could process fifty times the cotton that a (slave) laborer could in a day. Soon plantations and farms were supplying huge amounts of cotton to textile mills in England and in the Northeast of the United States where in 1790 another inventor, British-born industrialist Samuel Slater, had built the first successful American water-powered machines for spinning cotton cloth. Together the inventions founded the American cotton industry. Whitney struggled to protect his patent. His problem was getting Southern courts to enforce his patent. The courts, dominated by plantation interests, refused in every case to uphold his patent.

For the southern slaves, Whitney's invention was a disaster. Prior to the invention of the cotton gin a consensus had prevailed that slavery would fade away.

There were the moral objections to slavery (which, however, for the first 250 years of its existence in colonial and early republican America, never seemed to be quite persuasive enough to put an end to it). But there was also the fact that slavery was inefficient when applied to most kinds of agriculture or skilled production. Cotton, however, was a labor-intensive crop requiring large gangs of workers moving through the fields at different times in the growing cycle, planting, hoeing, and harvesting. With the invention of the "gin," cotton suddenly became a highly profitable cash crop. Although the Constitution had stipulated that the importation of slaves would end in 1808, now the price of slaves rose and the slave system was reinvigorated at the very time when it was being outlawed in most of the rest of the world.

See also: **King Cotton, Samuel Slater, Slavery, Textile Industry**

COUGHLIN, CHARLES EDWARD

Charles Edward Coughlin (1891–1979) is not a household name in the later part of the twentieth century, when talk radio has taken on such a prominent role in public discourse. But from 1926 to 1940, this name was well known as a radio voice with a mission. A Roman Catholic priest first, radio personality second, and political activist third, Charles Edward Coughlin was a pioneer in radio talk who used the medium to promote his church, his religious beliefs, and his political agenda.

Born on October 25, 1891, in Hamilton, Ontario, Canada, Coughlin was educated at Catholic schools and at St. Michael's College of the University of Toronto. He was ordained a priest in the Roman Catholic Church in 1916, and was assigned to assist parishes in the Detroit, Michigan, area. Coughlin was made a full parish priest (i.e. incardinated) by the Detroit diocese in 1923. In 1926 he was assigned his own church, the new Shrine of the Little Flower in Royal Oak, Michigan. Coughlin set about building the new parish by publicizing it. He began broadcasting a weekly show of religious topics over the local radio station, which proved to be widely popular, and within four years the show was picked up by the Columbia Broadcasting System (CBS) for national play.

Coughlin began his radio career speaking entirely on spiritual and religious matters. But by 1930 he spoke out strongly against communism. His denunciations gained him a reputation and earned him an

A cotton gin.

appearance before the Committee to Investigate Communist Activities of the U.S. House of Representatives. The Great Depression (1929–1939) had begun by the end of 1930, however, and Coughlin's attention over the air waves turned to matters of poverty and despair.

"The radio priest," as he was known, addressed social problems through the years of the Great Depression, and he attacked Bolshevism and socialism as enemies of social justice. His constant attacks on the Hoover administration (1929–1933) and other controversial subjects in his broadcasts caused CBS to discontinue them in 1931. Coughlin then put together an independent broadcast network that eventually grew to 26 stations.

Coughlin championed Franklin D. Roosevelt (1933–1945) in the presidential election of 1932, calling the choice "Roosevelt or ruin." In turn, Roosevelt cultivated Coughlin's support but did so without embracing the politics of the priest. Coughlin advocated a program for altering American capitalism keyed to monetary inflation, which was based upon a late nineteenth century Papal encyclical, *Rerum novarum*. When Roosevelt refused to fully accept his ideas, however, Coughlin turned on Roosevelt and became a bitter critic.

Coughlin formed the National Union for Social Justice in 1934, an organization dedicated to combating communism and fighting for currency inflation and government control of big business. By 1936 Coughlin's animosity towards Roosevelt had grown to the point that he not only actively spoke out against his reelection, but also made his National Union for Social Justice the nucleus for the Union Party, an independent opposition party. The Union Party, inheritors of the followings of the late Huey P. Long (1893–1935) and Francis E. Townsend (1867–1960), polled fewer than 900,000 votes in Roosevelt's landslide victory in 1936. The National Union died with the election.

Charles Coughlin's influence declined over the next several years. He established a magazine, *Social Justice*, which ran from 1936 to 1942. He organized a new vehicle for his ideas, the Christian Front, and publicly pushed for his program and opposition to Roosevelt. As the 1930s wore on, however, Coughlin concentrated more and more on Communists and Jews as the source of societal and economic problems. Eventually, his rhetoric embraced a program that was anti-Semitic and fascist. He advocated a corporate state under which most political institutions would be demolished.

Coughlin's controversial attitudes split the Catholic populace. In 1940 the larger radio stations in Coughlin's network of affiliates did not renew his contract. When he refused to moderate his positions against the government following Pearl Harbor in

> The great betrayer and liar, Franklin D. Roosevelt, who promised to drive the money changers from the temple, had succeeded [only] in driving the farmers from their homesteads and the citizens from their homes in the cities. . . I ask you to purge the man who claims to be a Democrat, from the Democratic Party, and I mean Franklin Double-Crossing Roosevelt.
>
> **Father Charles Coughlin, 1936**

World War II (1939–1945), his bishop officially silenced him. The U.S. Post Office banned his newsletter, and the last of the radio stations quit broadcasting his program. Still the good priest, Coughlin pulled back his activities to focus on the duties of running the parish.

For the remainder of his days, Coughlin accepted his less outspoken position and was effectively silenced. From the high days of his radio program, when he had to hire one hundred clerks to answer his mail and tabulate contributions, he remained the parish priest of the Shrine of the Little Flower until his retirement in 1966. From then until he died on October 27, 1979, he tended his home in Birmingham, Michigan, and wrote pamphlets denouncing Communism. A fiery, vibrant, and opinionated priest, he ultimately followed the orders of his church and restrained his own opinions.

See also: **Communism, Socialism**

FURTHER READING

Bowden, Henry Warner. *Dictionary of American Religious Biography.* 2d ed. Westport, Connecticut: Greenwood Press, 1993, s.v. "Coughlin, Charles."

Brinkley, Alan. *Voices of Protest: Huey Long, Father Coughlin and the Great Depression.* New York: Knopf, 1982.

Encyclopedia of World Biography. 2d ed. Detroit: Gale Research, 1998, s.v. "Coughlin, Charles."

Kyvig, David E. *Worldbook Multimedia Encyclopedia.* Chicago: World Book, Inc., 1998, s.v. "Coughlin, Charles."

Marcus, Sheldon. *Father Coughlin: The Tumultuous Life of the Priest of the Little Flower.* Boston: Little, Brown, 1973.

Tull, Charles J. *Father Coughlin and the New Deal.* Syracuse: Syracuse University Press, 1965.

COUNCIL OF NATIONAL DEFENSE

Council of National Defense (CND) was an executive branch committee charged with the duty of inventorying the nation's resources and reporting its findings and recommendations to the president during World War I (1914–1918). CND was required to appoint a seven-member advisory commission to carry out its functions. Later known as the National Defense Advisory Commission, this federal body was composed of cabinet members, industry executives, and labor leaders. They were asked to apply their specialized knowledge in mobilizing the military, governmental, commercial, and civilian sectors into a cooperative group aimed at bolstering the Allied cause through the exchange of information and materials. CND was established by the National Defense Act of 1916 during the presidency of Woodrow Wilson (1856–1924). Critics complained that CND lacked a clear mandate and was devoid of formal authority. Wilson, however, relied on CND in deciding how to allocate fairly scarce and valuable resources between the civilian and military production sectors. CND was briefly revived by President Franklin Roosevelt (1882–1945) in 1940 before it was replaced by the Office of Production Management in 1941, as the U.S. prepared to enter World War II (1939–1945).

See also: **World War I**

COVERED WAGON

The covered wagon came to symbolize America's pioneer days. (The term was in use by 1745.) It consisted of a wooden wagon with a canvas top, which was supported by a frame of either wood or metal. Depending on size and cargo, the wagon was pulled by one team or several teams of horses, oxen, or mules. Pioneers relied on their covered wagons for shelter during long cross-country journeys. Another name for the covered wagon was prairie schooner, because the white canvas cover resembled the sails of a ship as it moved slowly across the "sea" of grasslands.

Another type of wagon used during pioneer times was the Conestoga, so named for Pennsylvania's Conestoga Valley, where it was first built during the early 1700s. Alternately called the camel of the prairies, the Conestoga was an *uncovered* wagon, pulled by teams

A family poses with the covered wagon in which they live and travel during their pursuit of a homestead.

of four to six horses. This wagon had wide-rimmed wheels that prevented it from getting stuck in the mud. The wheels could also be removed so that the wagon could be used as a boat or barge. For this reason, the front and back of the Conestoga were built higher than its middle section.

See also: **Westward Expansion**

COW TOWNS

Cow towns were cities that sprang up at railroad terminals in the West. Abilene and Dodge City, Kansas, were two early and celebrated cow towns (also called cattle towns). Beginning in 1867, when the Union Pacific Railroad reached westward as far as Abilene, cowboys began driving large herds of cattle from Texas northward along the Chisholm Trail which were then loaded on trains and transported to markets in the eastern United States.

The cattle industry prospered in the years following the American Civil War (1861–65): demand for beef rose at the same time as large herds of cattle, the offspring of cows and bulls left behind by early Spanish settlers, roamed wild on the open range. Cowboys were hired to protect the herds from mountain lions and rustlers, round them up at the end of grazing season,

and drive them to railheads. At the end of the long trail drive, when the cowboys were paid, many of them went on spending sprees. With inns, saloons, and brothels that catered to the hard-working and free spirited cowboys, the cow towns were rough places. Many legendary lawmen, such as Wyatt Earp (1848–1929) and Wild Bill Hickock (1837–76), earned their fame trying to maintain law and order in the cow towns.

By the mid-1880s, changes on the frontier brought an end to the "Wild West." Settlers used barbed wire to fence in their lands, effectively closing the open range. Railroads also reached into formerly remote locations thereby eliminating the need for cattle drives. The days of the long cattle drives were over. But cow towns continued to prosper as trading posts, serving the interests of farmers and ranchers alike. Many of today's thriving cities in the West grew out of the cow towns of yesterday—including Wichita, Kansas; Fort Worth, Texas; and Cheyenne, Wyoming.

See also: **Barbed Wire, Cowboy, Chisholm Trail, Longhorn Cattle, Open Range, Prairie**

COWBOY

The cowboy, a person who rounded up and "drove" large herds of cattle, figured prominently in U.S. life

Cowboy with lasso working on the Sherman Ranch in Genessee, Kansas.

from the mid-1860s to the mid-1880s. During this 20-year period the cattle industry in the West grew rapidly.

After the Civil War (1861–65) demand for beef increased, and butchers in the East and North were willing to pay handsomely for it. At the same time, large herds of cattle, produced by bulls and cows left behind by the early Spanish settlers, roamed freely on the open ranges of Texas. Seeing the business opportunity, cattle ranchers hired cowboys to round up the cattle, brand them (burn the skin with a rancher's mark or symbol), release them again onto the open range, protect them from rustlers, and at the end of the grazing season, round them up. The cowboys then ran a trail drive—guiding the cattle as far as 1,500 miles (2,400 kilometers) to the nearest railhead, where the animals were loaded into railcars and transported eastward. The train terminals at Abilene and Dodge City, Kansas, made those cities into "cow towns," frontier boom towns of the cattle industry.

By 1870 cattle ranches had spread northward into present-day Kansas, Colorado, Wyoming, South Dakota, North Dakota, and Montana. Between 1860 and 1880, the cattle population in these areas increased from 130,000 to 4.5 million. Where the cattle went, so did the cowboys, conducting roundups twice a year. Though there were probably no more than 100,000 cowboys (also called cowpokes or cowhands) in the West, they captured the American imagination and came to symbolize the days of the "Wild West." (As many as 25 percent of the mounted cowboys were African Americans.) The innovation of barbed wire (1874) allowed ranchers to fence in their lands, and by the 1880s the railroads reached into previously remote

areas. The long cattle drives became a thing of the past and the need for cowboys declined.

See also: **Cow Towns, Barbed Wire, Open Range, Chisholm Trail, Prairie, Longhorn Cattle**

COXEY, JACOB SECHLER

Jacob Sechler Coxey (1854–1951) was a successful manufacturer and unusual reform leader. An advocate of pure paper currency and a champion for the unemployed, he was perhaps best known for organizing "Coxey's Army" of unemployed men to march on Washington, DC, in the first public protest of its kind.

Jacob Coxey was born on April 16, 1854 in Selinsgrove, Pennsylvania, the son of Thomas and Mary Sechler Coxey. His father worked as a sawmill engineer. When Jacob Coxey was six years old, the Coxey family moved to Danville, Pennsylvania, where the boy went to school. Coxey quit school at age fifteen to work in an iron mill as a stationary engineer. In 1878, at the age of 24, he started his own business as a scrap iron dealer. He moved to Massillon, Ohio, in 1881 and opened a sandstone quarrying factory. This business supported Coxey and his family, while the proceeds allowed him to pursue a second career in politics.

In 1877 Coxey joined the Greenback Party, which supported the idea of switching to a pure paper (green back) currency as opposed to one based on gold or silver. Coxey was a firm supporter of monetary reform, declaring that "the government should not only coin money but issue it and get it direct to the people without the intervention of banks." In 1885 Coxey ran unsuccessfully as a Greenback candidate for the Ohio State Senate.

Coxey's politics combined many of the ideas that were being pursued separately by the Greenbacks, Populists, and labor groups. Coxey believed that the combination of these ideas would restore the country to prosperity. He specifically supported a more plentiful currency, public works projects in cities, better transportation in rural areas, and jobs for the unemployed.

Following the financial panic of 1893 Coxey called for government investment in public works projects such as road-building. He particularly wanted Congress to adopt two bills. The first was the Good Roads Bill, which would require the government to issue $500 million of legal tender currency to improve county roads. The second was the Non-Interest-Bearing Bond Bill, which allowed any government body to obtain funds for public works through the issuance of bonds without interest. In addition, both bills required the government to employ any unemployed man who applied for a position, at a minimum wage of $1.50 per day, to work on these projects.

Coxey's ideals affected him personally when he was forced to lay off 40 laborers from his company. He then decided to become an advocate for the unemployed. Coxey joined forces with Carl Browne, a former radical politician and cartoonist from California. While Coxey was said to be soft-spoken and quiet, Browne was a flamboyant and eccentric character who dressed like Buffalo Bill. Together the two reformers organized a group of unemployed men to march across Ohio, Pennsylvania, and Maryland, to the capitol in Washington, DC, in an attempt to bring attention to their plight. "Coxey's Army" consisted of about 100 men when they left Ohio on Easter Sunday, March 25, 1894. When they arrived in Washington, DC, on May 1 that same year there were approximately 500 men. Coxey was not granted an audience with President Grover Cleveland (1885–1889, 1893–1897) but instead was arrested. Though Coxey did not succeed in his mission, he did introduce a new form of public protest—the march.

Despite this disappointment, Coxey continued to fight for his causes. In 1894 he ran unsuccessfully for Congress on the Populist ticket. Three years later he ran for governor of Ohio and was again defeated. In 1914 Coxey led another march on Washington, DC and this time he was allowed to speak to an audience from the Capitol steps. In 1922 he was given the opportunity to speak to President Warren Harding (1921–1923) and he argued for the abolition of the Federal Reserve System, which he believed to be a tool of the banking interests that he opposed.

Coxey continued to pursue political office in the early 1900s, running unsuccessfully for Congress, Senate, and President. He finally won a position as mayor of Massillon, Ohio in 1931, but lost his reelection bid in 1934. On the 50th anniversary of his first march on Washington, DC, May Day 1944, the 90-year-old Coxey was again given the opportunity to address a crowd from Capitol Hill. He died on May 18, 1951 in Massillon.

See also: **Federal Reserve System, Gold Standard, Greenback Party, Greenbacks, Unemployment**

FURTHER READING

Gustaitis, Joseph. "Coxey's Army." *American History Illustrated*, 29, March/April 1994.

Howson, Embrey Bernard. *Jacob Sechler Coxey: A Biography of a Monetary Reformer*. New York: Arno Press, 1982.

Schwantes, Carlos A. *Coxey's Army: An American Odyssey*. Lincoln: University of Nebraska Press, 1985.

Sweeney, Michael S. "The Desire for the Sensational: Coxey's Army and the Argus-eyed Demons of Hell." *Journalism History*, 23, Autumn 1997.

Vincent, Henry. *The Story of the Commonwealth*. New York: Arno Press, 1969.

CREDIT

Credit allowed consumers and borrowers the power to buy something or receive money in exchange for future repayment with added interest. Credit card companies extended credit to consumers that allowed them to be in possession of goods and services before they were paid for. Businesses often purchased their raw materials from other businesses in advance through "trade credit," the most common form of short-term credit.

Credit was extended by individuals, businesses, and governments to pay for a variety of projects or purchases. The provision of credit generated debt that had to be repaid within a specified period of time. To protect themselves from the risk that a borrower might never repay, credit lenders charged the borrower interest. Commercial banks were the most important source of credit in the United States; they had the power to expand the amount of credit available in the economy through their willingness to assume the risk of extending credit to individuals and businesses.

In 1913 the Federal Reserve System was given the power to raise or lower the interests rate that determined how "expensive" it was for banks to extend credit. When interest rates were low, banks were more willing to borrow money from the Federal Reserve, which increased the amount of credit they could extend to consumers and businesses.

The amount of credit extended to consumers and businesses grew enormously in the twentieth century. Credit growth was fueled by the introduction of the credit card and the adoption of sophisticated "credit scoring" techniques that helped lenders analyze the creditworthiness of borrowers. To help fund World War II (1939–1945) and the Korean War (1950–1953), the Federal Reserve imposed "selective controls" on the amount of credit that could be offered to consumers. However by the 1990s the willingness of U.S. lenders to extend credit and of consumers to take on credit debt created a credit crisis. In 1996 a record 1.35 million U.S. citizens filed for bankruptcy, and by mid-1996 U.S. credit card balances had reached $444 billion.

See also: **Federal Reserve System**

CREDIT UNION

Credit unions were not-for-profit financial institutions formed by people who, joined by a common interest, pooled their savings and made loans to each other at below market rates. There were three fundamental differences between credit unions and savings and loan associations. First, credit union members usually worked at the same company, lived in the same community, or belonged to some other common organization, like a church. The second difference was that the money that credit unions loaned was generally used for prudent, short-term consumer loans, such as medical procedures, car purchases, emergencies, or home improvements. Finally because credit unions were based on the notion that their members shared community ties, they took a more flexible, personal approach to evaluating the creditworthiness of those they loaned to.

The first credit unions appeared in Germany in the middle of the nineteenth century, but it wasn't until 1909 that the first credit union was established in the United States. In that year a credit union opened in Manchester, New Hampshire, and Boston businessman Edward Filene successfully convinced his state legislature to legalize credit unions in Massachusetts. In 1921 Filene founded the Credit Bureau National Extension Bureau (CBNEB) to promote credit union expansion nationwide.

The CBNEB was replaced in 1934 by the Credit Union National Association, and 41 of the 48 U.S. states made it legal to operate credit unions. In the same year the Federal Credit Union Act made it possible for credit unions to be established anywhere in the United States, and by 1969 there were almost 24,000 credit unions nationwide.

In 1970 two federal agencies helped to further legitimized the credit union industry. The National Credit Union Share Insurance Act extended federal deposit insurance coverage to include credit union assets. The National Credit Union Administration was also established to regulate the credit union industry.

Following federal moves to strengthen public trust in credit unions, the number of U.S. credit unions dwindled as smaller unions consolidated to offer more services. Nevertheless, the number of individual credit union members increased. By 1999 credit union membership in the United States had climbed to more than 72 million.

See also: **Savings and Loan Association**

CROLY, HERBERT

Herbert Croly (1869–1930) was a writer and editor best known for founding the politically influential journal called the *New Republic*. The magazine became the voice of the "New Nationalism" and was instrumental in delaying the entry of the United States into World War I (1914–1918). Croly also wrote books outlining his views for a strong central government.

Herbert Croly was born January 23, 1869 in New York City to a family of writers. His mother, Jane Cunningham Croly, was a successful writer and editor, and his father, David Croly, was an abolitionist and editor for the *New York Daily Graphic*. The Crolys sought a good education for their son. Herbert Croly first attended J.H. Morse's English, Classical, and Mathematical School for Boys. At the age of fifteen he enrolled in the City College of New York. Two years later Croly moved to Cambridge, Massachusetts, to attend Harvard University. His success at Harvard was mixed, and he was enrolled there on and off for fourteen years.

In 1888 Croly left school to work as his father's secretary. He then took a job as the editor of the *Real Estate Record and Guide*, a magazine issued to help real estate agents keep up with the rapid changes occurring in New York. Three years later, Croly switched jobs to work on the staff of the *Architectural Record*. In the same year, Croly married Louise Emory, the daughter of a moderately wealthy family. Croly returned to Harvard in 1892, where his studies were interrupted when he suffered a nervous breakdown. He and his wife then traveled to Europe for a year so that Croly could recover. He returned to Harvard again in 1895, studying philosophy. His classes introduced him to inspiring thinkers, such as psychologist William James and educational philosopher John Dewey, whose ideas would later influence Croly's writings.

In 1899 Croly again left Harvard to edit the *Architectural Record*. He demoted himself to associate editor in 1906 and worked part time so that he could write a book about his views on society and politics. The late 1800s were a time of great change as the United States became an industrialized society. Croly believed that the growth of big business needed to be guided by the government, and he supported a system with a strong and organized federal government. By 1909 Croly had written a 450-page book, *The Promise of America*, outlining his views on U.S. history. Croly explained in his book his belief that the years between the war of the American Revolution (1775–1783) and the American Civil War (1861–1865) were dominated by a pioneering spirit. When the wild frontier began to disappear people in the United States began to search for ways to put their country and their lives in order. As the country grew it was difficult for U.S. citizens to protect their interests under the weak central governments of Presidents Thomas Jefferson (1801–1809) and Andrew Jackson (1829–1837). The promise of America was being threatened by the closing of the frontier, powerful corporations, organized labor, and the growing role of the United States in world politics. The answer to this problem was a revival of U.S. nationalism and a government that served the people. A strong government would ensure that big business served national interests, preserve international peace, and redistribute wealth equitably among U.S. citizens.

While Croly's book was not a bestseller, it appealed to a number of intellectuals and politicians, including President Theodore Roosevelt 1901–1909). Roosevelt's ''New Nationalism'' reforms were strongly influenced by Croly's work. Due to the book's success, Croly was finally awarded a Bachelor of Arts from Harvard in 1910. Four years later, Croly joined Willard and Dorothy Straight in the creation of a new magazine dedicated to exploring the ideas outlined in Croly's book. Croly became the editor of the *New Republic*, which published its first edition on November 7, 1914, the day World War I began in Europe. Croly hired talented writers such as Walter Weyl, Walter Lippmann, and Felix Frankfurter, who were already well known champions of socialism. The provocative journal was an instant success and circulation reached 40,000 by the end of World War I.

Croly and the magazine became strong supporters of Woodrow Wilson's (1913–1921) presidency, and the magazine influenced Wilson's decision to delay the United States' entry into World War I. Despite this rapport with the president, Croly, in an editorial published by the magazine, denounced the Treaty of Versailles, which ended the war. This controversial position cost the *New Republic* half of its circulation.

Croly became very pessimistic about the policies and economy of the United States after World War I.

He eventually left the *New Republic* to write independently and became a political advisor. In the last years of his life Croly moved away from politics altogether and devoted his final years to studying religious and metaphysical questions. He died on May 17, 1930.

See also: **Publishing Industry, Socialism**

FURTHER READING

Dorreboom, Iris. *The Challenge of Our Time: Woodrow Wilson, Herbert Croly, Randolph Bourne and the Making of Modern America.* Amsterdam: Rodopi, 1991.

Levy, David W. *Herbert Croly of the New Republic: The Life and Thought of an American Progressive.* Princeton, New Jersey: Princeton University Press, 1985.

O'Leary, Kevin C. ''Herbert Croly and Progressive Democracy.'' *Polity*, 26, Summer 1994.

Pearson, Sidney A. ''Herbert Croly and Liberal Democracy.'' *Society*, 35, July/August 1998.

Stettner, Edward A. *Shaping Modern Liberalism: Herbert Croly and Progressive Thought.* Lawrence, Kansas: University Press of Kansas, 1993.

CROSS OF GOLD SPEECH

William Jennings Bryan (1860–1925), a populist firebrand, delivered his famous ''Cross of Gold'' speech at the Democratic Party's national convention held in Chicago in1896. The convention went on to nominate Bryan as the Democratic candidate for president. Bryan's speech, in which he declared that advocates of hard money should not be allowed to ''crucify mankind upon a cross of gold,'' was a dramatic expression of one of the central battles in the political history of the United States. The confrontation between hard and soft money proponents reached back to the American Revolution (1775–1783) and followed in large measure regional and class lines. By 1896, the clash over monetary policy had become one of the central issues in the presidential campaign.

Hard money proponents believed U.S. currency should be backed by the gold standard in the interest of economic security and stability. For this group, government debt and inflationary policies debased the currency and undermined confidence in the economy, leading to the flight of capital. The gold standard, which theoretically limited the amount of money in circulation to the supply of gold, restrained the power

> Having behind us the producing masses of this nation and the world, supported by the commercial interests, the laboring interests and the toilers everywhere, we will answer their demand for a gold standard by saying to them: You shall not press down upon the brow of labor this crown of thorns, you shall not crucify mankind upon a cross of gold.
>
> **William Jennings Bryan, Democratic Presidential Candidate, "Cross of Gold" Speech, 1896**

of government and of banks to trigger inflation with excessive emissions of paper money.

Bryan and other advocates of the free coinage of silver, or a "soft money" policy, believed that moderate inflation was not an economic evil but a vital boost to economic development. Indeed, in the context of 1896, Bryan and his followers argued that an increase in the supply of money, based on the unlimited coinage of silver at a ratio to gold of 16 to 1, was necessary medicine for the depressed economy after the Panic of 1893.

On the presidential stump in 1896, Bryan continually hammered at the monetary issue, portraying eastern stockbrokers, industrialists, and bankers as dangerous opponents of farming and labor interests. Bryan's brand of class warfare created a split in the Democratic Party. Although western and southern Democrats believed an increase in the money supply would eliminate the scourge of low agricultural prices, eastern "gold" Democrats were appalled by Bryan's rhetoric and position on silver. Many Democrats, including former president Grover Cleveland (1885–1897), refused to campaign on behalf of Bryan.

Although Bryan campaigned tirelessly and effectively, his Republican opponent, William McKinley (1897–1901), carried the day, with 7,036,000 popular votes to Bryan's 6,468,000 votes. Bryan's loss was not completely due to business and financial interests lining up solidly against him. Farming interests also voted for McKinley in large numbers, particularly in those states not severely affected by the agricultural depression, such as Michigan and Wisconsin. Most of the labor vote also voted Republican, impressed by McKinley's honesty and his long record of supporting the rights of industrial workers. While governor of Ohio, McKinley supported the arbitration of industrial disputes and upheld a law fining employers who prevented their workers from joining unions.

With their defeat in the election of 1896, the advocates of free silver faded in significance. Ironically, new gold discoveries in Alaska and South Africa, as well as new extraction techniques, led to a dramatic expansion of the money supply in the United States.

FURTHER READING

Ashby, LeRoy. *William Jennings Bryan: Champion of Democracy*. Boston: Twayne Publishers, 1987.

Cherny, Robert. *A Righteous Cause: The Life of William Jennings Bryan*. Tulsa: University of Oklahoma Press, 1994.

Glad, Paul W. *William Jennings Bryan and His Democracy, 1896–1912*. Westport: Greenwood Press, 1960.

Koenig, Louis. *A Political Biography of William Jennings Bryan*. New York: Putnam, 1971.

Werner, M. R. *William Jennings Bryan*. New York: Chelsea House, 1983.

CUMBERLAND GAP

The Cumberland Gap is a mountain pass in Claiborne County, northeastern Tennessee near the intersection with Kentucky and North Carolina. A natural low spot in the Cumberland Plateau range of the Appalachian Mountains, the gap rises only to 1,650 feet (500 meters). The gap was first discovered by European Americans in 1750 when land speculator and explorer Thomas Walker (1715–94) led a party to survey lands in the west. The Wilderness Road, forged between 1761 and 1771 by American pioneer Daniel Boone (c. 1734–1820), ran through Cumberland Gap. The gap became a strategic military objective for both sides during the American Civil War (1861–65). Today it is a National Historic Park.

See also: **Appalachian Mountains, Back Country, Daniel Boone, National Road, Wilderness Road**

CURRENCY

Currency refers to money in any form, either paper or coin, as long as it is in "current" use to pay for goods and services. Although it may have collector's value, money that is no longer accepted for payment, such as coins from ancient Rome, is no longer considered currency. Economists sometimes use the term currency in various specialized ways. A reserve currency, for example, is any medium of exchange, such

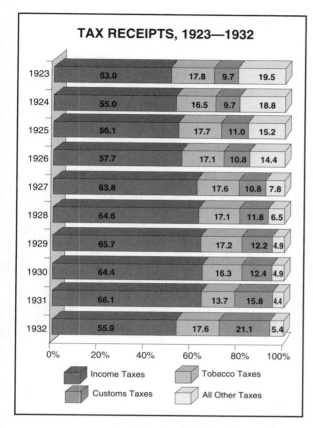

TAX RECEIPTS, 1923—1932

Year	Income Taxes	Customs Taxes	Tobacco Taxes	All Other Taxes
1923	53.0	17.8	9.7	19.5
1924	55.0	16.5	9.7	18.8
1925	56.1	17.7	11.0	15.2
1926	57.7	17.1	10.8	14.4
1927	63.8	17.6	10.8	7.8
1928	64.6	17.1	11.8	6.5
1929	65.7	17.2	12.2	4.9
1930	64.4	16.3	12.4	4.9
1931	66.1	13.7	15.8	4.4
1932	55.9	17.6	21.1	5.4

Tax receipts from 1923–1932 depicts the percentages of federal revenues collected including customs taxes. The custom tax is a charge collected by the federal government on goods brought into the U.S. from other countries.

as gold, that is used for settlement of international debts. The U.S. dollar, which serves as currency within the United States, also serves as a reserve currency to settle accounts which arise from trade among many nations.

See also: **Money**

CUSTOM DUTIES

Custom duties are charges or taxes collected by the federal government on goods brought into the United States from other countries. The tax rates are computed as a percentage of the price of the goods.

An agency of the Department of the Treasury, the U.S. Customs Service was established in 1789 to levy and collect custom duties. Prior to the advent of personal income taxes in the 1910s, various duties provided most of the federal government's revenue. In the 1990s the Service administered seven regions in the United States, Puerto Rico, and the Virgin Islands. Within the seven regions there are 300 ports of entry where agents inspect the baggage of all travelers returning from foreign countries. Returning travelers must declare any articles brought in from abroad. "Declare" means to identify and state the dollar value of the article. Amounts up to $400 are exempt from any duty tax. Amounts over $400 incur a duty. An individual may only claim the $400 exemption once every 30 days. Also, the individual's trip abroad must have lasted at least 48 hours. Trips to Mexico or the Virgin Islands do not fall under the 48-hour rule. If the traveler is not able to claim the $400 exemption because of the 30 day period or the 48-hour rule, they can claim a $25 exemption but must pay duties on all values over $25.

Customs prohibits illegal drugs, dangerous weapons, and obscene publications from entry into the United States. Custom duties produced little federal revenue in the 1990s, but they served as an important policing tool in preventing smuggling and enforcement of many federal laws concerning illegal substances.

See also: **Tariffs**

DE-INDUSTRIALIZATION

De-industrialization can be understood as the steady erosion of the industrial base of the United States, especially in the North-Eastern ''fertile crescent'' of heavy industrial investment from Chicago to New England. It is associated both with cheap industrial imports from newly industrialized countries as well as with the ongoing transformation of the maturing economy of the United States itself. The availability of import items (cars, for instance) at lower cost has created intensely competitive conditions for industrial employment in the United States. As the steel plants and automobile factories built in the early twentieth century got older and less efficient, jobs disappeared, and many U.S. blue-collar workers had to seek jobs outside of the traditional, often unionized and high-wage industries. They often found employment in mostly non-union, relatively poorly paying service jobs. In the 1970s, many U.S. corporations began to shut down their plants in high wage areas and relocated them in the newly industrialized, cheap labor areas of South Korea, Hong Kong, Taiwan, and Singapore. Low-skilled workers in U.S. industry have experienced the biggest losses. Workers displaced by foreign competition were forced to seek jobs in lower paying service industries, while industrial production in the United States eroded. De-industrialization, which began in the 1970s, the corporate merger-mania of the 1980s, and government neglect of trade policy all seem to have set the stage for a massive loss of high-paying jobs for millions of U.S. workers during the last three decades of the twentieth century.

See also: **Corporate Restructuring, Rust Belt**

DEBS, EUGENE VICTOR

Eugene V. Debs (1855–1926) was a pioneer labor organizer and five-time Socialist Party candidate for the U.S. Presidency. Debs advocated abolition of child labor, the right of women to vote, unemployment compensation, and a graduated income tax. His proposals were radical in the early twentieth century, but later became standard public policy for both major political parties.

Born on November 5, 1855 in Terre Haute, Indiana, Debs left home at age 14 to work in a railroad shop, where he was paid 50 cents a day for scraping grease and paint from locomotives. He later became a locomotive fireman, and in 1875 Debs helped organize a local lodge of the Brotherhood of Locomotive Firemen. An active union member, he became editor of the association's *Firemen's Magazine* in 1878 and was elected national secretary and treasurer of the union in 1880. He also served as city clerk of Terre Haute from 1879 to 1883 and as a member of the Indiana legislature in 1885.

Early in his career Debs gained recognition as an effective labor organizer. In addition to organizing numerous locals for the Brotherhood of Locomotive Firemen he was an organizer for other railroad-related labor organizations. They included the Brotherhood of Railroad Brakemen, the Switchmen's Mutual Aid Association, the Brotherhood of Railway Carmen, and the Order of Railway Telegraphers. Since these organizations failed to join together in their dealings with management, Debs found a union that would include all railroad workers, the American Railway Union in 1893. He later became its president. Against Debs's advice the new union participated in the Pullman Strike of 1894 in sympathy with Pullman Palace Car workers. One of the most famous strikes in U.S. labor history, it nearly paralyzed commerce in the western half of the nation before it was finally halted by a federal injunction. For his involvement in the strike, Debs was jailed for six months in 1895 in Woodstock, Illinois.

Debs spent much of his prison time reading and was deeply impressed by the works of Karl Marx. He became convinced that no single union could protect the rights of workers. In the presidential election of

1896 he campaigned for the Democratic-Populist candidate William Jennings Bryan, but a year later Debs announced his conversion to socialism.

For the next 30 years Debs was the leading spokesmen for democratic socialism to millions of U.S. citizens. He helped form the Socialist Party of America in 1898 and was its presidential candidate in 1900, 1904, 1908, 1912, and 1920. Debs attracted huge crowds during his energetic campaigns throughout the country; he was an exceptionally effective public speaker, winning wide support through his personal warmth, integrity, and sincerity. His speeches also raised much-needed funds for the Socialist Party. Though he failed to win a large percentage of the vote on election day, the number of people who voted for him was substantial, ranging from 96,000 in 1900 to 915,000 in 1920.

> DEBS ADVOCATED ABOLITION OF CHILD LABOR, THE RIGHT OF WOMEN TO VOTE, UNEMPLOYMENT COMPENSATION, AND A GRADUATED INCOME TAX. HIS PROPOSALS WERE RADICAL IN THE EARLY TWENTIETH CENTURY, BUT LATER BECAME STANDARD PUBLIC POLICY FOR BOTH MAJOR POLITICAL PARTIES.

Debs's writings and speeches spread his ideas far beyond the confines of a relatively minor political party. In 1912 he ran for president against future president Woodrow Wilson (1913–1921), former president Theodore Roosevelt (1901–1909), and incumbent president William Howard Taft (1909–1913). At the time Debs found that both Wilson and Roosevelt were advocating many of the ideas he had introduced in earlier campaigns. In a spontaneous speech after he won the Socialist Party nomination in 1912 he eloquently expressed his underlying philosophy: "When we are in partnership and have stopped clutching each other's throats, when we have stopped enslaving each other, we will stand together, hands clasped, and be friends. We will be brothers and sisters, and we will begin the march to the grandest civilization the human race has ever known." Although he again lost the election, Debs considered the campaign a moral victory.

Instead of running for the presidency in 1916, Debs waged an unsuccessful campaign for Congress. In 1920 he ran for president as a Socialist candidate for the last time. He campaigned from a prison cell where he was serving a 10-year sentence for sedition under the 1917 Espionage Act. His case became a rallying point for those who believed he should be freed as a matter of freedom of speech. He was released from prison by order of President Warren Harding (1921–1923) in 1921, but he never regained his citizenship, which was taken away from him at the time of his sedition conviction. It was restored in 1976, forty years after his death.

Following his release from prison, Debs spent the remaining five years trying to improve his impaired health and attempting to reconstitute the Socialist Party. Yet, in spite of the large and enthusiastic crowds that flocked to hear him, the 1920s was an era of capitalist domination and the Socialist Party was in decline. Although many of his followers had joined the Communist Party, Debs refused to do so because he opposed the Soviet system and its suppression of free speech.

In his final years he concentrated on prison reform, since he had firsthand experience about prison conditions. He also became interested in the trial of Sacco and Vanzetti, two Italian anarchists accused of murder. This case involved heightened public attention towards labor and political radicals. In the summer of 1926 Debs returned to a sanitarium where he had spent extended periods in 1922 and 1924. He died in Elmhurst, Illinois, on October 20, 1926.

See also: **William Jennings Bryan, Labor Movement, Pullman Palace Coach Company, Pullman Strike, Railroad Industry, Socialism, William Howard Taft, Woodrow Wilson**

FURTHER READING

Constantine, J. Robert, ed. *Letters of Eugene V. Debs.* Urbana: University of Illinois Press, 1990.

Constantine, J. Robert. "Eugene V. Debs: An American Paradox." *Monthly Labor Review,* August, 1991.

Debs, Eugene V. *Writings and Speeches of Eugene V. Debs.* New York: Hermitage Press, 1948.

Ginger, Ray. *The Bending Cross: A Biography of Eugene V. Debs.* New Brunswick: Rutgers University Press, 1949.

Salvatore, Nick. *Eugene V. Debs: Citizen and Socialist.* Urbana: University of Illinois Press, 1982.

DEBT

Individuals, businesses, and governments all incur debts, which are amounts owed to others. Household or consumer debt most commonly resulted from auto loans, home equity lines of credit, credit cards, and personal loans.

During the 1990s consumer debt climbed rapidly, rising 20 percent a year between 1993 and 1996 alone.

By the end of 1996 consumers' outstanding credit card debt alone was approaching $500 billion. Given these numbers, it is not surprising that between 1996 and 1997 the number of U.S. citizens filing bankruptcy claims climbed 25 percent—100 percent higher than in 1986.

Large corporations accrued debt in the form of short-term bank loans or longer-term debt like bonds in order to invest in their own futures, use their cash efficiently, or discourage other companies from considering a takeover. U.S. tax law encouraged firms to borrow money by allowing businesses to take tax deductions on the interest payments they make on their debts. When a corporation's debt came due, rather than pay it all off debt was generally rolled over by borrowing new funds—old debt was replaced with new debt.

Like individuals and businesses, governments got into debt when their expenses exceeded their revenues. Throughout U.S. history wars and recessions have been the largest causes of federal debt. The United States began with a $75 million debt that was used to the finance the American Revolution (1775–1783). Since only one quarter of the cost of the American Civil War (1861–1865) was paid using tax revenue, government budget surpluses for several years were used to pay off the $2.7 billion Civil War debt. The next major war, World War I (1914–1918) raised the federal debt to $26 billion, and the tax revenue the government lost because of the Great Depression (1929–1939) raised U.S. debt to $43 billion by 1940. But World War II (1939–1945) expenses dwarfed any public debt in the country's history. Where U.S. debt had never exceeded one third of Gross National Product (GNP) before the war, in 1945 the government's debt exceeded the entire national GNP by 29 percent. For the most part the government remained in debt after the war. It reached crisis proportions in the 1980s, but the government now hopes to retire the debt by 2015 because of cuts in spending and a thriving economy. Although almost all discussions of government debt focused on federal debt, the debt of U.S. state and local governments was also quite large and totaled some $454 trillion by the mid-1980s.

See also: **Credit, Deficit, National Debt**

DEERE, JOHN

With his invention of a practical steel plow John Deere (1804–1886) played a major role in opening up the Midwest in the United States to wide-scale productive agriculture. The pioneers' traditional iron and wood plows were no match for the rich, heavy soil of the Great Plains of the United States. Deere's modern steel plow could cut through the earth with speed and efficiency. As an inventor and manufacturer Deere helped enable the settling of the United States. He brought to the new frontier effective agricultural equipment for the first wave of hard-working productive farmers who populated and settled the wilderness of the newly-founded United States.

Deere was born in 1804 in Rutland, Vermont, the son of a tailor. He spent his boyhood and young adulthood in Middlebury, where he attended school and served a four-year apprenticeship as a blacksmith. In 1825 he became a journeyman blacksmith. His careful workmanship and ingenuity earned him respect throughout western Vermont, and he soon became a financial success as well. When hard times hit the region in the 1830s, Deere decided to leave his wife and family temporarily and venture west.

Deere traveled both overland and by canal and lake boats for several weeks before he arrived in Grand Detour, Illinois. It was a community settled by fellow-Vermonter Major Leonard Andrus and others from his native state. The need for a blacksmith was so great that two days after his arrival in 1836 Deere had built a forge and was busy at work.

Deere quickly realized the iron and wooden plows his customers brought from the East were unsuited to the heavy clay soil they found in the Midwest. The plowing was slow and frustrating because the area's rich soil clung to their plow bottoms, and after short intervals it was necessary to scrape the soil off. Deere set about to invent a new kind of plow to make the most of this fertile but formidable land.

From a broken saw blade, Deere fashioned a curbed plow blade, shaped by bending the material over a log. By 1838 he had made and sold three of these new plows. Continuing to refine his design he produced 10 improved plows in 1839 and 40 in 1840. Unlike other blacksmiths of his day who produced custom-ordered tools Deere went into the business of manufacturing plows before he had orders for them. He was more aggressive in selling them than any of his competitors, and his plows came to be considered the best available.

Deere's first plows had to be produced with whatever he could find at hand. By 1843 he had arranged for a shipment of special rolled steel from England. Shipped across the ocean and then up the Mississippi and Illinois rivers, the steel finally arrived at the little plow factory in Grand Detour by wagon. In 1846, when his annual output had grown to 1,000 plows, the first slab of cast plow steel ever rolled in the United States was

John Deere demonstrating his new plow.

made for Deere. It was shipped from Pittsburgh to Moline, Illinois. Deere moved there in 1847 to take advantage of the Mississippi River's water power and transportation potential.

The John Deere Company was officially organized in Moline in 1857. That year the company produced 10,000 plows that were carried in nearly every covered wagon heading further west across the prairie. The Deere plow became known as the ''singing plow'' because of the high-pitched humming sound it made while slicing through the dirt.

In 1858 Deere took his son Charles into partnership, and in 1868 the firm was incorporated as Deere & Company. The company soon expanded to manufacture cultivators and other agricultural implements. Deere remained president until his death at age 82.

See also: **Mississippi River, Steel Plow**

FURTHER READING

Arnold, Dave. *Vintage John Deere*. Stillwater, OK: Voyageur Press, 1995.

Broehl, Wayne, Jr. *John Deere's Company, a History of Deere and Company and Its Times*. New York: Doubleday, 1984.

Clark, Neil M. *John Deere, He Gave the World the Steel Plow*. Moline: Deere and Co., 1937.

Hofstadter, Richard. *The United States: The History of a Republic*. Englewood Cliffs: Prentice-Hall Pub., 1967.

Louis, Arthur M. ''The Hall of Fame for U.S. business leadership.'' *Fortune*, April 4, 1983.

''The Story of John Deere,'' [cited January 4, 1999] available from the World Wide Web @ www.deere.com/.

DEFENSE SPENDING

Defense spending has become an issue in the twentieth century economy of the United States because of the vastly increased inputs of wealth into modern warfare. The constantly evolving military technology also enhances the impact of war and defense preparedness on the national economy. The ''spin-offs'' of defense-related research and development technology into civilian use is another important aspect of defense spending. To avoid the large costs of war most nations seek to deter aggression, at the first level, by allocating resources for an ongoing minimum military capability, so that the costs to a potential aggressor of starting a war will far exceed any likely gains of aggression. The financial policies that a government uses to conduct war are collectively known as "war finances," a branch of "defense economics." The prime concern of defense spending is to determine what proportion of economic wealth a society must devote to war preparations and what is left over for the civilian sector of the economy. In the nuclear age economists concerned with defense spending have also had to plan for the allocation of resources for the different types of military confrontation that a country may face. Modern defense spending involves planning and weapons-development that pose extremely complex and problematic defense scenarios. For example, planners of defense procurement in the United States must decide how the government should spend its defense dollars. Should it invest on the "Strategic Defense Initiative" (SDI, or "Star wars") anti-missile defense system that was first proposed during Ronald Reagan's presidency? Should it concentrate on conventional warfare, or should it spend its money on counter-terrorism? The answers to these questions will shape the future of defense spending. It will establish the nature of the relationship between the government, the defense industry, and the research apparatus of major universities. It is a relationship that President Dwight Eisenhower (1939–1945) once identified as the emerging "military-industrial complex."

See also: **Military-Industrial Complex**

DEFLATION

Deflation is a general and sustained reduction in the level of prices. It is the opposite of inflation. Falling prices may seem to bring widespread benefits to society, making everything more affordable; in reality, deflation may pose serious dangers. Falling prices are usually a sign that economic activity is slowing down to an alarming degree. That means that companies take in less money and make less profit; therefore, they can hire fewer workers and they may have to lay off those they have. Falling prices also mean that fewer companies will be able to invest in new plants and equipment. Failures to modernize can often hurt companies in the long run. With smaller paychecks, families will buy less, which further dampens economic activity. Extreme examples of deflation, most notably the Great Depression (1929–1939) of the 1930s, have been marked

by hardship and high unemployment. In general, economists prefer that prices neither rise nor fall too quickly; they instead prefer to see prices remain steady over time.

See also: **Inflation, Price**

DELAWARE

Delaware, the second-smallest state in the nation, was once compared by President Thomas Jefferson (1801–1809) to a diamond—small, but highly valued. Through most of its history this diminutive state, located between the Atlantic coast and Delaware Bay, has rivaled many larger states in economic prosperity. This prosperity has largely been associated in the public's mind with the du Pont family, the entrepreneurs who created much of Delaware's wealth in the chemical industry.

Both the Dutch and the Swedes staked out colonies in Delaware in the seventeenth century, but it was the English who took over the colony in 1664. The Duke of York ceded the colony to a proprietor, William Penn (1644–1718), who kept Delaware closely tied to his family and to his beloved Pennsylvania until 1776. Delaware was the first of the new states to ratify the U.S. Constitution in 1787.

When it was still a colony Delaware depended on agriculture. Tobacco was a major crop in the colonial period; it was superseded later by corn, wheat, and peaches. Fishing was also an important economic factor during this period. The industrial development of the state really started with the construction of railroads, the first being the New Castle and Frenchtown Railroad completed in 1832. Finished in 1838 the Philadelphia, Wilmington, and Baltimore Railroad made the industrial development of northern Delaware possible.

By 1900 the population of Wilmington grew dramatically and comprised forty percent of the entire population of the state. Immigrants from Ireland and Germany in the mid-nineteenth century and from southern and eastern Europe in the early twentieth century helped to fuel this population growth and staff the developing industries. While the north developed rapidly the southern portion of the state remained agricultural and largely lacking in economic development. Farmers only gradually began to take advantage of new markets provided by the railroad.

Important Delaware industries in the nineteenth century, mostly centered in Wilmington, included flour and textile mills, shipyards, carriage factories, iron foundries, and morocco leather plants. Shipbuilding in

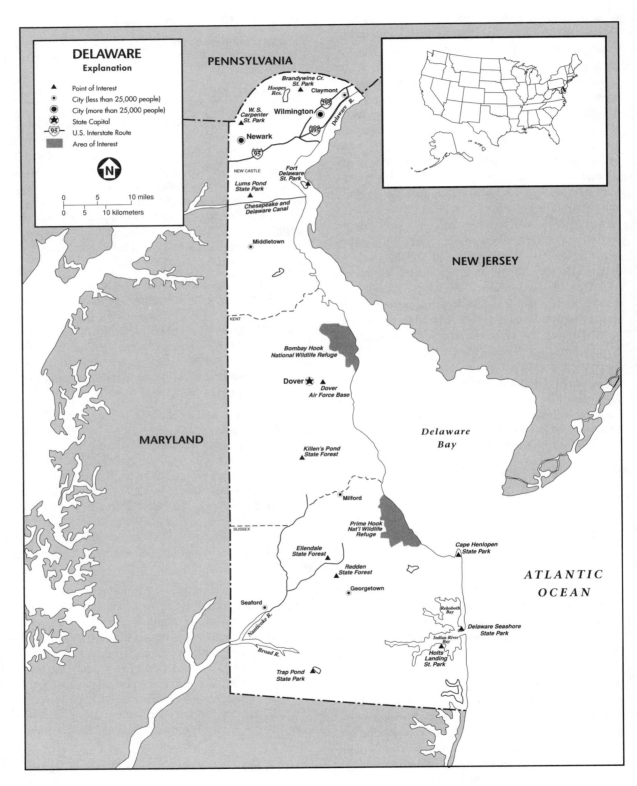

State of Delaware.

particular was a vital force in the economy during this time, with shipyards making wooden sloops, schooners, and fishing boats located in all the port towns along the Delaware and its tributaries.

In 1802 a French immigrantē named Eleuthère I. du Pont, found the right combination of a power source on the Brandywine River, a good location between Philadelphia and New York, and an adequate supply of timber, constructed a mill to produce gunpowder. His family's friendship with then-President Thomas Jefferson helped assure him of government contracts. The area of Wilmington around the Du Pont factory rapidly became a company town, encompassing a large house for the du Pont family, row houses for the workers and even dormitories for single workers and a Sunday school building. Work days were long (averaging 12 hours) and wages, never very high for men, were even lower for women.

Well before the railroad came to Delaware, Philadelphia businessmen saw the need for a better transportation route between Philadelphia and Baltimore. They encouraged the building of the Chesapeake and Delaware Canal, linking the Chesapeake Bay in Maryland with Delaware Bay via the Delaware River, which was completed in 1829. This three-hundred-mile-long canal benefited Delaware by circumventing the longer sea route from Philadelphia to Baltimore. By this time packet steamboats were plying the canal. Big sidewheelers were also a familiar sight along the Delaware.

Around 1900 the Du Pont Company employed only around four hundred people. It was no more important in Wilmington than a number of other companies. After Alfred I. du Pont, a descendant of the founder, along with his cousins T. Coleman du Pont and Pierre S. du Pont, took over the company, it became a major producer of explosives. During World War I (1914–1918) the company supplied nearly 1.5 billion pounds of explosives for the Allies, securing the fortunes of the company and making possible a postwar expansion into the chemicals industry. In the late 1990s Du Pont manufactured a host of products such as gasoline additives, antifreeze, dyes, nylon, and rayon; the company employed 11 percent of Delaware's total work force. It had only one major rival, Dow Chemical.

T. Coleman du Pont was also instrumental in promoting the state's first major highway project, begun in 1911, to connect the southern part of the state with Wilmington. The Du Pont Highway became the hub of a network of highways that eventually crossed the state. The trucking industry soon became a major economic force in the state, making possible a healthy

poultry industry and boosting the grain industry associated with it.

During the 1950s the population of Delaware grew by forty percent. Both the Wilmington area and the state capital of Dover grew, mostly because of its large air base. One of the impacts of the population's rapid growth was that it strained the state's infrastructure and social services. However because chemical plant workers fled to the suburbs, Wilmington proper actually decreased in population by thirteen percent between 1920 and 1960. Industry followed the same path, with a large General Motors and a Chrysler plant appearing in suburban Wilmington and Newark, respectively. Du Pont also located a huge experimental station near the site of the original powder mills, among other facilities. Another major economic impact was the new interstate, I-95, which was built in New Castle County in the 1960s.

Delaware's unique combination of heavy industry and coastal beauty has brought concerns to the fore regarding environmental protection. In 1971 a Coastal Zone Act was passed, outlawing all new heavy industry because it would be incompatible with the coastal environment. In 1979 this law was amended to allow offshore drilling and construction of coastal oil facilities. Environmentalists remain concerned about the dangers posed by oil tankers in Delaware Bay.

The 1980s were good to Delaware, bringing in an era of economic improvement. Unlike most of the rest of the recession-plagued nation, Delaware prospered during this time. In 1988 Delaware's unemployment rate was only 3.3 percent, the second lowest in the country. A 1981 state law raised the usury limits (interest rates allowable for money lending) and lowered taxes for large financial institutions. This encouraged over thirty banks to set themselves up in Delaware, including such large concerns as Chase Manhattan and Manufacturers Hanover. In addition, the state has been friendly to foreign corporations who seek to incorporate in the state. Since 1899 Delaware has also had an unusual law which allows companies to be incorporated and chartered in Delaware even if they actually do no business in the state and have stockholders' meetings elsewhere. Along with the efforts of Delaware Economic Development Office and the Delaware Innovation Fund (a private fund designed to encourage new companies), this law has helped to bring many new businesses to the state.

In the 1990s Du Pont remained the driving force in Delaware's economy, ranking as the tenth largest U.S. industrial corporation, with sales of $39,689 billion in

1997. A number of other sectors were contributing to the state as well. Other manufacturers were also flourishing, such as the Chrysler Corporation and those associated with the food products industry. Tourism was second only to manufacturing in importance, bringing in $836 million in 1993. Some of the most popular tourist venues include Rehoboth Beach on the Atlantic coast and the state's many historic sites.

Not surprisingly, along with its economic success, Delaware faces social welfare problems and other difficulties associated with industrial growth and decay and with urban blight. The state has lagged well behind many others in welfare benefits and has also experienced housing shortages, urban sprawl, and pollution problems. Since the mid-1970s, however, Delaware has maintained a position as one of the nation's most prosperous states. Delaware ranked fifth among all the states in per capita personal income in 1996, with average per capita disposable income at well over $23,000.

See also: **Chrysler Motors, Éleuthère Irénée du Pont, General Motors**

FURTHER READING

Federal Writers Project. *Delaware: A Guide to the First State*. New York: Somerset, 1958.

Hoffecker, Carol E. *Delaware: A Bicentennial History*. New York: Norton, 1977.

Mosley, Leonard. *Blood Relations: The Rise and Fall of Du Ponts of Delaware*. New York: Atheneum, 1980.

Munroe, John A. *History of Delaware*. Newark, DE: University of Delaware Press, 1993.

Vessels, Jane. *Delaware: Small Wonder*. New York: Abrams, 1984.

DELL, MICHAEL

Michael Dell (1965–) started Dell Computer from his dormitory room in 1984, when he was a college freshman. In only 14 years, Dell's revenues zoomed to $12 billion and the company became the third-largest computer maker in the world.

Born in 1965, Michael Dell appeared destined to be an entrepreneur from his early youth. When he was only 12 years old, he worked as a water boy and dishwasher at a Chinese restaurant and saved enough money to start a stamp collection. He turned the collection into $2000 via a stamp-trading enterprise he operated through the mail. In high school, while he worked as a newspaper delivery boy for the *Houston Post*, he expanded his roster of subscription clients by obtaining mailing lists of marriage license applicants. He then mailed personalized letters offering two weeks free service to newlywed couples. The enterprising teenager's paper route made between $18,000 and $20,000, which he used to buy his first BMW.

Dell's parents hoped their son would become a doctor. His father Alexander was an orthodontist. But soon after Dell entered the University of Texas in 1983, he was operating a business adding components to remaindered IBM and IBM-clone computers and selling them for a profit either by mail order or door-to-door on campus.

The summer following his freshman year at Texas, Dell was able to devote his full attention to his rapidly growing computer business. In the final month of his summer vacation he sold $180,000 worth of personal computers and convinced his parents to agree he could quit school. He incorporated his company, PCs Unlimited, and began operating out of a storefront. By the end of 1984, the company's sales reached $6 million.

By early 1985, PCs Unlimited had 30 employees, and in July of that year the company introduced its own computer, the Turbo PC. By the end of its second year of business, company sales reached $34 million. The company was renamed Dell Computer Company in 1987, and went public in 1988. By 1993 sales surpassed $2 billion.

Dell built his business by adhering to a few basic concepts. First, he realized that if he bought parts directly from suppliers and assembled computers himself, he could sell the finished products more cheaply. Dell also eliminated the middleman—the retail dealer—by selling directly to the consumer. This was another way to lower the price of individual units. He advertised in computer trade magazines and established phone numbers that customers could call to order a computer. Competitors scoffed at the idea that prospective buyers would make such a major purchase without first seeing the product. Dell, however, believed that experienced computer users would be comfortable ordering equipment over the phone or through the Internet, and those buyers comprised the market he was seeking to capture. Direct sales also appealed to corporations and government organizations, which comprised 90 percent of Dell's customers.

Dell backed up his direct sales model by guaranteeing that customer service on Dell PCs would be first-rate. He also made a practice of never manufacturing a computer until it had been ordered, thereby eliminating backlogs of unsold merchandise. Finally, because each component ordered indicated a user preference, he used customer orders as an automatic form of market research.

The path of Dell's success was not without its twists and turns. In the early 1990s the company tried to introduce a high-end product, the Olympic, but it proved to have little customer appeal. Dell canceled the line entirely, revamped the way the company approached new products, and used the best of Olympic's new technology in other products. As Dell wrote in his 1999 autobiography, *Direct from Dell*: "Thanks to our customers, we turned a potentially disastrous mistake into a great opportunity, and pushed the company to the forefront of technological development."

After steady growth over 14 quarters, Dell Computer posted two consecutive quarterly losses in 1993. Dell moved quickly to bring in experienced managers to reorganize the company's operations. The company again began to focus on the bottom line. By the end of 1993 Dell Computer was again turning a hefty profit, and in the next three years its revenues grew 50 percent a year. By the end of 1997 (after 16 consecutive quarters of growth in revenues and earnings) the company expanded into the server business to better compete in the corporate market. Michael Dell led his company in an international expansion during the late 1990s.

See also: **Computer Industry**

FURTHER READING

Dell, Michael, and Catherine Fredman. *Direct from Dell*. New York: Harper Business, 1999.

Palmer, Jay. "Selling To Veterans." *Barron's*, March 24, 1997.

1998 Current Biography. New York: H.W. Wilson, 1998, s.v. "Dell, Michael."

"Leadership Experts Explain the Secrets." *Forbes*, April 8, 1996.

"Michael Dell's Plan For the Rest of the Decade." *Fortune*, June 9, 1997.

DEMING, WILLIAM EDWARDS

William Edwards Deming (1900–1993) was largely responsible for introducing quality control to mass production. He developed his management theory while working as an economic consultant in Japan. Eventually his ideas took hold in the United States as well, and many major corporations began to incorporate quality control into their businesses through Deming's teachings.

William Edwards Deming was born October 14, 1900, in Sioux City, Iowa, the oldest son of Pluma Irene and William Albert Deming. When he was young, his family moved to Wyoming, where Deming graduated from high school in 1917. He then enrolled at the University of Wyoming. Deming worked his way through college as a janitor until he graduated in 1921. With a Bachelor of Arts in engineering, Deming started his career teaching mathematics. He taught physics at the Colorado School of Mines, while pursuing a Master of Science at the University of Colorado. He then taught briefly as an assistant in physics before accepting a scholarship to Yale University.

Deming pursued a Ph.D. at Yale and worked summers at the Western Electric plant in Cicero, Illinois. It was during this time that Deming learned the early quality control theories of Walter Shewhart, a physicist at Dell Laboratories. Deming earned his Ph.D. in 1928 and began working for the federal government. For the next 19 years he worked for various branches of the government—as a mathematical physicist for the Department of Agriculture, a lecturer in the National Bureau of Standards, the department head of the Mathematics and Statistics Division of the Department of Agriculture, and the chief mathematician and advisor in sampling and survey techniques for the Bureau of Census.

After World War II (1939–1945) Deming gave up his government career to start his own international consulting firm. His aim was to help war-torn countries rebuild their economies. Deming traveled to such diverse countries as Greece, Turkey, India, West Germany, and Mexico, and he even worked with the United Nations. However, it was in Japan that Deming made his biggest mark.

In Japan, Deming developed and implemented his approach to quality management. He combined Shewhart's statistical theories of controlling quality in mass production with his own thinking to create a specific philosophy for achieving practical quality control. This philosophy stressed cooperation among employees, rather than competition. In addition, it called for a continuous improvement in products and services and the use of statistical measurements to track the quality of products. Deming created what he called a "System of Profound Knowledge," which was a comprehensive theory for management.

Deming is probably best known for his "14 Points for Management." Among other things, this plan encourages leaders to stop doing business based on price alone, to constantly improve the production system, to utilize job training, and to encourage pride in workmanship. Deming also taught management leaders to encourage cooperation at all levels. In addition, he instructed them to assure job stability and to equally value all employees.

Deming is credited for contributing largely to the "Japanese Industrial Miracle," whereby Japan not only recovered from the damages of World War II, but quickly came out ahead as a world economic leader. Deming's teachings were such a great success that he was awarded the Secord Order Medal of the Sacred Treasure by Japanese Emperor Hirohito in 1960. It would, however, take twenty more years for his ideas to take root in his native country. Only in the 1980s, when the United States could no longer ignore Japan's economic successes, did U.S. business become interested in Deming's techniques.

Deming, along with Joseph Juran, launched the Total Quality Management (TQM) movement in corporate America. Deming was hired as a consultant by large companies like Ford, General Motors, Dow Chemical, and Hughes Aircraft, among others. It was Deming's philosophy that influenced Ford Motor Company chairman Donald Peterson to make quality an important part of his corporation, so much so that the company's new slogan became "Quality is Job 1."

Deming was finally recognized for his contributions in the United States in 1987, when he received a special award, the National Medal of Technology, at the White House. The award was in recognition of his determined support of statistical methodology, his contributions to sampling theory, and his advocacy of these methods to corporations. Deming continued to teach his business philosophy until his death in 1993. In that same year, the W. Edwards Deming Institute was founded to continue to teach quality control management to corporations around the world.

FURTHER READING

Aguayo, Rafael. *Dr. Deming: The American Who Taught the Japanese about Quality.* New York: Carol Publishing Group, 1990.

Gabor, Andrea. *The Man Who Discovered Quality: How W. Edwards Deming Brought the Quality Revolution to America.* New York: Times Books/Random House, 1990.

Gluckman, Perry. *Everyday Heroes of the Quality Movement: From Taylor to Deming, the Journey to Higher Productivity.* New York: Dorset House Publishers, 1993.

Scherkenbach, William W. *The Deming Route to Quality and Productivity: Road Maps and Roadblocks.* Washington, DC: CEEP Press Books, 1991.

Tetzeli, Rick. "Quality: A Day in the Life of Ed Deming at 92." *Fortune*, January 11, 1993.

DEPARTMENT STORE

Department stores emerged in the mid-1800s and offered a wide variety of goods for sale in various categories. Many were transformed general stores (which offered a variety of goods but were not divided into departments), while others evolved out of dry goods stores (which sold textiles and related merchandise). The first bona fide department store was established in Paris: the *Bon March* (French, meaning "good bargain") opened its doors in 1838.

Between the 1850s and 1880s, numerous department stores opened in U.S. cities. The department store Jordan Marsh was founded 1851 in Boston, Massachusetts. R.H. Macy's was founded 1858 in New York City and was known for its creative advertisements. Wanamaker's, founded in 1861 in Philadelphia, successfully implemented fixed pricing so that customers no longer haggled over price. Marshall Field was founded in 1881 in Chicago, Illinois, and within twenty-five years it became the world's largest wholesale and retail dry goods store. These pioneer department stores, multi-storied buildings located in downtown areas, introduced many innovations to merchandising, including the policy of returnable or exchangeable goods, ready-made apparel, clearly marked prices, and window displays.

By the early 1900s department stores could be found throughout the country. The timing was right for their emergence: urban centers grew rapidly at the end of the century, giving department stores a ready clientele. Also the advent of the telephone, electric lighting, and billing machines helped retailers conduct business efficiently. Transportation improvements allowed for

Marshall Field's store in Chicago, as it appeared in 1879.

the shipment of large quantities of goods, a variety of finished goods were mass produced (which increased supply and lowering production costs and consumer prices). By the 1910s the stores were part of a new mass culture, which centered in U.S. cities. During the twentieth century, department store sales typically generated between six and twelve percent of total annual retail sales.

See also: **Chain Store, Mail-Order House, Retail Industry**

DEPRECIATION

Economists use the term *depreciation* to refer to the loss of economic value suffered by business assets and equipment, consumer goods, and currency as time passes. The most common use of depreciation in economics is in business tax law. The Internal Revenue Service (IRS) allows businesses to lower the amount of taxes they owe by counting as a business expense the total depreciation of aging equipment and assets over the previous year. For example, if a business bought a photocopier in March, by December it will have declined in value by some amount. To claim this depreciation in value as an expense, the business must first determine the average "life span" of the photocopier, so it will know what percentage of the photocopier's total value has eroded in the past year. The two most common methods for determining how much assets have depreciated were the "straight-line" method and the "declining-balance" or "declining-charge" method.

During World War II (1939–1945), the U.S. government began to allow businesses to "accelerate" the depreciating value of their assets. For example, rather than telling businesses that typewriters had a "life span" of seven years, the IRS allowed businesses to claim that typewriters had a useful life of, say, five years. This meant that businesses could enjoy the tax savings they gained from the declining value of their typewriters in five years rather seven. Speeding up the depreciation of a company's assets in this way gave businesses more money in the short term to invest in expansion and new equipment. Among the first legislation of President Ronald Reagan's (1981–1989) administration was the Economic Recovery Tax Act of 1981, which attempted to encourage companies to expand by shortening the standard five-year depreciation for business assets to three years.

The term depreciation also referred to the decline in value of one currency against another. If one U.S. dollar bought 1.5 German marks one year but only 1.4 marks the next year, the dollar "depreciated" against the mark.

See also: **Appreciation**

DEPRESSION AND WORLD WAR II, 1929–1945 *(OVERVIEW)*

When Herbert Hoover (1929–1933) took the oath of office as president of the United States in March of 1929, he and most Americans were confident that the economic prosperity that had characterized the 1920s would continue indefinitely. Individual income had risen from $480 in 1900 to $681 in 1929. Purchasing power had increased even more as improvements in manufacturing methods and technology brought down prices for many goods. Yet, by the end of 1929, millions of Americans were unemployed and much of the nation's industrial capacity was idle. Hoover's promise that poverty was about to be eliminated from the nation was mocked through the name "Hooverville" attached to the many ramshackle camps of the dispossessed. The nation was mired in the Great Depression (1929–1939), which continued until preparations for World War II (1939–1945) began to revive the economy.

The causes of the Great Depression were complex and rooted in the transition of an economy based on the production of durable goods and building infrastructure to one based on the manufacture and sale of consumer goods. The introduction of a wide range of new consumer products after World War I (1914–1918) helped

Unemployed by the Great Depression, large numbers of people line up for food at a New York City relief kitchen.

end the post-war recession relatively quickly and firmly established the new economy.

Farmers had not shared in the prosperity of the 1920s. They were encouraged to expand production during World War I and had borrowed heavily to bring more land into production and to take advantage of mechanized farm equipment, especially the tractor. This created a problem when the end of the war came almost before the farmers could bring their new land and equipment into full use. As Europe recovered from the devastation of the war farm prices fell, leaving farmers with sizable gaps between their incomes and their expenses.

On the industry front, rising wages for workers during the 1920s were rooted in increasing efficiency. Industrial production increased faster than industrial employment; profits increased even faster. Fewer workers were needed to produce more goods. Much of the wealth created by the new economy was returned to shareholders as stock dividends. While this spurred reinvestment and kept the economy healthy when infrastructure and durable goods were its backbone, the new consumer products-based economy presented a different situation. Surpluses of inventory began to accumulate and many industries began to cut back on production and employment.

A third factor leading to the depression was the increase in consumer debt. For most of U.S. history

debt was seen as a negative thing. Except for a mortgage, most consumers avoided debt and saved for things they needed. The array of new products available during the 1920s, along with the introduction of the installment plan, broke down this traditional resistance to making payments over time and Americans accumulated unprecedented levels of debt.

A fourth factor was the interconnection of the U.S. and European economies. Following World War I the United States began lending money to Germany to facilitate the payment of war reparations. Germany paid England, France, and the other allies, who then repaid their war-time loans from the United States. When the European economies experienced economic crises in the late 1920s the cycle was broken and shortages of capital quickly hit the United States.

The final factor leading up to the depression was the national fascination with the stock market and large-scale speculation with borrowed money. The expansion of industrial production and profits made stocks an attractive investment. New companies (formed to manufacture new products) and established firms that expanded their sales offered very impressive returns on their stocks in the early 1920s. As stock prices rose steadily the market attracted investors who only intended to hold the stock until it turned a profit. The dividends, or actual return on the investment, became secondary to the market itself. The seemingly endless

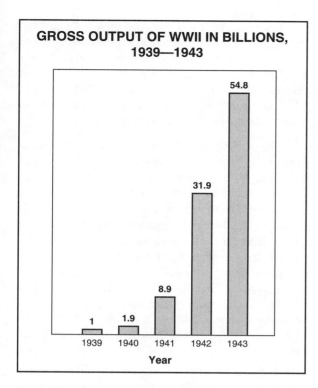

GROSS OUTPUT OF WWII IN BILLIONS, 1939—1943

The significant increase in war output from 1939 to 1943 greatly helped to revive U.S. industrial production, expand agriculture and stimulate the economy.

capacity of the market to rise lured millions of Americans to buy stock on margin, i.e., a credit loan with the promise to pay within a stipulated period, usually 30 days. As long as the stock increased in value everything was fine.

In October 1929 the stock market began to show signs of reversing its long upward trend. Many firms began to experience a decline in or slower growth in profits due to excess inventories caused by slowing sales. Declining stock prices forced those with margin contracts to sell their investments in order to minimize their losses. Stock prices, which had surged upwards steadily for years, now spiraled downward. J.P. Morgan and others tried to stabilize the market, but its crash wiped out many investors. The most serious consequence of the collapse of the stock market was that it became almost impossible for companies to use the sale of stock to raise capital or to cover their short-term needs. Massive layoffs and wholesale closures of plants followed rapidly after the market's collapse.

The economy now spiraled downward, seemingly out of control. Unemployment spread across the nation and banks began to fail as debtors defaulted and depositors withdrew their funds. Within weeks it was clear that the entire nation faced a grave economic crisis.

The Hoover administration did not see the depression as a reason to deviate from its basic economic policies and it attacked the depression with traditional remedies. Federal construction projects were moved ahead of schedule and Hoover urged state and local governments to do the same. The Agricultural Marketing Act was designed to encourage the organization of farm cooperatives to address the farmers' problems. Other federal legislation established the Grain Stabilization Corporation and the Cotton Stabilization Corporation to shore up prices of those key crops. Hoover and his administration tried to keep people's hopes up with frequent predictions of the imminent revival of the U.S. economy.

The Smoot-Hawley Tariff of 1930 raised tariff rates in an effort to promote the purchase of U.S. manufactured goods. By early 1931 there were signs that the economy was on an upward swing and that the Hoover administration's optimism and adherence to traditional policies were about to be vindicated. In March of that year, however, the European economic situation turned from bad to worse. Hurt by the loss of U.S. markets due to Smoot-Hawley and the resulting crisis, Europe's economic problems dragged the fragile U.S. economy down to new depths. A wave of bank failures further eroded public confidence in the economy and dried up sources of financing for businesses. Many individuals lost their life savings when banks failed.

Hoover responded by proposing the formation of the Reconstruction Finance Corporation (RFC). Chartered by Congress in January 1932, the RFC loaned funds to banks, railroads, and building and loan associations. This was followed by the expansion of funds available to Federal Land Banks and a liberalization of Federal Reserve requirements for banks. The Glass-Steagal Act released gold to meet foreign demands and the Federal Home Loan Bank Act tried to stabilize the mortgage market. Hoover, however, refused to agree to any more direct programs to help end the depression and vetoed the Garner-Wagner Act which would have provided direct relief and large scale public works. He did sign legislation allowing the RFC to lend money to states for self-liquidating public works projects and to help with relief when state and local funds were exhausted.

Despite Hoover's efforts the economy worsened and appeared headed for a shut down. At the beginning of the summer of 1932 iron and steel production, for example, stood at twelve percent of capacity, unemployment nationally approached 25 percent and was much higher in single industry towns. Businesses failed at record rates, banks closed their doors, and the once vibrant economy was moribund.

During the presidential election of 1932 Franklin Delano Roosevelt (1933–1945) campaigned on the promise of a New Deal, offering hope for an economic recovery. During the months between the November election and his March 4 inauguration, Roosevelt and his "Brains Trust" developed a legislative agenda to provide relief for those out of work, recovery for the economy, and reforms to prevent such a disaster in the future. The first three months of the Roosevelt administration, known as the 100 Days, saw an unprecedented volume of legislation move quickly though Congress.

Roosevelt's first priority was relief and a number of government agencies were formed to provide work. The Civil Works Administration (CWA), the Public Works Administration (PWA) and the Works Progress Administration (WPA) provided jobs initially on public works construction projects cosponsored with local governments. The WPA developed a wide range of projects that employed writers, actors, and historians, among others, to use their special skills and talents. The National Youth Administration (NYA) provided work and job training for young people and helped them stay in school to complete their education. The Civilian Conservation Corps (CCC) provided jobs for young men on conservation and reforestation projects. These programs and others, cumulatively, put millions of people back to work.

While New Deal employment programs gave people money to meet their needs, its recovery programs sought to allow the economy time to regain its strength. The National Industrial Recovery Act (NIRA) established a series of boards to oversee every industry in the country. Each National Recovery Administration (NRA) board established rules for its industry, setting hours of work, wages, prices, and many other details. The idea was to limit competition while the economy regained its strength. Businesses that subscribed to the NRA code for their industry received a "Blue Eagle" emblem and consumers were urged to buy where they saw the blue eagle. In 1935 the Supreme Court held the NIRA unconstitutional in the case *A.L.A. Schecter Poultry Corp. et. al. v. United States*.

A second recovery goal was solving the long-standing problems of farmers. The Agricultural Adjustment Act provided price supports for farmers linked to limits on production and paid for by a processing tax administered by the Agricultural Adjustment Administration (AAA). The Commodity Credit Corporation provide loans to farmers who agreed to take land out of production. Despite initial negative images of crops being plowed under and hogs and piglets slaughtered in 1933, the program succeeded in raising farm income and crop prices and reducing farm debt from their 1932 levels. In 1936 the Supreme Court held the processing tax unconstitutional in *United States v. Butler et al.* In 1938 a second AAA was created by Congress to address the continuing problems of farmers.

The third aspect of the New Deal was its attempt to reform the economy to prevent future depressions. Several agencies were created to address specific problems that were seen as major factors in bringing on the depression. The Securities and Exchange Commission (SEC) was established to regulate the stock market and the Federal Deposit Insurance Corporation (FDIC) insured deposits against loss if the bank failed. In 1935 Roosevelt proposed a social security system, financed by a payroll tax, to provide pensions for those over age 65. The Social Security Act also established unemployment insurance, aid to the disabled and blind, and to women with young children. In a more general way the New Deal established the federal government as a major participant in every aspect of the economy.

Despite all the New Deal programs the economy remained stalled and millions remained unemployed, underemployed, or employed in federal programs. The value of industrial production of consumer goods in 1937 was still only 89 percent of what it had been in 1929 and declined to less than 75 percent in 1938. Steel production in 1938 was half what it had been in 1929, having declined sharply after several years of recovery. Throughout the economy it was hard to find good news as 1937 turned into 1938.

German leader Adolf Hitler's (1889–1945) invasion of Poland in September 1939 brought war to Europe, a war the United States was determined to avoid. It became clear to Roosevelt and his advisors that with the fall of France U.S. neutrality was impossible, even if the country avoided combat. The war led Congress to authorize large sums to build up the nation's defenses—which helped revive industrial production. The defense build up also included expanding the armed forces and equipping them. In September 1940, Congress authorized a military draft. Beginning with the Lend-Lease program the United States gradually began to supply the British and later acted to defend ships carrying the weapons and other war materiel to them. War preparations brought mines and factories back in to operation, provided markets for farm production, and put people back to work.

The revival of the U.S. economy was impressive for its scale and its speed. Manufacturing production had an index value (a measure of production) of 58 in 1929 and had fallen to 46 in 1938, by 1940 it had reached 66, and rose to 110 by 1942 and 133 in 1943. Steel production, to cite a key industry, passed its 1929 level of 56 million tons in 1940 and reached 80 million tons in 1944. Unemployment fell from 19 percent in 1938 to 1.2 percent in 1944. Average weekly earnings in manufacturing more than doubled between 1938 and 1944. The challenge facing the economy changed from a shortage of jobs to a shortage of workers. The demand for workers in defense industries created new opportunities for women, Hispanics, and African Americans. The expansion of industrial production not only revived existing industrial operations and fields but saw new plants built, usually by the government, for war production in existing industrial areas. In addition, plants were built in new areas to disperse production of war materiel in case of sabotage or bombing. This policy decision greatly expanded the industrial capacity of the United States and spread it over a much wider area of the country.

Manufacturing was not the only segment of the economy to benefit from the war-time demands for increased production. Agriculture also expanded tremendously. The parity ratio, which compares farm prices with farm expenses, had edged downward from 1917 through 1941, falling from 120 to 93, with a low of 58 in 1932. The parity ratio rose to 113 in 1942 and remained above 100 until 1953. Farm wages rose from an index figure of 89 in 1932, to 208 in 1942, and 366 in 1945.

The revival of the economy during the war combined with the manpower demands of the armed services brought the various New Deal employment programs to an end. The federal government, however, remained heavily involved in the economy and a number of regulatory and coordinating agencies were created. Not only did defense contracts drive the manufacturing sector, but the government provided draft deferments for those working on farms or with critical industrial skills and mounted an advertising campaign encouraging women to work in the defense industry. The government also coordinated industrial production through the War Production Board, while the National War Labor Board set wages, hours, and working conditions and the War Labor Disputes Act allowed the government to seize factories in case of strikes. There were also price controls and extensive rationing of consumer goods including tires, gasoline, coffee, shoes, canned foods, sugar, and others administered by the Office of Price Administration. The War

Food Administration worked to reverse the AAA's efforts to limit agricultural production to meet increased demand.

As the end of the war drew near there was concern about the conversion to a peacetime economy. The return of millions of servicemen seeking jobs during the conversion potentially compounded the problem. The Servicemen's Readjustment Act of 1944 (popularly known as the GI Bill of Rights) provided unemployment insurance, business loans, low-cost home mortgages, and educational assistance to returning veterans. The program spread the reentry of veterans into the workforce over a number of years and stimulated the home building industry. The GI Bill was an important factor in avoiding a post war recession.

At the end of the war there was tremendous demand for consumer goods that people had not been able to purchase for some time, first because of the depression and then because of the conversion of the economy to war production. Combined with the accumulated savings from money invested in war bonds and in savings due to the lack of goods during the war, the economy was poised for a period of prosperity.

See also: **Civilian Conservation Corps, GI Bill, Glass-Steagal Act, Great Depression, Lend-Lease Act, National War Labor Board, New Deal, Office of Price Administration, Rationing, Reconstruction Finance Corporation, Franklin Delano Roosevelt, Smoot-Hawley Tariff, Social Security Act, Speculation, Stock Market, Stock Market Crash of 1929, War Production Board, Works Progress Administration, World War II**

FURTHER READING

Blum, John Morton. *V Was For Victory: Politics and American Culture during World War II.* New York: Harcourt Brace, 1976.

Brinkley, Alan. *The End of Reform: New Deal Liberalism in Recession and War.* New York: Knopf, 1995.

Leuchtenburg, William E. *The Perils of Prosperity, 1914–1932.* Chicago: University of Chicago Press, 1958.

———. *Franklin D. Roosevelt and the New Deal, 1932–1940.* New York: Harper and Row, 1963.

Watkins, T.H. *The Great Depression: America in the 1930s.* Boston: Little, Brown and Company, 1993.

DEVOS, RICHARD

Richard DeVos (1926–) founded Amway, the largest direct-sales company in the world. The privately-owned firm sells more than 450 personal care, nutrition, home, and commercial products through three million distributors (many of whom work part-time) to customers in more than eighty countries and territories. A billionaire, DeVos's personal wealth made him one of the richest men in the United States in the last decade of the twentieth century.

DeVos was born in 1926 and grew up in Grand Rapids, Michigan, in a devout fundamentalist Christian family. Church attendance was a requirement, twice each Sunday. DeVos credited the values he learned there, including piety and a sound work ethic, as defining influences in his life. Throughout his life he was a devout churchgoer; in the 1990s he gave $14 million to a Florida church.

DeVos met his lifetime friend in high school, fellow conservative Christian and business partner Jay Van Andel. Company legend has it that their friendship actually began with a business proposition that DeVos struck with Van Andel for a ride to school in return for 25 cents a week. Both entered the military during World War II (1939–1945), and they vowed to start a business together as soon as the war was over. Their first joint venture was a drive-in restaurant.

In 1948 the two young men took off in a sailboat from Connecticut, hoping to see the world. Their boat sank off the shores of Cuba and they later returned to Grand Rapids, Michigan. Back home, DeVos and Van Andel went to work as sales agents for Nutrilite, a California-based vitamin company that marketed products directly to customers. Van Andel and DeVos (who was a natural salesman) were both successful in the firm's direct sales environment. They broke away from Nutrilite in 1959 to found their own company, Amway. "We call our company Amway because the American way of private ownership and free enterprise is the best way," DeVos said at the time. The new company, patterned on Nutrilite's multilevel, commission-based model, was headquartered in the basements of the founders' homes in Ada, Michigan.

DeVos and Van Andel developed a complex, and sometimes controversial, company structure, involving salespeople who convinced others to join the sales force through the purchase of a starter kit which consisted of Amway products and sales information. After a salesperson signed up a requisite number of new recruits, he or she became a "distributor," entitled to a percentage of every sale that the new members

of the team subsequently made. Despite revival-like techniques, including many motivational tapes recorded by DeVos himself, most of Amway's approximately 2.5 million-member sales force earned comparatively little for their efforts.

The company, however, prospered, posting record growth in the final decades of the twentieth century. In 1998 alone sales were up five percent over the preceding year, totalling $5.7 billion. This success was not without its difficulties. Beginning in the 1970s, Amway was taken to court for allegedly overstating the earnings potential of its salespeople. In 1983, charged with customs fraud in Canada, the company paid a $25 million fine. Three years later, in 1986, Amway paid another $100,000 in fines as a result of an investigation by the U.S. Federal Trade Commission. In the 1990s a class-action suit in a Pennsylvania district court was open to anyone who had been an Amway distributor between 1990 and 1996.

The company survived these lawsuits and expanded into money management with its stock fund, Amway Mutual. It also continued to improve its products. From the start, Amway attempted to create and market products that did not harm the environment. The company's first products were household cleaners, including a biodegradable soap. In the 1990s almost all of Amway's products were biodegradable, including their packaging. For its consistently forward-looking approach to environmental issues, Amway was awarded the Environmental Programme Achievement Award from the United Nations in 1989.

Though liberal on the environment, DeVos and Van Andel became noted for their staunch conservatism in regards to other issues. Van Andel, for example, built the Arizona-based Van Andel Creation Research Center to support Creationism, the belief that Man was a creation of god and not a result of evolution. DeVos was a major contributor to the Republican Party. He donated $2.5 million in 1994 to pay for the television broadcast costs of the party's 1996 national convention, and in 1997 he donated $1 million to cover Republican debts from the 1996 election.

Edward DeVos and his partner Jay Van Andel retired and focused their efforts on charity; each man was reported to have a private fortune of more than $1.4 billion. When DeVos retired from day-to-day operations at Amway in 1992, he underwent triple-bypass heart surgery. The DeVos and Van Andel families retained ownership of Amway. Edward DeVos's son Dick became president and Co-CEO with Steve Van Andel, the son of Jay Van Andel.

FURTHER READING

"Our Story" [cited April 14, 1999] available from the World Wide Web @ www.amway.com/.

Butterfield, Stephen. *Amway: The Cult of Free Enterprise*. Boston: South End Press, 1985.

DeVos, Rich. *Compassionate Capitalism*. New York: Dutton Books, 1993.

"The Forbes 400: The Richest People in America." *Forbes*, October 12, 1998.

Guest, Larry. "Rich DeVos on Road to Recovery with New Heart." *Saturday Evening Post*, September/October, 1997.

DINGLEY TARIFF

Passed by Congress in July 1897, the Dingley Tariff Act increased duties by an average of 57 percent. Tariff rates were hiked on sugar, salt, tin cans, glassware, and tobacco, as well as on iron and steel, steel rails, petroleum, lead, copper, locomotives, matches, whisky, and leather goods.

Protective tariffs figured prominently in nineteenth century political debates. Tariffs were used in the United States as early as the 1790s. In 1828 Congress passed a bill (called the "Tariff of Abominations" by its opponents) levying government taxes on imported goods as a way of protecting the nation's burgeoning industrial interests. Thereafter tariffs were adjusted depending on current economic conditions and the political atmosphere. Republicans came to stand for higher tariffs, while the Democrats, leery that such protectionism favored monopolistic business practices in U.S. industry, championed lower rates. Since the Republicans controlled the government for most of the period between 1860 and 1890, tariffs remained high.

The presidential election of 1896, which pitted Republican candidate William McKinley (1843–1901) against Democrat William Jennings Bryan (1860–1925) was dominated by the debate over Free Silver, but the subtext of the debate centered about the tariff issue. Since they knew him to be a strong advocate of protection, the Republicans chose McKinley as their candidate. (Indeed, in 1890, McKinley had sponsored a high tariff, which bore his name.) McKinley saw the collection of tariffs as an effective way to replenish the U.S. Treasury. After winning the election he wasted no time in bringing the issue to the fore.

Calling a special session of Congress in March 1897, President McKinley (1897–1901) worked with House speaker, Thomas Brackett Reed (1839–1902), and the Ways and Means Committee Chairman, Nelson Dingley (1832–1899), to pass tariff-increase legislation in near-record time: three weeks after convening, the House passed the bill. When it reached the Senate, the moderate increases sought by McKinley were raised sharply, to an average 57 percent. The rate hike was the result of a coalition formed between eastern and western senators who agreed to higher rates on goods produced by their respective regions in exchange for the support of another region. The Dingley Tariff was the highest protective tariff in U.S. history. The legislation's effect was to raise the cost of living by nearly 25 percent between 1897 and 1907. The cost of living was mitigated only by an influx of gold from the Klondike (Yukon Territory, Canada), which helped end a four-year economic depression and begin a decade of prosperity.

The tariff was not lowered until 1913 when the Underwood Tariff reduced rates to approximately 30 percent. That same year, the ratification of the Sixteenth Amendment, which provided for a federal income tax, helped alleviate pressure for high tariffs by providing the federal government with another stream of revenue.

See also: **Tariff, Underwood Tariff**

DISCOUNT RATE

The discount rate is the interest rate charged member banks for loans from Federal Reserve Banks (FRB). The Federal Reserve System (FRS), established in 1913, has 12 FRBs in 12 districts and 25 FRB branches. All national commercial banks are required to be members of the FRS. Just as individuals use the banking services of a local bank, member banks use the banking services of the FRB in their district. The Federal Open Market Committee (FOMC) determines the interest rate or discount rate member banks pay when borrowing money from the RRB. The FOMC meets ten times a year, and depending on the monetary needs of the country, it adjusts the discount rate up or down.

A decrease in the discount rate increases the money supply by making money less expensive. This allows member banks to borrow more money, which is then made available in their localities. Member banks pass on the savings within a few days or weeks by lowering rates on loans to businesses. Likewise, rates on home mortgages, consumer loans, and credit cards began to fall, stimulating borrowing and spending. Businesses began growing and more jobs become available. When spending exceeds business' ability to produce goods, the price of goods goes up thereby increasing the rate of inflation. The FOMC may then find it necessary to increase the discount rate. The increased discount rate decreases the money supply by making money more expensive. This, in turn, discourages borrowing and spending, and the economy slows down.

When the FRS first began operating, the discount rates constituted the FRS' primary, almost exclusive, means of monetary control. By the second half of the twentieth century, the FRS influenced the flow of money to promote economic stability in three ways. It could change the discount rate, conduct open market operations (the sale or purchase of government securities), and change reserve requirements (the percentage of deposits all commercial banks are required to set aside). The discount rate is used to signal overall changes in the Federal Reserve monetary policy.

The discount rate ranged between 1.5 percent and 8 percent from 1922 to 1978, and then climbed to an all time high at 14 percent in 1981. With the economy faltering, the RFS lowered the rate in an effort to stimulate business activity. The rate fell relatively steadily to 4 percent in 1994, remaining between 4 and 5 percent through 1998.

See also: **Federal Reserve System, Inflation, Interest**

DISCRIMINATION

When two individuals with equal productivity receive significantly different wages for doing similar work, discrimination is said to exist. In addition to wage discrimination, inequalities in employment are reflected in the higher unemployment rates of minorities and young persons when compared to the unemployment rates of adult white males and females. The unequal treatment is based on worker's personal characteristics, unrelated and irrelevant to productivity. Discrimination issues center on differential treatment by race or ethnic group, gender, age, or handicap.

Economists speak of two types of discrimination: pure and statistical. Pure discrimination involves personal taste or preferences. Some employers may prefer not to be associated with members of a certain group such as minorities, women, young people, old people, or persons with disabilities. They tend simply not to hire that group. Statistical discrimination involves eliminating people from consideration who, as a group, have unstable work histories or poor work habits. This type

of discrimination assumes all members of a group are less qualified because their group's education or training is widely perceived as inferior. A firm may be able to lower its recruiting costs by limiting its search to adult, white, married males. But, not hiring from certain demographic groups limits the pool of candidates in very competitive markets and can be costly to a business.

Since the early 1960s federal legislation in the United States prohibits job discrimination based on race or national origin, sex, age, religion, or handicap. The seven major laws are: Title VII of the Civil Rights Act of 1964, Age Discrimination in Employment Act of 1967, Equal Pay Act of 1963, Title I of the Americans with Disabilities Act of 1990, Civil Rights Act of 1991, and Section 501 of the Rehabilitation Act of 1973. In the 1970s the government also began a program called affirmative action, to counteract past discrimination by giving preferential hiring to disadvantaged groups.

Despite extensive legislation, statistics show continued inequality in employment practices and wages. Employment figures from the Bureau of Labor Statistics show that black unemployment is more than double the rate of unemployment for whites in 1997. Concerning wages, statistics show that in 1997 women's overall earnings was seventy-four percent of men's earnings. Although legal gains are considerable, longstanding discrimination in job opportunities and wages persisted toward the conclusion of the twentieth century.

See also: **Affirmative Action, Americans with Disabilities Act**

DISINCENTIVES

A disincentive causes certain actions or activities to not be profitable, thereby decreasing motivation to carry them out. Typical disincentives in the United States revolve around the income tax structure. Income taxes cause work disincentives. With marginal rates of tax, people have less incentive to earn more dollars because they will have to pay more of it in taxes. Although few people choose the poverty of unemployment to avoid paying income taxes, some evidence indicates people may decide not to work overtime or take a second job. Married women may prefer not to work outside the home. Research shows that work disincentives are not strong influences for the majority of taxpayers. In fact, data indicate that many low and middle income groups, trying to meet their family budgets, work longer hours so their net income will be higher.

Effects of tax disincentives most often appear at very high income levels and at very low levels. At the highest levels those subject to the highest marginal tax rates may increase their leisure time rather than work to earn more. At the lowest levels individuals may fall into a poverty trap. Certain benefits paid by the government such as free school lunches for children, medical care, or supplemental income, will be reduced or not paid at all if a person reaches a certain income level. Individuals will choose to not work or work only enough so that their income stays at a very low level.

The tax system creates disincentives to save. Savings are an important source of funds for investment in the United States. Interest earned on savings accounts must be declared to the Internal Revenue Service each April when filing taxes. A family's gross adjusted income is raised by interest on savings, increasing their tax bill. Reporting interest income therefore acts as a disincentive to save.

Economists also look at the home mortgage deduction allowed as a disincentive to save. The yearly home mortgage interest deduction represents large tax savings to families. This tax saving encourages them to go into debt, the opposite of saving, for the purchase of large homes. If this deduction were eliminated, people would demand smaller houses to save more of their income. Less money would be invested in housing, making more funds available for lending to other industries.

See also: **Incentive, Mortgage, Profit, Savings**

DISNEY, WALTER ELIAS

Walt Disney (1901–1966) was a major business pioneer of the twentieth century. He created cartoons, live-action movies, imaginative theme parks, and wholesome family entertainment on a global scale. Having himself grown up almost without a childhood, Disney found a way to find the child in everyone by making cartoons and filling them with amusing characters like Mickey Mouse and Donald Duck.

Born in 1901, Walt Disney had a difficult upbringing. His father Elias, a restless and unsuccessful carpenter and farmer, was a stern religious fundamentalist who readily disciplined his children with his belt. He also denied the children toys, games, and sporting

Walt Disney brushes up on his Spanish with the help of Mickey Mouse and Donald Duck.

equipment. This experience may have had an impact on his son's later determination to look on the sunny side of life. As the father changed jobs, the family moved frequently: from Chicago to Marceline, Missouri, to Kansas City, Missouri, and back to Chicago. Because of the family's constant traveling and the necessity for the children to contribute to the household's income, Disney's formal education ended at the ninth grade. At age 16, hoping to become a newspaper cartoonist, he joined an art class at the Academy of Fine Arts to develop his drawing skills.

In 1919, after a stint as a driver in the Red Cross Ambulance Corps during World War I (1914–1918), Disney moved to Kansas City, Missouri. There he worked at a variety of jobs as a commercial artist and cartoonist. With another young artist, Ub Iwerks, he formed his first small cartoon-film production company in the early 1920s. Along with brief animated advertising films, the company produced a series of animated fairy tales, "Alice in Cartoonland." With Disney's brother Roy as business manager, the little film company moved to Hollywood and produced 56 "Alice" films in three years. They also introduced the

"Oswald the Rabbit" series, producing 26 of these cartoons in less than two years.

Mickey Mouse came to life in 1928, first as an airplane pilot, then as an adventurer and a sort of pirate-character. After viewing the first sound movie, "The Jazz Singer," late in 1928, Disney decided to make the first talking-and-music cartoon: Mickey Mouse as "Steamboat Willie." (He used his own voice for Mickey.) Soon, Mickey was joined by a girlfriend, Minnie. Their popularity led to the invention of such familiar characters as Donald Duck, Pluto, and Goofy. By 1936, eight years after the mouse with human characteristics appeared on the scene, Mickey Mouse had become one of the most widely recognized personalities in the world. Throughout the 1930s Disney continued to make both long and short cartoon features, many of which later became classics, including "Snow White," "Pinocchio," and "Dumbo."

In the 1940s, despite his many successes, Disney produced a series of financial failures, notably "Fantasia," a very different animated film set to classical music and later regarded as a classic. Disney was devastated when "Fantasia" did poorly at the box office and when half his artists went on strike to protest his dictatorial style. The training films combining live action with cartoon characters that he made for the federal government during World War II (1939–1945), however, turned Disney in a new and very successful direction.

Following the war, Disney made many films combining live-action and cartoons, including "The Song of the South." His company also produced very popular full-length animated films, including "Cinderella," "Alice in Wonderland," and "Peter Pan." In the early 1950s Disney made a popular series of nature films. His film career was capped by "Mary Poppins" in 1964, for which he won five Academy Awards.

By the mid-1950s Disney had begun to produce such television shows as "Davy Crockett" and "The Mickey Mouse Club." At the same time, he was also developing the first of his famous Disneyland theme parks. The first Disneyland, near Los Angeles, California, opened in 1955. Disney's brilliant move was to integrate all his business ventures, using his television programs to motivate people to visit Disneyland, intending Disneyland to inspire parents and children to attend family-oriented Disney films. Disneyland was such a success that later the Disney company opened another theme park, Disney World, near Orlando, Florida.

By the 1960s Disney had created a very diversified entertainment empire, built on cartoon themes, animal icons, nostalgic sentiment, and a high level of quality

control. His imagination, highly-developed merchandising skills, and uncanny ability to tap into the fantasies of children of all ages ensured that his company would thrive long after his death from lung cancer in 1966.

See also: **Amusement Parks, Entertainment Industry, Movies**

FURTHER READING

Finch, Christopher. *The Art of Walt Disney: From Mickey Mouse to the Magic Kingdoms*. New York: Abrams, 1995.

Mosely, Leonard. *Disney's World*. New York: Stein and Day, 1985.

Schickel, Richard. *The Disney Version*. Chicago: Ivan R. Dee, 1997.

Thomas, Bob. *Walt Disney: An American Original*. New York: Simon and Schuster, 1976.

"Walt Disney: A Biography." [cited July 12, 1999] Available on the World Wide Web @ disney.go.com/disneyatoz/read/walt.

Watts, Steven. *The Magic Kingdom: Walt Disney and the American Way of Life*. Boston: Houghton Mifflin, 1997.

DISPOSABLE INCOME

Disposable personal income, or take-home pay, is the income received by households after personal income tax and social security contributions are paid. The income may result from wages in payment for labor and/or from government transfer payments. Government transfer payments are payments from the government and include social security, Medicaid, and unemployment benefits. Disposable income is the amount of income that households can spend or save. Historically, people spend approximately ninety percent of their disposable income. When disposable income increases, consumer spending increases. Personal consumption expenditures constitute approximately sixty-seven percent of the Gross Domestic Product (GDP), a measure of the total production of an economy. The GDP serves as an assessment of the health of the economy as a whole, the nation's economic report card. When disposable income grows and spending increases, overall level of demand rises, the GDP grows, and economic forecasts are positive. Conversely, when disposable income is flat or decreases, consumers spend less, slowing economic growth. Overall, consumers spend less when anxious about the future, but release their pent-up spending urges during boom times.

See also: **Gross Domestic Product**

DIVIDENDS

Dividends are a sum of money paid to stockholders out of a corporation's earnings. Once a dividend has been declared, the percentage of dividend that stockholders receive is based on a dollar amount per share of stock owned by the stockholder. Preferred stockholders generally have a prior right to dividend payments over common stockholders. Dividends are usually paid in cash. However, they can also be distributed in other forms: stock dividends and stock splits; scrip, which is a company's promise to pay in the future; or property, such as inventory goods. Most commonly, corporations declare dividends at regular intervals, such as monthly, quarterly, or annually. Before a dividend is paid, the board of directors must make a dividend announcement. This announcement sets the amount of the dividend, the date of record, and the payment date. The date of record is important as all stockholders have the right to receive the dividend on that date. By law, dividends can be paid only from corporate profits; they can not be paid from a corporation's capital. This measure, known as the impairment of capital rule, is intended to protect the corporation's creditors.

See also: **Capital, Stock**

DIVISION OF LABOR

Division of labor refers to the specialization of jobs in any complex economy, particularly in a manufacturing enterprise. Since the British writer Adam Smith (1723–1790), economists have noted that division of labor is the most important feature of modern capitalism. Smith showed how several people with different skills are required to manufacture even a simple object like a pin; each person specializes in his own aspect of the job. Division of labor allows workers to become expert at a single task and to perform it very quickly; therefore, it allows great precision in the manufacturing process. Division of labor makes the modern consumer economy possible, because a person can use the wages from one specialized job to buy all the other products he or she needs, rather than trying to produce everything themselves. A downside of division of labor is can lead to mind-numbing, even dehumanizing, factory work. An assembly line worker, for

example, does nothing by tighten the same bolts all day long.

See also: **Assembly Line, Mass Production, Adam Smith**

DIX, DOROTHEA LYNDE

Dorothea Lynde Dix (1802–1887) was born to Joseph and Mary Dix on April 4, 1802, in Hampden, Maine. Her father was a farmer but became an itinerant Methodist preacher when he failed at farming. Dorothea Dix spent her early years in poverty, moving frequently and living a life she saw as bleak and lonely. At age twelve she moved to live with her grandparents in Boston. This was the first of several dramatic turns she was to experience in life.

Dix enjoyed and excelled at learning, and set up her first school at age fourteen. While she displayed a joy in teaching, she was also strict—she did not shy away from humiliating disobedient children. Dix operated her first school for three years in her aunt's home in Worcester. She closed the school to return to Boston and her own studies. In 1821 Dix opened another school in her grandmother's Boston home. After a year she added a free charity school for poor children.

Even while her schools were successful, ill health plagued Dix. Typically, Dix overworked herself and was forced to temporarily abandon teaching. She took to writing children's books while convalescing from frequent attacks of chronic lung disease. Her writing included textbooks, hymnbooks, and poetry.

Dix was attracted to the Unitarian Church. She admired Boston activist, (Unitarian) William Ellery Channing (1818–1901), whose children Dix tutored. Catering to Boston's Unitarian community, Dix revived her school in 1831, but she was forced to close it in 1835, again because of ill health. She moved to England to recover.

Dix returned to Boston in 1841 and began working as a Sunday school teacher in the women's jail at East Cambridge, Massachusetts. The conditions at the jail disgusted her, especially the treatment of mentally ill inmates. Dix took the jailer to court to improve conditions and won the case, beginning her life-long passion: championing the rights of the mentally ill.

Dix's work began in the Commonwealth of Massachusetts, where she brought attention to the plight of the mentally ill. To further her cause she became one of the first to gather and publish social statistics. In 1845

Dorthea Dix.

her statistically supported presentations secured reforms from the state legislature. Encouraged, Dix spread her crusade across the country, founding new hospitals or additions in fifteen states and Canada. In 1848 Dix lobbied Congress for legislation endorsing the sale of public lands to provide revenue for asylums, but the measure was defeated. Discouraged, she left for Europe on a tour of its hospitals and asylums. There, she observed the work of Florence Nightingale (1820–1910), whom she admired.

The American Civil War (1861–1865) brought Dix back to the United States, where she was appointed Superintendent of Women Nurses. Dix attempted to replicate for the U.S. Army Nightingale's work in the Russian Crimea. She was not popular with the U.S. government bureaucrats but nevertheless served her complete term before returning to her reform efforts. Chronic ill health forced her retirement in 1870. She retired to an asylum she had designed and built forty years earlier and died there in 1887.

Dorothea Dix lived her life at extremes: poverty and wealth, periods of great effort and success punctuated by ill health and infirmity, success in her teaching and her reforms punctuated by often deep opposition to her strident and strict ways. But because of her efforts, the number of mental hospitals in the United States increased from only thirteen in 1841 to 123 at the time of her death.

FURTHER READING

Commire, Anne, ed. *Historic World Leaders*. Detroit: Gale Research, 1994, s.v. "Dix, Dorothea Lynde."

Encyclopedia of World Biography. Detroit: Gale Research, Second Edition, 1998-1999, s.v. "Dix, Dorothea Lynde."

Marshall, Helen E. *Dorothea Dix: Forgotten Samaritan*. Chapel Hill, NC: University of North Carolina Press, 1937.

Tiffany, Francis. *Life of Dorothea Lynde Dix*. Boston: Houghton, 1891.

DOLLAR DIPLOMACY

The concept of the U.S. government protecting U.S. commercial enterprises abroad and offering political loans to foreign governments is not unique to any specific time period. The term "Dollar Diplomacy," however, became particularly associated with the policies of President William Howard Taft (1909–13) that were designed to further U.S. interests in Latin America and China. Taft sought to use U.S. economic aid in order to coax underdeveloped countries to follow U.S. political leadership and at times accept a U.S. military presence.

Almost a century earlier in 1823 President James Monroe (1817–25) established what became known as the Monroe Doctrine. While Spain was involved in the Napoleonic Wars in Europe, a number of New World countries proclaimed their independence. Concern rose in the United States that Spain might attempt to reassert its colonialist control in countries of the Western Hemisphere following the war. Anticipating increased economic trade prospects with newly independent Latin American countries, Monroe held that the hemisphere was closed to further European colonization. Any efforts by European nations to reestablish political control would be considered a threat to U.S. security. President Theodore Roosevelt (1901–09) later broadened the Doctrine by asserting that the United States had the right and obligation to intervene when Western Hemisphere nations became so politically or economically unstable that they were vulnerable to European control. However Roosevelt's forceful intervention with several countries stirred considered hostility in the region.

As Secretary of War in Roosevelt's administration, Taft oversaw construction of the Panama Canal and establishment of the U.S. Canal Zone. In his later role as president, Taft and his advisors, including Secretary of State Philander C. Knox, became concerned over security of the canal and how to protect it from foreign encroachment. Heavily indebted to European nations, the overwhelmingly poor Latin American countries experienced continual economic and political unrest. Fearing that European nations might forcibly intervene in Latin American affairs while seeking repayment of outstanding loans, Taft and Knox sought to promote an aggressive program of economic and political stability.

> **UNDER TAFT, PAN-AMERICANISM MADE NO PROGRESS. WHILE BRAZIL ATTEMPTED AT THE FOURTH PAN-AMERICAN CONFERENCE AT BUENOS AIRES IN 1910 TO WIN AN ENDORSEMENT OF THE MONROE DOCTRINE, THE DELEGATES MADE IT QUITE CLEAR THAT THEY WISHED TO LIMIT UNITED STATES INFLUENCE IN THE CARIBBEAN.**
>
> Paolo E. Coletta, *The Presidency of William Howard Taft*, 1973

Chief targets for Dollar Diplomacy included Colombia, Honduras, and Nicaragua. Dollar Diplomacy consisted of Taft and Knox lobbying private U.S. bankers to "invest" in these nations. The bankers would provide the countries with loans so they could pay off their debts to European nations. The U.S. was to control investment markets of the Latin American nations, thereby eliminating economic competition while incorporating the countries' economies into the political and economic world of the United States.

Taft began putting Dollar Diplomacy into action, but he ran into many obstacles. Colombia, heavily in debt to European banks but still bitter from the loss of the land surrounding the Panama Canal, refused U.S. economic advances without first settling the loss of Panama. Taft also lobbied U.S. bankers in 1909 to loan money to Honduras so that it could pay its debt of $110 million, which was primarily owed Britain. After Taft successfully persuaded J.P. Morgan (1813–90) and others to participate, Congress failed to approve the plan. Revolution erupted in Honduras, leading to U.S. armed intervention. Fearful of the political instability and Honduras' refusal to fully cooperate, the companies withdrew their loan offers and the proposal died. Nicaragua, holding an alternative canal route to the Panama Canal, antagonistically threatened the United States that it would sell canal rights to Great Britain or Japan. Taft sought to have U.S. bankers loan Nicaragua

$20 million, but Congress withheld approval until after Taft left office. Dollar Diplomacy in Latin America was a failure.

Taft and Knox also attempted to apply Dollar Diplomacy to the Far East in 1910. Knox was convinced that European funding of major railway construction in China threatened U.S. access to free trade. Taft again arranged for financier J.P. Morgan to establish a syndicate of U.S. bankers to enter the project. Though loans were made, little profit resulted. Concern also arose over possible Japanese and Russian involvement in railroad construction in Manchuria. Taft arranged for U.S. bankers to form a six-nation consortium to fund the project. Both of Taft's efforts in Asia failed.

Taft had been unabashed in his efforts to expand the U.S. economy through international trade, reporting to Congress a $300 million gain in exports in 1910 and another $200 million in 1911. Taft even suggested that Congress establish U.S. banks abroad.

Dollar Diplomacy failed as a crudely designed foreign policy. Critics saw it as economic imperialism replacing territorial imperialism. Indeed Taft himself described it as "substituting dollars for bullets." The strategy's blatant nature brought the policy into disrepute and was bitterly debated at home and abroad. Many viewed with alarm use of government employees, such as diplomats and consuls, to establish new inroads for private U.S. commercial enterprise. The term itself became a derogatory description of international economic coercion. Following Taft in the White House, President Woodrow Wilson (1913–21) explicitly repudiated Dollar Diplomacy in 1913. The United States continued to pursue programs of political intervention by providing economic and military aid to Latin American countries, but with less blatant economic gain in mind. In 1965 President Lyndon Johnson (1963–69) unsuccessfully tried similar tactics in Southeast Asia when he offered $1 billion in aid in an attempt to avoid armed conflict.

See also: **Big Stick Diplomacy, William Howard Taft**

FURTHER READING

Drake, Paul W., ed. *Money Doctors, Foreign Debts, and Economic Reforms in Latin America from the 1890s to the Present.* Wilmington, DL: SR Books, 1994.

Harrison, Benjamin T. *Dollar Diplomat: Chandler Anderson and American Diplomacy in Mexico and*

Nicaragua, 1913–28. Pullman, WA: Washington State University Press, 1988.

May, Ernest R. *The Making of the Monroe Doctrine.* Cambridge, MA: Harvard University Press, 1992.

Minger, Ralph E. *William Howard Taft and United States Foreign Policy: The Apprenticeship Years, 1900–08.* Urbana: University of Illinois Press, 1975.

Munro, Dana G. *Intervention and Dollar Diplomacy in the Caribbean, 1900–21.* Princeton, NJ: Princeton University Press, 1964.

DOW, CHARLES HENRY

Charles Henry Dow (1851–1902), co-founder of Dow, Jones and Company, Inc. and first editor of *The Wall Street Journal*, was a journalist and financial analyst. He created an index of a dozen leading stocks, mostly railroads, that eventually became the Dow Jones Industrial Average (DJIA), the most popular and widely-read of all stock measurements.

Born in 1851, Dow's only formal education took place in a one-room village schoolhouse in Connecticut. He left home at age sixteen to work as an apprentice printer and reporter and began a newspaper career that took him to Springfield, Massachusetts, Providence, Rhode Island, and finally to New York City in 1879.

Writing for the *Providence Journal*, Dow filed a series of stories from Leadville, Colorado, about a huge silver strike that brought thousands of speculators, miners, and gamblers to the area. He realized he had a talent for financial reporting and analysis, and upon returning from the West, he decided to relocate to New York. Within months, Dow had a job as an editor with the Kiernan News Agency, a firm that wrote and delivered handwritten, brief news bulletins to banks and brokerage houses. At the same time, a former newspaper colleague, Edward D. Jones (1856–1920), also joined Kiernan as a reporter.

In November 1882, Dow and Jones left Kiernan and formed their own financial news service, Dow Jones and Company. They were a well-balanced team. Jones was a first-rate financial reporter with excellent sources. Dow's strength was his thoughtful analysis of companies, industries and market trends. They set up a news bulletin service in a small room next door to the New York Stock Exchange. Throughout the day, their boy messengers rushed "flimsies" (bulletins handwritten with a stylus on thin paper to make multiple copies) containing business news and analyses reported and written by the two partners to subscribers in

Charles Henry Dow.

banks and brokerage houses throughout the financial district.

On July 3, 1884, Dow and Jones began to publish a two-page afternoon newsletter with the average closing price of representative active stocks, including nine railroads and two industrials. Twelve years later, the Dow Jones Industrial Average, limited to 12 representative industrial stocks, appeared. Both lists were determined by Dow's research to be reliably indicative of market trends.

The first issue of *The Wall Street Journal*, published by Dow Jones and Co., appeared July 8, 1889. Charles Dow was the editor. The new daily afternoon paper cost two cents a copy, but reduced rates were offered to bankers and brokers, and the paper was delivered free to subscribers of the company's news bulletin service. Correspondents from London, Boston, Washington, D.C., and Chicago regularly wired news stories by telegraph from those cities.

By the turn of the century, *The Wall Street Journal* was clearly headed for success. Its circulation reached 10,000 in 1899, and Dow sought to expand its readership from Wall Street insiders to the general public. On April 21, 1899, he introduced a regular column, "Review and Outlook," in which he attempted to educate readers on the stock and bond markets. These essays provided an analysis of stock market behavior that remained valid and became the basis for what was later called the Dow Theory. Charles Dow died in 1902, having firmly established the Dow Jones Industrial Average and *The Wall Street Journal* in the American financial and investment markets.

See also: **Dow Jones Industrial Average, Stock Market, Wall Street, Wall Street Journal**

FURTHER READING

Bishop, George W., Jr. *Charles Dow and the Dow Theory.* New York: Appleton, Century Crofts, Inc., 1960.

———. *Charles H. Dow: Economist.* Princeton, NJ: Dow Jones Books, 1967.

''Charles Henry Dow'' [cited March 19, 1999], available from the World Wide Web @ averages.dowjones.com/chDow.html/.

Scharff, Edward E. *Worldly Power: The Making of The Wall Street Journal.* New York: Beaufort Books Publishers, 1986.

Wendt, Lloyd. *The Wall Street Journal: The Story of Dow Jones and the Nation's Business Newspaper.* Chicago: Rand McNally and Co., 1982.

DOW JONES INDUSTRIAL AVERAGE (DJIA)

A measure of stock prices of important industrial companies, the Dow Jones Industrial Average (DJIA) was first printed in the *Wall Street Journal* in 1897. The average is an indicator of the overall stock market and is used, along with other indexes, by investors, stockbrokers, and analysts to make investment forecasts and decisions.

In 1882 Dow, Jones and Company (the comma between the two names was later dropped) was founded by financial reporters Charles Henry Dow (1851–1902) and Edward Davis Jones (1856–1920). Since the founding of the New York Stock Exchange (NYSE) in 1792, business reporting had been largely based on rumor or speculation. Dow and Jones were determined to provide U.S. businesspeople and investors with up-to-date and accurate reporting on the stock market.

Dow, Jones and Company began publishing composite lists of major stocks in 1884. In 1897 the Dow Jones Industrial Average made its first appearance in the *Wall Street Journal*. Dow and Jones had conceived of the index as a summary measure of the market, which could be used to analyze past trends, indicate

current trends, and even predict future ones. The first DJIA averaged the prices of 12 major companies. The list had been expanded since—in 1916, it averaged the stock prices of 20 companies, in 1928, 30 companies were averaged. Adjustments were made as the result of company mergers and dissolution. Though it was a measure only of the New York Stock Exchange, the Dow Jones Industrial Average has been called a barometer of the stock market. News of fluctuations in the DJIA can affect market prices around the world.

See also: **Charles Dow, New York Stock Exchange (NYSE), Wall Street Journal**

DRED SCOTT CASE

After a lifetime of slavery, Dred Scott (1795?–1858), who had been born a slave in Southampton County, Virginia, sued the state of Missouri for his freedom in April 1846. He argued that he had traveled with his owner in Wisconsin and Illinois, states where slavery had been prohibited by the Missouri Compromise of 1820. By the compromise, Congress decided to admit Missouri as a slavery state and Maine as a free state, and declared that, with the exception of the state of Missouri, the territories north of the 36th parallel (present-day Missouri's southern border) were free.

The case, which hinged on Scott's travels in free territories in the North, went through two trials. (The second trial was granted because of a procedural error in the first.) In 1850 at the conclusion of the second trial, a Missouri jury ruled Scott a free man. This decision was based on his prior residence in a free territory or state, which according to precedent, resulted in his emancipation, regardless of the fact that Missouri itself was a slave state. John F. A. Sanford, the lawyer for Scott's owner, immediately appealed the decision before the Missouri Supreme Court, where a pro-slavery judge reversed the ruling, rescinding Scott's freedom. But the case did not end there.

Sanford filed the court papers under Scott's own name rather than that of Scott's former owner; thus, the case of *Scott* v. *Sanford* took an interesting twist. As a litigant, Scott had legal status. Scott hired a new lawyer who was able to have the case heard before the federal court. Sanford had moved to New York, and because the appellant (Scott) and the registered defendant (Sanford) were now residents of different states, the case came under federal purview. In 1854 a circuit court in St. Louis again heard Scott's case, but he was again denied his freedom. The decision was appealed to the United States Supreme Court, which began hearing the case in 1856.

In March 1857 the Supreme Court, which had a Southern majority, ruled that Scott's residence in Wisconsin and Illinois did not make him free. The court ruled that an African American (a ''Negro descended from slaves'') had no rights as an American citizen and therefore could not bring suit in a federal court. Further, the court ruled that Congress never had the authority to ban slavery in the territories. The decision pronounced the Missouri Compromise unconstitutional, deepened the divide between North and South, and helped pave the way for the American Civil War (1861–65). Dred Scott died the following year.

See also: **Abolition, Missouri Compromise, Slavery**

DREW, DANIEL

Daniel Drew (1797–1879) grew up under difficult financial circumstances in the early 1800s, but he grew to become an extremely wealthy and notorious stock manipulator. In an era noted for ''robber barons'' Drew used every means available, including fraud and deception, to make a fortune in investments in the transportation industry. In the end, however, Drew became of victim of his own game, and died a poor man.

Daniel Drew was born on July 29, 1797 in Carmel, New York, the son of Gilbert Drew and Catherine Muckleworth. Drew's father owned a modest hundred-acre cattle farm. He died when the boy was only 15, and left the family in poverty. Drew then enlisted in the War of 1812 (1812–1814) as a substitute for someone who sought to avoid military service and could afford to pay Drew $100 to act as his replacement. After his brief military service, Drew worked with a traveling zoo before finding work as a cattle drover.

Drew began his business career by buying cattle and sheep in New England and the Midwest and selling them to butchers in New York City. He received some financial assistance from a wealthy businessman, Henry Astor. Drew, however, quickly gained a reputation on his own as a sharp dealer. For example, it was believed that Drew would have his cattle over-drink before their sale, so that they would look healthy and weigh more. Through this shrewdness Drew established himself as a capable businessman. In 1820 he married Roxanne Mead, and the couple had one son. By 1829 Drew had moved his young family to Manhattan, where he established the headquarters of his livestock business.

In the 1830s Drew became interested in the steamship industry. In 1834 he used the profits from his livestock trade to invest in a steamboat fleet that ran on Long Island Sound and the Hudson River. This business venture brought Drew into direct competition with Cornelius Vanderbilt (1794–1877), a shrewd businessman who liked to monopolize the industries in which he invested. Drew and Vanderbilt became lifelong business adversaries.

After a decade in the steamboat business, Drew had earned a fortune. He used these profits to open a Wall Street banking and brokerage firm in 1844, called Drew, Robinson, and Company. Within a decade Drew's business partners had died and, left to himself, he became an aggressive stock manipulator. He specialized in railroad stock and became involved in the Erie Railroad in 1853. In 1857 Drew took advantage of a financial panic to make himself director of the railroad. This brought him once again into direct competition with Cornelius Vanderbilt, who had also developed an interest in the railroad industry.

In 1864 Vanderbilt tried to drive Drew out of the railroad business. Vanderbilt failed, but he nonetheless caused Drew to lose $500,000. In 1866 Drew joined forces with James Fisk (1834–1872) and Jay Gould (1836–1892) to drive Vanderbilt out of their business. Drew was treasurer of the Erie Railroad, and he advanced company money for 50,000 newly printed shares of fraudulent stock. This move drove up the value of the stock. Drew then sold the fraudulent stock on the resulting bull market for a huge profit. As the price of stocks fell, Drew continued to make money by manipulating the bond market. In doing so, he further angered Vanderbilt and set himself up for a showdown.

Vanderbilt lost a considerable amount of money in the so-called Erie War and, in 1868, he persuaded a judge to order the arrest of Drew, Fisk, and Gould for their questionable stock market activities. To avoid arrest, the three ran off to a hotel in New Jersey, where they continued to run their business. The group never faced prosecution for their illegal dealings because Gould was able to bribe judges and state legislators to legalize the fraudulent stock issued by Drew.

Though Drew gained a fortune through the Erie War, he soon lost it because of the unscrupulous dealings of his business partners. After their joint defeat of Vanderbilt, Fisk and Gould betrayed Drew. In 1870 they sold Erie Railroad stock in England, driving down the value of Drew's holdings. Drew lost $1.5 million from their misdeed. Soon afterward, he lost the rest of his fortune in the nationwide financial panic of 1873. He was forced to declare bankruptcy in 1876. Shortly thereafter, Drew retired to New York, where his son William H. Drew helped to support him.

Notwithstanding his sly and often unethical business dealings, Drew was a pious man who contributed generously to the Methodist Church. In 1866 he founded the Drew Theological Seminary (now Drew University) in Madison, New Jersey, with an endowment of $250,000. He also founded Drew Seminary for Young Ladies in Carmel, New York, though he went bankrupt before he could give the seminary all the money he had pledged. Daniel Drew died on September 18, 1879, in New York City, leaving behind an estate worth less than $500.

See also: **Jay Gould, Cornelius Vanderbilt**

FURTHER READING

Browder, Clifford. *The Money Game in Old New York: Daniel Drew and His Times.* Lexington: University of Kentucky, 1986.

Fisher, Kenneth L. *100 Minds That Made the Market.* Woodside, CA: Business Classics, 1995.

Geisst, Charles R. *Bull and Bear; Wall Street: A History.* Cambridge: Oxford University Press, 1988.

Gordon, John Steele. "Businessmen's Autobiographies." *American Heritage*, May/June 1995.

White, Bouck. *The Book of Daniel Drew: A Glimpse of the Fisk-Gould-Tweed Regime from the Inside.* Burlington, VT: Fraser Publications, 1996.

DRUCKER, PETER FERDINAND

Peter Drucker (1909–) is considered to be the founding father of modern management. In a career that spanned most of the twentieth century Drucker has remained a highly influential writer, teacher, and philosopher of business management principles. The author of more than 30 books that have been translated into at least 25 languages, Drucker's contributions to management have been likened to Isaac Asimov's influence on astronomy.

Born in Austria as the eldest son of a liberal civil service official, Peter Drucker grew up among a cultured society that admired the city of Vienna before World War I (1914–18). After high school Drucker left war-torn Austria to take an apprentice job at an export firm in Hamburg, Germany. To please his father he also enrolled in University of Hamburg to study law. Although young Drucker worked during the day, the University offered no evening classes. He passed his courses by taking final exams without attending a single class. That was not to say that he did not study; many of Drucker's evenings during his college years were spent reading library books printed in various languages.

In 1929 the twenty-year-old Drucker published his first article, in which he confidently predicted that the stock market would rise. A few weeks later the market crashed. Having learned a lasting lesson about the unpredictable nature of stock markets, an older and wiser Drucker confessed that this was the last financial prediction he ever made. "Fortunately, there is no copy of the journal left," he stated in his book *The Concept of a Corporation*.

Drucker earned his doctorate in public and international law from the University of Frankfurt while working as an editor and financial writer. Shortly after the Nazis came into power in 1933, Drucker was offered a job as a writer by the Ministry of Information. Because he was opposed to Nazism, Drucker dared to publish a pamphlet that ridiculed that party's oppressive, totalitarian politics. The Nazis banned and burned the pamphlet. Drucker soon left Germany for England, where he took a job at an insurance company as a securities analyst.

While attending a Cambridge University seminar led by the famous economist John Maynard Keynes (1883–1946) Drucker suddenly realized his interest was in people, not economics. He shifted his focus of study to management. In 1937 he came to the United States as the correspondent for British financial newspapers. Drucker's first book, *The End of Economic Man: The Origins of Totalitarianism*, was published in 1939. In his lifetime more than 30 well-received books would follow.

In 1943 General Motors allowed Drucker to study their management practices. His observations of GM set the tone for *The Concept of a Corporation*, the first book to treat a business enterprise as a political and social institution. *Concept of a Corporation* became one of the most popular management books in history. It advocated the emerging era of cooperation between labor and management by explaining one of Drucker's most famous ideas—employees having managerial responsibility in job structure and the performance of major tasks, as well as decision–making power over schedules, safety codes, and work benefits. But when Drucker first proposed these ideas during the 1940s, they were considered a rebellious challenge to managerial authority.

Drucker has said that writing is the foundation of all his work. His topics are varied and include advice to managers in *Managing for Results* (1964) and *The Effective Executive* (1966); general management in *Management: Task, Responsibilities, Practices* (1974);

social and political analysis in *The Age of Discontinuity* (1969); essay collections such as *The Ecological Vision* (1993), and two novels. His famous autobiography was titled *Adventures of a Bystander* (1979).

Along with his books Drucker also wrote articles for the world's most respected business journals, including *Forbes, Inc.*, *New Perspectives*, *The Atlantic Monthly*, *Esquire*, *Harvard Business Review*, *Foreign Affairs*, *The Public Interest*, and *The Economist*. From 1975 to 1995, he wrote a monthly column in the *Wall Street Journal*.

Drucker spent his life teaching others as a consultant and as a professor. He served on the faculties of Sarah Lawrence, Bennington College, New York University, and the Claremont Graduate School. He taught not only management and economics but also government, statistics, religion, philosophy, and literature. Every three to four years of his teaching career he would take on a new subject, ranging from Japanese art to sixteenth-century finance. Drucker said that in more than half a century of teaching he never found a subject that did not spark his interest.

Sixty years after the publication of his first book, Peter Drucker remained a mentor to generations of managers. He was respected for his past insights and the originality of his contemporary ideas. As he approached the age of 90, Drucker appeared on the cover of *Forbes* magazine with the caption ''Still the Youngest Mind.''

FURTHER READING

Beatty, Jack. *The World According to Peter Drucker*. New York: The Free Press, 1998.

Drucker, Peter. *Adventures of a Bystander*. New York: Harper & Row, 1979.

Galagan, Patricia A., and Stephen H. Rhinesmith. ''Peter Drucker: Interview with Management Guru.'' *Training and Development*, September 1998.

Johnson, Mike. ''Drucker Speaks His Mind.'' *Management Review*, October 1995.

Tarrant, John J. *Drucker: The Man Who Invented Corporate Society*. Boston: Cahners, Books, Inc., 1976.

DRY FARMING

Dry farming was an agricultural method that allowed crops to be cultivated on the prairie, which typically received low levels of rainfall and endured very hot summers and harsh winters. Growers who practiced dry farming cultivated some fields while allowing others to lie fallow, so that a field only supported crops every other year. In the off-year, the soil stored up enough moisture and nutrients for the following growing season. Another method of dry farming called for the soil to be tilled, rather than plowed, to a depth of only three or four inches (eight to ten centimeters).

While there was evidence that American Indians on the Great Plains and in the Southwest practiced dry-farming techniques, settlers of European descent did not adopt the method until late in the nineteenth century, when increasing westward expansion necessitated it. Ample enticement to move westward was provided by the Homestead Act of 1862, which granted settlers up to 160 acres (64 hectares) of frontier land as long as the settler built on it or cultivated it. Population growth in the East, largely the result of increased immigration in the late-1800s, also spurred westward migration during the last two decades of the nineteenth century. By 1900, more than a half million families had settled in the West under the Homestead Act. Determined to settle the prairie lands of the Great Plains (in present day Oklahoma, Kansas, Nebraska, South Dakota, and North Dakota), homesteaders experimented with dry farming; they found that wheat was particularly well-suited to the method. Early in the twentieth century, the Great Plains, which received many of the settlers, became one of the world's leading wheat-producing regions.

The widespread practice of dry farming had a catastrophic effect in the 1930s: the Dust Bowl. By the end of the nineteenth century Great Plains farmers, aided by steel plows, uprooted most of the native prairie grass, which held moisture in the soil. Strong winds and extended droughts had not disturbed the land when the grasses covered it. Because the demand for wheat increased after World War I (1914–1918), Great Plains farmers responded by planting more than twenty-seven million new acres of wheat. By 1930 there were almost three times as many acres in wheat production as there were ten years earlier. In 1934 drought, high winds, and the stripped land combined to create the Dust Bowl in the Plains. The situation prevailed into 1937, at a dear cost to crops and livestock. This combined with the effects of the Great Depression (1929–1939) to cause great hardships. Though many homesteaders abandoned their lands, other stayed and eventually replanted the Great Plains. The region was spared a recurrence of the Dust Bowl due to conservation efforts, which staved off over-planting and restored some prairie lands to their natural states.

See also: **Dust Bowl, Homesteaders, Prairie**

DUKE, JAMES BUCHANAN

James Buchanan Duke (1856–1925) was a driving force in the development of the U.S. tobacco industry. Through innovative marketing and production techniques Duke popularized cigarettes in the United States and abroad. He also made his mark in the electric power and textile industries. As a successful businessman Duke shared his good fortune through generous philanthropy, most visibly in his endowment to Duke University in North Carolina.

James Buchanan Duke was born on December 23, 1856 on his parents' farm in Durham, North Carolina. He was one of five children born to Washington and Artelia Duke.

While his father was away fighting for the South in the American Civil War (1861–1865) Union soldiers destroyed much of the 300-acre Duke farm. The farm had produced corn, oats, wheat, and tobacco crops, but only some stored leaf tobacco escaped destruction.

The Duke family then turned to the tobacco crop and subsistence farming for their survival. Because so much tobacco was destroyed throughout the South during the Civil War, demand for tobacco skyrocketed once the fighting stopped. Sensing the demand for tobacco and its greater market potential, Duke's father sold the family farm in 1874 and set up business in a tobacco factory in downtown Durham. James joined the family business, W. Duke and Sons, after completing business training at a New York school. It was there that the younger Duke began to seek creative ways to promote and improve the family business.

James Duke developed innovative marketing and production techniques that helped propel his family business to success. One of these innovations was the 1884 acquisition of the Bonsack cigarette-rolling machine, which allowed mechanized mass production of cigarettes. Before the Bonsack machine was introduced cigarettes were hand-rolled and difficult to mass produce. They were not very popular. Once Duke set mass production in motion, he directed his efforts to capturing public attention. In 1884 he moved to New York City and opened a company office. He studied the operations of retail stores in the city and planned his strategy based on his findings.

As a promotional effort Duke offered free samples of his cigarettes to new immigrants, hoping they would come back for more as paying customers. He advertised on billboards and posters, as well as in newspapers and magazines. He used the Duke family name to support sporting events and included coupons inside packets of Duke cigarettes.

Duke's aggressive marketing techniques were unprecedented in his day and they paid off. By 1889 the business, now called W. Duke, Sons and Company, produced 45 percent of all cigarettes sold in the United States. Duke's attempts to win an ever-greater share of the growing tobacco market culminated in an 1889 merger with four other major tobacco manufacturers. The American Tobacco Company was thus born. It controlled 90 percent of all tobacco sales in the United States.

As president of the company, James Duke became the dominant leader in the tobacco industry. He was determined that the company retain market and industry superiority. Duke closed less efficient factories and discontinued unpopular cigarette brands. He undercut the retail prices of his remaining competition and hired non-union labor at low wages. He also signed a contract with the Bonsack Company to restrict its sales of the automatic cigarette-making machine to any company other than the American Tobacco Company. By 1898 the American Tobacco Company had almost eliminated its competition. In 1910 the company expanded to the overseas market.

The United States government watched the business practices of the American Tobacco Company for several years. As early as 1907 the company faced lawsuits alleging violations of anti-trust regulations. In 1911 the federal government charged American Tobacco with violations of the Sherman Anti-Trust Act, inhibiting fair and reasonable competition in the marketplace. Ultimately, the U.S. Supreme Court determined that much of the American Tobacco Company's business was pursued with illegal secret agreements and false public promotions. Its practices were ''unreasonable'' in the fair U.S. marketplace. To encourage competition, the Supreme Court ruled the tobacco giant be broken up into four smaller firms, the American Tobacco Company, Liggett and Myers, P. Lorillard, and R.J. Reynolds.

Duke remained president of the American Tobacco Company, now at 40 percent of its previous size. His attention, however, turned to more diversified business interests. He invested heavily in hydroelectric power plants, founding the Southern Power System in 1905. Southern Power built eleven plants (1907–1925). At the same time Duke invested in textile mills producing cotton and wool. The mills ran on power supplied by Duke's hydroelectric plants. The Southern Power System eventually became known as the Duke Power Company.

Duke shared his good business fortune with the public through his generous philanthropy. In 1924 he established the Duke Endowment with $40 million. A portion of the endowment went to Trinity College in North Carolina. The school was later renamed Duke University. The Duke Endowment was also established to support other educational institutions, health care organizations, children's homes, and churches.

James Buchanan Duke pioneered the development of the U.S. tobacco industry and made significant contributions to philanthropy and business. He died in 1925.

See also: **American Tobacco Company, Mass Production, Sherman Anti-Trust Act, Tobacco, Tobacco Industry, Tobacco Trust**

FURTHER READING

Armentano, Cominick T. *Antitrust and Monopoly: Anatomy of a Policy Failure.* New York: John Wiley and Sons, 1982.

Cox, Reavis. *Competition in the American Tobacco Industry, 1911–1932.* New York: Columbia University Press, 1933.

Durden, Robert F. *The Dukes of Durham: 1865–1929.* Durham, NC: Duke University Press, 1975.

Jenkins, John Wilber. *James B. Duke: Master Builder.* New York: George H. Doran Co., 1927.

Porter, Earl W. *Trinity and Duke, 1892–1924: Foundations of Duke University.* Durham, NC: Duke University Press, 1964.

Tilley, Nannie May. *The Bright-Tobacco Industry: 1860–1929.* Chapel Hill, NC: University of North Carolina Press, 1948.

Winkler, John K. *Tobacco Tycoon: The Story of James Buchanan Duke.* New York: Random House, 1942.

DUPONT COMPANY

E.I. du Pont de Nemours & Company, better known as DuPont, developed from a family business, which manufactured gunpowder and explosives, to a multinational corporation that produces petroleum, natural gas, chemicals, synthetic fibers, polymers, and various other products. DuPont brand names—such as nylon, Teflon, Lycra, and Mylar—are part of the everyday vocabulary of people across the world. At the end of 1998 DuPont employed about 84,000 people in 70 countries and was the sixteenth largest industrial service corporation in the United States.

The founder of the company was the French nobleman with the impressive name of Éleuthère Irénée du Pont de Nemours, who had studied with the famous chemist Antoine-Laurent Lavoisier. Du Pont came to the United States in 1797 and built a gunpowder factory on the Brandywine River in Delaware. His sons continued producing superior gunpowder after his death and also manufactured smokeless powder, dynamite, and nitroglycerine.

When competition in the early twentieth century became fierce, shareholders of the company voted to sell the company to the highest bidder. Alfred I. du Pont and two of his cousins, Pierre S. du Pont and Thomas Coleman, acquired the company in a leveraged buyout in order to keep it in the family. Pierre du Pont and Coleman, with Alfred in a lesser role as vice president, guided DuPont to unprecedented success, acquiring 54 other companies within three years. By 1905 DuPont held a 75 percent share of the U.S. gunpowder market and had become a major producer of explosives and one of the nation's largest corporations. With laboratories in New Jersey and Wilmington, Delaware, it was one of the first American companies to devote itself heavily to research. DuPont had also become the economic lifeblood of the state of Delaware.

Much of the company's success was due to its efficient structure, which designated different levels of management. In this sense, DuPont profoundly influenced the way U.S. corporations were run. Too much success, however, ultimately worked against the company. DuPont controlled so much of the explosives market that in 1912 the U.S. government ordered it to divest itself of a number of its assets. Adding to the company's troubles was a continuing feud between Alfred du Pont and his cousins, who eventually took away all of Alfred's real responsibilities within the organization.

DuPont continued to diversify in the early 1900s. Pierre Samuel du Pont began to buy General Motors (GM) stock in 1914, and he soon became embroiled in a struggle for power within that company. William C. Durant (1861–1947), founder of GM, fought to maintain control of the company, which he later lost. Pierre du Pont eventually acquired enough stock to be a dominant force within the company during the 1920s. This facilitated an economic relationship between General Motors and DuPont, and DuPont began selling to GM its Duco paint, antifreeze, and lead additive for gasoline.

DuPont also expanded into the textile business, manufacturing artificial fibers for use during World War I (1914–1918). When the company acquired rights from the French to manufacture cellophane in the 1920s, it began manufacturing rayon and developed a stronger version of the cord used in automobile tires. By far the most important of DuPont's creations was nylon, developed in 1930 by a research group headed by Wallace H. Carothers. DuPont's thermoplastics division spun off all kinds of products, including shower curtains, radio dials, eyeglass frames, and screwdriver handles.

In many ways, DuPont contributed to the American effort to win World War II (1939–1945). Through a partnership with the U.S. government, DuPont established an atomic bomb research center in Hanford, Washington. After the war women lined up to purchase DuPont-produced nylon stockings, which had been unavailable during wartime. Some of DuPont's other product innovations included neoprene, Lucite, Orlon, and Dacron, products that revolutionized the global consumer industry.

DuPont's string of successes came to a halt in the mid-1970s, when the demand for artificial fibers began to decline, and the costs of raw materials increased. DuPont's concentration on rebuilding its old business rather than branching out into new areas cost it dearly; moreover, a recession in 1980 hurt the company. In that same year, however, the development of a product called Kevlar brought renewed success. Kevlar was a light, strong polymer with five times the tensile strength of steel. It could be used for such products at fire-resistant clothing, tire reinforcements, and bulletproof vests. Its cost, however, was high since it was derived from petroleum.

Mergers and acquisitions in the 1980s helped bring DuPont out of the recession. The most important of these was the acquisition of Conoco, which provided DuPont with oil at competitive prices. DuPont also involved itself in joint ventures with such companies as P.D. Magnetics, the Sankyo Company (pharmaceuticals), the Mitsubishi Rayon Company, and British Telecom (optoelectronic components). The company, moreover, began to branch out from stock chemicals and petrochemically based fibers into the life sciences, taking on such fields as genetic engineering and the

manufacture of heart medications and the cancer-fighting drug interferon. In addition, DuPont took part in the development of pesticides and electronics parts supplies. By the mid-1980s DuPont owned about 90 businesses that sold a wide range of products.

In the late 1980s, however, management at DuPont decided that the company should begin concentrating on its most profitable areas—oil, healthcare, electronics, and specialty chemicals. While divisions such as pharmaceuticals and electronics were losing money, textiles continued to be its most successful product line, and the company began to publish a consumer products catalog featuring items made from its well-known fibers, such as Lycra, Zytel, and Supplex. The stretch polymer Lucre, favored by many fashion designers, became a big seller.

During the late 1980s and early 1990s DuPont paid particular attention to pollution control and clean-up, gradually replacing its environmentally harmful chlorofluorocarbons with safer chemicals, at a cost of $1 billion. The company also began to market safer pesticides and entered the growing recycling market.

With the exception of a temporary rise in profits for Conoco as a result of the Persian Gulf War (1991), most of DuPont's operations lost ground during the early 1990s. The company began restructuring, divesting itself of unprofitable components and reducing staff levels. DuPont also concentrated more on its chemicals and fibers divisions, acquiring polyester technology from ICI; meanwhile, ICI bought out DuPont's acrylics business.

In the 1990s DuPont began to recover from the downturn of the 1980s. The company posted record profits in 1994 and 1996, and stock prices rose. New joint ventures in the areas of synthetic fibers, chemicals, and agricultural products continued to turn profits. In 1997 DuPont purchased a division of Ralston Purina that manufactured soy products, and also bought out Merck's share in the DuPont Merck Pharmaceutical Company. In an effort to concentrate on its core businesses, DuPont divested itself of Conoco in 1998. In that year DuPont had a net income of $4.7 billion. Nearing the close of the twentieth century, the company could safely boast that DuPont products had become inseparable from the everyday life of most societies in the world.

See also: **E.I. du Pont, William C. Durant**

FURTHER READING

Colby, Gerald. *Du Pont Dynasty*. Secaucus, NJ: Lyle Stuart, 1984.

Hess, Glenn. "DuPont Vows to Double Value Within Five Years." *Chemical Market Reporter*, March 3, 1997.

Hoffecker, Carol E. *Delaware: A Bicentennial History.* New York: Norton, 1977.

Lenzer, Robert, and Carrie Shook. "There Will Always Be a DuPont." *Forbes*, October 13, 1997.

Meikle, Jeffrey L. *American Plastic: A Cultural History.* New Brunswick, NJ: Rutgers University Press, 1996.

DU PONT, ÉLEUTHÈRE IRÉNÉE

Éleuthère Irénée du Pont (1771–1834), a French refugee in the early days of the American republic, founded an international industrial giant, E.I. Du Pont de Nemours and Company. Begun as a small gunpowder mill on Brandywine Creek near Wilmington, Delaware, his company became a leading manufacturer of chemicals, plastics, and synthetic fibers and was one of the older continuously operating industrial enterprises in the world.

Du Pont was born in Paris, France, in 1771, the son of Pierre Samuel du Pont, a French nobleman. His mother died when the boy was fourteen. With his older brother, Victor, du Pont grew up at Bois-des-Fosses, a family estate sixty miles south of the French capital.

The political turmoil of revolutionary France strongly influenced du Pont's early life. His father was politically active, sharing the title of commander of the National Guard with the Marquis de Lafayette, the French general and statesman who came to the aid of the American army during the American Revolution (1775–1783). The elder du Pont, together with Lafayette, founded the conservative *Société de 1789* to promote a constitutional monarchy. The son aligned himself politically with his father. On August 10, 1792 the du Ponts led a sixty-man private guard to defend the king's palace from an assault by radicals dedicated to ending the monarchy. But their success on that occasion did not change the inevitable; the king, queen, and many supporters were later imprisoned and guillotined.

Among the many men and women put to the guillotine was Antoine Lavoisier (1743–1794), known as the father of modern chemistry. Lavoisier was one of

Éleuthère Irénée du Pont.

the greatest scientists of his day and a close friend of Pierre du Pont. He was also in charge of the royal gunpowder mills and, in that role, he taught the young du Pont the craft of gunpowder-making.

When the future emperor Napoleon Bonaparte (1769–1821) seized power in 1799, both Pierre and Éleuthère du Pont were imprisoned for their opposition to his autocratic rule. They were released when they pledged to leave France. The du Pont family arrived in Newport, Rhode Island, on December 3, 1800, it was in the United States that Éleuthère du Pont would thrive.

It was soon apparent to du Pont that gunpowder was a much-needed commodity in his adopted land. Guns were needed on the frontier. Settlers hunted for meat and skins and gunpowder was also used to clear land to build homes and roads. Although some gunpowder was produced locally, ninety percent was imported from France.

On July 19, 1802, du Pont purchased land on Brandywine Creek near Wilmington, Delaware, with $36,000 in capital from a group of French investors, and he set about building his first black powder factory. In the spring of 1804 the first du Pont gunpowder was sold. The business was an immediate success and it became highly profitable during the War of 1812 (1812–1814).

Following the teachings of his mentor, Lavoisier, and the scientific method the great chemist advocated, du Pont brought to the United States new ideas about the manufacture of consistently reliable gun and blasting powder. Unlike much of the black powder then available, du Pont's product ignited when it was supposed to. In 1811 former President Thomas Jefferson (1801–1809) wrote to du Pont to express his appreciation of the quality of the gunpowder he had purchased to clear the land for his new estate, Monticello.

DU PONT BROUGHT TO THE UNITED STATES NEW IDEAS ABOUT THE MANUFACTURE OF CONSISTENTLY RELIABLE GUN AND BLASTING POWDER. UNLIKE MUCH OF THE BLACK POWDER THEN AVAILABLE, DU PONT'S PRODUCT IGNITED WHEN IT WAS SUPPOSED TO.

Du Pont gave careful attention to preparing his raw materials. Saltpeter was thoroughly cleaned in du Pont's mills, no matter what the state of the material's cleanliness when it arrived at the plant. Sulfur was not used unless pure and clear in color.

Du Pont always sought ways to improve the quality of his product and the company's manufacturing methods. He was also a man of exemplary ethics. In March 1818, for example, an explosion killed 40 men and ruined his mills. Even though there were no laws requiring it, and it was not the business practice of the day, du Pont took it upon himself to compensate the families of the victims. He pensioned the widows, gave them homes, and took responsibility for the education and medical care of the surviving children.

Du Pont spent 32 years as president of his very profitable enterprise. At the time of his death in 1834 the privately owned company he had named E.I. du Pont de Nemours and Company had become highly successful. Following his death the company was passed down to his sons and, until 1940, the enterprise was headed by a member of the du Pont family.

See also: **DuPont Chemical Company**

FURTHER READING

Colby, Gerald. *Du Pont: Behind the Nylon Curtain.* Englewood Cliffs, NJ: Prentice-Hall, 1974.

Dorian, Max. *The Du Ponts: From Gunpowder to Nylon.* Boston: Little, Brown and Co., 1961.

Du Pont De Nemours, E.I. *Du Pont: The Autobiography of an American Enterprise.* Wilmington, DE: E.I. Du Pont de Nemours and Co., 1952.

Du Pont de Nemours, Samuel Pierre. *The Autobiography of du Pont de Nemours.* Wilmington, DE: Scholarly Resources, 1984.

Gates, John D. *The du Pont Family.* Garden City, NY: Doubleday, 1979.

Winkler, John K. *The du Pont Dynasty.* New York: Blue Ribbon Books, 1935.

DURABLE GOODS

Durable goods are tangible commodities that will last more than a year with normal usage. Durable goods comprise two categories: consumer and producer durables. Examples of consumer durables are cars, boats, furniture, televisions, appliances, and fine jewelry. Producer or capital durables include machinery and equipment.

In the 1920s immediately following World War I (1914–1918) the United States witnessed a consumer durables revolution. Businessmen invested sharply in production facilities of many kinds. New manufacturing plants made possible a huge expansion in the output of durable goods, particularly automobiles, refrigerators, radios, washing machines, and vacuum cleaners. Individuals no longer restricted their spending to the amount of cash they had on hand. They bought on time. Finance companies specialized in providing installment credit, and buyers made wide use of the technique to purchase durable goods.

The role of durable goods in the business cycle, the ups and downs of business activity in the United States, are extremely important. The output of durable goods shows greater variability over the business cycle than output of other goods. An automobile is a "big ticket" item and lasts a number of years. Since it is a long lasting good, its purchase can usually be postponed for long periods. The purchase is usually with borrowed money involving the payment of interest. In a recession, usually accompanied by high interest rates, purchases of durables will fall dramatically. In contrast during a time of expansion with low interest rates, durables are in high demand. On the other hand, the purchase of non-durables, like bread, milk, and beer, will change minimally over the business cycle.

Key statistics, or indicators, are used to analyze and forecast changes in the business cycle. The Gross Domestic Product (GDP) is the market value of all final goods and services produced within a certain time period. A key component of the GDP is personal consumption expenditures, which include durable goods expenditures. Durable goods alone accounted for approximately 8 percent of the GDP in the 1990s. Increased spending for durables contributes to a positive economic forecast whereas a decrease points to an economic slowdown.

See also: **Capital Goods, Consumer Goods**

DURANT, THOMAS CLARK

As a financier and an executive of the Union Pacific Railroad in the early 1860s Dr. Thomas C. Durant (1820–1885) was instrumental in building the first railway spanning the western United States. He ended his career, however, in scandal and financial disaster, having greatly enriched himself at the public's expense.

The Durants were a wealthy and distinguished western Massachusetts family. Bowing to the wishes of his parents, Thomas Durant graduated from Albany Medical College in upstate New York in 1840. But he never practiced medicine, choosing instead to devote his career to business.

After a period of working in his uncle's grain and flour export business, Durant moved to New York City and became involved in the stock market. The 1850s saw the wide-spread building of railways, the ''super-highways'' of that time. Durant recognized railroads as a good investment, and soon he began to concentrate his entire resources on financing railroad construction.

Together with engineer Henry Farnum, he orchestrated the construction of numerous major rail lines, including the Mississippi and Missouri railroad across Iowa. In 1862 he negotiated a contract with the U.S. government to build the Union Pacific. a rail line that would go westward from Omaha, Nebraska. It was expected to join the Central Pacific, which was moving eastward from California to create a transcontinental railroad. Durant joined the company as vice president and general manager mainly in order to protect and extend his own financial interests.

The Union Pacific soon fell into financial difficulties. Durant attempted to solve the problem by creating a construction and finance company called the Crédit Mobilier of America to complete the building of the railroad. The Crédit Mobilier was a complex and corrupt scheme in which a small group of financiers contracted with themselves or their associates to construct the railroad, charging exorbitant prices for their services. Durant and his cronies pocketed huge profits for construction that was often faulty. Crédit Mobilier became a symbol of corruption in an era when illegal manipulation of large contracts was often the standard operating procedure.

Durant was instrumental in obtaining support and financing at every level of government. He lobbied President Abraham Lincoln (1861–1865) and both houses of Congress and with every favorable decision he pocketed more cash. He played on the fascination with the West during the war-torn 1860s and also exploited people's ignorance of the value of the vast area of land between the Mississippi River and California, which maps called the ''Great American Desert.'' Therefore he was able to persuade Congress to pass the Pacific Railway Act of 1862 with a promise that the railroad would receive 10 square miles of land for every mile of track it laid.

In 1864 Crédit Mobilier took over the Union Pacific's construction contracts. Durant persuaded Congress to double the size of the land grants the railroad was previously awarded. He later sold some of this land but retained much more. This land holding added greatly to his wealth as did an elaborate scheme for padding his expenses. The original estimates for construction of the Union Pacific line had accurately set the cost at around $30,000 per mile of track. The Crédit Mobilier doubled this figure, with Durant and a few others pocketing the difference. Construction methods were shoddy. Shortly after the 1869 track completion ceremonies construction crews were forced to undertake several years' worth of additional work rebuilding the tracks.

Durant's reign as the leading robber baron of the Union Pacific and Crédit Mobilier did not last long. In 1865 Durant and his associates faced a severe financial problem, which Oakes and Oliver Ames, who amassed a fortune in the pick and shovel business, promised to ameliorate. They invested more than a million dollars of their own money in the railroad and raised an additional $1.5 million upon the credit of their businesses. Shortly thereafter it was discovered that Oakes Ames, a member of Congress from Massachusetts, distributed shares of Crédit Mobilier stock as political favors. He and a colleague were censured by the House of Representatives. Vice President Schuyler Colfax, Speaker of the House James C. Blaine, and future U.S. President James A. Garfield (1881) were all implicated but were later absolved in the scandal.

Durant had managed to accumulate some $23 million by defrauding the railroad's investors with his Crédit Mobilier scheme. An associate later called him "the most extravagant man I ever knew in my life." But, deeply involved in the worst financial scandal of his time and justifiably accused of bribery and fraud, Durant saw his fortune dwindle to virtually nothing following the financial Panic of 1873. He spent his latter days living quietly on his property in upstate New York, where he died on October 5, 1885.

See also: **Oakes Ames, Oliver Ames, Central Pacific Railroad, Mississippi River, Panics of the Late Nineteenth Century, Transcontinental Railroad, Union Pacific Railroad, Westward Expansion**

FURTHER READING

Ames, Charles Edgar. *Pioneering the Union Pacific: a Reappraisal of the Builders of the Railroad.* New York: Appleton-Century-Crofts, 1969.

Galloway, John D. *The First Transcontinental Railroad: Central Pacific, Union Pacific.* New York: Arno Press, 1981.

Ingham, John N. *Biographical Dictionary of American Business Leaders.* Westport: Greenwood, 1983, s.v. "Durant, Thomas."

Johnson, Allen and Dumas Malone, eds. *Dictionary of American Biography.* Volume 5, Cushman-Eberle. New York: Scribner's, 1930, s.v. "Durant, Thomas."

McCabe, James Dabney. *Behind the Scenes in Washington: Being a Complete and Graphic Account of the Crédit Mobilier Investigation.* New York: Continental, 1873.

DURANT, WILLIAM CRAPO

Born in Boston, Massachusetts, on December 8, 1861, William Crapo Durant (1861–1947) grew up in Flint, Michigan. His parents divorced after his father went bankrupt in the late 1860s, and his mother moved the family to Michigan. There she reunited with her father, who had prospered in the lumber business and served as mayor of Flint and governor of Michigan. Durant left high school early to work in his grandfather's lumberyard and at various other jobs. One of those jobs was as a salesman for a local cigar manufacturer.

Durant was a natural salesman. "Let the customer sell himself," was his stated philosophy. In 1885, after finding a unique suspension system that minimized bounce, he organized the Durant-Dort Company to make carriages. This company was his first success, and it became one of the leading manufacturers of horse-drawn carriages. By 1900 the company was the largest carriage manufacturer in the United States.

But Durant saw that the future of transportation rested in the automobile rather than the horse-drawn carriage. In 1904 he took over management of the Buick Motor Company, which had financial problems. That year, he arranged for Buick to participate in the New York Automobile Show and took orders for 1108 cars, more than 25 times the number of cars the company had ever manufactured. To raise the capital necessary to respond to this increased need, Durant sold Buick stock to anyone in Flint who was interested in buying. Production at the Buick Company went from 725 cars in 1905, to 1400 in 1906, to 4641 in 1907. Buick reached the position of number one in the country in 1908, with a production of 8820 cars, outselling Ford Motor Company and Cadillac combined.

Durant tried to buy Ford in 1907, but the bid failed when Henry Ford (1863–1947) insisted on being paid in cash. The next year Durant formed General Motors Company in response. Durant's concept for his new company was to be a total supplier of automobiles from the car itself to its parts and service. Durant added Cadillac, Oldsmobile, Oakland (Pontiac) and other lesser companies to the original Buick at General Motors. Durant was a great salesman, but not so great at purchasing companies. Many of his acquisitions were over-priced or ill advised. In 1910 General Motors was heavily in debt and under a cash crunch. Bankers rescued the company from its financial predicament, but the price was a loss of control for Durant.

Still believing in the automobile, Durant joined forces with race car driver Louis Chevrolet (1879–1941) and established Chevrolet Motor Company in 1911. Chevrolet was an instant success with the Model

490, which cost more than Ford's Model T, but offered greater refinements and comfort. The loan the bankers had made to General Motors expired in 1915, and with it, Durant's prohibition from involvement in the company. With the help of the Du Pont family, Durant was able to regain control of General Motors in 1916. Chevrolet was brought into the General Motors family of automobiles, and the company prospered.

Durant, however, was unable to effectively deal with the company's stock price problems during the Panic of 1920. General Motors stock fell from $42 per share in March to just $14 per share in October. Durant felt personally responsible to many of the shareholders, as he had made personal commitments to friends and neighbors to sell the stock. He tried valiantly to prop up the stock price and save his friends' investments, but he failed.

When the Du Ponts discovered Durant's position, they forced him out of General Motors in order to protect their own investment. Oddly, Durant could have weathered all the problems with stock prices and the company if he had just left the situation alone. By 1926, just six years later, General Motors stock was trading at $210 per share. From April to November of 1920, Durant lost over $90 million. Adjusted for inflation, that amount would have been over $1 billion in the 1990s. Many believe this to be the largest relative loss of money in the history of the stock market.

Durant made another attempt to succeed in the automobile industry, starting Durant Motors in 1921, but it failed to establish itself in the market. By the time of the stock market crash of 1929, Durant Motors was already shaky and it lost ground steadily until its dissolution in 1933. By 1935 Durant had declared bankruptcy. He dabbled in a number of other business ventures, including a bowling alley, but none were particularly successful. He died in New York on March 18, 1947.

See also: **Automobile Industry, General Motors Corporation**

FURTHER READING

Bowman, John S., ed. *The Cambridge Dictionary of American Biography*. Cambridge: Cambridge University Press, 1995, s.v. "Durant, William C."

Encyclopedia of World Biography. Detroit: Gale Research, 1998, s.v. "Durant, William C."

Gordon, John Steele. "Paper Losses, Real Losses." *American Heritage*, February-March 1996.

"Trailblazer Buick Put Premium Cars on the Sales Chart Hit Parade." *Automotive News*, April 29, 1996.

Weisberger, Bernard A. *The Dream Maker: William C. Durant, Founder of General Motors*. Boston: Little, Brown, 1979.

DUST BOWL

Farmers across the Great Plains longed for rain during the spring of 1934. But day after day, the weather offered no relief, only intense sun, wind, drought, more sun, then gale-force winds. On April 14, massive clouds of dust blotted out the sun over western Kansas. At first the wind raced along the surface, tearing at the stunted wheat and licking up the topsoil. Then the dust thickened into low, heavy, dirt-laden clouds. From a distance, the storm had the appearance of a cumulus cloud, but it was black, not white; and it seemed to eat its way along with a rolling, churning motion. As the storm swept toward Oklahoma and Texas, the black clouds engulfed the landscape. For those at the storm center there was an eerie sensation of silence and darkness. There was little or no visibility, and wind velocity hit 40 to 50 miles per hour. The next month was exceedingly hot with a temperature above 100 degrees Fahrenheit every day. On May 10, the gales returned, this time from the west. Unlike the previous storm, these winds whipped up a formless, light-brown fog that spread over an area 900 miles wide and 1500 miles long. The next day an estimated 12 million tons of soil fell on Chicago, Illinois, and dust darkened the skies over Cleveland, Ohio. On May 12, dust hung like a shadow over the entire eastern seaboard. By the time they were over, these two storms alone blew 650 million tons of topsoil off the Great Plains.

The Dust Bowl covered 300,000 square miles of territory located in Kansas, Texas, western Oklahoma, eastern Colorado, and New Mexico. In the hardest-hit areas, agriculture virtually ceased. With successive storms, the wind and the flying dust cut off wheat stalks at ground level and tore out the roots. Blowing dirt shifted from one field to another, burying crops not yet carried away from the wind. Cattle tried to eat the dust-laden grass and filled their stomachs with fatal "mud

Children at a water pump shielding their faces against swirling dust. In 1935, 650 million tons of topsoil eroded in the Central Plains states. The nation's farmland endured intense dust storms, during time known as, "The Great Dust Bowl."

balls.'' The dust banked against houses and farm buildings like snow, and buried fences up to the post tops. Dirt penetrated into automobile engines and clogged the vital parts. Housewives fought vainly to keep it out of their homes, but it seeped in through cracks and crevices, through wet blankets hung over windows, through oiled cloths and tape, covering everything with grit. Hospitals reported hundreds of patients suffering from "dust pneumonia." The black blizzards struck so suddenly that many farmers became lost in their own fields and suffocated, some literally within yards of shelter. More than 350,000 people fled the Great Plains during the 1930s. These "Okies" loaded their meager household goods and struck out along famous highway Route 66 for California.

Fifty years earlier, a strong, protective carpet of buffalo grass had covered the Great Plains. The grass held moisture in the soil and kept the soil from blowing away. In dry years, the wind blew out huge craters, later mistakenly called "buffalo wallows," but as long as the turf remained, the land could recover. In the last two decades of the nineteenth century, farmers began staking out homesteads in regions once considered too

arid for anything other than range. Wherever they went, farmers plowed under the buffalo grass. During World War I (1914–1918) the demand for wheat, along with the invention of the tractor, meant plowing larger areas of the virgin grassland. Between 1914 and 1917, the area of wheat planted increased to 27 million acres, much of which (more than 40 percent) had never been plowed before. After the war, the plowing continued. Larger tractors and combines, new machines that could harvest and thresh grain in one operation, inaugurated the age of the wheat kings. By 1930, there were almost three times as many acres in wheat production as there had been a decade earlier, and that number was steadily increasing. The plow exposed the land to rain, wind, and sun. By 1932, the earth on the plains was ready to blow away.

The Dust Bowl sped the development of long-range federal programs in the new field of soil conservation. A veteran conservationist, President Franklin D. Roosevelt (1933–1945) in late 1933, created the Soil Erosion Service, later the Soil Conservation Service (SCS), with Hugh Bennett as its head. The SCS's task was to supply technical assistance and leadership, while local soil conservation districts carried out Bennett's program of strip crops, contour plowing, stubble-mulch farming, and terracing. More dramatically, the Forest Service under Ferdinand A. Silcox in 1934 started planting a "shelter belt" of trees, within a 100-mile wide zone, from Canada to the Texas Panhandle. Ten years later, more than 200 million cottonwoods and other varieties of trees were serving as wind breaks and helping to conserve moisture. In 1936, the Agricultural Adjustment Administration (AAA), directed by Chester Davies, adopted soil conservation as a subterfuge to get around an unfavorable Supreme Court decision; but on the Great Plains, soil conservation was a legitimate part of the AAA program. Farmers received government checks for both acreage reductions and wind control practices.

After 1936, the New Deal added little to its conservation program. Roosevelt did appoint two special committees under the chairmanship of Morris L. Cooke, one to study Dust Bowl conditions and the other to recommend specific legislation. Congress passed a water storage bill along the lines that the latter committee had suggested, but did little else. In 1939 Harlan H. Barrows reported for the Committee on the Northern Great Plains but again, little was done.

Although it achieved less than it might have, the New Deal did much to hasten recovery in the Dust Bowl; more importantly, the rains began anew. As the buffalo grass spread again, the bowl area rapidly shrank from 8.727 million acres in 1938 to 1.2 million in 1939. Yet there remained the danger that farmers would forget the terrible lessons from the drought and that the Dust Bowl would once again reappear.

See also: **Agricultural Equipment Industry, Agriculture Industry, Colorado, Kansas, New Mexico, Oklahoma, Texas**

FURTHER READING

Bennett, Hugh Hammond. *Elements of Soil Conservation*, 2nd ed. New York: McGraw-Hill Book Co., 1955.

Sears, Paul B. *Deserts on the March*. Norman: University of Oklahoma Press, 1947.

Steinbeck, John. *The Grapes of Wrath*. New York: Viking Press, 1939.

Svobida, Lawrence. *An Empire of Dust*. Caldwell, ID: Caxton Printers, 1940.

Johnson, Vance. *Heaven's Tableland : The Dust Bowl Story*. New York: Farrar, Straus, and Giroux, 1947.

EARLY REPUBLIC TO CIVIL WAR, 1815–1860 (OVERVIEW)

At the end of the War of 1812 (1812–1814) the U.S. economy was overwhelmingly agricultural. It had a small industrial base concentrated in the Blackstone and Merrimac river valleys of New England and the Delaware River valley between Philadelphia and Wilmington, Delaware. The largest manufacturing industry was flour milling, followed by the production of leather goods, and then other food processing, including distilling. The iron, chemical, paper, and textile industries were very small.

During this period most industry was still carried out by the putting out system (in which craftsmen and their families did work in their homes). In 1810 ninety percent of the textile production in the nation was still done in homes, even though the textile industry was among the most industrialized in the nation at the time. The total value of manufacturing production was approximately $200 million.

By 1860, however, there were over 140,000 manufacturing establishments employing more than 1.3 million people to produce just under $2 billion in products. Very little of this output was produced by the putting out system, except in the shoe industry. Nearly all of this industrial growth took place north of Chesapeake Bay. By this time the United States was second in the world in manufacturing production behind only Great Britain. Between 1810 and 1860 the nation's population increased over four-fold, from 7.2 million to 31.5 million, with most of the growth occurring in the industrializing areas.

The economy in 1815 was not only largely agricultural, but it was also very localized due to poor roads. It was difficult to move bulky goods over any significant distance, with few alternatives for transportation outside the areas that could ship by river or sea. Steamboats, however, began sailing rivers in 1807 and

by the 1840s they carried 10 million tons of freight a year on the Ohio, Mississippi and other western rivers. Steamboats were much faster than sailboats, but their period of dominance was brief due to the rise of canals and railroads.

In 1825 the Erie Canal connecting New York City to the Great Lakes at Buffalo opened. Its immediate success led to a boom that saw canal construction increase dramatically. By 1840 there were 3,300 miles of canal in operation. However a decade later canal construction plans were being abandoned due to competition from the railroads. In the 1830s railroads began to appear and by 1860 the nation had over 30,000 miles of rail in operation. Local, state, and federal governments subsidized both canal and railroad construction as well as river and harbor improvements to facilitate transportation. The construction of this transportation network was a major factor in the economy, employing large numbers of people and facilitating the movement of raw materials and manufactured goods. Most importantly it allowed the inexpensive and efficient movement of food from the west to the industrial cities of the northeast.

Plantation slavery dominated the South during this period. The invention of the cotton gin in 1793 by Eli Whitney increased the potential profit in growing the short-staple cotton that grew well in the interior parts of the South. The expansion of the textile industry both in England and the northeastern United States provided a large and expanding market for the crop. Cotton production increased from just 209,000 bales in 1815 to almost 5.4 million in 1859. Planters moved their slaves in large numbers to the interior of Virginia, North and South Carolina, Georgia, Alabama, Mississippi, Arkansas, Louisiana, and Texas. World demand for cotton kept pace with increasing production and cotton plantations were highly profitable during most of the period leading up to the American Civil War (1861–1865). Tobacco growing did continue in Virginia and North Carolina as well as sugar cane and rice growing in coastal Carolina, Georgia, and Louisiana. But cotton

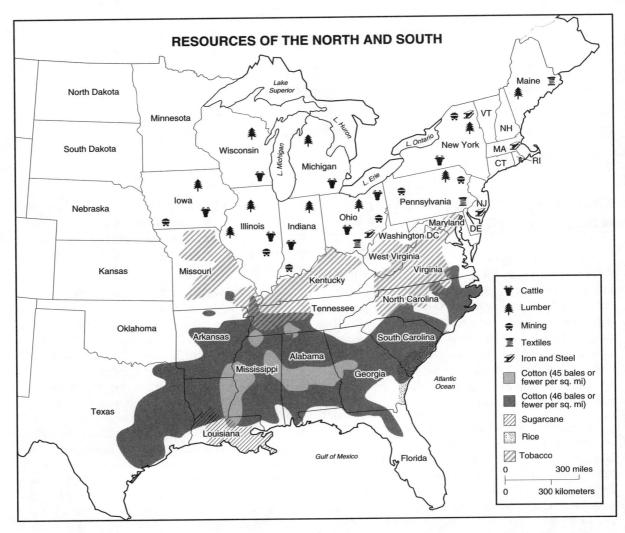

RESOURCES OF THE NORTH AND SOUTH

This map depicts the major resources of the Northern and Southern states in 1860. The North's economy was industrialized and dependent on a free immigrant labor force. The relatively independent economy of the South was primarily based on staple crop production and slave labor forces.

dominated the Southern economy and drove the political agenda of the Southern states. For example, railroad development in the South focused on short transport routes that moved cotton to the nearest river rather than an integrated system tying the region together. (Integrated transportation systems were only beginning to appear when the Civil War began.)

Cotton plantations were highly specialized: nearly all available land was planted in cotton while food and other goods were purchased from those areas in the upper South that were not well-suited to cotton, particularly Kentucky. Slavery was only marginally profitable in those areas that did not grow cotton, but the demand for slaves in the cotton areas kept slave prices high. A large internal slave trade developed rapidly after the importation of slaves ended in 1808. Southern capital was largely invested in land and slaves for the

production of cotton and the economy of the region was highly specialized by 1860.

Industry in the Northeast began to develop in several areas, initially using waterpower. For generations northerners had ground grain into flour, fulled cloth, and cut lumber using water-powered mills. There was an extensive community of millwrights familiar with water-powered machinery and who had worked on ways to mechanize work in those mills. For years northern merchants had traveled all over the world carrying world commerce and accumulating capital. In 1790 Samuel Slater brought detailed knowledge of the new British textile technology to the United States. With the support of Moses Brown he built a wool mill and a machine shop at Pawtucket, Rhode Island. Slater's venture was almost immediately successful and gave the community of millwrights enough information to not only replicate the British machinery, but to begin independently improving it.

After the War of 1812 capital in the United States began to shift away from trade to domestic manufacturing. The Tariff of 1816 was the first truly protective tariff; it provided a secure environment for investment in factories. As a result, the textile industry, especially cotton textiles, began to expand rapidly. Cotton textile production increased from 600,000 yards in 1810 to 141.1 million yards in 1830, and ultimately reached over 857 million yards in 1860.

The scale of textile factories changed during this period. The small mills with a few dozen spindles and looms that characterized the initial period of the industry gave way to larger complexes. This pattern began with the Boston Associates complex at Waltham, Massachusetts. Waltham itself soon appeared small as the Boston Associates developed Lowell on the Merrimac River. The population of Lowell increased from 2,500 in 1826 to 35,000 in 1850. The Lowell Machine Shop became a center for innovation not only in textile machinery but waterpower technology as well. It also trained a generation of industrial engineers that spread throughout the economy. Lowell attracted further international attention because of its labor system that employed young women housed in corporate boarding houses with an extensive corporate welfare and cultural program.

The expansion of textile manufacturing was not only important in its own terms but also as a stimulus to the machine tool industry. This industry began developing machinery for a wide range of industrial activities, as well as iron and steel production. A key element of the machine tool industry was its emphasis on interchangeable parts for machinery. Known as the American system of manufacturing, it entailed an increasing range of products manufactured by machines that turned out identical objects and could be operated by a minimally skilled operator. The skill needed was built into the machine.

The increased demand for iron led to the expansion of what had been a small industry making iron with charcoal at a large number of small-scale furnaces and forges spread across the country. The new furnaces and forges were much larger in scale and capitalization, and they increasingly used coal to produce higher quality iron and steel. They used the Bessemer Process discovered by William Kelly (1811–1888), a west Kentucky iron master. The discovery of extensive deposits of rich iron and copper in the Upper Peninsula of Michigan further contributed to the rapid development of the iron and steel industry. The completion of locks at Sault Ste. Marie in 1855 removed a major obstacle in the shipping of iron ore and copper to Cleveland and to the emerging iron and steel center at Pittsburgh.

The growth of large cities in the industrial northeast created a tremendous demand for food. The Erie Canal allowed the relatively inexpensive transport of bulky foodstuffs from western New York, Ohio, Indiana, and Illinois. Feeder canals and eventually railroads within those states expanded the transportation network, moving larger and larger amounts of food to the growing industrial cities. Agriculture in the Midwest was a large-scale commercial activity raising crops and livestock for sale to the east. The transportation system involving railroads, canals, and the Great Lakes linked the east and the Midwest, binding them together into a single economic unit. As commercial agriculture expanded in the Midwest farming declined in the northeast and the scale of farms increased. While 70 percent of the North's population lived on farms in 1820, by 1860 this figure was down to only 41 percent.

An important element in the development of the northeastern manufacturing economy was the large number of immigrants who arrived in the country during the 1820s. With the exception of a few southern seaports like Savannah most immigrants came to the North because of the greater economic opportunity there. Between 1820 and 1860 some five million people came to the United States, the vast majority of them derived from western Europe: as much as 85 percent came from Ireland, Germany, and Great Britain. Immigrants provided labor for expanding industries and for the construction of canals and railroads. The rapid expansion of population in the emerging industrial cities was a further stimulus to the economy, creating a tremendous demand for housing and other infrastructure.

During this period there were two largely separate economies north and south of the Ohio River. There were some connections between the two—northern textile mills used southern cotton and the South imported some manufactured goods from the North. But otherwise the two economies were almost entirely independent of one another. This can be seen clearly in their transportation systems, each built to facilitate the operation of its economy. The two systems connected at only one point in 1860: Bowling Green, Kentucky.

The economy in 1860 was not only much larger than it had been in 1810, it also produced a much wider range of products than ever before. The industrialization of the economy changed the material lives of people living in the United States. This involved new products and improved every day items, as well as lower prices due to the increasing efficiency of industrial production.

FURTHER READING

Bruchey, Stuart. *The Roots of American Economic Growth, 1607–1861*. New York: Harper and Row, 1965.

Cochran, Thomas C. *Frontiers of Change: Early Industrialism in America*. New York: Oxford University Press, 1981.

Heilbroner, Robert and Aaron Singer. *The Economic Transformation of America, 1600–Present*, 4th ed. New York: Harcourt Brace Jovanovich, 1998.

Sellers, Charles. *The Market Revolution: Jacksonian America, 1815–1846*. New York: Oxford University Press, 1991.

Willis, James F. and Martin L. Primack. *An Economic History of the United States*, 2nd ed. Englewood Cliffs, NJ: Prentice Hall, 1989.

EASTERN WOODLANDS INDIANS

The Eastern Woodlands Indians were native American tribes that settled in the region extending from the Atlantic Ocean in the east to the Mississippi River in the west and from Canada in the north to the Gulf of Mexico in the south. (The Woodlands Indians are sometimes divided further into the Northeastern Indians and the Southeastern Indians.) A majority of Eastern Woodlands tribes spoke Iroquoian or Algonquian. The Iroquois speakers included the Cayuga, Mohawk, Oneida, Onondaga, Seneca, and Huron. The Iroquoian tribes were primarily deer hunters but they also grew corn, squash, and beans, they gathered nuts and berries, and they fished. The Algonquian speakers included the Abenaki, Chippewa (or Ojibwa), Delaware, Mohegans (or Mohicans), and Pequot. The Algonquian tribes also cultivated corn, beans, and squash. While the northerly tribes relied more heavily on hunting, the tribes that settled in the fertile region of the Ohio River Valley and southward through the Mississippi Delta (the Cherokee, Choctaw, Natchez, and Seminole) developed a farming and trading economy. These groups were also Mound Builders—they erected huge earthworks as burial grounds.

The Eastern Woodlands Indians traveled on foot and in birch-bark canoes. In the north, they wore deerskin clothing and they painted their faces and bodies. In the southern region, they wore little clothing and they often tattooed their bodies. The Eastern Woodlands Indians of the north lived predominately in dome-shaped wigwams (arched shelters made of a framework of poles and covered with bark, rush mats, or hides) and in long houses (multi-family lodges having pole frames and covered with elm shingles). The tribes in the south lived in wattle and daub houses (wooden framed houses covered with reed mats and plaster). The Eastern Woodlands Indians built walls and fences around villages for protection. Warfare sometimes broke out among the tribes. The Indians used bows and arrows as well as clubs to defend themselves and their lands.

The Eastern Woodlands tribes that lived along the Atlantic Coast were the first native Americans that had contact with Europeans. Friendships were made; alliances forged; land deals struck; and treaties signed. But as settlers in increasing numbers encroached on tribal lands, conflicts arose. These conflicts were between white settlers and the Indians and between Indians and other Indians, as native inhabitants took sides in the conflicts. The Huron and some Algonquian groups allied themselves with the French. The fierce Iroquois League (made up of the Cayuga, Mohawk, Oneida, Onondaga, and Seneca tribes) sided with the British. When the American colonies waged a battle for freedom from Great Britain, the American Revolution (1775–83) divided the tribes of the Iroquois League. All but the Oneida allied themselves with the British. In the 1800s many Eastern Woodlands tribes were forced off their native lands by the U.S. government and were settled in Oklahoma and other western states. The 1838–39 migration of the Cherokee Nation is known as the Trail of Tears because not only did the Indians reluctantly leave their homeland, but many died along the way.

See also: **Choctaw, Corn, Iroquois, Trail of Tears**

EASTMAN, GEORGE

George Eastman (1854–1932) became fascinated with the hobby of photography in the 1870s, while working for a bank in Rochester, New York. At the time, taking and developing photos was a clumsy, cumbersome, time-consuming business limited to those who had the patience and the ability to deal with the expensive mechanical processes involved. When he failed to receive a promotion he believed he deserved,

George Eastman.

Eastman, still in his twenties, decided to quit banking and devote himself full-time to his all-consuming hobby.

Working in the kitchen of his widowed mother's boarding house, Eastman investigated the problems presented by photography's heavy plate-glass negatives, which required an immediate dipping in silver nitrate and processing on the spot. He began to experiment with various emulsions used to coat the "wet plates" on which most photographs of the time were taken. In his extensive reading on the subject Eastman came upon a formula for "dry plates" printed in an English almanac. The formula offered the opportunity to reduce the size and weight of the glass plates then in use. By 1880 Eastman had developed a gelatin dry plate that did not need to be immediately processed.

Eastman took out patents in England and the United States on his "method and apparatus for coating plates for use in photography," and he set himself up in business as the Eastman Dry Plate and Film Company to manufacture these dry plates. In 1884 he began searching for a way to produce a transparent and flexible film. The first commercial film, which his company began to produce a year later, was cut in narrow strips and wound on a roller device.

In 1888 Eastman introduced the first Kodak camera, a simple, hand-held box loaded with a 100-exposure film. Correctly guessing that "Kodak" would be

pronounced the same in every language, Eastman coined the word, which had no meaning. He reportedly chose "Kodak" because the letter "K" was the first letter of his mother's maiden name, Kilbourne, and he thought it was "strong and incisive." To acquire his patent in England, Eastman also needed to use a word not then existent in the English language. Leaving nothing to chance, Eastman also chose Kodak's eye-catching yellow packaging.

From the beginning, Eastman intended the Kodak camera for amateur photographers. It was made to be sent back to the factory for processing after its film was used. At $25 a roll, however, the film itself was too expensive for most U.S. citizens at that time. By 1896 Eastman was producing a smaller version of his original camera, and it sold for a much more affordable $5. Four years later he introduced the first of a long line of Brownie cameras, intended for use by children; the price tag: one dollar.

A brilliant marketer, Eastman promoted his cameras with the slogan, "You press the button, we do the rest," and began to sell cameras to millions worldwide. He adopted the strategy of constantly making improvements on cameras and film. This allowed him to introduce new and improved products well ahead of his competition.

In 1889 Eastman introduced transparent film. That same year, responding to a request by Thomas Edison (1847–1931) to come up with film for Edison's newly-invented movie camera, Eastman's chemists designed celluloid 33mm film, which remains the world standard today. Eastman incorporated his company in 1892 under the name Eastman Kodak Company.

At the turn of the twentieth century, Eastman began to buy out his competitors whenever possible. By 1927 Eastman Kodak controlled the U.S. market in cameras, plate cameras, printing paper, and motion-picture film. Eastman spent much of his later career embroiled in legal disputes related to his monopolistic activities and his alleged use of other inventors' ideas without proper acknowledgment. Although no longer a monopoly, Eastman Kodak retained its leadership in the photographic industry throughout the twentieth century.

George Eastman recognized early the value of retaining loyal employees. In an era when workers' rights were being defined by growing union activities, Eastman independently created many employee benefit programs. In 1910 he began to establish a profit-sharing program for all employees, and in the next decade he offered other progressive employee benefits.

Meanwhile, he had become one of the nation's wealthiest men. In 1905 he built a 50-room mansion in Rochester, New York. It included such amenities as a huge conservatory filled with plants and flowers, in which the lifelong bachelor breakfasted each day to organ music played on a full pipe organ by his private organist.

As the years went on, Eastman became a generous philanthropist, eventually giving away more than $100 million. Although he had left school at age thirteen, his largest gifts were to academic institutions, including the Massachusetts Institute of Technology, the University of Rochester (and its Eastman School of Music) and the predominantly black Tuskegee Institute. In 1932, at age 77, stricken with a crippling spinal disease, Eastman took his own life.

See also: **Eastman Kodak**

FURTHER READING

Adams, Susan. "As Convenient as a Pencil." *Forbes*, November 30, 1998.

———. "Photography and Lemon Pie in Rochester." *Forbes*, November 30, 1998.

Breyer, Elizabeth. *George Eastman: A Biography.* Baltimore, MD: Johns Hopkins Press, 1996.

Chandler, Alfred D. *The Visible Hand: The Managerial Revolution in American Business.* Cambridge, MA: Harvard University Press, 1977.

Collins, Douglas. *The Story of Kodak.* New York: Harry N. Abrams, 1990.

"George Eastman," [cited April 12, 1999] available from the World Wide Web @ www.invent.org/book/book-text/indexbyname.html/.

EASTMAN KODAK

Headquartered in Rochester, New York, the Eastman Kodak Company was one of the leading image photography businesses in the United States. The company had eight major divisions: Consumer Imaging; Kodak Professional, Digital and Applied Imaging; Entertainment Imaging; Health Imaging; Commercial and Governmental Systems; Business Imaging Systems; Office Imaging; and Global Customer Service and Support. Kodak was the top U.S. manufacturer of 35-millimeter (mm) film, capturing close to 75 percent of the market at the end of 1998 and 70 percent at the

beginning of 1999. But Kodak shared the lead with Fuji Photo in worldwide film sales. Kodak also manufactured cameras, information systems (including writable CDs and software), and medical imaging technology.

The Eastman Kodak Company traces its origins to 1881 when George Eastman (1854–1932) founded the Eastman Dry Plate Company. A bank clerk from Rochester, New York, Eastman had spent three years developing the dry-plate photography process, which was a vast improvement over the sloppy and awkward wet-plate process in use at the time. Determined to develop a camera that was as easy to work as a pencil, Eastman next produced a film consisting of gelatin coated paper packed in a roll that could be used in any dry-plate camera. In 1884 the company changed its name to Eastman Dry Plate and Film Company.

In 1888 the company introduced the first readily portable camera. Selling for $25, the camera held enough rolled film for 100 photographs. Customers developed the film by sending it back to Rochester, where the company printed the photographs and refilled the camera with a new roll. The product was advertised with the slogan, "You push the button, we do the rest." The small sized, easy to use camera revolutionized photography by opening it up as a hobby to thousands of people.

In 1892 Eastman renamed his business again, calling it the Eastman Kodak Company. Eastman chose the name "Kodak" after experimenting with combinations of letters starting and ending with the letter "k," which the founder thought was a "strong, incisive sort of letter." In addition, to register his cameras for trademark protection in Britain, Eastman needed to use a word that did not already exist in the English language. By 1897 Eastman Kodak had manufactured 100,000 cameras, but Eastman wanted to make photography more convenient and less expensive. In 1900 he did so, introducing the first Brownie Camera. It sold for $1 and used a 15-cent roll of film.

During the next two decades Eastman Kodak continued introducing new products and technologies. In 1902 it offered a machine that developed film without a dark room. During World War I (1914–1918) Eastman Kodak developed products to help U.S. troops fighting in Europe, including aerial cameras and an unbreakable lens for gas masks. In the 1920s Eastman Kodak rolled out 16-mm motion picture film, a 16-mm motion picture camera, and the Kodascope projector. Despite George Eastman's death by suicide in 1932, Kodak continued to thrive. In 1935 the company introduced Kodachrome film, the first commercially successful amateur color film.

Kodak's success, however, was not without some mistakes in judgment. During the 1940s the company rejected Edwin Land's offer to have Kodak market the instant camera he had invented. Land later went on to found a firm that competed with Kodak, the Polaroid Corporation. Bouncing back in the 1950s, Kodak brought out the inexpensive Brownie hand-held movie camera and the Brownie projector. In 1953 Kodak formed the Eastman Chemical Products Company to produce chemicals, plastics, and fibers used in film production, poising itself to serve the burgeoning new market of photofinishing. Five years later Kodak unveiled the first fully automated slide projector.

In 1963 Kodak again revolutionized amateur photography with its introduction of the Instamatic camera that used a film cartridge instead of a roll, eliminating the need to load film in the dark. Within ten years Kodak had launched five different, immediately successful pocket models of the Instamatic. By 1976 the company had sold about 60 million such cameras, 50 million more than the nearest competitor.

Kodak's commercial success was tempered by its legal setbacks. In the early 1970s several smaller companies filed a series of antitrust lawsuits, alleging that Kodak had illegally monopolized the photography industry. The most famous of these cases involved Berky Photo, which accused Kodak of conspiring with Sylvania Companies and the General Electric Company in developing two photographic flash products. The case was settled for $6.8 million in 1981. Kodak also lost a patent infringement suit instituted by Polaroid during the 1980s. As a result, Kodak was forced to pay $925 million in damages, cease production of instant cameras, and recall all instant cameras that had been sold to customers. In 1997 the World Trade Organization (WTO) denied Kodak's claim that it had been refused fair access to Japanese markets.

As its market share began dwindling in the 1990s, Kodak took several actions to reverse its fortunes. The company first began selling its peripheral businesses in chemicals, pharmaceuticals, and household products. Kodak then refocused its energies on its core imaging business, investing heavily in digital photography. In 1992 Kodak introduced the Photo CD system, allowing photofinishers to record 35-mm images on compact discs, and enabling customers to view the images on their televisions and personal computers.

Kodak also formed a strategic research alliance with some of its competitors, including Fuji Photo, Canon, Inc., Nikkon Corporation, and Minolta, Co., Ltd. This endeavor resulted in the 1996 release of the Kodak's Advanced Photo System (APS), featuring a drop-in film cassette, a choice of print formats, and improved picture quality. But sales continued to decline, and in 1997 Kodak announced a restructuring program whereby it would reduce the company's workforce by 20 percent before the end of the century. By 1999 Kodak could boast that it manufactured a line of digital cameras among the best in the world. But the cost of such cameras, between $700 and $1000, was too high for most consumers.

See also: **George Eastman**

FURTHER READING

''Pretty Picture.'' *Discount Merchandiser*, February 1, 1999.

Dickinson, Mike. ''RPD's focus on combating crime turning digital.'' *Rochester Business Journal*, November 6, 1998.

Garfinkle, Simson L. ''Not Exactly Picture Perfect, Kodak Digital Cameras Among Best Around But Very Expensive.'' *The Boston Globe*, April 8, 1999.

''Eastman Kodak Company,'' [cited April 10, 1999] available from the World Wide Web @ http://www.hoovers.com/.

ECONOMIC DEVELOPMENT, FEDERAL INVOLVEMENT IN (ISSUE)

While it may have certainly escalated with President Franklin D. Roosevelt and the New Deal and grown even more in the last half of the twentieth century (some economists say to the point of gross intrusion), federal involvement in economic development actually began with the earliest English settlements. Throughout American history, the federal government intervened in response to political pressure exerted by state, local, and national constituencies for such things as the capturing and preservation of rents, the mediation of market failure, and the attainment of private goals when private action proved impossible. But what has changed from the nineteenth to the twentieth century is that while government intervention was once seen as a question of last resort, today on the eve on a new millenium, it is too often seen as the first fix.

During the colonial period, government at all levels acted in the public interest, and could set the ''just'' price for milling and the price of bread, regulate the purity of beer, establish reasonable ferry charges and grant monopoly franchises. They could set wages and even require work. In the process, many colonial regulations were established into the "common law." To enforce this web of complex rules and regulations, colonial governments used constables, wardens and even gaugers. While many of the colonial regulations had disappeared by the time of the American Revolution (1775–1783), the Revolution itself did little to interrupt institutional continuity, and English common law remained the foundation of American law, as the Supreme Court repeatedly affirmed. The American Revolution only changed the form but not the nature of government.

While some economists see a period of laissez faire in the late eighteenth and early nineteenth-centuries and mark the period as that of a "market revolution," the federal government remained a potent force in the economy nonetheless. Nowhere was this more clearly demonstrated than in the history of banking. The federal government established the First and Second Banks of the United States as central banks with effective power to regulate commercial banks chartered and licensed by state governments. The existence of a "national" or "central" bank raised numerous issues of constitutionality, states rights, federal power, scope and purpose, and national currency. After the Bank War, the Panic of 1837, and the demise of the Second Bank of the United States, the question of a central bank wasn't seriously raised again until the financial insecurities and social displacements of industrialization at the beginning of the twentieth century forced the government to establish the Federal Reserve Bank in 1913.

But for well over a century, the dispute raged between advocates of a decentralized banking system and proponents of a strong central bank. The former argued that a national bank was dangerous because it concentrated the power of granting loans and expanding currency into the hands of a relatively small group of men who would follow private rather than national interests. But proponents of a central bank disagreed. They argued that a central bank was necessary to enlarge the national manufacturing base, maintain a stable currency, and keep up with the demands of a country whose boundaries and peoples increasingly pushed westward. For them, a central bank could keep the amount of currency in circulation flexible and provide the capital and credit needed to meet the demands of population increases, territorial expansion, and heavy industrialization.

As the central bank today, the Federal Reserve, established after the Panic of 1907, has two basic functions. Along with other federal agencies, it helps assure the financial soundness of private banks. As lender of last resorts, it protects banks against insufficient funds (liquid assets) when those banks are forced to cover the withdrawal demands of their depositors. Secondly, the Federal Reserve monitors and controls the national money supply. It can order changes in the percentages of bank assets held as reserves which in turn changes the ability of banks to create money by making loans. Moreover, it can change the money supply directly by buying and selling government bonds in the market.

By the time the Federal Reserve System was established in 1913, the financial insecurities and social displacements of industrialization appeared to have settled the long pressing questions of constitutionality, and state rights, but no one could have imagined the degree to which the government would become involved in the economic development of the United States at the end of the twentieth century.

One way it was assisted in this role at the beginning of the century was its regulation of the railroad industry and in breaking up monopolies. When the National Grange, Farmers' Alliance, Greenback Party and eventually the Populist Party flexed their political muscles in the last two decades of the nineteenth-century, Congress finally responded in 1887 with the Act to Regulate Commerce. It assigned the federal government the role of market arbiter. The act prohibited rate discrimination among rail shippers buying identical service, and also forbade rate discrimination between long and short hauls unless a specific exemption was granted. It also established the Interstate Commerce Commission to ensure enforcement. Between 1903 and 1913, Congress passed a series of laws, especially the Elkins Act, the Hepburn Act, and the Mann-Elkins Act, that broadened considerably the ICC's statutory authority.

In addition to regulating commerce, the federal government also became involved in trade and breaking up monopolies. On October 15, 1914, Congress passed and President Woodrow Wilson signed the Clayton Antitrust Act which was designed to strengthen the Sherman Antitrust Act of 1890 by fully codifying specific illegal antitrust activities. The Clayton Act forbade a corporation from purchasing stock in a competitive firm, outlawed contracts based on the condition that the purchaser would do no business with the seller's competitors, and made interlocking stockholdings and directorates illegal. It also contained provisions designed to make corporate officers personally responsible for antitrust violations. The Clayton Act also declared that labor unions were not conspiracies in restraint of trade, thus exempting them from provisions of the bill. To carry out and enforce the

Clayton Act and the Sherman Act, Congress created the Federal Trade Commission in a related measure.

With the advent of New Deal legislation, the federal government passed comprehensive legislation affecting the nations banking, industry, agriculture, and labor that were all directed primarily toward one of three goals: recovery, reform, or relief during the Great Depression. The National Industrial Recovery Act (NIRA) and the Agricultural Adjustment Act (AAA) addressed recovery; the Civilian Conservation Corps (CCC) and the Federal Emergency Relief Administration (FERA) relieved some of the suffering of the unemployed and destitute; and the Securities and Exchange Act of 1934 and the Glass-Steagall Act of 1933 attempted to reform institutions that were considered "failed." Most economists agree that many of the New Deal's structural reforms were misguided or inefficient. For example, minimum wages eliminated jobs for some unskilled workers. And farm programs have led today to a situation twhere there are more employees of the Department of Agriculture than there are full-time farmers. Moreover, the farming industry has still not contracted sufficiently to bring supply and demand into equilibrium.

The New Deal did however mark a watershed period for national economics. Not only was the scope of the government forever increased, the New Deal also represented a complete restructuring of the American economy and a complete reform of its institutions. From the New Deal onward, the federal government assumed responsibility for the relief of the poor and for unemployment. It gave farmers protection from foreclosure, and it guaranteed farm prices rather than allowing the market to do so.

Today, perhaps no other issue has raised as much concern over the federal government's involvement in economic development as the military-industrial complex. It is industry which has devoted itself to the production of goods to supply weapons and other materials to the Pentagon, and it has formed a matrix of government spending, foreign initiatives, and ideological commitments. Within both the government and the market, the voices of private business and the military have only grown stronger since World War II (1939–1945). By the 1970s private business and the military had developed a formal and comfortable relationship of mutual support. Since the 1950s especially, military calls upon national resources have vastly increased, and for the most part, leading corporations have been the principal beneficiaries of that demand. While payrolls, research grants and political influence have been large enough to ensure a consensus for the system, the whole complex has been underwritten by a popular and almost unassailable anticommunist ideology. But some conservatives fear that the military-industrial complex keeps military spending at a level higher than that dictated by the strict needs of national defense. They claim that it leads to economic dislocation at home and dangerous tensions abroad, and that the separate parts of the military-industrial complex will prove countervailing.

With these and other issues that tie the federal government's role more intricately into economic development, any attempts to diminish their size or existence will meet with sustained and continued opposition.

See also: **Glass-Steagal Act, Greenback Party, Hepburn Act, Mann-Elkins Act, Military Industrial Complex, National Grange, New Deal, Populist Movement**

FURTHER READING

Kolko, Gabriel. *The Triumph of Conservatism: A Reinterpretation of American History, 1900–1916.* New York, Free Press of Glencoe, 1963.

Link, Arthur S. *Wilson: The New Freedom.* Princeton: Princeton University Press, 1956.

Melman, Seymour. *Pentagon Capitalism.* New York, 1970.

Pursell, Carroll W., Jr., ed. *The Military Industrial Complex.* New York, 1972.

Thorelli, Hans B. *The Federal Antitrust Policy: Origination of an American Tradition.* Baltimore: The Johns Hopkins University Press, 1955.

ECONOMIC GROWTH

Economic growth is the increase in an economy's output of goods and services over an extended period of time. The term *economic growth* refers to a much broader period of prosperity than the narrow expansion phase of the traditional business cycle since an economy can still be in a period of long-term economic growth while undergoing a recession. Periods of economic growth are marked by rising standards of living, increases in the variety and number of goods and services, and improving rates of productivity. The first analysis of economic growth was provided by the Scottish economist Adam Smith (1723–1790). In *The Wealth of Nations* Smith argued that an economy's growth depended on its ability to engage in large-scale production, which depended in turn on the adoption of refined manufacturing methods and the division of labor into highly specialized craftsmen. Perhaps the greatest economist of economic growth in the twentieth century was Joseph Schumpeter (1883–1950), who argued that the real sources of growth are the technological innovations of entrepreneurs. In his theory of "creative destruction," successful entrepreneurs create an economy of copycats who strive to duplicate the entrepreneurs' success but eventually wind up causing a depression by overinvesting. Economic growth continues again after these depressions, however, when the entrepreneurs' new technologies make possible new phases of ever higher productivity.

Several factors combined to make the economic history of the United States perhaps the greatest historical example of economic growth. From the start, U.S. businesses benefited from the English work ethic, technological ingenuity, and principles of economic and political freedom. Fueled by a steady stream of enterprising immigrants, the U.S. labor force grew faster than in most other developed countries. Americans benefited from a large geographical territory with superior natural resources, and the country's founding fathers put in place a system that encouraged the development of public infrastructure, education, technological innovation, and capital accumulation. Within half a century of its independence, the United States had already one of the richest and biggest economies in the world, and between 1840 and 1960 the United States maintained a 3.6 percent annual growth rate, which economist Robert E. Gallman has described as "extraordinarily high" by historical standards. More recently, between 1950 and 1990 the United States remained a model of strong economic growth, with its gross national product (*GNP*) growing at a very healthy 3.1 percent annual rate.

See also: **Joseph Schumpeter, Adam Smith, Work Ethic**

ECONOMIC OPPORTUNITY ACT

In 1964 President Lyndon Johnson (1963–1969) announced in his first State of the Union address: "This administration today, here and now, declares unconditional war on poverty." This announcement was predated a few months earlier by a wave of urban riots in U.S. cities. The announced "War on Poverty" became a reality in August 1964 when Congress enacted the Economic Opportunity Act (EOA). This federal act created the Office of Economic Opportunity (OEO) and gave it the responsibility of administrating the Community Action Program (CAP) and the Job Corps. The CAP was designed to administer services to the poor, coordinate poverty functions of the federal, state, and local governments, and to create areas in the program where the poor would have some direct responsibility and power over those new programs. The Job Corps as another part of the EOA was a job training program aimed at disadvantaged youth in the United States. Though both programs were theoretically color-blind the EOA seemed likely to focus on the needs of many urban African Americans. Despite the major initiatives of the EOA the threatening racial tensions in the United States only worsened. Despite urban riots that began in 1967 and continued through the rest of the 1960s President Johnson continued in his efforts to wage war on poverty in the United States through the EOA. Responding to the riots in Detroit, Michigan, in 1967 he said that the only long-range solution for urban poverty was to continue EOA efforts to reduce the conditions of poverty: "ignorance, discrimination, slums, disease, and the joblessness." EOA efforts disappeared with the Richard Nixon (1969–1974) presidency.

See also: **Great Society, Poverty**

ECONOMIES OF SCALE

Economies of scale allow businesses to reduce their per-unit fixed costs by making more of their products. Fixed costs include expenses such as insurance, rent, shipping, and administrative expenses, which are not affected by increases or decreases in sales or production. For example, suppose a stapler manufacturing company paid $50,000 a month in fixed costs, and its monthly production was 15,000 staplers. For each stapler the company sold, $3.33 went toward paying the company's fixed monthly business costs. If the company increased its monthly production to 20,000 staplers, however, its fixed costs per mouse would have dropped to $2.50—a cost savings of eighty-three cents per mouse. By increasing the "scale" or volume of its production, the company achieved an "economy" or efficiency in its per-unit fixed costs. Thus, the more staplers the company produced in one month, the more staplers sold in that month, and fewer dollars per unit spent on fixed costs.

In his landmark study of the capitalist system, *The Wealth of Nations*, Scottish economist Adam Smith (1723–1790) showed that economies of scale make businesses more efficient. Throughout the economic history of the United States, businesses used the benefits of economies of scale to justify expanding their production capacity. However, there is a point, called the "minimum optimal scale," beyond which the per-unit cost of stepping up production begins to rise again. For example, the stapler manufacturer may have found that if it increased the number of staplers the plant manufactured per month to 20,000, it would have to keep the plant open longer every week and pay more in shipping charges. Both of these actions would increase the company's fixed costs and, as a result, the per-stapler fixed costs could climb back to $3.33, or even higher. When expanding production increases per-unit fixed costs "diseconomies of scale" are the result. Companies with large production capacities or vast production resources are said to have the advantage of economies of scale over smaller competitors who can not increase their production as easily. The advantages of size, however, are not unlimited.

See also: **Adam Smith**

EDISON, THOMAS ALVA

As one of history's great inventive geniuses Thomas Alva Edison (1847–1931) secured patents for more than a thousand inventions. His patents include the incandescent electric light bulb, the phonograph, and the motion picture projector. Edison was a classic example of the nineteenth-century American success story. Through talent, energy, and hard work, he rose from poor beginnings in a small Midwestern town to a position of eminence and wealth.

Born in Milan, Ohio, the seventh and youngest child of Samuel and Nancy Edison, Thomas was taught at home by his mother. With her encouragement he began his lifelong habit of voracious reading. One of his textbooks included instructions for several physics and chemistry experiments. By age 10 he set up a chemistry laboratory in the cellar and conducted original experiments.

Edison's restless entrepreneurial spirit surfaced at an early age. At 12 years of age he took a job on the Grand Trunk railroad branch line that ran between Port Huron and Detroit, Michigan. He sold newspapers, magazines, candy, apples, sandwiches, and tobacco on the train. Identifying a potential market of readers among the line's regular passengers, he set up a small printing press in an empty baggage car. There he produced a small newspaper at a subscription of eight cents per month. He also used the baggage car as a

Thomas Edison with his favorite invention, the phonograph.

chemistry laboratory. During long daily layovers in Detroit he read every book he could find.

As a teenager Edison was fascinated by the telegraph. He mastered telegraphy quickly and for the next few years worked as a telegraph operator in towns throughout the Midwest. In 1868 he became an expert night operator for the Western Union Telegraph Company in Boston, Massachusetts. Instead of sleeping during the day he experimented with electrical currents.

The first invention resulting from these experiments was a device for electronically recording voice votes taken by a legislative body. Edison received his first patent for this device, which raised little interest on the market. Thereafter he operated as a freelance inventor.

In June 1869 Edison was in New York City, desperately poor and looking for work. His first successful invention was the Edison Universal Stock Printer. This machine, together with several other derivatives of the Morse telegraph, produced the $40,000 he needed to set himself up as a manufacturer in Newark, New Jersey. There he produced stock tickers and high-speed printing telegraphs. His firm quickly employed 50 consulting engineers. During the next six years Edison was granted about 200 new patents for inventions he and others made there.

In 1876 Edison began constructing a large new plant at Menlo Park, New Jersey. Here the "Wizard of Menlo Park" accomplished some of his most important work. This included the phonograph (1877), a primitive instrument in which sound vibrations were transferred by a steel stylus to a cylinder wrapped in tin foil. Despite enormous popular interest in Edison's new toy, which he actively promoted, the inventor did not envision its commercial potential right away and abandoned its development for 10 years.

Meanwhile he worked hard to invent an economical, practical, and durable incandescent lamp. On October 21, 1879, Edison first demonstrated in public an incandescent light bulb made with charred cotton thread sealed in a vacuum that could burn for several hours. This time, Edison realized the immense implications of his discovery, and he spent the next few years adapting his invention for large-scale use. On December 17, 1880, he founded the Edison Electric Illuminating Company of New York, which evolved into the present-day Consolidated Edison Company. In 1882 his company began operating the world's first electric power station, which supplied power to 400 incandescent lamps owned by 85 customers.

In 1887 Edison constructed a large laboratory in West Orange, New Jersey (since 1955, the Edison National Historic Site). The laboratory eventually employed 5,000 persons to produce a variety of new products, including improved phonographs that used wax records, mimeographs, alkaline-storage batteries, dictating machines, and motion picture cameras and projectors. Edison's best known invention from this period was probably the kinetograph, a primitive moving picture. Edison produced *The Great Train Robbery*, one of the first movies ever made, using this technology. By 1913 he developed a prototype of the "talking picture."

During World War I (1914–1918) Edison served as president of the U.S. Navy Consulting Board and contributed many valuable discoveries to the war effort.

Edison's inventions have had a profound effect on modern society. No other man has ever been responsible for inventing products with such influence on so many lives around the world. In recognition of his accomplishments Edison was appointed Chevalier of the French Legion of Honor in 1878 and promoted to Commander of the Legion in 1889. In 1892 he was awarded the Albert Medal by the Society of Arts of Great Britain. In 1928 he received the Congressional Gold Medal for "development and application of inventions that have revolutionized civilization in the last century."

Edison married twice and was the father of six children. He maintained residences in West Orange, New Jersey, and Fort Myers, Florida. He died in West Orange on October 18, 1931.

Automotive pioneer Henry Ford credited Edison with encouraging his early work on automobiles. Ford purchased the Menlo Park Laboratory complex in 1928, and moved it to his new historic park, Greenfield Village, in Dearborn, Michigan. The Henry Ford Museum and Greenfield Village complex is officially called the Edison Institute, in honor of Thomas Edison.

See also: **Henry Ford, Western Union, World War I**

FURTHER READING

Baldwin, Neil. *Edison: Inventing the Century*. New York: Hyperion, 1995.

Conot, Robert. *A Streak of Luck*. New York: Seaview, 1979.

Josephson, Matthew. *Edison: A Biography*. Reprint Edition. New York: John Wiley & Sons, 1992.

Millard, Andre. *Edison and the Business of Innovation*. Baltimore: The Johns Hopkins University Press, 1990.

Vanderbilt, Byron. *Thomas Edison, Chemist*. Washington, D.C.: American Chemical Society, 1971.

EFFICIENCY

Efficiency, or allocative efficiency, is a central concept of economic theory. If one plan produced a product with fewer resources than another plan, it is said to be more efficient. A system that produces maximum output from minimum input of resources is efficient. Resources, including natural resources from the earth, labor, and technology, are considered finite or limited. To reach technical efficiency, they must be allocated or distributed so that the best use of available resources is made without waste, undue effort, or cost. Technical efficiency must result in the consumers' wants being satisfied within their economic purchasing power.

Increased efficiency is closely tied to improvement in technology. When a business adopts a new technology or improved plan of production to produce more of a product with fewer resources yet maintains the product's quality, then an efficient change has been made. A classic example occurred in the early 1900s when Henry Ford (1863–1947) developed a new method for producing cars, the assembly line. Rather than a group of workers making a complete car one at a time, each worker performed one task and cars were mass produced. This approach greatly reduced the time and cost needed to make a car. Resources saved would ideally be used in other areas.

In a perfectly efficient economic system resources are allocated into their highest-valued uses as evidenced by consumers' willingness to pay for the final product. While furniture or flooring made of oak garners a high price, no one would pay extra for shipping pallets or matchsticks made of oak. In a free market economy as in the United States the forces of supply and demand guide resources to their most efficient uses. In other words profits signal moves in resources to their highest valued use. A central government allocates resources in a command or planned economy as in the former Soviet Union.

See also: **Assembly Line, Mass Production, Productivity**

EIGHTEENTH AMENDMENT

The Eighteenth Amendment to the U.S. Constitution (1790) forbade in all territories within its jurisdiction making, selling, or transporting "intoxicating liquors" in the United States. This controversial amendment was proposed in Congress on December 18, 1917, and ratified on January 16, 1919. Though Congress provided states with a period of seven years in which to ratify the amendment, approval took just over a year, such was the prevailing spirit among lawmakers. In the early decades of the twentieth century the Temperance Movement (which advocated abstinence from alcohol) was steadily growing: Thirteen of 31 states had outlawed the manufacture and sale of alcohol by 1855.

During the 1870s temperance also became one of the cornerstones of the growing women's movement. As the nation's women, joined by other activists, mobilized to gain suffrage (the right to vote), they also espoused sweeping cultural changes. Outlawing the manufacture and consumption of alcoholic beverages, which were viewed by many women to be a corrupt influence on American family life, was one such initiative. In 1874 a group of women established the Woman's Christian Temperance Union (WCTU); in 1895

Government official destroying a barrel of liquor during the prohibition era.

the Anti-Saloon League was formed. Such societies found increasing support and eventually influenced legislators to take action, many of whom were "dry" (anti-alcohol) candidates that the societies had backed. Even President Woodrow Wilson (1856–1924) supported Prohibition, as one of the domestic policies of his New Freedom program.

After the amendment was passed, Congress passed the Volstead Act to enforce the law. But enforcement proved difficult for the government. There was a proliferation of bootleggers (who made their own moonshine—illegal spirits, often distilled at night), rum runners (who imported liquor, principally from neighboring Canada and Mexico), and speakeasies (underground establishments that sold liquor to their clientele). More, organized crime soon controlled distribution of liquor in the country. Citizens had not lost their taste for alcoholic beverages.

The government now found itself with a bigger problem than prohibition of alcoholic beverages. As the Federal Bureau of Investigation (FBI) and police worked to control and end mob (organized crime) violence, and as the country suffered through the early years of the Great Depression, lawmakers in Washington reconsidered the amendment. On February 20, 1933, the U.S. Congress proposed that the Eighteenth Amendment be repealed. Approved by the states in December of that year, the Twenty-First Amendment declared the Eighteenth Amendment null. The manufacture, transportation, and consumption of alcoholic beverages was again legal in the United States; thus ended the 13-year period of Prohibition. Franklin Delano Roosevelt (1933–45), president at the time of repeal, called Prohibition a ''noble experiment.''

See also: **Black Market, Prohibition, Twenty-first Amendment**

EISNER, MICHAEL D(AMMANN)

Michael Eisner (1942–), a shrewd businessman in a tough industry, chairman of the board at the Walt Disney Company, became one of the most important and most highly compensated figures in U.S. business by the end of the twentieth century. Eisner turned Walt Disney Company into what *Fortune* magazine called ''the Cinderella story of Hollywood.'' By 1998 Disney's annual sales and earnings had grown to $22.9 billion and $1.9 billion, respectively. The wealth of Disney's shareholders increased more than $80 billion during Eisner's tenure as chairman. Through bonuses and stock options, in addition to an annual compensation of $764,423, Eisner became one of the nations most highly paid executives. In 1997, for example, he sold 5.4 million Disney stock shares, which at the time had a market value of $514 million. In June 1998 *Fortune* estimated the total value of Eisner's exercised and unexercised stock options to represent $1.43 billion.

The son of wealthy parents, Eisner was born in 1942. He was raised in suburban New York and educated at the Lawrenceville School and Denison University. His first brush with the entertainment industry was through a summer job as a page at NBC studios in New York. Following his college graduation in 1964, he worked briefly in low-level clerking jobs at NBC and CBS. Dissatisfied with these positions, Eisner mailed out 200 resumes. The only response was from a young ABC programmer, Barry Diller, who persuaded his network bosses to hire Eisner as assistant to the national programming director.

Eisner produced his first special, ''Feelin' Groovy at Marine World,'' in 1967. The program was a success, and in 1968 Eisner became ABC's director of program development for the East Coast, responsible for Saturday morning programming. Among the projects he developed were animated programs based on the Jackson Five and the Osmond Brothers singing groups. Eisner's fast-paced career track took him through vice president for daytime programming (1971), vice president for program planning and development (1975), and senior vice president for prime time production and development (1976). During these years, ABC moved from third to first place among television networks.

In 1976 Eisner was offered the position of president and CEO at Paramount Pictures. Again, his track record was phenomenally successful. Costs were down and profits up. During Eisner's eight years at the helm, Paramount moved from last place to first among the six major studios. In October 1978, half the top ten box office attractions were Paramount films. Films produced by the studio during the Eisner years included *Saturday Night Fever, Raiders of the Lost Ark, Bad News Bears, Grease, Heaven Can Wait*, and *Beverly Hills Cop*.

In 1984 the Disney Company was looking for new direction. Since the death of its founder, creative genius Walt Disney (1901–1966), the studio had continued to earn profits on its theme parks and merchandising, and it had chalked up some box office successes. However, many analysts believed the company had failed to keep pace with changes in popular culture. With its earnings declining for three straight years, the company was vulnerable to corporate raiders.

Eisner's contract to join Disney in 1984 made him the highest-paid executive in the motion picture industry. With his colleague, Frank Wells, Eisner lost no time in demonstrating that his creativity and drive were worth the price. Within months, Disney began to turn around, and within a few years Eisner had transformed the company into an industry leader. New blood was brought into the management team; the Disney film archives were used to their fullest capacity; the theme parks were restored to profitability with attendance again rising annually; the animation division of Disney returned to feature-length films; and stocks rose dramatically in value.

Among Eisner's box office and merchandising triumphs in his first ten years at Disney were *Down and Out in Beverly Hills* (1986), *Who Framed Roger Rabbit* (1988), *The Little Mermaid* (1989), *Beauty and the Beast* (1991) (the first animated feature to be nominated for an Academy Award as Best Picture), *Aladdin* (1992), and *The Lion King* (1994). Disney returned to television with the hit show ''The Golden Girls'' and the ''Disney Sunday Movie.'' Disney diversified through

Immigrants arrived in the U.S. at its port of entry, Ellis Island, New York, from January 1, 1892 until its closure November 29, 1952.

its Hollywood Pictures subsidiary and, in order to produce films for a more sophisticated urban market, expanded through the acquisition of independent motion picture maker Miramax. A new amusement park, Euro Disney, was opened outside of Paris, France. In a move that positioned Eisner as the most powerful executive in the international communications industry, Disney acquired Capital Cities, which owned ABC television and the cable sports network ESPN. Revenues and stock market value skyrocketed.

In 1998 Disney launched a chain of interactive game attractions in major cities: Disney's Animal Kingdom (near Walt Disney World in Florida), the Disney Cruise Line, and Disney Quest. The company also financed renovation of Anaheim Stadium, home of the Disney-owned Anaheim Angels baseball team, and it purchased an Internet technology company, Starwave, as well as a search and information site, Infoseek. These investments dragged earnings down in 1998, but in a letter to stockholders published in Disney's 1998 annual report, Eisner promised that "in the long run (which is all that really matters), we believe they will enrich our company."

See also: **Walt Disney, Entertainment Industry**

FURTHER READING

Eisner, Michael D. *Work in Progress*. New York: Random House, 1998.

Current Biography Yearbook 1987. New York: H.W. Wilson, 1987, s.v. "Eisner, Michael D(ammann)."

Flower, Joe. *Prince of the Magic Kingdom: Michael Eisner and the Re-making of Disney*. New York: J. Wiley, 1991.

Grover, Ron. *The Disney Touch: Disney, ABC and The Quest for the World's Greatest Media Empire*. Chicago: Irwin Professional Publications, 1997.

Rose, Frank. "The Eisner School of Business." *Fortune*, July 6, 1998.

ELLIS ISLAND

Ellis Island is situated in the New York Harbor, off the southern tip of Manhattan. It was named for Samuel Ellis (n.d.), a merchant and farmer who owned the island during the late 1700s. New York acquired the land and, in 1808, sold it to the federal government. The site served as a fort and later, as an arsenal. By the end of the century record numbers of immigrants prompted the federal government to establish a bureau to process the new arrivals, the vast majority of whom entered the country at its largest port, New York City. On January 1, 1892, the Federal Immigration Station opened on Ellis Island—in the shadows of the Statue of Liberty (dedicated 1886 on nearby Bedloe Island). The

Ellis Island facility, which by 1901 consisted of thirty-five buildings, was the country's chief immigration station. Its heaviest use was in processing the influx of immigrants who arrived between 1892 and 1924. The majority of new arrivals were European, but immigrants also came from the West Indies, Asia, and the Middle East. More men than women arrived at the immigration depot.

New arrivals (mostly third-class passengers; first- and second-class passengers were processed aboard their ships) were ferried from their transatlantic vessels to Ellis Island, where they disembarked and were guided into registration areas in the Great Hall and questioned by government officials who determined their eligibility to land. Upon completing the registration process newcomers were ushered into rooms where physicians examined them. The process, extremely business-like to the point of being dehumanizing, typically took between three to five hours. Ninety-eight percent of those arriving at Ellis Island were allowed into the country; two percent were turned back for medical reasons (as U.S. health officials tried to keep out infectious diseases) or for reasons of insanity or criminal record. Other facilities at the Ellis Island Immigration Station included showers, restaurants, railroad ticket offices, a laundry, and a hospital. At its peak the Ellis Island station processed some five thousand immigrants and non-immigrating aliens (visitors) daily.

The facility was closed on November 29, 1954—immigration quotas had drastically reduced the number of incoming people, eliminating the need for the mass processing center. On May 11, 1965, Ellis Island was designated a national historic site. During the 1980s it was extensively restored. More than twelve million people first entered the United States through Ellis Island; their descendants account for an estimated 40 percent of the nation's current population.

See also: **Immigration**

EMANCIPATION PROCLAMATION

President Abraham Lincoln's (1861–1865) Emancipation Proclamation, which freed the slaves of the rebelling Confederate states during the American Civil War (1861–1865), was signed on January 1, 1863. At first glance, the proclamation was a paradox. Although Lincoln abhorred slavery, he did not attempt to abolish

it after taking office or after the Civil War began in April 1861. Indeed, Lincoln initially stated that the Civil War was being fought to preserve the Union, not to end slavery in the South.

There were several factors behind Lincoln's reasoning. First, he felt duty-bound to honor the Constitution, which safeguarded slavery in any state whose citizens supported the institution. Instead, Lincoln favored gradual emancipation, voluntarily accepted by the states, with federal compensation to slaveholders. Second, after the start of the Civil War, Lincoln avoided policies aimed at abolishing slavery, fearing that the four pro-slavery border states that remained loyal to the Union—Missouri, Kentucky, Maryland, and Delaware—would withdraw their allegiance. Finally, Lincoln was intent on maintaining the solidarity of the political coalition of Republicans and Northern Democrats. Although anti-slavery sentiment was strong in the Republican Party, the Northern Democrats were split on the issue. Irish Democrats were particularly opposed to fighting a civil war whose purpose was to end slavery.

> **THAT ON THE 1ST DAY OF JANUARY,** A.D.
> **1863, ALL PERSONS HELD AS SLAVES**
> **WITHIN ANY STATE OR DESIGNATED PART**
> **OF A STATE THE PEOPLE WHEREOF SHALL**
> **THEN BE IN REBELLION AGAINST THE**
> **UNITED STATES SHALL BE THEN,**
> **THENCEFORWARD, AND FOREVER FREE.**
>
> **President Abraham Lincoln, Emancipation Proclamation**
> **speech, 1863**

As the war continued, Lincoln eventually altered his public stance on slavery. He was influenced by a number of considerations. Perhaps most important, Lincoln was swayed by the strategic value of proclaiming the emancipation of the slaves. Slavery was an important asset for the South's military machine. Slaves tilled southern farms, worked in its munitions factories, and built the fortifications of the Confederate Army. Calling an end to slavery would demoralize the South and encourage Southern slaves to rebel or attempt escape to Union Army lines. Such calculations became especially important in 1862, when Northern armies were faring poorly on the battlefield.

Lincoln also quite rightly expected emancipation to generate much needed political capital. To be sure, an anti-slavery proclamation would alienate many Northern Democrats, but it would also strengthen Lincoln's support among his vital Republican constituency, which was increasingly anxious over the president's failure to move against slavery. Emancipation would also obtain foreign support for the Northern cause and discourage European intervention on the side of the South.

Despite the incentives to accept emancipation, Lincoln would have supported the preservation of slavery in the core southern states if they had ended their secession. After the Battle of Antietam on September 17, 1862, Lincoln decided to leave the matter to the rebelling states. He publicly stated that unless the southern states returned to the Union by the end of the year, he would declare their slaves to be free. None of the Southern states returned to the Union, however, and Lincoln issued the Emancipation Proclamation on New Year's Day 1863.

The proclamation had an important and positive effect on Northern prospects of winning the war, which was now transformed into a moral crusade, reviving support for the Northern war effort. The proclamation also gained international approval and undercut support for Confederate independence. For example, British support for diplomatic recognition of the Confederate States began to decline after the Emancipation Proclamation cast the conflict not only as a struggle for national unity, but as a noble war in support of basic human rights. Equally important for the outcome of the war, the proclamation invited free Blacks and newly freed slaves to join the ranks of the Union Army. By the end of the war in April 1865, more than 190,000 Black men had enlisted.

See also: **Civil War (Economic Causes of), Civil War (Economic Impact of), Slavery**

FURTHER READING

Donald, David. *Lincoln Reconsidered: Essays on the Civil War Era.* New York: Vintage: 1989.

Franklin, John Hope and Alfred A. Moss, Jr. *From Slavery to Freedom.* New York: Knopf, 1994.

McPherson, James M. *Abraham Lincoln and the Second American Revolution.* New York: Oxford University Press, 1992.

———. *The Struggle for Equality: Abolitionists and the Negro in the Civil War and Reconstruction.* Princeton: Princeton University Press, 1995.

Sandburg, Carl. *Abraham Lincoln: The War Years.* New York: HarcourtBrace, 1976.

Stewart, James Brewer. *Holy Warriors: The Abolitionists and American Slavery.* New York: Hill and Wang, 1997.

EMBARGO

An embargo is a formal policy by a government to prevent the movement of exports either out of its own ports or into another country. It differs from a boycott in that it only involves the interruption of exports, not other financial or commercial transactions. A civil embargo is directed against one's own shippers to prevent them from shipping vital materials to warring nations. A hostile embargo is directed against the economic well-being of a foreign power.

Because of the central role of the U.S. economy in global trade, the United States frequently uses embargoes as effective, nonviolent tools of foreign policy. Although the United States declared its neutrality when Great Britain and France went to war in the early 1800s, both of the warring countries blocked U.S. merchant ships. And in 1807 a British warship killed three U.S. citizens while forcing four British-born ''deserters'' to rejoin the British Navy. In response, President Thomas Jefferson (1801–1809) convinced Congress to pass the Embargo Act of 1807, which banned all U.S. ships from trading in foreign ports. French and British ships continued to attack U.S. ships, however, and the damaging affects on the U.S. economy forced Jefferson to repeal the embargo in 1809. When Great Britain continued violating U.S. neutrality and commandeering U.S. sailors, Congress passed the Embargo Act of 1812 to block all trade between the United States and Great Britain.

During the American Civil War (1861–1865) the Confederacy considered placing an embargo on cotton shipments to Great Britain, to force Great Britain to enter the war as an ally. The Confederate Congress never passed the embargo, but Confederate state governments and individual citizens imposed a voluntary embargo on cotton exports to England. The British remained neutral throughout the war, and the Southern economy suffered greatly from the North's embargo on exports to the South.

In 1941 the United States imposed an embargo on German, Italian, French, and Danish ships in U.S. ports before it was finally forced to enter World War II (1939–1945) after Japan's attack on Pearl Harbor. As a member of the United Nations, the United States used embargoes against North Korea and China during the Korean War (1950–1953), against Iraq after the Gulf War (1991), and against the former Yugoslavia in the 1990s. In June 1960 President Dwight D. Eisenhower (1953–1961) imposed the longest-running embargo in

U.S. history by blocking all exports (except food and medicine) to Cuba because of Fidel Castro's (1926–) hostile actions against U.S. interests.

See also: **Embargo Act, OPEC Oil Embargo**

EMBARGO ACT

On December 22, 1807, President Thomas Jefferson (1801–09) signed the Embargo Act, which prohibited from leaving the United States ships destined for any foreign port. The legislation had been drawn up to pressure France and Britain. Those two countries were then at war and had been seizing United States merchant ships to prevent each other from receiving goods.

After the French navy was crushed at the Battle of Trafalgar (October 1805) by the British under Admiral Horatio Nelson (1758–1805), French ruler Napoleon Bonaparte (1769–1821) turned to economic warfare in his long struggle with the British. He directed all countries under French control not to trade with Britain. With an economy dependent on trade, Britain struck back by imposing a naval blockade on France, which soon retaliated by interfering with U.S. shipping.

The United States tried to remain neutral when the struggle began in 1793. But the interruption of shipping to and from the Continent and the search and seizure of ships posed significant problems to U.S. export business. The Embargo Act was an attempt by Jefferson to solve these problems without getting involved in the conflict. The effort failed.

The embargo made sales of United States farm surpluses impossible. New England shippers protested the act and were joined by southern cotton and tobacco planters in their opposition. Still, the embargo remained in effect for 14 months, during which time the U.S. economy suffered. Many ships resorted to smuggling. In 1809 Congress passed the Non-Intercourse Act, which limited the shipping embargo to France and Britain; all other foreign ports were again open to American ships.

Despite efforts to remain neutral, the United States was ultimately drawn into the conflict three years later and fought with the British in the War of 1812 (1812–14).

See also: **Embargo, Thomas Jefferson, Napoleonic Wars (Economic Impact of)**

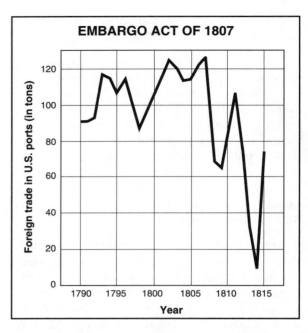

EMBARGO ACT OF 1807

The significant reduction of foreign trade in U.S. ports brought about the Embargo Act of 1807.

EMERGENCY PRICE CONTROL ACT

Emergency Price Control Act (EPCA) was a federal law that created the Office of Price Administration (OPA) to fix maximum prices and rents for the duration of World War II (1939–1945). Passed by Congress in 1942, EPCA directed OPA's Price Administrator to establish prices that ''in his judgment'' were ''generally fair and equitable'' and would effectuate the purposes of the act. The Price Administrator was also required to consider the prices prevailing in a two-week period during the fall of 1941 when wartime inflation was imminent, and make adjustments for national fluctuations in the cost of production, distribution, and transportation. Persons aggrieved by the maximum prices set in their trade or industry were authorized to file a protest with the Price Administrator. A special tribunal called the Emergency Court of Appeals was given exclusive jurisdiction to hear challenges to Price Administrator rulings. Violators who sold their commodities in excess of the prices set by the OPA could be prosecuted in criminal court or sued in civil court. Violators, however, were typically dealt with lightly, as less than two-percent of prosecutions resulted in prison sentences, and the normal civil remedy was a court order forbidding further transgressions. Some enterprises were entirely exempt from price regulation under the EPCA, including newspapers, magazines, and other print media. In August of 1945 price controls were removed from petrol, fuel, oil, and processed foods. By the end of the year very few price limits remained. EPCA expired by its own terms on June 30, 1947. Before it expired the U.S. Supreme Court upheld its constitutionality against complaints that it abridged the Due Process Clause of the Fifth Amendment to the federal Constitution. Citing the language of the act, the Supreme Court said that EPCA was necessary to the effective prosecution of the war, as it helped stabilize the economy, protect persons with fixed incomes, prevent speculative increases in prices or rents, and eliminate profiteering, hoarding, and other disruptive market conditions.

See also: **Office of Price Administration, Wage-Price Controls, World War II**

ENCOMIENDA

Encomienda is a Spanish word meaning ''commission.'' It refers to a system that was used by Spain in the New World to reward the conquistadors (conquerors). The encomienda dates back to earlier times. It was developed in feudal Spain, when the Moors (North African Muslims) occupied parts of the Iberian Peninsula (present-day Spain and Portugal). An encomienda was booty given to a Spaniard who conquered a Moorish province. It was usually the land that had belonged to the Moorish leader of the conquered territory. This practice made its way to the West Indies (Caribbean islands) by 1499: Christopher Columbus (1451–1506), who is believed to have opposed the traditional feudal system, nevertheless conceded encomiendas to his men. After Spain conquered Mexico and Peru in the mid-1500s, the system was established on the mainland as well. Spaniards were awarded the lands occupied by the Native Americans whom they had conquered. The native inhabitants, who were *encomendado* (meaning ''commended'' or ''entrusted'') to the Spaniards, were expected to pay tribute to the Spaniards and to work for them in the fields or mines. The encomienda system came close to slavery. It proved disastrous to the native populations. Mistreated by their supposed protectors and exposed to European diseases (such as smallpox, and measles) to which they had no immunity, the Indians died in large numbers. As the population declined the Spanish government made regulations to do away with the system. The encomienda became increasingly rare throughout the sixteenth century, and by the end of the following century it had disappeared altogether. The encomienda

system was at least partly responsible for the emergence of a new mixed population called Mestizos—people who are of white European and American Indian descent.

See also: **Mestizo**

ENTERTAINMENT INDUSTRY

The entertainment industry in the United States is a multi-faceted combination of a wide variety of disciplines. Radio, insurance, publishing, merchandising, television, film, music, and the computer industries are only a few of the elements that make up this immense industry. Any attempt to cover every aspect of this topic in less than five hundred pages would be foolhardy to say the least. However, it is possible to highlight specific elements of this industry and show how they have influenced U.S. economic history, particularly marketing and advertising.

Live entertainment became popular in the United States during the late nineteenth century. Two types of theater developed: the ''variety'' theater, offering comedy, musical performances, stage magic, and other spectacles at low prices; and the ''legitimate'' theater, which presented serious literary works for what were considered more ''sophisticated.'' The ''variety'' theater crossed ethnic and economic boundaries, emphasizing topics such as action and comedy. This form of theater was the model for vaudeville, a popular form of entertainment that existed in various forms from the early 1900s until the mid-1940s. Radio, and then television, pulled audiences away from the theater. This was due partially to the convenience of entertainment being provided in the home. Ironically, many of the performers from vaudeville successfully made the transition to these new media, thus regaining their audience. But this was far from the end of theater. Though vaudeville found an audience via mass communication, the ''legitimate'' theater thrived through the likes of Broadway, and through smaller venues across the country.

The film industry was born in 1889, when William Kennedy Laurie Dickson, working out of Thomas Edison's laboratory, developed a motion picture camera and a primitive projection device known as a kinetoscope. 1896 saw the arrival of the first commercial film projector, designed by C. Francis Jenkins and Thomas Armat. As there were no movie theaters in existence, films were shown in vaudeville houses and in a variety of other locations. The mass production of films did not begin until the early 1900s. The subsequent boom that followed would have a massive impact on the U.S. economy. From the 1920s to the

The enormous success of television changed American life and the entertainment industry forever. Watching television was often considered a family event in the 1940s.

1940s, Hollywood, California was the capital of the global movie producing market. One key to this industry's success was the manner in which it adapted when faced with economic and technological changes. Antitrust and patent infringement suits, the Great Depression, World War II, and other factors managed to damage the industry's financial status, but it always recovered quickly. Instead of bowing down, the film industry simply expanded. Initially the cameraman wore many hats, acting as director, producer, editor, distributor, and in other capacities. Mass production changed that; as more films were produced, it became necessary to delegate responsibility to several individuals.

This diversification led to the creation of many jobs, and opened up a new market for numerous existing jobs as well. By the 1990s, literally hundreds of people worked on each film produced. These artisans ranged from directors, cinematographers, and marketing specialists to insurance representatives, carpenters, and caterers. Production companies themselves had branched out into three different types: the majors, the mini–majors, and the independents. The majors are built up of large companies such as Disney or Sony, and usually handle not only film production

but also distribution and marketing. Mini–majors such as Orion Pictures Corporation, tend to specialize in specific film genres and have limited distribution ability. Lastly, the independents generally have no distribution power. In the mid–1990s, independent films were becoming more and more popular, as directors were able to apply more creative control to these pictures with very little corporate intervention. Regardless of the production company type, the film industry continued to prosper. Feature films produced in the United States earned approximately $4.6 billion worldwide in 1991.

Radio started as a hobby in the early 1900s and grew to become the world's first "instant" mass medium. As early as 1921, radio stations were being constructed and broadcasting such programming as religious services, news, and sporting events. With the inception of the National Broadcasting Company (NBC) in 1926 and the Columbia Broadcasting System (CBS) in 1927, national broadcasting networks came into being. In 1927, the Federal Radio Commission (FRC) began regulating the content of the airwaves. However, these regulations did not hinder the marketing of commercial products to mass culture. Indeed, commercial radio broadcasting became the number one way to advertise products of all types, including films—*King Kong* was the first motion picture to be promoted via the radio, in 1933.

However, this national mass media dominance came to an end in the late 1940s with the advent of television. However, the Federal Communications Commission (FCC) continued licensing new radio stations—so much so that between 1945 and 1960 the number of stations had increased from 973 to 4,306. Throughout the 1940s and 1950s radio stations developed a new marketing strategy; instead of targeting a national market, each station approached specific niche markets based on audience age, location, and other elements. A variety of musical forms such as country, jazz, and rock n' roll could now be represented over the airwaves, catering to specific target audiences. Advertisers were able to promote their products based on the station's audience type. This type of marketing remained the radio standard through the 1990s.

Many parallels can be drawn between radio and its successor— television. As with radio, television began its reign under the control of large national networks (NBC, CBS, and ABC). By 1955 over half of the homes in the United States had a television. Both radio and the stage lost a sizable share of audience, while radio suffered the added burden of losing some of its advertising to the visual mass medium.

In the 1950s, ABC found itself in a ratings slump. The network began experimenting with more risky programming designed to capture a specific audience—much in the same way that radio had begun to broadcast to specific niches of the market. *Maverick*, starring James Garner, was the first of these edgy shows. The gamble paid off and soon ABC was running programming that was heavy with sex and violence, such as *The Untouchables* and *77 Sunset Strip*. This would set a standard for the television industry that would continue through the 1990s. During the 1960s and 1970s, the other two networks (CBS and NBC) also began to angle their programming at target audiences as well.

The mid-1970s gave rise to a new threat to the networks: cable television. Home Box Office (HBO) and what would eventually become the Turner Broadcasting System offered a wider variety of programming. The Fox network was started by Rupert Murdoch in the mid-1980s with a goal of presenting programming that would push the barriers of good taste. Much like the "variety" theater of the past, the Fox network broadcast mostly low–brow comedies and action dramas.

The success of the Fox network spurred tremendous growth of the cable industry in the late-1980s through the 1990s. The major networks began to lose ground as numerous cable stations were launched. The Golf Channel, the Family Channel, the Arts & Entertainment Network, and Comedy Central offer just a few examples of the choices viewers had in 1999. This type of specific marketing approach became known as narrowcasting. As with radio, television found itself catering to specific markets in order to increase advertising sales.

The television medium also provided additional outlets for the film industry: television programming and video tape sales. Major movie studios provided approximately half of all prime-time network programming in the early 1980s. By the 1990s, major film production companies were buying up television stations throughout the United States. Paramount Pictures Corporation, Disney Studios, joined Twentieth Century Fox as major players in the television industry.

Amusement parks offer many elements of the entertainment industry in one central location. The origin of the amusement park is rooted in medieval history, when European cities would host "pleasure gardens" alive with fireworks, games, dancing, rides, and other diversions. The 1800s saw America as the primary developer of amusement parks. This was due in part to the development of the trolley. In order to boost business trolley companies would construct amusement parks at the end of their line. This industry continued to grow and by 1919 over 1,500 amusement parks existed in the United States.

Unfortunately, World War II disrupted the industry's success, causing many parks to close. This trend continued into the early 1950s, as television and other factors began to draw people away. However, with the opening of Disneyland in 1955, the theme park had arrived. Upon its success, theme parks began to spring up across the country. In the 1990s many amusement parks were associated with film and television companies—so much so that several offered attractions based on motion pictures. The two most prominent parks of this type were Disney/MGM Studios and Universal Studios. Both produced film and television material and also offered extensive entertainment facilities such as rides, restaurants, shows, and more.

By the late 1990s, the rapid advance of technology found many aspects of the entertainment industry receiving a facelift. Digital technology was changing the nature of film; from special effects to editing to projection, this high–tech approach opened a new realm of visual freedom to filmmakers and improved image quality in theaters as well. High Definition Television (HDTV) was in the works, offering drastic improvements in picture quality. Small satellite dishes that offered a wide variety of programming for less cost to the user were rapidly replacing cable. Cable companies, in turn, were hedging their bets on the Internet—the cable modem, allowing for faster access speeds and greater reliability. The World Wide Web became a global hub of home entertainment, allowing for global broadcasts of talk radio programs, theater and movie ticket purchases, television listings, and much more. Who can say where technology will take the entertainment industry in the future?

See also: **Amusement Parks, Vaudeville, Jack L. Warner**

FURTHER READING

"The Amusement Park Industry: A Very Brief History," [cited April 20, 1999] available from the World Wide Web @ www.carousel.org/ amusement.html.

Bordman, Gerald. *American Musical Theatre: A Chronicle*. New York: Oxford University Press, 1995.

Harmon, Renee. *The Beginning Filmmaker's Business Guide: Financial, Legal, Marketing, and Distribution Basics of Making Movies*. New York: Walker & Co., 1994.

Hartwig, Robert L. *Basic TV Technology: A Media Manual (Media Manuals)*. New York: Focal Press, 1995.

Resnick, Gail and Scott Trost. *All You Need to Know About the Movie and TV Business*. New York: Fireside, 1996.

ENTREPRENEURSHIP

In French, to be an entrepreneur is to be "one who undertakes a task or project." Thus, entrepreneurship has come to be defined as the act of risking capital and resources to identify and implement a solution to a problem with the goal of turning a profit. The eighteenth-century Irishman Richard Cantillon first used term *entrepreneur* in a business context to describe businessmen who bought goods and services only in order to resell them later at a higher price. This idea of risking one's fortune for the possibility of a large but uncertain future gain is still the central meaning of *entrepreneurship*.

In 1904 the German sociologist Max Weber (1864–1920) described the entrepreneur as a heroic, energetic figure whose "Protestant work ethic" relied on thrift

and hard work to make possible economic innovation and growth. The leading economist of entrepreneurship, Austrian Joseph Schumpeter (1883–1950), argued that in every capitalist society great risk-taking entrepreneurs arise who have the vision and energy to create new technologies and industries. But when lesser imitators attempt to recreate the success of these entrepreneurs, the economy becomes glutted with over-investment and eventually collapses into recession. Eventually a new generation of entrepreneurs arises to fuel a new boom in innovation.

The strong tradition of property rights in the United States created an ideal environment for the first great period of U.S. entrepreneurship. Between 1789 to 1932 U.S. entrepreneurship enjoyed its "classical" age. During this time business risk-taking and economic growth occurred largely through the efforts of individual men such as Andrew Carnegie (1835–1919), John D. Rockefeller (1839–1937), Thomas Edison (1847–1931), and Henry Ford (1863–1947). These entrepreneurs and many like them accumulated the capital, identified the opportunities, organized the resources, and crushed their competition to build vast corporate empires. Since 1933 the federal government has played a much larger role in ensuring that pure entrepreneurship doesn't harm the public interest.

To some people, the rise of Bill Gates (1955—) and the Microsoft Corporation in the 1980s represented the birth of a new age of corporate-style entrepreneurship. Some U.S. economists attributed the explosion in new Internet and technology companies in the 1990s both to the emergence of a new class of managers and risk-takers trained to pursue innovation and to economic conditions that created a large pool of investment capital for these entrepreneurs to draw on. But at the close of the twentieth century entrepreneurship means everything from starting a small home-based business to developing and marketing a new product or technology to establishing an entire corporation or industry

See also: **Capital, Capitalism, Microsoft, Joseph Schumpeter, Work Ethic**

ENVIRONMENTALISM

The environmental movement in the United States was born in the 1960s and it gathered strength in the 1970s, when a growing populace took interest in curbing the effects of industrial and agricultural practices on the natural environment and on public health. The literature written and the legislature passed during this period led to many changes in the way that manufacturing and farming were conducted throughout the country. Federal regulations and agencies were established to restrict the use of harmful chemicals and their release into the environment. While certain companies found that they had to resort to costly measures in order to comply with these regulations, other manufacturers managed to find inexpensive or even money-saving solutions. Nevertheless, the new emphasis placed on environmental awareness altered the way in which many businesses were to operate nationwide.

Scientist and author Rachel Carson was a key figure in the early environmentalist movement: Her groundbreaking 1962 book *Silent Spring* alerted U.S. citizens to the hazards of several widely used pesticides and herbicides. Her arguments caused uproar among chemical manufacturers and created a stir in political circles around the country. Carson named specific chemicals responsible for contaminating the natural environment, for spreading disease among humans, and for killing birds, fish, and other wildlife. She painted a chilling futuristic picture of a world unfit to support life—of the silence of a spring without songbirds.

In addition to the appearance of this highly influential book, three events contributed to the rise of environmentalism in the 1960s United States: an oil spill in the Santa Barbara channel blackened the shoreline in Southern California; the chemically contaminated Cuyahoga River in Cleveland, Ohio spontaneously caught fire; and an active afternoon at the steel mills of Pittsburgh, Pennsylvania caused a temperature inversion in the city, which grew so dark and polluted that street lights and drivers' headlights were turned on at midday. Media coverage of these incidents increased public awareness about the dangers of certain chemicals and toxic substances widely used by industries. Concerned citizens and legislators called for action, asserting that industrial practices throughout the country would have to change.

WE ARE SUBJECTING WHOLE POPULATIONS TO EXPOSURE TO CHEMICALS WHICH ANIMAL EXPERIMENTS HAVE PROVED TO BE EXTREMELY POISONOUS AND IN MANY CASES CUMULATIVE IN THEIR EFFECTS. THESE EXPOSURES NOW BEGIN AT OR BEFORE BIRTH AND—UNLESS WE CHANGE OUR METHODS—WILL CONTINUE THROUGH THE LIFETIME OF THOSE NOW LIVING.

Rachel Carson, *Silent Spring*, 1962

In 1969 lawmakers passed the National Environmental Policy Act (NEPA), the first of a series of legislation designed to protect the environment. The

NEPA required federal agencies to submit statements about the environmental effects of their activities. In the same year Congress established the Environmental Protection Agency (EPA), which monitored federal agencies' compliance with the NEPA and with later legislation. The following year Congress introduced both the National Institute of Occupational Safety and Health, which conducted research on workers' exposure to harmful substances in the workplace, and the Department of Health and Human Services, which set on-site business standards for health and safety. The Clean Air Act (1970) called upon manufacturers to safeguard against the release of air pollutants in their vicinity and the Clean Water Act (1972) forbade manufacturers from contaminating nearby bodies of water. Many more acts and agencies were introduced throughout the 1970s, 1980s, and 1990s, and all were born out of the tremendously effective environmentalist movement.

After the regulations went into effect, the United States saw much improvement in air and water quality, as well as in the management of toxic substances, pesticides, and waste. In ''Twenty-Five Years of Environmental Progress at a Glance'' the EPA reported that between 1970 and 1994 emissions of six common air pollutants decreased by 24 percent and emissions of lead dropped by 98 percent. The EPA also noted that during the same period wastewater standards prevented more than one billion pounds of toxic substances from contaminating bodies of water. Considering that in the same amount of time the nation's economy grew by 90 percent; the population increased by 27 percent; and the number of motor vehicles driven rose by 111 percent, the environmental improvements achieved were quite dramatic.

Because environmental legislation targeted corporations in particular, many manufacturers had to spend a lot of money creating devices and conducting tests that would control the use and release of harmful substances. The EPA estimated that in 1997 U.S. corporations spent $170 billion in efforts to comply with federal regulations. Critics of environmentalism noted that this figure represented 2.2 percent of the country's gross domestic product, a proportion that exceeded what was spent on environmental safety in other countries. Whether or not the benefits of the regulations merited this considerable expense was becoming a topic of heated debate.

Throughout the 1990s economics played a growing role in environmental policymaking, as powerful corporations had a great impact on the passing of legislation. Environmental policymaking became a struggle between big business, which wished to curb the spending required by federal regulations, and the proponents of environmentalism, who strove to continue improving air and water quality and enhancing public health. Those who straddled between economic and environmental interests believed, perhaps idealistically, that the two forces would keep each other in check and that taking both interests into account would lead to cost-conscious approaches to environmental protection in the United States.

FURTHER READING

Carson, Rachel. *Silent Spring*. 1962. Reprint, Boston: Houghton Mifflin, 1994.

DiLorenzo, Thomas J. "Federal Regulations: Environmentalism's Achilles Heel." *USA Today*, September, 1994.

"Silent Spring Revisited," [cited May 25, 1999], available from the World Wide Web @ www.pbs.org/wgbh/pages/frontline/shows/nature/disrupt/sspring.html/.

Portney, Paul R. "Counting the Cost: The Growing Role of Economics in Environmental Decision making." *Environment*, March, 1998.

The Reader's Companion to American History. Boston: Houghton-Mifflin Co., 1991, s.v. "Conservation and Environmental Movements."

"Twenty-Five Years of Environmental Progress at a Glance," [cited May 25, 1999], available from the World Wide Web @ www.epa.gov/25year/intro.html/.

EQUAL OPPORTUNITY ACT

In the shadow of the Great Depression (1929–1939), the New Deal programs of President Franklin D. Roosevelt (1933–1945) expressed a new, broader vision of the social contract between the people and the government: from now on, the national governments of industrial societies were responsible for assuring the welfare of citizens unable to provide for themselves. This definition of the welfare state was largely put into practice in Western Europe after the war. But even as early as the later 1930s, this confident vision of the welfare state had begun to run aground on a politically conservative Congress and Supreme Court intent on dismantling the New Deal safety net. Given the national priority of fighting the World War II (1939–1945), social activism lost the compelling momentum that it had exhibited in the 1930s. But reform was not dead. Even as the patriotic consensus of World War II was

followed by the repressive anticommunist consensus of the early Cold War, the New Deal coalition of Democrats, organized labor, ethnic and racial minorities forged in the 1930s stayed in touch and waited for the opportunity to put forward its agenda.

The rise of the Civil Rights Movement in the mid-1950s appeared to signal this opportunity. Though not the full-throated liberal that his Vice President, Lyndon Johnson, was, newly elected President John F. Kennedy (1961–1963) embraced the ideals of social justice as he proposed education, health, and civil rights reforms. In the tradition of the New Deal, Kennedy tried to outline this program, which he called the "New Frontier." However, given his razor-thin victory over Richard Nixon in the 1960 election plus the non-cooperation from Congress, Kennedy was cautious in what he proposed. In 1963, Kennedy began to focus on poverty, requesting his Council on Economic Advisors to develop proposals for legislation for 1964. The president's assassination in November 1963 cut short his leadership in social reform, but he succeeded in raising public awareness of pressing social issues and stimulated greater political activism.

Kennedy's successor and vice president, Lyndon B. Johnson (1963–1969), grew up in the hills of central Texas. His family was not poverty stricken, but he had seen plenty of poverty when, as a young man, he bummed around and took jobs on highway crews and as a teacher in a largely Mexican-American school.

In contrast to Kennedy, Johnson knew how to get what he wanted from Congress. He could intimidate as well as flatter. He had been a leader in both houses of Congress. Johnson began by defining Kennedy's political testament in such a way that helped move legislation through Congress. Taking advantage of national sympathies over Kennedy's sudden death as well as the rise of non-violent leadership in the Civil Rights Movement, Johnson shepherded a series of social reform measures through Congress, including the landmark Civil Rights Act of 1964. Continuing the study of the poverty problem begun by Kennedy, in his State of Union address to the nation in January of 1964 Johnson declared war on poverty. He proposed a comprehensive domestic agenda.

A few months later Johnson began referring to the need to build America's "Great Society." The time appeared right to pursue domestic policies. In spite of the widening war in Vietnam, the public still backed Johnson, perhaps because the economy was booming.

By August 1964 Johnson signed the Equal Opportunity Act (EOA) into law, the legislative vehicle for his war on poverty. Rather than directly providing money and jobs perpetuating welfare dependency, the focus was on helping individuals develop skills through education, job training, and community development, to break out of the cycle of poverty permanently. The act established the Office of Economic Opportunity (OEO) to administer a variety of antipoverty programs. The programs included Head Start for preschool children, the Job Corps providing vocational training to high school dropouts, Upward Bound assisting poor high school students entering college, work-study programs for college students, job-training for adults, grant and loan programs to farmers and businesses willing to hire the previously unemployed, and a domestic volunteer program patterned after Peace Corps called Volunteers in Service to America (VISTA). A central feature of EOA was creation of community action programs (CAP) that politically empowered residents of poor neighborhoods to create and implement specific programs tailored to their community's needs. But CAPs proved of limited effectiveness. Unforeseen conflicts arose with established local political regimes and traditional social service organizations who saw grassroots empowerment as a threat to their turf.

Other related legislation passed in 1964 included the food stamp program, a program providing free legal counsel for indigents, and programs for urban renewal and mass transit to revitalize inner cities. In the fall of 1964, Johnson won the presidential election with over 60 percent of the popular vote. The landslide victory significantly changed the political complexion of Congress establishing Democratic control in both houses. With the Democrats in control, Congress proceeded to pass almost one hundred bills in 1965 and 1966 building an extensive social reform program. Added was health insurance for the aged, health care for the poor, voting rights for minorities, funding for education programs, and environmental protection. The federal government had become a key player in promoting the quality of life in the United States.

This socially progressive agenda came to a quick end, however, as the Vietnam War escalated. Funding demands of the war and public disillusionment with urban riots between 1965 and 1967 led to funding declines for OEO and other social programs. OEO's budget fell from $4 billion in 1966 to less than $2 billion in 1967. The war on poverty made only modest gains.

Major political changes followed Johnson's presidency with conservative Republican control of the White House or Congress through most of the remainder of the twentieth century. Crime-fighting measures gained priority as white middle and upper class opposition to expensive welfare programs, extensive federal regulation, and affirmative action began to threaten those who viewed the programs as altering the terms of a ''zero-sum-game.'' However, the Johnson domestic agenda, driven by social activism at its height in the 20th century, made a lasting mark on U.S. society as many of the individual programs of OEO continued, though often scaled back from original forms.

See also: **Civil Rights Movement, Great Society, New Frontier**

FURTHER READING

Andrew, John A. *Lyndon Johnson and the Great Society.* Chicago: I.R. Dee, 1998.

Bernstein, Irving. *Promises Kept: John F. Kennedy's New Frontier.* New York: Oxford University Press, 1991.

Bornet, Vaughn D. *The Presidency of Lyndon B. Johnson.* Lawrence, KS: University Press of Kansas, 1983.

Langston, Thomas S. *Ideologues and Presidents: From the New Deal to the Reagan Revolution.* Baltimore: Johns Hopkins University Press, 1992.

Patterson, James T. *America's Struggle Against Poverty, 1900–1994.* Cambridge, MA: Harvard University Press, 1994.

Simon, Barbara L. *The Empowerment Tradition in American Social Work: A History.* New York: Columbia University Press, 1994.

EQUITY

Equity, in economic and financial terms, stands for ownership or a share of ownership in property, a corporation, or other asset. Equity oftentimes is represented in the form of stock. A stock represents a claim on a portion of a corporation's assets and profits. It may be purchased on a securities market such as the New York Stock Exchange (NYSE), the National Association of Securities Dealers Automated Quotations (NASDAQ), and the American Stock Exchange (AMEX).

If, for example, one wishes to acquire equity in a new technology company listed on one of the securities markets, one will place an order to purchase a certain number of stock shares. Once the purchase is complete, the individual retains part ownership in the technology company until the stock is sold. With this ownership, the individual may become the recipient of dividends, a small amount of the companies profits distributed on a regular basis to shareholders in the form of cash or additional stock shares.

Equity is also a technical term representing the value of a property minus the owner's outstanding debts, including a mortgage balance. A mortgage is money loaned to a borrower at a set interest rate in exchange for a portion of the profits when the borrower sells the mortgaged property. When the mortgage and all other debts are completely paid off, the owner retains 100 percent equity in the property.

See also: **Asset, Dividends, Mortgage, National Association of Securities Dealers Automated Quotations (System), New York Stock Exchange, Stock**

AN ERA OF ECONOMIC INSTABILITY, 1897–1920 (OVERVIEW)

The period in U.S. economic history between 1897 and 1920 was marked by prosperity and expansion. U.S. industry (especially the new industries that took advantage of new sources of power and new organization of labor) experienced giant gains in productivity. Agriculture also experienced productivity improvements because of the use of the internal combustion tractor and other mechanized farm implements. It was an era of mergers and the business sector expanded by consolidating clusters of sizeable businesses into monster corporations. The government set out to establish safe investment havens for U.S. corporations in Central and South America with the resulting rise in foreign trade. The national economy boomed during World War I (1914–1918). But nearly every period of expansion was countered by a downturn. Unbridled business expansion also brought governmental regulation and monitoring agencies. World War I stimulated the economy, especially heavy industry. After the war the agricultural sector of the economy began to experience weakness in some areas and the polarization of wealth began negatively to affect the domestic market. The nation as a whole vacillated between prosperity economic instability.

By 1890 the United States had conquered a contiguous stretch of the North American continent. The Bureau of the Census announced in 1890 that the frontier, as a line of settlement, no longer existed. As the economy continued to expand, business and political interests began to worry about an economy that was so productive that the domestic market was insufficient

to soak up the product. They began to look to international investments and international markets to solve the problem of "overproduction." In 1898 the United States intervened in a Cuban revolt against Spain. During the ensuing Spanish American War (1898), the United States conquered Cuba, Puerto Rico, Guam, and the Philippines. When the war was over the United States had its own empire: it retained control of Puerto Rico, Guam, and the Philippines, and established dominance over independent Cuba. (The Philippines was granted independence in 1946, but Puerto Rico and Guam remain U.S. possessions. Dominion over Cuba was relinquished in 1934.)

During the early twentieth century the U.S. expansionist agenda continued. In 1903 the United States encouraged Panama to separate from Columbia and form a new republic. Then under a treaty signed late in the same year the United States was given the right to build and control a canal in Panama. In addition the United States intervened in the Dominican Republic in 1905, Nicaragua in 1912, and Haiti in 1915. These interventions resulted in the U.S. taking financial control of these countries and retaining control into the 1930s. A period of prosperity followed the Spanish American War, and the U.S. economy was bolstered by profits from these newly acquired holdings in South and Central America.

Prosperity in the early 1900s was linked to additional, domestic factors. The United States officially went on the gold standard in 1900. Prices began to rise for two reasons: new discoveries and increased mining expanded the gold supply, and the government issued more bank notes. Thus the per capita circulation of money increased from $23.85 in 1893 to $33.86 by 1907. Moreover the general price level rose 70 percent between 1896 and 1914, and per capita income rose from $480 to $567 between 1900 and 1920. During roughly the same period the population increased 40 percent from 76.2 million to 106 million, the number of factories increased 32 percent, capital investments soared by 250 percent, and the value of products rose 222 percent. Prosperity carried over to farmers, too. Between 1910 and 1920 gross farm income rose from $7.4 billion to $15.9 billion, and the value of farm property shot up 400 percent.

Prosperity was accompanied by the growth of super-large corporations and consolidations in the business world. There was a wave of consolidations (or mergers) between 1897 and 1904 that fundamentally changed the nature of the U.S. corporate system. By 1904 there were 236 giant industrial corporations with total capital of more than $6 billion. In addition, 95 percent of railroad track in the country had come under the control of six groups, and 1,330 public service companies had been consolidated into a mere handful.

Consolidation mania was a response to unbridled competition; business owners sought to establish some control over an unstable market and wild price fluctuations. One solution was merger and monopoly. Corporate heads and financiers were impressed by the results of three early mergers—Standard Oil, American Tobacco, and American Sugar. All three consolidated corporations had prospered handsomely. It seemed clear that through consolidation competition could be reduced, prices controlled, and markets equitably divided. Assisted by professional promoters and investment bankers, competitors in many industries narrowed their differences and combined their strengths. The steel industry, the copper industry, the smelting and refining industry, and the meat packing industry were among the business sectors that most actively merged assets and production processes. The consolidation movement paused in 1904 because by then almost all of the major industries were consolidated, and because the federal government began to accuse the resulting corporations of violating anti-trust laws.

It was this emergence of government regulation that offered another solution to the instability and erratic economic climate of unrelenting competition. Smaller would-be competitors found the regulated economy more difficult to break into. As the giant business consolidations emerged there arose a simultaneous demand for their regulation. The public appreciated the vast array of products and services provided by business, but they feared the great wealth and power of the corporate leaders. Political leaders responded and the result was a renewed interest by the federal government in controlling, or at least overseeing the relationship between business and society. These government efforts toward regulating business characterized the Progressive Era. The Progressive Era (roughly 1901 to 1920) was associated with the presidencies of Theodore Roosevelt (1901–1909), William Howard Taft (1909–1913), and Woodrow Wilson (1913–1921).

Roosevelt was regarded as the most progressive of the three. He used the Sherman Anti-Trust Act of 1890 to dissolve several large corporations, and he favored the passage of several regulatory laws. The Hepburn Act of 1906 increased the power of the Interstate Commerce Commission (created in 1887), The Pure Food and Drug Act of 1906 created the Food and Drug Administration (FDA) to define and enforce quality standards in products manufactured for human consumption. Roosevelt also placed great emphasis on the conservation of national resources. By presidential decree he added millions of acres to the protective status of national parks and forests, and he prohibited the exploitation of certain important oil and coal lands by private enterprise. But there were limits to Roosevelt's radicalism. Though he knew there was a need for tariff revision (tariff rates were very high) and banking reform, Roosevelt did not touch these issues for fear that a conservative reaction would split the Republican party.

Few reforms occurred while Taft was in office (although Taft continued to prosecute anti-trust cases), but under Wilson there were several notable achievements. Tariffs were reduced and Congress passed the Clayton Anti-Trust Act (1914) and the Federal Trade Commission Act (1914). These were designed to alleviate certain unfair business practices in an effort to inhibit corporate mergers. They marked an important step forward for those who favored the regulation of business, but in the long run were not very effective. Business consolidations continued to be an important element of the U.S. economy.

Wilson's most important contribution was the Federal Reserve Act. The Federal Reserve System was designed to eliminate the defects of the most recent reform in the banking system—back in 1863. Chief among these defects was the inelasticity of currency—meaning, the money supply did not fluctuate with the needs of business. Instead the money supply fluctuated with the needs of the government because the amount of currency in circulation was directly tied to the volume of government bonds sold to the banks. Banks could only issue currency amounts equal to the value of the bonds they owned.

The Federal Reserve System divided the country into 12 districts, each with a Federal Reserve Bank. These were ''bankers' banks;'' that is, they did not deal directly with the public. They loaned money to commercial banks, governed the interest rate, and issued Federal Reserve Notes. The result of the Federal Reserve System was that the volume of currency in circulation tended to fluctuate with the needs of business as determined by a governing board in Washington, D.C.

In the same year that the Federal Reserve Act passed through Congress, 1914, war broke out in Europe. The U.S. did not enter World War I until 1917, but the war had a significant effect on the U.S. economy from the outset. The United States served as the major source of raw materials, foodstuffs, and supplies to Europe; thus the war generated enormous industrial and agricultural expansion. The Gross National Product (GNP) increased by 15 percent between 1914 and 1918. During the same period the production of all types of metals increased substantially and there was an agricultural boom. Cotton prices rose from 8.5 cents to 35.9 cents per pound and wheat rose from 97 cents to $2.73 per bushel. However, inflation became a serious problem. Between 1914 and 1920 the cost of living index increased from 100 to 200.

When the United States entered the war in 1917, the economy had to be mobilized. This meant a sudden and considerable increase in government activity and a shift from peacetime to wartime production. Mobilization went reasonably well and the United States was able to orchestrate its role in the war without disturbing economic growth or stability. Under authority provided by Congress the government created several special boards to administer the war effort. The most important of these was the War Industries Board, which had the power to control industrial production. It could determine priorities, fix prices, and even take over factories. Other boards with similar powers included the Food Administration, the Fuel Administration, the Shipping Board, and the Railroad Administration (which actually took over the railroads until the end of the war).

The increased needs of the wartime economy created a greater demand for labor at the very same time that the number of available workers declined. This was caused by a decrease in immigration, coupled with the fact that nearly four million men enlisted in military service. The overall effect of this worker shortage was to strengthen the position of labor. Wages rose significantly, from an index of 100 in 1913 to 234 by 1920. Labor unions also benefited—membership rose from 2.77 million in 1916 to 4.12 million in 1919. In addition, the government created the War Labor Board to settle disputes between workers and employers.

The United States financed as well as fought in the war by loaning the Allies more than $10 billion. In order to cover its expenses the U.S. government resorted to a dual strategy: one-third of the cost of the war was funded through tax revenue, and the remaining two-thirds was financed through loans. Most of the loan money was generated through the sale of Liberty Bonds—in five issues the government raised $25 billion. Additionally there were tax increases on liquor and tobacco, luxuries, and "excess" profits. Taxes rose from $735 million in 1914 to $4.64 billion in 1919. In some income tax brackets the tax rose as high as 70 percent.

Economic expansion during the war had long-term effects. In industries like coal, textiles, agriculture, and shipbuilding, expansion extended production capacity far beyond what the nation's postwar economy demanded or could support. Thus key industries were permanently weakened. Moreover sudden wage deflation after the war set the stage for major labor disputes and the opening of a new and turbulent era.

See also: **Federal Reserve Act, Lever Food Control Act, Model T, War Industries Board, World War I**

FURTHER READING

Hays, Samuel P. *The Response to Industrialism, 1885–1914*. Chicago: University of Chicago Press, 1957.

Kennedy, David. *Over Here: The First World War and American Society*. New York: Oxford University Press, 1980.

Link, Arthur S. *American Epochs*. New York: Alfred Knopf, 1963.

Vatter, Harold G. *The Drive to Industrial Maturity: The U.S. Economy, 1860–1914*. Westport, CT: Greenwood Press, 1975.

Wiebe, Robert H. *The Search for Order, 1877–1920*. New York: Hill and Wang, 1967.

ERIE CANAL, BUILDING OF

The Erie Canal was one of the largest and most controversial construction projects undertaken in the United States during the nineteenth century. It linked the navigable part of the Hudson River in eastern New York State with the Great Lakes. Western farmers were able to ship their produce directly to American markets without having to go through Canadian waters. The Erie Canal also symbolized the unification of the nation, binding the western frontier to the eastern markets by ties that were stronger than the East's historic links to Canada or its former economic links to markets on the Mississippi River. But, the canal also raised important political questions about public versus private funding of infrastructure. Within New York itself, the canal became a heated point of debate between the major political parties, the Federalists and the Democratic Republicans. Later canal issues, such as the act to enlarge the waterway in 1835, divided the New York government against itself.

The concept of a canal linking the Hudson River valley with the Great Lakes was proposed during the first decades of independence following the American Revolution (1775–83). Before the war the area had been the home of the Iroquois Federation or Six Nations. During the war the future canal route through the Mohawk River valley had been the scene of many battles between British troops, Canadian irregulars,

Drawing of the opening of the Erie Canal, October 26, 1825.

and Native Americans on one side and the American rebels on the other. In 1783, after resigning his commission as general of the Continental Army, George Washington (1732–1799) made a tour of western New York and recommended linking eastern New York with the Ohio River and Lake Erie. In 1792 the New York legislature authorized the incorporation of the Western Inland Lock Navigation Company for the purpose of linking Albany on the Hudson River with Lake Ontario. By 1798 the company's progress on the canal made it possible for large boats carrying up to 16 tons of cargo to move alongside the Mohawk River to Rome, New York, a town about 75 miles west of Albany. It cut the cost of moving cargo between Albany and Seneca Lake (at least 80 miles west of Rome) by two-thirds and reduced the cost of moving cargo between Albany and the Niagara River on the Canadian border by half. Canal operations, however, were inefficient due to poor engineering, unreliable management, and scarce, expensive labor. One company supervisor was accused of embezzling funds and some locks were so poorly constructed that they had to be rebuilt four times. Nonetheless, the canal formed the nucleus of the future Erie Canal.

At the beginning of the nineteenth century Lake Ontario was still believed to be the logical endpoint of an internal New York canal. In 1800, however, Gouverneur Morris, the former Minister to France, foresaw the creation of a canal linking the Hudson River with Lake Erie. Such a canal was formally proposed in 1807–08 by Jesse Hawley, a merchant

from western New York who was in prison at the time because he was unable to pay his debts. At the same time, President Thomas Jefferson's (1801–1809) Secretary of the Treasury Albert Gallatin and surveyor James Geddes independently proposed canals that would link New York seaports to western markets, although they both preferred the Lake Ontario route. New York land speculators and politicians, such as future Governor De Witt Clinton, supported the prospect of federal dollars to pay for these internal projects. By 1810 they had revitalized the Western Inland Lock Navigation Company and launched plans to explore western New York for the best canal tracks.

> **I SHOULD LIKE TO KNOW WHETHER MY LITTLE FARM IN THE COUNTY OF JEFFERSON HAS GOT TO BE TAXED FROM YEAR TO YEAR, FOR THE PURPOSE OF ENABLING THE FARMERS ON THE SHORES OF LAKES ERIE, HURON AND MICHIGAN TO BRING THEIR PRODUCE TO MARKET FOR NOTHING.**
>
> "Peter Ploughshare" [pseudonym of Samuel Beach], *Considerations Against Continuing the Great Canal West of the Seneca,* 1819

The high hopes among New Yorkers for federal assistance in canal construction were soon dashed. Before the funding could pass through Congress, the United States declared war on England, launching the War of 1812 (1812–14). The war tied up funds for the canal and for other internal improvements. By 1815 it appeared that the canal idea had failed. This perception continued through 1816 when President James Madison vetoed the "Bonus Bill" that would have provided federal money for the Erie Canal. Fortunately, state money was substituted instead, thanks in large part to the support of DeWitt Clinton, who campaigned successfully for governor the following year on a canal platform. New York politicians quickly made the canal an issue in their campaigns and Democratic Republicans split between those in favor of the Lake Erie route (led by Clinton) and those opposed (led by future president Martin Van Buren, 1837–1841). Some landowners in southern New York objected to the canal project, seeing it as an excuse to tax them for the benefit of the rest of the state. Clinton's opponents, who drew some of their support from these people, formed the nucleus of the organization that later became known as Tammany Hall, a political force which controlled New York politics for most of the nineteenth century.

Paradoxically, the War of 1812 created strong nationalistic feelings among New Yorkers that boosted regional support for canal construction. The failed invasion of Canada in 1812 made Midwestern Americans aware of the dangers of shipping their produce through Canadian waters. It also made plain, to even the most hawkish Americans, that although much produce traveled to market via the St. Lawrence River, it would never be United States territory. The theater of war in the west centered on the Great Lakes—particularly Lake Erie—and brought public attention to the area. By the spring of 1816 construction on the canal was back on schedule.

Construction of the Erie Canal officially began on July 4, 1817 at Rome, New York. For almost nine years, teams of up to 3,000 workers cut a 40-foot wide, four-foot deep trench through 364 miles of wilderness. The Erie Canal crossed rivers and valleys; it included 18 aqueducts, 84 locks (each 15 feet wide and 90 feet long), and more than 300 bridges. Much of the work was done by immigrant Irish and Welsh laborers, who were poorly paid and often sick. Wages averaged fifty cents a day. A report from 1819 stated that about a thousand men were unable to report for work because of sickness. Nonetheless, the project was an unqualified success. The canal cut the cost and time of shipping freight from Buffalo to New York City from $100 per ton and twenty days to $5 per ton and 6 days. The canal cost $7,143,789 to build, but by the time it opened on October 25, 1825, it had already earned $1 million in tolls. The Canal was enlarged between 1835 and 1862 to meet the demands of increased traffic, even though by that time the railroads were beginning to crowd out canal freight. Even so, the peak year for use of the New York canal system was 1872.

The Erie Canal opened the New York interior to commerce and immigration. Before 1820 the population of the westernmost portion of the state was just over 23,000. By 1850 the state's population had ballooned to over three million. Equally important, the canal forged strong economic and political links between the west and the east. Before the Erie Canal opened, the western states tended to side politically with the South; their freight went down the Ohio and Mississippi Rivers to New Orleans and other southern ports. The Erie Canal changed the direction of western commerce from the slave-holding South to the industrial North. It helped equate western interests with northern interests and insured western support of the North in the American Civil War (1861–65).

See also: **American Revolution, Civil War, Thomas Jefferson, James Madison, Mississippi River, New Orleans, War of 1812, George Washington**

FURTHER READING

Cornog, Evan. *The Birth of Empire: DeWitt Clinton and the American Experience, 1769–1828.* New York: Oxford University Press, 1998.

Goodrich, Carter, editor. *Canals and American Economic Development.* New York: Columbia University Press, 1961.

Shaw, Ronald E. *Erie Water West: A History of the Erie Canal, 1792–1854.* Lexington, KY: University of Kentucky Press, 1966.

Shaw, Ronald E. *Canals for a Nation: The Canal Era in the United States, 1790–1860.* Lexington, KY: University of Kentucky Press, 1990.

Sheriff, Carol. *The Artificial River: The Erie Canal and the Paradox of Progress, 1817–1862.* New York: Hill & Wang, 1996.

EUROPEAN LOANS

European loans were critical to the patriotic cause of the American Revolution (1775–83). Had it not been for foreign aid, it is unlikely that the United States would have won the war of independence. When the fighting began at Lexington and Concord, Massachusetts, in April 1775, the colonies were hardly prepared to sustain war against the powerful British. But the nation's founding fathers rose to the occasion. Assembling in Philadelphia, Pennsylvania, in May 1775, the delegates to the Second Continental Congress quickly issued articles of war against Britain and named George Washington (1732–99) commander in chief of the Continental Army. After declaring independence from the mother country in 1776, the Congress turned its attention to financing a fight with Britain, which not only had the advantage of a highly trained military but also had tremendous material resources. To fund the war effort, Congress issued paper money, called Continentals, which it used to purchase supplies, ammunition, and pay its soldiers. But as the government issued more Continentals, the bills eventually became worthless.

The early days of fighting were grim: The mighty British navy readily claimed ports up and down the Atlantic seaboard; ground troops of the Continental Army were poorly supplied; and a financial crisis was evolving as the U.S. currency continued to devalue. The autumn of 1777 proved to be the turning point for the Americans. Victories at Trenton and Princeton, New Jersey, and at Saratoga, New York, encouraged

France, which had been quietly and cautiously supporting the patriots' cause, to establish an open alliance with the United States. Other countries—also foes of Great Britain—soon committed their support as well. After suffering a brutal winter in 1777–78, when Washington's troops at Valley Forge, Pennsylvania, went hungry and were in rags, foreign aid began to stream into the United States in the spring of 1778. In addition to clothing, food, muskets, and gunpowder, the United States now received borrowed money and cash gifts from France, the Netherlands, and Spain. With this assistance the Americans were able to muster a decisive victory over the British at Yorktown, Virginia. Within months the British government expressed its willingness to make peace. After two years of negotiations and intermittent fighting, both countries signed the Treaty of Paris in 1783, officially ending the American Revolution.

See also: **American Revolution, Continental Congress (Second), Continentals**

EVANS, OLIVER

Oliver Evans (1755–1819) was born in Newport, Delaware, on September 13, 1755. Evans was apprenticed to a wagon maker, or wheelwright, as a young man. But beyond the apprenticeship, he was a self-taught, natural mechanic who was good at figuring things out. Evans began his career as an inventor at the age of twenty-one, when he began work on a machine to make the toothed cards used to brush wool prior to spinning. In just a year, he perfected the process and had an operational machine.

Married in 1780, Evans moved to Wilmington, Delaware, to join two brothers in a flour milling business. Within five years, he had analyzed the milling machinery and built automatic machinery to mill grain in one continuous process. The machinery he invented included the grain elevator, conveyor, drill, hopper boy, and descender. With these improvements, grain could be milled and the process completely controlled by one person. Moreover, the end product was much cleaner than in the old process.

The legislatures of Maryland and Pennsylvania granted Evans exclusive rights to use this machinery, and in 1790, he was granted patents by the U.S. Congress. Evans' patent was the third ever granted by the U.S. government. However, he had trouble enforcing his rights and was unsuccessful at profiting from the inventions.

Evans moved to Philadelphia and established a manufacturing company to build and sell mill equipment. The next project Evans tackled was the steam engine. James Watt (1736–1819) introduced a low-pressure steam engine in 1802. In the Watt engine, condensing steam created a vacuum that "pulled" the piston. Evans worked on a high-pressure engine that used the expansion of steam to "push" the piston, a more efficient method of converting heat energy into work. A parallel effort in England at the same time is often credited with this particular improvement to the steam engine. However, British inventor Richard Trevithick had access to Evans' plans and drawings, and Evans grieved that others got credit for his work.

Evans built a steam-powered amphibious vehicle in 1804 to dredge mud and silt from the Schuylkill River. This vehicle was likely the first steam-powered vehicle on either land or water in the United States. Named the *Oruketer Amphibolos*, or amphibious vehicle, by Evans, the device moved over land with wheels and was propelled in the water with a paddle wheel. Evans lobbied for the first railroad, believing that the propulsion device could be adapted to moving vehicles over land on rails made from either wood or iron. Evans' plan was to run rails from Philadelphia to New York, but the first commercial railroad was not in place until years after Evans died. He continued to refine his design and work on the steam engine throughout his life.

Evans published books on his inventions and engineering. His *The Young Millwright and Miller's Guide* (1797), *The Young Engineer's Guide* (1805), and *The Abortion of the Young Steam Engineer's Guide* (1805) were early handbooks on these subjects. They were translated into French and published in Paris as well.

His iron foundries in Philadelphia and Pittsburgh, the Mars Iron Works, were founded in 1807. By the time of his death, they were producing mill equipment, steam engines, and other types of ironwork. Oliver Evans died in New York City on April 21, 1819.

FURTHER READING

Bathe, Greville and Dorothy. *Oliver Evans: A Chronicle of Early American Engineering*. Philadelphia: The Historical Society of Pennsylvania, 1935.

Bowman, John S., ed. *The Cambridge Dictionary of American Biography*. Cambridge: Cambridge University Press, 1995, s.v. "Evans, Oliver."

Encyclopedia of World Biography. Detroit: Gale Research, Inc., 1998, s.v. "Evans, Oliver."

Percell, Carroll W., Jr. *Early Stationary Steam Engines in America: A Study of the Migration of a Technology.* Washington: Smithsonian Institution Press, 1969.

World of Invention. Detroit: Gale Research, Inc., 1994.

EXCHANGE RATE

The price of one country's currency described in terms of another country's currency is known as the foreign exchange rate. The rate is a mechanism used to convert the value of one country's currency into the currency of another. The rate is expressed in terms of the currencies of both countries such as dollars per pound, francs per dollar, or yen per franc. A U.S. citizen who buys a product from France would pay in dollars, but the French would want francs. The dollars are converted into francs at the current exchange rate. If the exchange rate is one dollar per five francs, the U.S. citizen would pay nine dollars for a French product that costs 45 francs.

The kind of exchange rate system countries choose to operate under determines exchange rates. Historically three choices have been available: a fixed rate, a flexible or floating rate, and a managed flexible or managed floating rate. A fixed or pegged exchange rate is a system where governments of different nations agree to a set (''par'') value for their currencies. The price of one currency is fixed in terms of another so the rate does not change. Before 1914 all countries had fixed systems defining their currency in terms of a given amount of gold. If one ounce of gold were worth $20, but four British pounds, then the exchange rate would be $20 per four pounds, or five dollars to one pound. In a flexible rate system the market sets the value of currencies based on supply and demand. Under a managed floating rate countries are on a floating rate system, but if the exchange rate for their currencies rises or falls too far, the central banks intervene or manage the rate.

Difficulties with the fixed gold standard led to the Bretton Woods System immediately after World War II (1939–1945). Under this system countries maintained a fixed exchange rate with each other but based their currencies on the U.S. dollar which was fixed at $35 per ounce of gold. All nations could trade their currencies for dollars and then buy gold at a rate of $35 per ounce from the United States. The Bretton Woods agreement also created the International Monetary Fund, an international economic ''police'' organization. By 1971 President Richard Nixon (1969–1974) announced the United States would no longer redeem

EXCHANGE RATES

United States	$1
Great Britain	0.618 Pound
Canada	1.461 Dollar
China	8.277 Renminbi
European Union	0.941 Euro
Germany	1.841 Deutsche Mark
Japan	121.506 Yen
Mexico	9.145 Pesos
Russia	26.24 Rubles

This is an example of the exchange rate. The exchange rate measures the value of national currencies. These rates change daily.

dollars for gold and since then the world has been on a managed floating exchange rate system.

See also: **Bretton Woods Agreement, Currency, Gold Standard, Money**

EXCISE TAX

An excise tax is a tax on the sales of specific commodities and on certain privileges. Goods and privileges taxed include alcohol and tobacco, gasoline, and specific licenses. Local, state, and federal governments can levy excise taxes. The government sets excise taxes on a per unit basis, such as by the gallon for gasoline, or as a certain percentage of the sale price of an item. In contrast to direct taxes, such as income tax, which is assessed directly on individuals, excise taxes are considered indirect taxes. They are levied against the goods rather than the individual, and the business passes the collected tax onto the government. Nevertheless the real burden is on the consumer who must pay higher prices. Since low-income families spend a greater percentage of their income than high-income families to purchase the same amount of goods, excise taxes tend to be regressive. This means that a greater burden is placed on lower income families.

Excise taxes on the sale of alcohol and tobacco are sometimes called the ''sin'' taxes. Gasoline is taxed at the pump and the revenues are used for highway construction and maintenance. License taxes include marriage and hunting licenses. Franchise taxes, also a form of excise tax, are licenses to operate certain types of businesses. Other types of excise taxes are severance taxes which tax the processing of a natural resource such as timber or petroleum, taxes levied on airways and airports, and taxes on telephone services.

Article I, section 8, of the *Constitution of the United States* gave Congress the power to collect excise taxes. Opposition to the Excise Law of 1791, which placed a tax on whiskey, led to the Whiskey Rebellion in western Pennsylvania in 1794. By the end of the American Civil War (1861–1865), Congress had revised the tax system to incorporate more and larger excise taxes. Between 1870 and 1900 almost all federal internal revenues were raised through excise taxes and tariffs and most of those through excises on alcohol and tobacco. In 1913 the income tax amendment was passed and direct taxes on individuals and businesses quickly became the chief source of revenue. By 1997 excise taxes accounted for only four percent of federal receipts.

See also: **Regressive Tax, Revenue**

EXODUSTERS

Exodusters were African American homesteaders who moved westward during the last decades of the nineteenth century to settle the Great Plains. After federal troops withdrew from the South in 1877 at the end of the twelve-year period of Reconstruction (1865–1877), civil rights for African Americans began to erode. Southern state legislatures adopted laws, so-called "black codes," to restrict the movement, prosperity, and freedom of African Americans. A campaign of intimidation led by the Ku Klux Klan was intended to keep former slaves "in their place," a sentiment that seemed precariously close to the pre-Civil War slave-owner mentality. The system of sharecropping, whereby plantation owners—out of economic necessity—divided up their lands for former slave families to farm, resulted in numerous former slaves being indebted to landowners. State laws, such as poll taxes, literacy tests, and grandfather clauses, were also designed to keep African American citizens from voting, and effectively disenfranched them. Unable to improve their economic conditions, severely oppressed by the terror of the Ku Klux Klan, and unable to participate in government, southern African Americans became disillusioned—the American Civil War (1861–1865) had seemingly done little to change their quality of life. This situation prompted a mass exodus of blacks from the South during the last two decades of the nineteenth century.

While many southern African Americans migrated to cities in the North, in 1879 a major migration onto the dusty plains of Kansas began a flow westward as well. By the end of the 1800s, "all-black" towns could be found in Oklahoma and other western states. Some who migrated onto the Great Plains took advantage of the Homestead Act of 1862, which allowed them to settle up to 160 acres (64 hectares) of land, and lay claim to it after a period of five (and later just three) years. These homesteaders braved the harsh climate of the open plains to carve out a living for themselves. The exodusters ("exodus" since they had left the South en masse, and "dusters" since they settled the dry prairie region) helped transform the Great Plains into a prosperous agricultural region.

See also: **Black Codes, Homestead Act, Homesteaders, Westward Expansion**

EXPANSIONISTS

Soon after the colonies won the American Revolution (1775–83) and founded the United States of America, nationalist fervor emerged. Eager to spread "American ideals," expansionists looked westward, northward, and southward to expand the territory of the Union beyond the original 13 states. They favored the settlement of the frontier—some advocated seizure of the Southwest (from Spain and later from Mexico), Florida (from Spain), the Louisiana Territory (from France), and the Northwestern Territories and even Canada (from Britain). By the 1840s the doctrine of Manifest Destiny took hold. (A doctrine which held that the United States had a God-given right and duty to expand its territory and influence throughout North America).

The fires of expansionism were fueled by population growth during the 1800s. Pioneer settlement of the Plains and the Old Northwest (present-day Ohio, Michigan, Indiana, Illinois, Wisconsin, and part of Minnesota) resulted in an increase in farmland and overall crop production. Inventions such as the cotton gin and the McCormick reaper improved the processing and harvesting of raw materials such as cotton and grain, and a continuous influx of immigrants from Europe supplied labor for the factories that had opened across New England and the Mid-Atlantic. All these factors combined to create a rapid population growth. In the two decades between 1840 and 1860 alone, U.S. population more than doubled, increasing from about 17 million to more than 38 million. Though the eastern seaboard cities grew, a system of new canals, steamboats, roads, and railroads also opened up the interior to increased settlement. By 1850 almost half the population lived outside the original 13 states.

Though Canada remained in the hands of the British, the spirit of expansionism resulted in a rapid acquisition by the United States of North American territories that had belonged to Spain, Mexico, France, and England. By 1853 the United States owned all the territory contained in the present-day contiguous states. By the end of the century, the United States owned all the territory of its present-day states— which included Alaska (purchased from Russia in 1867) and Hawaii (annexed in 1898).

See also: **Alaska, Hawaii, Manifest Destiny, Old Northwest, James Polk**

EXPORTS

Exports are goods and services that are produced in one country but shipped to another country for consumption. Some examples would be lumber grown in the United States but shipped to Japan; U.S. wheat shipped to Russia; Hollywood movies sent around the world; and U.S. jet fighter planes made here but sold to allied nations such as Israel and Saudi Arabia.

The United States exports thousands of types of goods and services. The United States, however, exports a relatively small portion of its total output, generally less than 10 percent, compared to some other nations. Some European nations, for example, export 25 percent or more of their total production. Where there is a difference between the amount that a country imports and the amount it exports, a trade imbalance exists.

The United States, which has the wealth to import a vast array of goods from around the world, typically runs a rather large trade deficit with other nations. This deficit worries many government officials who fear that U.S. citizens are supporting foreign workers with their dollars, but not workers at home. Because of such fears, many governments try to increase the export of their own goods and decrease imports. There are various ways to do this. Nations may give exporting companies tax breaks to encourage them to send their products overseas. Or they may create special banks whose job is to loan money to firms that export goods.

See also: **Balance of Trade, Imports, Trade**

EXTERNALITIES

Externalities are economic benefits or costs that affect people who are not directly part of an economic activity. In a way externalities can be thought of as economic "black holes" that have economic effects that are hard to determine because so many people are affected indirectly. For example, if a chemical company has to store all its manufacturing waste in metal drums, it will incur the cost of buying the drums, putting the waste into the drums, and allocating the land to store the drums. Because this will be expensive the company may have to cut back on its production to keep its waste disposal costs under control, thus losing profits. If the company simply dumps its waste into a nearby river, however, its waste disposal costs would be smaller. From the standpoint of the company there is greater economic incentive to pour the waste into the river than to store it in drums, but to the people who live along that river, the company's waste will become a major environmental hazard. This is a "negative externality": a collision of the "private benefit" of one party (the company that pollutes) with the "public cost" to society. To prevent the company from polluting the river, the people must force it to do something detrimental to its profits. Since the company has an economic incentive to continue polluting, the people must convince the company to change its policy by boycotting its products or by passing legislation against pollution.

An example of a "beneficial externality" is a company that hires and trains unskilled workers when it would be more efficient and profitable to hire trained workers. The company incurs a "private cost" (the expense of training unskilled people) and provides society with a "public good" (employed people learning new skills). Since society gains more skilled and employed workers at the company's expense, it is an externality that is beneficial to the economy as a whole, but it is difficult to measure.

EXXON CORPORATION

The Exxon Corporation grew out of another oil company giant, Standard Oil Company, founded by John D. Rockefeller (1839–1937) in 1870. Standard Oil's monopoly over the oil business in the early twentieth century led to a series of attacks on that company from journalists and politicians. Likewise, Exxon's reputation in the late twentieth century has been damaged by the environmental havoc created by a massive oil spill in Alaska from the tanker *Exxon Valdez* in 1989. Still, Exxon remains the third largest company in the United States and the seventh largest in the world.

In the 1860s Rockefeller foresaw the potential of refining Pennsylvania crude oil. Though internal combustion engines were not yet developed, kerosene oil could be used, among other things, to fuel lanterns.

When Standard Oil was formed, it integrated all of the docks, railroad cars, warehouses, lumber resources, and other facilities it needed into its operations. Because of its size it was able to make lucrative deals with railroads. The result was to drive smaller refiners out of business.

Standard Oil became the foremost monopoly in the country. It was so big that it more or less dictated to the railroads what it would pay in freight rates. Although this practice was abandoned because of public pressure, by 1878 Rockefeller and partner Henry Flagler (1830–1913) were in control of most of the nation's oil refining business. Rockefeller's business successes had made him one of the five wealthiest men in the country. Those same monopolistic business practices that gave him such monetary success were also a source of criticism from many quarters in industry and government.

In 1882 Rockefeller and his associates established the first trust in the United States, which consolidated all of Standard Oil Company's assets in the states under the New York Company, in which Rockefeller was the major shareholder.

In the 1880s Standard Oil began producing as well as refining and distributing oil. It also began an overseas trade, particularly in kerosene to Great Britain. The trust encountered difficulties with the Sherman Antitrust Act of 1890, followed by an 1892 Ohio Supreme Court decision which forbade the trust to operate Standard of Ohio. The company then moved its base of its operations to New Jersey, which in 1899 became home to Standard Oil of New Jersey, or Jersey Standard, the sole holding company for all of Standard's interests. Jersey Standard later became Exxon Corporation. In the first decades of the twentieth century Jersey Standard was banned from holdings in several states. Instead, it acquired companies in Latin America in the 1920s, particularly in Venezuela, and also expanded its marketing companies abroad.

As the supply of crude oil began shifting from the United States and Latin America to the Middle East in the 1920s, Jersey Standard and other companies effectively used the same monopolistic practices that John D. Rockefeller had used 50 years before to establish a foothold in the region. Middle East production was stepped up following World War II (1939–1945) and Standard Oil exploited its rich resources in Iraq, Iran, and Saudi Arabia. Oil prices stayed low and the United States and Europe became extremely dependent on oil fuels for industry and automobiles.

During the 1960s growing nationalism in the Middle East brought much resentment against the western companies dominating Middle Eastern oil. The Organization of Petroleum Exporting Countries (OPEC) was formed to protect the interests of the producing countries. As OPEC became more assertive, Jersey Standard sought other sources of crude oil. The company discovered oil fields in Alaska's Prudhoe Bay and in the North Sea. Around the same time, in 1972, Standard Oil of New Jersey officially changed its name to Exxon Corporation.

Financial difficulties beset the company in the 1970s, as the OPEC-induced oil shortage depleted much of Exxon's reserves. Long lines formed at gas stations in 1973 and again in 1979, lights were turned out across the nation (even at the White House), and low and moderate income families struggled to heat their homes in the winter. The oil crisis even helped to derail President Jimmy Carter's (1977–1981) bid for a second term in office in 1980.

In 1989 the company was shaken by the *Exxon Valdez* disaster. A drunk Captain of the oil tanker *Exxon Valdez* ran aground in Alaska's Prince William Sound, doing immeasurable damage to the wildlife and to the company's public image. Eleven million gallons of oil spilled in the Alaskan harbor. The state of Alaska conducted public hearings and Exxon was deemed to have been ''reckless'' by an Alaskan Grand Jury. Exxon lost a share of the world oil market to its competitor, Royal Dutch/Shell in 1990. Still, teamed up with Pertamina, the Indonesian state oil company, Exxon in the 1990s developed the Natuna gas field. Exxon also agreed to a $15 billion development of three oil wells in Russia. A large oil discovery in 1996 in the Gulf of Mexico also allowed Exxon to court expansion plans far into the future.

Thus, neither the oil crisis nor the oil spill destroyed the company's profitability. While ordinary people worried, Exxon continued to reap major profits, reaching the $800 billion mark by 1980. Two hundred sixty thousand barrels of crude oil were spilled in Alaskan waters by the *Exxon-Valdez* ship, costing Exxon billions of dollars to clean up Prince William Sound and spawning hundreds of lawsuits from individuals and state and local governments. But, although the spill caused a public relations debacle, Exxon actually improved its financial status in the early 1990s, when other oil companies were losing money. To enhance profitability, the company engaged in cost-cutting, eliminating thousands of jobs and cutting spending for exploration. In 1997 the company's gross profit was $43 billion. By 1998, when oil prices had again sunk to record low levels, Exxon reported a resource base of 1.2 billion barrels of newly discovered resources.

Since the *Exxon Valdez* incident, Exxon has attempted to improve its image by emphasizing its efforts to produce environmentally sound products and contribute to environmental causes. Still, the outcries from the residents of Prince William Sound continued to be heard through the end of the 1990s. The 1994 federal jury verdict held Exxon liable for $5.2 billion in punitive damages—a verdict Exxon is still working to overturn.

Though Exxon began as an American company, it participates in a worldwide market. As a result, the company also has a successful European affiliate, Esso. Operating from its base in Germany, where it is the third largest oil and gas company, Esso manages over 1,500 gas stations in Germany. It also has interests in the Czech Republic, Hungary, Poland, and Slovakia. Esso, like Exxon, explores, produces, and manufactures gasoline, other fuels, chemicals, and lubricants.

See also: **Kerosene, Monopoly, OPEC Oil Embargo, Petroleum Industry, John D. Rockefeller, Sherman Anti-Trust Act, Standard Oil Company**

FURTHER READING

Clarke, Jim. "Exxon to Appeal $5 Billion Oil Spill Judgment." *San Diego Daily*, February 13, 1997.

Nevins, Allan. *Study in Power: John D. Rockefeller—Industrialist and Philanthropist*. 2 vols. New York: Charles Scribner's Sons, 1953.

Sampson, Anthony. *The Seven Sisters: The Great Oil Companies and the World They Made*. New York: Viking, 1975.

Strauss, Gary. "10 Years Later, Case Is Hardly Closed: Exxon's PR Mess Still Isn't Cleaned Up." *USA Today*, March 4, 1999.

"Pumping Up Profits for Years." *Fortune*, April 28, 1997.

Wall, Bennett H. *Growth in a Changing Environment: A History of Standard Oil Company (New Jersey)*. New York: McGraw-Hill, 1988.

FAIR EMPLOYMENT PRACTICES

Beginning in the 1960s Congress passed a series of laws prohibiting employment discrimination based on a variety of factors. These laws are the underpinnings of fair employment practices in the United States. Title VII of the Civil Rights Act of 1964, besides prohibiting employment discrimination on the basis of race, color, religion, sex, or national origin, also established is the U.S. Equal Employment Opportunity Commission (EEOC). Congress charged the EEOC with enforcing fair employment practices.

Additional laws the EEOC enforces are: (1) the Equal Pay Act of 1963 (EPA), an amendment to the Fair Labor Standards Act of 1938 that prohibits discrimination on the basis of gender in compensation for similar jobs under similar conditions; (2) Age Discrimination in Employment Act of 1967 (ADEA) prohibiting job discrimination against persons 40 years of age and older; (3) Section 501 of the Rehabilitation Act of 1973 prohibiting employment discrimination against federal employees with disabilities; (4) Title I of the Americans with Disabilities Act of 1990 (ADA) prohibiting employment discrimination on the basis of disability in both public and private sectors, excluding the federal government; and (5) the Civil Rights Act of 1991 that includes provisions for monetary damages in cases of intentional discrimination.

The EEOC has 50 field offices throughout the United States. It investigates complaints of job discrimination filed by individuals or groups such as labor unions and employment agencies. If the EEOC finds ''reasonable cause'' that discrimination occurred and it seeks voluntary resolution of the dispute. If voluntary resolution is unsuccessful the EEOC may bring suit in federal court.

The EEOC issues guidance in interpreting the laws it enforces, administers the federal sector employment discrimination program, and provides extensive education and outreach with seminars and with information on the Internet. It provides funding and lends support to approximately 90 state and local fair employment practices agencies that process discrimination claims under federal laws as well as state and local employment discrimination charges.

See also: **Americans with Disabilities Act, Fair Labor Standards Act**

FAIR LABOR STANDARDS ACT OF 1938

The Fair Labor Standards Act of 1938 (FLSA) originated in President Franklin Roosevelt's (1933–1945) New Deal. It was a landmark piece of legislation that had a significant impact on the labor movement in the United States. The FLSA set nationwide standards for employees of organizations engaged in interstate commerce, operations of a certain size, and public agencies. Still active today, it affects millions of full and part time workers in the private sector and the federal, state, and local governments.

Under the Fair Labor Standards Act, the first minimum wage (25 cents per hour) was established. The work week was limited to 44 hours per week, which was revised in 1940 to 40 hours per week. Standards were developed to keep records of hours worked and wages paid. These same standards allowed employers to keep track of overtime owed to employees who exceeded the standard work week.

Perhaps most significantly, the Fair Labor Standards Act banned child labor. Children under age fourteen were no longer legally allowed to work. Exceptions were made for the agricultural industry and some family businesses. Children under age eighteen were restricted from ''hazardous'' jobs, including mining and some factory jobs. The ban on child labor

In 1938, the Fair Labor Standards Act was passed, addressing the need to cease childhood exploitation in the workforce. This landmark piece of legislation is still in effect today.

greatly decreased the number of children harmed by bad working conditions.

A 1963 amendment to the FLSA called the Equal Pay Act prohibited differences in pay based on sex. Under this provision women who were often paid wages lower than a man in the same position could now demand equal pay. The Equal Pay Act was an important step in leveling the often uneven work field in which women competed with men for the same jobs but had to settle for making less money.

Over twenty amendments have been made to the Fair Labor Standards Act. Most of these were made to increase the minimum wage, which has gone from 25 cents in 1938 to $5.25 in 1998.

Enforcement of FLSA standards is handled by the U.S. Department of Labor's Employment Standards Administration, Wage-Hour Division. The Equal Pay Act is an exception; it's enforcement was transferred to the Equal Employment Opportunity Commission in 1979.

See also: **Child Labor, Interstate Commerce, Minimum Wage, Franklin Delano Roosevelt**

FALLEN TIMBERS, BATTLE OF

The battle of Fallen Timbers (1794) and the Treaty of Greenville (1795) that followed it marked the successful conclusion of a long struggle for control over the Ohio country—the region between Lake Erie and the Ohio River. Since the 1740s, the territory had been the site of numerous battles between Native Americans, French Canadians, and British and Colonial troops. Although the Treaty of Paris (1783) ended the fighting between England and the United States in the American Revolution (1775–1783), the struggle between the new country and its Native American neighbors continued. Despite the provisions of the Treaty of Paris and the Treaty of Ft. Stanwix (in which the Iroquois Confederacy relinquished its claim on the Ohio country to the United States), Great Britain still wanted the area. Great Britain had excluded its Indian allies from the treaty negotiations that ended the American Revolution. Some British politicians believed the Indians might continue the war on the frontier and bring the area back under British influence. The British built Fort Miami, near modern Toledo, Ohio, to help support the Native American effort in the Ohio country.

Matters came to a head in the early 1790s, in the conflict known as Little Turtle's War (1790–1794). As more white settlers flooded into the area following its partition under the Land Ordinance of 1785, the Native Americans were forced westward. The Miami commander, Michikinikwa (Little Turtle), led a confederation of tribes against U.S. expeditions led by General Josiah Harmar in 1790 and General Arthur St. Clair in 1791, defeating them both. Both Harmar's and St. Clair's armies consisted largely of untrained militia, frontiersmen with guns but little discipline, who often broke ranks and fled when confronted by Native American warriors.

In late August 1794, Little Turtle and his Shawnee ally, Weyapiersenwah (Blue Jacket), faced a new U.S. Army, including a core of nearly 5,000 professionals trained and led by General ''Mad'' Anthony Wayne. Wayne had spent the better part of two years training and disciplining his troops. On June 30, 1794, Wayne's army drove off a Native American attack from Fort Recovery, the site of St. Clair's defeat three years before. By August 20, his force confronted the Native Americans outside modern Maumee, Ohio. A tornado had recently knocked down many of the trees in the area, and about 2,000 Native Americans used them as cover to attack Wayne's group of 900 (thus the name Fallen Timbers). Within a few hours, however, Wayne's army rallied and drove the Indians from their cover, killing about 200 and forcing the others to seek refuge at Fort Miami. Official American casualties numbered 107 dead.

The battle of Fallen Timbers had ramifications that stretched all the way to Europe. News of the American victory helped negotiator John Jay secure a treaty with the British that promised British withdrawal from the frontier forts—securing the area for the Americans. The Treaty of Greenville, negotiated between Wayne and Little Turtle the following year, secured most of what is now Ohio for American settlement. The victory calmed the fears of frontiersmen about Indian raids and secured the area's allegiance to the United States. From a long-term perspective, the battle of Fallen Timbers secured American access to the western Great Lakes and the western Ohio River valley, giving farmers in the area access to international markets for their produce.

See also: **Land Ordinance of 1785, Ohio**

FURTHER READING

Axelrod, Alan. *Chronicle of the Indian Wars: From Colonial Times to Wounded Knee.* New York: Prentice-Hall, 1993.

DeRegnaucourt, Tony. *The Archaeology of Camp Stillwater: Wayne's March to Fallen Timbers, July 28, 1794.* Arcanum, OH: Upper Miami Valley Archaeological Research Museum, 1995.

Knopf, Richard C., editor and transcriber. *Anthony Wayne, a Name in Arms: Soldier, Diplomat, Defender of Expansion Westward of a Nation; The Wayne-Knox-Pickering-McHenry Correspondence.* Westport, CT: Greenwood Press, 1975.

Nelson, Paul David. *Anthony Wayne, Soldier of the Early Republic.* Bloomington, IN: Indiana University Press, 1985.

Slaughter, Thomas. *The Whiskey Rebellion: Frontier Epilogue to the American Revolution.* New York: Oxford University Press, 1986.

FAMILY AND MEDICAL LEAVE ACT

President Bill Clinton's (1993–) first legislative action after taking office was the Family and Medical Leave Act (FMLA), which went into effect August 5, 1993. According to the Commission on Family and Medical Leave, the act was developed to ''support families in their efforts to strike a workable balance between the competing demands of the workplace and the home.'' This action was significant because previously, the United States was the only industrialized country that did not guarantee job protection when employees needed work leave that exceeded company vacation or sick-leave allowances.

The FMLA, which applies to all school, public agency and private sector employers with 50 or more employees, allows up to 12 weeks of unpaid leave in a 12-month period for certain family and medical reasons. The law also requires employers to maintain the employees' health benefits during leave and to restore the employee's job after the leave. Under FMLA guidelines the 12-week leave is allowed for the birth of a child; adoption or foster care of a child; care for a spouse, child or parent with a serious health condition; or for employees who cannot work due to a serious health condition.

After legislation was passed in 1993 conflicting reports emerged about the effectiveness of FMLA. In 1996 a government-sponsored Report to Congress, called ''A Workable Balance,'' concluded that ''the FMLA has not been the burden to business that some feared. For most employers compliance is easy, the costs are non-existent or small, and the effects are minimal.'' As a result of this report, an amendment was introduced in 1997 to expand the FMLA. The amendment extended coverage to 13 million more employees by requiring employers with 25 or more employees to provide FMLA benefits in addition to those with 50 or more employees already covered by existing legislation. In 1997, a second independent survey contradicted the Report to Congress with evidence that the FMLA was fraught with compliance and implementation problems. This study resulted in action by a bipartisan group in 1998 to introduce the Family and Medical Leave Clarification Act, an amendment that would make the FMLA easier for employers to understand and use.

What could account for the difference in opinion between the two surveys? According to some experts it may have been a matter of timing. The Report to Congress survey was conducted between January 1994 and June 1995, before the Department of Labor implemented final regulations. These regulations included several changes, such as the definition of a serious health condition, which made the mandate more difficult to manage. Indeed, when Human Resources professionals were asked in the 1997 independent survey about changes that would make the FMLA more user-friendly, respondents cited tightening the definition of a serious health condition. Some stated that FMLA actually cost companies money because it was costly and time-consuming to contest poorly documented medical claims. Also, some employers noted an increase in absence rates as a result of FMLA.

While the controversy continued regarding the FMLA, both sides agreed that the legislation was well-intentioned. Though most members of the Labor Policy Association (LPA), a Washington, DC-based employer association that focused on employment policy issues, considered the law an inconvenience rather than a threat to business, they would have liked the problems with FMLA corrected before it was expanded.

See also: **Women in the Workplace**

FURTHER READING

Papa, Jeri White, Richard E. Kopelman, and Gillian Glynn. "Sizing Up the FMLA." *Workforce*, August 1998.

Raizel, Michelow. "Family Leave Act Presenting Problems." *Crain's Cleveland Business*, November 3, 1997.

Ruhm, Christopher J. "Policy Watch: The Family and Medical Leave Act." *Journal of Economic Perspectives*, Summer 1997.

Unowsky, Keri G. "The FMLA at Five Years: The Courts Struggle to Define the Parameters." *Employee Relations Law Journal*, Autumn, 1998.

"The Family and Medical Leave Act Summary of Provisions." *Congressional Digest*, May 1997.

FAR WESTERN INDIANS

Far Western Indians were those tribes living west of the Sierra Nevada Mountain range before European incursion. This group is also called the California Indians. It included the Pomo, Hoopa (or Hupa), and Serrano tribes. These Indians lived in an area that stretched from the southern part of Oregon and extended south to northern reaches of Mexico's Baja Peninsula. At least five language groups were represented in this region. The tribes hunted deer, elk, bighorn sheep, and rabbits. They also fished for salmon and collected clams and other shellfish, and they gathered acorns (which were pounded to make flour for bread), pine nuts, grass seeds, fruits, and berries. The Pomo were known for their watertight baskets. In the north, people lived in wooden plank houses. To the south, the Pomo lived in cone-shaped shelters constructed of rush mats, brush, and bark covering pole frames. Some lived in pit houses (semi-subterranean, circular shelters).

The Spaniards, arriving in the 1500s, were the first Europeans in the region. By the 1700s they had established missions. In addition to converting many Indians to Christianity (these people became known as Mission Indians), the Spaniards also taught them to farm and raise livestock. Diseases devastated the Indian population, and U.S. settlers arriving in the early 1840s pushed Indians off their lands. The California gold rush (1848) caused further displacement.

See also: **Gold Rush of 1849**

FARM CREDIT ADMINISTRATION

In 1933 the United States was mired in the Great Depression. President Franklin Roosevelt (1933–1945) instructed Congress to create the Farm Credit Administration (FCA) to assist agricultural workers who found loans and credit increasingly hard to come by during the difficult economic times.

Still functioning to this day, the FCA supervises the institutions that grant credit to farmers and ranchers and also coordinates the Farm Credit System. The Farm Credit System is a centralized banking system designed to serve U.S. agricultural interests by granting short- and long-term credit through regional banks and local associations.

The Farm Credit System was established in 1916. Its purpose is to provide dependable credit to agricultural workers. When the Great Depression arrived in the 1930s, farmers were hit hard. Farm property values dropped sharply and debt delinquencies grew quickly. Many of the loan companies involved with agricultural workers failed. Thus, when the Farm Credit Administration was created, the banks and associations comprising the Farm Credit System were supported completely by the federal government in an attempt to give the agricultural economy more stability in the uncertain day of the Depression. Today, these organizations are financed entirely by the sale of stock.

Franklin Roosevelt developed the Farm Credit Administration to unify all government farm credit programs under one agency. In addition to overseeing the Farm Credit System, the FCA also sets regulations, ensures compliance with established procedures, and has the authority to intervene when an institution violates those regulations.

See also: **Great Depression, Franklin Delano Roosevelt**

FARMERS' ALLIANCES

National organizations of U.S. farmers, the farmers' alliances were founded in the 1870s. The alliances grew out of the increasing unrest in rural areas due to a depressed economy, falling farm prices, and increasing farming costs. Most growers experienced a decline in their standard of living; many were debt-laden while others teetered on the brink of foreclosure. Farmers began meeting to discuss their problems. As the groups became more organized, they established cooperative programs to help bring down costs and secure the highest possible price for farm products. Alliances ran cooperative stores and grain elevators, purchased machinery directly from manufacturers, collectively marketed crops, and eventually (after 1890) offered members reduced-rate insurance plans. But such efforts only managed the impending agricultural crisis; alliance members realized that to effect change they would need to work inside government.

The 1880s began a period of political activism for the alliances. Members protested against banks (for charging high interest rates) and against railroads (for charging high freight rates). Others lobbied politicians or ran for office themselves. In the mid-term elections

of 1890, the Farmers' Alliance managed to elect several governors and 30 U.S. Congressmen (all members of the Democratic and Republican parties) to office. In Kansas, "America's breadbasket," the Alliances won control of the state legislature. The following year, 1891, the People's (or Populist) Party was formed, absorbing many of the agrarian interests of the Farmers' Alliances in its platform. The third party supported its own political candidate, the former Greenback candidate James B. Weaver (1833–1912), for president in the election of 1892. Though Weaver lost, the Populists remained a strong force. In the next presidential election, of 1896, Populists backed Democratic candidate William Jennings Bryan (1860–1925), a self-proclaimed commoner, who was sympathetic to the causes of the Farmers' Alliances and the National Grange (another reform-minded agricultural organization). Bryan lost to William McKinley (1897–1901), and soon after the Populist Party began to fall apart, disappearing altogether by 1908. Nevertheless, the party's initiatives continued to figure in the nation's political life for the next two decades. (These included free coinage of silver, the government issue of more paper money, a graduated income tax, direct popular election of U.S. Senators, passage of anti-trust laws, and implementation of the eight-hour workday.) Many Populist ideas were eventually made into laws.

See also: **William Jennings Bryan, Cross of Gold Speech, Free Silver, Greenback, Populist Movement, National Grange**

FARMERS' PROTEST MOVEMENTS, 1870–1900 (ISSUE)

After the American Civil War (1861–1865) agricultural prices began a long decline that lasted for a generation. Between 1870 and 1897 wheat fell from $106 per bushel to $63; corn fell from $43 to $29; and cotton fell from 15 cents a pound to five cents. At the same time farmers' costs of operation remained constant or increased. These costs included freight rates, interest on loans, and the cost of machinery and other needed commodities.

The cause of the farmers' troubles was overproduction occasioned by the expansion of the agricultural domain—it doubled during the same period—coupled with more efficient methods. Increased production overseas also contributed. However, U.S. farmers did not recognize the complexities of the matter. They believed they were the victims of a conspiracy generated by the railroad companies, the bankers, the grain elevator operators, and conservative politicians who favored a money system based on the gold standard. The latter was an outgrowth of the specie theory of money which held that precious metals must stand behind the circulating medium (money) to give it value. This system tended to keep money scarce and prices low. The farmers and their political leaders, on the other hand, adhered to the quantity theory of money which held that the amount of currency in circulation should be flexible (based on production) in order to meet the needs of all producers and debtors as well as creditors. A system based on this theory would tend to enlarge the money supply and make credit more easily available. It would also tend to drive prices up.

Farmers sought redress of their grievances through organization. There were three major efforts: the Grange, the Farmers' Alliance, and the Populist Party. Each had a platform consisting of several demands, but two demands received more emphasis than others: government regulation of the railroads and currency and banking reform.

U.S. FARMERS . . . BELIEVED THEY WERE THE VICTIMS OF A CONSPIRACY GENERATED BY THE RAILROAD COMPANIES, THE BANKERS, THE GRAIN ELEVATOR OPERATORS, AND CONSERVATIVE POLITICIANS WHO FAVORED A MONEY SYSTEM BASED ON THE GOLD STANDARD.

The first farmers' organization of the post-war period was the National Grange of Patrons of Husbandry, better known as the Grange. Founded in 1867 by Oliver H. Kelley, it was established as a social club that allowed farmers and their families to improve their lives through mutual aid. By 1875 the Grange claimed a membership of 800,000, mostly in the Midwest and South. By this time also, the organization had shifted its focus from social to political and financial matters and had become a lobby. The Grangers advocated railroad regulation by the states and they wanted the federal government to leave in circulation large amounts of paper money that had been issued during the Civil War.

On the latter issue, the Grange and other groups that wanted to inflate the currency had no success because the government brought paper money to a par with gold in 1875 through the Specie Resumption Act. However, their efforts aimed at railroad regulation were more promising. Beginning in 1871, several states led by Illinois passed laws controlling railroad freight rates and grain elevator charges. The railroads fought these measures, which they called "Granger

Laws," in federal court, where they were ruled unconstitutional. Though the Granger Laws were declared unconstitutional, they marked the beginning of a new era in which government would assume more responsibility for regulating the actions of common carriers and their associated businesses.

In addition to their political ventures the Grangers went into business. They set up cooperative creameries, elevators, and warehouses; they also organized insurance companies and attempted the manufacture and sale of farm machinery. Eventually, most of these ventures failed because of intense competition or mismanagement. By the late 1870s the Grange was declining; its business activities disappeared and it ceased to be an aggressive political and financial lobby. Nevertheless, Grange social activities continued and it remains in existence.

The Grange was replaced at the forefront of the agrarian revolt by the Farmers' Alliance. Between the mid 1870s and 1880 two Alliances emerged: the Northwestern, or Northern Alliance, and the Farmers' Alliance and Industrial Union, better known as the Southern Alliance.

The Northern Alliance was founded in Illinois in 1880, and soon spread to other Midwestern states, especially Nebraska, Kansas, and Iowa. By 1882 the Alliance claimed to have 100,000 members. After that it declined for a while, but hard times in the late 1880s spurred further growth. By 1890 the Northern Alliance had become a force to be reckoned with.

The Southern Alliance began in Texas in 1875. Originally a cattlemen's association in Lampasas County, it soon grew into a statewide organization with both a social and political agenda. By 1886 it seemed on the verge of dissolution because of disagreements about whether or not to enter into politics, but then Charles William Macune became president. His leadership not only averted the split, but launched the Alliance on a course of expansion. By the end of 1887 the Alliance had spread to every southern state. It appealed to farmers because it was portrayed as a cooperative business venture. With cotton prices collapsing this idea seemed to offer a ray of hope.

By the end of the 1880s both national Alliances had identical platforms. They called for government regulation or ownership of the railroads, currency reform, abolition of the national banks, and abolition of alien land ownership. As their goals were similar there was talk of union, but it never occurred. This was because of the race issue—the Northern Alliance allowed black farmers to join—and because the Southern

Alliance was larger. Northern leaders feared they would lose their positions in a combined Alliance.

Like the Grange, the Alliances had a social program designed to improve the lives of farmers and their families. It consisted of meetings, picnics, debates, musical performances, and the like. There was an educational program carried on through lectures and publications, and the Alliances also entered business, usually by forming cooperatives to buy and sell products and insurance. These efforts were temporarily successful but eventually most of them failed.

More important was the Alliances' entry into politics. They wanted reforms and pursued them by attempting to influence politicians in the major parties to adopt their platforms. In 1890 numerous Alliance men were elected to office in states like Kansas, Nebraska, South Dakota, South Carolina, and Georgia. However, there were not enough of them to achieve all their goals and this led many to consider the creation of a national third party.

The Peoples' party—better known as the Populist party—was born at a meeting in St. Louis in 1891. It held its first national convention in Omaha the following year and nominated James B. Weaver of Iowa for president. The party platform reflected the demands of the Farmers' Alliances but there was a major change in the money plank. It now called for the remonetization of silver in order to expand the money supply. Silver had been demonetized in 1873, restored in 1878, and demonetized again in 1893. Demonetization means that silver was dropped as a basis for the value of currency.

In the election of 1892 Weaver polled nearly a million votes, mostly in the Midwest. During the next four years the party flourished. It elected numerous members to state legislatures and several governors. Free and unlimited coinage of silver at 16 to one became the party's battle cry. This meant the Populists wanted the United States' Treasury to buy all the silver produced by U.S mines, peg its value at 1/16th that of gold, and mint as much silver coinage as possible. They believed that this formula would create a financial system that would meet their needs by producing a controlled inflation.

In 1896 the Democrats, led by William Jennings Bryan (1860–1925) of Nebraska, adopted the Populist platform for the presidential campaign. The Republicans, led by William McKinley (1843–1901), supported the gold standard. McKinley won and after his victory farm prices began to improve. This was because new discoveries of gold increased the supply and because the Treasury put more banknotes into circulation. The Populist party collapsed and the farmers' revolt was over.

The early years of the twentieth century and the years of World War I (1914–18) were fairly prosperous for U.S. farmers but the twenties were not. Once again overproduction and falling prices combined to wreak havoc in the agrarian community, but this did not lead to the rise of national protest movements like the ones in the late nineteenth century.

During the Great Depression (1929–39) conditions worsened and before President Roosevelt's (1933–45) New Deal there were some efforts to organize. The best known of these was the Farm Holiday Association (FHA) in Iowa in early 1933. Led by Milo Reno, the FHA wanted to persuade farmers to withhold their produce from the market until prices went up. In some cases there were efforts to force farmers to comply, and in March 1933, the FHA threatened a nationwide farmers strike. They also sought to intimidate sheriffs and judges from exercising foreclosure sales. When President Roosevelt made it clear that he intended to assist farmers as soon and as much as possible, the movement quickly declined.

See also: **Farmers' Alliance, National Grange**

FURTHER READING

Buck, Solon J. *The Granger Movement: A Study of Agricultural Organization and its Political Economic and Social Manifestations.* Lincoln: University of Nebraska Press, 1913.

Goodwyn, Lawrence. *Democratic Promise: The Populist Movement in America.* New York: Oxford University Press, 1976.

Hahn, Steven. *The Roots of Southern Populism: Yeoman Farmers and the Transformation of the Georgia Upcountry, 1850–90.* New York: Oxford University Press, 1983.

Hicks, John D. *The Populist Revolt: A History of the Farmer's Alliance and the People's Party.* Minneapolis: University of Minnesota Press, 1955.

McMath, Robert C. *Populist Vanguard: A History of the Southern Farmers Alliance.* New York: Norton, 1975.

Weinstein, Allen. *Prelude to Populism: Origins of the Silver Issue.* New Haven: Yale University Press, 1970.

FEDERAL DEBT

The federal debt is the amount of money that the federal government has borrowed and not yet paid back. The government pays for most of its operations by raising money through taxes, but when tax revenues are not enough to cover everything the government wants to do, it borrows the rest. In that sense, it is like a family borrowing something extra each month to pay its bills. The government borrows by selling bonds, notes, and Treasury bills to investors. These debts pay a rate of interest to the lender. As may be expected, the federal debt rises in times of war and other calamities, when the government is borrowing heavily to accomplish its ends. The debt then tends to shrink back down after the crisis passes as the government gradually pays off what it borrowed. Intense public debate has raged in recent decades over how large the federal debt should be. Economists who favor an expansive government role argue that some federal debt is no problem. For example, in times of unemployment the government should borrow more and then spend the money on job-producing programs. On the other hand, fiscal conservatives maintain that too high a federal debt is bad for the economy. When the government competes for dollars with all other borrowers, interest rates tend to rise dampening economic activity. In the recent history of the United States, the federal debt was very high during World War II (1939–1945); it fell in the years after that and rose again in the 1980s during the military build-up during the final stages of the Cold War; then it began to fall again during the economic boom of the 1990s.

See also: **Keynesian Economic Theory**

FEDERAL DEPOSIT INSURANCE CORPORATION

"Deposits insured by the FDIC." Many banks today promote the insurability of customer deposits with this simple slogan, but this wasn't always the case. Prior to 1933, people depositing their money into a bank had no guarantee that their money was safe. From the stock market crash of 1929 to the first years of President Franklin Roosevelt's (1933–1945) administration, nine thousand banks collapsed, and depositors lost $1.3 billion.

Public confidence in the banking system collapsed along with the banks. In the hard times of the Great Depression, the government needed to bolster public confidence and maintain financial stability in the nation. The Federal Deposit Insurance Corporation (FDIC)

was an effort to do just that. When the Glass-Steagall Act became law in 1933, it provided for the creation of the FDIC, which provides insurance coverage for bank deposits.

The FDIC insures deposits in national banks, Federal Reserve member state banks, and state banks that have applied for federal deposit insurance and meet FDIC qualifications. After its inception, the FDIC tried to repay all deposits, regardless of whether they occurred at an insured bank or were over $100,000. This method was felt to be the best way to keep public confidence in the banking system high.

In the 1980s, however, the country experienced a savings and loan crisis. Between 1980 and 1990, 1,110 banks failed. Their failure was caused in part by bad loans in a weak real estate market and also by risky loans to developing countries. Until this time the Federal Savings and Loan Insurance Corporation handled insured deposits at savings and loan associations. With the FDIC Improvement Act of 1991, the FDIC was given authority to insure deposits at savings and loan associations and new restrictions were made on how the organization repaid lost deposits.

The FDIC now operates by a "least-cost" method. If an insured bank collapses, the FDIC pays up to $100,000 of a depositor's claim. It is not allowed to cover uninsured depositors unless the president, the secretary of the treasury, and the FDIC jointly agree that failing to do so would seriously effect the economic conditions of the nation or the community.

See also: **Federal Reserve System, Glass-Steagal Banking Act**

FEDERAL RAILROAD ADMINISTRATION

For many years the economic practices of the transportation system in the U.S. were unregulated. In 1887, railroads came under federal regulation to curtail abuse of railroad monopolies. The U.S. railroads were the first large monopolies in the U.S., and society was not certain how to protect itself from them. Regulation of the railroads, first enforced by the Interstate Commerce Commission, controlled rates, and provided that railroads could not charge more for a short haul than for a long haul over the same route. Regulators tried to make railroads set rates that were "fair" to all users, communities, and industries served by the railroads. After World War II (1939–1945), it was clear that federal regulation of railroads was not working well.

Trucking and airline industries took much business away from the railroads. Most of the railroads in the Northeast were bankrupt. One of those bankruptcies, Penn Central, was the nation's largest bankruptcy to date. Circa 1970, many of the regulatory shackles were removed from the nation's carriers, including the railroads. In 1966, the Department of Transportation created the Federal Railroad Administration (FRA). The FRA, operating within the U.S. Dept. of Transportation, sets train regulations, including transportation safety, and movements of hazardous materials. The FRA has also moved in the direction of creating partnerships among rail labor, rail management, rail suppliers, passenger and freight railroads, and state and local governments, and the federal government.

See also: **Free Trade, Monopolies, Railroad Industry**

FEDERAL RESERVE ACT OF 1913

On December 23, 1913, President Woodrow Wilson (1913–1921) signed the Federal Reserve Act, and thereby created the Federal Reserve System. The Federal Reserve Act was intended to prevent a national financial crises and promote economic stability. The legislation established a national system for governmental regulation of currency supply and federal distribution of currency to banks. The Act also relocated supervision of the banking system from the private sector to the federal government. After years of popular national opposition to the federal government's involvement in the banking system, the passage of the Federal Reserve Act was a turning point. The Act represented a recognition that banking and currency would remain unstable without a unifying regulatory system at the national level.

Opposition to a federal banking system dated back to the United States' beginnings. The newly formed United States was largely agrarian, with little banking experience and a deep distrust of any central government activity. Nevertheless, many congressional members believed that a banking system was crucial to the fledgling nation's economic development. Under leadership of the first Secretary of the Treasury, Alexander Hamilton (1755–1804), Congress established the First Bank of the United States in 1791. However the First Bank (and its successor the Second Bank, established in 1816) fell prey to fears that the federal government's power was excessive at the states' expense. As the nation expanded a stampede ensued to establish state

banks under numerous state laws. These banks wildly vacillated between freely issuing bank notes and lending money, to tightening down on the money supply. Bank failures and loss of depositors' savings were widespread.

Not until the nation was faced with the financial demands of the American Civil War (1861–1865) did the government attempt to intervene in the financial sector again. Congress passed National Bank Acts in 1863 and 1864. The acts created a system of privately owned banks called "national" banks because they were chartered and regulated by the federal government. The national banks issued a uniform currency nationwide, but the national bank system was not equipped to meet the money supply needs of a rapidly expanding economy.

> [THE STRUGGLE THAT PRODUCED THE FEDERAL RESERVE ACT] IS NOT MERELY A CHAPTER IN FINANCIAL HISTORY; IT IS ALSO AN ACCOUNT OF THE FIRST BATTLE IN A CAMPAIGN FOR SAFE AND SCIENTIFIC BANKING.
>
> H. Parker Willis, first Secretary of the Federal Reserve Board, 1923

A series of devastating cash panics between 1873 and 1907 focused public attention on the need for more extensive banking and monetary reform. The Aldrich Vreeland Act of 1908 provided temporary issues of emergency currency. In 1910 the National Monetary Commission began extensive investigations of the banking system, laying the groundwork for the system's reform. After much Congressional debate and compromise, the Glass-Owen bill—the Federal Reserve Act—was passed and signed into law in 1913.

Careful to avoid the label "central bank," the Federal Reserve Act diffused bank supervision by creating 12 Federal Reserve Districts. Each district had a Federal Reserve Bank and a Federal Reserve Board to oversee and coordinate operation for the entire system. To ensure that commercial bankers throughout the country would have a voice, the Federal Advisory Council was established and composed of twelve members, one from each Federal Reserve district and elected by member banks of that District.

All national banks had to belong to the entire system. Member banks also included a small number of state-chartered banks that were willing and qualified to join. The required investment of each member bank was six percent of its capital. Each member bank received an annual dividend of six percent of the amount it invested in the Reserve Bank.

Passage of the Federal Reserve Act began a long organizing process. Section 10 of the act charged the Federal Reserve Board with establishing a centralized banking system to meet the challenging and changing needs of the U.S. economy. The board, based in Washington, D.C., consisted of seven members serving 10-year terms. The board members were: the Secretary of the Treasury, the Comptroller of the Currency, and five members appointed by the President of the United States with consent of the Senate. In order to avoid potential domination by any region, the act specified that no more than one of the five appointed members could be from any one Federal Reserve District. To eliminate partisan pressures the framers of the act intended that the appointees be public figures who could not financially benefit from board decisions. The act also required that at least two board members be knowledgeable in banking and finance so that the commercial and financial needs of the nation were addressed according to scientific principles. To insulate the board from the legislative branch, all expenses were paid from Reserve Bank earnings rather than congressional appropriations. Once they were appointed, board members were neither directly responsible to the president nor to any other branch of the federal government.

The Federal Reserve Board was charged with establishing and overseeing the twelve Reserve Banks. In addition, the board would examine the accounts, books, and affairs of reserve and member banks, and review discount rates (the rate charged to member banks for loans from Reserve Banks) set by each Reserve Bank. The Federal Reserve Board was also charged with oversight of currency circulation. This included regulating the amount of gold reserves held against Federal Reserve notes (paper money), supervising the issue and retirement of notes, serving as a central clearinghouse for checks, and executing various supervisory and regulatory functions pertaining to Reserve Banks.

Conflicts arose between the Federal Reserve System and U.S. Treasury. The Banking Act of 1935 diffused the discord by removing the Treasury Secretary and Comptroller of the Currency from the Federal Reserve Board. All seven board positions became presidential appointees. The 1935 act also established the Federal Open Market Committee (FOMC), a group consisting of the seven board members and five of the twelve Reserve bank presidents. For over fifty years the powerful FOMC held complete control over the country's money supply.

By the end of the twentieth century the Federal Reserve System remained largely an independent agency of the government. At that time the system controlled the flow of money and credit in three ways. First the Federal Reserve System conducted open-market sales or purchases of government securities; second, the system raised or lowered the discount rate. Finally the Federal Reserve System changed reserve requirements—the percentages of deposits that a member bank must hold as currency in their vaults or as deposits in their district Federal Reserve Bank. The Federal Reserve System continued to grow and undergo adjustments, assuring economic stability in the United States.

See also: **Bank of the United States (first), Bank of the United States (second), Woodrow Wilson**

FURTHER READING

Broz, J. Lawrence. *The International Origins of the Federal Reserve System.* Ithaca, NY: Cornell University Press, 1997.

McCulley, Richard T. *Banks and Politics During the Progressive Era: The Origins of the Federal Reserve System, 1897–1913.* New York: Garland Publishing, 1992.

Timberlake, Richard H., Jr. *The Origins of Central Banking in the United States.* Cambridge, MA: Harvard University Press, 1978.

Toma, Mark. *Competition and Monopoly in the Federal Reserve System, 1914–1951: A Microeconomics Approach to Monetary History.* New York: Cambridge University Press, 1997.

West, Robert C. *Banking Reform and the Federal Reserve, 1863–1923.* Ithaca, NY: Cornell University Press, 1977.

FEDERAL RESERVE SYSTEM

The Federal Reserve System, also known simply as "the Fed," is a U.S. central bank. Its primary role is to influence the amount of money and credit circulating in the economy in order to promote full employment, stable prices, and economic growth. It also regulates and supervises the U.S. banking industry, distributes currency and coins, clears checks, and handles some electronic funds transfers. Unlike traditional banks, the Fed's purpose is not to make a profit but to serve the national interest. Moreover, its customers are not individual citizens but the roughly 4,300 banks that make up its members. The Fed is governed by a seven-member Board of Governors appointed by the President of the United States and it is led by the Board's chairperson, who since 1987 has been Alan Greenspan

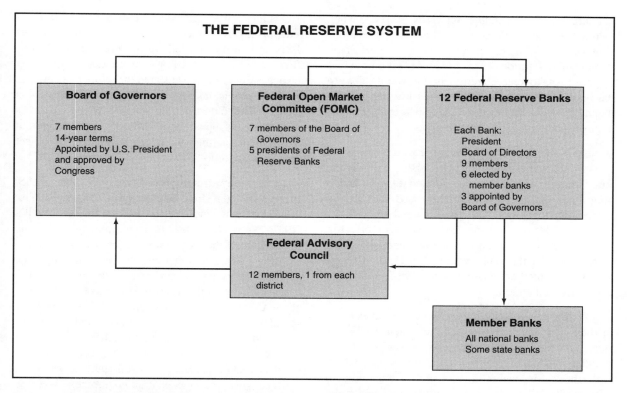

THE FEDERAL RESERVE SYSTEM

Board of Governors

7 members
14-year terms
Appointed by U.S. President
and approved by
Congress

Federal Open Market Committee (FOMC)

7 members of the Board of Governors
5 presidents of Federal Reserve Banks

12 Federal Reserve Banks

Each Bank:
President
Board of Directors
9 members
6 elected by
member banks
3 appointed by
Board of Governors

Federal Advisory Council

12 members, 1 from each district

Member Banks

All national banks
Some state banks

The Federal Reserve System is the central bank of the United States. This non-profit, semi-public organization is run by presidential appointees. Its main function is to influence the amount of money and credit circulating in the economy to insure economic stability.

(1926—). Although the Board determines the Fed's policies, the twelve district Federal Reserve banks, located in major cities across the United States, perform its day-to-day operations.

The Federal Reserve System came into being after four financial panics destabilized the U.S. economy between 1873 and 1907. Congress established the National Monetary Commission to determine what made the U.S. banking system so susceptible to these periodic crashes. The commission's report led directly to the Federal Reserve Act of 1913, which created the Federal Reserve System. Initially, the Fed performed only the narrow functions of lending money to banks when they could not get loans elsewhere, supervising the banking industry, and increasing or decreasing the money and credit supply in response to changing economic conditions. However, many believed that the Great Depression of the 1930s occurred in part because the Fed did not provide banks with enough reserves to make loans that would have increased the money supply and kept the economy from contracting. In response, Congress passed the Banking Act of 1935 to give the Fed greater controls over the minimum amount of reserves each member bank needed to make loans. The Full Employment Act of 1946 empowered the Fed to make full employment and stable prices explicit

goals of its policy, and the Full Employment and Balanced Growth Act of 1978 required that the Fed publicly state what the objectives of its monetary and credit policies are. In the 1980s, under President Ronald Reagan (1981–1989), the Fed adopted a monetary policy of maintaining specific rates of growth in the money supply.

See also: **Central Bank, Federal Reserve Act of 1913, Financial Panic, Alan Greenspan**

FEDERALISM *(ISSUE)*

Federalism is the division of powers and duties among various levels of government. In the U.S. context federalism refers to the division of powers and duties among the state governments and the federal, or national, government.

Ever since the founding of the British North American colonies in 1607, the United States struggled with federalism in five distinct phases. During the colonial era, federalism's first phase, colonial governments controlled local affairs but deferred to Britain to set policies for the whole British Empire. The question on where to draw the lines of power between a central government and the colonial/state governments arose beginning with the Stamp Act crisis in 1765, when colonists first started to question the imperial relationship with the United Kingdom, through to the era of the American Revolution (1775–1783). At that time, a first response was to keep governmental power as close to the people as possible, which meant leaving governmental power in the localities and transforming colonial government into state governments.

Still some central government proved necessary to carry on the war effort against Great Britain during the Revolution, and also to conduct foreign relations and to secure foreign aid. To meet this need the Second Continental Congress (an *ad hoc* national body) drafted the Articles of Confederation which took effect in 1781. In this second manifestation of federalism, power remained in the states which confederated themselves for limited national purposes stated in the Articles of Confederation.

A flaw developed in this scheme: the states acted in their own interests often at the expense of other states and any national interests. As a result, the Articles of Confederation seemed inadequate which led to the drafting and ratification of the Constitution in 1787–1788. When the first Congress met under the new Constitution in 1789, Americans experienced a new form of federalism. States retained large powers over their populations and some concurrent powers with the federal government, while the central government possessed enumerated powers to both defend itself against the states *and* check any excess of power in the states. Scholars describe this phase of federalism as dual federalism.

Over time, defenders of minority interests began to claim that not only did states have rights, but they were also sovereign. Southerners, in particular, argued in favor of this state sovereignty position to defend their declining numbers in the country, their lifestyle, and their form of property (slaves). Was the United States a national Union or a mere confederation of the states? Southerners answered this question by claiming to secede to form their own confederation in 1861, while Northerners and Midwesterners believed that secession from a national Union was impossible; the result was the American Civil War (1861–1865) and Reconstruction (1865–1877).

With the end of the war and the process of Reconstruction under way, the nation adopted the Fourteenth Amendment to the Constitution on July 9, 1868. This amendment, which marks the beginning of federalism's fourth phase, rearranged the division of powers and duties among the levels of U.S. government. With the Fourteenth Amendment national power prevailed

over state power. An understanding of this form of federalism can be seen in a key U.S. Supreme Court decision that defined federalism after the Civil War, *Texas v. White* (1869). For a unanimous Court, Chief Justice Salmon P. Chase stated that ''the Constitution in all its provisions looks to an indestructible Union composed of indestructible states.'' While the states would not disappear or be absorbed by the central government, neither would they be as free to set policies as prior to the war.

States played an important role in the lives of U.S. citizens up to the Great Depression (1929–1939). With the Depression and President Franklin Roosevelt's (1933–1945) New Deal to overcome the economic catastrophe of the Depression, federalism shifted into its fifth phase. National power came to dominate American lives in ways never before imagined because bureaucratic federalism emerged. In this form of federalism, Congress, federal agencies, and federal bureaus set national policies and mandates, and the states complied. The states deferred to national authority as more power shifted to the national government. This trend slowed during the 1980s and 1990s when public concern grew that the central government was too powerful and the states too weak. As a result, in the late 1990s federalism might be shifting back towards a more balanced national picture of federal power co-existing with viable and responsible state governments.

See also: **Constitution (Economic Benefits of), Stamp Act, States' Rights**

FURTHER READING

Hyman, Harold and William M. Wiecek. *Equal Justice Under Law: Constitutional Development, 1835–1875.* New York: Harper and Row, 1982.

Kelly, Alfred H., Winfred A. Harbison, and Herman Belz. *The American Constitution: Its Origins and Development.* 7th ed. New York: W.W. Norton and Co., 1991.

Levy, Leonard W., Kenneth L. Karst, and Dennis J. Mahoney, eds. *Encyclopedia of the American Constitution.* New York: Macmillan Publishing, 1986.

FIELD, MARSHALL

Marshall Field (1834–1906), the founder of one the world's largest department stores, represented for many U.S. citizens of his generation an example of the

Marshall Field.

classic rags-to-riches success story. Field, the tenth richest man in U.S. history, originated the "customer is always right" policy and introduced many other now-standard retail practices including liberal credit, openly displayed prices, an in-store restaurant, and acceptance of returned merchandise.

Field was born in 1834 and raised on a farm near Pittsfield in western Massachusetts. He left school at age 17 to work in a local dry goods store. After five years his employer offered him the opportunity of an eventual partnership in the store, but Field declined, deciding that opportunities for an ambitious young man lay further west. In 1856, at age 22, armed with a reference from his boss describing him as "a young man of unusual business talent," Field left New England for Chicago, then a rude, muddy, and vibrant city that had just produced its first generation of millionaires. Field's older brother, Joseph, helped secure him a job with Cooley, Wadsworth and Co., the city's largest dry goods store. The small, serious, and polite Marshall Field arranged to live and sleep in the store, and thus he managed to save half of his small income. Field, who came to be known as "silent Marsh" because of his retiring social manner, was determined to make a success of himself. In less than four years, he had become a full partner in the store.

When Cooley retired in 1864, the store became known as Farwell, Field, and Company. Field soon left the store to join with a partner, Levi Leiter, in a new and expanded dry goods business, which they called Field, Leiter. The firm grossed $9 million in its first year (1867). Field worked day and night to build his business and make it a success.

The firm's first major building, a grandiose edifice at the corner of Washington and State Streets in downtown Chicago was only three years old when it went up in smoke in the Chicago Fire of 1871. Field was back in business in a new building by the following year. In 1877 Field, Leiter was again devastated by fire. The building was a total loss, but Field, more than adequately insured, was again able to immediately rebuild.

THE CUSTOMER IS ALWAYS RIGHT.

Marshall Field

At a relatively young age, Field had become well known for his hard work, shrewdness in business, honesty, merchandising skills, and penny-pinching personal habits. In 1881 he bought out his partner, Leiter, for $2.5 million. By 1888 he was an extremely rich man and a director of least 28 major corporations. His store continued to thrive during Field's lifetime and throughout the twentieth century. At his death in 1906, Field left an estate valued at $125 million, the equivalent of $40.7 billion in 1998, according to *American Heritage*. Among his bequests were substantial gifts to the University of Chicago and the museum that later became the Field Museum of Natural History.

See also: **Chicago Fire of 1871, Department Store**

FURTHER READING

Becker, Stephen. *Marshal Field III*. New York: Simon and Schuster, 1964.

Klepper, Michael, Robert Gunther, Jeanette Baik, Linda Barth, and Christine Gibson. "American Heritage 40: A Ranking of the 40 Wealthiest Americans of All Time." *American Heritage*, October 1998.

Pierce, B.L. "Rise of a Modern City, 1871–1893." *History of Chicago*, vol. 3, New York: Alfred A. Knopf, 1957.

Twyman, Robert. *Marshall Field and Co., 1852–1906*. Philadelphia: University of Pennsylvania Press, 1906.

Wendt, Lloyd. *Give the Lady What She Wants*. Skokie: Rand McNally and Co., 1952.

FIFTEENTH AMENDMENT

The Fifteenth Amendment to the U.S. Constitution (1789) guarantees that an American citizen cannot be discriminated against in exercising the right to vote. The amendment was proposed in Congress on February 26, 1869, and ratified by the required number of states on February 3, 1870. The amendment states that the ''right of citizens of the United States to vote shall not be denied or abridged by the United States or by any state on account of race, color, or previous condition of servitude.'' Though the language applied to people of all races, it was sometimes called the Black Suffrage (right to vote) Amendment because, during the period in which it was passed, legislators intended to prevent southern states from denying African American citizens the right to vote.

After ratification of the Thirteenth Amendment (1865), which outlawed slavery throughout the Union, the U.S. Congress made approval of the Fourteenth and Fifteenth amendments a prerequisite for reentry to the Union. Before a southern state could be readmitted, its legislature had to approve both amendments. Congress thus assured that former slaves would be made citizens of both the United States and the state where they lived, that equal rights would be granted to all citizens, and that suffrage (the right to vote) was extended to African American men. Under these conditions all southern states were readmitted to the Union by July 15, 1870.

By the end of the 1800s, however, state legislatures in the South had devised ways to prevent their African American citizens from voting. Methods included instituting a poll tax (requiring a voter to pay a fee in order to cast his vote) and literacy tests, which had to be passed as a prerequisite for voting. Most states also adopted legislation by which voting rights were extended only to those citizens who had been able to vote in 1867—a date when few if any African Americans would have had the right. Because these laws also established high voting requirements for the descendants of men who could not vote in that year, they were called ''grandfather clauses.''

Attempts to deny citizens the right to vote were made unlawful in 1964 by the Twenty-Fourth Amendment to the U.S. Constitution. (One of the features of that Amendment outlawed the poll tax in federal elections and primaries.) Moreover, in 1966, poll taxes at state and local levels were also declared illegal. Literacy tests and grandfather clauses were also struck down as unconstitutional.

See also: **Poll Tax, Thirteenth Amendment**

FINANCIAL PANIC

A financial panic is a sudden, drastic, widespread economic collapse. All at once, many people become convinced their money or investments are at risk and rush to the institutions holding their assets. Unable to pay back all their customers at once, the institutions go bankrupt, starting a domino effect that brings down the whole economy. Typical ''symptoms'' of a panic are many bankruptcies, loan defaults, or bank failures at the same time; It also includes a period of intense stock market or real estate speculation followed by a steep decline in prices; and/or a sudden run on banks by large numbers of people trying to withdraw their deposits.

Between 1790 and 1907 there were 21 financial panics in the United States. The first major panic occurred in 1819, when the Bank of the United States, the nation's central bank, tried to reduce the number of new speculative banks being founded in the United States. The bank called in its loans to the new speculative banks and required them to redeem their paper bank notes for hard gold and silver. Many of these banks had printed far more notes than they had real reserves and quickly failed. The Panic of 1837 was also the result of the government's attempt to control the rapid spread of bank notes not backed up by hard currency. The Panic of 1857 came about when U.S. banks overextended themselves loaning money to railroads, and railroads defaulted on their bonds. Several hundred U.S. banks failed.

Other painful panics followed in 1893 and 1907, but it was the anxiety brought on by the stock market speculation of the 1920s that caused the most destructive panic in U.S. history—the stock market crash of 1929. By October 1929, the stock market had climbed to new heights in part because anyone could buy a stock by putting down only a fraction of its face value. Many investors became wealthy on paper but there were few real assets behind the speculative frenzy. When millions of investors simultaneously began selling their shares, the prices of stocks plummeted and many paper fortunes were wiped out sparking the Great Depression (1929–1939). Because of the severity of the panic of 1929, the U.S. government implemented fundamental reforms that have prevented the recurrence of a major financial panic through the end of the twentieth century.

See also: **Currency, Money, Panic of 1919, Panic of 1837, Panic of 1907, Panics of the Late Nineteenth Century, Stock Market Crash of 1929**

FIRESTONE, HARVEY SAMUEL

Harvey Samuel Firestone (1868–1938) was an inventor and innovator, as well as a shrewd businessman. The company he founded in 1900 has been one of the largest in its industry, surviving two world wars and the Great Depression. Firestone personally pushed many of the industry's innovations, including vertical integration of rubber production in tire manufacturing and product retailing strategies.

Harvey Firestone was born December 20, 1838, in Columbiana, Ohio. His parents, Benjamin Firestone and Catharine Flickinger, were farmers from an Alsatian family residing in Ohio since 1807. Young Firestone was educated in a one-room schoolhouse. Uncommon in pioneer families, Firestone graduated from high school and completed a business college course in Cleveland before working as a bookkeeper and a salesman. His lifetime career in transportation and tires began with a job at the Columbiana Buggy Company, where he worked for his uncle, Clinton Firestone.

Firestone's salesmanship abilities earned him district responsibilities, and by 1892, he was in charge of the Michigan district. The buggy company went bankrupt in 1896, and Firestone decided the future was in wheels rather than carriages. With a friend's help and investment, Firestone established a rubber wheels company in Chicago in 1896. He sold the company in 1899 and pocketed $40,000. Taking this cash and a patent for attaching rubber tires to wheels, Firestone moved to Akron, Ohio, then the center of rubber tire manufacturing. With $10,000 of his own cash and his patent, he established the Firestone Tire and Rubber Company, retaining 50 percent ownership of the company.

For the first few years, Firestone had others manufacture his tires, and the company did not do well. In 1903 the company began to manufacture its own product and improved its performance. Firestone decided to cater to the needs of the fledgling automobile industry, and he began to produce a pneumatic tire for autos. In 1906 Henry Ford (1863–1947) placed a large order for tires for his new automobiles, and Ford and Firestone established a sound personal and business relationship that would last for many years.

Firestone's innovations included the 1907 "dismountable rim," which allowed the wheel and tire to be removed together. The spare tire was born. Firestone promoted his tires through support of the racing industry, piggy backing his product with the rising popularity of the new sport. By 1913 the Firestone Tire and Rubber Company's sales topped $15 million, and it joined the ranks of the "Big Five" of the tire industry, along with Goodyear, Goodrich, U.S. Rubber, and Fisk.

After World War I (1914–1918), the depression of 1920–1921 hit Firestone Tire and Rubber hard. The company had a debt of $43 million, and Firestone's answer was to cut prices to increase sales, while cutting wages to decrease costs. Decreasing wages was, of course, unpopular, but Firestone was still able to forestall unionization until the 1930s. By 1924 the debt was paid off, and Firestone's company was again in good financial shape.

Firestone promoted the use of motor driven trucks, the building of the American highway system, and the elimination of railroad grade crossings. In 1923 he introduced the balloon tire, which shortly became the standard for motor vehicles. From 1922 to 1924 the price of rubber became a critical problem for the tire and automobile industries. Great Britain controlled a majority of the world's rubber supply via the Crown Colonies, and it tried to restrict rubber production to drive up prices. To combat the problem, Firestone and Henry Ford worked together to develop rubber plantations in the African nation of Liberia.

Firestone's efforts in Liberia helped break the rubber cartel. It also made him a major player in the economy of the African nation. Firestone made improvements to the harbor in Monrovia, loaning the Liberian government millions of dollars, and built quarters for his workers that included sanitation. Despite his efforts there, allegations of slave traffic and worker exploitation were made against Firestone and his operation in Liberia. At the end of the controversy, a 1930 League of Nations inquiry exonerated Firestone and his labor policy.

Another of the innovations Firestone brought to the tire and rubber industry was that of the "one-stop master service store," which he designed to provide tires, gasoline, oil, batteries, and brake service through a single outlet. Firestone's plan, which was first put in place in 1928, was to build these establishments throughout the country. Eventually, the stores included auto parts and provided even more services.

Through sound business management, the Firestone Tire and Rubber Company made it through the Great Depression (1929–1939) without suspending dividend payments. Firestone even managed to expand his operations through the 1930s, and by 1937, his firm had one-quarter of the tire market in the United States and showed over $9 million in profits on sales of over $156.8 million. Firestone Tire and Rubber Company had twelve factories in the United States and five plants abroad making rubber, steel, and textile products.

Firestone stepped down as president of his company in 1932, but remained chairman of the board until his death in 1938.

Harvey Firestone was active in Republican politics and the Episcopal Church. He served as president of the Ohio Federation of Churches. He married Idabelle Smith in 1895, and they had five sons: Harvey S. Jr., Russell Allen, Leonard Kimball, Raymond Christian, and Roger Stanley. All of Firestone's sons were active in his business. Harvey Firestone died February 7, 1938, in Miami Beach, Florida.

See also: **Tire and Rubber Industry**

FURTHER READING

Bowman, John S., ed. *The Cambridge Dictionary of American Biography*. Cambridge University Press, 1995, s.v. ''Firestone, Harvey.''

Encyclopedia of World Biography. Detroit: Gale Research, 1998, s.v. ''Firestone, Harvey.''

Ingham, John N. *Biographical Dictionary of American Business Leaders*. Westport, Connecticut: Greenwood Press, 1983, s.v. ''Firestone, Harvey.''

Lief, Alfred. *Harvey Firestone: Free Man of Enterprise*. New York: McGraw-Hill, 1951

The McGraw-Hill Encyclopedia of World Biography. New York: McGraw–Hill Book Co., 1973, s.v. ''Firestone, Harvey.''

FISCAL POLICY

Fiscal policy concerns the federal government's use of taxation and public spending to affect the general flow of the economy. If, for example, the government wanted to stimulate consumer spending it might cut taxes and spend more on government programs, which would have the effect of giving consumers more cash. If, however, the government wished to cool off an economy that was in danger of inflation, it might raise tax rates and cut government spending to dampen economic activity. During the 1950s and 1960s many economists, especially followers of the British economist John Maynard Keynes (1883–1946), believed that fiscal policy could be used to fine-tune the economy. Some believed, for example, than the government might achieve a certain level of unemployment or gross domestic output through fiscal policy.

However, later economists came to discredit this notion. They believed that government attempts to fine-tune the economy through fiscal policy were more likely to create problems than solve them.

See also: **Keynesian Economic Theory**

FISHING INDUSTRY (COMMERCIAL)

Although the U.S. commercial fishing industry had seen many changes since its earliest days, it has remained an important part of the economy for many communities, states, and countries. Throughout the twentieth century, an ever-increasing population fueled many changes in the industry, including technological advances in fishermen's ability to catch, successfully transport, and sell products. It also caused a constant increase of the number of fishing fleets around the world. These changes were a mixed blessing for the industry. A widespread demand in the use of ocean products (ranging from the use of fish protein as an additive in livestock feed to fish burgers at the local drive-through window) made the industry extremely profitable. On the other hand, this increase in demand also meant an increase in the number of fleets, industry investors, and fisherman, which eventually ended in the world's oceans becoming over-fished.

The first fishing vessels were powered by sail, and they were developed to fill the needs of the particular fishing region. This meant that the design of boats from different regions varied according to a particular environment or fishery. In the nineteenth century larger steam-driven winches replaced sailboats, allowing for heavier fishing gear and larger crews. By the end of the nineteenth century the internal combustion engine supplanted steam, and in the early twentieth century the inboard diesel engine had become accepted worldwide as the propulsion of choice.

These improvements in the overall size, speed, and range of fishing vessels led to advances in the methods used by fisherman to increase fish hauls. Larger catches, translating into larger profits, could now be obtained by increasing the number of hooks per line from one to over one thousand. Single traps were networked into a system of hundreds of connected traps. Nets became much larger, and their development even initiated a sub-industry in support of commercial fishing. Net-making is an industry that evolved from the making of nets from linen and hemp to the making

Fishing trawlers harvest many of the ocean products that are in demand in the U.S. as well as abroad.

of nets from cotton and hard fibers woven by rapidly moving machines. Small family fishing boats and cast netters were finding it tough to compete with the volume and subsequent lower price produced by the larger commercial fishing fleets.

Several developments during the 1940s and 1950s had a very significant impact on the profitability and stability of the commercial fishing industry. Mechanization made significant advances in netting methods when the power block was invented, which made it easier for fishermen to haul and store gear while purse seining (a method of fishing using a net that is weighted at the bottom and has floats along the top). Also important was the introduction of devices such as the power-driven drum designed to carry and store seine nets, gill nets, purse seines, and even the large trawl nets. Perhaps the most important development of the decade came with the invention of stern trawlers that processed their catch on board. Developed by the British, this idea was eagerly copied by many countries, including the Soviet Union, Japan, Poland, and Spain. The importance of this technology went beyond the vast quantities of ocean products that could now be processed at sea and sold more quickly back on land. The new technology brought about the collapse of some resources harvested by these highly efficient seiners and with it the realization that these resources were not limitless and needed to be protected.

In 1972 Iceland became the first country to claim an extended fisheries limit of 50 miles. In 1975 it extended this limit to 200 miles. Several countries followed Iceland's lead and soon the Law of the Sea was passed. This allowed for an exclusive economic zone of 200 miles off the coast of each country.

Many coastal communities in the United States are today supported by the commercial fishing industry, which became the largest private employer in states such as Alaska. According to government statistics printed in *U.S. Industry Profiles* in 1995, 364,000 people were employed in fishing industries in 1988. Of that number, 274,000 were fishermen and 90,000 were shore workers.

Although the industry is quite large in certain areas, pay levels are low. Compensation of fishermen is usually based on the percentage of the catch brought in by their captain's boat. Based on the earnings information of 1988, published in *U.S. Industry Profiles*, an inshore fisherman working within three miles of shore received an average salary of between $15,000 and $20,000, while an off-shore fisherman working outside the three mile limit earned an average of $30,000.

Not all of the profits generated from the commercial fishing industry come from the sale of ocean products. Freshwater fishing, carried out in lakes, rivers, or streams, does contribute a small percentage of the fish consumed globally. Fresh water fisheries tend to be more specialized depending on the species of fish they are producing. Fish such as the salmon and sturgeon that live in the sea but spawn in fresh water, and the eel that lives in fresh water but spawns in the sea, have forced these fisheries to become as specialized as they are. Other contributions to the specialty of fresh water fishing are the variations in the physical and chemical properties of fresh water in different areas and the overall size of the body of water itself.

Fish farming in aquatic hatcheries is another form of revenue supporting the fishing industry. Fish farming is the practice of raising generations of fish in controlled environments free from predators and maintained in optimal conditions. These fish farms supply plants and animals for a variety of purposes, including the production of animals for live bait, stocking purposes for sport fisheries, as well as the needs of the pharmaceutical industry. Many of the products of fish farms are the high-priced species that are sold as fresh products. Among these are shrimp, salmon, and oysters. The depletion of natural sources has helped provide more demand to support these hatcheries and it has allowed them to expand their production to other species, some of which are fresh water varieties, like catfish and trout.

Although fish farms offered the fishing industry several alternative methods of production, industry experts maintained concern with the depletion of resources in the world's oceans. Traditional techniques for managing fishery resources remain under close scrutiny, and calls for greater regulation of the industry have grown in number. According to Amos Eno, spokesperson for the National Fish and Wildlife Association, marine fisheries were the single most threatened resource in the United States in the late 1990s.

FURTHER READING

Bay-Hansen, C. D. *Fisheries of the Pacific Northwest Coast: Traditional Commercial Fisheries*. New York: Vantage Press, 1992.

Cheney, Daniel P., Thomas Mumford, and Thomas Mumford, Jr. *Shellfish and Seaweed Harvests of Puget Sound*. Seattle, WA: University of Washington Press, 1987.

Maril, Robert Lee. *The Bay Shrimpers of Texas: Rural Fishermen in a Global Economy*. Kansas City, MO: University of Kansas Press, 1995.

Oakley, Barbara A. *Hair of the Dog: Tales from Aboard a Russian Trawler*. Pullman, WA: Washington State University Press, 1996.

Sainsbury, John C. *Commercial Fishing Methods: An Introduction to Vessels and Gears*. Boston: Blackwell Science Inc., 1996.

FIVE CIVILIZED TRIBES

Five Civilized Tribes is a name white settlers gave to the Chickasaw, Choctaw, Cherokee, Creek, and Seminoles in the 1800s after these Native American tribes adopted Christianity and European customs. When the colonists arrived on the North American mainland, these native peoples were living in the southeastern United States. They had settled there in small villages and farmed and hunted for subsistence.

The Indians were not immune to many illnesses the settlers brought to the new world. Smallpox, measles, pneumonia, and other sicknesses claimed many lives and reduced the populations of these tribes by an estimated 75 percent in less than two hundred years. Thus, by the time colonists won the American Revolution (1775–1783), relatively small numbers of Chickasaw, Choctaw, Cherokee, Creek, and Seminoles survived; of necessity they began to adapt to the

growing culture around them. They attended church services, sent their children to school, and even bought plantations. Nevertheless, under the Indian Removal Act of 1830 the U.S. government claimed the lands of the five tribes in Kentucky, Tennessee, North Carolina, South Carolina, Georgia, Florida, Alabama, and Mississippi.

The government moved the tribes westward to "Indian Territory" in Oklahoma. The forced migration along the Trail of Tears, which claimed four thousand lives, was completed by 1842.

Installed in their new lands, each of the Five Civilized Tribes was given the status of a nation. While they lived on communally held land, each tribe drew up its own constitution, formed its own government, and set up schools. They successfully farmed the rich soil of their new lands in peace, but their independence was again threatened by the further encroachment of white settlers, who moved ever westward in what finally became the Land Rush (of 1889). Eventually the Oklahoma lands were opened to white settlers; the Five Civilized Tribes became increasingly assimilated into the culture around them. In 1907 the state of Oklahoma (which is a Choctaw word meaning "red people") was created by merging Indian Territory with the Oklahoma Territory.

See also: **Native American Policy, Oklahoma, Trail of Tears**

FIXED INCOME

A fixed income is one in which earnings remain constant and do not fluctuate in relation to the current price levels in the economy. When the gain or yield of an investment has a more or less uniform rate of income or return every year, it is said to have a fixed income. Bonds, money market instruments, annuities, and preferred stocks all pay a specific interest rate or dividend and are examples of fixed income investments. People living on a fixed income have a difficult time when prices rise; an example is a retired person living off of a pension in a period of inflation.

FLAT TAX PROVISION *(ISSUE)*

A flat tax taxes everybody at the same tax rate. A graduated tax taxes at different tax rates. In the late-1990s flat tax proposition generated heated discussions not only about the legitimacy of the flat tax but also

> I think that we are seeing Americans becoming better educated about the flat tax, about its pluses and minuses. I mean, even the Democrats have suggested various versions of a flat tax. I'm thinking of Congressman Gephardt's tax proposal. . . . So, whether you agree with the details of Steve Forbes's plan or not, he's certainly forced that issue in the American political agenda. I think we'll be hearing a lot more about it in the next couple of years.
>
> **David Yepsen, *Des Moines Register*, on C-SPAN, January 15, 1996**

about the income tax itself and the Internal Revenue Service (IRS) that administers, regulates, and enforces it. That the system needed reforming was clear to almost every U.S. citizen. It was riddled with exemptions for everything under the sun. Most economists acknowledged that it stifled investment and entrepreneurship and that it was difficult to understand. But the pressing question was what should be done.

The Founding Fathers were opposed to any politics based on income differences because they feared it would lead to class distinctions in the law. They believed that comity and tolerance among the states and classes were the preconditions for a unified country. They forbade direct taxes unless apportioned among the states in order to prevent states from ganging up and placing the tax burden on outvoted regional interests. They preferred taxes, such as import tariffs and excise taxes, that are reflected in the price of a good and paid indirectly by consumers.

The revulsion that people felt toward direct taxation prevented the enactment of a federal income tax until the American Civil War (1861–1865). As the Union broke apart, so did constitutional scruples about income taxation. In 1861 Congress enacted the first federal income tax, at a rate of three percent on net incomes over $800 and 1.5 percent on income from government bonds. The next year Congress passed another income-tax law. This one strengthened enforcement powers. The Revenue Act of 1862 also included explicit progressive taxation, applying higher rates to higher incomes. The rate schedule taxed incomes between $600 and $10,000 at three percent, between $10,000 and $50,000 at five percent, and over $50,000 at 7.5 percent. Although the income tax provided almost $350 million in war financing, the public never liked it. Several anti-income-tax leagues were

formed and public discomfort led Congress to repeal the first federal income tax in 1870.

Agitation in the West in reaction to hard economic times was the impetus for the second federal income tax. In the generation after the Civil War, the West was pitted against the Northeast over the money supply and tariffs. Westerners resented having to make mortgage payments for their farms and ranches to Wall Street financiers and having to buy goods from New England industries protected by high import tariffs, while they had to sell their commodities in the competitive market and absorb high railroad shipping rates. The anger swelled when economic downturns caused commodity prices to fall, especially in the late 1880s, culminating in the formation of the Populist Party in Omaha, Nebraska in 1892. Populists advocated ending the gold standard, reducing tariffs, and implementing a graduated income tax.

The Populists represented a threat to the Democrats, who had captured the White House and both houses of Congress in 1892 on a platform of lower tariffs. Although the Populist Party won only nine percent of the presidential vote, Populist ferment did not subside. Were it not for Democratic support for segregation, party strategists knew, many Southern votes would have gone Populist. The income tax became the instrument to keep Populist-inclined voters in the Democratic camp.

The income tax reappeared in 1909, when President William Howard Taft (1909–1913) wanted an increase in tariffs. To get the tariff through, Taft and Senate Finance Committee Chairman Nelson W. Aldrich agreed to accept the income-tax amendment to the Constitution because they did not think it would be ratified by the state legislatures, of which Republicans controlled a majority. But they underestimated the progressive swing in the country and the split in the Republican Party between Taft and Theodore Roosevelt (1858–1919). On February 3, 1913, Delaware, New Jersey, New Mexico, and Wyoming put the amendment over the top.

The states followed the federal example and by 1970 almost all of them had their own income tax. In the late 1990s, although the rich paid a disproportionate share, the bulk of the income-tax revenues came from the middle class. In the beginning the income tax was explicitly directed at the rich, and even at the end of the twentieth century any across-the-board reduction in marginal income-tax rates was denounced by some as "trickle-down" economics. But the income tax ceased to be an elite tax during World War II (1939–1945), when the need for revenues caused the rich man's tax to be applied to 64 percent of the population. Since then, middle-class U.S. citizens have found themselves taxed at rates once thought excessive even for millionaires.

With countless loopholes, an army of income tax bureaucrats in the IRS, complex instructions, increased taxation year by year, and the poor and middle-classes forming the bulk of the tax burden, U.S. citizens agreed that something had to be done. The only real question was what to do about it. Modeled on a tax blueprint first developed in the mid-1980s by Stanford University economists Robert Hall and Alvin Rabushka, the flat tax provision gained considerable momentum in the late 1990s. According to proponents, it would abolish virtually all deductions and loopholes, terminate tax withholding, end the double taxation of savings and investment, shorten the income-tax form to the size of a postcard, and eliminate the capital-gains and estate taxes.

Flat taxes combine a consumer-income scheme tax which taxes at the household level and a value-added tax (VAT) that taxes at the business level. Income from employment is taxed at its destination (households); income from capital, net of investment, is taxed at its source (businesses). The business part of the tax is similar to a VAT. But besides subtracting its input costs and investment from total sales, each company deducts its labor costs as well. Labor income is then taxed at the same rate as at the household level. In effect, a flat tax of this kind is just another variant of a consumption tax. Proponents claimed that it was easy to implement and that it offered the best of both worlds (VAT and consumer-income tax).

Supporters argued that, like a VAT, a flat tax made the tax on capital income easier. Businesses do not have to worry about how their decisions affect the taxes of their myriad shareholders, each with different incomes and personal circumstances. Proponents claimed that there was no need to file countless forms certifying the amount of dividends that companies had paid out to each shareholder and they also claimed that the IRS was spared the chore of verifying how much people saved. Moreover, supporters claimed that a flat tax, like a consumed-income tax, was also easy to make progressive. Since labor income was taxed at the household level, the government could offer generous personal exemptions on a big chunk of each taxpayer's wages. It was estimated that a flat tax raising as much revenue as the existent system could combine a rate of 19 percent with an exemption of about $28,000 for each family of four (with other families getting bigger or smaller exemptions depending on their size). This would allow a family's average tax rate (i.e. its total taxes as a share of its total income) to increase with its

income. Whereas the current graduated-income-tax system has multiple tax rates, the flat tax has only two: zero and, whatever the decided rate, say 19 percent. Although the flat-tax curve is not as steep as that for the current system, the tax burden still rises fairly sharply with income.

Supporters claimed that the flat tax may be the United States' best bet politically as well. They said that it would no longer be possible for politicians to confuse voters with mind-numbing details and competing forecasts. Voters would need to ask only two questions. How much income is excluded? And what is the tax rate? Political debate might then have a better chance of focusing on political issues.

Even with such optimism, the flat tax provision was in for a bumpy ride at the end of the last decade of the twentieth century. No matter how simple the scheme, arguments about taxes tended to become complicated. Opponents of the flat tax reform raised numerous flags. They claimed that it would benefit the rich at everyone else's expense. They claimed that because it fell on consumption, a flat tax bore heavily on the elderly and people in retirement. Unlike younger people, the retired tend to consume all their income. Indeed, most consume more than their income by running down their stock of savings. Any consumption-based tax therefore hits them especially hard. Opponents also argued that the flat tax did not sufficiently address investment income. At the very end of the century the fate of the flat tax provision was uncertain.

FURTHER READING

Armey, Dick. *Flat Tax*. New York: Fawcett Press, 1996.

Hall, Robert E. and Alvin Rabushka. *Low Tax, Simple Tax, Flat Tax*. New York: McGraw Hill, 1983.

———. *The Flat Tax*. Washington: The Hoover Press, 1996.

Hicko, Scott E. *The Flat Tax: Why It Won't Work for America*. Omaha, NE: Addicus Books, 1996.

Sease, Douglas R. and Herman. *The Flat-Tax Primer*. New York: Viking, 1996.

FLORIDA

The state of Florida still has a certain exotic reputation. With its balmy climate, Spanish influences, citrus groves, and miles of beaches and tourist attractions, Florida continues to draw both visitors and new

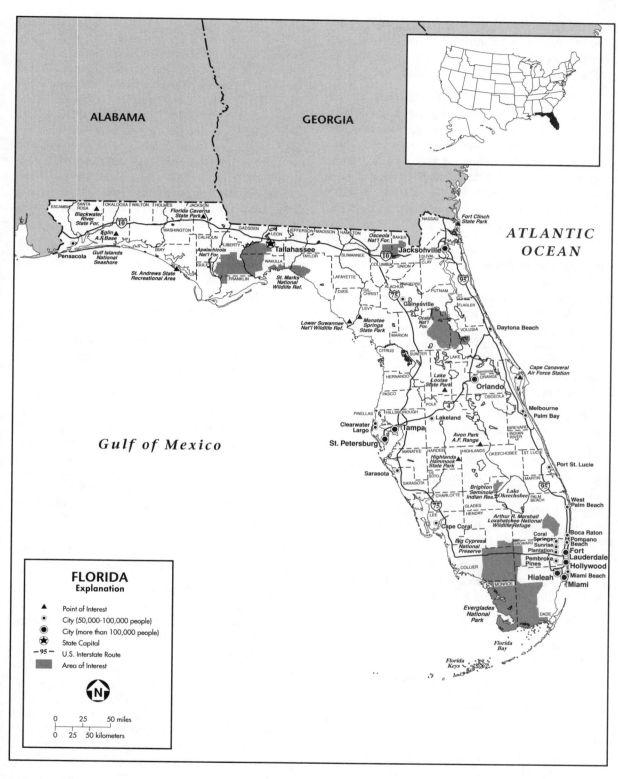

State of Florida.

residents. Florida is a very modern state, however, with a manufacturing and commercial base to match its tourist attractions and, at the same time, environmental problems brought on by its rapid growth.

In 1513, Ponce de Leon (1460–1521) was the first European to sight Florida, claiming it for Spain. Hernando de Soto (c1500–1542) later tried to establish a colony in Florida but abandoned hope for finding wealth there. In 1565 the Spanish successfully defended French claims in Florida and made St. Augustine a military outpost to protect Spain's interests. In 1763 Spain ceded Florida to the British in exchange for Cuba.

The Spanish who came to Florida found nearly 100,000 Native Americans living there. Franciscans soon began to establish missions up and down the coast. In addition to attempts to convert the native population, the Spanish used the Indians to assist the Spanish in growing food, supplying labor, and defending the province. As in other areas where Europeans came to dominate, the Indian population was gradually decimated by disease or by wars with whites or other Indians. The Seminole War of 1835–1842 finally eliminated most of the Indians in Florida.

When the British took over the area, Florida's territory spanned from the Atlantic Ocean to the Mississippi River and eventually split into two colonies, East and West Florida. Settlers established farms and began to be self-sufficient. During the American Revolution (1775–1783), Florida became home to thousands of Loyalists to the British crown. In 1781 Spain successfully attacked and captured Pensacola; in 1783 Great Britain returned Florida to Spain.

Though the Spanish were formally in control of the region, several cultures clashed in the territory during this time. In addition to the Native Americans, runaway slaves, renegade whites, pirates, and other adventurers roamed the land. British influence was strong, and the United States continued to penetrate into the territory. By terms of the Louisiana Purchase (1803), all of Florida west of the Perdido River was taken over by the United States in 1810. What later became the state of Florida was finally ceded to the United States in 1821. The first military territorial governor was Andrew Jackson (1767–1845), who had led a successful expedition against the Seminoles and their British allies. Tallahassee was set up as the first capital, and soon the middle region of Florida became known for its slave-owning cotton plantations. Settlement was hindered for a time by the war to remove the Seminoles and by the Panic of 1837, but in 1845 Florida entered the Union as a pro-slavery state.

Florida did not remain part of the Union for long. In 1861, at the start of the American Civil War (1861–1865), the state seceded and became part of the Confederacy. Florida at that time had only around 140,000 people—40 percent of them slaves—no manufacturing, and only a few hundred miles of railroad. After Reconstruction (1865–1877), conservative Democrats governed Florida for the remainder of the century. These politicians were pro-business, promoted the expansion of railroads, and kept taxes low. Although cotton production did not return to its prewar levels, Florida became known for its citrus and vegetable farms, cattle raising, forestry, and phosphate mining, as well as for a growing tourist industry.

Both tourists and developers were helped by the railroad builders who appeared in the late nineteenth century. By far the best known of these entrepreneurs was Henry M. Flagler (1830–1913), who completed an East cost railroad line that ended in Daytona, Florida, in 1890. Despite numerous construction difficulties, a line was completed to West Palm Beach in 1894, and later to Miami. Flagler's most ambitious project was a railroad all the way to Key West.

Flagler and other railroad magnates built magnificent hotels in Florida, which attracted many of the tourists who began to trek to the state to enjoy the sun. More important, the railroads brought in more settlers, who soon began to transform the swamps and sand dunes of southern Florida into an important agricultural and commercial area. Key West cigar makers transferred many of their operations into mainland factories in Tampa. The Spanish-American War (1898) stimulated the economy, since Tampa was the point of embarkation to Cuba. Many soldiers returning from the war also eventually settled in the state.

The cities of St. Petersburg, Clearwater, Sarasota, Palm Beach, Fort Lauderdale, and Miami soon began to thrive. Orlando became the largest city in south central Florida. When parts of the Everglades were drained, towns sprouted up in the Lake Okeechobee area. Governor Napoleon B. Broward, who took office in 1905, emphasized drainage projects. Thousands of acres were drained and made available for agriculture over the next 20 years. By 1920 the farms of the state were producing more than $80 million in income, with oranges as the single largest crop. Other agricultural products included grapefruit, potatoes, cotton, tobacco, domestic animals, and meat. The fact that no one crop was dominant made the risk of economic disaster less likely.

During the 1920s Florida's population soared by almost 50 percent, starting a land boom. The 1930s saw alternate periods of depression and recovery. Despite the difficulties of the nationwide Great Depression (1929–1939), Florida created some new sources of income in paper mills and a type of betting known as pari-mutuel. During World War II (1939–1945), several Army and Navy bases in the state also stimulated growth.

Though agriculture, especially citrus farming, was basic to the postwar economy, during the period between 1947 and 1963, Florida manufacturing also grew considerably. The most important manufacturing sectors were foods, chemicals, paper, publishing, and electrical machinery. By 1963, moreover, the value of retail trade had increased 225 percent since 1948. Adequate power and water, as well as the convenience of Florida ports to fuel supplies, was beneficial to commerce in the state during this time.

Tourism continued to thrive in Florida, bringing in an era of expansion in spectator sports and amusements. In addition, the increasing demand for government services brought a 37 increase in government employees between 1960 and 1965. Federal facilities expanded as well, the most famous of which became the Air Force Missile Test Center on Cape Canaveral, home base for future space exploration.

In 1971 the Disney World theme park opened its doors, becoming one of the biggest economic booms to Orange and Osceola counties. It is estimated that nearly 60 percent of the millions of tourists who visit Florida come specifically to visit Disney World. In 1986 the number of people visiting the park equaled the number who visited the entire state 14 years earlier.

Environmentalists continued to be concerned about the rapid development of Florida. Thousands of acres of former forests, agricultural fields, and orange groves have been destroyed to make way for commercial development. Natural water drainage patterns have been altered, often creating problems for both human consumption and animal habitats. Of particular concern has been the disruption of the wetlands known as the Everglades. Contamination of the groundwater that supplies nearly all of Florida's water has also been aggravated in recent decades. After the settlement of a federal lawsuit, the Florida Department of Environmental Protection and other agencies have undertaken a program for restoration of several watersheds.

Some natural upheavals beyond human control are the hurricanes that periodically wreak havoc on the Florida coast. A hurricane in 1926 brought a land boom to an early halt; in the late 1930s, another destroyed most of the Florida East Coast Railroad line to Key West, leading to the building of a modern highway along the old railroad lines. In 1960 Hurricane Donna caused extensive damage to the Tampa and Orlando areas, as well as along the southwest coast and in mid-Florida. In 1992 Hurricane Andrew caused more than $10 billion in damage to southern Florida, and Hurricane Opal caused $2.1 billion in losses in the Pensacola area in 1995.

Contemporary Florida is rather vulnerable to recession because of its many visitors and part-time dwellers, who bring many dollars to the state but do not create a permanent tax base. The economic downturn of the early 1980s hit Florida especially hard, especially in the housing industry. The aerospace and electronics industries, however, were aided by the defense buildup during the administrations of President Ronald Reagan (1981–1989). The Miami area has also benefited from an influx of Latin American investment funds. Floridians are less proud, however, of the state's so-called "underground economy," which provides unreported low-wage income to many illegal immigrants and also funnels large amounts of cash into the state from the illegal drug trade.

FURTHER READING

Derr, Mark. *Some Kind of Paradise: A Chronicle of Man and the Land in Florida*. New York: William Morrow, 1989.

Gannon, Michael, ed. *The New History of Florida*. Gainesville: University Presses of Florida, 1996.

Hanna, Kathryn T. Abbey. *Florida: Land of Change*. Chapel Hill: University of North Carolina Press, 1948.

Jahoda, Gloria. *Florida: A Bicentennial History*. New York: Norton, 1976.

Patrick, Rembert W. *Florida Under Five Flags*. Gainesville: University Presses of Florida, 1960.

FOOD PROCESSING INDUSTRY

Food processing techniques have been evolving since the Stone Age. But it was not until these procedures met with the machinery, scientific discoveries, mass production, and population changes of the nineteenth century that the activity of food processing surged ahead and became the basis for a sophisticated and far reaching industry. By the middle of the twentieth century, this industry included everything from the most basic preparation of foods to canning, freezing, otherwise preserving, and packaging of finished products for distribution throughout the world.

In the nineteenth century the United States experienced an expansion of industrial cities, similar to the pattern that Great Britain had experienced in its industrial revolution. But the United States had an additional factor: westward expansion and settlement. The geographic relationship between the western plains and eastern urban centers was crucial for the beginnings of the food processing industry. This relationship led to inventions, discoveries, and manufacturing systems that would determine the industry's evolution. In the United States the need for food was driven by the concentration of population on the eastern seaboard. Westward expansion into the plains opened a vast area where farmland was abundant and livestock breeding was inexpensive. Transportation and communication systems connected the urban centers with the developing west. Such connections ultimately provided the industry with the means of getting food that was produced in the west to the areas of need in the east. Also, manufacturing centers in the east provided the food processing industry with the labor, machinery, and the manufacturing systems necessary to mass-produce food.

Transportation links between the regions and advanced production techniques were possible because of the on-going revolution in technology and scientific discovery. The invention, in 1850, of the horse-drawn reaping machine made large-scale farming in the vast plains possible because it simplified the ages-old task of cutting wheat by hand. It would soon be followed by the steam-powered reaper and, later, the tractor and the combine. The transport of slaughtered meat across significant distances was possible because of the emergence of refrigerated railway cars after 1869 when George Hammond improvised refrigerated transport. Finally, in 1940, the self-propelled combine machine reduced harvesting time for one acre of wheat from 14 hours to 30 minutes. This sequence of inventions shaped the emergence of the mass-production and movement of huge amounts of food.

Other inventions and discoveries were more specific to the processing of food. In the early 1800s Nicolas Appert, a French chef, started the process of canning. That technique would be patented in the United States in 1815, and in 1847 the mass production of tin-plated steel cans would emerge. These canned goods were consumed by soldiers during the American Civil War (1861–1865), and the Union commissaries were freed from concerns about storage and safe supplies of food. In 1861 Louis Pasteur's discovery of the process of ''pasteurization'' was an important contribution to reliable food preservation. Food was heated to kill dangerous microbes and then sealed in an airtight container. In 1906 modern freeze-drying techniques were being used in France. Home refrigerators emerged in the United States in 1913, and in 1920 American Clarence Birdseye invented the process of deep-freezing foods. The Swiss invented instant coffee in 1937, which led to the future production of powdered food products. In 1973 the era of biotechnology began, when scientists demonstrated how genes could be split and merged to engineer superior products. The scientific contributions to the processing of food escalated as the industry evolved and helped raise the standard of safe food preservation to the point that food could be processed and even manufactured on a mass scale.

Also important to large-scale production of food intended for mass consumption was the evolution of the factory. As the site of bringing into play the efficient combination of labor and capital, factories emerged in the 1820s. They were substantially enhanced in the 1880s with the discovery of electricity. They refined the processes of production and instituted brand names for various foods that would enhance consumer demand. Food processing factories enjoyed a very high ratio of capital to labor. Companies opted to build plants of the greatest possible size in order to benefit from economies of scale and to minimize overhead costs. They created national and international advertising apparatus and retailing centers for the sale and distribution of groceries. This was especially important with meat processors, who required slaughterhouses and warehouses for the fast and efficient processing and sale of their perishable goods. These factories made use of the principles of mass production of the time: the division and specialization of labor and the use of standardized parts and processes. (In fact, the process also worked in reverse as Henry Ford is said to have been inspired to develop the automobile assembly line after visiting a Chicago exposition which featured the ''disassembly line'' of modern meatpacking.)

Other developments were necessary for the food processing industry to fit into mass production systems. Before the advent of large-scale factory processing and transport of food (which were both made possible by food preservation technology), individual growers and processors sold their products in local stores. In the early 1800s small manufacturers had appeared, but they were often without the capital to start larger factories which would yield greater profits. As the merger movement of the nineteenth and early twentieth century brought together the factors of production, many small-scale processors merged with others, forming the big conglomerates that would push the food processing industry into the powerful position it maintained throughout the twentieth century. Companies such as Quaker Oats (the result of a merger of three producers in 1901), General Mills (a 1928 merger), and Del Monte (a series of mergers beginning in 1899) built strong and long-lasting businesses out of small but reputable beginnings.

From its beginnings the industry was a concern for the U.S. government—not only in terms of safety regulations, but also in the area of research and development. The U.S. Department of Agriculture (USDA) was established under the Organic Act of 1862, which charged the commissioner ''to collect new and valuable seeds and plants . . . and to distribute them among agriculturalists (sic).'' The USDA would soon take on far broader authority such as meat inspection and the approval of certain chemical processes used in growing and producing foods. Food safety anxieties were first addressed in the Pure Foods Act and Meat Inspection Act of 1906. Those laws were the result of the exposé of the unsanitary practices in the Chicago meatpacking industry depicted in Upton Sinclair's novel, *The Jungle*. This issue of food safety and the public demand for government regulation of processed food became more pronounced throughout the twentieth century.

At the end of the century of boom for the food processing industry, consumers, governments, and consumer advocates also called for more accountability on the part of the industry. Food-borne disease reached an all-time worldwide high as people became increasingly concerned about the chemicals and processes used in food production. The United Kingdom, the European Union, and the United States called for higher measures of food inspection and safety. Nutritionists, wary of the industry's use of health trends to promote products, called for a definition of food terms in 1997. Under a decidedly skeptical eye, the industry would increasingly face the challenge of giving consumers more convenient and inexpensive food, while gaining public trust in a globally competitive market by ensuring real food safety and honest sales.

See also: **Agricultural Equipment, Assembly Line, Merger, Economies of Scale, Upton Sinclair**

FURTHER READING

Connor, John, and William Schiek. *Food Processing: An Industrial Powerhouse in Transition.* New York: John Wiley and Sons, 1997.

''Food Industry Snapshot,'' [cited April 5, 1999] available from the World Wide Web @ www.hoovers.com/features/industry/food.html/.

Lacey, Richard. *Hard to Swallow: A Brief History of Food.* Cambridge: Cambridge University Press, 1994.

Multhaup, Robert, and Gunther Eschenbrenner. *Technology's Harvest: Feeding a Growing Population.* Houston, TX: Gulf Publishing Company, 1996.

Ruiz, Vicki, and Cicki Ruiz. *Cannery Women, Cannery Lives: Mexican Women, Unionization, and the California Food Processing Industry.* Albuquerque, NM: University of New Mexico Press, 1987.

Stromquist, Shelton, and Marvin Bergman, eds. *Unionizing the Jungles: Labor and Community in the Twentieth Century Meatpacking Industry.* Iowa City, IA: University of Iowa Press, 1997.

FOOD STAMPS

Food stamps are vouchers issued to low-income households that are redeemable only for food at retail stores. The Food Stamp Program in the United States is administered by the Food and Nutrition Service unit of the Department of Agriculture and financed through the Social Security Administration. The program is operated by state and local welfare offices and is available in all 50 states, the District of Columbia, Guam, and the U.S. Virgin Islands. The objective of the Food Stamp Program is to end hunger and improve nutrition and health by assisting low-income households in obtaining a nutritionally adequate diet. Participants in the program use food stamps to supplement what they would normally spend on food. Both low-income families with dependent children and households without children can be eligible for food stamps. The quantity of Food Stamps an eligible household is entitled to depends on the amount of income the household has available and the number of people in the household.

See also: **Social Security Act, Welfare Policy**

FORBES, MALCOLM STEVENSON

Millionaire Malcolm Forbes (1919–1990), the publisher of *Forbes* magazine from 1957 to 1990, converted a business publication his father started into one of the most influential in the United States. The younger

The Food Stamp Program is one of the government's tools to end hunger and improve nutrition and health in low-income households.

Forbes' exuberant lifestyle, combining business and pleasure, and his unabashed enjoyment of his wealth, made him a singular personality in the normally staid business community.

Forbes inherited his wealth from his father, who established his son as owner and publisher at the *Fairfield Times*, a weekly newspaper in Lancaster, Ohio, only days after his graduation from Princeton University. In later life he was fond of saying that he had been loaded with "sheer ability (spelled i-n-h-e-r-i-t-a-n-c-e)." That quip belied his real talent and ability. At Princeton he was awarded the Class of 1901 Medal as a member of the class of 1941 who "contributed the most to Princeton as an undergraduate."

Forbes was also a genuine war hero of World War II (1939–1945) who was wounded in combat and received both the Bronze Star and a Purple Heart for his service as an infantry staff sergeant of a heavy machine gun section serving in France, Belgium, Holland, and Germany. Following his discharge from the Army in 1945 he joined *Forbes* magazine. He successively held positions as associate publisher, publisher, editor, editor-in-chief, vice president, and president.

During the 1950s Forbes was also active in politics. In 1951 he was elected to the New Jersey State Senate; in 1957—the year he became editor-in-chief and publisher of *Forbes*—he made an unsuccessful run for the New Jersey governorship. In 1964 he took over the family business as president of Forbes, Inc.

According to *Advertising Age*, Forbes "expanded the magazine his father created in 1917 into a publishing powerhouse—whether measured in circulation, advertising revenue, or the trepidation with which CEOs awaited stories about their companies." With a circulation of 750,000 copies (of which 250,000 were reported as sold to millionaires), *Forbes* became one of the most influential and successful business magazines in the United States. In the early 1960s the publication's advertising revenues stood at nearly $2 million; at the time of Forbes's death this expense was well beyond $150 million. Forbes's own net worth, which he never included in his magazine's annual list of the nation's four hundred richest citizens, was estimated between $400 million and $1 billion.

Forbes's lavish lifestyle and charismatic personality were central to the success of his company. His well-publicized hobbies and interests included his notable collection of Faberge eggs, expensive motorcycles, and opulent retreats in France, Tangiers, and Fiji, as well as a Colorado ranch and a New Jersey estate. He used his lavish parties, ballooning adventures, and trips on his luxurious yacht *Highlander* to woo advertisers and top executives. "On the *Highlander*, we entertain anywhere from thirty to fifty CEOs and their wives," he said in a 1989 interview in *Forbes*. "The event is the medium's message bearer. Nobody makes a direct pitch. It's a group sell, but the real selling is done one-on-one when the salesman with the account calls on the agency media buyers, and the account executives and the higher men in the hierarchy call on the directors.''

All the publicity about Forbes' lifestyle masked his hard work and dedication to the magazine. He was usually in his office by six a.m. ''It's fun to be at your desk when you're the boss,'' he said in the same *Forbes* interview. ''You can't be successful if you don't love what you're doing. Whatever really turns you on does it. Psychic income is what real income is used for anyway.'' Malcolm Forbes died in 1990.

See also: **Publishing Industry**

FURTHER READING

Buckley, William F. ''Malcom Forbes, RIP.'' *National Review*, March 19, 1990.

Current Biography 1975. New York: H.W. Wilson, 1975, s.v. ''Forbes, Malcolm Stevenson.''

Gschwandtner, Gerhard and L.S. Gschwandtner. ''Selling with Style, Wit and Class.'' *Forbes*, July 24, 1989.

''Malcom Forbes: He Practiced What He Preached.'' *Forbes*, April 30, 1990.

Pearl, Jayne. ''The Forbes Mystique.'' *Forbes*, October 22, 1990.

FORD, HENRY

Henry Ford (1863–1947) launched the era of the mass-produced automobile. He provided tools such as the moving assembly line to enable the fast mass-production of cars and other consumer goods. Ford founded the Ford Motor Car Company, which remained the second largest car and truck manufacturer in the world through the 1990s. He is regarded as one of the great industrialists and automobile innovators of the twentieth century. Ford was also a generous philanthropist.

Henry Ford was born in Dearborn, Michigan, into a farming family. The first child of William and Mary Ford, he was taught largely by his mother, who instilled in him a strong sense of responsibility, duty, and self-reliance. As a young man he became an excellent self-taught mechanic and machinist. At age 16 he left

the farm and went to nearby Detroit, a city that was process of becoming an industrial giant. There he worked as an apprentice at a machine shop. Months later he began to work with steam engines at the Detroit Dry Dock Co., where he first saw the internal combustion engine, the kind of engine he would later use to make his automobiles.

When he was 28 Ford took a job with Thomas Edison's (1847–1931) Detroit Illuminating Company, where he became chief engineer. In his spare time he began to build his first car, the Quadricycle. It resembled 2 bicycles positioned side by side with spindly bicycle-like wheels, a bicycle seat, and a barely visible engine frame. Some said it bore a resemblance to a baby carriage with a two-cylinder engine. In June 1896, Ford took an historic ride in his first automobile that was observed by many curious Detroit on-lookers. The Quadricycle broke down in a humiliating scene.

By 1899 Ford created a more proper-looking motorcar with the help of wealthy businessman William Murphy. It had high wheels, a padded double bench, brass lamps, mud guards, and a ''racy'' look. In the same year Ford founded the Detroit Automobile Company. Within 3 years Ford had built an improved, more reliable Quadricycle, using a four-cylinder, 36 horsepower racing engine. In 1901 his car beat what was then the world's fastest automobile in a race before a crowd of eight-thousand people in Grosse Pointe, Michigan.

The publicity he received for this victory allowed Ford to finance a practical laboratory for refining his auto ideas. In 1903 Ford launched his own car company, The Ford Motor Car Company, and by January 1904 he had sold 658 vehicles. By 1908 he built the famous Model T, a car that was affordable to the middle class. The automobile was no longer the toy of the rich. Sales of the Model T increased to 720,000 by 1916.

Ford was able to make a reliable and inexpensive automobile primarily because of his introduction of the innovative moving assembly line into the process of industrial manufacturing. The assembly line is a system for carrying an item that is being manufactured past a series of stationary workers who each assemble a particular portion of the finished product. The assembly line was undoubtedly Ford's greatest contribution to industry. It revolutionized manufacturing and made it possible to make uniform products quickly and affordably.

Ford personally controlled most aspects of his company operations. He shocked the industrial world

Henry Ford in his first car, the Model A.

in 1914 by paying his workers the very high wage of $5 a day. In exchange for this high wage Ford demanded of his employees regular attendance at work, as well as a serious and sober private life. He required all immigrant laborers learn English and become citizens of the United States.

Ford was intrigued by the ideas of Frederick Taylor (1856–1915), the founder of Scientific Management. It was a philosophy of standardizing the behavior of workers to increase efficiency and production. Ford designed his factories to fit human performance, but then demanded his workers perform according to the factory design. He was one of the first to introduce time clocks into his business operations to monitor the exact minute a worker arrived at his job, took his lunch, and when he left his job. Ford began treating the worker like a living machine, and he attracted heavy criticism for this. The most enduring indictment of Ford's totalitarian business style was created by Aldous Huxley (1894–1963) in his classic novel *Brave New World*.

Ford was criticized for more than his totalitarian business practices. It was shocking for most people in the United States to read of Henry Ford's anti-Semitism,

which he published weekly for 2 years in unsigned articles in his own newspaper, *The Dearborn Independent*. Oddly, many of his best friends were Jewish. An example is Albert Kahn (1869–1942), the great architect who designed Ford's factory in Highland Park, Michigan. Despite his controversial and at times publicly unpleasant views, some people thought enough of Ford to encourage him to run for president in 1922. They quickly retracted their support when they discovered Adolph Hitler (1889–1945) had a picture of Ford on his wall and often cited Ford as an inspiration. Ford was the only U.S. citizen mentioned in Hitler's *Mein Kampf*.

Driven by his childhood sense of duty and obligation, Ford was also an active philanthropist throughout his life. He built a hospital for his employees in Detroit, and in 1936 established the Ford Foundation for the purposes of ''advancing human welfare.'' Since its founding the Ford Foundation has issued more than $8 billion in grants worldwide.

This complex farmer's son from Michigan, who made automobiles affordable to the masses, died at his estate, Fairlane, in Dearborn, Michigan in 1947 at the age of 84.

See also: Assembly Line, Automobile, Automobile Industry, Ford Motor Company, Frederick Winslow Taylor

FURTHER READING

Bryan, Ford R. *Beyond the Model T: The Other Ventures of Henry Ford.* Detroit: Wayne State University Press, 1990.

Lasey, Robert. *Ford: The Men and the Machine.* Boston: Little, Brown and Co., 1986.

Lee, Albert. *Henry Ford and the Jews.* New York: Stein and Day, 1980.

Nevins, Allan and F. E. Hill. *Ford: The Times, the Man, the Company.* New York: Scribners., 1954.

Wik, Reynold M. *Henry Ford and Grass-roots America.* Ann Arbor: University of Michigan Press, 1972.

FORD MOTOR COMPANY

Ford Motor Company is the largest manufacturer of trucks in the world and the second largest manufacturer of automobiles, behind only General Motors Corporation (GM). Headquartered in Dearborn, Michigan, Ford has plants in 19 countries and facilities in more than 100 others. The company markets vehicles under the brand names of Ford, Lincoln, Mercury, Jaguar, and Aston Martin. Ford owns a controlling interest in Japanese automaker Mazda Motor Corporation and in the Hertz Corporation, the world's number one rental-car company. Ford Credit, one of the company's subsidiaries, is the world's leading provider of automotive financing.

Henry Ford (1863–1947) founded the Ford Motor Company on June 16, 1903. The company was launched from a small converted wagon factory in Detroit, and its assets initially consisted of tools, appliances, machinery, blueprints, patents, and a few models. Henry Ford experimented with a number of early automobile designs during the 1890s, developing a reputation as a pioneer in the area. This reputation grew with Ford's release of the Model A, a two-cylinder, eight-horsepower design that sold 1,708 models in the company's first year of operation. Over the next five years Ford engineers feverishly developed 19 different models, designating each by a letter between *B* and *S*. Some models succeeded, some failed, and some never left the plant. The most successful of the group was the Model N, a small four-cylinder car that sold for $500. The biggest failure was the Model K. At $2,500 it priced most consumers out of the market.

The Model K's failure fueled Ford's desire to design an inexpensive and reliable car that could be mass produced. The 1908 Model T was the answer. Affectionately dubbed the "Lizzy" by U.S. car buyers, Ford's Model T came to symbolize low-cost, and durable transportation. The four-cylinder vehicle, which could travel at a top speed of 45 miles per hour, sold 10,660 units in its first year. As demand climbed, Ford invented the world's first moving automobile assembly line in 1913. Henry Ford believed that automobile production would become more efficient if all employees were assigned one place to work, where they could focus on a specific task to accomplish in a diligent manner.

Within 12 months of the invention, Ford workers had reduced the time during which a chassis could be assembled from 12 hours and eight minutes to one hour and 33 minutes. Ford manufactured 308,162 cars in 1914, more than all 299 other car manufacturers combined. The Model T's success and the use of the assembly line allowed Ford Motor Company to drop its price from the original sticker of $850 to $350. It could also double its employees' minimum wage to five dollars and open new factories in the United States, Canada, Europe, Australia, South America, and Japan. It also provided Ford with revenue to purchase luxury carmaker Lincoln Motor Company in 1922.

FORD MOTOR COMPANY IS THE LARGEST MANUFACTURER OF TRUCKS IN THE WORLD AND THE SECOND LARGEST MANUFACTURER OF AUTOMOBILES.

Consumer interests gradually shifted in the 1920s. Competitors began rolling out more powerful and stylish cars. To stem dwindling profits Ford discontinued production of the Model T in 1927 and closed plants around the country so the company could retool. When Ford opened its doors six months later it unveiled a vastly improved Model A. Featuring hydraulic shock absorbers, automatic windshield wipers, a gas gauge, and a speedometer, the Model A sold more than 4.5 million units in four years. Now refusing to sit idle in face of increasing competition, Ford pushed aside the Model A in 1932, introducing the world's first V-8 engine block that was cast in a single piece. Six years later Ford introduced the Lincoln Continental and a new line of Mercury automobiles.

The 1930s and 1940s also marked a time of transition for the automaker. Ford's market share slipped behind those of GM and the Chrysler Corporation. An avowed opponent of labor unions, Ford was forced to recognize the United Automobile Workers of America (UAW) as the collective bargaining representative for all of the company's workers. In 1941 Ford shut down its civilian automobile production to manufacture B-24 bombers, aircraft engines, tanks, jeeps, trucks, munitions, and equipment for the Allies during the balance of World War II (1939–1945). When the war ended, most of Ford's contracts with the government terminated, and the car company soon started suffering losses of $10 million per month. In 1947 founder Henry Ford died, four years after the premature death of his 49-year-old son Edsel, who had succeeded his father as the company's president in 1918.

Henry Ford II, Edsel's eldest son, took over as president in 1945. For the next three decades he helped modernize Ford and return it to profitability. In 1955 Ford introduced the Thunderbird. The sleek and sporty two-seat roadster sold more than 16,000 units in its first year, while Chevrolet sold comparatively meager 657 Corvettes. In 1956 Ford Motor Company went public. In the largest stock sale ever at the time, Ford sold 10.2 million shares to 250,000 investors for $657 million, or 20 percent of the family's business. In 1956 Ford created an aerospace division, and two years later the company announced its entry into the heavy and extra-heavy truck market. In 1963 Ford debuted the highly successful Mustang sports coupe, which remains one of the company's most popular muscle cars.

The reign of Henry Ford II as president was not one of uninterrupted success. In 1958 the company released the Edsel, a 410-horsepower, 17-foot sedan that generated losses of $250 million in just two years. During the 1960s Ford's management fought bitterly over the company's direction, changing executives throughout the decade. In the 1970s Ford Motor Co. was named as a defendant in a series of wrongful death lawsuits stemming from numerous incidents when the gas tanks on its subcompact Bobcat and Pinto models exploded during rear-collisions. The OPEC oil embargo of the 1970s also made Ford's bigger, gas-guzzling vehicles a liability, and many U.S. citizens started turning to smaller, more fuel-efficient Japanese vehicles.

The 1980s brought downsizing to Ford. After losing $3.2 billion from 1980 to 1982, the company reduced its workforce by one-third and closed 15 plants. Ford diversified during this period as well. Its 1986 purchase of the Sperry Corporation's New Holland tractor division helped Ford become the world's third largest maker of agricultural equipment. Ford also purchased First Nationwide Financial Corporation and U.S. Leasing in the mid-1980s. On December 26, 1985, Ford introduced the Taurus, an affordable midsize vehicle that was named car of the year in 1986. By 1987 the Taurus was outselling every other car in the United States. The Ford F-Series pickup truck and subcompact Escort were also gaining in popularity as the decade ended, when Ford was reporting record profits.

Ford continued restructuring in 1990s. It gradually dropped out of the heavy-truck business during this period and consolidated its operations in North America and Europe. In 1994 Ford introduced its year 2000 initiative, under which the entire Ford family of enterprises would be organized into a single operation by the beginning of the next millennium. Ford also announced a plan to make all of its vehicles more environmentally safe before the twenty-first century. Emissions for sport utility vehicles (SUVs) would be reduced to levels required for new cars, while new car emissions would be decreased by 70 percent. In 1999 Ford teamed with DaimlerChrysler AG and the state of California to test zero emission cars powered by fuel cells that produce electricity through the chemical reaction of hydrogen and oxygen. At the same time Ford announced its plan to purchase auto junkyards over the Internet and to recycle undamaged car parts to mechanics.

These announcements, however, were tempered by Ford's plans to roll out the industry's biggest SUV to date. A 3.5-ton, six-door, 19-foot long colossus was scheduled to go on sale for about $50,000 in the fall of 2000. The environmental group, the Sierra Club, described the SUV as a ''tanker'' that will ''guzzle enough gas to make Saddam Hussein smile.'' Such criticism has concerned the Ford family, which still owns a controlling interest in the company. But the family also recognize that the company's success has always been linked to meeting consumer demands.

See also: **Assembly Line, Automobile Industry, Automobile (origin of), Henry Ford, Model T**

FURTHER READING

Collier, Peter. *The Fords: An American Epic.* New York: Summit Books, 1987.

''Ford Motor Company,'' [cited May 25, 1999] available from the World Wide Web @ www.hoovers.com/.

''Ford Motor Company,''[cited May 25, 1999] available from the World Wide Web @ www2.ford.com/.

''Ford Takes Control of Mazda.'' *St. Petersburg Times*, April 13,1996.

''GM, Ford Still Top Fortune 500 List.'' *The Detroit News*, April 7, 1999.

Langworth, Richard, M. *The Complete History of Ford Motor Company*. New York: Beekman House, 1987.

FORDNEY-MCCUMBER TARIFF

After President Warren Harding's (1921–1923) inauguration in 1921 he asked Congress for emergency tariff legislation, stating ''I believe in the protection of American industry, and it is our purpose to prosper America first.'' By the following year Congress completed a comprehensive tariff revision, The Fordney-McCumber Tariff Act. The law represented a return to pre-World War I (1914–1918) protectionism of the United States amid fear that European producers could undersell U.S. manufacturers. The Fordney-McCumber Tariff raised average duties (import taxes) on all imported goods 15.2 percent in 1922, and up to 36.3 percent in 1923. The tariff effectively raised the average import tax on goods 138 percent in two years. All data collected about the impact of the Fordney-McCumber Tariff suggests it did not have the desired effect on the U.S. economy. In fact the quantity of imports continued to rise. Analysis suggests that global economic conditions in the world after World War I exerted a greater negative impact on trade than did the high Fordney-McCumber ''protective'' tariff. This measure is perhaps the most blatant example of the Harding administration's efforts to make the United States ''The Unconditional Most Favored Nation'' in the world, seeking both to reduce the profitability of foreign imports and to pursue retaliation against other countries that sought to limit U.S. exports.

See also: **Protectionism, Tariff**

FOREIGN INVESTMENT IN THE UNITED STATES *(ISSUE)*

Since World War II (1939–1945), and especially in the 1950s and 1960s, the United States dominated world-wide foreign investment. But with the advent of the energy crisis and the oil shortages in the early 1970s the situation was reversed. The United States became the recipient of large investments from Great Britain, the Netherlands, and especially Japan. Although the 1980s witnessed unusually rapid growth in worldwide foreign direct investment, from approximately $55 billion in 1980 to $137 billion in 1987, world output rose by only 20 percent and the volume of world trade by 28 percent. During the 1980s the United States became the largest recipient of foreign direct investment and Japan became the leader in direct investment abroad. Since 1985 foreigners, especially the Japanese, have increased their acquisitions in the United States or have expanded or established businesses in the United States.

The reasons for this surge in investments were varied and complex. Some foreign companies felt they must have a position in the U.S. market, which was still the richest and largest consumer market in the world. U.S. political stability and the appreciation of foreign assets made U.S. assets relatively attractive and cheap. For example, Mitsubwashi purchased Rockefeller Center in downtown Manhattan (New York) for approximately $850 million, a fraction of what a similar piece of real estate in downtown Tokyo would have cost. In addition the lure of overseas profits pushed many multinational companies into staking out international claims. Exporting countries could frequently work around other countries' protective legislation by establishing factories within that country's borders. Honda, a case in point, now produces more cars in the United States than it does in Japan.

Another attractive feature for foreign investment was that the new global economy emphasized consolidation and bigness. Mergers and acquisitions occurred six times more frequently in the United States than in foreign counties. Mammoth deals in pharmaceuticals, media, and food industries helped set a new record of $144 billion for the combined value of the fifty largest annual acquisitions and mergers in 1989. Moreover the scientific, industrial, managerial, marketing, financing, advertising, insurance, and especially research and development systems in the United States had all developed and matured to make the United States very attractive for investors.

Foreign investment in research and development experienced especially explosive growth. From 1987 to 1995 investment in research and development rose from $700 million to more than $17 billion. In addition to investment foreign companies by the end of the 1990s employed more than 150,000 U.S. citizens in research and development activities at hundreds of research laboratories and manufacturing facilities across the country. The growing presence of foreign companies conducting research and development in the U.S. reflected a fundamental trend in the world economy, the globalization of innovation. Multinational enterprises had long operated international networks of manufacturing plants, but during the 1990s these multinational companies added a new dimension to their activities—an increasing capacity for research and development and innovation in various locations outside their home countries.

In addition to the debate over foreign investment in general, the relatively new phenomenon of foreign-owned, U.S.-based research and development programs also provoked controversy. Proponents believed foreign-owned laboratories contributed to the U.S. science and technology base, and that the government should encourage their development. Critics however argued that the facilities were merely skeleton research operations designed to monitor the U.S. research scene, or even pirate ideas developed within U.S. borders. Part of the controversy stemmed from the startlingly rapid growth of foreign research and development programs. Until recently most multinational companies conducted virtually all of their research and development at home. The 1990s however saw an explosion of international research and development activities by large multinational firms. The magnet that drew research and development to the United States was talent. Companies opened labs in the United States to gain access to world-class researchers. (Thus, the proximity of many labs to major research universities, which were regarded as a key source of commercial innovation.) The NEC Research Institute, for example, was able to recruit renowned computer scientists partly because it was adjacent to Princeton University. When Canon established a research center for work on optical character recognition, image compression, and network systems, the company chose Palo Alto to be close to Stanford University and Xerox's famed Palo Alto Research Center. Mitsubwashi Electric Research Laboratory, which conducted research and development on a range of information technology including computer vision, was next door to MIT.

In the automotive industry foreign laboratories geared their work to supporting U.S. manufacturing plants and customizing products for the U.S. market. Nissan Design International's close ties to the U.S. market enabled them to realize that Nissan could attract U.S. car buyers by adding a stylish body to a pickup truck platform. The result, the Pathfinder, launched the sport utility craze and transformed the entire automotive market.

While the funding for these research labs came from abroad, the style of work in them was very U.S.-oriented. Offshore companies generally recognized that to recruit and retain U.S. researchers required

adoption of a U.S. style of management. In this respect these labs differed markedly from foreign-owned manufacturing facilities. Japanese companies that ran U.S. factories, for example, typically sought to transfer and transplant to their U.S. facilities manufacturing practices honed at home. On the other hand foreign laboratories in the United States were organized much like leading research centers of U.S. universities. These labs encouraged scientific and technical staff to work autonomously and publish widely. They sponsored visiting scholars and hosted seminars and symposia.

But critics saw a threat to U.S. technological leadership by giving international companies easy access to U.S. technology. For them foreign research and development facilities were skeleton operations designed to monitor and pirate U.S. ideas. They believed that federal policymakers should tilt the rules of innovation to benefit U.S. companies over foreign competitors, or develop rules and regulations that reward "good" U.S. companies (those that invest in the United States) over "bad" ones (those that invest abroad). Proponents of foreign investment counter this argument and believe that although such policy proposals were well-intentioned and sought to protect U.S. investments, they were completely out of touch with the reality of a global system of innovation. According to proponents of foreign investment, financing of U.S. research and development by foreign corporations strengthened U.S. science and technology, especially when government and private sponsorship of U.S. research was being cut back. Proponents also pointed out that these labs churned out patents at rates that exceeded those of U.S. industrial research and development. They also argued that foreign laboratories also added considerably to the stock of new scientific and technical knowledge by reporting their findings in scientific and technical journals. They claimed that they published an average of 10 journal articles per 100 scientists and engineers per year, better than the rate for industrial research and development by U.S.-owned companies.

FURTHER READING

Finkelstein, Joseph, ed. *Windows on a New World: The Third Industrial Revolution*. New York: Greenwood Press, 1989.

Henderson, D. F. *Foreign Enterprise in Japan*. Chapel Hill, NC: University of North Carolina Press, 1973.

Nawasbitt, John. *Megatrends 2000*. New York: Morrow, 1990.

Porter, Michael. *The Competitive Advantage of Nations*. New York: The Free Press, 1990.

Reich, Robert. B. *The Work of Nations: Preparing Ourselves for 21st Century Capitalism.* New York: Knopf, 1991.

FOREIGN INVESTMENT OF U.S. COMPANIES ABROAD (ISSUE)

Foreign investment of U.S. companies abroad has changed drastically in the last half of the twentieth century. Since World War II (1939–1945) and especially in the 1950s and 1960s, the United States dominated world wide foreign investment. But with the advent of the energy crisis and the oil shortages in the early 1970s, that situation reversed. The United States became the recipient of large investments from Great Britain, the Netherlands, and especially Japan. Yet recently American ''indirect'' investment abroad has begun to rise dramatically and in 1998 foreign ''indirect'' investment hit a record of more than $250 billion, climbing sharply during the entire decade. Europe was the prime destination, with the pharmaceutical and telecommunications industries dominating, along with banking and electricity, gas and water utilities. In 1998 U.S. investment abroad doubled to $97 billion—higher than the world direct investment total less than a decade ago. During the 1980s the United States became the largest recipient of foreign direct investment and Japan became the leader in direct investment abroad. Since 1985 foreigners, especially the Japanese, have increased their acquisitions in the United States or have expanded or established businesses there. That kind of investment from Japan and other countries has ''trickled'' down to include foreign investment of U.S. companies abroad.

Many economists argued that foreign investment, both inward and outward, has been fundamental to the prosperity of the United States. In 1996 flows of foreign direct investment (FDI) into the United States reached $78.1 billion, while FDI outflows reached $85.6 billion; economists argued that in a globalizing world economy U.S. firms need a global presence in order to sell effectively. Service industries especially, which accounted for $236.8 billion in exports in 1996, almost always needed a physical presence on the ground. These economists contended that a foreign presence is necessary to effectively market exports of goods, arguing that approximately 26 percent of U.S. exports are channeled through foreign-based affiliates of U.S. companies. They also argued that over the past several years developing countries have become more interested in and more receptive to foreign investment. They said that foreign countries recognize the benefits of foreign investment to their economies and people and that private foreign investment flows have substantially outpaced foreign assistance funds. They also contended that the interest of developing countries in attracting foreign investment can be seen in the explosion of bilateral investment treaties globally since the beginning of the 1990s—from 435 in 1990 to some 1,300 in 1999. But others disagree. Those in other countries argued that the Multilateral Agreement on Investment (MAI) would legalize and dramatically increase the capabilities of multinational companies to place every small business in participating countries under the real threat of closure, take-over, or bankruptcy. They maintained that foreign small businesses were the backbone of their respective economies and were one of the few remaining reliable sources of tax revenue because multinational companies paid little or taxes under the International Tax Agreement Act of 1953. And finally they declared that the consequence of the MIA and the continued non-payment of tax by multinationals, the reduced tax revenue from small business as a result of corporate take-over or decimation, and the reduction in the number of ''pay-as-you-earn'' or PAYE taxpayers through unemployment would threaten foreign tax bases with total collapse.

Opponents in the United States argued that the MAI, NAFTA-GATT, and other trade deals had sold out U.S. workers, ravaged the manufacturing base, provoked serious ''protectionists'' issues including software piracy and national security, and caused disruption in small towns and farming communities. They held that ''trading partners'' continued to impose 40 percent tariffs on U.S. agricultural goods and that since 1992 the United States had run a trillion-dollar trade deficit—$200 billion with Communist China, which used U.S. currency to expand its military, steal U.S. technology, and buy weapons to target U.S. military establishments.

In the late 1990s countries included in the Organization for Economic Cooperation and Development (OECD) included Australia, Austria, Belgium, Canada, the Czech Republic, Denmark, Finland, France, Germany, Greece, Hungary, Iceland, Ireland, Italy, Japan, Korea, Luxembourg, Mexico, Netherlands, New Zealand, Norway, Poland, Portugal, Spain, Sweden, Switzerland, Turkey, the United Kingdom, and the United States. Proponents argued that additional members could enhance the agreement's attractiveness as the sound investment policies and the commitments to other policy objectives encompassed in the MAI were embraced by a wider group of countries.

FURTHER READING

Finkelstein, Joseph, ed. *Windows on a New World: The Third Industrial Revolution*. New York: Greenwood Press, 1989.

Henderson, D. F. *Foreign Enterprise in Japan*. Chapel Hill, NC: University of North Carolina Press, 1973.

Naisbitt, John. *Megatrends 2000*. New York: Morrow, 1990.

Porter, Michael. *The Competitive Advantage of Nations*. New York: The Free Press, 1990.

Reich, Robert. B. *The Work of Nations: Preparing Ourselves for 21st Century Capitalism*. New York: Knopf, 1991.

All persons born or naturalized in the United States are subject to the jurisdiction thereof, are citizens of the United States and the State wherein they reside. No State shall make or enforce any law which shall abridge the privileges or immunities of citizens of the United States; nor shall any State deprive any person of life, liberty, or property, without due process of law; nor deny to any person within its jurisdiction the equal protection of the laws.

Fourteenth Amendment, *U.S. Constitution*

FOURTEENTH AMENDMENT

The Fourteenth Amendment to the U.S. Constitution is a product of the post–Civil War Reconstruction (1865–1877) effort to protect the rights of the former slaves. It is best known for its definition of citizen, which it defined as a person born in the United States or ''naturalized'' (granted citizenship). It also bestowed on U.S. citizens equal rights under the law. The result was to limit drastically the power of states to define citizenship or to treat their citizens in a discriminatory fashion. Thus, the states were prohibited from denying a person equal protection under the law. The meaning of this development in the long-term debate over federalism versus states' rights was that henceforth the federal government would assume the ultimate responsibility for protecting the civil rights of citizens. As part of this ruling, the Fourteenth Amendment also declared that states must respect every person's right to due process of law.

The Fourteenth Amendment touched on several other matters that had great relevance at the time of the amendment's enactment, although they are less well-known at the close of the twentieth century. One was the provision that reduced the number of representatives and presidential electors apportioned to a state if that state refused to allow any of its male citizens over the age of 21 the right to vote. This language was intended to prevent the former states of the Confederacy from gaining political power as a result of the freeing of the slaves if those states prevented their former slaves from voting. (Under the ''three-fifths compromise'' in the Constitution, each slave had been

counted as three-fifths of a citizen for the purpose of determining the number of congressmen and presidential electors that the states could claim. Now that the slaves were declared free under the Emancipation Proclamation and the Thirteenth Amendment, they each counted as a full citizen. This had the unintended effect (from the standpoint of most of the northern members of Congress) of increasing the political power of the former Confederate states. The Fourteenth Amendment attempted to redress the balance by ruling that if a state were guilty of denying the voting rights of any of its citizens, its entire population of former slaves would now not be counted for the purposes of figuring out the number of presidential electors or representatives that the state could have.

The Fourteenth Amendment also denied former Confederates the right to hold office in federal or state governments. In addition, this amendment established the validity of the country's public debt. It also stated that the United States would not assume responsibility for the debts of the former Confederate government or of the states that had participated on the South's side in the American Civil War (1861–1865). The amendment also stated that the federal government would not compensate former slave owners who had been deprived of their slaves as a result of the war or in accordance with the Thirteenth Amendment.

The Fourteenth Amendment had several unforeseen consequences. Whereas the Constitution and the Bill of Rights had tried to protect the individual from the power of the federal government, the Fourteenth Amendment sought to protect the individual from the power of the state. Yet it was purposely vague on some crucial matters. One was the question of African Americans in the North. There were enough congressmen who thought that something should be done to protect the ex-slaves in the South, but who feared to offend white supremacy in the North. They spoke in generalities about reducing the total apportionment of representatives and presidential electors if the state violated the voting right of male citizens. The result was that several northern states still denied the right to vote to their African American residents because there were so few African Americans in the North that the penalty was negligible. The language was, however, gender-specific and implicitly denied the vote to women, a fact that attracted the attention of feminist activists.

The most ironic consequence of the Fourteenth Amendment was that throughout the later years of the nineteenth century it was invoked more often in defense of corporate America than in defense of black America. The railroad companies' trial lawyers, for instance, convinced the courts that the Fourteenth Amendment's clause that no state ''shall deprive any person of life, liberty, or property, without due process of law. . .'' could be invoked to protect the corporations, which, they argued, were legally ''persons,'' against the regulation of the industry on the state level.

Just as the language banning ''restraint of trade'' in the Sherman Anti-Trust Act of 1890 was most frequently used against picket lines and strikes rather than against monopolies, the Fourteenth Amendment's language was often used by corporate lawyers to protect the emerging post–Civil War concentrations of economic power.

See also: **Sherman Anti-Trust Act, Thirteenth Amendment**

FURTHER READING

Berger, Raoul. *The Fourteenth Amendment and the Bill of Rights.* Norman, OK: University of Oklahoma Press, 1989.

Graham, H. J. *Everyman's Constitution: Historical Essays on the Fourteenth Amendment, The Conspiracy Theory, and American Constitutionalism.* Madison, WI: State Historical Society of Wisconsin, 1968.

James, Joseph B. *The Framing of the Fourteenth Amendment.* Urbana, IL: University of Illinois Press, 1956.

Nelson, William E. *The Fourteenth Amendment: From Political Principle to Judicial Doctrine.* Cambridge, MA: Harvard University Press, 1988.

Ten Broek, Josephus. *The Anti-Slavery Origins of the Fourteenth Amendment.* Berkeley, CA: University of California Press, 1951.

FRACTIONAL RESERVE BANKING

In the United States banks operate under the fractional reserve system. This means that the law requires banks to keep a percentage of their deposits as reserves in the form of vault cash or as deposits with the nearest Federal Reserve Bank. They loaned out the rest of their deposits to earn interest. Such banking practices formed the basis for the banking system's ability to ''create'' money.

To illustrate the creation of money, suppose an individual deposited one thousand dollars in a bank and the reserve requirement is 20 percent. The bank was required to keep $200 on reserve but could loan out $800. The $800 loan paid for a television and was deposited in another bank, which, in turn, kept 20 percent but loaned out $640 to someone else. At that point, $1440 had been created and used for purchases.

The Federal Reserve System affects the nation's money supply directly by adjusting the amount of reserves it requires member banks to keep. If a 15 percent reserve requirement was lowered to 10 percent, more money was available to businesses and individuals for loans. The money supply could increase. In contrast, if the reserve requirement was raised to 30 percent, less money could be loaned, and the money supply shrank.

The first banks in the United States were chartered by the states and were not required to keep reserves. By 1820 a few New York and New England banks entered into redemption arrangements provided that a sufficient deposit of gold was maintained in their respective vaults to guarantee their paper money. In essence these gold deposits represented the first required reserves. Most states still had no reserve requirement when the American Civil War (1861–1865) began in 1861. In 1863 the National Bank Act established reserve requirements to ensure liquidity, the ability to satisfy a customer's cash demands, especially during times of financial panic. A series of bank runs in the late nineteenth and early twentieth centuries demonstrated that reserve requirements helped little in providing liquidity. The Federal Reserve System created in 1913 became the lender of last resort, capable of meeting cash needs. The notion of reserves meeting liquidity demands all but vanished. Instead reserve requirements evolved into a monetary policy tool of the Federal Reserve System for controlling the nation's money supply and credit conditions.

See also: **Federal Reserve System, Federal Reserve Banking Act**

FRANCHISE

A franchise is the business resulting when permission or authorization is given to someone to sell or distribute a company's products in a given location. Sometimes the geographic territory itself is called a franchise. A franchisee is a person who operates under such authorization.

Franchises are extremely common in the economy of the latter-half of the twentieth century. Most fast-food restaurants, retail shops, and other common businesses operate as franchises. Typically, the parent company that authorizes the franchise also develops the concept, designs the store, markets the product nationally, and trains the local franchisee, all in exchange for a fee and perhaps a percentage of profits. The parent company may also insist that certain standards of product quality be met, and that employee uniforms and the like be similar to those in the company's other franchises. In the largest such companies, a single parent corporation operates through thousands of franchise outlets.

Critics complain that franchises lead to a loss of distinctive regional identities because all businesses tend to look the same all over the country. Defenders, however, contend that society benefits because a parent company can demand a level of quality higher than might be found in most small, local operations.

FRANKLIN, BENJAMIN

Benjamin Franklin (1706–1790) was an American Renaissance man, knowledgeable on a variety of subjects and active in many careers throughout his lifetime. Famous for his involvement in writing of the Declaration of Independence and the U.S. Constitution, as well as for his experiments with lightning, Franklin's lesser known accomplishments include work as a writer, a publisher, and a businessman.

Benjamin Franklin was born January 17, 1706, in Boston, Massachusetts, the fifteenth child and youngest son in a family of seventeen children. Because his family was not wealthy, young Franklin was only afforded two years of formal schooling. At age ten he was apprenticed to his father's business, a tallow shop, where he was to learn the craft of candle and soap making. Franklin disliked the work and sought an apprenticeship as a printer with his older brother, James. Franklin spent five years working and learning under James and became an expert printer.

Benjamin Franklin.

Franklin described himself as a printer for the rest of his life. In the eighteenth century printers were more like today's publishers than simple typesetters. A successful printer needed to be a researcher, writer, and editor as well as the technician who set the type and printed the page. Franklin excelled at this craft and learned to write well on many subjects. He published at age twelve his first of many works and continued to write until his death.

At age seventeen Franklin left his work with brother James and moved to Philadelphia. His brother had spent time in prison for criticizing the government and Franklin learned to love the freedom he found running the paper in James' absence. Franklin found employment as a printer in Pennsylvania, but left for England in 1724. He lived there for five years, writing and improving his skills as a printer. Franklin was a supporter of the English crown in his early years and appreciated the lifestyle of London and the European continent.

But Franklin did not make his life in Europe. He returned to Philadelphia in 1729 and purchased the *Pennsylvania Gazette*, a bankrupt newspaper that he turned into the principle publishing house in the state. Franklin's printing business extended to partnerships with printers from Nova Scotia to the West Indies. He began a famous publication, *Poor Richard's Almanack*, which was very popular with the public. Franklin also operated a bookstore, became clerk of the Pennsylvania Assembly, and served as postmaster for Philadelphia.

During his business career and later in life Franklin maintained an avid interest in science. His curiosity and inventiveness produced the Franklin Stove, a practical device that allowed the more efficient heating of larger rooms during winter. His study of electricity included the famous kite experiment by which he proved that lighting was electricity. This discovery led to his invention of the lightning rod, which soon appeared on buildings all over the world. His scientific efforts also included works in ship design and meteorology, and a theory of heat. In addition, he invented bifocal vision lenses and even a harmonica.

The child of humble origins and with only two years of formal schooling, Franklin achieved much of success. He was awarded multiple honorary degrees from institutions of higher learning. He took great pride in these awards, which included Masters of Arts from Harvard (1753), Yale (1753), and The College of William and Mary (1756), and doctorates from St. Andrews (1759) and Oxford (1762). As a result of his scientific labors, he was elected to the Royal Society in 1756.

Franklin became involved in civic affairs in 1727. He formed a club of tradesmen called ''Junto'' to work on civic improvements. Under Franklin's leadership, Junto sponsored a library, a fire company, an insurance company, a hospital, and a college to help bring about improvements within the community. In addition, the streets were paved, cleaned, and lighted because of Franklin's efforts.

Deborah Read became Ben Franklin's common-law wife on September 1, 1730. In a practical manner typical of Franklin, he refused to formally marry her in order to avoid responsibility for Read's debts from her first marriage. Franklin and Read had two children together: Francis Folger, who died of smallpox in 1736 at age four, and Sarah, born in 1743. Read and Franklin also raised an illegitimate son, William, fathered by Franklin around 1729 or 1730.

Franklin's business interests were so successful that he was able to sell them at age 42 and live comfortably on the proceeds for the next twenty years. From this retirement Franklin pursued civic and governmental affairs for the remainder of his life. He represented Pennsylvania interests in the English parliament and served as the colonial agent for Georgia, New Jersey, and Massachusetts. After serving in the Second Continental Congress and assisting in the drafting of the *Declaration of Independence*, Franklin was sent to Paris to negotiate a treaty of alliance with France at the start of the American Revolution (1775–1783). He served as a liaison in France for nine years before returning to Philadelphia, where he assisted in the drafting of the *U.S. Constitution* in 1787.

Benjamin Franklin spent his final days living with his daughter and her family on Market Street in Philadelphia. He died on April 17, 1790. Twenty thousand people honored him in attendance at his funeral.

See also: **American Revolution, Continental Congress (Second)**

FURTHER READING

Becker, Carl L. *Benjamin Franklin*. Ithaca, NY: Cornell University Press, 1946.

Commire, Anne, ed. *Historic World Leaders*. Detroit: Gale Research Inc., 1994, s.v. ''Franklin, Benjamin.''

Garraty, John A., and Jerome L Sternstein. *Encyclopedia of American Biography*. New York: HarperCollins, 1996, s.v. ''Franklin, Benjamin.''

Hutson, James H. *The World Book Multimedia Encyclopedia*. Chicago: World Book, Inc., 1998, s.v. ''Franklin, Benjamin.''

Van Doren, Carl. *Benjamin Franklin*. New York: Viking, 1938.

FREE ENTERPRISE

Free enterprise refers to an economy that allows private businesses the freedom to organize and operate competitively for a profit without government interference, regulation, or subsidy. The main characteristics of a free enterprise economy are market competition, generation of profit, and the law of supply and demand. Competition forces businesses to manufacture goods with available raw materials and means of production at the lowest cost possible. In order to generate a profit, businesses must then be able to sell their products at a price higher than the cost of production. Pricing of goods in a free enterprise economy is based on both the supply of goods available in the marketplace and the demand for those goods from consumers. If the supply is greater than the demand, the resulting surplus causes prices to decrease. If the demand is greater than the supply, the resulting shortage causes prices to increase. Eventually, an equilibrium price is reached when supply meets demand.

See also: **Capitalism, Supply and Demand**

FREE SILVER

A U.S. political movement of the late 1800s, "Free Silver" advocates argued for unlimited government coinage of silver. Like members of the Greenback Party, Free Silver supporters included many farmers who, in the 1870s, found themselves in debt from the effects of a drop in farm prices and an increase in costs. The agrarians were joined in their fight by silver mining interests in the West and members of the People's (Populist) and Democratic parties. "Silverites" believed the government purchase and coinage of silver would have an inflationary effect which would raise prices and put more money in circulation thereby allowing debts to be paid. In 1878 Congress passed a compromise to appease the Free Silver alliance: The Bland-Allison Act required the U.S. Treasury to buy silver bullion and coin in the amount of two to four-million dollars worth each month. Nonetheless the Free Silver forces continued lobbying for an unlimited coinage of silver.

Though they were opposed by gold-standard interests, mostly creditors who were opposed to any silver coinage, silver supporters got another boost. In 1890 Congress passed the Sherman Silver Purchase Act which doubled government purchase of silver to increase the money in circulation. The legislation backfired: The resumption of silver as a monetary standard increased the overproduction in western silver mines; thus, prices collapsed. Americans responded by trading their silver for gold dollars thereby draining federal reserves. In 1893 the Sherman Silver Purchase Act was repealed and the United States returned to the gold standard. The presidential election of 1896, which pitted Republican candidate William McKinley (1897–1901) against Democrat William Jennings Bryan (1860–1925) was dominated by the debate over Free Silver. The silverite candidate, Bryan, lost. An increase in the world supply of gold and a return to prosperity made the silver issue moot for the next three decades: Gold remained the monetary standard until 1933.

See also: **Bland-Allison Act, Gold Standard, Gold Standard Act, Greenback Party, Sherman Silver Purchase Act**

FREE TRADE *(ISSUE)*

Free trade was arguably one of the founding principles of the United States. The colonies grew up under the Mercantilist system of international commercial competition between the great trading nations of the time: the Dutch, the French, and the English. (By the eighteenth century Spain was already in decline as a trading nation.) The role of the colonies in a Mercantilist economy was to provide staple goods—agricultural commodities or raw materials like cotton—for the mother country; a market for finished goods produced by the mother country; and a tax base to help pay for the administrative and military costs of imperialism. Mercantilism, as practiced by the main commercial nations of Europe, required government granting of monopolies, government checking for "quality control" in the colonies' commercial products, government stipulation of trade routes, and government imposition of tariffs (import taxes).

Mercantilism was the opposite of the free trade system advocated by economist Adam Smith in the late eighteenth century. Adam Smith, in his brilliant summary of the free trade system, *The Wealth of Nations* (1776), argued that the government only got in the way of wealth creation under a capitalist economy. Much of what Smith said was true, but the inertia of government policy steered the colonial policy of the British Parliament in the direction of greater government intervention and regulation of the economy. The Navigation Acts of the late seventeenth century had already required the American merchant marine to channel its trade with Europe through English ports, where the goods were taxed.

After the exhausting Seven Years War (1754–1763), the Board of Trade in victorious England attempted to spread the costs the conflict among the colonies by taxing everything from sugar to stamps. It was this internal system of taxation that rankled the American commercial and consuming classes and moved the country in the direction of Revolution. But after the colonists won the revolution one of the first pieces of legislation to be passed by the first Congress in 1789 was a tariff act whose purpose was to raise revenue.

The debate between free trade or protectionism became one of the most contentious and long-standing issues in the politics in the new republic. It was central to the argument between the Federalists and the Republicans over economic policy. Alexander Hamilton (1755–1804) held an American mercantilist position—promoting, in his *Report on Manufactures* (1791), a policy of protective tariffs and federal subsidies to foster a domestic manufacturing base for the U.S. economy. James Madison (1751–1836) and Thomas Jefferson (1743–1826), who represented the dominant agricultural side of the economy, attacked Hamilton's farsighted reforms, arguing that any measure which increased the power of the central government would not be in the national interest.

Over the next century the leaders in the U.S. government espoused global free trade in principle, but in practice they raised trade barriers to protect import-sensitive sectors of the economy. Tariffs became an integral part of the conflict between the North and South that led to the American Civil War (1861–1865). In 1828 the Tariff of Abominations placed tariffs on almost every imaginable manufactured good. Southern politicians feared and resented the tariffs because they raised prices for goods that the South needed, and displayed the growing political power of the North—a development the South feared because it seemed to indicate a more powerful might impose further restrictions on slavery.

As the U.S. economy became more productive it encountered the problem of over-production. This meant that the domestic market could not absorb the goods that industry and agriculture were producing. The obvious solution was to encourage trade with the markets of other countries. But this could not be accomplished if the United States was maintaining high tariffs keeping other countries from penetrating the its market. Potential trading partners would simply raise their own tariff walls and foreign trade would wither. This became clear in 1930, early in the Great Depression (1929–1939). The agricultural sector of the U.S. economy had been in a depression for the better part of a decade when President Herbert Hoover (1929–1933) attempted to protect U.S. farmers from international competition through the Smoot-Hawley Tariff. Passed in 1930, the Smoot-Hawley Tariff raised the protective barrier to an average of 53 percent of the commodity price—an unheard of level. Hoover had hoped the bill would convince the commodity exchanges to buy domestic agricultural products. Instead, foreign governments retaliated with higher tariffs and quotas of their own. Foreign governments saw Smoot-Hawley as a hostile act, yet another symbol of U.S. isolationism. It provoked a global trade war, which led to a fall in the volume of international trade and resulted in national economies plummeting into a worldwide depression. Scholars estimate that, largely as a result of Smoot-Hawley, the value of world trade in 1933 was one-third what it was in 1929. This demonstrated the perils of protectionism and the virtue of free trade.

Hoover's successor to the presidency, Franklin D. Roosevelt (1933–1945), marked a turning point in U.S. trade policy. With the encouragement of the Secretary of State, Cordell Hull, Roosevelt pushed the Reciprocal Trade Agreements Act of 1934. For the first time in history the executive branch was given authority to reduce tariffs up to fifty percent if the other country reciprocated. Also for the first time, as a step in the direction of expanding global production and employment, the government engaged in continual bilateral negotiations to reduce trade barriers. U.S. trade negotiators signed about twenty-five bilateral trade agreements by the early 1940s. Despite the disruption of trade relations by World War II (1939–1945) the Roosevelt administration had begun the process of trade liberalization that continued with the United States serving as the dominant postwar global economic power.

> **[T]HE U.S. GOVERNMENT ESPOUSED GLOBAL FREE TRADE IN PRINCIPLE, BUT IN PRACTICE THEY RAISED TRADE BARRIERS TO PROTECT IMPORT-SENSITIVE SECTORS OF THE ECONOMY**

By 1950 the United States had implemented a trade policy which favored Western Europe and Japan, with massive financial assistance to rebuild their war-torn economies. In the hope of integrating industrialized democracies into a stable and peaceful international economic order the United States gave Western Europe and Japan permission to protect their rebuilt industries with high tariffs against U.S. goods. The United States supported regional economic cooperation among Western European countries even though they maintained protective tariffs against U.S. exports. This free trade umbrella evolved into the European Economic Community and, eventually, in the 1990s, into the European Union. Meanwhile, successive U.S. administrations used trade policy as a foreign policy tool to contain the expansion of communism. Communist countries were excluded from the "free world's" trading system.

In the 1960s the John F. Kennedy (1961–1963) administration developed a plan to create a more integrated Atlantic Community. Using the concept of "trade or fade," the Kennedy administration pushed for the passage of the Trade Expansion Act of 1962, which authorized reciprocal across-the-board tariff cuts of up to fifty percent. It also authorized negotiations of total tariff elimination on a reciprocal basis when the United States and European Economic Community (EEC) made up at least eighty percent of world trade for a product. As a result, the Europeans and the United States signed an agreement that was the largest round of tariff cuts in history, about thirty-five percent globally.

The 1970s brought a new phase of international economic relations, with U.S. competitiveness decreasing despite the nation's continued political and military world hegemony. Observers expressed doubts about the soundness of a liberal trade policy as the nation's trade surplus continued to diminish. In 1971 the most powerful labor organizations in the United States, the American Federation of Labor-Congress of Industrial Organization (AFL-CIO), adopted a protectionist stance. The labor movement was losing members in droves as early as the 1960s due to de-industrialization, which business analysts attributed to the unwillingness of government policymakers to protect American industry from rising imports and increased overseas investments by U.S. corporations.

The pendulum swung back towards protectionism under President Richard M. Nixon (1969–1974). The Nixon administration brought protectionism back in full swing with the announcement of the New Economic Policy in 1971, which imposed a ten percent surcharge on all import duties and terminated the U.S. obligation to convert dollars held by foreign banks into gold at a fixed price. But the free-trade forces in Congress passed the Trade Act of 1974, which authorized the president to reduce tariffs.

The Trade Act of 1974 had two important and seemingly contradictory legacies. One was the completion of a Tokyo round of multilateral trade negotiations. Marking the decline of unilateral U.S. economic dominance, the industrialized nations indicated their intention to help the economies of less developed countries by authorizing "more favorable treatment" to these economies. Among other things, this meant facilitating increased investment in low wage economies.

Second, the Trade Act of 1974 gave more protection to U.S. interests desiring import relief, mostly from Japan and the newly industrializing nations of Korea, Singapore, Taiwan, and Hong Kong. The United States and the EEC practiced "the new protectionism," reaching a compromise between the protectionism of the 1930s and the internationalist trade liberalization of the 1960s.

During the 1980s Reaganomics had a substantive impact on U.S. trade policy. The Ronald Reagan (1981–1989) administration reduced taxes, brought about a rising budget deficit, and allowed the largest trade deficit in the nation's history. With the continued appreciation of the U.S. dollar many sectors of U.S. industry and agriculture were unable to compete in the international market.

In response, the Reagan administration attempted to increase exports rather than reduce imports. The United States introduced the policy of "reciprocity," a rejection of the U.S. postwar policy of ignoring what the administration considered other countries' unfair trade barriers. Reagan announced in 1985 that he would not "stand by and watch U.S. businesses fail because of unfair trading practices abroad." When other nations were unwilling to "voluntarily" reduce their trade barriers the United States threatened retaliation as it did with Japan and China in 1995.

In the 1990s the successive George Bush (1989–1993) and William Clinton (1993—) administrations concluded negotiations for the North American Free Trade Agreement, an historic accord establishing a free trade block between the United States, Canada, and Mexico. Even though the United States carved out a free trade system on the North American continent, it applied selective import restrictions for the rest of the world. While proclaiming its adherence to free trade policies the United States more often than not instituted protections against selected imports that undermined domestic industrial development. Thus, the United States has continually maintained a complicated and contradictory relationship between protectionism and free trade internationalism throughout its history.

See also: **De-industrialization, Foreign Investment in the United States, Foreign Investment of U.S. Companies Abroad, Mercantilism, Protectionism, Report on Manufactures, Smoot-Hawley Tariff, Tariff**

FURTHER READING

Bairoch, Paul. *Economics and World History: Myths and Paradoxes.* Chicago: University of Chicago Press, 1993.

Blecker, Robert A., ed. *U.S. Trade Policy and Global Growth: New Directions in the International Economy.* Armonk, New York: M. E. Sharpe, 1996.

Cohen, Stephen D., Joel R. Paul, and Robert A. Blecker. *Fundamentals of U.S. Foreign Trade Policy: Economics, Politics, Laws, and Issues.* Boulder, CO: Westview Press, 1996.

Dudley, William. *Trade: Opposing Viewpoints.* San Diego, CA: Greenhaven Press, Inc., 1991.

Miller, Henri, ed. *Free Trade Versus Protectionism.* New York: The H.W. Wilson Company, 1996.

Depicted in this drawing is Gen. Oliver O. Howard, the first commissioner of the Freedman's Bureau. He is shown protecting the gap between angry southern white men and the newly freed black men.

FREEDMEN'S BUREAU

After the end of the American Civil War (1861–1865) in April 1865, the newly reunited United States faced a humanitarian disaster on a scale not before seen. In the battle-torn South, cities, plantations, and crops had been burned, railroads were destroyed, and hundreds of thousands of whites and newly freed blacks suffered from disease and hunger. Also, most of the four million newly freed slaves were illiterate and largely incapable of succeeding in the postwar economy. In response to the suffering and the need to reintegrate the rebel states back into the Union, the U.S. government introduced an unprecedented bureaucracy of relief effort. The most important arm of this bureaucracy was the Freedmen's Bureau.

The Freedmen's Bureau was established by Congress as the Bureau of Refugees, Freedmen, and Abandoned Lands on March 3, 1865, to aid and protect former slaves after the end of the war. Its original charter was for one year. On July 16, 1866, the Bureau was reorganized under the U.S. War Department, which gave it the backing of military force. The 200,000 federal troops occupying the southern states helped

establish military law and order. As a result of its military ties, the Freedmen's Bureau became one of the most powerful tools wielded by the federal government during Reconstruction (1865–1877).

The first commissioner of the Freedmen's Bureau was General Oliver O. Howard, who had the power to organize the former slave regions into a structure that the Bureau could oversee. Howard created ten districts out of the slave-holding states, including those slave-holding states that had remained in the Union during the war. The work of the Freedmen's Bureau was concentrated to five areas: relief work for all citizens in war-torn areas; regulation of black labor; management of abandoned and confiscated property; administration of justice for blacks; and the education of former slaves. The Bureau compiled an impressive record in the first and last of these areas, but it had little success in setting up former slaves as landowners. During the summer of 1865 alone, the Freedmen's Bureau distributed 150,000 food rations daily—50,000 of those to white refugees. During the life of the Bureau, more than 22 million rations were given out.

The lack of success in setting up former slaves as landowners came as a result of President Andrew

Johnson's (1865–1869) May 29, 1865 Proclamation of Pardon and Amnesty to all southern citizens who would take an oath of allegiance. It applied to everyone except military officers and government officials. The amnesty restored property rights, excluding slaves, to all those owning property worth less than $20,000 and, thus, reduced the land pool preserved for distribution to freed slaves. General Howard at first refused to give back property to whites, but on August 16, 1865, President Johnson ordered him specifically to do so. Regardless of the Radical Republicans' intentions, which were to transfer massive amounts of land from former slave owners to freedmen, their efforts were largely a failure.

Finally, the Bureau operated as a patronage machine for the Republican Party. They traded favors to freedmen in the South in exchange for votes. This, along with the fact that the Bureau was instrumental in helping former slaves get elected to political office, helped to create political hatreds that lasted well into the twentieth century. The Freedmen's Bureau was also the focus of political troubles in places outside the South. Congress passed a bill in 1866 to increase the powers of the Bureau and extend its life indefinitely. President Johnson vetoed the bill on February 19, 1866, on the grounds that it was an unconstitutional continuation of the war and that it was too soon to extend the full rights of citizenship to blacks. The veto escalated Johnson's long and ultimately futile battle with the Republican Congress over Reconstruction policy. Congress passed another bill extending the Freedmen's Bureau for three years, overriding Johnson's veto on July 16, 1866. The majority of the work of the Freedmen's Bureau was discontinued on July 1, 1869, though the educational activities continued until 1872, when Ulysses S. Grant (1869–1877) was elected president.

See also: **Civil War (Economic Impact of), Reconstruction, Slavery**

FURTHER READING

Foner, Eric. *America's Reconstruction: People and Politics After the Civil War*. New York: HarperCollins, 1995.

Genovese, Eugene. *Roll, Jordan, Roll: The World the Slaves Made*. New York: Pantheon, 1974.

McPherson, James M. *Ordeal by Fire: The Civil War and Reconstruction*. New York: Knopf, 1982.

FRÉMONT, JOHN CHARLES

John Charles Frémont (1895–1983) not only explored the American West, he played an important role in popularizing it. The tales of his exploits made the very idea of settling the West an exciting and popular idea, and those tales made him a national hero. Frémont made scientific contributions that were recognized nationally and internationally, and won him gold medals from the Royal Geographical Society of London and the Prussian government.

Frémont was born in Savannah, Georgia, on January 21, 1813. He was the illegitimate son of Charles Fremon, a Frenchman, and Anne Beverley Whiting Pryor, who had left her elderly husband to run away with Fremon. The union of Fremon and Pryor produced another son and daughter, and the family was a scandal in Richmond, Virginia. The Fremons were poor and moved frequently. When Charles Fremon died in 1818, Pryor took the family to Charleston, South Carolina. No one knows when John Frémont added the acute accent to the ''e'' and the ''t'' to his name.

The lawyer for whom Frémont had been a clerk sent him to private school at age fourteen. Afterwards, Frémont enrolled in the Scientific Department at the College of Charleston, but in 1831 was dismissed for ''habitual irregularity and incorrigible negligence,'' just three months from graduating. Five years later, Frémont petitioned the college for his degree, and it was granted. The family was still poor, however, and despite frequent moving and determined efforts, John Frémont was unable to break out of poverty until he got his first big break. Joel Poinsett, an influential South Carolina politician, helped Fremont obtain an appointment as a teacher of mathematics to the midshipmen on the *U.S.S. Natchez.* Poinsett then helped Frémont gain employment, surveying land for the Charleston, Louisville, and Cincinnati Railroad, and for the Cherokee Indian lands in Georgia, Tennessee, and North Carolina. The survey work concerned mountainous country and forests, and Frémont was to later write he had ''found the path which I was 'destined to walk.'''

Again due to the influence of Poinsett, Frémont was commissioned a second lieutenant in the U.S. Corps of Topographical Engineers in 1838. His first assignment was to accompany French scientist Joseph Nicolas Nicollet on a reconnaissance of the region between the upper Mississippi and Missouri rivers. Frémont learned sophisticated methods of geodetic surveying, the use of the barometer in measuring altitude, and how to take astronomical observations from the French scientist. He also learned how to manage an expedition and to construct a map.

Back in Washington, D.C., Frémont met Jessie Benton and the two eloped on October 19, 1841. Jessie was the daughter of Senator Thomas Hart Benton of Missouri, and only 17 years of age when the couple eloped. Senator Benton's support was important to Frémont's career, and his wife became his collaborator in chronicling his journeys. Frémont took command of an expedition to survey the Platte River in 1842. In 1843, he again led a survey mission into the West, linking up with the Pacific Coast survey headed by Charles Wilkes (1798–1877). Christopher (Kit) Carson was Frémont's guide for these trips, and he was accompanied by German cartographer Charles Preuss.

Reunited with his wife in St. Louis, the couple wrote captivating accounts of his adventures—accounts that had much to do with glamorizing the exploration of the West and encouraging settlement of the area. Frémont laced his accounts with an enthusiasm for nature, as well as the pure adventure of shooting river rapids, traversing the Great Salt Lake in a rubber boat, and fighting snow to cross the Sierra Nevada mountains in mid-January. His stories were detailed and fun, but they also provided very useful information concerning terrain, campsites, water, vegetation, wildlife, and weather. Countless settlers used this information after Congress ordered Frémont's maps and reports published. As a result, Frémont became a national hero.

While on his third expedition to the West and California, Frémont was commissioned a lieutenant colonel in the Mounted Rifles. During that third expedition, American settlers in California mounted the Bear Flag Rebellion against Mexico, and Frémont became involved with a battalion of volunteers. Frémont and his California Battalion served under Robert F. Stockton during the Mexican War (1848), and Stockton rewarded Frémont with the governorship of California. Caught in a power struggle between Stockton and Brigadier General Stephen Watts Kearny, however, Frémont came out on the wrong side and was court-martialed and convicted on charges of mutiny, disobedience, and conduct prejudiced to military discipline. President James K. Polk (1845–1849) remitted the penalty and ordered Frémont to duty, but unable to deal with the original decision, Frémont resigned from the army.

Frémont's major life accomplishments occurred prior to the age of forty, with his explorations and writings on the West. He mined gold on his 44,000–acre estate in California. Though he reportedly made millions, he lost control of the property in 1864, along with his money. In the interim, he did serve a brief term in the United State Senate, representing California from 1853 to 1854. In 1856, he was the first nominee of the Republican Party for president and did nearly well enough to win the election. During the American Civil War (1861–1865), he served a brief term as a major general in command of the Western Department, headquartered in St. Louis. President Abraham Lincoln (1861–1865) fired him for a declaration Frémont made on August 31, 1861, freeing the slaves of Missouri rebels. Frémont also served as commander of the Mountain Division at Wheeling, West Virginia, during the Civil War, but Frémont again chose wrongly in his political affiliations and resigned.

After the war, Frémont bought a home on the Hudson River and became involved in railroad promotion. He lost everything in a failed attempt to finance and build a railroad from Norfolk, Virginia, to San Diego, California. In 1878, friend and President Rutherford B. Hayes (1877–1881) appointed him territorial governor of Arizona. Extended absences from the territory, along with conflicts of interest, prompted President Chester A. Arthur (1881–1885) to ask for his resignation, which Frémont submitted on October 11, 1881. Frémont wrote an autobiographical account, *Memoirs*, but the book did not address the more recent events in his life, and did not sell well.

In 1887, John and Jessie Frémont moved to Los Angeles, hoping to profit from a real estate boom. Their spinster daughter, Elizabeth, accompanied them, while sons John Charles, Jr., and Frank Preston, served in the Navy and the Army respectively. Frémont died July 13, 1890, in a New York boarding house while on a business trip. He and his wife are buried in a Rockland Cemetery overlooking the Hudson River.

See also: **Westward Expansion**

FURTHER READING

Encyclopedia of World Biography. Detroit: Gale Research, Inc. 1998, s.v. ''Frémont, John.''

Goetzmann, William H. *The World Book Multimedia Encyclopedia*. Chicago: World Book, Inc. 1998, s.v. ''Frémont, John.''

Jackson, Donald, and Spence, Mary Lee. *The Expeditions of John Charles Frémont*. Urbana: University of Illinois Press, 1970–84.

Nevins, Allan. *Frémont: Pathmarker of the West*. Lincoln: University of Nebraska Press, 1992.

Spence, Mary Lee, and Anne Commire, editors. *Historic World Leaders*. Detroit: Gale Research, Inc., 1994, s.v. ''Frémont, John.''

FRENCH AND INDIAN WAR (1754–1763)

The French and Indian War (1754–1763) was the last of a series of great colonial wars that stretched for almost a hundred years and disrupted settlements throughout North America. It marked the end of the French empire in North America and the beginning of English domination of the continent. It also emphasized the differences between Englishmen and colonists and laid the groundwork for the drive toward independence, culminating in the American Revolution (1775–1783).

The events that sparked the French and Indian War had their origin in the trade with Native Americans. The French had claimed the territory surrounding the Great Lakes and had established Christian missions and trading posts throughout the area. They hoped to profit from the trade in furs that they maintained with the Indians. By the 1740s, British traders were entering the nearby same area of what became the state of Ohio, crossing over the Appalachian and Allegheny mountains and competing with the French. Because British trade goods were cheaper and better made than those the French offered, many Native Americans—including the Wyandot chief Memeskia, the Shawnee, and the Delaware, chose to break with the French and establish links with the English instead. The Six Nations, also known as the Iroquois League, retained their alliance with the English, which was formed almost a century earlier. The French responded by beginning the construction of a network of forts stretching from Lake Erie to the Ohio River. They also warned the Native Americans that the English were more interested in their lands than they were in the items the Indians had to trade.

The French were telling the truth about the British desire for land. In 1749, King George II authorized the charter of the Ohio Company, a coalition of British and Virginian traders and speculators, and gave the new company title to enormous territories in the Ohio valley. King George required the company to establish a settlement in the area and to build a fort for its protection within seven years. From 1750 to 1752, Ohio Company agent Christopher Gist traveled the area, looking for suitable areas to place such a settlement. Between May and July 1752, Gist concluded the Logstown Treaty at Ambridge, Pennsylvania, between the colony of Virginia and the Six Nations of the Iroquois, Wyandot, Delaware, and Shawnee, which opened the Ohio country to English trade and settlement.

The negotiations at Logtown were disrupted by news that a coalition of French-allied tribes, led by a French Indian agent named Charles Langlade, had attacked the town of Pickawillany (modern Piqua, Ohio), which was the major center of English trade in Ohio. Memeskia, a long-time British friend and collaborator, was killed by Langlade and ritually eaten. As a result of the news the Seneca asked the Virginians to build a fort at the junction of the Monongahela and Allegheny rivers—known as the Forks of the Ohio—to protect them from the French and their Indian allies and to give them access to English goods.

Partly because of this request and partly because of the forts the French were building in the area and political pressure in the British Cabinet, in 1753 Virginia governor Robert Dinwiddie sent George Washington (1732–1799)—the brother of an Ohio Company investor, who had trained as a surveyor—on a mission to the French at Fort LeBoeuf (modern Waterford, Pennsylvania). Washington demanded the French evacuate the fort, which (the English claimed) was built on Virginian territory. The French commander, Captain Legardeur de Saint-Pierre, refused and Washington, unable to force his compliance, returned to Dinwiddie. The governor then commanded Captain William Trent to begin work on the fort requested by the Seneca. On April 17, 1754, a French force of 600 captured the fort and its 41-man English garrison. On May 28 Washington, who had been sent by Dinwiddie with 150 reinforcements for the fort, surprised a French reconnaissance party and killed several of its members, including Ensign Joseph Coulon de Villiers de Jumonville, an officer the French regarded as an ambassador.

Washington's fight marked the opening of the French and Indian War, even though it would be another two years before the English and the French governments formally declared war in 1756. In the meantime, the brother of Ensign Coulon de Villiers forced the surrender of Washington's party and the makeshift fort Washington built at Great Meadows. Washington's defeat and the fall of the fort effectively ejected the English from the Ohio country. It also helped alienate many Native Americans who had been English allies. Most of the Ohio Indians, won over by military successes, returned to their traditional relationships with the French.

By the time the Albany Congress was convened in mid-summer of 1754, the Iroquois were the only Native American allies left to the English. Although the

British General James Wolfe was killed during a victorious battle with the French at Quebec in 1759. This event led to the end of the French and Indian War.

Congress was intended to promote unity among colonies and to conclude a treaty with the Iroquois, it had almost the opposite effect. Although a treaty was signed, Conrad Weiser of Pennsylvania and Joseph Lydius of Connecticut bribed and cheated Iroquois chiefs into ceding thousands of square miles of land in western Pennsylvania and southern New York. The Oneida sachem Concochquiesie complained to Indian agent William Johnson that Lydius "is a Devil and has stole [sic] our Lands. He takes Indians slyly by the Blanket one at a time, and when they are drunk, puts some money in their bosoms, and perswades [sic] them to sign deeds for our lands." The Iroquois Confederacy declared itself officially neutral in the war, but many of their tributary tribes allied themselves with the French.

English policies in the early years of the war met with resistance from white settlers as well. Merchants in the north, especially in New York, had created a close (and illegal) trade with Canada based on smuggling. These businessmen took exception to the difficulties the war created and opposed British efforts to deal with the risks the French posed. Colonists who served in the armed forces resented the strict discipline, harsh punishments, and contempt in which British officers held them, despite the fact that provincial forces and their Indian allies won British victories while regular commanders were defeated. Major General Edward Braddock, for instance, lost the Battle of

the Wilderness (July 9, 1755) and drove the Delaware into a French alliance in part due to his refusal to pay attention to his colonial advisors. Provincial forces also played important roles at the Battle of Lake George (September 7–8, 1755), and the relief of Fort Oswego (July 3, 1756).

The fortunes of the English began to shift with a change in government. When William Pitt became Prime Minister of Great Britain in December of 1756, he promised a much more aggressive promotion of the war. Despite the victories of the talented French commander the Marquis de Montcalm, most notably at Fort William Henry (August 1757), Pitt increased financial and military support for the British forces in the colonies. By the summer of 1757 Pitt's efforts had begun to be felt, and in October, 1758, a new Indian treaty signed at Easton, Pennsylvania, brought many French Indian allies into the British camp. In September, 1759, the town of Quebec fell to an assault by General James Wolfe, and in 1760 Montreal fell. The war in the American colonies was essentially over.

The aftermath of the French and Indian War had a great economic effect on the colonies. With battlefields spreading over much of the Pennsylvania, New York and New England frontier districts, the war left colonial economies in ruins. Many backwoods families had been forced to abandon their homes and, according to the terms negotiated between the British and the Indians, they would never be allowed to return west of the Appalachians. Although England had won great territories by forcing the French out of Canada, they had also created a huge national debt in fighting the war. The means of financing and repaying this debt—and for paying the salaries of the thousands of soldiers needed to keep peace between frontiersmen and Indians on the Appalachian borders as well as in Canada—brought Great Britain and her American colonies to the brink of war a little more than a decade later.

See also: **George Washington**

FURTHER READING

Jennings, Francis. *Empire of Fortune: Crown, Colonies, and Tribes in the Seven Years' War.* New York: W. W. Norton, 1988.

Middleton, Richard. *The Bells of Victory: The Pitt-Newcastle Ministry and the Conduct of the Seven Years' War.* New York: Cambridge University Press, 1985.

Newbold, Robert C. *The Albany Congress and Plan of Union of 1754.* New York: Vantage Press, 1955.

Schwartz, Seymour I. *The French and Indian War, 1754-1763: The Imperial Struggle for North America.* New York: Simon & Schuster, 1994.

Walton, Gary M., and James F. Shepherd. *The Economic Rise of Early America.* New York: Cambridge University Press, 1979.

FRIEDMAN, MILTON

Born July 31, 1912, in Brooklyn, New York, Milton Friedman (1912–) was raised in Brooklyn and Rahway, New Jersey. He was educated at Rutgers University, where he received his Bachelor's in Economics in 1932. In 1933, he received a Masters of Arts from the University of Chicago, where he worked as a research assistant for two years. Friedman then took a series of positions in government service which shaped his economic theories.

Friedman worked from 1935 to 1943 as an economist for the National Resources Committee, the National Bureau of Economic Research, and the Department of the Treasury. For the 1940–1941 school year, he took a break from his government jobs in Washington, D.C., to serve as visiting professor of economics at the University of Wisconsin. In 1943 he resumed his work on a doctorate degree at Columbia University, where he received his degree in 1946. He spent one year on the faculty of the University of Minnesota before joining the University of Chicago as associate professor of economics. Friedman became a full professor at the school in 1948.

Milton Friedman began writing shortly after completing his first two degrees, publishing many articles and books. Through his writing, Friedman became an advocate of the monetarist school of economics. In this economic theory, the business cycle is influenced more by the supply of money and interest rates than the fiscal policy of the government. As such, Friedman was opposed to the prevailing thoughts of his day, which were guided by the theories of John Maynard Keynes (1883–1946), the British economist who championed the role of government expenditures and taxes in influencing economic cycles.

Friedman married Rose D. Friedman, also an economist, who collaborated on some of his works. He was on the editorial boards of the *American Economic Review* from 1951 to 1953 and the *Econometrica* from 1957 to 1968. He was named the Paul Snowden Russell Distinguished Service Professor at the University of Chicago in 1962. In 1967 he began a ten year run as a regular columnist in *Newsweek* magazine. In 1976 Friedman was awarded the Nobel Prize for Economics.

Senator Barry Goldwater (1909—) used Friedman as an economic policy advisor in his unsuccessful 1964 presidential campaign. President Richard Nixon (1969–1974) sought Friedman's advice frequently. But perhaps Friedman's greatest influence with presidential politics occurred during the administration of President Ronald Reagan (1981–1989), when monetary policy and ''supply side'' economics gained influence with Washington policymakers. Friedman retired from his position at the University of Chicago in 1979 to become a senior research fellow at a conservative think tank, the Hoover Institution, at Stanford, California.

Friedman's published works include *Capitalism and Freedom*, written in 1962 with his wife. This book advocates a ''negative'' income tax or guaranteed income to replace welfare, which Friedman accused of destroying traditional values of individualism and work. In addition, Friedman published *A Monetary History of the United States, 1867–1960* (1963), and *Monetary Trends of the United States and the United Kingdom* (1981). Other works include *The Great Contraction*, with A. J. Schwartz (1965), *The Balance of Payments* with R. V. Roosa (1967), *Dollars and Deficits* (1968), *The Optimum Quantity of Money and Other Essays* (1969), *Bright Promises, Dismal Performance: An Economist's Protest* (1983), and *Money Mischief: Episodes in Monetary History* in (1992).

See also: **Keynesian Economic Theory, Monetary Theory**

FURTHER READING

Frazer, William. *The Friedman System.* New York: Praeger, 1997.

Friedman, Milton. *Bright Promises, Dismal Performance: An Economist's Protest.* New York: Harcourt Brace Jovanovich, 1983.

————. *Money Mischief: Episodes in Monetary History.* New York: Harcourt Brace Jovanovich, 1992.

Garraty, John A. and Jerome L. Sternstein, eds. *Encyclopedia of American Biography.* New York: Harper Collins, 1995, s.v. "Friedman, Milton."

Van Doren, Charles, ed. *Webster's American Biographies.* Springfield: Merriam-Webster Inc., 1984, s.v. "Friedman, Milton."

FRINGE BENEFIT

Next to wages, fringe benefits are the most important method businesses use to entice workers to accept or stay in jobs. Fringe benefits, also known as "employee benefits," can be provided voluntarily by employers, required by law, or won through collective bargaining negotiations between companies and employees. Fringe benefits can be generally divided into those offered individually, such as 401(k) retirement plans, and those offered to employees as a group, such as daycare facilities or free lunch. Most employee benefit plans traditionally offered three basic benefits: health insurance, a retirement plan or pension, and additional benefits, such as stock option plans or life insurance. A crucial advantage of fringe benefits to businesses was that the Internal Revenue Service (IRS) allowed firms to deduct benefits as an employee compensation expense from the taxes they owe. Similarly while employees had to pay taxes on any increases in their salaries, their benefits were not taxed.

In the late 1990s, medical benefits and flex-time—allowing workers to choose their daily work schedules—were the two most important fringe benefits for U.S. job seekers. Medical benefits comprised the single most costly benefit for employers. A special class of fringe benefits were "perks" (short for *perquisites*), which were usually offered only to senior-level employees. Perks included mobile car phones, executive parking, company cars, and even chauffeured limousines or a company jet.

In the United States, fringe benefits became much more common after collective bargaining became common in the 1930s and 1940s, giving workers the power to persuade businesses to improve working conditions. During World War II (1939–1945), government-mandated wage and price controls prevented companies from giving raises, so they relied on fringe benefits to recruit and reward employees. Fringe benefits accounted for 17 percent of the total compensation of blue-collar workers by 1951, and 30 percent by 1981. In the 1980s employee benefit reforms introduced by President Ronald Reagan (1981–1989) had the unintended effect of complicating the national fringe benefits system, and in the 1990s innovations like customizable "cafeteria" health, insurance, vacation plans, and SIMPLE (Savings Incentive Match Plan for Employees) benefits simplified benefits choices. During the tight job market of the 1990s, employers began offering a more creative mix of fringe benefits, including club memberships, legal services, home offices, and errand services. Among the most sought-after benefits were stock options, or shares in an employer's stock. During the stock market boom of the 1990s some fast-growing companies boasted that their stock options had turned secretaries and other non-management workers into millionaires.

FUGITIVE SLAVE ACT OF 1850

The roots of the American Civil War (1861–1865) were complex, but the conflict-ridden issue of slavery is rightly given prominence by most scholars. At its base, the Civil War pitted fundamentally different regional and socio-economic forces against each other. Although agriculture had dominated the economy of the early American republic, its importance varied by region. Farming defined the economy of the South, which evolved into an agricultural aristocracy based on slavery. The states of New England, however, were shaped by very different natural forces. Deprived of fertile soil, society in New England developed an energetic mercantile culture in sharp contrast with the lifestyle of the South. The Northern region gave birth to influential merchant and business classes, whose wealth had little or no connection to the land. Although the middle colonies enjoyed a more mixed economy, they were inevitably influenced by the great trading and business centers of New York and Philadelphia.

Understandably, both the Northern and Southern cultures viewed its rival as a significant, if not mortal, threat to its way of life. As the first half of the nineteenth century drew to a close, many Southerners tightly embraced safeguards to their way of life as they felt increasingly threatened by the dynamic and often turbulent urban culture of the North. One such safeguard was the cluster of constitutional and legal provisions that mandated the return of runaway slaves to their legal owners.

As part of the sectional compromise that ensured the ratification of the *Constitution*, Article IV, section 2 of the document directed that ''no person held to service or labor in one state, under the laws thereof, escaping into another, shall, in consequence of any laws or regulation therein, be discharged from such service or labor, but shall be delivered up, on claim of the party to whom such service or labor may be due.'' Congress subsequently enacted the Fugitive Slave Act of 1793 to specify procedures to aid in the recovery of runaway slaves.

Although slaveholders possessed formal legal remedies to recover runaway slaves, these measures, including the Fugitive Slave Act of 1793, were routinely scorned in the North, where anti-slavery sentiment was generally strong. Ironically, Southern slaveholders, who routinely invoked the doctrine of states' rights to help protect the institution of slavery, were often frustrated in the recovery of runaway slaves by personal liberty laws enacted by the legislatures of several northern states. In one variant, personal liberty laws forbade state officials from participation in efforts to return fugitive slaves.

The question of runaway slaves was again placed before Congress in the famous Compromise of 1850. The compromise attempted to solve growing North-South tensions over the extension of slavery, specifically into newly annexed Texas and the territory gained by the United States in the Mexican War (1850–1853). The compromise measures originated largely from Stephen A. Douglas (1813–1861) and were sponsored in the Senate by Henry Clay (1777–1852). The compromise called for the admission of California as a free state, the use of popular sovereignty to decide free or slave status for New Mexico and Utah, the prohibition of the slave trade in the District of Columbia, and the passage of a stricter fugitive slave law. The prospects for the acceptance of these proposals were reinforced by the powerful speeches of statesman Daniel Webster (1782–1852), and the presidency of Millard Fillmore (1850–1853), a supporter of the compromise who stepped into office after the death of President Zachary Taylor (1784–1850). The proposals were passed as separate bills in September 1850.

The Fugitive Slave Law was arguably the most controversial part of the Compromise of 1850. The law carried a number of provisions that strengthened slaveholders in their pursuit of runaways. Federal commissioners were to be appointed with the power to issue warrants and mobilize posses. Suspected runaways were denied due process of law, and could be sent to the South on the basis of an owner's affidavit.

Southern opinion had been inflamed by a long record of Northern obstruction of the recovery of runaways. The so-called Georgia Platform adopted in late 1850 held that the fate of the union itself now depended on the North's faithful observance of the new fugitive slave act. Such cooperation was not forthcoming. Popular opposition to the recovery of slaves received frequent coverage in northern and southern newspapers. At the same time, a number of northern states passed stronger personal liberty laws. In Wisconsin, a reporter was arrested for encouraging a mob to free a captured runaway. The state court released him on a writ of *habeas corpus* (a court order determining an individual was confined illegally) and held the Fugitive Slave Act unconstitutional. Although the Supreme Court upheld the law in *Abelman v. Booth* (1859), the effort provided Southerners little comfort.

The single greatest blow to the Fugitive Slave Act and to the Southern cause came from northern printing presses. The passage of the Fugitive Slave Act prompted Harriet Beecher Stowe (1811–1896) to write her famous novel, *Uncle Tom's Cabin*, published in 1852. The novel was a powerful and convincing indictment against slavery, and over 300,000 copies of the novel were sold in a year, an astronomical amount for that time. Although the injustices of the Fugitive Slave Act and the emotions stirred by Stowe's novel did not likely convince most Americans that the abolition of slavery would justify a civil war or the dissolution of the Union, the outcomes of the Fugitive Slave Act did lead many Americans to reject any future efforts at political compromise over differences between the North and South.

See also: **Civil War (Economic Causes of), Slavery, States' Rights**

FURTHER READING

Berlin, Ira. *Many Thousands Gone: The First Two Centuries of Slavery in North America*. Cambridge: Harvard University Press, 1998.

David, Paul A. et al. *Reckoning With Slavery: A Critical Study in the Quantitative History of American Negro Slavery*. New York: Oxford University Press, 1976.

Elkins, Stanley. *Slavery: A Problem in American Institutional and Intellectual Life*. Chicago: University of Chicago Press, 1959.

Franklin, John Hope and Schweninger, Loren. *Runaway Slaves: Rebels on the Plantation*. New York: Oxford University Press, 1999.

Gutman, Herbert G. *The Black Family in Slavery and Freedom, 1750–1925*. New York: Pantheon, 1976.

FULL EMPLOYMENT ACT OF 1946

The Full Employment Act of 1946 sought to strengthen the economic gains to the U.S. economy that had resulted from massive government spending during World War II (1939—1945). Applying the theory of British economist John Maynard Keynes, who argued that intensive government spending was necessary to end economic depression, President Harry S. Truman (1945–1953) proposed a 21-point program in 1945 to boost the U.S. economy. The plan called for full employment legislation, an increased minimum wage, and better unemployment and social security benefits as well as housing assistance. Truman believed the bill would ensure that the country would not slip back into depression because it allowed the initiation of remedial action, such as tax cuts and spending programs if economic indicators shifted downward.

The Full Employment Act as initially proposed won the strong support of labor as well as liberal politicians, but was fiercely opposed by industry. The National Association of Manufacturers condemned the bill as a socialist measure and argued that government intervention would threaten free enterprise. To placate the business community, Congress cut several key elements of the bill before finally passing a severely truncated version of Truman's proposed legislation. The Full Employment Act passed by Congress in 1946 created a Council of Economic Advisers to report to the president, but failed to authorize governmental intervention to maintain full employment when economic indicators signaled a recession. Instead of giving government the strong role that Truman wanted, the act allowed it only a modest role in economic planning.

See also: **Keynsian Economic Theory, Harry S. Truman**

FULLER, RICHARD BUCKMINSTER, JR.

Poet, philosopher, writer, designer, engineer, teacher, futurist, cartographer, geometrician, inventor, and businessman were all terms applied to Richard Buckminster Fuller, Jr., (1895–1983) a nonconformist known for unorthodox ideas about the world. Fuller was an original thinker. He was an environmentalist decades before it became popular.

Richard Buckminster Fuller, Jr. was born July 12, 1895, in Milton, Massachusetts. He was well educated as a young man and entered Harvard University, where he was twice expelled. Fuller never finished college. His family were well-known Nonconformists, and his great aunt Margaret was cofounder of *The Dial*, a publication of the Transcendentalist movement.

Fuller served in the U.S. Navy during World War I (1914–1918), commanding a crash-boat flotilla. He invented special lifesaving equipment while in the Navy, and, as a reward, was granted an appointment to the U.S. Naval Academy at Annapolis. Buckminster "Bucky" Fuller married Anne Hewlett in 1917. The daughter of a well-known architect and muralist, Anne was herself an inventor who created a modular construction system using compressed fiber block. After the war Fuller was employed briefly at Armour and Company, then went to work for his father-in-law in 1922. This venture involved the formation of Stockade Building System, which utilized the building material invented by his wife. The experience of building and dealing with building tradesmen convinced Fuller there were better ways to use Earth's resources.

In 1922 tragedy came to the Fuller family when their first daughter, Alexandra, died at the age of four from successive bouts with influenza, polio, and spinal meningitis. Fuller concluded that his daughter's death was the fault of inadequacies in the environment in which she lived. He believed that this environment could be controlled through comprehensive anticipatory design. Fuller set out to devote his life to understanding this holistic approach to designing and building strategies that would maximize the efficient use of the planet's resources.

Fuller's comprehensive design theory blended mathematics, engineering, and philosophy. He invented a series of products, which he labeled "Dymaxion" for *dynamic* and *maximum* inventions. He built a house in 1927 that was spacious, comfortable, and portable. It was financially inexpensive and was physically supported by a single column at the center of the home. In 1933 Fuller's Dymaxion automobile was developed to

Richard Buckminster Fuller shown here with a playsphere made with two of his geodesic domes.

achieve a speed of 120 miles per hour and a gas mileage of 30 to 40 miles-per-gallon. It was able to traverse rough terrain and could turn 180 degrees and park within the length of the vehicle itself. The Dymaxion Corporation, founded by Fuller, was unable to achieve commercial success with his inventions, and after two false starts, it was finally disbanded at the beginning of World War II (1939–1945).

Fuller's most famous invention, however, was the geodesic dome. The dome was constructed using what Fuller called ''Energetic-Synergetic geometry.'' In this structure, the dome is constructed by many series of tetrahedrons (a pyramid shaped cube) interlocked with octahedrons (eight-sided shapes). This building scheme provided for the most economical means of enclosing a space, and it also served to disperse architectural stresses in the most efficient way ever conceived. Geodesic domes were built all over the world for many purposes, from commercial applications to remote military enclosures in hostile environments. The largest geodesic dome was built in 1958 in Baton Rouge, Louisiana, 384 feet in diameter and 116 feet (about 10 stories) in height.

In addition, Fuller developed a system of cartography that allowed for the printing of land masses without distortion, die-stamped prefabricated bathrooms, underwater farms enclosed within geodesic domes, and floating cities. Fuller never saw himself as an inventor, however, and as he grew older, he spent more time philosophizing, writing, and teaching. What Fuller saw was a world of limited resources in materials and energy, but with unlimited potential for knowledge to make use of those resources. He believed in making comprehensive, long range technological and economic plans for man's place in the universe. Fuller lectured and wrote extensively on this subject. He coined the phrase ''a passenger on spaceship Earth'' to describe our place on this planet and in the universe.

Fuller was never particularly successful in business, although he tried several times to succeed with his building companies and Dymaxion. He did flourish in the academic environment, teaching at various times at Yale, Cornell, and Princeton Universities, and at the Massachusetts Institute of Technology. He also gained a lifetime appointment to a professorship at Southern Illinois University in 1968. Fuller was a prolific writer.

In *Nine Chains to the Moon* (1938), Fuller proposed a general strategy for maximizing the social applications of Earth's energy resources. He continued to refine these ideas in *No More Secondhand God* (1962), *Utopia or Oblivion* (1969), *Operating Manual for Spaceship Earth* (1969), *Earth, Inc.* (1973), and *Critical Path* (1981).

Fuller was internationally recognized for his work. Queen Elizabeth II awarded Fuller the Royal Gold Medal for Architecture, and he also received the 1968 Gold Medal Award of the National Institute of Arts and Letters. In 1979 he was granted membership in the American Academy and Institute of Arts and Letters.

Richard Buckminster Fuller was the darling of the youth culture, the environmentalists, and the futurists of the 1960s and 1970s. His nonconformist views were provocative to those who were looking for different answers to old problems. Fuller died in Los Angeles on July 1, 1983.

FURTHER READING

Baldwin, J. *BuckyWorks: Buckminster Fuller's Ideas for Today.* New York: John Wiley, 1996.

Encyclopedia Britannica. Chicago: Encyclopedia Britannica, Inc., 1994, s.v. "Fuller, Jr., Richard Buckminster."

Garraty, John A. and Jerome L. Sternstein. *Encyclopedia of American Biography.* 2d ed. New York: Harper Collins, 1996, s.v. "Fuller, Jr., Richard Buckminster."

Snyder, Robert. *R. Buckminster Fuller: An Autobiographical Monologue.* New York: St. Martin's Press, 1980.

Van Doren, Charles, ed. *Webster's American Biographies.* Springfield, Mass.: Merriam-Webster Inc., 1984, s.v. "Fuller, Jr., Richard Buckminster."

FULTON, ROBERT

Robert Fulton (1765–1815) was not the first inventor to turn his attention to the concept of the steam boat. He was the first, however, to successfully couple steam engines with a boat that could be commercially viable. Robert Fulton was a multitalented individual who began his adult career as an artist, but he showed inventive talent for most of his life.

Robert Fulton was born on November 14, 1765, on a farm in Lancaster County, Pennsylvania, near the town of Little Britain. He grew up in Lancaster, and was a clever child, showing an inventive trait by fashioning lead pencils, household utensils, and sky-rockets. For his rowboat, he put together a hand-operated paddle wheel. He also designed and built a rifle with an original bore and sight. Moving to Philadelphia at age 17, Fulton apprenticed to a jeweler and did well painting miniatures and portraits—well enough to buy a farm for his mother just outside of Philadelphia.

Fulton moved to England in 1786 to study painting with Benjamin West. He made a moderate living in England as an artist. But his true interest was in science and engineering. After 1793 he devoted his efforts to science and engineering, and relegated his painting to that of a hobby. Water transport was his main interest, and Fulton studied the problems of canals and shipping. He worked on the design of canal boats, and a system of inclined planes to replace canal locks. At the same time, Fulton invented machines for rope making and spinning flax. He made a device that cut marble, and he invented a dredging machine for cutting canal channels. In 1796, he published a work on his canal investigations, *A Treatise on the Improvement of Canal Navigation.*

Next Fulton turned his attention to the development of underwater warfare devices and equipment. He worked on the submarine and explosive torpedoes. Like many idealists, Fulton believed the development of efficient warfare appliances would make warfare so terrible it would no longer be pursued. This rather naive idea has been held by many who dabbled in instruments of war. Fulton was successful in some torpedo development, and built a semi-functional submarine. In 1801 his *Nautilus* diving boat could descend 25 feet underwater and return to the surface. Fulton attempted to enlist the patronage of the French government for his research, but was unable to demonstrate success in sinking British ships. He then attempted the same deal with the British, but failed for the same reason.

The problem of underwater propulsion frustrated Fulton and many others who came before him. For centuries sail or oar had propelled ships along the water's surface. Several men had experimented with placing steam engines on ships for propulsion, but unsuccessfully. In 1802 Fulton partnered with Robert

R. Livingston (1746–1813) to work towards a practical and commercial application of steam engines on boats. Livingston was to be a key supporter and benefactor. Fulton's experimental boat sank in Paris in 1803 because of problems with the weight of the engine. But he was more successful with a second attempt.

Finally, in 1806 Fulton ordered a quality steam engine from the British firm of Boulton & Watt. Previous attempts at coupling steam engines with boats had failed, Fulton believed, because of the lack of a well-designed engine. Previous inventors had attempted to build the steam engine as well as the boat. Fulton decided to purchase a quality engine from a reputable firm and couple it with a decent boat. The result of this effort was the construction of the first successful steamboat in New York in 1807.

The ship was registered as the *North River Steam Boat* but it was popularly called the *Claremont* after Robert Livingston's home. On August 17, 1807, the paddle wheel driven steamboat made its maiden voyage up the Hudson River to Albany at an average speed of five miles per hour. The *Claremont* was a technical success, but more importantly, a commercial success. Fulton insisted that the ship be well attended and that the needs of its passengers be tended to.

Fulton set about expanding the steamboat business. He obtained monopolies from state legislatures. His steamboat *New Orleans* was the first steamboat on the Mississippi River. He erected a large shipyard in New Jersey, which built 17 steamboats as well as a ferryboat and a torpedo boat. Fulton had designed and was building a steam powered warship, *Fulton the First* when he died on February 24, 1815.

See also: **Steamboats**

FURTHER READING

Bowman, John S., ed. *The Cambridge Dictionary of American Biography*. New York: Cambridge University Press, 1995, s.v. "Fulton, Robert."

Dickinson, H.W., *Robert Fulton, Engineer and Artist: His Life and Works*. New York: John Lane Company, 1913.

Encyclopedia of World Biography. Detroit: Gale Research, 1998, s.v. "Fulton, Robert."

Flexner, James T. *Steamboats Come True: American Inventors in Action*. Boston: Little, Brown, 1944.

Philip, Cynthia Owen. *Robert Fulton, A Biography*. New York: Franklin Watts, 1985.

FURNITURE INDUSTRY

The furniture industry has a long history. From the ancient Greeks, Romans, and Egyptians through the Middle Ages, the craft of furniture making has evolved with technology. Where once furniture was necessarily crafted by hand, the twentieth century has seen technological advancements that allow all manner of furniture items to be automated and mass-produced. In the United States, the furniture industry began with the traditional methods of hand crafting. As the division of labor (task specialization) method was applied in the nineteenth century, furniture production began to increase, and the division between furniture manufacturing and sales developed.

Furniture sellers developed the practice of buying furniture at wholesale prices from manufacturers and selling them in showrooms, which gained popularity in the mid-1800s. Large stores kept their own workshops for specialty items. With the rapid development of retail trade the direct link between the customer and the furniture maker began to disappear. By the early 1900s mass production of furniture was well established in the United States, with principal manufacturing centers at Jamestown, New York; High Point, North Carolina; and Grand Rapids, Michigan.

Grand Rapids initially developed a reputation for high-quality, high-end living room and dining room furniture. In the 1920s the city became well known for inexpensive but reliable furniture. Due to the continued need for hand-crafted items, furniture factories never became very large, and usually employed about 100 people.

Before and after World War II (1939–1945) there was a shortage of wood products, and hard times hit the furniture industry. The industry recovered slowly in the 1950s with the introduction of new wood materials, woodworking machinery, adhesives, and wood finishes. It became increasingly difficult to discern whether a piece of furniture was made commercially or crafted by hand. Larger furniture factories were laid out with conveyor belts to enable the high-volume mass production needed to fill a constant supply of orders.

In attempts to generate more sales many manufacturers entered agreements with retailers to showcase

Showroom at a furniture store.

their products. The concept proved successful as the manufacturer had access to a dedicated retail outlet, and the retailer received proprietary rights on the goods. A vendor-ship program was also created, allowing consumers to choose the furniture in a showroom and then having the manufacturer ship these items directly to their household; this allowed the showroom to carry less inventory. Wholesale distribution of furniture became divided into two categories: household/garden and office/business.

History has shown that interest rates and housing sales affect the furniture industry. When economic indicators are strong, the furniture industry has higher retail sales. Between 1992 and 1993 a five to six percent growth occurred in upholstered wood furniture, expanding the market for manufacturers. Statistics compiled by the U.S. Department of Commerce in 1987, listed 6,819 wholesale furniture distribution establishments with combined sales totaling $18.63 billion. By 1996 sales had increased to $28.78 billion with an estimated 7,194 establishments. Employment in the furniture industry increased from about 69,000 in 1992 to about 81,000 in 1996. By the late 1990s much of the industry growth came from sales to offices, hotels, and restaurants.

FURTHER READING

Agins, Teri. "Marketing—Home Furnishings." *Wall Street Journal*, November 22, 1993.

Andersen, Arthur and Co. *Facing the Forces of Change 2000*. Washington, D.C.: Research and Education Foundation, 1992.

Encyclopedia of American Industries. Farmington Hills: The Gale Group, 1998, s.v. "Furniture."

U.S. Department of Commerce. *1987 Census of Wholesale Trade: Geographic Area Series*. Washington, DC: GPO, October 1989.

U.S. Industry Profiles. Farmington Hills: The Gale Group, 1995, s.v. "Furniture, Household."

GADSDEN PURCHASE

The Gadsden Purchase of 1853 was the last territory acquired by the United States within the boundaries of the lower 48 states. In 1853, President Franklin Pierce (1853–1857) instructed James Gadsden, his minister to Mexico, to buy as much of the northern Mexico territory as possible, with the idea of using it as a southern route for a transcontinental railroad. Gadsden, a former railroad administrator from South Carolina who had long supported a southern railroad linking the Gulf Coast with California, was given instructions to offer Mexican leader Antonio Lopez de Santa Anna (1794–1876) up to $50 million for some 250,000 square miles—including the Gila River basin in modern Arizona, parts of Baja California, and the bits of northern Mexico that had not been annexed in the Mexican War (1846–1848).

THE ONLY EXPANSIONIST ACHIEVEMENT OF THE PIERCE ADMINISTRATION WAS THE GADSDEN PURCHASE. AND EVEN THAT CAME TO LESS THAN SOUTHERNERS HAD HOPED.

James M. McPherson, *Battle Cry of Freedom: The Civil War Era*, 1988

The purchase was part of Pierce's plan to unite a divided country by expanding American interests aggressively into foreign territories, a plan known as ''Young America.'' The Gadsden Purchase was opposed by Northern antislavery senators, who suspected Pierce's long-range plan was to obtain land for the expansion of slavery—an explosive political issue in the early 1850s. It was also opposed by some southern senators who wanted even more land. Unable to stop the deal, these senators managed to limit Pierce's purchase to 55,000 square miles for $15 million.

The Gadsden Purchase added to U.S. territory, but it also emphasized the gulf that separated North and South. Some northern senators who opposed the Purchase were under pressure to do so from northern railroad interests. By December 1853, a rail route that ran through the Gadsden Purchase had already been completed, and the northern interests were campaigning hard for territory north of the Missouri Compromise line to be organized. This led to the Kansas-Nebraska Act of 1854, which broke the Compromise and allowed expansion of slavery into areas from which it had legally been excluded 34 years earlier. The northern railroad was finally established in the Pacific Railway Act (1862), which set aside public land for the building of the first transcontinental railroad, completed in 1869.

See also: **Transcontinental Railroad**

FURTHER READING

Cochran, Thomas Childs. *Frontiers of Change: Early Industrialism in America*. New York: Oxford University Press, 1981.

Garber, Paul Neff. *The Gadsden Treaty*. Philadelphia: Press of the University of Pennsylvania, 1923.

Nevins, Allan. *Ordeal of the Union*. New York: Collier Books, 1992.

Potter, David Morris. *The Impending Crisis 1848–1861*. New York: Harper & Row, 1976.

Taylor, George Rogers. *The Transportation Revolution, 1815–1860*. New York: Rinehart, 1951.

GALBRAITH, JOHN KENNETH

John Kenneth Galbraith (1908–) was one of the more influential economists of the post–World War II era. Galbraith was an economic advisor to many Democratic party candidates and officeholders, with his influence peaking as advisor to President John F. Kennedy (1961–1963). Kennedy rewarded Galbraith with an ambassadorship to India, a country in which he had a personal interest.

> There must be, most of all an effective safety net [of] individual and family support for those who live on the lower edges of the system. This is humanely essential. It is also necessary for human freedom. Nothing sets such stern limits on the liberty of the citizen as the total absence of money.
>
> **John Kenneth Galbraith**

John Kenneth Galbraith was born in southern Ontario, Canada, on October 15, 1908 to a Scottish farming family. He attended the Ontario Agricultural College, which at the time was part of the University of Toronto but is now the University of Guelph. He graduated with distinction in 1931, having studied agricultural economics. He then moved to Berkeley and studied agricultural economics at the University of California, where he received his Ph.D. in 1934. His dissertation was on public expenditures in California counties, a subject that presaged his career in public service.

As soon as he graduated, Galbraith began his career teaching at Harvard University, where he remained, albeit with interruptions, until he retired in 1975. Galbraith became a citizen of the United States in 1937. He worked in the Department of Agriculture for President Franklin Roosevelt (1933–1945) and was a proponent of the New Deal. During World War II, he served in the Office of Price Administration and Civilian Supply. John S. Gambs said Galbraith was "virtually the economic czar of the United States" until he left the position in 1943. As a result of his experience during the war, Galbraith published *The Theory of Price Control* in 1953.

Galbraith worked for the Office of Strategic Services after the war ended, studying the effectiveness of the strategic bombing of Germany. He was one of the founders of Americans for Democratic Action, a liberal interest group, in 1947. He worked as a speech writer for Senator Adlai Stevenson (1835–1914) during his presidential campaigns, then chaired the Democratic Advisory Council during the presidency of Dwight D. Eisenhower (1953–1961). In 1960, he campaigned for the successful presidential candidacy of John F. Kennedy.

Having visited India in 1956 and finding the country fascinating, Galbraith was rewarded for his efforts in the Kennedy campaign by an appointment as U.S. Ambassador to India. He held the post from 1961 to 1963. Galbraith's political leanings were decidedly toward liberal causes and candidates of the Democratic Party. He was an outspoken critic of the U.S. involvement in Vietnam, and campaigned for anti–war candidates Eugene McCarthy (1916–) in 1968 and George McGovern (1922–) in 1972. In 1976, he worked for the presidential campaign of Congressman Morris Udall and in 1980, for the presidential campaign of Senator Edward Kennedy.

Galbraith was a thoughtful educator and an observant writer. He published over twenty books, two novels, coauthored a book on Indian painting, and wrote memoirs, travelogues, and political tracts. In 1977 he collaborated on the writing and narrated a Public Broadcasting System television series, "The Age of Uncertainty." His first major book, *American Capitalism: The Concept of Countervailing Power* was published in 1952. In it Galbraith argued that the growth of economic power in one area breeds countervailing power from those who must bargain with the powerful. For example, powerful manufacturers are counterbalanced by the rising power of organized labor. Galbraith's view was that the government had a role in supporting the countervailing powers for the good of the economy.

Of all his writings and publications, three stand out as major works of economic thought. *The Affluent Society* was published in 1958, and put forth the proposition that economic progress is impeded by the more–is–better mentality. Galbraith further postulated that progress could be extended by putting affluence to better use than purchasing goods propped up by artificial techniques such as advertising and salesmanship. He also argued in support of the view that culture and history have a significant role in economic life. *The Affluent Society* was a best seller, and served to place Galbraith in the forefront of economic thought.

The second of Galbraith's three important works was *The New Industrial State*, published in 1967. In it he argued for a concept, which he called *revised sequence*. Revised sequence simply means that the order of control and economic power is reversed in certain situations. Normally price competition is the dominant force controlling the economy. In instances where businesses control consumers through advertising and salesmanship, the forces controlling the economy are reversed. It is this revised sequence that is at the core of Galbraith's economic thinking, explaining distortions in the economy, which he saw as stemming from this reversal of control. *The New Industrial State* was also a best seller and proposed a plausible explanation of the power structure in the American economy.

The third book in Galbraith's trilogy of economic thought was *Economics and the Public Purpose*, and it continued the thinking from his earlier works. In this book, however, Galbraith goes on to argue the conventional economic model produces an "imagery of choice" that obscures the true sources of power within the economy. This situation prevents policymakers and citizens from understanding the true sources of decisions and the true seats of power, making the establishment of sound economic policy problematic. Galbraith believed any economic model should pass the "test of anxiety," or the ability of the economic system to allay fears and anxiety within the populace. It was Galbraith's contention that conventional economic systems did not meet that test.

Following his years in public service, Galbraith returned to Harvard University. He continued even in semi–retirement to critique conventional economic thought. He continued to propose "there must be, most of all an effective safety net [of] individual and family support for those who live on the lower edges of the system. This is humanely essential. It is also necessary for human freedom. Nothing sets such stern limits on the liberty of the citizen as the total absence of money."

FURTHER READING

Bowman, John S., ed. *The Cambridge Dictionary of American Biography*. New York: Cambridge University Press, 1996.

Encyclopedia of World Biography. Detroit: Gale Research, 1999, s.v. "Galbraith, John Kenneth."

Galbraith, John Kenneth. *The Affluent Society*. Boston: Houghton, 1958.

———. *A Life in Our Times*. Boston: Houghton Mifflin, 1981.

Who's Who. New York: St. Martin's Press, 1998, s.v. "Galbraith, John Kenneth."

Kretsler, Harry. "Intellectual Journey: Challenging the Conventional Wisdom." *Conversations with History*. Berkeley: Institute of International Studies, University of California, 1986. Available from the World Wide Web @ (http://globetrotter.berkeley.edu/convresations/Galbraith)

GALLUP, GEORGE HORACE

George Gallup (1901–1984) invented a reliable statistical technique from which he could discover the views of his fellow citizens on everything from corn flakes to religious convictions by sampling the opinions of only a limited number of typical respondents.

Gallup financed his college education at the University of Iowa with scholarships and a variety of jobs. During one summer vacation he worked for the St. Louis *Post-Dispatch*, going door-to-door surveying readers about their feelings toward the newspaper. After a few days Gallup asked himself whether or not there wasn't an easier, more efficient way to get the responses the paper needed. His answer to that question would become his life's work.

After graduating from the University of Iowa in 1923 with a Bachelor of Arts in journalism, Gallup went on to earn a Master's in psychology and, in 1928, a doctorate in journalism. His doctoral dissertation, "A New Technique for Objective Methods for Measuring Reader Interest in Newspapers," forecast his future career interests.

IF GOVERNMENT IS SUPPOSED TO BE BASED ON THE WILL OF THE PEOPLE, THEN SOMEBODY OUGHT TO GO OUT AND FIND OUT WHAT THE WILL IS.

George Gallup, in an interview with historian Richard Reeves

Gallup taught for brief periods on the faculties of Drake, Northwestern, and Columbia universities. Meanwhile, he was conducting reader-interest evaluation surveys for a number of major Midwestern newspapers. In 1932, at the age of 31, he accepted a position as director of research at a rising New York advertising firm, Young and Rubicam. The firm's clients were eager for data concerning public reaction to various products. Gallup, who became vice president of the firm in 1937, remained with Young and Rubicam for more than a decade.

In 1935 while he was still associated with Young and Rubicam, Gallup founded the independent American Institute of Public Opinion in Princeton, New Jersey, to gather information about public attitudes regarding a variety of topics. That year he also published the first random-sample opinion poll in a newspaper column, "America Speaks." The column was eventually distributed to 200 subscribing newspapers. Audience Research, Inc., was formed in 1937 and was an organization devoted primarily to assessing public reaction to movie titles, casts, and stories. It is said that Walt Disney (1901–1966) decided to go forward with producing "Alice in Wonderland" on the strength of Gallup's research.

Convinced that his sampling methods were as valid for politics as they were for marketing choices Gallup boldly and correctly predicted that Franklin Roosevelt (1933–1945) would win the 1936 presidential election over Alf Landon. Although in 1948 Gallup, like other pollsters, incorrectly picked Governor Thomas Dewey to win over incumbent President Harry Truman (1945–1953), his polling techniques changed the political landscape forever. By the turn of the century it would be unthinkable that any political campaign would be undertaken without extensive polling.

Toward the end of his life, in an interview with historian Richard Reeves about the effect that polling had on a democracy, Gallup said, "If government is supposed to be based on the will of the people, then somebody ought to go out and find out what the will is. More and more people will be voting on more and more things, officially, and unofficially in polls, on issues as well as candidates. And that's a pretty good thing. Anything's good that makes us realize that government is not 'them.' We are the government. You either believe in democracy or you don't."

Although Gallup's fame rested on his political predictions, his personal fortune was built on his ability to accurately assess middle America's reaction to new products and entertainment vehicles. That work continued after his death in 1984. In addition the Gallup Organization's periodic opinion surveys on cultural attitudes provided a running historical commentary on how U.S. views on such topics as religion, education, and the role of women both changed and remained the same over the last half of the twentieth century.

FURTHER READING

Current Biography 1952. New York: H.W. Wilson, 1952, s.v. "Gallup, George."

Gallup, George. *The Miracle Ahead*. New York: Harper Bros., 1964.

Gallup, George and Saul F. Rae. *The Pulse of Democracy: The Public Opinion Poll and How it Works*. New York: Simon and Schuster, 1940.

Gallup, George and John O. Davies. *What My People Think*. New York: American Institute of Public Opinion Press, 1971.

"Dr. Gallup's Finger on America's Pulse." *The Economist*, September 27, 1997.

Reeves, Richard. *Fifty Who Made a Difference*. New York: Villard Books, 1984.

GATES, WILLIAM HENRY III

William "Bill" Henry Gates III (1955–) started his first company at age 14; he later dropped out of college to launch Microsoft Corporation, which was to become the largest computer software company in the world. Labeled the richest man in the America in 1997, Gates' estimated net worth was more than $37 billion.

The second child of William Henry Gates Jr. and Mary Maxwell, Gates was born on October 28, 1955, in Seattle, Washington. Though he would later be known as Bill, his family called him Trey after the "III" in his name. His older sister, Kristi, would become his tax accountant. The elder Gates, a prominent Seattle attorney, and Gates' mother, a former school teacher, enrolled their son in the private Lakeside School in an attempt to stimulate and challenge him, as he displayed an uncommon curiosity and intelligence at an early age.

At Lakeside Gates befriended Paul Allen (1953–), who would later become his business partner. While in school Gates developed an interest in computers; he eventually worked to debug programs for the Computer Center Corporation's PDP-10. He also helped computerize electric power grids for the Bonneville Power Administrations and, with Allen, founded a company called Traf-O-Data to analyze local traffic patterns. Traf-O-Data earned $20,000 in fees while the boys were still in high school, but their contract was cancelled when the clients learned that Gates was only 14 years old.

I CAN DO ANYTHING IF I PUT MY MIND TO IT.

Bill Gates, quoted in *Hard Drive*, 1993

Among the more dubious of Gates' early accomplishments was the first computer virus. Gates used Computer Center Corporation's PDP-10 to install a program that copied itself to other computers via the Cybernet national network, ruining data and making computers crash. Gates was caught, reprimanded, and banned from computers through his junior year at Lakeside. During his senior year, however, he was back at the computers with Allen, programming class scheduling for the school. In a typically impish manner Gates used the program to ensure his class schedule included all the right girls.

Gates entered Harvard University in 1973, but left after a year and a half. Meanwhile, Allen had driven to Harvard and shown Gates a January 1975 issue of *Popular Mechanics* that focused on an inexpensive

Bill Gates.

microcomputer. Gates and Allen wrote a BASIC interpreter for the Altair computer and, in typical fashion, sold it to Altair manufacturer MITS before the program was even finished. Fortunately for Gates, the demonstration worked. Gates then dropped out of Harvard, and he and Allen formed Microsoft Corporation. Their first work was writing programs for the early Apple and Commodore machines and expanding BASIC to run on microcomputers.

The most significant break in Gates' career occurred in 1980, when he approached IBM to offer help on Project Chess, an IBM effort to build a personal computer (PC). Gates developed the Microsoft Disk Operating System (MS-DOS) to be the programming platform upon which the computer would run. But more importantly, he convinced IBM to open the specifications for the computer and its operating system to everyone. This move opened the market for software developers to work on IBM machines; in turn, the proliferation of software development established the IBM PC as the prevailing model in the computer industry. By the early 1990s Microsoft had sold more than 100 million copies of MS-DOS, becoming the all-time leader in software sales.

Gates took Microsoft into multimedia in 1987, promoting the CD-ROM—an optical storage medium easily connected to the PC. A boon to the computer industry, CD-ROM technology greatly expanded the capacity to store information on disks, enabling encyclopedias, feature films, and complex interactive games to be brought more easily to the PC.

Gates has always been well known as a fiery competitor who does not like to lose. His drive incorporates a belief that ''I can do anything if I put my mind to it,'' as he has been quoted as saying in James Wallace and Jim Erikson's book, *Hard Drive* (1993). He has a temper, although he encourages dissent in his company in the quest for the best solution to problems. Allen, who also made a fortune with Microsoft, left the company to enter the world of venture capital. He did, however, maintain a seat on the Microsoft's board of directors.

Microsoft hiring practices encourage brilliant minds and creative thinking. Gates does not mind being told he is wrong by his subordinates, and he thinks nothing of engaging in shouting matches during meetings. His business competitors are critical of his ethics and accuse him of using Microsoft's position as maker of the PC operating systems to an unfair advantage. To many outsiders and detractors, Gates is cold, ruthless, and relentless; to his friends, he is humorous and loyal. Several lawsuits came up against Microsoft in the 1990s, but Gates and his company were largely successful in the results.

Gates married Melinda French, a Microsoft manager, on New Year's Day in 1994. Many say that the tycoon relaxed after his marriage to French and the birth of their first child in April 1996; a second child was born in May 1999. Gates has stated that he will continue to run Microsoft until approximately 2010, when he will retire and turn his efforts to philanthropy—an effort he has already begun, giving millions of dollars to educational institutions such as schools and libraries.

See also: **Paul Allen, Computer Industry, Microsoft Corporation**

FURTHER READING

''Chairman Gates, Up Close and Personal.'' *U.S. News & World Report*, October 19, 1998.

Current Biography Yearbook. New York: H.W. Wilson Co., 1991, s.v. ''Gates, William Henry.''

Encyclopedia of World Biography. Detroit: Gale Research, 1999, s.v. ''Gates, William Henry.''

The World Book Multimedia Encyclopedia. Chicago: The World Book Company, 1998, s.v. ''Gates, William Henry.''

Isaacson, Walter. ''In Search of the Real Bill Gates.'' *Time*, January 13, 1997.

Samuelson, Robert J. ''A Tycoon for Our Times?'' *Newsweek*, November 16, 1998.

Wallace, James and Jim Erickson. *Hard Drive: Bill Gates and the Making of the Microsoft Empire.* New York: HarperBusiness, 1993.

GENERAL AGREEMENT ON TARIFFS AND TRADE (GATT)

Prior to World War I (1914–18), world trade flourished and international monetary relations were healthy. After 1860 a network of bilateral treaties based on most-favored-nation principals (MFN) governed trade relationships. Nations had flexibility to set and revise tariffs as long as they (tariffs) were consistent with MFN ideals. (A tariff is a special tax applied to imports to protect a domestic market from a competing foreign products or sometimes simply to raise

revenue for the government.) Tariffs increase the costs of imports by foreign competitors or by a company domiciled in the U.S. but which exports from another country, thus making it more difficult for the company to be competitive. Besides tariffs, few other trade barriers existed during this early period.

World War I severely undermined existing trade networks as countries charged higher tariffs and introduced import quotas and other controls. These trade barriers persisted after the war, because there was no central authority to reestablish prior order to world trade. Trade reform was an international focus until the Great Depression (1929–1939) struck in 1929. The 1930s witnessed greater protectionism measures, discriminatory trade practices, and other trade actions that impeded international commerce. As a result, during the 1930s world trade stagnated, not keeping pace with increased economic production. Another complicating factor was that the Peace Treaty of Versailles that ended the First World War allowed the Allies (especially France and Great Britain) to receive huge payments of war reparations from Germany. The final amount of reparations, established in 1921, was $56 billion. These reparations cut into the financial resources of central Europe. In addition, the erection of protective tariffs, hobbled Europe's economic recovery, perpetuated poverty, and probably contributed to the rise of fascist nationalistic movements in Italy and Germany during the 1920s and 1930s.

To insure that the World War I precedent of war reparations and protectionism was not renewed at the end of World War II (1939–1945), the United States and Great Britain immediately took steps to arrive at international cooperation among the non-socialist economies of post-war Europe. Rather than further drain Europe's devastated economies, the United States injected much needed economic assistance in the form of the Marshall Plan, which was an attempt to help reconstruct Europe in order to neutralize the considerable political appeal of socialist and communist parties after the war. As part of the economic program for the Western Allies after World War II, trade barriers were reduced and discriminatory tariff preferences were eliminated wherever possible.

It was in this political and economic climate that the General Agreement on Tariffs and Trade (GATT) resulted from a 1947 meeting of 22 nations (representing 80 percent of world trade) in Geneva, Switzerland. GATT, a specialized agency of the United Nations, comprised a system of international obligations to limit tariffs on particular items consistent with a set schedule. GATT's primary goal was to raise living standards and seek full employment by establishing mutually beneficial trade arrangements. GATT sought to reduce or eliminate tariffs and prohibit other trade controls such as import quotas.

Thus, unlike post–World War I experiences, the world economy following World War II witnessed expanding international commerce with lowered trade barriers. The extent to which GATT contributed to the economic success was a subject of debate. Many believed the organization's successes at periodically reducing trade barriers had greater influence on the post–World War II economic boom than other institutions including the World Bank and the International Monetary Fund. With the United States taking the lead, tariffs of industrialized countries fell from approximately 40 percent immediately following World War II to about five percent in the mid-1990s.

The history of GATT was marked by a series of eight negotiating rounds aimed at steadily reducing trade barriers. Some rounds took years to reach signed agreement. The first five rounds, occurring in 1947–1962, expanded membership but they did little to further tariff reduction or eliminate import quotas. Trade reform and, correspondingly, post-war economic recovery were slow through the 1950s. The sixth round, known as the Kennedy Round, lasted from 1962–1967, producing the most substantial tariff reductions of the post-war period. The following Tokyo Round of 1973–1979 added more reductions, and it also developed a code of conduct and made progress on other barrier restrictions.

The eighth series of negotiations, the Uruguay Round, led to more than 20 separate agreements in 1994. The 124 participating nations made substantial progress in several areas. Notably, the 47-year-old GATT organization was replaced by the newly created World Trade Organization (WTO). Unlike GATT, WTO was provided international dispute resolution authority. The participants established more stringent rules on investment and trade in service industries. (Service includes engineering, tourism, accounting, and construction industries.)

The WTO recognized intellectual property rights: trademarks received seven years of protection, patents 20 years, and copyrights 50 years. Inclusion of such property rights was a major benefit to U.S. software industry. It protected books, computer software, film, and pharmaceutical products from piracy. The agreements further reduced tariffs overall by a third. While industrialized nations agreed to completely eliminate some tariffs by 2005, developing countries agreed to hold tariff rates to set levels. This reduction was the largest at that time. Tariffs eliminated by developed

countries included a range of products such as construction, agricultural, medical equipment, steel, alcoholic beverages, paper products, and pharmaceuticals. Provisions were made to allow nations to withdraw from agreements based on environmental protection concerns.

Occasionally the hardship of structural relocation of industries in order to arrive at a global division of labor produced political backlash that impeded the implementation of GATT goals. For instance, the U.S. textile industry, which had helped to define the regional economies of the Northeast and Southeast and the West, resisted being phased out to developing nations. The result was the continued protection of U.S. textiles, with tariffs in place as social factors outweighed economics. However, prior protectionist agreements, such as the Multi-Fiber Agreement, established that U.S. import quotas would eventually be phased out. Officials continued to expect that developing countries would eventually take over textile and apparel production.

GATT/WTO supporters estimated U.S. income would be boosted by $122 billion by 2005 and exports would double to one trillion dollars by 2010. U.S. manufacturers thought to benefit most from the Uruguay round were producers of food and chemical products, industrial machinery, computer and telecommunications equipment, and scientific instruments.

Many U.S. jobs in industries previously protected by tariffs migrated to the cheap labor markets of developing countries and Eastern Europe. The U.S. workers who used to fill those jobs could only hope that the promise of new business opportunities and new jobs through expanded international trade would be fulfilled.

See also: **Foreign Investment in the United States, Foreign Investment of U.S. Companies Abroad, North American Free Trade Agreement**

FURTHER READING

Bhagwati, Jagdish, and Mathias Hirsch, eds. *The Uruguay Round and Beyond: Essays in Honor of Arthur Dunkel*. Ann Arbor, MI: University of Michigan Press, 1998.

Hoekman, Bernard M., and Michel M. Kostecki. *The Political Economy of the World Trading System: From GATT to WTO*. New York: Oxford University Press, 1995.

Jackson, John Howard. *The World Trading System: Law and Policy of International Economic Relations*, 2nd ed. Cambridge, MA: MIT Press, 1997.

Jackson, John H., and Alan O. Sykes. *Implementing the Uruguay Round.* New York: Oxford University Press, 1997.

Martin, Will, and L. Alan Winters, eds. *The Uruguay Round and the Developing Countries.* New York: Cambridge University Press, 1996.

Preeg, Ernest H. *Traders in a Brave New World: The Uruguay Round and the Future of the International Trading System.* Chicago: University of Chicago Press, 1995.

GENERAL ELECTRIC COMPANY

The General Electric Company (GE) is the fifth largest business in the United States. Headquartered in Fairfield, Connecticut, GE was valued at more than $350 billion in the late 1990s. The company's operations span many different areas, including manufacturing, technology, network and cable television, financial services, leasing, loan and information services, electricity distribution hardware, plastics and silicone production, medical diagnostic equipment, and utility, industrial, and marine power systems. GE does business in over 100 countries and maintains approximately 250 plants worldwide.

Established in 1892, GE was the result of a merger between the Thomson-Houston Company and the Edison General Electric Company. Charles Coffin was GE's first president, and inventor Thomas Edison (1847–1931) served as a director until 1894. Lightbulbs, elevators, trolleys, electric motors, generators, and locomotives were among GE's earliest products. In 1900 GE built a research laboratory in New York. The laboratory contributed to a number of breakthroughs, including X-ray tubes, high-speed steam public utilities, photoelectric relay (to control the flow of electricity), gas-filled incandescent lamps, and electrically propelled ships.

GE soon began diversifying its business. In 1918 the company purchased Hughes Electric Heating Company, the maker of an electric cooking range, and Pacific Electric Heating Company, the manufacturer of America's then most widely used appliance, the iron. The following year it teamed with Westinghouse Electric and American Telegraph and Telephone (AT&T) to found the Radio Corporation of America (RCA). In 1922 it debuted one of the country's first radio stations, WGY, in Schenectady, New York. Over the next 20 years GE introduced a series of appliances that quickly became fixtures in the American home. Refrigerators, toasters, food mixers, fans, air conditioners, vacuum cleaners, and washing machines were perennial money makers for the company.

Other advances included GE's 1940 development of frequency modulation (FM) radio transmission, considered a vast improvement over the existing amplitude modulation (AM) mode. GE's innovation proved to be an asset to Allied forces during World War II (1939–1945). The company produced more than 50 different types of radar for the armed services, and more than 1,500 marine power plants for the Navy. America's first jet airplane, the Bell XP-59, and its largest battleship, the *North Carolina*, were both powered by GE parts and ingenuity. In the late 1940s GE initiated a project to harness nuclear power for civilian and military use. This project bore fruit in 1955, when the Navy unveiled its first nuclear submarine powered by a GE reactor. Two years later the Atomic Energy Commission granted GE a license to operate the first privately owned nuclear reactor. By the end of the 1950s GE was boasting record profits.

GE's dominance in so many areas raised a number of anti-trust concerns. Both competitors and the federal government made efforts to ensure that GE did not hold a monopoly in any one industry. Between 1911 and 1967 GE was named as a defendant in 65 anti-trust lawsuits and formal complaints. Some of the legal actions resolved themselves without great cost, as when GE sold its interest in RCA in 1930 to loosen its grip on the fledgling recording industry. Other lawsuits were more injurious to the company. For example, in 1961 the U.S. Department of Justice indicted GE for fixing prices of electrical equipment. GE was fined nearly $500,000 and required to pay damages of approximately $50 million. Three GE managers faced jail sentences and other executives were forced to quit.

Despite its recurring anti-trust problems, GE continued to enjoy success, tripling its earnings during the 1970s. In 1976 GE made what was then the largest corporate purchase in U.S. history, paying $2.2 billion for Utah International, a major mining company and producer of natural gas and oil. The 1980s marked a period of transition for the company. In 1981 John (Jack) Welch took over as president with the goal of making GE number one or number two in every field of operation. He decentralized operations and sold $10 billion worth of the company's less profitable business, including its air-conditioning, housewares, and semiconductor sectors.

GE used the proceeds from these sales to purchase Employers Reinsurance, a financial services group, in 1984; RCA and the National Broadcast Company

General Electric workers are shown completing construction of the world's first large generator with liquid-cooled stator in 1955.

(NBC) in 1986; CGR medical equipment in 1987; and investment bankers Kidder, Peabody in 1990. The Employers Reinsurance acquisition made the company's financial services division, known as GE Capital, enormously profitable. The NBC acquisition paid dividends in the 1990s, when it aired a number of critically acclaimed and popular primetime programs on network television and debuted CNBC and MSNBC on cable.

GE's fortune and profitability continued to climb in the late 1990s. In 1997 the company reported revenues of $90.8 million. That same year GE became the first company in the world with a market value exceeding $200 billion. Since surpassed by the Microsoft Corporation's $479 billion market value, GE held on to second place with a market value of approximately $375 billion as of April 1999.

Regardless of its profit margin in any particular year, GE has a strong reputation for community involvement. In 1994 GE received the President's Volunteer Action Award for its charitable work. A year later its College Bound program for underprivileged youth received national recognition. In 1996 the company and its employees donated $75 million to philanthropic organizations around the world. At the end of the twentieth century GE announced that during 1998 its employees had logged 1.3 million volunteer hours doing various acts of good will in communities where the company is present.

See also: **Thomas Edison**

FURTHER READING

''General Electric Company.'' *Hoover's Online*, [cited May 1, 1999] available from the World Wide Web @ www.hoovers.com.

''General Electric Company's Homepage,'' [cited May 1, 1999] available from the World Wide Web @ www.ge.com.

''GE Top Dog on Forbes List.'' *Sun-Sentinel*, April 2, 1999.

Microsoft Encarta Online Encyclopedia, available from the World Wide Web @ encarta.msn.com/ EncartaHome.asp/.

Slater, Robert I. *The New GE: How Jack Welch Revived an American Institution*. Homewood, Illinois: Business One Irwin, 1993.

GENERAL MOTORS CORPORATION

Founded in 1908, General Motors Corporation (GM) is the largest industrial company in the United States. Known primarily as a manufacturer of American cars and trucks—including such standard nameplates as Buick, Chevrolet, Oldsmobile, Pontiac, GMC, and Saturn—GM also takes part in the manufacturing and marketing of Isuzu, Saab, and other foreign and domestic vehicles. In addition to its vast interests in the automobile industry, GM produces locomotive components, products and services for telecommunications and space, consumer electronics, and financial and insurance services.

The history of GM begins in 1892, when Ransom E. Olds raised enough capital to start a business building horseless carriages, working in a converted factory that belonged to his father. Within two years Olds' facility had become the first American factory in Detroit, Michigan, involved exclusively in the manufacturing of automobiles. It was not until 1901, however, that this business, the Olds Motor Vehicle Company, introduced its first model: the curved-dash Oldsmobile buggy. Meanwhile, other car manufacturers were cropping up in Detroit around the turn of the century; David Buick formed the Buick Motor Company in 1897, while Henry Leland founded the Cadillac Automobile Company in 1901.

A new market, the automobile industry was financially unstable, and before long these Detroit companies had no choice but to consolidate to stay afloat. Henry Ford (1863–1947) was winning American consumers' hearts with his Model T, and competition was beginning to intensify. The man responsible for bringing together the individual companies was William Durant (1861–1947), the son of a Michigan governor and a director at Buick. In 1908 Durant combined Oldsmobile and Buick, calling the new business General Motors; he introduced Cadillac and Oakland (later known as Pontiac) to the consortium in the following year. The mergers attracted little media attention at the time. Quick to turn a profit nonetheless, GM was off to a strong start.

Durant established a corporate base in Flint, Michigan, where he aimed to produce a variety of models based on those developed by the original companies. Within a few years, he put together a core staff of specialists to oversee and coordinate production throughout the company's various units and factories. Charles Kettering's 1911 breakthrough, an electric self-starter that would replace the arduous hand-crank mechanism, brought technological innovation to GM, which would later install the device in its Cadillacs. GM promptly invited Kettering to join its ranks, and he eventually took charge of the company's research and engineering programs. By 1920 GM had acquired more than 30 automotive businesses, including Chevrolet, which it procured in 1918.

When the United States entered World War I (1914–1918), GM stepped up to wartime levels of production. During the last two years of the war, 90 percent of GM's trucks went to the armed forces. Cadillac manufactured war materials like the V-8 engine and the mortar shell, while Buick built tanks, ambulances, and airplane motors. With the Ford Motor Company swelling to mammoth proportions, GM emerged from the 1910s as a potential competitor.

The Great Depression (1929–1939) hit the country in the late 1920s, threatening to ravage the automotive industry. GM responded to the crisis by recruiting the corporate management talents of Alfred Sloan Jr., who at his previous position at Hyatt Roller Bearing Company had transformed a $50,000 investment into a $3.5 million enterprise. Sloan helped to steer GM through the country's crisis, developing a strong management structure that other companies sought to replicate. Under the new system, GM's market share rose from 12 percent in 1921 to 44 percent in 1941.

With the United States entering World War II (1939–1945), GM again increased production. War materials from GM factories included 1,300 airplanes and one-fourth of all U.S. aircraft engines. In total, the company's contribution to the war effort was worth approximately $12 billion. After the war the automotive industry benefited from the rejuvenated national economy. But while many American families looked to buy a second car, market trends indicated a growing consumer preference for smaller European models. GM responded by developing more compact cars, but these did not gain the favor of American buyers. In 1959 the company's market share remained high, however, at 42 percent.

The 1960s brought turbulence in Detroit: Riots and other expressions of civil unrest compelled GM to recognize urban poverty and to revise its hiring practices to include minority workers. The expansionist policies of Presidents John F. Kennedy (1961–1963) and Lyndon B. Johnson (1963–1969) fostered such efforts toward diversity in businesses nationwide. Finding that change helped the company to grow and prosper, and GM developed new interests in home appliances, electronics, locomotives, insurance, banking, and financing at this time. But the 1970s brought costly changes to the company as it rose to meet national demands to control pollution and conserve resources. By 1977 GM had spent $4.5 billion meeting local, state, and federal requirements regarding pollution control.

Consumer demand for fuel-efficient cars led GM to spend billions more redesigning many of its once-popular models. Two significant purchases in the 1980s—the acquisitions of Hughes Aircraft and Electronic Data Systems—further depleted the company's financial resources. As a result of this period of heavy spending, GM reported a decrease in earnings between 1985 and 1992. And from 1990 to 1992 GM reported losses totaling $30 million.

The time was ripe for change at GM, and a new CEO, Jack Smith Jr., ushered in reformed policies. In 1993 Smith moved toward downsizing the company, paring down operations and slimming the corporate staff. Unveiling a plan to close 24 plants by 1996, Smith promised $3.9 billion in benefits to those made jobless and raised the salaries of blue-collar workers. Smith negotiated with the United Auto Workers as he made these changes, but the group remained disgruntled. A 54-day strike ensued in June 1998.

Meanwhile, GM rallied to retain its market share. When vans, trucks, and sports-utility vehicles came into vogue in the 1990s, GM followed the trend. Japanese manufacturers went after the same market, but a weakened dollar made imported cars more expensive than their domestic equivalents. GM benefited from the financial trend, pulling in hefty earnings from 1993 to 1995. Introducing the first electric car built for consumers in 1996, GM went on to announce more plans for change within the corporation and for innovation in the automotive field. As the slimmed-down company entered a new century, it showed no signs of giving up its role as an industry leader.

See also: **Automobile Industry, Automobile (Origin of), William C. Durant, Alfred Sloan**

FURTHER READING

Hamper, Ben. *Rivethead: Tales from the Assembly Line*. New York: Warner Books, 1992.

Howes, Daniel. "GM Now Running Leaner, Faster." *Detroit News*, November 2, 1997.

Keller, Maryann. *Rude Awakening: The Rise, Fall and Struggle for Recovery of General Motors*. New York: Harper Collins, 1990.

Sloan, Alfred, Jr. *My Years with General Motors*. New York: Doubleday, 1964.

Weisberger, Bernard A. *The Dream Maker: William C. Durant, Founder of General Motors*. Boston: Little, Brown, 1979.

GEORGIA

Georgia is located in the southeastern United States, where it is bordered in the north by Tennessee and North Carolina, in the south by Florida, in the west by Alabama, and in the east by South Carolina and the Atlantic Ocean. The country's twenty-first largest state, Georgia has a total area of 58,910 square miles. In the 1990s Georgia's estimated population of 7.64 million ranked it tenth among the fifty states. During the nineteenth century the state boasted a thriving agricultural economy, but by the end of the twentieth century Georgia's manufacturing and service industries were its most successful and buoyant. The state's economic center is located in Atlanta, which is both Georgia's largest city and its capital.

The colony of Georgia was founded in 1733 by James Oglethorpe, a soldier, politician, and philanthropist who had been granted a charter to settle the territory by Great Britain. Named after the English King George II, Georgia was the last of the 13 British colonies established in the United States. Georgians were among the first colonists to sign the *Declaration of Independence*. Following the American Revolution (1775–1783) Georgia was the fourth state overall and the first southern state to ratify the federal *Constitution* in January of 1788.

Georgia's support for the federal government began to wane during the early 1800s, when Congress proposed legislation to outlaw slavery in the Western territories. Georgia's rich cotton and rice plantations depended on slavery, and Georgians feared that the abolition movement would eventually reach their state. The Missouri Compromise (1820), which designated the states and territories in question as slave or free states, was passed by Congress largely through the

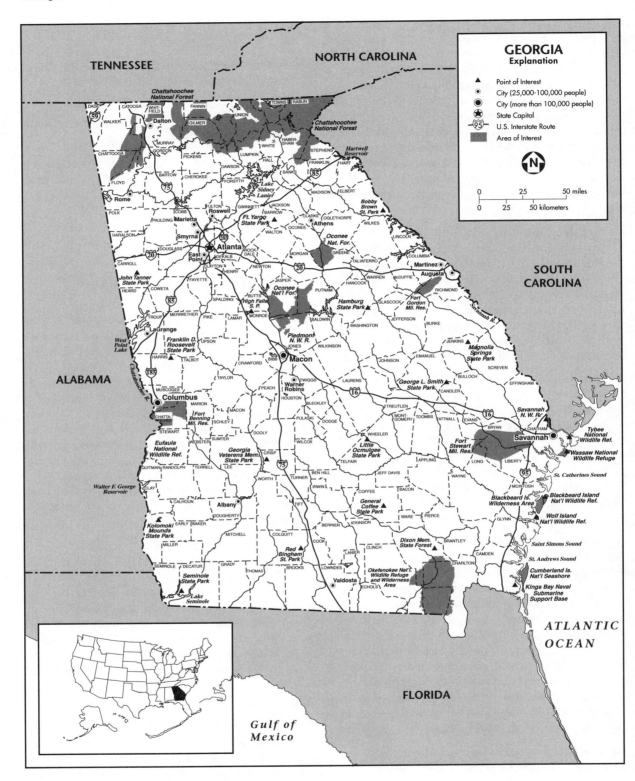

GEORGIA
Explanation

▲ Point of Interest
⊙ City (25,000-100,000 people)
◉ City (more than 100,000 people)
⊛ State Capital
〰95〰 U.S. Interstate Route
▨ Area of Interest

Ⓝ

0   25   50 miles
0   25   50 kilometers

TENNESSEE

NORTH CAROLINA

SOUTH CAROLINA

ALABAMA

ATLANTIC OCEAN

FLORIDA

Gulf of Mexico

State of Georgia.

efforts of Georgia Representatives Alexander H. Stephens, Robert Toombs, and Howell Cobb. This legislation helped calm tempers in the South, but it was only a temporary fix. On January 19, 1861 Georgia became one of the eleven Confederate states to secede from the Union. Less than three months later the nation was at war.

The American Civil War (1861–1865) left much of Georgia in ruins. Union General William T. Sherman (1820–1891) captured Atlanta in September of 1864, and began his famous "march to the sea" in November. Before his troops overtook Savannah in December, houses were looted, bridges were burned, and railroads, factories, mills, and warehouses were destroyed. Georgia residents were not the only ones in their state to suffer during the war, almost 50,000 Union soldiers were held prisoner at a camp in Andersonville, Georgia. Approximately one-fourth of those prisoners died from exposure, malnutrition, starvation, and filth. The prison superintendent was later convicted of war crimes before a U.S. military court and hung.

Georgia was readmitted to the Union on July 15, 1870 after it ratified the Thirteenth, Fourteenth, and Fifteenth Amendments to the federal *Constitution*. Those amendments abolished slavery and guaranteed the former slaves equal protection under the law and the right to vote. The amendments did not, however, protect thousands of black Georgia residents from being persecuted by white terrorists. Nor did they prevent the state government from enacting so-called Jim Crow laws that legalized segregation in Georgia. Such laws remained on the books until Congress passed the Civil Rights Act of 1964, which outlawed segregation in all public places. Georgia native Dr. Martin Luther King, Jr. (1929–1968) played an essential role in bringing about the passage of that civil rights law.

Other famous Americans have also hailed from Georgia. Jimmy Carter (1924–) is the only U.S. president who claims Georgia as his birthplace. Supreme Court Justice Clarence Thomas (1948–) is one of four Georgians to have sat on the nation's high court. Baseball players Raymond "Ty" Cobb (1886–1961) and Jack Roosevelt "Jackie" Robinson (1919–1972) are among the legendary Georgia athletes. Eli Whitney (1765–1825) may be the most famous Georgian from before the twentieth century. Whitney's invention of the cotton gin in 1793 made cotton so efficient to clean that the crop became the foundation for Georgia's economy in the nineteenth century.

Cotton would not have the same importance to the Georgia economy of the twentieth century. In the 1920s the boll weevil decimated the state's cotton industry. The Great Depression (1929–1939) further weakened the cotton farmer and by 1940 the old plantation system was gone. At the same time, World War I (1914–1918) and World War II (1939–1945) hastened the growth of manufacturing in Georgia. Federal dollars poured into state businesses that built and sold airplanes, ships, and munitions for the war effort.

By the end of the twentieth century manufacturing was the state's leading revenue-generating activity, with the textile industry being its oldest and largest such business. Of the almost four million persons employed in Georgia during the early 1990s, however, about 25 percent worked in the services sector, 23 percent worked in wholesale or retail trade, and only 15 percent worked in manufacturing. Three percent of Georgia residents worked on farms where cotton was only one of several crops grown for a profit. Tobacco, peanuts, peaches, and watermelons have also proven lucrative to grow in the state.

Tourism was another revenue-generating activity for the state in the twentieth century, with visitors to the state spending nearly $9.2 billion annually. The state's several national parks and forests, 100-mile oceanic coastline, balmy winter temperatures, and verdant plant life make it a nationwide attraction. In 1996 Atlanta attracted millions of people from around the world for the summer Olympics, which were generally considered a success despite a bombing that killed two people.

Both residents and visitors have contributed to the host of nicknames by which the state of Georgia is known. Unofficially called the Peach State, Georgia has also been affectionately referred to as the Peanut State, the Buzzard State, and the Empire State of the South. Over the past quarter-century Georgia has become known in some parts as the Bulldog State acquiring that moniker in conjunction with the successful academic and athletic programs at the University of Georgia, where the school mascot is a bulldog.

See also: **Boll Weevil Infestation, King Cotton, Sherman's March on Georgia**

FURTHER READING

Hepburn, Lawrence R. *The Georgia History Book*. Athens, GA: University of Georgia Institute of Government, 1982.

Lane, Mills. *The People of Georgia: An Illustrated History*, 2nd ed. Savannah, GA: Library of Georgia, 1992.

"Microsoft Encarta Online Encyclopedia, 1999," [cited May, 12 1999] available from the World Wide Web @ encarta.msn.com/EncartaHome.asp/.

Sams, Cindy. "Georgia Farmers Find Peanuts Still the Crop to Grow." *Knight-Ridder Tribune Business News*, October 8, 1998.

"State of Georgia Homepage," [cited April 20, 1999] available from the World Wide Web @ www.state.ga.us/.

GERBER PRODUCTS COMPANY

When Gerber's baby food was first introduced in 1928 the company was still known as the Fremont Canning Company. Based in rural Fremont, Michigan the company was started in 1901 by Frank Gerber and his father. The original idea of manufacturing and selling strained baby foods came from Dorothy Gerber, wife of Frank's son Daniel, who reasoned that such a product would help end the tedious chore of cooking, mashing, and preparing solid foods for infants.

Before launching the product Frank and Daniel Gerber undertook an extensive marketing research campaign. They tested the product, contacted nutrition experts, distributed samples, and conducted follow-up interviews. The Gerbers' careful implementation of the "baby food" concept laid a solid foundation for the company that would dominate baby products for the rest of the century.

The company's first-year sales of the baby food were boosted by an innovative coupon redemption program. The campaign resulted in national distribution of the product within six months, and first-year sales of 590,000 cans generated revenues of $345,000. The Gerbers created a new industry that had previously been served by pharmacists, and soon there were numerous competitors. By 1935 more than 60 other manufacturers had introduced their own baby food products.

Fremont Canning was able to hold its market lead because it had established the Gerber brand's reputation for quality and expert-backed research. The product's logo, the "Gerber Baby," was already famous and the company's research and education department flooded the market with useful pamphlets on parenting, feeding, and child psychology. Dorothy Gerber became a model spokesperson through her widely read newspaper column, "Bringing Up Baby."

The baby-food producer matured in the 1940s and in 1941 the company name was changed to Gerber Products Company. With the post-World War II baby boom, Gerber went from selling one million cans of baby food a week in 1941 to two million cans a day in 1948. It was during the 1940s that Gerber began packaging baby food in jars instead of in tin cans.

During the 1950s Gerber added three production plants. Frank Gerber died in 1952, and Daniel Gerber assumed leadership of the company. Under Daniel Gerber the company began advertising on television, launched a toy line in 1955, became listed on the New York Stock Exchange in 1956, opened a Mexican subsidiary in 1959, and introduced a line of baby-related products in 1965. In the 1960s Gerber introduced "safety button caps," the first tamper-evident caps of their kind. When Daniel Gerber died in 1974 the company was the world's largest baby-food manufacturer with sales of $278 million and a domestic market share of nearly 70 percent.

In the late 1970s the company successfully defended itself against a hostile takeover. In 1979, with birth rates declining, it launched a major diversification campaign acquiring freight carrier, furniture, toy, and other subsidiaries. By 1989, however, Gerber had divested most of these fringe ventures to refocus on its core business: baby food, baby care, and baby clothing.

Perhaps the biggest threats to Gerber during the 1980s were two public relations crises in 1984 and in 1986, both involving allegations of the presence of glass fragments in jars of baby food. In the first instance Gerber regained public confidence by recalling 550,000 jars in a 15-state region as a cautionary action. In the second instance the company chose the less popular tactic of cooperating with investigators, but otherwise remaining silent. As a result, profits dropped from $69 million in 1985 to $54 million in 1987.

During this time the company's leadership changed hands several times with former Carnation senior vice president Alfred A. Piergallini eventually taking over as chief executive officer (CEO) in 1988. He sustained Gerber's reorientation through a "superbrand" marketing strategy. A new Tropical line of baby foods was introduced in 1991, and the Gerber Graduates line for children past 15 months of age was introduced in 1992. Gerber also entered international markets in the early 1990s, noting that 98 percent of the world's births took place outside the United States.

By 1994, after struggling with severe price-cutting by its competitors and unprofitable sidelines, Gerber was ready for a takeover. After seeking a suitable buyer, Gerber announced that it would be purchased by Sandoz Ltd., a Swiss pharmaceutical giant, for $3.7 billion. Gerber was sold for a high premium, with

In 1928, Dorothy Gerber proposed adding a line of strained infant foods to the inventory of her husband's cannery, the Fremont Canning Company. They made "baby food" into a scientific and nutritious industry, and won the gratitude of many parents.

Sandoz paying more than 50 percent above the going price for the company's stock.

In 1995 Gerber entered the adult nutrition market with a nutritional supplement drink called Resource. The product had originally been marketed by Sandoz to hospitals and nursing homes. In 1996 Gerber's sterling reputation was challenged by the Center for Science in the Public Interest, which disputed some of Gerber's health claims. As a result, Gerber announced it would reformulate its recipes taking out starch and sugar. In 1997 Gerber updated its labels and introduced a new organic line of baby food. A 1998 survey commissioned by the WPP Group concluded that Gerber had the highest consumer loyalty rating in the United States. At the end of 1998 Gerber announced it was moving its corporate headquarters from Fremont to Summit, New Jersey, as part of a reorganization by its parent company, Novartis AS.

FURTHER READING

Brooks, Geraldine. "From the Mouths of Babes." *Good Housekeeping*, September 1997.

Cardona, Mercedes M. "WPP Brand Study Ranks Gerber 1st in U.S. Market." *Advertising Age*, October 5, 1998.

Gerber Products Company. *Fifty Years of Caring: Our Golden Anniversary Year, 1928–1978*. Fremont, MI: Gerber Products Company, 1978.

McDonald, Barbara. "Gerber Celebrates its 70th Anniversary." *Supermarket News*, August 10, 1998.

Teegardin, Carol. "Gerber Will Move Headquarters and Managers to NJ." *Detroit Free Press*, October 2, 1998.

GETTY, J(EAN) PAUL

In 1957 J. Paul Getty (1892–1976), an American expatriate living in England, was named the richest man in America by *Fortune* magazine. His net worth at the time was said to be between $700 million and $1 billion. Getty made his fortune by purchasing oil leases cheaply, then drilling and watching his oil wells yield huge profits. He is also remembered for his disastrous family life; his eccentric habits, which included forcing guests to use a pay phone at his baronial English country estate; and his coterie of mistresses.

Born in 1892, Getty began his career as a wildcatter in Oklahoma in 1914, with a stake from his oilman father, George F. Getty. The young Getty bought leases at giveaway prices on land believed to be barren of oil.

His wells struck rich oil beds, however, and Getty made his first million by the time he was 23. During the 1920s, constantly on the hunt for bargains, he bought leases and drilled for oil in the rich fields opening up along the California coast. By the time his father died in 1930, Getty was worth $3 million—a remarkable fortune in the first year of the Great Depression (1929–1939).

I JUST FLEECED MY MOTHER.

J. Paul Getty, alleged comment to an acquaintance, quoted in *The Great Getty*, 1986

Throughout the Depression, with many businesses desperate for cash, Getty realized that he could buy shares in oil companies for a fraction of what the oil in the ground was worth. He staked everything he owned or could borrow on his determination to acquire oil company stocks. He even persuaded his mother to give him control of her trust fund. (According to biographer Robert Lenzner, he then boasted to an acquaintance, ''I just fleeced my mother.'')

In the early 1930s Getty bought the Pacific Western Oil Corporation, a holding company with large oil reserves. In 1932 he began to buy stock in Tide Water Associated Oil, then one of America's best-known oil companies, which owned more than 1,200 service stations. Within 20 years, he had voting control of the company.

Following World War II (1939–1945), on the basis of good geological information, Getty became interested in the potential of oil fields in the Middle East. In 1949 he obtained a concession to drill for oil in an area then called the neutral zone, between Kuwait and Saudi Arabia. Drillers struck oil in 1953, vaulting Getty into the ranks of the world's richest oil barons. His Getty Oil Company, which concentrated on oil exploration and production, remained hugely profitable for the rest of his life. In the last full year of his life, Getty made $25.8 million in company dividends.

In his biography of Getty, Robert Lenzner reports that the oil mogul was a poor company manager whose autocratic and eccentric style attracted only those mediocre managers who could stomach the boss's mean and vindictive ways. Getty's personal life was no better: He had five wives and five sons, and was said to have treated them all very badly. He changed his will 21 times, using each revision as a means to punish various family members. He was too busy to attend the funeral of one son who died at age 12; he allegedly drove another to suicide. After his death, the infighting among the remaining three sons left the company,

which Getty had worked so hard to build, vulnerable to a successful takeover by Texaco.

At least partly to escape paying U.S. taxes, Getty moved to Europe permanently in 1952, settling in 1960 on Sutton Place, a historic country estate 23 miles outside of London. Typically, he prized the large and elegant mansion for the bargain price he had paid for it. There, he amassed an important art collection, the cornerstone of what is now the J. Paul Getty Museum in Los Angeles. The museum grew from a small collection of Greek and Roman antiquities, eighteenth-century French furniture, and European paintings that Getty had established at his home in Malibu, California, in 1953. At the same time, he founded a charitable trust to maintain the collection. Following his death in 1976, the trust received $1.2 billion, which endows the much-expanded museum and funds many other activities that support the arts.

See also: **Petroluem Industry, Robber Barons**

FURTHER READING

Glassman, James K. ''Billionaire and Bore.'' *The New Republic*, March 31, 1986.

Lenzner, Robert. *The Great Getty: The Lives and Loves of J. Paul Getty, the Richest Man in the World*. New York: Crown Publishers, 1986.

Lubar, Robert. ''The Great Getty: The Lives and Loves of J. Paul Getty, the Richest Man in the World'' (book review). *Fortune*, March 17, 1986.

Miller, Russell. *The House of Getty*. New York: Henry Holt, 1985.

Pearson, John. *Painfully Rich: The Outrageous Fortune and Misfortunes of the Heirs of J. Paul Getty*. New York: St. Martin's Press, 1995.

GHETTO

After World War II (1939–1945), millions of African Americans sought to escape poverty in the rural south by moving to northern cities where they hoped to find better paying jobs. But, they encountered housing discrimination that forced them into racially separate neighborhoods known as ghettos. Ghetto populations soared during the 1950s, when the black population of major cities grew quickly. During that timeframe Detroit's black population increased from 16 percent to 29 percent, while Chicago's grew from 14 percent to 23 percent. Boston's increased from five to 10 percent, and the District of Columbia's rose from 35 to 55 percent. At one time during this period, more

Low income children playing behind a tenement building in one of the ghetto neighborhoods of New York City.

than 2,200 African Americans moved to Chicago each week. This rapid population shift severely strained housing and urban services and created a set of circumstances that made ghettos, which had first appeared in the early decades of the 1900s during the Great Migration, an entrenched feature of almost every major city in the United States.

One of the most significant factors in the creation of ghettos was the mass movement to the suburbs of middle-class whites. At the same time, expansion of highway construction and the growth of the automobile industry enabled companies to move away from cities to areas where they could operate more cheaply. Thus, just as millions of blacks were moving to cities, jobs there were disappearing, as were tax revenues that could support decent services such as schools and sanitation. Housing in ghettos deteriorated badly, and high unemployment and limited social services combined to create blighted areas where crime rates soared. Yet blacks found it extremely difficult to escape from these areas because they were consistently denied the opportunity to purchase homes in white neighborhoods. Even after passage of the Fair Housing Act in 1968, which prohibited discrimination in the sale, rental, or financing of housing units, most African American families in urban areas had no choice but to

live in ghetto neighborhoods. By the late 1960s ghetto residents were extremely frustrated by the slow pace of change as advocated by civil rights leaders. In 1965, the Los Angeles neighborhood of Watts erupted in violence as thousands of African American residents burned stores and looted the area. The riots, which lasted from August 11 to August 16, caused 34 deaths and injured more than 1,000. Devastating riots also broke out in Detroit. These riots traumatized the nation and brought significant public attention to ghetto conditions. Though ghettos were beset by poverty and other problems, however, they also fostered racial pride and provided an important base for black businesses.

See also: **Discrimination, Suburbs**

GI BILL

The GI Bill has been called the single most significant legislation passed by Congress in the twentieth century. It created benefits for veterans of U.S. military service, including financial assistance for higher education. The GI Bill is composed of two pieces of legislation, the Serviceman's Readjustment Act of 1944 and the Montgomery GI Bill. It is intended to help veterans leaving military service readjust to civilian life and to encourage qualified individuals to volunteer for military duty.

When World War I (1914–1918) ended, millions of veterans returned from fighting overseas and were faced with unemployment and homelessness. The country went into an economic recession. Twice as many veterans returned from World War II (1939–1945), creating a concern that the economy would be even harder hit by economic difficulties. In order to keep the economy strong and to help returning veterans, the American Legion, led by former Illinois governor John Stelle, proposed and drafted the Serviceman's Readjustment Act. The bill unanimously passed both houses of Congress in 1944.

This was the original GI Bill. Among its benefits, veterans were eligible for up to $500 in educational costs, a monthly allowance, and mortgage subsidies. Despite initial concerns that college campuses would become overcrowded, the bill was a success. Not only did it positively affect education, but it also changed the face of society as well.

Colleges benefited from the high increase in student enrollments, which assured them financial security for years to come. Over 2.2 million of the 7.8 million World War II veterans receiving benefits used the program for higher education. All eligible veterans could now go to college. As a result, education became more equal, less divided by restrictions of class, race, or religion. The increase in education and skill led to an increase in average taxpayer income, which in turn increased federal income.

The mortgage subsidies provided through the Serviceman's Readjustment Act increased demand for housing and led to development of the suburbs. One fifth of all single-family homes built in the twenty years after World War II were financed with the assistance of the GI Bill's loan guarantee program. All of these factors led to the creation of a new middle class in the United States.

After the Vietnam War (1964–1975) and the end of the draft in 1973, the number of qualified adults willing to serve in the military declined. Representative G.V. "Sonny" Montgomery, chairman of the House Veterans' Affairs Committee, proposed a new GI Bill in 1984 to encourage military service, even in times of peace. That same year, President Ronald Reagan (1981–1989) signed the Montgomery GI Bill into law.

The Montgomery GI Bill is a voluntary plan. Upon entry into military service, a participant may elect to have $100 deducted from pay each month for the first twelve months of service. In return, the participant is eligible to receive up to $400 per month, for a period of thirty-six months, toward educational expenses. The federal government does not set standards or administer the plan. The Veterans' Administration determines candidate eligibility and schools handle admission and track expenditures.

See also: **Recession, Suburbs, World War II**

GIANNINI, AMADEO PETER

Widely recognized as the father of modern banking, A.P. Giannini (1870–1949) built the world's largest privately held bank, the Bank of America, by lending to ordinary citizens solely on "a man's face and signature." He pioneered mortgages for working class homeowners and loaned as much as $300 or as little as $10 to anyone with a job. His personality and career were the inspiration for the character George Bailey in the film, *It's a Wonderful Life*.

Born to a poor immigrant Italian family in San Jose, California, in 1870, Giannini left school at age thirteen. His father, a truck farmer, had been murdered in a dispute with a worker over $2 in wages when Giannini was seven. Giannini's first job was as a fruit and vegetable broker, working on commission for his stepfather. At age fifteen he was driving through the California valleys and successfully competing with veteran buyers for farm produce. The boy was exceptionally ambitious and hard working. By carrying a loaf of bread and a hunk of cheese with him, for example, Giannini said he saved time that might otherwise have been spent stopping for meals. He became a partner in his stepfather's food brokerage firm when he was only nineteen years old.

At the turn of the twentieth century, Giannini, then thirty-one, decided to retire as a food broker and sold his half-share of the fruit and vegetable business to a group of employees for $100,000. When his father-in-law died the following year Giannini took his place on the board of directors of the Columbus Savings and Loan Society in San Francisco. In 1904, frustrated by the bank's unwillingness to lend to small borrowers, he and a group of other directors founded a new bank, the Bank of Italy, with a capitalization of $300,000.

The bank's immediate success was almost entirely due to Giannini's unorthodox focus on the ordinary wage earner. He made loans to small farmers and fishermen, and even went door to door in the North Beach neighborhood, explaining how banking could help immigrant families realize their dreams. When the San Francisco earthquake devastated the city in 1906, Giannini commandeered a wagon and two horses and concealed nearly $2 million of the bank's gold and securities under a blanket of oranges. Two days later, as more traditional bankers declared a bank holiday for the duration of the emergency, he set up a temporary office on a wharf and began to lend money to anyone who needed it to rebuild.

The Bank of Italy continued to thrive during the first decades of the century. Bankrolling the movie industry at a time when the success of filmmaking was not assured, Giannini funded thousands of films, including *Snow White and the Seven Dwarfs* and *Gone with the Wind*. He was also instrumental in helping the California wine industry get its start and, in the worst years of the Great Depression, financed construction of the Golden Gate Bridge.

In 1909 California adopted a law that allowed banks to open branches throughout the state. In less than ten years the Bank of Italy had opened 24 branches. By 1930, when its name was changed to Bank of America, the bank was one of the largest in the country. When Giannini died in 1949, his bank had $6 billion in assets, 522 branches, and was the largest commercial bank in the world.

Giannini's personal estate, however, was a modest one. He established two foundations and directed his fortune to them and to other charities. Although he could have been many times a millionaire, he never wanted to be a rich man. He believed that great wealth would force him to lose touch with those he served. "No man actually owns a fortune," he is reported to have said. "It owns him."

See also: **Great Depression**

FURTHER READING

Dana, Julian. *A. P. Giannini, Giant in the West.* New York: Prentice-Hall, 1947.

Gordon, John Steele. "The People's Banker." *American Heritage.* September, 1998.

Kadlec, Daniel. "America's Banker: A. P. Giannini." *Time.* December 7, 1998.

Radin, Harvey. "Bank of America Founder A. P. Gianinni Named One of the 100 Most Important People of the 20th Century." Press Release, "Bank of America." December 2, 1998.

GILLETTE COMPANY

One summer morning in 1895 an ambitious traveling salesman found that the edge of his straight razor had dulled. King Camp Gillette (1855–1932) later said that the idea for an entirely new kind of razor with a disposable blade flashed into his mind as he looked in irritation at his dull blade. Gillette had been searching for the right product, one that had to be used and replaced regularly, around which to build a business. His innovation in shaving technology was just such a product. Another safety razor, the Star, was already on the market at the time, but like the straight razor it was meant to replace, its blade needed to be sharpened with a strop before each use and eventually had to be professionally sharpened. Gillette envisioned an inexpensive, double-edged blade that could be clamped over a handle, used until it was dull, and then discarded.

Gillette spent the next six years trying to perfect his safety razor. The scientists and toolmakers he consulted were pessimistic and thought the idea was impractical. Gillette did not give up—he was 40 years old at the time and a successful salesman, inventor, and writer. In 1901 he joined forces with William Nickerson, a Massachusetts Institute of Technology educated machinist. Nickerson developed production processes to make Gillette's idea a reality while Gillette formed the American Safety Razor Company to raise the estimated $5,000 they needed to begin manufacturing the razor. Production of the razor began early in 1903.

The renamed Gillette Safety Razor Company began advertising its product in October 1903, with the first ad appearing in *Systems Magazine*. The company sold 51 razor sets at $5 each and an additional 168 blades, originally at 20 for $1, during the first year. In 1904 Gillette received a patent on the safety razor; sales rose to 90,884 razors and 123,648 blades that year. In the following year the company bought a six-story building in South Boston. During the years leading up to World War I (1914–1918) Gillette steadily increased earnings through print advertisements that emphasized how with his razor men could shave themselves under any conditions without cutting or irritation.

During World War I the U.S. government ordered 3.5 million razors and 36 million blades to supply all its troops. In order to meet military supply schedules, shifts worked around the clock and Gillette hired over 500 new employees. Gillette thus introduced a huge pool of potential customers to the still new idea of self-shaving with a safety razor. After the war ex-servicemen needed blades to fit the razors they had been issued in the service.

In 1921 Gillette's patent on the safety razor expired, but the company was ready for the change. It introduced the "new improved" Gillette razor, which sold at the old price, and entered the low-priced end of the market with the old-style razor, renamed the Silver Brownie razor. Gillette also gave away razor handles as premiums with other products, developing customers for the more profitable blades. Expansion and growth continued.

In the early 1930s Gillette made a bold advertising move: the company admitted that the new blade it had brought out in 1930 was of poor quality. The company then announced what became its most recognizable product, the Gillette Blue Blade, promising uniformly high quality. The Blue Blade kept Gillette the leader in the field, but profits remained disappointing throughout the Great Depression (1929–1939), as men increasingly turned to bargain blades.

In 1939 the company began heavy broadcast sports advertising and purchased the radio broadcast rights to the 1939 World Series for $100,000. Despite a short series in which the Cincinnati Reds lost four straight games to the New York Yankees, sales of Gillette's World Series Special razor sets were more than four times the company's estimates. This success encouraged more sports advertising. By 1942 Gillette-sponsored events were grouped together as the "Gillette

Cavalcade of Sports.'' Although it eventually included college football's Orange Bowl and Sugar Bowl, and horse racing's Kentucky Derby, in addition to the World Series and baseball's All-Star Game, the ''Cavalcade of Sports'' became best known for bringing boxing to U.S. audiences. Sports programs continued to remain an important vehicle for Gillette advertising.

During World War II (1939–1945) foreign production and sales declined, but domestic production more than made up for those losses. Almost the entire production of razors and blades went to the military. In addition Gillette manufactured fuel-control units for military plane carburetors. The backlog of civilian demand after the war led to consecutive record sales until 1957.

The company changed its name to the Gillette Company during the 1950s, at the same time when it began diversifying its product line. By the end of the twentieth century half of the company's profits were still derived from shaving equipment. Gillette generated the remainder from a variety of consumer product areas, including writing instruments (Paper Mate, Parker, and Waterman brands), correction products (Liquid Paper), toothbrushes and other oral care products (Oral-B), alkaline batteries (Duracell), and toiletries (Right Guard, Dry Idea, White Rain). The company's products were sold in more than 200 countries and territories, with more than 60 percent of sales occurring outside the United States.

See also: **King Camp Gillette**

FURTHER READING

Adams, Russell B., Jr. *King C. Gillette: The Man and His Wonderful Shaving Device*. Boston: Little, Brown, 1978.

Flaherty, Robert J. ''The Patient Honing of Gillette.'' *Forbes*, February 16, 1981.

Gillette Company. ''The Gillette Company, 1901–1976.'' *Gillette News*, 1977.

Grant, Linda. ''Gillette Knows Shaving—and How to Turn out Hot New Products.'' *Fortune*, October 14, 1996.

McKibben, Gordon. *Cutting Edge: Gillette's Journey to Global Leadership*. Boston: Harvard Business School Press, 1998.

Miller, William H. ''Gillette's Secret to Sharpness.'' *Industry Week*, January 3, 1994.

Ricardo-Campbell, Rita. *Resisting Hostile Takeovers: The Case of Gillette*. Westport, CT: Praeger, 1997.

Symonds, William C. ''Gillette's Edge: The Secret of a Great Innovation Machine? Never Relax.'' *Business Week*, January 19, 1998.

GILLETTE, KING CAMP

Before the beginning of the 1900s, when the only means of shaving a beard was the straight razor, shaving was a nuisance and even dangerous. That changed, however, in 1903, when the disposable razor made its debut. No one has done more to alter the face of men's fashions than King Camp Gillette (1855–1932), inventor of the disposable razor.

Gillette was born in Fon du Lac, Wisconsin, on January 5, 1855, and raised in Chicago, Illinois. His family lost everything in the Chicago Fire of 1871, and he was forced to go to work. For the next 20 years Gillette worked in a succession of jobs ranging from traveling salesman to hardware store employee. A turning point came in 1891, when Gillette's current employer, William Painter, the inventor of the crown bottle cap, encouraged him to begin working on a product that would be thrown away after its use, thereby keeping consumers returning for more. It took Gillette four years to come up with his invention.

Seeing the need for a better way to shave, Gillette took the straight razor and improved upon it. He created a razor that housed a double-edged, thin metallic blade between two metal plates, which were then attached to a T-shaped handle. A crude first version of the razor was ready by 1895, but early proposals for the product met with skepticism. Nevertheless, he pushed on with the manufacturing of the razor, founding the Gillette Safety Razor Company, later renamed the Gillette Company, in Boston, Massachusetts, in 1901. In 1903 the company's first sale consisted of only 51 razors and 168 blades, but the razor was an instant success. Gillette went on to produce 90,000 razors and 12,400,000 blades by the end of his second year in business. The disposable razor was such a sweeping success that sales quickly grew into the millions. Beards, once common on men, were soon on the decline as it became increasingly fashionable for men to be seen well shaven.

Even though he retired in 1913 and moved to Los Angeles, Gillette remained president of his company until 1931. Although he continued to function as director, he shifted his focus to writing books; in these pages, he publicized his views on utopian socialism. Gillette believed that competition was a waste of time and resources. Instead he proposed that society should be restructured to adopt a system in which engineers plan out and organize all economic efforts. His views were similar to those expressed by Edward Bellamy, who envisioned a system based on the sharing of domestic functions within huge residential units, the planned utilization of advanced technology, and the organization of labor into efficient production groups. Although such views were never widely popular, Gillette did live to see his once small business expand into an enormous and successful company.

Gillette died in Los Angeles on July 9, 1932.

See also: **Chicago Fire of 1871, Gillette Company, Utopian Communities**

FURTHER READING

Adams, Russell B. *King C. Gillette, The Man and His Wonderful Shaving Device*. Boston: Little, Brown, c1978.

The Encyclopaedia Britannica. Chicago, IL: Encyclopaedia Britannica, Inc., 1994, s.v. "Gillette, King Camp."

"Gillette, King C(amp)" [cited on June 30, 1999], available on the World Wide Web @ search.biography.com/.

Gillette, King Camp. *World Corporation*. Boston: New England News, c1910.

Webster's American Biographies. Springfield, MA: Merriam-Webster, Inc., 1984, s.v. "Gillette, King Camp."

GLASS-STEAGALL BANKING ACT

In the early 1900s, commercial banks established security affiliates to underwrite securities, such as stocks and bonds. A commercial bank is an institution that accepts demand deposits, such as a check, and makes commercial loans. Underwriting is the bank's guarantee to furnish a definite sum of money by a certain date to a business or government entity in return for the entity's issue of bond or stock. Commercial banks were heavily involved in securities underwriting until the 1929 stock market crash.

In 1930 the Bank of the United States failed, allegedly because of the activities of its security affiliates. In 1933 all banks nationwide closed for four days because of the Great Depression. Four thousand of

these banks never opened again. This apparent collapse of the U.S. financial structure eroded public confidence that was already shaken from the hard times of the Depression. The failure of so many banks in such a short time frame was a fearful symbol to the public.

Responding to the public's lack of confidence in banks, President Franklin Roosevelt (1933–1945) proposed the Glass-Steagall Act as part of his New Deal program. Also known as the Banking Act of 1933, Glass-Steagall prohibits commercial banks from engaging in the investment business. Initially an emergency measure, the Act became permanent in 1945.

The Glass-Steagall Act established tighter regulation of national banks by the Federal Reserve System and created the Federal Deposit Insurance Corporation, which insures bank deposits with a pool of money supplied by the banks. It also prevented commercial banks from underwriting securities, except for a limited number of asset-backed securities, such as corporate bonds and U.S. Treasury and federal agency securities. The underwriting of securities was now almost strictly left to investment banks, which are unable to accept deposits. Investment banks are also authorized to set up corporate mergers, acquisitions, and restructuring, and provide brokers or dealers in investment transactions.

Succeeding legislation has relaxed the initial tenets of the Act. Commercial banks may now offer advisory services to customers regarding investments and buy and sell securities for them. Any information gathered through advisory services, however, can not be used by the bank when it acts as a lender.

See also: **Federal Deposit Insurance Corporation, Great Depression, New Deal, Stock Market Crash of 1929**

GLOBAL ECONOMY

Global Economy was a concept associated with the twentieth-century evolution of financial markets and institutions, where traditional geographic boundaries did not restrict economic transactions and consumer activities. The global economy applied to the increasingly international transaction characteristics of banks, industries, businesses, and other economic institutions. A global economy of financial markets was attributed to international deregulation of financial markets; technological advances to provide for the careful monitoring of world markets; and increased institutionalization of worldwide economic institutions. In a global economy investors and lenders viewed international loans and securities as comparable to domestic or local transactions. Banks and other financial institutions in a global economy participated in both foreign and domestic markets. A global economy was encouraged by advances in data-processing and telecommunications monitoring, liberalization of worldwide capital funds, deregulation of local capital markets, and increased international competition among markets and economic institutions.

silver dropped. Americans exchanged their silver dollars for gold, and the gold reserve in the U.S. Treasury was depleted. After the financial panic of 1893, the Sherman act was revoked that same year. In 1900 the Gold Standard Act reaffirmed gold as the standard unit of value for the nation's currency.

See also: **Bland-Allison Act, Free Silver, Gold Standard Act, Sherman Silver Purchase Act**

GOLD RESUMPTION ACT

Passed by Congress in 1873, the Gold Resumption Act officially revoked the bimetallic standard that was adopted by the U.S. government in 1792. The legislation was passed in recognition of the fact that by 1873 there were few silver coins in circulation. One hundred years earlier, in adopting the bimetallic standard (by which both gold and silver coins are minted), the legal mint ratio of 15:1 was established—silver coins contained 15 times as much silver as the gold coins contained gold. But, during the nineteenth century, fluctuations in the market prices of the two metals wreaked havoc on the supply of coins in circulation. (Whenever silver's value was higher on the open market than it was at the mint, people would hoard their silver coins for sale on the open silver market, effectively taking them out of circulation.) Even after the ratio was adjusted to 16:1, silver continued to be undervalued by the mint. Due to the under-valuation of silver—and the discovery of gold in California in 1849—gold gradually replaced silver in the nation's money supply. In passing the Gold Resumption Act of 1873, Congress put into law what had long ago been put into practice: silver coins were no longer considered legal tender. But shortly after enacting the law, political factions began agitating for the government to resume issue of silver coins. The Free Silver forces, mostly silver miners in the West, indebted farmers, and poor workers, believed the depressed economy of the 1870s would improve if silver coins were issued. This action, they said, would increase the supply of money to produce a mild inflationary effect, which would raise prices and allow debtors to pay their loans. The silver interests succeeded in influencing government: In 1878, five years after taking silver coins out of circulation, Congress passed the Bland-Allison Act which required the government to purchase and mint between two- and four-million dollars in silver each month. This amount was increased by the Sherman Silver Purchase Act of 1890; an enormous quantity of silver was put into circulation. As a result the value of

GOLD RUSH OF 1849

On January 24, 1848 a New Jersey prospector James Marshall discovered gold on the American River in northern California, while he was working on a sawmill owned by John Sutter. When news of the discovery leaked out, there was a mass migration to California, and in subsequent years a fortune in gold was mined. Historian Malcolm J. Rohrbough called the Gold Rush the most significant event in U.S. history between the Louisiana Purchase and the outbreak of the Civil War. It had important economic, social, and political implications for the United States.

In 1848, when President James K. Polk (1845–49) notified Congress of the discovery in his annual message, gold fever broke out. Thousands of people made arrangements to go to the West Coast either individually or as a member of a group. These associations, which were called companies, helped lessen the cost of the trip, and they often but not always disbanded when they arrived in California. Some Argonauts, as the miners were called, took overland routes; others sailed around Cape Horn or booked passage to Panama, where they crossed the isthmus and took another ship to California. Disease and attacks by hostile natives often made the trip perilous, and many died on route.

MAKE A DOT THERE AND LET ME INTRODUCE A MAN, WELL-KNOWN TO ME WHO HAS WORKED ON THE YUBA RIVER SIXTY-FOUR DAYS AND BROUGHT BACK AS THE RESULT OF HIS INDIVIDUAL LABOR FIVE THOUSAND THREE HUNDRED AND FIFTY-SIX DOLLARS.

Walter Colton, Mayor of Monterey, California, August 16, 1848

It was the greatest mass migration in American history and completely transformed California. Until the Gold Rush the population of the future state hovered at 13,000, about half of whom were Californios, people of Spanish or Mexican descent. The natives were submerged by the flood of 80,000 people, who

African American gold miner in Auburn Ravine, California, in 1852 during the Gold Rush, which helped to settle much of the western territory.

arrived in 1849, and who swelled to 300,000 by 1854. The immigrants were mostly young and mostly male. Because of the vast wealth that could be made, the Gold Rush cut across social classes. Both professional men and unskilled laborers could be found in the gold fields, working side by side.

The cities grew dramatically. At the beginning of 1849 San Francisco was sleepy little village of 800, but in the summer of that year, one contemporary observed that it had compressed 50 years growth into four months. San Francisco's population reached 20,000 by 1850 and 50,000 by 1860. Other towns, like Marysville, Sacramento, and Stockton, also expanded, becoming supply centers for the miners, and hundreds of smaller mining camps appeared. The large influx of people from the United States probably accelerated the move to statehood. California had been seeded to the United States after the Mexican War (1846-1848), and a constitutional convention was called in September of 1849. It became a state in 1850.

The amount of gold available and the ease with which it could be obtained seemed fanciful to those who first heard the stories in the East. But all one needed was a pick, pan, shovel, and the determination to go to California. Gold was deposited in streambeds,

which could be harvested by poking around with a knife and digging it out with a spoon. Water, which originally deposited the gold, was also used to mine for it. Flowing through a tin pan, the water would carry off the lighter particles of dirt and leave the heavier gold. At a time when farm hands would earn $1.00 and skilled craftsman about $1.50 for a 12-hour day, a miner could earn $16.00 a day by panning an ounce of gold. In 1847 Eddin Lewis, a successful farmer in Sangamon County, Illinois made $350.00 for the year by selling beef, pork, lard, and corn. In the fall of 1850, C.C. Mobley, a California miner, wrote in his diary that the men in his company made an average of $350.00 each in a two-week period. From 1849 to 1855 $300 million was taken from the California gold fields.

The vast amount of wealth inflated prices. A miner from New York and his partner had a large but ordinary breakfast at a boarding house near the mines that cost the $43.00. Although the men did not complain, the miner noted that the usual price for such a meal was $5.00. The cost before the Gold Rush was 25 cents. In spite of high prices that could be ruinous, there was a considerable fortune to be made, if one was provident and avoided gambling and ''fancy'' women. In fact, there was very little for the miners to buy. The men wore shabby clothing that was often patched, lived in tents or lean-tos, and ate the same drab food. Appearances could be deceiving, and clothing ceased to be a mark of distinction. Walter Colton the mayor of Monterey described a man who looked like he had just climbed out of an animal's lair, but who carried a sack containing $15,000 in gold dust. Since at first there were no banks, miners usually kept their wealth on their person or left it at their campsite. The early miners had a reputation for honesty and generosity.

I SOON SHALL BE IN FRISCO. AND THERE I'LL LOOK AROUND, AND WHEN I SEE THE GOLD LUMPS THERE I'LL PICK THEM OFF THE GROUND

''Oh California,'' miners' song sung to the tune of ''Oh Susanna''

The great wealth attracted many people who hoped to profit indirectly. A New England dentist set up practice in Northern California and returned to New Hampshire four years later after having earned a profit of $2,800.00. Although only a few women worked in the gold fields, many moved to California in the hope of marrying a miner or providing some domestic service the miners needed. In 1850, women in Sacramento could make $150.00 a month doing housework, while men were being hired for $75.00 a month to build levees. In that same year, when the average farm laborer in the United States earned only $10.85 a month with board, one enterprising woman made $100.00 a week by washing clothes. Managing a rooming house in Sacramento for three months brought Emeline Day $184.00 in addition to her room and board. Lucy Stoddard Wakefield opened a pie shop in the mining town of Placerville, from which she grossed $240.00 a week.

Within a couple years of the initial strike, the gold that was easy to find had already been mined, and it became more difficult for a miner to realize his dreams of wealth. Gold production reached its peak in 1854, when $81 million was taken from the gold fields. The amount declined every year until 1857, when it leveled at $45 million, an average it kept until the end of the Civil War. Large companies that could afford the capital investment began to dominate the industry, and they hired miners for wages. By 1854 miners who could obtain jobs were averaging only $75.00 a month. More than a few left in bitter disappointment.

The discovery of gold had both a national and an international impact. The United States provided 45 percent of the world's gold production between 1851 and 1855. The nation was thus able to export gold, which helped offset the country's negative balance of payments in the 1850s. This abundance was also important in allowing the government to mint $40 million in gold coins during that decade. On the other hand, the discovery caused U.S. commodity prices to leap and compelled workers in the east to strike in order to protect their standard of living.

See also: **California**

FURTHER READING

Holliday, James S. *And the World Rushed In: The California Gold Rush Experience.* New York: Simon & Schuster, 1981.

Maffly-Kipp, Laurie F. *Religion and Society in Frontier California.* New Haven: Yale University Press, 1994.

Rodman, Paul. *The California Gold Discovery: Sources, Documents, Accounts, and Memoirs Relating to the Discovery of Gold at Sutter's Mill.* Georgetown, Calif.: The Talisman Press, 1966.

_____. *The Beginning of Mining in the Far West.* Cambridge, Mass.: Harvard University Press, 1947.

Rohrbough, Malcolm J. *Days of Gold: The California Gold Rush and the American Nation.* Berkeley and Los Angeles: University of California Press, 1997.

GOLD STANDARD *(ISSUE)*

The gold standard was first put into operation in Great Britain in 1821, but the full international gold standard lasted from about 1870 until World War I (1914–18). Great Britain re-established its gold standard in 1928.

During the colonial period, American commerce was hindered by the absence of an adequate, standard medium of exchange. It was impossible to establish a gold or silver currency because colonists did not have natural supplies of these metals and had to rely on foreign trade to acquire them. Some Spanish and Portuguese coins made their way into the English colonies. These coins were exchanged for goods and paper money, but the value of the coins varied because the colonies competed with one another and overvalued the specie.

After Independence, the Constitution provided for the establishment of a national currency. The Mint Act of 1792 adopted the decimal system as the medium of reckoning, established the dollar as the basic unit of value, and created a bimetallic currency with a mint ratio of 15 to one. Authorized gold coins were the $10 eagle, the $5 half-eagle, and the $2.50 quarter-eagle. Silver coins were the dollar, half-dollar, and quarter. Copper coins were the penny and the halfpenny. This bimetal system would last for the remainder of the nineteenth century until the passing of the Gold Standard Act of 1900.

The bimetallic coin production system met with many early difficulties. From roughly 1792 until 1834 the market ratio of silver to gold rose above the fixed mint ratio. Silver's resulting domination drove gold out of circulation. But merchants found that it was possible to gain a silver premium by exchanging U.S. silver dollars for slightly heavier Spanish silver dollars. This in turn caused a drain on U.S. currency. Accordingly the United States discontinued the minting of the silver dollar from 1806 to 1840 and the half-dollar became the principal coin in use. The resulting shortages of U.S. specie compelled the United States to grant legal tender status for foreign coins. This status lasted a short time since it was assumed that U.S. currency would soon replace the foreign coins.

The Coinage Act of 1834 was intended to bring gold back into circulation. With the mint ratio adjusted to 15.988 to one, silver was undervalued at the mint and forced out of circulation. Discoveries of gold in California and Australia further debased gold and increased the supply of gold coins. In an effort to prevent silver from disappearing altogether, Congress passed the

Subsidiary Coinage Act in 1853 which reduced the weight of subsidiary silver coins. But despite these attempts at keeping the dual system alive, opposition and opinion against bimetallism mounted.

During the 1870s demand for the free coinage of silver increased, especially among Western farmers who had been adversely affected by falling prices and the "demonetization" of silver. After the American Civil War (1861–1865), the worldwide output of gold slowly diminished, silver production greatly increased, and the value of silver—relative to gold—declined. In 1873 the government removed the silver dollar from the list of coins to be minted. A year later the commercial ratio of silver to gold rose to over 16 to one, and many Western farmers (then a growing political force) felt that it would have been profitable to coin silver dollars at the mint ratio. Forming a Populist agenda, farmers called the "demonetization" act the "crime of 73" and pushed for the coinage of free silver to push prices up. With the passing of the Bland-Allison Act, the government agreed to purchase between $2 and $4 million worth of silver to be coined into silver dollars.

During the 12 years the Bland-Allison Act was enforced, 378 million silver dollars were coined. Pushed by Populist demands, the Republicans agreed to pass the Sherman Silver Purchase Act in 1890 which required the United States Treasury to buy 4.5 million ounces of silver monthly. During the three-year period of the Purchase Act's operation, the government bought nearly $156 million of silver. This endangered the gold standard, and eventually gold was forced out of circulation. During the Panic of 1893, President Grover Cleveland (1885–89) and (1893–97) called a special session of Congress during which the Sherman Silver Purchase Act was repealed. Between 1894 and 1896, the government maintained the gold standard through the purchase of over $200 million in gold, paid for with four and five percent bonds.

While the agitation surrounding silver coinage continued for a while, it never again became so important an issue as in the election of 1896. During the presidential election of 1896, Democratic candidate William Jennings Bryan (1860–1925) was heavily influenced by the Populist demand to inflate silver's value in order to raise prices for their crops. Bryan campaigned for the free coinage of silver at the ratio of 16 to one. But Bryan's opposition, Republican candidate William McKinley (1897–1901), called for the maintenance of the gold standard. After a heated contest between the two candidates, William McKinley was elected president. Reasons for McKinley's victory were twofold: conditions for farmers began to improve in 1896, and voters distrusted Bryan's financial policies.

When the U.S. Congress passed the Gold Standard Act in 1900, many of the monetary questions that had plagued the U.S. economy for over a century appeared to be settled. The Gold Standard Act established a full gold standard, and provided the free coinage of gold and full convertibility of currency into gold coin. But the Great Depression caused the collapse of the gold standard and reopened the issue of a currency standard for the United States. In response Congress passed the Gold Reserve Act in 1934 which put the country on a modified gold standard and stipulated that gold could not be used as a medium of domestic exchange. This legislation paved the way for the end of a gold-based monetary system altogether in domestic exchange. Under the Gold Reserve Act, the dollar was legally defined as having a certain, fixed value in gold. Thus, although gold was still considered to be important for the preservation of confidence in the dollar, its connection with the actual use of money remained vague.

After World War II (1939–1945), most exchange rates were pegged either to gold or to the dollar. In 1958 another type of gold standard was established in which major European countries had free convertibility of their currencies into gold and dollars for international payments. But there was no restoration of a pure international gold standard as such and many wanted a more clearly defined relationship between gold and the dollar. Later attempts were made to make the dollar less dependent upon gold for its value. In 1971 President Richard M. Nixon (1969–1974) ended the convertibility of the dollar into gold. Following Nixon's action, practically all U.S. currency, paper or coin, was essentially fiat money, and gold became no more than a commodity traded on international markets.

A gold standard had both advantages and disadvantages. On one hand, it provided a fixed pattern of exchange rates for international trade. Under normal circumstances, the value of gold did not fluctuate greatly over short periods because of the relative stability of demand and supply. Over longer periods however, the effects of cumulative production in relation to immediate demand resulted in an unstable value, which caused difficulty in gold management in relation to price stability.

Many economists believed that the disadvantages of a gold standard far outweighed the advantages. Because of the limited supply of gold, a gold standard inherently limited flexibility in the money supply; thus, it hampered the growth and expansion of the economy. A gold standard also limited the power to create money, which in turn caused inflation. Moreover, since gold was a commodity, its value increased or decreased according to supply and demand for it which caused destabilization and consumer uncertainty. And finally, the gold supply benefited some countries at the expense of others. Some countries controlled large supplies of gold and affected the operation of other economies, either through natural supply or acquisition of gold.

See also: **William Jennings Bryan, Cross of Gold Speech, Free Silver, Gold Resumption Act, Gold Standard Act, Sherman Silver Purchase Act**

FURTHER READING

Friedman, Milton, and Anna Schwartz. *A Monetary History of the United States, 1867–1960*. Princeton: Princeton University Press, 1963.

James, John A. ''The Development of the National Money Market, 1893–1911.'' *Journal of Economic History*. 36 (1976): 878–97.

———. *Money and Capital Markets in Postbellum America*. Princeton: Princeton University Press, 1978.

Mitchell, Wesley C. *Gold, Prices, and Wage under the Greenback Standard*. Berkeley: University of California Press, 1908.

Shannon, F. A. *The Farmer's Last Frontier: Agriculture 1860–1897*. New York: Farar, Straus, and Young, 1945.

GOLD STANDARD ACT

In 1900, following more than a century of wild fluctuations in the valuation of U.S. currency, Congress adopted gold as the nation's monetary standard. In passing the Gold Standard Act, lawmakers rejected the bimetallic standard originally adopted in 1792: silver was no longer legal tender and paper currency (greenbacks) was now backed up by gold alone. The move to gold was inspired by the tumultuous monetary system of the late-1800s, when Free Silver advocates urged the government to issue an unlimited supply of silver coins to produce a mild (and, they believed, beneficial) inflationary effect.

Gold standard advocates believed the nation's money supply would never be stabilized under the bimetallic standard. They contended that because the open market value of each metal (gold and silver) was constantly fluctuating, the under valuation or over valuation of either metal by the mint would impact the supply of coins in circulation. For example, when the U.S. mint undervalued silver coins, savvy people opted to sell their silver coins on the open market for more than their face value. When silver was over produced

and the government issued too many silver coins (as was the case after the Sherman Silver Purchase Act of 1890), the price of silver dropped and people eagerly traded in their silver coins for gold coins and thereby exhausted federal reserves.

In the election of 1896, the Free Silver forces supported Democratic candidate William Jennings Bryan (1860–1925); Republican candidate William McKinley (1897–1901) ran on a platform that included backing paper money with gold. McKinley was supported by businessmen who believed the adoption of the gold standard would stave off inflation and help the country achieve economic prosperity—McKinley won the election. In 1900 he made good on his campaign promise, signing the Gold Standard Act into law. Gold remained the standard of the U.S. monetary system until April 1933, when, in the midst of the Great Depression (a worldwide economic downturn) Congress abandoned the gold standard because the U.S. could no longer guarantee the value of the dollar in gold. The legislation enabled the Federal Reserve to expand the nation's money supply without regard to gold reserves.

See also: **William Jennings Bryan, Cross of Gold Speech, Free Silver, Gold Resumption Act, Gold Standard, Sherman Silver Purchase Act**

GOMPERS, SAMUEL

Samuel Gompers (1850–1924), the best known and most influential U.S. labor leader in the late 19th and early 20th century, was the first president of the American Federation of Labor (AFL). In an era when armed physical combat between employers and workers often characterized labor relations, Gompers acted on the principle that unions should instead employ strikes, boycotts and other non-violent strategies to gain their ends.

The eldest of nine children, Gompers was born on January 27, 1850, in London, England, in a working-class tenement area. He attended school for only four years when financial considerations forced him to apprentice with his father, a cigarmaker.

In 1863, when the boy was 13, the family emigrated to New York City. Father and son immediately pursued work as cigarmakers. By 1864, at the age of 14, Samuel had joined the Cigarmakers' Union. In his autobiography written years later, he wrote, ''All my life I had been accustomed to the labor movement and accepted as a matter of course that every wage-earner should belong to the union of his trade.''

Samuel Gompers.

Gompers had a great thirst for knowledge and spent his spare time reading and attending public lectures and debates. In the cigar shop where he worked, he was able to test many of his ideas with fellow workers who often discussed issues of the day as they worked together. Gompers later claimed that these workplace discussions were like debating societies and that they honed his reasoning, as well as his persuasive and speaking skills.

Beginning in the 1870s, Gompers became actively involved in reorganizing the largely ineffective Cigarmakers' Union. He joined in a demonstration for the eight-hour day in September 1871, and from then on, became a tireless advocate of the benefits that would accrue to workers from shorter working hours. Taking on leadership of the union, he advocated raising union dues to build a strike fund and to support a benefits program including out-of-work, sickness, and death payments. Strikes were carefully controlled. Gompers believed in building unity based on a common form of skilled work and then binding workers to the union through a strong benefit plan. He veered sharply away from becoming involved with socialism and later became hostile to socialists who attempted, unsuccessfully, to take over leadership of the union movement.

By 1877, Gompers had been able to introduce many of his theories into the Cigarmakers' International Union, which had become a model of militant, principled, persistent unionism. In 1886, under Gompers, the cigarmaker's union, along with other trade unions, formed the American Federation of Labor, (AFL). Except for one year (1895), Gompers remained president of the AFL until his death in 1924.

Gompers gave the growing union movement a moral gravity and a conservative approach. He supported craft as the basis for the organization of workers and argued that the labor movement should look first to organizing skilled workers. Suspicious of easy solutions and ideological answers, he held the union back from radical actions and irresponsible strikes that he believed would tarnish the unionism movement overall. He also distrusted the influence of intellectuals and outside reformers. Gompers was tireless in keeping the national union together through good times and bad and building it into an effective organization. By 1894, the AFL had more than 250,000 members.

Gompers accepted the capitalist system as a practical reality. But he did not trust the government, which he believed to be a tool of the moneyed classes, to look out for the needs of workers; in fact, he believed the state would use its power at the expense of the working class. Because he distrusted government so deeply, he even opposed progressive legislative initiatives concerning hours, wages, and unemployment and health insurance for men. (He did, however, approve of labor legislation to protect children and women, who were not part of organized labor.)

Gompers argued that trade unions were the only dependable working class institution in American society. His theories, called ''voluntarism'' held that workers should depend on their voluntary membership in trade unions to protect them instead of relying on the government. Many state and local union leaders split with Gompers on the voluntarism issue, choosing instead to seek legislative redress for labor issues.

Gompers also believed in keeping the unions out of partisan politics. In his view, political action had to yield to strikes and boycotts as a bargaining tool. Although, like most labor leaders, he had advocated neutrality in the early days of World War I, he was staunchly supportive of the participation of the United States by the time it entered the war in 1917. In fact, he headed the effort against those in the labor movement, chiefly socialists, who continued to oppose the war.

Gompers spent his final years attempting to shore up the labor movement which was losing influence in the 1920s. In 1924, in a speech to the AFL quoted in the

July 1989 *Monthly Labor Review*, he summed up his career this way: "I want to live for one thing alone—to leave a better labor movement in the America and in the world than I found it when I entered, as a boy. . . . He died in San Antonio, Texas, a few weeks later.

See also: **American Federation of Labor, Capitalism, Labor Movement, Labor Unionism, Socialism, Trade Unions**

FURTHER READING

Dubofsky, Melvyn and Warren Van Tine, eds. *Labor Leaders in America.* Urbana: University of Illinois Press, 1987.

Gompers, Samuel. *Seventy Years of Life and Labor.* New York: ILR Press, 1984.

Kaufman, Stuart B. *Samuel Gompers and the Origins of the AFL.* New York: Greenwood Press, 1973.

Kaufman, Stuart B., ed. *The Making of a Union Leader 1850–1886.* The Samuel Gompers Papers, Vol. I. (Urbana, Ill.: University of Illinois Press, 1986.

Kaufman, Stuart B., ed. *The Early Years of the American Federation of Labor 1887–1890.* The Samuel Gompers Papers, Vol. II. (Urbana, Ill.: University of Illinois Press, 1987.

Livesay, Harold. *Samuel Gompers and Organized Labor in America.* Boston: Little, Brown, 1978.

Yellowitz, Irwin. "Samuel Gompers: a half century in labor's front rank." *Monthly Labor Review*, July 1989.

GOODYEAR, CHARLES

Charles Goodyear (1800–1860) did not prosper in his lifetime, but the industry he helped to found has played a major role in the development of the world's economy. Goodyear failed at business, spent many years in and out of debtor's prison, and left his family destitute, but his persistent work at developing rubber as a commercial product launched an entire industry.

Born in New Haven, Connecticut, on December 29, 1800, Charles Goodyear was son to a father who worked as a manufacturer, an inventor, and a merchant of hardware, particularly of farm tools and implements. Goodyear attended public schools and was sickly as a child—a problem he was never to overcome. At age 17 he moved to Philadelphia, Pennsylvania, to learn the hardware business as a salesman, but ill health forced his return to New Haven in 1822, where

Charles Goodyear.

he became his father's partner. At age 24 he married, and he and his wife Clarissa later had six children.

In 1826 Goodyear and his wife opened the first American hardware store in New Haven. Four years later, two events occurred that would shape Goodyear's life—both he and his father went bankrupt, and, on a trip to New York City, he visited a store that sold goods made of India rubber. Excited by the possibilities of goods made of rubber, Goodyear purchased a rubber life preserver from the Roxbury India Rubber Company. The only problem was that India rubber goods were frail; they became brittle when exposed to cold, and sticky when exposed to heat. Goodyear quickly invented an improved valve for the life preserver, but he was rebuffed by Roxbury and told that if he really wanted to improve the life preserver he would need to work on the rubber, not the valve.

So began a life's work that would consume Goodyear. He spent all of his time and resources working with rubber, trying every imaginable method to improve the quality of the material. He had no money, little knowledge of chemistry, and few resources for experimentation, yet he continued to persevere with his experiments, using trial and error to see what would work. He mixed rubber with anything and everything, from witch hazel to castor oil, from acids to cream cheese. Throughout his efforts, Goodyear was in poor financial condition. While his family often lived on the charity of friends, he zealously pursued his dream of developing rubber. He worked on his processes even while in debtor's prison.

Goodyear thought that he had secured acceptable results for treating rubber with nitric acid laced with sulfuric acid, but the financial panic of 1837 wiped out his fledgling company. Undaunted, he kept on with his work, wearing a suit of clothes made from rubber as a gimmick to gain attention. Shortly after the panic, Nathaniel Hayward partnered with Goodyear, and it appeared that their venture would be successful: The U.S. Post Office ordered 150 mailbags made of Goodyear's treated rubber. Unfortunately, the bags disintegrated in the summer heat and the venture failed. Goodyear persevered. His breakthrough came quite by accident in 1839, when he spilled a rubber and sulfur mixture onto a hot stove. Expecting the rubber to melt, Goodyear was surprised to see that the rubber had only charred on the edges. The areas that had not burned retained their elastic properties. Exposed to cold, this fragment continued to maintain its flexibility.

Goodyear had discovered the key to the process he called *vulcanization*, which was to cure the rubber-acid mixture with heat. He obtained a patent for the process on June 14, 1844; however, his typically poor business sense led him to license the patent at ridiculously low prices. Moreover, industrial pirates preyed on the patent and used it without authorization. Goodyear eventually retained famed attorney Daniel Webster (1782–1852) to represent him and secure his rights, but Webster's attorney fees exceeded the amount that Goodyear had made from his patent. He also had trouble obtaining a patent abroad, since Thomas Hancock had already patented the process in Great Britain.

Still attempting to make good on his dream of manufacturing rubber products, Goodyear borrowed money for extravagant displays of his products in London in 1851, and in Paris in 1855. He earned nothing from these attempts and spent another round in debtor's prison as a result of the Paris show. Nevertheless, while in debtor's prison he was awarded the Cross of the Legion of Honor for his efforts.

Goodyear returned home sick, feeble, and broke. When his daughter was dying in 1860, Goodyear traveled to New Haven to visit her, but he died en route in New York in 1860, leaving his family more than $200,000 in debt.

See also: **Tire and Rubber Industry**

FURTHER READING

Allen, Hugh. *The House of Goodyear: A Story of Rubber and Modern Business*. New York: Arno Press, 1976.

Encyclopedia of World Biography. Detroit: Gale Research, 1998, s.v. "Goodyear, Charles."

O'Reilly, Maurice. *Goodyear Story*. New York: Benjamin Co., 1983.

Quackenbush, Robert M. *Oh, What an Awful Mess: A Story of Charles Goodyear*. Englewood Cliffs, NJ: Prentice-Hall, 1980.

Travers, Bridget, ed. *World of Invention*. Detroit: Gale Research, 1994.

GORMAN, LEON ARTHUR

Leon Gorman (1934–) was president of L.L. Bean, the world's largest supplier of outdoor clothing and active gear. The company's business, founded by Gorman's grandfather, L.L. Bean, in 1912, was built on catalog sales and a reputation for conservative styling, high quality merchandise, and customer satisfaction. L.L.Bean's guarantee was unconditional; no matter how long a customer owned a product it could always be exchanged for a replacement or for a refund.

When Gorman became president of the privately-held family company in 1967, L.L. Bean was in serious trouble. Throughout the last years of his grandfather's life, he had made sure his company retained its old-fashioned business practices, limited growth, and only slowly accommodated to modern technology. According to John Skow, writing in *Sports Illustrated*, the company "had fallen into a prolonged snooze." Sales had dropped to $3.5 million and profits to a mere $60,000.

Gorman found that employee performance was poor partly because nearly everyone was of retirement age or older. The products the company sold were outdated; quality had slipped. L.L. Bean's landmark store in Freeport, Maine, had become shabby. Under Gorman, L.L. Bean was completely overhauled as he boosted advertising budgets, conducted marketing research and expanded the company's traditional mail-order sales base. Gorman spent $12 million in modernization, streamlined the company's operations, and introduced a retirement policy. Along the way he increased benefits and wages to boost morale and attract new workers.

For more than two decades, the company's revenues soared. L.L. Bean posted double-digit revenue growth in the 1970s thanks to a boom in outdoor sports. The company followed that up with more growth in the 1980s when the "preppy look" enjoyed widespread popularity. Strong international sales of its products, particularly in Japan, also helped make L.L. Bean an industry giant. By 1985 Gorman had boosted company sales to $300 million. In 1992 he received the Entrepreneur of the Year award from Ernst and Young.

By 1999 the company had grown into one of the world's leading international mail-order firms with sales of some $1 billion a year. L.L. Bean was selling more than 16,000 products through catalogs, the Internet, a retail operation in Freeport, eight retail stores in Japan, and nine factory outlet stores. More than 4.5 million customers placed orders from all over the world; as many as 180,000 orders a day were received by phone. Yet growth slowed significantly throughout the 1990s. After dropping in 1996 sales grew by only a sluggish 2.9 percent in 1997. According to *Business Week*'s William Symonds, L.L. Bean was "firmly stuck in the past."

Analysts placed the blame partly on the conservative styles of L.L. Bean's khakis, parkas, and sweaters, on Gorman's reluctance to move into children's clothing, and retail outlets that operated outside of Maine and Japan. As L. L. Bean's sales slowed, other retailers in the often-cutthroat mail-order businesses, such as Lands' End and J. Crew, caught up and passed the venerable company in some areas of its business. According to *Business Week*, the overall number of catalogs mailed out each year in the U.S. jumped from 7.8 billion in 1982 to 13.9 billion by 1998 making the Bean catalog easily lost in the pile. In addition, other rivals, such as The Gap, gained a very strong foothold in retail stores.

Gorman vowed to fight back and his goal, he said, was to add $300 million in sales by 2001 and triple pretax profits. He announced plans to locate a 100,000-square-foot superstore along with several smaller nearby satellite shops in the Mid-Atlantic region. A full fashion update of Bean's standard clothing line was on the books as was a specialty catalog, Freeport Studios, featuring dressier clothes for women of the baby-boom generation. Gorman also pledged to double marketing spending, including its biggest ever television advertising campaign, to $26 million. He also reorganized L.L. Bean's corporate structure into business units responsible for specific sales areas.

See also: **Leon Leonard Bean, Mail-Order House**

FURTHER READING

"Bean Sticks To His Backyard." *Economist*, August 4, 1990.

Brubach, Holly. "Mail Order the United States." *New York Times Magazine*, November 21, 1993.

Skow, John. "Using the Old Bean." *Sports Illustrated*, December 2, 1985.

Symonds, William C. "Paddling Harder at L.L. Bean." *Business Week*, December 7, 1998.

"The Company Behind the Catalog: The Story of L.L. Bean," [cited July 21, 1999] available from the World Wide Web @ www.llbean.com/.

GOULD, JAYSON "JAY"

Jayson Gould (1836–1892), known as Jay, was born in Roxbury, New York, on May 27, 1836. A farmer's son, he attended a local academy for schooling and also learned surveying skills. From ages 18 to 21, Gould helped to prepare maps of New York's southern counties; he later worked as a clerk and a blacksmith. When he and a partner were able to put together a stake of $5,000, he went into the leather-tanning business in northern Pennsylvania.

Gould eventually moved to New York City, where he sold leather goods and, in 1859 and 1860, began speculating in the stock market. Ruthless in his stock market dealings, Gould made great profits from Pennsylvania, New York, and Ohio railroad stocks. Financial markets were unregulated at that time, and Gould became a master at maneuvering stocks for his own gain.

Trading in the securities of his own companies, exploiting banks, and corrupting legislators and judges were all strategies employed by Gould. He became a power on Wall Street as he learned to manipulate the intricacies of corporate management and security trading. Gould was not above savaging companies and driving investors to ruin if it would make him a profit. The first financing he obtained was from a man who committed suicide after being wiped out. Gould himself was to earn and lose millions of dollars several times in his career.

Gould obtained a position on the board of directors of the Erie Railroad in 1867. He planned to control the railroad, and wanted to expand it to Chicago. His opponent in this scheme was famed industrialist Cornelius Vanderbilt (1794–1877). Gould schemed behind the scenes, using front persons in what became known as the Erie War with Vanderbilt. Illegally

Jay Gould.

converting debentures to stock, Gould bribed legislators in Albany to legalize his actions. Eventually, Vanderbilt left the Erie to Gould, who then sought to expand the railroad. At the same time, he increased the company's debt as he traded in Erie stocks, making a fortune before driving the railroad into bankruptcy in 1875.

While working on the expansion of the Erie, Gould bought controlling shares of the Wabash Railroad, which was principally a carrier of wheat. Gould hatched a scheme to increase wheat purchases—and therefore Wabash freight revenues—by manipulating the price of gold to make American wheat more attractive to foreign purchasers. His plan involved pushing the price of gold up by secretly buying the metal on the market. But on September 24, 1869, the date known as Black Friday, the U.S. Treasury dumped gold on the market to bring the price back down, and the sudden drop in gold prices created a panic on Wall Street. Gould lost a fortune in the panic, as all stock prices came tumbling down. However, continued successful speculation brought Gould back to the ranks of the rich by 1872, and he set out on another scheme to manipulate railroad stocks. In the meantime, one of his

partners, James Fisk, was murdered by his mistress's pimp.

Although Gould had lost the Erie, he added the Texas and Pacific, Missouri Pacific, and Union Pacific railroads to his interest in the Wabash. He followed the time-honored practice of buying up large amounts of shares when the prices are low. In another shrewd move, he purchased independent lines and feeder lines that added to the larger railroads' clout. The railroad companies then saw great increases in their stock prices, and Gould sold out his interests during the strong market of the early 1880s, making another fortune. Gould's tenure as the business leader of railroads was not solely self-serving, however: He added 2,500 miles of track to the Missouri Pacific from 1879 to 1882, and he forced shipping rates down by waging relentless war on his competitors. Between 1885 and 1889, he reacquired and reorganized the Wabash and the Texas and Pacific railroads, then merged them with his Missouri Pacific system.

Two more of Gould's interests would eventually add much to his estate. He used the Manhattan Elevated Railroad of New York to establish a monopoly on Manhattan's rapid transit system. He also purchased the American Union Telegraph company in 1879 and consolidated with Western Union in 1881. In 1888 he added the telegraph network of the Baltimore and Ohio Railroad; by the end of the 1880s Western Union had no real competition in railroad telegraphy and the transmission of wire stories to newspapers via the Associated Press.

Biographers have described Gould as somber, joyless, diabolical, and fiendishly clever at making money through stock manipulations; many refer to him as a "robber baron" who liked only money, books, and gardening. In 1863 he married Helen Day Miller and the couple had six children. At his death in New York on December 2, 1892, his estate was worth $77 million. His children, having inherited great wealth, lost or squandered a good deal of the money, although some philanthropic activities did take place in later years.

See also: **Railroad Industry, Robber Barons**

FURTHER READING

Encyclopedia of World Biography. Farmington Hills, MI: Gale Research, 1999, s.v. "Gould, Jayson."

Gale, Robert L. *The Gay Nineties in America: A Cultural Dictionary of the 1890s*. Westport, Connecticut: Greenwood Press, 1992.

Grodinsky, Julius. *Jay Gould: His Business Career, 1867–1892*. Philadelphia: University of Pennsylvania Press, 1957.

Hoyt, Edwin P. *The Goulds: A Social History*. NY: Weybright & Talley, 1969.

O'Connor, Richard. *Gould's Millions*. Garden City, NJ: Doubleday, 1962.

GOVERNMENT FARM POLICY (ISSUE)

Farming has little concrete meaning for many Americans. Society is so urbanized that the ordinary citizen's notions of farm life are highly abstract and usually inaccurate. The farm does have a secure position—perhaps even a mythic status—in the national culture, however. This status has shaped American political rhetoric from President Thomas Jefferson (1801–1809) to the present time. Discussion of the "plight of the farmer" and the "disappearance of the family farm" in modern America are usually coded language for the crisis that besets middle-class urban or suburban families who see their personal freedom diminishing in relation to economic developments over which they have no control—just like the farmer.

Such thinking about the plight of the farmer has a New Deal ring to it. Although the Democratic President Bill Clinton once declared that "the era of big government is over," many Americans who think about the problems of rural America seem to assume the necessity of an active role for the federal government. This belief that it is the responsibility of the government to take care of the farmer dates back to the early 1920s, when rural parts of the United States went into a depression almost 10 years before the rest of the country followed suit.

During World War I (1914–1918) the federal government encouraged farmers to increase production. When farmers maintained wartime levels of production in the postwar period, the result was a sharp drop in farm prices. Farm income plunged from almost $1,400 in 1917 to a little over $500 in 1921. In order to pay their mortgages and costs of production, farmers demanded a government subsidy, which they called "parity." The Agricultural Credits Act, passed in 1923, was one of several attempts to bolster the farm commodity price levels. However, it failed to deploy enough resources to solve the problem of low farm prices.

In 1929 President Herbert Hoover (1929–1933) signed the Agricultural Marketing Act, which established the Federal Farm Board with a fund of $500 million. The Farm Board helped to found farming cooperatives and set up stabilization boards; such boards would regulate the prices of grain and cotton by making purchases on the open market. Such purchases, however, only encouraged farmers to put more land in cultivation in expectation of greater profits. Consequently, the Farm Board failed and had to sell its holdings at a loss of $200 million.

The Agricultural Adjustment Act (AAA) of 1933, one of the first pieces of legislation passed under President Franklin Delano Roosevelt (1933–1945) in his New Deal program, attempted to control farm prices by reducing and controlling the supply of basic crops. The AAA empowered the Secretary of Agriculture to fix marketing quotas for major farm products, to take surplus production off the market, and to decrease production of staple crops by offering producers payments in return for voluntarily reducing the acreage devoted to raising such crops. The Commodity Credit Corporation (CCC), also created in 1933, began making loans to farmers on agricultural products. The CCC granted loans only to farmers who agreed to sign production-control agreements. Farm prices steadily improved, and between 1932 and 1937 the prices for major farm products increased by almost 85 percent. But in a major setback, the U.S. Supreme Court declared certain production control features of the AAA unconstitutional.

Large crops of wheat and cotton led to passage of the Agricultural Act of 1937. In its amended form, this act provided the framework for the major farm programs that are still in effect today. The act made price-support loans by the CCC mandatory on the designated basic commodities of corn, wheat, and cotton, and it authorized optional support for other commodities. Under this act and subsequent legislation, the CCC supported more than one hundred different commodities, including fruit, vegetables, and various types of seed.

From 1941 to 1948, during and just after World War II (1939–1945), surpluses were rapidly utilized, and price supports became an incentive to stimulate production of agricultural commodities. In 1948 price-support levels were lowered for most of those commodities. By 1949 the agriculture of war-devastated Europe and Asia had recovered to a significant extent, and the demand for American farm products declined considerably. At the same time, however, crop production in the United States had greatly increased; as a result, farm commodity prices dropped and surpluses began to build up again. Rigid support levels were once

Many crops were ruined because they were unprotected outdoors. The lack of proper storage space for new harvests was an important issue during the Farmer's Protest Movement.

again enacted, but when the Korean War (1950–1953) strengthened farm prices, most CCC stocks were sold. Mounting surpluses and increased costs of government programs led to the enactment of a flexible price-support program (1954) and of the Soil Bank program (1956). These programs offered direct payments to farmers only if they agreed to reduce their acreage of major supported crops and to leave fallow the land removed from production. Ultimately, these control programs did not achieve the desired effect, since improved technology made it possible for farmers to greatly increase their yields per acre.

In the early 1960s price supports on major commodities were pegged at or near market-clearing prices, and producers' incomes were protected by direct payments on fixed quantities of products. Direct payments to farmers have greatly increased since the 1960s, with the feed-grain, cotton, and wheat programs accounting for most of this increase. Yet once introduced, federal subsidies to maintain prices have proved extremely difficult to end. In 1989 the U.S. Department of Agriculture paid farmers more than $10.8 billion in various subsidies. In France, farmers have vigorously protested an imminent decrease in the subsidies ($34 billion in 1989–90) that have made them the world's second largest food exporter after the United States.

Agricultural subsidies in the United States, Japan, and Europe were issues of contentious debate during Uruguay's round of international trade negotiations under the General Agreement on Tariffs and Trade (GATT) in 1990.

Some economists have argued that U.S. export expansion policies have undermined foreign production capacity, altered consumer preference, and consequently created dependence on imports of wheat and other grains. They argue that domestic U.S. farm policies have aggravated supply and price volatility for wheat and other cereal crops and that developing nations are pressured during trade negotiations to exchange domestic food security policies for access to the world trade market and debt-servicing arrangements. Unable to compete with U.S. production resources and U.S. Treasury–subsidized cereal prices, farmers in many poorer nations find that the prices they receive for their crops don't cover their costs. Economists point out that as early as 1965, food aid to India had driven down the price of domestic wheat and curtailed native production. Similar problems have occurred during the past three decades in nations throughout Africa, Latin America, and Asia.

A growing number of economists claim that small-scale farming must be made economically viable again so that established small farmers can survive and new ones can get started. They argue that this can be accomplished either by eliminating the favors the federal government bestows on large farms and corporate farming; or else by enacting labor laws that guarantee a minimum wage to farmworkers that is equal to that of other workers; or finally by writing legislation that makes the willful and acknowledged employment of illegal aliens punishable by imprisonment.

Still others claim that subsidy programs should be revised. They argue that when farm subsidies began during the New Deal, they were intended to help the impoverished small farmer. But because they were pegged to total marketing and total acreage rather than to personal income, they ended up lining the pockets of the wealthy. These same economists argue that if farm subsidies are continued—as the economists think they should be in order to stabilize farm income—they ought to be strongly weighted in favor of small farmers. They contend that no farmer should receive subsidies for crops grown (or not grown) on land in excess of a certain acreage, and that farm subsidies could be completely detached from crops and related to income instead. Farmers could sell on the open market, with federal payments making up the difference, if any, between earnings and a minimum livable income. Aiming to protect the small farmer from the conglomerates, they also support protective legislation that would work like a forceful antitrust policy for agriculture.

There is yet another school of thinking: some claim that the current federal agricultural policy should include a redistribution of land. These critics explain that the guiding principles behind redistribution are that land should belong to those who work and live on it and also that holdings should be of reasonable, not feudal, proportions.

Many economists believe that federal farm programs have been rationalized in the past based on public interest or ''market failure'' grounds, and that government intervention has been justified because agricultural markets do not conform to an ideal level of competition. But conservatives claim that government failure—rather than market failure—better explains the persistence of wasteful and inconsistent farm programs. Whatever the position, the issue of agribusiness will only get more controversial as e-commerce, the global marketplace, and increases in the world population further complicate the debate.

See also: **Agriculture Industry, Farm Credit Administration, General Agreement on Tariffs and Trade, Government Land Policy**

FURTHER READING

Benedict, Murray. *Farm Policies of the United States, 1790–1950.* New York: Twentieth Century Fund, 1953.

Davis, Joseph S. *On Agricultural Policy, 1926–1938.* Stanford: Food Research Institute, 1939.

Hamilton, David. *From New Day to New Deal.* Chapel Hill: University of North Carolina Press, 1991.

Kirkendall, Richard. *Social Scientists and Farm Politics in the Age of Roosevelt.* Ames, Iowa: Iowa State University Press, 1982.

Nourse, Edwin G. *Marketing Agreements Under the AAA.* Washington, DC: Brookings Institution, 1935.

GOVERNMENT LAND POLICY (ISSUE)

The Treaty of Paris of 1783, which brought the Revolutionary War to a close, ceded to the United States an area that became known as the Northwest Territories, and later, the ''Old Northwest,'' which included all lands south of Canada, east of the Mississippi River, and north of the Ohio River. At the time of the treaty the eastern third of the area east of the Mississippi was occupied. The land west of the Appalachian Mountains remained virtually untouched by European settlement until after 1800, when waves of settlers flooded into the area. The Louisiana Purchase in 1804 nearly doubled the size of the country, and the public domain of the United States tripled. Subsequent treaties and purchases continually added new land faster than the sales of the land could diminish it. By 1850 the federal government of the United States held 1.2 billion acres in the public domain.

For Congress, land represented wealth, and the question to be decided was, who should profit from the public domain? One option was to sell the land at full value and retain the wealth for the benefit of the country. Congress could also choose to give the land away and distribute the wealth to those whom it deemed worthy. Before the American Civil War (1861–1865), Congress tended to follow the first option but failed to implement it fully; as a result, the government received only a portion of the value while the rest went to purchasers. After 1862 Congress tended to follow the second strategy, but it again failed to ensure that the policy achieved its goals.

The Federalists (the party of Washington, Hamilton, and John Marshall, who favored a strong central government) viewed the public land primarily as a source of revenue that would give the federal government a chance to expand its role in the economy. For Secretary of the Treasury Alexander Hamilton, the sale of public land at high prices and in large lots would secure the maximum advantage for the public treasury. It would also discourage settlement, limit agricultural expansion, and indirectly encourage manufacturing by turning labor and capital away from the frontier and farming.

But Thomas Jefferson, James Madison, and the Republicans disagreed. They saw the sale of public land as an opportunity to create a nation of small landed farmers that would become the bulwark of democracy and a protection against the arbitrary power of the federal government. Jefferson proposed that the land be sold in small lots and on credit at low prices (if not given away) so that it would fall within the financial means of the largest number of people.

According to the Land Ordinance of 1785, all territory west of the Appalachian Mountains was to be settled in an orderly, systematic fashion. The land was to be surveyed prior to its sale and settlement, and was to be established along a rectangular grid and divided into townships six miles square. In turn, each township was to be subdivided into 36 sections one mile square. The initial terms of the ordinance represented a victory for the Federalists. Prices were set high and the minimum acreage was large. Alternating townships were to be sold whole or by sections consisting of 640 acres. All sales were to be held at public auction in order to ensure that the Treasury obtained the land's full market price as well as its reservation price of $1 per acre.

According to the Northwest Ordinance of 1787, Congress would appoint a governor until a population of five thousand voting-age males could elect its own territorial legislature. When the population reached sixty thousand, the territory could form a state that would be accepted with complete equality among the existing states. The legislation created five states, provided for civil and religious liberties in the respective states, and prohibited slavery within the territory.

Legislators had envisaged an orderly transfer of secure land titles from public to private hands; however, such transfers were often disrupted by eager settlers who already occupied some of the best land in the territory. These "squatters" posed a serious dilemma for government land policy. On the one hand, they contributed to the value of the land by converting it to farmland. On the other hand, they often encroached on the rights of Native Americans, fueling other debates about U.S. policy regarding the Native American population. Moreover, by taking the best properties, squatters

made the land unavailable to those who chose to follow federal guidelines. Finally, a system adopted in 1841 allowed squatters to purchase up to 160 acres of land at the minimum price of $1.25 an acre.

In 1854 Congress passed the Graduation Act, which addressed the problem of selling government land surrounded by private property and worth less than the reservation price. The Graduation Act provided for a progressive reduction in the price of unsold public lands to a minimum of 12.5 cents per acre for land that remained unsold for more than 30 years.

On May 20, 1862, President Abraham Lincoln (1861–1865) signed the Homestead Act, which gave settlers who had lived on land five years or more the rights to acquire a full title of 160 acres of land from the public domain. Those eligible would pay only a $10 registration fee. This "free" land for the cultivator seemed to bring America closer to Jefferson's ideal republic—but the reality fell short of the dream. As settlers moved farther west, water became scarce, and the land in general was less suitable for farming. One hundred and sixty acres proved inadequate for family self-sufficiency. Some scholars have argued that the Homestead Act induced many individuals and families to enter farming when they might have found more lucrative employment elsewhere. More liberal homestead acts followed, and between 1863 and 1900 there were close to 1.5 million entries for homesteads. Settlement and agriculture expanded, but western farmers remained disgruntled and eventually soon sought political solutions to their economic problems.

Another aspect of the government land policy was the land subsidies given to the transcontinental railroads that spanned the nation from the 1860s to the end of the nineteenth century. Motivated, as it turned out, by bribes paid by railroad promoters to congressmen as well as by a legitimate appreciation of the potential importance of railroads to the national economy, the Congress not only granted generous loans for construction of the rail lines, it also gave huge grants of land. The government gave the railroad companies not only the right-of-way for the line for free, but for each mile of track, a grant of twenty square miles of land grouped in an alternating checkerboard pattern along the right-of-way. Because of its proximity to the railroad, this land immediately became more valuable. Soon, the state governments were also granting favorable loans and land grants to railroads. By the end of the century, the federal government had given 130 million acres to the railroads, while the states had given an extra 50 million acres. Historians note that in some cases the subsidies exceeded the cost of construction of the rail lines.

The Land Ordinance of 1785 and the Northwest Ordinance of 1787 provided a foundation for the orderly and systematic expansion of the United States through land acquisition and settlement. After its creation in 1812, the General Land Office transferred vast quantities of land from the public domain to private ownership. Government initiatives such as these had a marked and lasting impact upon the division of land and the size distribution of farms throughout the territories to which it applied. By 1860 in the Northeast, farm sizes varied as a result of sales and subdivisions among heirs. In the Midwest, on the other hand, farms were much more consistent in size. For specific states, the impact of land act provisions is apparent in the size distribution data. For example, in Ohio, Indiana, and Illinois, states where settlement occurred when the minimum purchase was 80 acres, 80-acre farms were the model size. In Michigan and Wisconsin, states where settlement occurred after the 1832 revision had cut the minimum purchase to 40 acres, 40-acre farms were the model size.

The impact of these land sales and transfers has generated exhaustive debates among scholars. These kinds of government land policies have often been criticized for inhibiting growth and for being inefficient. Many scholars have argued that sales of land increased too rapidly, bringing too much labor and capital into agriculture and starving manufacturing of these resources. Some have argued that by establishing minimum rather than maximum acreage, the public land policy promoted speculation, concentration of ownership, and tenancy rather than individual small holdings.

But other scholars argue that the release of western land from the public domain induced westward migration and population growth, increased wage rates, increased the gross national product, and redistributed income regionally and between different socioeconomic groups.

See also: **Homestead Act, Land Ordinance of 1785, Louisiana Purchase, Northwest Ordinance, Old Northwest**

FURTHER READING

Brinkley, Alan et al., eds. *American History: A Survey*, 8th ed. New York: McGraw Hill, 1991.

Dennen, A. Taylor. "Some Efficiency Effects of Nineteenth-Century Federal Land Policy: A Dynamic Analysis." *Agricultural History*, 1977.

Fogel, Robert W. and Jack Rutner. "The Efficiency Effects of Federal Land Policy, 1850–1900." In *Dimensions of Quantitative Research in History*. William Aydelotte et al., eds. Princeton: Princeton University Press, 1972.

Gates, Paul W. "The Homestead Law in an Incongruous Land System." *American Historical Review*, 1936.

Hibbard, Benjamin H. *A History of the Public Land Policies*. New York: Macmillan Co., 1924.

Robbins, Roy M. *Our Landed Heritage*. Princeton: Princeton University Press, 1942.

GRAND BANKS

Grand Banks are a shallow section of the northern Atlantic Ocean, lying east and south of Newfoundland, Canada, and extending about 350 miles (563 kilometers) from east to west. The ocean is shallow here because of underwater plateaus, called banks. After the Vikings explored the region around A.D. 1000, fishermen from Basque (northern Spain) also sailed the Grand Banks as they searched for whales. In the late 1300s other European fishermen may have sailed here as well, skimming the coast of Newfoundland and Nova Scotia, and possibly going ashore for food, to make repairs, or to trade with the natives. By the early 1500s more fleets were attracted to the rich fishing grounds. By the end of the century fishing villages were established on Newfoundland. American and Canadian fleets relied on the Grand Banks as a major source of codfish during colonial times. The area is still fished today, but the Canadian government carefully monitors it to avoid depletion of its stock.

See also: **Fishing (Commercial), L'Anse aux Meadows**

GRAYING OF AMERICA (ISSUE)

At the beginning of the twentieth century retirement was practically unheard of. Pension plans were a rarity and Social Security did not yet exist. People typically "died working." It was only after President Franklin D. Roosevelt's New Deal, especially the Social Security Administration, that the concept of retirement became rooted in the American psyche. Beginning in the 1950s, as a result of government-encouraged corporate pension plans and the Social Security Administration, older workers were rapidly leaving the work force. In fact, they were leaving so rapidly that they threatened to bankrupt the Social Security System. The key statistic here is the ratio of

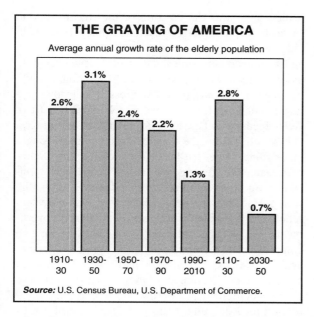

THE GRAYING OF AMERICA

Average annual growth rate of the elderly population

2.6%	3.1%	2.4%	2.2%	1.3%	2.8%	0.7%
1910-30	1930-50	1950-70	1970-90	1990-2010	2110-30	2030-50

Source: U.S. Census Bureau, U.S. Department of Commerce.

The historical and projected annual growth rate of the elderly population is depicted in the graying of America. There should be an increase of elderly citizens between 2010–2030 due to the aging of the "Baby Boomers."

workers paying FICA taxes to retirees. A high ratio leaves the system solvent; a low ratio bankrupts it. At the close of the century the ratio of workers to retirees was decreasing at an alarming rate. In 2010 the ratio was projected to hover around four to one. By 2020 the estimated ratio would decline to three to one. By 2030 the ratio would be nearly two to one; moreover, the trend was not expected to reverse itself for decades to come.

In addition, the retirement system drains the economy of skilled workers. Some economists believed that in order to foster the growth of the labor supply and increase the level of experienced workers the Congress needs to amend the Social Security laws and eliminate income restrictions on recipients. Older workers, they argue, need an incentive to work. But in the late 1990s most post-retirement workers had to sacrifice a significant portion of their Social Security income once they started getting a paycheck again. If the retiree was under age 65 with earnings in excess of $7,680, one dollar in benefits was deducted for each two dollars earned above $7,680. From age 65 to 70, one dollar in benefits was deducted for each three dollars earned above $10,560. Above age 70 the Social Security benefits were not affected.

Other economists disagreed with Social Security reform. They argue that the older worker needs to be able to retire after a life of work. For them the only problem with the retirement system is that the Social

Security program is so popular that it is running out of money and needs to be refunded. The advocates of refunding tend to believe that there should be a tax on the working population to cover the retirees' Social Security and Medicare.

Proponents of an elderly work force pointed to studies suggesting that aging baby boomers were not looking to spend their twilight years working in high school level jobs at minimum wage, nor were they as concerned with advancement as their younger counterparts. These studies suggest that older workers want to "enjoy" themselves on the job more: they wanted stability, a good rapport with coworkers, and also a liberal amount of discretionary time. In other words, older workers enjoy both the social aspects of working and the challenge of work, in addition to the pay.

Economists believed that this was a motivational characteristic that blended well with the growing popularity in the late twentieth century of mentoring, flextime, and part-time positions. They argued that many older workers tended to be more focused and conscientious and that they exhibited greater feelings of company loyalty and maintained better job morale. These proponents of fostering an elderly work force discounted various charges: that older workers were less creative, that they were less likely to keep up with new developments in their fields, and that they were more difficult to supervise. These workers seemed to enjoy a working environment consisting of both younger and older workers.

But will there be enough older workers to fill any expansion in the work slots set aside for older workers? A potential problem for the U.S. labor force during the first few decades of the twenty-first century is that the baby-boomer generation, beginning to retire in substantial numbers around the year 2020, would be followed by a much smaller generation of workers who, because of their relatively small number, might not have the skills to pull the economy forward. Some predicted a significant shortage of qualified workers, old or young, as early as 2000.

This touches on the general problem of training. The shift from heavy industry and agriculture to an information and services society will probably increase the need for a more highly skilled, technically adept and "agile" work force, able to fill multiple functions on the job. But the U.S. educational system had not caught up with growing needs. If the schools did not provide new workers with technical skills to fill the wave of future job markets, how can we expect older workers to step in and fill that need? But some economists thought that older workers might help to staunch the hemorrhaging of skills that will take place when experienced workers leave work for early retirement.

See also: **Human Capital, Social Security Act**

FURTHER READING

Crampton, S., J. Hodge, and J. Mishra. "Transition-ready or Not: The Aging of America's Work Force." *Public Personnel Management*, 25, 1996.

D'Amico, Judy, R. *Workforce 2020: Work and workers in the 21st Century*. Indianapolis, IN: Hudson Institute, 1997.

Menchin, R. *New Work Opportunities for Older Americans*. Upper Saddle River, NJ: Prentice Hall, 1993.

Parnell, D. *Dateline 2000: The New Higher Education Agenda*. Washington, DC: The Community College Press, 1990.

Rifkin, J. *The End of Work: The Decline of the Global Labor Force and the Dawn of the Post-market Era*. New York: G.P. Putman's Sons, 1993.

GREAT DEPRESSION

The stock market crash on October 29, 1929, sent the United States careening into the longest and darkest economic depression in American history. Between 1929 and 1933, all major economic indexes told the same story. The gross national product (GNP), the total of all goods and services produced each year, fell from $104.4 billion in 1929 to $74.2 billion in 1933, setting back the GNP per capita rate by twenty years. Industrial production declined 51 percent before reviving slightly in 1932. Unemployment statistics revealed the impact of the Depression on Americans. In 1929, the U.S. Labor Department reported that there were nearly 1.5 million persons without jobs in the country. After the crash, the figure soared. At its peak in 1933, unemployment stood at more than 12.6 million without jobs, although some estimates placed unemployment as high as 16 million. By 1933, the annual national combined income had shrunk from $87.8 billion to $40.2 billion. Farmers, perhaps the hardest hit economic group, saw their total combined income drop from $11.9 billion to $5.3 billion.

For the first two years of the Depression, which spread worldwide, President Herbert Hoover (1929–1933) relied on the voluntary cooperation of business and labor to maintain payrolls and production. When the crisis deepened, he took positive steps to stop the spread of economic collapse. Hoover's most important

achievement was the creation of the Reconstruction Finance Corporation (RFC), a loan agency designed to aid large business concerns, including banks, railroads, and insurance companies. The RFC later became an essential agency of the New Deal. In addition, Hoover obtained new funds from Congress to cut down the number of farm foreclosures. The Home Loan Bank Act helped prevent the foreclosure of home mortgages. On the relief issue, the President and Congress fought an ongoing battle that lasted for months. The Democrats wanted the federal government to assume responsibility for direct relief and to spend heavily on public works. Hoover, however, insisted that unemployment relief was a problem for local, not federal, governments. At first, he did little more than appoint two committees to mobilize public and private agencies against distress. Yet after a partisan fight, Hoover signed a relief bill unmatched in American history. The Emergency Relief and Construction Act provided $300 million for local relief loans and $1.5 billion for self-liquidating public works. Tragically, the Depression only worsened. By the time Hoover's term in office expired, the nation's banking system had virtually collapsed and the economic machinery of the nation was grinding to a halt. Hoover left office with the reputation of a do-nothing President. The judgment was rather unfair. He had done much, including establishing many precedents for the New Deal; but it was not enough.

What happened to the economy after the stock market crash of 1929 left most people baffled. The physical structure of business and industry was still intact, undamaged by war or natural disaster, but businesses closed. Men wanted to go to work, but plants stood dark and idle. Prolonged unemployment created a new class of people. The jobless sold apples on street corners. They stood in breadlines and outside soup kitchens. Many lived in "Hoovervilles," shantytowns on the outskirts of large cities. Thousands of unemployed men and boys took to the road in search of work, and the gas station became a meeting place for men "on the bum." In 1932, a crowd of 50 men fought for a barrel of garbage outside the back door of a Chicago restaurant. In northern Alabama, poor families exchanged a dozen eggs, which they sorely needed, for a box of matches. Despite such mass suffering, for the most part there was little violence. The angriest Americans were those in rural areas, where cotton was bringing only five cents a pound and wheat only 35 cents a bushel. In August 1932, Iowa farmers began dumping milk bound for Sioux City. To dramatize their plight, Milo Reno, former president of the Iowa Farmers Union, organized a farm strike on the northern plains and cut off all agricultural products from urban

Work was scarce during the Depression. Workers and families struggled to survive in the uncertain economy.

markets until prices rose. During the same summer, 25,000 World War I (1914–1918) veterans, led by former sergeant Walter W. Waters, staged the Bonus March on Washington, DC, to demand immediate payment of a bonus due to them in 1945. They stood passively on the Capitol steps while Congress voted it down. After a riot with police, Hoover ordered the U.S. Army to clean the veterans out of their shanty-town, for fear they would breed a revolution.

The Great Depression was a crisis of the American mind. Many people believed that the country had reached all its frontiers and faced a future of limited opportunity. The slowdown of marriage and birth rates expressed this pessimism. The Depression smashed the old beliefs of rugged individualism, the sanctity of business, and a limited government. Utopian movements found an eager following. The Townsend Plan, initiated by retired California physician Francis E. Townsend, demanded a monthly pension to people over age 65. Charles E. Coughlin (1891–1979), a radio priest in Royal Oak, Michigan, advocated the nationalization of banks, utilities, and natural resources. Senator Huey P. Long (1893–1935), Governor of Louisiana, led a movement that recommended a redistribution of the wealth. All the programs tapped a broad sense of resentment among those who felt they had been left out

of President Franklin Roosevelt's (1933–1945) New Deal. Americans did gradually regain their sense of optimism. The progress of the New Deal revived the old faith that the nation could meet any challenge and control its own destiny. Even many intellectuals who had "debunked" American life in the 1920s began to revise their opinions for the better.

By early 1937, there were signs of recovery in the American economy. Business indexes were up—some near pre-crash levels. The New Deal had eased much of the acute distress, although unemployment remained around 7.5 million. The economy again went into a sharp recession that was almost as bad as 1929. Although conditions improved by mid-1938, the Depression did not truly end until the government launched massive defense spending in preparation for World War II (1939–1945).

See also: **Great Depression (Causes of), Hoovervilles, New Deal, Recession, Reconstruction Finance Corporation, Franklin D. Roosevelt, Stock Market Crash of 1929, Unemployment**

FURTHER READING

Phillips, Cabell. *From the Crash to the Blitz, 1929–1939.* New York: The Macmillan Co., 1969.

The Great Depression drove millions of Americans out of their homes in search of work. This mother and her children left Oklahoma in search of work picking cotton in California.

Schlesinger, Arthur M., Jr. *The Age of Roosevelt.* Boston: Houghton Mifflin Co., 1957.

Shannon, David A. *The Great Depression.* Englewood Cliffs, NJ: Prentice-Hall, 1960.

Terkel, Studs. *Hard Times: An Oral History of the Great Depression in America.* New York: Pantheon Books Inc., 1970.

Wecter, Dixon. *The Age of the Great Depression, 1929–1941.* New York: The Macmillan Company, 1948.

GREAT DEPRESSION, CAUSES OF *(ISSUE)*

After the presidential election of Herbert C. Hoover, (1929–33) in November, 1928, it seemed that all was well in the United States. The economy was prosperous and the stock market was booming. The President had promised that economic gains would continue and that poverty would disappear. Most people believed Hoover and they looked forward to a bright future. But already there were signs that the economic system was not as sound as it appeared to be—soon the great collapse began.

The most crucial barrier to U.S. economic health was the unstable character of the international economy following World War I (1914–1918). Before World War I the United States had been a debtor nation, but between 1914 and 1919 there was a major change. The United States had become the world's leading creditor; the war also propelled most of Europe's economies into a state of collapse and they could not pay their debts. By the end of the war the private debt owed by Europeans to the United States equaled nearly $3 billion, and the public debt owed by foreign governments to the U.S. government was $10.3 billion.

To deal with this potentially disastrous situation the United States could have forgiven public debts and adopted a trade policy designed to encourage exchange, but the policy that was followed was exactly the opposite. The United States demanded that foreign governments pay their debts in full. At the same time, the United States raised tariff rates, which undermined trade. This resulted in a favorable balance of trade for

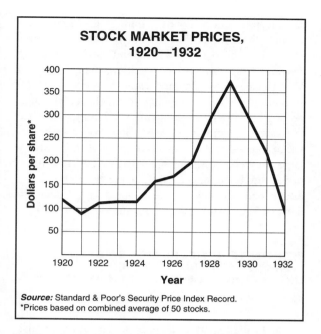

STOCK MARKET PRICES, 1920—1932

Source: Standard & Poor's Security Price Index Record.
*Prices based on combined average of 50 stocks.

Stock market prices from 1920 to 1932, which peaked in 1929 after two years of wild trading, then suddenly fell, causing the market to crash and contribute to a world wide depression.

the United States and an increasing trade deficit for Europe. It was only because of massive investments by U.S. businesses, which amounted to about $1 billion per year between 1919 and 1930, that Europe was able to make up the deficit. Thus the international financial structure came to be almost entirely dependent upon U.S. businesses and banks. This European reliance on U.S. investments was a system that could operate successfully only as long as the outflow of U.S. capital continued.

The perpetuation of such a system required that the U.S. economy remained healthy and, although it appeared to be robust, there were critical problems. The agricultural sector of the economy had never fully recovered from the recession of 1921–1922 and the industry operated at a net loss throughout the balance of the 1920s. When crops yielded precipitously declining prices in 1929, economic sectors that were linked to farming suffered similar losses.

Another critical problem was a longstanding maldistribution of income. By 1929 a substantial 26 percent of national income went to *only* two percent of income receivers. Moreover businesses tended to plow enormous portions of their profits into expansion and to increase wages at a lower rate than the economy demanded. This led to overproduction and a dangerous rise in consumer credit. (During the twenties, to purchase consumer goods, real estate, and automobiles, people went more deeply into debt than ever before.)

Thus an economic scenario evolved that could only last as long as there was continued growth. Unfortunately, the growth of the period had a fragile base.

The unrealistic and unstable nature of the U.S. economy was evident in the stock market's behavior during the late 1920s. Between 1927 and 1929 trading on the stock market increased sharply and prices soared. Referred to as a "bull market," it was characterized by rigorous buying and selling—not necessarily for long-term investment, but to make a quick profit while prices continued to rise. This type of speculation was very dangerous because it was often accomplished using borrowed money. In 1927 alone, brokers' loans—using the stocks themselves for collateral—increased from $3 billion to $4.5 billion, while the volume of shares traded increased from 451 million to 577 million. This behavior drove stock prices up, far beyond any realistic connection to the value of the businesses the stocks represented. By early 1929, for example, many share issues were selling at more than sixteen times their earnings whereas the safe maximum ratio was said to be 10 to one. Between 1925 and 1929 the average price of common stock increased some 300 percent and the volume of trade more than doubled. Bank loans that were used to finance speculation rose during the same period from $3.5 billion to $8.5 billion.

Exactly why this irrational boom of borrowing and trading took place is hard to explain. Part of the blame lay with businesses that continued to produce even after there were signs that the market for their products was becoming saturated. Blame also lay with the banking community for making enormous unsound loans, and with the investors themselves who were greedy for profit. Another contributing factor might have been the fact that there were few government regulations over business, the stock trade, and banking in the period preceding the market boom and during the subsequent collapse.

By the summer of 1929 the system was out of control and stock prices had reached levels that could not be maintained. The market collapse began in September 1929, when the Bank of England raised interest rates, pushing bank clients to withdraw several hundred million dollars from New York banks. This caused stock prices to falter slightly and large investors began to unload some of their holdings quietly. Then on October 24, 1929, panic seized the stock market. On that day, known as "Black Thursday," 12 million shares were exchanged and stock prices collapsed. Business and government leaders reassured the public that this catastrophe represented only a "market adjustment" and for a few days conditions stabilized.

Then on October 29, the bottom fell out again. Following this the market entered a long period of general decline that seemed to represent the virtual collapse of the financial system.

The prosperity of the twenties was dependent upon the smooth inter-working of world trade, domestic capital investment, the construction industry, and manufacturing—especially of automobiles. The key ingredient in this mix was confidence that goods could be sold and that investments would yield profits. The stock market crash severely weakened the confidence of the business community, causing purchases to decline and foreign investments to dwindle. This, in turn, led the already rickety European economy to collapse, putting an even greater strain on U.S. businesses and banks. Thus was generated an irreversible downward economic spiral which enveloped the entire industrialized world. By 1931 the Great Depression (1929–1939) was in full swing—the worst of its kind in recorded history.

See also: **Hoovervilles, New Deal, Stock Market Crash of 1929**

FURTHER READING

Bernstein, Michael L. *The Great Depression: Delayed Recovery and Economic Change in America, 1929–1939*. Cambridge: Cambridge University Press, 1989.

Faulkner, Harold Underwood. *American Economic History*. New York: Harper and Row, 1964.

Friedman, Milton, and Anna Jacobson Schwartz. *The Great Contraction, 1929–1933*. Princeton, NJ: Princeton University Press, 1991.

Galbraith, John Kenneth. *The Great Crash, 1929*. Boston: Houghton Mifflin Company, 1997.

Garraty, John Arthur. *The Great Depression: An Inquiry into the Causes, Course, and Consequences of the World Wide Depression of the 1930s, as Seen by Contemporaries and in the Light of History*. New York: Doubleday Press, 1986.

Link, Arthur S. *American Epoch: A History of The United States Since 1890s*. New York: Alfred A. Knopf, 1955.

GREAT MIGRATION (1630–1640)

Soon after the establishment of the English colonies of Virginia and Massachusetts Bay in the early seventeenth century, floods of immigrants began arriving in both places. Although some of these immigrants (especially those in New England) arrived seeking freedom from religious persecution, many others in Virginia and New England came for economic reasons—looking for easy money from tobacco planting, or escape from a failing cloth market, inflation, and bad harvests. The immigrants, who came from a variety of social classes and occupations, arrived in relatively large numbers, averaging 4,000 each year. This migration strongly influenced the character of the newly established colonies and contributed to the development of long-lasting English institutions.

"[I]NFINITE NUMBERS MAY BE SET TO WORK" IN AMERICA, "TO THE UNBURDENING OF THE REALM AT HOME."

Richard Hakluyt, *Discourse of Western Planting*, **1584.**

In the early part of the period, most of the English immigrants to the colonies headed for New England. There were several reasons for this: a sizeable number of them were religious non-conformists who objected to the governmentally enforced rites of the Church of England, and who came to Massachusetts Bay in whole congregations, ministers and all. They hoped to join or establish their own religious settlements as the Pilgrims had done before them. These same immigrants, however, faced economic as well as religious discrimination. They were mostly middle-class and well-educated, but were limited in the occupations they could pursue and were taxed more heavily than their Anglican neighbors. In addition, they faced rising prices and a depression in the cloth trade, which they had hoped to escape in the colonies. At the height of New England immigration in the 1630s, an average of 2000 English men, women, and children arrived in Massachusetts Bay colony each year. The Parliamentary victory in the English Civil War (1642–1649) eased pressure on non-conformists, and immigration to New England virtually stopped after 1640.

In the later part of the period, Virginia was the destination of many new settlers to the country. Before the 1640s, many of the Virginian immigrants were adventurers looking for a quick profit from the New World. After the establishment of tobacco as the colony's major product, however, the need for labor brought people to Virginia as indentured servants. Between 1635 and 1705, about 2000 persons arrived from England each year, most of them contractual laborers bound to serve Virginian planters without wages for a period of years, in exchange for their transportation to the colony. They ranged from lower-middle-class to laborers, but they all arrived with the idea of serving out their contracts and winning land of their own in the colony. Perhaps as much as 75 percent of Virginia's colonists by the end of the seventeenth century had originally arrived as indentured servants. Some of these came unwillingly, practically kidnapped by sea captains and labor contractors.

The other major group of immigrants to the colonies during the seventeenth century were Africans. From 1619—when a Dutch warship brought the first load of African laborers—to 1670, the African population of Virginia grew to more than 2000. At first, Africans were treated about the same as English indentured servants. Some Africans even managed to end their terms of servitude and buy and farm land of their own. But by about 1650 a color bar had risen that kept Blacks from sharing in colonial prosperity. Thus, one of the largest immigrant groups was effectively prevented from sharing the economic benefits of settling in America.

See also: **Africans Arrive in Virginia, Indentured Servants**

FURTHER READING

Anderson, Robert Charles. *The Great Migration Begins: Immigrants to New England, 1620–1633.* Boston: New England Historic Genealogical Society, 1995–.

Anderson, Virginia DeJohn. *New England's Generation: The Great Migration and the Formation of Society and Culture in the Seventeenth Century.* Cambridge: Cambridge University Press, 1991.

Bailyn, Bernard. *The Peopling of British North America: An Introduction.* New York: Alfred A. Knopf, 1986.

Cowing, Cedric B. *The Saving Remnant: Religion and the Settling of New England.* Urbana: University of Illinois Press, 1995.

Ransome, David R. "'Shipt for Virginia': The Beginnings in 1619–1622 of the Great Migration to the Chesapeake." *Virginia Magazine of History and Biography*, October, 1995.

GREAT MIGRATION, 1910–1920

In 1914, 90 percent of African Americans lived in the states of the former Confederacy, where so-called Jim Crow statutes had legalized the separation of Americans by race. These statutes were validated by a series of Supreme Court rulings during the 1890s, culminating in the famous 1896 "separate but equal" doctrine of *Plessy v. Ferguson*, which made segregation legal in the United States. But between 1910 and 1920, the percentage of African Americans living in the South began to fall. By 1930, more than 21.2 percent of African Americans lived outside of the South.

Historians continue to debate why African Americans failed to leave the South in large numbers at the end of the American Civil War (1861–1865). Migration itself is a result of both push and pull factors—prejudice, better economic opportunities, discrimination, etc. While the South certainly provided push factors, the North offered strong pull elements for Southern African Americans, appearing to have a more open society and better economic opportunities, though it still had its share of prejudice and discrimination.

Some historians argue that European immigration accounts for the slow start of the Black exodus. The huge demand for labor in the heavily industrialized North was met mostly by massive European immigration. Irish and German laborers first filled many of the urban factory jobs, and the remaining jobs tended to go to southern and eastern Europeans. Had Northern industries not met their demand for labor with European immigration, some historians argue that employers would have more actively recruited Southern Blacks.

World War I (1914–1918) greatly accelerated the migration of African Americans out of the rural South, where agriculture had been plagued by floods and crop failures, including a devastating plague of boll weevils that decimated the cotton crop. With greater demand for the war effort, factory owners in northern cities sent recruiters to draw workers northward with glowing reports of high wages and good living conditions. During the decade between 1910 and 1920, the African American population of the North and West grew by 333,000.

Once in Northern urban areas, however, African Americans were segregated in urban slums, where they continued to be objects of race hatred by their white neighbors, especially unskilled workers who viewed them as competitors for their jobs. A growing number of African Americans during this time began to demand the rights long denied to them, particularly higher wages, equal protection under the law, and the chance to vote and hold political office. Leading the increasingly militant National Association for the Advancement of Colored People (NAACP), W.E.B. DuBois (1868–1963) took on all of these aims as key goals for the group.

Turning to terrorism, lynch mobs in the South murdered more than 70 African Americans in 1919, ten of them World War I veterans in uniform. The new Ku Klux Klan, committed to the intimidation of African Americans, gained more than 100,000 members. In 1919 the country saw the worst outburst of racial riots in American history up until that time. Two of the most tragic occurred in Washington, DC, where a majority of the offenders were white veterans; and in the Chicago slums, where for thirteen days a mob of whites fought African Americans. Before the year ended, twenty-five race riots had resulted in hundreds of deaths and injuries, and millions of dollars worth of property damage.

Most African Americans resisted their attackers, as the NAACP advised them to do, and liberal whites organized to fight intolerance and to lobby for anti-lynching laws, but by and large African Americans were neither hopeful of remedy nor ready to campaign on their own behalf. Instead, by 1923, about half a million African Americans had joined the Universal Negro Improvement Association led by Marcus Garvey (1887–1940), a Jamaican Black nationalist who proposed to create a new empire in Africa with himself on the throne. Though Garvey's plans for an empire collapsed, his movement met the powerful African American need for self-identity, racial pride, and an escape from a society that denied them dignity, opportunity, and personal safety.

See also: **Jim Crow Laws, Ku Klux Klan, Plessy v Ferguson, Slum**

FURTHER READING

Grimshaw, Allen D., ed. *Racial Violence in the United States.* Chicago: Aldine Pub. Co., 1969.

Franklin, John Hope. *From Slavery to Freedom: A History of Negro Americans.* New York: Alfred A. Knopf, 1980.

Nieman, Donald G. *Promises to Keep : African-Americans and the Constitutional Order, 1776 to the Present.* New York: Oxford University Press, 1991.

Schaffer, Ronald. *America in the Great War: The Rise of the War Welfare State.* New York: Oxford University Press, 1991.

GREAT RAILROAD STRIKE OF 1877

In July 1877 West Virginia was the scene of a railroad strike that soon became the first nationwide strike in United States history. The trouble began when an economic depression led railroad companies to cut wages. Workers in West Virginia withheld their labor, and paralysis quickly spread to railways in the East and the Midwest in what became known as the Great Railroad Strike of 1877.

In reaction to a business slump, the Baltimore and Ohio Railroad in West Virginia cut wages for all employees by ten percent, including the president of the company. During the nineteenth century wages for unskilled laborers were meager, averaging $10 per week, although skilled workers could earn $20 per week. Since a 10 percent cut in pay caused a financial crisis for the families of many railroad workers, a number of train firemen refused to accept the wage cut and went on strike. The Great Railroad Strike of 1877 began.

The Baltimore and Ohio Railroad firemen were soon joined by the employees of other rail lines in a sympathy strike. The railroad network itself insured that sympathizers stretched beyond the state of West Virginia, and strikes later broke out in Illinois, Indiana, Kentucky, and Pennsylvania. It wasn't long before over half of all American railway line were closed.

In Martinsburg, West Virginia, a small number of local volunteer militiamen tried to break strike against the Baltimore and Ohio. Several strike leaders were arrested, but a supportive crowd quickly rescued them. West Virginia's governor Henry Matthew attempted to send in more military support for the beleaguered town. But the militia company called to suppress the strike would not mobilize, since many of its volunteers were railroad workers or had family ties to railroad workers. West Virginia had four organized militia units, but since two of them sympathized with the strikers, the state had need of re-enforcement. Governor Matthews requested federal troops from President Rutherford B. Hayes (1877–1881) to help end the strike. The state's appeal was followed by similar requests from Kentucky and Pennsylvania. President Hayes had the resources and complied. Federal troops were available because the end of Reconstruction saw the withdrawal of many soldiers from the South.

The worst violence took place in Pittsburgh, where local militia ordered to break the strike instead sided with the workers. Federal troops arrived, and ten strikers were killed when violence erupted. Enraged by the deaths of the strikers, a crowd attacked the federal troops, driving them from the city. The mob then turned to destroying railroad property. Additional strikes occurred along the nation's railroad lines, and federal troops continued to provide assistance to beleaguered

The first train containing meat for the marketplace departs the Chicago stockyards with cover from the U.S. Cavalry following a strike by railway workers. This labor protest is believed to be the first nationwide strike in U.S. history.

states unprepared to deal with the strikers and their widespread support.

At the height of the 1877 strikes, eleven states called 45,000 Guardsmen into service. The War Department committed 2,100 regular troops. By August 2, 1877, the strikes were over. Order was restored and the trains were running again. Military force, assisted by managerial restraint, ended the walkout. The wages of railroad workers were restored or at least not cut further.

Newspapers blamed the strike on Communists and Communist sympathizers. President Hayes, however, was just as quick to deny the involvement of Communists. The attacks, he said, were directed against the railroads and not against property in general, as one would expect if the strike was Communist inspired.

Hayes was both praised and criticized for his use of federal troops. Striking workers and their sympathizers, many of whom were Civil War (1861–1865) veterans, deeply resented his employment of federal troops to break the strike. On the other hand, the president's supporters pointed to his cautious use of the troops and his reluctance to cause bloodshed. Critics,

including Pennsylvania Railroad president Thomas Scott, charged that the president waited too long to call in the troops and that the wide scope of the strike was a result of the government's failure to protect the private property of the corporation and its shareholders.

Regardless of blame, the Railroad Strike of 1877 revealed serious labor unrest throughout the nation. The railroad industry targeted unions as a main source of their labor problems, and states re-examined their need for a well-equipped and trained militia. This widespread strike was among the first acts of what was to become a national labor movement.

See also: **Baltimore and Ohio Railroad, Labor Movement, Railroad Industry, Reconstruction**

FURTHER READING

Collins, Holdridge. *History of the Illinois National Guard, 1874–1879.* Chicago: Black and Beech, 1879.

Foner, Philip Sheldon. *The Great Labor Uprising of 1877.* New York: Monad Press: distributed by Pathfinder Press, 1977.

The Great Serpent Mound, a quarter mile long, appears as an uncoiling snake when viewed from above, and was constructed by Indians near Hope Well, Ohio.

Rich, Bernard. *The President and Civil Disturbances*. Washington, DC: Brookings Institute, 1941.

Scheips, Paul. *Benevolence and Bayonets and Civil Military Relations in the United States*. Evansville: University of Evansville, 1988.

Yeller, Samuel. *American Labor Struggles*. New York: Harcourt Brace and Co., 1936.

GREAT SERPENT MOUND

Near Hopewell, Ohio, an early group of Indians, called Mound Builders, constructed an earthworks that looks like a huge snake when viewed from the sky. The Great Serpent Mound is one-quarter mile (just under one-half kilometer) long and was built by the Fort Ancient group. These Indians were descendants of the Hopewell, an earlier culture that dominated the Ohio River Valley until about A.D. 500. The ruins of the Fort Ancient people indicate that they were hunters and gatherers like the Mississippian people to their south and west, but they also fished and cultivated some crops including beans, corn, and squash. The Fort Ancient people lived in stockaded villages like that found in southwest Ohio, overlooking the Miami River. The site is called Fort Ancient (after its name the

prehistoric Indian group was named), and it is a fortification surrounded by an earth wall, ranging from six to ten feet (two to three meters) in height and it is over 3.5 miles (5.6 kilometers) long.

See also: **Mound Builders, Ohio Valley**

THE GREAT SOCIETY

The United States mourned when President John F. Kennedy (1960–1963) was assassinated on November 22, 1963. But despite the tragedy, the country was experiencing an era of unprecedented economic health. President Kennedy had already proposed a series of government-funded programs aimed at spreading U.S. prosperity to people still mired in poverty, such as the residents of Appalachia or of the urban ghettoes. When Kennedy's Vice President, Lyndon B. Johnson (1963–1968) assumed the presidency, he pushed to make many of Kennedy's proposals into law. Capitalizing on U.S. stability, as well as the emotions of Kennedy's death, Johnson proposed anti-poverty, civil rights, education, and health care laws. In a speech at the University of Michigan in May 1964, Johnson said he hoped these programs would help create a ''Great Society.''

Great Society programs, as they came to be known, assisted millions, but they were very controversial. In the short run, funding for these costly programs decreased, as the United States spent more and more fighting the Vietnam War (1964–1975). In the long run, many critics have charged that these initiatives resulted in high taxes, "big government," and that they actually hurt the very people they were designed to help. Nonetheless, Great Society programs such as Medicare, which assists the elderly with medical expenses, remained popular and in the late 1990s they were still a crucial part of many Americans' lives.

Great Society programs were not the first large scale effort by the federal government to aid the disadvantaged. President Franklin D. Roosevelt (1932–1945) promised a "New Deal" to all Americans when he was elected. This "New Deal" was a long list of employment, income-assistance, and labor legislation, and it also had many critics.

But President Roosevelt's New Deal came at a time of mass poverty, when the United States and the world were living through the tough economic times of the Great Depression (1929–1939). Having emerged from World War II (1939–1945) as the world's most powerful nation, the United States experienced astounding economic growth in the 1950s and 1960s. Many Americans who barely had enough to eat during the Depression, now found themselves living in brand new homes and driving automobiles.

THE GREAT SOCIETY RESTS ON ABUNDANCE AND LIBERTY FOR ALL. IT DEMANDS AN END TO POVERTY AND RACIAL INJUSTICE, TO WHICH WE ARE TOTALLY COMMITTED IN OUR TIME. BUT THAT IS JUST THE BEGINNING.

President Lyndon Baines Johnson, 1964

President Kennedy believed this national wealth could be used to uplift those who had not yet shared in the good economic times. Particularly disadvantaged were African Americans, who faced legal segregation in the South and poverty and discrimination in the North. In the tradition of Roosevelt's New Deal, Kennedy proposed employment, education, and health care legislation.

This was the legacy President Lyndon Johnson (1963–1969) hoped to fulfill with his Great Society. A masterful politician, Johnson may have lacked Kennedy's public grace, but he made up for it with political savvy. A former leader in the Senate, Johnson would need these skills to enact his ambitious programs which faced serious opposition in Congress.

During the summer of 1964 Johnson challenged Congress to pass the Economic Opportunity Act, the foundation for what came to be known as the "war on poverty." Johnson also proposed the Civil Rights Act of 1964, which combated racial discrimination. Johnson said enacting these bills would be a fitting tribute to Kennedy.

Johnson's initiatives seemed to be popular with voters. He won the 1964 election in a landslide. Capitalizing on what appeared to be a mandate from the American people, Johnson quickly proposed a wide range of programs for mass transportation, food stamps, immigration, and legal services for the poor. Bills aiding elementary, secondary, and higher education were also passed. Medicaid and Medicare were established to assist the poor and elderly, respectively, with medical treatment.

Other initiatives created the Department of Housing and Urban Development, aimed at improving housing conditions, particularly in crowded cities, and Project Head Start, which aided poor children in their earliest years of education. The National Endowment for the Humanities and the Corporation for Public Broadcasting were created in an effort to expand access to culture.

These programs cost billions of dollars but Johnson presented them not only as moral and just but also as a way to further expand the U.S. economy using education, job training, and income assistance. Johnson's party, the Democrats, won big again in the 1966 elections. However, forces were already converging, which would make it difficult to carry out Great Society programs. Across the country cities were exploding with demonstrations and even riots. Some wondered why problems seemed to be getting worse, just as billions of dollars had been committed to solving them.

A more daunting problem lay halfway around the world. The War in Vietnam claimed an increasing amount of Johnson's attention. And the war became just as controversial as Johnson's War on Poverty. It was also becoming more and more expensive as troops and supplies poured into the region to combat the "Viet Cong" guerilla fighters and the North Vietnamese Army. Johnson was pressured to hike taxes to cover the soaring costs of the war and his Great Society measures. Johnson's need for a tax increase gave political opponents leverage to demand domestic spending cuts. By 1968 Johnson's top economic and political priority was the increasingly unpopular war in Vietnam. This commitment ultimately led to him refusing to seek reelection as the Democratic presidential candidate.

That year also saw California Governor Ronald Reagan (1911–) fail in his bid to become the Republican presidential candidate. But twelve years later, when the nation's economy was stagnant, Reagan was elected president on a platform that identified many of Johnson's programs as the source of the nation's economic woes. Republicans like Reagan claimed the burden of Great Society initiatives on taxpayers had become too great while poverty only seemed to worsen. "It was 25 years ago that Lyndon Johnson announced his plans for 'The Great Society,'" the conservative magazine *National Review* wrote in 1989. "Today the phrase refers only to a bundle of welfare programs that have helped make the federal budget a chronic problem."

Republicans stepped up their attack into the 1990s and in 1994 they won majorities in both houses of Congress. They continued to criticize federal spending on programs such as Aid to Families with Dependent Children, more commonly called welfare, which were greatly expanded under the Great Society. Some Democrats said the attacks unfairly singled out society's most vulnerable citizens. Republicans argued that such social programs lead to dependency, which creates problems for both the beneficiary and the nation. Even President Bill Clinton (1993—), a Democrat, declared an "end to welfare as we know it."

Despite the criticism a diverse selection of Great Society programs, from Medicare to public television, remain politically popular. The ultimate legacy of the Great Society will surely be debated for decades to come.

See also: **Medicaid, Medicare, Franklin D. Roosevelt, Vietnam War**

FURTHER READING

Brown-Collier, Elba K. "Johnson's Great Society: Its Legacy in the 1990s." *Review of Social Economy*, Fall, 1998.

Dallek, Robert. *Flawed Giant: Lyndon B. Johnson, 1960–1973*. Oxford: Oxford University Press, 1998.

Fraser, Steve, and Gary Gerstle. *The Rise and Fall of the New Deal Order, 1930–1980*. Princeton: Princeton University Press, 1989.

Moore, Allison. "From Opportunity to Entitlement: The Transformation and Decline of Great Society Liberalism." *Yale Law Journal*, December, 1996.

Unger, Irwin. *The Best of Intentions: The Triumph and Failure of the Great Society Under Kennedy, Johnson and Nixon*. New York: Doubleday, 1996.

Wilson, William Julius. *The Truly Disadvantaged: The Inner City, the Underclass, and Public Policy*. Chicago: University of Chicago Press, 1987.

GREENBACK PARTY

The Greenback Party was founded in 1874 in Indianapolis, Indiana. Following the panic of 1873, an economic downturn hit the nation's agricultural sector: farm prices dropped but growers' costs (including rail freight rates) remained stationary or rose. The amount of money in circulation decreased and interest rates increased. Farm families were caught in the middle— those unable to pay their mortgages faced bank foreclosure. Rural America was in crisis. The greenback forces, mostly western and southern farmers, reasoned that putting more money into circulation would have an inflationary effect: Farm prices would rise thereby putting more cash in farmers' pockets and allowing them to pay off their debts.

Originally called the Independent National Party, the Greenbackers advocated the government issue of more greenbacks (the paper currency printed to fund the American Civil War 1861–65). When the party assembled its first convention in 1876, it nominated American inventor and industrialist Peter Cooper (1791–1883) as its presidential candidate. Receiving only 81,837 votes, Cooper's run for office was a failure. But in the midterm elections of 1878 the party united with workers to form the Greenback-Labor Party. Capturing more than 1 million votes, the independent political party placed 14 members in Congress. For the presidential election of 1880, the party nominated Congressional leader James B. Weaver (1833–1912) in order to broaden their political platform to support women's suffrage, a graduated income tax, and the eight-hour work day (then a popular initiative among the nation's laborers). The Greenbackers received few votes and lost seats in Congress, in part because the economy had rebounded.

The Greenback-Labor Party dissolved following the 1884 election. Some of its members joined the People's (Populist) Party. But the nation's monetary crisis was far from over. The greenback forces, which consisted largely of debtors, were later replaced by the Free Silver supporters who advocated government coinage of silver to expand the nation's money supply and produce inflationary effects. Until the mid-1890s the Free Silverites struggled against gold standard forces, (mostly New England creditors who favored a limited money supply).

See also: **Bland-Allison Act, Free Silver, Gold Resumption Act, Gold Standard Act, Greenbacks**

GREENBACKS

Greenbacks were the paper money printed and issued by the U.S. government during the American Civil War (1861–65). The financial demands of the war quickly depleted the nation's supply of specie (gold and silver). In response the government passed the Legal Tender Act of 1862, which suspended specie payments and provided for the issue of paper money. About $430 million in notes were issued. The notes were legal tender—money that had to be accepted in payment of any debt. Because the bills were supported only by the government's promise to pay, it was somewhat derisively observed that the bills were backed only by the green ink they were printed with on one side. (Hence the name greenbacks.) The value of the notes depended on the peoples' confidence in the U.S. government and its future ability to convert the currency to coin. As the fighting between the Union and the Confederacy raged, confidence in government fluctuated: When the Union suffered defeat, the value of the greenbacks dropped—one time to as low as 35 cents on the dollar.

Greenbacks remained in circulation after the fighting ended; they finally regained their full value in 1878. After the financial crisis in 1873, many people—particularly western farmers—clamored for the government to issue more. Advocates of the monetary system formed the Greenback Party, which was active in U.S. politics between 1876 and 1884. The party believed that by putting more greenbacks into circulation, the U.S. government would make it easier for debts to be paid and prices would go up—resulting in prosperity. At the end of the twentieth century, the system of paper money remained based on the government's issue of notes (greenbacks), which was made necessary by the Civil War.

See also: **Confederate dollars, Free Silver, Gold Standard, Greenback Party**

GREENSPAN, ALAN

Alan Greenspan (1926–), chairman of the Federal Reserve Board since 1987, has sometimes been described as the second most powerful person in the

Alan Greenspan.

world. Greenspan's slightest utterance could directly affect the lives of millions of citizens and could alter the monetary policies of governments on six continents. His tenure at the Federal Reserve has been marked by low unemployment, near-zero inflation, a strong dollar, and unprecedented prosperity.

The only child of divorced parents, Greenspan was born and raised in New York City where he attended public schools. He enrolled in the prestigious Juilliard School of Music but, after a year he left to play tenor saxophone and clarinet on the road with Henry Jerome's swing band.

Toward the end of World War II (1939–1945), he entered New York University where he received a Bachelor of Arts in economics in 1948 and a Master's in economics in 1950. He studied for a doctoral degree at Columbia University but left in 1953 before completing work on it. (In 1977, based on his impressive career as an economist, New York University awarded him a Ph.D. in economics without a formal dissertation.) At Columbia he became close friends with economist Arthur Burns, who later became Chairman of the Federal Reserve Board from 1970–1978.

In the early 1950s he came under the intellectual influence of novelist Ayn Rand, the author of *The Fountainhead*. Gloria Borger in *U.S. News and World Report* reported that Greenspan said of Rand, "What she did was to make me see that capitalism is not only efficient and practical, but also moral." With this view in mind Greenspan virtually invented the business of providing economic analyses specifically for senior business executives. He and William Townsend founded the economic consulting firm of Townsend-Greenspan & Co., Inc. which provided industrial and financial institutions with forecasts and other business-related services. The firm was immediately successful and Greenspan became a wealthy man. He was soon in demand as a forecaster and adviser and was named to the boards of such prestigious companies as Alcoa, Capital Cities/ABC, J.P. Morgan & Co., and Mobil Corporation.

In 1968 Greenspan was recruited to serve as an adviser to then presidential candidate Richard Nixon (1969–1974). In 1974 Greenspan's friend, Arthur Burns, urged him to serve as chairman of the Council of Economic Advisors. Burns felt it was Greenspan's "patriotic duty" to combat the inflation was threatening capitalism. Greenspan accepted the position and began his battle against inflation on September 1, 1974. For the next three years, under his leadership, the rate of inflation dropped from eleven percent to six-and-a-half percent. Ten years later, then Treasury Secretary James Baker (1985–1988) nominated Greenspan to the chairmanship of the Federal Reserve. Little wonder Greenspan was the only nominee for the position.

The Federal Reserve system ("the Fed") is a complex organization of independent parts. It is made up of twelve regional Federal Reserve banks, each with a president, board of directors, officers, and research staff. In Washington DC, a board of governors also maintains a staff of top economists. Chairman Greenspan exercised strong and effective leadership of the Fed. Greenspan's personal charm and his mastery of data helped secure his position as undisputed chief.

Greenspan's steady hand calmed uncertain domestic and global economic markets. From 1989 to 1992 he tightened lending practices but also injected cash into the U.S. economy to ensure recovery from the post–Cold War economic downturn. He also refused to inflate the money supply in reaction to a temporary worldwide price hike for oil; thus price stability remained. By 1992 the economy was on an upward trend. In 1994 Greenspan raised interest rates several times in a successful effort to thwart possible inflation. The ultimate result, despite what critics warned, was a very low 4.7 percent unemployment rate. Over the next few years the Fed gradually decreased the prime lending rate. As a result, the economy boomed at an historic pace, the federal budget balanced, and the nation's inflation rate fell below two percent.

By the accounts of his contemporaries, Greenspan was considered the best chairman the Federal Reserve Board had ever seen. In 1998 a Louis Harris survey of 400 senior executives gave Greenspan a favorable rating of 97 percent. Economists at all points along the theoretical spectrum awarded him high marks. The 1990s, as a period marked by peace and prosperity in the United States, could easily be called the Age of Greenspan.

See also: **Federal Reserve System, Inflation, Ayn Rand**

FURTHER READING

Borger, Gloria. "The politician-economist: walking the fine line between the public White House and the private Fed, Chairman Alan Greenspan looks to the numbers for answers." *U.S. News and World Report*, July 1, 1991.

Foust, Dean. "Alan Greenspan's Brave New World." *Business Week*, July 4, 1997.

Kudlow, Lawrence A. "Four more years." *National Review*, March 9, 1998.

Moritz, Charles, ed. *Current Biography Yearbook, 1989*. New York: H. W. Wilson Co., 1990, s.v. "Alan Greenspan."

Norton, Rob. "In Greenspan We Trust." *Fortune*, March 18, 1996.

Who's Who in America, 1988–1989. New Providence, NJ: Marquis Who's Who, 1989, s.v. "Alan Greenspan."

GROSS DOMESTIC PRODUCT

Gross Domestic Product, or GDP, represents the total output of goods and services produced by a nation. In the United States for example, GDP includes all the corn and wheat grown by farmers, all the movies filmed in Hollywood, all the automobiles built in Detroit, all the meals served in restaurants, all the money spent on school books; in other words, every item produced for sale in the United States is represented by the GDP. Obviously millions of products and services go into the GDP of a modern industrial economy. Government economists keep track of output and release a measure of the GDP four times a year. These

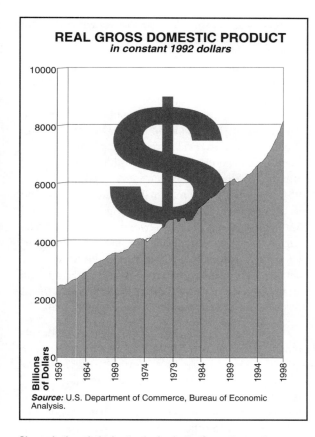

REAL GROSS DOMESTIC PRODUCT
in constant 1992 dollars

Source: U.S. Department of Commerce, Bureau of Economic Analysis.

Shown is the relatively steady rise in the Gross Domestic Product (GDP), represents the total annual value of all goods and services produced in the United States.

figures try to capture the amount that the economy is growing or shrinking. For example the government may report that the economy grew three percent in a given year. When the GDP figure is rising, the nation is in a positive economic upswing. In such times, more workers are being hired, and paychecks are getting bigger. But when the GDP begins to shrink, it means the nation is entering a recession. More people lose their jobs, and families have to tighten their belts. In general GDP growth in the range of three to five percent a year in the United States is considered healthy; growth of one or two percent a year is considered slow; and any decline in GDP is considered cause for alarm.

See also: **Gross National Product**

GROSS NATIONAL PRODUCT

There are many ways to measure the economic health of society. The best available indicator of the

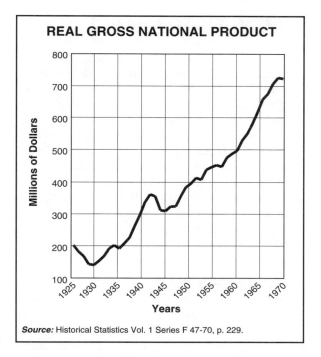

REAL GROSS NATIONAL PRODUCT

Source: Historical Statistics Vol. 1 Series F 47-70, p. 229.

This graph depicts the generally healthy growth of the Gross National Product through 1970. The Gross National Product is an annual measure of all goods and services produced by U.S. industries.

economy's overall health is its annual total output of goods and services. To calculate the output of goods and services, economists use two closely related basic national income accounting measures of the full goods and services output. One is the gross national product (GNP), and the other is called the gross domestic product (GDP). Both of these measure the total market value of all goods and services produced in the economy in one year. The difference between the GNP and the GDP is in how the economy is defined.

The GNP consists of the total output produced by land, labor, capital, and business talent supplied by U.S. industries. Since 1992 the GDP has generally replaced the GNP and comprises the value of the total goods and services produced within the boundaries of the United States, whether by U.S. or foreign-supplied resources. Measuring the overall production performance of the economy as a whole does what accounting does for an individual business enterprise: it tells the government executive how well the business of the country is performing. Whether one uses the GNP or the GDP, such measuring provides national income accounting, so as to keep a finger on the economic pulse of the nation, compare annual figures over time, and help plan for future budgeting and the creation of new public policies to improve economic performance.

See also: **Gross Domestic Product**

GRUEN, VICTOR DAVID

An architect who first brought the modern shopping mall to the sprawling, growing, and scattering suburbs, Victor Gruen (1903–1980) was both a successful businessman and an influential urban planning theorist. Known as a practical visionary Gruen attempted an alternative to both post–World War II suburban sprawl and dying center cities. In the early 1950s he designed two major Midwest shopping malls: Northland outside Detroit, Michigan; and Southdale near Minneapolis, Minnesota. Both projects strongly influenced countless suburban malls built in the last half of the twentieth century by integrating architecture, art, and landscape which, in turn, had an immeasurable impact on U.S. society and culture of the period.

Born in Vienna, Austria, in 1903, Gruen was the son of a successful lawyer. He grew up in a cultured home, enjoying the excitement of a vibrant, beautiful city and visiting relatives in all the capitals of Europe. He especially loved the theater. His father had many clients in the arts, and the boy loved to watch directors organize stage sets and place actors within pleasing backdrops. David R. Hill, writing in the *Journal of the U.S. Planning Association*, suggested that these early experiences may have influenced Gruen's later insistence on designing architectural spaces in which human beings were integral players.

After studying architecture at the Vienna Master School for Architecture of the Academy of Fine Arts after World War I (1914–1918), Gruen began his career with a German architectural firm, Melcher and Steiner, in Vienna. After nine years with the firm he opened his own architectural offices. It was not an auspicious moment to strike out on his own. Austria was hard hit by the Great Depression (1929–1939) and the family fortune was lost. The young architect's projects were limited to retail storefronts and building rehabilitation. However with two friends he won a competition for the design of a public housing project. And he had just received his largest commission for a store building when Nazi troops arrived in Vienna.

After three terrifying months spent as a Jew in occupied Vienna, Gruen fled to the United States in 1938 with only eight dollars in his pocket. Beginning with design work on stage sets for Broadway shows he was soon designing commercial spaces, progressing from small shops to commissions from Macy's for major new department stores in Kansas City and San Francisco. Moving to Los Angeles he established Victor Gruen Associates, Architects, Planners and Engineers. The firm would soon expand to five partners, 50

professionals, and some 200 employees with offices in Los Angeles and Detroit.

A brilliant, energetic man with a pronounced talent for business, Gruen had amassed 21 state architecture licenses, given 225 speeches and lectures, published 75 articles, coordinated two hundred important projects for his firm, and completed two major books within 20 years after his arrival in the United States. Gruen's first shopping mall, Northland, outside of Detroit, Michigan, was begun in 1952 and opened in 1954. It was the largest mall in the world at the time and has been called "a classic in shopping center design." Northland was soon followed by the 70-store Southdale near Minneapolis, Minnesota, the nation's first completely enclosed mall. Southdale introduced the concepts of a climate-controlled shopping space and the associated development of office buildings, apartment houses, and parks connected to the shopping mall.

Gruen subsequently turned to downtown redevelopment planning. An important breakthrough came with his 1956 plan for Fort Worth, Texas. He envisioned a downtown with a ring freeway and parking just off the freeway ramps. Commuters and shoppers, after parking their cars outside the urban area, would take minibuses to offices and retail establishments in the city center. Trucking and mass transportation would go underground. Pedestrians would be able to walk everywhere. Although his plan was never implemented urban designers around the world took pieces of it and adapted it to local needs. Gruen's firm, meanwhile, took on assignments for additional shopping centers, regional health complexes, major office buildings and parking garages, as well as urban renewal projects. Among these were the cities of Kalamazoo, Michigan; Fresno, California; St. Petersburg, Florida; and Cincinnati, Ohio.

Gruen continued to crusade for a comprehensive metropolitan approach to city planning in which automobiles would not dominate. He believed that the business centers of modern cities should adopt the organizing concepts behind medieval marketplaces. According to this concept, shops should be arranged in logical sequences and shoppers should walk instead of ride between them. In books, articles, and lectures Gruen promoted his theories. At age 65 he returned to Vienna, where he opened a European branch of his firm. He consulted on major European planning projects and continued to write prodigiously until his death in 1980.

See also: **City Planning**

FURTHER READING

Current Biography. New York: H.W. Wilson, 1959, s.v. "Victor Gruen."

Current Biography. New York: H.W. Wilson, 1980, s.v. "Victor Gruen."

Gruen, Victor. *The Heart of Our Cities: The Urban Crisis: Diagnosis and Cure*. New York: Simon and Schuster, 1964.

Gruen, Victor. *Shopping Towns U.S.A.: The Planning of Shopping Centers*. New York: Reinhold Publishing Co., 1960.

Hill, David R. "Sustainability, Victor Gruen, and the Cellular Metropolis." *Journal of the U.S. Planning Association*, Summer 1992.

"Victor Gruen: Architect," [cited April 20, 1999] available from the World Wide Web at: www.uwyo.edu/ahc/digital/gruen/.

GUGGENHEIM, DANIEL

Daniel Guggenheim.

Daniel Guggenheim (1856–1930) dominated the U.S. mining industry in the first half of the twentieth century. One of ten surviving children in an immigrant household, he took over his father's successful mining interests and turned them into one of the great U.S. family fortunes.

Guggenheim's father, Meyer, emigrated with his family to the United States from Switzerland in 1847, and settled in Philadelphia. With his father, Simon, Meyer worked as a peddler, carrying packs of household goods into the coal-mining region of Pennsylvania. Soon realizing that stove polish was the most popular item he sold, he located a chemist who taught him how to make the product. Simon then stayed home to produce stove polish while Meyer sold it at a substantial profit. Within four years Meyer made enough money on his peddling business, stove polish, and a product called "coffee essence" to marry and open a grocery store.

During the American Civil War (1861–1865) Meyer speculated successfully in supplies required by the Union troops and began to accumulate a comfortable nest egg. His subsequent business ventures in spices, lye (needed for the manufacture of soap), railroads, and imported Swiss lace and embroidery were each more successful than the last. By 1880, a little more than thirty years after arriving penniless in the United States, Meyer had put together an $800,000 bank account.

As a teenager, Daniel Guggenheim, the second son in a family of eleven children, was sent to Switzerland to learn the lace and embroidery business. Like his brothers, he later joined the family embroidery and lace importing firm, M. Guggenheim's Sons. Beginning in the early 1880s Meyer began to invest money in two Leadville, Colorado, lead and silver mines. According to Guggenheim family biographer, John H. Davis, the mining operation hit a great silver lode in 1881. The strike produced nine million ounces of silver and 86,000 tons of lead by 1887, earning Meyer Guggenheim about $750,000 per year. Meyer closed the embroidery business and invested everything he had in mining and the refining of metals. He acquired a smelter and channeled the efforts of his seven sons into the new family enterprise.

Of all the sons, Daniel Guggenheim was the most energetic and ambitious. Together he and his brothers sought to dominate the Western mining industry. Both their mines and the smelter were immensely profitable. But they took no chances. They beat back the railroads on transportation charges, aggressively evicted miners who squatted on their property, and used armed thugs to force striking mineworkers back to work. The brothers also expanded into Mexico, where Guggenheim had managed to obtain a concession for the family to "undertake the exploration and exploitation of any mine they may want to lease or buy." By 1895, due to the great success of the smelters they built in Monterey and Aquascalientes, the Guggenheim family established a strong industrial presence in Mexico.

In 1891 the Guggenheims formed a trust, the Colorado Smelting and Refining Company, to consolidate their various enterprises. They were now faced with competition for control of the U.S. mining industry. A rival trust, the American Smelting and Refining Company (ASARCO), was formed with the financial backing of the Rockefellers. Daniel Guggenheim led his brothers in several battles for power against the new trust. By 1901 he won the struggle. The Guggenheim family assumed control of ASARCO and achieved dominance over the U.S. mining industry, including its largest metal-processing plants, for the next two decades.

Until 1919 Daniel Guggenheim was chairman of the board and president of ASARCO. He convinced financiers J. P. Morgan (1837–1913) and Jacob Schiff (1847–1920) to form a syndicate to mine the great copper deposits at Kennecott Creek in Alaska. By the end of 1912 the Kennecott copper mine had paid dividends of $3 million to Morgan, Schiff, and the Guggenheim family. Meanwhile the Guggenheims were mining tin in Bolivia, diamonds in Africa, and copper in Utah. Their worldwide domination of the mineral industry gave them great international power. It was said that Daniel Guggenheim could make or break a government with one telegram.

Because the family controlled so many essential natural resources the Guggenheims emerged from World War I (1914–1918) with a fortune estimated between $250 million to $300 million, enough to rank them second only to the Rothschilds as the richest Jewish family in the world. In 1923, although the brothers no longer involved in the day-to-day administration of ASARCO, the family still controlled vast international holdings. They sold a large copper mine in Chile to the Anaconda Copper Corporation for $70 million in cash, the largest private sale of a mining property in world history at that time. With that sale the surviving Guggenheim brothers retired from active business and turned to philanthropy.

By the last half of the twentieth century the scale of the family's charitable activities through their various foundations became their greatest legacy. Medicine, education, and the arts all benefited from their largesse. Among them was the Daniel and Florence Guggenheim Foundation, established in 1924 to advance the "well-being of mankind throughout the world." The Foundation supported Robert Goddard's work on the development of liquid-propelled rockets and established many research centers and scholarly activities concerned with the aerospace sciences and exploration. Daniel Guggenheim died in 1930, a successful businessman who led his family to success in American industry.

FURTHER READING

Davis, John. *The Guggenheims: An American Epic.* New York: William Morrow, 1978.

Hoyt, Edwin P., Jr. *The Guggenheims and the American Dream.* New York: Funk and Wagnalls, 1967.

Lomask, Milton. *Seed Money: The Guggenheim Story.* New York: Farrar, Straus, and Giroux, 1964.

O'Connor, Harvey. *The Guggenheims: The Making of an American Dynasty.* New York: Covici, Friede, 1937.

HALPIN, JAMES

James F. Halpin (1951–) led computer superstore CompUSA, Inc. out of the financial troubles it found itself in at the beginning of the 1990s. After a period of dramatic growth during the 1980s, CompUSA began to lag in the marketplace. The multi-billion dollar retailer known as "America's Computer Superstore" was lethargic and its bloated bureaucracy brought it to the brink of declaring Chapter 11 bankruptcy. When CompUSA's chief executive officer (CEO) resigned in the last few weeks of 1993, James Halpin was left with the daunting task of turning the company's fortunes around. His efforts helped turn CompUSA into a strong competitor that, in the late 1990s, dominated the fast-paced world of computer retailing.

James F. Halpin was born in 1951 in Chicago, Illinois, to Irish Catholic parents with a strong blue-collar background. Because of the family's lack of money Halpin never attended college; he instead went directly to work after graduating from high school.

At age twenty-one Halpin got a job unloading trucks for the Boston-based retailer Zayre Corporation for $2.60 an hour. He quickly showed initiative and his hard working style quickly caught the notice of his employers. He did not stay on the loading dock for very long, but began moving up through the ranks of the company. By 1984 Halpin had been promoted to the position of Vice President and senior merchandising manager for the Zayre department store chain. His leadership at Zayre soon attracted the attention of others, and in 1988 Halpin left Zayre to become the president of BJ's Wholesale Club. Two years later, in 1990, Halpin moved BJ's Wholesale Club to head Waban Inc. In 1991, he left the presidency at Waban for the same position at Home Base, a home improvement retail chain based in Irvine, California.

Meanwhile CompUSA, the company Halpin would lead out of hardship, was establishing itself as a leader in its industry. Founded as Soft Warehouse in Dallas, Texas, in 1984, CompUSA was the first to adapt the "superstore" idea to the home computer and peripherals market (the "superstore" idea was pioneered by companies such as Office Depot). In January of 1989 a group of investors acquired CompUSA and placed the company under the leadership of former Home Depot executive Nathan Morton. Under Morton's control the company grew rapidly. In just two years, from 1988 to 1990, sales increased from $66 million to $600 million. In December 1991, the company began selling stock to the public.

But there were signs of stress on the horizon. Despite its strong growth during the 1980s, the first quarter of 1993 reported a loss of nearly $1 million for the company. Although this was not an enormous amount in proportion to the company's volume, Morton resigned, paving the way for Halpin to come in and face the challenge of turning CompUSA around.

From his position at Home Base Halpin was recruited to become president of CompUSA in May of 1993. Halpin felt CompUSA was focusing too much of its corporate energy on promotion and advertising and not enough on the bottom line. He immediately made changes.

Like his predecessor Nathan Morton, Halpin came to CompUSA from a hardware superstore company. He decided to apply a different strategy and he got vastly different results. While competitors such as Best Buy, Neostar, Wal-Mart, and the Tandy Corporation experienced shrinking profit margins, CompUSA grew steadily under Halpin's leadership. Whereas in 1994 CompUSA posted a $16.8 million loss on $2.1 billion in sales, by 1996 it had an estimated $56 million profit from $3.8 billion in sales.

One of Halpin's first actions as president of CompUSA was to end the company's racing car sponsorship and sell its cable television show. He next fired 2000 of the company's store managers, replacing them with more experienced employees from other successful chain stores. This move raised the average age of a

CompUSA store managers from twenty-six to thirty-seven, an oddity in the young computer industry. Halpin's new managers did well. Halpin also initiated an incentives system that enabled some of his store managers to earn in excess of $100,000 a year.

By 1994 Halpin had turned over the assembly of CompUSA's Compudyne brand computers to an outside contractor and was promoted to CEO of the company. He replaced seventeen of the twenty top management positions in the company and eliminated some of the sideline businesses, such as software publishing, that the previous CEO had established. Only once these actions were done and the company had stabilized did Halpin consider opening more stores.

He revamped the new CompUSA stores, redesigning the layout and requiring an increase in the level of employees' technical education. His goal was to create an exciting and interactive stores that would appeal to consumers.

In October 1995 Halpin took a seat on the board of directors at Invincible Technologies Corporation with the title of Outside Director. Invincible is a Massachusetts-based computer company specializing in security applications, file servers, and data storage solutions for businesses that use large computer networks. Halpin's knowledge of both business and the computer industry helped Invincible rise to the top quickly as growing numbers of businesses sought to make their computer networks safe, fast and efficient.

Facing pressure from other computer chain stores, such as Dell Computer Corporation, Halpin introduced a system of direct marketing. CompUSA began selling custom-designed computers for a reasonable rate according to customer specifications. Halpin hoped this system would allow CompUSA to tap into the 25 percent of the market then firmly controlled by independent vendors who built customized computers. Halpin called these vendors "the wicked screwdriver guys," and he introduced his company's build-to-order service in late 1997. This service allowed customers to order a computer over the telephone according to their specifications and pick it up or have it delivered to them within a few days.

Halpin's custom-design innovation was a success. Instead of building the computers itself, CompUSA subcontracted the task to independent contractors, who delivered the finished product to a CompUSA store for installation or delivery. This method cut down on CompUSA's costs and increased its profit margin dramatically over companies such as Dell who built custom-made computers itself.

By 1997 CompUSA had 134 stores nationwide and its net income rose 57 percent to $93.9 million and net sales had topped $4.6 billion. In the late 1990s every CompUSA store generated sales of $1,388 per square foot of floor, two or three times more than other consumer electronics and office supply chains. This allowed CompUSA to employ a further 5,000 employees than before Halpin's cuts and restructuring. CompUSA appeared at number 329 on *Fortune* magazine's list of the top 500 companies in the United States for 1998.

By the late 1990s all CompUSA stores contained a computer repair shop and computer training classrooms for customers who had problems learning how to operate their computers. The company also offered a delivery service that included a crew to install computer service. Along with a direct sales force soliciting corporate, government, and educational customers directly, these improvements made CompUSA an industry leader in computer sales and dramatically increased computer literacy rates throughout the nation.

Halpin has become one of corporate America's most powerful people. In 1997 he appeared at number seventeen on *Forbes* magazine's list of the top corporate executives in the retailing industry. His annual salary was over $2 million. Halpin's efforts to create a focused, consumer-oriented, interactive store were successful. His vision and leadership has lead "America's Computer Superstore" through the twentieth century.

FURTHER READING

International Directory of Company Histories, Volume 10. Detroit: St. James Press, 1995, s.v. "CompUSA."

"CompUSA Seeks Profit Boost." *Business Marketing*, January, 1994.

"Executives Step Up To Meet Tough Challenges In 1994." *Computer Reseller News*, January 3, 1994.

"Getting the Bugs Out." *Business Week*, July 22, 1996.

"James Halpin." *Computer Reseller News*, November 18, 1996.

Who's Who In America 1997. New Providence, NJ: Marquis, 1996, s.v. "Halpin, James."

HAMILTON, ALEXANDER

Alexander Hamilton (1755–1804) was the first Secretary of the Treasury of the United States and a primary contributor to *The Federalist Papers*. Among the founding fathers, he was the man whose vision was largely responsible for the creation of the American nation as it is today. Samuel Eliot Morison wrote in *The Oxford History of the American People* that it was Hamilton's genius that enabled the new government to function successfully.

Born in 1755, Hamilton was an illegitimate child. He had a difficult upbringing in the West Indies. His father, an aristocratic but unsuccessful Scottish trader, abandoned the family when the boy was about 10 years old. At age 11 Hamilton began work in the West Indies office of a New York mercantile firm. When his mother died in 1768, he was taken under the wing of her relatives. They and other sponsors recognized the boy's exceptional intelligence and energy and arranged for him to attend preparatory school in New Jersey; he was then enrolled at King's College (now Columbia University) in 1773.

As a student Hamilton wrote and published three brilliant pamphlets. He defended the colonists' cause in protesting the actions of the British government which brought on the War of Independence and he upheld recent decisions of the Continental Congress. These very influential writings brought the young man to the attention of General George Washington (1732–1799). At only age 22 Hamilton joined the general's military staff as aide-de-camp with the rank of lieutenant colonel. Remaining on the staff for four years, he became indispensable to Washington. Hamilton was entrusted with his general's correspondence, sent on many sensitive missions, and eventually made Washington's liaison with French military commanders who supported the Revolutionary army. At Yorktown, in the final battle of the war, Hamilton led a successful assault on a key British position.

Following the war, Hamilton married Elizabeth Schuyler, a member of one of New York's wealthiest and most distinguished families, and he settled down to practice law in New York City. He was soon, however, caught up in national politics. He recognized almost immediately that the *Articles of Confederation*, which defined the relationships among the states, were weak and unenforceable. As a delegate to the 1787 Philadelphia meeting of the Constitutional Convention, Hamilton argued for a strong national government with almost unlimited power over the states. His views were in the minority and were particularly unpopular in New York, where the prevailing sentiment was in favor of political power remaining with the individual states.

With James Madison (1751–1836), a delegate from Virginia, and John Jay (1745–1829), the secretary for foreign affairs, Hamilton wrote a series of essays

which were published in a New York newspaper between October 1787 and May 1788. These essays, comprising *The Federalist Papers*, effectively argued the case for a strong national government. They were enormously influential among the framers of the Constitution and they remain relevant more than 200 years later. Hamilton is credited with two-thirds of the 85 essays. In his essays he described the proposed powers of the executive, legislative, and judicial branches of government. He also explained how, as a final check on legislative powers, the Supreme Court would be able to declare unconstitutional even those laws passed by Congress and signed by the executive.

Named by President George Washington (1789–1797) to be the first Secretary of the Treasury, Hamilton acted swiftly to establish a strong economy. The country's foreign debt was repaid by the end of 1795; the national domestic debt was paid off by 1835. The Bank of the United States was chartered and funded under Hamilton's watch. By August 1791, U.S. currency was strong on domestic and world markets.

Hamilton's three great reports to Congress (the Report on the Public Credit of 1790, the Report on the Bank of the United States of 1790, and the Report on Manufactures of 1791) laid down the basic economic principles on which the U.S. government has, in general, operated ever since. Hamilton believed that the states should be subordinate to the federal government. The federal government, in turn, should protect the states from foreign intervention and from each other through a single military force.

An important duty of the federal government, Hamilton argued, was to promote a strong capitalist economy through a strong currency and public investment in infrastructure. He encouraged new industry in both the South and the North by protecting infant U.S. industries until they were able to compete on an equal basis with imports.

Hamilton was the opposite of a populist. The government, in his opinion, should not be run by amateurs but by a trained and educated elite. In many of his views he was strongly opposed by Thomas Jefferson (1743–1826), the author of the *Declaration of Independence* and future president, who believed that the American republic rested firmly on an agrarian democracy.

Hamilton's last years were spent in the midst of political turmoil. Through various political intrigues he managed to sow dissension in his own Federalist party and to incur the enmity of several important political leaders in both the Federalist and Republican parties. Along with Jefferson, these included John Adams

(1735–1826), a Federalist and the second president of the United States, and Aaron Burr (1756–1836), a Republican and Jefferson's Vice President. In 1804 Hamilton opposed Burr's unsuccessful bid to be governor of New York. On the grounds of some insulting remarks Hamilton had allegedly made about him, Burr challenged his old rival to a duel following the election. Hamilton died in the duel at Weehawken, New Jersey, on July 11, 1804.

See also: **Bank of the United States (First National Bank), Thomas Jefferson, Report on Manufactures**

FURTHER READING

Cooke, Jacob E. *Alexander Hamilton, a Biography.* New York: Scribner's, 1982.

Hendrickson, Robert. *Rise and Fall of Alexander Hamilton.* New York: Van Nostrand Reinhold, 1981.

Lind, Michael. "Hamilton's Legacy." *The Wilson Quarterly*, Summer 1994.

Mcdonald, Forrest. *Alexander Hamilton: a Biography.* New York: Norton, 1979.

Miller, John C. *Alexander Hamilton: Portrait in Paradox.* New York: Harper, 1959.

Morison, Samuel Eliot. "Alexander Hamilton." *The Oxford History of the American People.* New York: Oxford University Press, 1965. ·

Rossiter, Clinton. *Alexander Hamilton and the Constitution.* New York: Harcourt, Brace and World, Inc., 1965.

HAMMER, ARMAND

It is the dream of some Americans to become rich and powerful, to live a jetset lifestyle and to brush shoulders with the great leaders of the world. Armand Hammer (1898–1990) lived the American Dream.

Armand Hammer was born on May 21, 1898, in New York. His father Julius Hammer was a Russian immigrant, a doctor, a socialist activist, and the first card carrying member of the U.S. Communist Labor Party.

Armand Hammer was working toward his medical degree at Columbia University when he made his first $1 million through his father's pharmaceutical company. He received his medical degree from Columbia

Armand Hammer.

University in 1921. After he earned his degree, Hammer took his money and journeyed to the Soviet Union to give medical aid to famine victims.

While there, Russian leader Vladimir Ilyich Lenin (1870–1924) took a personal interest in Hammer and persuaded him to apply his business talents to Russia. In 1925 Hammer, with a concession from the Bolsheviks, began to manufacture pencils for the Soviet Union. Soon thereafter, his firm became the largest supplier of inexpensive and durable pencils in the Soviet Union. By the late 1920s the Soviet's bought out Hammer's businesses, and he returned to the United States in 1930. He returned to the United States with many paintings, jewelry, and other art pieces said to be formerly owned by the Romanov imperial family. During the 1930s Hammer sold most of these items and turned the profits into business ventures that became profitable after the Prohibition era. Among these ventures included cattle raising, the building of whiskey barrels, and the production of whiskey.

In 1956 Hammer retired, having grown tired of his hectic business lifestyle. In the same year, however, he was approached by a friend who persuaded him to finance two wildcat oil wells being drilled in Bakersfield, California, by Occidental Petroleum Corporation, which was near bankruptcy. With Hammer's financial support, Occidental began drilling the wells. Unexpectedly, the wells struck oil. Hammer immediately increased his interests in Occidental. By 1957 he was the corporation's chief executive officer (CEO) and chairman of the board. Hammer remained chairman of the board and CEO for the next 33 years, turning the once near bankrupt company into a billion-dollar conglomerate.

Hammer, using his long-standing relations with the Soviets, helped to champion U.S.-Soviet relations throughout the Cold War. He was able to promote cultural and commercial exchanges, as well as represent the United States in trade negotiations. He often became an unofficial ambassador during complicated moments between the two superpowers. In 1986 Hammer personally financed the dispatch of a relief team of physicians to the Soviet Union to assist in the wake of the Chernobyl nuclear disaster.

Incredibly rich, Hammer made many donations to Columbia University, the National Gallery, and the Metropolitan Museum of Art. He also supported numerous philanthropies through the Armand Hammer Foundation. In Los Angeles he founded the Armand Hammer Museum of Art and Cultural Center, which housed the bulk of his art collection.

Often praised for his humanitarianism while he was alive, Hammer has been criticized since his death. It is now believed that Hammer may have been a Soviet spy. The Central Intelligence Agency (CIA) and the Federal Bureau of Investigations (FBI) suspected him of being a full-fledged Soviet agent. It is also believed that his ventures in the petroleum market may have found success, due in some part to of his ability to bribe officials and leaders in Libya. After bribing his way into a favorable position, Hammer would then offer a humanitarian act to sweeten the deal, such as drilling water wells for the King of Libya's parched ancestral village.

Armand Hammer died in Los Angeles, California, on December 10, 1990.

FURTHER READING

''Armand Hammer,'' [cited June 30, 1999] available on the World Wide Web @ www.biography.com.

Blumay, Carl. *The Dark Side of Power: The Real Armand Hammer*. New York: Simon & Schuster, 1992.

Epstein, Edward Jay. *Dossier: The Secret History of Armand Hammer*. New York: Random House, 1996.

Farnham, Alan. ''Armand Hammer: Tinker, Traitor, Satyr, Spy.'' *Fortune*, November 11, 1996.

Weinberg, Steve. *Armand Hammer: The Untold Story*. Boston: Little, Brown, 1989.

HANCOCK, JOHN

Although many saw John Hancock (1737–1793) as nothing but a vain and pompous merchant, he was nonetheless a key figure in securing American independence and creating the republic of the United States. His capacity to sidestep controversy made him an ideal presiding officer. He displayed this skill in the Provincial Conventions, the Continental Congress, and as governor of Massachusetts. Though he was largely an uninspired leader, generally lacking personal style, Hancock became famous for the enormous signature he affixed to the *Declaration of Independence* as one of the nation's founding fathers.

John Hancock was born in Braintree (present-day Quincy), Massachusetts, in 1737, the son of John and Mary Hancock. Hancock's father was a minister who died when his son was only seven. His widowed mother took him and her two other children to live in Lexington, Massachusetts, with her father-in-law. In 1795 Hancock was sent to live with his uncle and aunt, Thomas and Lydia Hancock, in Boston. His uncle was one of Boston's wealthiest businessmen, and so John Hancock grew up in wealth, living in the Beacon Hill area.

Hancock attended Harvard College as part of the class of 1754; after graduating, he returned to Boston and joined his uncle's import-export business. Hancock's return to the family business coincided with the outbreak of the French and Indian War (1754–1763)— for the next six years the House of Hancock, as the business was called, became busy fulfilling government contracts. During this time Hancock learned a great deal about the business. In 1759, to cement business ties and to introduce the young Hancock to a wider world, his uncle sent him to England for a year. On his return in 1761 Hancock found his uncle in poor health and began to take more responsibility in the business and, when his uncle died in 1764, Hancock assumed full responsibility.

Although the young man began life with many advantages, he was not a gifted businessman, and Hancock lost the House of Hancock business eleven years later in 1775. Despite the fact that his uncle had left him a thriving business which Hancock was unable to adequately manage, the loss was not completely his fault. English rule made it very difficult for anyone to run a profitable import-export business.

It may be said that the business world's loss was a gain for the movement of rebellion in America. Hancock subsequently immersed himself in politics and won election to the General Court of Massachusetts. He blamed British colonial rule for his business disasters and, in 1768, when British troops stationed in Boston Harbor seized his ship (the *Liberty*) for smuggling, Hancock was drawn deeper into the movement for independence. He increasingly adopted the revolutionary perspectives of Samuel Adams (1722–1803) and Thomas Paine (1737–1809).

By 1775 Hancock had become such an irritation to the British that they tried to seize him along with Samuel Adams. Hancock avoided arrest and escaped to Philadelphia as a Massachusetts delegate to the Continental Congress. He was elected president of the Congress and held that position for three years. But in spite of his prominence in that service, Hancock contributed little of note to its efforts. Most of the Congress' work was accomplished through committees, which created a patchwork of enormous inefficiencies.

Hancock's greatest moment as a member of the revolutionary movement came on July 4, 1776, when he was asked with others to sign the *Declaration of Independence*. With his characteristic flair for the grand gesture Hancock signed the document first, with an oversized signature.

Hancock was becoming an annoyance to other members of the Continental Congress, as well as to his constituents back home. In 1777 he announced that, for reasons of health, he was returning to Boston. Still, he delayed his return until the summer of 1778. Back in Massachusetts, Hancock worked in concert with the French navy to commanded 5,000 Massachusetts militiamen in an attempt to capture Newport, Rhode Island, from the British in 1778. The expedition was a failure.

Hancock was elected as the first governor of the Commonwealth of Massachusetts after the American Revolution (1775–1783). He continued as governor until 1785, when he retired purportedly because of poor health. Insiders knew that Hancock's mismanagement of Massachusetts' finances had put the state in financial peril. Hancock left in time to avoid the uprising of small farmers (including many revolutionary veterans) who, during the post-war depression, were losing their land for non-payment of taxes. Hancock's successor had the unhappy task of suppressing the rebellion.

In spite of his fiscal and governmental misadventures Hancock was elected delegate to the state ratifying convention for the new Constitution, which was written in 1787. He made public speeches in favor of ratifying the new Constitution. Many felt that without his support the Constitution might never have been ratified. Perhaps this was Hancock's finest moment in a life otherwise filled with failures and missteps. With the ratification of the Constitution, George Washington (1789–1797) was elected president. Contrary to his hopes Hancock was not elected as Vice President. John Adams (1735–1826) was instead awarded the post.

Hancock served as governor of Massachusetts from 1780 to 1793 (with the exception of two years, 1785 to 1787). He died in Boston in October of 1793.

See also: **American Revolution**

FURTHER READING

Baxter, William T. *The House of Hancock: Business in Boston*. Cambridge, MA: Harvard University Press, 1945.

Becker, Carl L. *The Declaration of Independence: A Study in the History of Political Ideas*. New York: Vintage Books, 1958.

Fehrenbach, T.R. *Greatness to Spare: The Heroic Sacrifices of the Men Who Signed the Declaration of Independence*. Princeton, NJ: Van Nostrand, 1968.

Fowler, William M. *The Baron of Beacon Hill: A Biography of John Hancock*. Boston: Houghton Mifflin, 1979.

Magill, Frank N., ed. *Great Lives from History*. Pasadena, CA: Salem Press, 1990. s.v. "John Hancock."

Sears, Lorenzo. *John Hancock, the Picturesque Patriot*. Boston, MA: Gregg Press, 1972.

HANNA, MARCUS ALONZO

Marcus Alonzo Hanna (1837–1904), was a wealthy businessman from Ohio and a leading spokesman for enlightened capitalism (the cooperation of business, labor, and government to help improve economic and social conditions.) He appreciated the importance of the relationship between business and politics and lent his organizational skills to the campaigns of Ohio Republicans. He is best known for managing successfully the presidential campaign of William McKinley (1897–1901), and later serving as United States Senator.

Marcus Hanna was born in New Lisbon (now Lisbon), Ohio in 1837. He moved with his family to

Cleveland, where his father ran a wholesale grocery business. Hanna became a partner in this business after his father's death in 1862. In 1864 he married the daughter of Daniel P. Rhodes, a coal and iron magnate. Hanna joined his father-in-law's company and had such success in business dealings that the company reorganized as M. A. Hanna and Company in 1885. He also supported other business interests in Cleveland, such as a bank, a newspaper, the Opera House, lake transportation, oil refining, and the street railway system.

Hanna's ideal of capitalism included the support of large-scale production, tariff protection, and the gold standard. He was an unusual capitalist in that he did not oppose labor organizations. He saw it as a necessary means to settle industrial disputes in a quick and efficient manner. More importantly, Hanna appreciated the inevitable link between business and politics. He assumed that the Republican party would be a valuable ally for his business endeavors and became actively involved in the campaign of the Ohio Republicans who sought the presidency between 1880 and 1890: James A. Garfield (1881), John Sherman, and William McKinley. Hanna applied his business skills, such as corporate assessment and merchandising techniques, to the campaign process.

As the chairman of the Republican National Committee, Hanna successfully organized the campaign to elect William McKinley as president in 1896, and remained one of McKinley's closest advisors during his presidency. In 1897 he was appointed U.S. Senator from Ohio to replace John Sherman, who became McKinley's Secretary of State. Hanna then won full-term Senate elections in 1898 and 1903. When McKinley was assassinated in 1901, Hanna served as an advisor to President Theodore Roosevelt (1901–09), though he disagreed with many of Roosevelt's policies.

A successful businessman and U.S. Senator, Hanna died in 1904.

See also: **Gold Standard, Theodore Roosevelt**

FURTHER READING

Beer, Thomas. *Hanna*. New York: A. A. Knopf, 1929.

Croly, Herbert David. *Marcus Alonzo Hanna: His Life and Work*. Hamden, Connecticut: Archon Books, 1965.

Garraty, John A., and Jerome L. Sterstein, eds. *Encyclopedia of American Biography*, 2nd edition. New York: HarperCollins Publishers, Inc., 1996, s.v. ''Hanna, Marcus Alonzo.''

O'Brien, Steven G. *American Political Leaders from Colonial Times to the Present*. Santa Barbara: ABC-CLIO, Inc., 1991.

Stern, Clarence Ames. *Resurgent Republicanism: The Handiwork of Hanna*. Ann Arbor, MI: University of Michigan Press, 1963.

HARLEY-DAVIDSON, INC.

Harley-Davidson, Inc. began in 1903 as the Harley-Davidson Motor Company, the brainchild of three young mechanics—William Harley and brothers Walter and Arthur Davidson. The men began by building a three-horsepower motorized bicycle in a backyard shed in Milwaukee, Wisconsin. Demand and production grew, and they began to advertise in 1907. Throughout the course of the company's history, Harley motorcycles have grown to become an industry classic.

The V-twin engine that produced the signature Harley-Davidson sound was introduced in 1909. It enabled riders to reach then unheard of speeds of 60 miles per hour, setting the company apart from its competition. By 1911 there were 150 companies manufacturing motorcycles, which had not yet been replaced by automobiles as an affordable, utilitarian means of transportation.

Police forces throughout the United States adopted Harley-Davidson motorcycles for their use, as did the U.S. military. The company prospered during World War I (1914–1918), making 20,000 machines for the U.S. infantry. Officers also rode Harley-Davidson motorcycles while patrolling the border between the United States and Mexico.

During the 1920s Harley-Davidson took the lead in innovative engineering by introducing such new features as the teardrop gas tank and front brakes. In 1921, for the first time, a Harley-Davidson motorcycle achieved speeds greater than 100 miles per hour. That year, however, the company's production fell to 10,000 machines, its lowest level in ten years. Henry Ford (1863–1947) had perfected assembly line production methods, and inexpensive Model T automobiles were flooding the market, with other automobile manufacturers following suit. In 1924 a basic Model T retailed for $265, while a comparable Harley-Davidson fetched $325. As workers and businesspeople opted to buy automobiles for daily use, motorcycles began to acquire the status of recreational vehicles.

The Great Depression (1929–1939) had a profound effect on the motorcycle industry. Among its

Harley-Davidson motorcycle used by the New York Police Department, circa. 1927.

competitors, Harley-Davidson was one of only two manufacturers that survived. The company relied on its strong dealer network; its use by police, the military, and the U.S. Post Office; and strong exports to Canada and Europe. And better days came toward the end of the decade: Like many other manufacturing companies, Harley-Davidson prospered during World War II (1939–1945). Devoting itself entirely to the war effort, the company shipped nearly 100,000 machines overseas. After the war a healthy economy found consumers with enough money to spend on recreation, including motorcycles. In 1947 the company purchased additional manufacturing capacity to keep up with demand.

Harley-Davidson's main competitor, Indian Motorcycle Company, experienced a streak of engineering and production difficulties in the 1940s and 1950s. Indian struggled with debt before breaking up in the early 1950s, allowing Harley-Davidson to become the veritable "king of the road." The second generation of the founding families became managers at the company, which continued to stress design innovations. Introduced in 1957, the Sportster model marked the start of the superbike era. During this period, leather-clad biker gangs became popular, spawning a stereotype that the company has continually attempted to dispel.

In 1965 the two families, Harley and Davidson, decided to raise additional capital by going public and putting their stock on the open market. However, they effectively maintained a dominant interest in the company by purchasing many of the shares themselves. Sales had dropped for several years, profits were flat, and the company held a mere six percent of the domestic retail market. With proceeds from the sale of stock, the company introduced its first electrically started motorcycle, the Electra Glide. While the Electra Glide became one of the most sought-after full dresser models over time, in the short run its technical problems did not benefit the company.

By 1967 Harley-Davidson was on the brink of ruin: Its Juneau Avenue factory in Milwaukee was small and outdated, and the company had not recently invested in new models. Japanese and British manufacturers filled segments of the market in which there were no Harley-Davidson models to compete. With liquidation a distinct possibility, executives sold the company in 1969 to American Machine and Foundry Company (AMF), a leisure equipment manufacturer headed by Harley-Davidson fan Rodney C. Gott.

AMF used its financial resources to help Harley-Davidson meet the new competitive threat from Japanese manufacturers such as Honda, Kawasaki, and Suzuki. In 1974 a Harley-Davidson assembly plant opened in York, Pennsylvania. Although the company would continue to manufacture its engines in Milwaukee, it would assemble its motorcycles in the York plant. Vaughn Beals was put in charge of the company, and 36-year-old Jeff Bleustein was named chief engineer.

The late 1970s brought problems for Harley-Davidson. Improvements had added about $1,000 to the cost of each motorcycle; meanwhile, AMF management began to seek a higher sales volume. Pressure to increase sales resulted in quality-control problems. Production standards dropped, and parts were often in short supply. In some cases manufacturers accidentally shipped incomplete bikes. By 1979 Harley-Davidson's share of the U.S. motorcycle market for super-heavy-weight machines (with engines 850 cubic centimeters or larger) fell to 20 percent from 80 percent a decade ago. Compounding Harley-Davidson's problems was the 1981 recession that nearly finished the company.

With financial support from Citicorp, Beals and 13 Harley-Davidson executives effected a leveraged management buyout of the company. On June 16, 1981, they took control of the company at a cost of $81.5 million. The new owners focused on turning around the company by adopting new management techniques copied from their Japanese competitors. Also influencing their thinking was the success of the new General Motors Saturn plant and the concept of worker empowerment. The company soon found that increased worker involvement resulted in increased productivity. In addition, Harley-Davidson introduced two new developments: a just-in-time inventory control program called MAN, or ''Materials As Needed,'' and a statistical operator control system designed to improve quality control.

In 1982, after Japanese manufacturers had swamped the U.S. market with their surplus inventory of heavy-weight motorcycles, Harley-Davidson won an antidumping judgment from the International Trade Commission. President Ronald Reagan (1981–1989) was then able to impose on these imported models an additional 45 percent tariff, which was designed to decrease gradually over the next five years. Although the Japanese manufacturers often sought to avoid some of the tariffs by building more motorcycles in the United States, by 1986 Harley-Davidson's share of the U.S. super-heavyweight market had risen to 33.3 percent, ahead of Honda for the first time since 1980.

The company gained back some of its market share by investing in marketing programs, establishing the Harley Owners Group (HOG) in 1983. In addition, manufacturers designed new models to appeal to a broader range of customers. In 1984, however, the company faced another crisis when Citicorp withdrew some of its financial support. By October 1985 Harley-Davidson was ready to file for bankruptcy protection,

but at the last minute an interested lender approached the company to offer help. Heller Financial Corporation agreed to buy out Citicorp's stake for $49 million, forcing Citicorp to take an $18 million write-down on its original agreement.

With profits topping $4.3 million on sales of $295 million in 1986, Harley-Davidson went public, raising $20 million through the sale of stock and $70 million through the sale of unsecured subordinate notes. The company used some of the proceeds to diversify its manufacturing efforts and to acquire motor-home maker Holiday Rambler Corporation for $156 million. Also at this time, Harley-Davidson won a government contract to produce military hardware.

By 1990 sales reached $864.6 million, and the company had a 62.3 percent share of the U.S. heavy-weight motorcycle market. Harley-Davidson's come-back was complete. Over the next few years the company acquired Eagle Credit, which would provide financing and insurance for its dealers, and a 49 percent stake in Wisconsin-based Buell Motorcycle Company, which specialized in performance bikes. In 1996 the company divested the money-losing Holiday Rambler operation for $50 million, substantially less than it had paid for it.

Under the leadership of Richard Teerlink and, later, Jeff Bleustein, Harley-Davidson achieved record sales and earnings levels throughout the 1990s. The company's merchandising strategy paid off, as dealers and other retailers began to devote more space to just about anything with the Harley-Davidson logo on it. In 1998 the company celebrated its 95th anniversary with a weeklong gathering of its fans in Milwaukee. Its two assembly plants in York and Kansas City were producing 137,000 motorcycles annually and struggling to keep up with consumer demand.

FURTHER READING

''Bleustein Elected Chairman of Harley-Davidson Board of Directors.'' *PR Newswire*, December 9, 1998.

Green, William. *Harley-Davidson: The Living Legend.* New York: Crescent Books, 1991.

Gross, Daniel. ''The Turnaround at Harley-Davidson.'' In *Forbes Greatest Business Stories of All Time.* New York: John Wiley & Sons, 1996.

Reid, Peter. *Well Made in America: Lessons from Harley-Davidson on Being the Best.* New York: McGraw-Hill, 1990.

Taylor, Rich. "The Mystique." *Popular Mechanics*, November 1998.

Wagner, Herbert. *Harley-Davidson, 1930–1941: Revolutionary Motorcycles and Those Who Rode Them.* Atglen, Pennsylvania: Schiffer, 1996.

Wright, David. *The Harley-Davidson Motor Company: An Official Ninety-Year History.* Osceola, Wisconsin: Motorbooks International, 1993.

HARPERS FERRY ARMORY

In 1796, Harpers Ferry, Virginia (the city is now in West Virginia) became the site of the second of two arsenals selected by President George Washington (1732–1799); the first was established in 1794 at Springfield, Massachusetts. The Virginia town, situated in the Blue Ridge Mountains, at the confluence of the Potomac and Shenandoah rivers, was considered a safe and central place for military stores. Harpers Ferry developed as a center for the manufacture of rifles, but production remained inadequate. In 1798, Congress passed an act appropriating funds to purchase weapons from private armories. By the 1820s, according to *American Machinist Magazine* ("An Industry Evolves," August 1996), private manufacturers such as Remington and Colt's Patent Fire Arms Manufacturing, "managed to develop, through a series of painful stages, an effective combination of machines and gages to provide true interchangeability of parts" to allow for efficient mass production. One important stage of the development process occurred at Harpers Ferry Armory between 1819 and 1826: John Hall, who had established an independent rifle works within the armory, developed milling machines that produced truly interchangeable parts. This technology combined with the factory system to create the American System of Manufactures, which soon spread from Virginia to New England (via Springfield) and then to Europe—giving Harpers Ferry the reputation as the birthplace of the system.

The Harpers Ferry Arsenal became a strategic point for both sides during the American Civil War (1861–1865), changing hands several times before the conflict ended. But the town is also noted for the raid that occurred there just over a year before fighting broke out between Union and Confederate forces.

In fall 1859 American abolitionist John Brown (1800–1859) led a group of twenty-one men, black and white, on a raid of the government armory at Harpers Ferry, Virginia. Brown believed the action would inspire a general insurrection of southern slaves.

On October 16, 1859, the band took control of the village and seized the U.S. arsenal. Ten of Brown's followers, including two of his sons, were killed or injured, and on October 18 the band surrendered to federal troops under Colonel Robert E. Lee (1807–1870). Brown was tried for treason and convicted. He was hanged on December 2, 1859, a martyr for the cause. The raid on Harpers Ferry heightened tensions between the pro-slavery South and the free North, which would only be resolved by further bloodshed.

See also: **American System of Manufactures, Harpers Ferry Raid, Springfield Armory**

HARPERS FERRY RAID

John Brown (1800–1859) was an American abolitionist and insurrectionist whose violent raid on the federal arsenal at Harpers Ferry, Virginia, in 1859 played a key role in sharpening the regional tensions that led to the American Civil War (1861–1865). John Brown was born at the turn of the nineteenth century in Torrington, Connecticut, and spent his childhood in Ohio, where he encountered and absorbed strong anti-slavery sentiments from the local population. Over the next three decades Brown raised a large family, but failed at a series of businesses. By 1855, Brown's antislavery stance had evolved into the conviction that God had chosen him to free the slaves from bondage. He followed five of his sons to Kansas to join the growing struggle between pro-slavery and Free Soiler forces over the legal status of slavery in the territory. (The Free Soil party was a U.S. political party with a main objective to prevent the extension of slavery to newly acquired U.S. territories.)

Angered by the ravaging of the Free Soiler town of Lawrence, Kansas, by pro-slavery guerrillas in May 1856, Brown and four of his sons launched a brutal retaliatory raid three days later. In a nighttime attack on a pro-slavery settlement on Pottawatomie Creek, Kansas, Brown and his followers killed five settlers. The murders inflamed the conflict in Kansas as hundreds of settlers rushed to arm themselves. By the end of 1856, at least 200 Kansas citizens lay dead. The tragedy in Kansas ignited the national debate over slavery. Animosities hardened, and in Washington, D.C., pro-slavery and anti-slavery congressmen hurled curses and threats at each other in the Capitol over responsibility of the "bleeding Kansas." President Franklin Pierce (1853–1857) made matters much worse. An advocate of Southern interests, he refused to intervene when intimidation and fraud led to the election of a pro-slavery legislature.

For many Northerners, including respected intellectuals such as Ralph Waldo Emerson and Henry David Thoreau, John Brown was considered a hero, praised for his righteous and uncompromising stand against slavery. To Southerners, Brown was a loathed and feared abolitionist who threatened a core institution of Southern society. He personified the horrible fate that awaited if the North was able to dictate its will on the issue of slavery.

Encouraged by his celebrity, but alarmed by the apparent victory of pro-slavery forces in Kansas, Brown next conceived a plot to strike a mortal blow against slavery. With a group of 18 white and black followers, Brown attacked and seized the federal armory at Harpers Ferry, Virginia. Brown hoped the assault would inspire slaves to join his cause. Arming the slaves in his group with weapons from the arsenal, Brown then intended to establish a Negro republic in the woods of Virginia. From this stronghold he planned to wage war against the South, his forces continuously strengthened by slave rebellions and private Northern assistance.

The failure of the raid was inevitable. The local population and militia quickly mobilized against the group, which failed to recruit a single slave to its side, let alone spark a general rebellion. The raid's fate was sealed when a company of United States Marines under the command of Army Colonel Robert E. Lee, ordered to the site by President James Buchanan (1857–1861), charged the engine house in which Brown and his followers had barricaded themselves. Ten of his group were killed and Brown was wounded and captured.

Brown's grand scheme lasted only 36 hours, but the impact of his raid on Harpers Ferry was far reaching. Although Brown was tried, convicted, and ultimately hanged for treason, he conducted his defense with uncharacteristic dignity and muted religious conviction, inspiring a wellspring of sympathy and support in the North. In death, Brown did more to provoke the dispute over slavery than he accomplished alive. Not surprisingly, Brown's raid heightened the sense of threat in the South, where many concluded the North approved his behavior, and that secession was the only viable solution to the great struggle over the future of slavery.

See also: **Bleeding Kansas, Civil War (Economic Causes of), Harpers Ferry Armory**

FURTHER READING

Connelley, William Elsey. *John Brown*. Topeka, KS: Crane and Company, 1900.

Fried, Albert. *John Brown's Journey: Notes and Reflections on His America and Mine*. Garden City, NY: Anchor/Doubleday, 1978.

Keller, Allan. *Thunder at Harper's Ferry*. Englewood Cliffs, NJ: Prentice-Hall, 1958.

Nelson, Truman. *The Old Man: John Brown at Harpers Ferry*. New York: Holt, Rinehart, and Winston, 1973.

Oates, Stephen B. *To Purge This Land With Blood: A Biography of John Brown*. New York: Harper and Row, 1970.

Villard, Oswald Garrison. *John Brown, 1800–1859: A Biography Fifty Years After*. Gloucester, MA: Peter Smith, 1965.

HARRINGTON, EDWARD MICHAEL

Michael Harrington (1928–1989) was one of the few writers who could claim to have affected business and economic history. Born at the beginning of the Great Depression, Harrington retained youthful memories of that difficult period, and by the time he was 33, he had written one of his more important works, *The Other America* (1962). His book spoke about the "invisible poor" living in America at a time when most Americans were busy celebrating the country's wealth. In speaking out on behalf of the poor, industrial rejects, migrant workers, minorities, and the aged, Harrington drew the attention of at least two presidents to focus on the legislative issues of poverty in America: President John F. Kennedy (1961–1963), and President Lyndon Johnson (1963–1969).

Harrington was born in St. Louis, Missouri, and grew up in a middle-class Irish-Catholic family whose political affiliations were with the Democratic Party. He was heavily influenced by his Jesuit teachers, who maintained that all people can become successful if they are only given a chance. In college Harrington was drawn to the political left and he became a socialist. Over the 30 years that followed he was one of the most eloquent voices of socialism in America.

Harrington lived his adult life as a self-described agitator and organizer. He worked as a political and social activist who tried to achieve the greatest benefits for the poorest Americans. His goal was to create greater economic justice for those who lived in poverty in America, the richest country in the world. In his first autobiography, *Fragments of the Century*, he expressed this view of socialism in capitalist America: "To be a socialist . . . is to make an act of faith, of love even, toward this land. It is to sense the seed beneath the snow; to see, beneath the veneer of corruption and meanness and the commercialization of human relationships, men and women capable of controlling their own destinies. To be a radical is, in the best and only decent sense of the word, patriotic."

TO BE A SOCIALIST . . . IS TO SENSE THE SEED BENEATH THE SNOW; TO SEE, BENEATH THE VENEER OF CORRUPTION AND MEANNESS AND THE COMMERCIALIZATION OF HUMAN RELATIONSHIPS, MEN AND WOMEN CAPABLE OF CONTROLLING THEIR OWN DESTINIES.

Edward Harrington, *Fragments of the Century*, 1973

Harrington spoke directly to American business, asking for the creation of a truly "good" society. He was a writer of books, a lecturer, and the co-chairman of the largest socialist organization in America, the Democratic Socialists. Harrington advocated working with the Democratic Party to achieve liberal economic and business reform. He felt gradual, liberal reform would bring about social justice in a capitalist economy, which he feared would become susceptible to revolutionary overthrow if economic justice for all was not a part of the American way. As a principled anti-Communist, Harrington sought to help create ongoing reform in the existing system that would lead to full employment, the abolition of poverty, and a national health care system.

A scholar, a man of religious principle, a political and economic socialist, Harrington helped forward the principles of progressivism and equality in the twentieth century. He was an idealist who fought throughout his life for social justice in America, who fought for socialist reforms, but who, in the end, died of cancer in 1989 in the midst of a conservative turn in American politics.

See also: **Great Depression, Socialism**

FURTHER READING

Contemporary Authors. Farmington Hills, MI: The Gale Group, 1999, s.v. "Harrington (Edward) Michael."

Fermain, Louis A. and Joyce Kornbluh, eds. *Poverty in America: A Book of Readings*. Ann Arbor: University of Michigan Press, 1965.

Harrington, Michael. *Fragments of the Century: A Social Autobiography*. New York: MacMillan, 1973.

Harrington, Michael. *The Other America: Poverty in the United States*. New York: MacMillan, 1965.

Howe, Irving and Michael Harrington. *The Seventies: Problems and Proposals*. New York: Harper & Rowe, 1972.

HAWAII

Hawaii's rich history, tropical climate, and beautiful scenery have made tourism the leading source of revenue in the state. While agricultural products and military bases also contribute to the growth of Hawaii's economic base, visitors to the islands spend millions annually to enjoy the Hawaiian culture and climate.

Of the 132 Hawaiian Islands located in the northern Pacific Ocean, the eight largest are Hawaii, Maui, Oahu, Kauai, Molokai, Lanai, Niihau, and Kahoolawe. All the islands were formed by volcanic eruptions. Mauna Loa on the island of Hawaii is the largest active volcano in the world. Because of volcanic eruptions, Hawaii's terrain and vegetation have changed over the years. There are only a few species of trees left that are native to the environment. Most of the unique trees and flowers were brought to the islands from other parts of the world since the 1800s. More than half of the vegetation is considered endangered and is protected by the government.

Polynesians from Southeast Asia or the Marquesa Islands in the South Pacific were the first to arrive in the Hawaiian islands, coming by canoe between 1000 and 1400 years ago. In 1778 Captain James Cook (1728–1779), an English navigator, was the first Westerner to see the Hawaiian Islands. When he saw Oahu and the surrounding islands, he named them the Sandwich Islands, after the fourth Earl of Sandwich, John Montagu (1718–1792). The islands were ruled by chiefs under a class system called *kapu*. But the *kapu* system would eventually be destroyed as European and American influences diluted the native culture.

After Captain Cook's landing, visitors to the islands were scarce until 1786, when ships from England, France, Russia, Spain, and the United States discovered that Hawaii was a convenient stop for water and supplies on the trade route between Asia and North America. During those first years, natives were able to sell sandalwood, Hawaii's first marketable natural resource, to foreigners for money and goods. In the

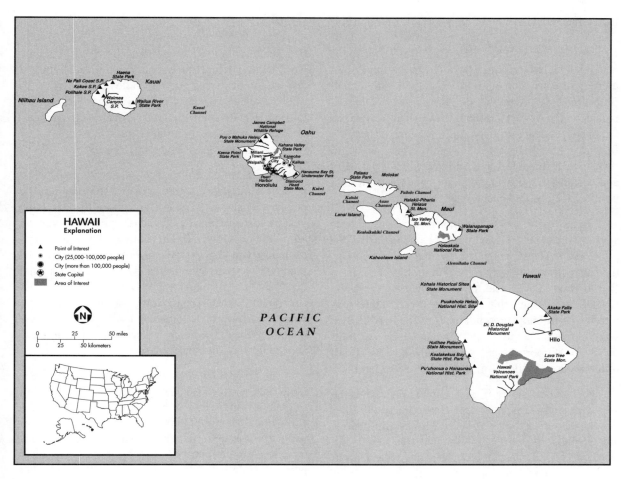

State of Hawaii.

1820s the demand for whale oil grew. Whaling was Hawaii's major source of income until 1860, when there were fewer whales to hunt. Petroleum and coal took the place of whale oil for fuel, and England stopped whaling during the American Civil War (1861–1865). During those years, Protestant missionaries and Roman Catholics arrived on the islands to spread Christianity and help establish public schools, a newspaper, a legislature, and the first sugar plantation.

During the 1850s, Chinese laborers were brought to the islands under five-year contracts to work on Hawaiian sugarcane plantations. Some left Hawaii after their work contracts expired, but others stayed and opened successful small businesses. More laborers were needed as the sugar industry grew, so Polynesians were brought to Hawaii in 1859. In the late 1860s Japanese laborers arrived. In the 1870s German and Portuguese immigrants worked the sugar plantations.

After the Civil War, sugar became the primary source of revenue for Hawaii. As pioneers moved westward in the United States, they provided a market for almost all the sugar produced in Hawaii. American sugar planters became powerful on the islands, exerting pressure for a trade agreement with the United States. In 1875 the United States lifted a tax on shipments of sugar to the United States. This reduced the price of sugar for Americans and solidified the market for Hawaiian-grown sugar. In return, Hawaii allowed only the United States to use its ports.

Americans enjoyed increasing power and influence in Hawaiian politics and society. In 1891, Queen Liliuokalani took the throne and made efforts to restore Hawaii to its native people. Unfortunately, visitors brought with them diseases that proved deadly to the natives, including smallpox, leprosy, cholera, and measles. In 1778 there were nearly 300,000 natives on the islands, but by the 1890s there were fewer than 60,000. And almost all the land and all the power was held and controlled by foreigners.

Two years later, a European and American led revolution overthrew Queen Liliuokalani, and a temporary government was formed, led by Sanford B.

Dole. The new leaders immediately asked for annexation by the United States, but were denied by President Grover Cleveland (1885–1889, 1893–1897), an opponent of U.S. expansion. Hawaii's government then drafted its own constitution on July 4, 1894, and proclaimed the Republic of Hawaii, with Dole as president. On August 12, 1898, Hawaii was recognized as an independent territory, and Dole became Hawaii's first governor in June 1900. A few sugar plantation owners made huge fortunes during the territorial years and became the most influential powers in Hawaiian politics, society, and business circles.

In the early 1900s the pineapple industry was started by James D. Dole, Sanford Dole's cousin. The pineapple business generated revenue second only to the sugar crop. New groups of immigrants came from Puerto Rico, Korea, and the Philippines to work the plantations. During this time, the United States expanded its military presence in Hawaii. Fort Shafter was the first built and, in 1908, a naval base was built on Pearl Harbor; others soon followed. By 1990, military bases would cover 25 percent of the land.

Hawaii became more accessible to the rest of the world as communication and transportation further developed during the 1920s and 1930s. Radio stations and telephone systems were brought to the islands and airplanes could transport people and goods. Hawaii became a convenient stop between continents for air travel as well. Like on the mainland, the Great Depression (1929–1939) put many people out of work in Hawaii. People stopped buying pineapples and travelers stopped vacationing in Hawaii, which significantly affected Hawaii's economy.

In the midst of World War II (1939–1945), on December 7, 1941, the Japanese attacked the Hawaiian port of Pearl Harbor. The United States' Pacific fleet was severely damaged, and Hawaii was placed under martial law due to distrust of Hawaiians of Japanese descent. Thousands of citizens who were of Japanese heritage living in western states such as California and Oregon were rounded up and sent to internment camps. In Hawaii, however, where 40 percent of the population was Japanese, the decision was made not to relocate the Japanese because they were integral to Hawaii's economy. Servicemen stationed in Hawaii doubled the territory's population in four years as Hawaii became the central location of the Pacific war operations.

After World War II (1939–1945) efforts resumed to secure statehood for Hawaii. President Dwight D.

Eisenhower (1953–1961) signed the bill to let Hawaii enter the Union on March 18, 1959, and Hawaii became the fiftieth state on August 21, 1959. After the war, Hawaii's tourism industry grew as additional airports, built during the war, allowed for more air traffic. Airfare was less expensive than ocean-liner fare, and enabled more people to travel. As the number of visitors grew, so, too, did the construction business as hotels and shopping centers were built.

By the 1980s, the service industry employed 80 percent of the state's workers. In 1990 tourism was the largest industry in Hawaii, with more than 100,000 visitors to the islands daily, and revenues of more than $4 billion annually. Government was the second-largest industry in Hawaii, with more than 65,000 Department of Defense employees. Of the manufactured goods that make up about 5 percent of Hawaii's gross state income, sugar production is still most important, with pineapple production second. Additional products manufactured in Hawaii are macadamia nuts, clothing, and stone, clay, and glass products.

The population of Hawaii continued to grow rapidly after it achieved statehood, primarily through migration from Asia and the U.S. mainland. Since the early 1970s, about 40,000 people have moved to Hawaii from the U.S. mainland each year. Nearly half, however, were military personnel stationed there temporarily while in the service. Between 1980 and 1990 the population of Hawaii increased 15 percent, and according to the 1990 U.S. census, nearly four-fifths of the population lived on Oahu in the metropolitan Honolulu area. Honolulu is the state capital.

While the number of inhabitants increased, annual personal income grew at a much lower rate than the national average, although the cost of living in Hawaii is much higher than on the United States mainland. Between 1995 and 1996, Hawaii saw only a 1.7 percent income increase, compared to the national average of 4.5 percent. The average personal income in Hawaii was listed as $25,159. Hawaii's personal income tax rate is one of the highest in the nation, ranging between two and ten percent. In 1995, 10.3 percent of Hawaii's residents were living below the federal poverty level.

FURTHER READING

Beckwith, Martha. *Hawaiian Mythology*. Honolulu: University Press, 1982.

Tabrah, Ruth. *Hawaii, A Bicentennial History*. New York: Norton, 1980.

Thompson, Kathleen. "Hawaii." In *Portrait of America*. Steck-Vaughn Publishing, 1996.

Worldmark Encyclopedia of the States. Detroit: Gale Research, 1998, s.v. "Hawaii."

HAY, JOHN MILTON

John Milton Hay (1838–1905) was born on October 8, 1838, in Salem, Indiana, and raised on a small town on the Mississippi River. He graduated from Brown University and decided to enter law. In 1858 Hay was studying law at his uncle's law firm in Springfield, Illinois, when he made friends with an interesting neighbor, Abraham Lincoln (1809–1865). Already a Republican, Hay became an assistant private secretary to Lincoln and followed the president-elect to Washington, DC. Hay served with Lincoln until the president's assassination in 1865.

Hay was then appointed secretary to the legation in Paris in March 1865; he moved on to Vienna in 1867, then finishing this tour of duty from 1868 to 1870 in Madrid. Returning to the United States in 1870, Hay took a position on the editorial board of the New York *Tribune*. In 1871 he published a book of poems, *Pike County Ballads and Other Pieces*. Soon afterward he published a travel book based upon his days in Spain, *Castilian Days*. In 1875 Hays moved to Cleveland, Ohio, until President Rutherford B. Hayes (1877–1881) appointed him Assistant Secretary of State, an office he held from 1879 to 1881. In 1881 Hay returned to the New York *Tribune* as editor. For the next 15 years he worked at the *Tribune* while concurrently traveling and writing.

John Hay anonymously published an anti-labor novel, *Bread-Winners* in 1884, and his most famous published work, *Abraham Lincoln: A History*, in 1890. Written in collaboration with John G. Nicolay (1832–1901), the ten volume *Abraham Lincoln* was the standard biography on the famous president for many decades. Hay continued to write, but his career took another turn to public service in 1897 when President William McKinley (1897–1901) appointed Hay as U.S. ambassador to Great Britain.

Hay arrived at the Court of St. James sharing expansionist views that were held by another important politician, Theodore Roosevelt (1858–1919). Like Roosevelt, Hay supported the American entry into the Spanish-American War in 1898. After initially believing the Philippines should not be completely annexed by the United States, he shifted his position to support the full annexation of the islands as a means of balancing the political power in Asia with that of Japan and Russia.

President McKinley appointed John Hay to serve as Secretary of State in 1898, a position Hay maintained when McKinley was assassinated and Theodore Roosevelt became president (1901–1909). He held this position until his death. Hay presided over two extremely important episodes in the history of the United States: the Open Door policy with China and the Panama Canal Treaty. In 1899 and 1900, Hay issued two "open door" notes that called for all foreign powers to respect the territorial rights of China. His goal was to encourage free trade in China without that country being partitioned by European or other powers. The Boxer Rebellion of 1900 presented just such an opportunity to these powers, but Hay's influence was able to keep China open.

Hay was also a firm advocate of a canal that would connect the Atlantic and Pacific Oceans. There were several plans afoot at the time for an inter-oceanic canal in either the Isthmus of Panama or in Nicaragua. Hay negotiated a treaty with Columbia in January 1903 to pay $10 million and an annual rental of $250,000 for a ninety-nine year lease on property in Panama. Columbia initially rejected the offer, but in November 1903 Panama, assisted by machinations by Roosevelt and Hay, successfully rose up against Columbia and established itself as a sovereign nation. Hay then signed a treaty with the new Panamanian minister similar to the one made with Columbia.

John Hay was an excellent writer and a cultured man. He preferred the more erudite social scene of the East to the midwestern frontiers of his youth. In 1904 he fell ill, and he died in Newbury, New Hampshire, on July 1, 1905.

See also: **Open Door Policy, Panama Canal Treaty**

FURTHER READING

Dennett, Tyler. *John Hay: From Poetry to Politics*. New York: Dodd, Mead and Co., 1933.

Encyclopedia Britannica. Chicago: Encyclopedia Britannica, Inc., 1994, s.v. "Hay, John."

Garraty, John A. and Jerome L. Sternstein. *Encyclopedia of American Biography*. New York: HarperCollins, 1996, s.v. "Hay, John."

Hay, John. Edited by Tyler Dennett. *Lincoln and the Civil War in the Diaries and Letters of John Hay.* New York: Dodd, Mead and Co., 1939.

Van Doren, Charles, ed. *Webster's American Biographies.* Springfield, MA: Merriam-Webster Inc., 1984, s.v. ''Hay, John.''

HAYMARKET BOMBING

As industrialization escalated following the American Civil War (1861–1865) many corporations gained substantial power. Working conditions in many factories became increasingly dismal, leading workers to organize into unions seeking better conditions and higher pay. While the United States wrestled with the slavery issue, socialism influenced by the writings of Karl Marx (1818–1883) and others gained strength in Europe. Immigrants to the United States from Europe brought these political and economic ideals with them, leading to the creation of socialist labor organizations such as the National Labor Union in 1866. Though short-lived, the union gained eight-hour workdays for federal workers and established a tie between socialism and labor in the United States.

The first national influential labor union in the United States was the Knights of Labor, established in 1869 in Philadelphia. Before long the Knights grew into a large diverse membership including skilled and unskilled workers, African Americans, immigrants, and women. Given this diversity of membership, disagreements over labor tactics deepened, especially with respect to the use of strikes. The union leadership preached nonviolence and gradual reform through education. However in the 1870s unrest escalated, highlighted by violent clashes between hostile police and some of the more militant union members. Labor achieved some successes through strikes against railroads, which substantially increased the Knights' membership to 700,000 by 1886. As with other labor organizations key issues for the Knights included eight-hour work days and government restriction of the growing number of powerful business trusts or monopolies. But the organization's effectiveness declined as the Knights' size reached beyond the number that could be effectively controlled.

By the 1880s labor unions were not well respected by the general public and were feared by management. To gain a more effective voice, skilled workers in various occupations organized into the American Federation of Labor (AFL), which was founded in 1886.

> Through the mid-1870s both union and radical activity, and the level of rhetorical and physical violence on all sides, rose sharply in response to layoffs and wage reductions. Labor advocates and agitators . . . predicted class uprisings against ''arrogant capitalism,'' while the major dailies, influential periodicals, and business and political leaders became more shrill in throwing immigrants, tramps, union organizers, and communism together as enemies of public order whose activities must be answered with force.
>
> **Carl S. Smith,** *Urban Disorder and the Shape of Belief: The Great Chicago Fire, the Haymarket Bomb, and the Model Town of Pullman,* 1995

The organization, adopting a conservative policy seeking gradual improvements, pursued issues including shorter hours, improved wages, and safer working conditions. Unskilled laborers had no strong unions representing their interests. Discontent and the struggle for recognition led to radical actions by some labor organizers as thousands of workers were periodically involved in localized strikes across the country.

In 1886 a broad labor movement brought the campaign for eight-hour workdays to the forefront. In Chicago labor leaders and militant anarchists called a strike against the McCormick Harvesting Machine Company. The company hired strikebreakers to replace striking workers. On May 3 Chicago police were brought in to protect the strikebreakers from the strikers. With tensions high, four strikers were killed in the violence that erupted. In reaction to the killings, radicals and union leaders called for a rally the following day at nearby Haymarket Square. The gathering remained peaceful during the speeches, but when police moved in to break up the rally, an unidentified person tossed a dynamite bomb into the crowd, which killed seven policemen and injured 60 others. In the mayhem that ensued police fired their pistols into the crowd—ten people were killed and approximately 50 wounded.

Numerous arrests followed as police targeted hundreds of known radicals. Eight anarchist labor leaders, including August Spies and Albert Parsons, were indicted for the death of one of the policemen killed at the Square. Seven of the eight were foreign born. Their trial began on June 21, 1886. They were found guilty of conspiracy against police authorities despite the fact that authorities never identified the actual bomber or their connection to the unknown person. Seven of the

On May 4, 1886 a rally was called to protest the police actions revolving around the striking McCormick Harvesting Machine Co.

eight were sentenced to death and the eighth to fifteen years in prison. In September 1887, the Illinois Supreme Court upheld their convictions on appeal; two months later authorities hanged Spies, Parsons, and two others. Another committed suicide shortly before his execution date. In 1893 the Illinois governor pardoned the three surviving convicted union members on grounds of insufficient evidence—a decision that was applauded by members of organized labor.

The Haymarket bombing incident increased antiunion sentiments in the United States. Radical elements lost power as more conservative labor strategies were adopted. Much of the blame for the violent incident was inappropriately directed toward the Knights of Labor, which led thousands of workers to resign. Public disdain for unions was compounded in the 1890s by government application of the Sherman Antitrust Act toward union activities allegedly inhibiting business competition rather than at endemic business consolidations. When the socialists attempted to establish various company unions and the Socialist Labor political party, they met stiff resistance and were largely unsuccessful.

See also: **Knights of Labor, Cyrus McCormick, Sherman Anti-Trust Act, American Federation of Labor**

FURTHER READING

Avrich, Paul. *The Haymarket Tragedy.* Princeton, NJ: Princeton University Press, 1984.

Dubofsky, Melvyn. *Industrialism and the American Worker, 1865–1920*, 2nd ed. Arlington Heights, IL: H. Davidson, 1985.

Greene, Julie. *Pure and Simple Politics: The American Federation of Labor and Political Activism, 1881–1917.* New York: Cambridge University Press, 1998.

Jacoby, Daniel. *Laboring for Freedom: A New Look at the History of Labor in America.* Armonk, NY: M. E. Sharpe, 1998.

Nelson, Bruce C. *Beyond the Martyrs: A Social History of Chicago's Anarchists, 1870–1900.* New Brunswick, NJ: Rutgers University Press, 1988.

HEALTH MAINTENANCE ORGANIZATIONS (HMOS)

Health Maintenance Organizations (HMOs) in the United States have their roots in the first decades of the twentieth century. In the early 1900s millions of Americans belonged to fraternal orders and mutual benefit societies which provided prepaid medical care to their members. Many large companies, particularly those where injuries were commonplace such as railroads, created medical departments to care for their workers.

One of the first true HMOs was established by an agreement between the employees of the Los Angeles Department of Water and Power and practice of two doctors, Donald Ross and H. Clifford Loos. This agreement exhibited the basic traits that came to distinguish HMOs. The employees paid the doctors set fees, regardless of the state of their health. In return for these payments, the doctors provided whatever medical care was necessary for the employees or their families. This was as compared to traditional fee-for-service health care, in which a patient pays no money to a doctor unless he goes in to visit, but then has to pay that doctor for the cost of their particular treatment. In essence, the employees who joined the Ross-Loos plan were agreeing to pay smaller fees for health care that they might never need, rather than risk needing to pay a large fee, a fee which conventional health insurance might not cover entirely, if they became seriously ill. In return, Ross and Loos received a solid base of patients and a steady income.

In 1938, Henry J. Kaiser (1882–1967) established an HMO for workers at his shipyard. This plan, originally known simply as Dr. Garfield and Associates, was opened to the general public after World War II (1939–1945). Renamed Kaiser Permanente in 1955, it became the first large, national HMO. At this time, there was a widespread feeling among both doctors and the general public that arrangements such as Ross-Loos and Kaiser Permanente led to inferior care, and fee-for-service care and traditional health insurance continued to dominate the U.S. health care system.

All of this began to change in the 1970s. By this time, the cost of health care had risen to the point that it was becoming difficult for some to afford. It was also placing a strain on the federal government's new Medicaire and Medicaid programs. Many began touting systems such as Ross-Loos and Kaiser Permanente as a way to control medical costs and ensure that Americans received adequate care. It was at this time that the term HMO came into use to describe such managed care systems. In 1973 Congress passed the Health Maintenance Organization Act, which removed many legal barriers to the development of HMOs, leading to the formation of more than 200 HMOs by the end of the decade.

HMOs remained a minor part of the U.S. health care system at the beginning of the 1980s. Only four percent of the U.S. population belonged to an HMO, approximately half of which were in Kaiser Permanente. As the cost of health care in the United States, already the highest in the world, continued to rise during the decade, Americans began joining HMOs in large numbers. By 1995 three-quarters of all doctors were providing service as part of a managed care plan, and nearly three-quarters of all working Americans were members of such a plan.

As HMOs rose to dominate the U.S. health care system, attention turned from their supposed benefits to their perceived flaws. HMOs gave patients little choice over which doctors they could see, a fact that made many uncomfortable. New types of managed care, known as Preferred Provider Organizations (PPOs) and Point of Service (POS) plans became increasingly popular as systems which provided many of the cost-reducing benefits of HMOs while leaving members with some options as to what doctors to see.

Yet other problems, however, remained. HMOs and other forms of managed care generally had guidelines and standards of treatment that they expected participating physicians to follow. Some patients feared, and some doctors complained, that these guidelines were more concerned with keeping HMO costs low than with ensuring patients received the best possible treatment. And while HMOs were undoubtedly less expensive for many Americans than more traditional types of insurance, they remained too expensive for most to join except as part of a plan sponsored by their employer. Smaller businesses, their employees, and the self-employed remained largely unable to join HMOs.

See also: **Henry J, Kaiser, Medicare, Medicaid**

FURTHER READING

''Health Maintenance Organization,'' [cited March 30, 1999] available from the World Wide Web @ www.encyclopedia.com/.

''Health Maintenance Organization,'' [cited March 30, 1999] available from the World Wide Web @ www.eb.com:180/bol/topic?eu=40537&sctn=1#s_top/.

''The HMO Page,'' available from the World Wide Web @ www.hmopage.org/

Jones, Rhys W. *The Ultimate Hmo Handbook: How to Make the Most of the Revolution in Managed Care.* T.T.M. Publishers, 1994.

''Managed Care Guide,'' [cited July 15, 1999] available from the World Wide Web @ www.helix.com/pathway/mangcare.htm/.

HEARST, WILLIAM RANDOLPH

"Yellow journalism" was a phrase coined in the early twentieth century to describe a type of journalism that was principally developed by William Randolph Hearst (1863–1951). The term described a newspaper that focused on sensationalism to sell papers, including frenzied reporting of sports, crime, sex, and scandal. Writer Arthur James Pegler said, "A Hearst Newspaper is like a screaming woman running down the street with her throat cut." But this legacy does not begin to describe the complex and talented William Randolph Hearst.

George Hearst made a fortune in the California gold rush, bought huge tracts of land, and became a U.S. Senator. His wife Phoebe Apperson Hearst gave birth to their son, William Randolph Hearst, on April 29, 1863, in San Francisco. A schoolteacher, Hearst's mother ensured her son received the best education his father's wealth could buy. Young Hearst went to private schools, had private tutors, and was given tours of Europe. Eventually, Hearst entered Harvard University, but he was expelled from the school for misconduct after only two years.

While at Harvard, Hearst was the student editor of the *Lampoon*, spent time at the *Boston Globe*, and afterward served as a cub reporter for Joseph Pulitzer (1841–1911) at the *New York World*. Hearst's father had purchased the financially ailing *San Francisco Examiner* in 1880. In 1887 the younger Hearst asked his father for ownership of the paper, and it was given to him. This newspaper was William Randolph Hearst's start as a newspaper mogul. At the *Examiner*, Hearst began his run at faking news and using sensationalism to sell papers. He paid top wages, attracted the best journalism talent, and sold newspapers.

Moving his base of operations to New York City in 1895, Hearst took a $7.5 million gift from his mother (taken from his father's estate) and purchased the failing *New York Morning Journal*. Within a year, Hearst's style of shock news ran the circulation from 77,000 to over one million. In New York he continued his penchant for paying top dollar for talent. Hearst supported the Democratic Party with his newspapers, although he had little in common with either his newspaper's readers or the party's candidates and workers. Hearst opposed Democratic candidate William Jennings Bryan (1860–1925) in the presidential campaign of 1896, and backed the Spanish-American War in 1898. During that war, Hearst spent a half million dollars covering the news of military actions.

William Randolph Hearst.

In 1900 Hearst established the *Chicago American* and, in 1902, the *Chicago Examiner*. He added the *Boston American* and *Los Angeles Examiner* in 1904. His media empire was expanding rapidly, but by this time the acquisition of newspapers was more than a business ploy. It was an attempt to control the news to further Hearst's rising political ambitions. William Randolph Hearst wanted to be president of the United States. Hearst won election to the U.S. House of Representatives in 1902 and 1904 as a Tammany Democrat, but he was not a good congressman. Chronic absenteeism from Congress, which he found necessary to run his newspaper business and campaign for president, cost him his political support. He ran for mayor of New York in 1905 and for governor of New York in 1906 but lost both races. These loses finished him as a candidate in politics. Hearst then went on to use his newspapers and wealth to influence political decisions as best he could behind the scenes.

Hearst married Millicent Willson in 1903. He was 40; she was 21 years old. They had five boys, several of whom followed their father into journalism. But in 1917 Hearst followed his father's lead of unfaithfulness and took a young mistress, 20-year-old actress Marion Davies. Hearst continued his relationship with Davies until his death, and settled her in the castle he built on his father's land at San Simeon, California.

The $37 million castle, which he stocked with many pieces of his $50 million art collection, was an ostentatious display of wealth, even for the flamboyant newspaper publisher. Hearst used the castle for opulent parties, wining and dining the rich, famous, and powerful. (After his death, the Hearst family gave the castle to the State of California, who operates it as a public park, providing guided tours of the castle and its mostly intact art collection.)

At the height of his career in 1935, Hearst owned 26 daily and 11 Sunday newspapers in 19 cities, with nearly 14 percent of the total U.S. daily circulation. He owned the King Features syndication service and the International News Service. He owned a Sunday supplement, the *American Weekly*, and International News Reel. He owned six magazines, including *Cosmopolitan*, *Harper's Bazaar*, and *Good Housekeeping*. He had lesser holdings in radio stations, and had spent millions in Hollywood, much of it to promote the career of Davies. Hearst possessed over $50 million in New York real estate, the castle at San Simeon, and homes in several locations. His art collection was the largest ever assembled by a single individual.

Hearst turned more conservative in his older years. He fought with progressive Democrats, though he had little to do with Republicans either. He fought against an emerging writers' union, the American Newspaper Guild and opposed U.S. involvement abroad until the Japanese attach on Pearl Harbor, Hawaii, in 1941, changed his mind. Hearst was strongly anticommunist.

Scandal, including a famous 1927 incident where Hearst newspapers printed, unchecked or unverified forged documents alleging Mexican government bribery of U.S. Senators, made no dent in Hearst's empire. But the Great Depression (1929–1939) did have an enormous impact on the Hearst holdings. By 1937 Hearst's two corporations were $126 million in debt. He had to relinquish control of his empire in order to save it, and he lost much of his personal fortune in the process. He died on August 14, 1951, with his newspaper holdings down to just eight papers. Breaking with their father, his five sons, who continued in the newspaper business, worked to give the remaining papers credibility and shed the yellow journalism label. The Hearst Foundation continues to provide scholarships to journalism students.

See also: **James Gordon Bennett, Muckrakers, Joseph Pulitzer**

FURTHER READING

Bowman, John S., ed. *The Cambridge Dictionary of American Biography*. Cambridge: Cambridge University Press, 1995, s.v. "Hearst, William Randolph."

Encyclopedia of World Biography. Detroit: Gale Research, Inc., 1998, s.v. "Hearst, William Randolph."

The Media in America. Santa Barbara: ABC-CLIO, Inc., 1995.

Street, Sarah. "Citizen Kane." *History Today*, March 1996.

Swanberg, William A. *Citizen Hearst*. New York: Scribner, 1961.

H.J. HEINZ COMPANY

The Heinz ketchup bottle and the company slogan, "57 Varieties," are familiar to any American who eats in a restaurant or shops for food. The H.J. Heinz Company today manufactures thousands of food products in plants across the world and remains one of the world's leading food companies. Some of the best-known Heinz brands—such as Skippy peanut butter, StarKist tuna, and Ore-Ida Tater Tots—do not carry the Heinz name. Heinz's divisions include food service, infant foods, ketchup and condiments, pet foods, tuna, and weight-control products.

The company's founder, Henry John Heinz, grew up not far from Pittsburgh, Pennsylvania. After working as a bookkeeper in his father's brickyard he and a partner, L.C. Noble, began to sell bottled horseradish, sauerkraut, vinegar, and pickles, naming their business Heinz, Noble & Company. This enterprise ultimately failed after the Panic of 1873, but Heinz and some of his relatives later organized a new business, which became known as the H.J. Heinz Company in 1888. The Pittsburgh business prospered and the nation came to know Heinz as the famed "pickle king." He also produced jams, jellies, and condiments, always packed in clean conditions and made from the freshest ingredients.

Heinz promoted his products skillfully and with great zeal. Noting that the American diet at this time was quite bland, he coined the "57 Varieties" slogan to spark an interest in changing people's eating habits. The slogan logo appeared everywhere—in newspapers and magazines and on streetcars, billboards, and even large concrete figures along highways. At the 1893 World's Fair in Chicago he introduced "pickle pins," a fad which soon swept the country. In 1900 he put up the first electric advertising sign, representing a 40-foot pickle, in New York City. A religious man, Heinz

An executive of the H. J. Heinz Company, presents a bottle of their ketchup with one of the estimated 60,000 entries in a 1997 product label design contest.

never allowed such advertisements to appear on Sundays. His plants were known for their humane treatment of workers and there was never a strike against the company while Heinz was president.

By 1905 Heinz had opened a factory in Great Britain, beginning what would become a global operation. In 1906, unlike many other American food manufacturers, he supported the Pure Food and Drug Act, which regulated the production of processed foods to make them safer to eat. By the time of Heinz's death in 1919, the H.J. Heinz Company employed 6,500 people and ran 25 branch factories. He was succeeded by his son, Howard, who remained president until his death in 1941. Heinz continued to produce its traditional condiment lines, though in 1931 it added a baby food division, which, along with canned soups, helped keep the company afloat during the Great Depression (1929–1939). By 1937 the company's business had doubled.

H.J. Heinz II, known as Jack, took over as president after his father's death, leading the company in once again doubling its sales over the next five years. Jack Heinz was active in food relief efforts during World War II (1939–1945); during this time, many more women took jobs in Heinz plants as men went to war. Sales abroad increased substantially in the 1940s, ketchup and baked beans were particularly popular in England. Heinz went public after the war and continued to expand during the 1950s and 1960s, opening plants in the Netherlands, Venezuela, Japan, Italy, and Portugal. It also bought Reyumer & Bros., Inc., Hachmeister, Inc., StarKist Foods, and Ore-Ida Foods. Throughout the latter half of the twentieth century, Heinz weathered many changes in the food industry, as distributing and marketing systems adapted themselves to the new supermarket chains.

R. Burt Gookin succeeded Jack Heinz as CEO, and J.F. O'Reilly, president of the company's British subsidiary, took over as president of the parent company in 1973. He changed the company's emphasis by cutting back on traditional business while introducing new products. During O'Reilly's tenure Heinz acquired Weight Watchers International and several other companies, and ceased trying to compete in the soup market with the Campbell Soup Company. O'Reilly, who became CEO in 1979, also instituted a cost-cutting policy, downsizing some product packages and pressuring plants to be more productive. Although the Justice Department prohibited Heinz's bid to purchase Bumble Bee Seafoods in 1988, the company reorganized StarKist Foods and Heinz Pet Products in an effort to increase sales abroad.

Heinz began to expand into Third World countries and also reached into China, Korea, and Thailand. These new strategies succeeded, doubling Heinz's sales from $2.9 billion in 1980 to $6.1 billion in 1990. During these years Heinz was investing almost as much overseas as in the domestic economy. It controlled 29 percent of the worldwide infant food market, challenged only by the U.S. leader, Gerber Foods. Heinz also had begun investing in the Asia-Pacific market with the acquisition of Wattie's Limited in New Zealand. A recession in the early 1990s, however, combined with increased competition caused a slowdown which decreased the company's stock value. A number of divestments, staff reductions, and decreases in advertising outlays helped to minimize the losses in the domestic market.

Despite continuing market challenges O'Reilly insisted that Heinz would prosper if it remembered its dedication to niche markets—condiments, tuna, frozen potatoes, and weight-control products—and to what he called ''constant rebirth.'' The company acquired the pet food division of Quaker Oats Company in 1995 and increased its market share of the tuna business to 46 percent by 1997. O'Reilly instituted a major restructuring plan called Project Millennia, which would eliminate 25 plants, cut 2,500 jobs (6 percent of the total workforce of 43,000), and take a charge against earnings of $650 million. O'Reilly said that the move would make Heinz, along with Campbell Soup Company and Sara Lee Corporation, one of the three most important food companies in the world. Indeed, the company came close to its 1997 goal of $9.5 billion in sales, pulling in actual sales of $9.3 billion. Although O'Reilly was criticized by some industry observers for raising product prices and reducing advertising support for some of the Heinz brands, he had helped the company to grow from $1 billion in net worth in 1979 to nearly $20 billion in 1998.

In 1997 Heinz divested itself of the Ore-Ida food service operations business and scaled down its Weight Watchers division. Under the leadership of William Johnson, the company president who succeeded O'Reilly as chairman, Heinz considerably enhanced its advertising and marketing efforts. After a drop in 1998 sales, in February 1999 the company announced another cost-cutting plan that would eliminate 4,000 jobs and close an additional 20 factories.

See also: **Campbell Soup Co.**

FURTHER READING

Alberts, Robert C. *The Good Provider*. Boston: Houghton Mifflin, 1973.

Alexander, Keith L., and Baker, Stephen. ''The New Life of O'Reilly.'' *Business Week*, June 13, 1994.

A Golden Day, A Memorial and a Celebration, 1869–1924. Pittsburgh: H.J. Heinz Company, 1925.

''Heinz to Close or Sell 25 Plants, Eliminate 2,500 Jobs.'' *Minneapolis Star Tribune*, March 15, 1997.

''H.J. Heinz Company.'' *1998 Quarterly Report*. Pittsburgh: H.J. Heinz Company, 1998.

In Good Company: 125 Years at the Heinz Table. Warner Books, 1994.

Murray, Matt. ''Era Is Nearing an End As Heinz's Johnson Assumes More Control.'' *Wall Street Journal*, March 10, 1997.

HELMS-BURTON ACT

Despite vigorous opposition from the main trading partners of the United States, including the European Union and Canada, the Helms-Burton Act was signed into law by Congress on March 12, 1996. The law extended sanctions to all non-U.S. companies that did any business with Cuba, and allowed U.S. citizens (including naturalized Cuban exiles) to sue foreign companies for dealing in confiscated U.S. property in Cuba. The Helms-Burton Act (also known as the Cuban Liberty and Democratic Solidarity Act) was perhaps the most assertive move of the United States during the 1990s designed to further isolate Cuba, to strengthen the trade embargo against it, and to extend U.S. legislation to punish foreign companies investing simultaneously in the United States and Cuba.

Cuba, the island-Socialist republic, located 90 miles south of the tip of Florida, had made efforts in 1975 to soften its relations with the United States, but these efforts ceased in 1996, following an incident in February of that year in which two aircraft, piloted by Cuban exiles living in Miami, Florida, were shot down in the Caribbean Sea off the northern coast of Cuba, killing four men. The United States maintained that the planes had been shot down over international waters and reacted strongly to the incident. The reaction included the creation of the Helms-Burton Act of 1996, named after the bill's co-authors, Senators Jesse Helms of North Carolina, and Dan Burton of Indiana.

See also: **Embargo**

HEPBURN ACT

Passed by the United States Congress in June 1906, the Hepburn Act gave the Interstate Commerce Commission (ICC), established in 1887, the authority to compel railroads to abide by the regulatory agency's standards and rulings. Rail companies that chose to challenge the ICC in court continued to be subject to all ICC regulations while the legal proceedings were going forward; in other words, the fact that a trial was underway did not exempt any rail company from abiding by all ICC rules. The Hepburn Act gave the ICC the right to fix rail rates, investigate rail trusts, and expanded the agency's purview to include interstate transportation terminals, bridges, rail sleeping cars, express companies, and ferry services. The bill, also called the Railway Rate Regulation Act, was sponsored by representative William Peters Hepburn (1833–1916) of Iowa. The legislation was one of several congressional acts to broadened the jurisdiction and increased the power of the Interstate Commerce Commission, which originally gave the agency control over interstate rail rates and practices.

See also: **Interstate Commerce, Interstate Commerce Commission, Railroad Industry**

HERSHEY FOODS CORPORATION

Milton S. Hershey, the founder of Hershey Foods Corporation, was born in 1857 in central Pennsylvania. As a young boy Hershey was apprenticed to a Lancaster, Pennsylvania, candy-maker for four years. When he finished this apprenticeship in 1876, at age 19, Hershey went to Philadelphia to open his own candy shop. After six years, however, the shop failed, and Hershey moved to Denver, Colorado. There he went to work for a caramel manufacturer, where he discovered that caramel made with fresh milk was a decided improvement on the standard recipe. In 1883 Hershey left Denver for Chicago, Illinois, then New Orleans, Louisiana, and New York, New York, until in 1886 he finally returned to Lancaster. There he established the Lancaster Caramel Company to produce "Hershey's Crystal A" caramels that would "melt in your mouth." Hershey had a successful business at last.

In 1893 Hershey went to the Chicago International Exposition, where he was fascinated by some German chocolate-making machinery on display. He soon installed the chocolate equipment in Lancaster and in 1895 began to sell chocolate-covered caramels and other chocolate novelties. At that time Hershey also began to develop the chocolate bars and other cocoa products that were to make him famous.

In 1900 Hershey decided to concentrate on chocolate, which he felt sure would become a big business. That year he sold his caramel company for $1 million, retaining the chocolate equipment and the rights to manufacture the chocolate products he had developed. He decided to locate his new company in Derry Church, the central Pennsylvania village where he was born, and where he would have a plentiful milk supply. In 1903 Hershey broke ground for the Hershey chocolate factory, which today is still the largest chocolate-manufacturing plant in the world.

Before this factory was completed in 1905 Hershey produced a variety of fancy chocolates. But with the new factory he decided to mass-produce a limited number of products, which he would sell at a low price. The famous Hershey's Milk Chocolate Bar was born, the first mass-produced chocolate product in the United States.

In 1906 the village of Derry Church was renamed Hershey. The town was not simply named after the man or the company: it was Milton Hershey's creation, the beneficiary of and heir to his energy and his fortune. At the same time he planned his factory, Hershey began planning a whole community that would

These are some of the miniature products manufactured by Hershey Corp.

fulfill all the needs of its inhabitants. A bank, school, recreational park, churches, trolley system, and even a zoo soon followed, and the town was firmly established by its tenth anniversary. One of Hershey's most enduring contributions was the Hershey Industrial School for orphans, which he established in 1909 with his wife Catherine. After Catherine's death in 1915 the childless Hershey gave the school Hershey stock, valued at about $60 million. Today the school, which became the Milton Hershey School in 1951, still owns 31 percent of Hershey Foods Corporation's stock and controls 76 percent of the company's voting stock.

In 1907 Hershey's Kisses were first produced, and the next year the Hershey Chocolate Company was formally chartered. In 1911 it had sales of $5 million, more than eight times what it had earned 10 years earlier. The Hershey company continued to prosper, producing its milk chocolate bars (with and without almonds), Kisses, cocoa, and baking chocolate. In 1921 sales reached $20 million, and in 1925 Hershey introduced the Mr. Goodbar Chocolate Bar, a chocolate bar with peanuts. In 1927 the company listed its stock on the New York Stock Exchange.

By 1931, 30 years after the company was established, Hershey was selling $30 million worth of chocolate a year. As the Great Depression (1929–1939) cast its shadow on the town of Hershey, Milton Hershey initiated a "grand building campaign" in the

1930s to provide employment in the area. Between 1933 and 1940 Hershey's projects included a 150-room resort hotel, a museum, a cultural center, a sports arena (where the Ice Capades was founded), a stadium, an exotic rose garden, and a modern, windowless, air-conditioned factory and office building. Hershey liked to boast that no one was laid off from the company during the Great Depression.

Though Hershey's intentions seem to have been wholly sincere there was always some suspicion about his "company town." Labor strife came to the company in 1937, when it suffered its first strike. Though bitter, the strike was soon settled, and by 1940 the chocolate plant was unionized.

In 1938 another famous chocolate product was introduced, the Krackel Chocolate Bar, a chocolate bar with crisped rice. The next year Hershey's Miniatures were introduced, bite-sized chocolate bars in several varieties.

During World War II (1939–1945), Hershey helped by creating the Field Ration D for soldiers, to sustain them when no other food was available—a four-ounce bar that provided 600 calories and would not melt easily. The chocolate factory was turned over to the war effort and produced 500,000 bars a day. Hershey received the Army-Navy E award from the quartermaster general at the end of the war. Hershey died soon after, on October 13, 1945.

After Milton Hershey's death, the chocolate company continued to prosper and maintain its strong position in the chocolate market. By the 1960s Hershey was recognized as the number one chocolate producer in the United States. In the middle of that decade the company began expanding beyond candy for the first time, acquiring two pasta manufacturers, San Giorgio Macaroni and Delmonico Foods Inc., in 1966. The company changed its name to Hershey Foods Corporation in 1968. An end of an era was marked in 1969 when the company raised the price of Hershey's candy bars to 10 cents. The bars had been priced at five cents for the past 48 years. Another key change came in 1970, when Hershey launched its first-ever national advertising campaign, having previously relied mainly on word of mouth advertising.

In 1977 Hershey bought Y&S Candies, Inc., the nation's leading manufacturer of licorice. Hershey acquired Peter Paul/Cadbury in 1988, thereby gaining such brands as Peter Paul Mounds, Almond Joy Candy Bars and York Peppermint Patties. Through the 1996 purchase of the North American operations of Leaf, Inc., Hershey gained the Good and Plenty and Jolly Rancher brands. By 1999 the company decided to concentrate solely on chocolate and candies, and it sold its pasta business that year. At the end of the twentieth century Hershey Foods was the number one candy manufacturer in the United States.

FURTHER READING

Altman, Henry. "Hershey's 'New' Ingredient." *Nation's Business*, June, 1983.

Brenner, Joel Glenn. *The Emperors of Chocolate: Inside the Secret World of Hershey and Mars*. New York: Random House, 1999.

Castner, Charles Schuyler. *One of a Kind: Milton Snavely Hershey, 1857–1945*. Hershey, PA: Derry Literary Guild, 1983.

Hershey Chocolate Corporation. *Hershey's 100 Years: The Ingredients of Our Success*. Hershey, PA: Hershey Chocolate Corporation, 1994.

———. *The Story of Chocolate and Cocoa: With a Brief Description of Hershey, "the Chocolate and Cocoa Town," and Hershey, "the Sugar Town"*. Hershey, PA: Hershey Chocolate Corporation, 1926.

Heuslein, William. "Timid No More." *Forbes*, January 13, 1997.

HILL, JAMES JEROME

James J. Hill (1838–1916) rose above a childhood of poverty in Canada to become one of the great U.S. empire builders and one of the wealthiest men of the nineteenth century. Hill founded the Great Northern Railroad, which by 1893 connected St. Paul, Minnesota, to Washington's Puget Sound. Hill also acquired a reputation as a "robber baron," and the Supreme Court ruled in 1904 that his railroad system was an illegal monopoly.

Hill was born in 1838 and grew up in Ontario, Canada. His father, who had secured only occasional employment as a farmer, died when the boy was only 14. While his mother kept an inn, young Hill worked as an assistant to a grocer and studied with the Rev. William Wetherald, a schoolmaster who taught him algebra, geometry, literature, and grammar.

In 1856 Hill moved to St. Paul, Minnesota, and began work as a clerk for a firm of shipping agents who served a fleet of Mississippi steamboats. In addition to keeping the books, he handled freight and performed other manual tasks. Hill arrived in St. Paul around the same as the Old Northwest, including Minnesota and Wisconsin, was experiencing explosive growth. Over

James Jerome Hill.

the next several years Hill worked for a succession of shipping firms. The ambitious young man had exceptional energy and drive, and he developed a reputation for hard work and shrewd judgement.

In partnership with two associates, Hill formed the James J. Hill Company in 1866. He soon negotiated an exclusive arrangement as a forwarding agent for the St. Paul and Pacific Railroad, under which his firm would transfer produce from riverboats to the westward-oriented railroad. He built a large warehouse, and the business began to prosper. Simultaneously, Hill expanded his business to include fuel. With two other partners he formed Hill, Griggs and Co., which first concentrated on firewood but quickly shifted to coal. It was Hill's rise to the top of the local coal business that formed the cornerstone of his fortune.

By 1872 Hill, Griggs and Co. dominated the Twin Cities coal market, selling 5,000 tons of anthracite annually. Four years later, after organizing his company with its chief competitors in a market-sharing consortium, Hill left the independent coal business.

His attention began to focus on railroads. Together with three Canadian capitalists he purchased the financially troubled St. Paul and Pacific Railroad in 1878. The line was subsequently reorganized as the St. Paul, Minneapolis, and Manitoba Railway Company ("the Manitoba"). Hill became the railroad's president in 1882 and began to extend the line north to the Canadian border. After linking up with a Canadian railroad to

Winnipeg, Hill expanded the Manitoba westward, reaching Great Falls, Montana, in 1887, and Everett, Washington, in 1893. The rail system was renamed the Great Northern Railway Company in 1890.

Hill was not content to simply construct a railroad. He recruited thousands of homesteaders to settle and establish small towns in the Dakotas and Montana. To develop markets for goods to be carried on his railroad, Hill found buyers in the Far East for U.S. cotton, flour, and metals; the Great Northern also carried Pacific timber and minerals east to the Midwest and the Mississippi.

Together with financier J.P. Morgan (1837–1913) of the Northern Pacific Railway Company, Hill acquired control of the Chicago, Burlington and Quincy Railroad Company in 1901. Hill's railroads now had complete access to cotton and other commodities grown in the South, as well as to the natural and manufactured products of the Northwest, the Plains, and the Midwest. In that same year Hill formed and became president of the Northern Securities Company, a holding company that consolidated the Great Northern, the Northern Pacific and the Burlington lines. In 1902 Northern Securities was sued at the behest of President Theodore Roosevelt (1901–1909) as a violation of the federal Sherman Anti-Trust Act. The president's attack on the holding company won him popular acclaim as a "trustbuster." In 1904 the Supreme Court ordered that the company be dissolved. Nevertheless the three railroads involved remained under the control of the same group of investors.

According to biographer Michael P. Malone, Hill was "without peer, the preeminent builder of the frontier economy of the Northwest. By controlling the transportation structure of the region. . . he exercised more sweeping economic power than did any other industrialist, even the lumbermen and mining barons." James Hill died in 1916.

See also: **Northern Securities Case, Railroad Industry, Robber Baron**

FURTHER READING

Bruchey, Stuart, ed. *Memoirs of Three Railroad Pioneers*. New York: Arno, 1981.

Holbrook, Stewart H. *James J. Hill: A Great Life In Brief*. New York: Knopf, 1955.

Kerr, Duncan J. *The Story of the Great Northern Railway Company and James J. Hill*. Princeton, NJ: Princeton University Press, 1939.

Malone, Michael P. *James J. Hill: Empire Builder of the Northwest*. Norman, OK: University of Oklahoma, 1996.

Martin, Albro. *James J. Hill and the Opening of the Northwest*. Minnesota Historical Society, 1991.

HILTON, WILLIAM BARRON

William Barron Hilton's (1927–) name has become nearly synonymous with the word "hotel." The son of Conrad Hilton (1887–1979), he was arguably one of the founders of the U.S. hotel tradition. Hilton struggled with tough competitors, like Marriott and Hyatt, but with the record and reputation of his own father. For several years Hilton was told that if business was good, it was because of the assets his father put together, and if business was bad, then it was William Hilton's own fault. However, Hilton's assumed control of the family-owned Hilton Corporation in 1979, after his father's death, and the company prospered to the point where, in the late 1990s, it ranked as one of the country's largest holders of real estate.

William Barron Hilton was born in Dallas, Texas, in 1927. His father, Conrad Hilton, was the legendary founder of the Hilton hotel chain. When William was eight, the Hilton family relocated to southern California in the midst of the hotel chain's enormous growth. Before growing into manhood the young Hilton watched his father go through two divorces.

As a young man Hilton showed little interest in taking up the family business. Instead, he joined the Navy and served as a naval photographer during World War II (1939–1945). After the war he started his own business selling orange juice products in California; he was soon the owner/operator of his own citrus distributorship. It wasn't for another five years that Hilton considered joining his father's business. When he did, in 1951, he started in the operations department of the Hilton Hotel Corporation, at the bottom of the corporate ladder. Hilton showed an early talent and initiative for the work in the hospitality business, and in 1954 he assumed the role of vice president of the corporation, with his father in the role of president.

Variety in business ventures seemed important to the younger Hilton. In 1960, while still vice president of the company, he turned his attention to establishing the Los Angles Chargers football team, a team of the American Football League. The following year he moved the team to San Diego, California, and served as its president until 1966.

That same year he took on the role of president and chief executive officer (CEO) for the Hilton Hotels. In 1970 he bought two Las Vegas hotels, beginning the company's involvement in the gaming industry. Gaming interests grew rapidly, and within 25 years they accounted for 46 percent of the firm's revenues.

With the death of his father in 1979, Hilton became chairman of the board of the company's operations. The will of the senior Hilton specified that the bulk of his estate go to the Conrad Hilton Foundation, a charity to aid Catholic nuns. William Hilton fought successfully to alter the terms of the will, and he obtained sufficient shares of Hilton Hotel stock to control 25 percent of the company.

Only after a long struggle did William Hilton come to be seen as the company's master strategist. During the 1970s, when other hotel chains plunged ahead with the development of luxury hotels and vacation resorts, Hilton sat back and watched his competitors' successes and failures before making any of his own moves. He was also cautious during the 1980s, when it seemed that everyone else in the business was either buying or selling.

Hilton made the move, finally, to sell off his less profitable hotels and retain choice properties like New York City's famed Waldorf-Astoria. He decided also to manage and franchise the rest of the hotels bearing the Hilton name. His cautious yet strategic maneuvers caused the company stock to rise while other hotel operations were seeing a downturn. William Hilton obtained the reputation of a cautious, prudent, and savvy strategist in real estate dealings.

During the 1990s, however, he became aggressive about the gaming industry and led the pack with construction of new casinos and proposals for gambling complexes. In 1996 Hilton began expanding internationally. His aim was to bring his total hotel room capacity to 100,000 by the year 2000—by 1997 he had already reached his goal. By the late 1990s the Hilton Corporation operated 16 casinos and 240 hotel properties, and in 1996 Hilton bought the Bally Entertainment Corporation for $43 billion.

At the close of the twentieth century, as owner of more than 25 percent of the company's shares William Barron Hilton was president of a vast hospitality empire employing 62,000 people. His personal wealth was estimated to be over $600 million, which made him a regular on *Forbes* magazine's list of the "400 Richest People in America" since 1982.

FURTHER READING

"Dr. Jekyll and Mr. Hilton." *Financial World*, May 26, 1992.

"New Baron Now Calls Hilton Shots." *Hotel and Motel Management*, March 4, 1996.

"New Hilton Chief: Chain Will Grow by Investing in Hotels and Gaming." *Travel Weekly*, May 27, 1996.

"Rumors at the Inn: The Wall Street Sharks are Circling Hilton Hotels, Eager to Break up the Family Dynasty." *Financial World*, April 4, 1989.

"The Son Also Rises." *Forbes*, January 25, 1988.

HIRES, CHARLES ELMER

Charles Elmer Hires (1851–1937) was the first soft drink entrepreneur. Before industry giants like Coca-Cola and Pepsi, there was Charles Hires and his "root beer," which he created in 1875. An entrepreneur at 24, Hires went on to develop a second successful business in the manufacturing of condensed milk.

Charles Hires was born on August 19, 1851, in Roadstown, New Jersey, the son of a farming couple. At age 12, after a meager early education, Hires moved from his parents' farm to begin a four year apprenticeship as a pharmacy clerk. He completed the apprenticeship at age 16 and moved to Philadelphia, where he worked for a pharmacist and attended evening classes at Jefferson Medical College and the Philadelphia College of Pharmacy.

At age 18, Hires opened his own pharmacy in Philadelphia. Oddly, his first successful business venture involved the purchase and resale of a kind of clay (fuller's earth) that Hires recognized as having solvent properties. He renamed the common substance "Hires' Potter's Clay" and made several thousand dollars selling it to various wholesale drug houses, to whom he advertised it as a successful grease and spot remover.

Hires first tasted the drink that would bring him fame and fortune while staying at a New Jersey boarding house during his honeymoon. The drink, "root beer," was served to him by the landlady. It was a beverage made from sassafras bark and herbs. Hires loved the taste and, so the story goes, wanted to produce it himself.

After conversations with chemist friends and his own experiments with sarsaparilla root and other ingredients, Hires finally created what came to be known as root beer. Originally, he intended to call the beverage a tea, hoping to sell it among Pennsylvania miners as a substitute for an alcoholic drink. A friend told him bluntly that miners would never drink his concoction if it were called tea. His friend further instructed him to call it a beer, root beer, if he expected it to sell to men.

During the Philadelphia Centennial Exposition of 1876 Hires took the opportunity to sell his root beer to the millions of fair visitors. Their response was immediately favorable and it led Hires to begin marketing and packaging his root beer. He first sold it in bulk, dried, for 25 cents. It could be brewed at home by mixing it with water and a few other ingredients and it made about five gallons of the drink. In 1893 he began to produce root beer in liquid form, packaged in three ounce bottles.

Root beer began to sell extremely well at soda fountains which were popular during that era. The drink became popular among industrial workers as an alternative to water, tea, and alcohol, and it also became popular among the middle class as a universal beverage available to children, adolescents, and adults.

Hires advertised his product extensively in newspapers and national magazines. By 1890 he was able to organize all his business efforts into the Charles Elmer Hires Company. Starting with an original capital investment of $300,000 Hires watched his company's value rise to more than $2 million by 1921.

In addition to root beer, Hires made considerable money from the manufacture and distribution of condensed milk. The venture began in 1899 and blossomed into a wholly separate business for Hires. He eventually sold this condensed milk company to the Nestle Company in 1918, after having built more than 20 milk plants in various regions of the United States and Canada.

Hires spent much of his leisure time supporting the work of the Society of Friends, a Quaker organization he joined during the last half of his life.

By the end of the nineteenth century Hires Root Beer was known as a favorite American soft drink. Hires' success made U.S. business realize there was a large market for an alternative to tea, coffee, alcohol, and fruit drinks. It did not take long for Coca-Cola and other soft drink manufacturers to follow in Hires' footsteps and create the enormous world market for bottled soft drinks. The founder of root beer died in 1937.

See also: **Coca Cola**

FURTHER READING

Fucini, Joseph J., and Suzy Fucini. *Entrepreneurs: The Men and Women Behind Famous Brand Names and How They Made It*. Boston: G.K. Hall, 1985.

Ingham, John N. *Biographical Dictionary of American Business Leaders*. Westport, CT: Greenwood, 1983, s.v. ''Hires, Charles Elmer.''

Schuyler, Robert L, ed. *Dictionary of American Biography*. s.v. ''Hires, Charles Elmer.''

Van Doren, Charles. *Webster's American Biographies*. Springfield, MA: G & C Merriam Co., 1984, s.v. ''Hires, Charles Elmer.''

Who Was Who in America. Chicago: Marquis, 1998, s.v. ''Hires, Charles Elmer.''

HOFFA, JAMES RIDDLE

During the mid-twentieth century James Riddle Hoffa (1913–1975) rose to become one of the most powerful figures in the U.S. labor movement. In 1932 Hoffa began his involvement in the unions. He organized for the Teamsters during the Great Depression and by 1935 was president of the local Detroit, Michigan, chapter of the International Brotherhood of Teamsters (IBT). During the ten years that followed he brought many smaller unions into the IBT through his organizing skills, ''street smarts,'' and personal charisma. Hoffa was elected president of the IBT in 1959, becoming the head of the largest, richest, and most powerful labor union in the United States. At the time the IBT represented a membership of two million blue-collar truckers and transportation workers. While historians have disagreed about his contributions to the labor movement, none have questioned his legacy of power and influence, or his status as a legend.

Jimmy Hoffa was born in 1913 in the small town of Brazil, Indiana, one of four children. His father was a coal miner who labored long hours to support his family and died young of a lung disease associated with working conditions in the mines. Hoffa's mother was employed as a domestic worker and a cook, and took in washing to make ends meet. She moved the family to Detroit, Michigan, four years after the death of her husband.

Jimmy Hoffa attended school until the tenth grade, when he dropped out to help his family meet the severe economic conditions of the Great Depression. He took a full-time job as a stock boy at Kroger's, a Detroit grocery store chain. The low pay, poor working conditions, and the impact of the Great Depression all contributed to making the young Hoffa conscious of workers' problems.

Hoffa began to demonstrate his organizing skills as a young man. At age seventeen he led four of his co-workers in a successful strike against the Kroger Company. Hoffa's synchronized the strike with the delivery of a large trailer of fresh strawberries to the Kroger loading docks. Kroger's business managers knew it would not take long for the strawberries to spoil and they desperately needed the loading dockworkers to unload the shipment. Within one hour a new union contract was reached and within one year Jimmy Hoffa's ''Strawberry Boys'' joined Teamsters Local 674, which later merged with Truck Drivers Local 299. Hoffa transformed the local from a 40-member unit with $400 in its coffers to a 5000 member unit with $50,000 in the bank.

The early U.S. labor movement was volatile and Hoffa's involvement with the IBT during the late 1930s resulted in many threats to his life. Hoffa's car was bombed, his office was searched, and he was once arrested eighteen times in a single day. Hoffa once recalled, ''When you went out on strike in those days, you got your head broken. The cops would beat your brains out if you even got caught talking about unions.'' Undeterred, at the age of twenty-eight Hoffa became vice president and chief negotiator for the IBT.

During the 1950s the federal government began promoting strong attacks against organized crime such as the Mafia. Hoffa had never made a secret of his relationship with the Mafia and the federal government's intense focus on organized crime, combined with the resistance of business to his unionizing, squeezed Hoffa at both ends. The government, for criminal reasons, and business, for labor reasons, both sought Hoffa's downfall.

During the 1960s, after numerous charges of corruption in the Teamsters, Hoffa faced several felony trials. He was convicted of jury tampering and fraud in two separate trials in 1964, and was sentenced to a 15-year prison term. President Richard Nixon (1969–1974) commuted Hoffa's sentence in 1971, but banned him from any union activity. Hoffa had remained president of the Teamsters Union throughout the five years he served in jail, but upon his release from prison he stepped down.

Hoffa appealed to the courts to regain his union presidency but the Supreme Court denied his motion. Hoffa continued to be unofficially involved with the Teamsters union, and with organized crime. On a July afternoon in 1975, Hoffa disappeared after a luncheon meeting. He was never seen again. His colorful life and mysterious disappearance have created an enduring historical legend about the man who served at the

James R. Hoffa.

forefront of the U.S. labor movement in the mid-twentieth century.

See also: **Labor Movement, Labor Unionism**

FURTHER READING

Clay, James. *Hoffa! Ten Angels Swearing*. Beaverdam, VA: Beaverdam Books, 1965.

James, Ralph C. *Hoffa and the Teamsters: A Study of Union Power*. Princeton: Van Nostrand, 1965.

Moldea, Dan E. *The Hoffa Wars: Teamsters, Rebels, Politicians, and the Mob*. New York: Paddington Press, 1978.

Sheridan, Walter. *The Fall and Rise of Jimmy Hoffa*. New York: Saturday Review Press, 1972.

Zagri, Sidney. *Free Press, Fair Trial*. Chicago: C. Hallberg, 1966.

HOLLERITH, HERMAN

Herman Hollerith (1860–1929), an American engineer and inventor, made a major breakthrough that paved the way for the invention of the modern digital computer. He invented a punch-card system in 1890, first used widely by the federal government, that was the beginning of all modern data processing in business. His invention of the punch-card tabulating system, still used in many voting machines in the United States, became the foundation of a company that evolved into the International Business Machines Company (IBM).

Hollerith was born in 1860, and raised in Buffalo, New York. In 1879 he graduated at the age of 19 from Columbia University with a degree in mining engineering. He then went to work for the United States Census Bureau's Division of Vital Statistics, compiling mountains of census information into readable data. At the time, information was processed by hand. It was costly, time consuming, and very slow.

In the late 1880s the Census Department determined that the upcoming 1890 census would include data from over 62 million Americans. The department's traditional census tabulating measures were so time consuming that it had little hope of compiling the information into any useful format until well after the 1900 census. By that time the data would be of little value. Working on a solution, Herman Hollerith designed a machine to tabulate the large amounts of census data in a shorter time period. His automatic machine was based on electrical impulses, which transmitted only when holes in punched cards passed over the electrical contacts. The signals were then fed into electrical-mechanical tabulators to be counted, like those in old-fashioned adding machines. Hollerith's tabulating machine quickened the Census Department's ability to compile data and, for the first time, allowed the census data to record new details, such as the number of doctors working in a particular state who were married with one child and owned their own home.

Hollerith patented later models of his machine, ones that could count, add, sort, and which used automated card-punching to make the right holes in the cards to provide the right electrical signals in the right places. He sold his first machine to the United States Army to help in their compilation of medical statistics. He then obtained a contract from the Census Bureau to provide machines to be used in the census count of 1890.

According to evaluations made of the value of his early tabulating machines, Hollerith's tabulators saved the Census Bureau $5 million for the 1890 census and did in one year what would have taken eight years of hand-tabulation. Hollerith's invention was the beginning of modern data processing. His humble ''press'' machine, using paper cards with punched holes in them, became the beginning of an electronic way for all businesses to efficiently keep track of thousands of business transactions.

It did not take long for businesses and industries to find uses for Hollerith's tabulators. Business could keep track, easily and quickly, of the amount of stock they had in different departments and keep more adequate supplies on hand for consumers. The business tabulator was an important advancement in business, especially for large companies that dealt with mass markets where significant amounts of information needed to be processed quickly.

When Hollerith was 36 years old, he had enough demand for his tabulating machines to found the Tabulating Machine Company, where he continued to improve his machines. In 1911 Hollerith sold his share of this company, retiring in his mid-fifties. The company name changed, and by 1924 it merged with others to become the first giant in computer tabulating companies—IBM, the International Business Machine Corporation.

Herman Hollerith's modest punch-card press tabulator changed the face of American business by allowing for the creation of high-speed, efficient ways to keep track of all aspects of business transactions, enabling businesses to grow significantly without losing control of daily information crucial to the maintenance of business.

Hollerith died in 1929 at the age of 70, having no idea he would later be regarded by many as the grandfather of the modern computer.

See also: **Computer Industry, International Business Machines**

FURTHER READING

Austrian, Geoffrey. *Herman Hollerith, Forgotten Giant of Information Processing*. New York: Columbia University Press, 1982.

Bohme, Frederick G. *100 Years of Data Processing: The Punchcard Century*. Washington, DC: U.S. Dept. of Commerce, Bureau of the Census, Data User Services Division, 1991.

Cortada, James W. *Historical Dictionary of Data Processing—Technology*. New York: Greenwood Press, 1987.

Fisher, Franklin M. and John J. McGowan. *Folded, Spindled, and Mutilated: Economic Analysis and U.S. v. IBM*. Cambridge: MIT Press, 1983.

Watson, Thomas J. *A Business and Its Beliefs: The Ideas that Helped Build IBM*. New York: McGraw Hill, 1963.

HOME FRONT

Home front is a term that describes domestic civilian activity during times of war. During World War II (1939–1945) the U.S. home front was marked by a national purpose that united Americans behind the efforts of the Allied Powers (United States, Great Britain, Russia, and China, among others) to defeat the Axis Powers (Germany, Italy, and Japan). Sacrifice and patriotism of average Americans combined with the dynamism and flexibility of private enterprise to galvanize domestic war production. More than 7 million of America's 8 million unemployed persons in 1940 returned to work by 1944. Nearly 3.5 million of the newly employed were women. The popular image of Rosie the Riveter working on planes, tanks, and ships embodied the contribution made to industrial war production by female laborers. Jobs were paying both sexes 25 percent more at the end of the war than they had at the beginning. However, inflation was spiraling upward so rapidly that the federal government placed a ceiling on prices, wages, and rents. Congress also established the nation's modern tax structure during the war, imposing a steeply graduated income tax that

Americans were patriotic during the war, and more united than ever before. To increase productivity factories stayed open for a second or third shift, and workers added long hours of overtime. Roosevelt's promise in 1940 to build 50,000 aircraft was received with amazement. In the end 300,000 were built. The gross national product doubled from $101 billion in 1940 to $214 billion in 1944. Egalitarianism was the rule in the war years, reinforced by rationing, shortages, price controls, and the universalism of the draft.

Oxford Companion to World War II, 1995

for the first time covered most middle-income and lower-income groups. As a result, the number of families paying income tax quadrupled, and the amount of tax they paid increased twenty-fold.

Governmental rationing of scarce and valuable commodities, such as gasoline, rubber, meat, sugar, and leather, also tested the resolve of civilians on the home front. But the ingenuity and entrepreneurial spirit behind America's capitalistic system helped civilians look past the daily inconveniences to see the bigger picture. For example, the Allies had to devise an efficient way to transport personnel, vehicles, and equipment across the oceans in order to invade Europe, Africa, and the South Pacific. Andrew Higgins, a Louisiana boat manufacturer, convinced reluctant Navy officials to turn production of transport vessels over to him. He integrated a workforce of 30,000 blacks, women, and men, and paid top wage without regard to sex or skin color. A huge sign hung over the assembly lines: ''The Man Who Relaxes is Helping the Axis.'' Higgins' factory produced more than 20,000 transport vessels in four years. General Dwight D. Eisenhower (1890–1969) later credited Higgins and his workers with winning the war.

Hundreds of other American industries also converted civilian business to wartime manufacturing, churning out 44 billion rounds of ammunition, 20 million small arms, 2.5 million trucks, 300,000 planes, 100,000 tanks, and 90,000 ships. But single-minded zeal was not always an asset. To minimize domestic sabotage and espionage, President Franklin D. Roosevelt (1882–1945) issued an executive order in February 1942 authorizing the forcible removal of approximately 110,000 Americans of Japanese descent. There were transferred from strategic locations around the country

to inland relocation camps, where they were detained like prisoners without a hearing or trial. Despite their mistreatment many of the detained Japanese Americans maintained their patriotism, raising the Stars and Stripes every morning at camp and singing the national anthem. Some detainees contributed to the war effort, helping develop a synthetic rubber to augment the Allies dwindling supply of natural rubber. More than 17,000 Japanese Americans were released from detention to join the U.S. Army. During one campaign in Italy Japanese-American soldiers earned 3,000 Purple Hearts, 810 Bronze Stars, 342 Silver Stars, and 47 Distinguished Service Crosses in the field of battle. Although the U.S. Supreme Court upheld the constitutionality of the forcible relocation and detention, in 1988 the federal government issued an apology for the episode and offered to pay money damages to the victims and their families.

See also: **Liberty Ships, Rationing, Rosie the Riveter**

HOMESTEAD ACT (1862)

The Homestead Act, passed by the Republican-dominated Congress during the American Civil War (1861–1865), was intended to place public land in the hands of western settlers. It stated that any adult citizen (or a person who declared an intention to become a citizen) who was the head of a family could lay claim to 160 acres of public land. The only payment required was a small registration fee. The claimant was required to live on the land for a five-year period while improving it by building a house measuring at least 12 by 14 feet and farming at least ten acres. The period of residence was reduced to six months if the settler was willing to pay a price of $1.25 an acre. Within three years of the act's passage, more than 15,000 claims on public lands had been registered with the federal government.

The passage of the Homestead Act represented the culmination of 30 years' work by Republicans and their Whig predecessors. When the United States purchased the Louisiana territory from France in 1803, it acquired a huge tract of federally administered land. President Thomas Jefferson (1801–1809) envisioned this territory divided into small farms, whose owners could follow his rural vision of American democracy. Over the next few decades, Congress was split on the question of what to do with this land. Southern legislators feared that homestead laws, which divided public lands into small farms rather than large plantations,

Women working on an assembly line, mass producing planes on the home front during World War II.

would attract immigrants and others who were opposed to slavery. Some of their northern counterparts, especially from the industrialized northeast, feared that the lure of free land would drain cheap immigrant labor from the factories to the frontier. Others, such as Senator Thomas Hart Benton, supported free farms as a means of encouraging democratic growth.

> **I SOLD MY PENNSYLVANIA FARM WITH ITS STUMPS AND STONES AND STINGY SOIL THAT YIELDED SO GRUDGINGLY TO THE TOIL I HAD GIVEN IT. MY WIFE, SUSIE, AND I DECIDED TO GO TO KANSAS AND TAKE UP A GOVERNMENT CLAIM.**
>
> Warren P. Trimm, Kansas homesteader

The problem became especially acute after the Mexican War (1846–1848), when transportation of both people and produce became cheaper because of new canals and railroads. So important was the issue that one party, the Free-Soilers, made distribution of public lands the major plank in their campaign platform during the 1840s. Although bills offering public lands to settlers were passed by the House of Representatives in 1852, 1854, and 1859, they were all defeated by the southern-dominated Senate. When an

1860 homestead bill was finally passed by both houses of Congress, President James Buchanan (1857–1861) vetoed it.

Although the Homestead Act was intended to benefit the homeless immigrants of the east, those who gained the most from it were native-born Americans and land speculators. Immigrants were mostly too poor to afford the stake needed to move west and take up a claim. It was typically second- or third-generation Americans who sold their farms to head west with their families. Most of these farmers, however, were poorly prepared for farming on the Great Plains. The quality of land allotments open to farmers varied considerably, and good claims were quickly taken up. Accustomed to plenty of water and wood for cooking and heating, as well as plentiful grass for their livestock, many were unable to cope with the arid conditions of the West. Many original homesteaders were unable to live on their new land long enough to complete their claims. These farmers often sold their claims to land speculators, who resold them to latecomers at a profit. Some land speculators also bought abandoned land and hired claimants to file false claims.

Those homesteaders who remained on their claims found new opportunities, as well as challenges. Federally funded railroads spanned the continent by 1869, opening isolated farms to markets and manufactured goods and bringing new settlers to the prairie. These pioneers built schools, churches, and towns, as well as homesteads. Within 40 years of the passage of the Homestead Act, most of the territories opened to settlement had either entered the Union as states or filed for statehood.

See also: **Homesteaders, Westward Expansion**

FURTHER READING

Lee, Lawrence Bacon. *Kansas and the Homestead Act, 1862–1905*. New York: Arno Press, 1979.

Potter, Lee Ann, and Wynell Schamel. ''The Homestead Act of 1862.'' *Social Education.* October 1997.

Soza, Edward. *Mexican Homesteaders in the San Pedro River Valley and the Homestead Act of 1862, 1870–1908.* Altadena, CA: E. Soza, 1994.

Tatter, Henry. *The Preferential Treatment of the Actual Settler in the Primary Disposition of the Vacant Lands in the United States to 1841.* New York: Arno Press, 1979.

Trimm, Warren P. ''Two Years in Kansas.'' *American Heritage*, February/March 1983.

HOMESTEAD STEEL STRIKE

The industrialization of the United States in the second half of the nineteenth century involved a complex and unsettling social and economic transformation of U.S. society. The spread of factory towns, urban living, transportation networks, and new technologies were catalysts for the reorganization of American life. So, too, were the emergence of the American corporation, which concentrated industrial wealth and power in the hands of a new economic elite, and the mass labor union, which sought to protect the burgeoning ranks of factory workers. The Homestead Steel Strike of 1892, which pitted the industrialist Andrew Carnegie (1835–1919) against the Amalgamated Association of Iron and Steel Workers, was one of the most dramatic expressions of the sharpening conflict between the corporation and the union—between capital and labor—on the terrain of industrializing America.

Homestead, Pennsylvania, was the center of Andrew Carnegie's enormous steel empire, the Carnegie Steel Corporation, which produced fully one-quarter of the world's steel by 1892. Its work force was concentrated in Homestead, a town of 12,000. Most of the steelworkers belonged to the Amalgamated Association of Iron and Steel Workers. With 24,000 members, the union was one of the most important members of the American Federation of Labor (AFL).

Carnegie himself, along with most other business leaders of the time, possessed a deep opposition to unions. He viewed the Amalgamated as a dangerous organization that not only weakened his ability to treat labor as a freely disposed commodity, but also resisted his attempts to introduce technological advances. Carnegie was also well aware that the threat of a strike, which was fully endorsed by the AFL, could cripple his steel empire if it was carried out effectively. For their part, the Homestead workers, reflecting the attitudes of other steelworkers of the time, believed Carnegie was generally insensitive to their needs. In particular, they were upset that he refused to share the profits of more efficient production techniques.

In July 1892, as his contract with the AFL was about to expire, Carnegie decided to crush the steel workers union. He instructed his general manager, Henry Clay Frick, to announce that the steel mill would now employ non-union workers and pay lower wages. This started a general strike by the Amalgamated, which set up committees to run the strike and prepare the town. Carnegie, who left on vacation for Europe, transferred operational control to Frick, whose hatred of unions was well known. Frick proceeded to employ 300 company guards hired through Pinkerton's National Detective Agency to seize the millworks from the strikers. On July 5, the guards used river barges in an attempt to land near the factory under the cover of night. The strikers were waiting for them and a battle lasted for eight hours. When it was over, 35 men lay dead and 60 others were seriously wounded.

Even before the violent clash, public opinion was running against the strikers through no fault of their own. An agitator named Alexander Berkman had earlier attempted to assassinate Frick in his office. The failed attack brought much sympathy for Frick and significant discredit to the strikers. The news of the deadly confrontation between strikers and Pinkertons further turned opinion against the Amalgamated. Pennsylvania sent 4000 militiamen to occupy the factory, which was soon turned over to management. Nonunion workers were hired and the millwork resumed normal operations. Four months later, the Amalgamated voted to end the strike, but the organization was now crushed, effectively ending unionism in the steel industry. More important, the struggle crippled the AFL and weakened efforts to organize labor throughout the United States.

See also: **American Federation of Labor, Andrew Carnegie, Labor Unionism, Pinkerton, Strike**

FURTHER READING

Demarest, David and Weingartner, Fannia, eds. *The "River Ran Red": Homestead 1892.* Pittsburgh: University of Pittsburgh Press, 1992.

Krause, Paul. *The Battle for Homestead 1880–1892: Politics, Culture, and Steel.* Pittsburgh: University of Pittsburgh Press, 1992.

Livesay, Harold. *Andrew Carnegie and the Rise of Big Business.* New York: Harper Collins, 1975.

Serrin, William. *Homestead: The Glory and the Tragedy of an American Steel Town.* New York: Vintage Books, 1993.

Trachtenberg, Alan. *The Incorporation of America: Culture and Society in the Gilded Age.* New York: Hill and Wang, 1992.

HOMESTEADERS

Homesteaders, sometimes credited with settling the West, were people who took advantage of the Homestead Act of 1862. The first family to do so was that of Daniel Freeman (1826–1908), who made a land claim on January 1, 1863, the day the law went into effect. Freeman settled near Beatrice, Nebraska.

The Homestead Act of 1862 and its later modifications were collectively known as the Homestead Laws. During the mid-1800s, a debate arose over what the federal government should do with its newly acquired lands in the West. Those supporting the free land movement, led by the Free Soil Party, believed the government should grant lands in the West to whoever settled them. Conservatives believed the government should sell the lands to raise revenue. Southerners opposed free-soil policy, which they felt did not benefit their interests: they not only viewed the spread of agriculture in the West as a threat to their economic prosperity, but they feared that territories settled under a free-soil policy would eventually oppose slavery. Northerners tended to support the free-soil initiative, because the region's growing industrial sector would need new domestic markets for finished goods produced by the (industrialized) North.

Free land legislation that would improve the allowances of the earlier Pre-Emption Act of 1841 were introduced in Congress in 1851, 1852, and 1854; Southern Democrats succeeded in blocking passage each time. When the Republican Party was formed in 1854; in absorbing the Free Soil Party and its agenda, the Republicans proclaimed they would enact a "complete and satisfactory homestead measure." Soon after Republican presidential candidate Abraham Lincoln (1809–65) won the election in 1860. In response, the Southern states made good on their threat to secede from the Union if the Republican party put its candidate in the White House. With Southern lawmakers out of Congress (with the exception of Tennessee Senator Andrew Johnson (1808–75), who had long supported free-soil initiatives and did not join his fellow Southerners in the act of secession), the Homestead Act was introduced and passed in Congress.

The legislation provided that anyone who was head of a family, or 21 years of age, or a veteran of just 14 days of active service in the U.S. armed forces, and who was a citizen or intended to become a citizen of the United States could receive up to 160 acres (64 hectares) of land. A homesteader was required to build on the land or cultivate it for a period of five years. Having only paid the initial, nominal filing fees, at the end of the five-year period the homesteader received a title to the land. In 1912, the required period of settlement was decreased to three years. Other modifications opened forest and grazing land for settlement and increased the maximum acreage to 640.

The Homestead Laws encouraged the rapid settlement of lands held in the public domain outside of the original 13 states (as well as Maine, Vermont, West Virginia, Kentucky, Tennessee, and Texas.) By 1932 more than one million homesteaders had developed more than 270 million acres (109 million hectares) of formerly public lands. In 1935 the remainder of public domain was withdrawn from homestead settlement. By 1962 all agricultural land that had been set aside for homesteading had been settled. Congress repealed the Homestead Laws in 1976 (except for laws pertaining to Alaska).

See also: **Dry Farming, Homestead Act, Land-Grant Colleges, Prairie, Slavery, Sod Houses**

HOOVERVILLE

Hooverville was a derogatory term used to describe the ramshackle towns that were built and inhabited by millions of homeless and unemployed people in communities across the United States during the Great Depression. Named after Herbert Hoover (1874–1964),

Trash-laden shacks at a Hooverville, a temporary shantytown outside a factory during the Great Depression.

who was president from 1929–1933, when the Depression began, Hoovervilles typically consisted of makeshift homes made from cardboard, tin, crates, scrap lumber, and other discarded materials. Hoovervilles generally sprang up within the inner cities of the country's most populated metropolitan areas. For daily subsistence residents depended on the charity of nearby bakeries and produce houses that would make periodic deliveries of stale bread or gristly meat. Soup kitchens were established in several Hooverville communities. Residents cooked their food in cans when they cooked it at all. Newspapers used to keep the residents warm were called "Hoover blankets."

Health, fire, and law enforcement officials closely regulated many Hoovervilles, enacting requirements that tenements be above ground, have a certain number of windows, and be kept clear of debris and human waste. Some Hoovervilles assembled a rudimentary government of their own, electing a mayor, city council, and police chief. Hooverville tenements were bought and sold like other homes, though prices rarely exceeded $30. By the onset of World War II (1939–1945) most Hoovervilles had disappeared, as the nation's

unemployed and homeless began returning to an economy that was mobilizing for military production. A number of Hoovervilles, however, lingered through the early 1950s.

See also: **Great Depression, Poverty**

HOPKINS, HARRY LLOYD

Harry Hopkins (1890–1946) was one of the major architects and managers of the New Deal during the Great Depression (1929–1939) and he was a major U.S. policymaker during World War II (1939–1945). Brought to Washington, DC, by President Franklin D. Roosevelt (1933–1945) to administer public relief programs during the Depression, Hopkins went on to become one of Roosevelt's closest advisors during World War II.

Harry Lloyd Hopkins was the younger of two children born to David and Anna Hopkins. He was born in Sioux City, Iowa, in 1890, and grew up largely in Grinnell, Iowa.

His father was a moderately successful traveling salesman who apparently communicated to his son his competitive style, good nature, and early loyalty to the Democratic party. His mother, a deeply religious woman, impressed on Harry the values of strict honesty and moral principles. Hopkins was also exposed to his sister Adah's enthusiasm for social work.

In 1912 Hopkins graduated from Grinnell College, where he studied social work. He then left Iowa for New York City and a career in the same field, rising rapidly to the administrative ranks of his profession. From 1915 to 1930 he held a wide variety of difficult high-level positions in social work, always initiating new, creative, and useful programs.

Hopkins became active in social movements, especially those focused on political action to create pensions for widows with children and relief for the families of servicemen who had fought during World War I (1914–1918). Hopkins was one of the founders of the American Association of Social Workers, the first national professional organization for social workers.

Though Hopkins achieved much in social work, he would achieve a great deal more in the years ahead. His reputation as a fine administrator reached the ear of New York's governor Franklin Delano Roosevelt, who brought Hopkins into his administration. Hopkins' job was to help develop relief programs for New York state residents during the early years of the Great Depression.

After Roosevelt became the president of the United States, Hopkins was invited to join Roosevelt in Washington, DC. He was appointed head of the Federal Emergency Relief Administration (FERA), an agency which granted federal money to individual states for unemployment relief.

Hopkins was never able to resolve any of the large issues of the Great Depression, but he did create many useful programs that eased the pain and suffering of millions of Americans during that time. He demonstrated a consistent genius for creatively dealing with social emergencies.

In 1935 Hopkins began to build the Works Progress Administration (WPA), which became a major effort to combat unemployment during the Depression. Admittedly, it was a temporary "make work" government-supported program, but its focus on getting the average American back to work through socially useful jobs was enormously popular. It gave faith and hope to Americans looking for some relief from the devastation of the Depression.

The results of the WPA enriched U.S. society. Thousands of miles of roads were built during this time, as well as bridges, parks, playgrounds, schools, airports, post offices, and other public buildings. Though the WPA was a federal program Hopkins had the foresight to operate it in a decentralized fashion, with many decisions made at state and local levels. The WPA did not have the "feel" of a huge, faceless, federal bureaucratic program, largely because it was administered by local areas which defined their own needs, projects, and means by which to manage WPA monetary allotments.

Health problems caused Hopkins to resign from government service in 1940. Yet within a year he was back in service because Roosevelt's desperate need for someone with strong administrative and leadership skills during World War II. Despite his weakened health, Hopkins returned to work and supervised Roosevelt's controversial lend-lease program to the British. In this role Hopkins became a kind of unofficial roving ambassador for Roosevelt, providing him with impressions, observations, insights, and advice. Hopkins quickly familiarized himself with most aspects of the war effort and became a close working-partner with Winston Churchill (1874–1965), the Prime Minister of Great Britain. He also conferred with Russian leader and then-U.S. ally Joseph Stalin (1879–1953) and had a well-informed and motivated staff to assist him.

It has been said that as the United States entered the war in December of 1941, Harry Hopkins likely knew more about the details of U.S. war-making capacity that any other American. His actions in the administration of World War II, despite his ongoing poor health, marked the highpoint of Hopkins' career as a public servant.

Although Hopkins was officially behind the scenes in much of what happened during the war, he was praised worldwide by Allied Forces for his always creative and honest approach to the war effort. He also was known for his help in sustaining the confidence of Americans to overcome the crises of war and economic downturns.

His increasingly poor health and the death of his friend President Franklin Roosevelt, in 1945, did not deter Hopkins from playing an important role in winning congressional approval for the establishment of the United Nations, an international cooperative organization. For his service to the United States, President Harry Truman (1945–1953) awarded Hopkins the Distinguished Service Medal, the nation's highest civilian honor. Hopkins died months later, in January 1946, an American hero.

See also: **Great Depression, Lend Lease Act, New Deal, Works Progress Administration, World War II**

FURTHER READING

Adams, Henry H. *Harry Hopkins: A Biography*. New York: Putnam, 1977.

Kurzman, Paul A. *Harry Hopkins and the New Deal*. Fairlawn, NJ: R.E. Burdick, 1974.

McJimsey, George T. *Harry Hopkins: Ally of the Poor and Defender of Democracy*. Cambridge: Harvard University Press, 1987.

Schwartz, Bonnie. *The Civil Works Administration, 1933–1934*. Princeton: Princeton University Press, 1984.

Tuttle, Dwight W. *Harry L. Hopkins and Anglo-Soviet Relations, 1941–1945*. New York Garland Publishing, 1983.

HORSES

The horse originated in the Western Hemisphere but it became extinct there at the end of the ice age (around 10,000 B.C.). Horses had migrated into Asia before this time, and there the species continued. From Asia horses spread both northward and westward, and they were domesticated by man by 4350 B.C.. Between A.D. 900 and 1000 horses came into widespread use throughout Europe. When Christopher Columbus (1451–1506) landed at Hispaniola (present-day Santo Domingo, Dominican Republic) in 1492, he brought with him horses and cattle. These were the first seen in the New World in 7,500 years; the Native Americans had no beasts of burden prior to the arrival of the Europeans. In 1540 Spanish explorer Hernando de Soto (1500?–42) landed on the Gulf coast of Florida with more than six hundred men and two hundred horses. Also in 1540, Spanish explorer Francisco Vasquez de Coronado (c. 1510–54), who was looking for the Seven Cities of Cibola (mythical cities thought to contain vast treasures), arrived in the American southwest and brought with him the first horses and livestock ever seen in the region.

The introduction of the horse had a profound effect on North and South America. The Spanish conquistadors rode on horseback in battle against the native inhabitants, and they could easily subdue them and claim their lands. (The Spaniards also had guns, which combined with the horse to give them the advantage over the Native American warriors.) The American Indians that survived European incursion learned how to raise and use horses themselves. This knowledge enabled them to hunt game such as buffalo more effectively. The horse allowed the European settlers to expand westward via stagecoach and covered wagon and to convey messages cross country (by Pony Express).

Until the advent of the train (called the "iron horse") in the mid-1800s, the horse was the primary means for overland travel in the United States. It also figured prominently in the nation's military history, including the American Revolution (1775–83) and the American Civil War (1861–65). In 1811 construction began on the first federal road, the Cumberland Road (also called the National Road). Beginning in Cumberland, Maryland, the road continued west to St. Louis, Missouri. As a result, St. Louis received an influx of immigrants and became a vital trade center later that century.

See also: **Columbian Exchange, National Road, Mesoamerica**

HOWARD JOHNSON INTERNATIONAL, INC.

When 27-year-old Howard Johnson (1896–1972) bought a drugstore-newsstand outside of Boston in Wollaston, Massachusetts in 1924, he added more to his debt than to his assets. The $28,000 obligation that the new acquisition brought added to Johnson's already-existing debt of $10,000, which was left over from a failed joint venture in cigars with his father. Two innovations, however, quickly made Johnson's new business a success. First, he devised a home delivery service to peddle newsstand products in Wollaston and surrounding communities. His annual profits for the newsstand reached $30,000 in a few years. Although this money helped Johnson get out of debt, it was his interest in ice cream that had the biggest impact on his business.

An ice cream fanatic, Johnson wanted to use the drugstore's soda fountain to sell the best ice cream in town, which in his opinion was the ice cream being sold by a local pushcart vendor. Johnson paid the vendor $300 for the recipe (which yielded an extremely rich ice cream because it called for twice the butterfat of other commercially produced ice creams). Eventually Johnson began to experiment with other flavors, adding each one he liked to the soda fountain's menu. His 28 flavors were so popular that they became the Howard Johnson trademark.

These relatively small experiments began an early expansion and formed the basis for what would soon become a very big business. Howard Johnson was so pleased with the success of his ice cream that he decided to expand its sale outside of his drugstore. He put up small ice cream stands along the beaches of south Boston suburbs. The stands were a huge success; on one extremely hot August day alone, he sold 14,000 ice cream cones. In 1928 the profits from all Howard Johnson ice cream sales totaled $240,000.

Emboldened, Howard Johnson decided to open a family restaurant in 1928. The restaurant, in Quincy, Massachusetts, enjoyed only a short-lived popularity and closed in 1929 at a loss of $45,000 for Johnson. The Quincy restaurant, however, was not an entire loss. In 1929 a family friend, Reginald Sprauge, wanted to open a restaurant on a nearby highway. Sprauge knew that Howard Johnson's name and ice cream would boost the restaurant's visibility and popularity. The two men entered into an agreement that stipulated the following: Johnson would allow Sprauge to use the Howard Johnson name. In return, Sprague agreed to pay Johnson a cash fee, to sell only Howard Johnson brand ice cream, and to allow Howard Johnson to set the standards for all foods served at the restaurant. It all made perfect sense for Johnson who, in light of his earlier debts and failed restaurant, could not obtain bank loans to start new restaurants himself.

This is generally viewed as the birth of the first U.S. franchise restaurant chain. Under this system, independent businessmen called licensees owned and operated the restaurants, not Howard Johnson or his company. The licensees had the right to use the Howard Johnson name, but they paid the start-up costs for their properties, including an initiation fee paid to the company. They also had to purchase their food and other products from the Howard Johnson company, which was the main method by which the Howard Johnson company made money on these ventures.

Johnson had no trouble finding other takers for his franchise system. By 1935 there were seven Howard Johnson restaurants in Massachusetts. In 1940 there were 135 restaurants that extended down along the East Coast as far as Florida. That same year Howard Johnson won a bid to put 24 restaurants along the Pennsylvania Turnpike, where he would maintain a restaurant monopoly until 1979. Howard Johnson favored well-traveled automobile routes for his restaurants, knowing that the increasing popularity of cars would draw people out of population centers onto the roads. He hired 27 architects to design new properties. The trademark buildings each had bright orange roof tiles (orange being the color most likely to be seen by motorists) and a New England-style cupola in bright blue topped with a weathervane. Howard Johnson maintained high standards—he devoted two days a week to conducting unannounced inspections. He institutionalized novelties like the children's portion to attract families. The company provided the chain restaurants with elements of guaranteed success and it continued to grow.

World War II (1939–1945) brought gasoline rationing, and by 1944 only 12 out of about 200 restaurants were still open. Some restaurants were converted to cafeterias for workers in war plants. After the war Johnson decided to build smaller restaurants, leaving behind the grand roadside mansions of the pre-war years. In the summer of 1947, the company was building 200 of these new restaurants, which would extend into the southeast and Midwest. By 1954 there were 400 Howard Johnsons in 32 states, and the company was also adding a motel business. Some of these were franchises, others were owned directly by the Howard Johnson company.

In 1959 Howard Johnson Senior turned the company's presidency over to his 26-year-old son, Howard Johnson Jr. The company's headquarters remained in Wollaston, but executive offices were moved to Rockefeller Center in New York City. The company continued to expand and in 1961, when its stock went public, there were 605 restaurants, 10 Red Coach Grills, 88 motor lodges, 17 manufacturing and processing plants, net sales of $95 million from 1960, and a net income of $2.3 million. Between 1961 and 1967 Howard Johnson Sr., his son, and his daughter sold around two million shares of stock for $1 billion. When Howard Johnson, Sr. retired as chief executive officer and executive treasurer in 1964, his company was the country's third largest food distributor, behind only the navy and the army.

Although the company continued to grow—becoming a coast-to-coast chain with properties in California in the mid 1960s and adding Ground Round restaurants in 1969, it was now facing new problems and competition. Holiday Inns, Ramada Inns, and Marriott hotels were becoming increasingly popular with people who once stayed at Howard Johnson's motor lodges. Howard Johnson restaurants were increasingly perceived to be out of date in terms of their looks and their frozen food, which compared poorly to McDonalds and Burger King fast food franchises. Management was accused of being too cheap to upgrade the company's image. The company responded by introducing 24 hour service in over 80 percent of company-owned (not licensees') restaurants. Also, soda fountains were replaced with cocktail lounges in

100 company-owned locations. Seating capacity was expanded; special menu promotions were added; and new properties were concentrated in population centers as opposed to major highways. Howard Johnson continued to have record high sales and share earnings.

In 1979 Imperial Group Ltd. of Great Britain bought Howard Johnson for $630 million. It liberated the past controls over restaurants and motels, allowing them to buy food from a variety of sources and not just from the Howard Johnson company. Imperial also offered new food and lodging packages, entrees, and low cholesterol breakfasts. To attract business travelers, Imperial offered corporate discounts. Licensees were given the choice of refurbishing their existing properties by 1987, with low-interest loans from the company, or losing their franchises. Imperial also started a new Plaza Hotel chain in 1983. It was mid-priced and also geared toward business travelers, with restaurants and lounges, banquet and meeting rooms, and executive accommodations.

Despite its changes, Imperial was unsatisfied with Howard Johnson's performance and it sold the company to Marriott Corporation in 1985 for $314 million. Marriott divided the company, selling the franchise system and company-owned lodgings to Prime Motor Inns Inc. for $97 million. Prime assumed the company's $138 million debt but also took the Howard Johnson trade name and trademark. Both purchasing companies wanted to get rid of the independently owned properties after their franchise agreements expired.

This opened an interesting chapter in the company's history. To protect their interests, the franchisees threatened a class-action lawsuit against Marriott and Prime. In 1986 Franchise Associates, Inc., a company formed by the franchisees, won a perpetual exclusive license to the Howard Johnson name for restaurants in the United States, Panama, and the Bahamas. Franchise Associates, Inc. also obtained exclusive rights to use the trade name for Howard Johnson Signature Food Products and the free use of Howard Johnson recipes. By 1991 Franchise Associates owned and operated 85 of the 110 Howard Johnson restaurants.

The story of the lodging branch of the company took a different turn. In 1990 Prime sold its Howard Johnson lodging properties to an affiliate of Blackstone Group for $170 million. Blackstone renamed the Howard Johnson Franchise Systems subsidiary to Howard Johnson International Inc. in 1996. By the mid-1990s Howard Johnson lodging was expanding to worldwide locations under the leadership of president and chief operating officer Eric Pfeffer. Its intent was to fill the gap in international lodging between high-priced hotels and youth hostels. The company was operating over 600 hotels worldwide, with international locations in Columbia, the United Arab Emirates, and India.

See also: **Franchise**

FURTHER READING

Cahill, Timothy Patrick. *Profiles in the American Dream: the Real-life Stories of the Struggles of American Entrepreneurs.* Hanover, MA: Christopher Publishing House, 1994.

''Prime Motor Inns, Marriott to Acquire Howard Johnson's Motels, Restaurants.'' *Wall Street Journal*, September 21, 1985.

''Tintin Supermarkets with Orange and Blue.'' *Business Week*, July 2, 1966.

Wagner, Grace. ''A Natural Extension.'' *Lodging Hospitality*, November 1995.

''Virtual HoJo,'' [cited April 20, 1999] available from the World Wide Web @ ic.net/~dover/hojo.htm/.

HOWE, SAMUEL GRIDLEY

Samuel Gridley Howe (1801–1876) was a key figure during the nineteenth century in helping disabled people lead productive, dignified lives. Howe was a physician by profession and worked primarily with people who were blind or otherwise disabled. His activism spread to broad segments of the population. Through his efforts he demonstrated that people with a variety of physical and emotional disorders could become economically and socially functional. The disabled, his claimed, did not need to be abandoned or shut away in institutions.

Samuel Howe was born in Boston in 1801 to middle class parents. In 1824 he obtained a medical degree from Harvard University at age twenty-three. He then went to Greece and became involved in that country's war against Turkey. He spent five years in Greece as a surgeon and likely developed his ideas about disabilities during this time.

When he returned to Massachusetts Howe opened a new school for the blind. He aggressively pursued a philosophy of ''overcoming obstacles'' when it came to teaching the blind. This may have been based on his observations of how the disabled in Greece functioned during a time of war. He inspired educators of his time with the articles and reports he wrote about the disabled. His writing was filled with educational theories, positive principles of human psychology, and a good dose of hope.

Howe soon became the leading spokesperson for the needs of and the possibilities for the disabled in the United States during the nineteenth century. He increasingly asserted through his work and his writings that the disabled should be treated with confidence rather than pity. He developed a system of raised-print writing which was used by the blind to read until the simpler Braille method was invented by Louis Braille (1809–52).

OBSTACLES ARE THINGS TO BE OVERCOME.

Samuel Gridley Howe

Howe joined a variety of reform movements. He advocated better public schools, as well as enlightened treatment of the mentally ill and the developmentally disabled. He worked to reform prisons and end the institution of slavery.

Throughout his life Howe opened and organized schools designed to integrate disabled students into society. At the beginning of the twentieth century the trend in the United States was against isolating the blind and other disabled persons in institutions. A new social tendency arose to provide for the disabled a way to participate fully in everyday life.

At one point in his life Howe ran unsuccessfully for Congress as an antislavery candidate. He was among the most active of the New Englanders who worked to keep the state of Kansas from permitting slavery. He supported John Brown's (1800–1859) raid on Harper's Ferry in 1859. During both the American Civil War (1861–1865) and the Reconstruction era (1865–1877) Howe served on national commissions and agencies concerned with providing aid for freed slaves.

Howe died on January 9, 1876 at the age of seventy-five. His wife carried on his fight for the rights of slaves and the disabled. Julia Ward Howe also wrote the words for the famous "Battle Hymn of the Republic."

Howe is regarded as the father of the modern Disability Rights Movement (DRM). The movement advocates that people with disabilities be treated with appropriate techniques and education, allowing them to become active in the routine work and business of their communities.

Howe helped create an understanding that the blind, the deaf, and others with disabilities were not mentally or otherwise inferior. Howe's vigorous reform efforts at first focused on the blind, and later expanded to include former convicts, African slaves, the emotionally impaired, and the developmentally disabled. All of his efforts eventually focused on the fundamental humanity of all people. Howe championed the right of all people to be treated equally as their abilities allowed, and not their disabilities. He was among the first to aggressively confront U.S. society with the motto: "Obstacles are things to be overcome."

See also: **Americans with Disabilities Act**

FURTHER READING

Meltzer, Milton. *A Light in the Dark: The Life of Samuel Gridley Howe*. New York: Crowell, 1964.

Pelka, Fred. *The ABC-CLIO Companion to the Disability Rights Movement*. Santa Barbara: ABC-CLIO, 1997.

Schwartz, Harold. *Samuel Gridley Howe: Social Reformer, 1801–1876*. Cambridge: Harvard University Press, 1956.

Shapiro, Joseph P. *No Pity: People With Disabilities Forming a New Civil Rights Movement*. New York: Times Books, 1993.

Solinger, Richie, ed. *Abortion Wars*. Berkley: University of California Press, 1998.

HUGHES, HOWARD ROBARD

Howard Robard Hughes (1905–1976) was born into great family wealth, and despite his flamboyant lifestyle as a playboy, tycoon, and eccentric, he nevertheless enjoyed a remarkable business career that made him a billionaire. He was successful in many endeavors. He was a test pilot, the majority owner for years of TWA airlines, a movie producer, and a real estate developer. Oddly, Hughes is perhaps best remembered not for his successful business enterprises but for his bizarre and reclusive behavior. In his later years, his paranoid concern for privacy became legendary.

Howard Hughes stands on the flight deck of his enormous eight engine flying boat, the *Spruce Goose*, observing a pilot at the control panel.

Howard Hughes, Jr. was born in Houston, Texas, the only child of Howard and Alene Hughes. His parents had grown wealthy because of his father's invention of a drill bit used in most gas and oil drilling. This invention brought vast revenues to the family's Hughes Tool Company, which manufactured the drilling bit. Howard attended private schools in California and Massachusetts, and later, Rice Institute in Houston, and the California Institute of Technology.

His mother died when Hughes was sixteen. Two years later, his father also died. At age eighteen Hughes inherited an estate of $871,000 and a patent for the revolutionary drill bit, which continued to bring large revenues to the Hughes Tool Company. Hughes left school to take control of the company after his father's death, using its profits to finance a variety of projects.

At the age of twenty, in 1925, he married and moved to Los Angeles. Two years later, Hughes put up the money for the first of several films he produced, a movie called ''Hell's Angels,'' about World War I (1914–1918) fighter pilots. It was the most expensive movie ever made at that time, and it did very well at the box office. He went on to produce other films, some of which are considered classics, including ''Scarface'' and ''The Outlaw.'' He discovered the actors Jean Harlow and Paul Muni, and made Jane Russell a Hollywood star. Hughes became romantically linked with a number of Hollywood stars.

Hughes continued to produce movies while he pursued an interest in aviation. He seemed to be driven to prove his excellence in whatever field he entered. Becoming a pilot in 1928, Hughes went on in 1932 to found the Hughes Aircraft Company, and to design, build, and fly record-breaking planes. He set the world speed record in 1935, transcontinental speed records in 1936 and 1937, and a world flight record in 1938. He was named to the Aviation Hall of Fame in 1973. Hughes built the largest aircraft ever, made out of wood. It flew one time, piloted by Hughes, and was known as ''The Spruce Goose.''

Hughes became a well known public figure, popular for his aviation and movie heroics. He seemed to embody the traditional American qualities of individuality, daring, and ingenuity.

His aircraft company became a major defense contractor after World War II (1939–1945), and as the profits of his company increased, Hughes became obsessed with ways to avoid paying taxes on his huge profits. In 1953 he created a medical institute designed to be a tax-shelter, to which he transferred the assets of his aircraft company. For a time in the 1950s, his fame increased, as he openly confronted the federal government. In 1956 he loaned future President Richard Nixon's brother, Donald, $205,000 in an apparently successful ploy to influence the Internal Revenue Service's rulings on the Howard Hughes Medical Institute. In the eyes of many, he was a lone hero fighting against the intrusion of federal bureaucracy and the Internal Revenue Service (IRS). In the eyes of the government, he was a tax-cheat.

Hughes continued investing with his tool company profits. He created Trans-World Airlines (TWA), one of the most famous mid-century world airlines. Because he failed to appear in court in a matter related to possibly illegal TWA operations, Hughes was forced to sell his TWA holdings in 1966. He invested all of the $566 million from the sale of TWA into Las Vegas hotels, gambling casinos, golf courses, a television station, an airport, and land in Las Vegas. He again increased the size of his fortune.

In 1970 Hughes left the United States. He traveled secretly throughout the world, arriving unannounced in luxury hotels. To the paparazzi, he took on the aura of a romantic figure, but in reality he was a profoundly ill man. His last act of business, before going into total seclusion and paranoid decline, was to sell off his Hughes Tool Division, the basis of his great fortune, and put the money into a building company he named Summa Corporation, located in Las Vegas.

At that point, the Hughes fortune became muddled. His money and business interests seem to have often been used for secret activities; some allegedly involved in Central Intelligence Agency (CIA) operations aimed against the former Soviet Union. One such operation involved the Hughes conglomerate designing and constructing a naval vessel to raise a sunken Soviet submarine. The Hughes organization was reportedly linked, along with the CIA, to the Watergate affair. Details of the end of the Hughes empire are shrouded in mystery and controversy. Howard Hughes' mental illness was progressive and characterized by his obsessive concern to control every aspect of his environment. He died April 5, 1976, on an airline flight to a hospital in Houston, Texas. Hughes left no direct heir or will to his great fortune. The U.S. government was the big winner in the contest for the Hughes estate.

Sixty percent of his fortune was taken as estate tax by the IRS.

FURTHER READING

Bartlett, Donald L., and James B. Steele. *Empire: The Life, Legend, and Madness of Howard Hughes.* New York: Norton, 1979.

Drosnin, Michael. *Citizen Hughes.* New York: Holt, Rinehart and Winston, 1985.

Higham, Charles. *Howard Hughes: The Secret Life.* New York: Putnam, 1993.

Maheu, Robert. *Next to Hughes: Behind the Power and Tragic Downfall of Howard Hughes by his Closest Advisor.* New York: Harper Collins, 1992.

Rummel, Robert W. *Howard Hughes and TWA.* Washington: Smithsonian Institution Press, 1991.

HUMAN CAPITAL

The quality of labor in a country's workforce can directly influence a nation's economic growth. Investment in vocational training and education, which improves the quality of labor, is called investment in human capital. As an individual becomes more skilled and educated, productivity or output of work may increase, along with income. The concept of human capital can provide justification for wage and salary differentials by age and occupation. Education and training in skill development can create human capital just as construction of a building creates physical capital.

Some economists assert that a society should allocate resources to educational and training services similar to the allocation of resources for physical capital. Costs would be incurred in expectation of future benefits. However, unlike physical capital, human capital is not a guarantee and cannot be repossessed in settlement of a debt. The key question has been whether or not benefits exceed expenditures by a sufficient amount.

Until the mid-nineteenth century, education expenditures were primarily generated by the private sector. By the 1850s all states had developed programs for funding public schools. As late as the early twentieth century, most people considered education that was beyond the primary grades to be a luxury—particularly among low-income groups. However literacy rates continued to move upward and since 1940, education levels have consistently climbed. In 1940 24 percent of the U.S. population had high school diplomas and 4.6 percent earned college degrees. By 1996 almost 82 percent had completed four years of high school and almost 24 percent had completed four or more years of college. By attending college or vocational training programs, individuals were able to invest in themselves. Firms invested in human capital with on-the-job training. Government invested in human capital by offering programs to improve health, quality free schooling, including vocational and on-the-job training, and by providing student loans.

See also: **Physical Capital**

IACOCCA, LIDO ANTHONY

Lee Iacocca (1924–) retired as the Chief Executive Officer (CEO) of the Chrysler Corporation in 1992. He had joined the corporation fourteen years earlier when Chrysler was on the edge of bankruptcy. The company was at the time one of the largest automobile manufacturers in the world, employing thousands of people. Upon entering the company Iacocca convinced everyone involved, including the United States government, to underwrite $1.2 billion in loans to rebuild the company. To obtain this critical support, Iacocca used the legendary salesmanship and public relations skills he had honed while president of the Ford Motor Company. Seemingly by sheer willpower, Iacocca saved Chrysler and its employees from financial ruin.

Lido Anthony Iacocca was born in 1924 in Allentown, Pennsylvania. He was the son of Italian immigrants. Lee, as he preferred to be called, learned about business from his father, Nicola, who was a businessman with many interests. Nicola was a cobbler, the owner of a hot dog restaurant, a theater owner, and the owner of one of the first car rental agencies in the country. Iacocca credits his father with passing on to him a love for the automobile.

Iacocca earned his Bachelor's degree from Lehigh University. He later earned a Master's in mechanical engineering, with a specialty in industrial engineering, from Princeton University. He decided early on to become an auto company executive. After graduating from Princeton in 1946 he joined the Ford Motor Company as an engineering trainee. Within a year he realized that he was far better at selling automobiles than at making them. Iacocca entered the fast-track of sales. In 1960, at age thirty-six, he sped into the vice presidency and general management of the company's most important unit, the Ford division.

In 1964 Lee launched the Mustang automobile. Its attractive styling and successful marketing introduced a new wave of sports cars to the Ford operation. The Mustang earned Iacocca instant fame as an industrial innovator. In 1964 his face was on the cover of both *Time* and *Newsweek* magazines. By 1967 he was the executive vice president of Ford Motor Company. In 1970 he became president of the company. His only superior was Henry Ford II (1917–1987), chairman of the board of Ford Motor Co. For reasons that were never made clear, Chairman Henry Ford II discharged Lee Iacocca in June 1978. It was a shock to many people who saw Iacocca as a natural heir at Ford.

Five months later Iacocca was named president of the rival Chrysler Corporation. He became chairman in 1979 and began turning around the failing corporation. At the time Chrysler was headed for bankruptcy. Iacocca took the number three automaker, deep in debt, and transformed it into a highly profitable enterprise. He began managing expenses by winning approval of over $1 billion in federal loan guarantees. He then sold off profitable units like the tank manufacturing division and introduced new products to the marketplace. He also brought the president of the United Auto Workers onto the company's board of directors.

Within six years Chrysler paid off its debts and posted a profit of $2.4 billion. In 1985 Chrysler bought the Gulfstream Aerospace Corporation for $637 million and the E.F. Hutton Credit Corporation for $125 million.

Under Iacocca's leadership the company put out innovative new vehicles and eventually bought out competitor American Motors Corporation. As Chrysler bounced back to life in the 1980s, Iacocca became an extraordinary business and corporate celebrity. Some of his detractors felt he was a self-obsessed egomaniac, but many analysts of his career regard him as an important U.S. industrial hero of the late twentieth century.

A key product to the resurgence of the Chrysler Corporation was Iacocca's promotion of the K-car ''minivan.'' It was a vehicle loved by the young family

Lee Iacocca.

in need of room and efficiency. The mini-van largely helped revitalize Chrysler and its public image. It clearly set the trend for the enormous popularity of the sports utility vehicle that claimed much of the auto industry's market in the late twentieth century.

Iacocca continued to be the successful and charismatic CEO of the Chrysler Corporation until his controversial retirement in 1992, during a period when Japanese auto competition was once again hurting Chrysler's profits. He moved into retirement reluctantly after spending much of the previous thirty years of his life as an automobile industry corporate legend. Iacocca remained a major stockholder in Chrysler and in 1995 he became involved in a battle to gain control of the company. In the unsuccessful attempt for control, Iacocca sided with Las Vegas financier Kirk Kerkorian and was strongly criticized.

Iacocca's impact on the auto industry was controversial, but undeniable. He saved the Chrysler Corporation and turned it into a profitable business. In 1998, even in retirement, Iacocca was still involved in the auto industry, investigating the market for electric cars in California.

See also: **Automobile Industry, Chrysler Corporation**

FURTHER READING

Gordon, Maynard M. *The Iacocca Management Technique*. New York: Dodd Mead, 1985.

Iacocca, Lee A., and William Novak. *Iacocca: An Autobiography*. Toronto; New York: Bantam Books, 1984.

Jefferys, Steve. *Management and Managed: Fifty Years of Crisis at Chrysler*. Cambridge; New York: Cambridge University Press, 1986.

Levin, Doron P. *Behind the Wheel at Chrysler: The Iacocca Legacy*. New York: Harcourt Brace, 1995.

Wyden, Peter. *The Unknown Iacocca*. New York: Morrow, 1987.

IDAHO

One of the most sparsely populated states, Idaho remained undeveloped until gold and silver strikes began to attract eager prospectors. Like other areas of the Great Plains and the West, Idaho was at first just a place to cross during a westward journey, not a place to settle. As mining and agriculture began to take hold and the transcontinental railroad made settlement and commerce more feasible more people began to make Idaho their new home. Contemporary Idaho has a number of important industries and significant agricultural products, especially potatoes. Idaho's tourist industry is also strong, attracting thousands annually to the state's ski resorts and scenic areas.

During the first quarter of the nineteenth century Idaho was part of the vast territory known as the Oregon Country, claimed at various times by the United States, Great Britain, Spain, and Russia. Until 1805 no known white explorers had disturbed the Native American tribes who were the only residents of Idaho. When Meriwether Lewis and William Clark's expedition reached the region that year the Native Americans helped supply the explorers for their journey to the Columbia River and the Pacific. Fur trappers and missionaries soon followed. Although the Oregon Trail crossed Idaho and the area officially became United States land in 1846, no one thought the territory worthy of settlement until 1860. In that year, Mormons established the first permanent settlement at Franklin and a gold rush began in northern Idaho. The Idaho Territory was organized in 1863. According to historian F. Ross Peterson, "It is a sad fact of American history that while hundreds of thousands of uniformed Americans in Virginia, Tennessee, and Maryland were trying to kill each other [in the American Civil War (1861–1865)], thousands of Americans in the West were running from creek to brook to river trying to get rich quickly."

In the following two decades Idaho grew rapidly with Boise established as the capital in 1863. The Boise Basin became the most developed part of the state, reaching a population of 6,000 by 1864. Two years later $24 million in gold was produced during the Boise Basin strike. By then more than $50 million in gold had been taken from the Idaho mountains with little regard for possible damage to the environment.

As mining boom towns came and went agriculture was becoming more important in Idaho. Telegraph service and the transcontinental railway reached the state, and the population increased twofold between 1870 and 1880. The Utah and Northern Railroad, owned by mogul Jay Gould, was the first major railroad in the state which hastened the settlement of northern Idaho. Many Mormons, encouraged by their Utah church leaders, migrated to Idaho during this time to establish farms and communities such as Blackfoot and Victor. The Oregon Short Line was completed through Idaho in 1884 and a traveler could now reach Portland, Oregon, from Omaha, Nebraska, in five days—a trip that had taken Lewis and Clark 18 months to complete in 1805. The Northern Pacific and the Chicago, Milwaukee, Saint Paul, and Pacific railroads also made possible the development of lead-silver lode mining in the area of the Coeur d'Alene Mountains. During the late 1870s, as in all territories settled by whites, Native American residents were gradually pushed off their land by a series of wars. The most famous Idaho battle was the Nez Perc war, after which Chief Joseph surrendered and his people were pushed onto reservations.

Another rush of prospectors came to Idaho between 1880 and 1884 after silver and lead were discovered in south central Idaho and the panhandle region. Idaho became the 43rd state in 1890, having reached a population of more than 88,000 that same year. During the 1890s Idaho was plagued with violent labor disputes in the mining regions and political bickering among Mormons and non-Mormons.

Further economic growth was made possible in the early twentieth century by federal land and irrigation projects. A very large sawmill at Potlatch was an indication of an increasingly prosperous timber industry, and agriculture also began to grow in importance in the state. The development of the russet potato in the 1920s gave Idaho its signature agricultural product. A farm depression in the 1920s, however, lasted through the Great Depression of the 1930s and did not end until World War II (1939–1945). Both agriculture and industry were important after the war, especially the fertilizer and potato businesses. Development was encouraged even more after the construction of a nuclear reactor testing and power plant at Idaho Falls in 1951, the first such generating station in the country. Idaho's mountains and open spaces also created a thriving tourist business. Today, the Sun Valley ski resort and other scenic areas attract thousands of tourists each year.

Contemporary Idaho faces new problems as the population expands and environmentalists push for better land use planning. Controversies also arise over mineral development and over water supply and dam construction. A major economic and human disaster occurred in 1976 when the new Teton Dam in eastern Idaho collapsed, causing loss of lives and $400 million in property damage.

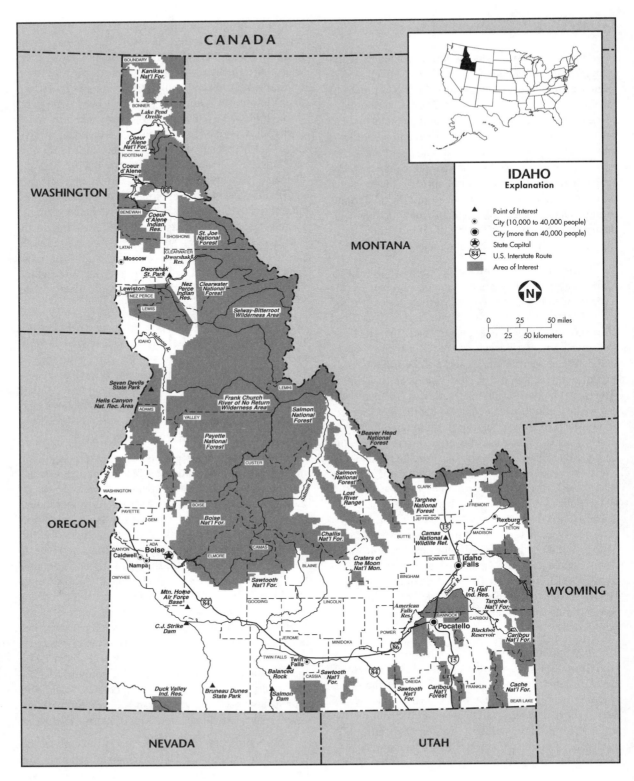

State of Idaho.

Idaho's economy in the 1990s was largely dependent on agriculture, mining, forest products, and food processing. Idaho is the nation's leader in potato production; most potatoes are grown in the Snake River plain, and about three-fourths of the crop is used for processed potato products such as french fries or instant mashed potatoes. Other important crops produced by Idaho include hay, wheat, barley, and sugar beets. This agricultural bounty is made possible because nearly 64 percent of all land used for farming in the state is under irrigation. Mining is only a small percentage of the state's annual gross product, but a variety of minerals, such as garnet, phosphate rock, construction sand and gravel, silver, lead, and pumice are produced. It is one of the few places that produces molybdenum, in a reopened mine at Thompson Creek.

Manufacturing in the state is concentrated in the resource industries—food processing, chemical manufacturing, and lumber production. In the late 1970s and early 1980s a number of northern California computer concerns, such as Hewlett Packard, opened or expanded plants in Idaho. The leading food producer is Ore-Ida Foods, and J.R. Simplot processes both food and fertilizers. Some of the wood products industries include Boise Cascade and Louisiana-Pacific.

The state survived a downturn during the recession of the early 1980s by restructuring its major industries. Although the number of workers employed in many industries in the state has shrunk, chemical manufacturing employment grew 36 percent during the 1980s, and paper industry employment rose by 30 percent. Between 1982 and 1991, tourism employment increased by 35 percent, and jobs in the high-technology industry increased by 50 percent between 1986 and 1990. In 1996 the average per capita income in the state was $19,539, ranking 43rd in the nation. Although Idaho was a pioneer in establishing fair labor practices only 8.1 percent of all workers belong to unions, and the state is now a right-to-work state.

FURTHER READING

Arrington, Leonard J. *History of Idaho*. Moscow, ID: University of Idaho Press, 1994.

Domitz, Gary, and Leonard Hitchcock, eds. *Idaho History: A Bibliography*. Pocatello: Idaho State University Press, 1991.

Beal, Merrill D., and Merle W. Wells. *History of Idaho*. New York: Lewis, 1959.

Peterson, F. Ross. *Idaho: A Bicentennial History*. New York: Norton, 1976.

Young, Virgil. *The Story of Idaho*. Moscow, ID: University of Idaho Press, 1984.

ILLEGAL DRUGS *(ISSUE)*

One of the most serious social problems in the United States since World War II (1939–1945) has been the trafficking in illegal drugs. These drugs—mostly derived from the opium poppy or from coca leaves—have powerful psychotropic (mind-altering) effects and are very addictive.

The U.S. government's attempt to deal with the drug problem has few defenders. The devastation that heroin and ''crack'' cocaine have imposed on the nation's already disorganized central cities and even on its affluent suburban high schools are widely acknowledged. There is less agreement on the root causes of this policy failure. Critics differ widely. Conservatives point to the weakening of family values. Liberals have no consolidated position on the drug problem. Some counsel a ''get tough'' policy of more vigorous enforcement of existing drug laws. Others go to the other extreme and favor the decriminalization of drugs. They point to the fact that the greatest growth in the U.S. prison population is from non-violent drug offenders. They argue that the result of the official U.S. policy banning drugs has been to turn addicts into criminals and to create a world-wide ''black market'' in illegal drugs.

As Adam Smith (1723–1790), the eighteenth century spokesman for free market economics, might have predicted, the constricted supply and growing demand of a banned substance inevitably increases the price and attracts entrepreneurs—in this case, organized crime. Or, as novelist William Burroughs once ironically remarked, the economic marvel of heroin is that the problem of slack demand never arises. Heroin is a very salable product: once introduced into the population, it needs no advertising; it not only sells itself, it drives the buyer to sell himself or herself.

As early as the second half of the nineteenth century, medical researchers recognized that opium and morphine combined beneficial pain-killing qualities with problems of addiction. In fact, when the German pharmaceutical company Bayer introduced heroin into the United States, it called the drug a non-addictive substitute for morphine. By the time government regulation arose during the Progressive period (1900–1920), the addictive qualities of these drugs

Policeman guarding 20 tons of cocaine in 1989, which at the time was the largest drug bust to date. The cocaine had a street value of $6.7 billion.

were better understood and the government banned them in the Pure Food and Drug Act of 1906 (which prevented Coca-Cola Co. from adding its most potent ingredient). By World War II, a growing number of drugs were ruled illegal. Still, the use of illegal drugs before World War II was minuscule by late twentieth century standards and confined to the margins of society.

In the first few decades after World War II the worldwide black market in illegal drugs grew steadily and sustained the profit margins of organized crime. Not since the Eighteenth Amendment to the U.S. Constitution prohibited alcohol in 1918 (followed by the repeal of Prohibition in 1933) had organized crime been able to corner the market on such an attractive commodity. Still, in spite of a growing underground drug culture in the 1940s and 1950s, there was little panic concerning drugs in mainstream society.

This all changed suddenly in the 1960s and 1970s, as rampant drug use (both marijuana and hallucinogenic drugs) by the young and a "tidal wave" of heroin inundated the United States. In contrast to earlier heroin, which originated in the opium poppy fields of Afghanistan, most of this new wave of drugs came from the "golden triangle" area of Laos, Burma, and Thailand in southeast Asia.

This was made possible by a remarkable set of military and political alliances between the Central Intelligence Agency (CIA) and the warlords that it recruited to fight covert anti-communist campaigns in

Laos, Cambodia, Thailand, and Burma during the Vietnam War (1964–1975). At that time, Congress had granted authority to President Lyndon Johnson (1963–1969) to wage limited war in Vietnam, but nowhere else. In order to generate funds for covert anti-communist warfare, the CIA allowed the Meo tribesmen of northern Laos, among others, to cultivate opium and to sell large quantities of drugs. Beginning in 1965, "Air America," a CIA-front operation, even participated in transporting drugs. A large portion of the drugs made their way into the United States, and through corruption among individual agents as well as South Vietnamese government officials, some went directly into the veins of U.S. soldiers in Southeast Asia,. The Corsican Mafia (the "French Connection") in Marseilles, France, also prospered from this glut of heroin.

In the late 1970s youth-culture drugs like LSD faded from the U.S. drug scene and the more addictive heroin once again become popular. The Sicilian Mafia, facing competition from the Corsican Mafia, stepped up its own drug operations, smuggling heroin from anti-communist guerrillas in Afghanistan. Thus, the connection between opium trafficking and Cold War anti-communist crusades clicked into place again as much of this new opium product was generated by the rebel Mujahadeen to fund their CIA-supported war against the communist government of Afghanistan. Anti-communist warlords needed money to fund their operations, and the CIA was willing to "look the other way" as they grew and sold prodigious quantities of drugs. These banner crops needed outlets, and U.S. organized crime was there to service the market.

Late in the 1970s the U.S. heroin market seemed finally to have reached its saturation point. New organized crime rings in Latin America began to step up production and distribution of a different, but equally addictive and destructive drug, cocaine. By the mid-1980s new, more potent methods of ingestion (freebasing) and forms (crack) appeared. Whereas heroin never lost its association with a low socio-economic consumer profile, cocaine appealed to a more "upscale" public. Hollywood stars like Richard Prior were quite open in their acceptance of the drug. Because of the few short-term side affects associated with its use, cocaine became the "drug of choice" during the 1980s. Sex was reportedly more enjoyable on cocaine. Long-term side effects like heart problems and sexual impotence did not become apparent until later, when millions of Americans found themselves addicted.

On January 30, 1982, President Ronald Reagan (1981–1989) mobilized his forces and announced a war on drugs. The First Lady, Nancy Reagan, took a high-profile position and sternly advised America's youth to "Just say no!" Vice President George Bush became the chief coordinator of drug policy. As former head of the Central Intelligence Agency, Bush was no doubt familiar with the problem. He targeted a prominent center of narcotics distribution, south Florida. Bush incorporated the U.S. Attorney's Office, the Drug Enforcement Agency, the U.S. Customs Service, the Federal Bureau of Investigation, the Bureau of Alcohol, Tobacco and Firearms, the Internal Revenue Service, the U.S. Border Patrol, and the Army, Navy, and Coast Guard into the fight. These agencies pooled resources, shared information, and coordinated a strategic assault to rid the United States of what many believed was a drug plague that caused crime, social dislocation, and demoralization.

During the first year of the war, the U.S. Attorney's Office reported a 64 percent increase in drug prosecutions. In 1983 six tons of cocaine were seized in south Florida; by 1985 such seizures snared twenty-five tons; in 1986, thirty tons. According to the DEA, this represented more cocaine than the drug cartels in Colombia had produced in 1980. While these arrests and seizures were touted as successes, many realized that more people were using cocaine, heroin, and other drugs than ever before. Even in south Florida, the primary theater of combat, illicit drugs were as easily available as over-the-counter varieties, and were often sold in the same places—openly and without fear of the law.

At the same time the new Latin American cocaine cartels were growing in power, the Reagan administration began to wage a covert war against the Cuban-supported Sandinista government of Nicaragua and to oppose all Marxist and communist influence in Latin America. In a post-Vietnam mood of disgust with waging wars against Third World countries, Congress forbid the use of public funds to overthrow the Sandinistas. The Reagan administration used covert methods, paid for with predominantly private funds. The resulting congressional Iran-Contra hearings investigated relations between the United States government, the Islamic fundamentalist regime in Iran, and the anti-Sandanista *Contra* forces in Nicaragua. Buried in this investigation was the question of whether drug sales helped fund the *Contras*.

Responding to public pressure, the Senate Foreign Relations Committee set up a special Subcommittee on Terrorism, Narcotics, and International Operations, chaired by Senator John Kerry, to conduct hearings into these matters. Its findings were clear: at the very least the CIA (and other U.S. agencies) had again looked the other way while the Colombian drug cartels provided millions of drug-generated dollars to arm the *Contras*.

The Kerry Committee also found instances of drug activities on the part of U.S. allies in the region, the most important of whom was General Manuel Noriega of Panama, known by U.S. drug enforcement agents since 1971 as a drug trafficker linked to the Colombian cartels. The Kerry Committee learned that the CIA had used Noriega to funnel secret arms to the *Contras*. As evidence uncovered by the Kerry Committee showed, Noriega had been on the payroll of the CIA since 1976, when he collected an annual fee of $110,000. By 1985 he was collecting $200,000 per year, all in secret cash deposits in the Bank of Credit and Commerce International (BCCI—which would figure prominently in new scandals in the early 1990s, including drug-money laundering). Ostensibly Noriega was "our man" in Central America serving in the war against communism. Yet in 1986, when the DEA proposed an undercover plan to unravel the mysteries of a multibillion-dollar drug money-laundering scam in Panamanian banks, it had to seek CIA approval. The go-ahead was given by the CIA, but with the stipulation that any information that exposed Panamanian government officials be dropped.

The DEA's findings in this regard may have been ignored, but the Kerry Committee's revelations were not. In 1988 the U.S. District Court in Miami issued an indictment against Noriega and a warrant for his arrest. Eventually Noriega was caught, tried, convicted, and imprisoned. During his trial, both the CIA and the National Security Council (NSC) refused to hand over files on Noriega, saying that to do so would compromise national security.

In late November 1997, under the administration of President Wiiliam Clinton (1993–2001), the United States and Mexican governments entered into an agreement to help control the weapons smuggling from the United States into Mexico. Under the agreement, the U.S. Federal Bureau of Investigations (FBI) and the Office of Alcohol, Tobacco, and Firearms (ATF) were to coordinate efforts with Mexico's Procuraduria General de la Republica (PGR) to stop illegal trafficking of arms. A U.S.-based ATF office and U.S. Customs personnel at the American Embassy in Mexico City were called upon to oversee the effort. Experts from the two countries conducted investigations to determine whether weapons sold legally in the United States were diverted to the black market, where drug traffickers in Mexico acquired them. The new accord was part of a sophisticated joint strategy to combat drug trafficking, a strategy which included the creation of a hotline between the U.S. Pentagon and Mexico's Secretary of National Defense to coordinate efforts to intercept drug shipments moving into the United States.

The joint U.S.-Mexico effort to control illegal sales of firearms was part of an ongoing campaign embraced by the Organization of American States (OAS) to reduce gun smuggling and reduce violence both in the United States and in Central and South America. The campaign, which was first proposed by Mexico, sought to tighten controls on weapons trafficking across national borders and impose restrictions on weapons production. According to a report from Mexico's drug enforcement campaign, customs and other law enforcement authorities confiscated almost 23,000 illegally imported weapons and 1.2 million munitions during 1996 alone. The report said at least one-third of the weapons and almost one-fifth of the munitions were destined for drug traffickers in the black market.

Ironically, the joint U.S.-Mexico effort followed reports that the Clinton administration had requested a threefold increase in the budget for exports of weapons and military equipment to Mexico. According to the non-governmental Federation of American Scientists (FAS), the Clinton administration requested $9 billion for sales of weapons, aircraft, radar units, and other military equipment to Mexico in the 1998 budget. The FAS, whose board of sponsors includes over 55 American Nobel Laureates, claimed that the United States domestic gun market was the principal source of weapons for the drug traffickers, and that both the Mexican

government and the drug traffickers were dependent upon the United States for guns. The FAS also warned that weapons originally exported to Mexico to combat drug trafficking would soon be diverted for other purposes.

Thus, as of the late 1990s, the ability of the U.S. government to control the black market in drugs and guns appeared to be limited by a set of strategies, reflexes, and relationships in place for generations.

FURTHER READING

Allen, David F. and Jekel, James F. *Crack: The Broken Promise*. New York: St. Martin's Press, 1991.

Belenko Steven R. *Crack and the Evolution of Anti-Drug Policy: Contributions in Criminology and Penology*, no. 42. Westport, CT: Greenwood Press, 1993.

McCoy, Alfred. *The Politics of Heroin in Southeast Asia*. New York: Harper & Row, 1972.

Harris, Jonathan. *Drugged America*. New York: Four Winds Press, 1991.

Scott, Peter Dale and Marshall, Jonathan. *Cocaine Politics: Drugs, Armies, and the CIA in Central America*. Berkeley: University of California Press, 1991.

ILLINOIS

Situated in the center of the Midwestern prairie, on the edge of Lake Michigan, the state of Illinois was always in a good position to benefit from its own natural resources. It is bounded on the west by the Mississippi River, while the Ohio runs along its southern border. Good land and water routes helped the state grow from an undeveloped territory into a powerhouse of agriculture and industry. Most notable of the land routes were the numerous railway lines running through the state. Illinois cities and farms, as well as its service industries continuously fostered a diverse economy. This eventually placed the state high in per capita income nationwide, with Chicago as its shining star.

The first white people to exploit the resources of Illinois were French fur traders who explored Illinois rivers in the seventeenth century. Although the British controlled the Illinois territory after the Treaty of Paris (1763), they made no attempt to establish permanent settlements. The state of Virginia claimed Illinois from 1778 to 1784 but gave up its claim to the area when Illinois became part of the new Northwest Territory. The Treaty of Greenville in 1795 gave the United

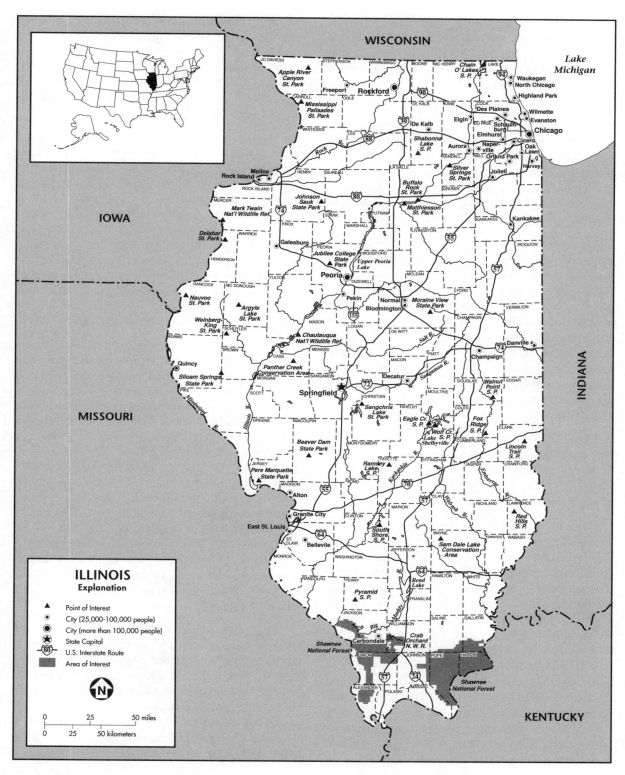

State of Illinois.

States the tract at the mouth of the Chicago River, which later became the site of Chicago. The Illinois Territory was created in 1809, and after the British were defeated in the War of 1812 (1812–14), Illinois formally became the twenty-first state in 1818.

After the final defeat of the Indians in the Black Hawk War of 1832 the Illinois prairie became open to settlement, especially by people from Kentucky. The term ''land office business'' certainly applied to Illinois during this time, as settlers, who were lured by cheap land prices, flocked into the new state. Farmers and entrepreneurs from the East found possibilities in the state's good soil and convenient water routes.

In the first part of the century, schemes to promote rapid economic development in the form of roads, canals, and railroads left the state in a debt so heavy that it would persist for 50 years. Yet, Illinois continued to grow rapidly, and northern and central Illinois were helped considerably when the short-lived Illinois and Michigan Canal opened in 1848. A network of railroads was built in the 1850s and allowed the state to prosper during the American Civil War (1861–65). It fostered continued growth after the war by providing easier routes to market for both farmers and manufacturers.

The early years of the industrial revolution helped both farm and city. The John Deere plow and McCormick reaper, both made in Illinois, revolutionized agriculture during the mid-nineteenth century and added to the increased prosperity of the state

The period after the American Civil War saw substantial economic growth, particularly in the city of Chicago. In the minds of its citizens, Illinois was soon divided into two parts: Chicago and ''downstate.'' Chicago became the central city of the Midwest; its development was spurred by its proximity to Lake Michigan and the Chicago River, and by the railroads, which brought farm products to the city. The great Chicago Fire of 1871 temporarily halted the city's growth. But it was soon brought into even greater prominence by steel mills, banks, new buildings, and transportation networks. The crown jewel in the latter part of the nineteenth century was the building of the ''White City''—the Columbian International Exposition of 1893. It showcased the technological achievements of a growing United States and highlighted the importance of the nation's second largest city at the time.

Foreign immigrants, so vital to the growth of the entire state, came at first from northern Europe and after 1890 from southern and eastern Europe. They developed prairie farms, small towns, and cities and eventually provided needed labor for Chicago industries. Chicago became a cradle of the labor movement; the Knights of Labor and the Chicago Federation of Labor, two of the earliest unions were originated in Chicago. The 1886 Haymarket riot and the 1894 Pullman Strike brought the labor problems of Illinois to national attention.

Most of Illinois prospered during the first 30 years of the twentieth century. The International Harvester Company became a major Chicago manufacturer of farm equipment. The Caterpillar Company, makers of earth-moving equipment, dominated Peoria. The Chicago steel industry, centered in Gary, Indiana, became second only to that of Pittsburgh. The state led the nation in food production, agricultural implement manufacture, and agricultural finance. World War I (1914–18) spurred economic growth in the state. War production demanded more the unskilled labor, which was again provided by European immigrants and also by African Americans coming from the South.

The pursuit of wealth preoccupied Illinois during the 1920s, highlighted by the violence and corruption surrounding the Prohibition era and the organized crime wave that accompanied it. The Great Depression affected Illinois as much as it did the rest of the nation. Farmers were the first to suffer; then industries began closing around 1930. Growth slowed drastically, and the Illinois coal industry suffered. The pro-business Republicans who had run the state since the 1850s suffered great losses in the 1932 election, as African Americans, white ethnic minorities, and factory workers responded to the economic hopes brought by Franklin D. Roosevelt's New Deal. The 1933 Chicago World's Fair (named ''A Century of Progress'') brought attention to Chicago and optimism to its citizens, despite depressed economic conditions. During World War II (1939–45) Illinois began to recover, helped largely by military contracts.

Prosperity reigned in Illinois during the 1950s. At that time the economy began its gradual shift from a manufacturing to a service economy. The negative effects of heavy industrialization began to appear as well. By the 1960s the state faced severe problems with air and water pollution, and urban decay. The Chicago stockyards closed in 1972. The yards had been a symbol of Chicago's preeminence in the meat-packing industry since 1865. A severe recession followed during the early 1980s, as industries like steel, machine tooling, and automobiles were facing increasing foreign competition and were forced to lay off workers. Many industries fled to the South, and by 1990 the unemployment rate in Illinois was 7.2 percent, in contrast to the national average of 5.2 percent. In 1992 the city of Chicago faced additional economic losses when water tunnels under the city ruptured. In 1993 flooding of the Mississippi and Illinois rivers caused 1.5 billion dollars of damage in western Illinois.

In the 1990s Illinois regained economic strength, ranking seventh in per capita income among all the states in 1996. It prospered in the service sector, the metals industry, and food processing, as well as in the manufacture of industrial and farm equipment, electric equipment, appliances, electronic components, and printing equipment. The 1989 Technology Advancement and Development Act aided companies that develop advanced technologies for commercial use. Labor unions in Illinois declined to little more than 20 percent of workers statewide, but continued to be strong in the Chicago area. Chicago remained the Great Lakes' busiest port and the leading wholesaling center of the Midwest, as well as Illinois's industrial center. The city was followed by Rockford, the East St. Louis area, Rock Island and Moline, and Peoria. The tourism industry also became an important economic boon to the state, with Chicago as a major tourist destination.

Led by the central and northern corn-belt counties, Illinois was one of the top five producers of agricultural products in the late 1990s. The total number of farms, however, declined significantly after World War II. Mining is also an important industry in the state. Illinois continued producing significant amounts of non-fuel minerals, including industrial sand and gravel, cement, and clays. The state was the only producer in the nation of fluorspar in 1995.

See also: **Black Hawk War, Caterpillar Company, Chicago Fire of 1871, John Deere, Haymarket Bombing, Knights of Labor, Cyrus McCormick, McCormick Reaper, Northwest Ordinance, Pullman Strike**

FURTHER READING

Carrier, Lois. *Ohio: Illinois: Crossroads of a Continent*. Urbana, IL: University of Illinois Press, 1993.

Howard, Robert P. *Illinois: A History of the Prairie State*. 5 vols. Grand Rapids, MI: William B. Eerdmans, 1972.

Illinois Department of Commerce and Community Affairs. *Illinois Data Book*. Springfield, 1994.

Jensen, Richard J. *Illinois: A Bicentennial History*. New York: Norton, 1978.

Petterchak, Janice A., ed. *Illinois History: An Annotated Bibliography*. Westport, CT: Greenwood, 1995.

IMMIGRATION *(ISSUE)*

Immigration is the influx of people to a country or region which is different from their country of birth. In the United States, immigration has been a basic part of life at least since the settlement of Jamestown in 1607 and remains part of American life today. One of the truisms of U.S. history, then, would seem to be that all Americans are immigrants or the descendants of immigrants.

While the early white settlers of America were largely English, there were significant numbers from other areas including Ireland, Scotland, and Wales in the British Isles, various German states, French Huguenots, as well as Dutch and Swedes who were absorbed when their settlements became English colonies. With the exception of the Huguenots who settled in Massachusetts and South Carolina, most of the non-English settlers were in New York, Pennsylvania, and Delaware. Immigration can be voluntary or involuntary. Africans, too, represented a significant portion of the immigrant colonial population, especially in Virginia and South Carolina. However, immigration was not a clear concept in the colonial period when all of the colonies were being settled. In fact, prior to 1820, no statistics were kept on immigration and regulation was largely left to the states. In that year the Department of State began to keep statistics. Thus, in the sense that immigration is an observed and recorded phenomenon, it can be said to have begun in the United States around 1820.

Emigration (the outflow of people from the country of origin) was characterized by two factors—push and pull. Push is shorthand for the various reasons people might want or need to leave their home country; the pull consists of the attractions that the United States offered. Famine, religious persecution, failed revolutions, and war have been strong factors "pushing" emigrants toward the United States. Low-cost land in the late nineteenth century, religious and political freedom, and economic opportunity have been the major "pull" factors which helped immigrants (people of foreign heritage newly-landed in the United States) achieve the promise of success in their new country.

U.S. immigration can be divided into several distinct phases based on the origins of those entering the country. Immigrants from the British Isles, including Ireland, and Germany heavily dominated the "old" phase of immigration, prior to the 1890s. The "new" immigration phase, from the 1890s to 1920, saw large numbers of immigrants from southern and eastern

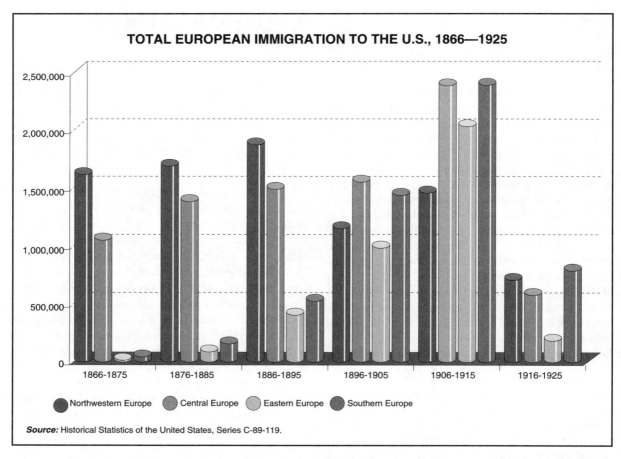

TOTAL EUROPEAN IMMIGRATION TO THE U.S., 1866—1925

● Northwestern Europe ● Central Europe ● Eastern Europe ● Southern Europe

Source: Historical Statistics of the United States, Series C-89-119.

Shown are the changes in European immigration to the United States. Prior to 1896 immigrants were primarily from Northwestern and Central Europe. Between 1896 and 1915 the number immigrating from Eastern and Southern Europe greatly increased.

Europe. From 1920 to 1965 there were nationality quota limitations on the number of emigrants from a particular country entering the United States each year. The post-1965 period continued limitations on the numbers entering the country each year, but abandoned nationality quotas.

Between 1830 and 1880 some 9 million people entered the United States. Most were from western and northern Europe. Irish and Germans were the two most identifiable groups, although equally large numbers came from Great Britain and smaller but steadily increasing numbers from Scandinavia. Repeated failure of the potato crop in Ireland beginning in the mid-1840s and the failure of the 1848 revolutions in Europe were events that led to dramatic increases in migration.

Many immigrants entered the United States through Castle Garden, New York City's immigration depot. In 1864 Congress established the Bureau of Immigration, but it was primarily concerned with collecting statistics. In 1882 the first comprehensive, national immigration law was passed, but primary responsibility still

lay with the states. In 1891 Congress established immigration as a federal responsibility and established formal procedures and standards for admission to the U.S. Since most immigrants were entering the country through the port of New York a processing center was established at Ellis Island in 1892.

Between 1880 and the outbreak of World War I (1914–1918) 25 million people entered the United States. Beginning in the late 1880s increasing numbers of immigrants derived from eastern and southern Europe. They were Italians, Poles, Russian and other eastern European Jews. These "new" immigrants supplemented rather than replaced emigration from northern and western Europe, which continued as before. The new immigrants were overwhelmingly non-Protestant and few spoke English. The new immigrants triggered concerns about the future character of the United States and how such different groups could be assimilated. There was also concern about Asian immigrants that led to the Chinese Exclusion Act of 1882 and the Gentlemen's Agreement between the United States and Japan in 1907. These concerns first led to demands for a literacy test for immigrants that was enacted over President Woodrow Wilson's (1913–1921) veto in 1917 and the establishment of quotas for various nationality groups based on the 1890 census, first enacted on a temporary basis in 1920.

The quota system was made permanent in 1924 and governed entry into the United States for forty years. Some countries rarely filled their quotas while others, in central eastern and southern Europe, often had long waiting lists. Latin American, Caribbean, African and Asian countries had minuscule quotas. The quota represented a significant reduction in the number of people allowed into the country. Between 1925 and 1929 the total quota was 164,667 people per year, a striking contrast to the 1.2 million immigrants in 1914, the last year before World War I. Some exceptions were made to the quotas for refugees from World War II through the Displaced Persons Act of 1948 and the McCarren-Walter Act (1952), but total immigration remained well below pre-quota levels.

In 1965 the Immigration and Nationality Act ended the national origin quota system and established new criteria for admission to the United States based on the need for certain skills in the workforce, refugee status, and the reunification of families. The changing nature of immigration is clear from the comparison between the origins of immigrants since 1820 and the origins of those arriving between 1981 and 1996. Seven out of the top ten nationalities represented in the emigration from 1820 to 1981 were European—Germany, Italy, the United Kingdom, Ireland, the former Soviet Union, Austria, and Hungary. The others are Mexico, Canada, and the Philippines. In contrast, no European nation appears in the list of most common nation of origin from 1981 to 1996. This group is dominated by Mexico, with nearly a quarter of all emigrants, along with Asian and Caribbean nations.

See also: **Tenements**

FURTHER READING

Bodnar, John. *The Transplanted: A History of Immigrants in Urban America*. Bloomington, IN: Indiana University Press, 1985.

Handlin, Oscar. *The Uprooted*. Boston, MS: Little, Brown and Company, 1951.

Hansen, Marcus Lee. *The Atlantic Migration, 1607–1860: A History of the Continuing Settlement of the United States*. Cambridge, MA: Harvard University Press, 1940.

Marzio, Peter C. ed. *A Nation of Nations*. New York; Harper and Row, 1976.

Reimers, David. *Still the Golden Door: The Third World Comes to America*. New York: Columbia University Press, 1985.

Thernstrom, Stephan, ed. *Harvard Encyclopedia of American Ethnic Groups*. Cambridge, MA: Harvard University Press, 1980.

IMPERIALISM (POSSESSION OF COLONIES) *ISSUE*

Imperialism is a policy aimed at the extension of political, economic, and cultural control over areas beyond a nation's boundaries. It can be accomplished in one of four ways: by military conquest; by treaty; by lending money to a weak country and then taking over control when the recipient country is unable to repay the debt; by economic penetration followed by intervention when the settlers from the expansionist country demand it. During the late nineteenth and early twentieth centuries the United States engaged in all these activities.

Modern imperialism was triggered by the Industrial Revolution, which so increased the productive capacity of the major European states that they were forced to seek overseas markets and sources for raw materials. This process began around 1870. The United States joined the competition late because the country had been preoccupied with westward expansion across the North American continent.

Until the 1890s overseas expansion was not a matter of high priority, interest in the acquisition of Cuba peaked from time to time, especially during the 1850s. The United States purchased Alaska from Russia in 1867, and established a presence in Samoa during the 1870s. The importance of Hawaii was recognized early in the nineteenth century; by 1875 a treaty made Hawaii a virtual protectorate of the United States and gave the country control of Pearl Harbor.

American imperialism received new impetus during with the Spanish-American War (1898), when the press stimulated a spirit of nationalism. Between 1895 and 1898 the native Cubans were in revolt against an oppressive Spanish regime. Major American newspapers gave the rebellion extensive and sympathetic coverage, which fueled demands for action. The United States demanded a settlement and sent the battleship *Maine* to Cuba to protect American interests. When it blew up in Havana harbor on February 15, 1898, hostilities became a certainty. The war in the Caribbean began in April and lasted only until August 1898. The conflict included U.S. invasions of Cuba, Puerto

Rico, Guam, and the Philippines. In addition, during the height of wartime enthusiasm, Hawaii was annexed. Early in the war the United States, by means of a law known as the Teller Amendment, had denied any ambition to take over Cuba. However, the actual conquest of Cuba during the war naturally raised the question of the status of the island in relation to the United States.

The war was formally concluded by the Treaty of Paris of 1898 in which Spain ceded Guam and Puerto Rico and sold the Philippines to the United States for $20 million. Spain also gave up her claim to Cuba which remained under American military occupation from 1898 to 1902.

During the war attitudes shifted among many groups in U.S. society and the desire for territorial expansion matured. It was especially well developed among business leaders, advocates of a large navy, and influential politicians like Theodore Roosevelt and John Hay. They came to be known collectively as the "Imperialists." They argued that territories won with U.S. blood should not be given up, that ownership of overseas territories would be good for business and trade, and that to be a great nation, the United States had to have a great navy (which, of course, required coaling stations and bases all around the globe).

Not everyone agreed with the Imperialists. The opponents of expansion, including former President Grover Cleveland, author Samuel Clemens, and Progressive Jane Addams, were given the name "Anti-Imperialists." They argued that conquest was incompatible with U.S. tradition, and that the economic advantages of overseas possessions would be offset by the dangers of potential conflict with other nations. The debate on Imperialism raged on until February 6, 1899, when the Treaty of Paris was narrowly ratified by two votes.

American expansion did not end with the conclusion of the war. In Cuba, a U.S. influence remained, although United States troops were withdrawn in 1902. Cuba was forced to accept the terms of the Platt Amendment, which permitted U.S. intervention and reduced Cuba to the status of an American protectorate. This relationship endured until 1934 and led to substantial U.S. economic penetration.

United States' expansion in the Caribbean continued. In 1903 the United States fomented a revolution in Panama, which separated the province from Columbia. The United States and the new Republic of Panama immediately concluded a treaty, which allowed the United States to build a canal in Panama on land leased

for 100 years. The Panama Canal was built over a period of 10 years from 1904 to 1914, and its very existence required a United States presence in the Caribbean. The importance of the region to the United States was also reflected in the so-called "Roosevelt Corollary" to the Monroe Doctrine. In 1904 President Theodore Roosevelt (1901–09) declared that the U.S. reserved the right to intervene in the affairs of smaller western hemisphere nations (whom the U.S. policy makers sometimes called "banana republics") should these smaller countries fail to meet their financial obligations to European creditors. The United States would reorganize the repayment schedule to prevent invasion by the European creditors. During the next few years this policy was applied in the Dominican Republic, Haiti, and Nicaragua.

The Dominican Republic went bankrupt in 1904. The following year the United States took over control of the country's customs houses and the administration of its finances. Marines were inserted in 1916 to maintain order and the Dominican Republic remained under American military government until 1924. Even after the marines were withdrawn, U.S. financial control continued until 1941. Meanwhile private U.S. interests gained control of the financial affairs of the country and 30 percent of the sugar industry.

In 1915, in order to prevent possible occupation by German creditors, the U.S. intervened in Haiti and remained there until 1934. The American presence was based upon a treaty that allowed for American control of Haiti's finances and defenses, but the intervention in Haiti was deeply resented by the Haitian people, even though it brought infrastructure repair and improved health standards.

During the early twentieth century U.S. Marines entered Nicaragua on several occasions, at the request of the government, to maintain order. Moreover, there was an extensive financial connection. By 1913 U.S. interests handled 30 percent of Nicaragua's imports and bought 56 percent of exports. During the next few years U.S. businesses assumed almost complete control of the nation's finances. President Calvin Coolidge sent the Marines back into the country in 1925 to help put down a revolution and to protect U.S. interests. The Marines did not leave again until 1933.

During the era of U.S. expansionist activities abroad there was also a vast increase in overseas investments, which rose by 500 percent between 1898 and 1914. Canada and Mexico were the leading targets for U.S. investments. In the former, where the major interests were manufactured goods, chemicals, and lumber, the increase was from $189.7 million to $867 million. In Mexico the increase was from $49 million to $336 million. There, investments were concentrated in extractive industries like mining and oil as well as in railroads. In Central and South America, U.S. investments totaled $458 million by 1914. The main interests in those regions were fruit and mining. Investments in oil did not begin to expand until later.

Investments in Asia also increased, but not to the extent predicted by the Imperialists of 1898, who had argued that possession of the Philippines would open vast markets and sources of raw materials, especially in China. However despite major efforts on the part of the U.S. government to promote trade and investments in the Far East, trade did not flourish. From 1898 to 1914, U.S. exports to Asia increased from $39.2 million to $380.2 million. Although the latter figure may seem large, it represented only 6.05 percent of all U.S. trade. U.S. economic penetration in the Far East did not develop to the level that had been predicted because of the poverty in the region and the determined opposition of competitive nations, especially Japan.

Overall, U.S. imperial expansion was not as successful as many people had hoped. The interventions were expensive and often frustrating because they caused bitterness and resentment among the people of the affected countries. Moreover, as U.S. productivity rose, businesses sought to expand their markets in the Western Hemisphere rather than in the Far East. This required the promotion of good will, not tension. So the Age of Imperialism waned.

In 1934 Congress passed legislation providing for Philippine independence in 10 years; in Latin America a new ''Good Neighbor'' policy replaced the Roosevelt Corollary. Troops were removed from the Dominican Republic, Haiti, and Nicaragua, and treaties with Cuba (1934) and Panama (1939) ended their protectorate status. At an international conference in Montevideo, Uruguay, in 1933, the United States formally renounced intervention.

But, after the 1959 revolution in Cuba, the Cold War priorities of the U.S. dictated a new round of intervention by the Central Intelligence Agency (CIA) in Cuba, Honduras, Chile, Nicaragua, and a number of other countries.

See also: **Big Stick Diplomacy, Dollar Diplomacy**

FURTHER READING

Beismer, Robert L. *Twelve Against Empire: The Anti-Imperialists, 1898–1900*. Chicago, IL: Imprint Publications, 1968.

Foner, Philip S. *The Spanish-Cuba-American War and the Birth of American Imperialism*. 2 Vols. New York: Monthly Review Press, 1972.

McCormick, Thomas J. *China Market: America's Quest for Informal Empire, 1890–1915*. Chicago: Quadrangle, 1967.

Munro, Dana G. *Intervention and Dollar Diplomacy in the Caribbean, 1900–1920*. Westport, CT: Greenwood Press, 1980.

Pratt, Julius W. *America's Colonial Empire*. Gloucester, MA: P. Smith, 1950.

Rosenberg, Emily S. *Spreading the American Dream: American Economic and Cultural Expansion, 1890–1945*. New York: Hill and Wang, 1982.

Williams, William A. *The Tragedy of American Diplomacy*. New York: Norton, 1972.

IMPORTS

Imports are goods and services that are brought from the country in which they are produced into another country for use by its people. Examples of goods that have been imported into the United States include oil from the Middle East, cars from Japan, wine from France, and bananas and coffee from South America. There are thousands of other imported goods, ranging from raw materials to finished products like computers, clothing, and jet aircraft.

Imports play an important role in the economy of virtually all modern industrial nations. In many leading industrial nations, 20 percent or more of all money spent was used for buying something produced in another country. The United States is one of the world's leading importing countries, which enables citizens to buy a wide range of goods and services.

Imports give citizens a broader range of products to choose, but they can be a source of political anxiety as well. Laborers who rely on sales of domestic-made products for job protection may complain that their fellow citizens are spending money on foreign-made products when similar products may be produced domestically. The higher the amount of imports, the greater the number of jobs that may be lost to foreign workers. In the 1970s for example, U.S. auto and steelworkers were losing jobs while record levels of foreign-made cars and steel were being imported to the United States. This anxiety led to calls for protectionist legislation—laws that restricted the flow of goods into a nation. Another source of anxiety from imports is the fear that one nation may develop too great a dependence on foreign goods. In the 1970s for example, Middle Eastern oil producers were able to create widespread shortages of gasoline and other energy products in the United States by temporarily halting oil shipments to the United States.

See also: **Exports, OPEC Oil Embargo, Protectionism**

INCA

The Inca were an American Indian people of western South America who settled in the altiplanos (high plains) of the Andean mountain region. Between 1200 and 1400 they subjugated neighboring tribes to form a vast and wealthy empire. Inca territory covered parts of present-day Colombia, Ecuador, Peru, Bolivia, Chile, and Argentina. The capital was at Cusco (in Peru). The civilization reached its peak during the latter part of the 1400s and into the early 1500s. The Inca had a multi-layered government in which the central authority of the emperor was balanced against the regional authority of chiefs. However, the emperor required absolute obedience from local rulers. Inca ruins indicate that they were accomplished engineers: They not only built an extensive system of roads and bridges to connect the provinces, but they built irrigation systems, temples, citadels, and terraced gardens on a grand scale. Machu Pichu, high in the Andes of Peru, is believed to be the last great city of the Inca. The Inca were skilled craftspeople who worked with gold, silver, and textiles (cotton and wool). The government controlled trade. There was no system of money; cloth, which was highly valued, was sometimes used as a medium of exchange. The Inca used llamas to transport goods. Canoes, rafts, and other boats were used in coastal areas and along rivers. Like the Aztec of central Mexico, the Inca were pantheistic (worshiped many gods), and they, too, at first mistook the Spanish explorers for gods.

The last of the great Inca rulers, Huayna Capac, died in 1525, and his sons subsequently fought over the empire. When the Spaniards, led by Francisco Pizarro (c. 1475–1541), arrived in 1532, they encountered a somewhat weakened Inca society. Nevertheless the people resisted the European incursion, and in 1536 they rose up in rebellion. The Inca were conquered by the Spaniards in 1537, and their vast territory came under Spanish colonial control.

See also: **Aztec, Maya**

INCENTIVE

Companies offer incentive plans to encourage employees to work harder. Incentive pay is a reward for employees or employee groups whose extra effort on the job results in higher production levels. For instance, incentive pay might be given to a sales department that exceeds its monthly sales goals. In addition to helping motivate employees, many companies believe that incentives improve recruiting and retaining high-quality workers, boost morale, and send a positive message about management's performance expectations.

Incentive schemes can be found at all levels of a company, from the shop floor to the boardroom. To be effective, an incentive plan must be clearly defined and the terms for payment understood and agreed upon by the employer and employees. There are several types of incentive schemes, which provide different ways to determine if an employee should receive incentive pay. The type of program will also affect how an employee's job performance will be measured. For example, factory workers might have their job performance rated according to their contribution to a team or the quality of the product they produce. On the other hand an executive's job performance might be based on company profit or cash flow. The outcome of these performance measures will determine whether an employee qualifies for incentive pay.

Incentives may be monetary or nonmonetary and may include cash or vest an employee in a profit-sharing plan. In some ways incentive pay is similar to an employee bonus program because compensation in both plans is based on exceptional job performance and paid in addition to an employee's basic salary. Bonuses, however, are usually given to employees only once a year, while incentive payment is made immediately after an employee becomes eligible for it.

Incentive programs are an outgrowth of the piece-rate system. The piece-rate system bases payment on the number of units that workers produce. The system began in the sixteenth century with the disintegration of the craft guilds. At that time, merchants hired people to work from their homes; home-based workers were then paid based on piecework. This piecework system was replaced by the rise of the Industrial Revolution in the late 1700s, which took production out of the home and into the factory. The use of incentives for factory work did not come about until the end of the 1800s, when scientific management theorists said that financial rewards could improve worker performance.

See also: **Industrial Revolution**

INCOME

Income is an important concept in economics as well as accounting. Accountants prepare an income statement to measure a company's income for a given accounting period. Economists are concerned with measuring and defining such concepts as national income, personal income, disposable personal income, and money income versus real income. In each field the concept of income is defined in slightly different terms.

For accounting purposes, income is distinguished from revenues. A company's revenue is all of the money it takes in as a result of its operations. On the other hand, a company's net income or profit is determined by subtracting its expenses from its revenues. Thus, revenues are the opposite of expenses, and income equals revenues minus expenses. When looking at a company's income statement, it is easy to distinguish between revenues, which appear at the top of the statement, and net income, which appears at the bottom. In other contexts, however, it is easy to confuse the two through improper usage. It is misleading to refer to revenues as income, for a company with revenues of $1 million is much different from a company with net income of $1 million.

For personal income tax purposes, gross income is money received by an individual from all sources. Many of the items that the Internal Revenue Code defines as income and that are called income on tax form 1040 are actually revenues, such as dividend income, investment income, and interest income. The Internal Revenue Code also provides for exclusions and exemptions as well as for nontaxable types of income to arrive at the concept of taxable income.

While accountants measure a single company's income for a specific accounting period, economists are concerned with the aggregate income for an entire industry or country. In looking at an entity as a whole, economists define its gross income as the total value of all claims against its output. That is, when goods are produced and services are rendered by the entity, workers, investors, the government, and others have a claim against those goods and services. Workers are paid wages or salaries, investors receive interest payments for their investment, and the government collects taxes. The total value of these claims represents the entity's gross income and is equal to the total value added through activities that have contributed to the production of the entity's goods and services.

In looking at the economy as a whole, economists view gross national income as the total of all claims on the gross national product. These include employee compensation, rental income, net interest, indirect business taxes, capital consumption allowances, incomes of proprietors and professionals, and corporate profits. National income includes all compensation paid to labor and for productive property that is involved in producing the gross national product. In addition, about 20 percent of national income includes such items as depreciation or capital consumption allowances, indirect business taxes, subsidies less surpluses of government enterprises (such as the U.S. Postal Service), and business transfer payments to employees not on the job.

Personal income includes all payments received by individuals, including wages, transfer payments such as sick pay or vacation pay, and the employer's contribution to Social Security. Personal income differs from national income in two important aspects: (1) some national income is received by entities other than individuals, and (2) some individuals receive personal income from social insurance programs that are not connected with producing the current gross national product.

Disposable personal income is the amount of personal income that remains after an individual's taxes have been paid. It is estimated that approximately 70 percent of the gross national income ends up as disposable personal income. The remaining 30 percent includes such items as depreciation, retained corporate profits, and the government's net tax revenue.

Economists also distinguish between money income and real income. While money income is measured in terms of the number of dollars received, real income is measured by the purchasing power of those dollars. After all, what is important is not how much money you earn, but how much you can buy with that money. Economists use a deflator based on a price index for personal goods and services to calculate an individual's real income from his or her money income. Since rising prices reduce the dollar's purchasing power, real income provides a truer measure of buying power than does money income.

See also: **Revenue**

INCOME GAP

In the United States, as in every nation, an income gap exists between the rich and poor. Income levels predict the ability to purchase goods and services. Economists analyze the distribution of income by ranking all family income levels from highest to lowest, then dividing the levels into fifths, 20 percent of

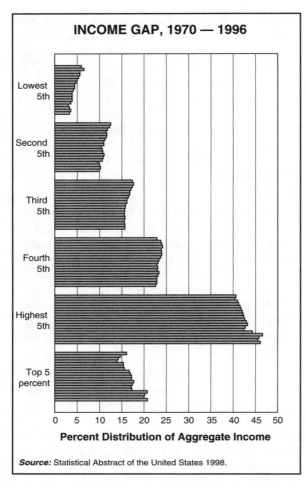

INCOME GAP, 1970 — 1996

Lowest 5th

Second 5th

Third 5th

Fourth 5th

Highest 5th

Top 5 percent

0   5   10   15   20   25   30   35   40   45   50

Percent Distribution of Aggregate Income

Source: Statistical Abstract of the United States 1998.

This graph depicts the share of total income received by U.S. families divided into five equal income groups and the top five percent. The income gap remained relatively the same, though the bottom 80 percent decreased, and the top 20 percent increased their shares.

families in each of five groups. (The same numbers of households are in each fifth.) The range of income for each fifth is then determined. In 1998 the lowest fifth's income ranged from $0 to $15,102, and their total income represented 4.6 percent of the entire income of all households in the U.S. That same year the highest fifth's income range was $55,907 and above. Their total income represented 44 percent of the entire income of all households.

In 1947 the lowest fifth received 5.1 percent of the entire income of all households and the highest fifth, 44.3 percent. Although the incomes of all families increased through the years, these figures illustrate that the income gap between the poorest and the richest, in percentage of all U.S. household income received, changed very little. Individuals at the lowest levels generally fall into the following categories: minorities, the elderly, young wage earners, households headed by

women, urban low-income-housing residents, and the rural poor.

Various factors, including education, inherited wealth, ability, experience level, and discrimination, contribute to the unequal distribution of income or the income gap. In addition, a self-perpetrating condition known as the cycle of poverty traps many individuals at the lowest income levels. People born into slums in large cities are likely to remain there the rest of their lives. High crime, poor living conditions, limited educational opportunities, and lack of adult role modeling all contribute to the perpetuation of the cycle. Wealthy families are more likely and able to send their children to expensive universities and thus help them obtain high-paying jobs.

INDENTURED SERVANTS

The arrival of indentured servants in the American colonies addressed a labor shortage that emerged in the early 1600s because of the success of a system of land distribution that was meant to encourage the establishment of farms. In 1618 the Virginia Company, a joint stock enterprise that wanted to settle and develop of Virginia, adopted a new charter based on the "headright system." Englishmen who could pay their own Atlantic crossing were granted fifty acres of land; each of their sons and servants were also granted an additional 50 acres. Other colonies were developed under the headright system in which the land amounts varied by colony. Soon there were more farms than there was labor to work the fields. The colonists solved this problem through the system of indentured servitude.

There were two kinds of indentured servants: voluntary and involuntary. Voluntary servants were people, often trained in a craft or skill, who could not afford passage to the colonies. In exchange for their passage, they agreed to work for a period of four to seven years for a colonial master. At the end of this period, the servant became a freeman and was usually granted land, tools, or money by the former master. Involuntary indentured servants were the impoverished, those in debt, or criminals whose sentence was a period of servitude. Most indentured servants in North America were voluntary. Their period of obligation to a colonial master was longer than that of a voluntary servant, usually seven to fourteen years. But, like their counterparts, the involuntary servants also received land, tools, or money at the end of their contract, called "freedom dues," and they also became freemen.

Certificate of Freedom for an indentured servant

Many indentured servants were drawn from England, Ireland, Scotland, and Germany. In European ports people contracted themselves or became involuntarily contracted to ship captains, who transported them to the colonies where their contracts were sold to the highest bidder. Roughly speaking, half of colonial immigrants were indentured servants. Colonial laws ensured servants would fulfill the term of their obligation; any servant who ran away was severely punished. Laws also protected the servants, whose masters were obligated to provide them with housing, food, medical care, and even religious training. The system was prevalent in the Middle Atlantic colonies, but it was also used in the South. When the economies of the Caribbean islands failed at the end of the century, plantation owners sold their slaves to the mainland. There the slaves worked primarily on southern plantations, replacing indentured servants by about 1700. In other colonies the headright system ended with the American Revolution (1775–1783).

See also: **Slavery**

INDEPENDENCE, ECONOMIC IMPACT OF *(ISSUE)*

Although the Treaty of Paris (1783) ended the American Revolution (1775–1783) and formally granted the newly formed state political independence from Great Britain, answers to the economic questions raised by its new-found freedom were not as easy to find. The former colonies had been an integral part of the British Empire and its vast transatlantic economy for nearly 200 years. Before any decisions could be made concerning the economic direction that the United States would take, serious political questions had to be settled first. But even after the Constitution of the United States was adopted in 1789, after the Articles of Confederation proved insufficient, economic problems still loomed large in the minds of many Americans. In the end, Americans were posed with two rather idealistic options. Would the United States seek self-sufficiency in an agrarian economy with small, independent self-sufficient farms, as Thomas Jefferson (1743–1826) advocated. Or would it seek a continuation of the international specialization and exchange it had grown accustomed to during the colonial era, as Alexander Hamilton (1755–1804) proposed? Before they could choose either one of these however, Americans had to deal more directly with the problems caused by the Revolution and its newly found political independence.

For many Americans, independence didn't provide all the solutions it appeared to have promised. For some, it only made things worse. The British Navigation Acts, although no longer restricting trade outside the Empire, were now applied to Americans who wished to trade in the Empire. Moreover, the mercantilist regulations of other European countries were often times more stringent than British laws had been. War-born industries found it impossible to match British efficiency. Cheap British manufactured goods began reappearing on the American market and the protection that American industries had enjoyed due to trade disruptions during the war, disappeared. Trade came to a standstill, domestic prices fell (farm produce brought the lowest prices) and unemployment among common laborers rose sharply.

Specie (coined money) balances that had accumulated in the last years of the war flowed out, back to England as payment for imports. During the war, Congress and the several states had issued almost $437 million in paper currency. Because of the magnitude of these issues as well as counterfeit currency, state monies had depreciated in varying degrees. Money issued by Congress (Continental currency) had become almost completely worthless and soon found it way into the hands of speculators. As money lost is value, business again, as it had during the colonial years, became dependent upon English, Spanish, French, and Portuguese coin. Currency became as scarce as it had ever been under British rule and the cry for paper money mounted, especially from the debtor class of farmers and common laborers. In many cases, the legal collection of farmer/laborer debts could only be settled by imprisonment or by stripping the debtors of real estate, cattle, or furniture.

Under the Articles of Confederation, which had been adopted in 1777 during the war, Congress had little authority and was unable to exert any effective control over the economic activity of the individual states, either in their relations with foreign countries or with each other. It could not levy taxes, issue money, or enforce a uniform tariff on imports and exports and could only ask the states for funds with which to carry out its duties. Under the Articles, some states could receive a higher percentage of foreign trade that would more than compensate for any loss either in manufacturing or employment.

But things weren't all bad under the Articles of Confederation. The break-up of some of the large estates previously owned by Tories (Loyalists) did allow states to provide some minor improvements in access to land and to flexibility of its use (although some tracts passed intact into the hands of wealthy patriots). Quitrent payments to colonial proprietors were abolished and laws restricting entail (which allowed heirs only the use but not the right to sell estates) and primogeniture (a policy which granted the eldest son exclusive rights to inheritance) were established. The Land Ordinances of 1784 and 1785 and the Northwest Ordinance of 1787 provided a highly favorable climate for westward movement and unwittingly eased transition to government under the soon-to-be ratified Constitution. By dictating the terms by which land could be sold and administered politically, the Ordinances settled many potentially serious problems. Land could be sold only after accurate surveys had been done and townships systems had assured secure land titles. In addition, because the thirteen states ceded their claims to western lands to the central government, new states could enter the Union on equal political footing, not as colonies.

Even so, with the central government facing no more urgent problems than those stemming from its financial difficulties, what little progress the Articles did achieve proved insufficient to reestablish public confidence and order. Shays's Rebellion in 1786 convinced many Americans that a stronger federal government was necessary.

But when the framers of the Constitution assembled in the spring of 1787, their emotions were still mixed. While they were compelled by the sobering experiences of what independence had brought so far, they were also moved by the revolutionary zeal of more

liberty and less government. In the end, the Constitution they produced reflected these tensions. It gave the federal government the powers to tax, borrow, and coin money, regulate foreign and interstate commerce, establish a postal service, and issue patents and copyrights, but it imposed constraints on the government's ability to regulate trade. The federal government could not impose duties on exports, could not discriminate against the ports of any state in its commercial regulations, could not restrict a carrier's freedom to enter or leave a state without stopping in another, and finally, could not extend any trade barriers between the states themselves.

In his Report on Public Credit (January 1790), Alexander Hamilton, Secretary of the Treasury under President George Washington (1789–1797), recommended that the federal government assume full responsibility not only for the outstanding debts incurred by Congress during the war but also for the debts accumulated by the states since 1775. By doing so, he wanted to ensure that the holders of public securities, most of whom were wealthy merchants and speculators, would have a significant financial stake in the survival of the national government. The new Congress accepted Hamilton's proposal and assumed the debts of the central government under the Articles of Confederation as well as the debts of the thirteen states.

To further promote economic development, Hamilton also presented to Congress a report on manufacturing. The report recommended that the government embark on a protective tariff policy that would tax imports in order to nurture infant industries, foster new ones, and stimulate domestic production. As a strong advocate of mercantilism, Hamilton was dissatisfied with the narrow economic base of merchants and farmers. He believed that manufacturing had to be developed, with the aid of the federal government, as soon as possible. Finally, Hamilton proposed that the creation of a national bank would provide the federal government with funds necessary to discipline irresponsible state banks, some of whom he believed could debauch the monetary system by issuing paper money.

The response to Hamilton's proposals was quick and immediate, mostly among farmers. They resented monetary curbs and saw a national bank as a successor to the Bank of England, which they felt, was too inclined to make monied men rich and landed men poor. They found their most ardent spokesman in Thomas Jefferson. Jefferson envisioned a rural democracy with an agrarian economy and believed that the United States should remain a nation of farmers. He argued diligently against the shackles of tyranny, which for him came in the form of a powerful central government. He spoke out against the "evils" of an urban economy and sought to uphold liberty at all costs. Hamilton, on the other hand, sought order and regulation and fought against political anarchy. He wanted to diversify economic life by encouraging shipping, manufacturing, and increased economic activity through the legislative powers of a strong federal government. While Americans remained skeptical about the extremes of both of these views, by the end of the nineteenth century, Hamilton's vision had been decided through the fires of political maturity, civil war, victory abroad, national aggrandizement, economic prosperity, and western expansion.

See also: **American Revolution, Alexander Hamilton, Thomas Jefferson, Mercantilism, Navigation Acts, Navigation Acts (Economic Burden on the American Colonies), Report on Manufactures, Specie**

FURTHER READING

Appleby, Joyce. *Capitalism and the New Social Order: The Republican Vision of the 1790s.* New York: New York University Press, 1984.

McCoy, Drew R. *The Elusive Republic: Political Economy in Jeffersonian America.* New York: Norton, 1980.

McCusker, John J. and Russell R. Menard. *The Economy of British America, 1607–1789.* Chapel Hill: University of North Carolina Press, 1985.

Peterson, Merrill D. *Thomas Jefferson and the New Nation.* New York: Oxford University Press, 1970.

Stourzh, Gerald. *Alexander Hamilton and the Idea of Republican Government.* Stanford: Stanford University Press, 1970.

INDIANA

The stereotypical picture of Indiana is one of rolling farm fields, open space, and small towns with picturesque courthouse squares. The state of Indiana is much more than this, however. It is as urban as it is rural, and has a highly diversified economy. The state's economy has a high proportion of agriculture, but the state also houses a large heavy industrial and high technology sector. The urban-industrial lifestyle in some parts of Indiana coexists well with the rural small-town ways of life in other parts of the state.

Europeans first ventured into Indiana in the 1670s. It was the Frenchmen Father Jacques Marquette (1637–75) and Robert Cavelier (1643–87) who first explored the region. Another Frenchman named Jean Baptiste Bissot lived in a Native American village at the present site of Fort Wayne. The French erected Fort Miami in 1720. Vincennes' son constructed another fort at the site of the town that later bore his name. The British vied with the French for control of the territory during this period, and the land was ceded to the British after the French and Indian War (1754–1763). During the American Revolution (1775–1783) George Rogers Clark (1752–1818) captured Fort Vincennes from a British garrison.

Future development in what would become Indiana was regulated by the Ordinance of 1785 and the Northwest Ordinance of 1787. The Northwest Territory was the area between eastern Pennsylvania and the Mississippi River. It was bounded on the south by the Ohio River and on the north by Canada. This region included the present-day states of Indiana, Ohio, Illinois, Michigan, Wisconsin, and parts of Minnesota. In 1794 General Anthony Wayne (1745–96) defeated the Native Americans in Ohio at the Battle of Fallen Timbers. The resulting Treaty of Greenville pushed many Native American tribes out of the territory. This encouraged the rapid settlement of the region by white Americans.

The first state to form out of the Northwest Territory was Ohio in 1803. By that time the rest of the Northwest Territory was called the Indiana Territory. The Michigan and Illinois territories soon separated from the Indiana Territory, and Indiana took on its present boundaries. In 1816 it became the nineteenth state of the union.

Indiana developed from south to north, largely because of the commerce made possible by the Ohio River. An increasing number of settlers established farms in the area as Native American tribes were driven out of the state. Trade in corn, hogs, whiskey, and timber flourished along the river. Indianapolis was a centrally located and planned city, being the capital of the state. It grew slowly, however. The major transportation arteries were located far away from it early on.

In the 1830s the state embarked on a massive internal improvements program that left it in severe debt. The Wabash Canal was built, largely using the labor of Irish immigrants. The National Road (now U.S. 40) reached Indiana in 1827, and the Michigan Road (now U.S. 421) was completed in the late 1830s. The first railroad in Indiana was completed in 1847. It ran from Madison to Indianapolis. Railroad building

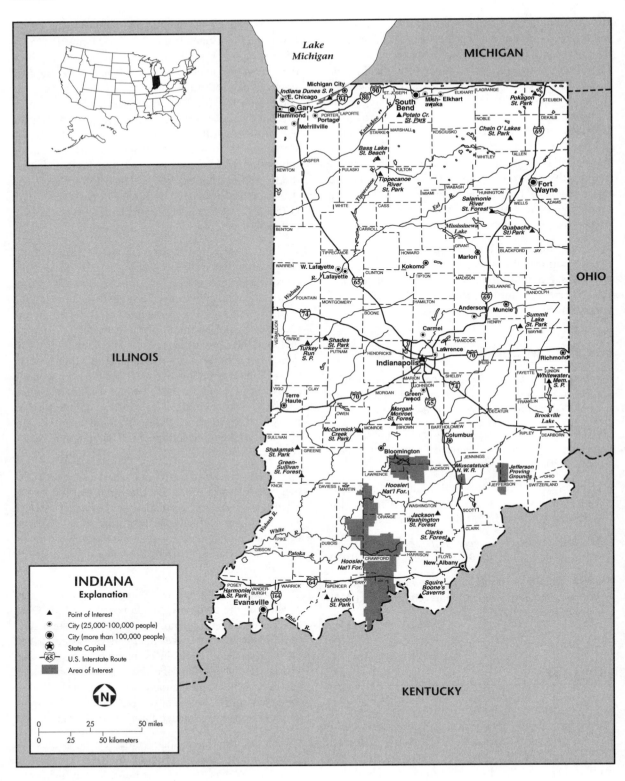

State of Indiana.

increased rapidly in the 1850s and continued to do so after the American Civil War (1861–1865).

Indiana was staunchly pro-Union during the Civil War. Primarily an agricultural economy when the war began, Indiana began to industrialize during the war. The industries included such enterprises as gristmills, sawmills, meat packing plants, breweries, furniture factories, and carriage makers. The Studebaker Company became well known for its wagon manufacture during the Civil War. The Van Camp Company was also important during the war for its canned pork and beans.

Industrialization and growth continued after the war. In 1867 the famous Eli Lilly drug company was established in Indianapolis. Glass factories proliferated in the 1880s in northeastern Indiana after the discovery of natural gas. New manufacturing towns like Terre Haute, Muncie, Fort Wayne, and South Bend began to grow. Steel manufacture became the lifeblood of Gary and an oil refining industry was centered in nearby Calumet. By the beginning of the twentieth century, Indiana had become a center for the developing automobile industry, with 375 manufacturers were turning out "horseless carriages." The popularity of cars in the state made possible the construction of a speedway at Indianapolis; the first Indianapolis 500 race was held in 1911.

Indiana industries were benefited by the onset of World War I (1914–1918). But things changed once the war was over. By 1920 the number of automobile manufacturers had declined to around a dozen. The only one to compete successfully with the "big three" automakers in Detroit was Studebaker. It grew to around 23,000 employees during World War II (1939–1945). Studebaker ceased manufacturing in 1965, but auto parts remained a large segment of Indiana's industrial base. By 1920 the urban population was beginning to outnumber the rural population.

World War II gave a strong boost to Indiana's economy. Most factories converted to production of war materials, and unemployment virtually disappeared in the state. DuPont and Goodyear built large powder plants near Charlestown. That virtually made the sleepy small town of just under 900 "explode" overnight. According to historian John Bartlow Martin, 45,000 were employed in the plants' operations and 15,000 managed to stay in Charlestown. Martin wrote: "The single liquor store reportedly earned more than one hundred thousand dollars net." The town was again virtually deserted after the war: "[T]housands of war workers hadn't even waited to be laid off; they just piled their mattresses, stepladders, and pots and pans onto their cars and put the kids in the back seat and went back across the river to the hills to stay."

The economy of Indiana remained strong even after wartime production ceased. The number of wage earners in Indiana nearly doubled between 1940 and 1950. Workers came in from other states. Labor unions grew despite Indiana's reputation as an anti-union state. National corporations like General Motors and Inland Steel were absorbing smaller companies. In 1984 General Motors was the state's largest employer, followed by Inland and U.S. Steel. The availability of natural resources such as coal, natural gas, and stone encouraged industrial development; good transportation networks also enabled industrial success. This was especially true in the northwestern part of the state.

The early 1980s were difficult economic times for Indiana. The state suffered a recession like many of the other "Rust Belt" states. In addition Indiana had been losing population since the 1960s as many workers migrated south. The state's economy began to improve as high-technology industries were brought in and the service sector expanded. That brought a net gain in population between 1990 and 1996. In 1995 Indiana's per capita income was over $21,000, ranked 28th in the nation. In 1997 there were six Fortune 500 companies with headquarters in Indiana. The state continued to rank among the top ten states in agricultural production, with cash receipts for all crops and livestock reaching $5 billion by 1995.

See also: **Northwest Ordinance, Rust Belt**

FURTHER READING

Barnhart, John D., and Donald F. Carmony. *Indiana from Frontier to Industrial Commonwealth,*. 4 vols. New York: Lewis Historical Publishing, 1954.

Latta, William C. *Outline History of Indiana Agriculture*. Lafayette, IN: Purdue University and Indiana County Agricultural Agents Association, 1938.

Martin, John Bartlow. *Indiana: An Interpretation*. New York: Knopf, 1947.

Starr, George W. *Industrial Development of Indiana*. Bloomington, IN: Indiana University Press, 1937.

Wilson, William E. *Indiana: A History*. Bloomington: Indiana University Press, 1966.

INDIGO

Indigo is a deep blue dye used to color cotton, wool, and other textiles. Today it is manufactured synthetically, but in earlier times it was derived from the indigo plant, a member of the legume family. The plant was chiefly grown in India (hence its name). In the Caribbean indigo was cultivated by European colonists. During the 1600s it was a principle item of export from the region. In the United States the indigo plant was cultivated in the low country of South Carolina and Georgia beginning in 1741. It was introduced by Elizabeth Lucas Pinckney (1722–93), the daughter of a plantation owner whose family later figured prominently in American politics. Pinckney had brought the plant with her from the Caribbean island of Antigua, where she had lived. Since indigo is a labor-intensive crop, plantations required numerous slaves to cultivate the plant. Growers sold indigo overseas to be used in the European dyestuffs industry. By the 1760s indigo had become an important crop for the southern plantation owners—its export value was on a par with rice and wheat. It continued to be grown in the region until the American Civil War (1861–65). Synthetic indigo was produced in 1880, and it was first used commercially in 1897. This launched a synthetic dye industry that completely eliminated the need for the dye to be derived from plants.

See also: **Plantations, Triangular Trade**

INDUSTRIAL POLICY

Industrial policy refers to organized government involvement in guiding the economy by encouraging investment in targeted industries. Such policy serves to allocate capital across manufacturing industries by a system of taxes, subsidies, and investment incentives designed to move the economy along a specific pathway. Although an industrial policy was in place since the 1950s in many developed countries including Japan, Germany, France, and Sweden, it continued to be hotly debated in the United States toward the end of the twentieth century.

Japan's successful industrial policy drew a great deal of attention. In Japan the Ministry of International Trade and Industry (MITI) orchestrated directed development of selected industries and products which it deemed necessary for Japan to compete in the international market. MITI only assisted the private sector in targeted industries. It generally financed no more than 50 percent of a project, leaving the rest to the private sector and market influences. The MITI is not autonomous but is overseen by various government agencies. Japan's automobile industry served as a highly successful model where a specific industry was targeted to assume an expanded role in world markets.

Advocates for an industrial policy in the United States pointed to four major issues. First, since the law of supply and demand in world markets is greatly skewed by various measures employed by nations to help particular industries, the U.S. needed to do likewise to compete. Second, an industrial policy could help ease the social costs when industries lost their competitive advantage by assisting in retraining workers for new jobs. Third, industrial policy could ease ''boom and bust'' cycles by planning tax incentives to stabilize regions. Finally, the United States already protected certain industries and special interest groups but in a haphazard manner with no organized social goals; an organized program was believed to be more effective.

Opponents cited the market as the most efficient allocation of resources, insisting the government could not do a better job. Interfering in the market process was generally less accepted in the United States than in other countries.

See also: **De-Industrialization**

INDUSTRIAL REVOLUTION

The advent of the Industrial Revolution towards the end of the nineteenth century raised numerous economic and political questions for the United States that neither the populace nor the government was prepared for. In the years following the American Civil War (1861–1865), the twin pillars of capitalism and industrialization catapulted the American economy to the forefront of world commerce. Oil, steel, rail, mining, and agricultural industries all enjoyed tremendous growth in the latter part of the nineteenth century as Americans exploited the riches of its natural resources, land, manufacturing technology, and a large labor pool from increased immigration. In cities across the United States, all of these elements came together to form the ingredients and the momentum behind the Industrial Revolution.

America's tremendous industrial and financial growth in the last decades of the nineteenth century were due in large part to the entrepreneurial boldness and business instincts of a number of industrial and financial tycoons who came to be known as the ''robber barons.'' J.P. Morgan, John D. Rockefeller, Cornelius Vanderbilt, Andrew Carnegie, James J. Hill, Jay Gould, and others guided their diverse business interests to unprecedented levels of profitability. The monopolies of the robber barons enabled them to eliminate less powerful competitors, raise prices, and subsequently realize huge profits that were pumped back into their businesses. The federal government gradually began to heed the voices of small business owners, who called for reform, and the cries of American workers, who had begun launching the country's first organized labor unions in the face of company-sponsored violence and public ridicule.

In 1890 the Sherman Anti-Trust Act was enacted in an effort to curb the power of the trusts, but the robber barons continued to maintain their privileged positions in the American system. Blessed with access to abundant natural resources, valuable technological advances, a growing labor force, and a congenial political environment, these men and the monopolies they held dominated the U.S. economy. So much so that, for a generation after the Civil War, political power of the presidency paled in comparison to the economic talent and power of the robber barons.

The railroad industry particularly transformed the business landscape of the United States. By the early 1850s several railroads had established lines that allowed them to transport freight back and forth between the Great Lakes region and the East Coast, and new railroad construction projects were generating across eastern America. This ever-growing network of rail lines, many of which spanned relatively short distances, came to be seen as a more timely, reliable, and inexpensive way to transport goods than other options previously available. The explosive growth of the railroad industry in the eastern states, coupled with the potential wealth contained in the country's western territories and the nation's accompanying desire to expand in that direction, convinced growing numbers of people that a transcontinental railroad stretching from coast to coast should be built. Begun in 1863, the effort was hampered by the Civil War and the daunting obstacles of western geography and weather, but on May 10, 1869, the rail lines of the Central Pacific and the Union Pacific railroads were finally joined in Utah. Celebrations of the epic achievement erupted across the nation as Americans hailed this giant step forward in the country's westward expansion.

Farmers benefited from increased mechanization, sophisticated transportation options, and scientific cultivation methods. Nonetheless, the financial situations of many farming families grew precarious in the 1880s and 1890s. Record crop yields resulted in lower prices while production costs increased, a combination that threw many farmers into debt. They responded by forming unions and alliances that insisted on populist reforms. Many of their themes, dismissed as outlandish when first expressed, later became cornerstones of progressive reform in the early 1900s.

The surging economic and technological growth of the United States caused tremendous changes in the character of American life during the last decades of the nineteenth century. The rural farming culture of previous generations gave way to an increasingly urban and industrial one, as manufacturing plants sprang up and cities mushroomed in size; the nation's urban population rose 400 percent between 1870 and 1910.

Still, for many Americans, city life was less an immediate experience than a distant and powerful lure. The attraction was powerful, for the drain on the countryside was particularly noticeable, especially in the Midwest and in the East. As the 1870s and 1880s witnessed the worst agricultural depression in the country's history, large numbers of farmers succumbed to the temptations of urban promises and packed their bags. Jobs, higher wages, and such technological wonders as electricity and the telephone gradually took its toll on rural defenses.

THE SURGING ECONOMIC AND TECHNOLOGICAL GROWTH OF THE UNITED STATES CAUSED TREMENDOUS CHANGES IN THE CHARACTER OF AMERICAN LIFE DURING THE LAST DECADES OF THE NINETEENTH CENTURY.

Joining these farmers were an increasing number of immigrants from eastern and southern Europe, who, like their American counterparts, came mostly from the countryside and knew very little of urban life. These "new" immigrants, as they were called—as opposed to the more established generation of largely Protestant immigrants from the western and northern European countries of Britain, Ireland, Germany, and Scandinavia—came largely from Italy, Austria, Hungary, Poland, Serbia, and Russia and were predominantly Catholic or Jewish. These "new" immigrants typically congregated in the urban centers of the East, particularly New York.

As Americans gradually came to favor urban over rural life, there was much about the Industrial Revolution that would justify the prejudices of the old rural ideals. Cities of the late nineteenth century grew without plan, with a minimum of control, and typically by the direction of industrial enterprise. Accordingly, American cities seemed to harbor all the afflictions that plague modern society: poverty, disease, crime, and decay. For members of the urban working class, life was often marked by hardship and uncertainty. Layoffs were common, and as much as 30 percent of the urban work force was out of work for some period during the year. Child labor was common as well, and in 1900 as many as three million of America's children were forced to work on a full-time basis to help support their families.

Living conditions in the cities were often deplorable, with thousands of families forced to reside in slums that were breeding grounds for typhoid, smallpox, cholera, tuberculosis, and other diseases that swept through the cities on a regular basis. City tenement housing quickly degenerated into slums that not only brought unsanitary living conditions, but also increased poverty, prostitution, and organized crime. In 1881 the homicide rate in America was 25 per million; in 1898, the rate had risen to 107 per million. Diseases such as cholera, typhoid fever, and diphtheria increasingly plagued cities and wreaked havoc on working-class populations. Several factors made many problems in American cities more pronounced. In the 1880s and 1890s the gulf between social classes was dramatically emphasized. The term ''Gilded Age,'' coined by Mark Twain, came into common use and indicated corruption, profiteering, and false glitter. In both Chicago and New York, elegant and lavish homes were often built on the same street or within view of the slums. A few blocks from New York's elite Fifth Avenue, the desolation of Shantytown, with its Irish paupers and roaming livestock, presented a sharp 60-block contrast. While a relatively high degree of residential mobility did exist, ethnic neighborhoods such as Little Italy, Polonia, and Greektown also served to highlight and define urban poverty.

The industrialization of the United States also produced a fundamental reorganization of public consumption. As the nation's manufacturing plants and farms produced greater quantities of goods and products, an increasingly consumer-oriented economy emerged. Products of convenience—such as processed and preserved foods, ready-made clothing, and telephones—appeared and were made available to a far greater number of consumers than ever before.

Leisure time activities blossomed as well. Revolutions in transportation, technology, and urbanization all fostered an environment favorable to the pursuit of recreational activities. Americans with money in their pockets and time on their hands looked to spend both on entertainment, and businessmen rushed to supply consumers in this newest lucrative economic niche. Organized sports, previously the territory of only the wealthiest American families, were embraced by all classes of spectators and participants. Circuses, vaudeville shows, theatrical dramas, and musical comedies attracted tens of thousands of citizens, too. As one commentator on the times noted, ''while telephones, typewriters, cash registers, and adding machines sped

and made routine the conduct of business, cameras, phonographs, bicycles, moving pictures, amusement parks, and professional sports defined the mass popular culture that still dominates our times.''

See also: **Child Labor, Immigration, Industrialization, Monopoly, Robber Barons, Sherman Anti-Trust Act, Slums, Tenements, Urbanization**

FURTHER READING

Bruchey, Stuart. *Enterprise: The Dynamic Economy of a Free People*. Cambridge, MA: Harvard University Press, 1990.

Cochran, Thomas. *Frontiers of Change: Early Industrialism in America*. New York: Oxford University Press, 1981.

North, Douglas. *The Economic Growth of the United States, 1790–1860*. Englewood Cliffs, NJ: Prentice-Hall, 1961.

Sellers, Charles. *The Market Revolution: Jacksonian America, 1815–1846*. New York: Oxford University Press, 1991.

Taylor, George Rogers. *The Transportation Revolution, 1815–1860*. New York: Holt, Rinehart, and Winston, 1951.

INDUSTRIAL WORKERS OF THE WORLD (IWW)

Founded in 1905 by the leaders of 43 labor organizations, the Industrial Workers of the World (IWW) was a radical labor union. The IWW pursued short-term goals via strikes and acts of sabotage and a long-term agenda to overthrow capitalism and rebuild society based on socialist principles. One IWW organizer proclaimed that the ''final aim is revolution.'' Though small in numbers because of their extremist views and tactics (its membership probably never exceeded 100,000), the IWW members, called ''Wobblies,'' attracted national attention. Railroad labor organizer and socialist Eugene Debs (1855–1926) endorsed the organization's anti-capitalist agenda and became one of its leaders.

Unlike the American Federation of Labor (AFL), the IWW organized skilled and unskilled workers by industry rather than by craft. Founded and led by miner and Socialist William ''Big Bill'' Haywood (1869–1928) and mineworkers agitator Mary ''Mother'' Jones (1830–1930), the IWW aimed to unite all workers in a camp, mine, or factory for eventual takeover of their employer's industrial facility. The union organized strikes in lumber and mining camps in the West, in the steel mills of Pennsylvania (1907), and in the textile mills of New England (1912). The leadership advocated the use of violence to achieve its revolutionary goals and opposed mediation (negotiations moderated by a neutral third party), collective bargaining (when worker representatives bargain with an employer), and arbitration (when a third party resolves a dispute). The group declined during World War I (1914–18), when the IWW led strikes that were suppressed by the federal government. The organization's leaders were all arrested and the organization dissolved. Haywood was convicted of sedition (inciting resistance to lawful authority), but managed to escape the country. He died in the Soviet Union.

See also: **American Federation of Labor (AFL), Knights of Labor, Textiles**

INDUSTRIALIZATION

In the years following the American Civil War (1861–1865), the twin pillars of capitalism and industrialization catapulted the American economy to the forefront of world commerce. Oil, steel, rail, mining, and agricultural industries all enjoyed tremendous growth in the latter part of the nineteenth century as Americans harvested the riches of its natural resources, land, manufacturing technology, and a large labor pool from increased immigration.

America's tremendous industrial and financial growth in the last decades of the nineteenth century was due in large part to the entrepreneurial boldness and business instincts of a number of industrial and financial tycoons who came to be known as the ''Robber Barons.'' J. P. Morgan (1837–1913), John D. Rockefeller (1839–1937), Cornelius Vanderbilt (1794–1877), Andrew Carnegie (1835–1919), James J. Hill (1838–1916), Jay Gould (1836–1893), and others guided their diverse business interests to unprecedented levels of profitability. The monopolies of the Robber Barons enabled them to eliminate less powerful competitors, raise prices, and subsequently realize huge profits that were pumped back into their businesses. But the federal government gradually began to heed the voices of small business owners who called for reform and the cries of American workers who had begun launching the country's first organized labor unions in the face of company-sponsored violence. In 1890 the Sherman Anti–Trust Act was enacted in an effort to curb the power of the trusts. But the Robber Barons continued to maintain their dominant positions in the American system. Blessed with access to abundant natural resources, valuable technological advances, a growing labor force, and a congenial political environment, these men and the monopolies that they held dominated the American economy. For a generation after the Civil War, the political power of the presidency paled in comparison to the economic power of the Robber Barons.

The railroad industry especially transformed the business landscape of America. By the early 1850s several railroads had established lines that allowed them to transport freight between the Great Lakes region and the East Coast, and new railroad construction projects proliferated across eastern America. This ever-growing network of rail lines, many of which spanned relatively short distances, came to be seen as a more timely, reliable, and inexpensive way to transport goods, compared to other options. The explosive growth of the railroad industry in the eastern states, coupled with the potential wealth contained in the country's western territories and the country's attendant desire to expand in that direction, convinced growing numbers of people that a transcontinental railroad stretching from coast to coast should be built. Begun in 1863, the effort was hampered by the Civil War and the daunting obstacles of western geography and weather. But on May 10, 1869, the rail lines of the Central Pacific and the Union Pacific were finally joined in Utah. Celebrations of the epic achievement erupted across the nation as Americans hailed this giant step forward in the country's westward expansion.

Farmers benefited from increased mechanization, sophisticated transportation options, and scientific cultivation methods. Nonetheless, the financial situations of many farming families grew precarious in the 1880s and 1890s. Record crop yields resulted in lower prices while production costs increased, a combination that threw many farmers into debt. They responded by forming farmers' alliances that insisted on populist reforms. Many of their reform themes, such as the institution of referendum, recall, and petition, and the direct election of senators were dismissed as outlandish when first articulated, later became cornerstones of progressive reform in the early 1900s.

The surging economic and technological growth of the United States engendered tremendous changes in the character of American life in the last decades of the nineteenth century. The rural agrarian culture of previous generations gave way to an increasingly urban and industrial one as manufacturing plants proliferated and cities mushroomed in size. The nation's urban population rose 400 percent between 1870 and 1910.

Still, for many Americans city life was less an immediate experience than a distant and powerful lure. Yet the attraction was powerful, for the population drain from the countryside was particularly noticeable, especially in the Midwest and East. As the 1870s and 1880s witnessed the worst agricultural depression in the country's history, large numbers of farmers moved to the city. Jobs, higher wages, and such technological wonders as electricity and the telephone gradually drew many failing farmers to the cities.

Joining these erstwhile farmers in the cities were an increasing number of immigrants from eastern and southern Europe, who, like their American counterparts, came mostly from the countryside and knew very little of urban life. These "new" immigrants—in comparison to the more established generation of largely Protestant "old" immigrants from the western and northern European countries of Britain, Ireland, Germany, and Scandinavia—were Italians, Austrians, Hungarians, Poles, Serbs, and Russians, mostly Catholic or Jewish. As the African American emigration out of the South to northern and midwestern cities, the "new" immigrants typically congregated in the urban centers of the East, particularly New York.

As Americans moved to the cities, they were not necessarily happy with the change. Cities of the late nineteenth century grew without planning, with a minimum of control, and typically by the dictates of industrial enterprise. U.S. cities seemed to harbor all the afflictions that plague modern society: poverty, disease, crime, and decay. For members of the urban working class, hardship and uncertainty often marked their lives. Layoffs were common, and as much as thirty percent of the urban work force was out of work for some period of the year. Even steady work brought frequently brought exhaustion. "Scientific Management," a phrase coined by Frederick Winslow Taylor, invaded the workplace and the disciples of efficiency used stop-watches to "time" the performance of a job in order to figure out how to get more productivity out of the workforce. Child labor was common as well, and in 1900 as many as three million of U.S. children were forced to work on a full-time basis to help support their families. Living conditions in the cities were often deplorable, with thousands of families forced to reside in slums that were breeding grounds for typhoid, smallpox, cholera, tuberculosis, and other diseases that swept through the cities on a regular basis. City tenement housing quickly degenerated into slums that not only bred vermin and rotten odors, but also brought poverty, prostitution, and organized crime. In 1881 the homicide rate in America was 25 per million; in 1898, the rate had risen to 107 per million. Diseases such as cholera, typhoid fever, and diphtheria increasingly plagued cities and wreaked havoc on the working-class population.

Several factors exacerbated the problems in American cities. In the 1880s and 1890s the gulf between social classes was dramatically widened. The term "Gilded Age," coined by Mark Twain, came into common use and indicated corruption, profiteering, and false glitter. In both Chicago and New York, elegant and lavish homes were often built on the same street or within view of the slums. A few blocks from New York's elite Fifth Avenue, the desolation of Shantytown with its Irish paupers and roaming livestock posed a sharp sixty-block contrast. While a relatively high degree of residential mobility did exist, ethnic neighborhoods like Little Italy, Poletown, and Greektown also served to highlight and define urban poverty.

In addition, the industrialization of the United States produced a fundamental reorientation of consumption. As the nation's manufacturing plants and farms produced even greater quantities of goods and products, an increasingly consumer–oriented economy emerged. Products of convenience—such as processed and preserved foods, ready-made clothing, and telephones—appeared and were made available to a far greater number of consumers than ever before.

Leisure time activities blossomed as well. Revolutions in transportation, technology, and urbanization all fostered an environment conducive to the pursuit of recreational activities. Americans with money in their pockets and time on their hands looked to spend both on entertainment, and businessmen rushed in to supply consumers in this newest of lucrative economic niches. Organized sports, previously the province of the wealthiest American families, were embraced by all classes as spectators and participants. Circuses, vaudeville shows, theatrical dramas, and musical comedies attracted tens of thousands of citizens.

See also: **Child Labor, City Planning, Immigration, Frederick Winslow Taylor**

FURTHER READING

Bruchey, Stuart. *Enterprise: The Dynamic Economy of a Free People.* Cambridge: Harvard University Press, 1990.

Cochran, Thomas. *Frontiers of Change: Early Industrialism in America.* New York: Oxford University Press, 1981.

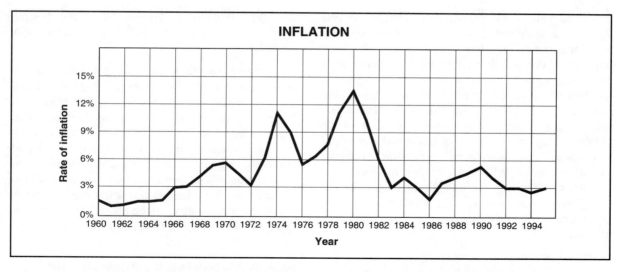

INFLATION

Graphing inflation, which is an economy-wide rise in prices that continue over time. Shown here, rates over a 35-year span, with a low rate of about two percent in 1960 and a high of about 13 percent in 1980.

North, Douglas. *The Economic Growth of the United States, 1790–1860.* Englewood Cliffs, New Jersey: Prentice-Hall, 1961.

Sellers, Charles. *The Market Revolution: Jacksonian America, 1815–1846.* New York: Oxford University Press, 1991.

Taylor, George Rogers. *The Transportation Revolution, 1815–1860.* New York: Holt, Rinehart, and Winston, 1951.

INFLATION

Inflation is a continuous rise in the price of goods and services. It is important to note that a rise in the price of just one or two items does not constitute inflation; nor does a one-time rise in all prices mark an inflationary period. To count as inflation, the price increases must be general throughout the economy and must continue over time. The hallmark of inflation is that money buys less than it once did. A cup of coffee that may have cost a dime at mid-twentieth century may cost a dollar some 50 years later.

Rising prices have been observed in most Western industrialized nations since the end of World War II (1939–1945). Economists, however, debate at which point inflation begins to pose a threat to society. If prices rise steeply and quickly enough, say, in the range of five to ten percent a year, inflation can undermine a nation's economic well being. The value of savings decreases, since the money saved will buy less and less over time. Senior citizens and others living on fixed incomes see their buying power erode.

Inflation also means business owners must pay a steadily rising price for labor and raw materials, which cuts into profits. Eventually, rising prices can choke off economic growth, and lead to a recession.

The government can fight inflation by restricting demand for goods and services, usually by raising interest rates or imposing new taxes. Such measures tend to lead to higher unemployment, which dampens demands for goods and services and, in turn, brings down prices. Economists debate whether the cost of fighting inflation, e.g., higher unemployment and less growth, is worth the pain. Certainly a moderate amount of inflationary price increases, in the range of one to two percent per year, is viewed by many economists as not worth worrying about.

Inflation is measured by the government's cost of living index. The opposite of inflation is deflation, a steady decline in the level of prices over time.

See also: **Cost of Living Index, Deflation**

INFORMATION SUPERHIGHWAY

As highways made out of concrete help people to physically transport themselves and their goods from one place to another, the Information Superhighway, (made out of telephones, computers, satellites, and other communication devices), helps people and businesses remain in contact with one another. The Information Superhighway is a phrase that describes the expansion of digital telecommunications, involving more and more people: locally, nationally, and globally. This superhighway, whether it involves making a cellular phone call to a friend, or e-mailing a business to order a product, is leading us in a direction of increasingly easier communication without regard for borders. The development of new methods, such as the Internet, to share information has triggered a revolution in global telecommunications. It began in the 1950s and continued to make dramatic and high-speed changes in the ways we communicate throughout the twentieth century. With each evolution in telecommunications technology, the Information Superhighway has grown in size, improving the connections between individuals and businesses next door and around the world.

See also: **Internet**

INFRASTRUCTURE

Infrastructure refers to the network of roads, bridges, railroad lines, water and sewage pipes, the electrical power grid, and all the other physical structures needed for the functioning of a modern industrial economy. Although some new roads and other projects are built each year, the crucial need of infrastructure in already industrialized countries is to repair and maintain what is already there. Governments at all levels, including federal, state, county, and local, must budget funds each year to maintain their infrastructure. Failing to do so means risking the deterioration of roads, bridges, and other structures essential to the orderly working of society. The existing infrastructure in the United States has been built up over many decades, and represents an investment by society that probably runs into trillions of dollars. Economists also sometimes use the word infrastructure to refer to the financial institutions that are needed in a modern economy, such as banks, stock and bond exchanges, and the like.

INITIAL PUBLIC OFFERING (IPO)

In order to raise capital, corporations offer their securities for sale to the general public. An initial public offering (IPO) is the first instance in which a corporation offers a specific, registered security for sale. An IPO of common stock converts a business owned by one person or several persons into a business owned by many. This practice provides an immediate injection of cash which can be used to increase the

company's prospects of growth and expand its equity base, increasing the possibility of stock value appreciation.

Corporations must go through the red tape of registration with the Securities and Exchange Commission (SEC), which sets standards and regulations for the investment market, before any offering can be made. In this process a corporation must reveal extensive information about its inner workings, develop an initial offering prospectus (a detailed brochure about the corporation's performance, management, and plan of use for the funds raised), and determine the price at which the new security will be offered on the market. Once the SEC has given its approval, the initial public offering may go forward.

See also: **Appreciation, Equity, Securities and Exchange Commission, Stock**

INTEREST

Interest is typically expressed as a quarterly or annual rate of percentage charged or earned on a sum of money. For example, if an individual borrows $2000 from a bank or lending institution and that institution charges an annual rate of six percent interest on the loan, the individual will pay the lender up to $60 a year for the use of the money. Paid interest is usually incorporated in monthly installments submitted by money borrowers in a scheduled repayment plan. The process is similar for interest earned. A bank may offer an annual earned interest rate of three percent to investors with a savings account. An individual with $100 in a savings account at that bank will earn $6 a year in interest.

Interest rates play an important role in lending and investment decisions. Money borrowers will look for the lowest interest rate they can find for their loan, whereas investors will look for the highest interest rate to better the return on their investments. In the economy the interest rate is often affected by factors such as a country's stage of development, productivity, and investment needs, among others. Internationally, fluctuating interest rates can cause flows of capital between financial institutions and different countries. For instance, if domestic interest rates are low in the United States and higher in Asia, investment capital will flow out of the United States and into Asia so that investors can take advantage of the higher interest rates on their investment moneys.

See also: **Capital Gain, Debt**

INTERNATIONAL BUSINESS MACHINES CORPORATION (IBM)

Around the year 1911 Charles Ranlett Flint (1850–1934) founded the Calculating-Tabulating-Recording (CTR) company. He merged two companies he had previously managed, International Time Recording Company and Computing Scale Company of America, with an unrelated firm called Tabulating Machine Company. A man named Herman Hollerith (1860–1929) had founded the Tabulating Machine Company. Hollerith was an engineer who invented a tabulator to punch, sort, and count cards. This merger was the beginning of IBM. It would eventually become the world's largest computer company.

The tabulator served the needs of the U.S. Census Bureau in the 1890 and 1900 censuses. It was used for processing large amounts of data. Other organizations with similar needs adopted the machine for their own use. In the early twentieth century society was becoming more urban and commercialized. Consequently the ability to process financial and other data became an important factor in running a profitable business.

CTR did not become focused on the tabulator as its primary product until John Watson (1874–1956) was hired as the company's general manager in 1914. Watson had worked at National Cash Register (NCR) for about 20 years. Although he rose to become the company's general sales manager, he was under a cloud when he came to CTR. He had been convicted along with his boss, John Patterson, of violating the Sherman Antitrust Act on behalf of NCR. When the government dropped its case against NCR in 1915, Watson was made president of CTR.

Watson understood that CTR's future lay in its tabulating division. The tabulator was a basic office tool that would be in ever-increasing demand as the number of office workers grew. He quickly established a well disciplined sales force. He hired many former NCR salespeople. They were courteous, well-dressed, and trained in selling a service, not just a product.

The nation's economy boomed in the 1920s. In 1924 CTR became IBM. By the end of the decade it was a dominant leader in providing large tabulating systems for public and private customers. The company was very profitable in the 1920s and 1930s. It operated in the less competitive business segment of large custom–designed systems. IBM's practice of leasing rather than selling its machines increased its profits. Its cross–licensing agreements with its chief competitor, Remington Rand, kept the two companies from antagonizing each other.

IBM also required its customers to use IBM cards for its tabulating machines. There were literally millions of such cards already in use. IBM was selling nearly 85 percent of all keypunch, tabulating, and accounting equipment in the United States. The company's growth remained unchecked despite a 1936 U.S. Supreme Court ruling that ordered IBM to lift its restriction that customers use only IBM cards.

Demand for IBM's products increased when President Franklin Roosevelt's administration (1933–45) inaugurated the New Deal during the mid–1930s. The newly created federal bureaucracy needed IBM's calculating machines. The newly formed Social Security Administration placed an order for more than four hundred accounting machines and 1,200 keypunchers. IBM had successfully carved out a market niche that addressed the need of large–scale organizations that required machines capable of massive amounts of calculations.

World War II (1939–1945) saw IBM's sales more than triple. They reached $141.7 million by the end of the war. Demand was high in both governmental and private sectors. The company's machines were used to monitor the manufacture and movement of numerous products used in the war effort. The military had a need for high–speed calculators. This resulted in IBM creating the Mark I, a machine that is considered by many to be the world's first computer. It used IBM punch cards for large calculations. It also retained a set of rules to apply to future input. Practically, it was the first calculator with memory. The Mark I had 765,000 parts and 500 miles of wire, yet it was still less powerful than the kind of hand–held calculators which were common in the latter half of the twentieth century.

IBM was involved in other computer–related projects during World War II and after. But in 1951 its old rival Remington Rand took the lead by marketing the UNIVAC. IBM remained cautious about entering the computer market. At the time IBN punch cards were used even by electronic computers and the company still controlled 85 percent of their market.

In 1952 Thomas Watson, Jr. (1914–1993), succeeded his father as president of IBM. The new president led IBM into the computer market; IBM's first business computer, the 701, was introduced in 1951. As IBM marketed new models its customers began switching from IBM tabulating equipment to IBM computers.

IBM also began to expand internationally. In 1949 it established a new subsidiary for international sales, IBM World Trade Corporation. Thomas Watson's younger brother, Dick Watson, headed the subsidiary. While World Trade had sales of only $6.3 million in 1949, it operated in 58 countries, giving the company a base for future expansion. In many countries IBM set up local subsidiaries to sell IBM products and conduct further research and development. As those countries adopted computers IBM was able to achieve dominance on those markets. Only Japan and the United Kingdom produced local competitors for IBM. This left IBM with a 33 percent market share in those two nations. World Trade eventually surpassed the domestic IBM in sales.

Computers began developing more rapidly in the late 1950s. In 1958 Sperry Rand and Control Data Corporation (CDC) introduced the second generation of computers. The new machines featured transistors instead of vacuum tubes. Then a third generation of machines using integrated circuitry was quickly introduced. IBM responded with a large capital–spending program. Six new plants were built and thousands of workers were hired. In 1965 IBM introduced its 360 line of small, fast computers with their own exclusive software. The 360s were immediately successful and resulted in IBM's dominance over the computer market for more than a decade. From 1965 to 1975 IBM sold 65 percent of all U.S. computers.

IBM's competitors challenged the company by specializing in different niches of the computer market. When the first microcomputers were introduced in 1960 IBM chose not to enter the market. IBM did not enter the personal computer market until 1980. By that time it was unable to achieve the dominance it had with its mainframes and minicomputers. Nonetheless sales of the 360 line and the subsequent 370 line continued to grow. In 1984 IBM achieved peak earnings of $6.6 billion on sales of $46 billion.

During the 1980s IBM was held up as a model of business excellence. But by the end of the decade the company needed an overhaul. Revenues and earnings were weak, and the company's stock price was in decline. Its worldwide market share had fallen from 36 percent to 23 percent. IBM could no longer keep its dominant position in the fast–changing world of computers simply by building bigger and faster machines. The corporation had to find other ways to compete.

IBM's turnaround began in 1993 when Louis Gerstner, former chair of RJR Holdings Corporation, took over as Chief Executive Officer (CEO). The measures he took to revive the company included de–emphasizing research and development, refocusing on services and systems, and cutting the work force. He also revived the company's faltering mainframe business.

IBM also embarked on a more aggressive acquisitions program. In 1995 it acquired the software company, Lotus, for $3.5 billion. Other software firms were bought. IBM also invested $1.2 billion in Prodigy with Sears, Roebuck, and Company before selling it at a loss to the company's management and other investors.

With computer networking becoming more predominant in the business world IBM began to make all of its products network-ready. Corporate use of the Internet also became more widespread. IBM sought to provide products for corporate intranets and new Web technologies. In 1997 it introduced a new line of lower–cost mainframe computers that promised the same speed as traditional mainframes. In 1998 it introduced a new line of so–called "e–business tools." These included servers, work stations, PCs, and notebooks. They were meant to facilitate business transactions over the Internet.

"Deep computing" was another area of emerging growth for IBM. It linked high–speed computers with analytical software. The U.S. Department of Energy and the National Aeronautical and Space Administration (NASA) were two major customers for this type of supercomputer.

As the 1990s drew to a close IBM was in a much stronger position. Despite it's poor market position in the computing industry at the beginning of the decade, IBM was being held up once again as a model of business excellence.

See also: **Computer Industry, Herman Hollerith, Microsoft**

FURTHER READING

Fisher, Franklin M. et al. *IBM and the U.S. Data Processing Industry: An Economic History.* New York: Praeger, 1983.

"IBM History," available from the World Wide Web @ www.ibm.com/ibm/history/.

Pugh, Emerson W. *Building IBM: Shaping an Industry and Its Technology.* Cambridge, MA: MIT Press, 1995.

Simmons, William W., and Richard B. Elsberry. *Inside IBM: The Watson Years, a Personal Memoir.* Bryn Mawyr, PA: Dorrance, 1988.

Watson, Thomas J., Jr., and Peter Petre. *Father, Son & Co: My Life at IBM and Beyond.* New York: Bantam Books, 1990.

INTERNATIONAL MONETARY FUND (IMF)

The International Monetary Fund (IMF) was a group of 182 countries that joined together to create a cooperative, stable system for buying and selling each others' currencies; monitoring the global flow of money; and fostering international trade and economic growth. To join the IMF, a country had to agree to contribute an amount of money (based on its economic size) to a general pool of funds. The IMF used this pool of money to make loans to member countries that fell behind in their financial obligations with other IMF countries, or that wanted to restructure their economies. Because it had the world's largest economy, the United States contributed the largest amount ($35 billion in 1998) to the IMF and therefore had the largest vote in how the IMF used its funds. The IMF had no power to enforce how its members spent the money loaned to them, but it could threaten to withhold future loans if a member country failed to live up to its obligations.

The IMF was formed in 1944 as the Allied countries began to write the rules that would govern the economic relationships between the nations after World War II (1939–1945). During the Great Depression (1929–1939) the sudden collapse in economic confidence around the world led many consumers to try to trade in their paper currency for gold. But many countries did not have enough gold on hand to meet this demand and were forced to break the longstanding connection between their currencies and their gold reserves. With some countries hoarding gold and others letting their currencies ''float'' unattached to gold, it was hard to determine how much one country's currency was worth compared to another's, and international trade suffered. The IMF rectified this situation by requiring that all member countries permit their currencies to be converted freely into other members' currencies, by establishing a definite value for each currency relative to others, and by eliminating policies that discouraged global investment and trade. The value of all world currencies was fixed in terms of the U.S. dollar, with $35 equaling one ounce of gold.

In 1971 President Richard M. Nixon (1969–1974) ended this system of defining the value of the dollar against gold, and the values of world currencies have since been defined more loosely. As a result the IMF maintained much closer supervision of its members' economic policies so exchange rates—the value of one currency relative to another—didn't fluctuate wildly. Although the IMF's main functions were to coordinate the economic policies of its members and to provide technical assistance, training, and consultation, it has been mostly known for the massive loans it made to its members. In 1995 for example, the IMF extended credits of $18 billion to Mexico and $6.2 billion to Russia to help them survive economic crises.

See also: **Currency, Exchange Rates, Mexican Bail-Out**

INTERNET

The Internet is an international system of interconnected computer networks of government, educational, nonprofit organization, and corporate computers. The computers and networks are connected to each other by high-speed data communications lines, and even dissimilar computers are able to exchange data with each other using a set of data communications protocols called TCP/IP (Transmission Control Protocol/Internet Protocol). TCP/IP supports Simple Mail Transfer Protocol (SMTP) to permit the sending of electronic mail (E-mail) messages, File transfer protocol (FTP) for moving files between computers, and telnet which makes it possible to log in and interact with a remote computer. TCP controls the transmission of data between computers, and IP controls the automatic routing of the data over what might be a chain of computers.

The Internet's structure is based on a predecessor network called ARPAnet, which was established by the U.S. Department of Defense's Advanced Research Project Agency (ARPA) in 1969 as an experiment to determine how to build a network that could withstand partial outages, such as from an enemy attack. Each computer on the network communicates with others as a peer instead of having one or a few central hub computers, which would be too vulnerable. In the late 1980s ARPAnet was replaced by NSFNET, run by the National Science Foundation, which expanded the network, replaced its telephone lines with faster ones, and funded more college and university connections to the network. Thus, educational institutions became the dominant users in the 1980s. Other organizations and corporations joined by linking their computers, local

This girl's computer is accessing the Internet, which is an interconnected international network linking together computers via high speed data communication lines.

area networks (LANs), and wide area networks (WANs) to the Internet and adopting TCP/IP to connect their computers. As a result, the Internet comprises some networks that are publicly funded and some of which are private and which charge network access fees. Consequently, different users pay different fees, or none at all, for the same services. In the 1990s corporations and consumers became the biggest users of the Internet.

See also: **Computer Industry**

INTERNET AND THE ECONOMY (ISSUE)

The Internet, an electronic form of communication that uses a computer, a modem, and a phone line, was developed in the mid-twentieth century. First established as a communications board for academics in the late 1960s, the Internet grew from a phenomenon found mainly in the halls of academia and government

to a worldwide source of information, "chat," and commerce. It has spawned the Information Superhighway, which allows for instant communication everywhere. It created a new arena for advertisements and opened a new avenue of commerce—E-commerce.

Twenty years after its development, the Internet grew from a small hobby of academics and government workers to a worldwide community of millions of Web users. Though industries were initially wary of using the Internet to promote their business to consumers, the continued growth of the World Wide Web and the temptation of reaching millions of users were undeniable. In the late 1990s it was estimated that the Internet doubled in size every three months. Though it grew worldwide, much of this increase was in the United States, where over half of the Internet's nearly seven million host computers were located.

As the Internet grew, service companies sprung up to offer online services (connections to the Internet) to users, encouraging the even further expansion. Companies like CompuServe, America On-Line, Netcom, and Prodigy took early advantage of the new market. By the mid-1990s the Internet had become an economic and social force. In the fall of 1995 the initial public offering of an Internet service company called Netscape Communications on the New York Stock Exchange created huge publicity. The stock opened for trade at around $14 per share, and the company's young founders soon found themselves millionaires. By July 1999, Netscape stock was trading at $97.63 per share.

Online service companies were not the only ones to profit from the Internet. By the end of the twentieth century, the United States was home to more businesses online than any other part of the world. It was also home to the highest number of computer owners, the most access nodes, and the lowest telecommunication rates. The Internet, however, was still a work in progress at the end of the twentieth century. Computer crashes, connectivity interruptions, slow transfers and downloads, and out-of-date or finding inaccurate information were common user experiences. But these problems did not slow the Internet's popularity or its development. Computer industry pioneers like Bill Gates have envisioned the Internet as a source for most avenues of communication, connecting computers, telephones, television, and radio.

One vision of the Internet—as a new market for business—was clearly being realized in the 1990s with the development of E-commerce. Businesses can post their advertisements online in hopes of wooing consumers to their products. By the click of a mouse on an online advertisement, a user can be taken to a business's website, see an image of the promoted product, read about its benefits, and often have the option to purchase that item online. The Internet is a forum in which small companies may be able to better compete in the global marketplace. It also removes many barriers of communication between customers and businesses, such as geography and time zones.

AVAILABLE 24 HOURS A DAY, SEVEN DAYS A WEEK, THE INTERNET PROVIDES A NON-STOP FORUM FOR BUYERS AND SELLERS TO INTERACT.

E-commerce has grown notably in the 1990s. Online companies such as Amazon.com have experienced large growth and surging popularity with users. Amazon.com provides the curious with book and music reviews, customer opinions, soundbites of song tracks, discounted prices, and ease of purchase. An online shopper at Amazon.com can read many opinions about a book or CD before deciding to purchase, add an item to his or her electronic shopping cart, and head to the never-a-line check-out (payment by credit or check only) all without the hassle of crowded malls or overeager salesmen. The benefits for a purely online company such as Amazon.com come in the low overhead costs of operation and the many consumers it can reach through its general reputation and extensive advertising network.

Books and music and online services are not the only areas of business to benefit from the Internet. Consumers can buy just about anything on the Internet, from food and clothing to cars and airline tickets. Looking for a new apartment? Go to apartments.com. A new job? Try careerpath.com. The options are endless for the diligent online consumer. The variety of choice and the ease with which consumers can communicate with one another present a challenge to businesses. While the Internet allows companies to talk directly with their customers without the aid of distribution channels and mass advertising or the mediation of the press, it also allows outsiders to more easily reach one another and talk about companies amongst themselves, without going through the same intermediaries. Received poor service from an online company? Post your complaint in chat rooms and on posting boards across the World Wide Web. Bad publicity from the average consumer has become more a threat for businesses due to the easy communication inspired by the Internet. Companies have less control over their public image. Anything and everything about a business can be known—and found out—on the Internet. While this may benefit consumers, it is a double-edged sword for companies.

Though E-commerce grew rapidly in the second half of the twentieth century, its actual successes have been questioned. Some economists claim E-commerce may diminish a company's profits. The Internet drops the cost per transaction, so it becomes practical to auction an item for dollars rather than thousands of dollars and still make money. A mass merchandiser like Internet Shopping Network, for example, can program its computers to accept the 3,000 best bids over $2.10 for 3,000 pieces of costume jewelry, rather than accept one set price for the jewelry, which would be common practice in a shop. In addition, as consumers use search engines to scour the web for the cheapest prices and the latest offers, rival competitors are only a mouse click away. The advantages of being the most well known company or the biggest advertiser are mitigated on the more level playing field of the Internet.

Available 24 hours a day, seven days a week, the Internet provides a non-stop forum for buyers and sellers to interact. The opportunities for profit, loss, problems, and rewards may be staggering and unpredictable, but E-commerce is clearly paving the way to a new economic road. Buy. Sell. Complain. Compliment. Do it all at your convenience on the Internet.

See also: **Computer Industry, Information Superhighway, Internet**

FURTHER READING

Manes, Stephen and Paul Andrews. *Gates*. New York: Doubleday, 1993.

Slater, Robert. *Portraits in Silicon*. Cambridge, MA: MIT Press, 1987.

Sussman, Vic. "Gold in Cyberspace." *U.S. News and World Report*, November 13, 1995.

Wallace, James and Jim Erickson. *Hard Drive*. New York: Wiley, 1992.

INTERSTATE COMMERCE COMMISSION ACT

The Interstate Commerce Commission (ICC), established by act of Congress in 1887, is responsible for regulating the rates and services of specified carriers that transport freight (goods, whether raw or finished) and passengers between states. ICC jurisdiction, expanded by subsequent acts of Congress, includes trucking, bus services, water carriers, expedited delivery services, and even oil pipelines. The regulatory agency, the nation's first such body, was borne of necessity during the late 1800s, when farmers and others charged the railroads with discriminatory freight practices.

With rail lines crisscrossing the nation, the question of who would control rates and monitor practices had become crucial. Many states, particularly in the Midwest, had set up regulatory boards but because the rail companies operated between states, enforcing state laws on them proved cumbersome and impractical. Meanwhile the railroads, operating without oversight by any effective regulatory body, set their own standards and practices, which resulted in many abuses.

In a U.S. Supreme Court ruling in 1877, in the case of *Munn v. Illinois*, the authority of the state boards to regulate the railroads was upheld. But less than a decade later, in the case of *Wabash, St. Louis and Pacific Railway Company v. Illinois*, the high court invalidated its earlier decision and proclaimed that only the U.S. Congress has the right to regulate interstate commerce. In issuing their decision the Court cited Section 8, Article 1 of the U.S. Constitution (1790), which states that "Congress shall have the power . . . to regulate commerce with foreign nations, and among the several states, and with the Indian tribes."

The Interstate Commerce Act was passed in 1887, creating the Interstate Commerce Commission to regulate the interstate railroads. The agency's purview was later expanded to include all ground and water carriers that operate on an interstate basis. In addition to controlling rates, the agency also enforced laws against discrimination. The ICC's authority was strengthened by congressional legislation including the Hepburn Act (1906) and the Mann-Elkins Act (1910).

See also: **Hepburn Act, Interstate Commerce: Regulation and Deregulation, Mann-Elkins Act, Munn v. Illinois, Wabash Case**

INTERSTATE COMMERCE: REGULATION AND DEREGULATION

In many ways the methods of transportation in the United States in the early nineteenth century would have been familiar to the medieval European. Overland transport was still largely by foot and four-legged beasts over poorly maintained roads. Mass amounts of freight could not be moved efficiently over very long

distances. But by the mid-1800s growth of a national railway system began to profoundly alter the country forever.

Although a few horse-powered railroads began operating in the United States in the early 1800s, steam-powered locomotives were not used until the 1830s. By the 1850s railroads were under construction in all states east of the Mississippi (many for only short distances), with most activity in the Northeast. Expansion of the rail network continued, peaking in the 1880s.

With rail lines crisscrossing the nation, the question of who would control rates and monitor practices had become crucial. Meanwhile the railroads, operating without oversight by any effective regulatory body, set their own standards and practices, which resulted in many abuses.

From the start, railroads were capital-intensive and demanded high-cost maintenance regardless of the fluctuations in the amount of business. The large amounts of money needed created the conditions for consolidation and merger, or at least for coordination of markets and services offered. This need for greater organization stemmed from railroads' increasing dependence on higher volumes of business to spread these fixed costs over as much traffic as possible. In addition, railroads often attempted to form cooperative "pools," or cartels to keep rates high. However, consistent and effective cooperation was not always feasible between competitors. Price wars did occur on lucrative high volume lines, such as links between Chicago and New York. Prices were frequently inflated on smaller branch lines with less competition. Rural areas tended to pay higher rates to subsidize higher volume lines connecting urban centers. This sometimes drove smaller customers out of business. The railroad's political power was also increasingly evident with the rise in corrupt and discriminatory practices mostly at the state level.

Consequently, the public, especially farmers and small independent manufacturers, became disenchanted with the railway companies. The platform of the Farmers' Alliance movement (1880–1896) included a reform of transportation costs, which led state legislatures to begin passing legislation to create commissions to oversee railroad business. These commissions were generally ineffective because of the railroad's pervasive economic and political power. As railway networks continued expanding across state lines, an individual state's power to regulate railroads diminished.

Thus, in the early days of the republic most trade did in fact occur within the borders of each state, but as systems of transportation and communication emerged in the nineteenth century, an increasing percentage of all economic transactions involved interstate commerce. Many states, particularly in the Midwest, had set up regulatory boards, but because the rail companies operated between states, enforcing state laws proved cumbersome and impractical. This meant that the role of Congress in overseeing the affairs of the economy was bound to grow.

For most of the nineteenth century, however, the U.S. Supreme Court assumed a very conservative posture and discouraged Congress from attempting to expand its authority in the economy. The Constitution itself actually offered guidance on this somewhat ambiguous point. Although it gave the states the power to regulate trade within their own borders, the so-called "commerce clause" of Article I gave Congress the power to "regulate Commerce . . . among the several states," i.e., trade that crosses the border between two states. *Interstate commerce* is the term used to refer to such trade.

Thus, the Supreme Court ruled in 1877, in the case of *Munn v. Illinois*, that the state regulatory boards had jurisdiction over the railroads. But less than a decade later, in the case of *Wabash, St. Louis and Pacific Railway Company v. Illinois*, the high court invalidated its earlier decision and proclaimed that only the U.S. Congress has the right to regulate interstate commerce. In issuing this decision the Court cited Section 8, Article 1 of the U.S. Constitution (1790), which states that "Congress shall have the power . . . to regulate commerce with foreign nations, and among the several states, and with the Indian tribes."

Thus, inevitably, as the country became more complex and interconnected, and as the railroad companies grew from small, local concerns into interconnected systems of rich and powerful corporations, the fight over regulation of interstate lines moved to Congress. As time went on, railroad interests actually preferred dealing on the federal level rather than fighting the same war in all the state legislatures. In addition, the railroads' feared the "ruinous competition" of the unregulated capitalist environment. Far from being free market capitalists, their goal was to become a government-sponsored cartel that would insure them a rational process of setting rates and a guaranteed profit. Thus, both the railroads and the anti-railroad forces pushed for regulation.

Finally, in 1887 Congress passed the Interstate Commerce Act, the first broadly regulatory act designed to establish government oversight over a major industry. Patterned after earlier state regulatory laws, the act created the Interstate Commerce Commission (ICC), the nation's first regulatory agency. The agency's original charge was to regulate railroad rates through court orders and to prohibit discriminatory practices including rebates to selected customers. The act originally provided for a commission of five, which eventually expanded to eleven.

The stated purpose of the ICC was to protect consumers and shippers from the monopolistic freight rate policies of the railroad industry, to control which companies gained entry into that industry, and to foster an efficient national transportation system. Other legislation expanded the scope and function of transportation regulation. Congress added telephone, telegraph, and cable service oversight to the ICC in 1888, followed by railroad safety in 1893. However, the ICC remained largely ineffective. During the President Theodore Roosevelt's (1901–1909) administration, the ICC's authority was substantially strengthened. Discriminatory practices against short haul routes were ruled illegal in the Elkins Act of 1903. The Hepburn Act of 1906 gave the ICC the authority to enforce approved rates without court orders and it also added pipelines to ICC oversight. The Sherman Anti-Trust Act of 1890 and the Clayton Act of 1914 further strengthened the federal government's role in interstate commerce by outlawing monopolies and business practices that tended to "restrain trade."

In 1902 President Theodore Roosevelt (1901–1909) persuaded Congress to create the Bureau of Corporations to inspect the financial books of any business involved in interstate commerce. In 1906 the powers of the ICC were expanded to include the regulation of oil pipelines, and in 1935, under the Motor Carrier Act, they were expanded again to include the trucking industry. The Transportation Act of 1920 further changed the ICC's charge from merely approving rates to actually setting them. The ICC now determined appropriate profit levels of railroads. It also granted the right to operate and it organized mergers. In 1938 the federal government was given regulatory power over the domestic airline industry and in 1940 and 1942 over the inland waterways and freight forwarding industries, respectively.

The monopoly of railroads in freight hauling came to a close in the 1930s with emergence of the trucking industry, which was also added to ICC responsibilities in 1935. In three Supreme Court decisions between 1936 and 1942 the commerce clause was reinterpreted to permit Congress to regulate virtually all commerce that had a national impact, even intrastate (within a state's borders) commerce. However, as the railroads failed to generate sufficient capital to meet increasing volumes, their political power declined, beginning in the 1910s. The ICC then sought rate stability to ensure the industry's survival and profitability.

During the Great Depression (1929–1939), the ICC assumed a publicly unpopular role of guaranteeing rates of return on railroad capital by raising freight rates despite declining freight volumes. No rate reductions occurred during the 1930s—a bitter pill for industries needing long-distance hauling of bulky commodities. In 1940 Congress added water carriers such as barges to ICC oversight; in 1970 Amtrak's passenger rail service was also added to ICC oversight by the Rail Passenger Act. The ICC thus had oversight over all surface common carriers.

By 1970, however, it was clear that federal regulation of interstate commerce had created its own problems, and Congress began deregulating such industries as airlines, railroads, freight carriers, household moving companies, and inter-city buses. Finally in 1996 Congress eliminated the Interstate Commerce Commission altogether.

The ICC's original goal had been to ensure the public "reasonable and just" rates that did not constitute a monopoly. The Interstate Commerce Act did not define exactly what that meant except that rate setting should not be used to suppress competition. Through the years ICC critics accused the agency of favoritism to the railroad industry by establishing high rates and discouraging lower priced competition. Others argued the railroads' monopolistic powers had so diminished by the 1930s that the ICC was no longer needed.

Other regulatory agencies took over some of the ICC's territory. In 1934 the Federal Communications Commission (FCC) assumed responsibility for telephones, telegraphs, and cable services. The newly formed Department of Transportation in 1967 took over safety concerns. Still, by the 1960s the ICC had 2,400 employees and its annual budget in the 1970s was $30 million. President Jimmy Carter's (1977–1981) administration greatly diminished the commission's powers to set rates by the 1976 Railroad Revitalization and Regulatory Reform Act. In December of 1995, through the ICC Termination Act, the ICC ended with some of its staff and functions transferred to the Surface Transportation Board.

See also: **Hepburn Act, Interstate Commerce, Interstate Commerce Act, Mann-Elkins Act, Munn v Illinois, Sherman Anti-Trust Act, Clayton Anti-Trust Act, Wabash Case**

FURTHER READING

Bryner, Gary C., and Thompson, Dennis L. eds. *The Constitution and the Regulation of Society*. Albany, NY: State University of New York Press, 1988.

Hoogenboom, Ari A., and Olive Hoogenboom. *A History of the ICC: From Panacea to Palliative*. New York: Norton, 1976.

Rothenberg, Lawrence S. *Regulation, Organizations, and Politics: Motor Freight Policy at the Interstate Commerce Commission*. Ann Arbor, MI: University of Michigan Press, 1994.

Stone, Richard D. *The Interstate Commerce Commission and the Railroad Industry: A History of Regulatory Policy*. New York: Praeger, 1991.

Wilner, Frank N. *Comes Now the Interstate Commerce Practitioner*. Gaithersburg, MD: Association of Transportation Practitioners, 1993.

INTERSTATE HIGHWAY ACT

By 1919 the need for a planned system of national highways became apparent with the increasingly common use of the automobile in the United States. The emergence of the trucking industry in the 1930s further increased calls for long-distance interstate superhighways. The limited-access German autobahn system provided a model concept for a similar system in the United States. President Franklin D. Roosevelt (1933–1945) envisioned highway construction as an ideal public works program, and Congress passed the Federal Aid Highway Act of 1938, which directed a feasibility study of a toll road highway network. The study concluded that a toll system was impractical, but it did recommend creating a 26,700 mile non-toll highway network. Roosevelt forwarded the proposal to Congress in 1939, but the nation was soon drawn into World War II (1939–1945), and Congress shelved the idea. Roosevelt, however, maintained an interest in the proposed highway program throughout the war, expecting that such a massive public construction program would help the postwar economy rebound. In 1941 Roosevelt established the National Interregional Highway Committee to further refine the concept. The resulting 1943 committee report recommended a 39,000 mile interregional highway system. Also focusing on urban freeways, the committee recognized the great influence such transportation networks would have on urban development and stressed the importance of careful design.

Further debate highlighted conflicting interests, such as urban versus rural needs, states with dense populations versus those with a sparse population, and state versus federal control. The resulting Federal Aid Highway Act of 1944 authorized a 40,000 mile interstate highway system connecting primary metropolitan areas and industrial centers, and serving national defense needs. But the act set no priorities for construction and, significantly, provided no special funding. It did require state and local governments to determine the most appropriate routes and to development national design standards. In 1945 the federal Public Roads Administration adopted a set of standards and, in 1947, designated almost 38,000 miles of routes for construction. With no special funding, however, the resulting construction was slow, as states were reluctant to divert funds away from other priorities.

The Cold War and the Korean War (1950–1953) emphasized the need for improved highways for military use. Consequently, the 1952 Federal-Aid Highway Act provided the first specifically authorized federal funds for interstate highway construction: $25 million to states on an equal match basis. By 1953 states had constructed almost 20 percent of the designated interstate highway system, at a cost of nearly $1 billion. Little of it, however, was considered of suitable quality for even existing use.

With newly elected President Dwight Eisenhower (1953–1961) taking special interest in the proposed system, Congress passed the Federal-Aid Highway Act of 1954, authorizing $175 million on a sixty-forty matching basis. Still disappointed with the meager funding commitment, Eisenhower formed an Advisory Committee on a National Highway Program to press for more sweeping legislation. Finally, overcoming opposition of the trucking industry to a proposed user tax to support the program, Congress passed the Interstate Highway Act in 1956. The act established a 40,300-mile national system of highways to be built over a 13-year period. The federal government would contribute 90 percent of construction costs, projected to exceed $30 billion, with states responsible for later maintenance costs.

Avoiding major debt, Congress created a pay-as-you-go program. The unique funding strategy included creation of the Highway Trust Fund and the Federal Highway Administrator position to manage the massive program. Funding was also provided to purchase right-of-way not already acquired by the states. Motorist-related user taxes on various fuels (including gasoline) and on truck use (including tire and equipment sales) formed the basis for funding. Those enterprises selling the taxed products, such as service stations,

paid the excise tax directly to the government and then were reimbursed through consumers' purchases the following year. The tax revenue annually raised more than the federal portion of construction expenses. The excess funds were invested in special U.S. Treasury securities, with the interest from the securities placed in a trust fund. The federal government reimbursed the states after the highway construction expenses were incurred, placing limits on how much states could spend annually. How these funding limits were apportioned to the various states, a very contentious issue during original passage of the act, was based on a formula taking into account populations served, total roadway mileage in a state, and the land area served.

The act stipulated uniform design standards to meet interstate demand projected through 1975, including fully divided highways with complete control of access, minimum distances between interchanges, and set lane widths. Use of overpasses or underpasses for road intersections and railroad crossings was required initially for only the more heavily traveled segments, but after 1966 was required for all interstates.

Upon passage of the 1956 act, the federal government provided over $1 billion to begin construction. The interstate legislation was hailed as one of the greatest public works programs in U.S. history. The unique numbering system and interstate marker designs were selected in 1957. In 1990 President George Bush (1989–1993) re-designated the system as the Dwight D. Eisenhower System of Interstate and Defense Highways. Although comprising only one percent of U.S. roadways, the interstates supported over 20 percent of vehicular traffic and almost 50 percent of trucking traffic.

The interstate program had substantial socioeconomic effects on U.S. society, some anticipated and some not. The cement and concrete industries boomed spurring advances in pavement technologies. Goods could be moved much more efficiently, and increased mobility allowed commuting workers to live in areas farther from their places of work. Not fully anticipated was the mass movement of city residents to the suburbs. The exodus left some cities with declining populations and a demise in the quality of life resulting from a substantial loss of tax revenue. In addition, the freeways undercut mass transit prospects in the United States.

By the mid-1990s, over 40,000 miles of the interstate system had been constructed, at a cost of $137 billion. The system extended across the lower 48 states, Hawaii, Alaska, and the Commonwealth of Puerto

Rico. Maintenance expenses and increasing congestion had become major concerns by the 1990s.

See also: **Suburbs (Rise of)**

FURTHER READING

Goddard, Stephen B. *Getting There: The Epic Struggle Between Road and Rail in the American Century.* New York: Basic Books, 1994.

Lewis, Tom. *Divided Highways: Building the Interstate Highways, Transforming American Life.* New York: Viking, 1997.

Rose, Mark H. *Interstate Express Highway Politics, 1941–1989.* Knoxville, TN: University of Tennessee Press, 1990.

Seely, Bruce E. *Building the American Highway System: Engineers as Policy Makers.* Philadelphia: Temple University Press, 1987.

St. Clair, David J. *The Motorization of American Cities.* New York: Praeger, 1986.

INTOLERABLE ACTS (1774)

The Boston Tea Party of December 16, 1773, helped unite American resistance to the British government. It also launched, however, a campaign in Parliament that was led by King George III's Prime Minister Lord Frederick North to punish the rebellious Bostonians. Between March and June of 1774 the government passed four bills aimed at ending dissent in the colony of Massachusetts. They are known collectively as the Intolerable Acts.

The Boston Port Act, passed in March of 1774, stopped all shipping into or out of the port of Boston until payment was received for the tea ruined in the Boston Tea Party and the tax that was due on it. Another measure, the Massachusetts Government Act, was passed in May 1774. The act altered the charter presented to the colony in 1691, changed the representative assembly to an appointed body, and gave much greater powers to the colony's governor Thomas Hutchinson, who was appointed by the king. When Hutchinson requested a leave of absence the government replaced him with a soldier who would unquestioningly obey orders: General Thomas Gage, commander of all British forces in North America.

The Administration of Justice Act, also passed in May, moved trials for capital offenses that involved British officials or soldiers out of Massachusetts. The British Parliament believed local juries would never render a fair verdict. Finally, the Quartering Act, passed in June, gave General Gage the power to house British soldiers in private homes, something forbidden in the previous Quartering Act of 1764. Although Gage had to pay fair rental prices for his soldiers' lodgings, the act's intent was to punish the people of Boston for the Tea Party. Gage received four regiments of soldiers to keep order in the town.

THERE IS NO ANIMAL, HOWEVER WEAK AND CONTEMPTIBLE, WHICH CANNOT DEFEND ITS OWN LIBERTY, IF IT WILL ONLY *FIGHT* FOR IT.

Samuel Adams, June 27, 1774

These four acts, all directed primarily against the people of Massachusetts and Boston in particular, constituted the Intolerable or Coercive Acts. The acts aroused little direct opposition because they were limited in scope to New England and did not affect the interests of the majority of colonists. Taken together, however, the statutes posed a threat to American interests and institutions throughout the colonies. They denied the power of local political organizations, supported military law over civil law, and changed customary judicial practices. The end result was that most colonists felt sympathy for the Bostonians. The colony of Virginia, for instance, observed a day of fasting and prayer to protest the closing of Boston Harbor.

Parliament's passage of another bill, however, sparked feelings of alarm throughout British North America. The Quebec Act, passed in June, 1774, created a government for the former province of French Canada. Part of the act established the rights of French-speaking residents to worship as Roman Catholics and created a royal governorship and advisory council for the area. The act also expanded the territory of Quebec south from the Great Lakes to the Ohio River. Although Parliament did not intend the Quebec Act to be part of the Intolerable Acts, colonial radicals grouped it with the others as a way of uniting opposition to the king's government.

If there was a single act of Parliament that was almost guaranteed to offend all the colonies, it was the Quebec Act. The measure took away all the claims that colonial governments had to western lands through their original charters. It also created a reserve area for Native Americans bordered by the Mississippi and Ohio Rivers in the west and by the Appalachian Mountains in the east. By stopping colonial expansion at the mountains, the act alienated both rich and poor

Americans. Impoverished settlers had been making homesteads west of the Appalachians since the end of the French and Indian War (1754–63). Richer colonists, including Benjamin Franklin and George Washington, had already laid claim to thousands of acres of these western lands and risked losing their private fortunes. George III's Solicitor General Alexander Wedderburn publicly acknowledged the anti-American bias of the Quebec Act. He declared in Parliament that the Quebec Act was meant to keep the colonies tied economically and politically to the sea, so that they would be easier to control.

In order to resolve the differences brought about by the Intolerable Acts, the colonists called the First Continental Congress (1774). Representatives from 12 of the 13 colonies (Georgia declined to participate) met in Philadelphia in September of that year. The delegates represented a complete spectrum of political beliefs, ranging from conservative loyalists to radical patriots. They joined together to petition the Crown for repeal of the acts. They split, however, over the question of what measures should be taken if the acts remained in effect. In a document known as the Suffolk Resolves, the Massachusetts delegation—including Samuel Adams and his cousin John Adams—called for a complete boycott of British goods and the training of local militia to resist British troops. The stage was set for the beginning of the American Revolution (1775–83).

See also: **American Revolution, Appalachian Mountains, Boston Tea Party, Benjamin Franklin, French and Indian War, Quebec Act, George Washington**

FURTHER READING

Ammerman, David. *In the Common Cause: American Response to the Coercive Acts of 1774*. Charlottesville, VA: University Press of Virginia, 1974.

Brown, Richard D. *Revolutionary Politics in Massachusetts: The Boston Committee of Correspondence, 1773–1774*. Cambridge: Harvard University Press, 1970.

Donoughue, Bernard. *British Politics and the American Revolution: The Path to War, 1733–1775*. New York: St. Martin's Press, 1964.

Thomas, Peter D. G. *Tea Party to Independence: The Third Phase of the Revolution, 1773–1776*. New York: Oxford University Press, 1991.

Wells, William V. *The Life and Public Services of Samuel Adams*. Boston: Little, Brown, 1865.

INVESTMENT

Investment refers to the acquisition of an asset for the sole purpose of producing future monetary income and/or capital gains. For an individual an investment may consist of the purchase of financial assets such as stocks, bonds, life insurance, and mutual funds, or physical assets such as a house or a car. Economists define investment as the increase in capital goods in an economy. Capital goods are the material or human resources that enable a business to produce a product or service. Investments in capital goods by businesses would include the purchase of factories, buildings, machinery, or a skilled and knowledgeable labor force. Businesses may also invest in research and development projects in order to improve their products or create new ones. For a business a successful investment is considered to be one that increases profits that can be passed on to shareholders which, in turn, raises the value of a company's stock.

A business's decision to invest in a particular item or project is based on two considerations. The first consideration is the expected rate of return on the investment, or how much profit the investment will generate for the business. The expected rate of return can be estimated based on forecasts of potential sales, profits, and expenses. The second consideration is how much risk is involved in obtaining the expected rate of return. Whether an individual or a business makes an investment, evaluation of risk is essential to successful investing. Practically every investment has some capacity for financial loss, but the degree of risk involved can vary greatly. Therefore investors need to estimate how much loss can feasibly be assumed and limit any risks accordingly.

See also: **Capital Goods, Profit, Speculation, Stock**

IOWA

Situated in the center of the nation and between two major rivers, Iowa had some built-in advantages as pioneers began to move westward to establish farms on the prairie grasslands. Spurred on by the development of railroads, more and more people came to this fertile territory. Although the economy of contemporary Iowa actually depends more on industry and the service sector than on farming, the image of Iowa as a state of rolling farmlands and small towns persists. As the diary of Elmer Powers, a 1930s rural Iowan, indicated, Iowa farmers take pride in ''[t]he responsibility of

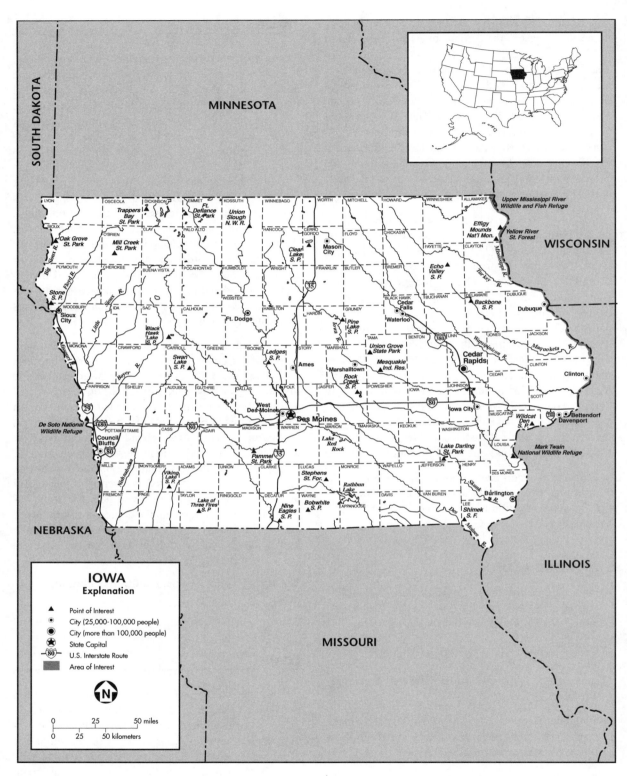

State of Iowa.

growing the food and flesh for a distant and often unappreciative city.''

A trip down the Mississippi River in 1673 made Father Jacques Marquette the first European to visit Iowa. The territory was inhabited by several Native American tribes. The only permanent white settler for many years was a French trapper, Julien Dubuque, who obtained the right from the Fox Indians to work the lead mines in the area, which later bore his name. Iowa came under United States control when France included it as part of the Louisiana Purchase of 1803. Meriwether Lewis and William Clark then went up the Missouri River on their famous expedition, stopping in Iowa and finding it a fairly empty region.

The westward wave of white settlement caused Winnebago, Sauk, and Fox Indians to flee to Iowa. Their stay was brief, however, as more whites moved into the territory and drove them out. Iowa was successively part of the Louisiana, Missouri, Michigan, and Wisconsin territories, becoming a separate territory in 1838. It entered the Union in 1846 as a free state at the same time Florida was admitted as a slave state.

Settlement in the territory proceeded at a rapid pace, since the new state boasted one-fourth of the nation's fertile topsoil. Farmers from Indiana, Ohio, and Tennessee, and from far-reaching states, such as Virginia, New York, and the Carolinas, came in droves. According to historian Joseph Frazier Wall, the convenience of waterways was important to the development of Iowa. Travelers from the East could come via canals to the Ohio River, and from there down the Mississippi to Davenport or Dubuque. ''The entire water trip,'' according to Frazier, ''might take a month, but this was lightning-quick compared to the wagon and cart journey from interior Pennsylvania or Ohio or even farther east across a third of the continent from the Great Smokies of Carolina or the Blue Ridge mountains of Virginia.'' These mostly Anglo-Americans made the state's culture quite homogeneous in religion and ethnicity. Later immigrants came from Germany, Ireland, and Scandinavia during the 1870s and 1880s. Iowa was the second-highest producer of wheat by 1870, but in the following decades the wheat belt moved farther west and Iowa began to produce more corn to feed cattle.

Despite the abundance of farmable land in Iowa, pioneers by no means had an easy time taming it. The high prairie grass with its extensive root system made it necessary in many cases to hire a professional ''prairie-breaker,'' a person who made his living by breaking up the soil with a team of oxen and a special, heavy-duty plow. According to Frazier, this process was effective but very costly to the average farmer who might have to work six to eight years to make his land claim pay for its cost. In addition farmers had to cope with periodic plagues of grasshoppers and plant diseases.

Some interesting sidelights in Iowa's history were the experimental socialist communities that developed in several areas of the state during the mid-nineteenth century, particularly the Amana colonies in Iowa County. In Amana, founded by a religious group called the Community of True Inspiration, all lands, mills, factories, tools, and livestock were held in common. While other utopian communities had failed, Amana flourished, growing to 26,000 acres of farmland and 1,800 inhabitants by the turn of the century. The communitarian character of Amana, however, was weakened by the Great Depression of the 1930s, and Amana soon became a capitalist corporation with each member a stockholder. Today it is a cooperative company town that has become famous for its manufacture of refrigerators, air conditioners, and microwave ovens, as well as for its tourist appeal.

Iowa supported the Union during the American Civil War (1861–1865), not only because of its anti-slavery sentiment but because of its strong desire to keep Mississippi River shipping alive during a time of crisis. Railroads were vital to the growth of agriculture in the state; the Mississippi and Missouri railroad was the first to cross the state, followed by the Chicago, Iowa & Nebraska, and later the Chicago & Northwestern railroads. Three other major railroads were the Chicago, Burlington & Quincy, the Illinois Central, and the Chicago, Milwaukee, St. Paul & Pacific. By the 1870s, despite the railroads' obvious benefits to commerce, Iowa farmers were against the high rates and monopolistic practices of the railroads. A powerful lobby in the state, the National Grange, succeeded in getting the legislature to pass the Granger laws to regulate railroads.

During the late nineteenth century Iowa was slowly becoming a center for much scientific experimentation in farming, especially in animal and plant genetics. Livestock and poultry were refined to meet the tastes of urbanized people who liked more tender beef and chicken. Soybeans were introduced from the Orient, and hybrid corn appeared early in the twentieth century, increasing corn yields significantly. Giant seed companies, such as Pioneer, DeKalb, and Cargill, grew rapidly to accommodate the farmers' increasing desire for the hybrids.

Because so much of Iowa's land was valuable for agriculture, towns and cities tended to stay relatively small. At first they grew up along the rivers—towns such as Dubuque, Burlington, Davenport, Bellevue, Keokuk, and Fort Madison. Railroads made possible the development of inland cities such as Grinnell and Waterloo. Still, the state did not develop major metropolitan areas comparable to Chicago or Indianapolis. Des Moines, the state's largest city, still has only around 200,000 people, and the second-largest city, Cedar Rapids, is only about half that size. Since much of Iowa's industrial production is related to agriculture no one metropolitan area dominates, nor is there any natural port of entry that would create a concentration of population and industry.

After World War I (1914–1918) prices for farmland rose considerably, forcing many cash-poor farmers to lose their land around the time of the Great Depression. A small number of farmers joined the Farmers Holiday Association, which staged a number of violent strikes in 1932. Most farmers, however, sought relief in political change within the system. Overwhelmingly, Democrats were elected to office in 1932 on all levels, and the state began to benefit from President Franklin D. Roosevelt's (1933–1945) New Deal programs. High demand for farm products improved the farmers' situation during World War II (1939–1945). After the war, however, the state's economy shifted emphasis from agriculture to manufacturing and service industries. Food processing and farm implement manufacture, early industries in the state, remain important to the economy. In the 1990s the service sector encompassed nearly 50 percent of the economy, with manufacturing at 25 percent, and agriculture at only nine percent.

Inflation plagued Iowa during the late 1970s, driving up the cost of fertilizers and farm equipment. Iowa also suffered during the recession of the 1980s, losing 7.9 percent of its population. A serious drought in 1988 prompted Iowa's governor to declare a state of emergency, as soybean and corn harvest dropped to their lowest levels in 14 years; this disaster was followed by an early frost, which further damaged the already ruined farmlands. Since 1970 the state has seen a loss of 41,000 family farms; more than 90 percent of all of Iowa's land, however, is still farmland. By the early 1990s diversification of businesses, industries, and agriculture had helped the state's economy to make a cautious recovery.

Iowa ranked well below the national average in unemployment, at 3.8 percent, in 1996. Its per capita income in that year was $22,560, placing it 28th among all states. Iowa's farm income, nearly $12 billion in 1995, came from the sale of livestock and meat products, feed grains, and soybeans. Some of the important industries in the state, all members of the *Fortune* 500,

include Caterpillar Tractor, General Motors, Mobil, General Electric, General Foods, Procter & Gamble, and U.S. Steel. Around 12.5 percent of all employees in the state are members of labor unions.

See also: **National Grange, Utopian Communities,**

FURTHER READING

Iowa Development Commission. *1985 Statistical Profile of Iowa*. Des Moines, 1985.

Powers, Elmer G. *Years of Struggle*. Ames: Iowa State University Press, 1976.

Sage, Leland. *A History of Iowa*. Ames: Iowa State University Press, 1974.

Swierenga, Robert P. *Pioneers and Profits*. Ames: Iowa State University Press, 1968.

Wall, Joseph Frazier. *Iowa: A Bicentennial History*. New York: Norton, 1978.

IRONCLADS

Ironclads were warships built of wood or iron and covered with thick plates of iron. During the 1820s naval guns that fired explosive shells (versus solid cannonballs) were developed. Because the new shells could easily destroy the hull of a wooden ship, the navy began developing ways to protect its battleships from this superior ammunition. Ships clad in iron could better sustain the fire of explosive shells.

The first battle between two ironclads was staged during the American Civil War (1861–65). On March 9, 1862, the Union's *Monitor*, originally built as an ironclad and equipped with a revolving gun turret, faced the Confederacy's *Virginia*. (The *Virginia* was made by raising the sunken federal boat the *Merrimack* and covering the wooden vessel with iron plates.) The ships met at Hampton Roads, Virginia, a channel that empties into Chesapeake Bay. Though the outcome was indecisive, the *Monitor*'s performance in the battle was sufficient to warrant the U.S. Navy's production of a fleet of ironclad ships. The March 1862 battle off the coast of Virginia marked the beginning of modern naval warfare.

The use of sturdier materials in shipbuilding, along with the steam-power and the screw propeller, all of which were used by Civil War ironclads, greatly improved the efficiency of maritime commerce after the war. In fact John Ericsson (1803–1899), the designer of the Monitor, had also developed the screw propeller.

See also: **Civil War**

IROQUOIS

The Iroquois, or Iroquois League, was an American Indian confederacy made up of the Cayuga, Mohawk, Oneida, Onondaga, and Seneca—Iroquoian-speaking Eastern Woodlands tribes that had settled in the area of present-day New York, west of the Hudson River. The confederacy was formed sometime between the late 1300s and mid-1400s as the League of Five Nations. Member tribes agreed they would not undertake war without the agreement of the other tribes. Within the confederacy each nation had a role; the Mohawks, for example, were charged with defending the eastern end of Iroquois territory.

The Iroquois were mighty warriors. Other tribes either looked to the league for protection or viewed them as a menace. Among the Iroquois enemies were the Huron, a tribe in the Great Lakes region. As the French and British encroached on Indian lands, the bond among the Five Nations grew stronger. In 1722 a sixth tribe, the Tuscarora, joined the league, expanding its territories and its number. (Thereafter the confederacy is alternately known as the League of Six Nations.)

When fighting broke out in the colonies between the French and the British, the Iroquois sided with the British, in what would be known as the French and Indian War (1754–1763). Some historians view the Indian-British alliance as the critical factor in the British victory in the conflict. These historians promote the idea that had it not been for Iroquois involvement, North America would have been divided between the French and British.

When the American Revolution (1775–1783) began, the Iroquois split their loyalties: All tribes except the Oneida sided with the British. During the course of the war, Mohawk chief Thayendanegea, better known as Joseph Brant (1742–1807), led the Iroquois in many raids including the massacre at Cherry Valley, New York, in 1778. The following summer an American army marched through upstate New York, devastating

Indian lands. After the war ended, most of the Iroquois were moved to lands in Ontario.

See also: **Eastern Woodlands Indians**

IRRIGATION

Irrigation is an artificial watering of the land to produce crops. Irrigation compensates for the lack of regular rainfall in the more arid regions of the world and requires large supplies of water. The two water sources are surface water in lakes, streams, and rivers, and groundwater stored beneath earth's surface in aquifers. Aquifers are natural underground reservoirs where water accumulates.

The two main types of irrigation making use of surface water are the basin system and the perennial system. Basin irrigation relies on annual flooding to fill canals dug adjacent to the overflowing river. The canals traverse through farmland, flooding the area with nutrient-rich water. The modern and widely used perennial system, utilizing reservoirs generally created by dams and extensive canal networks, allows water to be supplied at suitable intervals throughout the year. The other source of irrigation water, groundwater, is pumped to the surface from wells dug into aquifers. The well is placed as near to the land to be irrigated as possible and a system of canals or pipes carries water to the crops.

Recognizing the value of irrigation as an aid to permanently settling the arid American West, Mormon settlers in the Salt Lake Valley in present-day Utah built the first large scale irrigation canal system in 1847. Demand for food by the gold rush miners in California and Colorado in the 1840s and 1850s spurred development of ditch systems to irrigate bottomlands along streams. After the American Civil War (1861–1865), the great agricultural settlement boom, lasting from the 1870s to the 1940s, promoted more efficient irrigation institutions as a means of stimulating economic development of the West. Mutual irrigation companies, first formed in Utah, were followed by irrigation districts in California formulated through the Wright Act of 1887. The districts could levy taxes and issue bonds for irrigation development. With the Carey Act of 1894 and the Reclamation Act of 1902, the federal government began major dam construction efforts. The Reclamation Act established the Reclamation Service, later known as the U.S. Bureau of Reclamation. The agency planned the two largest irrigation systems in the United States, the Colorado River Project with Hoover Dam completed in 1936 and the Columbia River Basin Project with the Grand Coulee Dam completed in 1942. The projects transformed immense expanses of arid lands into productive farmland.

The development of deep-well turbine pumps in the 1930s and 1940s lead to a rapid increase in acreage irrigated by wells, particularly in the Great Plains and Texas.

See also: **Westward Expansion**

ISOLATIONISM *(ISSUE)*

From the time when George Washington (1789–1797) gave his farewell address at the end of his presidency, warning against "entangling alliances with Europe," through the nineteenth century, the United States maintained an almost steadfast policy of isolationism. But at the beginning of the twentieth century the United States began to turn away from the isolationism that preceded the Spanish-American War (1898). As a major industrial nation with expanding foreign markets, the United States was soon considered a world power. Global expansion meant increased wealth as raw materials became cheaper to acquire; prices were driven down and consumption was up. The new century saw American businesses prospering in many sectors, including oil, steel, textiles, railroads, and food products. This unprecedented technological progress was marked by the birth of the automobile and the aviation industries. But even with increased prosperity, the isolationist reflexes of the U.S. still shaped U.S. economic and diplomatic life until the advent of World War II (1939–1945).

In the first four decades of the twentieth century the United States clumsily attempted to ward off Japanese aggression in China, assumed a paternalistic administration of Philippine affairs and engaged in "dollar diplomacy" vis a vis its smaller neighbors in the western hemisphere. The most ambitious and idealistic diplomatic project that the U.S. attempted was to intervene in World War I for the most altruistic and idealistic of reasons but with little diplomatic success. In short, the U.S. had little to show for its diplomatic efforts before World War II. With very different policies, Theodore Roosevelt and Woodrow Wilson stand

out as the most internationalist presidents. Neither believed that the U.S. could go far with an isolationist foreign policy.

Teddy Roosevelt put forth a muscular, imperialist foreign policy, while Wilson tried a kind of "missionary" foreign policy—sacrificing 112,000 American deaths simply in order to participate in the peace treaty through which he tried to structure a post-war set of diplomatic relationships that would end all wars. Wilson stood for democracy as the most advanced, humane, and Christian form of government. For him all people were capable of being trained in the habits of democracy and it was the role of the United States to help them achieve democracy.

When the nations of Europe were drawn into World War I (1914–1918) the majority of U.S. citizens wanted their country to remain neutral. The national consensus was solidly isolationist. They approved of trade, but they feared being sucked into a war in which they could see no moral difference between the belligerents. The pattern of immigration led most Americans to sympathize with the British and the French, and they grudgingly accepted the British maritime blockade of trade with Germany. Wilson helped to create a pro-war national consensus based on the belief that German actions—especially its submarine warfare, were morally bereft and would, if left unchecked, eventually threaten the United States. U.S. trade with Germany declined from $169 million in 1914 to $1.2 million in 1916, but the flow of U.S. goods into Allied hands was overwhelming, rising from $825 million to $3.2 billion in the same period. The United States became a warehouse for the Allied powers and sent munitions, food, and goods to Europe.

World War I gave the Wilson administration unique opportunities to achieve its international economic goals. He was successful in getting the Allies to accept the concept of the League of Nations. But his arrogance in dealing with the Republican Senators, plus the isolationism that sprung up again with the end of the war led the Senate to reject the Treaty of Versailles. This resulted in a powerful swing back to isolationism in the years before World War II.

During the 1920s the nation's attention was directed towards internal changes rather than international affairs. In the opening years of what would be a decade of worldwide depression, President Herbert Hoover (1929–1933) made a series of proposals to quiet rising international tensions. In 1930 his administration extended the naval-limitations agreements of the early

1920s. In 1931 he proposed a moratorium on international debt while refusing to cancel the lingering World War I debts owed to the United States by the European powers. Hoover also pressed for an international agreement on arms limitation, but the World Disarmament Conference held in Switzerland in 1932 failed to achieve its goals. International economic and military pressures intensified. Fascism in Italy, Nazism in Germany, State Socialism in the Soviet Union, and militarism in Japan were ascendant, fueled by the global depression.

President Franklin D. Roosevelt's (1933–1945) early foreign policy achievements were mixed. His administration took an isolationist stance at the World Economic Conference in June, 1933, when U.S. representatives refused to cooperate in an effort to stabilize world currencies. In 1934 however Roosevelt took an internationalist stance in the U.S.-negotiated Reciprocal Trade Agreements on tariff reductions. His vacillating policies reflected his political priorities: at the beginning of his administration, domestic issues were much more important than foreign policy.

The predominant mood in the United States in the 1930s was deeply isolationist. Not only was the Great Depression (1929–1939) wreaking havoc domestically, but many citizens believed that the nation's losses during World War I far outweighed the gains. Between 1934 and 1936 discoveries made by a Senate investigating committee headed by Senator Gerald P. Nye further fueled the nation's mood of isolationism. Exposing war profiteering by banks and corporations during World War I, the Nye committee investigation led many to conclude that the interests of U.S. banks and corporations had driven the United States into a war the nation should have avoided. The notion that "merchants of death" were responsible for manipulating the United States into war was widespread.

Influential men such as Charles Lindbergh and retired U.S. Marine Corps Maj. Gen. Smedley D. Butler promoted the idea of "Fortress America," the notion that the United States was ensconced safely between the moats of the Atlantic and the Pacific, armed for defense against but not for intervention in the corrupt affairs of Europe. The Senate's refusal to allow the United States to join the World Court in 1935 was another indication of the country's, pervasive, isolationist mood. Fearful of being pulled into a war from which it would only suffer, Congress passed three acts that declared U.S. neutrality. In the event that a war broke out between other countries, the Neutrality

Acts of 1935 and 1936 made it clear that the United States would not supply either side with weapons or ammunition. The Neutrality Act of 1937 moved the nation further in the direction of isolation and asserted a "cash-and-carry" policy by which warring countries could purchase weapons (but not ammunition) in cash only. When the Spanish Civil War broke out in 1936, the United States remained on the sidelines.

Interventionists insisted that the future of the United States lay in establishing peace and stability abroad for the sake of trade and commerce. A world divided into closed and self-contained trading blocs was a world in which the United States would not prosper. Interventionists anticipated that renewed U.S. trade abroad might end the Depression. They believed that the United States had a vital stake in ensuring that the outcome of the war in Europe and Asia favored liberal democracies and market economic systems. However, not all interventionists advocated direct military involvement toward this end. Many argued that economic assistance, as in the case of the Lend-Lease Plan, would be enough to ensure the survival of western democracies. Others, however, insisted that liberal democracy and free enterprise would perish in a world dominated by authoritarian regimes. Such interventionists saw no alternative to military engagement.

In his first term Roosevelt worked closely with isolationist progressives such as Senators Robert La Follette, Jr., Hiram Johnson, George Norris, Burton K. Wheeler, and Gerald P. Nye. During his second term Roosevelt gradually broke with the isolationists as international tensions heightened. In October, 1937, Roosevelt's famous quarantine speech which called for international cooperation in bringing unspecified economic and diplomatic pressure to bear on aggressor-nations irritated the isolationists. Beginning in 1937 they increasingly turned against the president.

As the 1930s drew to a close the United States stood by while Hitler began his push eastward. As World War II began Roosevelt declared, "This nation will remain a neutral nation," but he called for a revision of the Neutrality Acts to allow the United States to sell England and its Allies weapons and ammunition. Congress skeptically allowed purchase of arms on a cash-and-carry basis.

Ironically, European orders for war goods sparked a phenomenal economic boom that brought the United States out of the Depression for good. Many believed that as long as the United States stayed out of the war both peace and prosperity were possible. But members of the Roosevelt administration leaned toward U.S. intervention in the European conflict. Economists within the administration warned that German success in Europe and Japanese victory in Asia would irrevocably close huge markets for U.S. goods. Unless the United States intervened in these conflicts, they argued, the economic future of the United States would be worse than the Great Depression. Such arguments, in concert with war atrocities on the part of Germany and Japan, convinced Roosevelt and his administration that the United States must set isolationism aside and take an active hand in the European and Asian wars. But the people of the United States still resisted. On December 12, 1937 Japanese airplanes sank the Panay, a U.S. gunboat navigating the Yangtze River in China. But people in the United States were ready to forgive the incident after a formal Japanese apology. The Japanese invasion of Manchuria remained a major cause of disagreement between the United States and Japan. But only the bombing of Pearl Harbor on December 7, 1941, effectively pulled the United States out of the isolationistic attraction.

See also: **Franklin D. Roosevelt, Woodrow Wilson, World War I, World War II**

FURTHER READING

Cole, Wayne S. *Roosevelt and the Isolationists, 1932–1945*. Lincoln, NE: University of Nebraska Press, 1983.

Divine, Robert A. *The Illusion of Neutrality*. Chicago, IL: University of Chicago Press, 1962.

Jonas, Manfred. *Isolationism in America, 1935–1941*. Ithaca, NY: Cornell University Press, 1966.

Keylor, William R. *The Twentieth-Century World: An International History*, 2nd ed. New York: Oxford University Press, 1992.

JACKSON, ANDREW

Andrew Jackson (1767–1845), the seventh President of the United States, grew to adulthood and public prominence as the emerging nation was undergoing profound social and economic changes. In the wake of those changes Jackson worried about the central government's propensity toward abuse of power and the accumulation of power in the hand of a small political and economic elite. As president, Jackson remained a strident and popular spokesperson for majority rule in the United States. He did, however, exert the power of the presidency over other government branches far more than any president before him, leading to charges that he was primarily interested in personal power. He was denounced as a fraud and an opportunist who nearly wrecked the credit and currency systems of the United States. But Jackson also took issue with members of the privileged elite who sought to use the government for their own selfish purposes and thereby endanger the integrity of democracy in the United States. For many in the United States Jackson came to symbolize the democratic advances of his time.

Andrew Jackson was born in March 1767, in a log cabin, the son of poor Scotch-Irish immigrants. He was orphaned at age 14 and spent his adolescence with his aunt in the frontier areas of the Carolinas. Jackson drifted from one job to another, squandered a small inheritance, and developed a lifelong interest in horseracing and cockfighting. His education was spotty and he never appeared to develop an affinity for formal learning.

In 1784, at the age of 17, Jackson moved to Salisbury, North Carolina, to study law. He worked as a clerk for two years, copying legal documents, running errands, cleaning the office, and reading law books. He finished his law training in the office of Colonel John Stakes, and in 1787 he became an attorney in North Carolina.

Shortly after his law training ended, Jackson moved to the territory that would become Tennessee, and he

Andrew Jackson.

was appointed the area's attorney general. While in this position Jackson bolstered his income by selling land to new settlers. He also built a mansion in Nashville called the Hermitage. Later, when Tennessee became the sixteenth state, Jackson represented the state in Congress, but he resigned after only two years in order to be a judge on the superior court of Tennessee.

When the War of 1812 (1812–1814) broke out against Great Britain, Jackson was dispatched by the governor of Tennessee to fight with the Tennessee militia against Creek Indians, who had used the war as an opportunity to attack the Southern frontier. Although he lacked military training and experience, Jackson soon became an excellent general. His leadership qualities emerged and he was highly regarded by other soldiers who gave him the nickname "Old Hickory" as a sign of respect. After leading a spectacular victory over a British invasion of New Orleans, Louisiana, in 1815, Jackson instantly became a national celebrity.

Distinguished as a popular military hero, Jackson was encouraged by his friends to bid for the U.S. presidency. After the War of 1812 ended, however, Jackson only briefly returned to Tennessee before resuming his military position in order to subdue raids carried out by Native Americans from Spanish Florida. After a series of controversial military moves made by Jackson, including the capture of Spanish cities, the United States and Spain negotiated their disputes, and the United States acquired land that would eventually become Florida. In 1821 Jackson become provisional governor of the new territory of Florida, but resigned from the position after only four months.

Upon returning to his home in Tennessee, Jackson was pushed once again to campaign for the presidency. Though he made an unsuccessful presidential run in 1824, losing to John Quincy Adams (1825–1829), Jackson ran again in 1828 and won the presidency at age 61. He rewarded many of his supporters with government jobs—then a common practice in state governments, but essentially new to the federal government. This so-called "spoils system"—where elected officials employed their friends as pay-off for campaign support—tended to guarantee that no appointed federal employee would have a lifetime "right" to his or her job. Jackson believed that this system of replacing staff made the government more democratic.

Jackson's administration was marked by his fight against the Second Bank of the United States, which was a federally chartered institution where government funds were kept. The Bank of the United States used these funds to pay the government's bills, but also to give loans to the public and other banks. It was not directly regulated by the government, but rather led by a board of shareholders, with Nicholas Biddle (1786–1844) as its head. Jackson disliked the bank for economic and political reasons. He felt that its shareholders used the bank's control of much of the money supply to benefit themselves. Jackson also distrusted the issuance of bank notes, which in his own experience led to excessive borrowing and debt. Like many other Americans, Jackson distrusted credit and banks in general, and favored the strict use of specie (coined precious metals).

When the Bank of the United States' charter was brought up for renewal in 1832, Jackson vetoed it. He criticized the bank for failing to establish a "uniform and sound" currency, and began to deposit government funds in other banks. Many of the leaders in the Senate opposed Jackson, and his position on the bank. Nevertheless, Jackson's successful veto of the rechartering of the bank in 1832 was arguably a major reason for his re-election to a second presidential term that same year.

Over the course of its remaining four years of existence, the Second Bank of the United States tried to use its power to force a reconsideration of its charter. It issued far more loans than it could support, helping to trigger a wave of real estate speculation on the frontier. Disturbed, Jackson issued the Specie Circular in 1836. The circular required that all purchases of frontier land, which was owned by the government, be paid for with specie. This stopped the speculation, but also bankrupted many investors who lacked sufficient specie to pay their obligations and helped to trigger a major depression.

Jackson's policy of fiscal restraint helped him accomplish one of his most cherished objectives during his second term: full payment of the national debt. This was the only time up to that point in U.S. history when the nation was free of debt and it was one of Jackson's proudest accomplishments.

As Jackson proceeded through his second term, he frequently used his executive power to veto proposed Congressional legislation. He believed that the president had the right to annul what he deemed harmful to the public interest, a departure from earlier presidents who only vetoed bills they thought were unconstitutional. Using his veto power creatively, Jackson vastly expanded presidential executive power in government.

Also during his second term, a concept called "Jacksonian democracy" emerged as Jackson developed and popularized his own notion of essential democratic elements. He preached about the importance of equality, freedom, and majority rule, and advocated a limited government, fiscal restraint, laissez-faire economics, and support of the individual states in their constitutional sphere of activity.

Throughout his political career Jackson was both a beloved and much-hated figure. During many reform periods in U.S. history Jackson was seen as a hero, and Jacksonian democracy was extolled as one of the great advances in the development of popular government. Yet Jackson was also denounced as a person out for his own political advantage, who mesmerized the public with populist rhetoric and behaved like an autocrat in his role as president.

When Jackson's friend Martin Van Buren (1837–1841) was elected president in 1836, Jackson retired to the Tennessee mansion, the Hermitage. He remained politically active until his death, at the age of 78, in 1845.

See also: **Bank of the United States (Second National Bank), National Debt, Spoils System, War of 1812**

FURTHER READING

Bugg, James L. *Jacksonian Democracy: Myth or Reality*. New York: Holt, Rinehart and Winston, 1962.

Remini, Robert V. *Andrew Jackson and the Bank War: A Study in the Growth of Presidential Power*. New York: Norton, 1967.

Schlesinger, Arthur M. *The Age of Jackson*. New York: Book Find Club, 1946.

Sellers, Charles, ed. *Andrew Jackson: A Profile*. New York: Hill and Wang, 1971.

Terrin, Peter. *The Jacksonian Economy*. New York: Norton, 1969.

JAPAN, OPENING OF

In 1638 the shogun Hideyoshi, a Japanese military and political leader, was determined to isolate Japan from growing European religious and commercial influences. Hideyoshi declared Japan closed to all foreigners and restricted the empire's contact with the outside world to a small group of Dutch traders. This policy of isolationism came to an end nearly 250 years later with the arrival of an American naval expedition led by Commodore Matthew Perry (1794–1858). His diplomatic efforts, backed by a military show of force, opened the Japanese empire to trade and political relations not only to the United States but to the rest of the known world.

Ships of the American whaling industry sailed in the northern Pacific ocean near Japan beginning in the late 1700s. Those unfortunate foreign sailors who were shipwrecked on the Japanese islands because of the region's violent storms were normally imprisoned, and in some extreme cases they were put to death. News of this mistreatment slowly trickled back to the United States, where Congress became increasingly agitated by the Japanese rulers' isolationist foreign policy. A movement to open diplomatic relations between the United States and Japan was further accelerated by the introduction of steam-powered ships.

By the mid 1800s the American sea–going fleet was converting from clipper ships whose sails relied on the wind to steam ships powered by coal-fueled furnaces. Because steam ships were not capable of carrying enough coal to complete the voyage across the Pacific, refueling ports were established along the Northern Pacific following a trail from the western United States, up through Alaska, and on through the northern border of Japan's empire. In 1851 the United States discovered that coal could be mined in Japan. If refueling stations could be established along the country's shores, the United States fleet could greatly increase its influence within Asia. The thought of establishing ports of call within the Japanese empire greatly appealed to the expansionist political philosophy popular at the time.

SO LONG AS THE SUN SHALL WARM THE EARTH, LET NO CHRISTIAN DARE TO COME TO JAPAN.

Hideyoshi, Japanese Shogun, 1638

The United States' first attempt to negotiate a treaty with Japan was met with an embarrassing defeat. An envoy led by U.S. Naval Commodore James Biddle (1783–1848) sailed into Edo (Tokyo) Bay in 1846. The Commodore's ship was quickly surrounded by Japanese guard boats and boarded by several of the shogun's emissaries who diligently studied every component of the ship. Once completed with their inspection, the Japanese officials provided Biddle with a letter from the shogun demanding he immediately set sail and not return. Six years would pass until the United States would once again attempt to establish a treaty with Japan.

In 1852 Matthew Perry was appointed as Commander in Chief of the United States Naval Forces stationed in the East India, China, and Japanese seas. Perry's naval career was primarily spent directing peacetime activities. Although Perry saw action during the War of 1812 (1812–14) and the Mexican War (1846–48), he was mainly known for his involvement in helping to establishing Liberia, a West African country where freed American slaves found sanctuary. A passionate believer in American expansionism, Perry was greatly concerned over the growing British trade presence in Asia. He expressed these concerns to President Millard Fillmore (1850–53) in 1852 after England gained control over Singapore and Hong Kong. President Fillmore heeded Perry's advice, and in 1853 he commanded Perry to implement a trade treaty with the Emperor of Japan.

Perry diligently studied the lessons learned from the United States first attempt at negotiations with Japan six years earlier. He believed Commodore Biddle's chief mistake was not demanding respect from the Japanese officials. A plan was set in motion to impress the Japanese by displaying America's technological advantages and military might. Perry set sail for Edo Bay with a contingent of four vessels which included the new steam driven paddle wheelers the *Susquehanna* and *Mississippi*. He also brought with him gifts for the Japanese Emperor to demonstrate the technology gap between the two countries. A scaled-down version of a steam-powered locomotive train, rifles, plows, and other American-engineered machines were stored on board the ships.

On July 8, 1853, Perry's small but impressive fleet entered Edo Bay. Once again the Japanese quickly surrounded the ships and demanded that they be allowed to board the vessels. Perry had anticipated this response. Orders had been issued by the Commodore not to allow any Japanese officials to board the ships until a qualified representative from the Emperor was present. His crew obeyed his commands and held off the Japanese at musket point. An American interpreter informed the officials that their commander had been ordered to present a letter to the Emperor or an appropriate representative. The military presence displayed by the fleet left little doubt the Americans would be easily rebuffed.

Intense negotiations took place between the two parties during the next five days. Finally, on July 14, Commodore Perry left his stateroom and came ashore along with 250 members of his crew. Attired in his dress uniform and accompanied by two armed black stewards, Perry presented the Japanese officials with the letter from President Fillmore. The Japanese also provided Perry with a letter demanding he immediately set sail and not return. Perry stated he would return the following year to accept the Emperor's response. The meeting was brought to a close and the American force sailed out of Japanese waters for the winter.

In February 1854 Perry returned to Edo Bay with a larger show of military might. His force consisted of more than 1,500 sailors serving on 10 ships. Once again intense negotiations took place over the trade concessions stated in President Fillmore's letter. After days of deliberation an agreement was reached between the two countries.

The official treaty ceremony with the presenting of gifts took place on March 13, 1854. The Japanese were enthralled with the scaled-down version of the steam locomotive presented by Perry. Equally impressive was the exhibition held by the Japanese sumo wrestlers.

Perry visited several other Japanese ports before returning to his command on April 14, 1854. His actions led to extensive negotiations between the United States and Japan. Townsend Harris, an American diplomat, spent the next 10 years attempting to finalize a trade agreement with the Japanese. Perry's treaty also opened the door for several other European nations to establish trade treaties with the formerly reclusive country. His efforts and the resulting trade with the western nations had a profound effect on the technological and military modernization of the Japanese empire, although the opening of Japan had little immediate economic impact on the United States.

See also: **Matthew Perry**

FURTHER READING

Buschini, J. *Expansion in the Pacific*. Andover, MA: Small Planet Communications, Inc., 1996.

Fallows, James. "After Centuries of Japanese Isolation, a Fateful Meeting of East and West." *Smithsonian*. July 1994.

The New Encyclopaedia Britannica. Chicago: Encyclopaedia Britannica, Inc., 1997, s.v. "Japan."

UMI The Answer Company. "Commodore Perry's Expedition to Japan 1853" [cited April 22, 1999] available from the World Wide Web @ www.umi.com/hp/Support/K12/GreatEvents/Perry.html/.

Weisberger, Bernard A. "First Encounter." *American Heritage*, December 1991.

JAY TREATY

The main problems confronting the second administration of President George Washington (1793–1797) were rooted in the conflict between England and France. The French Revolution in 1789 quickly moved from a period of moderate rule through ever more tumultuous stages. In 1793 King Louis XVI was guillotined and the monarchies of Europe mobilized for war with France. Until 1793 the revolution had little direct impact on the young American republic, although it is difficult to overstate how important the events in France were to Americans with respect to their political beliefs. Americans believed that their own revolution and republican institutions would serve as a guide for a world shackled by tyrannical government. For citizens of the United States, the revolution in France and the triumph of republicanism validated their own experiment with democratic government. Both the American and the French revolutions were seen as harbingers of a new golden age of worldwide individual liberty and representative government. These were lofty ideals and few held them more dearly than Thomas Jefferson (1743–1826) and his political supporters, who were loosely organized in the Democratic-Republican Party.

As head of state, Washington felt obliged to plot a moderate course for the United States. As Europe plunged into warfare, Washington labored to keep the fragile republic out of harm's way, convinced it would suffer great, perhaps irreparable, damage if it became entangled in the European war. This war, in a sense, was the first "world war" and it unleashed frightening levels of violence. Washington feared that the new nation might be caught underfoot in this elephant stampede. To this end, Washington addressed the delicate problem of the United States' relationships with France and with England. Under the alliance of 1778, the United States was obliged to defend the French West Indies "forever against all powers." Other treaty provisions allowed French privateers to equip themselves and operate in U.S. ports.

Even though France had been a critical factor in the Revolutionary War against Britain, Washington was unwilling to honor what he felt were unrealistic and dangerous obligations. On the one hand, he believed France was outnumbered on the European continent and would likely lose the war. More importantly, France was clearly weaker in naval power than Great Britain, and the United States had virtually no navy at all. Defending the French West Indies or allowing French privateers to operate out of U.S. ports appeared to be an unrealistic task. Furthermore, the European war brought Spain and Britain together as allies. Any official or unofficial aid to France ran the risk of bringing the weight of Spain and Britain—whose colonial possessions bordered the United States—and their numerous Native American allies against the United States.

Other calculations were also important. Even though the two nations had fought a war against each other, Great Britain was still the United States' main trade partner and eastern merchants lobbied against any action in support of France. Indeed, those who had commercial interests at stake usually supported the Federalist Party and the policies of Treasury Secretary Alexander Hamilton (1755–1781), which favored supporting Britain. After conferring with his advisors, Washington issued a proclamation of neutrality in April 1793.

Although the United States had no navy to speak of, it did have a large merchant marine, and British treatment of U.S. trading vessels made it difficult for Washington to maneuver safely among the belligerents. Great Britain rejected its former colony's definition of neutral rights, based on one strand of international law that held that "free ships make free goods." Instead, the Crown embraced a narrower definition that permitted the seizure of neutral ships' cargoes. Britain also regularly boarded U.S. merchant ships at sea and "impressed" (kidnapped) U.S. seamen who, they claimed, were deserters from the Royal Navy. This issue would foul Anglo-American relations until the War of 1812. Between 1803 and 1812, 8,000 American sailors were impressed by the British. But impressment was already an important complaint during the 1790s. Another issue between the U.S. and Great Britain was that the British forces had not vacated the forts in the Northwest Territories as they had agreed to do in the Treaty of Paris that ended the American Revolutionary War. They also foiled Washington's efforts to make peace with the region's tribes, who were reportedly told by the British Governor General of Canada to prepare for war with the United States.

Washington dispatched Chief Justice John Jay to Britain to negotiate a settlement. Jay's Treaty was signed on November 19, 1794. When it arrived in the United States in March of 1795, it re-ignited political warfare between the Republicans and the Federalists. The treaty failed to resolve the most divisive issue: Britain refused to recognize the United States' rights of neutrality. The treaty also prevented the United States from imposing discriminatory tariffs on British goods, and provided for the payment of pre-Revolutionary war debts still owed to British businessmen. For its part, Britain agreed to evacuate its forts in the disputed territories and to make compensation for U.S. ships recently seized in the West Indies.

Widely viewed as a humiliating and one-sided document, the treaty was unpopular and Washington suffered the indignity of scattered calls for his impeachment. Critics argued that the treaty stripped the United States of the weapon of trade sanctions, the only weapon that could persuade Britain to change its position on the neutrality issue. The Republicans also charged that the treaty was yet another effort by the Washington administration to bring the United States closer to Britain, albeit in a subordinate position, and away from any sympathetic treatment of France. Washington, however, supported the treaty, fearing war with Britain.

Amid renewed criticism of his judgment and character, Washington brought his still considerable prestige and power to bear on the issue of ratification and, with the aid of committed Federalists, secured passage.

But a high price was paid for the treaty in that it moved the nation further from Washington's long-standing hope that the republic, through the goodwill of its leaders, could achieve elite and popular consensus. The treaty further polarized elite and popular opinion. It also widened and hardened divisions in Congress between New Englanders and much of the Middle Atlantic states, on the one hand, and the South, on the other. In the vote in the House of Representatives over whether or not to support the treaty, 79 percent of those supporting the Jay Treaty were from New England or Middle Atlantic states, while over 73 percent of those rejecting it were from Southern states.

Despite its divisive political repercussions, the Jay Treaty must be judged as an important achievement. By working to normalize relations with Britain, the treaty helped protect American security and promote economic development during the vital formative years of the republic. One of its key provisions was the British agreement to turn over to the United States several military posts (including Detroit) that the British had illegally occupied since the Treaty of Paris (1783). The date for the Britain evacuation of the forst was July 1, 1796. Equally important, the treaty marked the advent of modern international arbitration. It authorized the formation of three boards or commissions of arbitration to resolve three important issues: the northeast boundary of the United States; the amount of losses and damages to British creditors who suffered breaches of lawful contracts due to the Revolutionary War; and compensation of U.S. citizens for losses sustained by the seizure of their vessels or cargoes by the Crown or its agents during the war with France.

Although the arbitration approach was important as a concept of international relations, the commissions formed to address the issues of the U.S. boundary and compensation to British businessmen were less than successful. The findings on the first matter were inconclusive, while the deliberations on the second matter were eventually deadlocked. The tribunal dealing with the claims of U.S. citizens against Great Britain, however, had lasting importance. Similar in structure to the other two commissions, it was comprised of two members appointed by both Britain and the United States. The final member was chosen by mutual consent, or in the case of disagreement, by the drawing of names submitted by each side.

Significantly, the commission was able to avoid deadlock over differing positions on substantive law by enlisting an outside expert to resolve the issue. This marked the beginning of the use of neutral, third parties to make binding decisions to resolve disagreements.

See also: **American Revolution, War or 1812, George Washington**

FURTHER READING

Combs, Jerald. *The Jay Treaty: Political Background of the Founding Fathers*. Berkeley and Los Angeles: University of California Press, 1970.

Flexner, James. *George Washington: Anguish and Farewell, 1793–1799*. Boston: Little, Brown, 1972.

Freeman, Douglas Southall. *George Washington, A Biography*, completed by J.A. Carroll and M.W. Ashworth. 7 vols. New York: Augustus M. Kelley, 1948–1957. Abridgement by Richard Harwell, New York: Scribner's Sons, 1968.

Reuter, Frank. *Trials and Triumphs: George Washington's Foreign Policy*. Fort Worth: Texas Christian University Press, 1983.

JEFFERSON, THOMAS

Thomas Jefferson (1743–1820) is best known as one of the founding fathers of the United States, a president, and the primary author of the *Declaration of Independence*. Less well known is the enormous range of Jefferson's other interests and talents. He was very well-read in science, ancient and modern history, philosophy, and literature, and was one of the best-educated and most knowledgeable people of his time in the United States.

From his intense reading in the philosophy and literature of his day, Jefferson adopted the elements of what became known as the eighteenth century Enlightenment. He believed that human nature was good, and rational laws governed the universe. He also believed in the freedom of all individuals to inquire into all things. He was convinced of man's inherent individual capacity for justice and happiness by the use of reason, the self-improvement of one's work, and progress.

Jefferson's political and business philosophy translated into fiercely democratic feelings about the new nation's destiny. He embraced the spirit of capitalism as long as everyone could participate in it equally. He fought tendencies of large property owners to behave like aristocrats and kings in the newly born United States. He expressed his philosophy and, indirectly, his view of life in the *Declaration of Independence*: ''We hold these truths to be self-evident, that all men are created equal, that they are endowed by their Creator with certain unalienable Rights, that among these are Life, Liberty and the pursuit of Happiness.''

Thomas Jefferson.

Jefferson was born into a social circle where he could have lived a life of ease and comfort. He was born in Shadwell, Virginia, in 1743 on a farm property that included five thousand acres of land. He entered the prestigious College of William and Mary at age seventeen. Although he enjoyed the study of science he decided there was no opportunity for a scientific career in Virginia at that time. He instead studied law and philosophy, and was admitted to the bar in 1767, at age twenty-four. Jefferson led a successful legal practice, which he abandoned in 1774 at the onrush of the American Revolution (1775–1783) to lend his support to the independence movement.

While he was a member of the Second Continental Congress in Philadelphia, Pennsylvania, Jefferson was asked to draft the *Declaration of Independence*. Other members of the Congress made many changes to his original draft; yet it clearly bore Jefferson's stamp. For the first time in history the basic written tenets of individual personal freedom were laid as the foundation of a nation. The principles of national equality, the rights of individual persons, the sovereignty of the people, and the right to revolution were all written into a single document that served as a theoretical basis for the United States government and national commerce.

After the American Revolution and the birth of the United States, Jefferson served in the U.S. Congress where he developed much of what became national policy on business and commerce. He drafted the first ordinance of government for the vast Western territory, which indirectly created free and equal republican states from the existing wilderness. By doing this Jefferson opened up new regions of land to U.S. commerce. Jefferson also paid attention to foreign trade and business, creating a liberal commercial policy to increase business with different European powers.

In 1785 Jefferson succeeded Benjamin Franklin (1706–1790) as minister to France. In Europe, he focused on commercial diplomacy with France and was also engaged in ongoing efforts to broaden U.S. commerce with many other European nations.

In 1789 President George Washington (1732–1799) asked Jefferson to become Secretary of State. He accepted. For the next three years Jefferson fought to increase commercial trade with France and develop more even-handed commerce. His strongest opponent was Alexander Hamilton (1755–1804), who was then Secretary of the Treasury. Hamilton promoted policies that interfered with free trade and enriched the few at the expense of the many. These policies encouraged fraud in commerce and broke down the restraints of the Constitution. Jefferson fought Hamilton, fiercely seeking a free trade situation in which all citizens could participate. This led to the formation of the modern political party now known as the Democratic Party. (It was ironically called the Republican Party at that time.) In 1800 the "man of the people" was elected to the presidency of the United States based on his democratic political principles.

Jefferson's presidency comprised a series of reforms. He restored freedom of the press, which had suffered from restrictions in early nationhood; scaled down the military forces; and abolished all internal taxes. He also began a federal fiscal program to end the national debt. Jefferson sought to create a national condition that would further not only peace, but also equality and individual freedom in business and most other matters. During his presidency he also expanded the size of the United States, purchasing 800,000 square miles of North American territory from the French in the Louisiana Purchase (1803).

Jefferson's legacy to the United States is large. He increased the physical size of the United States through land purchases and supported democratic participation of common people. As a founding father of the United States and a writer of the *Declaration of Independence*, Jefferson embodied the ideals and hopes that shaped a nation. He died at his home in Monticello, Virginia, on July 4, 1826.

See also: **Continental Congress (Second), Louisiana Purchase, George Washington**

FURTHER READING

Commager, Henry S. *Jefferson, Nationalism, and the Enlightenment.* New York: G. Braziller, 1975.

Ellis, Joseph J. *American Sphinx: The Character of Thomas Jefferson.* New York: Alfred A. Knopf, 1997.

Foner, Philip S., ed. *Basic Writings of Thomas Jefferson.* New York: Willey Book Co., 1944.

Kaplan, Lawrence S. *"Entangling Alliances With None": American Foreign Policy in the Age of Jefferson.* Kent, OH: Kent State University Press, 1987.

Spivak, Burton. *Jefferson's English Crisis: Commerce, Embargo, and the Republican Revolution.* Charlottesville: University Press of Virginia, 1978.

JIM CROW LAWS

In 1877, as the post–Civil War (1861–1865) era of Reconstruction drew to a close, the former Confederate states of the South were freed from the control of the occupation army of federal troops and carpetbaggers. They began to assert segregationist policies on the ex-slaves who had experienced only a fleeting taste of freedom. Although defeated, the white people of the former Confederacy considered African Americans inferior. Although the Thirteenth, Fourteenth, and Fifteenth Amendments to the Constitution had supposedly freed African-Americans from slavery and declared them citizens with enforceable rights, the concerted resistance of the old white South undid the few gains that Reconstruction policies had achieved.

In 1875 the U.S. Congress passed a Civil Rights Act guaranteeing African Americans access to public facilities. It was obvious, however, that even at the federal level the political commitment to equality was weakening, as the language to maintain integrated school systems was stripped from the bill before its passage. Still, when some minor efforts were made to enforce the already weakened law, Southern state legislatures reacted by erecting a legal system to separate the races in every aspect of daily life. The result was a web of public policies and practices through which a racial caste system emerged in the South. Under these new laws, which were called "Jim Crow laws" after the ubiquitous shuffling minstrel character of the same name, "persons of color" were relegated

> In the 1890s, poll taxes and literacy tests succeeded in disenfranchising all but a handful of southern blacks. America had once again walked away from an opportunity to achieve justice. In place of slavery came "Jim Crow" laws that governed almost every aspect of life for Black Americans living below the Mason-Dixon line. The insidious Jim Crow caricature of the Negro became a powerful barrier to legal and social equality.
>
> **Henry Hampton and Steve Fayer, *Voices of Freedom: An Oral History of the Civil Rights Movement from the 1950s through the 1980s,* 1990**

to second-class status and denied access to the public education and transportation institutions.

The emergence of a caste system in the South gained momentum from two Supreme Court decisions. In the 1883 *Civil Rights Cases*, the Court struck down the 1875 act as exceeding Congress' powers under Reconstruction. Then in 1896 the Court ruled racial segregation was legally acceptable. The 1896 ruling came from a Louisiana case, *Plessy v. Ferguson*.

In 1890 the state of Louisiana passed a law requiring "colored" and white persons be provided "separate but equal" railroad passenger car accommodations. In 1892 Homer Plessy, a person of acknowledged one-eighth African American descent, refused to leave the "white" car on the East Louisiana Railroad. He was arrested. The case eventually ended up in the U.S. Supreme Court. The Court ruled that the state law was a reasonable exercise of state police powers to promote the public good. The Court went further and held that separate facilities did not have to be identical. It turned out that the "separate but equal" doctrine was merely self-serving rhetoric. For the next six decades the reality was most often "separate and unequal" treatment. Because the races could not encounter one another on the grounds of a presumption of equality, the ideology of white supremacy was able to perpetuated itself from generation to generation. African Americans had to live with inferior facilities, access, and services.

As inequality became institutionalized, the Jim Crow laws required the separation of races in every facet of life including transportation, schools, lodging, public parks, theaters, hospitals, neighborhoods, cemeteries, and restaurants. Inter-racial marriages were prohibited. Business owners and public institutions were prohibited from allowing African American and white clientele to mingle. While the objective was to eliminate any contact between whites and persons of color as equals, the effect was to deprive African Americans of key economic and social opportunities, adequate food, shelter, clothing, education, and health care. In addition, between 1890 and 1908, every state of the former Confederacy acted laws to limit African American voting rights. With discriminatory voting requirements, such as literacy tests and poll taxes, African Americans (and many poor whites) were effectively barred from participation in the political arena.

The National Association for the Advancement of Colored People (NAACP), created in 1909, took the lead in combating Jim Crow laws. Successes in reversing Jim Crow laws were quite limited prior to World War II (1939–1945). Finally, the turning point came in 1954 when the Supreme Court struck down public school segregation in *Brown v. Topeka Board of Education*. Reversing the earlier *Plessy* decision, the Court asserted that the separate-but-equal doctrine was unconstitutional in regard to public educational facilities. Support for Jim Crow laws waned as the civil rights movement gained momentum in the following years. Finally, the Jim Crow era came to a close with a series of landmark federal laws passed by Congress during the 1960s. The most notable of the new federal laws were the Civil Rights Act of 1964, the Voting Rights Act of 1965, and the Fair Housing Act of 1968. Though formally ended, the Jim Crow era had lasted from the 1880s to the 1960s. Its legacy was a society still struggling with the effects of "separate and unequal."

See also: **Civil Rights Movement, Plessy v. Ferguson**

FURTHER READING

Adelson, Bruce. *Brushing Back Jim Crow: The Integration of Minor-League Baseball in the American South*. Charlottesville: University Press of Virginia, 1999.

Gilmore, Glenda E. *Gender and Jim Crow: Women and the Politics of White Supremacy in North Carolina, 1896–1920*. Chapel Hill: University of North Carolina Press, 1996.

Litwack, Leon F. *Trouble in Mind: Black Southerners in the Age of Jim Crow*. New York: Knopf, 1998.

McMillen, Neil R. *Dark Journey: Black Mississippians in the Age of Jim Crow*. Urbana: University of Illinois Press, 1989.

Oshinsky, David M. *Worse than Slavery: Parchman Farm and the Ordeal of Jim Crow Justice*. New York: Free Press, 1996.

Schneider, Mark R. *Boston Confronts Jim Crow, 1890–1920*. Boston: Northeastern University Press, 1997.

JOBS, STEVEN PAUL

Computer designer and corporate executive Steven Jobs (1955–) was the co-founder of Apple Computers. He helped create one of the first affordable personal computers for home use and launched one of the largest industries in the United States. Jobs, with his friend, Steve Wozniak (1950–), pioneered the design and development of desktop computers.

Born in 1955 and adopted by Paul and Clara Jobs of Mountainview, California, Steven Jobs grew up in the comfortable environment his adoptive parents provided. His father was a machinist, and his mother an accountant. Steve attended high school in Los Gatos, California, where his family had moved. While in high school he became involved with electronics projects and worked a summer job at a nearby computer firm, Hewlett Packard. After graduating in 1972 Jobs attended Reed College for two years before dropping out. He worked for the Atari computer company part time where he earned enough money to visit India to study Eastern spiritualism. While in India he practiced meditation and studied Eastern culture, but he became ill with dysentery after three months and was forced to return to the United States for adequate medical treatment.

In 1975 Jobs began associating with a group of computer aficionados known as the Homebrew Computer Club. There he met a technical whiz named Steve Wozniak, who was working on building a small computer. Jobs and Wozniak teamed up and formed Apple Computer Corporation in 1976. Wozniak finished the design of his small computer and, working out of Steve Jobs' parents' garage, the two men worked at refining and marketing their product.

Jobs saw a huge gap in the existing computer market at that time because no computer was yet targeted for home use. While Wozniak improved his initial computer, Jobs lined up investors and bank financing.

The redesigned computer, called the "Apple II," hit the marketplace in 1977. The first year sales reached $2.7 million and within three years had grown to $200 million. Jobs and Wozniak successfully and importantly opened an entirely new market—the home, or personal, computer. They brought the computational speed of business systems into people's homes and started a new era in information processing.

By 1980 the personal computer era was well underway and Apple had plenty of competition from Radio Shack, Commodore, and IBM. Fierce competition proved a good thing for the consumer public, but the Apple corporation stumbled in its efforts to stay ahead of the competition. When the Apple III was introduced to the public in 1980 it suffered from technical and marketing problems. In 1983 Jobs' introduction of the new computer Lisa failed in the marketplace because of its high price and stiff competition from IBM. Apple lost half of its market share in 1983. The Macintosh was introduced in 1984 and continued Apple's trend of poor marketplace performance. By 1985, following internal conflicts at Apple Corporation, Steve Jobs resigned from the company he had founded, retaining only his title as chairman of the board of directors.

That same year, Jobs sold his shares of Apple stock to launch another business in Redwood City, California, called "NEXT." The goal of NEXT was simple: to build a breakthrough computer that would revolutionize research and higher education. Jobs used $100 million of his own assets from Apple shares to start NEXT, and other entrepreneurs, like Texas billionaire Ross Perot (1930—), invested an additional $20 million in the project. Canon Corporation also invested heavily, $100 million in 1989, and an additional $15 million extended in credit to NEXT in 1992. The NEXT did not live up to its goals and Jobs was criticized by the business media as being more of a business huckster than a consistently productive business entrepreneur. However, lightning did strike twice for Jobs.

In 1986 Jobs had purchased a small firm from filmmaker, George Lucas (1945–), called PIXAR, a business specializing in computer animation. During the next six years Jobs put $40 million into PIXAR and set out to make the first-ever completely computer animated film. In 1996 the film "Toy Story" was released. Produced completely with PIXAR computer animation, it was an enormous success. PIXAR's market value for Steve Jobs, who owned 90 percent of the company, climbed suddenly to $1 billion.

Within a short time after PIXAR's success Jobs made headlines again. In 1995 Apple bought Jobs' NEXT company for $400 million and rehired Jobs as advisor to G.F. Amelio, the Apple chief executive officer (CEO). Jobs was also officially re-appointed to Apple's board of directors. Apple understood that it could not hope for a better salesman than Jobs. His genius for infecting others with his enthusiasm was recognized by critics and admirers alike.

By 1997 lightning struck Jobs a third time. Jobs and Bill Gates (1955–), CEO of Microsoft Corporation, announced that their companies were joining forces. Microsoft would invest $150 million for a nonvoting minority stake in Apple and the two companies would cooperate in several marketing and technology fronts. This alliance made Microsoft and Apple the two largest players in the still growing computer industry. Steve Jobs regained his former position as one of the richest and most successful people in the revolutionary marketplace of home and business computers.

See also: **Computer Industry, Stephen Wozniak**

FURTHER READING

Butcher, Lee. *Accidental Millionaire: The Rise and Fall of Steven Jobs at Apple Computer.* St. Paul, MN: Paragon House, 1987.

Encyclopedia of World Biography. Detroit: Gale Research, 1998, s.v. "Jobs, Steven."

Rose, Frank. *West of Eden: The End of Innocence at Apple Computer.* New York: Viking, 1989.

Sculley, John. *From Pepsi to Apple.* New York: Harper & Row, 1987.

Stross, Randall. *Steve Jobs and the Next Big Thing.* New York: Atheneum, 1993.

Young, Jeffrey S. *Steve Jobs: The Journey is the Reward.* Glenview, IL: Scott, Foresman, 1988.

JOHNSON, HUGH SAMUEL

Few have the opportunities to serve as did Hugh Samuel Johnson (1882–1942) in war and peace, in the military and in public service. And few who have served did so with as much distinction and universal praise. General Hugh Johnson served in the Army in the first great world war and in the government as an administrator, a critical position during the beginnings of the recovery from the Great Depression.

Hugh Samuel Johnson was born on August 5, 1882, at Fort Scott, Kansas. His father, Samuel Johnston, and mother, Elizabeth Mead, had moved to Kansas from Pontiac, Illinois, in order for the elder Johnston to practice law. Before Hugh's birth, his father dropped the "t" from his last name in an effort to separate himself from another lawyer with a similar name. Shortly after his birth, Hugh Johnson's family moved to Greensburg, Kansas, and the family was to continue moving regularly until 1893 when they moved to

Cherokee Strip in the Indian Territory, now Oklahoma. Johnson's father was appointed the postmaster of Alva, and there he remained for the rest of his childhood. Johnson rode horseback, hunted, and studied at local schools. He rubbed shoulders with frontiersmen and Indians.

Johnson studied at Northwest Normal School (later to be Oklahoma Northwestern Teachers College) until the start of the Spanish–American War, when he ran away to enlist in the Teddy Roosevelt's (1858–1919) Rough Riders. Brought back home by his parents, Johnson extracted a promise of an appointment to West Point, and his father was able to deliver, having become active in Democratic Party politics. Johnson did not have a very distinguished career at West Point, finishing in the middle of his class and graduating in 1903. After West Point, Johnson entered the cavalry service in Texas.

Immediately after the great San Francisco earthquake and fire in 1906, Johnson's 1st Cavalry was ordered to the area to administer relief. By coincidence, the two officers above him in the chain of command were transferred or taken ill, and he was left to feed, shelter, and cloth seventeen thousand destitute people. He did the job well. In addition, Johnson spent two years in the Philippine Islands from 1907 to 1909, was executive officer at Yosemite National Park from 1910 to 1912, and was superintendent of Sequoia National Park in 1911. After a short tour on the Mexican border in Arizona, Johnson received orders to Harvard Law School. When war broke out in Europe in 1914, Johnson was transferred to the University of California, where he finished a three year course of study in 19 months. Johnson received a Bachelor of Arts in 1915 and his Doctor of Jurisprudence in 1916 with the highest honors.

Armed with his law degree, Johnson reported to General John Pershing's command in Mexico. While there, he studied the problems of Mexico's form of government, and according to Johnson, he was to study "the whole body of constitutional, administrative, State and municipal law of both the United States and the Republic of Mexico." This study "soaked me through with the theory and practice of Federal, State and municipal political structure in the United States." This formed the basis for his next big assignment: the establishment of the Selective Service Administration.

Hugh Johnson was next ordered to Washington to serve as the assistant to the law officer of the Bureau of Insular Affairs. In this post, he prepared briefs for cases in the Supreme and Circuit courts. His superior, General Crowder, was assigned by President Woodrow Wilson

(1913–1921) to draw up a bill for organizing a large army in preparation for joining the war in Europe. Johnson was assigned the task, and wrote the draft version of the bill that would establish the draft in 1917. Moreover, as Deputy Provost Marshal General, he wrote the rules and policies under which the draft would be implemented, and was the executive in charge during 1917 and early 1918. Johnson established a draft system that was decentralized, placing much authority on local draft boards while making the entire system far more fair than draft systems had been before. Johnson's accomplishment was considered brilliant and he was awarded the Distinguished Service Medal.

Johnson wanted to serve in combat, however, and he made several attempts to see action in France. Appointed Colonel on March 20, 1918, however, he took over the Purchase and Supply Bureau of the General Staff as a Brigadier General just the following month. Johnson did another brilliant job of bringing order to chaos in the Army supply system. During this time, he also served on President Wilson's War Industries Board, where he made friends with an important person, Bernard Baruch. Yet Johnson still itched for combat, and on September 1, 1918, he was able to take command of the 15th Brigade, 8th Division, at Camp Fremont in California. Before he was able to get to France, however, the Armistice was signed and the war was over. Disappointed, Johnson resigned from the military and assumed a career in the civilian world of business.

During the 1920s, Johnson worked with the Moline Plow Company and the Moline Implement Company. He remained close to Bernard Baruch, and they worked together on plans for an economic crash they saw coming. Together they joined President Franklin Roosevelt's (1933–1945) "New Deal" brain trust. When Roosevelt was elected in 1932, Johnson was credited with many of the planks in Roosevelt's New Deal platform. General Johnson helped draft the National Industrial Recovery Act, and when it was passed into law, Johnson was appointed as the first head of the National Recovery Administration (NRA). As such, Johnson was in charge of establishing codes of fair practice for business (companies who complied were awarded the "Blue Eagle"), and in organizing industry throughout the country to create jobs. Sincerity, energy, and skillful administration characterized his work at the NRA and he was credited with creating nearly 2.8 million jobs worth about $3 billion in payroll. The NRA had a major role in abolishing child labor and sweatshops, and in regulating hours, wages, and working conditions. He resigned from the NRA on

October 15, 1934, and the Supreme Court overturned the NRA law shortly thereafter.

Hugh Johnson served as Works Progress Administrator in New York City from August to October, 1935, but never again held a position in public service. He increasingly broke ranks with the Roosevelt administration until ultimately he supported Wendell L. Willkie in the election of 1940. Johnson's opposition to involvement in the coming war in Europe and to Roosevelt stemmed from his belief that the United States military was unprepared for entry in World War II (1939–1945) and for what he termed "amazing blunders and failures" by the New Deal brain trust.

Johnson continued to be constructive, typically, even as the advent of the war approached. He wrote columns in the Scripps–Howard newspaper chain from 1934 until his death. He applied for reinstatement into the Army Reserve, and was saddened when the appointment was declined.

Hugh Johnson married Helen Kilbourne on January 5, 1904. They had one child, Kilbourne Johnston (who resumed using the "t" in the last name). Besides his service medals, Johnson was affiliated with both Phi Delta Phi and Phi Beta Kappa fraternities. He was an Anglican Catholic by religion. Johnson died on April 15, 1942, in Washington, D.C. He was buried in Arlington National Cemetery with full military honors.

See also: **National Recovery Administration, New Deal, Franklin Delano Roosevelt**

FURTHER READING

Columbia Encyclopedia. New York: Columbia University Press, 1993, s.v. "Johnson, Hugh."

Observer, Unofficial. *The New Dealers*. New York: The Literary Guild, 1934.

Ohl, John Kennedy. *Hugh S. Johnson and the New Deal*, available On Line @ www.mc.maricop.edu/ academics/soc_sci/history/johl/new_deal.html/.

Perkins, Francis. *Roosevelt I Knew*. New York: Viking, 1946.

Time Magazine's Man of the Year: "Recovery: Hugh S. Johnson."*Time*, January 1, 1934.

JOINT STOCK COMPANY

A joint stock company is a specific form of business organization that is structured like a corporation, but is treated like a partnership in the eyes of the law.

Such companies are no longer common in the United States, but are still frequently found in Europe. Like a corporation, a joint stock company has a legal identity distinct from the legal identity of whomever owns it. Its owners hold shares in the company that can be freely transfered to others, and the company continues to exist even if its original members no longer retain ownership of it. Like a partnership, the owners of a joint stock company have some limited liability if the company goes bankrupt or is sued. Joint stock companies are easier to establish than corporations, but they share the ability of corporations to raise large amounts of capital.

Even for the prosperous governments of Britain and the Netherlands in the seventeenth century, settling the North American continent was too expensive a proposition to shoulder on their own. Before Christopher Columbus's (1451–1506) discovery of the New World was a century old, the British government was granting exclusive charters to joint stock companies like the Levant Company and the Muscovy Company to establish colonies around the world. By pooling the wealth of many private businessmen, these companies could undertake the huge expense of funding colonial settlements until they became profitable. The first joint stock company in America, the Virginia Company of London, failed to produce a profit in Jamestown, Virginia. After 18 years of losses, Britain dissolved the company in 1624 and took over the settlement. The Plymouth Company, a joint stock company founded to settle New England, was a little more profitable, and the Massachusetts Bay Company (founded in 1629) successfully established a colony in Salem, Massachusetts; Boston; and Connecticut. Another joint stock company, the Dutch West India Company, settled present-day New Jersey and New York before England seized the territory from the Netherlands in the 1660s. The joint stock companies' charters gave them wide powers to recruit armies, establish political institutions, and collect taxes, and because all of its owners lived in the colony the Massachusetts Bay Company actually achieved independent self-management. This kind of independence made the British Crown very nervous, however, and in 1684 it cancelled the Bay Company's charter and ruled the colony directly.

See also: **Corporation, Partnership, Settlement and Economic Development**

JONES, MARY HARRIS

Mary "Mother" Jones (1830–1930) is one of the great legends of American progressive politics. After

Mary "Mother" Jones.

losing her own family to yellow fever, Mary Jones found in the lives of the downtrodden a new family to nurture and support. She did this for seventy years as a trade union organizer, a feminist, and a campaigner against child labor in America.

"Mother Jones" was born in 1830, near Dublin, Ireland to parents who were eager to emigrate. When Mary was five years old, her father came to America, where he went to work building canals and railroads, a job similar to the one he had held in Ireland. Once he became a naturalized American citizen around 1840, he sent for his wife and daughter.

The family first settled in Toronto, Canada, where Mary's father was working on one of the first Canadian railroads. They later moved to Michigan. Mary was an excellent student and she graduated with high honors from high school. She became a teacher at a Catholic school in Monroe, Michigan, soon after graduation.

She moved to Chicago to explore the possibilities of becoming a professional dressmaker, but, at age 30, returned to teaching, this time in Memphis, Tennessee. There she met and married Robert Jones, an iron

worker who was an enthusiastic member of the Iron Moulder's Union. During the first four years of their marriage they had four children. Work was plentiful in Tennessee, and for a time the family enjoyed a modest prosperity. But in 1867 a sudden yellow fever epidemic swept through Memphis, taking the lives of Mary's husband and all of her children. At 37, Mary Jones's life was devastated and she was completely on her own.

She returned to Chicago and worked as a dressmaker, but her bad luck continued when her dressmaking business was destroyed in the Chicago Fire of 1871. Homeless and penniless, she turned to her deceased husband's fellow union members for help. Their compassion towards her touched her heart. She felt that the union had saved her life. From that time on, she pursued union organizing with an astonishing enthusiasm that made her an American legend.

Mary Jones began working as a union activist with the Knights of Labor. This union was founded in 1869 in an attempt to unite all workers under a single organization. Mary discovered she had a real talent for inspiring others with her speeches. The Knights of Labor often sent her to particularly tense spots during strikes. She could inspire workers to stay with the union during the hard days of labor action, when there was neither work nor money.

Joining strikers in the coal mines of Pennsylvania in 1873, she witnessed conditions bordering on slavery and children near starvation. Her own Irish heritage caused her to work passionately on behalf of the mostly Irish workers. It was her kindly, protective concern for the workers in the Pennsylvania coal mines that earned her the nickname "Mother Jones."

Mother Jones moved from strike to strike. In 1877 she was involved in the nationwide walkout for better conditions for railroad workers. In 1880 she was in Chicago on behalf of workers trying to obtain an eight-hour day. She also took part in the strike at the McCormick-Harvester works, where a bomb killed several policemen and police fired randomly into a crowd of union workers, killing 11 people and wounding dozens of others.

In her 60s Mother Jones became an organizer for the United Mine Workers Union. Since judges were reluctant to jail such an elderly woman, her age was an asset to the union movement. As she grew older, her attention focused on securing laws that prohibited child labor. She made speeches and engaged newspaper writers to accompany her to places where children were working in slave-like conditions. She also became active in the movement to obtain the right of women to vote.

During the final years of her life, Jones continued to move around the country, giving fiery speeches and organizing workers. She was one of the founders of the Social Democratic Party in 1898 and of the Industrial Workers of the World in 1905. She helped to organize the coal fields of Pennsylvania in 1899. At age 82 she was arrested during a violent strike in West Virginia and sentenced to 20 years in jail. Public outcry was so loud that she was pardoned by the governor and released. She then went on to spend six days in Michigan's Copper Country in August 1913, supporting a copper miners' strike. A woman of astonishing vigor, she marched three blocks in a miners' parade at age 83. In her 90s, she returned to Chicago to work at organizing dressmakers.

On her 100th birthday Mother Jones was asked to speak on the radio about her experiences. She spoke long and well, denouncing the exploitation by business of the American worker and urging all her listeners to organize to transform an unjust society that had fallen into a great Depression. Unchanged by time and full of passion for justice for the American worker, Mother Jones died in Silver Springs, Maryland, in 1930. She became a legend in her lifetime.

See also: **Chicago Fire of 1871, Industrial Workers of the World, Knights of Labor, Labor Movement, United Mine Workers**

FURTHER READING

Fetherling, Dale. *Mother Jones, Miner's Angel.* Carbondale: Southern Illinois University Press, 1974.

Mooney, Fred. *Struggle in the Coal Fields.* Morgantown: West Virginia University Library, 1967.

Jones, Mary Harris. *Autobiography of Mother Jones.* Mary Parton, ed. Chicago: Charles H. Kerr, 1925.

————. *Mother Jones Speaks: Collected Speeches and Writings.* Philip S. Foner, ed. New York: Monad Press, 1983.

————. *The Correspondence of Mother Jones.* Edward Steel, ed. Pittsburgh: University of Pittsburgh Press, 1985.

Werstein, Irving. *Labor's Defiant Lady: The Story of Mother Jones.* New York: Thomas Crowell Press, 1969.

JONES, SAMUEL MILTON

Samuel Milton Jones (1846–1904) was born in the village of Ty Mawr, in Caernarvonshire, Wales, on August 3, 1846. Jones was brought to the United States at the age of three and raised in New York, where he received only about thirty months of schooling. At the age of 18, in 1864, Jones found work in the Titusville, Pennsylvania, oil fields. Jones did well in the oil business, and worked the industry in Pennsylvania, West Virginia, Ohio, and Indiana. In 1870 he became a producer himself.

When Jones' first wife died, he moved to Ohio in 1886 seeking some change in his life. He operated from a headquarters in Lima, Ohio, and operated his oil fields, which were the result of a big strike that year. Also in 1886 Jones met and married a woman from a prominent Toledo family, Helen W. Beach. They were to have three sons.

Jones studied oil field production. In 1893 he invented the "sucker rod," a device that permitted deep–well drilling. He made a fortune on the sucker rod by establishing a manufacturing plant in Toledo he called the Acme Sucker–Rod Company. Jones was an efficient business manager. But he was also a kind and benevolent employer who introduced many worker reforms such as the 8–hour day, paid vacations, and a minimum wage. He also eliminated child labor and piece–work. He instituted a five percent Christmas Bonus. Many of his competitors and political enemies called Jones "socialistic."

Jones hung a sign in his factory extolling the "Golden Rule" and encouraged all employees to honor it. He used the same Golden Rule in his own dealings and believed it worked. From this, his workers and the general public came to call him "Golden Rule Jones".

Golden Rule Jones entered politics in 1897. Running as a Republican, he was elected mayor of Toledo. But his political allies did not support the reforms he championed, and he fell out of favor. Jones's reforms included fighting against corruption, improvement of industrial conditions in the city, and the establishment of city parks. The Republicans refused to nominate Jones in 1899. But he ran as an independent and won by a landslide. Following this victory, Jones brought the 8-hour day and minimum wage to city workers.

Jones continued with his reforms as he won four successive elections. He pushed for municipal ownership of services and utilities, and the direct popular nomination of candidates for public office by petition (without the intervention of political party machinations). He added public services and established public parks and kindergartens. Jones died in office on July 12, 1904, but his reforms were carried on by his mayoral successor.

FURTHER READING

Biography.com. ''Samuel Milton Jones,'' available On Line @ www.search.biography.com.

Encyclopedia Britannica. Chicago: Encyclopedia Britannica, 1994, s.v. ''Jones, Samuel Milton.''

Killits, John, ed. *Toledo and Lucas County Ohio, 1623–1923*. Chicago: S.J. Clarke, 1923.

Van Doren, Charles. *Webster's American Biographies*. Springfield, Mass.: Merriam-Webster, Inc., 1984.

''Woodlawn Cemetery Necrology: Samuel M. Jones,'' available On Line @ www.history.utoledo.edu.

JUNK BONDS

Junk bonds are bonds issued at higher yields than investment grade bonds. The higher the yield, expressed as a percentage rate, the higher the risk of the bond. Two major rating services, Standard and Poor's, and Moody, have slightly different bond rating scales. Bonds rated lower than BBB on Standard and Poor's, or Baa on Moody are considered junk bonds. In comparison, Standard and Poor's rates investment grade bonds at BBB up to AAA.

Junk bonds, issued by companies without long track records of sales and earnings and/or with shaky credit ratings, must pay higher yields to off-set the real risk of nonpayment. They attract risk-oriented investors willing to gamble that companies issuing the higher interest rate bonds will be able to meet the terms of the bonds. The junk bond market is volatile and investment institutions with fiduciary responsibility, charged with investing wisely for a beneficiary's benefit, generally avoid junk bonds.

Racing into the U.S. investment scene in the 1980s, junk bonds allowed companies to raise funds cheaply. Legendary junk bond guru Michael Milken of the investment company Drexel Burnham Lambert had dazzling success raising enormous sums of capital for companies through the sale of high-yield junk bonds. Milken and Drexel were behind many junk bond finance attempts at company takeovers. In 1988, interestingly, the fortunes of many unsuspecting buyers were lost when the Securities and Exchange Commission charged Milken and Drexel with insider trading and stock fraud, which drove the company out of business.

In the late 1990s junk bonds underwent a reincarnation of sorts; they became a more acceptable part of a highly diversified investment portfolio. A number of professionally managed high yield junk bond funds emerged and offered investors a safer route than buying individual issues.

See also: **Bonds, Investment, Standard and Poor's**

KAISER, HENRY JOHN

During the first part of the twentieth century Henry Kaiser (1882–1967) became one of the most prominent business entrepreneurs in the United States. Because he built most of his businesses in the western United States, he played a major role in developing the economy of that region. By the end of his life he had founded Kaiser Paving, Kaiser Steel, Kaiser-Frazer Automobile Corp., Kaiser Aluminum and Chemicals, Permanente Cement, Kaiser Industries, and the Kaiser Health Plan, the largest health maintenance organization (HMO) in the United States.

Born in 1882 in upstate New York to German immigrant parents, Kaiser was the youngest of four children. He began working full time at age thirteen in a dry goods store in Utica, New York. His boundless energy, optimism, and creativity showed in most things he did. By age seventeen Kaiser had taken up photography, just as the nearby Eastman Kodak Company was pioneering major advances in photographic equipment. He began as a partner in a small photographic studio, and by age twenty-one had opened a successful string of photography shops on the east coast of Florida aimed at servicing the tourist trade.

Looking elsewhere for more business opportunities, Kaiser made his way to the west coast of Canada and started a cement paving company. Before long, he expanded his operations to Washington, Oregon, and California. Later his headquarters moved from Canada to Oakland, California.

Kaiser's major work began as an extension of his cement company. He earned a reputation for fast, high quality work as a road builder and expanded his operations to build highways. In 1931, Kaiser joined an incorporated consortium of contractors known as Six Companies in order to contract with the federal government to build the Hoover Dam. He served as a liaison between the contractors and the government bureaucrats. Later he was similarly involved in building major

portions of the Bonneville and Grand Coulee dams on the Columbia River.

With the outbreak of World War II (1939–1945), Kaiser recognized that the war would enlarge the prospects for business by increasing the need for raw-materials, such as aluminum, steel, and magnesium. Between 1939 and 1941, he advocated greater business involvement in war preparations. After 1939, Kaiser became heavily engaged in the shipbuilding industry, primarily the building of cargo ships. He attracted national attention during World War II, gaining the reputation of a "Miracle Man" and the "Number 1 Industrial Hero" because of the speed with which he built ships crucial to the war effort. Kaiser ignored the usual methods of building ships bottom up from the keel; instead he employed assembly-line methods. (His reputation was so well established that President Franklin Roosevelt (1933–1945) considered him as a vice presidential running mate in the 1944 election.)

Kaiser made his share of enemies in business. When eastern steel shortages began in the United States prior to the attack on Pearl Harbor (December 12, 1941), Kaiser began to make his own steel. The large steel industries of the east were outraged. After World War II began, however, much of the anger against him fell away as the nation entered into a spirit of business cooperation to support the war effort.

Kaiser joined in a business partnership with Joseph Frazer in 1945 to manufacture automobiles that featured streamlined body curves and eliminated old-style wheel fenders altogether. Kaiser-Frazer quickly became the fourth largest producer of automobiles in America. It was a short-lived enterprise, lasting only until the early 1950s. At that time Kaiser-Frazer could no longer compete with Detroit's Big Three: General Motors, Ford, and the Chrysler Corporation. Nonetheless, Kaiser-Frazer automobiles were visionary and changed the shape and design of modern cars. Though Kaiser's automobile business was a business failure, the company inspired car owners with a new vision of what cars could be. Moreover, despite dropping his car venture, Kaiser continued to develop his aluminum and chemicals companies which had been created to aid the production of his modern, lightweight cars.

Kaiser's aluminum company was, overall, his most profitable enterprise. After World War II, however, the Kaiser Corporation became a multi-faceted empire. His company's personal health care program, Kaiser Permanente, eventually grew to become the largest health maintenance organization (HMO) in the nation.

Kaiser was a successful and creative businessman who was known as a ''workaholic'' because of his addiction to his work. In 1954 he moved with his second wife to Hawaii but never retired; leisure did not interest him, and he had few hobbies. Though he remained seriously overweight, he enjoyed good health until near the end of his life. He died in Hawaii in 1967, at the age of 85, still involved with the many successful business projects he created.

See also: **Assembly Line, Automobile Industry, Health Maintenance Organizations, Liberty Ships**

FURTHER READING

Adams, Stephen B. *Mr. Kaiser Goes to Washington: The Rise of a Government Entrepreneur.* Chapel Hill: University of North Carolina Press, 1997.

Cobbs, Elizabeth A. *The Rich Neighbor Policy: Rockefeller and Kaiser in Brazil.* New Haven: Yale University Press, 1992.

Foster, Mark S. *Henry J. Kaiser: Builder in the Modern American West.* Austin: University of Texas Press, 1989.

Heiner, Albert P. *Henry J. Kaiser, American Empire Builder.* New York: P. Long Pub., 1989.

Loeb (Carl M.) Rhoades and Company. *Aluminum, an Analysis of the Industry in the United States.* New York: Loeb (Carl M.) Rhoades and Company, 1950.

KANSAS

Native Americans roamed the plains of Kansas at the time French explorers paddled the Mississippi River in the 1700s. The area now known as Kansas was part of the vast French holdings in central North America known as the Louisiana Territory. In 1803 Napoleon Bonaparte, Emperor of France, needed funds to support his European wars. U.S. President Thomas Jefferson (1801–1809) seized this opportunity and purchased Louisiana land for $15 million, doubling the size of the United States and bringing the region that would become Kansas and several other states under American control.

President Jefferson sent the Lewis and Clark expedition to explore the country from St. Louis to the Pacific Ocean. When the expedition reached Kansas, they described the country as ''delightful . . . the whole country exhibits a rich appearance.'' Although this account was favorable, other explorers reported Kansas to be a dry wasteland, and as a result migration to Kansas started out slowly compared to other parts of the country. However, the rich abundance of fur-bearing animals lured American trappers and traders to the area.

During the first half of the 1800s settlers started to migrate west to Kansas, at this point still an unorganized territory, in search of adventure and a new life. Missionaries also came to the plains and taught tribes of the region how to work the land. Eventually, the United States government would push all Native Americans westward onto reservations.

When gold was discovered in the 1850s in what is now Colorado, miners rushed across the country to seek their fortune. As mining grew in the west, transportation was needed to carry people and goods. The Leavenworth and Pike's Peak Express to Denver made 19 stops in Kansas along the route. Federal land grants were awarded to other companies to encourage more railroad building and settlement along the railroads. Over the next several decades about 200 companies built railroads across Kansas. Many towns sprang up along the track, together with hotels, gambling houses, and saloons.

The 1850s were also a period of political turmoil in Kansas. The passage of the Kansas-Nebraska Act in 1854 formally organized the territory of Kansas, and allowed for the people who lived there to determine if slavery would be permitted there. Previously, the Missouri Compromise had prevented slavery from spreading into Kansas, and the predominantly anti-slavery North was greatly angered by what they saw as an attempt by the South to expand its power and influence. Pro-slavery southerners and anti-slavery northerners flooded into the region in an effort to gain control. There was frequent conflict between the two sides, the area became known as ''Bleeding Kansas.'' The controversy over Kansas worsened the split between the

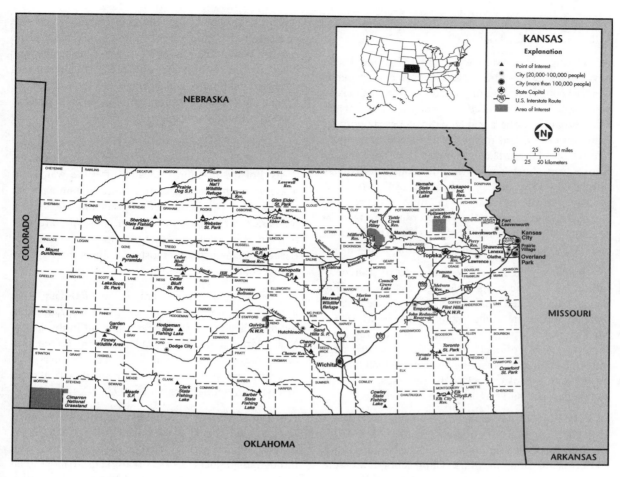

State of Kansas.

North and the South, was a major force behind the formation of the Republican Party, and helped drive the nation in the American Civil War (1861–1865). Kansas would eventually be admitted to the Union as a free state in 1861.

After the Civil War thousands migrated to Kansas to take advantage of the government's promise of free land. In a government-backed effort to encourage settlers to move west, the Homestead Act of 1862 allowed any citizen who paid a ten dollar filing fee to claim up to 160 acres of federal land as long as they farmed the land for 5 years. In 1873 the Timber Culture Act made the same promise to those who would plant trees on one-fourth of the land they claimed within four years. By that time new Kansas homesteaders had already claimed about 6 million acres.

After the Civil War the government also encouraged the development of railroads by giving the railroad companies land grants. More than 200 companies laid tracks that zigzagged across Kansas. As the railroads offered land grant acreage at low prices and reduced fares to new settlers, they helped to open the state for commerce and development.

The new settlers in Kansas were known as "sodbusters" because they cut up large squares of sod and, as lumber was scarce, used them to make walls and roofs for their new homes. They planted crops in place of the sod. They soon discovered how harsh life could be on the plains. "Rattlesnakes, bedbugs, fleas, and the 'prairie itch' were what kept us awake at nights and made life miserable," wrote W.H. Russell, a Rush County settler. Also, a grasshopper plague in 1874 destroyed crops on 5,000 square miles of farmland. In addition, the severe weather—blizzards, rainstorms, droughts, and prairie fires—stranded trains and destroyed crops and homes.

After the Civil War cattle was abundant in Texas but scarce in the north. Texas cattle ranchers took advantage of the demand from the north and began driving their cattle to the nearest railroad stations in Kansas. "Cow towns" were established at cattle shipping points. The cow towns played host to cowboys looking to spend their money in hotels, saloons, dance halls, and gambling houses.

During the boom years of the 1870s and 1880s new settlers were attracted to Kansas due to better weather conditions and improved farming methods as well as easy railroad access to outlying areas of the state. Wealthy farmers and land developers bought up land and established towns. At the same time, more than 15,000 former slaves traveled from the south to Kansas to establish a new way of life for themselves. A blizzard in 1886 and a drought in 1887, however, quickly caused the state to fall into a depression. Ranchers were forced to leave because more than 20 percent of the state's cattle herd perished in the blizzard and the farmers lost all their crops in the drought.

Farmers who stayed behind were frustrated by falling wheat prices and the high cost of shipping goods. They formed the Farmers' Alliance and became a major component of the Populist Party in the 1890s. Members of the party were voted into congressional seats of other political office. The Populists were instrumental in implementing laws that helped farmers by regulating banks, stockyards, railroads, telegraph companies, and building-and-loan associations.

The Populist movement gave way to the Progressive administrations of governors from 1905 to 1913. New reforms called for laws that reduced railroad fares and costs for shipping grain. Child labor laws were instituted along with workmen's compensation and further banking regulations. In addition, the use of machines such as tractors and threshers made farming easier and helped increase crop production. New crops such as sorghum, sugar beets, broomcorn, and alfalfa were harvested in the plains.

During World War I (1914–1918) Kansas stepped up production of wheat to feed the troops. After the war more roads were built to accommodate automobiles built by a Kansan Walter P. Chrysler (1875–1940), founder of the Chrysler Motors automobile company. This modest recovery, however, was only temporary. During the Great Depression (1929–1939) Kansas was devastated. The country suffered the worst depression in history; stock markets crashed and Kansas crop prices dropped. In 1932 a severe drought began and turned the area into a ''dust bowl. Governor Alfred M. Landon attempted to bring relief to farmers and businessmen by reorganizing state banks, cutting taxes, and halting mortgage foreclosures for six months. President Franklin D. Roosevelt's (1933–1945) New Deal provided jobs building libraries, schools, and post offices. The Agricultural Adjustment Act was also passed in 1933 as part of the New Deal. It sought to raise farm prices by encouraging farmers to reduce production. But true economic relief only came at the start of World War II (1939–1945). During the war plants in Kansas built more than 25,000 aircraft and produced munitions and artillery for the war effort. Wheat and soybean farming also stepped up to provide food for military personnel.

After the war, manufacturing growth steadily increased and people began to move from rural to urban areas. For the first three decades after the war, businesses grew in Kansas and meat packing, mining, flour milling, and petroleum refining became the largest industries in the state. In addition, more aircraft were built in Kansas than anywhere else in the country. Farming remained the most prominent part of the state's economy.

Farmers enjoyed prosperity in the 1960s and 1970s as feeds and improved fertilizers increased production, but they faced a crisis as a recession hit in the 1980s. Many farmers lost their land and were forced into bankruptcy. Kansas sought to expand its market of products and signed a trade agreement with the St. Petersburg region of Russia in 1993.

The 1990s also brought extremes in the weather. Drought and topsoil erosion damaged 865,000 acres, drove up prices, and depleted grain stores. From April through September 1993, floods caused more than $574 million worth of damage. Efforts to restore economic growth included the allocation of government block grants. In 1995 the median household income in Kansas was $30,346 and about 11 percent of all Kansans lived below the federal poverty level.

See also: **Bleeding Kansas, Cow Towns, Dust Bowl, Farmers' Alliance, Homestead Act, Homesteaders, Kansas-Nebraska Act, Lewis and Clark Expedition**

FURTHER READING

Anderson, George L. *Kansas West*. San Marino, CA: Golden West Books, 1963.

Aylesworth, Thomas G. *South Central: Arkansas, Kansas, Louisiana, Missouri, Oklahoma*. New York: Chelsea House Publishers, 1988.

Fredeen, Charles. *Kansas*. Minneapolis, MN: Lerner Publications, 1992.

Kummer, Patricia K. *Kansas*. Mankato, MN: Capstone Press, 1999.

Worldmark Encyclopedia of the States. Detroit, MI: Gale Research, 1998, s.v. ''Kansas.''

KANSAS-NEBRASKA ACT (1854)

The Kansas-Nebraska Act of 1854 was the one piece of legislation most responsible for bringing about the American Civil War (1861–1865). Within a year of the passage of the act, free-soil settlers and pro-slavery advocates were at war in Kansas—a confrontation known in the press as ''Bleeding Kansas''. That conflict continued throughout the Civil War, resulting in the death of hundreds of settlers and the destruction of thousands of dollars of property.

The federal government had been looking for a general solution to the conflict between those who wanted to see an expansion of slavery and those who wanted to see the abolition of slavery. The first serious attempt to resolve the issue was the Compromise of 1820, or the Missouri Compromise. This solution would have Missouri join the union as a slave state, while Maine would come in as a wage-labor state. Finally, no more slave states could be created north of Missouri's southern boundary (36 degrees; 30 minutes latitude). The slavery issue reemerged after the Mexican War (1846–1848), in which the United States won California, Arizona, and New Mexico—territory south of the Missouri Compromise line, but not specifically covered under the Compromise. The Compromise of 1850 tried to patch together a solution by admitting slave states and free states to the Union in pairs and passing a stronger federal fugitive slave law, among other items. By 1854, however, the flood of settlers heading west to the Nebraska territory exposed the failure of the Compromise and brought the slavery issue before Congress once again.

The Kansas-Nebraska Act was the brainchild of Senator Stephen A. Douglas (1813–1861), a Democrat from Illinois. Douglas proposed to split the Nebraska Territory into two states, Kansas and Nebraska, and to repeal the Missouri Compromise (which would have kept slavery out of both states). Douglas believed that sectional conflict between the North and the South over slavery could be avoided by adopting a policy he called ''popular sovereignty.'' Popular Sovereignty had been suggested by Michigan Senator Lewis Cass. It allowed the citizens of each territory to decide by referendum whether slavery could exist in their areas. Although the concept was fair in principle, it was very easy to abuse. Of the first three elections for congressional representatives in Kansas (each of which resulted in a pro-slavery victory) congressional examinations later found all of them to be fraudulent.

Instead of bringing the North and South closer together, Douglas's bill widened the gap between North and South. Many northern voters regarded his Kansas-Nebraska Act as a betrayal of their key principles of free soil and free labor. The Democratic Party now had very little appeal in the North. It became the party of the South and the party of slavery. The Democratic Party lost control of most free-state legislatures in the elections of 1854 while Free-Soilers, Whigs, and other opposition parties gained representation.

The Kansas-Nebraska Act drove the nation closer to secession. Organizations such as the New England Emigrant Aid Company were formed to promote free-labor settlement in Kansas. Among the provisions that they donated to the free labor forces in Kansas were rifles. Southerners responded with their own organizations, led by public figures like Senator David Atchison of Missouri, to intimidate the anti-slave forces and to insure a pro-slavery population in the territories. The end result of this process was the outbreak of civil war and the eventual admission of Kansas to the Union as a free state on January 29, 1861.

See also: **Bleeding Kansas, Civil War (Economic Causes of)**

FURTHER READING

Brown, Thomas J. ''Franklin Pierce's Land Grant Veto and the Kansas-Nebraska Session of Congress,'' *Civil War History*, 42:2, 1996.

Johannsen, Robert Walter. *The Frontier, the Union, and Stephen A. Douglas*. Urbana: University of Illinois Press, 1989.

Johannsen, Robert Walter. *Stephen A. Douglas*. Illini Books Edition. Urbana, Ill.: University of Illinois Press, 1997.

McPherson, James M. *Battle Cry of Freedom: The Civil War Era*. New York: Oxford University Press, 1988.

Wolff, Gerald W. *The Kansas-Nebraska Bill: Party, Section, and the Coming of the Civil War*. New York: Revisionist Press, 1977.

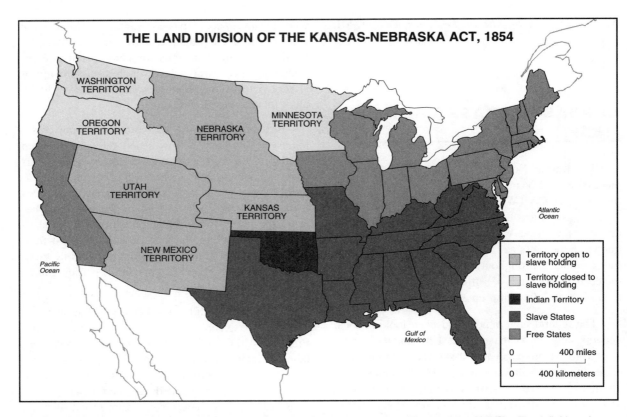

THE LAND DIVISION OF THE KANSAS-NEBRASKA ACT, 1854

WASHINGTON TERRITORY

OREGON TERRITORY

NEBRASKA TERRITORY

MINNESOTA TERRITORY

UTAH TERRITORY

KANSAS TERRITORY

NEW MEXICO TERRITORY

Pacific Ocean

Atlantic Ocean

Gulf of Mexico

Territory open to slave holding

Territory closed to slave holding

Indian Territory

Slave States

Free States

0　　　400 miles

0　　　400 kilometers

The land division detailed in the Kansas-Nebraska Act of 1854 was one of the events leading up to the Civil War. The definition of which states west of Missouri would be free and which would allow slavery aroused strong public feeling on both sides.

KEELBOATS

Keelboats were long, narrow crafts that come to a point at one or both ends (the bow and/or the stern). They linked the northwest and southwest frontiers of the United States and continued to do so even after the introduction of the steamboat in 1811.

Keelboats moved along waterway currents. Going downstream, a keelboat could carry up to thirty tons of cargo and travel at about five miles an hour. Traveling upstream was more difficult. Return trips, often from New Orleans to Pittsburgh, could take as long as four months, traveling sometimes at a pace of less than one mile per hour. The boatmen poled, paddled, or pulled the boat by hand.

Powering keelboats against the currents of the Mississippi, Ohio, or Allegheny Rivers required keelboat workers to have incredible strength and endurance. The boats frequently had to be towed with a rope or ''corde'' upstream, where currents were too strong for rowing. The crew climbed over rocks and cliffs and waded through swampy waters at the river's edge to pull the boat, always alert for venomous snakes, alligators, bears, wildcats, and wolves.

When snags or quicksand prevented keelboat crews from cordelling, they used the arduous technique of warping. Warping involves tying a rope to a tree, returning to the boat, and hauling it hand over hand up the river.

Through the determination and strength of keelboat workers in the 1800s, settlers, their belongings, livestock, and freight were transported throughout the nation's interior. Keelboat workers were paid an average of $10 to $20 per month and provided to a vital link to the nation's interior, contributing to the nation's westward expansion.

See also: **Westward Expansion**

KELLEY, FLORENCE

Florence Kelley (1859–1932) never saw the fruits of her efforts to agitate on behalf of working women and children in the United States. Her early efforts led to minimum wage legislation for women and children in 1937, and to the Federal Fair Labor Standards Act of

Florence Kelley.

1938. Most historians credit her with creating conditions for the legislative abolishment of unregulated child labor and establishing a minimum work wage for all U.S. citizens.

Florence Kelley was born to comfortable circumstances in Philadelphia, Pennsylvania on September 12, 1859, the daughter of U.S. Congressman William Darrow Kelley. Florence grew up in an intensely political household. She was exposed to talk about political changes occurring in the United States, including abolition of slavery and the women's rights movement which was then focused on passing a nineteenth amendment to the Constitution to guarantee the right of women to vote.

Kelley graduated from a Quaker-run school in Philadelphia and then entered Cornell University, graduating at age 23 with a bachelor of arts degree. She taught briefly after graduation, and then in 1883 went to Zurich, Switzerland for graduate studies.

In Switzerland at the age of 25 she met a young Russian medical student whom she married in 1884. While living and studying with her husband, Florence came into contact with a number of European socialists. She learned their new ideas about economics and social structure. At one point she received permission from Friedrich Engels (1820–1895), a collaborator and friend of Karl Marx (1818–1883), to produce an English translation of Engels' important book, *The Conditions of the Working Class in England*. Kelley and Engels corresponded regularly thereafter for several years, and Kelly was deeply influenced by Engels' socialist ideas.

Kelley and her husband returned to the United States in 1886. They had three children together, but the marriage ended in divorce in 1891. During her married life Florence Kelley embraced socialist economic ideas. After her divorce, while raising her three children, she began to put her ideas together with her work life.

Florence began her work life in 1891 as a special agent for the Illinois Bureau of Labor Statistics, inspecting ''sweat-shops''—small unregulated manufacturing companies usually in the clothing manufacturing business, where frequently 10-year-old girls worked 12 to 16 hours a day sewing for dismal wages. At this time in the 1890s, there were no restrictions or laws against these practices.

In 1853 Kelley was appointed by the newly-elected governor of Illinois, John Attgeld, as Illinois's chief factory inspector. In this position she was able to establish within certain factories a free medical examination center for working children. She also recommended legislation related to controlling dangerous machinery in the workplace. She also personally examined more than a thousand shops during a smallpox epidemic in Chicago, ensuring that contaminated garments of clothing were discarded. Unfortunately, after Governor Attgeld lost his re-election bid in 1897, most of Kelley's progressive programs were reversed or abandoned. An Illinois law Kelley had worked on which established an eight-hour workday for women, and banned employment of girls under age 14, was declared unconstitutional by the Illinois Supreme Court. Despite such reversals Kelley went on to become the General Secretary of the National Consumers League, continuing her fight against child labor and poor working conditions in factories.

During the 1920s Kelley came to realize that progressive political reform in the United States, popular in the pre-World War I (1914–1918) era, had changed; the United States had become more politically conservative. More and more people in the United States were associating social welfare programs with "radicals" and socialist subversion.

Florence Kelley died in 1921. Despite setbacks in the implementation of her ideas an astonishing number of them were eventually put into practice, mostly during the Great Depression era (1929–1939). In 1937 the U.S. Supreme Court reversed the Illinois Court decisions related to women's working conditions and millions of women achieved a minimum wage guaranteed by Federal legislation. Child labor was also abolished and maximum hours of employment were established and regulated.

Florence Kelley's "failures" during her lifetime likely represented a series of good ideas raised at the wrong time. During the 1920s, the peak activity of Kelley's work life, the forces of powerful unregulated business interests in the United States served to frustrate many social reforms aimed at improving the health and working conditions of millions of U.S. workers. Arguably it took a Great Depression in the United States to cause U.S. legislators and businessmen to see the values of social reform.

See also: **Child Labor, Fair Labor Standards Act, Women in the Workplace**

FURTHER READING

Blumberg, Dorothy. *Florence Kelley, the Making of a Social Pioneer.* New York: Augustus M. Kelley Press, 1966.

Forbath, William. *Law and the Shaping of the American Labor Movement.* Cambridge, MA: Harvard University Press, 1991.

Goldmark, Josephine. *Impatient Crusader: Florence Kelley's Life Story.* Urbana, IL: University of Illinois, 1953.

Lemons, J. Stanley. *The Woman Citizen, Social Feminism in the 1920s.* Urbana, IL: University of Illinois Press, 1973.

Tentler, Leslie. *Wage-Earning Women: Industrial Work and Family Life in the United States.* New York: Oxford University Press, 1979.

KELLOGG COMPANY

By the time Will Keith Kellogg (1860–1951) launched his cereal company—originally known as the Battle Creek Toasted Corn Flake Company—in 1906, he had already been in the cereal business for more than 10 years as an employee of his brother's Adventist Battle Creek Sanitarium. Dr. John Harvey Kellogg, a strict vegetarian and the sanitarium's internationally celebrated director, also invented and marketed various health foods. One of the foods sold by Dr. Kellogg's Sanitas Food Company was called Granose, a wheat flake the Kellogg brothers had stumbled upon while trying to develop a more digestible form of bread. The wheat flake was produced one night in 1894 following a long series of unsuccessful experiments. The men were running boiled wheat dough through a pair of rollers in the sanitarium basement. The dough had always come out sticky and gummy, until by accident the experiments were interrupted long enough for the boiled dough to dry out. When the dry dough was run through the rollers, it broke into thin flakes. Thus were flaked cereals born.

Commercial production of the Granose flakes began in 1895 with improvised machinery in a barn on the sanitarium grounds. The factory was soon in continuous production, turning out more than 100,000 pounds of flakes in its first year. A ten-ounce box sold for 15 cents, which meant that the Kelloggs collected $12 for each 60-cent bushel of wheat processed, a feat that did not go unnoticed around Battle Creek, Michigan.

Meanwhile, other cereal companies were growing quickly. Kellogg's most notable competitor was the Postum Cereal Company, launched by a former sanitarium patient, C. W. Post. Post added Grape-Nuts to his line in 1898 and by 1900 was netting $3 million a year, an accomplishment that inspired dozens of imitators and turned Battle Creek into the cereal-making capital of the United States.

In spite of the competition, Dr. Kellogg was slow in funding the company's expansion of cereal production. His brother, W.K. Kellogg assumed the leadership of that branch of the business and in 1902 Sanitas

Kellogg's CEO Arnold Langbo shakes the paw of "Tony the Tiger" after announcing that prices would be cut on their most popular cereals.

improved the corn flake that it had first introduced in 1898. The new product had better flavor and a longer shelf life than the unsuccessful 1898 version. By the following year the company was advertising in newspapers and on billboards, sending salesmen into the wholesale market, and introducing an ambitious door-to-door sampling program. In late 1905, Sanitas was producing 150 cases of corn flakes a day with sales of $100,000 a year.

The next year W. K. Kellogg went into business for himself and launched the Battle Creek Toasted Corn Flake Company. Kellogg recognized that advertising and promotion were key to success in a market flooded with look-alike products, so the company spent a third of its initial working capital on an ad in *Ladies Home Journal*. The result was that sales jumped from 33 cases per day to 2,900 cases per day in 1907.

In July 1907 a fire destroyed the main factory building. On the spot, W. K. Kellogg began making plans for a new fireproof factory, and within a week he had purchased land at a site strategically located between two competing railroad lines. Kellogg had the

new plant, with a capacity of 4,200 cases a day, in full operation six months after the fire. "That's all the business I ever want," he is said to have told his son, John L. Kellogg, at the time.

By the time of the fire, the company had already spent $300,000 on advertising but the advertising barrage continued. One campaign told newspaper readers to "wink at your grocer and see what you get." (Winkers got a free sample of Kellogg's Corn Flakes.) In New York City, the ad helped boost Corn Flake sales fifteen-fold. In 1911 the annual advertising budget reached $1 million.

By that time, W. K. Kellogg had finally managed to buy out the last of his brother's share of the company, giving Will Kellogg more than 50 percent of the company's stock. W. K. Kellogg's company had become the Kellogg Toasted Corn Flake Company in 1909, but Dr. Kellogg's Sanitas Food Company had been renamed the Kellogg Food Company and used similar slogans and packaging. Will Kellogg sued his brother for rights to the family name and finally prevailed in 1921.

In 1922 the company reincorporated as the Kellogg Company because it had lost its trademark claim to the name ''Toasted Corn Flakes,'' and had expanded its product line so much that the name no longer accurately described what the company produced. Kellogg introduced Krumbles in 1912, followed by 40% Bran Flakes in 1915 and All-Bran in 1916. Kellogg also made other changes, improving his product, packaging, and processing methods. Many of those developments came from W. K.'s son John L. Kellogg, who had been working for the company since its earliest days. J. L. Kellogg developed a malting process to give the corn flakes more of a nutlike flavor. He also saved the company $250,000 a year by switching from a waxed paper wrapper on the outside of the box to a waxed paper liner inside, and invented All-Bran by adding a malt flavoring to the bran cereal. He held more than 200 patents and trademarks.

In subsequent decades the company continued to add new products, but it never strayed far from the ready-to-eat cereal business. In the early 1950s Kellogg's continued success was tied to two external developments: the postwar baby boom and television advertising. To appeal to the younger market, Kellogg and other cereal makers brought out new lines of presweetened cereals and unabashedly made the key ingredient part of the name. Kellogg's entries included Sugar Frosted Flakes, Sugar Smacks, Sugar Corn Pops, Sugar All-Stars, and Cocoa Crispies. The company created Tony the Tiger and other cartoon pitchmen to sell the products on Saturday-morning television. Sales and profits doubled over the decade.

In the 1980s Kellogg targeted a more health-conscious market. The company spent $50 million to bring three varieties of Nutri-Grain cereal to market in 1982. Two years later, Kellogg sparked a fiber fad when it began adding a health message from the National Cancer Institute to its All-Bran cereal. By the late 1990s Kellogg held about one-third of the U.S. cereal market and produced 12 of the world's top 15 cereal brands.

See also: **Advertising, Will Keith Kellogg, Charles Post**

FURTHER READING

''Breakfast at Battle Creek.'' *Forbes,* September 13, 1982.

Carson, Gerald. *Cornflake Crusade.* Salem, NH: Ayer, 1976.

Hunnicutt, Benjamin Kline. *Kellogg's Six-Hour Day.* Philadelphia, PA: Temple University Press, 1996.

Kellogg Company. *The History of Kellogg Company.* Battle Creek, MI: Kellogg Company, 1986.

Powell, Horace B. *The Original Has This Signature: W. K. Kellogg.* Englewood Cliffs, NJ: Prentice Hall, 1956.

Serwer, Andrew E. ''What Price Brand Loyalty.'' *Fortune*, January 10, 1994.

KELLOGG, FRANK BILLINGS

Frank Billings Kellogg (1856–1937) emerged out of poverty and hardship to achieve a career as U.S. Secretary of State and a recipient of the Nobel Prize for Peace in 1929. Though Kellogg began his professional life as an awkward legal representative of some of the wealthiest Americans, his political and personal friendship with President Theodore Roosevelt (1901–1909) led Kellogg to become one of the most formidable and progressive attorneys in the federal government's efforts to break-up industrial monopolies. Kellogg was the first great prosecutor of the Sherman Anti-Trust Act, a federal law that prohibited an exclusive private monopoly or ownership of any single industry.

Kellogg was born in New York. He relocated to Olmsted County, Minnesota, with his family at age eight, part of the typical pioneering experience of his era, moving from the East Coast to the then mysterious West. Kellogg's father took the family to Minnesota to farm, but the endeavor was not prosperous. Kellogg worked on the family farm and managed to obtain six years of formal education, an accomplishment for children of hard-working farming families.

He determinably worked to be become a lawyer and escape the miseries of farm life. Kellogg passed the bar in 1877, and he described his success as ''a life line thrown to rescue me from a desperate struggle for a livelihood.''

As a young attorney, he took every case that came his way. In 1887, at age 31, Kellogg became a partner in a prestigious law firm in St. Paul, Minnesota, headed by his cousin, Cushman Kellogg Davis. There, Kellogg began a successful career. He took on railroad and iron ore litigation, connected with the exploitation of the great Mesabi mineral range in Minnesota, defending some of the titans of American business, such as John D. Rockefeller, Andrew Carnegie, and the railroad builder James Hill.

During business trips to Washington, D.C., Kellogg met Theodore Roosevelt, then a member of the Civil Service Commission. They became friends, and when

Roosevelt became president, Kellogg had an easy entree to the White House. His friendship with Roosevelt led to many court cases in which Kellogg, representing the federal government, fought many of the most formidable industrial figures of his day. Like Roosevelt, Kellogg was alarmed by the sudden increase in corporate mergers, the formation of huge entities that often resulted in near-total monopolies on industries in the United States.

Appointed as Special Assistant Attorney General, Kellogg began fighting the paper trust, known as the General Paper Company, and won. In 1906 he began prosecution of the Union Pacific Railroad, which was eating up its competition at an alarming rate. These government victories led to the greatest single trust case of the era, the prosecution of the Standard Oil Company for violating the Sherman Anti-Trust Act. Kellogg won a Supreme Court interpretation of his case in 1911, which forced Standard Oil to break-up into smaller, competitive companies. This victory inspired newspapers to describe Kellogg as "the trust buster." Though Kellogg was a largely uneducated, nervous, hot-tempered, outspoken, and undiplomatic man, he had become a winner in the eyes of the public through his work at keeping monopolies from dominating American big business.

In 1912, Kellogg was elected president of the American Bar Association. By this time, Kellogg had undergone a conversion in political thinking. He began his career as a Republican conservative, but by 1912 he admonished his fellow lawyers to "stand for modern economic legislation, necessary to the development of the people."

In 1916 Kellogg was elected as a Republican Senator to the U.S. Congress, representing the state of Minnesota. He was, however, defeated in his 1922 bid for re-election.

President Calvin Coolidge (1923–1929) also liked Kellogg, and saw his usefulness during a prosperous post-war period. In 1925 Coolidge named Kellogg Secretary of State. In this position, Kellogg worked to aid in the reconciliation of German reparation debts to the United States and helped arrange loans to Germany for that country's post-war recovery.

Kellogg's diplomatic successes were modest, and not truly comparable to his important success as a "trust buster" for Theodore Roosevelt, fighting the industrial monopolies of pre-World War I America. Yet, he was also a success as Secretary of State, always striving to convey the spirit of American good will in foreign affairs. In 1929 Kellogg was awarded a Nobel Prize for Peace in honor of his diplomatic success with France, creating the Kellogg-Briand Pact of 1928 in which the signing nations renounced war "as an instrument of national policy," with the hope that it might prevent future war. Frank Billings Kellogg died in 1937.

See also: **Sherman Anti-Trust Act**

FURTHER READING

Armentano, Dominick T. *Antitrust and Monopoly: Anatomy of a Policy Failure*. New York: Holmes & Meier, 1990.

DuBoff, Richard B. *Accumulation and Power: An Economic History of the United States*. Armonk, N.Y.: M.E. Sharpe, 1989.

Ellis, Lewis E. *Frank B. Kellogg and American Foreign Relations, 1925–1929*. New Brunswick, N.J.: Rutgers University Press, 1961.

Ferrell, Robert H. *Frank B. Kellogg*. New York: Cooper Square, 1983.

McChesney, Fred S., and William F. Shughart II, eds. *The Causes and Consequences of Antitrust: The Public Choice Perspective*. Chicago: University of Chicago Press, 1995.

KELLOGG, WILL KEITH

Will Keith Kellogg (1860–1951) was a pioneer producer of health and breakfast foods born in Battle Creek, Michigan. He was the seventh son of John and Ann Kellogg. Kellogg's family background includes noted lithographer Elijah C. Kellogg, well-known physician Albert Kellogg, and diplomat Frank Billings Kellogg (1856–1937), who won the Nobel Peace Prize in 1929.

Will Kellogg's start in life was modest. He attended public school until age fifteen. He then began to work as a salesman for his father's broom company. He attended Parsons Business School in Michigan for three months. In his late teens Kellogg took a job as an assistant to his flamboyant brother Dr. John Kellogg. John Kellogg was a health food crusader and the creator of a health sanitarium in Battle Creek, where Will Kellogg worked as a bookkeeper, shipping clerk, cashier, and troubleshooter. He helped his brother bring the health sanitarium to national prominence.

At the same time Kellogg developed his business skills while by running a subscription service for his brother's health books and managing his brother's Sanitas Food Company. They developed a cooked and flaked wheat cereal which became very successful.

In 1906 Kellogg decided to launch his own breakfast food company. It was first known as the Battle Creek Toasted Corn Flake Company. With an intensive advertising campaign, Will Kellogg built his company into a national corporation, but it had its problems. Kellogg's brother John was the owner of the original patent for the wheat flake cereal. John Kellogg fought his brother in court from 1908 to 1920, challenging Will Kellogg's right to have an independent breakfast cereal company. In 1920 Will Kellogg won the legal battle and claimed exclusive ownership and copyrights to his own cereal products and his company name, the W.K. Kellogg Company.

The wheat and corn flakes were originally developed as health foods to be sold by mail to users of health products. Will Kellogg's later enterprises, however, led him to sell the corn flake products as healthy, enjoyable, and convenient breakfast foods for everyone. Kellogg was enormously successful targeting the mass public this way. At the time, people living in the United States traditionally ate heavy, hot breakfasts. Kellogg achieved a minor revolution when his corn flakes and other cold cereals began to replace the traditional fare.

Will Kellogg was a driven and aggressive man, with whom it was difficult to work. Kellogg groomed his son John to become his successor, but fired him after seventeen years, during which John obtained more than 200 patents for Kellogg's company. Kellogg's grandson was also groomed for the company presidency, but he too was demoted, and later quit the company.

Kellogg broke easily from his parents' Seventh Day Adventist religious faith, but turned much of his early religious training into business and charitable endeavors. During the 1920s he created one of the largest charitable foundations in the nation, the W.K. Kellogg Foundation. Its mission is "to help people help themselves through the practical application of knowledge and resources to improve their quality of life and that of future generations." It is active to the present day.

As a multimillionaire Kellogg purchased a 377-acre ranch in California in 1925. There he raised Arabian horses of the best stock from all over the world. The ranch had high-quality animals and striking architecture and attracted regular visits by world leaders and movie stars during the 1920s.

Will Kellogg was blind for the last ten years of his 91-year life. The creator of the modern breakfast food industry died in 1951. He was known for hard work, a missionary zeal for the possibilities of the future, and an intolerance for people who didn't see the world his way. He left behind a worldwide industry that continued to thrive long after him.

See also: **Charles Post**

FURTHER READING

Hunnicutt, Benjamin K. *Kellogg's Six-Hour Day*. Philadelphia: Temple University Press, 1996.

Kellogg Company. *A Citizens Petition: The Relationship Between Diet and Health*. Battle Creek, Mich.: Kellogg Co., 1985.

Numbers, Ronald L. *Prophetess of Health*. New York: Harper & Row, 1976.

Powell, Horace B. *The Original Has This Signature-W.K. Kellogg*. Englewood Cliffs: Prentice-Hall, 1956.

Quelch, John A. *Behavioral and Attitudinal Measures of the Relative Importance of Product Attributes: The Case of Cold Cereals*. Cambridge: Marketing Science Institute, 1978.

KELSEY-HAYES

Kelsey-Hayes was established in 1927 through the merger of Kelsey Wheel and Hayes Wheel. Both companies were founded in 1909, and both had made early advances in the wooden wheel industry. Kelsey and Hayes had important connections in automobile manufacturing, which helped them succeed as automotive parts suppliers. In 1909 the Ford Motor Company purchased three-fourths of the wheels produced by the Kelsey Wheel Company. Similarly, Hayes President and founder Clarence B. Hayes' early experiences in the wheel industry put him in contact with W.C. Durant (1861–1947) who eventually founded General Motors. Thus, even before the merger both companies had strong positions in the industry.

Fearing that Kelsey Wheel Company might become too dependent on the Ford Motor Company, John Kelsey sought to diversify his company's product line and customer base. Kelsey reduced business with Ford from three-quarters to less than one-third of total sales in 1910. By 1915 Kelsey produced wheels for 15 to 20 percent of the automobile industry. The Kelsey Wheel Company also produced 80 percent of artillery wheels during the World War I. By the end of the war Kelsey was turning consistent profits. During the same period, Clarence Hayes was supplying over half of the American automobile business with his wheels. In the 1920s the advent of the wire wheel required dramatic changes for these wooden wheel producers. Although both companies expanded into wire wheel production, they chose to face this new challenge together, and in 1927 they formed the Kelsey-Hayes Wheel Company.

Litigation against John Kelsey over the patent for wire wheels clouded the merger. The Wire Wheel Corporation of Buffalo, New York, disputed Kelsey right to produce the wheel. When Kelsey died in 1927, his successor George Kennedy bought the Wire Wheel Company in an effort to solve the problem. It was eventually decided, however, that the patent was owned by the Packard Motor Company, a car manufacturer, not the Wire Wheel Corporation. Kennedy paid Packard $500,000 so that Kelsey-Hayes could continue with wire wheel production. By 1929 the company was making 10,000 wire wheels per day; by this time the manufacturer had also added brakes to its product line.

Kelsey-Hayes endured great challenges in the 1930s. Economic crises overshadowed the purchase of General Motor's subsidiary Jaxon Steel Products Company of Jackson, Michigan. The company had very costly debts that resulted in approximately $2 million in losses for Kelsey-Hayes. They eventually survived these troubles by restructuring their finances and lowering expenses. But in the meantime a challenge from another quarter arose. The United Auto Workers (UAW) sought to organize the Kelsey-Hayes workers in Detroit, Michigan, who made and supplied brakes for Ford cars. The union struck the company in 1936. The company established a 75-cent minimum hourly wage but still refused to recognize the union. By 1938 and 1939, Kelsey-Hayes was showing profits again. By this time the company was selling newly developed hydraulic brakes to Ford (which had become standard equipment on Ford cars). Kelsey-Hayes also came out with a new brake drum.

During World War II (1939–1945), Kelsey-Hayes contributed to the war effort by producing machine guns. Kelsey-Hayes also manufactured tank components and aircraft wheels. The company acquired French and Hecht, Inc., an already successful manufacturer of wheels for agricultural and construction machinery. In 1946 labor strikes surged throughout the country and Kelsey-Hayes was shut down for six weeks. Nevertheless the same year brought successes when Buick and Chrysler began buying power brakes from Kelsey-Hayes. In 1947 Kelsey-Hayes bought a manufacturer of brake components—the Lather Company. By the 1950s Kelsey-Hayes was enjoying its highest profits in history.

During the Korean War Kelsey-Hayes produced parts for the aircraft industry. They also promoted specialty products for the automobile industry such as chrome-plated and aluminum wheels. In 1958 the company's research and development department began looking into anti-lock brake systems (ABS) for automobiles—prior to this, the ABS was only used in aircraft. With so much diversification of its product line, Kelsey-Hayes Wheel Company saw fit to change its name to Kelsey-Hayes Corporation in the late 1950s.

The company continued to broaden its product line beyond wheels; in the years that followed, the biggest successes were in non-wheel products. Kelsey-Hayes pioneered disc brake systems—standard equipment on Lincoln Continentals and Thunderbirds in the 1960s. But by the 1970s eighty-five percent of U.S. cars were equipped with Kelsey-Hayes disc brakes. Also at that time, nearly every jet engine contained some parts manufactured by the Kelsey-Hayes Corporation. During and after an oil crisis in the 1970s, the market demanded smaller cars that would be cheaper to operate. Kelsey-Hayes took researched and designed new components that would be lighter and more economical. Fewer people were buying new cars during this period; instead, they opted for used ones. Kelsey-Hayes sensed this and in 1978, as new automobile sales declined, they began manufacturing replacement parts.

In spite of these successes Kelsey-Hayes' stock was falling and its credit was overextended during the early 1970s. There was fear of a takeover; in 1973 the company became a subsidiary of Fruehauf Corporation. Kelsey-Hayes quickly recovered from its financial setback and consistently brought Fruehauf its best profits. In the late 1970s Kelsey-Hayes acquired Compositek Engineering Corporation whose history of producing fiber-reinforced plastics brought new opportunities for producing light-weight wheels. At the end of the decade Kelsey-Hayes was producing all types of wheels. The merger did not appear to diminish Kelsey-Hayes' success.

The Federal Trade Commission, however, (FTC) reviewed Fruehauf's acquisition of Kelsey-Hayes and decided that the merger violated anti-trust laws by discouraging competitive trade. Kelsey-Hayes had been a supplier to Fruehauf and, after the merger, Fruehauf was less inclined to buy from other suppliers. The FTC ruled that this was a restraint of trade. Also, prior to the merger, Fruehauf had itself manufactured products similar to those that Kelsey-Hayes produced. After the merger, Fruehauf had discontinued its own production of those products, and the FTC ruled that this was a limit on the diversity of available goods. Fruehauf was forced to divest itself of some of its Kelsey-Hayes holdings.

The problems for Fruehauf did not end there. Fruehauf was dismantled during a lengthy, unfriendly takeover in the mid-1980s. Kelsey-Hayes was independent again and was renamed the K-H Corporation. But K-H was short-lived, since debt and interest payments diminished any possibility for growth. In 1989 K-H sought out the Toronto-based Varity Corporation and arranged for a friendly buyout. Under this new owner the company became the Kelsey Hayes Group of Companies, and by organizing itself into business units, the company made it easier to focus on distinct product lines. One year after the merger Kelsey-Hayes showed $1 billion in revenues.

The Kelsey-Hayes story is about a company in the midst of a competitive environment that was able to survive and build itself up by furnishing the parts needed by big customers like General Motors, Ford, and U.S. government contractors. Although other parts suppliers tried to do the same thing, Kelsey-Hayes was successful because of its ability to read the market and to develop new products that were ahead of their time. The company also understood its limits and subsequently built relations with other companies, either by purchasing or merging. Such strengths contributed to Kelsey-Hayes' ability to issue innovative parts, such as aluminum wheels, disc brakes, and anti-lock braking systems—quite a change from the days of the wooden wheel.

See also: **W. C. Durant, Henry Ford, United Auto Workers**

FURTHER READING

"1936: Could Workers Stand up to a Powerful Company?" [cited April 14, 1999] available via the World Wide Web @ uaw.org/History/wh_kelsey2.html/.

A Billion Wheels Later. Romulus, Michigan: Kelsey-Hayes Company, 1984.

"Bad Brakes," [cited April 14, 1999] available via the World Wide Web @ www.kwtv.com/investigators/brakes.htm/.

Calahan, J. M. "Life After Buyout." *Automotive Industry*, August, 1987.

"Image Program for Kelsey-Hayes," [cited April 14, 1999] available via the World Wide Web @ www.franco.com/kelsey.html/.

May, George S. *A Most Unique Machine: The Michigan Origins of the American Automobile Industry.* Grand Rapids, MI: Eerdmans, 1975.

KENTUCKY

British and American surveyors, Thomas Walker and Christopher Gist first explored eastern and central Kentucky in 1751. As part of what was then called "the West," Kentucky held great promises for the use of its fertile land and abundant hunting grounds. Despite a British ban on western migration, settlers gradually began coming to Kentucky. In 1774 Harrodstown (now Harrodsburg) became the first white settlement in the region.

The Transylvania Land Company, assisted by famous frontiersman Daniel Boone (1734–1820), bought up a large tract of land from the Cherokee Nation and founded Fort Boonesborough in 1775. The colony of Virginia claimed Kentucky as part of its territory at this time. During and after the American Revolution (1775–1783) immigrants streamed in to the region, coming down the Ohio River or through the Cumberland Gap, as Kentucky became the principal route for migration into the Mississippi Valley. The settlements grew, and Kentucky strained at its bonds to Virginia. In 1792 Kentucky entered the Union as the fifteenth state.

Agricultural and processing industries enabled Kentucky to prosper over the next few decades. Kentucky was tied to the lower South economically, especially after the construction of a canal around the Ohio River Falls at Louisville in 1829. Kentucky supplied hemp, used to make ropes and bagging for cotton bales, as well as producing hogs, mules, workhorses, corn, flour, salt, and prepared meats. The state also became a large grower of tobacco, which by 1860 accounted for half the agricultural income in the state. Whiskey production began in the 1860s, with the most popular brew taking the name of the county where it was produced: Bourbon. Horse breeding and racing also developed during this period and became the trademark industry in the Bluegrass area near Lexington.

Kentucky was one of the border states with divided loyalties during the American Civil War (1861–65).

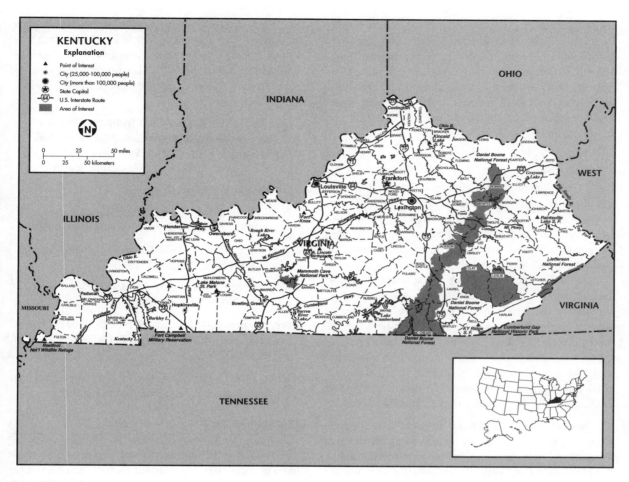

State of Kentucky.

Although the state ultimately backed the Union, thousands of soldiers from Kentucky also fought on the side of the Confederacy. A period of unrest and chaos followed the war during the Reconstruction (1865–1877) period.

By the 1870s economic health was gradually being restored in Kentucky. Liberal tax laws helped railroad construction to increase dramatically, and eastern Kentucky saw extensive development of timber and coal reserves. Many rural people moved into the cities of Louisville and Lexington as industrial growth flourished. In 1900 Kentucky held first place in per capita income among the southern states.

A bleaker picture, however, faced farmers in the state. The "dark-leaf" tobacco farmers of eastern Kentucky, as well as other farmers, experienced long-term price depression. Good land was also becoming hard to come by, as the size of the average family farm dropped to less than ten acres, and many were forced to become tenant farmers. New social movements aimed at farm unrest, including the Grange, the Farmers'

Alliance, and the Populist Party, found many supporters in Kentucky.

Another of Kentucky's most important industries, coal mining, was going through hard times at the beginning of the twentieth century. By the late nineteenth century lower-sulfur coal had been mined out of the Cumberland coal reserves in the Appalachian region. Distant corporations with a highly developed profit motive employed many but did little to improve the ordinary lives of the people they employed. As mechanization of coal mining increased, jobs in the mining areas of the state became increasingly hard to come by. Deep mining began to give way to strip mining during this period.

During the 1920s a great deal of economic change hit Kentucky. The development of modern highways brought the political power center of the state to the Highway Commission. Political patronage under Governor Flem Sampson controlled nearly all the highway jobs until Sampson's ouster in 1931. Meanwhile, in the distillery industry, the enactment of Prohibition in

1918 had put thousands out of work. Coal mining experienced a boom in the early twenties, but declining prices after 1927 put thousands more into unemployment lines. Violent confrontations between mine owners and workers became common during this time. In Harlan and Bell counties hostilities were especially rampant and caused property destruction and many deaths.

During the dark days of the Great Depression (1929–1939) in the 1930s, Governor Albert B. (''Happy'') Chandler brought a kind of ''conservative progressivism'' to the state after years of factional party politics. He used federal dollars from New Deal programs to cancel the state sales tax in favor of a progressive income tax and controversial taxes on cigarettes, whiskey, and beer. An unfortunate consequence of the sales tax loss prompted a downhill slide in funding for education and health care in the state. Adding to the state's woes, there were a number of violent confrontations during the 1930s between the United Mine Workers (UMW) and mine owners in eastern Kentucky. By 1940 Kentucky had acquired a negative image nationwide because of political corruption, poverty, and labor unrest. In that year the state ranked last among 48 states in per capita income.

World War II (1939–45) brought an economic boost to the state's economy by increasing the demand for coal and farm products, and also by stimulating the development of industry. As industries grew over the subsequent decades the percentage of people employed in farming decreased. Between 1945 and 1980 the farm population was reduced by 76 percent. Companies such as General Electric and Ford in Louisville and Rockwell International in Clark County helped bring Kentucky industry into the twentieth century. Lexington in particular changed from a farm and college town into a fast-growing metropolitan era, beginning with the arrival of International Business Machines (IBM) in 1956. A good measure of Kentucky's rise from the economic doldrums came from a steady influx of workers from 1970 on, after years of population loss.

Though still a poor state, economic conditions in Kentucky were greatly improved by the end of the twentieth century. The Bluegrass area and industrial cities were generally the most prosperous parts of the state. Despite federal programs that began in the 1960s to raise incomes in the eastern coal mining regions, income there was still lower and unemployment higher than in other areas of the state. A far higher percentage of the population in the Appalachian counties fell below the federal poverty level than in other counties. Though manufacturing cities, primarily along the Ohio River, provided high levels of employment, the state as a whole ranked only 42nd out of 50 states in per capita income with an average of $19,687 in 1996. Coal was still an important product of Kentucky, with over 114 million tons mined in 1996. A more recently discovered resource was petroleum, extracted mostly in Henderson County.

See also: **Daniel Boone, Coal Industry, Farmer's Alliance, International Business Machines, National Grange, United Mine Workers**

FURTHER READING

Alvey, R. Gerald. *Kentucky Bluegrass Country*. Jackson, MS: University Press of Mississippi, 1992.

Axton, W.F. *Tobacco and Kentucky*. Lexington: University Press of Kentucky, 1976.

Channing, Steven A. *Kentucky: A Bicentennial History*. New York: Norton, 1977.

Harrison, Lowell Hayes, and James C. Klotter. *A New History of Kentucky*. Lexington: University Press of Kentucky, 1997.

Kleber, John E., ed. *The Kentucky Encyclopedia*. Lexington: University Press of Kentucky, 1992.

KEROSENE

A flammable hydrocarbon oil, kerosene is a petroleum product primarily used for fuel. In 1854 Canadian geologist Abraham Gesner (1797–1864) discovered a process for distilling fuel from petroleum (initially, coal oil). He found the derived substance to be a superior lighting oil. In 1859, when the first successful oil well was drilled near Titusville, Pennsylvania, the shale oil was found to also be an excellent, and then plentiful, source of kerosene. Kerosene illumination caught on quickly. Until the advent of the incandescent lightbulb, invented by Thomas Alva Edison in 1879, kerosene lamps remained the primary source of artificial lighting.

See also: **Black Gold**

KEYNES, JOHN MAYNARD

Considered one of the most important economic theorists of the modern era, John Maynard Keynes (1883–1946) was a genius who used his extraordinary gift for mathematics to deepen his understanding of economics. He helped to revolutionize modern thought about the workings of the free-trade marketplace and modern industrial capitalism. He is credited with helping to pull the United States and much of Western Europe out of the Great Depression and with creating a kind of capitalism that works with the federal government to stabilize the ups and downs of a market economy.

John Keynes was the only son born to John Neville Keynes and Florence Keynes, on June 5, 1883. His father was a lecturer at Cambridge University, England, and became the top administrative official at Cambridge. As young John grew up, his parents doted on him, and his mother kept a thorough file of his early achievements.

Keynes was a brilliant student at Saint Faith's Preparatory School. Later, at Eton, he finished first in his class in the classics (the study of the language and culture of ancient Greece and Rome) and second in mathematics. He later went on to Cambridge University to complete his formal education, where, at age sixteen, he decided to pursue the study of economics.

His first job out of college was in India, working as a junior clerk for the British civil service for two years. Keynes then took a position back in England as an economics lecturer at King's College. In 1911, at age twenty-eight, he was named editor of the prestigious *Economic Journal* published by the Royal Economic Society, a position he retained for the next 33 years.

In his mid-30s, Keynes married a ballerina, Lydia Lopokova, and they remained together until his death in 1946. They had no children.

Keynes worked on international aspects of the economy for the British Treasury office in 1917, and in 1920 he began his own career speculating successfully on foreign exchange and commodities. Later that same year Keynes joined the board of directors of the National Mutual Life Insurance Company, where he became the board director in 1923, a position he held until 1938.

JOHN MAYNARD KEYNES WAS. . . CREDITED WITH HELPING TO PULL THE UNITED STATES AND MUCH OF WESTERN EUROPE OUT OF THE GREAT DEPRESSION.

Throughout his life Keynes occupied a variety of influential posts where his economic and financial advice was sought. During World War II (1939–1945), both English Prime Minister Winston Churchill, and U.S. President Franklin Delano Roosevelt (1933–1945) sought his advice.

Outspoken and controversial, Keynes wrote books on all aspects of economics, beginning with his small classic titled *Indian Currency and Finance* (1913), and ending with his last book, *How to Pay for the War*

(1940). In 1936 he published his major work, *The General Theory of Employment, Interest, and Money*. With respect to its importance in economic literature, this work has been compared to Adam Smith's *The Wealth of Nations*, and Karl Marx's *Das Kapital*. It was a shrewd analysis of how economics works in daily life.

Keynes' book contained little on sociology, philosophy, or ideology. He supported capitalism and focused on resolving the question of how a capitalist economy could recover from a depression, which seemed to be an inevitable affliction in the free market system. The answer Keynes proposed may have helped the capitalist world pull itself out of the Great Depression, as well as provided a way for capitalist societies to normalize after war. Keynes theorized that economic difficulties were not the result of overproduction, as was commonly believed, but rather of problems in the distribution of goods. He further stated that it was the shortage of money that prevented goods from being distributed properly during a depression. The solution was the government involvement. Keynes believed that if the government put money into the economy, without taxing citizens, the economy would experience some temporary debt, but the stimulation would bring the stagnant capitalist economy back to life.

Other economists were skeptical of Keynes' ideas, but eventually came to accept them as they saw the U.S. and European economies improve, behaving as Keynes had predicted. Keynes gave to capitalists a method to help economies rebound after periodic downturns.

Unlike most economists before him, Keynes analyzed problems in the economy as if they were arithmetic and not social. He had little use for ideas that glorified either the businessman or the common worker. He believed that the success of an economy depended on following certain basic rules that he had described in his writing. Keynes died in 1946.

See also: **Capitalism, Free Trade, Great Depression, Great Depression (Causes of), Keynesian Economic Theory, Adam Smith**

FURTHER READING

Collins, Robert. *The Business Response to Keynes.* New York: Columbia University Press, 1981.

Harrod, Sir Roy. *Life of John Maynard Keynes.* New York: Avon Books, 1971.

Heilbroner, Robert. *The Worldly Philosophers.* New York: Touchstone Press, 1992.

Hession, Charles. *John Maynard Keynes*. New York: MacMillan Pub., 1984.

Muggridge, D. E. *John Maynard Keynes*. New York: Penguin Books, 1976.

KEYNESIAN ECONOMIC THEORY

Until the onset of the Great Depression (1929–1939), it was conventional wisdom in classical economics that the best way to manage the economy was to take a laissez-faire, or "hands off," approach. Classical economists believed that, left to their own devices, economies tended toward full employment on their own, and that the best way to deal with a depression was to expand the money supply and wait for the economy to return to "equilibrium."

In his landmark 1936 book, *The General Theory of Employment, Interest, and Money*, the English economist John Maynard Keynes (1883–1946) argued that the classical economists had it all wrong. Some depressions were so severe that consumer demand needed to be artificially stimulated by government fiscal policies such as deficit spending, public works programs, and tax cuts. During deep depressions, Keynes believed, when the government expanded the money supply pessimistic consumers would simply hoard the money rather then spend it. As proof that Keynesian economic theory was true, economists pointed to the fact that the U.S. economy recovered from the Great Depression only through heavy deficit spending during World War II (1939–1945). Keynesianism became official government policy when the Employment Act of 1946 gave the federal government the explicit responsibility to use fiscal policy to maintain full employment as a way of keeping consumer demand and economic growth strong.

During the administrations of Democratic Presidents John F. Kennedy (1961–1963) and Lyndon B. Johnson (1963–1969), Keynesian economic theory guided government policy. A major tax cut in 1964 that spurred economic growth seemed to prove again that Keynes' faith in government fiscal measures had more validity than laissez-faire economics. By the early 1970s even Republican President Richard M. Nixon (1969–1974) admitted, "We are all Keynesians now." However the 1970s introduced a new phenomenon that Keynesian economic theory seemed to have no answer for: high inflation together with high unemployment—a phenomenon known as "stagflation." Keynes and all other economists had believed that when unemployment is low, inflation would be high because a fully employed economy consumes a lot, thus, prices would be driven upward. Stagflation seemed to leave the government without options: if it stimulated demand to reduce unemployment inflation would climb, but if it dampened demand to fight inflation unemployment would rise.

Stagflation turned out to be so difficult a problem that by the time President Ronald Reagan (1981–1989) entered office he was calling Keynesian economic theory "a failed policy." In a return to laissez-faire economics, he proposed that the government stop deficit spending and grow the money supply at a stable rate. The currency growth has been kept under control, and with budget cuts and an expanding economy, the budget was balanced under President William Clinton (1993-2001).

See also: **Inflation, John Maynard Keynes, Laissez Faire, Stagflation**

KIMBERLY-CLARK CORPORATION

Kimberly-Clark Corporation was established in 1872 in Neenah, Wisconsin, as Kimberly, Clark, and Company. The business was a partnership of four men—John A. Kimberly, Charles B. Clark, Frank C. Shattuck, and Kimberly's cousin, Havilah Babcock. The company established its first paper mill in Wisconsin; their first product was newsprint made from linen and cotton rags. Within six years the company expanded by acquiring a majority interest in the nearby Atlas paper mill, which converted ground pulpwood into manila wrapping paper. The business was incorporated in 1880 as Kimberly and Clark Company. In 1889 the company constructed a large pulp and paper-making complex on the Fox River.

In 1906, after the deaths of three of the four founders, the company was reorganized and renamed Kimberly-Clark Company. In 1914 researchers working with bagasse, a pulp byproduct of processed sugar cane, produced creped cellulose wadding, or tissue. During World War I (1914–18) this product, called cellucotton, was used to treat wounds in place of scarce surgical cottons. At that time field nurses also discovered that cellucotton worked well as a disposable feminine napkin. The company later recognized the commercial potential of this application and in 1920 introduced its Kotex feminine napkin.

Four years later the company introduced another disposable tissue product, Kleenex, to replace the face towels then used for removing cold cream. A survey showed, however, that consumers preferred to use Kleenex as a disposable handkerchief, prompting the company to alter its marketing strategy entirely. Nationwide advertisements promoting Kleenex for use as a facial tissue began in 1930; sales doubled within a year. In 1928 the company was reincorporated as Kimberly-Clark Corporation and became a publicly traded firm. During World War II (1939–1945) Kimberly-Clark contributed to the war effort by making M-45 anti-aircraft gun mounts, fuses for heavy shells, and other military products.

Introduced in 1968, Kimberly-Clark's first foray into the disposable diaper market, Kimbies, was withdrawn from the market in the mid-1970s because of poor sales and leakage problems. Much more successful were Huggies, the premium diaper introduced by Kimberly-Clark in 1978. Featuring an hourglass shape, elastic at the legs, and refastenable tapes, Huggies were an instant hit and had captured 50 percent of the higher quality disposable diaper market by 1984.

In 1980 Kimberly-Clark launched its Depend line of adult incontinence products through an aggressive television advertising campaign. Just as it had decades before through its promotion of once unmentionable feminine hygiene products, Kimberly-Clark again took on a taboo subject. The company was once again successful. Depend quickly became the best-selling retail incontinence brand in the United States and Kimberly-Clark now had a line of products serving the needs of absorbing bodily fluids which stretched from cradle to grave.

In 1985 Kimberly-Clark relocated its headquarters from Wisconsin to Texas. The company found new product success again in 1989, when Huggies Pull-Ups disposable training pants were introduced. Pull-Ups helped propel Huggies into the number one position in the disposable diaper market. In 1995 Kimberly-Clark merged with Scott Paper Co. in a $9.4 billion deal that created a global consumer products company with annual revenue of more than $13 billion. The new Kimberly-Clark emerged from their union with Scott with a roster of leading consumer brands, including Kleenex, Huggies, Kotex, Depend, Pull-Ups, and the Scott brand of bathroom tissue and paper towels.

FURTHER READING

Briggs, Jean A. "The Paper Chase." *Forbes*, November 10, 1980.

Forest, Stephanie Anderson, and Mark Maremont. "Kimberly-Clark's European Paper Chase." *Business Week*, March 16, 1992.

Glowacki, Jeremy J. "Kimberly-Clark Corp.: Accelerates Global Expansion with Scott Merger." *Pulp and Paper*, December, 1995.

Ingham, John N., ed. *Biographical Dictionary of American Business Leaders*, vol. 2. Westport, CT: Greenwood, 1983, s.v. "Kimberly, John Alfred."

Spector, Robert. *Shared Values: A History of Kimberly-Clark*. Lyme, CT: Greenwich Publishing, 1997.

KING COTTON

Until the 1790s growers were limited to producing the quantity of cotton that could be processed by slaves. Separating the seeds from cotton was time consuming and labor intensive. The bolls (cottonseed pods) were dried in front of a fire, and the seeds were picked out by hand. In 1793 American inventor Eli Whitney (1765–1825) introduced the cotton gin. A revolutionary laborsaving machine, it could clean 50 times more cotton fiber in one day than a human. Though Whitney patented the machine in 1794, imitations were quickly put into production by shrewd businessmen who realized the impact the gin could have on the nation's cotton industry. Just before Whitney developed the gin another inventor, British-born Samuel Slater (1768–1835), introduced the first successful water-powered machines for spinning cotton at a Rhode Island mill in 1790.

There was no shortage of demand for the fiber. As the 1800s dawned, machinery had made cotton the center of the nation's emerging textile industry. Soon New England was dotted with textile factories. Growers in the South increased cotton production to keep up with factories' demands. Slave labor and excellent growing conditions in the southern states (especially Alabama, Mississippi, Georgia, and South Carolina) combined to dramatically increase production. By 1849 annual cotton exports had reached $66 million and accounted for roughly two-fifths of total U.S. exports.

Cotton came at a dear price: laborers in the North's textile factories worked under difficult and sometimes dangerous circumstances, in the South cotton crops were planted and harvested by slaves. As abolitionists became increasingly vocal and demanded that the U.S. government legislate the end of slavery, southern growers defended the system, saying that their livelihoods and the South's economy depended on it.

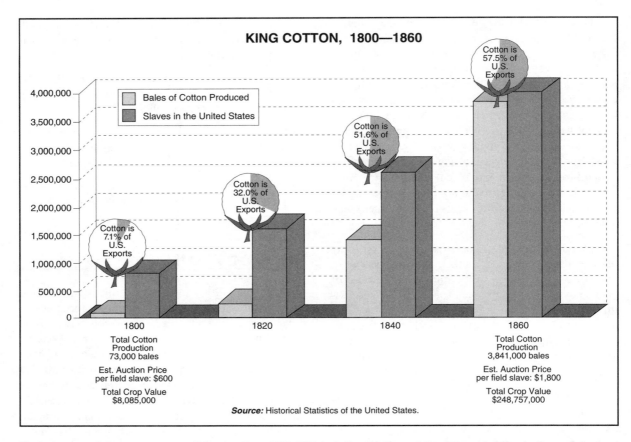

KING COTTON, 1800—1860

Cotton is 57.5% of U.S. Exports

Cotton is 51.6% of U.S. Exports

Cotton is 32.0% of U.S. Exports

Cotton is 7.1% of U.S. Exports

- Bales of Cotton Produced
- Slaves in the United States

4,000,000
3,500,000
3,000,000
2,500,000
2,000,000
1,500,000
1,000,000
500,000
0

1800   1820   1840   1860

Total Cotton Production 73,000 bales

Est. Auction Price per field slave: $600

Total Crop Value $8,085,000

Total Cotton Production 3,841,000 bales

Est. Auction Price per field slave: $1,800

Total Crop Value $248,757,000

Source: Historical Statistics of the United States.

The importance of the cotton crop as a U.S. export from 1800–1880, including the close relation between bale production and slave population.

King cotton became an expression coined during the mid-1800s when the economies of southern states were heavily dependent on the cotton industry. In 1858 South Carolina Senator James Henry Hammond (1807–64) taunted northern sympathizers, saying ''You dare not make war on cotton—no power on earth dares make war upon it. Cotton is king.'' Hammond was not the first to use the phrase; it was coined three years earlier in the title of a book. The South's dependence on cotton contributed to the deepening North-South divide in the nation. By the time the Civil War (1861–65) began, the southern United States supplied two-thirds of the world's cotton.

See also: **Abolition, Cotton Gin, Samuel Slater, Slavery, Spinning Mills**

KING, MARTIN LUTHER, JR.

During the last half of the twentieth century in the United States, Martin Luther King, Jr., (1929–1968) emerged as the major leader of the modern civil rights movement. He organized large numbers of African Americans in the 1960s to aggressively pursue non-violent civil disobedience in pursuit of racial justice and economic equality. Until his assassination in 1968, King remained a steadfast leader committed to the radical transformation of society through persistent, non-violent activism.

In 1929 Martin Luther King Jr. was born in Atlanta, Georgia, the son of Michael and Alberta King. King was born into a family with deep ties to the African American church. His father was a Baptist minister in Atlanta. King's maternal grandfather, Reverend Adam Williams, had served as the pastor of The Ebenezer Baptist Church in Atlanta since 1894.

King grew up during the Great Depression, a direct witness not only to racism in the South but to bread lines and social injustice. These experiences heightened his awareness of economic inequalities. He watched his father campaign against racial discrimination in voting and in salary differences between white and African-American teachers. His father's activism provided a model for King's own politically engaged ministry.

> But we refuse to believe that the bank of justice is bankrupt. We refuse to believe that there are insufficient funds in the great vaults of opportunity of this nation. So we have come to cash this check, a check that will give us upon demand the riches of freedom and the security of justice.
>
> **Martin Luther King, Jr., "I Have a Dream" speech,
> August 28, 1963**

King attended Morehouse College from 1944 to 1948. The president of Morehouse, Benjamin E. Mays, strongly influenced King's spiritual development by encouraging him to view Christianity as a potential force for social change in the secular world. King struggled with mixed feelings about religion during his college years, but decided to enter the ministry after graduation, responding to what he called an "inner urge" calling him "to serve God and community." He was ordained during his final semester at Morehouse. King later continued his religious education at Boston University's School of Theology; where he completed a doctorate in theology in 1955.

Accepting a 1954 offer to become pastor of Dexter Avenue Baptist Church in Montgomery, Alabama, King quickly came into contact with the many problems of the modern South. In December 1955, Montgomery African American leaders formed the Montgomery Improvement Association to protest the arrest of National Association for the Advancement of Colored People (NAACP) member Rosa Parks (1913–) for refusing to give up her bus seat to a white man. They chose King to head the new group.

During a year-long boycott African Americans in Montgomery avoided using the bus system. In his role as spokesman, King utilized the leadership abilities gained from his religious background and forged a distinctive protest strategy involving the mobilization of African American churches and skillful appeals for broad-based public support. In his organizing, King began to use the precepts of East Indian leader Mohandas Gandhi, combining Gandhi's non-violence with Christian principles.

After the U.S. Supreme Court outlawed racial segregation in 1956, King's victory spurred him on to expanding the non-violent civil rights movement. In 1957 he founded the Southern Christian Leadership Conference (SCLC), to coordinate civil rights activities throughout the South.

On September 20, 1966, Martin Luther King Jr. (*center*), escorted these young children to a recently integrated school.

By the time he moved to Atlanta, Georgia, in 1960, King was known nationwide for his book on civil rights advocacy, *Stride Toward Freedom*, and through his work to increase African American voting registration in the South. He also worked with a student-oriented group of civil-rights workers known as the Student Non-Violent Coordinating Committee (SNCC) in an effort to desegregate restaurants in the South with a series of non-violent sit-ins.

In 1963 King was part of the civil rights struggle in the Birmingham, Alabama, campaign. These demonstrations called for a variety of changes in the treatment of African Americans and resulted in King's arrest and brief imprisonment. The arrest brought international attention to him and to the civil rights movement. King spoke bravely and intelligently in speeches that invoked Biblical and Constitutional principles. His activities caught the attention of President John F. Kennedy (1961–1963), who introduced significant civil rights legislation.

That same year, in front of 200,000 people gathered in Washington, D.C., King delivered a speech, known today as the "I Have A Dream" speech. It marked a high point in King's crusade and served as an inspiration for civil rights supporters. Televised throughout the world, his speech electrified those who heard those words and saw the thousands who had marched on Washington in support of the civil rights movement.

Largely for his advocacy and his use of non-violent social activism in the United States in pursuit of justice for racial and economic minorities, King was awarded the Nobel Peace Prize in 1964. During the late 1960s, he remained a voice of moderation in an increasingly diverse and militant African American movement. The civil rights campaign of the early 1960s became a militant mass movement later in the decade, seeking economic and political gains in the workplace.

King continued to leave his mark on the social protest movements that arose throughout the 1960s. Women's groups formed and used non-violent militancy to achieve progress in what came to be called the modern feminist movement of the 1970s. Social and economic injustices throughout the country were being addressed with King's civil disobedience tactics. The American Indian Movement (AIM) became re-activated, as did the labor organizing movement of American Hispanics involved in migratory labor disputes.

On April 4, 1968, while King was working with striking sanitation workers in Memphis, Tennessee, he was assassinated by a white segregationist, James Earl Ray. King's kindling of social activism if ordinary citizens during the mid-twentieth century greatly affected civil rights in the United States, as well as the working conditions of nearly all minorities who were seeking equality and social justice. His legacy is perhaps best illustrated by the Civil Rights Act of 1964.

See also: **Civil Rights Movement**

FURTHER READING

Branch, Taylor. *Pillar of Fire: America in the King Years, 1963–65*. New York: Simon & Schuster, 1998.

Fisher, William H. *Free at Last: A Bibliography of Martin Luther King, Jr.*. Metuchen, NJ: Scarecrow Press, 1977.

Garrow, David J. *Bearing the Cross: Martin Luther King, Jr., and the Southern Christian Leadership Conference*. New York: Vintage Books, 1986.

Reddick, Lawrence D. *Crusader Without Violence: A Biography of Martin Luther King, Jr.*. New York: Harper, 1959.

Washington, James M., ed. *A Testament of Hope: The Essential Writings of Martin Luther King, Jr.*. San Francisco: Harper & Row, 1986.

KING, RICHARD

Richard King (1825–1885) became a legend of U.S. business when he created the largest cattle ranch in the United States during the 1850s. At its height the ranch extended over 1.25 million acres in South Texas, close to the Gulf of Mexico. King and his wife Henrietta founded the famous King Ranch with a purchase of 75,000 acres of land. They started with one small rugged house, which they constantly protected from thieves, cattle rustlers, hostile Native Americans, and a variety of trespassers. At his death in 1885 King's wife inherited the ranch and added thousands of acres to its region. Later heirs to the King Ranch continued to expand it until it became larger than the state of Rhode Island early in the twentieth century.

Richard King was born in 1825, from humble circumstances in Orange County, New York. At the age of eight his parents sent him to be apprenticed to a jeweler. The jeweler's harsh treatment caused King to run away, and he boarded a ship bound for Mobile, Alabama, where he signed on to become a cabin boy on a steamboat. During his time as a cabin boy he obtained eight months of formal education, the total extent of his schooling.

In 1847, at age twenty-two, King was drawn to the state of Texas. In Texas, King served as a pilot on a government steamship on the Rio Grande River. He later bought his own small steamer and engaged in trade on the Rio Grande. In 1850 a friend joined the venture, and they purchased 22 vessels. During the American Civil War (1861–1865) he traded with Mexico, exchanging cotton for supplies that would be given to the Confederate army. King spent 20 years as a steamboat captain in Texas. During that time he began plans for a great ranch in a region of Texas between the Nueces and the Rio Grande rivers.

In 1852 King purchased a 75,000-acre tract of land southwest of Corpus Christi, Texas, formerly known as the Santa Gertrudis Ranch. King bought the land at a cheap price because it was situated in a perilous region of Texas. The area had once been a part of Mexico and many Mexicans still maintained it was rightfully theirs. The same area was also claimed by Native Americans, who said the land historically belonged to them. A lengthy struggle ensued over ownership, but no clear legal claim was established. Into this controversy stepped Richard and Henrietta King.

The Kings were tough and determined to survive. They did not let the controversy over the land dissuade them from the purchase. Once their ownership was established the Kings set up residence, ready to fight off trespassers. Richard King erected rendering houses on his ranch before the northern markets were open for Texas beef. He used animal fat to make candle tallow and sent the tallow and animal hides to market by ship. Cowboys later drove thousands of his cattle over the long trail from Texas to Kansas, where they were put aboard trains to be shipped East.

By 1876 King greatly increased the size of his ranch through land purchases. The number of cattle raised on the ranch also grew. At the same time he constructed his own railroad, which he used to ship cattle from his ranch to Laredo, Texas. From Laredo his train joined the main train routes to the east and north. His holdings at that point numbered 100,000 Texas Longhorn cattle, 20,000 sheep, and 10,000 horses.

King died in 1885 on his half-million acre ranch. The King family was then cross-breeding Brahman cattle with English shorthorns. They produced a new and popular breed of cattle called Santa Gertrudis, which was able to mature to full size while eating less range grass.

King's wife survived him and remained on the ranch. Henrietta King founded the Texas town of Kingsville on the King estate. She also built houses, schools, and churches. She gave a tract of land for the establishment of the Texas-Mexican Industrial Institute. The Kings' five children continued to manage the ranch successfully.

By the middle of the twentieth century the King Ranch supplied much of the food and cowhide in the United States. It became a regional hub in Texas, where it transformed wild prairie into a populous and prosperous farming region.

See also: **Cattle Drives, Cowboys, Westward Expansion**

FURTHER READING

King Ranch: 100 Years of Ranching. Corpus Christi: Caller-Times, 1953.

Cypher, John. *Bob Kleberg and the King Ranch: A Worldwide Sea of Grass.* Austin: University of Texas Press, 1995.

Lea, Tom, Holland McCombs, and Francis L. Fugati. *The King Ranch.* Boston: Little Brown, 1957.

Melouf, Dian Leatherberry. *Cattle Kings of Texas.* Hillsboro, OR: Beyond Words Pub., 1991.

Monday, Jane C. and Betty B. Colley. *Voices from the Wild Horse Desert: The Vaquero Families of the King and Kenedy Ranches.* Austin: University of Texas Press, 1997.

KLONDIKE GOLD STRIKE

In 1896 the discovery of gold along the valleys of the Yukon and Klondike rivers launched a great stampede of prospectors north to Alaska and the Yukon territory of Canada. Although gold had been found all across Alaska since the 1870s, it was news of a huge gold strike at Bonanza Creek in August 1896 that launched the frenzy of the last great gold rush. The outside world learned of the riches of the Yukon Valley in the summer of 1897, when two ships arrived in San Francisco and Seattle loaded with about $1.1 million in Alaskan and Canadian gold. By the time winter cut communications, 2,000 prospectors had gathered in Canada at the former fishing camp of Dawson, at the head of the Yukon, with several thousand others on their way. Dawson profited from the influx of prospective miners. By the summer of 1898 it had a population of 30,000, making it the largest Canadian city west of Winnipeg. A few of the immigrants settled in the area, but most fled for richer fields elsewhere in Alaska. The gold boom lasted only a few years, but the social, political, and economic impact of the gold rush continues to this day.

The Klondike strike was one of the best-publicized events of its time. Because of improved communications linking the Atlantic with the Pacific Coast, the news reached New York and Europe almost as soon as it reached the West Coast. New infrastructure unavailable in previous gold strikes, such as the transcontinental railroad completed in 1869, helped bring prospectors from all over the world. In addition to their money and their labor, these people brought their diseases, their language, and their drinking to the area. These took their toll on the native population of the Yukon. Alcoholism, smallpox and tuberculosis, and residential schools that operated only in English stripped many Native Americans of their lives and their culture.

The population of the Yukon never recovered from the boom years of the gold rush. A hundred years

Missionaries in camp on the way to the Klondike to preach to the miners during the Gold Rush, in Alaska, 1897.

after the Klondike strike, the total population of Yukon territory was only 33,000, only a little more than the town of Dawson in the boom years at the end of the nineteenth century. Gold production began again in the Yukon in 1996. But the production was expected to be no more than 125,000 ounces per year, far short of the one million ounces produced in 1900.

GOLD! WE LEAPT FROM OUR BENCHES. GOLD! WE SPRANG FROM OUR STOOLS. GOLD! WE WHEELED IN THE FURROWS, FIRED WITH THE FAITH OF FOOLS.

Robert Service, a poet who lived in the Yukon

There are some direct links between Klondike gold and modern American business. John W. Nordstrom, a Swedish immigrant, used his gold stake to found the shoe store that still bears his name. The economic impact of the Klondike strike was usually less direct. Of the 100,000 hopeful prospectors who left for the Yukon in 1896–1897, only about 30,000 were able to complete the journey. Many of them passed through Pacific ports such as Seattle on their way home from the gold fields. These towns absorbed many of those miners, with or without their stake. According to *The Economist* magazine, the willingness

to take a risk—to persist in a difficult situation and, if the desired result does not materialize, to move on to another project—has become a characteristic of modern firms whose origins lie in the Pacific northwest. Businesses like Microsoft, Boeing, and Starbucks created corporate cultures that operate the same way that the successful Klondike miners did.

See also: **Alaska, Gold Rush of 1849**

FURTHER READING

Bergman, Brian. ''Golden Days on the Last Frontier: A Century After the Great Rush, the Yukon Is Still a Land of Dreams.'' *Maclean's*, August 19, 1996.

Craig, Simon. ''The Golden Dream.'' *Geographical Magazine*, October 1997.

''The End of the Trail.'' *History Today*, August 1997.

''The Heirs of the Klondike.'' *Economist*, February 15, 1997.

Sherwood, Morgan B. *Exploration of Alaska, 1865–1900*. New Haven, CN: Yale University Press, 1965.

Wharton, David. *The Alaska Gold Rush*. Bloomington, Indiana: Indiana University Press, 1972.

KNIGHTS OF LABOR

An American labor union, the Knights of Labor organization was founded in 1869 as a secretive fraternal society (the Noble Order of the Knights of Labor) in Philadelphia, Pennsylvania. A garment worker Uriah Stephens (1821–1882) and several of his colleagues banded together and opened membership to anyone except physicians, lawyers, bankers, professional gamblers, stockbrokers, and liquor dealers. After a relatively slow start in the depressed economy of the 1870s, when it spread mostly to coal-mining regions of Pennsylvania, the Knights of Labor's membership grew dramatically from fewer than 10,000 members in 1879 to 730,000 members in 1886. Recruiting women, blacks, immigrants, as well as unskilled and semiskilled workers alike, the Knights of Labor began working for reforms, including better wages, hours, and working conditions. The open-membership policy provided the organization with a broad base of support, something previous labor unions, which had limited membership based on craft or skill, lacked.

At a general meeting of its members in Reading, Pennsylvania, in 1878, the organization set its objectives. It wanted an eight-hour workday, prohibition of child labor (under age fourteen), equal opportunities and wages for women laborers, and an end to convict labor. The group became involved in numerous strikes from the late-1870s to the mid-1880s. At the same time, a faction of moderates within the organization was growing, and in 1883 it elected American machinist Terence Powderly (1849–1924) as president. Under Powderly's leadership, the Knights of Labor began to splinter. Moderates pursued a conciliatory policy in labor disputes, supporting the establishment of labor bureaus and public arbitration systems. Radicals not only opposed the policy of open membership, they strongly supported strikes as a means of achieving immediate goals—including a one-day general strike to demand implementation of an eight-hour workday.

Violence that sometimes attended labor strikes not only hurt the cause of organized labor in the country, it further divided the Knights: In May 1886, workers demonstrating in Chicago's Haymarket Square attracted a crowd of some 1,500 people; when police arrived to disperse them, a bomb exploded and rioting ensued. Eleven people were killed and more than a thousand were injured in the melee. For many Americans, the event linked the labor movement with anarchy. That same year several factions of the Knights of Labor seceded from the union to join the American Federation of Labor (AFL). The Knights of Labor remained intact for three more decades, before the organization officially dissolved in 1917, by which time the group had been overshadowed by the AFL and other unions.

See also: **Haymarket Bombing, Labor Movement, Labor Unionism, Terence Powderly, Strike**

KNOPF, BLANCHE

A leading U.S. publisher, Blanche Knopf (1894–1966) played a key role in twentieth century book publishing. By promoting books of controversial European authors, in English translation, and the books of U.S. minority groups (African American, Hispanic, and feminist authors), Blanche Knopf aggressively advocated a new cultural and intellectual climate for U.S. reading audiences, one that powerfully impacted, challenged, and changed their view of the world around them.

Born on July 20, 1894, in New York City, Blanche Wolf was an only child born to wealthy parents. As well as sending her to the elite Gardner School in New York, her parents provided the cultural and language training of her own French and German-speaking governesses.

Blanche grew up a keenly intelligent, aggressive, and demanding young woman, with high personal standards for intellectual excellence. At age twenty-two she married Alfred A. Knopf, whom she met at age seventeen and steadily dated thereafter. Alfred was a writer, editor, and a new publisher.

Together with her husband, Blanche Knopf founded and began building the publishing house Alfred A. Knopf Publishers, in 1915. By 1921, Blanche was director and vice president of the Knopf Publishing Corp.

Because she was perhaps the first woman of high position in a U.S. publishing firm, Blanche encountered sexism and personal censure in her professional life. She was openly denied membership to two powerful publisher's clubs—The Publisher's Lunch Club, and The Book Table, based on her sex. Despite certain closed doors, her flair for fluid social interaction, as well as a love for tough negotiating and strategic bargaining, proved great assets in difficult business situations. Without those personal qualities and her first-rate intelligence, she might have dismally failed in the highly competitive, male-dominated, publishing world of her day.

Blanche Knopf became one of the formidable publishers of her time, specializing in new material for the reading public. She sought out and discovered much new talent in Europe and Latin America and also began to publish the works of little known U.S. minority writers, like poet Langston Hughes and writers of the Harlem Renaissance. In publishing their works, Knopf provided a venue for many writers who had never before received much public attention. In doing so, she indirectly challenged contemporary U.S. thought.

Presenting to the public the words and ideas of African American and other minority writers, Knopf introduced a new world of expression to the literary mainstream—views of society by frequently suppressed minorities. She also introduced the new writings of Europeans in translated versions. Knopf introduced existentialism to the United States, publishing the works of Jean-Paul Sartre, Albert Camus, and Simone de Beauvoir. She also published other European giants such as Andre Gide, Thomas Mann, and the controversial psychiatrist, Dr. Sigmund Freud.

Publishing Simone de Beauvoir's work allowed Knopf to bring to U.S. readers one of the central works of mid-twentieth century feminism: *The Second Sex*. The book discussed the powerful and provocative issues of lesbianism, prostitution, and the nature of sex-role limitations, challenging the social conventions of the day.

Through her work Knopf assisted in the dissemination of ideas and issues that revolutionized thinking in the United States in the mid-twentieth century. Her efforts were regarded as controversial and, at the same time, emancipating because many of the books that caused such calamity in social circles were released at a time when the public was most conspicuously conservative in its sentiments (the late 1940s and 1950s).

Knopf and her husband continued to publish the best of foreign-language and minority writing, and the best of U.S. literature throughout their careers. They prided themselves on publishing books that were physically well-made, colorful—always with the hope that each book would challenge the ideas and imaginations of readers.

Blanche Knopf died in New York City on June 4, 1966. She continued to work as an editor until her death, despite losing much of her eyesight in middle age. Although not able to read new manuscripts in later life, she had many of them read aloud to her and retained the final say on what books were to be published.

FURTHER READING

Fadiman, Clifton. *Fifty Years: Being a Retrospective Collection*. New York: Alfred A. Knopf, 1965.

Flora, Peter. "Carl Van Vechten, Blanche Knopf, and the Harlem Renaissance." *Library Chronicle of the University of Texas* vol. 22 (1992).

Kaufman, Stanley. "Album of the Knopfs." *The American Scholar* vol. 56 (Summer, 1987).

Lewis, Randolph. "Langston Hughes and Alfred A. Knopf Inc., 1924–1935." *Library Chronicle of the University of Texas* vol. 22 (1992).

Postgate, John. "Glimpse of the Blitz." *History Today* vol. 43 (1993).

KOREAN WAR

In 1948 as part of the boundary adjustments following World War II (1939–1945), Korea was supposedly temporarily divided for occupation by the Soviet Union and the United States as victorious former allies against Japan. The Korean peninsula, whose reclusive history in the seventeenth and eighteenth centuries led it to be called the "Hermit Kingdom," had been under Japanese control since the end of the Russo-Japanese War (1904–1905). The division following World War II was at the 38th parallel, a temporary line of demarcation with no other cultural or geographic significance. Like the artificial divisions of Germany and of Berlin in 1945, as well as the supposedly temporary division of North and South Vietnam in 1954, this bifurcation of the Korean nation was a result of the Cold War rather than internal developments.

In their zone lying north of the 38th parallel, the Soviets organized a socialist regime under the Communist Party. Established in 1948 as the Democratic People's Republic of Korea, the regime was headed by Kim Il Sung, a long-time leader of the Communist Party. In the South, various factions vied for power, until the party of the "father of Korean nationalism," Syngman Rhee, won a United Nations–sponsored election. On August 15, 1948, Rhee became President of the Republic of Korea. His regime was about as dictatorial as that in North Korea, and was implicated in corruption and in the repression of internal political opposition.

Both Korean governments were determined to achieve unification on their own terms. Shortly after partition, North Korea supported large-scale guerrilla incursions into the south, and retaliatory raids by South Korean forces kept the divided country in a state of crisis. Despite this situation, American troops were withdrawn in June 1949, leaving behind only a small group of technical advisers. South Korea, whose army was small, poorly trained, and poorly equipped, faced

KOREAN WAR

Soviet Union

People's Republic of China

Yalu River

NORTH KOREA

Sea of Japan

• Pyongyang

Panmunjom

Seoul

Inchon

SOUTH KOREA

Yellow Sea

Pusan

Korea Strait

Japan

— Truce line, July 1953

0   100 miles

0   100 kilometers

The Korean peninsula was the scene of intense warfare between 1950 and 1953.

an adversary with an army of 135,000 men, equipped with modern Russian weapons, and between 150 and 200 combat airplanes. Although South Korean leaders and some Americans feared that North Korea might attack across the 38th parallel at any time, Secretary of State Dean Acheson, declared that Korea was not within the "defensive perimeter" of America's vital interests in the Far East.

The attack came on June 25, 1950. North Korean armed forces—armored units and mechanized divisions supported by massive artillery—struck without warning across the demarcation line. Meeting little resistance, within thirty-six hours North Korean tanks were approaching the outer suburbs of Seoul, the capital of South Korea.

Contrary to Korean and Soviet expectations, the United States reacted swiftly and with great determination. Immediately after the attack the United States requested that the UN Security Council hold a special session which passed a unanimous resolution calling for the end of hostilities and the withdrawal of North

Korean forces to their former positions north of the 38th parallel. The Soviet Union would probably have vetoed such a resolution but the Soviets were boycotting the Security Council to protest the failure of the UN to include Communist China in its deliberations. In any case, the resolution was ignored by the North Koreans and the Security Council met again on June 27 and passed another resolution recommending that "the members of the United Nations furnish such assistance to the Republic of Korea as may be necessary to repel the armed attack." On June 27, U.S. President Harry S Truman committed U.S. Air and Naval forces to the "police action" (a war was never formally declared) as well as ground forces stationed in Japan.

The North Koreans, however, continued their advance. By the end of June, more than half of the Republic of Korea (ROK) Army had been destroyed, and American units were forced to fight countless rearguard actions in the retreat southward. In early August, a defense perimeter was created around the important port of Pusan at the extreme southeastern corner of the peninsula. After violent fighting, a stable defense line was established. As American forces and contingents from fifteen other nations poured in, General Douglas MacArthur, Commander-in-Chief of U.S. forces in the Far East and Supreme Commander of the UN forces, decided on a daring amphibious landing at Inchon, a west coast port just a few miles from Seoul. The brilliantly conceived operation, launched on September 15, 1950, proved successful, and the North Korean Army, was forced to retreat back across the 38th parallel. Pressed by public demands for a complete victory, the Truman Administration gave General MacArthur the go-ahead to pursue the enemy across the demarcation line, justifying the decision with the UN Security Council's authorization. The first crossings took place on October 1. United Nations and ROK forces moved north, and by late November they were nearing the Yalu river boundary between North Korea and Communist China.

The seesaw struggle was reversed once again by the entry of Chinese "volunteers" into the war. Chinese leaders had warned that they would not allow North Korea to be invaded and would come to the aid of the North Koreans. By late October, thousands of Chinese soldiers had crossed the Yalu. One month later, they struck at the exposed flank and rear of MacArthur's overextended armies. By early December, UN troops were again in headlong retreat, a withdrawal marked by great heroism but resulting in near disaster.

This created a crisis of the first order for President Truman. Truman wanted to stabilize the battle lines and negotiate an end to the war. General MacArthur wanted to attack China, possibly using tactical nuclear weapons. He said as much in a letter to House Republican leader Joseph W. Martins. Truman could not brook this challenge to his authority and, on April 11, 1951, he relieved MacArthur of command. Although the public clearly sided with MacArthur, Truman's strong stand settled the question of civilian control over the military.

A new battle line was organized south of the 38th parallel, and through the remaining winter and early spring months the lines fluctuated from south of Seoul to north of the parallel. Stalemate finally was achieved in July 1951. The conflict settled down to trench warfare, at which the Chinese were particularly adept, and was marked by indecisive but bloody fighting. This conflict lasted for two cruel years, during which time, more than a million Americans served in Korea.

For much of this period, talks proceeded at P'anmunjom, Korea near the 38th parallel. These talks opened on July 10, 1951 at the suggestion of the Communists. Welcomed by the most Americans, these negotiations were designed to achieve a cease-fire and an armistice. They were broken off repeatedly as germ warfare charges and difficulties over prisoner-of-war exchanges clouded the atmosphere.

The stalemate in Korea was a source of mounting frustration in the U.S., where it heightened the "red scare" and furnished ammunition to Senator Joseph McCarthy in his quest to purge leftists from the government and from influence in the society at large. The Korean War also helped elect Dwight D. Eisenhower to the Presidency. The Republican nominee won support by promising to go to Korea if elected. Eisenhower kept his pledge, but the visit had no noticeable effect on the peace talks.

The Communists finally modified their position on forcible repatriation of prisoners, and a final armistice agreement was signed at P'anmunjom on July 27, 1953. It resulted in a cease-fire and the withdrawal of both armies two kilometers from the battle line, which ran from coast to coast from just below the 38th parallel in the west to thirty miles north of it in the east. The agreement also provided for the creation of a Neutral Nations Supervisory Commission to carry out the terms of armistice. The armistice called for a political conference to settle all remaining questions, including the future of Korea and the fate of prisoners who refused to return to their homelands. In succeeding months, the United Nations repatriated more than 70,000 North Korean and Communist prisoners but received in return only 3,597 Americans, 7,848 South Koreans, and 1,315 prisoners of other nationalities. The political conference was never held, and relations between North and South Korea remained hostile.

The Korean War cost the United States approximately 140,000 casualties including some 22,500 dead, and $22 billion. The results were somewhat inconclusive, but the war did prevent the Communist conquest of South Korea, and it demonstrated that the United States would fight to prevent the further spread of Communism. The war did change U.S. foreign policy. It marked a shift in military strategy from aiming for total victory to one of fighting limited wars.

The Korean police action also brought about a quick reversal of the policy of down-sizing the military. Major national security expenditures rapidly increased as a result of the war; national defense expenditures rose from four percent to 13 percent of gross national product in 1953. Defense spending revived inflationary impulses in the economy until the imposition of direct controls in January 1951 stabilized prices. In general, the Korean conflict changed the policy of containment from a selective European policy into a general global policy, and it contributed to the development of the military-industrial complex in America.

See also: **Cold War**

FURTHER READING

Berger, Carl. *The Korea Knot: A Military-Political History.*, revised ed. Philadelphia: University of Pennsylvania Press, 1965.

Oliver, Robert T. *Syngman Rhee: The Man Behind the Myth.* New York: Dodd, Mead & Co., 1954.

Leckie, Robert. *Conflict: The History of the Korean War.* New York: G. P. Putnam's Sons, 1962.

Paige, Glenn D. *The Korean Decision, June 24-30, 1950.* New York: The Free Press, 1968.

Rees, David. *Korea: The Limited War.* New York: St. Martin's Press, 1964.

KRESGE, SEBASTIAN SPERING

There are certain businesses that have shaped and reshaped the American landscape: the automobile business, the radio and television industry, and what is called ''the variety store industry.'' The variety store was a social invention of S. S. Kresge (1867–1966), the man who, at the turn of the twentieth century, began building so-called ''five-and-dime'' stores. By the mid-century these stores had evolved into the Kresge ''variety stores'' found in most American towns. They later became major innovators in retailing, operating huge discount retail stores known as K-Mart.

Sebastian Kresge was born in a small community in Pennsylvania in 1867. He was studious as a youngster and attended Fairview Academy, Gilbert Polytechnic Institute in Pennsylvania, and Eastman Business College in New York state. From an early age, he knew how to negotiate a business deal. When his parents had severe financial problems during his school years, Kresge made a deal with them: if they would finance his education, he would, as repayment, turn his entire salary over to them until he reached age twenty-one.

During his late teens, Kresge taught classes and worked as a deliveryman and clerk. By age twenty-three he was in the business world, working as a bookkeeper, selling industrial insurance, and investing in a half-share of a bakery.

The 1890s, for most Americans, were a time of economic depression. During this period of ''hard times'', Kresge had the idea of starting a chain-store operation based on low-end products. By 1899 Kresge and his partner J. G. McCrory opened stores in Memphis, Tennessee, and Detroit, Michigan. During 1899 Kresge traded his interest in the Tennessee store to McCrory and took full possession of the Detroit store. The Detroit store was a starting point of the largest chain-store company in America, the S. S. Kresge Co.

The large sign on the Detroit store read: ''Nothing Over 10 Cents in Store'' and customers poured in. Kresge opened another store with his brother-in-law in Port Huron, Michigan, about 150 miles from Detroit. By 1907 Kresge had created S. S. Kresge stores in Indianapolis, Indiana, in Toledo, Columbus, and Cleveland, Ohio, and in Chicago.

I NEVER MADE A DIME TALKING!

Sebastian Kresge

While making a fortune by selling his inexpensive products under one roof, Kresge was also developing a reputation as a miser. Though he became a millionaire while quite young, he still wore his suits until they became threadbare and he often lined his old shoes with paper instead of resoling them. He was a devout Methodist and Republican who never used alcohol or tobacco and who refused to be charitable toward anyone who did drank or smoked. Kresge was once asked to give a speech to a school of business administration. The speech, aimed at business students, was stunningly short and to the point. It had only 6 words: ''I never made a dime talking!''

Kresge was able to maintain the ten-cent limit in his stores until 1920, when he began selling items worth up to one dollar. After World War II he began selling a range of goods at various prices. His store became a ''variety store,'' but he was still holding on to the inexpensive end of the product market. By 1961 Kresge approved an $80 million deal to finance a line of stores called K-Mart and another discount chain, to be located in deteriorating neighborhoods, known as Jupiter stores. By 1966 the Kresge chain stores were the second largest in the country, with annual sales of $850 billion.

Though Kresge lived much of his personal life like a pauper, his consistent philanthropy, which became evident when he started the Kresge Foundation in 1924, served as an example for other benevolent foundations. Kresge explained his philanthropic spirit simply: ''I can get a greater thrill out of serving others than anything else on earth. I really want to leave the world a better place than I found it.'' Since its founding in 1924, with an initial endowment by Kresge of $1.3 million, the Foundation has generously helped children's organizations, colleges, universities, and many other causes. By the time of his death (in 1966, at age 99), Kresge had endowed the Kresge Foundation with over $275 million.

Kresge was a businessman who aimed his business at those who were not rich, and he made a fortune by doing so.

See also: **Chain Stores**

FURTHER READING

Dictionary of American Biography, Detroit: Gale Research Co., 1974, s.v. ''Kresge, Sebastian Spering.''

''The Kmart Story,'' [cited March 8, 1999] available from the World Wide Web @ http://www.kmart.com/d_about/index.htm/.

Kresge Foundation. *The First Thirty Years: A Report on the Activities of the Kresge Foundation, 1924–1953*. Detroit: The Kresge Foundation, 1954.

Kresge, Stanley Sebastian and Steve Spilos. *The S.S. Kresge Story*. Racine, WI: Western Pub. Co., 1979.

KROC, RAYMOND ALBERT

Raymond Albert Kroc (1902–1984)had the energy, the salesmanship, and the inspiration to build the greatest international restaurant chain empire in the world, McDonald's Corporation. He was a genuine pioneer of the modern fast-food restaurant business. He took the assembly-line methods of big industry and applied them to a restaurant franchise business that produced a small, standardized menu at low cost to the consumer. Kroc was a super salesman who, at age 52, bought ''the golden arches'' symbol and the name from the McDonald's brothers drive-in restaurant of San Bernardino, California, to build the McDonald's chain of restaurants. Based on the concepts of a limited menu of controlled quality and predictable uniformity, Kroc's restaurants operated on the credo of ''quality, service, cleanliness, and value,'' and used a massive advertising campaign to promote itself.

In 1902 Kroc was born in Chicago, Illinois, the son of relatively poor parents. He went to public school in the Chicago suburb of Oak Park, but did not graduate from high school. Instead, he left school to open his own music store. When World War I (1914–18) began, Kroc lied about his age in order to serve as an ambulance driver for the American Red Cross (like his neighbor in Oak Park, author Ernest Hemingway).

Kroc, passionate about music as a young man, returned to Illinois after World War I to become a jazz pianist, playing with at least two well-known jazz orchestras. He also became the musical director of one of Chicago's pioneer radio stations, WGES.

Yet, in 1924, a restless Kroc, dissatisfied with the outlook for a career in music, decided to become a salesman. During a period of booming development in Florida, he left Chicago to try his hand at selling real estate in Fort Lauderdale. The boom collapsed in 1926, and Kroc returned to Chicago with his first wife and their child. In Chicago, Kroc became a salesman for the Lily Tulip paper cup company, where he later became Midwestern sales manager, and developed strong promotional and sales skills.

I PUT HAMBURGERS ON THE ASSEMBLY LINE.

Raymond Kroc

In 1937 Kroc ran into an invention that captured his imagination—a machine called a ''multimixer'' that could make five milkshakes at a time instead of just one. At a time when milkshakes were very popular,

Kroc saw the potential in this invention. By 1941 he had left Lily Tulip and founded his own company to serve as the exclusive distributor for the multimixer. It was a successful business that made Kroc modestly wealthy, but it was not the one that would bring him legendary greatness as an entrepreneur.

Kroc became intrigued with one of his multimixer clients, the McDonald brothers, who owned a drive-in restaurant in San Bernardino, California. The brothers used eight of his mixers at once. A curious Kroc traveled to California in 1954 to find out why so many mixers were being used by this single drive-in.

Kroc discovered the brothers McDonald sold just three items: hamburgers, French fries, and milkshakes. Moreover, the ''restaurant'' only had walk-up windows. The McDonald brothers were specializing in the first ''fast food'' service.

Kroc marveled at the efficiency of the operation. He was certain he had stumbled on that ''once in a lifetime opportunity.'' The McDonald brothers agreed with Kroc's suggestion that he should open a national chain of their restaurants. The energetic 52-year-old veteran salesman entered into a franchise arrangement with the brothers and in 1955 opened his first store in Des Plaines, Illinois. Kroc quickly opened many franchises and oversaw quality control with an iron hand. His practice of purchasing the land used by the franchises for their operations, not leasing, eventually made McDonald's one of the largest real estate owners in the world.

By 1971 Ray Kroc had bought out the McDonald brothers' share of the business and became the sole owner of McDonald's Corporation. Kroc publicized his business relentlessly using every kind of advertising. Early in his career as Chief Executive Officer (CEO) of the business Kroc said, ''I put hamburgers on the assembly line.'' His stores were not restaurants. Instead they were designed for frequent customer turnover. He forbade the installation of telephones, jukeboxes, or anything that encouraged loitering in the establishment.

Kroc opened his ''McDonald's University'' in 1972, where every new franchise owner trained in McDonald food production techniques. The school became known as ''Hamburger University.''

The company used national advertising in every available medium during the 1960s, when McDonald's clown-spokesman, ''Ronald McDonald,'' was born.

Raymond Kroc.

Television advertising was aimed at both children and adults. The McDonald's brand name had an enormous impact on America's cultural fabric. The golden arches became the second most widely recognized trademark, behind Coca Cola.

The company is striking success. Some labor experts estimated that McDonald's was the first place of employment for one in fifteen Americans. Fast-food industry observers estimate that 96 percent of Americans have eaten at McDonald's at least once.

The company founded its international division in 1969. At the end of the twentieth century the international division provided 50 percent of McDonald's operating income, putting the "golden arches" into 85 countries, and adding $30 billion to its annual income.

McDonald's is also known for its philanthropy, including the creation of Ronald McDonald Houses, which provide live-in facilities for family members of seriously ill, hospitalized children. These residences, which are often near hospitals, have been a great help to the parents of the terminally ill.

In 1984 Ray Kroc died of heart failure at the age of 81. He was survived by his third wife. One of America's most successful entrepreneurs, Kroc is often thrust into the pantheon of American business world that includes Henry Ford, Andrew and Dale Carnegie, John D. Rockefeller, and J.P. Morgan.

See also: **Assembly Line**

FURTHER READING

Byers, Paula K., and Suzanne M. Bourgion, eds. *Encyclopedia of World Biography.* " Detroit: Gale Research, 1998, s.v. "Kroc, Raymond Albert.

Emerson, Robert L. *The New Economics of Fast Food.* New York: Van Nostrand Reinhold, 1990.

Kroc, Ray. *Grinding it Out: The Making of McDonald's.* Chicago: H. Regnery, 1977.

Love, John F. *McDonald's: Behind the Arches.* New York: Bantam Books, 1986.

Reiter, Ester. *Making Fast Food: From the Frying Pan into the Fryer.* Buffalo: McGill-Queen's University Press, 1991.

KROGER COMPANY

The Kroger Company traces its roots back to 1883, when Bernard H. Kroger began the Great Western Tea Company, one of the first chain store operations in the United States. Kroger left school to go to work at age 13 when his father lost the family dry goods store in the financial panic of 1873. At age 16 he sold coffee and tea door-to-door. At 20 he managed a Cincinnati grocery store, and at 24, he became the sole owner of the Great Western Tea Company, which by the summer of 1885 had four stores. Kroger's shrewd buying during the panic of 1893 raised the number of stores to 17, and by 1902, with 40 stores and a factory in Cincinnati, Kroger incorporated and changed the company's name to The Kroger Grocery and Baking Company.

Kroger Company historians characterize B.H. Kroger as somewhat of a "crank," fanatically insistent upon quality and service. Profanity was called his second language; he often advised his managers to "run the price down as far as you can go so the other fellow won't slice your throat."

Part of Kroger's success came from the elimination of middlemen between the store and the customer. In 1901 Kroger's company became the first to bake its own bread for its stores, and in 1904 Kroger bought Nagel Meat Markets and Packing House which made Kroger grocery stores the first to include meat departments. This important innovation, however, was not easy. It was common practice at that time for butchers to short weigh (give a customer less than the stated weight) and take sample cuts home with them, practices that did not coincide with B. H. Kroger's strict accounting policies. When Kroger installed cash registers in the meat departments, every one of them inexplicably broke. When Kroger hired female cashiers, the butchers opened all the windows to "freeze out" the women and then let loose with such obscene language that the women quit in a matter of days. When Kroger hired young men instead as cashiers, the butchers threatened them with physical force. But Kroger was stubborn, and in the long run his money-saving, efficient procedures won out.

From the beginning Kroger was interested in both manufacturing and retail. His mother's homemade sauerkraut and pickles sold well to the German immigrants in Cincinnati. And in the back of his store, Kroger himself experimented to invent a "French brand" of coffee, which is still sold in Kroger stores. The Kroger Grocery and Baking Company soon began to expand outside of Cincinnati; by 1920, the chain had stores in Hamilton, Dayton, and Columbus, Ohio. In 1912 Kroger made his first long-distance expansion, buying 25 stores in St. Louis, Missouri. At a time when most chains hired trucks only as needed, Kroger bought a fleet of them, enabling him to move the company into Detroit, Michigan; Indianapolis, Indiana; and Springfield and Toledo, Ohio.

After World War I (1914–1918), the company continued to expand, following Kroger's preference for buying smaller, financially unsteady chains in areas adjacent to established Kroger territories. In 1928, one year before the stock market crashed, Kroger sold his shares in the company for more than $28 million. One of his executives, William Albers, became president. In 1929 Kroger had 5,575 stores, the most there have ever been in the chain.

During the Great Depression (1929–1939), the company maintained its business. By 1935 Kroger had 35 "supermarkets," adopting the format that had debuted earlier in the decade, consisting of a bigger self-service grocery store featuring large quantities of food at low prices. Frozen foods and shopping carts were introduced in the 1930's. And, instead of going through the usual channels for buying produce, the Kroger Grocery and Baking Company began to send its buyers to produce farms so they could inspect crops to ensure the quality of the food their stores sold. This counteracted the frequent complaint that chain stores sold low-quality foods. This policy eventually resulted in the formation of Wesco Food Company, Kroger's own produce procurement organization.

Following World War II (1939–1945), the company changed its name to the Kroger Company. The postwar period was a time of rapid growth for supermarkets. Between 1948 and 1963, the number of supermarkets in the country nearly tripled and Kroger participated in this fast growth. In 1960 the company began its expansion into the drugstore business, with an eye on the potential for drugstores built next to grocery stores. To increase the accuracy and speed of checkout systems, in 1972 Kroger, in partnership with RCA, became the first grocery company to test electronic scanners under actual working conditions. Also during the 1970s Kroger moved more towards the "superstore" concept of one-stop shopping, testing additional in-store specialty departments such as beauty salons, financial services, cheese shops, and cosmetic counters. By the late 1990s Kroger was the largest grocery retailer in the United States with 1,400 stores located in 24 states.

See also: **Chain Stores**

FURTHER READING

Cross, Jennifer. *The Supermarket Trap: The Consumer and the Food Industry*. Bloomington, IN: Indiana University Press, 1976.

Danielson, Rikki. "Kroger Dodging Volleys from All Sides." *Advertising Age*, April 18, 1985.

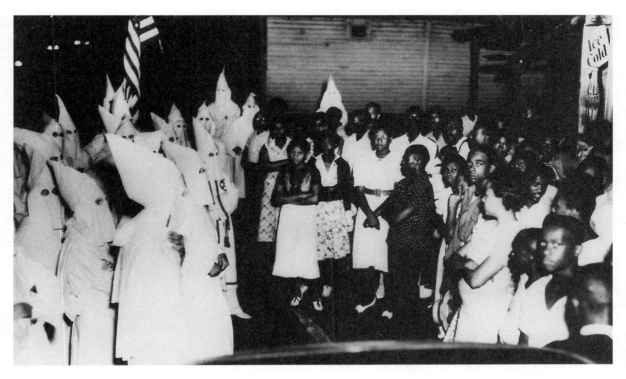

The Ku Klux Klan and African Americans confront each other in the South, 1938.

Kroger Company. *The Kroger Story: A Century of Innovation.* Cincinnati, OH: Kroger Company, 1983.

Lebhar, Godfrey M. *Chain Stores in America.* New York: Chain Store Publishing, 1963.

Saporito, Bill. "Kroger: The New King of Supermarketing." *Fortune,* February 21, 1983.

Tosh, Mark. "Kroger: Under Pressure." *Supermarket News,* January 18, 1993.

KU KLUX KLAN

The Ku Klux Klan (abbreviated KKK) is a white supremacist group—members believe in the superiority of whites over other races. The first part of the name ("Ku Klux") is derived from the Greek word *kyklos*, meaning circle. Klan is a derivative of the English word "clan," meaning family. The group was originally formed in 1865 in Pulaski, Tennessee, when Confederate Army veterans formed what they called a social club. The first leader (called the "Grand Wizard") was Nathan Bedford Forrest (1821–1877), a former general in the Confederate Army, who, on April 12, 1864, in the final days of the American Civil War

(1861–1865), led a massacre of three hundred African American soldiers in service of the Union Army at Fort Pillow, Tennessee.

As the unofficial arm of resistance against Republican efforts to restore the nation and make full citizens of its African American (formerly slave) population, the Ku Klux Klan waged a campaign of terror against former slaves in the South. Klan members, cloaked in robes and hoods to disguise their identity, threatened, beat, and killed numerous African Americans. While the group deprived its victims of their rights as citizens, their intent was also to intimidate the entire African American population and keep them out of, or in some cases remove them from, politics. People who supported the federal government's measures to extend rights to *all* citizens also became the victims of the fearsome Klan. Membership in the group grew quickly and the Ku Klux Klan soon had a presence throughout the South.

In 1871 the U.S. Congress passed the Force Bill, giving President Ulysses S. Grant (1869–1877) authority to direct federal troops against the Klan. The action was successful, causing the group to disappear—but only for a time. The society was newly organized at Stone Mountain, Georgia, in 1915 as a Protestant fraternal organization (called "The Invisible Empire, Knights of the Ku Klux Klan, Inc."), this time widening its focus of persecution to include

Roman Catholics, immigrants, and Jews, as well as African Americans. Members of all of these groups became targets of KKK harassment, which now included torture and whippings. The group, which proclaimed its mission to be "racial purity," grew in number and became national, electing some of their members to public office in many states (and not just Southern states). The KKK's acts of violence, howveer, raised public ire, and by the 1940s, America's attention focused on World War II (1939–1945) and the Klan died out or went completely underground. The group had another resurgence during the 1950s and into the early 1970s, as the nation struggled through the civil rights era. The Klan still exists today, fostering the extremist views of its membership and staging marches to demonstrate its presence on the American landscape. Such demonstrations are often attended by protestors, with violence being the sad outcome.

See also: **Reconstruction**